HUNTS' GUIDE TO MICHIGAN'S

UPPER

PENINSULA

Second Edition

Mary Hoffmann Hunt and Don Hunt

MIDWESTERN GUIDES

Albion, Michigan

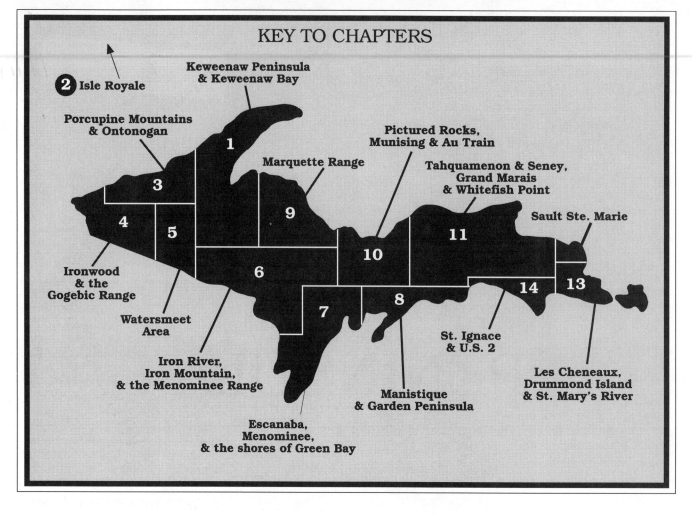

KEY TO CHAPTERS

② Isle Royale

Keweenaw Peninsula & Keweenaw Bay

Porcupine Mountains & Ontonogan

Pictured Rocks, Munising & Au Train

Marquette Range

Tahquamenon & Seney, Grand Marais & Whitefish Point

Sault Ste. Marie

Ironwood & the Gogebic Range

Watersmeet Area

St. Ignace & U.S. 2

Iron River, Iron Mountain, & the Menominee Range

Les Cheneaux, Drummond Island & St. Mary's River

Manistique & Garden Peninsula

Escanaba, Menominee, & the shores of Green Bay

Copyright 2001 by Mary Hoffmann Hunt and Don Hunt
Published by Midwestern Guides, 506 Linden Avenue, Albion, MI 49224
www.huntsguides.com; e-mail huntsguides@yahoo.com

ISBN 0-9709094-0-3

Maps by Don Hunt

Credits for illustrations

Many, many thanks to everyone who generously shared illustrations with a wider public! Uncredited photos were taken by the authors. Uncredited illustrations are from the author's collection of printed ephemera or from copyright-free clip art publishers, often Dover Publications, an outstanding resource for any publisher.
Chapter 1: p. 9 (above) Travel Michigan; p. 14 Betty Gabe; p. 19 Alan Pape, Hanka Homestead; p. 32 & 33 State Archives of Michigan; p. 37 drawing by Jan Manniko, photo from archives of Gerald Kinnunen, Modern Portrait Studio, Ironwood; p. 38 Shute's 1890 Bar; p. 39 Travel Michigan; p. 42 Belknap's Garnet House; p. 45 Copper Country Archives, M.T.U.; pp. 47, 48 Jan Manniko; p. 50 Sand Hills Lighthouse B&B; p. 53 The Lake Breeze. **Chapter 2:** Isle Royale National Park.
Chapter 3: p. 71 Dan Urbanski; p. 75 Porcupine Mts. State Park; p. 81 collection of Winifred Neph, Adventure Mine. **Chapter 4:** p. 87 archives of Gerald Kinnunen, Modern Portrait Studio, Ironwood; p. 88 State Archives of Michigan; p. 89 Old Depot Park Museum; p. 92 Norm Bishop; p. 92 Elk & Hound; p. 97 Norm Bishop. **Chapter 5:** p. 104 Travel Michigan; p. 108 Iron County (MI) Museum; p. 116 **Chapter 6:** Michigan DNR; p. 117 Jack Deo, Superior View; p. 120 State Archives of Michigan; p. 124 Iron County (MI) Museum; pp. 127-8 Crystal Falls Museum Society; p. 140 Travel Michigan. **Chapter 7:** p. 152 Hoegh Pet Casket; p. 155 John Franzen, Hiawatha National Forest; p. 157 Anne

Okonek, Hiawatha National Forest; p. 164 Linda Murto; p. 166 Marinette County Logging Museum. **Chapter 8:** pp. 173, 175 State Archives of Michigan; p. 178 drawing by Michele Earle-Bridges; p. 182 Gulliver Historical Society. **Chapter 9:** p. 186, Jack Deo, Superior View, p. 198 State Archives of Michigan; p. 204 Dover Publications Statue of Liberty coloring book; p. 208 Dean Sandell, Michigan State Forests; p. 210 Jack Deo, Superior View; p. 211 Thunder Bay Inn; p. 217 Jack Deo, Superior View; p. 219 Red Dust. **Chapter 10:** p. 231 Dean Sandell; p.233 Northern Waters Sea Kayaking; p. 237 John Franzen, Hiawatha National Forest; p. 242 Travel Michigan;p. 246 Morgan Country Store; p. 249 Anne Okonek, Hiawatha National Forest. **Chapter 11:** p. 255 Ted & Jean Reuther, friends of the Seney Refuge; p. 262 Grand Marais Historical Society (top) and Karen Brzys; pp. 265, 267 Pictured Rocks National Lakeshore; pp. 269, 274 Carol Taylor/Charles Sprague Taylor/Robert Nelson. pp. 277, 279 Travel Michigan; p. 284 Great Lakes Shipwreck Museum. **Chapter 12:** p. 291 Roger LeLievre; p. 295 State Archives of Michigan; p. 296 Gary Wright, Whitefish Point Bird Observatory; p. 297 Roger LeLievre; p. 301 photo by Joe Pedalino, Parks Canada/Sault Ste. Marie Canal NHSC;; p. 304 Canadian Bushplane Heritage Centre; p. 309 Travel Michigan. **Chapter 13:** p. 315 Les Cheneaux Historical Museum, Oliver Birge; p. 317 Les Cheneaux Historical Museum; p. 319 Hollyhocks & Radishes; p. 327 Dean Sandell, Michigan State Forests. **Chapter 14:** p. 332 State Archives of Michigan; p. 335 Museum of Ojibwa Culture.

CONTENTS

IT'S BEEN A PRIVILEGE to have a chance to explore the Upper Peninsula and share what we've learned with our readers — not just the well-known highlights but the interesting towns, low-key vacation areas, and wild places. The variety and richness of what's there has made for a longer book than expected. We hope you use it and other information tools to make your own discoveries about this unusual part of the United States. The U.P. is a thinly settled area where nature is always close at hand.

For many travelers, it is the more obscure, quirkier destinations that are most fondly remembered. We found that many of the most interesting places were created by a person with a dream who made it happen. Also, many places, from historic neighborhoods and old restaurants to wild landscapes with old-growth trees, have a special magic because of they go back in time and take visitors to another era. Family ties are more clearly visible here, and many summer resorts have been handed down and preserved from generation to generation.

Thanks to the hundreds of local people in every area who helped us out. Our book would be a very different thing without them. Forest service and DNR staff were exceptionally helpful, as a glance at the photo credits indicates. Don't buy into the stereotype of government employees as bureaucrats feeding on the public dole. Most parks and rec people we've met are public servants in the best sense of the word.

A few important reminders:

◆ **No one paid to be included in this book,** nor are there any commercial tie-ins with editorial content. In every entry we try to give enough candid information for you to decide if a destination suits you. Our research goes well beyond heavily promoted points of interest.

◆ **Prices, seasons, hours, and other important information change over time.** Our information was fresh as we went to press. It's still a good idea to call ahead if you need to be sure of circumstances before setting out. We include phone numbers for every place mentioned, and websites when possible.

◆ **What has been included in this book and why.** What we've described reflects our interests, our perceptions of our readers' interests, and what we have had the time and energy to investigate. Some worthwhile places are not in this book. It's just not possible to do everything. We hope our citations of other books and

information sources can helpfully supplement our offerings. Remember, your best research tools are perceptive eyes, an inquiring mind, and a willingness to ask questions locally!

About our choice of restaurants, lodgings, and campgrounds

Important considerations are scenery, local color, a historic setting, and/or a pedestrian-friendly location. **Location** and **setting** are very important factors. (AAA and Mobil guides evaluate facilities and typically consider locations in terms of access to highways and commercial strips.) Auto-dominated commercial strips are negatives in our selection process. If all other things are equal, we'll choose a restaurant or lodging that takes visitors to an interesting area that can be explored on foot. Everybody knows their favorite chain restaurants from home. The fun of traveling is coming upon regional variations and idiosyncratic, personal places. The U.P. is full of these!

Restaurants and lodgings have been chosen to reflect a variety of price points and tastes. We always look for good choices for families on budgets. We also seek out the upper end of offerings in each area.

◆ **Quoted nightly rates** for lodgings assume two-person occupancy with one and two beds. Sometimes a single person is charged less. Many lodgings charge more for each extra person, even children, reflecting increased costs for linens and hot water. Most lodgings offer weekly rates, often 10% less, sometimes a seventh night free. Many offer discounts for senior citizens, AAA members, and other affiliation groups — even Audubon Society members at some Paradise lodgings. Rates are subject to change.

What do our symbols mean?

⚐⚐⚐ means family-friendly. These restaurants have children's menu or some items that most kids like. For lodgings, we indicate whether there's an extra charge for children above two people per room. Incidentally, **many bars are family-friendly** to the point of having booster seats. In sparsely settled areas, eateries are multi-purpose.

♿ means wheelchair-accessible. Most restaurants are accessible, if not to current ADA standards, at least functionally. Where small restrooms are a problem, with older restaurants, we say so.

H.A. Stands for **handicap access.** In the U.P., many lodgings are older and therefore not wheelchair accessible. They may be suitable for mobility-impaired people

but too tight for wheelchairs. We note accessibility and often advise prospective guests to discuss their individual requirements with lodgings operators. **Advance reservations** are best if you want a **wheelchair-accessible room.**

🐕 : **pets** are accepted, often under certain circumstances. Often pets are taken only in rooms where smoking is permitted. Often an extra cleaning fee is required. It's best to **call first.** *Never leave a pet unattended in a room.*

TIPS for TRAVELING WITH DOGS. With experience, dogs can come to regard the car or van as their kennel/home. They can be quite happy there if the windows are left open, and if they get enough water and attention. Bring a six-foot leash (required in campgrounds and state and national parks), food, a water bowl and container, and plastic bags and paper towels to pick up poop. Relatively speaking, the **U.P. is a dog-friendly place.** A sociable, well-mannered dog enjoys camping. Older motels and resorts are more likely to take dogs. Dogs *love* hikes to waterfalls and elsewhere. M-DOT rest stops, often quite picturesque, almost always have dog runs. What doesn't work is getting out to see museums and shops when it's hot, there's no shady area, or you feel you need to roll up the windows and lock the car.

About smoking

This issue is a hard one in the U.P. Small restaurants and small motels in small areas often can't afford to exclude many of their potential customers. We try to note when smoke is bad by our own non-smoking standards. However, *if you are allergic to smoke,* make sure to inquire and reserve a no-smoking room. **Every bed and breakfast in our book is smoke-free inside.** More lodgings have mostly no-smoking rooms. Daily cleaning can remove a smoky smell, often by using sprays which may cause problems for some.

Most restaurants with bars have a smoke-free dining room. A good smoke-sucker can take away most smoke. If you need a totally smoke-free environment, you will miss out seeing the local social scene.

Cell phones? Don't count on them

Some places they work if you're on high ground. Some places (like Copper Harbor and Isle Royale) they don't work at all. Cell phone coverage in major towns is usually OK, though microenvironments like bluffs may interfere with reception on low shoreline areas. **If you must use your cell phone,** call about local coverage.

Four campground systems and four different styles

Campsites differ from system to system, and so does the clientele. These observations may be helpful. First, there's a **convenience-privacy tradeoff.** When you get electricity and other amenities of a modern campground (flush toilets, hot showers, pay phones, vending machines), you give up space between sites and usually a natural setting. The campground may resemble a subdivision. Rustic campers, who expect to pump water and do for themselves, can be "the aristocrats of campers, no matter what their income level," as one state park manager observed. Still, some private campgrounds have quit taking tent campers after too many problems.

Second, **destination campgrounds** that are somewhat hard to reach, down a long gravel road, for instance, have **fewer loud weekend campers** — a crew of young people off work, say. The closest campgrounds to populated areas have more weekend. A campground with a fair number of long-term, older campers is likely a quiet campground. Campgrounds with campground hosts are even better.

NATIONAL PARKS and LAKESHORES
www.nps.gov/piro (Pictured Rocks)
www.nps.gov/isro (Isle Royale)

Unusual scenery or history are criteria for becoming part of the national parks system. The National Park Service operates campgrounds at Pictured Rocks National Lakeshore and Isle Royale National Park. The Porcupine Mountains *almost* became a national park but World War II came up. Michigan's NPS campgrounds are all rustic (no showers, electricity, or flush toilets, first-come, first served). The natural setting is excellent; no little strips of lawn. National park visitors often come from farther away. Staff come from everywhere and may move around a lot. This is not a plus. Nature walks and evening programs are funded better than a few years ago. Hiking trails are scenic but often heavily used.

MICHIGAN STATE PARKS
www.dnr.state.mi.us/(info & online reservations); (800) 44-PARKS

High funding levels during Michigan's boom years have made developed Michigan's state park campgrounds with electricity and other conveniences, sometimes to the detriment of natural setting. This widely publicized system is so popular, it's increasingly hard to get a campsite in summer without reservations. The new site-specific system being implemented in more and more parks means it's easier to

Kids care more about little things — seeing more of the Milky Way in a dark sky; the smell of woodsmoke; beachcombing for rocks; investigating the life in the water (like this boy at the Au Train River mouth) — than checking off lots of well-known sights. The U.P. is a great place to slow down and get in touch with the natural world. Look in the index for canoe liveries. Try to minimize time spent in a car or in crowds.

plan ahead and get a choice site. Summer **Adventure Ranger programs** aimed at families are often excellent. Every park has at least a short hiking trail; often trails are outstanding. All parks (but not necessarily all campgrounds) are on water. Note: first fee is for 2001, second for 2002.

MICHIGAN STATE FORESTS
www.dnr.state.mi.us

These less publicized campgrounds are hidden treasures for people who like privacy and off-the-beaten path places. Like Michigan's national forests, they are managed for multiple uses (mostly timber, hunting, and other recreation) and made up mostly of tax-reverted cutover land on which owners didn't pay taxes, after logging or during the Depression. Land swaps consolidated federal Forest Service management in some areas, state DNR management in others. Land trust purchases from gas and oil drilling proceeds have allowed for some subsequent state land purchases of choice property. Michigan has more public land than any other state east of the Mississippi because so much was first owned by lumber and mining companies and then discovered to be unsuitable for agriculture. State forest campgrounds are all rustic (no

electricity or running water) and first-come, first-served. All are on lakes, rivers and remote Great Lakes beaches. They have large, private sites, often laid out with an artist's sensibility. Ask for a helpful locator map from Michigan Welcome Centers (see below). Some printed info on recreational opportunities is available from local offices listed in this book.

HIAWATHA and OTTAWA NATIONAL FORESTS
www.fs.fed.us/r9/ottawa or hiawatha

Campgrounds are rustic, with large sites, on lakes or rivers. See above for background. Ottawa is in the western U.P., Hiawatha in the central and eastern U.P. Some administrative offices double as visitor centers with **nature bookshops**. (See index under "Hiawatha" and "Ottawa.") Interesting info sheets on camping and recreational opportunities from camping to berry-picking are at offices and at Michigan Welcome Centers.

Our website keeps you up-to-date and adds special-interest info

One of the frustrating things about a book is its finite deadline and length. Our website,

www.huntsguides.com

lets us reflect changes in the U.P. tourism world and address special users. We have a list of destinations especially well suited to **HANDICAPPED TRAVELERS.** We have a map and comparative information on every **DESTINATION SKI HILL** in and adjacent to the U.P. We have a section on **FALL COLOR** and a list of **RECOMMENDED BOOKS**.

Michigan's #1 overnight destination is **MACKINAC ISLAND**. Nominally it is part of Mackinac County and the Upper Peninsula, but to us it's somewhere very different. It's been a tourist mecca for well over a hundred years. Go there without a clear sense of priorities and you'll get swept into a crowd scene with too much shopping— which admittedly some people really like. It can be easy to miss the best things about this beautiful island, which was the center of the fur trade on the Upper Great Lakes. The same thing is true of Mackinaw City, now that it's been Bransonized and Disneyfied. Our now out-of-print *Hunts' Highlights of Michigan* had three candid, helpful chapters on enjoying the Straits of Mackinac. We have revisited Mackinac Island recently. By 2002 we will have updated it on our website.

Tips: Don't miss Market St. The bike ride around the island is easy and fun; stop at the nature center on British Landing.

Our index: helpful and rich

Destinations for many activities — **canoeing** and kayaking, **cross-country skiing**, fishing, and **hiking**— have been indexed. So has every town or village, plus many rivers and lakes. You'll find listings of **gardens** open to the public and places where you can hear **live music** (summer band concerts, regular venues, and festivals). **Lighthouses**, **waterfalls**, maritime museums, **rock** and **mineral destinations**, and shipwrecks are other headings. You can find offices and visitor centers for the **national forests** plus **Michigan Welcome Centers**. Starting on page 356 is a separate index by chapter of every restaurant, lodging, and campground.

"Ethnic groups" (including Native American peoples) and **"religious denominations"** illuminate the rich cultural backgrounds that make the Upper Peninsula a special place. Look up **"trees, old-growth"** to find a dozen places with big, old-growth trees. The index lets you get the most out of this book.

Michigan Welcome Centers: personal and super-helpful

Michigan Welcome Centers are located at every major entrance to Michigan except Detroit, and within the state at Clare, Mackinaw City, St. Ignace, and Marquette. They are marked on state highway maps.

The supply of printed brochures and booklets is **vast. And** the year-round staff is typically well informed about detailed local information and about distant state-wide attractions, too. Welcome Centers are part of Travel Michigan. Welcome Center staffers belie the common notion that government is inefficient and unresponsive. If you need more information than UPTRA or MITS (below) can supply, Welcome Centers can respond to phone requests by mailing you specific brochures! **Welcome Center staff** know a lot about the entire state, no matter where they are, and most are **locally extremely well informed**, and not limited to giving info only about members, as Chambers of Commerce are. Responding to countless questions keeps them up on what visitors want to know about.

Here are Upper Peninsula Welcome Center locations and phone numbers, arranged from west to east like our book: **Ironwood**, 801 W. Cloverland/U.S. 2, (906) 932-3330, **Iron Mountain**, 618 Stephenson/U.S. 2, (906) 774-4201;

For backpacking beginners or for the season's first trip, it's a good idea to plan a campground just a mile or two away from the trailhead and take day hikes from camp. Staff at state and national forests and parks or Pictured Rocks (here) can advise.

Menominee, 1343 10th Ave. by the Interstate Bridge, (906) 863-6496; **Marquette**, 2201 U.S. 41 South, (906) 249-9066; **Sault Ste. Marie**, 943 Portage Ave. West off I-75 by International Bridge, (906) 632-8242; **St. Ignace**, Northbound I-75 off Mackinac Bridge, (906) 643-6979. Look for signs to Welcome Centers on major highways.

U. P. Travel Planner and custom U.P. travel info

www.uptravel.com; can customize

The **magazine-format publication** is packed with color photographs and helpful information The broad-based membership votes on the "finest attractions" highlighted in the central section. Nearly half the publication is devoted to compact summaries of lodgings, resorts, restaurants, and other attractions, written and paid for by owners and arranged by place. The Travel Planner is free upon request by phoning (800) 562-7134, faxing (906) 774-5190, visiting the website, or writing UPTRA, Box 400, Iron Mountain, MI 49801. It's published by the Upper Peninsula Travel & Recreation Association (UPTRA), a membership organization going back to efforts to develop tourism in the early 20th century in the wake of diminishing employment in logging and mining.

MITS: Customized travel information about Michigan

(888) 78-GREAT; TDD (800) 722-8191
www.michigan.org

M-F 8 a.m.-9 p.m, Sat. 9-5. Sun. closed.

You can request a basic information packet (**state map**, calendar of seasonal events, glossy annual *Michigan Travel Ideas* magazine). It is mailed third-class from Flint the next day and may take up to 10 days or more to arrive. Second, you can ask a real person for specific customized information. The operator then consults the MITS computer database to answer your questions. The results depend on which destinations have responded to MITS' requests for information. The customized computer info is faxed or e-mailed. When this service was begun, it was done in-state and got all screwed up. Now the operators are on Prince Edward Island. For some questions, they will refer callers to 800 numbers at local visitors' bureaus.

Drunk driving strictly enforced

The days are long gone when drunk driving in the U.P. was tolerated by local custom and lax enforcement. Sure, bars remain a social center, and alcohol abuse is too much a part of the local culture, associated with long winters, short days, isolated areas, and Scandinavian populations. But enforcement has become so rigorous that some local people carry around a tent and camping gear just in case they have a few too when many visiting friends or family. Lodgings with on-site bars are increasingly in demand. And snowmobilers are changing their ways.

Watch out for deer!

Not just in fall is it more dangerous to drive near dawn and dusk. Car-deer collisions are a major risk of highway driving throughout Michigan. Keeping deer populations in check and healthy is one reason why wolves are being de facto encouraged. It only makes sense to drive defensively, paying attention and maintaining a speed at which deer can be avoided. Remember, it's better to hit a deer than to swerve and hit another car.

Weather-wise what to expect

Summer can be surprising. Yes, the U.P. is generally cooler than down below, and summer is a magical time, with long days and wonderful berries and wild-flowers. But inland areas *can* get hot, and even the Keweenaw, surrounded by water, has its 90° days. On the other hand, nights can be cold and frost has occurred in every month. Campers along Lake Superior should come prepared with sleeping bags, cool-weather jackets, and layerable sweaters, no matter what the month. Kayakers and canoeists know enough to bring along warm clothes and windbreakers. A U.P. state forester recalls the naive surprise of visiting managers from Lansing who came totally unprepared for bone-chilling cold on a June camping trip on the big lake.

Winter is a six-month affair, and **bug season** is from mid-May into July. Not that you shouldn't come — just come prepared. (See details below.) **September** can be a fabulous month, with most visitors gone, but later in the month along Lake Superior it can get cold and even snow.

Winter temperatures are actually warmer where it's snowiest because Lake Superior moderates the temperatures. The Keweenaw Peninsula is, surprisingly, in the same hardiness zone as southern Michigan. It's colder inland, near Crystal Falls and Iron Mountain. The coldest areas are the Huron Mountains and related highlands between L'Anse and Michigamme. Herman is Michigan's icebox. Near Three Lakes along M-28, an early snow can cover the autumn foliage when it's relatively warm at lower elevations.

Snow removal is a top priority of local government and it's very good. But in winter, all engagements are considered tentative and weather-dependent.

Beating the bugs:
be flexible and experiment

Adapted with permission from the
Porcupine Mountains Companion
by Michael Rafferty and Robert Sprague

From the tail end of May through mid July is **bug season** in the Porkies. In some parts of the U.P., like the upper Keweenaw, most bugs are gone by July 4. Learn to deal with bugs and you'll enjoy spring wildflowers and orchids, hawk and warbler migrations, peak seasons for steelhead, brook trout, and waterfalls, and good canoeing on shallower streams. Also, you'll avoid crowds of other visitors.

Snowshoes are the traditional way to explore the winter woods: aerobic exercise with no lessons required. Bob Zelinski of Sylvania Outfitters, who spends a lot of time doing outdoors work in deep snow, swears by the classic wood snowshoes (here), made in the U.P. by Iverson's. Why? See page 247.

Follow these strategies to deal with bugs from a position of strength.

◆ Plan on accepting them and understanding them.

◆ Get a **bug hat with a mesh veil** at a good outdoor store. Bug hats from discount stores are mostly junk. Get dark mesh so you can see better, with less reflected light. Bring a **bandanna**, too, for times when a bug hat isn't needed.

◆ Most soft-bodied flies require high humidity to thrive and function. Then they will get busy seeking food to complete their life cycle. **Activity will be minimal if spring weather is cool and dry**, influenced by high pressure and cool air coming across Lake Superior.

◆ Wear **loose-fitting long clothes.** Color is a factor. **Avoid blue**, even navy. It has ultraviolet pigment that makes you more visible to bugs as they scan the environment for anything alive and breathing. They "see" you better if you're sweating, too. **Neutral colors** like khaki are good. White isn't so good. Bob and Mike never hike in shorts. Long pants protect against abrasion and sunburn, too.

◆ Avoid using laundry brighteners. they have UV pigments, too.

◆ Hunting catalogs offer sprays that deter ticks and some bugs. Allow time for spray to dry.

◆ Avoid perfumed personal care products that may attract bugs.

◆ **Black flies**, active from mid May to mid June, can fly up your pants legs and into the opening where your shirt sleeve buttons. Cover exposed skin. Tuck your pants into your boots. Some people use Lycra leggings beneath shorts. Black flies propagate in clean, cool rivers. They don't buzz to warn you, and you can't feel them bite. The ensuing itch is irritatng. They usually don't bite after dark.

◆ **Experiment with protective gear** and repellant *before* an extended overnight, especially with kids. Every body is different. What works for some people doesn't work for others. **DEET** is a powerful and effective general repellant but absorbed through the skin. That's especially a concern for children. DEET can be applied to clothing. **Citronella oil** is a "natural" repellant coming back into favor. **Avon Skin-So-Soft** is a north-woods standby against black flies. Other effective black fly repellants are **evergreen repellants** with DEET and "**Black fly solution**" brand.

◆ Get **No-See-Um netting** (a denser weave) on your tent to avoid these tiny evening insects whose bites itch and burn. Don't leave lights on at night.

◆ **Horse flies** and **deer flies** are in woods, especially near streams, in June and early July. **Keep covered up.** Their numbers are small enough that you can kill them off as they find you.

◆ **Stable flies** are the hardest to avoid or kill. They invade in huge numbers, up to two or three days, perhaps five or six times from June to mid July. Their proboscis has evolved to penetrate cows' backsides, and they flourish in dairy country, never bothering farmers because they find plenty of cows. They hitch rides on winds, fanning out in all directions for hundreds of miles, in their search for fresh prey. When the wind is out of the southwest, they **collect along the Lake Superior shore** because the lake acts as a barrier. When the weather changes to warm and humid, they move into action. Nothing will reduce their numbers to an acceptable level. **The only solution is avoidance**: head inland into the woods, or take a sightseeing trip. When the wind comes from the north, they'll hitch another ride, looking for fresh sustenance to complete their life cycle, and be gone.

◆ In late summer, **hornets** can be a problem along the trail. Hungry bears, skunks, and coons can invade their nests for larvae at night, when the mature hornets are inactive. They next day, when it warms up, they are agitated. They can attack hikers, especially those bringing up the rear. Long pants and shirts are the best protection.

A rich musical tradition

Many elements combine to give the Upper Peninsula a distinctive musical heritage, including the isolation of its rural communities and the ensuing need for homegrown entertainment, its many ethnic groups, and the fiddling at Finnish farm halls and dances. Consult **"music"** in our index for **music festivals**, for **summer concerts**, and for **regular venues**. Many summer concerts feature U.P. musicians who play to keep alive musical traditions they learned from family and neighbors.

It can be fun to listen to recordings with regional music and stories on vacation drives. **White Water**, an eclectic, folk-flavored family quartet inspired by handed-down stories of farm-hall dances in Amasa, has become quite well known. See page 131. Visit the performance and recordings section of its website, www.white-water-associates.com. Their CDs, available by mail, would make wonderful drive-time listening on a U.P. trip. The website links with other traditional U.P. performers. Click on Finnish-American music, and you're in a whole separate world! Dean and Bette Premo, White Water founders, started popular **Second Sunday folk dances** and potlucks held from October through April at 4 p.m. at the Fortune Lake Lutheran Camp three miles west of Crystal Falls on Bible Camp Road. White Water and friends like Helmer Toyras, an old-time Finnish fiddler from Aura, always play at the Aura Jamboree (page 13). **Richard Debelak** of Munising, a recent inductee in the polka division of the Michigan Music Hall of Fame, gets together a polka trio a few times a year at fundraisers with his second cousins Mike Klobucher of Engadine and Matt Spear of downstate Albion. They continue the spirit of Slovenian-style button-box accordion they knew and loved growing up in Engadine. No matter that they were mostly Croatian.

The Finnish musical and comic tradition has gone in different directions with two nationally known groups: **Da Yoopers** of Ishpeming, now more of a comedy act (see page 219-20), and their friends Les Ross and **Conga Se Menne**,

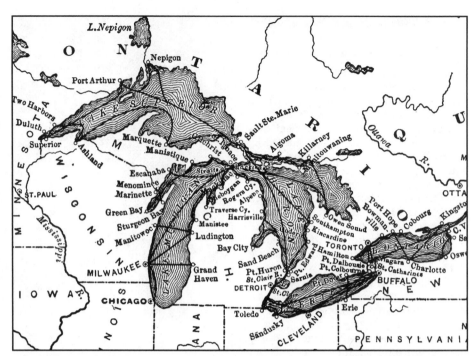

Of all the steamship lines shown on this 1890 map, one remains: the enjoyable Lake Michigan Carferry across Lake Michigan between Ludington, Michigan, and Manitowoc, Wisconsin. Note the site of Toledo, the reason for the Upper Peninsula being given to Michigan, and Isle Royale off the Ontario shore at Port Arthur (now Thunder Bay). At various times the U.P. has been closely connected by ship to Cleveland (headquarters of Cleveland-Cliffs Iron, with mining operations in Marquette County), Dearborn/Detroit in Henry Ford's day, and Gary, Indiana, near Chicago, and U.S. Steel.

a musically more sophisticated group from Negaunee that mixes reggae, calypso, and Finnish northwoods lyrics (in "We Go Green Bay" and "Guess Who's Coming to Sauna?"). The result is a "tropical sauna beat band" that's less unlikely than it seems. The Finnish-Latin connection goes way back; Finns long for sunshine during a long, dark winter. Conga Se Menne's busy time is playing tropical theme parties to chase away cabin fever. Their success has inspired Les's father, retired accountant Les Ross Sr. to launch a late-life performing career as a folk harmonica virtuoso. Nine other musicians teamed up on his *Hulivili Huuliharppu* album on a wide variety of polkas, rocking schottisches, soulful waltzes, and more. Visit www.congaonline.com for info on his and Conga Se Menne's albums.

The **Keweenaw Symphony** and chorus perform classical music in Houghton during the academic year. Michigan Tech's new, state-of-the-art **Rozsa Performing Arts Center** reflects the area's growing support for the arts. From mid June through late July the **Pine Mountain Music Festival**, founded in 1991 by Chicago musician Laura Deming, now presents six weeks of high-

caliber, mostly classical music including chamber music, soloists, symphony concerts, and **two complete, fully produced operas**. The accessible programs and informal, intimate setting bring out town and gown, arts enthusiasts and engineers. Most perfomances are in Houghton and Iron Mountain, with some also in Escanaba and Marquette.

How the Toledo War gave the U.P. to Michigan

Physically and culturally, the Upper Peninsula is much closer to Wisconsin. Why isn't it *in* Wisconsin? Because of politics from when before Wisconsin was a state. Fuzzy language and inadequate surveys were behind the 1805 establishment of the Michigan Territory's southern bounday, then at the southern tip of Lake Michigan. Twenty years later, Ohio wanted the "Toledo Strip," a slice of southern Michigan Territory, because Ohio wanted the site at the mouth of the Maumee River, a strategic site for economic development at the northwest end of Lake Erie — the future site of Toledo. In 1835 the populous state of Ohio had , more political clout in Congress than

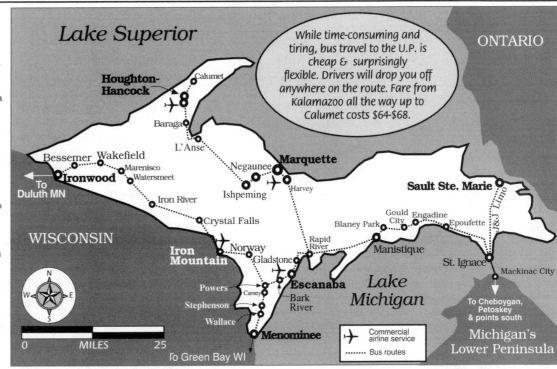

Lake Superior

ONTARIO

While time-consuming and tiring, bus travel to the U.P. is cheap & surprisingly flexible. Drivers will drop you off anywhere on the route. Fare from Kalamazoo all the way up to Calumet costs $64-$68.

Houghton-Hancock
Calumet
Baraga
L'Anse
Bessemer Wakefield
Marenisco
Ironwood
Watersmeet
Negaunee **Marquette**
Ishpeming
Harvey
Iron River
Sault Ste. Marie
Crystal Falls
Gould Engadine
Blaney Park City Epoufette
WISCONSIN
Rapid River
Iron Mountain
Norway
Gladstone
Manistique
St. Ignace
Mackinac City
Powers
Carney
Escanaba
Bark River
Lake Michigan
Stephenson
Wallace
To Cheboygan, Petoskey & points south
Menominee
Michigan's Lower Peninsula

To Duluth MN
To Green Bay WI

N E S W

0 MILES 25

Commercial airline service
...... Bus routes

Upper Peninsula Bus, Airline, and Carferry Service

Michigan, still a territory. Michiganders in Monroe County, on the border, prepared to fight, but a compromise was soon worked out. Ohio won the Toledo Strip. Michigan received the Upper Peninsula as a consolation prize. (Wisconsin didn't grow big enough to become a state until 1845.

At first the remote, unmapped peninsula was considered worthless. But Douglass Houghton and Henry Schoolcraft explored it, creating interest that lead to the discovery of iron and copper deposits in the 1840s.and copper for decades.

The spiritual side of travel

The Upper Peninsula's real magic is in some of its people, in its beautiful natural environment, and in its opportunities for solitude, or for being with friends or family, in a natural setting. The tradition of contemplation and renewal in the forest and near water goes way back. (See p. 281.) A soul-satisfying trip up north takes far less

time and money than, say, going to Asia. It's all a matter of preparing mind and body. There's also a natural zen in canoeing, camping, and hiking, from packing to facing the elements.

Leigh Wall of Sweet Violets bookshop in Marquette recommends *Gutsy Mama* and other Traveler's Tales imprints for women (www.travelerstales.com) and three books on spiritual journeys that needn't be to faraway places: *The Way of the Traveler: Making Every Trip a Journey of Self-Discovery* by Joseph Dispenz, *The Mindful Traveler: A Guide to Journaling and Transformative Travel* by Jim Currie, and (a favorite of ours) *The Art of Pilgrimage: The Seeker's Guide to Making Travel Sacred* by Phil Cousineau, native Detroiter, filmmaker, and biographer of Joseph Campbell. His descriptions of pilgrimage include a soul-restoring fishing trip to northern Michigan, his mother's sustaining novenas at her parish church, his friend's life-enhancing investigation of the dark side of his family's histo-

ry, and pilgrimages to Cooperstown, to the Cousineau family's ancestral village in Quebec, to Angkor Wat, Crete, and Ireland. *The Art of Pilgrimage* is not at all *about* the U.P., but it's quite relevant, a good warmup for a refreshing or even healing trip.

To find cheap ($2 and less), lightweight editions of works by Thoreau, or Wordsworth's poems, or selections from that pilgrimage classic *Canterbury Tales*, see www.doverpublications.com/retail. Sisters of the Earth Adventures (616-695-1201) leads outdoor trips in Michigan for women and girls. They are not nuns. *Real* nuns often give programs on eco-spirituality from Christian and other perspectives. These sisters are down-to-earth and not what most people would expect. Look up Sisters of St. Joseph of Kalamazoo, Adrian Dominicans, Grand Rapids Dominicans, Sisters of the Immaculate Heart of Mary in Monroe (all in Michigan). Or ask similarly inclined motherhouses in your neck of the woods.

Back then [in 1917] the forest belonged to everyone, or so we felt. The whole U.P. was dotted with cabins built by men who didn't possess a square foot of it. There were no "No Hunting" or "No Trespassing" signs. When Cyrus McCormick, the millionaire from Chicago, put up a steel gate across his entrance, someone shot off its hinges, hauled it half a mile, and threw it in the river. Hunting cabins were never locked, so that anyone who needed shelter could have it, and always there was coffee and korpua [cinnamon toast] in a mouse-proof can to be freely consumed. . . .

Although many changes have come to the U.P. . . . , the huge wilderness that was ours still remains. From a plane it is still a vast forest of green dotted by innumerable lakes and streams, and the hardy people who live in it still have that wonderful feeling that it is theirs. They can hunt in it, fish in it, or just walk in it without ever having to get permission. No wonder youth born in the U.P. leave it reluctantly when they have to go Down Below to get jobs; no wonder they dream of it and return when they are older.

— Cully Gage
A Love Affair with the U.P.
Quoted with permission of Avery Color Studios

As the late Cully Gage (Charles Van Riper) pointed out in the 1970s, much Upper Peninsula land to which the public has access is privately owned. The Porcupine Mountains are public land today largely because of the efforts of the late Genevieve Gillette (left), landscape architect and citizen volunteer who devoted a lifetime to building support for state parks. She and other advocates for public access deserve our thanks and our support.

Keweenaw Peninsula & Keweenaw Bay

THE KEWEENAW PENINSULA, that long finger of land poking into Lake Superior, is **one of the most remarkable, remote, and distinctive regions in the Middle West**. It has spectacular views and a colorful, important history. The Keweenaw is also called **"Copper Country"** for its glory days when it was the world chief supplier of that increasingly important metal. Its many mines drew tens of thousands of European immigrants from Finland to Italy and the Balkans. Their cultures, especially that of the most numerous Finns, have added exotic foreign touches to a place already full of striking features.

Keweenaw is Ojibwa for "place of the crossing," referring to a shortcut, a natural waterway that sliced almost entirely through the peninsula, passing today's Hancock and Houghton. It allowed Indians in canoes to bypass the peninsula's tip, with its dangerous rocks and reefs. Traveling west from Keweenaw Bay, Ojibwa canoes went across this Portage Waterway, then made a short portage to Lake Superior south of present-day McLain State Park.

In 1873, after massive amounts of copper began to be shipped from the region, the **Portage Canal** was cut through the remaining two miles of land. The canal made an island of the peninsula's northeastern part, which contains most of its old copper mines and the area's most scenic attractions as well. The upper Keweenaw is linked to the rest of the U.P. only by the impressive lift bridge on U.S. 41 between Houghton and Hancock.

Today this area is a **very special place** for lovers of nature and **wild places**, for **rockhounds** and geologists, for **kayakers**, and for fans of historic architecture and cultural history. Visually and culturally, it's quite a contrast to places like southeast Michigan, Milwaukee, and Green Bay.

A thousand million years ago, repeated volcanic eruptions deposited mineral-rich lava that forms a rocky spine along the Keweenaw's central axis. Today forests soften the jutting spine, but sweeping vistas and occasional dramatic rocky outcrops are visible to motorists along M-26 and U.S. 41. These highways fol-

Where spectacular rocky shorelines & Copper Country's rich mining & ethnic history come together. In the south, many waterfalls, the rugged Huron Mountains, and remote, scenic shores.

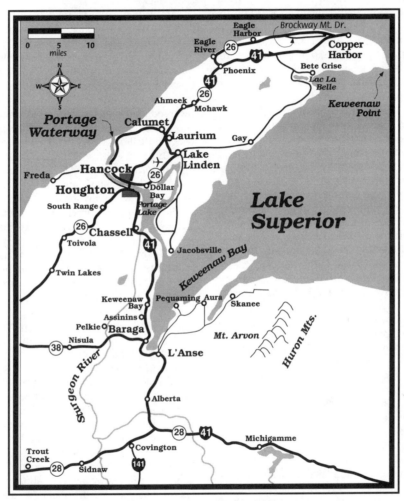

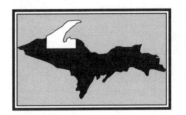

low the **Keweenaw's rugged fault line** from Mass City (in Ontonagon County to the south) to Copper Harbor at the Keweenaw's eastern tip. The ultimate place to take in the breathtaking sweep of this uplift is at the top of **Brockway Mountain Drive** near Copper Harbor. There you can see the rocky spine extend for many miles and tilt down into Lake Superior. On a clear day, Isle Royale, out in Superior at the other rim of the basin, can be seen almost 50 miles away.

The aftermath of those ancient eruptions brought copper to the surface — masses of pure copper in some areas. For hundreds of years Native American miners mined these surface deposits and used the copper in trade. Tools and ornaments of Keweenaw copper have been found as far as the Gulf of Mexico. Early French, British, and American expeditions eagerly learned about the copper locations from the Ojibwa they met. In the 1840s and 1850s, American investors from the East Coast and Lower Michigan started mining. At that time the remote region was well beyond any other American settlements. To supply the mines, export the copper, and feed the miners required treacherous boat shipments.

But by the 1870s this wild, snowy region was settled and shipping billions of pounds of copper. Mining companies had created a string of mining towns along the fault from Copper Harbor to Houghton. It was dangerous and unpleasant work for those who toiled long shifts down dark shafts, some of which extended almost two miles deep. That depth spelled the eventually doom of Keweenaw mining. Huge deposits of copper remain here, but for decades it has been much cheaper to strip mine the ore, first in Montana and Arizona, now in places like Chile, Australia, and Peru.

Beginning in the 1860s the demand for Keweenaw copper was so great that Eastern owners of the most successful Keweenaw mines had to recruit workers from Europe to work in their mines. The Cornish, seasoned miners from the spent-out tin mines of Cornwall in southwestern England, were mining professionals who accepted its risks with stoicism and a measure of fatalism. They typically rose to management ranks. Other ethnic groups disliked working underground and got out of mining when they could get better jobs, working above-ground in stamping mills or smelters, or getting a small business or farm. The mining companies' **corporate paternalism**, apparently generous and high-minded, came to be seen by workers as arrogant and manipulative, with good reason. Thus mining companies had to find fresh generations of underground workers from new waves of poor immigrants without prospects. First came the Cornish, Irish, Germans, and Scots, then various Scandinavians including the earlier wave of Finns, followed by Italians, Slovenians, Hungarians, Croatians, and more Finns after 1900. .

Finns became the largest immigrant group and today give the western U.P. much of its idiosyncratic character. Copper Country is the **Finnish-American heartland** for hundreds of thousands of far-flung Finns scattered from Massachusetts to Montana and Arizona. Hancock is home to the only American college with Finnish roots, formerly Suomi College, now Finlandia University.

Copper mining died slowly here. The last mines closed in 1968, but competition from Western U.S. mines meant that Keweenaw copper was already declining by the time of the **legendary 1913 strike**. It was brought about by workers' resentment of mining companies' efficiency measures to maintain profits in the face of rising costs. As mining declined, Copper Country became more and more a depressed backwater. Many of its children went off to earn their fortunes elsewhere.

Big money was made in Keweenaw copper, especially between 1890 and 1905, creating fortunes for the fortunate shareholders of the few mines that proved highly profitable. Some copper money stayed in the Keweenaw, in **ornate buildings** like the Calumet Theater, downtown business blocks, and mansions, and with high-earning local people who were mine managers or business people. But most of the money went east to Boston, where it built up the coffers of wealthy institutions like Harvard University and the Boston Symphony.

Few Finns gained even a modest fortune from the Keweenaw. Many yearned to have their own small farms, and when they had saved enough up, they bought land. They managed to make a living dairying and growing crops like potatoes, wheat, rutabagas, and later strawberries. That harsh, simple farm life can still be seen at the **Hanka Homestead farm museum** between Keweenaw Bay and Chassell. A good example of an isolated, mostly Finnish farming community still exists in Pelkie, west of Baraga and two miles north of M-38. Finns were pioneers of the cooperative movement in this country. The building of the Pelkie Cooperative Society, part of the widespread **co-op movement** of the upper Midwest, can be seen today. A one-room schoolhouse is held open from 11 to 4 Sundays from summer into fall.

Baraga and **L'Anse** are in the midst of a large **Ojibwa** community once served by Father Baraga, the "Snowshoe Priest." Baraga County was settled by European-Americans because of lumber and fishing, not copper. Fishing by Ojibwa and Scandinavian fishermen was an economic mainstay for years.

Today there is a gently faded, island atmosphere to the Keweenaw, akin to the mood of old mining boom towns in the West. Common sights are rusted hulks of massive old mining buildings, stamping mills' imposing concrete foundations along the water, and rows of company houses built for miners, some remodeled, others abandoned. Built around mine shafts, these housing developments were called "locations," and their residents were unusually close-knit.

The contemporary Keweenaw's tone is set by the simple lifestyle of local residents. They're a special breed that includes natives who have come back to retire or start second careers, a dwindling number of onetime miners, and a growing contingent of nature-lovers, downstate retirees, artists, old hippies, and New Age-ers.

Many first came to attend **Michigan Technological University** in Houghton, mostly to study engineering. Tech was founded as the state mining school in 1885. Other transplants came to love the area from childhood summers visiting grandparents. Ask summer vacationers where they're from, and you'll discover over half of them have Copper Country roots a few generations back.

Many historic buildings have been preserved by local pride and by the relative lack of development pressure. However, historic townscapes are increasingly dotted with vacant lots and even manufactured housing. Town life, once vibrant, has suffered now that more of the outdoors-loving populace commutes from homes on the water or in the country.

Lately decades of Keweenaw population loss has been reversed with modest gains in Houghton, Keweenaw, and Baraga counties. It's part of a nationwide pattern as more Americans become disillusioned with the lifestyle of an ever more materialistic, hurried culture. This area can seem calmer, saner, slower place. Sprawl happens here, too, however. The Houghton Wal-Mart is a busy place, and the strip along M-26 leading up from the Portage Waterway toward South Range is still growing.

Suddenly **land development issues** and zoning, long ignored as irrelevant, have become a **matter of widespread concern.** The big recent Mount Bohemia ski project at Lac La Belle divided summer people and transplants, generally against it, from local residents who welcomed added business from skiers. Lake Superior Land Company, a successor to Calumet & Hecla Mining, is selling off its prime property— places like Hunter's Point on Copper Harbor's west side that everyone treasures. Under the Commercial Forest Reserve Act, people had grown accustomed to having access to mining and timber lands for hunting, fishing, and hiking, and regarding them as public property. Increasingly that freedom to roam is threatened.

In reaction to this confining trend, a public access coalition is bringing together various business and environmental groups, from the Copper Harbor Improvement Association to Trout Unlimited and The Nature Conservancy. Its new website, www.publicaccesskeweenaw.org, keeps abreast of developments.

Keweenaw life is about nature, history, and outdoor recreation, with an increasing measure of art and music thrown in. It's definitely not about fashion, shopping, or showing off. The area exercises a powerful appeal for many people. But only a few except retirees can figure out how to accomplish the big move to the Keweenaw in an area with few employment opportunities.

Despite current trends, Copper Country remains a proud and idiosyncratic backwater. "Living up here is like living in the 1950s or 1960s," says Lake Linden's dentist. He likes to boast that he has the lowest income and best lifestyle of anyone in his University of Michigan dental school class. "The old values are important. Most people are honest. But you have to make your own activities — there's not much entertainment here. A lot of newcomers don't understand that."

TO FIND OUT MORE: Two websites have a wide variety of articles of visitor interest: **www.keweenawtraveler.com**, published by Charles Eshbach, a respected outdoorsman and photographer, and **www.keweenawtoday.com,** funded by downstate businessman Gary Kohs, owner of the Mendota Lighthouse and anti-Mount Bohemia activist. The *Daily Mining Gazette* in Houghton and the *L'Anse Sentinel* have online editions. . . For the L'Anse/Baraga/Skanee Huron Mountains area, contact the **BARAGA COUNTY TOURIST & RECREATION ASSOCIATION** at (800) 743-4908, (906) 524-7444, or www.destinationmichigan.com/baraga. Its L'Anse office, clear-

ly signed, is at 755 E. Broad at U.S. 41, open weekdays mostly from 8 to 4. . . All of Houghton and Keweenaw counties, including Houghton, Calumet, and Copper Harbor, is served by the helpful **KEWEENAW TOURISM COUNCIL**, (800) 338-7982, (906) 482-2388 or www.keweenaw.org. Phone assistance is available weekdays from 8 to 5, plus weekends 10-6 in summer. Its drop-in offices are in **downtown Houghton** (326 Shelden Ave., near the downtown McDonald's, open Mon-Fri 8-5; park in rear structure) and in **Calumet** on U.S. 41 at Lake Linden Road. The Calumet office, well stocked with a very wide variety of free walking tours, maps, and more, is open Mon-Fri 8-5 plus weekends 10-6 in summer. Its lobby is open 24 hours a day . . . The **Copper Harbor Improvement Association** publishes a helpful area map available at local businesses. Its beautiful website is www.copperharbor.org. . . . **www.publicaccesskeweenaw.org** has lists of many favorite places that are off the beaten path, in addition to wading into local development issues. . . .**Rock and mineral-related websites**, some quite outstanding, are easily entered via the links at **www.copperconnection.com**

LODGINGS TIPS: Sometimes Baraga County lodgings fill up with conventions, snowmobilers, or gambling, so reservations are a good idea. . . . The time when the Houghton area is full is for the **fabulous Michigan Tech winter carnival** in February. . . . Summer lodgings on the water are at a premium in Copper Harbor, Eagle Harbor, and Eagle River requiring advance planning, though last-minute cancellations do occur. . . . Copper Country campsites are also in short supply because there are no national or state forest campgrounds north of Twin Lakes. . . **Last-minute campers** could do way worse than the conveniently located city campgrounds in Lake Linden and Hancock, not likely to fill. **Baraga State Park** often isn't full, either, and **Curwood Park** in L'Anse, scenic and quiet, never fills. . . . Attractive rustic state and national forest campgrounds that seldom fill are between Skanee and the Huron Mountains and outside Sidnaw and Kenton along M-28 . . The **Best Western Copper Crown motel** in Hancock is a very good value, and it has an indoor pool. . . . **Twin Lakes Resort**, midway between Houghton and Ontonagon, makes a pleasant base camp for day trips to the Adventure Mine and Old Victoria to the south and Houghton and Calumet, and Copper Harbor. A bit farther south and in the Ontonagon/Porkies chapter are campgrounds near Greenland and Mass City.

PUBLIC LAND: South of M-38 (the highway from Baraga to Ontonagon) are large areas of public land, mostly in the **OTTAWA NATIONAL FOREST**. Campgrounds are on the Sturgeon River near a wilderness area and on several small lakes. Weekdays you can call or stop at its district office in on M-28 in Kenton (906-852-3501; TTY: 906-852-3618). Basic info is at www.fs.fed.us/r9/ottawa/. . . . Scattered areas of state land, including several campgrounds, are part of the **COPPER COUNTRY STATE FOREST**. They around Twin Lakes and in Baraga County. Big Eric's Bridge campground near Skanee is in a beautiful, remote area near the Huron River mouth, the Huron Mountains, and several waterfalls. For info, call or stop by the **DNR Baraga office** on U.S. 41 about half a mile north of M-38 (east side of road). (906) 353-6651. Currently the DNR website, www.dnr.state.mi.us/ has very little on state forests, but that may change. North of the Portage Waterway most state land is part of McLain State Park and Fort Wilkins State Park.

GUIDES, CHARTERS and RENTALS: Fisher Price Charters (906-523-0044) based in Skanee offers Lake Superior fishing charters to area fishing hot spots and to Stannard Reef, an outstanding lake trout fishery 50 miles north of Marquette . . . **Fred's Charters** (906-482-0884) is based in Copper Harbor. . . . **Indian Country Sports** on the L'Anse harbor covers the bases from fishing and hunting to canoeing, kayaking, and camping. Steve Koski is extremely knowledgeable about the area. Call (906) 524-6518. www.indiancountrysports.com . . . . The 110-foot *Keweenaw Star* (906-482-0884) offers 2 1/2-hour cruises of the Keweenaw Waterway from Dee Stadium in Houghton, usually west to McLain State Park, evenings at 7 for $15, or $31 for the Friday dinner cruise (reservations preferred). The most interesting scenery is right in Houghton and Hancock. The $25 Ojibwa Casino cruise ($5, reservations advised) passes interesting sandstone bluffs on the way to Baraga and includes $20 of casino chips. It leaves Sunday afternoon and Tuesday evening. . . .**Jim Rooks' Keweenaw Bear Track Tours** in Copper Harbor gives a variety of short eco-tours and geology tours and rents canoes. (906) 289-4813. **Keweenaw Adventure Company** in Copper Harbor **rents kayaks** and **mountain bikes** and leads **kayak tours** to rugged, roadless areas between Copper Harbor and Keweenaw Point. This extremely scenic, little-known area is the geological mirror of Isle Royale, with sea stacks and 600' cliffs. Keweenaw Adventure also leads area mountain bike tours. Call (906) 289-4303, visit www.keweenawadventure.com, or stop by the shop in downtown Copper Harbor. . . . In downtown Houghton, **Down Wind Sports** at 303 Shelden Avenue rents cross-country skis, kayaks, and snowshoes. (906) 482-2500; www.downwindsports.com . . . . Rick Oikarinen at **Cross Country Sports** in Calumet, a leader in area bicycling and cross-country skiing, rents cross-country skis and snowshoes. Call (906) 337-4520. www.crosscountrysports.com

EVENTS HIGHLIGHTS: Consult the tourism offices' websites for more complete events listings or call for details. Often more details are in this book, too, in the places where events occur. . . . Varied Thursday-evening **summer concerts at L'Anse's waterfront park** end in mid August with a White Water concert. . . . The **Aura Jamboree** — traditional-flavored acoustic music — is the third Saturday of July. . . . The **Keweenaw Bay Indian Community's powwow** is on the first weekend of August. . . . **Chassell's** big event is the **Strawberry Festival** on the second weekend of July. . . . Michigan Tech in Houghton has events throughout the school year; visit www.mtu.edu for its calendar. The **Rozsa Center for the Performing Arts** box office is (906) 487-3200. **Ice hockey** is hugely important. The **Parade of Nations** in late September is a fun international event with food from many countries and participation from Tech's sizable international community. . . . **Finlandia University** in Hancock hosts occasional music groups from Finland. Call North Wind Books, 906-487-7217 or try visiting www.finlandia.edu. . . . The **Fourth of July** is a big homecoming event in **South Range** and **Lake Linden**. Fireworks over the harbor at **Copper Harbor** are in a spectacular natural setting. . . . The **Pine Mountain Music Festival** has expanded into much of June and July, with high-caliber classical and other music, including two **operas**, at Houghton's Rozsa Center and in the Calumet Opera House. Call (877-746-3999) or visit www.pmmf.org. . . . Rocks and minerals take center stage at the **Copper Country Rock and Mineral Club's Keweenaw Week**, formerly the Red Metal Retreat, in early August. See www.geo.mtu.edu/museum/. . . . **Art in the Garden**, the Copper Country Arts Council's big fundraiser on the last Saturday in July and the following Sunday, takes visitors to beautiful varied Copper Country gardens. The free-

wheeling **yard art** and **wildflower** component is fun and refreshing. . . .The historic **Calumet Theater** produces a historical play each summer and hosts many musical acts; call (906) 337-2610 or visit www.calumettheater.org. The village of **Calumet's** new **Heritage Days** with games, ethnic food, and tours, is the last weekend in June. . . **Laurium's Daniell Park** hosts varied music concerts on summer Thursdays at 7. . . . **Keweenaw Krayons Arts Alive** brings summer music and more to Mohawk, Eagle Harbor, and Copper Harbor. Visit www.keweenawkrayons.com or ask around locally. . . . Copper Harbor's excellent website, www.copperharbor.org, details its many special-interest events. Fort Wilkins bustles with the **Civil War encampment** on the first weekend of August.

HARBORS with transient dockage: The **L'Anse marina** has a few overnight slips but no harbormaster. In **Baraga** (906-353-9916; off season 906-353-6237; lat. 46° 46' 39" N, 88° 28' 48" W) with showers. **Upper Entry of Keweenaw Waterway** near McLain State Park: lat. 47° 14' 08" N, long. 88° 37' 50" W. **Lower Entry of Keweenaw Waterway** near Chassel: lat. 46° 57' 40" W. In Ripley/Hancock (906-482-6010; off-season 482-8307) with showers. In **downtown Houghton** (day-use only). In Eagle Harbor (906-289-4416; alt. 906-289-4215; lat 47° 27' 52" N, long. 88° 09' 33" W) with showers. In **Copper Harbor** (906-289-4966; alt. 906-289-4215; lat. 47° 28' 42" N, long. 87° 51' 50" W) with showers, picnic tables. In **Lac La Belle** (906-289-4215; lat. 47° 22' 30" N, long. 87° 57' 40" W). On **Grand Traverse Bay** of the Keweenaw's south shore (twp. phone 906-296-8721; lat. 47° 11' 18" N, long. 88° 14' 00" W).

PICNIC PROVISIONS and PLACES: Pat's Foods on U.S. 41 in **L'Anse** is a competent supermarket. Copper Country's big supermarkets, all with good produce sections, are Festival Foods and Econo Foods on the M-26 strip in **Houghton**, Pat's Food off U.S. 41 on **Hancock's Quincy Hill**, another Pat's in **Calumet** on the Sixth Street Extension just west of U.S. 41, and the Econo Foods on M-26 between **Lake Linden** and Hubbell. In Keweenaw County the only grocery with fresh meat and much produce is the **Mohawk Superette** on U.S. 41. . Truly gourmet takeout fare is available in **Houghton** at Marie's Deli (see Houghton Restaurants) and in **Hancock** at the Keweenaw Co-op with its famous deli with meats, cheeses, and salads, and its outstanding beer and wine selection. Excellent bread and sandwiches are at The Bakery (see Houghton Restaurants. . . . Any area supermarket has a good selection of smoked fish and pretty good fresh fish, too. Fresh whitefish or lake trout is easy to grill. **Specialty fish markets in Hancock** are **Peterson's** (482-2343), easy to find on U.S. 41 on Quincy

Hill, and **Lake Superior Fisheries** (482-2710) by the hospital off M-203 on the way to McLain State Park, half a mile west of the intersection with U.S. 41. **Jamsen's Fish Market** in **Copper Harbor** (seasonal) is by the Isle Royale ferry dock.

◆ The **L'Anse waterfront park** downtown has it all: picnic area, great view, play equipment, and path to nearby waterfalls.

◆ Alongside the **Baraga County Historical Museum** on U.S. 41 are picnic tables with a fine view of Keweenaw Bay.

◆ A few miles north just off U.S. 41 at **Assinins**, plans for Father Baraga's Historical Mission and Native Genealogical Center include a picnic area. It's a special place with a striking view. There's already a pretty walk through the woods to the ancestral Ojibwa cemetery.

◆ Just north of the **Community of Keweenaw Bay**, the Michigan Department of Transportation Center **roadside park** by U.S. 41 has another beautiful bay view.

◆ **Chassell's Centennial Park** off U.S. 41 also has a kids' garden.

◆ **Houghton-Hancock's nicest picnic area** is the **waterfront park** just west of downtown along the Portage Waterway. Look for the turn along the water where M-26 turns and begins to go up the hill. Here are picnic tables, a swimming beach, and a most elaborate chutes-and-ladders playground.

◆ **McLain State Park** west of **Hancock** on M-203 has a beautiful picnic area in a natural setting, with a grand view of the setting sun over Lake Superior.

◆ **Lake Linden's waterfront park** and picnic area lacks shade but offers swimming and a playground.

◆ Off U.S. 41 at **Phoenix** a picnic table is by the little church.

◆ In **Eagle Harbor**, a most scenic picnic area is on a sunny, rocky promontory next to the **Eagle River Lighthouse**.

◆ **M-26** between Eagle Harbor and Copper Harbor has two of the most charming picnic spots anywhere — masterpieces of 1930s picturesque rustic design, Civilian Conservation Corps projects on especially beautiful stretches of rocky shore. **Esrey Park** comes first, five or six miles east of Eagle Harbor. A ways farther, just three miles west of Copper Harbor, is **Hebard Park.** These M-DOT parks also have grills.

◆ Just east of **Copper Harbor**, part of Fort Wilkins State Park, is a delightful **picnic area** where **Fanny Hooe Creek** enters the harbor, opposite the Copper Harbor Lighthouse.

◆ Finally, coming down the steep hill from U.S. 41 to Lac La Belle, turn right at the lake and in half a mile you'll see **Haven Falls** to your right. Here Haven Park has picnic tables and grills.

The Keweenaw chapter begins with places in the southern parts of Baraga and Houghton counties and then moves to L'Anse and Baraga, Chassell, South Range, Freda, and Twin Lakes. Houghton, Calumet, Copper Harbor, and other well-known Keweenaw places come later.

Covington

Covington itself is a small place in an area of **Finnish farms** and **dairying**. Its Lutheran church has a **handsome polygonal belfry**. Local people who owned a big sawmill in lumbering days built the large family home and farm

that's now the Covington Rest Home, on the north side of M-28.

If you want to **see a moose**, consider making this out-of-the-way trip. Go along M-28 to Covington, then drive 8 1/2 miles south along U.S. 141 until you get to Tracey Creek. (The creek crosses the highway about two miles north of the Iron County line.)

Each year, when the DNR sends a helicopter out to locate moose before netting, collaring, and tagging them, huge numbers of moose are seen in the wetlands along Tracey Creek east of U.S. 141. Be prepared to go back in on rough logging roads, and take a compass! Plan

your trip for the few hours after dawn or before dusk.

Sidnaw (pop. 100)

Sidnaw (pronounced "Sid NAH"), 20 miles southwest of L'Anse as the crow flies, boomed from logging in the 1890s. Now it has become mostly a retirement town. At the moment its remaining businesses are a convenience store/gas station and a bar. They're busy — and noisy — with snowmobilers in winter because Sidnaw is on the **U.P.'s main east-west snowmobile trail**, and one of the few places to gas up in a rather remote area.

Sturgeon River Gorge, Sturgeon Falls & Silver Mountain

Gorges and canyons up to 300 feet deep — the **deepest valley in Michigan** — have been formed by the Sturgeon and Little Silver rivers as they flow north to Keweenaw Bay. This rugged, remote **Ottawa National Forest** land is along the Baraga-Houghton county line between M-28 at Sidnaw and M-38 at Nisula and Alston. Here **over 14,000 acres** along the Sturgeon river and west of it, largely **old-growth red and white pine and hemlock**, have been designated the **Sturgeon River Gorge Wilderness Area** by the federal government. The Sturgeon here is part of the National Wild and Scenic River system. At the north end of the gorge, south of Silver Mountain, is an impoundment formed by Prickett Dam, owned by Wisconsin Electric Power. There's enough sugar maple, birch, and other broadleaf trees to make for **spectacular fall color**, as seen from **scenic overlooks** at the gorge, from the very steep and difficult 3/4 mile **trail to Sturgeon Falls**, or from nearby **Silver Mountain**.

Sturgeon River Gorge and Falls are among **Michigan's most memorable and remote scenic attractions**. A visit is at least a half-day outing, not to be rushed. bringing a sack lunch is a good idea. Don't undertake this trip without taking several things into consideration. First, although nice big brown Forest Service signs announce the turnoffs from the state highways, once you set off on the twisting, narrow gravel interior roads, you can't depend on signage because of vandalism. So pay attention to the road's twists and turns on a map. The *DeLorme Michigan Atlas* map works fine. Active logging is over for now. Sight lines aren't the greatest, so drive slowly enough that you'll have time to stop if you suddenly see another vehicle heading toward you. Also, you'll see some really ugly clear cuts from recent logging. (National forests are managed for multiple uses that include logging as well as recreation, hunting, and fishing.) Even without interruptions, the drive to the trailhead down to Sturgeon Falls is over 30 minutes. You may well want to stop a few times, partly to observe the river in its changing guises, and partly to keep from getting carsick.

Forest highways 2200 and 2270, on the high rim east of the Sturgeon River Gorge, provide access to parts of the gorge by vehicle and foot. One high overlook is even wheelchair-accessible. The designated wilderness area itself is by definition without roads and trails.

Topographical maps and a compass or GPS system are recommended for backcountry adventures.

Here are highlights and notes for the Sturgeon River Gorge area, from south (M-28) to north.

◆ Take FR 2200 north from Sidnaw. A little over two miles north of M-28, FR 2200 forks east. Be sure you make this turn. The sign currently is missing.

◆ Sturgeon River Campground. Here the river is a **pretty, rocky stream** in a fairly broad valley with a **ferny floor**. Also see Sidnaw camping. 6 miles north of M-28.

◆ **Pullover** with warnings and tips for prospective canoeists and interpretive signs about the gorge. The **river is quite pretty** at this logical put-in place for canoes. However, water volume can suddenly increase to over ten-thousand times what it is at low-flow levels. Though the river here is rated intermediate in terms of skill levels, it soon becomes difficult for the half mile before the falls, suitable only for canoeists with excellent whitewater skills. "Flattened canoes and lost equipment is regularly recovered from the banks," warns the sign. *7 miles north of M-28 on FR 2200.*

◆ **BEAR'S DEN Scenic Overlook**. A short drive leads to a **favorite beauty spot**, recently redeveloped by the Forest Service. Here you are very high up on a

The story behind the Sturgeon River canyon

As written on a Forest Service sign: "From here to Lake Superior the Sturgeon River flows over bedrock of ancient slate, sandstones, and basalt [of volcanic origin]. Sturgeon Falls is formed where the river flows over an erosion-resistant ridge of basalt. Above bedrock are thick deposits of glacial outwash, silt and sand carried as the last continental glacier around 10,000 years ago. The top of this outwash forms the nearby Baraga Plains. Much of the Sturgeon River Gorge was cut by the Sturgeon River over many thousands of years since the glacier left.

"Sturgeon River Gorge is a place of constant change. Floodwaters erode away the bases of high sand banks, causing them to collapse and form bare sand bluffs up to 250 feet high. Lowering water levels have left easily visible river terraces [in places]. Periodically the river will change its course, leaving castoff meanders with horseshoe-shaped oxbow lakes."

Sturgeon River fishing

Brook trout, brown trout, and rainbow trout spawn above Sturgeon Falls. Below the falls are smallmouth bass, walleye, and northern pike.

steep bank, looking down and out across the Sturgeon River Gorge onto a sea of green tree tops. A wood cross and plastic flowers are a memorial to a kayaker who perished in the river below here. A subtle gravel path from the north side of the parking area is a short, wheelchair-accessible trail to the overlook. *About 11 miles north of M-28 on FR 2200.*

◆ **Trailhead to STURGEON FALLS**. Stay straight (northwest at this point) where Forest Road 2200 makes a sharp right. You will now be on Forest Road 2270. Go .6 miles to the parking area on the right. The trailhead is on the left. This is the very difficult but **spectacular trail** down to the falls 3/4 of a mile — and back up. Descending, hikers first look down on treetops, then see the first falls, a short drop where the river is spread out. Downstream a short way, the river is forced to cut a narrow gorge. The waterfall is on Wisconsin Electric Power land, open to the public through the Commercial Forest Reserve Act.

◆ **SILVER MOUNTAIN**, a **splendid mountaintop lookout**, is reached by a trail that's mostly stairs. The parking area is off FR 2270, four miles northwest of the Sturgeon Falls trailhead. The vista looks across old-growth hardwood forests; a fire tower used to stand on the summit. The national forest doesn't publicize the lookout because it's actually on land owned by Wisconsin Electric Power and open to the public under the Forest Reserve Act. The land is managed in cooperation with the USDA with wilderness ethics in mind.

◆ About a mile north of Silver Mountain, stay on FR 2270. (Another road intersects on the left.) FR 2270 goes northeast for about five miles before joining Prickett Dam Road. It goes north two miles to M-38.

For an established rustic campground, see below. The **North Country Trail** parallels the Sturgeon River Gorge with a short connector to Sturgeon Falls. Excellent notes and photos are on the Western U.P. Peter Wolfe Chapter web site, www.northcountrytrail.org/pwf/

An **alternate route from the north** and M-38: about 9 miles west of Baraga or 3 miles east of Alston, turn south on

Prickett Dam Road (clearly marked). Proceed southwest around Prickett Lake on FR 2270 to Silver Mountain and, 4 miles beyond it, to Sturgeon River Gorge. *The gorge is in the national forest's Kenton Ranger District, (906) 852-3500.* ♿: Bear's Den trail. A few roadside pullovers. See above.

SIDNAW AREA CAMPING

STURGEON RIVER Campground/ Ottawa National Forest
(906) 852-3501. TTY: (906) 852-3618
www.fs.us.fed.us/r9/ottawa

This is the only developed campground near the Sturgeon River Wilderness Area on the way to the Sturgeon River Gorge (see above). Most of the nine rustic, non-reservable campsites have excellent locations, flat and private, along the Sturgeon River in an flat area of young trees. The campground may fill on July 4 and on nice summer weekends, but on a midweek visit in early August it was practically empty. Trailers over 14' aren't recommended here because of difficulties caused by the curving access road. *Directions: 6 miles north from M-28 on Pequet Lake Rd./FH 2200. Open from mid May thru Nov. $6/night.* **H.A.**: call.

NORWAY LAKE Campground/ Ottawa National Forest
(906) 352-3501. TTY: (906) 852-3618.

Travelers heading to or from the Porkies on M-28 might find this **pleasant, 28-site rustic campground** (no showers, vault toilets) handy. Space is usually available, though it fills on July 4 and occasional nice summer weekends. Norway Lake is a very small lake with a beach and boat launch. It is a destination family campground far **away from the sounds of civilization**. The **Deer Marsh Interpretive Trail** makes a three-mile loop from the campground, explaining about wildlife and wetlands along the way. Some of it is boardwalk. Wheelchairs can use it with some assistance if it's not too soft and wet. The pavilion with fireplace is used for family reunions. The shady campground can handle larger RVs. Not reservable. *8 miles south of Sidnaw. On a map, it's where Houghton, Baraga, and Iron counties come together. Go 6 miles on Sidnaw South Rd., turn east on Norway Lake Rd. $7-$9. Open from mid May thru Nov.* **H.A.**: call.

Kenton

In 1889, when the Duluth, South Shore, and Atlantic came through this area, the white pine was cut. Farming followed logging. Today Kenton consists of two bars, a store, and a trim Forest Service office on the north side of M-28.

KENTON CAMPING

TEPEE LAKE Campground/Ottawa National Forest
(906) 352-3501. TTY: (906) 852-3618.

This is another good family campground on a small lake south of M-28, midway between the Porkies and Marquette. Just don't go until early July, when the bugs are largely gone. **17 shady rustic sites** (no showers, vault toilets) are near a **sandy beach** and boat launch. Not reservable. It seldom fills except for holiday weekends. *7 miles south of Kenton on FH 16 (a paved road), then 1 mile east to campground. (906) 352-3501. TTY: (906) 852-3618. $7. Open from mid May thru Nov.* **H.A.**: call

Trout Creek (est.. pop. 480)

Thick stands of white oak growing in the sandy soil here once made Trout Creek a bustling lumber town. But those days are long past. When the tavern burned down a few years ago, it relocated to Bond Falls Flowage south of town, where there was more potential business. Trout Creek today does have a very good little restaurant and a quaint grocery. It makes for a pleasant stop for motorists between Ironwood or Duluth and Marquette.

The village core, first settled in 1888, is a few blocks north of M-28, along the one-time Duluth, South Shore & Atlantic tracks just inside Ontonagon County. The **White Door General Store** has a **vintage interior**. Hawaiian décor reflects the favorite vacation spot of the grocery's owners. Like the restaurant next door, the grocery is both community service and business. If it's Saturday morning or Tuesday afternoon, you can take a look at the **little museum** inside the Hazel Sliger Memorial Library just north of the tracks. Its displays revolve around the railroad and logging. Or you could see if Shirley Zimmer would let you in; she's at 852-3326.

TROUT CREEK RESTAURANT
The **LITTLE OLD SCHOOLHOUSE** restaurant, cheerful and cozy, was started by four retirees from Illinois who felt that Trout Creek needed a gathering place with good food. They proceeded to renovate the former schoolhouse and create just such a place, where the food really is good, and made on the premis-

es, too. It's also a **bakery** that produces bread, cakes, cookies, and **pies**, currently $1.75 a slice. The menu consists largely of soup and sandwiches, salads, lunch specials, and breakfasts like the $4.75 A+ (eggs with onions, green peppers, and cheese in addition to bacon, sausage, or ham). *Turn north at the Trout Creek "exit." Restaurant is before the tracks, on the east side of the road. 852-3620. Open daily except Tuesday from 8 a.m. to 6 p.m.* ♿

Alberta

This **picture-perfect sawmill and village** were built in 1935 as part of Henry Ford's idealistic (and expensive) village industries concept. Ford wanted to revitalize the rural life his own automobiles and huge assembly plants had done so much to disrupt. Of some two dozen village industries, this model village is the only one in which the entire village was built from scratch. Ford chose the location not just for its proximity to lots of hardwoods and the big Ford planing mill and dry kilns at L'Anse, but for its visibility, right on U.S. 41, the main route from Marquette or Iron Mountain to L'Anse and Houghton.

To earn a living, Ford employees in Alberta were to farm as well as work in the village sawmill. The elderly Ford had the resources to turn his dreams into first-rate reality. When he built Alberta in the wilderness, he installed a new water and sewage system, sidewalks, lighted boulevards, a church, a school, and a fire department. Explains the 1941 WPA guide to Michigan, "The 12 houses are set in a horseshoe formation opening on the main road. Surrounded by a virgin hardwood forest [owned by Ford], unbroken for miles by any sign of settlement, the new homes, neat streets, and well-kept lawns have on first sight an appearance of unreality."

Canyon Falls Roadside Park & Canyon Falls

It's about a mile walk from the pleasant roadside park, with its picnic tables, grills, and restrooms, to the **Upper Falls** of the Sturgeon River. The trail takes about a quarter mile to get to the river, then follows it downstream, first past rapids and little drops, until the stream drops directly into the canyon. That's Canyon Falls. When the trail seems to stop at a boulder, go around the huge rock and pick up the path again, follow-

immigrant urban proletariat he had attracted and created. His creative mind set to transplanting **America's self-reliant rural roots** into the **industrial age** he had done so much to develop. The **Greenfield Village** museum in Dearborn was one such result of Henry Ford's thinking; his money-draining **village industry concept** was another. Most village industries were in old southern Michigan spots (Dundee, Tecumseh, Manchester, Northville, Milford, Plymouth, and many more), tucked away on dam sites where they could generate their own power. (Ford was enthralled with the notion of having self-sufficient power sources.)

Alberta was consciously sited to be a showplace. By 1923 E. G. Kingsford, the Iron Mountain Ford dealer who was married to Henry Ford's cousin, had purchased for Ford Motor 400,000 acres of timber land in Baraga, Marquette, Iron, and Dickinson counties. Ford came to own the mill and village of Big Bay; a hydroelectric plant, sawmill/chemical processing plant, and iron mine at Iron Mountain/Kingsford; and sawmills at Munising, Sidnaw, L'Anse, and Pequaming.

Motoring along U.S. 41 between his summer home near Big Bay and his L'Anse facilities, Ford is said to have stopped his driver here by Plumbago Creek and exclaimed how this would be a fine spot for a mill pond and factory. "The mill and houses were in full view of passing motorists, demonstrating how a lumber mill operation should be managed," wrote Ford historian and relative Ford R. Bryan in *Beyond the Model T: The Other Ventures of Henry Ford.* "Signs along

the road for miles made it clear that the village and surrounding forests were the property of Ford Motor Company. Visitors were welcome to picnic on the neatly mowed grounds beside the mill pond and visit the immaculately clean mill in operation." On a few occasions Henry Ford himself greeted visitors. There's still a picnic area and nature trail by the mill pond, on the east side of the highway. In summer, 2000, it was a bit overgrown and neglected.

Wood was used for Ford bodies until 1937, when Ford switched to steel. Ford station wagons or "woodies" continued to have wood bodies and sides. Ford's U.P. lumber operations were just one part of Henry Ford's program to acquire his own supplies of raw material, from iron and coal to timber and rubber. He revived one mine in Michigamme and started a new one. "On these ventures it is certain Ford wanted his source of supply primarily for reliability rather than for profit," Bryan wrote.

Band saw, log carriage, edger, trimmer are all in place — everything except the engines, which are at Henry Ford Museum complex in Dearborn. It's all in tip-top shape, meticulously painted, just the way Henry Ford expected all his far-flung properties to be maintained.

The Alberta tour will appeal to people interested in mechanical technology, lumber, and Henry Ford's idiosyncratic approach to industry and social planning. A bolt chain lifts sample logs from the "hot pond," here represented by sand. It was a pond of heated water six feet deep where ice and dirt could be cleaned off logs throughout the winter. Large window areas allow for lots of nat-

From the roadside park by U.S. 41, follow the path among fragrant pines along the high bank of a wild canyon and you'll soon reach Canyon Falls.

ing the high bank along a dramatic, wild canyon where fragrant pines and balsam grow out of mossy stone walls. Just before the Upper Falls, the stream slides over a smooth trough it has made in the rock before it splits and drops in several extended cascades.

The park is on the west side of U.S. 41, 1 1/2 miles south of Alberta or about 23-24 miles west of Michigamme

Alberta Village Museum/ Ford Historic Sawmill

Summer visitors can now take a half-hour tour of Henry Ford's model sawmill and village. The 30-minute tour includes not only the sawmill and its intact machinery, but the grounds of the 12-house wilderness village. Its Cape Cod houses have charming individual details, quite unlike typical Upper Peninsula company housing for workers. Sawmill workers were required to raise much of their food on garden plots, two acres a family.

Alberta was part of Henry Ford's idealistic "village industries" of rural factories where workers could live close to the land — "one foot in industry, one foot in the land" — in contrast to the hundred thousand workers at Ford's giant Rouge complex in Dearborn. When the Rouge was finished, Ford quickly soured on the

Energetic, restless, idealistic, controlling, Henry Ford owned model factories in remote places, from the Amazon to several U.P. towns. His Alberta village and sawmill south of L'Anse is now open to the public. The tour conveys Ford's intense interest in social planning. Aldous Huxley picked up on Ford's impact and thinking and gave it a hedonistic spin when he made Fordism the central religion of the controlled mass society in his futuristic novel of 1948, *Brave New World.*

ural light into the factory. Ford corporate historian Bob Kreipke has prepared excellent signs, photos, and descriptions of each stage of sawing and milling wood. His **video** is quite interesting. The **nifty gift shop** has inexpensive scale models of woodies, relevant books including wildlife (Henry Ford loved birds), and bird's eye maple and other wood products, often made by Alberta's last sawyer, who sometimes gives tours.

When Henry Ford II took over from his senile grandfather, he quickly closed old Henry's beloved village industries. In 1954 Ford Motor gave the Alberta facility to Michigan Technological University. Tech's School of Forestry and Wood Products continues to use its **Ford Forestry Cente**r and 4,000-acre forest as a teaching and research facility with overnight housing. Other groups can rent it, too. Call (906) 524-6181.

On U.S. 41 nine miles south of L'Anse and five miles north of the U.S. 141/M-28 turnoff. (906) 524-7900. Open for tours from June thru color season. In July & August open daily 9-3. Otherwise closed Tues & Wed. Group tours at other times by appointment. $3/adult, $2/students. ♿: except for mill's second floor

L'Anse (pop. 2,107)

At the head of 30-mile-long Keweenaw Bay, this unassuming village and county seat is one of Michigan's very old European settlements. In 1660 a French Jesuit priest started an Indian mission here. L'Anse, pronounced "LAHNce," is French for "the bay." The settlement later became a trading post and, in 1871, a station on the railroad line between Houghton and Marquette. With the railroad, the port, and trees to be logged in most directions, L'Anse boomed briefly in the 1870s before the national economy went into a tailspin.

Freighters can sometimes still be seen up the bay from L'Anse. They have not come to deliver cargo, for L'Anse is no longer a commercial port. Instead they arrive seeking refuge from the fierce Lake Superior storms of early spring and late fall. L'Anse's harbor filled in over time but was dredged for the recent **municipal marina**, which can handle the biggest Lake Superior pleasure boats, up to 40'. Thanks to ongoing improvements including a lighted harborfront walkway and path to the Falls River Falls, the waterfront is again an active community focus.

Northeast of L'Anse, cottages line much of the Lake Superior shore along the Abbaye Peninsula and Huron Bay,

---

Waterfalls near L'Anse & Skanee
Waterfalls — over 20 of them, mostly on private land — are common in the area where the Silver, Slate, and Huron rivers descend from the Huron Mountain highlands east of L'Anse and Skanee. A **map** to Baraga County's most worthwhile waterfalls is available from the tourist bureau at Broad and U.S. 41 in L'Anse (906-524-7444). A series of outstanding waterfalls are right in town along the Falls River.

---

with old farms nearby. But just three or so miles to the east begin the ancient **Huron Mountains, once higher than the Rockies**, now worn down. It is the highest land in Michigan. The ground rises steadily, if undramatically, and is heavily wooded. East of L'Anse and Skanee are **many beautiful forest waterfalls**, some quite remote. But the most beautiful waterfalls of all are right in L'Anse, upstream from the big BPB Celotex ceiling tile plant and within a mile of U.S. 41. Just west of the plant, biting into the red rock bluffs, is an old **sandstone quarry** that yielded Jacobsville sandstone, also known as brownstone, a favorite building material for late 19th-century Romanesque Revival and Renaissance Revival architecture.

L'Anse is located in between two historic centers of the U.P.'s economy, Keweenaw's famous Copper Country and the rich iron ranges to the south and east. The village has been something of a backwater. Some residents here commute to work in the Tilden and Empire mines 60 miles to the southeast.

The maximum-security 589-inmate prison, built on Wadaga Road in Baraga in 1993, has created a small building boom to house some of its 502 employees. On the site of a former Ford sawmill, where the Falls River empties into Keweenaw Bay, is BPB Celotex, L'Anse's largest employer. The plant, purchased in 2000 by the British firm BPB, started three decades ago. The plant's 200 workers make ceiling tile for houses, now using mineral wool instead of wood pulp.

L'Anse and Baraga are surrounded by **Finnish farm country**, and people of Finnish ancestry outnumber all others. French, Ojibwa, and other Catholics are numerous, too, and the **impressive Sacred Heart Church** on the Sixth Street hill going into town is a memorable landmark. Many Finns have intermarried with Ojibwa members of the **Keweenaw Bay Indian Community**,

---

creating new generations of so-called **"Finndians"** who may have blond hair or blue eyes. It's not such an improbable combination, considering how in these parts both groups share a closeness to the land and love of fishing, hunting, and the woods. Baraga and L'Anse schools may be unique in providing enrichment classes in both Ojibwa and Finnish. Residents with French blood are almost as common as the Finns.

Scattered tribal lands extend from around tribal headquarters in Baraga to land around the old Ojibwa community of Zeba, on the shore road halfway from L'Anse to Pequaming to the north.

Front Street Park

The L'Anse waterfront enjoys a **grand view across Keweenaw Bay** to Baraga and beyond. No longer an active port, today it has been all spiffed up by the Downtown Development Authority with a combination of state grants and tax-increment financing.

Everybody appreciates the way the park has transformed drab city property used for parking. It now has lots of attractive features for visitors: a **playground**, restrooms, a **1,500-foot lighted walkway**, and a new marina. Most every kind of Great Lakes fish, including salmon and perch, can be caught from the **fishing pier** and breakwall. Everything's wheelchair-accessible, and downtown is just a block away. **Summer concerts**, from hymns to rock, are held Thursdays at the bandshell from early July into late August. It's become a tradition for the extremely popular traditional music group Whitewater to close out the season. (See Amasa in the Menominee Range chapter for more on this family foursome, two environmental scientists and their children.) A **paved path** goes east along the bay for about a half mile. At the park's west end a nature trail curves south along the Falls River alongside a striking series of **easy-to-reach waterfalls** (see below). For weary highway travelers, the park and its picnic tables offer a relaxing rest stop. Consider a picnic with subs from Subway or a takeout sandwich or salad from a downtown restaurant.

From U.S. 41, head down Broad Street at the main Y. Proceed a block past the Main Street business area to the park. ♿

Falls River waterfalls

These **wonderful, complex waterfalls** in a piney forest are not overrun with visitors, and they aren't impossibly difficult

to reach, either — though the river tumbles down a sizable hill the entire way. The eight falls are not far from U.S. 41, either within L'Anse or just outside it. The Penroses, authors of the highly recommended *Guide to 199 Michigan Waterfalls*, write, "If we had to recommend just one river to visit in all of Michigan, this would be it." For maps to the upper falls, get their book, or stop at the tourist bureau (see above).

From U.S. 41 outside L'Anse, take Broad St. into town down the hill. At the blinker light on Main St., go left. Do not cross the river. Park by the river next to the Celotex plant in the new lot connected with the waterfront park. The trail begins between the river and the plant's chain link fence and goes upstream. &: from parking area to first falls.

Indian Country Sports

Owner Steve Koski, avid hunter, fisherman, and outdoorsman, son of one of the area's last families of commercial fishermen, is a dedicated booster of all that his native Baragaland has to offer. First he developed and expanded his harborfront outdoors store into a complete outdoors destination for locals and visitors alike. Steve and his wife, Anne, built the expanded new store largely themselves, with friends' help. It deals with archery, hunting, **fishing**, **camping** and tents, skating, canoes, kayaks, **cross-country skiing**, and snowshoeing, and never in a trivial way. Indian Country Sports is an excellent place to stop for **detailed information about the area's outdoor recreation opportunities**, plus licenses, bait, nautical charts, plat books — everything but USGS maps. If it's Saturday and the tourism office is closed, this is the place for info on reaching the **high point at Mount Arvon**, on cross-country skiing on the attractive Pinery Lakes Trails, and on scenic highlights on the improved Big Bay Road through the rugged highlands of Huron Mountains and the Yellow Dog Plains.

After finishing the store, the Koskis went about creating a new landmark for the L'Anse harbor — a **full-scale, working lighthouse**. The tower and beacon rises 44 feet above street level. The lighthouse, recognized by the Coast Guard as a private aid to navigation, has become a destination for lighthouse fans. The light came on in March, 1997. Powered by diesel, gas, electricity, or solar, it's **visible for five miles**, recognized by its pattern of one second on, 2 1/2 seconds off. Steve Koski, a natural marketer, is con-

tinuing his efforts to put L'Anse on the map and foster improvements that take advantage of its natural beauty. (Not surprisingly he majored in marketing at Northern Michigan University.) He's an active member of the Downtown Development Authority, responsible for the new waterfront park, marina, and dock. *17 S. Front at Baraga, at the harbor and a block west of Broad Street (the street that leads down the hill from U.S. 41 to downtown L'Anse). (906) 524-6518. www.indiancountrysports.com Open year-round. Mon-Sat 8 a.m. to 5 p.m., Fri to 6.* &

Shrine of the Snowshoe Priest

This **7-foot bronze statue** celebrates a remarkable Catholic priest, one whose kindness and good works are so renowned that his church may some day declare him a saint. Between 1831 and 1843 Frederic Baraga founded missions near Grand Rapids, at L'Arbre Croche near Harbor Springs, at Sault Ste. Marie, Manistique, La Pointe in the Apostle Islands, and here just north of Baraga. Sent to the north woods by an Austrian missionary society, Baraga found his life's work in ministering to the needs of the Ojibwa people, whether or not they converted to Catholicism. He thought nothing of walking many miles on snowshoes to keep in touch with distant communities. He completed the **Ojibwa-English grammar and dictionary still used today** and translated and wrote many books in Ojibwa. His work to help Indians get title to their land made him unpopular among government Indian agents, including Michigan state booster Henry Schoolcraft. Fur traders didn't like Baraga either, because of his active support for Indian temperance. (Traders relied on alcohol as a trade good and negotiating tool.)

The Bishop Baraga Association erected this memorial on a hill overlooking Keweenaw Bay. Perched on a little cloud at the intersection of **five leaping arches** (one for each mission he founded), the unsmiling statue of Baraga looks out across Keweenaw Bay. Illuminated at night, it can be glimpsed from U.S. 41. The statue is a cold depiction of a warm, deeply caring person, some of Baraga's admirers feel. When Baraga's likeness was made, he couldn't smile — he had had a stroke. A tour with Elizabeth Delene, the Baraga Association's historian/archivist in Marquertte, can offer a fuller look at the life and work of the man once celebrated in Paris as a famous Indian missionary and still championed in his native

Slovenia and in Great Lakes Slovenian communities. Call (906) 227-9117). The association's chief purpose is research to find evidence of the two documented miracles necessary for sainthood in the Roman Catholic Church.

In a blend of altruism and self-interest, the original owners of the Shrine gift and pasty shop here donated the two acres on which the landscaped shrine sits. The gift shop is a homey, busy place, patronized by visitors and local people including a fair number of Native American ancestry. It has a good selection of religious medals, statues, and books, and also Ojibwa books and music.

The road up to the shrine is on the south side of U.S. 41 a mile west of the turnoff to downtown L'Anse. The outdoor shrine is never closed. For gift shop/restaurant hours, look under L'Anse restaurants. Free admission. &

James Oliver Curwood Park

The hemlocks and pines on the **bluff overlooking Keweenaw Bay** create a serene setting for this well-maintained L'Anse Township park. The view can be enjoyed from a **pleasant picnic area** near swinging benches and a playground. Small shelters for anyone to use have grills. The gated drive down the hill leads to Pequaming Road; walk across it to a rocky beach. The hemlocks' dense shade makes the forest here so clear of underbrush that formal trails aren't needed for a walk in the woods. The modern campground is a real find.

Look for entrance on west side of Skanee Rd. (the continuation of Main St.) 2 miles northeast of downtown L'Anse. 524-6985. Open mid-May to mid-Oct. &: call.

Mount Arvon

Generations of Michigan schoolchildren learned that **Michigan's highest point**, here in the Huron Mountains, was **Mount Curwood**, elevation 1,978.24 feet above sea level. It was named after James Oliver Curwood, the best-selling outdoor adventure writer of the 1920s and 1930s, who had a wilderness retreat in the vicinity. Then, in 1982, a U.S. Geological Survey team made new measurements and discovered that nearby **Mount Arvon** was actually **higher by nearly a foot**.

Neither high point in this heavily forested area offers any kind of panoramic view, though the scenery in this rugged area is enjoyable and there are a few views along the way. Views don't matter to members of the nation-wide **Highpointers' Club**, who aim to visit the highest point of every state. The Baraga County tourism office gives out a brochure and map to Mount Arvon. It's a **complicated route to the top** over old logging roads; the route changes with logging activities in the area. The tourism staff has thoughtfully installed a **mailbox at the top** where visitors can leave their impressions and stories of their ascent. The way to Mount Arvon may be impassable when it's muddy, and even snowmobiles will find the going tough if not impossible in winter.

L'Anse Restaurants

TK'S VILLAGE RESTAURANT is the locals' favorite spot to meet and eat. It's known for big breakfasts with toast of homemade bread, good chili, pasties (sold Tuesdays only), tuna sandwiches, and a full homestyle menu with daily specials. The price is right — as indicated by all the vehicles parked outside, winter and summer. *11 South Main downtown. To reach downtown from U.S. 41, turn onto Broad at the curve, go down the hill (northwest) to Main, then right. 524-5455 Open year-round. Mon-Sat 6 a.m. to 9 p.m., Sun 8-1.*

To the delight of travelers and local people alike, the **SHRINE GIFT & COFFEE SHOP** at the Shrine of the Snowshoe Priest has been revived and is now operated year-round. The **Shrine pasty** made famous by the original owners of the Shrine coffee shop, Pat and Myra Ellico, has been duplicated by current owners Judy Layle and Linda Garver. It wasn't an easy job, since there was no written recipe. But the Ellicos' last cook worked for a month with Judy and Linda to get it right. It's $3.50 with a side of slaw. Second only to the pasty in favor is the **"Indian taco"**: deep-fried Indian fry bread piled high with lettuce, onions, ground meat, and cheddar cheese.

The Shrine's menu goes way beyond that of a simple pasty shop to include homemade soups, chef salad, chili, sloppy joes, and a **hot meatloaf sandwich**. The **bakery** produces breads, muffins, cookies, and various **scones** (blueberry, nut, etc.). For some reason, scones are hugely popular in Wisconsin but virtually unknown in Michigan except for upscale enclaves. Being on the snowmobile trail enables the coffee shop to stay open year-round. "Each year is better," Judy says. *The road up to the shrine is on the south side of U.S. 41 a mile west of the turnoff to downtown L'Anse. 524-7021 Open year-round. From Mem. Day through color sea-son open daily at least from 10 a.m. to 6 p.m. In the off-season open 11-5, usually closed Wed & Thurs.*

At the **CANTEEN BAR & GRILL** you can sit at the bar, eat an excellent burger, and **look out at Keweenaw Bay**, thanks to a horizontal window behind the bar at this well-run, well-ventilated bar-restaurant. Its extensive menu includes baby-back ribs, Mexican specialties, salads, homemade soups, chili, and 1/3-pound burgers (around $3.50 with chips and pickle). *On the L'Anse waterfront at 9 Front Street, a block north of downtown 524-6211. Open Mon-Sat 7 a.m. to 2 a.m., Sun noon to closing.* Full bar

The **HILLTOP RESTAURANT** has been a favorite stopping place for motorists for years because of its **glazed donuts, famous cinnamon rolls** (really one-pound loaves of bread), and large portions of homestyle fare. It's a big, busy, spiffy place that's also very friendly. Non-diners are welcome to use the rest rooms. Construction workers stop by for **daily lunch specials**. Lunch specials (around $5) are things like taco salads, meatballs and mashed potatoes, sandwiches and fries. The extensive dinner menu ($8 to $12, served starting at lunchtime) includes fried chicken, meat loaf, steamed salmon, pasties, fajitas, and much more, all including potato plus soup and a big salad bar with fresh vegetables, pickled pollack, pasta salad, slaw and such, all made here. The salad bar alone is $6. **Weekend buffets** are at breakfast ($6) and from noon to 7. *On U.S. 41 a mile south of L'Anse. 524-7858.www.sweetroll.com From mid May thru mid Nov open daily 6 a.m.-8 p.m. Otherwise open daily 7 a.m. to 7 p.m.* Full bar

TONY'S STEAKHOUSE enjoys a big reputation for steaks (all are fresh cut just before serving), Italian food, and a good salad bar, in a fine dining setting with a separate lounge. Highlights include a filet mignon, fresh whitefish and lake trout, ribs, and crab legs. Dinners ($12 to $20) come with potato, soup and salad bar with tuna and four other salads, and garlic toast. For vegetarians, there's cheese ravioli and the salad bar ($7 alone). *On U.S. 41, 2 miles south of L'Anse. 524-9900. Open daily, 7 days a week, at 4 p.m. Kitchen closes at 10 p.m, Sunday at 9.* Full bar

L'Anse Lodgings

L'ANSE MOTEL & SUITES
(906) 524-7820; 800-800-6198 (reserv. only); www.discovermichigan.com — see

Baraga County

The **"Mackinac Look"** — flowery, fresh, romantically decorated, with a covered walkway with nouveau gingerbread trim and artificial flowers — has been effectively applied to this concrete-block motel from an earlier era. The two single-story buildings sit well back from the busy highway, behind some mature willows and spruces and some **picnic tables**. The 21 very pleasant drive-up units are newly decorated, with scrubbed pine furniture for a warm look. Rates for two in 2000: $40 and $46. Single-room suites ($56 for two) sleep up to 5 with a queen and double bed, sofa-sleeper microwaves and fridges. All rooms have phones, with free local calls, cable TV and free HBO. Close to Hilltop Restaurant. On snowmobile trail. Free casino shuttle service. *On U.S. 41, half a mile south of downtown L'Anse. Open year-round.*

: $2/extra person

HILLTOP MOTEL (906) 524-6321; 800-424-2548 (reserv. only); www.up.net/~hilltop/

Adjacent to the Hilltop Restaurant but under separate ownership, this single-story motel has 20 drive-up units with a mix of bed configurations. Two-person rates in 2000 were $37-$43. Newer and older furnishings included some shag carpet seen on a fall, 2000 visit. Basic amenities are up-to-date (direct-dial phones with free local calls; cable TV with ESPN, Disney, and free HBO, air-conditioning, no-smoking rooms available). On snowmobile trail. Credit cards not accepted after 11 p.m. check-in.

On U.S. 41 a mile south of downtown L'Anse. **H.A.**: call : $3/extra child; $5/extra adult : no

L'Anse Camping

JAMES OLIVER CURWOOD PARK
(906) 524-6985; not reservable

The modern campground in this **blufftop park overlooking Keweenaw Bay** is a real find. It's quiet, pretty, and shaded by pines and hemlocks. 30 sites ($10/ and $12/night) are rarely full. The services of a state park (showers, electricity, flush toilets, dump station, playground) are here without the crowds. It is very, very seldom full. *2 miles northeast of downtown L'Anse. Look for entrance on west side of Skanee Rd. (the continuation of Main St.) 2 miles northeast of downtown L'Anse. Open mid-May to mid-Oct.* **H.A.**: call.

Zeba

Zeba, halfway to Pequaming on the shoreline road northeast of L'Anse, was the site of **Father Baraga's first mission** in the area, built in 1831. The old mission churches are still there today — the Catholic church on the Pequaming Road and the Methodist church on the bluff above. In the nearby Ojibwa cemetery from the 1840s, **spirit houses** (tiny houses used instead of European-style cemetery markers) have been rebuilt and maintained. The cemetery is about a half-mile walk through the woods from the end of the Indian Cemetery Road off Skanee Road two miles outside L'Anse. It's also on the **Pinery Lakes Trail**, an attractive eight-mile series of cross-country ski loops groomed by the Baraga County Tourist & Recreation Association

Pequaming

In the 1870s Englishman Charles Hebard built a town on this distinctive **mushroom-shaped peninsula**, called a tombolo, jutting out into Keweenaw Bay. (Water currents can form a tombolo by joining an island to the mainland with a sandbar that enlarges.) The community Hebard created was unique in the U.P.— a **version of an English village**, complete with oak-shaded streets, board sidewalks, wide lawns with shingled homes, and a Gothic-style church.

Today it takes a practiced eye to discover vestiges of Hebard's Pequaming. Hebard and his son built and operated a Pequaming sawmill and an even larger one in L'Anse, where Celotex is today. In 1913 Hebard also built for himself a large, **secluded nine-bedroom bungalow on Keweenaw Bay**. Eleven years later **Henry Ford** bought the entire Pequaming peninsula; remodeled the town; and had the sawmill provide flooring for Ford floorboards, truck boxes, and wood panels for station wagons. He used the bungalow for a few days each summer and for "household arts training" for local children during the school year, according to Ford Bryan's *Beyond the Model T: The Other Ventures of Henry Ford*. Today the **Ford Bungalow** (906-524-7595) can be rented for reunions and such. It sleeps up to 20.

After the Ford era, Pequaming languished to the point that it was mistakenly considered a ghost town. But today it has the look of a resort and retirement community of more recent vintage. An increasing number of homes are being

Many families in L'Anse, Baraga, and Skanee earned their livelihood through commercial fishing up until a generation ago. Now Fisher Price Charters out of Witz's Marina in Skanee takes people fishing by the Huron Islands and Stannard Reef, where tremendous lake trout catches are the rule.

built by people commuting to L'Anse. The water tower and some buildings from the old sawmill complex remain, privately owned by the people who operate the boat launch and Pequaming Marina (906-524-6413) with its transient slips. A **pleasant place to picnic and swim** is the Second Sand Beach Park on the northeast shore of the peninsula.

Aura

A jig and a jog to the northeast of Pequaming, and you reach Aura, a rural **Finnish farming community** with its own community hall on Townline Road. Not so very long ago dances with fiddling were regular events at farm halls like these. Since 1976 the **AURA JAMBOREE** has been held the third Saturday of July next to the hall here. It began as a fiddlers' jamboree with traditional music from many countries. The event has evolved into a sort of **annual musicians' picnic and dance** with over a hundred invited musicians, all unpaid, all playing acoustic instruments, and an audience of thousands. In 2001 it cost $10 to attend. Musicians from southern Michigan and many parts of the U.S. treasure its noncommercial atmosphere. Regulars include the popular U.P. folk quartet White Water, their friend Helmer Toyras (his roots are in genuine old-time Finnish fiddling), and Art Moilanen of Mass City, the U.P.'s premiere accordionist. Stage performances are from 10 a.m. to 5 p.m., followed by a dance. Each invitee gets about 15 minutes; jam sessions form on the grounds. Though Finnish fiddling is still a big part of the festival, music ranges from traditional to folk to jazz to bluegrass. A neighbor makes his **orchard available for camping**; consult this book for other campgrounds. Call (906) 524-7842 for info.

To reach Pequaming, follow Front Street and the shore road northeast out of L'Anse for eight miles.

Skanee

On Lake Superior's Huron Bay near the Huron Mountains, this **dispersed rural community** on the road to nowhere once was the center of an apple- and potato-growing area. More moisture and moderate temperatures along the shoreline climate helped grow bountiful crops. Many old apple orchards can still be seen, but there's no commercial agriculture left in these remote parts. Skanee is now a summer resort and retirement community, with cottages along the shore and good hunting and fishing.

First homesteaded by Swedes in 1871, Skanee was named for a Swedish province. The **deep, protected harbor** here was a major factor in choosing this site, as was the valuable timber. In the 1870s thousands of Swedes immigrated to the U.S. because of crop failures at home. For just $26 they could homestead and eventually own 160 acres in Michigan. Initially, the only access to Skanee was by boat or by an old Indian trail to L'Anse. After the timber gave out, people relied for employment on fishing, farming, and jobs at the **slate quarry** at the end of Arvon Road. Its slate was shipped for roofs of grand buildings throughout the Midwest. Farmers used oxen to grow potatoes and apples, which were shipped by tug to Houghton. Read about the ill-advised railroad from Skanee to Michigamme's mines at the end of the Marquette chaper.

There's not much Skanee left. But if you drive out Skanee Road 15 miles northeast of L'Anse (it starts in town as Main Street), turn left onto Town Road, and go down the hill, you'll pass some **old houses** and a few commercial buildings from the 19th century and come to the intersection of Park Road. Park leads down to the **Arvon Township Park** and its beach and boat launch. That intersection, the center of Skanee, has the post office and an **impressive Colonial Revival township hall/community building** from 1915. North of Town Line Road on the water is **Witz's Marina** (524-7795) with a boat launch, docks, and campground.

Silver Falls

Visiting this waterfall in a rocky forest is an **interestingly complex experience**. The trail from the parking area leads to a **dramatic overlook** onto river and falls from a rock shelf. Go down the trail to the base of the falls, and you're surrounded by dark rock, close to the rushing water that has worn two channels in the stone. The pool just below the falls is fine for fishing or just getting your feet wet. (A **popular swimming hole** is farther downstream; beyond is a second waterfall.)

From downtown L'Anse, take Main St./Skanee Rd. up the hill and out 6 miles. A sign to Silver Falls, on the right, marks Falls Rd. Parking is in less than a mile. &: no.

Slate River waterfalls

The short Slate River makes **three visitable waterfalls** as it flows down into Huron Bay from its sources near Mount Arvon. Closest to Skanee Road is the Slate River Falls, where the river rushes over a slanting mass of rough, dark rock. Just east of the river (it's about 12 miles from L'Anse and about 3 1/2 miles southeast of Town Road in Skanee), turn south off Skanee Road (away from the bay) into the parking area. A **trail** along the river bank leads a half mile to the falls.

Two unspectacular but idyllic woodland falls are in the same area. Black **Slate Falls** and **Quartzite Falls** are near the end of Arvon Road, an unpaved road just west of the Slate River off Skanee Road. Take it 3.3 miles until you see a trail on the left. Look for a short trail that goes to the river. (If the road takes a hard right turn, you have gone a little too far.) Black Slate Falls is just upstream from where the trail reaches the river, and Quartzite Falls is just downstream. If you want to seek out the **old Arvon Slate Quarry**, continue upstream from Black Slate Falls.

Big Eric's Bridge

The Huron River, also known as the Big Huron, empties into Lake Superior just four miles away as the crow flies from Big Eric's Bridge and the **beautiful rapids** just downstream from it. To the immediate east, the Huron Mountains rise precipitously above Lake Superior. The prime fishing lakes of the exclusive Huron Mountain Club near Big Bay are not even ten miles east of here. This is part of the **Copper Country State Forest.** Anglers fill the campground here in spring and fall. In his helpful map/guidebook *Fish Michigan: 50 Rivers*, noted fishing writer Tom Huggler says the Big Huron is one of the **two best steelhead streams in the entire Upper**

Peninsula. Summer visitors may enjoy exploring the **three attractive waterfalls** in the vicinity and admiring the series of small falls, rocky rapids, and pools just below Big Eric's Bridge. Big Eric, incidentally, was a lumberman whose company logged in these parts fifty years ago.

Though it's not easy to carry a canoe down to the water, the Huron River can be canoed from below the first downstream waterfall to its mouth. (The mouth can also be reached via about two miles of unimproved road. Take Portrice Road north from Skanee Rd. near Big Eric's Bridge, go east on Huron Road. Do not cross river. At the next two intersections, take the right road.) The Huron River mouth is a **very beautiful area,** where sand piles up on the beach like waves. The bayou behind the sandbars at the river mouth is a contemplative, restful place, a favorite of paddler Dean Sandell, a recreation planner for the state forest system.

Go toward Skanee (see page 000 and continue out on Skanee Road past Town Rd. and Skanee. The road turns east and the pavement ends at Big Eric's Bridge. (906) 353-6651. Open from late April to first snowfall or end of deer hunting seson. &: no.

Huron Island & Lighthouse

From the Huron's mouth, it's possible to see the **high granite rocks** of the Huron Islands. Most of the islands are a designated national wildlife refuge and therefore not open to camping or public visitation of any kind. A **lighthouse** was built on West Huron Island in 1868 to warn sailors away from the dangerous waters. It marked the turn for ships entering Huron Bay, Keweenaw Bay, or the Portage Entry, waters that became increasingly busy in the late 19th century with vessels carrying copper, lumber, and sandstone.

The westernmost island, known as Lighthouse Island, can be visited during the day. (There's no camping, however.) Any boaters should be forewarned that winds can change quickly at this place, and calm water can turn to whitecaps, regardless of what the weather radio says about general conditions. Duncan Price offers **fishing charters to the Huron Islands area** as Fisher Price Charters (906-523-6393). On the island's southwest side there's a dilapidated but usable dock. A **steep short path** goes up to the lighthouse, built of red granite gained when the building site was leveled. The roof of the handsome

This granite lighthouse was built in 1868 to warn ships away from the rocky Huron Islands, three miles offshore between L'Anse and Big Bay, The lighthouse was in jeopardy until L'Anse and Skanee-area people teamed up with the National Wildlife Service to undertake repairs. Boaters can visit West Huron Island, where the lighthouse stands. The other islands are a wildlife refuge off limits to the public.

building has been repaired, thanks to a joint project by island managers (the Seney National Wildlife Refuge) and a group of mostly local volunteers, the **Huron Island Lighthouse Preservation Association** (Box 381, L'Anse 49946). The association has been successful in gaining government cooperation in its preservation efforts. Donations gladly accepted.

SKANEE LODGINGS

AURORA BOREALIS RESORT
(906) 524-5700;
www.uppermichigan.com/aurora

Arlene and Harold Ripple enjoyed their vacations here so much that when this old resort went up for sale, they bought it. In 1992 they built their retirement home on the Huron Bay lake frontage, and worked at totally transforming the four simple cottages into some of the most **comfortable and distinctive lodgings imaginable**. They are rented at remarkably reasonable rates, from $55 to $75 a night for up to four. Harold loves to remodel and do cabinetry; Arlene is the decorator and craftsperson. Amenities include beautiful kitchenettes; cheerful wood-burning stoves; chunky log beds with quilts; and antiques like Scandinavian painted cupboards and

chests. Two cottages sleep three in a single room with separate sitting and eat-in kitchen areas. A third now has two bedrooms. The largest cottage sleeps four or more on two levels. The cottages don't have lake views. But guests have the use of the a beautiful outdoor sitting area and **swing underneath a big pine** by the perennial and herb garden. There's a **sandy beach** and an L-shaped dock. Kids like the carved wood animals in the woodland garden by a creek. *On the north end of Park Rd. (which is along the shore south of the Community Building and Town Line Rd.) Call about winter dates.* **H.A.** : one cottage ADA accessible : $5/extra person over 4

GABE'S SUMMER SUITES

(906) 524-6619; e-mail: jgabe@up.net

It's hard to believe that a place as remote as Skanee could have two such attractive small resorts as Gabe's and Aurora Borealis — attractive in different ways. Both are on Park Road in a **beautiful, wooded shoreline cottage area**, and both have extensive lawns and a natural setting. The Ripples' style is a sophisticated urban take on rural living. (He's a retired physician from Milwaukee.) Joe and Betty Gabe are also artistic and versatile, but in an unusually rooted way. Their handsome home and resort are on the property where Betty Gabe grew up and where her father had his commercial fishing operation. Like her Finnish-American parents, Betty likes to sketch, photograph, and paint. Her drawings and paintings of area scenes have been reproduced on T shirts and notecards for local causes, and her trim signage creates a pretty, natural image for the place.

The resort has **200 feet of Huron Bay lakeshore**, a **gradually sloping sandy beach** with a **bonfire circle**, a fish-cleaning station, outdoor games, and a **creek** running through a small woods. Here are three newish cottages with **water views** and pleasantly country-rustic decor. The one-bedroom cabin sleeps four and rents for $65 for two, with $5 per extra person. The two-bedroom cottages ($72/night) sleep five to six . All have a living-room sofa bed, new kitchen with microwave and small appliances, color TV, and a deck, chairs, picnic table, grill. There's a **dock** for boats up to 16' long, and a boat for rent. Ask about remodeled summer homes, similarly furnished, off the property. *On Park Road (see directions for Aurora Borealis). One cabin stays open in winter.* **H.A.**: call

SKANEE CAMPING

WITZ'S MARINA and CAMPGROUND
(906) 524-7795
A **pleasant, wooded campground** wraps around this well-sheltered 70-slip marina on Huron Bay. The 50 campsites ($10/night) are definitely rustic, with vault toilets and no showers, but there is water and electricity. There's a **small store** with snacks, ice, pop, and tackle, but no groceries. This place is for anglers, not families. There are no playgrounds or such for children. *In Skanee. From the Community Building on Town Line Road, veer right (northeast) along the lake.*

BIG ERIC'S BRIDGE Campground/ Copper Country State Forest
(906) 353-6651. Not reservable. www.dnr.state.mi.us/
20 rustic campsites (vault toilets, no showers, hand pump) are up on a b**eautiful wooded bank** by the Huron River and Big Eric's Bridge. Downstream, at its mouth, there's a scenic, primitive beach campground in the pines. For directions, see previous page about Big Eric's Bridge and The Huron's mouth. *Serviced from May thru Nov. $6/$10 fee at rustic campground.* **H.A.**: no.

Baraga (pop.1,285)

Tucked at the bottom of a hillside going down to the west shore of Keweenaw Bay, Baraga is located at one of those **congenial protected spots** along the Great Lakes that the fur-trading French voyageur liked to use for camps back in the 18th century. While Baraga's small downtown, up the hill from U.S. 41, is none too healthy looking, a maximum-security prison built in 1993 has created jobs and brought new people to the area. The prison's 830 inmates are among the toughest to handle in Michigan's vast prison system. Those housed in five of the seven cell blocks are so unmanageable that they are "in segregation," i.e., allowed outside their cells only an hour a day for showering and exercise.

The town's biggest private employer, Pettibone, with 160 employees, was created when a local resident invented an exotic machine akin to a forklift truck that could lift heavy loads of steel and timber. The Pettibone plant, just south of downtown on Superior (the main street), also makes a $90,000 telescopic boom that can lift pallets of building materials as high as five stories. Terex, a rival company founded in 1984, is also in Baraga. Its 60 employees make extend-

able boom forklifts for rough terrain.

The forestry industry is a big part of the U.P. economy, and Baraga is home to one of the dozen or so large sawmills up here, Besse Forest Products. Its 20 employees saw six million board feet of hardwood a year, 65% of it hard maple. Furniture makers buy their top grades, leaving the rest for pallet manufacturers.

The town and county are named after Bishop Frederic Baraga, the famous "snowshoe priest." In 1843 Baraga established the last of his Michigan and Wisconsin Indian missions near here, two miles north of town at Assinins. When the area was organized, local people wanted to name both town and county after Captain James Bendry, an English immigrant, for his instrumental role in developing the area. In the early years of copper mining, Bendry's ships, based in Sault Ste. Marie, had transported material and supplies to the mines around Copper Harbor. Late one season in the 1850s, he was about to sail off to Copper Country. His resourceful Native American wife, Charlotte, fearing he would be stranded, bundled up the whole family and came along. Sure enough, they were forced to spend the winter here. Captain Bendry then became familiar with the area's possibilities. He bought land in the area, started a sawmill and brick yard, and founded the settlement. Bendry, a Catholic, became friends with Father Baraga, who was in the area a lot before becoming a bishop. Bendry preferred that Baraga village and Baraga County be named after his saintly friend. Bendry's journals are a treasured part of the collection of the Baraga County Historical Society Museum.

The **Keweenaw Bay Indian Community** has its tribal center, educational programs, law enforcement, and housing on the highway just north of Baraga. In fact, the tribe's police force of ten cars is five times the size of Baraga's. Tribal enrollment is 3,500, but only 1,100 of the 7,000 who live on the reservation are Indians. To be enrolled, a tribal member must be quarter blood — that is, one grandparent or two great-grandparents must be descended from people listed on the area's 19th-century allotment rolls.

The tribe's reservation land outside Baraga and L'Anse is extensive. Its casino has had a huge impact on the area today. The bingo games started in tribal leader Fred Dakota's garage have grown into the 550-employee **Ojibwa Casino and Resort**, (800) 323-8045. It's up the hill on M-38 a mile west of U.S. 41. A bowling alley is part of the complex.

Dakota, considered the **pioneer of Indian gaming in Michigan**, held to his dream of developing this legal gambling loophole into the kind of profit center his people had never known before.

More recently, a dissident group of tribal members, known as Fight for Justice, occupied the tribal center for over a year in 1995 and 1996 under the leadership of Father John Haskell, a Catholic priest of native ancestry then at Most Holy Name of Jesus at Assinins. But loyalty to Dakota was strong enough to reelect him chairman in 1996, despite charges that he and his associates diverted tribal gambling profits. Fred Dakota served a brief jail sentence for tax evasion.

Now that the tribe is functioning routinely again, its **popular Powwow** (906-353-6623) is again held on the last full weekend in July at the bayfront campground on the north edge of Baraga. One of the region's most popular powwows, it has grand entry marches, drumming and dancing, plus crafts and food booths, but only one small dance competition. Grand entry marches and dances are held at 7 p.m. Friday and Saturday, and at 1 p.m. Saturday and Sunday.

Baraga State Park

Travelers can take an easy break here, right off U.S. 41, at the **beach with picnic area and bathhouse** on Keweenaw Bay — or on an **interesting 3/4 mile trail** along old beach ridges and past a beaver pond, away from highway noise. Swimming on Keweenaw Bay is iffy, but the **view is great**. Eagles and herons are sometimes seen, looking for fish. See below for camping.

On U.S. 41, 1 1/4 miles south of M-38 in Baraga or 2 1/2 miles west of L'Anse. (906) 353-6558. State park sticker required: $4/day or $20/year. &: call.

Baraga County Historical Society Museum

This museum goes out of its way to collect artifacts and papers pertaining to the wide-ranging history of Baraga County. **Railroading** and **logging** are major themes of the permanent collection, as is a display on the lives of town founders Captain James Bendry and his Indian wife, Charlotte (see above). Time sheets for the Arvon slate quarry are here. The most striking artifact is a **beautiful globe** almost five feet high, made and painted by Francis Jacker, a German immigrant, at his home at Portage Entry. Chris Anderson is making cabinets to house his **outstanding bot-**

tle collection of area bottles, going back to the 1860s and including L'Anse brewery bottles, milk bottles, and pop bottles from L'Anse and Baraga pop bottlers. Each year there's a special theme exhibit. For 2001 it's Baraga County firefighters.

Next to the museum is a **picnic area** with a **grand view of Keweenaw Bay**. Here are an early Pettibone Cary-Lift, a Baraga product used in logging and industries, and a **big wheel** once used with horses to move logs over frozen ground. It was pulled out of a river where logging companies kept their equipment submerged when not in use so the wood spokes and axles would remain swollen and tight.

In a new log building on U.S. 41 in Baraga, just north of the Best Western Lakeside Inn. (906) 353-8444. Open from June thru September and probably thru color season. Mon-Sat 11-3. Call to confirm fall hours. $2/adult, $1 for ages 12 to 18. Large family discount. &

BARAGA RESTAURANTS

The hotel dining room at the **BEST WESTERN BARAGA LAKESIDE INN** enjoys a **beautiful setting** and has popular prices (around $4 for a cheese omelet with homefries and toast, $4.50 for a deluxe 1/3 pound burger with fries, $6 for whitefish or trout at lunch with potato or a prime rib sandwich). Every table has a **good view of Keweenaw Bay**, with nighttime lights twinkling across the water. There's a **terrace** where you can take your food out, too. The down side of this attractive restaurant is the smoke — not terrible, but unavoidable — that almost inevitably comes with gambler guests. Dinners (mostly around $11 to $16, with some entrées $8 and under) come with potato,

soup or salad, and bread loaf. Pizza, stir fries, and lighter fare dinners are served in the evening. A limited sandwich and salad menu is available any time. The separate lounge has no view. *On U.S. 41 4/5 mile south of M-38. 353-7123. Sun-Thurs 7 a.m.-8 p.m., Fri & Sat to 10 p.m. In July and August open daily 7 a.m. to 10 p.m. & ♿ Full bar*

IRENE'S PIZZA is a simple little place with **good pizza tacos, burritos, and sandwiches** like Italian beef and **cudighi** (that Italian sausage patty from the Marquette Iron Range). There are salads, too, like the $3.05 taco salad and a $3.85 shrimp salad. The **pizza log** is something like a pasty with pizza filling. Vegetarian pizzas and sandwiches are also available. Windows look out on Keweenaw Bay, and **picnic tables with a bay view** are on the deck. *On U.S. 41 south of Baraga, almost opposite Baraga State Park. Open daily from 4 p.m. to 11 p.m. or on Fri & Sat to midnight. &*

BARAGA LODGINGS

The area may fill up for special events, conferences, and conventions.

BEST WESTERN BARAGA LAKESIDE INN (906) 353-7123
Nearby gambling at the Ojibwa Casino enabled this attractive hotel to be built. Each of its 36 rooms on three floors **overlooks Keweenaw Bay**, as does its **indoor pool** and restaurant, open daily for three meals. (There's also a **bar** with no view. A sauna and whirlpool are part of the pool area.) The **view is striking**, especially at dawn and dusk. There's a also a **pleasant outdoor sitting area** by the bay. One drawback: smoking is permitted in many common areas (there are nonsmoking rooms), and nonsmokers

The pride of Baraga: this over $300,000 "high lifter" was invented in Baraga and has been manufactured for years at the Pettibone plant just south of downtown. Used in lumber yards and industrial plants, the Cary-Lift can lift up to 70,000 pounds. This unit was bound for Nigeria.

are likely to find it smoky. The front desk competently serves as a **local information center** for skiing, snowmobiling, ice fishing, and points of interest. Standard rooms: $69 for two in 2000. Deluxe corner rooms with whirlpool tub, sink, refrigerator, connection to adjoining rooms: $85, $10/extra person. *On U.S. 41 4/5 mile south of M-38.*

H.A. 👫🚶: 16 and under free, $5/extra person

SUPER 8 MOTEL   (906) 565-0500

There's nothing special about this 40-room motel's setting, surrounded by parking, across the road from the casino. But it, Carla's in Keweenaw Bay, and the Best Western Copper Crown in Hancock are the only places from L'Anse to Hancock to take pets of any kind. 2000 rates for two were $53. *On M-38, a mile from U.S. 41.* **H.A.** 🐕

BARAGA AREA CAMPING

BARAGA STATE PARK

(906) 353-6558. Reserv: (800) 44-PARKS; (800) 605-8295 TDD; www.dnr.state.mi.us/

Traffic on U.S. 41 whizzes right by the **shady campground** here, without a ridge or woods to buffer the noise. But campers do get to look out past the highway to Keweenaw Bay. A **beach** is across the road; a short trail through a natural area begins at the campground. 108 modern sites are here ($11/$14 night), one mini-cabin ($35), and 10 semi-modern sites with no electricity ($9). Except for the July 4 weekend and the powwow weekend (the last full July weekend), campsites have been available any time. Convenient as an overnight stop going to or from the northern Keweenaw, the park has lately attracted campers who stay the week and make day trips nearby and to the Porcupine Mountains, Calumet, and Copper Harbor. *On U.S. 41, 1 1/4 miles south of M-38 in Baraga or 2 1/2 miles west of L'Anse. Open year-round. Water and showers available May 15-Oct. 15. State park sticker required: $4/day or $20/year.* ♿: call.

Assinins

Assinins was the last mission Father Frederic Baraga, the "snowshoe priest" from Slovenia, established before becoming bishop of the Upper Peninsula. Chief Assinins wrote to get Father Baraga to come to the area, and he was the first to be baptized here. The **little school** here was built under his direction; the nails used seem to be the ones he arranged to

get from Europe. It's part of what was once an extensive mission center. Today Assinins has the Most Holy Name of Jesus Church and a former convent that serves as a parish hall. (Holy Name is a joint parish, twinned with Blessed Kateri Tekakwitha Church in Zeba northeast of L'Anse. It's one of Michigan's few Roman Catholic parishes with a Native American focus. Non-Indians are also members.) The **panoramic view** across the bay to the Huron Mountains is beautiful. Some homes and the cemetery are along the high road that parallels U.S. 41.

A large sandstone orphanage building, erected in 1881, is now a ruin. It was Assinins' principal landmark. According to some tribal members, the orphanage here was much more benign than the notorious Indian schools at Harbor Springs and Mount Pleasant, among other places, which aimed to strip young people of their native culture and remove them from family influences deemed injurious. During hard times this orphanage housed up to 950 children, half of them white. In recent times the impressive stone building was the property of the Keweenaw Bay Indian Community and housed various tribal services. That was before the 1990s, when Father John Haskell, a priest of native ancestry then at the Most Holy Name of Jesus, led an unsuccessful reform movement aimed at replacing tribal chairman Fred Dakota. Haskell's Fight for Justice divided the parish and the tribe. Tribal leaders let the roof of the historic building go. Now three tribal parishoners want to revive Assinins as a cultural center combining Ojibwa and Roman Catholic faith traditions. Plans for a museum also call for a picnic area.

Assinins is 2 1/2 miles north of Baraga off U.S. 41. It's the first place north of Baraga where Keweenaw Bay is in view. The community is up on the hill. A crucifix and white statues of Father Baraga and an Ojibwa man and girl can be seen from the highway. (In fact, they're illuminated at night.) Turn west (up) here to find the church, school, and old convent.

Father Baraga's Historical Mission & Native Genealogical Center

Three parishoners of the Most Holy Name of Jesus Church here are working to turn Father Baraga's simple school into a visitor destination that tells Baraga's story and helps far-flung descendants of the area Ojibwa band to research their roots. They are doing what needs to be

done, from hammering underlayment on the roof to writing grants and holding an annual **thanksgiving harvest feast and pow wow** in September (the public is invited). John Cadeau, Mike Cardinal, and Steve Hadden, working in cooperation with the Bishop Baraga Association in Marquette, hope to open the museum and gift shop in 2002. "The greatest accomplishment local native people feel Father Baraga did for them was to prevent their removal and relocation from their homeland to reservations out west," the museum pamphlet says. "He did this by establishing self-government and purchasing deeded land in their own names."

Today a **clear path** leads through the woods behind the school to a **cemetery** about a quarter-mile away. Here are some 850 burials without headstones; the men and their families are working to fund a more permanent monument with names, akin to the Vietnam Memorial but in a medicine wheel form.

Some day John, Mike, and Steve want to establish little spiritual buildings with silent retreats back here, kind of like a spiritual campground. Back near the cemetery, near an old baseball diamond, the dome framework for a sweat lodge already is used for sweats for people with ancestral roots in the Ojibwa community here. For a **sweat ceremony**, the dome is covered with canvas, rocks in the center are heated (they are the "grandfathers"), and cedar boughs are laid down over the hot rocks. Hot water is then poured on the rocks. The setting helps participants have visions and spiritual experiences. "When you believe, there's no denying something happens," says John Cadeau. "We had a son from Texas and a mother from California come back. They had lived as white people. For them the sweat was a breathtaking experience that really meant a lot to them."

The school-museum is on your right. To find out about upcoming events, future museum hours, etc., send e-mail to frbaraga@up.net

Most Holy Name of Jesus Church

This s**imple, beautiful church building** of squared logs was erected in 1982. The design incorporates nature and Ojibwa motifs in a contemporary manner that is in tune with many other Catholic church remodelings, like those of the Adrian Dominican architect-nuns who design and remodel churches. Here clear glass windows bring the natural surroundings

into the sanctuary. In a tribute to Father Baraga, snowshoes at the altar are mounted on blocks of sugar maple wood. Moving to maple sugar camps was an important community event in Ojibwa life here, because the trees produced the sugar that was used in barter. The **traditional medicine wheel** in this church interior reinforces the Catholic liturgical cycle. Its four colors and four directions represent the circle of life: red (east) is youth, blue (south) is new life and woman, yellow (west) is healing, and black or white (north) is the elders, winter, aging, dying, passing on.

White parishoners have helped steady the church after it was nearly torn apart by the intense tribal conflict. Now it has had a succession of priests, often foreigners, and a core of parishoners have provided direction and continuity. All are welcome at Mass, which blends Ojibwa customs with contemporary Catholic ritual. For instance, holy water is the age-old symbol, upon entering church, to acknowledge one's sin and purify oneself. Here, at the beginning of Mass, a smudge of dry cedar is lit instead, and an eagle feather is used to move the smoke in a circular motion to purify the Eucharist, the priest, and each member of the congregation.

Mass is at 6 p.m. Saturday and 11:30 a.m. Sunday. See directions for school. The church is across the road from it. ᕒ

Keweenaw Bay

In the 1930s, when U.S. 41 was rerouted as a scenic highway with a bay view, it bypassed the village of Keweenaw Bay up on the bluff. You'll find the village if you turn west and go up the hill where the highway sign says "Community of Keweenaw Bay." There's a new fire house and a community hall where many plays are performed because it has the only proscenium and stage curtain in Baraga County. Founded as a French farming community, Keweenaw Bay boomed briefly after the Mass Mining Company built its stamp mil here. Copper-rich rock mined at its Mass City mines was hauled 35 miles by rail to be pulverized and turned into copper ingots. Pilings from a long dock just south of the Michigan Department of Transportation roadside park can still be seen. Thousands of pounds of fish a week used to be shipped to Chicago from here. Many old-timers from Houghton and L'Anse remember coming to dance at the Michigan Ballroom just north of the docks.

KEWEENAW BAY RESTAURANT

Fresh fish, from-scratch cooking, and a cozy atmosphere with a good Keweenaw Bay view make **CARLA'S RESTAURANT** an attractive stopping place for travelers headed up the Keweenaw Peninsula along U.S. 41. It's a simple little restaurant and bar, warm with knotty pine, accented by copper and plants. Locally caught whitefish or trout dinners are $10, char-broiled steaks $10 to $14. Dinners include potato and vegetable, plus soup and salad bar. Unlimited salad bar alone: $8. Sandwiches ($4-$5) are served any time. Desserts are homemade; shortcake with local berries or apples is served in season. Smoking is allowed only at the bar. *On U.S. 41 six miles north of Baraga. 353-6256; www.carlasinn.com. Open year-round, but only Fri & Sat, 4-9 p.m., in the off-season (Dec. 1 to April 15 or so). Bar and grill stays open somewhat later. In season open daily except Sunday at 4 p.m., to 9 weekdays, 10 Fri & Sat.*

H.A.: restaurant yes; bathroom no.

KEWEENAW BAY LODGING

CARLA'S LAKESHORE MOTEL
(906) 353-6256; www.carlasinn.com

This older motel with 10 small, clean, **attractive rooms** adjoins the very good Carla's Restaurant. Each room ($45 for two, $55 for four) is individually decorated and **overlooks Keweenaw Bay and the Huron Mountains**. Rooms have phones (free local calls), TVs with 5 channels. (A satellite allows for a choice of one extra channel, beamed to every room.) There's a **sauna,** and a small terrace area with outdoor furniture and that **grand bay view** across the highway. A **beach** is accessible across highway; it's sandy some years and other years more rocky. On snowmobile trail. Two beachfront cabins a half down the road, not on the highway but off a quiet access road 35' from the shore, rent for $300/week. *On U.S. 41 six miles north of Baraga. Open year-round.*

H.A.: call. ♿👫: 12 & under free, $5/extra person 🐕:$5 extra

KEWEENAW BERRY FARM RESTAURANT & BAKERY is now open as a seasonal restaurant, **bakery, ice cream parlor** with Jilbert's ice cream, gift shop, fish market, and **petting zoo** with a few other shops — everything but a farm market with berries, which it started out from. Owner Janelle Kotila is the founders' daughter. It still makes for a great stop for car-weary travelers bound for Houghton and beyond, with asphalt walks through the landscaped area out back where the animals are. The restaurant offers a varied menu from burgers, soups, fresh fish, pasties every day, and changing specials that are about $5 on weekdays (for more of a lunch) and $8 To $10 for weekend whitefish, turkey, and steak. **Pannukakku** (Finnish oven egg pancakes) are a favorite for Sunday breakfast. *On U.S. 41 about 18 miles north of Baraga near the Portage Entry Road. 523-4271. Open May through October, possibly later, daily from 7 a.m. to 8 p.m.* ᕒ

Hanka Homestead

Though the Finnish influence is everywhere in the Keweenaw Peninsula, pure Finnish survivals are rare. Probably the most remarkable is this **self-sufficient pioneer farmstead on a beautiful, remote hillside** near the peninsula's base. Its farmhouse and nine outbuildings are carefully crafted Scandinavian log construction. The Hanka farm has been restored to the way it was in its prime in 1920, when it was the home of Herman Hanka, a disabled miner, his wife, and their four adult children. On the farm they continued the Old World ways they had brought with them to the U.S.

By the time you get to the Hankas' place, you've gone down five miles of country road off U.S. 41; turned at a fire tower near the top of a long, high hill; and driven down a rugged gravel road through a mile of forest. It's quite remote from the outside world, just as the Finns were who homesteaded in this neighborhood in the 1890s. The **log house** (now a century old), **two-story log barn**, **sauna**, and other small outbuildings sit in an 18-acre clearing, surrounded by forest. The Huron Mountains are blue in the distance across nearby Keweenaw Bay. The scene looks like something you'd expect to find in a remote hollow of the Smoky Mountains.

One mainstay of **self-sufficient local economies** like these was **cooperation**. Neighbors traded and shared harvest work and other skills and products. The disabled father, Herman Hanka, tanned hides and made shoes for neighbors. His son Jalmar tinkered and fixed things; in the early days of automobiles he became a local legend as a self-taught auto mechanic. The family boarded logging horses, which needed intermittent rest between periods of strenuous work. In winter Jalmar and his brother Nik, the farm manager, worked in logging camps, where their sister, Mary, cooked. One neighbor went to town every Saturday to

shop for the neighborhood.

People raised their own grains and vegetables, kept chickens and sometimes a pig. The Hankas depended on the Jersey cow and her rich milk for butter and cheese. And they hunted rabbits, partridges, and deer. Such a short growing season (an average of 85 frost-free days) made farmers focus on cold-resistant root crops like turnips, rutabagas, and potatoes. Preserving and preparing food took up an immense amount of time. Social life consisted of the weekly Saturday sauna, visiting, and music. Nik played a homemade kantele, a kind of zither that's the Finnish national folk instrument. Occasional dances were held at a pavilion that stood near where the fire tower is.

Finland's shifting 19th-century economy had transformed many independent farmers into a class of industrial workers and landless tenants without opportunities. Only the oldest son could hope to farm his own land. Finns emigrated to the northern U.S., largely to work in mines. Inexperienced as miners, they did the lower-paying work timbering and tramming. Between the peak emigration years of 1899 and 1914, over 200,000 Finns came to the U.S., largely from two rural counties, Vaasa and Oulu. On the edges of U.P. mining towns, miners farmed smaller plots to support their large families. It was a big step up from working in the dangerous mines to buying a 40-acre farm under the Homestead Act and becoming a full-time farmer.

For farms like the Hankas,' **everything changed in the 1920s**. New sanitation policies allowed the sale only of Grade A milk, which had to be produced and cooled under super-sanitary, refrigerated conditions. Grade B milk produced at farms like theirs could be sold only as cheese. Phone service in this remote neighborhood, unreliable to begin with, became so expensive as the population shrank that customers dropped it and lines were removed. Forests reclaimed many fields. Sons went into the army and saw a bigger world. Beginning when the 1913 strike disrupted mining, many went to work in Detroit's auto factories, like Mary's son, Arvo. **Detroit** even had **a Finnish neighborhood** around Livernois and Six Mile. The emigrant children came back to the U. P. only to retire.

The Hanka farm stopped being improved in 1923, when Nik, its energetic manager, died. Gradually most of the Hankas died off, but easygoing Jalmar lived on here until his death in1966. His needs were simple, and he didn't have the ambition to modernize.

The Hanka Farm
• SUMMER 1920 •
• Askel Hill, Pelkie, Michigan •

The remote, picturesque Hanka Homestead farm museum is an original Finnish farm from 1920. Rugged immigrants and their adult children lived in an almost completely self-sufficient rural community.

The farm pretty much remained a **time capsule of old Finnish folkways**.

Scouts from Old World Wisconsin, an outdoor museum of pioneer ethnic farm buildings in southeastern Wisconsin, came up here to buy the barn and move it. But they were so impressed with the unaltered condition of this classic Finnish farm that they encouraged a local group to preserve it as a museum. (Call 262-544-6300 or visit www.shsw .wisc.edu/sites/oww/ for details on visiting **Old World Wisconsin**.)

The tour is strong on explaining the how-tos of a subsistence lifestyle: how fish was smoked in the sauna, which was then prepared for the family's bath; how rag rugs were woven on looms passed around the neighborhood; how grain and food were stored. A satisfying amount of information on the people

who lived here is available to the patient reader in a somewhat tedious $6 book.

Some years **demonstrations and music** have been featured on special days each year, including Juhannus (St. John's Day, June 24, which Finns traditionally celebrate with bonfires. Call for this year's schedule.

From U.S. 41 about 10 miles north of Baraga, turn west onto Arnheim Road. As you pass the fire tower, continue straight onto the gravel (the blacktop turns west). Follow the gravel road left (east) to the farm. All this is signed. Open from Memorial Day through Labor Day, possibly later, on Tues, Thurs, Sat, and Sun from 12-4. If scheduled times don't fit your travel plans, call (906) 334-2601 for tours by appointment. $3/adults, $1.50/children 5-12. ♿: call. Ground is uneven, and most buildings have a step up.

Chassell (pop. 800)

Chassell is the village everyone drives up through if they enter Houghton and Copper Country by way of U.S. 41 along Keweenaw Bay, coming from L'Anse, Marquette, or Iron Mountain. First settled by French farmer John Chasell in 1867, it grew into a substantial place in the 1880s because of its location on a railroad and on Pike Bay. Lumber drives all along the Sturgeon River south to Covington and beyond floated logs to booms in Pike Bay, where they waited to be sawn. Over 15 fishing boats were busy during the fall herring run. The Dormer Fish House, active from 1930 to 1968, was busy cleaning, salting, and packing fish.

Chassell's history is well told in words and photos at the Chassell Heritage Center. The **Chassell Classic Cross-Country Ski Trail** starts and ends at the parking lot of the Chassell Heritage Center in the old school (see below). Trails wind along the wooded hillside, with views of the Portage Waterway.

Chassell is still known for its strawberry farms, now down to half a dozen. Its lively **strawberry festival,** held the first weekend after the Fourth of July, features tasty strawberry shortcake and a wonderful small-town parade Saturday at 11 a.m. Chassell is today a bedroom community. The success of Einerlei gift shop and garden, started in 1975 in one of Chassell's rundown commercial buildings, has inspired additional antique and crafts shops to occupy some of the town's old commercial buildings.

Sturgeon River Sloughs Natural Area

Slow down and enter the natural world by stopping at this convenient roadside stop. The grueling drive to get to the Keweenaw Peninsula can leave you spinning. The sloughs (pronounced "slews") are a good place to start unwinding on the last leg of your trip. There are a **lookout tower** and **picnic tables** by the roadside parking area.

The view of sweeping marshland and sky is relaxing. The slough had been pastureland so wet it could only be farmed by horses. Now channelization and flood control structures regulate the Sturgeon River to avoid spring flooding. The slough of onetime farmland is managed as a **stopover spot for migrating waterfowl and a nesting spot**. The aim is to increase the Upper Peninsula's resident goose population for hunting.

The **De Vriendt Nature Trail**, with interesting interpretive signs, uses boardwalks in part to make a 1.5-mile loop through the slough, now a nesting site for Canada geese, mallards, wood ducks, black ducks, and blue-winged teal. Eagles, great blue herons, and osprey can often be seen here. So can beavers and muskrats, especially at dawn and dusk.

On U.S. 41 about 18 miles north of Baraga and one mile south of Chassell. 353-6651. &: *trail, picnic area.*

The Einerlei

This **restful, pretty gift shop, greenhouse, and garden** has grown into a handsome, rambling series of indoor and outdoor spaces. Good design and natural themes are the rule. Here are cards, stationery (often on recycled paper), and candles, and a floral room with garden accents. **Regional items** are everywhere, from thimbleberry jam and cookbooks in the **well-stocked kitchen shop** to T shirts and sweatshirts to books to hand-thrown pots and posters by area artists. Other book sections are gardening, nature, and Native American cultures. There's comfortable, easy-care **natural-fiber clothing** for men and women. Customers are welcome to sit and relax on the rear deck. It overlooks the tightly planned **rear garden** and sales area for organically grown herbs, flowering perennials, and scented geraniums. The greenhouse is disguised as a summer house. A **beautiful perennial and wildflower display garden** is up front. There's so much on the first level, it's easy to miss the tabletop, toiletry, sauna, and home accessory area upstairs where local couples' bridal registry choices are individually displayed — a window on area taste. The second floor also has a cozy corner for browsing in books about women's concerns, from child-rearing to menopause.

Nancy and Bill Leonard started Einerlei in 1975 after quitting their jobs in Indiana (he was a civil engineer, she taught special ed) and spending a year exploring the Middle West and Canada. "Einerlei" means "one and the same" in German; the Leonards chose it because they wanted an integrated life in which their work and play were one and the same.

Look for the green awnings on the west side of U.S. 41 in the center of Chassell. (906) 523-4612. www.einerlei.com Open year-round. May-Dec: Mon-Sat 9-6, Sun 11-5. Jan-April: Mon-Sat 10-5, closed Sunday. &: *first floor, gardens.*

Chassell Heritage Center

Though its hours are limited, this local museum is worth seeking out because it does such a good job of interpreting the area's history and pre-history. It's a **good model for small museums** that aspire to tell their community's story, in contrast to the more typical "community attic" museum. One room in this handsome former elementary school coordinates enlarged photos and excellent captions with artifacts and a big map of Chassell to create the **Chassell Township Timeline Exhibit**. It lets visitors "read" the past and its vanished places with reference to present landmarks. The timeline begins with **pottery in the Laurel style** (up to 500 AD). Here are descriptions (often illustrated) of old Indian fishing sites, the lumber mill, the fishing docks and fish packing plant. Memorabilia have been chosen for the stories they tell — like the **wicker trunk of an immigrant family**.

A separate room houses each year's exhibit of the **Friends of Fashion**, a group that not only collects and preserves vintage clothing but uses it for public education, especially in **women's history**. Each year's exhibit interprets garments in terms of the lives of area women who wore them, using old family photographs and stories whenever possible. For 2001 the show is "Women Who Made a Difference": teachers, World War II veterans, adventurers, and more. The Friends also stage **educational fashion shows** for other museums and groups — Roaring Twenties, 100 Years of Bridal Customs, Historical Review, and more. Pick up an annual schedule at Einerlei shops in Chassell or Houghton, e-mail Nancy Leonard at nancy@einerlei.com, or call her at (906) 523-4612. The schoolhouse itself, set up on a hill away from busy U.S. 41, sheds a different perspective on the town.

The museum is a block up (west) from U.S. 41 on Second Street. Look for the sign at the north end of the village. (906) 523-1155. Regular hours during July and August Tuesdays 1-4, Thursdays 4-7, during the Strawberry Festival the Saturday and Sunday after July 4, and for a pre-Christmas event. Or call for an appointment. &: *too many stairs.*

Chassell Centennial Park & Mystic Meadow Children's Garden

Not obviously visible from the highway, this **well-equipped park** offers a **swim-**

ming beach and **peaceful view** across the Keweenaw Waterway. There's a **chutes-and-ladders playground**, a boat launch, full-size volleyball and basketball courts, picnic tables and grills and a gazebo, and a big new pavilion that's used as an ice rink in winter. Don't expect much shade; it's an open place. Mystic Meadow Children's Garden, a project of the Michigan State University Extension office, is a smaller North Country version of the hugely popular children's garden at the MSU Horticultural Gardens in East Lansing. Here are a **pasty garden** (with potatoes, rutabagas, carrots, and onions), a pizza garden, a **water pond**, a berry patch, and more. The garden is **at its peak in August**. Volunteers meet at 7 p.m. Mondays to weed. *Off U.S. 41 at the north end of Chassell, just south of the Chippewa Motel, at the foot of Third Street.*

CHASSELL LODGINGS

PALOSAARI'S ROLLING ACRES B&B
(906) 523-4947

To experience a **working Finnish-American dairy farm** today, stay at this homestay B&B not too far from the Hanka Homestead. Cliff and Evy Palosaari are no part-time hobby farmers but **third-generation farmers**. They have seven grown children, mostly in the area. Gary now runs the farm, with nearly a hundred head of dairy cows, and is buying the farm from his father. Cliff still grows strawberries.

The Palosaaris are warm, unpretentious hosts who enjoy sharing stories and philosophizing with their guests. Their 1940s Cape Cod farmhouse is a trim, efficient farm headquarters. Guests use upstairs bedrooms (2 small, one large, $50 for two people) with one shared bathroom upstairs, another bath and a half downstairs. phone in upstairs hall. Big front porch. Guests have own living room with a satellite TV. A **large country breakfast** is served in the pleasant new eat-in kitchen. Evy, active in many farm organizations, is also an **expert baker** well versed in the old Finnish ways. It's a 1/4 mile walk to the Palosaaris' **beach picnic area** at Portage Entry on Keweenaw Bay. 1 mile to the public boat launch. Kids are welcome to this thoroughly child-proofed home— provided they're well-behaved and any bedwetting problems are taken care of. At 67, Evy wants to be able to take some time off, so advance reservations are somewhat provisional. Guests can make a **self-guided farm tour** of outbuildings and equipment, from plows to combines

and large round balers. *Berry-picking in season. On North Portage Entry Rd., 1.3 miles off U.S. 41, 4 miles south of Chassell.* **H.A.**: no 👫🧍👫: $7-$15/extra person

HAMAR HOUSE BED & BREAKFAST
(906) 523-4670

Lumber was half of what built up Chassell (commercial fishing was the other half). Hamar House was built in 1903 by Edward Hamar, superintendent of the big lumber company. Now it's a homestay bed and breakfast complete with two toy poodles. Three guest rooms share a bath and a half. Lots of guests are repeat visitors connected with MTU in some way, and they manage to work out sharing showers. The guest rooms ($38 for one person, $58 for 2) are surprisingly private; one, with twin beds, has a **glassed-in rear sunporch**; another with a double bed has an **adjoining side sunporch**, unheated, with a daybed and **grand view of the waterway** in front and the wooded ravine alongside the house. No air-conditioning, but fans in rooms. Guests share a phone, have use of the living room with Mediterranean furniture, and music room with stereo. Decor ranges from interesting photos of the lumber company and other Chassell history to Precious Moments figurines and newish crystal chandeliers. Guests can use the TV in the Wilsons' den for special sports events. **Continental breakfast** with fresh muffins, juice, and fruit, s served in the dining room. A small enclosed front porch (where smoking is permitted) overlooks the town. Pleasant walks up the hill and adjoining neighborhood can begin from the back garden. Hosts Barbara and Harry Wilson, formerly of Dayton, Ohio, loved fishing in the area and decided to retire here. Harry sells reproductions of his pen and ink drawings of rural scenes. Open year-round. *502 Willson Memorial Dr./U.S. 41.*

H.A.: no 👫🧍👫: $10/extra person

CHIPPEWA MOTEL   (906) 523-4611; www.exploringthenorth.com

This one-floor, 15-room motel offers **big rooms** and a highway location immediately adjacent to Chassell Park on Portage Lake. The park (see above) has a **swimming beach**, **picnic area**, and boat launch. The Chippewa Restaurant next door, known for home cooking with a good view, was destroyed by fire but will probably be rebuilt soon. Motel owners Al and Betty Kotila plant **beautiful flowers** and have furnished some rooms individually with some antiques. Extras include coffee in the office, frequent home-baked

treats delivered most evenings to guests' doors, **bikes** to use at no charge, and **picnic tables** and grills in back that offer a **fine view across the park and waterway**. Rooms are air-conditioned with 40-channel cable TV. High, small rear windows mean there's effectively no water view. Guests may use the office phone or courtesy phone in the breezeway. Bed arrangements vary. Three rooms have fully equipped kitchens, walk-out back doors, and their own picnic tables and grills for $10 extra. Rates vary seasonally; high season is from mid June through September and then in snowmobile season. Here are some examples from summer, 2000: one queen $45 or two twins $45, two doubles $55. *On U.S. 41 at the north end of Chassell. Open year-round.*

H.A.: call. 👫🧍👫: no extra charge

South Range

Platted by a mining company in 1902, South Range was named for its location at the southernmost end of the Copper Range Mines just southwest of Houghton. The town became the business center for smaller clusters of miner homes on the South Range. In 1913 the range's Copper Range Company was one of the Keweenaw mines' biggest employers, second only to Calumet and Hecla.

Today South Range goes all out for the Fourth of July and puts on the **Keweenaw's biggest parade**, with personalized floats, dancing and other festivities, and fireworks on the ball field. Call 482-6125 for exact day and time.

One mile north of South Range on M-26 is one of the U.P's **most important sawmills**, Northern Hardwoods, owned since 1999 by the Connecticut firm Rossi. Logging trucks arrive daily from the vast surrounding forests. It produces pulpwood and veneer as well as over 22 million board feet a year of lumber, including white hard maple, red leaf maple, yellow and white Birch, red oak, soft maple, cherry, and basswood. 30% of the hardwood is exported overseas. Some 60% of exports are maple, the most prized of which is **rare bird's-eye and curly maple**. It's still a mystery why these beautiful woods are more abundant in the U.P. than anywhere else in the world. Stress on trees from hard winters may be a factor. One 10-foot log of bird's-eye maple sold for $7,000. Most of these choice logs are not sawn here but sent by freighter to Italy, Germany, and Japan, where precision machines cut paper-thin veneer. The best maple also goes to make musical instruments, especially guitars and violins.

Copper Range Historical Museum

The onetime bank houses a newish local museum that focuses on various aspects of life in these parts. "A day in the life" is illustrated with **wonderfully detailed room-size scenes** done fresh each year by the Bergdahl sisters. They are "display artists" in the words of museum organizer Karen Laitila Johnson. The hands-on Whatisit? table for kids changes yearly, too. The miners' life exhibit with personal lunch buckets and hats is always up. The museum occupies part of the historic Kaleva Building, erected circa 1910 by a Finnish fraternal group; its women's club remains active today.

On M-26 at Champion Ave. in the center of South Range. 482-6125. Open from Mem. Day weekend thru mid October, Mon-Sat 11-4 and by appointment for groups. $1/adult; children free. &: four steps.

Etc. Etc.

A museum-like consignment collection of things made or saved by a hundred contributors. Owner Karen Laitila Johnson likes it that the shop enables people to decorate their homes for little money. Expect to find **vintage clothing and jewelry**, hand-painted sweatshirts, some furniture, copper minerals, old bottles, historical books, Tauno Kilpela's information-packed maps about the area and its mining history, and a some offbeat things like the book "Goldilocks and the Three Little Bears" in Finnish.

42 Trimountain/M-26. 482-9171. From Mem. Day weekend thru mid October: Mon-Sat 11-5. Otherwise Thurs-Sat 12-5. &: three steps.

Freda

Named for the daughter of a mining company owner, Freda sits on a **high sandstone bluff overlooking Lake Superior** west of Houghton. It's one of several Keweenaw shoreline settlements that grew up around a stamping mill. Copper mining companies had to take copper-bearing rock brought up from the mines and concentrate the ore into much purer ingots which could be shipped long distances to customers. This required a stamping plant to grind up the rock. The process uses lots of water to separate the copper from other

materials. So stamping mills were sited along lakes.

The Copper Range Company built the Freda stamping mill below the big bluff in 1899. The company also laid out the village, built employee housing, installed water mains, and created a fire department. By 1910 Freda had 500 residents. Freda's park, long since abandoned, was once a popular weekend destination by train for people in the area. The stamping mill finally closed in 1967, leading to the loss of the post office. Today the stamp sands are a Superfund site for environmental cleanup.

Freda is literally at the **end of the road**. The only way out is back the way you came from Beacon Hill and Redridge. It's called Covered Road because of the way trees arch over it and form a tunnel. In fall color season it's a **popular excursion** to drive out this way to Freda, enjoy the view, and have a meal or piece of pie at the Superior View Restaurant.

FREDA RESTAURANT

The **SUPERIOR VIEW RESTAURANT** is in a cheerfully remodeled old copper company office overlooking Lake Superior. It has built a good business with home cooking and daily dinner specials (about $6-$7.50 including homemade bread or potato or onion rings, and salad). There's turkey on Thursday, lake trout or cod on Friday, BBQ ribs Saturday, baked ham Sunday, and Salisbury steak Monday. The menu ranges from sandwiches (the burger is under $2), soups, chili, and meal-size salads to dinners ($7 to $10) of steamed cod, fried chicken, steak, and beef tenderloin. **Homemade pies** are about $1.75/slice. Dessert specialties include a **baked crust vanilla pudding** and the Chipper Special, a **three-layered torte**. Brothers Clyde and Leo Durocher started the restaurant in 1974. Leo has died, but Clyde and Leo's wife continue to run it today. Photos from Freda's mining boom are on the walls, along with pictures of all the sixth-grades Clyde has taught. No alcohol or credit cards. At the entrance to Freda, about 14 miles west of Houghton. *Take Hougton Canal Rd. northwest along the Portage Waterway, turn west on either Smelts Rd./Covered Rd. or on Liminga Rd. 483-7563is Open from 1st weekend of May through 2nd week of October. From Father's Day to Labor Day open Thurs-Mon noon to 9. In spring and fall, open Fri 5-9, Sat 4-9, Sun noon to 9. &*

Twin Lakes

Twin Lakes is a dispersed resort community on and near U.S. 41, 13 miles north of M-38 near Mass City and 23 miles south of Houghton. It has a convenience store and the Golden Hearth bar and restaurant on U.S. 41. Its homes are mostly cottages clustered around Lake Roland and Lake Gerald, the "twin lakes." **Twin Lakes State Park** is between Lake Roland and U.S. 41. It gets a lot of road noise. A secluded **state forest campground** is on smaller **Emily Lake** south of town.

Twin Lakes' mailing address is Toivola, 10 miles to the north on U.S. 41, a former logging camp and stop on the Copper Range Railroad. In Finnish **Toivola** means **"city of hope."** North of Toivola the Misery Bay Road leads to one of the Keweenaw's magical, tucked-away spots with agate beaches and a 25-site primitive campground. A bonfire is held there in honor of Juhannes, St. John's Day, a feast day near the summer solstice.

TWIN LAKES RESORT (906) 288-3666; www.exploringthenorth.com

Twin Lakes Resort is beneath big oaks and maples on Lake Roland. The site is even hillier site than the state park. The resort has a **sandy beach** with two fire pits and a modest dock. Four of the 9 housekeeping cottages have **lake views**. Two have three bedrooms; the rest have two. All have complete kitchens, and each comes with a 14' aluminum boat. (One small cottage without a kitchen is rented for overnights.) All linens except towels are provided. No TV and no phones. You can use the office phone; cell phone coverage isn't the best. The cottages date from many eras; some have knotty-pine walls, and one has a rustic log interior. The owner can direct guests to local beauty spots. Reservations of 7 days and more are preferred. $400-$700/week. Not necessary to rent in full-week increments.

Using Twin Lakes as a base camp could give visitors a **peaceful, private lakeside housekeeping cottage** within an easy drive of many different destinations: the Adventure Mine and Old Victoria, the Porkies, the Seaman Mineralogical Museum in Houghton, even Copper Harbor for a long day's drive. Right in the neighborhood are the sporty, **9-hole Wyandotte Hills Golf Course** and the **remote agate beaches** of Misery Bay on Lake Superior. *Open from June through Sept. Call for extend-*

Downtown Houghton with its towers and spires is striking when viewed from across the Portage Waterway from the Quincy Hoist's tram car or from a window of the Best Western Copper Crown or Ramada hotels. Hancock is similarly picturesque seen from across the waterway.

ed season rentals. On North Parkside Drive north of Twin Lakes State Park on Lake Roland

H.A.: call

Houghton (pop. 7,010)

Built on a steep slope, Houghton has some of the most interesting and dramatic views in the Midwest. It's a **visual treat** to look across the wide Portage Waterway at its twin city, Hancock, and the surrounding green hills. You can see the **mining captains' mansions** of East Hancock. Much more visible is the **ski hill** east of Hancock at Ripley. Along the waterway at Ripley are the **evocative brick ruins** of the Quincy Mining Company's old copper smelter..

On the far skyline across the waterway you can see the **silhouette of the Shaft No. 2 hoist house** at the legendary Quincy Mine. It's the quintessential landmark symbolizing copper's central role in the twin cities' history. The rebuilt tram railway with big windows and a clear top connects the hoist area and visitor center at the top of Quincy Hill with a side mine entrance near East Hancock. The tram offers a fine opportunity to take in the extraordinary panorama of Houghton and the Portage Waterway. A scenic highway turnoff, on U.S. 41, has the same remarkable view.

The waterway, once a frequently-used short-cut for freighters, **slices the Keweenaw Peninsula in two**. The **unusual lift bridge** at Houghton is the only crossing point, making for occasional traffic jams during construction season, an oddity in this lightly populated part of the state. Unlike a drawbridge, the bridge's midsection rises vertically to allow freighters and tall sailboats to pass.

Houghton's **downtown** is both **handsome and lively**. Good views pop up in many places. The waterfront, which forms the city's northern boundary, is an interesting succession of docks. One the berth of the National Park Service's impressive165-foot passenger and supply ship, *Ranger III*, which makes regular trips to Isle Royale 60 miles away to the northwest. A seaplane is anchored west of the bridge.

Before this area became a mining region, giant hemlocks covered it. The first bridge connecting Houghton with Hancock was completed in 1876. This was three years after the Hancock side of the Keweenaw Peninsula was separated from the mainland by a two-mile-long canal, creating a western outlet from the Portage Waterway to Lake Superior. The canal allowed ships to avoid the lengthy and at times treacherous trip around Keweenaw Point, 50 miles to the north, and made an island of the peninsula's copper-rich northern section.

Central to Houghton's identity and economy today is not copper but education. The **well-regarded Michigan Technological University** is one of the top 50 state universities in the country, second in the state only to Ann Arbor's University of Michigan in admissions standards. Its campus is the first part of Houghton you see as you arrive from the south. Bristling with boxy newish buildings funded largely by the state's recent economic prosperity, the Tech campus spans both sides of U.S. 41 on the big bluff above the Portage Waterway. With 418 faculty and 1,035 staff, it's by far the region's largest employer.

Three-fourths of Tech's mostly undergraduate student body of 6,300 is male, and about the same proportion are engineering majors. The school brags that it's located in the "safest college town in Michigan." Geology and engineering, not surprisingly, are the fields for which Tech is well known nationally, but there's increased emphasis on a broader range of subjects in the sciences: communication, business, technology, and forestry. Tech has also played a big role in developing Michigan high school talent in science, technology, the environment, and the arts, through its popular **Summer Youth Program** (906-487-2354). A shining addition to cultural life in the western U.P. is the **Rozsa Center for the Performing Arts**,

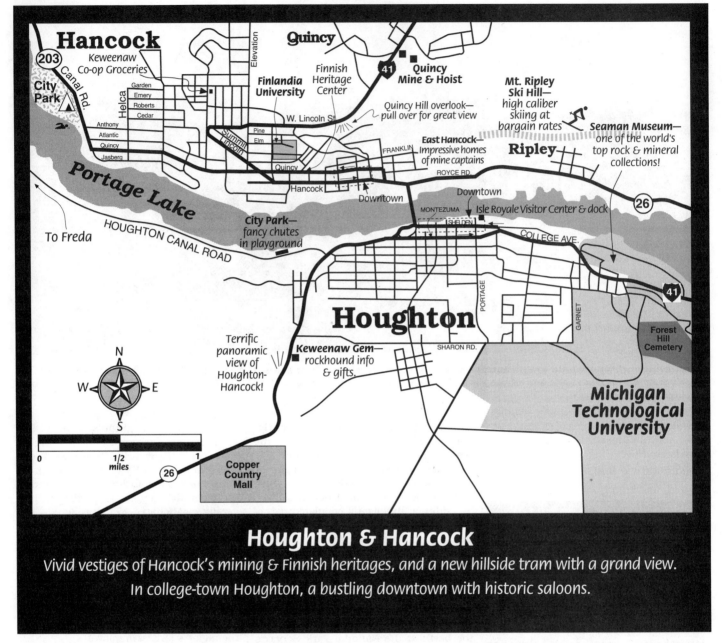

Houghton & Hancock

Vivid vestiges of Hancock's mining & Finnish heritages, and a new hillside tram with a grand view.
In college-town Houghton, a bustling downtown with historic saloons.

a state-of-the-art facility

Highway 41 turns into College Avenue as you reach the university. West of the university it is lined with impressive mansions, now often used as fraternities. A few blocks farther you enter the city's splendid downtown.

Downtown Houghton

Downtown along Shelden Avenue is distinctive and **architecturally rich**, a college town full of surprises to reward the perceptive pedestrian. Lavishly ornamented buildings from the mining boom climb a steep hillside. Interconnecting walkways make it easy to go from store to store in winter. The **balanced retail mix** is unusual for today: restaurants

and specialty shops, and still a hardware store, clothing stores, and a movie theater. Up the hill southwest of town along M-26 are Houghton's discount stores and the Copper Country Mall with its modest collection of national specialty chains.

Tech students and faculty, together with summer visitors, help sustain the bustling downtown. Two taverns have **opulent historic interiors and elaborate bars and back bars** that go back to mining boom times. If you're strolling around, take a peek. They also serve food; see restaurant listings below. The **Douglass House Saloon**, the oldest bar in town, is at downtown's east entrance, in the handsome orange brick Douglass House hotel, a local landmark with its

square corner towers. It was erected in 1900 by local businessmen who wanted a first-class hotel for their town. Original Tiffany-type chandeliers hang from the saloon's coffered ceiling with its rich woodwork. On downtown's other end at 126 Shelden, the **Ambassador** has a back bar with a vintage landscape mural populated by cavorting and carousing gnomes. A third memorable beer-drinking setting (with good hamburgers, too) is the **Downtowner Lounge's outdoor deck** overlooking the Portage Waterway, behind the bar at 100 Shelden.

Here are some noteworthy downtown businesses, arranged from east (closer to Tech campus) to west (the lift bridge). Shelden is one way from east to west. The other direction, west to east, is one

street up the hill, along Montezuma. There's plenty of parking on decks entered north (toward the waterway) off Shelden or from the street below it.

◆ **Isle Royale National Park HOUGH-TON VISITOR CENTER & Isle Royale Natural History Association STORE.** By the dock of the *Ranger III*, this space accommodates both a **nature bookstore** and a **staffed information center** where park rangers with detailed maps can answer some of the questions prospective visitors have. The shop offers a tightly focused selection of books, brochures, maps, videos, and posters either about Isle Royale or about subjects pertaining to it, such as wolves, moose, field guides, and Indian culture. Some poster images are from the natural history association's artist-in-residence program. A substantial portion of all merchandise profit goes to the national park. Mail orders are welcome; call (800) 678-6925. For the complete online catalog, visit www.irnha.org. Adjoining the shop are offices of National Park Service Isle Royale staff. *By the dock at 800 E. Lakeshore. From Shelden Ave./U.S. 41, look for signs, turn north just before entering downtown at the tall Franklin Square Inn. National Park (906) 482-0984. Natural History Assn.: (800) 678-6925. From mid June thru late August: open Mon-Sat 8-6. From late August thru mid Sept. closes at 4:30. From late Sept. to mid June: open Mon-Fri 8-4:30.* &.

◆ **EINERLEI UP NORTH** is an offshoot of the popular Chassell store. Northwoods contemporary is the look, in handmade jewelry, functional and fine art from regional artists, accessories for the home and bath, tees and sweatshirts, and natural-fabric clothing by Andrea Baldridge of Distant Drums and other area designers. Upstairs the card and paper loft has an expanded selection of stationery and rubber stamps. *520 Shelden at the light, before the Lode Theater. 482-9911 June-Dec open Mon-Sat 10-6. Jan-April Mon-Sat 10-5. Open Sundays for special events. Open some summer evenings.* &: main floor, not mezzanine.

◆ **LODE THEATER.** Three screens. *510 Shelden. 482-0280.* &: except toilets.

◆ **BOOK WORLD.** This lively, well-stocked general book shop, part of a chain based in Appleton, Wisconsin, has a good regional section, strong nature and children's books, and the best magazine selection in town. It also stocks premium cigars and imported cigarettes. *515 Shelden across from the Lode. Mon-Sat 9-9, Sun 9-5.* &.

◆ **MOTHERLODE COFFEEHOUSE** in its new location is more of a lunch spot and a study spot as well as a gathering spot and art gallery. Artist-entrepreneur Tom Ex offers estate-grown, hand-selected coffees, coffee drinks, and teas; soups, salads, sandwiches, and locally famous house-made scones; and a new, nutritious smoothie with tofu and yogurt instead of ice cream — good for breakfast. Some weekends bring **live acoustic music** — jazz, blues, bluegrass, and folk — mellow enough not to overwhelm conversation. *52 North Huron, next to Suomi Home Bakery. From Shelden Ave./U.S. 41, turn north at Superior Music, go under the viaduct. 487-JAVA. Mon-Sat 7 a.m.-11p.m. Sun 9 a.m.-11 p.m.* &.

◆ **KEWEENAW TOURISM COUNCIL/ Keweenaw Peninsula Chamber of Commerce.** This is a handy source of better-than-average free travel literature for this richly diverse area. *326 Shelden, after Swift Hardware. Sits back from street. 482-2388. Mon-Fri 8-5.* &.

◆ **The TOSH GALLERY.** Now by appointment only. Sculptor Tom Ex decided to focus on making art and overseeing his Motherlode Coffeehouse (see above). He started this high-caliber gallery in 1994, after the art world had temporarily hit the skids in the early 90s and his own nationwide gallery sales dwindled. The gallery's emphasis: **upper-end art, inspired by the North Country**, often spiritual, that "speaks to humankind's origins and destinies . . . and to our relationships with the environment." Expect variety, from nature images (and lots of **fish**) in wood engravings by internationally known Ladislav Hanka, a high school chum of Tom's in Kalamazoo, to Tom's own sculpture, mainly in wood. In his words, it's "non-representational, spiritual in intent, with suggestions of ancestral images and ritual objects." Check it out at Tom's coffeehouse or Larry Bell's Eccentric Café at the celebrated Kalamazoo Brewing Company. Larry commissioned Tom's large "Keeper of the Spirits" sculpture for the brewery's 10th anniversary in 1994. *315 Shelden. 482-2287. By appointment only.*

◆ **DOWN WIND SPORTS.** More bases are covered here than at any other Keweenaw outdoor store: **climbing, kayaking** and canoeing, mountain biking, **backpacking**, downhill and cross-country **skiing, snowshoeing**, snowboarding, and skijouring. Store hours accommodate last-minute purchases by people going to Isle Royale on the twice-weekly *Ranger III*. The staff is involved in all these sports. Under new ownership (the three owners of the Down Wind Sports in Marquette plus a local partner), there's much more inventory and more **scheduled programs** and **events**, publicized in the newsletter or on the website. The new downtown location allows for convenient demos of mountain bikes on the path out back, and of kayaks (call for weekly time) so various models can be test paddled. Now cross-country skis, kayaks, and snowshoes can be rented — giving prospective buyers a chance to test different models. *808 Shelden/U.S. 41, two blocks past the Lode Theater, across from Hunan Restaurant. 482-2500; www.downwindsports.com From May thru Sept. open Mon, Wed, Thurs 9:30-6, Tues 8-6, Fri 8-8, Sat 9:30-5, Sun noon to 4. Oct-April: open Mon-Fri 9:30-6, Sat to 5, Sun noon to 4.* &.

◆ **SURPLUS OUTLET Outdoor gear** that works in the U.P. is the stock in trade here, now that genuine military surplus is hard to come by. Here are Columbia for the whole family, Carhartts, wool Malone bib overalls, Woolrich, Duofold and Wigwam. There's an extensive work store with work boots and winter boots, a large camping department, and lots of Keweenaw T shirts and sweatshirts. *200 Shelden. 482-2550; 888-840-1950; www.surplusoutlet.net. Mon-Thurs 9 a.m.-6 p.m., Fri to 8:30, Sat to 5, Sun noon to 4 in winter, 10 to 2 in summer.* &.

Ranger III
Portage Waterway Cruise

Every Thursday night from mid June through Labor Day weekend, the National Park Service's big 165-foot *Ranger III*, which makes two round trips a week to Isle Royale, takes an excursion to one entry to the Portage Waterway or another, alternating weeks. People seem to get a kick out of experiencing the big boat. The narration on the 2 1/2 hour cruise deals with the waterway's natural history and evocative historic industrial sites. Eagles are sometimes pointed out. The ship goes out into Lake Superior, past the lighthouses at the end of either pier, and turns around. (The narration on the other waterway cruise, the *Keweenaw Star,* was disappointing, in its 2000 version, at least.) The South Portage Entry tour to the southeast is more interesting. It misses the setting sun but includes a spectacular farm near Chassell and the memorable Jacobsville sandstone bluffs, striped red and cream, near the once-active stone quarries.

Leaves from the dock by the Isle Royale Visitor Center (see above) on Thursday at 6 p.m. from mid June to Labor Day week-

end. (906) 482-0984. Adults $13, 12 & under $5. ⟨⟩

A.E. Seaman Mineral Museum/Michigan Technological University

Rockhounds and artistic or visual types will be dazzled by the sumptuous patterns and colors of this **very large, artfully displayed collection of minerals** from around the world. The collection grew as an educational tool of the geology department, a key component of this onetime mining college. In 1990 an act of the state legislature made the Seaman Museum the official mineralogical museum of Michigan.

"There are very few mineral museums left in universities today," says Tech geology professor Bill Rose. "Geology is not so central to most universities' missions. The only university geology museum today that's clearly better than ours is Harvard's." Here at Tech geology remains important. Furthermore, many avid amateur mineralogists and people interested in copper either live in the area or come here on collecting expeditions. So the Seaman Museum today is in expansion mode, thanks to a greatly increasing number of donors and friends. "Most of the great mineral collectors in North America think of this as a possible future home for their vast collections," says Rose.

The museum is raising funds for a new museum, much more visible and convenient for visitors, on Quincy Hill outside Hancock. The Quincy Mining Company was the second-richest in Copper Country. The tour of Quincy's giant steam hoist and part of a mine is one of the most educational and striking visitor attractions in Copper Country.

Current popular highlights of the Seaman Museum's extensive collection include:

◆ a **complete collection** of specimens from the mineral-rich Upper Peninsula

◆ **dramatically illuminated fluorescent minerals** under black light.

◆ the Keweenaw Gallery with some spectacular specimens, including native copper and **rare naturally occurring silver crystals** from the nearby Kearsarge Lode.

◆ the **Lake Superior gemstones exhibit** which includes datolites, Thompsonites, agates, and greenstones (Michigan's official gemstone, usually found on Isle Royale).

Of great interest to confirmed rock hounds are the museum's outstanding systematic collection of world minerals.

The museum and its helpful staff are a good starting place for Keweenaw rock collecting trips. An expanded **gift shop sells some interesting specimens** from $1 to $1,000 and up: fossil fish, copper and half-breeds (copper and silver in the same rock), agates, slabs of iron ore, and more. Also: jewelry, children's books, and soap and candy that look like granite stones. By appointment and for a small donation, the staff will identify minerals people bring in.

The museum's web site, www.mtu .edu/museum/index.html, connects with area mineral clubs and events, including the Keweenaw Week 2001 (formerly the Red Metal Retreat), a week of shows and collecting field trips in early August.

1400 Townsend Dr., on the 5th floor of the EERC building, the 2nd tallest building on the Michigan Tech campus. It's in the center of campus next to the library. Parking is a problem. Look for visitor parking signs off U.S. 41. Handiest: metered visitor parking by the Van Pelt Library. Free: lot by Hamar House, but you must get a permit from Public Safety across U.S. 41 in the Wadsworth Hall dorm. (906) 487-2572. Open year-round Mon-Fri 9-4:30; also generally open Sat. 12-4 from mid-June through Oct. Call to confirm Saturday hours. Admission: 13 and over, $3, seniors 55 and over $2, 12 and under free. ⟨⟩

Michigan Technological University Archives

The third floor of the Van Pelt Library is a treasure trove for history-minded visitors because of its large collection of **historic photographs**, part of the Copper Country Historical Collection. Anyone can look through the files and have **photographs made from negatives of historic photos** for a reasonable cost. Also of special interest is the **map collection.** Property can be researched. The archives also collect Michigan Tech and local history materials, including genealogical materials. **Railroad history** is another strong point. As the official respository for state archives of the Western Upper Peninsula, the archives also house occasional donated official records from a much wider area. Visit the online guide to the collections at www.lib.mtu.edu, then choose "archives."

Look for the three-story white Van Pelt Library in the center of campus. The drive off U.S. 41 by the big MTU sign brings you to the $2 all day parking lot. (906) 487-2505. Open Mon-Fri 8 a.m. to 4:45 p.m. except for national and university holidays. ⟨⟩

Keweenaw Gem & Gift

Gemologist Cindy Flood and her geologist husband Ken provide all manner of expert assistance at this **large Copper Country gift shop and jewelry studio.** They can point rockhounds in the right direction with free maps, rent them **a metal detector** for $15 a half day, sell them hammers and tools, help identify found stones, and fabricate and repair jewelry. Books pertaining to U.P. geology and minerals are for sale. **Jewelry using greenstone** (Michigan's state stone) and local agate and copper are a specialty. At Ken's fabricating studio in Dollar Bay slabs of copper are sawn and polished for use as bookends and clocks, and freeform copper crystals are "grown" on straw into fanciful shapes. Visitors are welcome; ask for directions.

The Floods have an **outstandingly helpful Michigan mineral website**, www.copperconnection.com, with an illustrated primer on U.P. minerals, answers to frequently asked questions, and many helpful tips on finding agates, cleaning copper, and much more. The store has a **very large selection of copper wall hangings, containers, and other copper accessories**, and specimen minerals from the U.P. and beyond. Currently on display is the Point Mills Nuggett, a **float copper mass** twice the size of the famous Ontonagon Boulder that launched early copper explorations. A logger unearthed it near Dollar Bay. Other even larger copper masses have been found elsewhere, too large to be removed.

On West Memorial Drive/M-26 just south of

Seen from the water, the remains of the smelter in Ripley, just east of Hancock, have a haunting, poetic quality. Industrial ruins from copper processing are a hallmark of many waterfront locations in Copper Country.

the blinker at Sharon Ave. by Pizza Hut. Look for the green tower. (906) 482-8447. (800) 554-8447. Open Mon-Fri 10-6, Sat to 5. From May thru Dec. also open Sun 1-5. &

HOUGHTON RESTAURANTS

Restaurants are arranged from downtown to the strip and then along U.S. 41 going to Chassell. See also: Hancock, Freda, Kearsarge, and Lake Linden.

ARMANDO'S RESTAURANT and the **DOUGLASS HOUSE SALOON** have a barroom from the glory days of copper mining, in Houghton's most conspicuous downtown landmark building, the orange brick Douglass House hotel with its corner towers and white cupolas. The food, priced for student budgets, is strong on tasty Italian dishes. Armando's distinctive pasta sauce is thick and tomatoey, used in vegetarian and optional meat dishes. Friday brings the **fish buffet** with three kinds of fish and salads ($7). Saturday is the **pasta buffet** with ravioli, lasagna, shrimp or chicken alfredo, homemade gnocchi, and various sauces (also $7). Sunday brunch ($5.50) is from 11 to 2. The full dinner menu includes steak, chicken, seafood, and vegetarian dishes. Lunch offers a big sandwich menu, with soup and half a sandwich for $4. Armando's is a smoke-free family restaurant. The same menu is served in The Douglass House Saloon, the oldest bar in town, where smoking is permitted. Original **Tiffany-type chan-**

deliers hang from the coffered ceiling with its **rich woodwork**. A Tech ritual is stopping at the Douglass House on Fridays for french fries, pickled eggs, and beer. *517 Shelden/U.S. 41 at Isle Royale on downtown's east side. 482-2003. Regular hours: Mon-Thurs 7 a.m. to 9 p.m., Fri & Sat to 10, Sun 8 a.m. to 9 p.m. In summer (from July into early October) stays open to 10 weekdays.* &: one step. Assistance provided.

At **MARIE'S DELI & GOURMET RESTAURANT**, Marie Catrib has retired, and Victoria Williams, who worked for Marie for over ten years, has taken over. The menu — an eclectic and inspired mix of **Middle Eastern, vegetarian, deli fare, and home cooking** — is the same, and Victoria can turn out **meat pies and spinach pies** like a good Lebanese housewife. (Marie, who is Lebanese, couldn't cook until she came to the north country.) "I miss Marie, but this is still a happy and special place," writes one fan. "Still the best home cooking," proclaims another. Both recommend the **Siberian turkey sandwiches** (with homemade Russian dressing, Swiss, and coleslaw, on grilled challah bread). Victoria is the one who kept the breakfast special (two eggs with homemade toast and terrific spicy-hot potatoes) at $2 because "college kids need good food. Parents worry about their kids eating well." Other breakfast favorites are the **Lebanese omelet** with sausage in an

open pastry shell and stuffed French toast with strawberries and bananas ($3.75). Marie's can supply a fabulous picnic: Lebanese-style spinach pies (no rich phyllo dough), tabooli, hummus, chicken salad, broccoli-cauliflower salad, and over a dozen other salads. Popular lunch buffets on Wednesday ($5) and Friday ($6) are worth going out of your way for. The price includes a main dish, salads and soups, and dessert, and chicken on Friday. Dinners ($8) include soup, salad, and dessert.

Marie's offers table service both in the front deli booths and the rear dining area with a view of the Portage Waterway. Portions are large, with ample leftovers. Marie's will ship some items to homesick patrons. *www.pasty.com/ marie 519 Shelden two doors east of the Lode Theater. 482-8650. Mon-Thurs 7-6, Fri 7-8, Sat 7-5. Closed Sunday.* & 🚶🚶🚶

Rebuilt after a fire destroyed its original quirky digs, **THE LIBRARY RESTAURANT, BAR & BREW PUB** is now much larger and more impressive, thanks to shiny fermenting tanks by the entrance and its big window-wall looking across the Portage Waterway to the mansions of East Hancock. Its offbeat coziness is gone. As of fall, 2000, service had suffered to the point that one former fan has stopped going altogether, after three bad experiences. Nevertheless, it's "still the hottest spot around," says a Tech

professor, "especially when the students are in town." He recommends "great white bean chicken chili, Swiss onion soup au gratin, fresh catch of the day, and beer fries." A favorite sandwich is Sicilian steak; favorite appetizers are bean dip, fried shrimp and mushroom hors d'oeuvres. *61 Isle Royale St. (west side) just downhill from Shelden in the heart of downtown. 482-6211. Kitchen open Mon-Wed 11:30-10, Thurs-Sat 11:30 to 11, Sun 5-10.* ♿ 👫 Full bar

MOTHERLODE COFFEEHOUSE (see page 25) has soup/sandwich/salad fare. *52 N. Huron next to Suomi Bakery.*

SUOMI HOME BAKERY & RESTAURANT is known for its homestyle cooking, the area's **widest selection of Finnish specialties**, plus a very friendly atmosphere and constant refills on coffee. **"Great people-watching!"** comments one patron. There is a back room for non-smokers, but most of the action is out front, especially when the old-timers get together for morning coffee. Breakfast is served all day; prices include coffee. Especially recommended: **pannukakku** (a custardy, oven-baked pancake with fruit sauce, $3), huge pancakes, homemade pies ($1.60 a slice), **nisu toast** with cinnamon and cardamom. For lunch there are pasties (under $3), burgers, homemade soups, and daily specials ($4.35). It's a plain place from an earlier era, with lots of old photos, and mining and logging equipment. No credit cards; out-of-town checks OK. *54 N. Huron off Shelden/U.S. 41 downtown. One street past the Douglass House orange brick historic hotel, turn down under covered street toward waterway. 482-3220 Mon-Fri 6 a.m.-6 p.m., Sat to 5 p.m., Sun 7 a.m.-2 p.m. Closed major holidays.* ♿: two steps

Copper Country has all too few places that serve food outside — a shame, considering how long and lovely the summer evenings are. The **DOWNTOWNER LOUNGE** has a **rear deck** that takes advantage of its location overlooking the lift bridge. "Eat on the deck on a warm day and watch the boaters go under the lift bridge," says a Michigan Tech professor who goes there for good burgers ($3.75 for 1/3 pound) and beer. "The bar reeks of cigarettes and dried beer, so hold your nose as you walk through to the deck." A vegetarian who eats out a lot likes their recently introduced veggie sandwiches and generous salads. Homemade soups like turkey sausage gumbo and, in winter, chili are good here, too. *100 Sheldon Ave./U.S. 41 close to the lift bridge, behind the Downtowner Motel. 482-7305. Closed Sunday. Kitchen open from 11 a.m. to midnight Mon-Sat.* ♿ 👫 Full bar

The **AMBASSADOR RESTAURANT** is a **favorite hangout**, great for atmosphere and for healthy bar food — no burgers, nothing fried, just crusty subs, big salads like beef vinaigrette or Italian tuna, nachos and other Mexican favorites, and thin-crust pizza. The name and front barroom date from the repeal of Prohibition in 1933. It has original booths and a landscape mural behind the back bar where gnomes cavort and carouse by beer barrels from Bosch Beer of nearby Lake Linden. **Big windows** in the smoke-free rear dining room look out onto the Portage lift bridge and the mansions of East Hancock. A cultural historian who eats out a lot says "this is where I take people when they come up to visit. It's a shame the keen booths are reserved for the smokers. Best pizza in the area." **Garlic chicken pizza** is a customer favorite; so is the veggie pizza with zucchini, broccoli, carrots, and garlic olive oil. Italian sausage is made on the premises. *126 Shelden/U.S. 41, past McDonald's, the big parking ramp, and St. Vincent De Paul's, kitty-corner from the Best-Western. 482-5054. Kitchen open Mon-Thurs 11-11, Fri & Sat 11 to 12:30 a.m., Sun 4:30 to 11.* ♿: not men's room.

THE BAKERY, the successor to Johnson's Bakery in Copper Harbor, makes sandwiches to order on your choice of bread, and has a few tables for eating in. Turkey, chicken salad, garlic pepper beef, hot Italian beef, veggie avocado — there are lots of alternatives to the fast food on the nearby strip. The **soup** is very good, too. The Bakery turns out an **impressive array of bread**, the area's best: crusty French bread, the best-selling 10-grain bread, true sourdough bread, even sourdough bagels that are boiled and baked. Come early for best selection, or get day-old bread for half off. Bread is delivered to the Keweenaw Co-op three days a week. The **pecan rolls** — big, rich sticky buns famous in Copper Harbor — are just as gooey and rich as ever. Coffee cakes, Danish, muffins, and doughnuts also satisfy the local taste for sweet rolls to go with lots of coffee. *901 Sharon in the Sharon Centre strip mall just east of the M-26 strip at the blinker light. Behind Pizza Hut and Blockbuster Video. 487-6166. Mon-Fri 7:30 a.m. to 6 p.m., Sat 8 a.m. to 6 p.m.* ♿

Michigan Tech's many Chinese faculty eat out a lot at **MING GARDEN** because of its peaceful mood, crunchy vegetables, generous portions, and food that measures up to that in better big-city Chinese restaurants. The waterfalls and serene atmosphere are great for unwinding. Most dishes are between $8 and $10; two dozen house specials are from $10 to $12. Lunch specials from 11:30 to three (around $5 to $6) come with soup, crab rangoon, and tea. *Off M-26 West up the hill a little before Wal-Mart, same side. 428-8000. Open daily from 11:30 a.m. to 9 p.m., to 10 Fri & Sat, to 8 Sun.* ♿ 👫 Beer & wine

A discriminating local diner and a summer visitor both point to the steaks at the **PILGRIM RIVER STEAKHOUSE** as extraordinary. Filets, strips, T bone, Delmonico — there's quite a variety, and there's seafood, too. The prime rib, offered all the time, is the biggest draw. It's $12 and $14 at dinner, which includes soup, salad, and potato. Chef Ken Steiner is the one who moved the Keweenaw Co-op's deli into its current fabulous mode, before he took over here. This steakhouse is about much more than meat: **great homemade soups**, especially the mushroom soup, "awesome" spinach salad, interesting lunch options, homemade fries, things like bourbon sauce on filets. Dinners, served all day, range from $13 to $24 for the surf and turf bonanza: a half-pound of crab legs and a six-ounce filet. The recent emphasis is on changing specials like whitefish with citrus cilantro or trout Italiano. Friday's seafood platter is a great value at $13. For lunch, there are those excellent soups ($3.25/bowl), a half-pound burger with homemade fries ($6) and other sandwiches, lunch specials, and a very good caesar salad with chicken or steak ($7). Don't expect elegance; diagonal wood siding and booths give the place more of a cozy ski lodge feel. Casual dress OK; reservations recommended, especially on weekends. *On U.S. 41 (side away from water), 1 mile south of MTU campus, 5 miles north of Chassell. 482-8595 Mon-Sat 11-10:30, Sun noon to 10.* ♿ 👫 Full bar

STEAMERS is the new restaurant that opened in fall, 2000, in the gorgeous spot overlooking Portage Lake where The Summer Place used to be. It's the "only trendy place" in Copper Country, and the only place to take seafood seriously, according to a transplant from Massachusetts. She loves their **crabcakes** (2 for $9), softshell crab, and fresh tuna. Popular dishes are Key West shrimp and scallops ($19) and a pound of crab legs (422). Fresh catch of the day ($17) is the best value. Dinners include choice of potato and salad. Carnivores won't be disappointed. The presentation is pretty, too. Reservations recommended. *250*

U.S. 41, 4 1/2 miles south of Houghton. Look for the sign by the long drive up the hill. 523-2722. Current hours: Mon-Thurs 4 p.m. to 9 p.m., Fri & Sat 4-10, Sun brunch 10-2. Call for possible longer summer hours. Full bar

HOUGHTON LODGINGS

Arranged from southeast (toward Chassell along U.S. 41) to northwest.

PORTAGE LAKE CABINS

(906) 482-8755; fax (906) 482-0585; e-mail mromps@up.net

Five completely renovated units offer **very attractive lodgings** looking out across Portage Lake's Torch Bay to Bootjack, and also southeast from the Portage Entry to the distant Huron Mountains. Ample porches have been added to the three attached units and two freestanding cottages. On the lawn, each has a picnic table, lawn chairs, and grill. There's a horseshoe pit and a built-up **sandy beach**; the sand extends quite a ways out. Guests can use the **boat launch**, dock, and paddle boats.

Inside, each cabin is carpeted and finished in drywall with oak and birch ceilings. All have queen beds, cable TV, new oak furniture, and full kitchens with microwaves, coffeemakers, etc. Four units are one room and sleep up to four with a sofa bed. The fifth unit has three separate bedrooms and air-conditioning. Smoke ionizers effectively get rid of smoke. Phone in office or jack outside. Rentals, by the week only in summer ($400-$700), are reserved starting a year ahead. Daily off-season rates range from $50 to $85 for the smaller units (ski and snowmobile season is higher), and $80 to $125 for the large cottage. On a snowmobile access trail, and quite close to Portage Lake Golf Course. *On U.S. 41 4 miles north of Chassell and 4 miles south of downtown Houghton. Close to MTU. Open year-round.* **H.A.**: call

VACATIONLAND MOTEL (906) 482-5351;
(800) VAC-EASY (reserv. & info)

This well-run, **peaceful older motel** sits well back from the highway at the east outskirts of Houghton. Three separate buildings are grouped around a 20' x 40' **outdoor swimming pool** with diving board. Picnic tables are out front. The 10 rooms in the two-story section are bigger. All 24 rooms have picture windows, paneling, and a tailored, outdoorsy, tasteful look circa 1970. All are air-conditioned, with phones, free local calls, cable TV with ESPN and Disney. 2000 rates for two people were $44 and $56 in summer, $39 and $46 otherwise. The lobby and seating area offers free coffee,

tea, hot chocolate, and a **continental breakfas**t. There's a **wax room** for skiers. The motel is on a snowmobile access road and across the road from an **informal bike trail** on a rail bed that goes from Chassell to Houghton. The Portage Lake Golf Course and excellent Pilgrim River Steakhouse are nearby. *On U.S. 41, 2 miles south of the Tech campus and 5 miles north of Chassell.*

 : call : under 4 free, 4-12 half off, 12 & up $5/extra person

MICHIGAN TECH VISITOR HOUSING
(906) 487-2543

Most visitors to Houghton don't know that the five guest rooms in the **Memorial Union Building** can be used by any visitor, and in summer they're not apt to be full. Two queen rooms are $50/night. Three suites ($80) have a bedroom and a living room with pullout sofa and fridge. All have coffeemakers and cable TV. The building also has a cafeteria, bookstore, game room, and bowling alley. Other indoor sports facilities are available for a fee. Free parking is provided. **H.A.**: call

Participants or relatives in any MTU-sponsored summer activity, including the Summer Youth Program, can rent **semi-furnished apartments** (487-2727) or dorm rooms (487-2963). At the center of the MTU campus. Park in visitor parking to the north off U.S. 41.

SUPER 8 MOTEL

(906) 482-2240; (800) 800-8000 (reserv. only); www. keweenaw.org

A **quiet location on the Portage Waterway**, away from U.S. 41, makes this two-story, 86-room hotel stand out. (In snowmobile season it may be not so quiet, however.) Half the rooms overlook the water, the Mt. Ripley ski hill, and the historic Ripley smelter. **Picnic tables** and grills overlook the waterway. The city boat dock is just outside. A **waterfront bike trail** goes west to downtown and the waterfront park, and east past the Tech campus. There's a **long indoor pool**, sauna, and whirlpool. Free continental breakfast with cereal is served in lobby. Standard rooms for two: $70 lakeside or $65 (by parking lot). The two-

> *Use Tech's indoor sports facilities for $5/day*
>
> The **SDC** (Student Development Complex) has a big indoor pool, gym and track, weight room, sauna, and racquetball, all open to the public. Call 487-2578 for details.

room whirlpool suite ($90) sleeps four and has a kitchenette. *1200 E. Lakeshore. Driving through the Tech campus on U.S. 41, just after the highway is no longer divided, go right on the first street to the right (Lake Ave.) and go right again.* **H.A.**: 3 rooms : 12 & under free

CHARLESTON HOUSE HISTORIC INN
(800) 482-7404; (906) 482-7790; www.charlestonhouseinn.com

The **epitome of Houghton elegance** is this 1900 Classical Revival mansion with original fixtures, woodwork and beveled glass. It's furnished with period reproductions. See photographs on website. Guests share the library, dining room and double veranda. The six air-conditioned guest rooms ($238 in summer, $138 otherwise) have phones, color cable TV, and canopy beds. Four have **waterway views**. There's a microwave and refrigerator in the upstairs hall; wine and other snacks and refreshments are complimentary. The **full breakfast** with changing hot entrée can be delivered to your room or eaten in the dining room. *On U.S. 41 in the College Avenue historic district, between campus and downtown. 918 College Ave.* **H.A.**: call

BEST WESTERN KING'S INN
(906) 482-5000; reserv. only (888) 482-5005; www.keweenaw.org

This 69-room hotel is right in downtown Houghton, near the lift bridge and an easy walk to the Lode movie theater and many restaurants and shops. The fourth and fifth floors (entered from Montezuma Ave. uphill in the back) offer **excellent views** of the bridge, Quincy Hill, and the Mount Ripley ski hill. These rooms, with one mirrored wall, are **premium executive rooms** ($71-$82 in 2000) with a king bed, queen sofabed, and mini-fridge. Since the hotel is built into the hillside, this back section is not connected to the elevator, and it's a something of a hike to the front three floors facing Shelden Avenue, with the desk and street lobby. The front section has glass-enclosed hallways and, on the third floor, an attractive indoor pool room with a **40' pool, sauna,** and whirlpool. Wood trusses and cedar siding give the pool room a warm, airy look. Tables and chairs — and a view of downtown — make it a **nice place to hang out,** All rooms have coffeemakers, phones with free local calls, cable TV, and at least one queen bed. Ask about **two two-room suites** in a separate building with full kitchen, whirlpool, and living area with pullout sofa (up to $108 in 2000). A free continental breakfast is served in a small, windowless interior room. Hunan Garden Chinese restaurant, McDonald's, and the Ambassador and Downtowner bar/grills are within half a block. For a half-mile walk to Houghton's waterfront park, go down to the waterway level and head west beneath the bridge. Three-season rate structure: late June-early Sept. ($69 for a standard double), Christmas through March ($61), and two shoulder seasons ($57). Single person $6 less. In summer, 3-day advance reservation is usually enough, except for holiday weekends. Books way ahead for MTU graduation, Winter Carnival. *215 Shelden Ave./U.S. 41.* **H.A.**: 1 room per floor 👪: under 18 free 🐕: $6

BAYSHORE INN BED & BREAKFAST

(906) 482-9010; www.bayshore-inn.com

This personal, homestay B&B with three guest rooms and shared baths doesn't fit easily in categories. It is, as advertised, "a waterfront country farm" on the Houghton side of the Portage Waterway. The house sits up overlooking a wide spot in the waterway, a **peaceful, idyllic view** marred only by one very plain trailer. The farm is said to be 150 years old, though the house, remodeled after a fire, looks more like a 1960s split-level on the exterior. Inside it's antique-filled and surprisingly plush and cushy in a comfy way, in tones of heather and green, with lots of patterned wallpaper, swags, paisleys and stripes. A highlight is the dining area and big deck with a **panoramic view of Portage Lake**. Guests also share an authentic wood-fired sauna and a cozy den with DVD/video player and **excellent video library**. The two upstairs guest rooms connect with a half bath; the downstairs bedroom is next to the full bath. All have water views. 2000 rates for one or two people were $50/night.

Innkeeper Pat Muller works with computers at Michigan Tech. She serves a continental breakfast. Guests, who range from MTU parents and alums to snowmobilers, are treated like family in this casual place. Internet and computer services are available upon request. Guests are welcome to visit the **horses** and **chickens** in the barn. A well-behaved Great Dane lives here, too. There's **fishing in the stocked trout pond** or from the waterway dock, where a boat can be moored. The paddleboat can be used on the pond or waterway. Water birds and other wildlife are plentiful. **Paths** are being developed through the 35-acre farm. About three miles away, where the Portage Waterway's west end meets Lake Superior, is the

small Stanton Township Park with a boat launch, a swimming beach, and picnic spot. Reserve ahead for good summer availability. Best time to call: 9 p.m.-11p.m. *On Bayshore Rd. off Houghton Canal Rd. about 8 miles northwest of Houghton.*

HA: call 👪: school-age children with good manners are welcome. Only one room is large enough for three.

HOUGHTON CAMPING

CITY of HOUGHTON RV PARK

(906) 482-8745. No reservations.

24 super-modern sites, paved and small, are right on the Portage Waterway a half-mile west of downtown. They are next to the municipal boat launch, fishing pier, swimming **beach**, and a most elaborate **chutes-and-ladders playground**. No tents. Each site has full hookups, cable TV, picnic table, fire ring. No shade. $15/night includes water, sewer, electricity, and TV cable. The park is usually full in July and August but there is a **holding area** without hookups where campers awaiting a spot can stay free of charge. Complimentary e-mail and e-mail address: rvpark@portup.com. *It's just west of town off M-26. Look for the turn along the Portage Waterway where M-26 climbs the hill to the strip.*

H.A. call 👪 🐕 ♿

Hancock (pop. 4,323)

Once you cross the bridge to Hancock from Houghton, it's a short but twisty path as you follow U.S. 41 to reach Hancock's main **shopping street**, Quincy, a one-way street heading west.

Hancock's siting on such a steep hillside did not prove ideal. Its north-south streets are a challenge in winter. Originally half a dozen large natural gullies made deep vertical cuts in the hillside. Laboriously the gullies were filled in, creating today's streets of Tezcuco, Ravine, and Montezuma.

Throughout the 20th century and today Hancock has been the **most Finnish city in America**. Now about 40% of its residents are of Finnish heritage. It was named after the famous colonial-era American, John Hancock, the 18th-century president of the Continental Congress. The frontier town was first settled in the 1860s. It grew large and prosperous with the Quincy Mining Company, nicknamed "Old Reliable" for the steady dividend checks paid to its fortunate stockholders.

Edward Steichen, the influential

American photographer, grew up in Hancock. Mary Chase Perry Stratton, founder of Detroit's illustrious Pewabic Pottery, lived here until the age of 10. Her childhood home at 222 Hancock, perhaps Hancock's oldest building, is being made into a museum.

Although Houghton, the county seat, is now larger, for a long time Hancock was more populous. In 1930 Hancock's population was 5,800, compared with Houghton's 3,800. But Houghton, with its state university, has grown in recent decades while Hancock has shrunk with the collapse of mining and the aging of its once fertile population.

The Quincy Mining Company just above Hancock on Quincy Hill was started in 1848 by Boston-based investors and closed in 1945. It had the longest mineshaft in America, 9,100 feet. By 1913 "the Quincy" employed 1,483. The smelter on the Portage Waterway in Ripley, just east of Hancock, was erected in 1861. Its ruins remain a local landmark. The beautiful old houses just east of the lift bridge in East Hancock were built by mining officials and prosperous businessmen. Most all of Hancock's large historic buildings make good use of reddish sandstone (commonly called brownstone) from quarries at nearby Jacobsville at the eastern entrance to the Keweenaw Waterway 20 miles away.

In the late 19th century, increasingly depressed rural conditions in Finland coincided with an acute need for workers in the expanding Keweenaw copper mines. Mining companies sent agents to Scandinavia to recruit. So many Finns came to the U.P. that they became the region's largest ethnic group. Without previous mining experience, Finns had the most mines' most menial and dangerous jobs. By 1910 Hancock had attracted so many Finnish mine workers that it had gained an overwhelmingly Finnish character, which it retains today.

Finlandia University

In Finland, churches had emphasized literacy, which eventually proved a great advantage to the immigrants. The Finnish Evangelical Lutheran Church, now merged with many other Lutheran churches, opened an academy in 1896 which became Suomi College, now known as Finlandia University. It's the only Finnish college in the U.S. and the **only private college in the U.P.** The name was changed as the college sought to market itself more broadly. Many non-Finns thought "Suomi," the Finnish name for "homeland," had Native Ameri-

can or even Asian origins. But the new name doesn't sit well with a wide variety of local people. The school recently changed from a two-year college to a four-year university. Enrollment has stabilized at around 400. Elementary education (the biggest major), nursing, and business programs draw students of many ethnic backgrounds. Students can also take Finnish language classes. The new fine arts curriculum in fiber arts, ceramics, and product design, was developed on the **model of Finland's leading design school**. The college's **new student union**, Kivi House, is on the hill above the west side of downtown. You can get a good meal at the dining hall, Mannerheim, on Franklin Street. It offers a **splendid view** across the waterway toward Houghton. Next to Kivi House is a well equipped recreation center which visitors can use for a nominal fee. It includes an indoor pool, basketball gym, and fitness center with weights and exercise machines. For a free campus tour, visit Finlandia House at 601 Quincy just west of downtown. For details call (800) 682-7604 or visit www.finlandia.edu/

Downtown Hancock

Hancock's downtown is on one-way Quincy Street that's also U.S. 41, the way to the vacation destinations in Calumet and Copper Harbor. The streetscape, with some empty storefronts, shows the effects of copper's collapse and the rise of strip retailing outside Houghton. Lately downtown Hancock is coming back some, partly because downtown Houghton has so little commercial space. An interesting printed **walking tour of historic Hancock** is distributed at Keweenaw Tourism Council and elsewhere.

Attractions are listed from east (nearer the lift bridge) to west.

◆ **TEMPLE JACOB.** The copper dome of this Jewish synagogue on the steep hillside beneath East Hancock is a familiar yet mysterious sight to motorists driving north off the lift bridge. Before 1912, when it was built, the area's then-numerous Jewish families, mostly merchants, had met for services in halls. The congregation of a hundred families named the temple after benefactor Jacob Gartner, owner of the large Hancock clothing and furniture store still operating under family ownership today. Today the Jewish community is much smaller, but Temple Jacob is used for High Holy Days and other occasions. Now a Reformed congre-

Culture observed above the bridge (that means above the lift bridge)

A Copper Country returnee, who himself lives above the bridge, reports on a recent conversation overheard in Jim's Pizza at 108 Quincy in Hancock "— though 'overheard' is perhaps a strong word, since the waitress was hollering across the restaurant to one of her regulars: 'Yeah, she did the whole shopping circuit, including the Houghton Vinnie's.'

"These are people for whom a trip across the bridge into Houghton is a special trip, saved up for shopping, when, in an orgy of consumerism, they blow their casino winnings on a spree at the St. Vincent de Paul resale store, of which we have several, along with a few Salvation Armies and a new Goodwill. This is in not in any way shameful or degrading.

"It's the way we live: some weird combination of frugal and loose, reserved and loquacious, parochial and fiercely loyal, resourceful when necessary but prone to binges of all sorts, trusting of neighbors but distrustful of authority and outsiders. Why spend hard-won dollars at Wal-Mart's when you can get it cheaper at Vinnie's? Why spend money on clothes and food when you can have snowmobiles and cable? They won't willingly give a penny more than necessary in taxes, but cheerfully pay the same government for lotto."

gation, it is regularly active with cultural and religious programs, though the building is closed in winter.

Visit www.uahc.org/mi/010 for happenings; call Harley Sachs at 482-8814 for a tour. His collection of interesting short stories, *Threads of the Covenant*, illuminates the lives of far-flung Jews in the Upper Peninsula and small towns in Lower Michigan. It's available at North Wind Books in Hancock.

◆ **MAXINE'S.** Over a third of the merchandise at this large gift shop is from Finland, including table runners, souvenirs, books, cookbooks, music, and a large selection of classics of contemporary Finnish design like **durable Arabia stoneware** (mugs are $17 to $20), **iittala contemporary glassware**, new iittala hand-blown collectors' vases and birds, and **Aarikka wood jewelry** ($11-$37) with simplified images of angels, birds, and more. *119 Quincy at Tezcuco, at the end of Quincy's first downtown block.*

482-5101. Mon-Thurs 10-5:30, Fri to 7, Sat to 5, Sun noon-3. &

◆ **COMMUNITY ARTS CENTER.** The attractive large gallery and studios of the Copper Country Community Arts Council are in this low orange building. **Changing exhibits** go beyond contemporary art and crafts to include architecture, antiques, and more. Stop by for a free copy of the council's busy arts calendar. The **gift shop** is worth checking out for unusual handcrafted items: Ojibwa baskets, blown and fused glass, wood, and much more. *126 Quincy/U.S. 41. 482-2333. Tues-Fri 10-6, Sat 10-4.* &

◆ **ST. VINCENT de PAUL RESALE STORE.** If you're an inveterate yardsaler, this large, well-organized store, formerly a Woolworth's, is worth a stop if you're passing by. There are many terrific bargains. The books almost always yield something worth reading, and customers are allowed to root around the basement, where larger things are sorted but not yet priced. Copper Country has lots of savers, and some good stuff eventually ends up here. *204 Quincy/U.S. 41. 482-7705. Open Mon-Fri 10-5.* &

◆ **FinPRO BAKERY & SHOP.** After retiring early from their Helsinki careers in advertising and publishing, Pekka Karstu and his wife, Arja, were persuaded by friends and relatives in the Keweenaw to move to the U.S. and start a store for Finnish products that are hard to get here. FinPro (for Finnish products) is the result. Now it has also become a **bakery** with **Finnish breads and tarts** and a business remodeling saunas and selling Helo **sauna kits**. (A 5'x7'x7' sauna and can be installed in two hours.) Imported sauna brushes, ladles, soaps, etc. are sold too, of course.

Stop by the bakery to sit down for a bite and you may well hear Finnish spoken. The Karstus bake authentic Finnish breads, typically $2.50 for a one-pound a loaf: **limppu** (a rye bread flavored with fennel, orange peel, and molasses), **nisu** (a popular braided **coffee bread** flavored with cardomom), barley bread, and **sour rye**. (It uses a starter that's at least a hundred years old). Individual sweets (60¢ to 90¢) include **ginger snaps**, **prune tarts**, and pirakka (individual barley sweets topped with rice pudding).

Their website, www.finpro.net, has interesting descriptions of their breads, Finnish regional costumes, saunas, and **Puuko knives** (a traditional, multi-purpose survival knife with a bone handle and distinctive leather sheaf). Mail order is available on all baked goods and merchandise. The book section features books translated from Finnish into English. Videos and music reveal some surprises. The tango, for instance, has long been big in Finnish popular music, and inventive students from the Sibelius Academy are known for using folk instruments in new ways. *208 Quincy/U.S. 41 downtown Hancock. Open Tues-Sat 10-5.* &

◆ **FINNISH-AMERICAN HERITAGE CENTER.** A beautiful exhibit gallery hosts changing exhibits of Finnish, Finnish-American, and regional artists and other subjects related to that culture. An extensive historical archive serves anyone interested in Finnish-American roots. Call for occasional special events. A lunchtime Campus Enrichment Hour is held at 11:30 on alternate Wednesdays during the school year. *601 Quincy/U.S. 41, between downtown and the Finlandia University campus. 487-7367. Mon-Fri 8 a.m.-4 p.m.* &

◆ **NORTH WINDS BOOKS and COFFEEHOUSE.** This personal bookstore, owned by Finlandia University, has select general reading and children's books in addition to its regional specialties: **Finnish and Finnish-American books,** history and literature of **the Upper Great Lakes and U.P.,** including maritime, Native American, copper mining, nature and the environment. The Hancock North Winds is the successor to Patricia and Peter Van Pelt's Eagle Harbor bookstore of the same name. It's next to the Finnish-American Heritage Center in a former church rectory that sits back from the street on a small plaza. The coffeehouse should be open by 2002, if not earlier. Manager Susan Ubbelohde keeps up on Finnish topics. She recommends Laila Hietamies' recent historical novel *Red Moon over White Sea* (in translation). It's set in Karelia, the Finnish cultural region on the Russian border at the time of Finnish independence during the Russian Revolution.

The conflict between Reds and Whites is still very much alive in many local families' memories. Mail-order is available; visit www.northwindbooks.com in the works. Call or consult the website for occasional special events. *437 Quincy/ U.S. 41. Parking is in the rear; turn right onto Ryan, which angles. (906) 487-7217. Open Mon-Sat 10-6.* &

◆ **HANCOCK PEWABIC HOUSE & MUSEUM.** Mary Chase Perry Stratton, whose famous Pewabic tiles are familiar architectural ornaments in many Detroit-area public buildings and grand homes of the 1920s, spent her first ten years, from 1867 to 1877, in this simple frame house, one of Hancock's few early buildings to have survived a fire. Her father, a doctor for the Quincy Mining Company, moved here in 1863. The idea for a **multifaceted local museum,** owned by the city of Hancock, came out of the Hancock Historic Preservation Committee. *Renovation/restoration work is still in progress, with a projected 2002 opening.* The museum is expected to include a display on the famous, persevering potter's life and career, a **working pottery,** a room about the history of Hancock, and a doctor's office with interpretation about health and working conditions in the mines. Perry Stratton named her pottery, famous for its iridescent copper glazes, after a Copper Country mine or possibly the Ojibwa word for clay the color of copper. She was an important part of Detroit's significant Arts and Crafts movement. Asian art connoisseur Charles Freer, who made a fortune as the finance man for a Detroit railroad car manufacturer, was the one who urged her to pursue her iridescent coppery glazes. For more Pewabic Pottery history, visit www.pewabic.com Donations of relevant artifacts or money will be much appreciated; call 482-9690. *222 Hancock, the eastbound part of U.S. 41 through Hancock. It's one street below Quincy. The museum is directly behind the Best Western Copper Crown motel. Call Hancock city hall, (906) 482-2720, for details.*

Keweenaw Co-op Natural Foods & Groceries

This is the place to stop for picnic and camping provisions, because of its convenience and outstanding selection. The co-op is definitely the Keweenaw's best specialty grocery, with an **outstanding deli section** It even has meat (verboten in many co-ops), a great wine, beer, and cheese selection, plus organic produce, good bread and crackers, dried fruit, gorp, nuts, local products like squeaky cheese, Asian and Middle Eastern ingredients, gourmet coffees and ice cream. Stop by for trail mixes and quality deli items before heading out to Copper Harbor, and you'll be prepared for impromptu picnics.

As you drive north out of Hancock, U.S. 41 swings hard right at Santori's Tire. To get to the co-op, don't go right, go straight up onto Ethel. Co-op is in 2 blocks at Ethel and Ingot. 482-2030. Mon-Sat 10-8, Sun 10-5. In July & August stays open an hour later. &

Quincy Mine Hoist, Underground Mine and Tram

The **best all-around underground mine tour in the Upper Peninsula** is based at this Keweenaw landmark on Quincy Hill above Hancock. (The Adventure Mine tour near Mass City and Ontonagon, also recommended, provides a good view of mining on an earlier, smaller scale.) Here you'll see the **monumental technology** mining companies developed to extract copper. The two-part tour lasts almost two hours. It begins with the giant hoist, a drum 60 feet high holding 13,200 feet of 1 5/8" cable.

There's a **surprising aesthetic power** to mining machinery and structures like this Nordberg steam hoist and the adjacent No. 2 shafthouse. Tour guides are articulate Michigan Tech engineering students, retired miners, and others, who are able to field all kinds of mining-related questions on

Mining companies provided housing at very reasonable rents to keep a stable work force of family men. Managers used better housing as an inducement for "a better class of workers," by which they often meant those from older ethnic groups, less likely to take up the cause of labor unions. These are Quincy Mining Company houses near Hancock.

The peak years of copper mining coincided with latter years of steam power, and the most profitable companies could afford colossal steam engines. Many were scrapped during World War II. The Quincy Hoist survives and is part of an outstanding mine tour. The huge steam engine powered the hoist, a spool-like 60' drum that pulled a thick metal cable 2 1/2 miles long. It brought copper-bearing rock and man-cars to and from the surface.

many levels. They give visitors an interesting overview of mining at this famous site. Engineering buffs of all ages, from upper elementary on up, are likely to enjoy the tour immensely.

From the hoist, tourgoers take a tram directly down the steep hill near East Hancock. (It's the **Midwest's only cog-wheel tram**, similar to those at Pike's Peak and Mount Washington.) The tram offers a **panoramic view of the canal**, the lift bridge, downtown Houghton, and the surrounding countryside. In the 1880s four such tramways transported copper ore from these mines to stamping mills on the Portage Canal in Ripley. Visitors can take the surface and tram tour alone for $7.50, or $3.50 for children. The tour's **underground portion** also takes visitors on a tractor-driven wagon into a hillside adit (a horizontal mine passage) for half a mile, where it intersects with the seventh level of Shaft No. 5.

The tour shows what a big-time operation Keweenaw copper mining once was. The hoist was designed to haul up a five-ton skip loaded with ten tons of ore at a speed of 36 mph from a **depth of almost two miles**. At the beginning and end of each shift, 30-man cars replaced the rock skips and took workers down into and out of the mines. This happened at the shafthouse, marked by the tall headframe that held the pulley rope. An informative six-minute film shows poignant glimpses of the men as they take their seats to be plunged to a dark, hot, and dangerous place of work.

The hoist operated from 1920 to 1931, at the end of the Copper Country's heyday. The Quincy Mining Company had the resources to build this largest-ever steam-powered hoist because it had mined **one billion pounds of copper**

In the Cornish mining hierarchy introduced to Copper Country, the underground miner was a "fairly exalted category, ranking below captains and bosses but ahead of trammers, timbermen, laborers, and 'boys.' Skill and responsibility were considerable. Income was based on the contract system. The more rock a miner brought out, the greater his pay." —Fred Bryant Jr., a miner's grandson

since opening in 1846. When the giant hoist was installed, the Quincy No. 2 shaft was already over a mile deep. Mine managers hoped that a much deeper shaft would be dug. The copper had become increasingly low-grade. Worldwide competition soon made it too expensive to extract. Only 40% of the copper has been removed. Today's copper comes from much cheaper open-pit mines in Utah, Arizona, Chile, and Australia. A new mine in Peru promises to surpass all the others.

The once-booming peninsula began its decline with the strike of 1913, which itself was brought about by local mining companies' unpopular efficiency moves. The Quincy mine closed in 1931 and reopened temporarily during World War II. Of its 92 levels, groundwater has flooded up to the eleventh level.

On the **underground copper mine tour**, visitors don coats and hard hats in this drippy environment, **always a chilly 40°** at this level. (At deeper depths temperatures became uncomfortably warm.) Loose rock has been bolted for safety. (The Keweenaw mines used to **lose a man a week** due to rockfalls and cave-ins.) Visitors enter a high, scaffolded "stope," dug out of the rock where copper deposits were found.

Be sure to allow time to see the **interesting videos and exhibits** in the hoist house, where the tour begins. Displays include a sampling of beautiful minerals from the Seaman Museum on the Michigan Tech campus; an exhibit on Native American use of Keweenaw copper 7,000 years ago; a video on Keweenaw mining; and models of a copper mine and equipment. A **realistic G-scale railroad model of the mine and mill** shows mining trains in action. The Quincy Mine Hoist Association, a volunteer group of mining enthusiasts, has restored the hoist, hoist house, and No. 2 shafthouse. Its website, www.quincymine.com, has many **historic photos** and **links** with other geology-related sites.

Located 1 mile north of Hancock on U.S. 41. (906) 482-3101. Open from mid April thru

October. From July probably thru color season hours are daily from 8:30 a.m. thru 7 p.m., with the last tour beginning at 6:30. Call for early and late-season hours. **Surface & underground tour with tram ride**: $12.50 adults, $7 children 12 and under. Under 6 free. **Surface tour and tram ride** *(no underground):* $7.50 adults, $3.50 children. &: call.

McLain State Park

Though the scenery isn't as spectacular as that along the rocky Superior shore at Copper Harbor, McLain has **beautiful areas of lakeshore and trees** with the advantage of a central location close to the many visitor sights and services of Calumet and Houghton/Hancock, each eight miles away. The day-use section of the 443-acre park has a **long, beautiful beach** — sand with some stones — backed by dunes and woods of maple, birch, oaks, and pine. It's a lovely place for fall color.

Sunsets over the big lake are spectacular. Benches with two seats flanking a small table make for a perfect spot for refreshments by the lake. The **West Portage Entrance Light** is at the end of a long, rocky pier, guiding pleasure boats into the Portage Canal and Keweenaw Waterway. Once a busy shipping channel, it now sees few larger vessels, mainly the *Ranger III* bound for Isle Royale in season, with an occasional cargo vessel seeking refuge from a storm. The **pretty picnic area** (&) is in a wooded area up on the bluff. A wheelchair-accessible **boardwalk** connects the parking area with the picnic grounds and, farther on, the new **picnic gazebo** (also &) with a view of the lighthouse. At the parking area's other end, the combined bathhouse/ concession stand and playground area perches above the **sandy swimming beach**, protected by the pier and sea wall. (Be advised, only the cold-tolerant will likely want to swim.)

A **trail** winds through the woods by the lake from the day-use area to the campground. Another easy path, the **Bear Lake Trail**, starts opposite the entrance drive, goes back from M-203 to shallow Bear Lake (fine for **children's fishing**). It then goes south a bit along the shore, turns north across M-203, and heads toward the end of the campground loop. In winter these trails and connecting drives are groomed (not tracked) to form **two easy cross-country ski loops**, starting at headquarters and totaling four miles. The park's **wildflowers** seen range from blooms of the spring woods to wetland blossoms and beach peas.

On M-203 at the entrance to the Portage Ship Canal, 8 miles north of Hancock and 8 miles west of Calumet. There M-203 is Pine St., a major cross street toward the north end of Fifth and Sixth. (906) 482-0278. *The park is open year-round. Flush toilets operate from May 15-Oct 15, weather depending. Otherwise, vault toilets are available.* &: restrooms, pavilion, picnic gazebo, connecting boardwalk.

HANCOCK RESTAURANTS

The restaurant in the Ramada Inn Waterfront, now called **THE UPPER DECK**, isn't what it was when the motel opened. Now it's worth visiting mostly for its setting, with a **big view of the Portage Waterway** just west of the lift bridge, and for its small outdoor **deck** — one of the few places with outdoor dining. Recommended: meal-size salads and chili. *99 Navy St. just west of the lift bridge. From Houghton, cross bridge, go right onto M-26, in 500 ft. right again , then right again under bridge. 482-8494. Restaurant open Mon-Thurs 11 a.m. to 10 p.m., Fri-Sun 8 a.m. to 10 p.m. Lounge open until 2 a.m. Patio service from both restaurant and lounge.* & 🚶🚶🚶 Full bar

GEMIGNANI'S ITALIAN RESTAURANT has highly recommended homemade specialties: **gnocchi**, and **ravioli** (meat, cheese, or a surprisingly good cheese and raisin; $6.50 and $8 à la carte). "This is the place for pasta," in the opinion of one food-lover and his vegetarian wife. The family recipe for the thick Northern Italian meat sauce is from the old Gino's, an area landmark. Garlic-cream sauce is a vegetarian option. Nice crusty dinner rolls. House salad is $1.50 extra. Big portions. Sandwich menu, too. Dishes like baked chicken with rosemary potatoes are on specials (always under $10). Homemade pies. Espresso drinks and Italian sodas. This small, homey spot may get too smoky for the sensitive. *512 Quincy/ U.S. 41 toward the west end of downtown Hancock, across from Finnish Cultural Center and Suomi College. 482-2920. Mon-Fri 11-9, Sat 5-9.* &: 1 step 🚶🚶🚶 Beer & wine

HANCOCK LODGING

RAMADA INN WATERFRONT
(906) 482-8400

This full-service hotel, new in 1997, is the only one in the area with its own dockage plus waterfront dining at The Upper Deck. Its **view** of the lift bridge and some of downtown Houghton is interesting. The county marina is within walking distance; so is downtown Hancock, up a steep hill. 51 rooms (half facing the water) are on two floors, with interior corridors. 2000 rates for two: $69 in summer and winter, $65 in off-season (standard double), $92 (whirlpool in corner), $113 suite with kitchenette. The medium-size **indoor pool** and whirlpool face the Portage Waterway and bridge. They have a sauna and outdoor terrace. **Free continental breakfast** in large lobby with fireplace. **Guest laundry.** *99 Navy St. From Houghton, cross bridge, go right on M-26, in 500 ft. right again to marina, then right again under bridge.* **H.A.** 🚶🚶🚶: 17 & under free; $5/extra person

BEST WESTERN COPPER CROWN
(906) 482-6111; (800) 528-1234 (reserv. only); www.bestwestern.com

This two-story, 47-room motel offers the area's best rates ($54-$60 in 2000, depending on season) for an **indoor pool** (medium-sized, with natural light) and **ample continental breakfast** with cereal. The downtown Hancock location is convenient for walks and drives through historic areas, from East Hancock to Quincy Hill. Cable TV includes ESPN, Disney, and free HBO. There's a garage for snowmobiles. *235 Hancock/U.S. 41.* **H.A.** 🚶🚶🚶: 12 and under stay free 🐕: two pet rooms

HANCOCK AREA CAMPING

McLAIN STATE PARK
(906) 482-0278; reservations (800) 44-PARKS; (800) 605-8295 TDD; www.dnr.state.mi.us/

103 modern campsites ($14/$19 night) plus 6 minicabins (in 2001 $32/night, sleep 4) are in long asphalt loops along Lake Superior. There are hookups for electricity but not water. A playground is near the picnic shelter by the main entrance and headquarters. **Spectacular sunsets** provide evening entertainment. The **beach,** which changes in depth and sandiness every year, can be reached from the campground.

Gradually erosion is claiming the campsites closest to the beach. Eventual plans call for moving the campground to the current day-use area and the adjoining property recently acquired along the canal. Then the day-use area would move east to what's now the campground. The **beach** along most of the 443-acre park is backed by **dunes and a woods**. See above for details on the trail system. For **winter camping**, two sites are plowed with electricity by headquarters; tent campers can hike in and use sites cleared by the wind. Vault toilets are available year-round. *On M-203 eight*

miles north of town at the entrance to the Portage Ship Canal. Open year-round. Flush toilets and showers function from May 15-Oct 15, weather depending.

H.A.: 1 shower stall. Picnic pavilion. Call for campsites.

HANCOCK CITY CAMPGROUND
(906) 482-7413;
off-season (906) 482-2720

Conveniently located on the Portage Waterway a mile outside Hancock, this pleasant 70-site campground ($14/night in 2001 for the 52 modern sites) offers good services (showers, cable TV, dump station, pay phones, asphalt drive, newspapers) in a grassy area with some trees. The 18 tent sites ($7) are well shaded and quite private. The adjoining Hancock town **beach** is about a quarter-mile walk through a woods. Reservations are a must for July 4 and advised otherwise, but often space is available here when there's none at nearby McLain State Park. *On M-203. 2 miles west of the lift bridge at Hancock. Open mid-May thru Sept, weather depending.*

H.A.: call : on 6-foot leash

Calumet (*pop. 879*)

Muted echoes of a booming past live on in Calumet, the commercial center of the northern Keweenaw Copper Range. In the early 1900s, Calumet Township's population was over 32,000, contrasted with today's 7,900. Downtown's main streets, Fifth and Sixth, looked like those in a big city more than in a remote mining town. Calumet had movie theaters, a grand opera house, electric lights, frequent trollies, and impressive four-story buildings of brick and sandstone. Evenings were as bright and busy as daytime, because miners worked round-the-clock shifts. Calumet was awash in money.

The **Calumet & Hecla** Mining Company here was the **richest and biggest mining company of them all**. Keweenaw

The copper-rich Keweenaw Fault

Mining historian Tauno Kilpela has found that "95.4% of the copper mined [by 1929] came from a strip of land three miles wide and 26 miles long, stretching from Mohawk [just inside Keweenaw County] to Painesdale [south of Houghton]." His extraordinarily informative map of Copper Country mining locations and geology is sold at stores specializing in minerals or local history.

mines had recruited workers from much of Europe. Many languages could be heard on Calumet's streets: Finnish, Italian, Croatian, Slovenian, French, Polish, Yiddish, German, Swedish, Norwegian, Greek, Arabic, English (spoken in Cornish, Irish, and Scottish accents), Gaelic, and Welsh. **Each major ethnic group had its saloons, over 70 in all**. Outsiders dared not venture into them as the evening wore on. Virtually every nationality had its **church**, often magnificent, built on land donated by the Boston-based Calumet and Hecla mining company.

Starting in the 1870s, the copper mines around Calumet (then known as Red Jacket) proved the most profitable the world had known. Copper's price appreciated as the metal became an increasingly vital component used in the booming electrical and plumbing industries of a rapidly modernizing world.

The region reached its economic peak well before the 1930s Depression. A 1968 miners' strike was the final nail in the coffin, closing the last of the long-declining mines here. A *Wall Street Journal* front-page article profiled Calumet as a town kept alive by its loyal old people, those who returned after retirement and those who never left.

But after decades of decline, the population is again increasing. The Calumet consolidated school district is the Keweenaw Peninsula's biggest. Calumet now even has a fast-food restaurant and a strip mall. History fans of many kinds were outraged when a respected local developer got federal funds to built the strip mall within the core of the fledgling Keweenaw National Historic Park, thereby obstructing one of Michigan's truly magical vistas — that of Calumet's many historic church steeples silhouetted against the evening sky. Now the site is just another a bit of standard-issue sprawl.

An economic bright spot locally has been Calumet Electronics, a manufacturer of electronic circuit boards on Depot Street. A local inventor founded it in the early 1970s to create jobs in the wake of the final mine closings. The company, currently expanding, can compete in this remote location because modems let its customers instantly send design specifications for its custom-made baseboards (components are added to the boards elsewhere), and the lightweight boards can be shipped cheaply by UPS. The circuit boards end up in all sorts of products, from personal computers to automobiles.

In 1992 the federal government, recognizing the Keweenaw's historic importance

Keweenaw cross-country skiing

is exceptional because the area has such beautiful terrain and so many ski enthusiasts willing to work cooperatively to groom trails. The premiere trail system is the beautiful **Swedetown Trails**, 18 miles of cross-country trails winding through small, rolling hills on the south side of **Calumet**. They're groomed, four to seven times a week, for traditional cross-country and ski-skating, and they're skiable well into April, after the snow cover has melted on south-facing slopes up here. A chalet is open daily from noon to 5, and some evenings.

On the northwest side of **Hancock**, the **Maasto Hiihto Trails** are mostly quite advanced. They wind through the steep hillside north of the Portage Waterway, with views across it. Signs show the way from U.S. 41. It's by the Houghton County Ice Arena. (Hancock's excellent website, www.cityofhancock.com, has a trail map.) A warming house has just been built.

A most helpful, annotated overview of 6 trails from Houghton to Copper Harbor, plus ski events and non-trail ski opportunities is **Ski Keweenaw Cross-Country**, a free guide from the Keweenaw Tourism Council (800-338-7982). It's also at **Cross-Country Sports** in Calumet and **Down Wind Sports** in Houghton. Both rent skis and snowshoes.

and responding to local lobbying, established the **KEWEENAW NATIONAL HISTORIC PARK** (337-3168). It's modeled after the urban industrial park organized around the textile mills of Lowell, Massachusetts. The national park boundaries include Calumet landmarks, plus the Quincy Hoist and smelter in Ripley to the south. It's more like a historic district with some protections than any expanse of federal property. In light of the strip mall fiasco and local political pressures, one might well wonder just how much protection and oversight the National Park can realistically provide. The park publicizes additional copper-related attractions as far north as the Delaware Mine and as far south as Old Victoria in Ontonagon County as Keweenaw National Historic Park participating sites.

Over 95% of Calumet will remain privately owned. The National Park Service hopes to use several million dollars to leverage strategic improvements that will help preserve and draw visitors to this imposing historic town. Development of the monumental legacy will occur slowly over the next 15 years. The National Park Service is in the process of purchasing and restoring historic buildings in key locations. The Park Service has bought the C&H administrative office building on Red Jacket Road just off U.S. 41 for use as its local offices. Across the street, the even more impressive **C&H Library** (see below) will be purchased and used to hold local archival materials. The Park Service has purchased the 1885 Union Building at the head of Fifth because it's at the entrance to downtown. Park funds have also gone to help restore the fine old fire station in partnership with a community group. Fifth Street's old paving bricks have been uncovered, giving it even more of a historic look even if it's somewhat bumpy.

National Park signs mark various park components. So far there's been little interpretation and no budget for a historian or for much of a staff until very recently. The good-looking interpretive signs scattered around C&H buildings from U.S. 41 along Red Jacket Road to Coppertown are not really very well thought out. They're too far apart to work as a walkway, and they don't relate their photographs with what is directly visible. The staff would do well to study the components of the timeline at the nonprofessional Chassell Heritage Center and apply that approach to Calumet.

Summer visitors drawn by the brand name of a national park have already helped make downtown Calumet a more vital place. It can be hard to find on-street parking on Fifth Street in summer. (There's plenty on side streets and along Fourth Street lots.) Owners are rehabbing storefronts. Upper-story apartments downtown are being re-occupied.

In exploring Calumet and Laurium it helps to have a local map because the towns spread out into adjoining smaller outlying communities, known as mining "locations." These consist of miners' houses clustered around mine shafts now abandoned and filled in: Tamarack, Centennial, Osceola, Red Jacket, Swedetown, and more. The mining companies built these standard, six-room houses; today they sell for $20,000 and under. Miners in outlying areas (especially Scandinavians) kept milk cows and chickens and big gardens out back to help feed their large families and make ends meet.

Keeweenaw Tourism Council

The local folks who promote tourism up

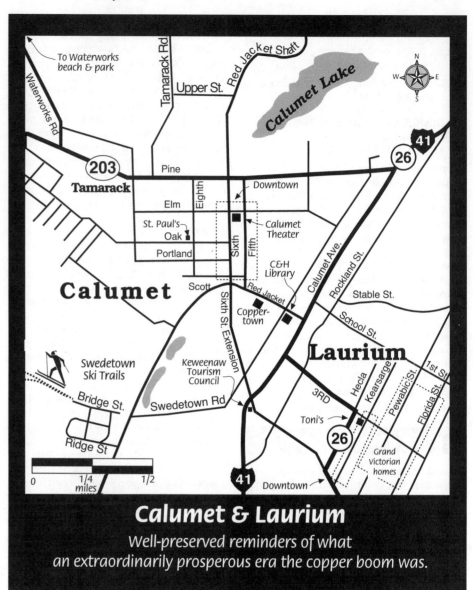

Calumet & Laurium

Well-preserved reminders of what an extraordinarily prosperous era the copper boom was.

here are unusually savvy and interesting in their tips — largely because they are participants and fans of what they write about. It pays off to spend some time picking up free info here or in Houghton. The **lobby** with its literature rack is **always open**. Call and they'll mail you travel publications, too.

U.S. 41 at Lake Linden Rd. (800) 338-7982. (906) 482-2388. Open Mon-Fri 8-5 plus weekends 10-6 in summer; 24-hour lobby. &

Calumet and Hecla Community Library

For extraordinarily beautiful and well-crafted stonework, this building is hard to beat. It was built because the Calumet and Hecla Mining Company and its longtime CEO Alexander Agassiz worked hard to develop a stable work force of family-oriented miners. Building this

library and giving land for churches furthered that goal. Altruism was far from Agassiz's only motivation, as Michigan Tech history professor Larry Lankton has pointed out in *Cradle to Grave: Life, Work and Death at the Lake Superior Copper Mines,* a revealing study for which he read much C&H internal correspondence. Miners who went to church, stayed home, played in bands, and avoided saloons were easier to control, especially when they rented company houses where they could be evicted with little notice.

The library is the striking building with the red and gray stone façade on Red Jacket at Calumet Ave./U.S. 41. Built in 1898, it was designed by a Boston architect related to the company's principal investor, Quincy Adams Shaw, and faced with mining waste rock in contrasting dark and light colors. The basement was a bath house for C&H

families. Reading rooms were on the second floor, including one where men could smoke, with a meeting room on the top floor. Library books were carefully reviewed by Shaw and the mine superintendent to be sure they did not contain material that would support union causes: worker safety, organizing, striking, and related issues. Muckraking authors like Upton Sinclair wouldn't be found here.

For years the library building has housed the offices of Lake Superior Land Company, now part of Champion Paper, which owns much of the land originally acquired by the mining company. The library building has been sold to the Keweenaw National Historic Park.

The interior remains very much as it must have looked when Calumet and Hecla reigned supreme in these parts. The varnished interior trim has never been painted or refinished. There are classic oak desks and map cases, cases of mineral specimens, and a big oil portrait of Alexander Agassiz, son of the famed Harvard botanist Louis Agassiz. Agassiz would rather have devoted himself entirely to scientific research. He was persuaded to spend part of his time for most of his life managing Calumet and Hecla while still living in Boston. Money from mining paid for his zoological and oceanographic investigations. C&H's Bostonian paternalism was widely resented here as controlling and condescending.

East of the office building is a big piece of **float copper** — pure copper formed in pockets created by volcanic bubbles. Such pure copper is found along the Keweenaw Fault, but almost

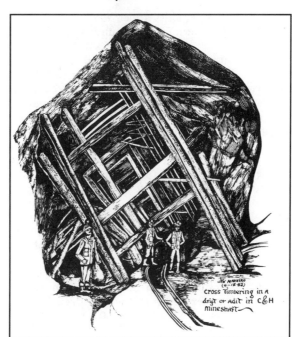

Massive quantities of logs were used in underground timbering to support tunneling for mine shafts, drifts, and stopes (enlarged areas where copper-bearing rock was removed). Rock layers in Calumet & Hecla's shafts, seen here in Jan Manniko's drawing, were steeply tilted. So many trees were cut for underground timbering and to fuel mines' steam engines that remaining forests consisted only of fast-growing sun-lovers like popple and birch.

nowhere else in the world. Outside is a **bronze statue of Alexander Agassiz,** C&H president from 1871 until his death in 1910. His **cold, analytical gaze** follows you unsettlingly as you shift your point of view.

On Red Jacket Road, just west of U.S. 41 by the turnoff to Calumet. 337-0202.

Coppertown Mining Museum

An excellent overview of copper mining, from both economic and social standpoints, is given by the **13-minute video** that starts a museum visit here. The rest of the museum, which includes a lot of

older and newer mining equipment, can be a little overwhelming if you don't pick and choose, and if you don't gain a conceptual framework through which to view all the details. You might even want to sit down, rest your feet, and see the video a second time.

Coppertown was started in the 1970s by local history enthusiasts who had largely worked for C&H. Many displays seem unprofessional by today's much slicker standards, but there's a lot of good stuff here. The **handmade model of Calumet** shows how the town grew up around mine shafts, which are no longer visible. The miners' point of view is con-

Much of the support for the 1913 strike came from women, whose daily parades through the streets encouraged strikers, and from trammers, who had good reason to turn to radical politics and unions. Most companies, including the wealthy C&H, used men as beasts of burden rather than exploring electric haulage, as Quincy did. So states Larry Lankton's detailed study of work in the copper mines, *Cradle to Grave.* The trammers pictured here (with a man who is apparently their supervisor) worked in an unidentified iron mine near Ironwood, but did the same work: in Lankton's words, they "continued to lift, fill, push, and unload vast tonnages of [rock]. Tramming remained the most physically demanding underground occupation." It fell to most recently arrived immigrant groups.

veyed in the display on the **Strike of 1913**. A recreated medical dispensary shows how general health care for miners, like many aspects of the mining system in Lake Superior mines, was a practice carried over from mines in Cornwall. If you're interested and patient, you can learn how usable copper was produced from copper-bearing rock, and understand crushers, smelters, and stamping mills.

The vacant space next to Coppertown used to be the grey iron foundry where C&H cast gears, bushings, and other parts for machinery used in mining and processing copper. A life-size room setting of its pattern shop clearly shows the steps in **casting iron in sand molds** — a vital part of many, many Michigan industries, yet invisible and unknown to the general public. Some old patterns are for sale. They're handsome wood objects painted black, russet, or tan, or left natural.

On Red Jacket Rd. between U.S. 41 and downtown Calumet. (906) 337-4354. Open from late May into early October. Mon-Sat 10-5. In July & August also open Sundays 12:30-4. Adults $3 (NPS passport $2), children 12-18 $1. Under 12 free. &

Downtown Calumet

Downtown Calumet is increasingly geared to the brief tourism season. Visitor-oriented stores cluster on Fifth Street, the main shopping street. It's one-way from the east as you enter downtown from U.S. 41. Oak developed as a business street, too, because it led downtown from the railroad station.

Here are downtown highlights, arranged from east to west.

◆ **KEWEENAW HERITAGE CENTER/ St. Anne's Roman Catholic Church.** This **splendid Gothic Revival church**, built of red sandstone in 1900 by French-Canadian immigrants, sits at the entrance to downtown Calumet. It's part of the cluster of churches and steeples — a wonderfully symbolic vista now marred by a strip mall. The church was deconsecrated in 1966 when ethnic Catholic parishes merged into larger churches. It fell into disrepair. Rev. Robert Langseth, then pastor of the Faith Lutheran Church in Calumet, conceived of the idea of preserving this key landmark as a **multi-ethnic heritage center**. A broad-based citizens' group has already raised $250,000 to help stabilize the building. They themselves have cleaned the interior to show the **beautiful stenciled Gothic patterns** on the walls. The **stained-glass windows** have been repaired, and their soft greens and blues bathe the interior in a diffuse light. It will be years until the building is restored and the permanent **"Steeples and Storefronts"** exhibit can be installed. It will "explore the lives of men, women, and children by looking at their homes, shops, bars, and churches," according to the brochure.

Meanwhile, volunteers hold the church open for visitors. Temporary exhibits have been quite interesting. 2001 showcases a school project in which sixth-graders photographed ways everyday life in 1900 differed from that in 2000. Advanced high school art students painted key local landscapes and buildings. **Donations** form seed money for matching grants and are much appreciated; make checks to Keweenaw Heritage Center, 106 Red Jacket Road, Calumet 49913. *Fifth St./Red Jacket Road ad Scott streets, downtown. 337-2534. Generally open from Mem. Day weekend thru color season, Mon-Sat 1-4:30. $1 donation requested to help pay for heat.* &: many steps. When renovated, a rear elevator will provide access.

◆ **COPPER WORLD.** The selection of copper items here is tremendous, almost overwhelming. Items range from copper teapots, plates, and molds to copper specimens, burnished sailboats, weathervanes, and copper jewelry. The hottest item at the moment: Don Korach's images of Keweenaw wildlife, lighthouses, and mines hand painted on turkey and other feathers. Second-generation owner Tony Bausano has an **excellent selection of videos and books about the region and about mining**; a video monitor lets you preview videos. *101 Fifth. 337-4016. From late June to Labor Day open Mon-Sat 9-8, Sun 1-4. Otherwise Mon-Sat 9:30-5.* &

◆ **HERMAN JEWELERS.** For this versatile, fifth-generation store, owner Ed LaBonte's father Herman makes jewelry of **Keweenaw greenstones** and half-breeds (copper and silver) and **Lake Superior agates**. There's also a **coin department**. Ed's repertoire of useful repairs includes fixing clocks and watches and soldering broken eyeglass frames. *220 Fifth. 337-2703. Mon-Sat 9:30-5 and by appointment.* &: one step.

◆ **THURNER BAKERY. Good pasties** ($3), fresh out of the oven every day but Sunday at around 10:30, and **saffron rolls**, another Cornish introduction, are among the products of this longtime local bakery. *319 Fifth, downtown Calumet. 337-3711.*

◆ **CROSS COUNTRY SPORTS.** Staffed by owner Rick Oikarinen and a crew of avid mountain bikers and cross-country skiers who helped develop the Swedetown Trails. They are happy to give visitors specifics on the area's fabulous mountain biking, cross-country skiing, and snowshoeing opportunities. Sales and rentals of cross-country skis, mountain bikes, and snowshoes. *Downtown at 506 Oak between 5th and 6th. (906) 337-4520. Open Mon-Fri 9:30-6, Sat to 5.* &:

Next to the Calumet Theater on Sixth Street is the lavish Shute's Bar, built in 1893 by Italian-born Marco Curto, after working for C&H. Today it's been restored to tip-top condition. It's open daily for drinks but not food. Another fabulous saloon interior is the Michigan House bar and restaurant down the street at Sixth and Oak. Calumet's 70+ saloons catered to specific ethnic groups, reinforcing social divisions.

Taxes on local saloons helped pay for the grand Calumet Theater. Visitors can tour the dressing room used by Sarah Bernhardt. Many summer performances take place here.

one step.

◆ The **MICHIGAN HOUSE**, the large railroad hotel, restaurant, and saloon from 1906, is reopening as a restaurant. The **original saloon interior** is well worth a look for its **elaborate tile floor** and massive bar with a **wonderful mural showing jolly German picnickers**, all drinking **Bosch Beer**, brewed in nearby Lake Linden. The greens and browns of **numerous stained-glass windows**, lamps, and backlit doors harmonize with the mural. Partners Tim Bies and Sue Kane, longtime Keweenaw visitors and fans, have moved from Alpena to rehab the building and launch the restaurant. They have hauled out over two tons of trash and bad plaster and they have installed a new ventilation system, which should do a lot to remove the smell of decades of beer and tobacco. They are making the third floor into their residence. Later they expect to create week-

end lodging on the second floor. *337-6849. At Sixth and Oak.* ♿: call

◆ **CALUMET POST OFFICE**. Inside is a **dramatic W.P.A. mural of broad-backed miners at work deep within the earth.** *Sixth at Portland.*

◆ **CALUMET THEATER and Village Hall.** The **handsome opera house** was built in 1900, part of a grand civic project that incorporated the existing Red Jacket village offices and council chambers. (Red Jacket consolidated with nearrby mining locations and became Calumet in 1929.) The first floor is faced in red sandstone from nearby Jacobsville, and the sandstone Renaissance Revival ornament of its arched entryway is continued on all window frames on and the four-story tower. Taxes on Calumet's busy and numerous saloons helped pay for the opera house.

Tours are held in the summer and fall. The **interior** has been **faithfully restored** to its original rich colors. The paintings on the proscenium arch are allegorical figures of the muses of painting, drama, poetry, sculpture, and music, with blue sky and puffy clouds behind them. In 1999 the proscenium murals were restored or recreated for the theater's centennial. The old theater still creaks enough to seem truly historic. Tourgoers get to visit the dizzying upper balcony and antiquated lights still in place. When you get to the **backstage dressing room** used by Sarah Bernhardt, among others, it's not hard to imagine the grueling life of rail travel that took the likes of John Philip Sousa and Douglas Fairbanks to such remote corners of the country.

For a century the 710-seat theater was the region's premiere performing venue. Now the much larger, air-conditioned, handicap-accessible, state-of-the-art Rozsa Center on the Michigan Tech campus has assumed that role. The Calumet Theater is booking more well-known perfomers and local and regional talent suited to this very special, more intimate venue. The theater is close to an ideal venue for music like Bolcom and Morris's concerts of American popular song from the 1890s on, and for the Chenille Sisters vocal trio. There'll be more shows for summer visitors, including specially produced historical revues like Copper Country Heritage in 2001. *Downtown at Elm and Sixth. (906) 337-2610. www.portupo.com~calthea The 40-minute guided tours begin in June (call for June hours) and run through color season, Wed-Sun 11-2. Self-guided tours ($2) are available at other times whenever the box office is open, which is Tues-Sat*

11-6. ♿: main floor only. Half the tour is not accessible

◆ **SHUTE'S 1890 BAR.** Next to the Calumet Theater, this **landmark saloon** has become a popular gathering spot. It still has the **magnificent original back bar** and all the trappings of boom-town saloons. The bar itself has a **splendid stained-glass canopy with vines**. Elaborate plaster caryatids frame the raised dance floor. The owner's restoration has won high praise. *322 Sixth, next to the Calumet Theater. 337-1998. Open daily, noon to closing (2 a.m. or whenever no one's there).* ♿: call.

◆ **UPPER PENINSULA FIREFIGHTERS' MEMORIAL MUSEUM.** The historic Red Jacket fire station is filled with exhibits and memorabilia. *Sixth St. across from the Calumet Theater. No phone. Early June thru Sept. Mon-Sat noon to 3. $2 adults, $1 ages 13-18, 12 & under free.* ♿: ground level only

◆ **Site of the 1913 ITALIAN HALL DISASTER.** A memorial park marks the site of a famous, horrible and needless tragedy. At the Italian social hall's 1913 Christmas party, during the fifth month of the bitter mining strike, someone yelled, "Fire." People rushed down the stairs, ignoring shouts that there was no fire, and 73 people, mostly children, died, trampled and smothered, in a stairwell whose doors opened inward and were locked shut. **"1913 Massacre," Woody Guthrie's moving song,** blamed mining bosses for the unsolved deed — a logical conclusion, though the perpetrators were never found. Filmmakers are making a film of the song and the story; their outstanding website, including photos and song lyrics, is at www.volcanomedia.com/lvg/calumet

The Italian Hall Disaster, together with the widely published photographs of dead girls looking like angels in the temporary morgue in the village hall, created widespread sympathy at every level of Copper Country society for the victims' families. Previously strikers had been successfully branded as socialist agitators by the local press, linked as it was with mining officials. Italian Hall was used for decades afterwards. Eventually it fell empty. Like so many other Calumet buildings, it was demolished in 1984, over much local opposition. Local people will describe the eerie scene of how the building refused to succumb quickly to the wrecking ball. *Downtown on Seventh near Elm.*

St. Paul the Apostle Church

Summer tours of the **unusually elaborate church** let you see the **beautiful stained glass windows**, altar, and paintings. It was built by Slovenian Catholics between 1903 and 1908. Today four historic congregations have joined together to worship here. In her monumental *Buildings of Michigan*, architectural historian Kathryn Eckert calls it "a double-spired Richardsonian red sandstone extravaganza. . . . which rises authoritatively over the village like a cathedral of medieval Europe." Go north on Eighth from here and you'll be in Calumet's most attractive residential district.

On 301 Eighth at Oak. (906) 337-2044. The church is generally open as early as 7 a.m. and closes at noon. During summer, parishioners serve as guides from noon to 3 p.m. Mass: Mon-Thurs 8 a.m., Fri 6:30 p.m., Sat 4 p.m., Sun 8 a.m. & 10 a.m. No charge; donations appreciated. &: no.

CALUMET RESTAURANTS

See Kearsarge and Laurium.

At press time, Calumet remains pretty much a dining wasteland. But things may improve when the **Michigan House**, a wonderfully preserved saloon and dining room at Oak and Sixth, opens up after renovations. 337-6849.

The **Evergreen Inn** at 108 Fifth is a charming vintage lunch counter with original booths and interior. It does well with breakfasts. 337-4700.

CALUMET LODGINGS

ARCADIAN MOTEL
(906) 482-0288
This older motel, set back from the highway with a big lawn, offers an **excellent value**. Each of the 13 nicely furnished standard rooms with two double beds ($40) has a phone, microwave, mini-fridge, and personal decorating touches from co-owner Barb Heinonen. (That's her country gift shop, Traditions, in an adjoining cottage.) Free morning coffee and rolls are served in the office. An upstairs kitchenette ($45), not quite so pleasantly furnished, has a good view. *On U.S. 41 four miles northeast of Quincy Hill and six miles south of Calumet.*
H.A.: call ♦♦♦: rates by the room

AmericINN
(906) 337-4990; (800) 634-3444 (reserv. only); www.americinn.com
The traveling public in the U.P. has welcomed AmericInn's format: a big, comfy entrance lounge with fireplace and breakfast area (where a free **continental**

breakfast with cereal is put out); **indoor swimming pool** room with big window-walls, whirlpool, and sauna; and attractive rooms with the requisite contemporary amenities (cable TV, phones) and luxuries. An addition soon followed. First-time Keweenaw visitors from down below often want the familiarity of a chain motel close to famous visitor attractions. The AmericInn, grown to 68 rooms in 2000, has made things harder for ma-and-pa motels deemed adequate by longtime Copper Country visitors. On our visit in fall, 2000, rates for two in a standard double (2 queens or one king) were $72; the same room with a whirlpool in the corner was $20 more. Ask about the executive room with mini-fridge, microwave, and pullout sofa. Expect higher rates on some weekends, lower rates after color season and in spring. All rooms have coffeemakers. *5101 Sixth St. Extension by the strip mall. From U.S. 41, turn west at Tourist Info office.* **H.A.** ♦♦♦: 12 & under free; $5/extra person 🐾

ELMS MOTEL   (906) 337-2620
www. keweenaw.org
Virtually the same room as the Americ-Inn, smack in the heart of historic Calumet opposite the theater and Shute's Tavern, can be had for around $41 (the rate in fall, 2000). Each of the 14 surprisingly pretty rooms in this two-story, exterior corridor motel has cable TV, free local calls and mini-fridges. In fall of 2000 there was a whiff of cigarette smoke; there were no smoke-free rooms. *335 Sixth Ave. at Elm at the west side of downtown Calumet.* **H.A.:** call ♦♦♦: $2/extra person

Laurium (pop. 2,126)

While Calumet was the business center of the northern Keweenaw mining range, its sister city of Laurium just across U.S. 41 developed more as a **bedroom community** of miners and higher-ups. Some blocks are lined with **fine old mansions** built by mining officials and prosperous merchants and bankers. Most of the town has simpler miners' homes. Laurium was platted by a minor mining company of the same name, borrowed from a famous mining site in ancient Greece.

The main street, Hecla, has a **fine red sandstone village hall**, re-faced from its original brick façade in 1914. Originally Osceola Street was the village's main thoroughfare. But late in the 19th century the Palace Hotel and assorted stores were built on less expensive Hecla Street. After the turn of the

century Hecle began to rival Calumet's main commercial boulevard, Fifth Street. There were once three banks on Hecla, several hotels, and the sizable Vivian's department store, now the local hospital's rehab center at Hecla and Fourth.

But Laurium's glory days began to fade with the bitter 1913 miners' strike. Its population once neared 9,000. But the turmoil of the strike prompted a sizable number of residents to move to Detroit, where Ford was paying $5 a day. In the aftermath of that long, slow decline, Laurium has become a commercial backwater compared to downtown Calumet. **THE YARD SALE**, a well-organized resale store, has taken advantage of the inexpensive space and built a thriving business in two buildings on opposite corners of Hecla at Third. Yard Sale furniture and many, many LP records occupy a former bank. *Hecla at Third. Open Tues-Sat 10-5 and occasional Mondays. 337-5012.*

Just east of downtown, along Tamarack, Pewabic, and Iroquois streets between Second and Fourth, is a **lovely, settled, neighborhood of turn-of-the-century homes**, built with style and comfort to compensate mine managers for the hardships of living in this remote region. Some of these **houses are quite grand**, with rear carriage houses, low red sandstone walls along the street, sweeping stairways, and stained-glass windows (if they haven't been removed by old-house strippers who came through the area several decades ago). Deep maple shade sets this part of Laurium apart from the sparse streetscapes of miners' homes.

For a **takeout picnic**, you can pick up pasties and other baked goods at Toni's Country Kitchen, nearby on Third at Kearsarge, and walk two blocks east to the pleasant, shady corner park at Third and Pewabic. Free Thursday-evening **summer concerts** featuring an interesting variety of top local talent take place in the band shell here at 7 o'clock. On the northeast corner of this intersection stands one of the most sophisticated of the area's grand historic mansions, the **1898 Vivian House**, built of red sandstone and shingles in the horizontal, asymmetrical Shingle Style.

At 320 Tamarack, year-round tours are available of the **LAURIUM MANOR INN**, a showy turn-of-the century mansion with huge columns and interesting interior murals. The stained glass and original lighting were sold off by a previous owner. 45-minute guided tours are from mid June thru mid October at noon, 1, 2, and 3 p.m. The cost is $4 for adults, $2 for children. In the off-season tours for $3 and $2 are self-guided. Call 337-2549 to make sure there isn't a conflict with a wedding or other events.

At the edge of this neighborhood, where Tamarack joins Lake Linden Road/M-26, the **GEORGE GIPP MEMORIAL** commemorates Laurium's most famous native son, better known as **the Gipper**, the Notre Dame football star whose deathbed scene gave Ronald Reagan his most memorable role. It is made entirely of football-shaped fieldstones. Jukuri's Sauna on M-26/Lake Linden Avenue at Iroquois, was one of the U.P.'s few remaining public saunas when it closed because the boiler gave out.

Northwest of stately Pewabic Street, fans of old houses may also enjoy seeking out the house at 101 Willow at First. Paul Roehm, "the region's preeminent stonemason and supplier," according to architectural historian Kathryn Eckert, used Portage Entry sandstone in his own 1896 house, a picturesque, simplified version of H.H. Richardson's Romanesque Revival.

LAURIUM RESTAURANT

Honors for **best Keweenaw pasty** are usually given to **TONI'S COUNTRY KITCHEN & BAKERY**. It's a very popular spot in a small, newish building. There are tables for eating in, and a huge carryout business, too. Breakfast is served all day. The one-pound pasty ($2.50 to go, $2.75 eat in) is made with coarse-ground chuck and rutabagas. Homemade soups are $1.50 a bowl. Sandwiches range up to $3.50 for the popular Reuben. The bakery is known for cookies and big cinnamon rolls, saffron bread, and other U.P. ethnic specialties. Eric Frimodig has owned Toni's for 19 years but kept the name of a previous owner, Antoinette Coppo. His late father, Mac Frimodig, was well known as a manager of Fort Wilkins State Park and as an authority on U.P. history and culture, though he would wince at being called an authority. Mac's notecards of sauna scenes with Finnish/English sayings are for sale here. No credit cards. Out-of-town checks OK. 79 Third St. next to post office on north end of downtown Laurium. *From U.S. 41 one block north of the Tourist Info office, turn east onto Third. 337-0611. June-Oct: Mon-Sat 7 a.m.-5 p.m. Closed Mondays in off-season. Closed most of January.* ♿ ♟♟♟

LAURIUM LODGINGS

LAURIUM MANOR INN
(906) 337-2549;
www.lauriummanorinn.com

A mining magnate's 45-room neoclassical revival mansion is now a bed and breakfast inn with 10 guest rooms. An earlier owner stripped and sold its fixtures, but original fireplaces and murals remain, along with **unusual wallcoverings like elephant hide** in the dining room and a **forest mural** painted above the library wainscoting. Advertising has enabled the innkeeper-owners, Michigan Tech alums, to position their two inns, the Laurium Manor and Victorian Hall across the street, as a luxury experience. A large inn operation like this is more like a small hotel than a typical B&B, and guests see more of the paid staff, less of the innkeepers. If you're thinking of relaxing during the day, be aware that group tours are given from noon to four. Though occupied guest rooms are off-limits, the common areas won't be very private. The 10 guest rooms, all large, have phones, 8 have private baths, most have TVs. Photos of each room are on the website. Typical rates: for standard room $79-$89 in season (late June-color season), $59-$69 otherwise. Rooms with shared bath: $55-59 in summer. Large suites with two beds: $119-$149 in summer, $89-$109 winter. Guests can use front parlor, music room, library, dining room, and the big front porch. Full buffet breakfast. No air-conditioning. *320 Tamarack, east of downtown Laurium and north of M-26/Lake Linden Rd.* ♿: no ♟♟: well behaved children over 4

VICTORIAN HALL   (906) 337-2549;
www.lauriummanorinn.com
The owners of Laurium Manor across the street have renovated this **1906 brick four-square late-Victorian mansion** in an historic manner. Each of the 8 guest rooms has a bath, **many have fireplaces**, and a few have whirlpools and TVs. Guests share the parlor, library, dining room, and porch, and have **full buffet breakfast** at Laurium Manor (see above). No tours of this inn are offered, which makes it quieter during the day. Same rates as Laurium Manor. Details, room photos, and rates are on the website. *Check in at 320 Tamarack (above).* ♿: no ♟♟: well-behaved children over 4.

WONDERLAND MOTEL & CABINS
(906) 337-4511

This **quaint little complex** (three attached motel units and several duplex cabins with **kitchens**) has real possibilities for thrifty travelers who enjoy **retro places**. Reservations may not be necessary, even in peak summer season. The cabins are clean and cute, if on the plain side: linoleum floors, wood kitchen cabinets, a two-burner gas stove and full refrigerator, a pleasant eating area and small back bedroom. Some cabins have two bedrooms. All bedrooms have two double beds. 2000 rate for all units: $35/night. Fans; no air-conditioning. There's a pleasant little lawn with seating in front, and M-26 here isn't too busy. The immediate neighborhood — ranch houses and gas storage tanks — is uninteresting, but the most beautiful streets of Laurium are just a few blocks away. Many guests come back again and again, but the owner may have to stop operating as a transient motel due to a changing market. *787 Lake Linden Ave./M-26, just over a mile east of U.S. 41 in Calumet. Open May through October at least.* **H.A.**: call   ♟♟♟: $5/extra person

Kearsarge

This old mining community on U.S. 41 just north of Calumet, was named after the *U.S.S. Kearsarge* by a former naval officer with the Calumet and Hecla Mining Company. Copper deposits here were discovered in 1882. The Centennial Mine was closed in 1930.

The Last Place on Earth

Idiosyncratic, truly personal shops like this are things to treasure, and they go against current trends, even in Keweenaw tourism. Here are Jan Manniko's memorable paintings and stationery, and wooden items, including wooden spoons, carved by her husband, Tom Manniko, in all sorts of functional shapes and sizes. Jan's portraits of Copper Country landscapes and people sometimes are done in loose, expressionistic brushstrokes and swirling color, sometimes in detailed pen and ink drawings. Folks at the morning kaffee klatsch, hunched over their mugs, smoking cigarettes, or old mining machines, or railroad engines — whatever the subject, they're all done with great affection that doesn't pretty up the subject. (Many are on view at the Copper Country Community Arts Council gallery/gift shop in Hancock.)

In the tradition of curiosity shoppes, here are antiques and collectibles including Copper Country bottles and old mining memorabilia, glassware and dishes and glass lampshades, even some books, and whatever new things Jan and Tom are creating. Right now she's doing papier-maché owls. The friendly wood stove adds to the mood.

The shop's poetic name goes back to 1968. Tom, a Calumet native, and Jan had decided to settle up here. (Jan was from Florida and met Tom at her parents' restaurant in Copper Harbor, the Coral Inn, which later became the Harbor Haus.) They were "sick of renting," so they bought this building, then quite decrepit, with a fallen-in floor and 40 windows that had to be replaced. After Tom and his father finished renovating it, he said, "I wouldn't do this again if it were the last place on earth!" That's the store name, said Jan. They live upstairs. Extremely simple living and the income from this summer business has enabled them to pursue their interests without resorting to day jobs. *59621 U.S. 41. Look for the two-story dark red cement block storefront at the bottom of the hill in Phillipsville, three miles north of Calumet. 337-1014. Open daily including Sunday 9-5 from Mem. Day weekend into late Sept or by appointment.* &

KEARSARGE RESTAURANTS

The HUT INN offers consistently good diner fare in a **remarkable owner-built setting** inspired by Frank Lloyd Wright. The founding owner started The Hut in 1952 as a drive-in hamburger stand. For the building material, he used "poor rock" (waste rock with no copper in it), and added on each winter when he closed. Wrightian touches include massive stone walls, a pool and waterfall, and low, angled ceilings with big beams. The trek to the restrooms is an adventure. Known for quarter-pound steakburgers ($2.75, or $5.75 with fries, applesauce or cottage cheese, choice of soup, salad, or tomato juice), daily specials ($3-$5), homemade pies ($2.25), and gingerbread with butterscotch sauce and whipped cream. The dinner menu ($6.25 to $10, including soup, salad or juice, potato, and bread basket) ranges from steaks, chicken, fish to vegetarian dishes like a **flavorful nut and cheese loaf** (made with walnuts, cashews, and cheeses, $6.25 served with salad and cottage cheese) and vegetable lasagna with fresh fruit ($6). *On U.S. 41 one mile north of Calumet. 337-1133. May thru color season: now open for break*fast. *Open daily except Mon 7 a.m. to 9 p.m. , to 8 p.m. Sun. Off-season: call about breakfast; may open at 11:30 a.m. except possibly for weekend breakfast. Occasionally closed in spring.* & ♟♟♟

Despite the new name and new menu, the **LOG CABIN INN** has the same owner-chef, Eric Karvonen, who was half the ownership team when this was known as the Old Country Haus. There's

The Garnet House bed and breakfast is a mining captain's house with its original lighting, woodwork, and leaded glass.

no more salad bar, and there's a single menu all day, with smaller and larger portions of many dishes, like fresh whitefish ($7.25 and $11.25) and steaks. A variety of homey entrées like lasagna, meat loaf, pork chops, shrimp scampi, and Southern fried chicken have replaced most of the German dishes, but two remain: Jaegerschnitzel (a breaded veal cutlet with mushroom sauce) and the Bavarian platter with sauerbraten and bratwurst. Entrées come with potato and tossed salad. Vegetarian entrées on request. All the desserts are made here; the amaretto Bavarian cream torte is Eric's favorite. The log interior features mounted game and an unusual back bar incorporating a long log with carved images of moose, dogs, bear, fish and a long 27-link chain carved of one piece of wood. *On south side of U.S. 41 2 miles north of Calumet. 337-4626. Mid-June thru color season: opens daily at 11:30, to 9 except for Sunday to 8. Off-season: closes at 8, or Fri & Sat at 9.* **H.A.** ♟♟♟ full bar

KEARSAGE LODGINGS

BELKNAP'S GARNET HOUSE
(906) 337-5607;
www.laketolake.com/garnet

The captain of the nearby Centennial Mine built this mansion in 1898, now **meticulously preserved** and furnished true to period by Debby and Howard Belknap. The Belknaps love people, old houses, canoeing, and the U.P. Their first restoration B&B project was the Hanson House, an outstanding lumberman's mansion in Grayling. Now they have moved their year-round residence from outside Saginaw to the U.P., and their **side yard perennial garden is fabulous**. Two guest rooms ($60) share a bath and two ($75) have private baths. A

suite ($90) includes a sitting room. All guest rooms now have air-conditioning and **cable TV and VCRs**, with an ample supply of feel-good movies. A full breakfast is served in the elaborately detailed dining room. Guests use dining room, two parlors, cable TV in the den, a phone in the hall, and a wonderful front porch. The wooded three-acre yard has interesting outbuildings, and wildlife seen from the porch. The Hut Inn restaurant is across the street; the Log Cabin is within walking distance. *On U.S. 41 one mile north of Calumet, across highway from The Hut. Open mid-June thru color season.* &: call ♟♟♟: well-behaved older children

Lake Linden (*pop. 1,081*)

Lake Linden and its sister city, Hubell, profited from their location on the shores of Torch Lake, first by shipping lumber, and then by being the site of copper stamping mill and smelters. Lake Linden was largely settled by French-Canadians who worked in the woods and lumber mill.

Torch Lake got its name from Indians who fished at night with torches and spears. It connects with the Portage Waterway and Lake Superior, so large vessels could travel all the way to Lake Linden docks. By the late 1870s the big white pines were gone. Finns turned the area's cut-over land into farms. In 1900 the French-Canadians built the **beautiful, twin-towered St. Joseph Catholic Church**, on the main street just north of downtown. Most of the church's original interior survives.

Calumet & Hecla's great innovation was to develop a process that extracted small amounts of copper deposits carried by much of the area's rock. A key to the process was a stamping mill to crush the rock brought up from the mines. C&H's first stamping mill, built in 1866, crushed rock transported by narrow-gauge railway from the company's Calumet-area mines down the steep hill to Lake Linden/Hubbell. A smelter then extracted copper from the crushed rock. By 1873 an astounding **10,000 tons a year of ingot copper were shipped from here**. The later stamping mill and smelter, whose remains are visible today, were among **the world's largest**. They finally closed during the 1968 strike.

The amount of tailings, a fine red sand left from the stamping the mined rock, was so great that it has filled in large parts of the western Torch Lake shoreline, mostly in Hubbell. Recently, a $15 million

At Lakes Dairyland in Lake Linden, you can get Jilbert's terrific ice cream (its Mackinac Island Fudge is way better than most) and take in the streetscape dominated by the cathedral-like spires of Saint Joseph Church. French-Canadian Catholics built it in 1900-1912. Lake Linden remains a noticeably French town.

EPA Superfund project has covered the tailings with sandy loam, resulting in grassy parkland along the shoreline. Today it's a favorite spot for geese to gather, and eagles are also commonly seen.

Most workers who live in Lake Linden now commute to jobs elsewhere. It is home to one of the U.P.'s more exotic businesses: Nitrate Eliminators Inc. on Calumet Street/M-26 across from the Lindell Chocolate Shoppe. Owned by a Michigan Tech professor and his wife, the biotech company has garnered substantial federal research grants for developing enzyme-based products for water testing and treatment. It also sells a home-nitrate testing kit for $12.95.

Lindell Chocolate Shoppe

This elaborate sweet shoppe has **survived pretty much intact from the 1920s**, the glory days of that restaurant genre. The marble counter on the soda fountain has given way to Formica, but the back booths and paneling are perfectly preserved. The interior is all aglow with golden oak, accented with little fringed lamps. Quick lunch counters and soda fountains like this thrived in newly industrialized areas, where workers had cash for inexpensive treats. Italian and especially Greek immigrants latched onto the sweet shoppe as a business opportunity where the whole family could work, making hand-dipped chocolates and ice cream, and where it didn't matter if their English was rudimentary. Here the Greek owners' names, Grammas and Pallas, are proudly spelled

out in tiles on the entryway. See below for food. *300 Calumet. 296-0793. Mon-Sat 6:30 a.m.-7 p.m., Fri to 8. Closed major holidays, last week in August.* &: one step.

LAKE LINDEN RESTAURANTS

See also Al's in Hubbell, Quincy's in Dollar Bay.

A 1922 Greek sweet shoppe in all its original glory. the **LINDELL CHOCOLATE SHOPPE** retains its fine golden oak wainscoting and booths with little fringed lampshades, its tile floor, mirrored back bar, fretwork, and stained and leaded glass. The ensemble cost $3,700 in 1922. Today the Lindell isn't just a visitor attraction but a popular hometown spot, where regulars meet for coffee and breakfasts like two eggs, sausage, from-scratch hash browns, and toast ($4.15). "Much better than average diner fare," proclaimed an Ann Arbor visitor who especially enjoyed her onion rings and sugary-crusted pie. Some call the food classic; others say it's uninspired. Changing daily specials and Friday evening fish fry. Rice pudding and ice cream (choclate, strawberry, and vanilla) are made on the premises. No credit cards or out-of-town checks. *300 Calumet/M-26 in downtown Lake Linden. 296-0793. Mon-Sat 6:30 a.m.-7 p.m., Fri to 8. Closed major holidays and the last part of August, the two weeks before and including Labor Day.* &: one step. 👫: $2.50 kids' special   Full bar

Stopping at **LAKES DAIRYLAND** is a regular summer ritual for Jilbert's ice

cream lovers (there's even fried ice cream). But it also has a full menu including breakfasts, four homemade soups, lots of sandwiches, meal-size salads ($5 and under), and good daily specials served in the dining area, with lots of booths. Lake Linden's schools are just down the street. This small-town gathering spot attracts just about every age group in town. Lots of fried appetizers are on the menu (onion rings, chicken nuggets, etc.) but there are always low-fat options like buffalo burgers, baked potatoes, and veggie and turkey sandwiches. No credit cards. *On M-26/Calumet Ave. at the north end of downtown Lake Linden. 296-0414. Open from April 1 into mid December, daily 7 a.m. to 10 p.m.* &

The utterly plain exterior of the **DREAMLAND HOTEL** would lead you to think it's just a bar. Actually, on winter weekends and every day in summer the kitchen turns out a full menu of steaks, delicious broiled shrimp dishes, fresh fish, salads, and more. Even the bar menu, served any time, offers better eating than many bars: pizza made on the premises, fresh burgers and steak and chicken sandwiches ($4 to $6), homemade soups, and fried chicken. Year-round there's fresh fish on Friday, either deep-fried or broiled — half a pound for $7.25 including potato and salad. Regular dinner entrées are mostly around $9 to $13. The side dining room is smoke-free.

Steamers used to take holiday-makers from Houghton and Hancock to the hotel, park, and dance pavilion here. Patrons can still arrive by boat and walk a block through the woods to the hotel. Norbert Sarazin, one of the original loggers of 19th-century Lake Linden and a major area landowner, started the resort and hotel in 1913, and it's still in the family. Jim and Gladys Sarazin have owned it since the late 1940s; their daughters Tina and Laurie run it today. The interior seems to be from the early 1950s. *Eight miles south of Lake Linden on Bootjack Road. Follow the east shore of Torch Lake until you reach the hotel. 296-3191. Bar open year-round Mon-Sat from 11 a.m. to 11 p.m., Sun noon to 10 p.m. Full menu served weekends year-round, daily in summer.* &: 2 steps, assistance provided. Rest rooms are tight.

LAKE LINDEN LODGINGS

LAKES MOTEL   (906) 296-9528
This simple, 8-room motel is between the Lindell restaurant (see above) and the village recreation area (see below for features). It could be a centrally located

backup option if better locations were full. Lake Linden itself has its small-town, walk-anywhere charms, and better restaurants than Calumet. Each room is much more pleasant than are suggested by the loose block step by the entrance encountered on a fall, 2000 visit. Rooms were clean and fresh, though none were no-smoking, and the decor was attractive in a retro way: plain white walls, maple furniture, white chenille bedspread. $45/night (one bed) and $48 (two beds). There's no outdoor sitting area of any kind, but the park is nearby. Cable TV. No phones. Rooms face the side street, not M-26. Open year-round. *301 Calumet/M-26 at Third in downtown Lake Linden.*

H.A.: call. Big step into room. 🚶🚶

LeBLANC MOTEL   (906) 296-0105

This 12-unit motel may interest boaters and anglers. It's way off the beaten path in Bootjack, a quiet rural area 3 1/2 miles south of Lake Linden, on the shore road toward Dreamland (where the old hotel serves good food) and Jacobsville. Rice Lake and Mud Lake, both known for fishing, are within four miles; Keweenaw Bay is just beyond them, with a boat launch on Grand Traverse Bay at the end of Rice Lake Road. An excellent swimming beach is 15 minutes away at Jacobsville. Rooms are good-size and nicely coordinated. None are smoke-free. All have coffeemakers and cable TV with ESPN. Rates in 2000 for 2: $31 (1 double bed), $36 (1 queen with kitchenette). Snowmobilers welcome. *On Bootjack Road. From M-26 in Lake Linden, turn at the north end of town, toward Gay, but stay along Torch Lake — that's Bootjack Road —for 3 1/2 miles.* **H.A.**: call 🚶🚶

LAKE LINDEN CAMPING

LAKE LINDEN VILLAGE REC. AREA (906) 296-9911 for info & reserv.

Part of a town park with volleyball, basketball, tennis, an elaborate playground, a picnic shelter, and a roller rink, this 20-site modern campground offers some advantages for those not in search of a quiet, remote, natural setting. There's a **swimming beach**, boat launch, dump station, and cable TV. All sites $11/night. Tents are welcome. It's right on Torch Lake and within easy walking distance of three restaurants, a good supermarket, and an interesting town to explore. Reservations advised but not always necessary from late June through mid-August. July 4 weekend is reserved way ahead by homecoming locals. *From*

M-26/Calumet St., turn onto Third opposite the Lindell Choc. Shop toward the lake. Park is in a block. Open from Mem. Day weekend thru Sept. 30. **H.A.**: yes. Sites are grassy and hardened with gravel. Paved walks connect park attractions to town. 🚶🚶 🐕: on leash

Dollar Bay

Three miles east of the lift bridge, Dollar Bay is an unincorporated place whose several streets strech between M-26 and the small bay off the Portage Waterway after which it is named. The bay is round like a dollar coin. The village sits on the isthmus to the Dollar Peninsula, over five miles long at its longest point, which forms Torch Bay and the marshy channel to Torch Lake, much used by copper stamping mills. Like its neighbor Lake Linden, Dollar Bay began as a lumber town. Today it is the home of Horner Flooring, makers of maple flooring for basketball courts and other uses.

DOLLAR BAR RESTAURANT

QUINCY'S RESTAURANT & LOUNGE is a very popular gathering spot for its **cozy atmosphere** and extensive collection of **mining memorabilia**, starting with the mining train in the parking lot (Quincy mine replaced tram cars with trains) and ending with murals of miners in the restrooms. The menu ranges from Chicago-style pizza and burgers to steaks to Mexican and daily specials, including **turkey dinner on Sunday** and **fish on Friday** — a little bit of everything, modestly priced for local customers. "Great fish fry, mobbed with locals," comments one area diner. Another writes, "I have never understood its appeal. I think the atmosphere is better than the food. My favorite is the **root beer on tap**." *On the lake side of M-26 in Dollar Bay, 3 miles east of the lift bridge and 7 miles south of where M-26 turns to go up the big hill in Lake Linden.* 482-2118. *Kitchen open daily 11:30 to 11.* 🚶🚶 Full bar

Hubbell

The long Torch Lake waterfront close to many mines made Hubbell the logical location for several stamping mills, where heavy stamping machines crushed copper-bearing rock to free its copper. Water flushed out the copper and rock onto mill equipment designed to separate copper from rock. The Quincy, Osceola, Tamarack, and Ahmeek mines all had stamp mills here,

and C&H also had a smelter.

Houghton County Historical Museum

The onetime Calumet & Hecla smelter office and medical dispensary now houses the collections of the Houghton County Historical Society. Representative shops, businesses, and rooms of homes from the early 20th century have been recreated using artifacts from the museum's extensive collection. On the grounds is Lake Linden's CCC-built log warming house for skating, with still more artifacts, perhaps more interesting for their randomness: a Soap Box Derby car, a license plate collection, old sleds, the switchboard controls first used on the lift bridge. This is definitely a "community attic" museum rather than a museum that uses artifacts to tell key stories in local history.

For **rail fans**, Copper Country has been a magnet, what with its short-line mining railroads and diverse engines and equipment. Some have ended up here. The Soo Line caboose that was on the last train to Copper Country in 1983 is now open to visitors here. Soon C&H Engine #3, used on the 36" track between Calumet and the Lake Linden stamping mill, will be under shelter on the grounds. The Traprock Valley schoolhouse is here. So is an old depot. The museum office is in C&H's fire hall, now shared by **COPPER LAND ARTS & CRAFTS** gift shop (296-9191).

On M-26 south of downtown Lake Linden. (906) 296-4121. Open from mid June thru color season, Mon-Sat 10-4:30, Sun 12-4. NOTE: if no one is in the museum by 3:30, volunteers start closing it up. Tours by appointment given any time of year. Adults $5, seniors & students $3, children 6 to 12 $1, under 6 free. ♿: ground level and most outbuildings.

Upper & Lower Hungarian Falls

The dropoff from Laurium to Lake Linden and Hubbell on Torch Lake is spectacularly steep and scenic because, with the lake just ahead, you're descending along the edge of the of tilted volcanic crust that broke off along the copper-bearing fault line. The drive along M-26 is dramatic. So are the hill's two series of waterfalls. Douglass Houghton Falls, on private property off M-26, has been closed to public access. But the various falls of Hungarian Creek, tucked above and behind a neighborhood in

Hubbell, are just as worthwhile a destination. Sudden dropoffs make it no jaunt for rambunctious children. Follow Hungarian Creek downstream past two unnamed falls in a shady canyon. After about 1/4 mile of steep, root-filled trail you will reach the dramatic, 15-foot Lower Hungarian Falls dropping across a series of rocky steps.

From M-26 in Hubbell, go up Sixth St. where there's a sign to a golf course. In 2 blocks take the left fork, park on your right. at the fork. Walk across the road over to the trail along the nearby creek. Walk upstream to the dam and Upper Falls, a sheer 25-foot drop. Walk downstream to the Lower Falls. &: no.

HUBBELL RESTAURANT

AL'S SUPPER CLUB/TROPHY LANES
A local man who eats out often from Houghton to Copper Harbor says Al's has the best pizza north of the bridge. His vegetarian-leaning wife likes the chicken picatta, part of the full menu. New owner Jim Goldsworthy, happy to have come back to Copper Country from specialty construction in metro Detroit, is moving away from the old-fashioned supper club concept, which implies that eating out is just for weekends. *1500 Duncan/ M-26 in a two-story building that's one of downtown Hubbell's few going businesses. 296-0128. Kitchen open daily from 4 p.m. to 10 p.m. except in May and early June closed Mon & Tues.* & ♟♟ Full bar

Jacobsville

One of the U.P.'s most remote communities, Jacobsville today is not so much a village as a scattering of homes around an historic church and an old lighthouse. But in the year 1900 it numbered over 600 people. Most were here because of the uncommonly high quality of local red sandstone. (Iron precipitate gave Jacobsville sandstone, also called brownstone, its red color.) At the quarries that flourished here, simple mechanical wooden pole cranes would load heavy slabs of this valuable building stone onto schooners for transport.

The cliffside views from Jacobsville east across Keweenaw Bay are striking. Nine miles away is the Abbaye Peninsula jutting into Lake Superior. South and east of it can be seen the irregular outline of the Huron Mountains, including Mount Arvon, Michigan's highest point.

Although Jacobsville is only a dozen miles southeast of Houghton, it's a 40-

From the 1870s into the 1890s, red Jacobsville sandstone widely used as a building material and architectural trim. Architects liked its rich color and the ease with which it could be carved into column capitals and other ornaments that were key components of the Renaissance and Romanesque Revival styles. This photo shows one of the quarries at Jacobsville, at the north side of the East Portage Entry across the Portage Waterway from Chassell. Huge blocks were taken by tram cars to docks. Steam-powered drills, hoists, and channeling machines enabled large blocks like this to be easily cut, hauled, and shipped. Kathryn Eckert describes the process in *The Sandstone Architecture of the Lake Superior Region.*

minute drive via Lake Linden because the Portage Waterway and Torch Lake have create an isolated peninsula. At first, residents could only get here by boat, but a road from Lake Linden was completed in 1888. Even then, for many years the mailman would boat across the waterway, get into another car, and deliver Jacobsville's mail.

Jacobsville sandstone quarrying began in 1883. In five years over a hundred homes were built here. The village soon had a hotel, two saloons, a drug store, and a general store, none of which remain. Huge quantities of the distinctive red sandstone slabs were quarried over the years. (The sandstone may also be striped, dotted, and spotted, depending on whether chemicals that repelled the red iron were also in the water that leached through the sandstone as it was being formed.) Most stone was shipped to Marquette and transported by rail as far away as New York City. Nearby, Calumet, Hancock, and Houghton have many impressive buildings of Jacobsville sandstone. (The entire rock formation, which goes well beyond Jacobsville, is known as the Jacobsville formation.) By

1900, the rich, dark colors of sandstone was losing favor as a building material. The dark rich colors of Jacobsville sandstone were becoming unfashionable. Influenced by the classic revival and Chicago's "White City" world's fair of 1893, architects came to prefer the whites and beiges of Indiana limestone.

As local quarries closed, the area's many Finns switched to farming. Jacobsville became known for strawberries. In the 1950s its strawberry festival drew big crowds until they became too large for the tiny community to handle. The festival moved across the Portage Entry to Chassell, where it is a high point of July.

Today Jacobsville offers the patient, pokey visitor a number of simple pleasures. To get there, drive southeast from Lake Linden around Torch Lake. At Dreamland (marked by the **quaint Dreamland Hotel** and bar), turn onto Dreamland Road, which veers left and away from the water. At its end, in about eight miles, you'll be at the end of the road in Jacobsville. Turn right and you'll soon pass the former Coast Guard station and come to the **WHITE CITY PUB-**

LIC BEACH, once a commercially operated beach and picnic grounds reached by excursion boat from Hancock. Here a long pier extends out into Keweenaw Bay, with the **PORTAGE RIVER LOWER ENTRANCE LIGHT**, a handsome four-story tower, at its end. The pier's smooth surface lets you walk far out, surrounded by water.

If, instead, you turn left from the end of Dreamland-Jacobsville Road, you'll soon pass the small white community hall and then see a sign on the left at the head of a quarter-mile-long driveway to the beautiful little **FINNISH EVANGELICAL LUTHERAN CHURCH**. This prim, white-frame church was built in 1886 by a carpenter known for his skill with houses, sailboats, and skis. Today summer people and local residents keep up the church and use it from summer through fall for **Sunday evening vespers**, held by volunteer clergy at 7 p.m.

Ahmeek (pop. 157)

The village grew up near the four shafts of the Ahmeek Mine, opened in 1903. The Kingston Mine and Allouez Mine were also nearby. "Ahmeek" means "beaver" in Ojibwa, and beaver were plentiful in the area. Ahmeek developed a small commercial area because of its location on the Mineral Range Railroad and later an interurban. Like several other Keweenaw County towns along U.S. 41, Ahmeek is looking perkier lately. Business from summer visitors has induced several people to restore old buildings and open shops. A coffeehouse/gift shop is the latest of these.

True North Antiques

Dan and Marge Contour have bought the large building erected in 1915 for the Glass Brothers General Store. It is in excellent condition and fun to visit. Their attractively displayed general line includes what's clearly the **largest collection of antique mining artifacts** for sale anywhere in the U.P. *1 Vivian St. From U.S. 41, turn west at The Station. 337-1961. Open year-round. From May thru Oct. open Tues-Sat 10-6, Sun noon to 5. Closed Mon. From Nov-May open Fri-Sun 10-6 or by appt..* &: all but upstairs

Keweenaw Handicrafts Shop and snow gauge

The entrance to Keweenaw County is marked by this charming stone shop

Most U.P. residents are proud of the amount of snow they endure. The snow gauge on U.S. 41 between Ahmeek and Mohawk posts the previous year's total. Snow compacts and melts, so there's never 300 inches, as indicated here, on the ground at any time. Five feet — that's another matter. Snow removal is a major government expense and a major domestic activity.

and the snow gauge on the opposite side of U.S. 41. The store building is one of Keweenaw County's many appealing W.P.A. relief projects from the 1930s. There are **woodland footbridges**, a **play battleship** made of mining poor rock in Mohawk, rock walls on Brockway Mountain and at the Keweenaw Mountain Lodge. Relief projects were widespread because of Keweenaw County's 85% unemployment rate during the Depression. Families who had moved downstate for factory jobs came back home when their jobs disappeared.

The shop, now run by the **Community Action Agency**, sells things made by around **200 craftspeople** from the region: wood toys, agate jewelry, quilts, Christmas decorations, afghans, and more. Among the ordinary dolls and kit crafts a few attractive, reasonably priced traditional crafts stand

out, including rag rugs and handmade children's sweaters under.

The much-photographed **snow gauge** in a roadside park records annual cumulative snowfall, often 250 inches. Because the accumulated snow continually compacts and melts, there's rarely more than five feet on the ground at any time, except in drifts. Snow removal is a major priority of local government. Residents don't usually have to wait long for the snow plow to come, but it's understood that all Keweenaw winter engagements are tentative, depending on the weather. *South of Mohawk on U.S. 41 just north of Ahmeek, where 41 swings east and Cliff Drive continues straight ahead. 337-5737. Open daily Memorial Day thru mid-October. In May & June: noon-5. Otherwise 11-5.* &: one step.

AHMEEK RESTAURANT

The interurban waiting room and generator station was a local gathering spot, grocery, and ice cream fountain when streetcars ran from Houghton to Mohawk, starting when the station was built in 1907 and ending with the streetcars' last run in 1932. The first phone in Ahmeek was here. **THE STATION** again serves Jilbert's ice cream and gets people together, not only for ice cream cones but for a limited menu of homemade sandwiches, soups, and salads. Owner Mark McEvers recommends the **classic Italian sub**, made fresh according to a recipe he brought from Detroit. **Picnic tables** are outside, but be sure to go inside, too. Check out the marble counter of the oak **soda fountain**, the back bar, the tongue-and-groove paneling, and the interesting collection of old sheet music, antique advertising signs, and **streetcar memorabilia** Mark has assembled. His diligent restoration work and historical research have earned The Station a place on the state and national registers of historic places, which he hopes will be an extra inducement for a future buyer to expand the restaurant into the generator room. The Station is for sale: building, food service, and Mark's sign and graphics business. *On U.S. 41. 337-0350. Currently the ice cream window opens on Mother's Day, the sit-down area opens the second week of June. Closes after Labor Day.* **H.A.**: outdoor seating only 🚶🚶🚶

Mohawk

This old mining town is the largest in a string of spare, plain mining settlements stretching along the central spine of the Keweenaw Peninsula north toward Copper Harbor. In all of Keweenaw County there are only 2,300 full-time residents. Mohawk, the county's biggest town, is the home of its biggest employer, the county road commission. It removes snow in winter and runs the Keweenaw Mountain Lodge in summer. The **MOHAWK SUPERETTE** (337-2102) at 158 Stanton, one street east of U.S. 41, is the county's only full-service grocery with meat and produce departments. It's a **handy picnic stop**.

Lately Mohawk has attracted the attention of even the most hurried motorists on their way to Eagle Harbor and Copper Harbor. Colorful versions of famous paintings have been painted on big plywood panels by children. This is one project of **KEWEENAW KRAYONS ARTS ALIVE**, which now sponsors **free concerts** in Mohawk and other Keweenaw communities, gives free art lessons to local children and retirees, provides free internet access to local kids, and more. It all happened by accident a few years ago when Carol Rose Fouts moved up to Copper Country to be near her grandchildren and bought a house and beauty parlor on U.S. 41. She started Ramblin' Rose Hair Care & Art Gallery. Kids started hanging out at the shop. Mohawk is a mile long and four blocks wide — a place where kids ride bikes and have unstructured time. Carol turned the back of the store into a free art studio for kids. She learned how to write grants to fund more Keweenaw Krayons activities. By 2000 it was clear that the future lay in arts programming Keweenaw-style — accessible without fees, since a fair number of people couldn't or wouldn't pay. Now the physical gallery has closed and gone online at **www.RamblinRoseArt.com**, and the arts programming has taken off. Pick up a schedule in the area, or visit **www.keweenawkrayons.com**

Within a block of downtown Mohawk, at 237 Fulton, is the home and shop of Philip Switzer, a Pentecostal Christian who **carves ornate crosses** and other objects. His crosses, ranging from three inches to five feet high, have been taken by missionaries to spots all across the globe. They sell for $20 to $100.

The Wooden Spoon

Owner Bruce Beaudoin bakes bread and cookies and sells jams made in part from berries he grows: strawberries, currants, gooseberries, raspberries, and more, some available in low-sugar versions.

Thimbleberry jam is far and away the biggest seller. **Breads** (currently $2.50 for a 1 1/2-pound loaf) include cottage cheese-dill bread, pilgrim bread (cornmeal, honey, rye, and wheat), **saffron bread**, and more usual varieties. Honey, syrup, candles, and soaps are locally made. The woodenware spoons are bowls are from cottage industries in Idaho and Vermont. Also sold here: **antique Munising Woodenware** products. *On U.S. 41 at the south end of Mohawk, east side of road. 337-2435. Open from Mem. Day thru mid Oct., Mon-Sat 10-5. Also sold mail-order and online at www.exploringthenorth.com, then see "The Wooden Spoon."* ♿

Superior Crafts

Resourceful locals make cedar rustics — classic outdoor furniture and lawn swings — in a former building of Mohawk 3 & 4 mines, the **"dry,"** where 300 to 400 miners at a time cleaned up and changed clothes after their grueling shifts. Signs about mine safety precautions are still on the walls. Furniture is boxed partly-assembled for convenient transportation. *On U.S. 41 just south of Mohawk. 337-0875. Mon-Fri 8-5, Sat 8-1.* ♿: no.

MOHAWK RESTAURANTS

Though redecorating has turned the visual atmosphere into more of a generic small-town country look, **SLIM'S CAFE** retains its special social ambiance as "the best place to see people who have never crossed the lift bridge in their whole life" — and perhaps even that's something of an exaggeration. The pies are "great," according to food sophisticates; the blueberry pie is "to die for." Only part of the dining room is smoke-free. *On U.S. 41 at the north outskirts of Mohawk. 337-3212. Open daily from 7 a.m. to 8 p.m. year-round. From late June thru Labor Day open to 9 p.m.* ♿

Phoenix

Here the volcanic crust fractured along the Keweenaw Fault becomes a **dramatic, sheer rocky precipice**. This cliff looms over the Eagle River, which cuts through the Cliff Range at Phoenix and tumbles down to Lake Superior. In 1844, the Cliff Mine near Phoenix became the Keweenaw's first mine to earn big profits. North of here to the Keweenaw's tip at Copper Harbor, copper deposits were closer to the surface, and in smaller amounts. Mining boomed early, in the 1840s, and played out soon.

The picnic table next to the **CHURCH of the ASSUMPTION** is a fine place to sit and take in the view of river valley and rocky cliffs. The simple wood Catholic church was built in 1858 to serve Irish workers at the Cliff Mine. Later it was moved east a couple of miles to here. The Keweenaw Historical Society maintains it as a historical site. Visitors can see the interior through plexiglass. *On U.S. 41 near M-26 junction. Viewable by visitors from mid-May thru color season, 10 a.m. to 8 p.m. Donation requested.* ♿: 3-4 steps.

If you turn west onto M-26, you'll be following the Eagle River. About 300 yards past U.S. 41, if you look up on the hill to the right, you'll see a red frame building. This is the **BAMMERT BLACKSMITH SHOP**, donated, complete with tools, to the Keweenaw Historical Society. It too can be viewed from behind plexiglass. *Open from mid June to early October, 10 a.m. to 5 p.m. daily. Donation requested.* ♿

Central

Here are the scattered and **exceedingly picturesque remains of a mining town** that numbered over 1,200 residents in 1880. Central Mine was organized in 1854 to mine a vein exposed by a pit dug by prehistoric miners. It closed in 1898, having paid dividends of nearly two million dollars on an original investment of $100,000. It and Cliff were the eastern Keweenaw's most profitable mines.

The **Keweenaw County Historical**

Artist Jan Manniko captured the mood of old houses at Central.

The Central Methodist Church was the social center of the mostly Cornish mining town. Once a year the church is again active for the Central Reunion. Now that the Central's residents have passed on, the Reunion service memorializes all mine workers and their "years of hard work, lives of pain and hope" — the subtitle of *Central Mine*, a compilation of interesting articles. This and other drawings by Jan Manniko are available at The Last Place on Earth shop between Kearsarge and Ahmeek.

Society has purchased 11 weathered frame houses and 38 acres of land at Central. It has opened a modest **visitor center** in one house near the highway. Central is a low-key destination, best enjoyed while walking. It combines wildflowers and gnarled old apple trees, hauntingly spare buildings and ruins, and **beautiful views** across to Mount Horace Greeley. In mining days the landscape was quite bare, in contrast. Directly off U.S. 41 just west of the road to the townsite, the **"towering pile of poor rock** dominates the landscape and is the physical and spiritual center of Central," wrote one Central summer resident. "It is a testament to the years of hard work that went into making a successful mine. And it it the place wehre many generations of rock hounds have spent countless happy hours — prospecting."

The street that goes farther up the hill passes the doctor's house, a simple place. If you turn east at the first cross street, you'll pass the paymaster's house (now one of Central's private residences) and come to the beautiful **stone ruins of Engine House #2**, which powered the mine's steam hoist. Beyond it is the business manager's imposing house.

Central's residents were largely Cornish. In 1868 they built the simple Methodist church with the fortress-like crenellated tower, in the style of old Cronish masonry churches. It was the community's social center; the basement held the Sunday school and library. You'll see it if you turn left at the cross street up the hill. The annual **Central Reunion** has been held at the church since 1907, when the new Keweenaw Central Railroad enabled the town's scattered residents to return for a homecoming. At early reunions "the hills were black with people." The Cornish were known for singing — like the Welsh, who were kindred Celts, Methodists, and miners. The mighty bass voice of one Central miner was said to penetrate 10 levels into a mine and 15 miles down the road. Hymn-singing and a cornet band were the preferred forms of musical expression among the largely teetotaling Methodists here. Choirs sang hymns competitively, with the yearly championship held in Calumet.

The Central Reunion is still held at the church on the last Sunday of July. It doesn't recreate an old-time Methodist service. But its well rehearsed choir includes some of the old hymns at both the 9 a.m. and 11 a.m. services.

Central is just north off U.S. 41, three and a half miles east of the M-26 junction. Look for the sign and go up the hill. Site open year-round. Visitor Center open from early June thru color season, 10 a.m. to 5 p.m. daily. &: buildings have steps.

Eagle River

Driving through this little village and summer resort today, it isn't evident what a wild past Eagle River has had, going back to the beginning of the copper boom in 1845. Over a **dozen copper mines** sprang up to the east of here, including Cliffs Mine, the Keweenaw's first profitable copper mine. Although Eagle River had no good harbor, it became an important port for provisioning the mines and shipping copper. Long docks had to be built out to reach deeper water in Lake Superior. Earlier, French-Canadian voyageurs camping here had given the place its name, after the many eagles they saw.

Eagle River, Copper Harbor, and Eagle Harbor, all near the Keweenaw's tip, are among the oldest European settlements in the western U.P. Many Eagle River houses and churches date from well before the Civil War. They're simple frame or log buildings — without any fancy trim of late 19th-century buildings in Calumet or Laurium, Houghton, or Marquette.

Eagle River soon became the county seat, first of Houghton County, then of Keweenaw County after Houghton County was split off. It grew to have two breweries and the well-known Eagle River Hotel that hosted American President James Garfield and influential newspaperman **Horace Greeley**, he who advised, "Go west, young man." Greeley was a shareholder and director of a Keweenaw mining company. By 1880 an Eagle River company that made fuses for mining explosives was making 50,000 feet of fuses a day.

Clarence Monette's interesting booklet on Eagle River tells how on Sundays the town attracted many workers from the surrounding mines. Lethal fights were common. Animosity between the skilled Methodist miners from Cornwall and the Irish Catholic laborers was tremendous. Eventually a sturdy attic jail was built in an attempt to quell the violence. But even that wasn't enough to hold a notorious brawler, a miner of Herculean strength named Jemmie Tresize. Desperate, the town council ordered a 200-pound ball from Detroit and attached it by chain to Tresize's ankle before he became too inebriated. He was left in a yard, but was later seen at a saloon, a drink in one hand, the iron ball in the other.

Here are some interesting places in Eagle River today:

◆ The worn monuments in the rustic **EAGLE RIVER CEMETERY** attest to the many dangers and accidents that cut

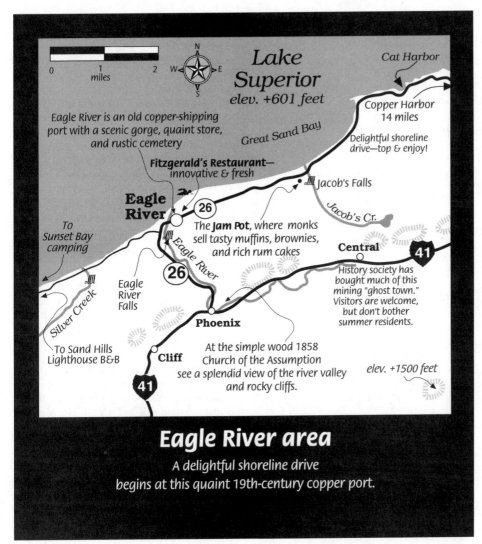

Eagle River is an old copper-shipping port with a scenic gorge, quaint store, and rustic cemetery

0   1   2 miles

N W E S

Lake Superior
elev. +601 feet

Cat Harbor

Copper Harbor 14 miles

Delightful shoreline drive—top & enjoy!

Great Sand Bay

Fitzgerald's Restaurant— innovative & fresh

Jacob's Falls

Jacob's Cr.

Eagle River

26

The **Jam Pot**, where monks sell tasty muffins, brownies, and rich rum cakes

Central

41

To Sunset Bay camping

26

Eagle River

Eagle River Falls

History society has bought much of this mining "ghost town." Visitors are welcome, but don't bother summer residents.

Silver Creek

Phoenix

To Sand Hills Lighthouse B&B

Cliff

41

At the simple wood 1858 Church of the Assumption see a splendid view of the river valley and rocky cliffs.

elev. +1500 feet

Eagle River area

A delightful shoreline drive begins at this quaint 19th-century copper port.

short miners' lives. *On M-26 south of town.*

◆ **DOUGLASS HOUGHTON MONUMENT.** Douglass Houghton, Michigan's state geologist and an early Detroit mayor, first drew attention to the Upper Peninsula's mineral riches. He combined the region's land survey with a geological survey. In a storm on one such expedition he drowned off the shore of Eagle River. He had ignored the recommendations of his French and Indian guides and decided to continue their canoe trip to keep an engagement. (His dog survived, and so did two guides, who told the story.) This dull monument commemorates his foolhardy death. The side street crosses the river to town and passes the 1874 Eagle River Lighthouse, now a private home, built in from the shore by the river. *On a corner on M-26 at the south entrance to Eagle River.*

◆ **KEEWEENAW COUNTY COURTHOUSE & JAIL.** Extensively remodeled in 1925, the courthouse resembles a frame Southern mansion, with massive columns and portico and a fanlight over

the door. Inside, you can get a useful **map of county highways and byways**. Government in this tiny county is an exercise in small-scale thrift and ingenuity. The jail next door, behind the sheriff's pleasant frame house, was temporarily closed for remodeling to bring it up to code so that the tiny county would no longer be forced to pay to transport prisoners considerable distances and jail them at approved facilities. Here prisoners (mostly arrested on alcohol-related charges) still eat good food prepared by the sheriff's wife for family and staff. *Where M-26 bends west after the falls and bridge, continue up the hill for one block. 337-2229. Open weekdays.*

◆ **EAGLE RIVER FALLS**. As you pass over the M-26 bridge across the Eagle River gorge, pull over to the right, walk over onto the old iron bridge, and look upstream for a **view of the waterfall rushing down the steep hillside** and the ruined dam of the Lake Superior Fuse Company. Downstream, see the **dramatic wood arches** supporting the new bridge.

◆ The **EAGLE RIVER STORE** was built in 1867 as the growing mining village's general store. The store has had a variety of occupants in recent years. In 2001 it sells not ice cream but **drums,** made by drumweaver Len Novak, dreamcatchers, and other Ojibwa handcrafts. *On Main St. at M-26, just east of the Eagle River. &: a few steps*

◆ **TOWN BEACH**. Just south of the Eagle River Inn and north of the Eagle River mouth is this simple public beach on Lake Superior. *At the foot of Main St. Turn at the Eagle River Store and continue down to lake.*

M-26 from Eagle River to Eagle Harbor

At Phoenix, M-26 turns west for about two miles, following the Eagle River to the village of the same name. Then it goes east along the Lake Superior shore to Copper Harbor. Beginning at Eagle River M-26 is **one of the most idyllic highway landscapes** in the United States. From here to Copper Harbor, the Lake Superior shoreline looks a lot like Maine — only without the summer crowds. **Rocky shores and islets** are interrupted by occasional crescent bays and beaches — some sandy, some rocky. Roadside parks have **benches, picnic tables, and occasional gazebos**. Tidy rustic signs hanging from brown cedar posts point out historic and scenic highlights. On the opposite, uphill side of the road, trails climb into ferny-floored forests of pine, balsam, and hardwoods.

Here, and at many sunny areas of birch and aspen in the Keweenaw, the landscape looks amazingly like Scandinavia. Thimbleberry bushes, with their velvety, maple-like leaves and bright red summer berries, border many roads and cover open woods. One house advertises **"Thimbleberry Jam for Sale."** The intensely-flavored spread is locally prized. The Jam Lady here is now a man, who has taken over his late wife's business. In a blind taste test at the U.P. Tourism & Recreation conference, **his jams were judged best**.

Signs sometimes point out the paths to waterfalls, formed as short creeks and rivers come cascading down to Lake Superior from the peninsula's high spine.

SAND DUNES DRIVE is the name of the **lovely eight-mile stretch** of M-26 between Eagle River and Eagle Harbor. It parallels the sandy beach of the **GREAT SAND BAY**. Frequent pullovers encourage motorists to get out and take a swim or walk down the beach. The tilted shelf of volcanic crust drops off so rapidly under water that the bay is 1,300 feet deep. On the opposite side of the road is the steep, dark, rocky forest, carpeted in pine needles. Delightful **JACOB'S FALLS** cascades right near the road, 2 1/2 miles east of Eagle River. Next to the scenic pullout, tucked away in the piney hillside, is The Jam Pot (see below).

The Jam Pot

To this idyllic spot next to Jacob's Falls, **three monks** (yes, monks — complete with hooded brown robes) withdrew from the world and their native city of far-away Detroit, to establish in 1983 the monastic community of the Society of St. John. Their mission, as explained in their online newsletter *Magnificat,* is "to embrace the struggle of life in a hard place; to heed the counsels of the monastic fathers [they mention the desert monks of St. Anthony, fleeing the corrupt and unnatural world created by man], to come to know God through personal and liturgical prayer, and to beg His mercy upon ourselves and upon the whole world." The Society is now affiliated with a small branch of the Christian Orthodox tradition, which historically looked both to the east and the west.

Things have worked out well for the monks. Their location on a beautiful road busy with summer visitors has enabled them to build a market, without a phone and without much advertising, for their jam and their **excellent muffins, breads, cookies, brownies, and giant chocolate chip cookies.** Summer business has led to lots of Christmas business shipping their jams and rich and **delicious rum cakes,** sold by mail and on the Internet via www.societystjohn.com (The website also gives retreat information.) They have no phone number. The long winter and physical bakery work meshes well with the traditional monastic life of contemplation. "The winter solitude and the healing presence of the Great Lake make this a good place to live out the monastic tradition," states the *Magnificat.*

Originally the monks gathered their own local berries for the jams and fruit butters they make. Some bakery customers become interested in the retreats they offer, focused on celebrating the Divine Office and Divine Liturgy for four hours a day, and then meditating and reflecting in silence and solitude except for meals. A continuing stream of publicity has, alas, necessitated a large parking lot which spoils The Jam Pot's early tucked-away mystique. Plans for an elaborate, onion-domed Holy Transfiguration Skete

have been circulated, and now new construction has begun.

Getting back to food, the **pumpkin muffin,** full of raisins and nuts and iced with lemon frosting, wins raves for its flavor and texture. Just one with milk and a piece of fresh fruit makes a good lunch. The cakes — things like walnut ginger cake, lemon pound cake, the Abbey Cake, rich with walnuts, raisins, molasses, and bourbon — are quite elaborate and costly. Order forms are sent in back of a newsletter filled with prayers, scripture, meditations, and reflections. An excerpt: "When we hear the comment at The Jam Pot, 'Well, you certainly do live in God's country,' we are likely to respond, 'Everywhere is God's country.' If we are feeling talkative, we may also add, 'But it is easier to see Him in some places than in others.'"

Open Mon-Sat 10-6 May through fall color season in early Oct. No phone. Mailing address:Society of St. John, Star Route 1, Box 226, Eagle Harbor, MI 49950. www.societystjohn.com Mailing address: The Society of St. John, Star Route 1, Box 226, Eagle Harbor, MI 49950.

Eagle River Restaurant

FITZGERALD'S RESTAURANT & LOUNGE is a destination because it's a beautiful place to watch the sun set over Lake Superior and enjoy the area's dinner specials ($14.50 to $20.50 in 2000) like pecan-crusted walleye with dried cherry butter. Dinners include a starch, bread basket, and soup or salad. "Not as good as they think they are," complain some diners, but others are most grateful for being able to dine with "a **great lake view** and decent food. Seems overpriced only by local standards. They have a **wonderful deck** outside, where they only want to serve drinks. Truly awesome if the lake breeze isn't too strong. In winter there are ice volcanoes right offshore." Reservations recommended. *From M-26 just east of the Eagle River, turn down toward the lake. In two blocks turn right at the end. 337-9959; 800-352-9228; www.eagleriverinn.com Current hours: June thru color season: open daily 5-9:30. Closed from the end of color season to mid-December, then open daily thru mid-March; after that, weekends only to June 1.* **H.A.**: call 👫👣 Full bar

Eagle River Lodgings

EAGLE RIVER INN

(800) 352-9228; (906) 337-9959; fax (906) 337-9959; www.eagleriverinn.com

Fitzgerald's restaurant and bar occupies

most of the downstairs of this contemporary building on the Eagle River beach. Each of the 12 pleasant, simple guest rooms has a lake view, phone, satellite TV, and 2 double beds or a double and queen. Summer rates are $77 to $92 with free continental breakfast. Winter rates are $65 and $75 with free full breakfast. 8-person whirlpool overlooks lake. Sauna. Sun deck. Ask about the one-bedroom condo. Not far from Eagle Harbor and Calumet ski trails. *From M-26 just east of the Eagle River, turn down toward the lake. In two blocks turn right to inn. Open year-round.* **H.A.**: call 👫👣: $5/extra person 🐕: call

THE OLD EAGLE HOTEL B&B

(906) 337-1392

In 1845, when this was built, the hotel was a pretty small and simple place. Today the desk and lobby remain pretty much as they were, with the hotel ledger, a parlor stove, and miners' cleat marks in the floor. The floors are all a little wavy. The place has been spiffed up, not rehabbed. The owners live in a separate newer wing connected with the old hotel. Homey antiques set the tone for the guests' front parlor, dining room, and **5 cozy, cheerful upstairs guest rooms.** The three with private baths are $60/night. The two with shared bath are often rented to family groups. A **full English-style breakfast** is served. It's one block from both beach and falls, and directly across from the old bridge across the Eagle River. *On Main St. From M-26, just east of the Eagle River, turn north at the Eagle River Store, go down a block. Open year-round.* **H.A.**: no 👫👣: no extra charge

SAND HILLS LIGHTHOUSE INN

(906) 337-1744; www.sandhillslighthouse.com

After 30 years of working to restore one of the Great Lakes' largest and newest

The Sand Hills Lighthouse south of Eagle River is now a luxurious B&B.

(1919) lighthouses, retired Dearborn portrait photographer Bill Srabotta has fulfilled his vision: to turn it into a luxurious B&B with outstanding food. The plain, almost modernistic exterior is quite a contrast to the **grand Victorian interior decor**, aimed at high drama. It has lots of reds and purples, and a few photographs of seductive beauties who were Srabotta's portrait models. Among assistant innkeeper Mary Mathews's duties are baking for breakfast and evening treats and sometimes playing soft background music on the grand piano in the cushy living room **overlooking Lake Superior**. The 35-acre property includes **3,000 feet of stony but accessible shoreline**. Guests can climb to the **lighthouse tower** and linger on the sizable roof outside it. Because it faces north, both **sunrises** and **sunsets** can be seen. In the works: small reading areas on the landings. Five of the 8 rooms (mostly $125/night) face the lake; the sixth has a side view. Two whirlpool rooms with balconies are $150. Two-night minimum from May through October. Air-conditioned and smoke-free. No TV — anywhere. One phone is for guests' use. An elegant breakfast is served at 9:30. Reserve well in advance, especially for specific dates. This place has been so popular through word-of-mouth and lighthouse fans that it's been full midweek in April. *4 miles west of Eagle River on the shore road. Open year-round.* **H.A.**: call

EAGLE RIVER CAMPING

SUNSET BAY
RV RESORT & CAMPGROUND
(906) 337-2494; Oct. thru May:
(941) 923-2378; www.sunset-bay.com

Right on Lake Superior, four miles south of Eagle River but away from summer's busy roads, this small (35 sites), low-key campground is a real find. The 70 acres include an **agate beach** and **picturesque point**; old logging trails lead back into the woods for miles. Campsites are under the pines, within view of the lake (most are on the other side of the drive, however) without shrubby natural buffers between sites. RV sites ($20/night in 2001) have electricity and water. Tent sites ($15/night) are larger. There are showers, a laundry, a dump station, and a fire pit, but not a lot in the way of entertainment other than nature (no playground, game room, etc.). Three cottages ($500/week) book very early. Visit the website for photos galore. Many family groups get together here each year; reservations are advised for

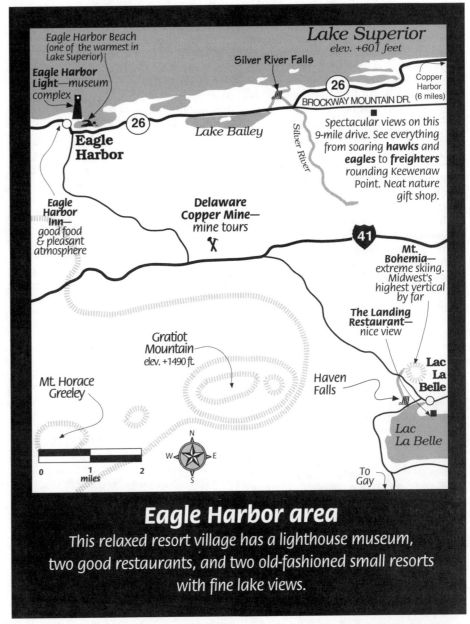

Eagle Harbor area

This relaxed resort village has a lighthouse museum, two good restaurants, and two old-fashioned small resorts with fine lake views.

July and August. *From Ahmeek and U.S. 41, turn north onto 5 Mile Point Road (marked by a brown sign). Sunset Bay is in about 7 miles. Or, from Eagle River, go south along the lakeshore 4 miles. It's a mile beyond the Sand Hills Lighthouse. Open from June through Sept.*

H.A.: call 🧑‍🦽🚶🚶 rates cover 4 persons/site; $2/extra person up to 6

Eagle Harbor

Situated on the western shore of an **beautiful horseshoe harbor** with a **lighthouse**, Eagle Harbor is today a summer resort. Ancient frame houses and newish cottages cluster around a shallow, protected harbor and beach that's one of **Lake Superior's most reliably warm places to swim**. Eagle

Harbor was first settled in 1845 as a port serving two important early inland Keweenaw copper mines, the Copper Falls and the Central.

It's is the prettiest village in the northern Keweenaw, with just enough attractions to make it a lazily interesting place to stay: two restaurants with pie and takeout food for a picnic; easy access to Brockway Mountain Drive and other excursions; several delightful local museums run by the Keweenaw Historical Society, an energetic group of old-timers and summer people. Note: Patricia and Peter Van Pelt no longer operate their memorable North Wind Books, formerly located in Eagle Harbor. It lives on as a general and regional bookstore next to Finlandia University's Finnish-American Heritage Center in downtown Hancock.

Cedar Creek flows into Eagle Harbor from a large cedar swamp south of town. About 4 1/2 miles east-southeast of Eagle Harbor, **LOOKOUT MOUNTAIN** rises 730 feet above Lake Superior. It is accessible by a foot trail that begins from a road just south of town.

Eagle Harbor Lighthouse and Museums

This **exceptionally picturesque** and much photographed brick lighthouse surveys the harbor from its rocky perch. Built in 1871, the keeper's dwelling is realistically furnished as it might have been in the 1930s by the Keweenaw County Historical Society (on the web at a newsy website, www.up.net/~ghite .kchs.htm). The society has purchased the light station complex here from the Coast Guard. It has developed several specialized museums in its various buildings. In 1999 a small **commercial fishing museum** was created in the assistant keeper's quarters next door. One building by the parking area houses the **surveying, smelting, and mining museum**. It includes a mineral collection, mining history, material on Daniel Brockway and the early days of Copper Harbor, and a fine exhibit on the Keweenaw's prehistoric copper culture. A separate **maritime museum** building covers **shipwrecks** in great detail. A patient, history-minded person could spend hours on a rainy day taking this all in. Many exhibits have signs that are dense reading, too much for casual visitors. But the museum is the best single place on the Keweenaw to assemble an overview of the area's history.

Outside are picnic tables on a sunny, rocky promontory. An overlook platform has a **grand view of the rocks** and, looking out into Lake Superior, of passing **freighters** as well.

At the west shore of the harbor. Follow signs from M-26 to lighthouse/museum. Summer phone: 289-4990. Keweenaw County Historical Open daily, mid-June thru Sept, noon-5. About $1/person. &: call. Lighthouse is not accessible. Mining and maritime museums are.

Rathbone School House

This simple, one-room schoolhouse has been preserved as the **birthplace of the Knights of Pythias secret fraternal society** that has grown to have some 2,000 lodges in the U.S. and Canada. While teaching here, Justus Rathbone dreamed up the rituals and founded the order in 1864. The ceremonies, based on the Roman story of the friendship of Damon and Pythias, celebrate the virtues of brotherly friendship and self-sacrifice. The Knights' elaborate ritual costumes include some fabulous fake jewels and embroidered satin robes. Mock-Roman tunics are decorated with hundreds of metal discs.

Two blocks west of the harbor on Center St., or one block south of St. Peter's-by-the Sea on M-26. Open daily 12-5, June through September at least. Donations welcome. &: several steps up.

M-26 from Eagle Harbor to Copper Harbor

These 14 miles of M-26/Lake Shore drive are **the Keweenaw's rockiest and most dramatic stretch of shoreline**. (Brockway Mountain Drive intersects M-26 here and offers a spectacular panoramic view of the shoreline and inland lakes that leaves you feeling you're floating above Earth's surface in a balloon. But that can be saved for a separate trip, timed at sunset, from Copper Harbor.)

Four and a half miles east of Eagle Harbor, a sign points out **SILVER RIVER FALLS**. By all means take the easy path through an overarching woods, both leafy and pleasantly piney. You'll hear and soon see the sparkling little river descending from a stone-arched bridge. Alternately it spreads out over rocky terraces and rests in a series of pools.

Soon you'll come to **ESREY PARK**, where picnic tables and grills overlook a particularly beautiful stretch of rocky shore. **Sunrises and sunsets are both beautiful** at this north-facing lakefront park. Stone steps go up to a rocky perch and a rustic gazebo — another charming Depression-era relief project in Keweenaw County.

Just west of the park is a Michigan Nature Association preserve. Look for the small signs that say "protected area." On the inland side of M-26, a posted **hiking trail** winds up to Brockway Mountain Drive through a **magically mossy forest** and loops across it. An unusual number of plants and lichens grow in this area, from the cracks in the wind-battered lakeshore rocks to the moist, protected areas in the woods. Inland, long strands of usnea lichen drapes over conifers. The MNA recommends taking a compass on this walk.

A few miles east of Esrey Park, M-26 runs right beside a place where big, bare slabs of ancient volcanic crust tilt right

Finding agates in Copper Country
These beautiful stones can be found on most of the north- and west-facing shorelines from Ontonagon to Keweenaw Point. Agates are formed in basalt rocks (usually grey, brown, or black in color) and are eroded out of the host rock. Conglomerate rocks (red nodules cemented together) yield no agates. Favorite beaches to look over are in the Silver City area, Misery Bay, Tamarack Waterworks, Seder Bay, Eagle River, Eagle Harbor, Agate Harbor, Hebard Park, Esrey Park, and many small gravel beaches from Eagle Harbor to Copper Harbor. Five Mile Point is good if you want to swim a little.

The best time to collect agates is after a storm with good waves that stir up the sands and gravels, exposing new material.

When you first check a beach for agate, look in the small 1/4" gravel. These small agates will be easier to find because they have been broken from bigger pieces and will show banding, translucency eyes, bold colors, and veining. Once you find small agates, then you can look at the larger gravels.

Wetting the rocks helps to see the patterns better. If you like to swim, you will find lots of treasures. A mask and snorkel work great!! A wet suit is a must early in the season.

Many rock and gift shops in Houghton, Calumet, and Copper Harbor will help you identify your finds. Happy hunting! Remember, good rockhounds respect private property!

— *Ken Flood, Keweenaw Gem & Gift*
Ken and Cindy's website is a wonderful introduction to area minerals. Visitors can ask questions, too.
www.copperconnection.com

into Lake Superior. A wide shoulder lets you get out and explore the rocks and the tiny lichen, tough little flowers and stunted trees that find sustenance in cracks in these rocks. The beaches in this area are known as **agate beaches**. Six miles east of here, **HEBARD PARK** is another simple little park with picnic tables, grills, outhouses, and wonderful view. Three more miles and you come to the village of Copper Harbor, Keweenaw County's tourism hub.

EAGLE HARBOR RESTAURANTS

Good home cooking and a friendly, retro atmosphere have made the **SHORELINE RESTAURANT** a memorably charming place. At this motel/gas station/restaurant on the Eagle Harbor beach, the pine-paneled dining room has a rock fireplace, a sofa for lounging, and reading material for guests. There's a counter and tables in the lunch room, which does a big business in Jilbert's and no-fat ice cream cones. New owners in 2000 seemed a little overwhelmed at the prospect of wearing so many hats. Ask around about how the food is this year. This has been the home-cooking restaurant option in Eagle Harbor, with pies and daily dinner specials. *On M-26 at the lake shore, on the east side of town. 289-4441. Open mid-June thru mid-Oct, daily 8 a.m. to 8 p.m.. Also open in snowmobile season.* &: call.

Nature themes set a relaxed and pleasant tone at the **EAGLE HARBOR INN**, where diners can enjoy some of the Keweenaw's best-prepared homemade food with a beer or drink. Pizzas ($15 and under) have homemade crusts, and pesto, Mexican, or regular toppings. The char-broiler is put to good use on the $4.25 hamburger, on steaks, and on the popular babyback ribs ($10 and $18 at dinner). Whitefish, trout, and perch are also served. Vegetarians love the pesto pasta and pizza. Dinners come with salad and potato. Good homemade pies and cheesecake. "Really worth a meal stop," comments one sophisticated local. Another recommends the BBQ chicken pizza. No reservations; come early or expect a wait. *On M-26 at the west end of Eagle Harbor. 289-4435. Closed April. From late June to Labor Day open daily 11:30-9 p.m. In spring and fall open weekends. In winter (after Xmas thru March) open daily except Mon 11:30-9 p.m.* & ♦♦♦ Full bar

EAGLE HARBOR LODGINGS

EAGLE HARBOR HOUSE
(906) 289-1039 in season;
otherwise (248) 363-6500

Summer people and locals are thrilled to see the transformation of this longtime tourist home (where co-owner Tom Westlake grew up) into a homestay B&B. It's furnished in a spare, simple style somewhat akin to that in 1845, when it was built as a **log boarding house** at the very beginning of the Keweenaw copper boom. Now the interior logs have been exposed. Eagle Harbor House is on Front Street (M-26), across from the village beach and harbor, so generations of passersby have been familiar with it as the yellow house with the big front porch. Tom grew up here when this was a tourist home; his mother fell in love with the

place on a trip to Copper Country during World War II, for which the Westlakes had carefully saved their gas rations, and was able to buy it with the financial support of her father-in-law. (Her husband didn't much like the idea.)

Tom's wife, Carol Ford, is responsible for the decor of the four antique-filled upstairs guest rooms. No fancy Victorian ornamentation here. Old house detectives will be fascinated to hear what the restoration project uncovered, from old partitions to a hidden attic with a barrel of handcuffs, acquired by an early resident who was the first Keweenaw County sheriff. Tom credits Carol with having the patience and persistence to comply with the state Bureau of History's exacting requirements to be awarded an official historical marker in front.

The Eagle Harbor House opened as a B&B in the summer of 2000. Rooms are only $65 (for front rooms with a harbor view) and $55 because they share a single bat. Only two rooms are rented at a time, unless a large group takes more and is willing to put up with the bathroom arrangement. There is a two-night minimum. A full breakfast is served to B&B guests, who have pretty much the run of the house, plus the porch with the grand harbor view. Four unrestored **housekeeping units** continue to be rented by the week for $350 (2001 rate). Two are in three-room cabins (they sleep four) behind the house, one is an apartment in the house, and one is a separate cottage on the hill toward the lighthouse.

Guests can hear what it was like for a boy to move from Trenton outside Detroit to Eagle Harbor. The tourist home stayed open through hunting season. Soon Tom's mother found work as a registered pharmacist in Calumet. Eagle Harbor was "a paradise for us kids," says Tom. They loved the sense of community, the pot lucks and picnics. Even winter brought its adventures, like

sneaking off and walking a mile out on Lake Superior ice, and rushing back when cracks sounded suddenly. about his boyhood in Eagle Harbor. His parents made the move after his mother made more money running the tourist home the first summer than his father made all year working at Great Lakes Steel in Ecorse.

It's a wonder that the house has survived, Tom says. Most of the other old rooming houses in town burned down over the decades, and several times neighbors alerted the Westlakes that buildup from their wood heater had started a chimney fire. Tom credits the Copper Country with his love of teaching junior high students earth science — an age group and subject most teachers would avoid — in Romulus, a racially mixed community of modest means. "Being from the U.P., you grow up with all sorts of people from many ethnic groups, many quite poor. You learn a perverse sense of humor which makes it easier to have good rapport with junior-high guys and get them to settle down." *On Front/M-26 at Center. Open regularly in July and August, in September by appointment.*

H.A.: B&B no; call for housekeeping units ♦♦♦: welcome. One B&B room sleeps 3 🐾: in cabins only

THE LAKE BREEZE
(906) 289-4514; winter (612) 721-5891

Fans of old summer resorts will treasure this place, with its vintage fireside gathering room, old rustic furniture, and display cases of birchbark curios, rock samples, and local memorabilia. The porch and sun porch have **wonderful views of Lake Superior's Eagle Harbor** with its rocks and waves. 10 second-story rooms, simple and pleasant, freshened in the 1980s, have private baths. Half ($79/night for two double beds) have lake views. The others are $59 (one

Eagle Harbor's Lake Breeze resort offers grand views of rocks and harbor, an old-fashioned fireside gathering room, and no TV anywhere.

double bed or two twins) and $72. Reserve way ahead; many regulars return each year. The Eagle Harbor lighthouse and natural area is two doors down. Phone in office. Not air-conditioned. No TV. Morning coffee provided. As a warehouse in the 1860s, this building handled outgoing copper and timber and incoming household goods. In 1922-23 the building was remodeled into a summer hotel and tearoom. Run by four generations of the Raley family. *Off M-26 on the west shore of Eagle Harbor; continue straight ahead when M-26 turns to parallel harbor. Open July-Labor Day.* **H.A.**: no 🚶🏻‍♂️🚶🏻: welcome

EAGLE HARBOR INN
(906) 289-4435

This refurbished older motel adjoins a very good restaurant (see above). It's a four-block walk from the Eagle Harbor beach. 8 rooms on one floor (4 have one bed, 4 have two doubles) are around $50/night, year-round. Decorated in simple, nature-loving style. Coffee in rooms. Cable TV with ESPN. Pay phone outside. Sauna. Not air-conditioned. *On M-26 at the west end of Eagle Harbor. Closed April.* **H.A.**: call. 🚶🏻‍♂️🚶🏻: usually $5/extra person

SHORELINE RESORT   (906) 289-4637
This simple 8-unit motel, under new ownership, is on a lawn right by the sandy town beach where the Lake Superior water is warmer than most places in this chilly lake. From the lawn chairs and from rooms it's a grand view of one of Michigan's most picturesque lighthouses across the bay. Small, simple rooms ($57-$70 summer AAA rates, $67-80 winter AAA rates) all have harbor views. Cable TV. Not air-conditioned. Phone and lounge area are in the adjoining restaurant. Marina a mile away. Four blocks to playground in town. Repeat customers make advance summer reservations a must. December & January aren't too early. *On M-26 at the lake shore, on the east side of town. Open mid-June thru mid-Oct and during snowmobile season.* ♿: call.

Copper Harbor

The mystique of being the Michigan's northernmost community belongs to this little resort near the Keweenaw Peninsula's tip. Love of nature is the common bond that knits together area businesspeople, visitors, and summer residents. Snowmobilers mean that two restaurants (The Pines and Mariner

North) stay open in winter. But the population dwindles to under 50.

Copper Harbor is where copper fever first began in the 1840s. Despite numerous efforts to strike it rich, no mines around Copper Harbor became nearly as productive as those a little ways west.

When the first prospectors came to the Keweenaw, it was a life-or-death matter that provisioning ships would arrive before the long winter set in, cutting off settlements from the rest of the world. This environment was challenging not only for its remoteness, but because the topsoil was too thin for farming. Food had to be shipped in for humans and farm animals alike.

Copper didn't come into great demand until it was needed for electrical wiring and plumbing later in the century. In the 1840s and 1850s it was mainly used to make cooking pans and ship sheathing. Still, when copper of a purity never before seen was found here, prospectors swarmed into the little harbor town. The U.S. Army was so concerned about maintaining law and order in this wilderness area that it built Fort Wilkins and garrisoned it with soldiers. However, prospectors soon found more copper farther down the peninsula. By the mid-1870s Copper Harbor was in decline. By the 1880s it numbered just half a dozen families. Fishing was Copper Harbor's mainstay until the tourist era.

Copper Harbor has always been a strategic location because it has the best harbor on the Keweenaw's long north shore. Early on it had been a fur-trading outpost. Lake Superior's first lighthouse was built here in 1849 to mark the harbor entrance. Many commercial fishing boats were based here.

Fort Wilkins State Park and Historic Complex

The 1843 Keweenaw copper rush in this distant area, way beyond the frontier of settlement, led to building this small fort. After the army abandoned it in the 1870s, it became a favorite picnic and camping destination because of its beautiful, forested location on Lake Fanny Hooe. (Named for an early visitor, it's pronounced "hoe" like the tool.) A bicycle club made regular visits starting in the 1880s, followed by auto jaunts circa 1910. In 1923 Fort Wilkins became one of Michigan's earlier state parks.

From 1844 to 1846 the fort was the area's only source of law and order. The government's greatest concern was friction between native Indians and unruly

Snow-covered balsams greet cross-country skiers on Fort Wilkins' groomed trails. Snowshoes are a good way to explore many of the area's scenic spots in winter.

miners. But little hostility actually broke out. By 1846 most of the small-time prospectors had left. Large mining companies had stabilized the region, so the fort was abandoned. It reopened after the Civil War, from 1867 to 1870, due to inadequate barracks facilities elsewhere in Michigan.

This was a typical 19th-century frontier garrison, the most northern in the U.S., 600 miles from Detroit. When the old fort became a state park, over two-thirds of the structures remained. Some buildings were rebuilt, starting as Depression make-work projects.

What you see today is the daily routine of military life as it was in 1869. A stockade surrounds 19 buildings: kitchen and mess room, hospital, bakery, company quarters, etc. The officers' quarters have fancy lamps and furniture befitting their higher status. Their wives here were supposed to bring civilization to the frontie here.. Structures have been restored or rebuilt and authentically furnished by the state's Michigan Historical Center. Many objects are replicas, so **the museum is becoming more**

Bring bikes for a relaxing stay in Copper Harbor. They're the perfect way to get around town, from Agate Beach by the marina to the state park to Manganese Falls. In the early morning, traffic is light along beautiful M-26 to Eagle Harbor.

hands-on, with fewer period rooms shielded by plexiglass. Now you can go in, sit down at a table, and look out the window. Some buildings have brief, to-the-point displays about how **archaeology** is being conducted here, about **the area's natural history**, and about **military life**. (Of the soldiers garrisoned here between 1844 and 1870, we learn that 8% died while in the army, half of natural causes, and 11% deserted.)

It's worth beginning your visit by seeing the **well-written tape-slide show**, played on demand in the visitor center in the second building as you enter the fort. It provides a fine introduction to the early history of Keweenaw copper-mining. (Just outside the fort is an abandoned mine shaft from the 1840s.)

Living history can be a real highlight of a visit. You may come upon a soldier's wife doing the post's laundry, or the schoolteacher, or an officer and his wife. Most years re-enactors, trained by Northern Michigan University, convincingly act as if it is the summer of 1867. (An occasional year has sub-par actors.) They stay in character as developed through historical research, using the language and accents of that time. Visitors can ask them about their life: where they're from, why they're in the army, what they eat, how long they work, how they spend free time. It's well worth overcoming any shyness and starting a conversation. Kids really enjoy this.

In the first building inside the fort, the **good, small BOOKSTORE** operated by the **FORT WILKINS NATURAL HISTORY ASSOCIATION** is open from July into October, 10 a.m. to 6:30 p.m. It has a **display of fresh wildflowers** currently blooming. Sales help pay for the association's publications and for park interpretive programs. The **larger gift shop** outside the fort is also a camp store. It has **nifty activity toys**, books, and games for children. Check at either shop for the summer events schedule. The **highly recommended evening lectures** (at 7:30 nearly every night in summer) attract local people as well as campers. Talks are indoors inside the West Barracks across the parade grounds from the entrance area. Speakers' specialties range from mining to moose and wolves.

Many happy hours could be spent exploring the features of the rest of the 700-acre park. A **pretty trail** through the woods **along Lake Fanny Hooe** connects the fort parking area with many park attractions: the interesting cemetery, the recently expanded and improved **playground** and **picnic area**, the fort, and the campgrounds. Don't miss the beautiful Lake Superior shoreline

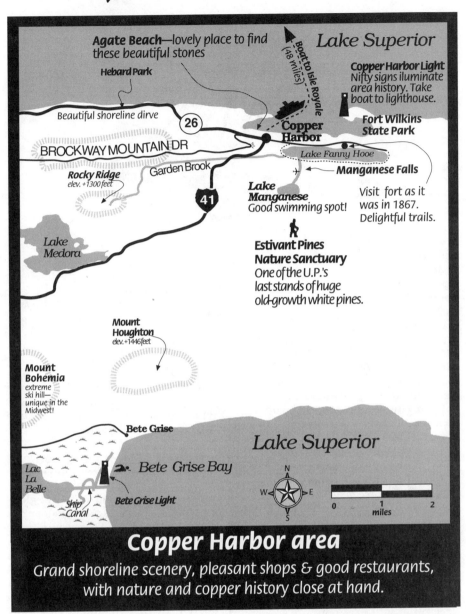

Copper Harbor area

Grand shoreline scenery, pleasant shops & good restaurants, with nature and copper history close at hand.

and lighthouse overlook across U.S. 41. On the south side of Lake Fanny Hooe over three miles of trail within the park and another 10 miles (the Kamikaze Trail, a favorite **mountain-biking** destination) are groomed for **cross-country skiing**.

1 1/2 miles east of Copper Harbor on U.S. 41. (906) 289-4215. TDD: (800) 827-7007. Park open year-round. Fort open mid-May thru mid-Oct, 8 a.m.-dusk. Park interpreters and living history is from the last week in June through the 3rd week in August, 9-5 daily. State park sticker required; $4/$5 a day, $20/$25 a year. &: now entirely accessible: fort, stores, campground, marina.

Lighthouse Overlook on Copper Harbor

Where Fanny Hooe Creek empties into the harbor, roughly across from the

entrance to Fort Wilkins, there's a small parking lot and a few **picnic tables**. The nearby red rocks offer a **grand view of the lighthouse**, especially beautiful as it catches the setting sun. The rocks are a fine place to sit and read or sketch. A **beautiful nature trail** winds among the cedars and pines, with interpretive signs provided by the Fort Wilkins Natural History Association. In the evening this is an enchanted place.

Off U.S. 41 just east of Fanny Hooe Creek. State park sticker required: $4/$5 a day, $20/$25 a year. &: picnic area can be used, not up to ADA code.

Copper Harbor Lighthouse

The brick lighthouse perched on the rocky peninsula that forms Copper Harbor has always been **one of the**

The April hawk migration viewed from Brockway Mountain is an annual highlight.

most picturesque on the Great Lakes. Now, thanks to recently installed exhibits in the buildings and on the grounds, it's more than just another pretty lighthouse. Two of the earliest and most significant events of the copper mining era occurred right here. They are vividly conveyed on the **interpretive foot trail** that goes through the woods and out onto the rocks, passing some shipwreck artifacts along the way. A **prominent blue-green vein of copper silicate** had made the rock here a voyageurs' landmark for 200 years. That's why the first Douglass Houghton expedition camped here in 1840. Their investigations prepared the geological report that would kick off the copper boom three years later, when the Keweenaw's first commercial mine shafts were sunk on this very site.

Even though the lighthouse and surrounding property is part of Fort Wilkins State Park, they must be reached by a **15-minute boat trip** because the adjoining cottage association has denied right-of-way by land. A Bureau of History guide meets visitors at the dock. By the boat dock is the very simple 1848 keeper's house, the **oldest lighthouse structure on the Great Lakes**. The period rooms in the 1866 lighthouse are now more engaging. Kids enjoy looking in drawers and investigating.

The tour and ferry ride takes 1 1/2 hours; if there's room on the next boat, you could arrange to stay on the picturesque point for three hours. In the summer season, more leisurely **sunset tours** ($15/person) take visitors to the lighthouse at an especially beautiful time and linger at the harbor entrance to enjoy the sunset over the water. For photos of the lighthouse tour, visit www.copperharborlighthouse.com. Advance reservations are for large groups only. All trips are weather-dependent and may be canceled because of electrical storms or high winds.

Leaves from Copper Harbor's municipal marina (on the west edge of town opposite the Brockway Mountain Drive entrance). Call the marina, (906) 289-4966, for current fees. (In 2001 the ferry ride is $12 for adults, $7 for kids.) Season: from Mem. Day through Sept. In July & August tours leave the marina on the hour from 10 to 5. Otherwise they're at 10, noon, 2, and 4. Sunset cruise leaves at 7:30 or earlier. ♿: *in part. Some of the interpretive trail. 1848 keeper's house is accessible. It has a video tour of the lighthouse.*

Brockway Mountain Drive

The highest highway between the Rockies and the Alleghenies offers **glorious sunsets, soaring hawks, and a splendid view** of the Keweenaw's rocky shore. Most spectacular of all Keweenaw County's Depression-era relief projects is this nine-mile road that twists and climbs to one of the peninsula's highest peaks, a thousand feet above Lake Superior. At the windswept Brockway Mountain Lookout, you're up so high that the view seems almost like a living map, occasionally punctuated by freighters rounding Keweenaw Point. Isle Royale, over 48 miles away, can be seen out of the lake on clear days.

The mountain's western slope goes down to Lake Superior. Inland to the east, the broken edge of volcanic crust along the north-south fault line becomes an almost vertical cliff that drops down to the river valley below. Each spring, peaking in mid-April, **hawks** migrate northeast along the entire Keweenaw Peninsula. They gather by these cliffs to ride the updrafts out to the peninsula's end — a final boost before their long flight across Lake Superior. Look down for them coming from the direction of Eagle Harbor. They concentrate at the west end of Brockway Mountain, away from its Lake Superior face.

The view from the lookout is so riveting, it's easy to forget about all the other remarkable features of this unusual road. The habitat toward the top is actually semi-alpine; the trees are stunted by the strong winds. (A windproof jacket is a good idea even in summer.) Visitors learn about the site from the elaborate rustic signs written and made by the Keweenaw Road Commission's talented signmakers. The **gift shop** at the summit has been known as the **SKYTOP INN** since its inception in 1934. It was the first gift shop in Keweenaw County. Today's unassuming building replaced the original log cabin; remains of its log fireplace can still be seen. It has a small but **very well chosen array of nature-related gifts and books**. When there's time, proprietor Lloyd Wescoat can field questions on natural history, good books to read, and good walks to take. A native Virginian, she has loved reading all her life. After majoring in environmental studies and political science at St. Andrew's College in North Carolina, she got a job waitressing at the Harbor Haus, fell in love with Clyde Wescoat and his home town of Copper Harbor, and has been here ever since. She has devoted more Skytop space to local-interest and children's books, now that she and Clyde sold their Brockway Inn motel and closed their shop by the former post office.

Brockway Mountain's many varied ecosystems are home to **lots of wild-flowers and berries** as well as trillium, orchids, wild strawberries, and thimbleberries — over 700 flowers in all, including many rare and endangered species, some found nowhere else in Michigan. Blooms peak in the month of June.

Here and all over the northern Keweenaw, the land seems like a vast park. Actually, most of it is onetime mining land now owned by Champion Paper. It can be sold and developed. In return for favorable commercial forest taxes, Champion's land is legally open to the public for recreational use, including rock-gathering, mountain-biking, and berry-picking. The Michigan Nature Association has purchased 200 prime acres on Brockway Mountain.

Plan to get out and walk at several places along the drive. There are many wildflowers along the road throughout the summer and in the woods in spring. A half mile or so east of the summit, the Michigan Nature Association's **Klipfel Memorial Nature Sanctuary** is a **popular overlook** for its grand views and its covering of Alpine grasses, ground cover, and sedge. The MNA guide *Walking Paths in the Keweenaw* states, "From the

Brockway Mountain offers outstanding panoramic views from the summit and (here) from the east end, overlooking the village of Copper Harbor. The harbor is the water body to the left. Lake Fanny Hooe is the long lake to the right. In the distance to the right are the rugged bluffs near Keweenaw Point.

point . . . one can watch the mist disappear from the valley shortly after sunrise. Soon the ravens rise from their overnight roost in the lowlands. Up and up they climb until they are soaring level with the mountain top." It's also fun to see the first evening stars. Another interesting overlook looks down on Copper Harbor, and Lake Fanny Hooe is 3 1/2 miles east of the summit. As far as other publicized MNA trails on Brockway Mountain, signage and directions are so confusing and trails so murky, it makes one wonder just how much the organization really wants the general public to find its natural areas.

For maximum enjoyment, devote an hour or two to the drive and stop frequently. Bring binoculars, and, if you want to hike in the forest, take along bug spray, a jacket, walking shoes, and a compass. Here at dusk, you'll witness a **sunset view** that's **hard to match**. Fall color season is even more glorious. It usually begins the second week of September and lasts into mid-October.

Drive entrances are off M-26. One is 5 miles northeast of Eagle Harbor. Another is half a mile west of Copper Harbor. The drive is not plowed in winter. It's open from the first snow-free days of spring (that's often in late May) up to the first snowfall. No admission fee.

Hunter's Point, Agate Beach & Copper Harbor marina

The beautiful natural areas that form the west side of Copper Harbor are long-time beauty spots enjoyed by local people and tourists alike. Hunter's Point and the agate beach along its north shore are now owned by a contractor. He is legally allowed to develop this prime site. The key natural area is now in jeopardy, but its future as public space open

to all looks promising. Public Access Keweenaw is working to make more natural areas permanently accessible to the public (www.publicaccesskeweenaw.org).

For a **rewarding hike to a remarkable beach**, start at the west end of the parking lot at the Copper Harbor marina and look for the trailhead to beautiful Agate Beach. The trail goes west through an evergreen forest close to Lake Superior's shore. In about 3/4 of a mile it forks. (Right takes you out along a beautiful narrow peninsula that forms the harbor, to Hunter's Point.) Turn left, and you cut across the peninsula's narrow base to come to Agate Beach, covered by pebbles and stones that sometimes include beautiful agates. A good time to find a fresh crop of agates is after storms, and in spring.

Explore the Michigan Nature Association's Keweenaw sanctuaries

This guide gets you focusing on the plants and rocks and natural areas near some much-visited places — Great Sand Bay, Brockway Mountain, the **Estivant Pines** (old-growth white pines), and the Lake Superior shore near Esrey Park. Look for *Walking Paths in Keweenaw* ($6.95) at Laughing Loon Handcrafts in Copper Harbor and some other area shops. The MNA has worked hard to acquire significant Keweenaw sites, sometimes paid for with bequests of suburban Detroit real estate. Most of these have trails.

Unfortunately, the trailheads of some MNA trails are so hard to find that it makes you wonder if they really do want the public to find them. Be prepared to hunt around a bit.

In winter these trails have been groomed for easy cross-country skiing.

Those with no boats can enjoy the harbor from the water by taking the **sunset tour of the Copper Harbor Lighthouse** (see above) or by taking Keweenaw Adventure's **harbor kayak paddle**. (No experience required; see below.)

Start at the Copper Harbor Marina, north off M-26 at the west end of Copper Harbor. Clearly signed. Marina phone: 289-4966.

A Superior Diver's Center/ Keweenaw Underwater Preserve

Head diver and agate-picker Jake Anderson grew up outside Copper Harbor (his parents owned the Lakeside Resort) and has been diving in the area and elsewhere for 45 years, since he was 11. He and his wife, Laura, offer classes and dives for all levels, rent and sell equipment for scuba diving (with air tanks) and snorkeling. They fill air tanks, too. A very popular **introduction to diving** is the Try It Class ($65) for ages 12 and up: two hours of instruction, largely through videos, followed by suiting up in $2,000 worth of gear and going on a 20' dive in Eagle Harbor. (Combine it with a second dive, for $100 altogether, and fledgling divers will have done two of the five dives required for basic certification that qualifies them to make dives up to 60'.)

The Andersons have set up a free basic-level **Compass Dive Trail** in Copper Harbor, where divers visit five stations, the last of which is the **anchor of the *John Jacob Astor***, the area's first wreck. Pick up the sheet at their shop. The area's popular basic-level dives, near Eagle Harbor, are to the *City of St. Joseph*, the *Tyoga*, and the

Moreland.

Agate-hunting while swimming is highly recommended because the agates are already wet and therefore the patterns are more visible, and the agates haven't been picked over as much. An extra plus for nearsighted swimmers: the water magnifies everything by 25%, making glasses less necessary. (It's possible to order a prescription scuba mask for $20 above the $80 regular cost.) Jake has combined rocks and diving in a **Diving for Agates** class ($35) for basic divers. First they learn about agates, then they take a one-tank dive (about an hour) at a good agate-collecting site, and take home an agate poster. Scott Wolter, author of *Lake Superior Agates*, has a new chapter in that popular book about diving with Jake. A **display case** is full of **agates in their natural state** to help people identify them. Some are up to 1 1/2 pounds.

The ill-fated buoy tender *Mesquite*, in 110 feet of water, is the Keweenaw's star diving attraction for advanced divers. In 1989 the *Mesquite* became hung up on a reef off Keweenaw Point. The Coast Guard cutter had been lifting the buoy that marked the reef when a navigational error was made by the Coast Guard officer on duty, an inexperienced person whom the captain should not have had in command in that situation. The commander's efforts to get off the reef only stuck the ship more.

That night, wind and waves from the southeast gave the ship such a pounding that the Coast Guard later decided to sink the aging ship instead of repairing it. "She was in a class of ships on its way out," said the officer investigating the incident. "The *Mesquite* was going in for an engine change-off anyway."

The waters here are **unusually clear**, and the underwater rocks and minerals are most unusual. But it's so cold that a dry suit is usually required. *At the west end of "downtown" Copper Harbor next to the red Country Village, just west of where U.S. 41 joins M-26. (906) 289-DIVE. Open from May thru mid-October. In July & August open 9-6, to 8 Fri & Sat. Call for off-season hours.* ♿ : 3" step

Copper Harbor shops

Especially for people interested in nature, Copper Harbor has some of the most interesting shops in the Upper Peninsula, an area unashamedly out of sync with trends and fashions. Almost every shop owner is quite familiar with the area's flora and fauna, its walks and beauty spots. They're happy to advise

visitors when time permits. Note: some times of the year the little village can seem too crowded with cars. You'll enjoy it more if you park your car and walk to shops of interest.

Here are some noteworthy Copper Harbor shops, arranged from east (toward Fort Wilkins) to west.

◆ **LAUGHING LOON:** Crafts of the North is run by dedicated naturalist Laurel Rooks. It carries many **nature-related gifts**, comical and serious, at all price levels: jewelry, T shirts, animal-design pottery, books on regional history and nature, and thimbleberry jam. Be sure to see the regional handcrafts including Ojibwa birchbark basketry, quillwork, and jewelry; prints of Bill Hamilton's watercolors of U.P. scenes; Diane Beier's pen-and-ink drawings of north country mammals on cedar rounds; and Steve Brimm's nature photography of the Lake Superior region. *On First at Bernard a block north of U.S. 41 at the east end of town. 289-4813. Open year-round, 10 a.m. til dark.* ♿: no

◆ **LOON OUTPOST** houses **canoe rentals** for nearby inland lakes and harbors of Lake Superior (they come with a car rack) and sign-up for **Bear Track Ecotours**, the guide service of Jim Rooks. It also offers Copper Harbor and Isle Royale visitors necessities they may not have brought along: camping supplies, windblock Polartec vests, jackets, and mittens (yes, mittens for July!) by Lake Affect; and wool socks, hats, neckwarmers, and headbands by Wigwam. It also sells maps and nature books: bird books, local bird checklists, and books on regional and Isle Royale geology, plants, and wildflowers. *Next to Laughing Loon on First at Bernard a block north of U.S. 41 at the east end of town. 289-4813. Open part-time from Mem. Day weekend thru mid Oct. Check at Laughing Loon for hours.* ♿: 1 step.

◆ **TRAPROCK VALLEY POTTERY** is the name of the tiny shop (it looks more like a porch) where biologist/park ranger Dennis Sotala makes and sells his pottery (both raku and salt-glazed) and baskets — sometimes to order. Dennis's exceptionally self-sufficient lifestyle and his interest in handcrafts were inspired by his hard-working Finnish forbears from this area. *On Gratiot/U.S. 41 across from the Pines. 289-4636. Off-season phone: (906) 337-6879. Open from mid June thru color season.*

◆ **SWEDE'S GIFT SHOP** carries Keweenaw minerals, copper items, original paintings by Linden Dahlstrom, and jewelry made with Keweenaw minerals. Alan

Billings, co-owner since the early 1980s, makes greenstone jewelry; his son Jim does scrimshaw on local datolite. *It's on Gratiot/U.S. 41 across from the community building. 289-4596. Open from May thru color season, daily from 9 to 5 at least.*

◆ **KEWEENAW AGATE SHOP**. Mineralogist-owners Les Tolenon Senior and Junior have a **splendid collection of mineral specimens** (datolite, greenstone, copper, and agates native to the area), books on area geology, and rockhound tools. **Maps of collecting sites** at beaches and mine rock piles can be purchased here. Visitors can watch a coppersmith make hammered candleholders, dishes, and more. *On Gratiot/U.S. 41 in Copper Harbor. 289-4491. Open daily from May thru September. Hours vary.* ♿

◆ **THUNDERBIRD GIFT CENTER & MUSEUM** is a rambling, old-fashioned souvenir shop with all the classics (rubber tomahawks, etc.), plus new and used books and antiques. The owner sells prints of her attractive drawings of local landmarks. The **fun, old-timey museum** feature antique dolls, Native American artifacts, and more. Admission is $2 for ages 12 and up. *In a white frame building connected to Minnetonka Resort on U.S. 41 in the center of Copper Harbor. 289-4449. Open May 15-Oct. 15,* *usually 9 to 9.*

◆ **THE ISLE ROYALE FERRY DOCK** has several interesting seasonal shops owned and managed by people whose roots in the northern Keweenaw often go way back. **JAMSEN'S FISH MARKET** (289-4285) sells fresh fish it catches and smoked fish, too. Proprietor Christine Jamsen grew up in Copper Harbor; her grandfather's commercial fishing tug was docked here. From late June through late August she comes back from California, where she teaches autistic children, and runs the fish market and **THE FISHERMAN'S DAUGHTER** handcrafts, which connects to the fish market. Her shop is devoted to handcrafts and nature-theme items, some that she makes (jewelry and stained glass), some made by others (rag rugs, fish-print T shirts, clothing, and soaps). Nature is also the inspiration of the hand-made jewelry, home accessories, sweatshirts, and watercolors at **ELIZABETH'S ON THE WATERFRONT** (289-4437). Elizabeth Kilpela is the mother of the Kilpela brothers who pilot the Isle Royale ferry. She also owns Ragamuffins on Copper Harbor's main street, which carries clothing for women and children. **HARBOR SIDE** (289-4437), which doubles as the *Isle Royale Queen III* ticket office, has a wide variety of books, gifts, T shirts, and more relating to Isle Royale, wolves, and moose. *The ferry dock is next to the Copper King motel in the center of Copper Harbor. To reach it from U.S. 41, turn north just east of the Minnetonka Resort. 289-4437. Jamsen's and The Fisherman's Daughter are open from late June thru late August and often in color season. Elizabeth's and Harbor Side are open from Mem. Day weekend thru Oct. 15 from 10 a.m. Open 'til 8 p.m. thru late Sept.* ♿

◆ **THE BERRY PATCH** serves up an unusual mix of pleasant things: ice cream (including **thimbleberry ice cream**), berry products, antiques, and gifts. The owners hand out a free info sheet on the tasty, tart thimbleberry with a jam recipe. *Next to the post office on M-26 near Brockway Mountain Dr. Open in summer only.*

Keweenaw Adventure Co. & harbor kayak paddle

Sam Raymond, a man of infinite patience with novice paddlers, and his friendly, committed crew lead a variety of kayak trips and also give lessons toward certification that include the Eskimo roll. Tours include basic instruction, and most can be done by people of almost any level of physical conditioning. All outings are weather-dependent, and all tours except the harbor paddle are by appointment. Kayaking experience isn't necessary to go on the **harbor paddle** ($26), given at 9:30, 1, and 7:30 (at 7 after August 1). A beautiful 2 1/2-hour introduction to an increasingly popular sport, it lets paddlers take sea kayaks into Copper Harbor's protected and scenic harbor, first to the uninhabited **Porter's Island** that buffers the harbor from Lake Superior, then past the **picturesque lighthouse** on its rocky point.

Half-day and all-day kayak tours go to the spectacular rocks and cliffs east of Copper Harbor around Keweenaw Point — scenery that's the equal and mirror of Isle Royale's more dramatic spots. To see photos of these outings, stop in the shop or visit www.keweenawadventure.com. The full-day **Horseshoe Harbor Paddle** ($95 with lunch) goes to a Nature Conservancy preserve with unusual rock formations. The half-day **Agate Harbor Paddle** ($65) goes along a chain of uninhabited islands to sheltered bays and Arch Rock. For well-conditioned paddlers, the **Bare Bluff Paddle** ($95) goes 14 miles and back to the sea caves, waterfall, and fishery at Keweenaw Point.

Mountain biking is Sam's longtime passion. He is working to establish an enpanded Copper Harbor trail system. The $95 "surf and turf" adventure combines biking and kayaking.

Keweenaw Adventures rents kayaks to qualified users (rates for Isle Royale are from $30 to $45 a day) and rents mountain bikes, too. The shop sells paddling gear, dried food, sunscreens, maps, and more. Ask about the ***Keweenaw Water Trail*** map that helps paddlers go around the peninsula in six or seven days. *On U.S. 41 in the center of Copper Harbor, across from the Pines. (906) 289-4303.* www.keweenawadventure.com *Open daily 9-8 in summer. Call for spring and fall hours.* ♿: for shop; call for tours.

Lake Manganese and Manganese Falls

This **beautiful, clear lake** in the hills just south of town is the area's favorite place to swim. The 52-acre lake has a long, **sandy beach**, a gradual dropoff, and water that's much warmer than Lake Superior, though cold enough for brook trout. There's no boat launch, but small boats can use the sand beach near the access drive from U.S. 41.

On the same road, closer to town, look for a pullover that marks the trail to the overlook for **beautiful Manganese Falls**. Go a little beyond where the road turns sharply right. The pullover is on the left. Head for the falls by following the sound; they're not far away. If you make your way down to the bottom of the gorge the falls has created, you'll find yourself in a **ferny, moist canyon** that creates its own small world, with only a patch of blue sky above.

From U.S. 41, take the road by the community building and The Pines. Go south and turn right to the lake when the main road veers left. Manganese Falls pullover is 7/10 of a mile from The Pines corner in town. The lake is beyond that; follow signs.

Sunset cruises on the *Isle Royale Queen III*

Enthusiastic narrator-skippers Don, John, and Ben Kilpela are longtime residents who know so much — about Great Lakes shipping, local history, ecology — that they can extemporize most effectively, never resorting to memorized scripts. Their 100-passenger *Isle Royale Queen III* goes to Isle Royale and back each day. The 1 1/2-hour evening cruise gets out onto Lake Superior to chase ships and to watch the sun set. **Ship-chasing** begins by scanning the radar to see what freighters are nearby, then choosing one to chase. Drawing up close to a big ocean-going vessel (called "salties'), with its six-story superstructure picked out in lights, is **spectacularly memorable** — like something from a Fellini movie. After a radio chat, visitors learn what it's carrying and where it's headed. A salty could be carrying sunflower seeds from Superior, Wisconsin, to Europe.

Come early to get a seat on the deck. Otherwise you'll be inside around a formica table (not a bad option on windy days). Make reservations on day of cruise.

The ferry dock is next to the Copper King motel in the center of Copper Harbor. To reach it from U.S. 41, turn north just east of the Minnetonka Resort. (906) 289-4437. Leaves at 8:30 p.m. from July 4 thru Labor Day weekend. $15/adult, $10 ages 12 and under. ♿: call.

COPPER HARBOR RESTAURANTS

See also Eagle Harbor, Lac La Belle.

THE PINES RESTAURANT & ZICK'S BAR is the ultimate northwoods gathering place and a **beloved local institution**, as welcoming for local work crews as for summer people. Diners get good from-scratch cooking at reasonable prices, served in a homey, knotty pine room with a big fireplace. The Pines opens in time for breakfast for visitors catching the Isle Royale ferry. In winter, townspeople sit in the kitchen chatting with Red Twardzik, proprietor and cook, and helping out. She and her husband, Ken, have been running The Pines restaurant, motel, and cabins since 1971. Now they have the place up for sale. After a few years of closing early, The Pines has started staying open for dinner, and the evening cook has added **Italian dishes** to the menu. Dinners include fresh fish ($10), liver and onions ($8), cheese ravioli, pasta primavera, homemade linguine with clam sauce, and spaghetti and meatballs. (Most dinners come with salad or soup and potatoes) The 1/4 pound cheeseburger (just $2.35) heads an ample basic sandwich menu. **Homemade soups** feature hearty basics like chicken and dumpling or beef barley. Famous for homemade **pies** and **cinnamon rolls** and Sunday turkey dinner (around $7). Dinners can also be served in the popular adjoining bar. The stone fireplace, copper accents, and interesting old photos of shipwrecks and snowstorms in the back hall set just the right tone. *On U.S. 41 at the east end of town. 289-4222. From mid-May thru mid-Sept open 6:30 a.m. to 3 p.m., Fri-Sun to 6 p.m. Otherwise opens at 8 a.m. Call for off-season hours.* ⎣ ⁙ Full bar

Good service, outstanding and imaginative food, and a fabulous view of the harbor make **HARBOR HAUS** one of Michigan's most memorable restaurants — "in a class by itself," as one fan says. The website shows the gorgeous view. The German atmosphere goes way beyond beer steins and the waitresses' dirndls to include terrific coffee and rich tortes from the pastry chef. The menu, which changes daily, includes the ever-popular **fresh planked whitefish** (highly recommended) and trout, venison or duck with lingonberry sauce (around $17), specials like **grilled rabbit with whiskey butter sauce**, and typical German specialties like knockwurst, sauerbraten, and wienerschnitzel with spätzle. Vegetarian and other special diets are gladly accommodated with creative, off-the-menu dishes. The authentic charcoal broiler uses varying woods (apple, hickory) for different flavors. Lunch entrées are about $6 to $10 with potato; sandwiches and salads are from $5 to $8. Vacationers could eat happily here every day and never be bored. Breakfast, an overlooked pleasure, brings pancakes with berries and simple surprises like perfectly cooked **scrambled eggs with smoked whitefish and green onions**. The entire restaurant and deck have the same **wonderful view**; the

Isle Royale boat always toots when it passes Harbor Haus. Big selection of German beers. *4 blocks east from the junction of U.S. 41 and M-26 at the harbor. Dockage for boats. 289-4222; www.harborhaus.com Open from Mem. Day to mid-Oct, daily 7 a.m.-9 p.m.* ⎣ ⁙ Full bar

KEWEENAW MOUNTAIN LODGE has been a dinner destination for generations. Its log lodge architecture, wooded setting, and rustic ambiance is as much an attraction as the food. WPA funds to create jobs during the Depression enabled Keweenaw County to build the lodge in 1933-37. The county had an extraordinarily high percentage of jobless male residents. A county road commissioner conceived the idea, and the commission still operates the resort. The pleasant grounds include a **9-hole public golf course** (which bears sometimes visit) and handsome stone walls like those in the county's smaller parks.. Trees block any vistas. Today the restaurant and lounge occupy nearly all the lodge's main floor, so it no longer has a central gathering area.

Food quality depends on who's cooking each year. **Prime rib** is a specialty, offered as a lunch sandwich (around $10), at dinner ($15.50), and on the $14 Saturday smorgasbrod. Dinner entrées ($10 to $18) include potato, soup and salad bar. The full menu also includes fresh fish and daily lunch and dinner specials. For lunch there's homemade soup, hamburgers and other sandwiches, salads, and entrées ($5 to $10). *Off U.S. 41 one mile south of Copper Harbor. Look for sign. 289-4403. Open mid-May to mid-Oct., 8 a.m. to 9 p.m.* ⎣: *use side entrance.* ⁙ Full bar

The **MARINER NORTH** is a very large place, rebuilt of logs after a fire, that combines a restaurant with a bar with cathedral ceiling and a game room. The casual dining room (dinner only) is separated from the bar and lounge, open for lunch. The bar is loudly convivial in the evening, when the action spills back and forth across the street to Zick's at The Pines. The place is so big and obvious, it fills up with tourists and becomes the happening spot.

Some winters, when the Pines has closed, The Mariner is the only place to eat, now that Johnson's Bakery has moved to Houghton. Being in a near-monopoly position hasn't been good for food or service, which is "overpriced and average," according to a Copper Harbor worker who has to eat there more than he'd like. The Mariner is known for big

sandwiches, pizza, a big salad bar at dinner, and Friday fish buffet and Saturday prime rib. Steaks and seafood are big items on the dinner menu. Occasional live music on weekends. *On M-26/U.S. 41 in the heart of Copper Harbor. 289-4637 In-season hours (from Mem. Day thru color season, also in snowmobile season): open daily 11 a.m.-10 p.m. in the lounge, 5 p.m. to 10 p.m. in the dining room. Off-season: open Friday thru Sunday only.* ⎣ ⁙ Full bar

COPPER HARBOR LODGINGS

BROCKWAY INN
(906) 289-4588; www.brockwayinn.com

Its location at the west end of Copper Harbor means this pleasant, six-room motel with enclosed front hall is away from midsummer congestion, but still an easy walk to shops and restaurants. Longtime owners Clyde and Lloyd Wescoat sold it in 2000 to Karen Trucks and Steve Karl, who have moved into the spot where Lloyd's bookstore and the post office was. The central lobby continues to be a gathering place, with morning coffee, hot chocolate and tea all the time, a microwave and fridge, and an extra cable TV. Each room has cable TV with ESPN; phones are a possibility. No air-conditioning — seldom needed. Rates in 2000: $40 for a small room with one double bed; $52 for a double and a single whirlpool; $66 for two double beds and a double whirlpool. Nature posters create a naturalist's atmosphere; Karen has added moose-silhouette lamps and more to enhance the cabin look. *On M-26 between "downtown" and the marina. Open year-round.* **H.A.**: call ⁙: no charge/extra person 🐕: call

BELLA VISTA MOTEL and COTTAGES
(906) 289-4213; www.bellavistamotel.com

This 1960s-era motel has an **ideal location**, centrally located but away from traffic, **overlooking the harbor**, close to the Isle Royale ferry dock. A big lawn by the water has a picnic area, and there is a dock. Nice flowers are a plus; renovations are ongoing. The main building's 13 rooms ($56) have sliding doors and a **deck overlooking the water**. In a second building, four larger upper rooms with two double beds ($58) have the same grand view. Five downstairs rooms have one queen ($54). All motel rooms and cottages have satellite TV. A phone and coffee are in the office. Eight cute cottages from the 1940s and later are on the street; their yards have little privacy or shade. They rent by the night or week. One-bed cottages are $40 or $240. Those with two beds and two to four rooms are $55 to $65 a night. Reserve by May or early June for best choice of accommodations. *On Sixth St. (the continuation of U.S. 41 north of the blinker toward harbor). Open mid-May thru mid-Oct,* &: call ♦♦♦♦: $4/extra person 🐕 : in cottages

LAKE FANNY HOOE RESORT
(906) 289-4451

The resort has always enjoyed an **outstanding location** at the west end of Lake Fanny Hooe. It's away from the busy main drag, yet just four blocks from Lake Superior. And it's the only Copper Harbor lodging or campground with a **swimming beach** on a warmer inland lake. In 1999 new owners Dawn and Ed Charbonneau moved up from northwestern Indiana, took over and started steadily improving the place — ,installing fire pits, a picnic area, and **playground** by the beach, and landscaping and cleaning up the property.

The two-story motel has 14 kitchenette units, all with balconies overlooking the lake. Each has two queen beds, a breakfast bar, and cable TV. A phone is in the office. No air-conditioning. There's a small dock and **lots of boat rentals**: canoes, motorboats, rowboats, paddleboats — everything but jet skis. Fishing in Lake Fanny Hooe has perch, walleye, bass, and trout. Garden Creek, a trout stream, runs through the campground into the lake. In the works: a volleyball court and horseshoe pit. An **extensive network of hiking, mountain-biking, and cross-country ski trails** begins next to the resort and extends over miles of state land along Lake Fanny Hooe to Manganese Falls. Motel rooms $63-$68/night. Ask about off-season rates and the two housekeeping cabins and one apartment. Reserve well ahead for July and August; it's half booked by January. *Just south of U.S. 41 at 505 Second. Turn at The Pines. Now open year-round.* **H.A.**: call ♦♦♦♦: 12 and under free 🐕: $5/pet/night

NORLAND MOTEL   (906) 289-4815

A delightful, quiet resort setting on Lake Fanny Hooe and lots of extras provided by hosts Gus and Heidi Koerschen make this a real find. Five simple, pleasant motel rooms ($35) have microwaves, coffeemakers, refrigerators and some kitchenettes. Three larger, more deluxe rooms **overlooking the lake** ($44) have sitting areas, decks, kitchenettes. Satellite TV. No phones; not air-conditioned. Here are horseshoes, a picnic area, grills, and a canoe to use. The window-lined summer house has games, books for general

use. Gus, an avid rockhound, will take guests on field trips for a small fee and tumble rocks for them. Reserve early for July thru color season. *Near the end of U.S. 41, 1 mile east of Ft. Wilkins. Open May into Oct.* **H.A.** ♦♦♦♦ 🐕: call

KEWEENAW MOUNTAIN LODGE
and Golf Course   (906) 289-4403; www.keweenawmountainlodge.com

Along with the legendary log lodge, 23 nifty log cottages were built in the 1930s. Some are duplexes; there are 34 cottage units in all. These rent for $75 (one bedroom, sleeps two) and $87 (two bedrooms, sleeps up to 4 or 6). A few are not vintage architecture. Most cottage units have **stone fireplaces**; all have phones, cable TV, and small porches. Reservations for fall color season should be made a year ahead; by spring, peak summer weeks are mostly booked. The newish 8-unit motel ($67/night, $5/extra person over two) has big rooms, phones, cable TV, but far less atmosphere. Mature trees screen potential views from this hillside setting. There's shuffleboard, a tennis court, and a **9-hole golf course**, where early golfers may be greeted by bears in the distance. *Off U.S. 41 a mile south of Copper Harbor. Look for sign. Open mid-May to mid-Oct.* &: two cabins, 1 motel unit.

EAGLE LODGE/LAKESIDE CABINS
(888) 558-4441; (906) 289-4294; www.eaglelodge-lakeside.com; e-mail cdjepj@up.net

New managing owners Doug and Liz Johnson and partner Bill Snyder have cleared away the dark cedars that mysteriously shrouded this longtime resort, perched on Lake Superior at the foot of Brockway Mountain. Now revealed are a lodge building (where plans call for a **restaurant**) and four cabins, three with kitchenettes. Only the two lighthouse inns have such a good location on Lake Superior. Here the surroundings are more **wild and natural**. The lodge and nine cabins sit on the seven acres (**660 feet of lakefront**) between M-26 and the lake, which is accessible though rocky here. There's 240° of visibility across open water — **great for seeing weather fronts move in and storms develop**. The north-facing orientation means you can see both sunrises and sunsets. Freighters rounding Keeweenaw Point are visible on the horizon. More resort acreage is across the highway, where informal **trails** lead up Brockway.

The cabins, already clean, have been winterized, and gas fireplaces are in the works. Some have drywall, some are knotty pine, and the large three-bedroom

cabin ($95 for up to 8) has the original log walls and wood-burning fireplace. They don't have TVs, phones, or air-conditioning (not needed). All towels and linens are supplied. Guests can use the office phone. Rates for 2001 are low, following the philosophy that it's better to be busy all the time than to get top dollar some of the time. Three one-bedroom cabins for two are $55, four two-bedroom cabins for up to four are $65, and the a small cabin without kitchen is $50 for two. $5 off for 5-night stay or more. Winter rates are $15 more to cover huge heating bills. Reserve early for peak seasons; word about these has gotten around fast locally. Doug and Liz, longtime U.P. visitors from Akron, Ohio, are glad to have found a way to live year year-round. *Open year-round. On M-26, three miles west of the Copper Harbor marina and 10 miles east of the Shoreline Resort in Eagle Harbor.* **H.A.**: call ♦♦♦♦: $5-$7/extra person above stated capacity 🐕: call

COPPER HARBOR CAMPING

FORT WILKINS STATE PARK
(906) 289-4215. Reserv.: (800) 44-PARKS; www.dnr.state.mi.us/

Campers here enjoy an unusually rich and interesting setting. The 165 modern campsites ($14/$17 a night) and 1 minicabin ($35) are in two wooded campgrounds right on Lake Fanny Hooe. Campsites are a short walk across U.S. 41 from the picnic area by the outlet of Lake Fanny Hooe Creek and the **dramatically rocky Lake Superior shore** looking out to the picturesque lighthouse. A short, easy walk through the woods along **Lake Fanny Hooe** and you're at the 1840s army fort, nifty playground, bookstore, snack bar, and camp store. It's an easy one-mile walk or bike ride to Copper Harbor's shops and restaurants. Campsites fill daily in July and most of August. If you reserve a month ahead, you'll probably get a site. For 2002 there will be more pull-through sites and probably fewer waterfront sites. *1 mile east of Copper Harbor on U.S. 41 Campgrounds open mid-May thru mid-Oct. State park sticker required: $4/$5 a day or $20/$25 a year.* &

Delaware

Established as a mining town in the 1840s, this ghost town declined as east Keweenaw mines proved unprofitable.

Delaware Copper Mine

This early Keweenaw copper mine was in operation from 1847 to 1887. Today it's privately owned and operated as a visitor destination. Visitors get to go underground. On the scenic grounds visitors can also see evidence of prehistoric mining pits made by the unknown ancient miners and the picturesque ruins of the pump house and hoist house made of grey amygdaloid rock from the first mine shaft. There's also a pen with miniature deer. The 40-minute tour takes visitors 110 feet into the first and second levels of the main shaft, involving a hundred feet of stairs. The tour isn't as generally informative about mining as the Quincy Hoist and Mine tour in Hancock or the Adventure Mine tour near Mass City in Ontonagon County. But it's an interesting place if you're in the area.

Take U.S. 41 to Delaware, 38 miles north of the Houghton-Hancock bridge or 12 miles south of Copper Harbor. 289-4688. Open daily from mid-May thru mid-Oct. **Guided tours** *from mid-June thru Labor Day; open 10-6 with last tour at 5:15. From Memorial Day to mid-June and from Labor Day thru Oct only* **self-guided tours** *are offered, 10 a.m. to 5 p.m. For both tours adults are $8, children 6-12 $4, children under 6 free.* &: no.

Lac La Belle

This resort enjoys an unusually picturesque setting on the north shore of Lac La Belle, a lake named by early French explorers. A village developed in the 1860s after a channel connected the lake with Lake Superior. A narrow-gauge railway brought ore from mines at Delaware and Medora to the lakeside stamping plant, now in ruins. It crushed rock so the smelter could extract the copper.

The **deep 1,100-acre lake** has a rocky bottom good for bass, muskies, perch, pike, and walleye. Picturesque **HAVEN FALLS** is in a **charming roadside park** with picnic area a half mile past where the road from Delaware turns west (right) at the lake. On the lakeshore near the train tracks stands one of the Keweenaw's oldest buildings, a two-story log house said to be over 200 years old. A popular local **swimming** spot is at **BETE GRIS BEACH** (locals say "BAY duh GREE"), east of Lac La Belle a couple of miles beyond the Lac La Belle Lodge resort. Lake Superior Land, owner of most former mining land, created the first big development controversy when it sold off much of the beach as lots. A

small part of the beach was saved for public use. Eagles nest at Bear Bluff across Bete Gris Bay and are seen here.

Just north of Lac La Belle, Mount Bohemia rises high above Lake Superior. The new **Mount Bohemia** extreme ski hill opened in December, 2000. Mount Bohemia introduced to the Midwest a new level of advanced wilderness skiing, taking advantage of very steep slopes and heavy lake-effect powder from three directions. Billed as **"the Rocky Mountain of the Midwest,"** Mount Bohemia had attracted ski fanatics before it even had lifts. Its previous owner had created a test ski slope in attempting to interest investors. Bohemia's remoteness proved too daunting until Crosswinds Communities, flush with money from suburban developments in southeast Michigan, bought the land and started the project. Mount Bohemia project became a **lightning rod for anti-development forces**.

LAC LA BELLE RESTAURANT

SEASONS at LAC LA BELLE is the new version of what used to be The Landing. The attractive space takes advantage of this beautiful spot. Cathy and Troy Westcott opened Seasons in time for Mount Bohemia's first ski season. The menu caters to a wide variety of customers. Seasons serves hearty breakfasts and from noon on, sandwiches (around $6, including reubens, honey-mustard chicken, and burgers), stone-baked pizza, and soup. After 5, dinner entrées are available, ranging from spaghetti ($9) to beef filet ($16). Big windows offer a **grand view of Lac La Belle and Gratiot Mountain** in the distance. There's bar and food service on the **deck**. The separate bar area means the dining room is smoke-free. **Takeout pizza** can be ordered up to 8:30. *On Lac La Belle. From U.S. 41 near Delaware, 12 miles west of Copper Harbor, look for the sign to Lac La Belle and turn south. At the lake, turn left, follow signs to Seasons and Lac La Belle Lodge. 289-4293. Open daily in summer and fall and in ski season from 9 a.m. to 9 p.m. Call for hours in the off-season.* & Full bar

LAC LA BELLE LODGING

LAC LA BELLE LODGE
(906) 289-4293; www.pasty.com
Four housekeeping cabins and two apartments are at what used to be called the Lac La Belle Resort (see above). The apartments are beneath the restaurant and store, where bait, tackle, and groceries are sold. See website for details. There's a dock and a newly improved beach and **picnic area** for guests. Consult website for details. Rentals are

by the week in summer, by the night other times. On snowmobile trail. *Open year-round.* &: call : call

Scenic South Shore drive

Often when it's cloudy or stormy on the rugged, north-facing side of the Keweenaw Peninsula's tip, the south shore, protected by the high central ridge, is sunny and relatively calm. Less spectacularly picturesque, the south shore has a **gentle beauty**, and it's much quieter than along M-26 on the north shore. Along the shore it's almost completely flat. There's very little traffic, which makes for wonderful, easy bicycling. The scenic shoreline drive from Lac La Belle to Gay passes many marshes, and shore birds are frequently seen. Wild blueberries can be picked from bushes near the road during most of August. A **roadside park** is at Betsy Bay, nine or ten miles south of Lac La Belle and about seven miles northeast of Gay.

The south shore drive can be reached from U.S. 41 by turning south at either Fulton (near Mohawk) on the west end by Gay, or at Delaware and Lac La Belle on the east end.

Gay

On an isolated stretch of the Keweenaw Bay's upper west shore, this hamlet, named after mining official Joseph Gay, has three distinctive landmarks:

◆ A **towering 256-foot-high smokestack** that can be seen from miles around. Its base alone is 30 feet in diameter. The stack is one of the few remnants of a huge smelter here, where crushed ore was heated to extract copper for copper ingots. Ore was shipped here from the Mohawk and Wolverine mines.

◆ An **eerie sight** along the Lake Superior's shore just east of town: a vast expanse of dark gray tailings, the remnants of finely crushed rock after the copper had been extracted. You can drive through this lifeless wasteland, a good half mile square, so inhospitable that even weeds can't take hold.

◆ The **GAY BAR** is the big draw these days, a classic U.P. bar owned by Bruce and Christine Fountain. It's located in the old home of the stamping mill superintendent and became a bar in the 1930s after the mines, mill, and smelter closed and Prohibition was repealed. Some come just to buy an "I've been to the Gay Bar" T-shirt. The **homemade pizza**, starting at $7.50, is popular, and the most requested beer is . . . Old Milwaukee. *296-0951.*

Isle Royale

TO EXPERIENCE NATURE in an especially remote, beautiful, and varied place, this roadless wilderness national park—on the biggest island in the world's biggest freshwater lake—is a very special, subtle place that exerts a powerful mystique. People who spend enough time on Isle Royale to accept it on its own terms usually want to return. **Wilderness solitude** is its attraction for many. **Adventure** and physical challenge in hiking or paddling is another part of its allure, though it's certainly possible to appreciate Isle Royale's unusual natural features in a less strenuous way. The island — an archipelago with over 20 smaller islands, properly speaking — is about **20 miles from the nearest shore**, in

The foggy magic of Lake Superior's rugged, remote wilderness island, includes wolves, moose, and striking volcanic and glacial landscapes

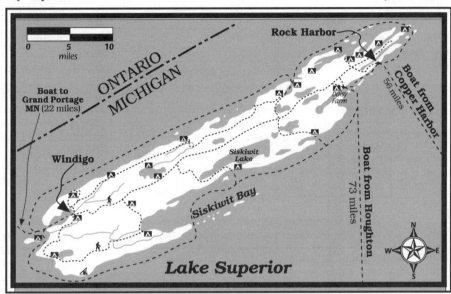

even at Rock Harbor, the island's most developed visitor base.

The 45-mile-long island is actually many different places because of its **ancient volcanic "ridge and trough" geological structure**. It was created by ancient lava flows, layered with softer sedimentary rock, that then uplifted at a slanting angle. When the Superior Basin sank, the layered rock tilted up at its edges. As the softer layers eroded away, the lava's hard basalt remained, creating the ridges. Isle Royale's geology mirrors that on the Keweenaw Peninsula, the corresponding shelf of uplifted rock on the opposite side of the Superior Basin. The island has long, rocky,

Canada, opposite the entrance to Thunder Bay, the natural harbor by the large industrial city of the same name. Getting to Isle Royale involves a 22-mile boat trip of two or three hours from Grand Portage, Minnesota, to Windigo near the island's western tip, or at least a 56-mile, 4 1/2-hour trip from Michigan's Keweenaw Peninsula to Rock Harbor, the main center of activity, with a hotel, housekeeping cabins, campground, boat rentals and charters, and sightseeing cruises. From early June through Labor Day both Windigo and Rock Harbor have **interesting nightly programs** about the island's natural and human history.

Often Isle Royale's shore is **enveloped in mist and fog**, which emphasizes the landscape's rocky forms and lets visitors know the limits of human activity. Sometimes the seaplane, the fastest and most expensive form of transportation to the island ($221 round-trip from Houghton), must wait for days to take off. Moose and foxes are often seen. Moose aren't shy, and they're amazing animals to watch, with their huge heads and antlers and thin legs. Foxes are the island's scavengers, hanging around campgrounds and docks hoping for a handout. Don't encourage them, and keep your food in your tent. There are no bears here. **Edible berries** near the trails in late July and August are a special treat. The **call of loons** reinforces the atmosphere of solitude. Theoretically, the howl of a wolf, among the most secretive of animals, can occasionally be heard — but what sounds like a wolf call almost always turns out to be a loon.

Fish species on Isle Royale are wild, evolved from the same genetic stock that has been here for thousands of years. Isle Royale has a special attraction for kayakers, canoeists, backpackers, boaters, anglers, botanists, birders, and geologists. (Taking rocks, flowers, plants, or driftwood in a national park is prohibited, however.) There's no TV and no reliable phone,

protected bays and inland lakes; exposed Lake Superior shore; and bogs and wetlands. High ridges and a few "mountains" and lookouts descend to Lake Superior on the island's northeastern end. There the **dramatic Five Fingers** trail off to form smaller islands and reefs, which caused several shipwrecks when mining was in full swing. Ten shipwrecks around different parts of the island are a **mecca for divers** today because Lake Superior's cold water preserves them in excellent condition. Of the **three lighthouses**, the Rock Harbor and Passage Island lights can be toured via the *M.V. Sandy* sightseeing boat.

The island incorporates **wetlands,** even old mines, and **fishery sites**. Before recorded history the island was used for thousands of years for hunting, fishing, and mining copper from surface deposits. Commercial copper mining occurred in the 1840s, the Civil War era, and again during the 1880s. Mines housing upwards of 80 men and their families were near McCargoe Cove, Windigo, and Siskiwit Bay. Many trees were cut for use underground and above ground. Isle Royale is not a place to see big old-growth trees, due to mining activities, forest fires, windy conditions, and rocky soil. Maples and yellow birch do well in the better soil at the island's southwest end. The outstanding Lake Superior fishery for lake trout led up to a hundred families of commercial fishermen to live here, usually only from spring through fall. Fishing peaked in the 1920s. In the 1930s falling prices triggered its gradual demise. The lives of these fishing families are conveyed in books of historical photographs and in the wonderful watercolors of Howard Sivertson, son of a commercial fisherman, who spent his boyhood here. His memorable *Once Upon an Isle* ($21) features facing pages of a written recollection and scenes painted from memory — being out in a fishing tug, for instance, or hanging out the wash and shooing away a moose.

In the early 1900s steamship companies build seven resort

hotels on Isle Royale and Washington Island just to the west, part of the North Woods resort boom fueled by well-to-do Midwestern urbanites seeking a cool, pollen-free climate and rustic fishing retreats. Individual families built cottages on the protected bays of the Five Fingers area, especially at Tobin Harbor, close to Rock Harbor on the other shore of a narrow, long peninsula. The Rock Harbor Lodge dining room, built as a guest house around 1900, is the best-preserved reminder of this era.

Summer people were the ones who successfully lobbied to have Congress pass a bill in 1931 to protect the island for future generations as a national park. In 1940 the **National Park Service** took over management of the island. The descendants of those resorters still form the core of the **Isle Royale Natural History Association** (www.irnha.org), which has published over 15 books on the island and its natural his-

tory, plus posters and note cards. Each summer the association's **artist-in-residence program** invites five artists or writers to spend two or three weeks apiece on the island, in return for giving a weekly presentation at Rock Harbor. The cottagers, so devoted to the island, are dwindling in numbers, since one provision of becoming a national park was that they sell their properties to the National Park Service in exchange for life leases for their descendants who were alive in 1940.

Three-fourths of the island's visitors are backpackers or paddlers who stay in the more remote back country. Some of those are in search of personal challenge. The steep ups and downs of the island's trail system are more challenging than many hikers expect. Some want to avoid the developed area around Rock Harbor. Others simply want to experience the island and can't find accommodations in Rock Harbor.

PLANNING AN ISLE ROYALE TRIP

For all prospective visitors, the National Park's free 12-page tabloid annual guide, **The Greenstone**, is an **essential planning tool**. It has a large map, planning tips, current fishing and other regulations, transportation schedules to the island, guidelines for **leave-no-trace wilderness use**, schedules of interpretive programs, and more. For current details about costs, request a separate info sheet.

The National Park Service has prepared a very helpful video, **Exploring Isle Royale: An Island Wilderness**, well worth its $18 price. It doubles as a souvenir of scenic spots. Any backpacker or paddler should get Jim DuFresne's **Isle Royale National Park: Foot Trails and Water Routes** (currently $12.95). It's a brief but complete guide to the island's human and natural history and to its hiking and water trails, recommended and sold by the National Park Service. It also outlines the options for day trips around Rock Harbor. **Superior Wilderness: Isle Royale National Park** by Napier Shelton (173 pp., $15.95) gives a good overview of island wildlife and ecosystems. **Isle Royale: Moods, Magic & Mystique** by Jeff Rennicke (40 pp., $11.95) is a briefer overview in photo-and-text format.

The following brief comments, gleaned from repeat Isle Royale visitors in many stages of life, are aimed the appreciative middle way of experiencing Isle Royale, somewhere between a wilderness physical challenge on the one hand and days of mostly planned group sightseeing activities on the other.

Surveys of Isle Royale visitors show that most want solitude — which turns out to be not all that easy between the Fourth of July weekend through mid August, when most visitors come. The island draws from 16,000 to 20,000 visi-

tors a summer. The average stay is four days, far longer than more widely visited national parks. The recently adopted general management plan is gradually implementing steps to separate user groups most likely to conflict, for instance, by keeping the often noisy powerboaters and youth groups away from small groups of wilderness-seeking backpackers and kayakers. The plan is already restricting boaters' former freedom to use generators and jet skis and to make wakes. The plan has been upheld in court. Backpackers tend to cluster at certain trails and campsites between major dropoff points. Divers are in their own fascinating world, as described in Nevada Barr's *Superior*

Fog and mist create haunting effects as they settle on the rocky landscape of the Isle Royale shore.

Death, featuring detective Anna Pigeon. (Her perceptive view of Isle Royale National Park Service personnel and visitors is considered on-target; after all, Nevada Barr herself is an NPS ranger. Of course, the story is fictitious, and no such murder occurred.)

Careful budgeting and planning is required for prospective visitors, starting with the **round-trip fare to the island** (at least $68 from Minnesota and $82 from Michigan for adults) and the $4 a day user fee. **Advance reservations for ferry service**, starting January 1 but at least a few months ahead, are recommended, especially if you want certain days at busy times. For people who suffer from motion sickness, vessel size is a factor if waves are high, and dramamine is recommended. The two Michigan boats allow up to 100 pounds of gear without charge; the Minnesota boats charge $27 for over 40 pounds. See *The Greenstone* for schedule and details for transporting other boats, fuel tanks, etc., or call.

At Rock Harbor, the destination of the two passenger boats from Michigan, a National Park concessionaire runs **Rock Harbor Lodge**, a 60-room hotel with public dining room and snack bar. It also books 20 private housekeeping units sleeping up to six in 10 duplex buildings. The **lodge rooms** are in four two-story buildings; half the rooms face the water. The **duplex cottages** are in the woods near the lodge. They are often booked way in advance for July and most of August, with sporadic openings. More cottages might be built, but that won't happen any time soon. There are too many more pressing needs for improving the developed area's infrastructure and notoriously shabby employee housing. The contract with the concessionaire may be renegotiated, too. (The Kentucky-based lodge management also operates facilities at Mammoth Cave.) All lodgings and meals are subject to a 17% utility charge, in addition to 6% Michigan sales tax. Lodge room rates include three meals a day. Including taxes and fees, they are currently $228 a day for two adults, $301 a day for two adults and two children. Housekeeping cabins for two, fees included, are $146, for four $208. Dining room meals including fees and tax but not tips are $10.49 for breakfast, $12.73 for lunch, and $24.54 for dinner. Fresh fish caught on the island is among the menu options.

GETTING THERE

◆ **From Copper Harbor, Michigan to Rock Harbor** (4 1/2 hours). The 81-foot, 100-passenger *Isle Royale Queen III* makes a round-trip at least five days a week from early June through Labor Day, daily in August, and on Mon & Fri from mid-May into early June and through most of September. Expect some interesting commentary from the three Captains Kilpela, brothers Don Junior, Ben, and John. One-way fares are $42 (adults), $21 (children 1-11), $20 for canoes and kayaks. (906) 289-4437. Fax:(906) 289-4952. E-mail: Captain@up.net. www. isleroyale.com

◆ From **Houghton, Michigan to Rock Harbor** (6 hours). The National Park Service's big, 165-foot, 126-passenger *Ranger III* leaves twice a week from June thru early September and returns the following day. It also carries supplies to the national park and concessionaires. **Ranger programs** and on-board campground registration are *Ranger III* extras. One-way fares: $48 (adult), $24 (children 1-11), $20 for canoes or kayaks up to 20'. (906) 482-0984. Fax: 482-8753. www.nps.gov/isro

◆ From **Grand Portage, Minnesota to Windigo** (2 hours) and Rock Harbor (5 hours). The 60-foot *Voyageur II* leaves mostly three times a week and goes around the island, also making stops at five smaller docks — a service much used by backpackers and paddlers. Its season begins in mid May and lasts through most of October. From late September on, the *Voyageur II* is the only boat to the island. One-way adult fares are $49 to Windigo, $56 to Rock Harbor and the other docks. Children are $32, canoes and kayaks are $28 to $32. (715) 392-2100. Fax: 392-5586. www.GRAND-ISLE-ROYALE.com

◆ From **Grand Portage to Windigo** (3 hours). The 63-foot *Wenonah* makes daily round trips from early June thru mid September. One-way fares: $34

Visiting the Edisen Fishery is like dropping in on a commercial fishing family in the 1930s. Fisherman Les Mattson has fished on Lake Superior all his life. In the 1920s Isle Royale had nearly a hundred families based at small fisheries like this. Their lives are depicted in detail in the watercolor paintings and text of *Once Upon an Isle*, by Howard Sivertson, who grew up in a family of commercial fishermen here.

(adult), $17 (children 4 thru 11), children 3 and under free. Most canoes and kayaks $28-$32. Phone and website same as for *Voyageur II* above.

PROS & CONS OF ROCK HARBOR VS. A BACK-COUNTRY EXPERIENCE

If solitude is definitely your goal, it's possible to adopt strategies to reduce the frequency of encounters with other people. Get away from the main harbors to less-used trails and campgrounds. "To get to isolated campgrounds, you need to leapfrog to get started" past each boat's wave of campers, says Chief Interpreter Smitty Parratt. "There are only a few on-ramps. Visitor flow patterns are being studied in for the upcoming Wilderness and Backcountry Management Plan." Consult Jim DuFresne's *Isle Royale National Park: Foot Trails & Water Routes* for more tips on finding less-used places. Or ask the ranger who issues your permit; rangers have a good idea of the current use pattern on the island just then. You could have the *Voyageur II* drop you off at McCargoe Cove, Belle Isle, Daisy Farm, or Chippewa Harbor or points in between. (This will cost an extra $32 to $42 and will require schedule coordination.) There's also a **water taxi** from Rock Harbor, which can take you and your canoe or kayak to shoreline places including campgrounds on smaller islands, subject to weather and lake conditions. Some sample one-way rates:

one to five miles (to Caribou or Tookers Islands or Three Mile Dock) $33 for two people up to $42 for six. 11 to 16 miles (to Duncan Bay or Chippewa Harbor campgrounds) $97 for two, $116 for six. A canoe or kayak counts as a person. A much cheaper alternative is the **"water bus service"** that's offered in conjunction with *M.V. Sandy* scheduled cruises (see below and in *The Greenstone*). The *Sandy* can drop off day-hikers or backpackers at its various destinations. Fare is modest $11.20 per adult in 2001.

On the other hand, you may find that the **advantages of staying close to the main visitor center at Rock Harbor** outweigh the attractions of solitude. The typical Isle Royale visitor is a fairly quiet nature-lover willing to forgo TV and other amenities. Staying near Rock Harbor spares visitors the planning logistics and physical work of carrying *all* their food and gear on steep trails or taxing portages. Even the nearby trails aren't crowded, and they're the island's most varied.

The Rock Harbor area is nothing like a summer visit to Tahquamenon Falls or Pictured Rocks. The Rock Harbor campground has 11 campsites and nine shelters, but campers can only stay here one night at a time. If you camp, you might want to coordinate your nights at Rock Harbor with evening programs or *M. V. Sandy* excursions of special interest. A hot shower every few days, available in the laundry building, can be nice even when you're camping. So can an occasional meal of fresh fish at the Rock Harbor Lodge. (Anglers are permitted to eat the fish they catch.) Especially if you're over 40, you may find that sleeping in a bed is much more restful than a tent, which is why the housekeeping cabins are so popular.

The National Park Service's **interesting nightly programs** about the **island's natural and human history**, held at Windigo and Rock Harbor at 8:30 or 8 p.m. from early June through Labor Day, have never been disappointing, says one woman who visits the island yearly with her geologist husband. The $11 **sightseeing cruises** on the 50-passenger *M.V. Sandy* out of Rock Harbor can expand your range and sometimes give you the option of hiking back. Often park rangers are their guides. Renting a kayak or canoe, or especially a boat and motor, can also expand your range.

ISLE ROYALE HIGHLIGHTS

In contrast to the wilderness experience, achieved by getting away from the shoreline areas and other people, these memorable outings to prime natural areas start from Rock Harbor. The schedule of *M.V. Sandy* cruises is fairly consistent from year to year but could change. Cruises are first-come, first-served and weather dependent.

◆ **LOOKOUT LOUISE** is the "Brockway Mountain" of Isle Royale — the northeastern end of Greenstone Ridge, with an **amazing, map-like view of many bays and islands**. It is a virtual microcosm of the island and its flora and fauna. It's especially beautiful in the fog. On a clear day the smokestacks of Thunder Bay's pulp and paper mills can be seen. Tuesday and Thursday mornings a the *M. V. Sandy* takes visitors four miles around Scoville Point from Rock Harbor to the trailhead at Hidden Lake, a place where moose are often seen. A park ranger leads a guided hike a mile to Lookout Louise, a 320-foot climb. (Cost in 2001: $11.20, half off for children under 12.)

◆ **RASPBERRY ISLAND,** opposite Rock Harbor, is a must. It's a **rugged outer island** with a **one-mile self-guided nature trail**. Its boardwalk crosses across a spruce bog walk past insect-eating plants. Make reservations at Rock Harbor Lodge for a shuttle to drop you off for a day ($9.20 in 2001). It's also an easy paddle on a calm day.

◆ The **EDISEN FISHERY** and **ROCK**

Isle Royale's wolf and moose populations: perfect material for a predator-prey study

In order to keep the island a natural wilderness, the island's guardians do not intervene to prop up a declining species or trim a burgeoning population, as is commonly done in wildlife management. The moose population grew to 2,400 in 1995 and then crashed to 502 in just two years. Part of the reason was the harsh winter of 1995-96, when deep snows had moose so starved that many fell to their deaths over shoreline cliffs trying to reach for tender twigs from trees with limbs hanging over the precipices.

Islands are ideal for scientific research because outside influences are more limited and fewer species live on islands. Wolves and moose are the predator and prey species on Isle Royale. Wolves arrived on the island over the ice during the winter of 1949 and have been studied by Michigan Tech professor Rolf Peterson with his mentor, Durward Allen, in the longest-running predator-prey study anywhere. It's documented in Peterson's interesting book, *The Wolves of Isle Royale: A Broken Balance*. Wolves help stabilize the moose population, but lack of genetic diversity seems to be hurting the wolves' ability to reproduce. The winter 2001 census revealed 19 wolves and about 900 moose. Air surveillance, radio collaring, and counting dead remains are chief research tools.

HARBOR LIGHTHOUSE, accessible only by water, can be visited via the *Sandy* on Thursday afternoon or Saturday morning. Cost in 2001: $11.20, or $5.60 for children under 12. The 1855 lighthouse, **one of the oldest navigational aids on Lake Superior**, and related exhibits are an interesting and much-photographed sight. The fishery, restored to the 1930s, is pretty much as it was left by commercial fisherman Pete Edisen, who lived here from the 1920s until 1978. Far and away the best thing about this excursion is the **presentation by resident fisherman Les Mattson** and having a chance to talk with him and his wife, Donna, afterwards. Les has been a commercial fisherman on Lake Superior since he

was a boy, nearly 50 years ago. Today his catch is for environmental sampling and for the restaurant at Rock Harbor Lodge. His perspective about his livelihood, the lake, and the environment are way **wiser than most any book**. Ask him about the unintended consequences of monofilament net.

◆ **PASSAGE ISLAND LIGHTHOUSE**, several miles off the island's east tip, is a one-of-a-kind lighthouse because of its **facing of Jacobsville sandstone**. A park ranger comes along on the *M.V. Sandy's* Monday and Friday afternoon trips and talks about the lighthouse, shipwrecks, and the island's unusual geology.

◆ The **SCOVILLE POINT TRAIL**, about a six-mile loop east from Rock Harbor, offers **beautiful, rocky vistas**.

◆ **CHIPPEWA HARBOR**, an inlet on the south shore, connects via portages to Siskiwit Lake. It is an **especially beautiful place to camp**. It has four shelters and two tent sites.

◆ The **FIVE FINGERS AREA** at the northeastern tip is known for its rocky scenery. The all-day *M. V. Sandy* **North Side Cruise** on Wednesday goes around the Five Fingers to McCargoe Cove for an optional steep, **three-mile hike to Minong Mine**, with a possible interpretive talk by a ranger. It's $18.15 for adults, $9.08 for children in 2001. Bring a lunch.

TIPS FOR VISITING ISLE ROYALE

◆ Don't expect wonderful rustic lodge architecture at Rock Harbor Lodge or the close-spaced housekeeping cabins. Built in the 1960s, they are utilitarian and institutional, more like rooms in a big college dorm. They do have picture windows. Half the rooms at Rock Harbor Lodge look out on Raspberry Island; the cabins look at trees. But they're **depressing at first**, according to a fit, fortyish graphics designer who has also camped at Isle Royale. "Then, after you put up your groceries, you get out onto the mossy forest trails, and the setting sun has a glowing effect. The beautiful, magical world hits you. As night sets in, when you get back to your cabin it feels **homey**. We had such deep sleeps. The cottages grow on you. It's *much* more comfortable than camping."

◆ The island stores at Rock Harbor and Windigo are very expensive and limited in their selection of groceries and trail food. **Plan on buying all your supplies on the mainland**. If you stay in a cabin, pack your groceries and gear in boxes.

Hundreds of moose live on Isle Royale. The huge, ungainly creatures don't avoid humans like their predator, the wolf. Visitors out and about, especially near dawn and dusk, are likely to see moose browsing shrubs or wading to eat submerged aquatic plants. Visitors are warned not to get too close to disturb moose. Cow moose with calves and bull moose in fall rutting season can be especially dangerous. Moose have reduced the diversity of plants on the main island. On a sightseeing trip to distant Passage Island more plants of the northern boreal forest can be seen.

They are delivered to cabins.

◆ Children who aren't already experienced backpackers will enjoy Isle Royale much more if their family stays in a cabin, and less hiking is expected of them. Try family backpacking somewhere else before going to Isle Royale.

◆ Renting a boat and motor ($47 a day in 2001) lets you get out to distant islands, a real plus for visitors interested in geology and botany. (Browsing by moose reduces the number of plant species on the main island.) Canoe rentals are $22 a day, but a canoe won't take you as far.

◆ Canoeists should be aware that conditions on Lake Superior can change quickly. Superior is so cold, it can quickly be **life-threatening** — a special danger to canoeists. Staying close to shore is essential. Lake Superior is for experienced canoeists. The island's north side is especially difficult.

◆ **No pets**; they could introduce disease to the wolves. Special arrangements can be made for seeing-eye dogs.

◆ To disturb the island as little as possible and to preserve its natural beauty, hiking here is more disciplined than most vacationers are accustomed to. **"Low impact"** is the watchword. That means, among other things: rigorously packing out all trash with you; wearing subdued colors of clothing; staying in the middle of trails to minimize erosion; and using backpacking stoves rather than making campfires.

◆ Mountain bikes or wheeled portage devices are not permitted in the wilderness national park.

◆ Isle Royale is a damp, misty place. The fog is beautiful. Come prepared for rain. **Get beyond the limitations of a fair-weather mentality.**

◆ Potable water is only available at Rock Harbor and Windigo. Otherwise, drinking water should be boiled at least two minutes, purified, or passed through a .4-micron water filter. Bring replacement filters.

◆ **Slopes on the island's north side are steeper** because they are at the tilted-up edge of the ancient lava flow. This is relevant planning information for hikers and canoeists. Trails and portages on the south side of Greenstone Ridge are more gradual.

◆ **Camping permits** are required for all campers and overnight boaters, who are asked to inform park rangers of their plans. They are issued on the *Ranger III* (the NPS boat from Houghton) or the Rock Harbor or Windigo visitor stations. Groups of six or fewer find campsites on a first-come, first-served basis. In the busy season, they may have to double up with other campers. Groups of seven to ten campers require advance reservations, or they need to split up into smaller groups with completely separate itineraries. Each campground has a limit of no more than five consecutive nights' stay, more often two or three, but only one night near Rock Harbor. Rangers who issue permits can help campers plan. **Back-country camping**, though difficult and only for experienced campers, is permitted; make arrangements when getting a permit.

◆ Currently 36 campgrounds are located on trails, docks and coves, and inland lakes. Most have a combination of tent sites and **screened three-sided shelters** without bunks (88 in all). Shelters usually get taken first. Hit them by 10:30 a.m. to increase your luck, but always carry a tent for backup. Sixteen shelters, six tent sites, and a dock are at the island's largest campground, **Daisy Farm**, a seven-mile paddle or hike from Rock Harbor. The shoreline path is narrow and rocky. Twice-weekly **evening program**s are held at Daisy Farm, and the Edisen Fishery and Rock Harbor Lighthouse are a one-mile paddle away (not accessible by land).

◆ **Hikers should plan conservatively**, start slowly, not push themselves, and plan to carry at least a half gallon of water per person. The biggest mistake backpackers make is **overestimating the number of miles they can hike in a day**. Five miles a day are plenty of exercise even without a heavy pack with gear and all your food. Ten miles a day is a lot for Isle Royale. Chief interpreter Smitty Parratt points out that east-west trails are up and down over a series of lava flow edges, going from 600 feet to 1,300 feet and back. "We recommend five to eight miles a day unless you've been here a lot," he says. Even the 40-mile **Greenstone Ridge Trail** down the island's long axis is criss-crossed with fault lines, making for lots of ups and downs. **Footing is often difficult**, due to an unusual number of roots and rocks and slanted bedrock that may be mossy and slick after a rain. On the roadless island, hikers who injure themselves are far from help. Marathons are for the mainland, advises the staff.

◆ **Lingering at the quiet inland lakes,**

mostly reachable by canoe, kayak, or hiking trail, can be "a soul-satisfying way to connect with the wilderness," in the National Park Service script to the *Exploring Isle Royale* video. Many inland routes are possible. Very fit, very experienced paddlers can take a big circle route that includes four inland lakes and some of the island's most striking scenery. Four lakes connect Rock Harbor with McCargoe Cove (five portages, two to three days of travel). It's 13 1/2 miles to take the challenging northern water route from McCargoe Cove through the Amygdaloid Channel and around the Five Fingers to Rock Harbor. Or you could take a water taxi back from McCargoe Cove.

◆ **All plans and schedules are provisional and weather-dependent.** If Lake Superior is too rough, vessels to and from the mainland may miss scheduled crossings, creating backups. Hikers and paddlers should take provisions for more days than they anticipate needing. You may want to stay longer — and you may be slowed down by bad weather. You can't count on getting a space on the next vessel back to the mainland, either.

◆ **Be prepared for cold, wet weather,** especially near Lake Superior. Stores in Houghton and Copper sell winter clothing to layer for prospective visitors who hear just how cold July can be.

◆ Conversely, the exposed rock portions of the Greenstone Ridge Trail can get **quite hot by 10 a.m.** Sunscreen is essential on the water or on the trail. Some paths grow thick with thimbleberries and other obstructions by August, so have long pants handy.

◆ **Come prepared for insects,** though they're not necessarily as bad as you might expect. "The bugs we've found

annoying are the stable flies on rocks by the shore," says a frequent visitor in late July. Gaiters to keep them away from your ankles are a good investment. On trails through bogs like Raspberry Island, mosquitoes can be fierce.

THE ISLAND IS OPEN TO VISITORS from mid April through October. However, transportation to the island is more limited. It's available from Minnesota from mid May through most of October. Scheduled transportation from Copper Harbor is from mid May through late September. Boaters are allowed earlier and later. Rock Harbor Lodge is open from June 12 or so through the first week of September. Cabins open in late May and close at the same time as the lodge. National Park Service visitor programming runs from June 9 through Labor Day.

HANDICAP ACCESS: A few rooms in Rock Harbor Lodge and some housekeeping units are wheelchair-accessible. The sightseeing boat *M.V. Sandy*, while not officially accessible, has taken people in wheelchairs. Trails are not generally handicap-accessible. Call the Isle Royale National Park for advice about individual cases.

CONTACTS:
PHONE, ON-LINE, AND IN PERSON

ISLE ROYALE NATIONAL PARK
Houghton Visitor Center.
(906) 482-0984. Visitor fax: 482-8753.
www.nps.gov/isro e-mail for info:
ISRO_ParkInfo@nps.gov

By the dock of the *Ranger III*, this office accommodates both a bookstore and a year-round staffed **information center** where park rangers with detailed maps can answer some prospective visitor questions (not about concessionaire

services, however) and provide some advice. The **Isle Royale Natural History Association Store** offers a tightly focused selection of books, maps, videos, and posters either about Isle Royale or about subjects pertaining to it, such as wolves, moose, field guides, and Indian culture. Some poster images are from the natural history association's artist in residence program. A substantial portion of all merchandise profits go to the national park. **Mail orders** are welcome; call (800) 678-6925 or e-mail irnha@ irnha.org. For the complete **online catalog**, visit www. irnha .org. Adjoining the shop are offices of National Park Service Isle Royale staff. *By the dock at 800 E. Lakeshore. From Shelden Ave./U.S. 41, look for signs, turn north just before entering downtown at the tall Franklin Square Inn. From mid June thru late August: open Mon-Sat 8-6. From late August thru mid Sept. closes at 4:30. From late Sept. to mid June: open Mon-Fri 8-4:30.* ♿

ROCK HARBOR LODGE
Summer: (906) 337-4993. Winter: general offices at Mammoth Cave, Kentucky. (270) 773-2191.

The lodge answers questions not only about lodgings but about sightseeing cruises, boat rentals, fishing charters, and other concession services.

FERRY SERVICES TO THE ISLAND: see bulleted items in main text. For more details, request *The Greenstone* from the Visitor Center.

Keep in mind that all prices and hours of operation are subject to change.

The Porcupine Mountains & Ontonagon

THE RUGGED PORCUPINE MOUNTAINS at the remote northwestern edge of the U.P. are **one of the Midwest's few great remaining wilderness tracts**. Long, high ridges have made the interior forests here too inaccessible and too expensive to log. The ridges are what remain of **once-towering mountains** formed when ancient, hard volcanic basalt was uplifted. The shape of the tree-covered ridges led local Ojibwa to call the area "*kaugabissing*"— the place of the porcupines.

Vast virgin forests, wonderful waterfalls and vistas, rugged hiking trails, and remote old mines in a distant place along Lake Superior

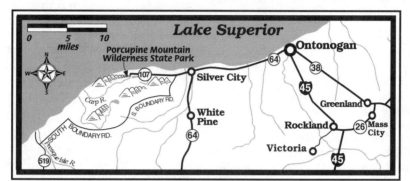

es, dozens of **beautiful waterfalls**, and **85 miles of hiking trails**. Winter means **42 kilometers of groomed cross-country ski trails** and **budget-priced downhill skiing** on slopes with 640' vertical drops and **terrific vistas**. (See separate skiing section.)

The rest of Ontonagon County also has its charms for people who enjoy getting off the beaten path. The town of **Ontonagon** has a mile of **beautiful, sandy Lake Superior beach** in its town park and an **excellent historical museum**. Finnish immigrants worked reluctantly in the mines, but many loved the self-sufficiency of farming and continue to operate farms today. Ontonagon County's many major highways pass through landscapes that are **surprisingly pastoral**, with grazing cattle and impressive barns. "Eat right with beef!" proclaims one sign.

The 35,000 acres at the heart of the 60,000-acre **Porcupine Mountains Wilderness State Park** have never been logged. What's even more unusual is that much of it is **old-growth forest**, where a favorable combination of rainfall, soil, and circumstances have enabled trees to grow very large. Dominant tree types here in the Porkies are hardwoods and eastern hemlock. Lots of **sugar maple** makes for **spectacular fall color**. Most of the Porkies has been spared the catastrophic natural fires that can make an old-growth forest little different in general appearance from a logged forest. Windstorms, while common here near Lake Superior's shore, are usually relatively small. Large wind events like the 1953 blowdown occur at intervals of 500 years or more on a given site.

Park ranger/naturalist Bob Sprague points out that **old forests of eastern hemlock** "capture the essence of what people expect to see in old-growth forests." **Dark and mysterious**, free of underbrush because of the dense canopy, hemlocks are the Midwestern forests most like the old-growth rain forests of the West Coast. They were the "forests primeval" described in Longfellow's "Evangeline," where "the murmuring pines and the hemlocks stood like Druids of eld." The trunks of hemlocks here are up to **three feet across**. A very large sugar maple, by comparison, is only two feet across. Old-growth forests of white pine or hardwood have an irregular, shaggy look in contrast to the hemlocks' thick, dark canopy. Hemlocks were often passed over by loggers because their wood splinters easily. A moist, shady microclimate perfect for hemlocks is created by the Porcupine Mountains' north-facing slopes, along with increased lake-effect precipitation from Lake Superior. Temperatures are more uniform than in nearby inland areas.

By the 1930s conservationists had recognized the Porcupine Mountains' rarity and value as a wilderness area. The Porkies became a state park in 1945. Only the 25-mile South Boundary Road connects the park's eastern end near Ontonagon with the western end around the Presque Isle River, reached from Wakefield near Ironwood. The Wilderness Natural Areas Act of 1972 quashed controversial proposals for more development and a through road along the lakeshore. Development threats have remained dormant ever since.

The park offers visitors a huge variety of experiences. There are **short hikes** and **scenic overlooks**, **Lake Superior beach-**

Some of the earliest serious mining took place around Rockland, Mass City, and Victoria, based on **mass copper outcrops and pits** made by the **mysterious ancient miners**. (Just who they were is a matter of great interest and scientific debate in Copper Country.) The **Ontonagon Boulder**, a great mass of copper well known by native people, created a sensation and ended up in the Smithsonian. Stories about the mis-named boulder created great excitement starting with 17th century missionary-explorers. It actually came from Victoria, south of Rockland, at a place near the West Branch of the Ontonagon River now covered by the reservoir of Victoria Dam. The quaint, **sleepy village of Rockland**, once a mining boom town, is an interesting place to explore on the way to The **Old Victoria Restoration**, which is rebuilding and furnishing log miners' houses as they were in 1900 and 1920. A few miles to the northeast, the **Adventure Mine** in Greenland offers a good underground tour of a copper mine akin to that in Victoria. The **Caledonia Mine** outside Mass City is still being mined— for specimens of copper and other minerals — and open to rockhounds by appointment.

A well-developed segment of the **North Country Trail** goes through this area from the Porcupine Mountains all the way to the Sturgeon River Gorge near Alberta south of L'Anse. It provides access to a **rugged, remote area** little penetrated by real roads, and it also connects several waterfalls, Old Victoria, lakes, a national forest campground, and the Sturgeon River Gorge and Wilderness Area.

TO FIND OUT MORE: The **ONTONAGON COUNTY CHAMBER OF COMMERCE** mails information and publicizes lodgings and events for all of Ontonagon County, including **Ontonagon**, the **Porkies**, and far-away places like Ewen, Bruce Crossing, and Trout Creek. (906) 884-4735. Their website is www.ontonagonmi.com It has an events calendar, too. They staff the **Tourist Information Center** *at M-64 and River Road just west of Ontonagon from Mem. Day through color season. At other times their office, open to the public, is in the River Pines RV*

Park at 600 River Road. . . . . The **PORCUPINE MOUNTAINS PROMOTIONAL CHAMBER** in Silver City responds to phone inquiries (906-885-5399), e-mail (dfubski@up.net) and has a website with Dan Urbanski's beautiful photographs, www.porcupinemountains .com For further inspiration, look in on www.quietlywild.com and investigate Dan's "**wilderness diary**" adventures. . . Rockland's new website is www.RocklandMI.org

PUBLIC LANDS: The **OTTAWA NATIONAL FOREST** has extensive holdings through the central part of Ontonagon County. Its Ontonagon District Office is at 1209 Rockland Road/U.S. 45. It's open weekdays from 7:30 to 4 Eastern Time. (906) 884-2411. TTY (906) 884-6577. Or look in at www.fs.fed.us/r9/ottawa . . . . From the Black River waterfalls just west of the Porkies all the way to the Sturgeon River Gorge near Alberta are 130 continuous miles of the **NORTH COUNTRY TRAIL** with just a mile along motor roads. The section from the hamlet of Norwich to Victoria is remote high land with some amazing vistas. Check out the **outstanding website** of the western U.P. Peter Wolfe chapter for many photos, complete trail notes, and current conditions, what's blooming, what's migrating, and more: www.northcountrytrail.org/pwf/

GUIDES: Don Scott (884-4866) guides for bear- and deer-hunting and for fishing on inland lakes. **Wilderness Adventures** in Silver City rents tents and backpacking gear.

LODGINGS TIPS: Cottages on the water are in limited supply and get booked up fast for July and early August, sometimes a year ahead. Call by January for good availability, and call early for fall color season and ski season weekends and Christmas week, too. . . . Similarly, call a year ahead for Porkies wilderness cabins in peak seasons. . . . Late August and early September, after kids are back in school and before color season, is a wonderful, unhurried time with good availability. Weather is iffy starting in late September; it could be balmy, or it might even snow. Attractive lodgings somewhat farther away, in Ontonagon, won't book as early. The same goes for the **former Konteka Lodge** in White Pine, which may be reopening as we go to press. Call the local chamber at 906-885-5399 for details. . . . In spring, you get wildflowers and no crowds if you can deal with the bugs. June's a spring month, too.

EVENTS: For exact dates and a full calendar, look in on www.ontonagonmi.com . . . . In **ONTONAGON** Riverfest on the second weekend of June coincides with free fishing weekend. It brings contests, arts and crafts, a pig roast, and more. A medieval reenactment group adds dancing and fighting demonstrations of the Robin Hood era, circa 1200. Ontonagon also holds a Labor Day Festival. . . . **WHITE PINE** and **BRUCE CROSSING** celebrate July 4. . . . The Ontonagon County Fair comes to Adventure Mountain in **GREENLAND** in late July or early August. . . . In **OLD VICTORIA** the Craft Fair is the third Sunday of August. . . . **EWEN** holds its Log Jamboree the third weekend of September. . . . The Porkies Fest is on Labor Day at the **PORCUPINE MOUNTAINS** Wilderness State Park.

HARBOR with transient dockage: In **Ontonagon** (906-884-9950, 906-884-4225; lat. 46° 52' 57" N, 89° 19' 58" W) with showers.

PICNIC PROVISIONS and PLACES

◆ The county's two supermarkets with substantial deli sections are Pat's Foods (formerly Fraki's) on M-38 outside **ONTONAGON** and the Settler's Co-op on M-28 at U.S. 45 in **BRUCE CROSSING**.

◆ In **ONTONAGON**, the township park on Lake Superior just north of town has a **beautiful beach and view**, with shade beneath tall pines. Riverfront Park in town on M-64 by the marina has a boardwalk but no shade. On M-64 halfway to Silver City, Green Park has a pretty picnic spot by the Lake Superior beach.

◆ There's a **delightful rest stop and picnic area** where U.S. 45 crosses the Middle Branch of the Ontonagon River, a few miles south of **ROCKLAND** and **MASS CITY**.

◆ In **SILVER CITY**, some picnic tables are nestled in the woods where the Iron River meets Lake Superior.

◆ The **PORCUPINE MOUNTAINS WILDERNESS STATE PARK** has picnic tables along the entrance road by Lake Superior, at the Lake of the Clouds overlook, at the Presque Isle River Mouth campground, and by the parking lot near Summit Peak (a less scenic option). It would be nice to take out chicken from the Rainbow Lodge restaurant, but as we go to press the proprietors feed bears, which puts them on the wrong side of the serious nuisance bear issue.

Porcupine Mountains Wilderness State Park

The park's true highlights are the **hiking trails** leading into the **old-growth forests**, especially when they also lead to one of the park's **over 30 waterfalls**. The Porkies are one of the **Midwest's premiere places to backpack**. To really experience the Porkies, try to plan spending a day — or better yet, at least two days and a night — hiking and camping in the wilderness, away from the busy visitor spots and modern campgrounds. Campers must be prepared to deal with **hungry, clever black bears**. (A detailed pamphlet, "Preventing Bear Problems in Michigan," is given out at the Visitor Center or headquarters. It makes fascinating reading.) Some two dozen or more bears live in the park.

The park has **16 frontier cabins**, one wheelchair-accessible, the others on trails at least a mile from parking. They are arranged so they can be used for a three- or four-day backpack trip. Their popularity means they must be reserved well ahead in peak seasons.

In fact, this huge park can seem crowded due to clustering of visitors at certain times (summer, fall color season, winter weekends and Christmas week in the ski areas) and in certain places like scenic overlooks and campgrounds. To experience **wilderness solitude**, consider coming at attractive off-season times. In mid to late May wildflowers are out. **Warblers** fly through in mid-May, just when black flies are getting bad. In early October most leaves have fallen but some are left. Mid-May through mid-June are generally worst times for black flies. These nasty pests remain longer when heavy snows cause lots of moisture.

PLANNING YOUR TRIP

Free telephone planning help is available year-round from the park's extremely helpful staff. For a **visitor packet** including camping at the park, area lodgings, and handouts customized to your interests, call (906) 885-5275 or write Porcupine Mountains Wilderness State Park, 412 S. Boundary Rd., Ontonagon, MI 49953.

For advance planning, there are two recommended book-length guides, each excellent in its way. Veteran Michigan outdoor writer Jim Du Fresne's

The forest primeval: The Porkies' rugged terrain enabled hardwoods and white pine to escape logging. The splintery wood of hemlocks were not attractive to loggers (their main economic use was tanbark for tanneries). Old-growth hemlocks are really impressive to visitors. These old hemlocks at Overlook Falls on the Little Carp River are reached by an easy, short, fairly level trail. It's a good place for hurried visitors to experience the old-growth forest.

Porcupine Mountains Wilderness State Park (Thunder Bay Press, 159 pp., $11.95) provides a quick, convenient overview from someone with a lot of hands-on visitor experience. The fascinating if somewhat unwieldy *Porcupine Mountains Companion* (328 pp., around $12-$14) conveys a vast knowledge of all aspects of the Porkies, compiled by naturalists who work here year-round. It's available at the visitor center or from Nequaket Natural History Assn., Box 103, White Pine, MI 49971. It details trails, cabins, waterfalls, local history of Ojibwa (18 pp.), mining (22 pp.), geology (22 pp.), botany, wildlife, nearby day trips, and even a quick constellation guide. Richly illustrated, it's the perfect book for a long backpacking trip.

Serious backpackers can plan many different several-day adventures along the Porkies' **85 miles of trails**. In this rugged wilderness, steep grades and unbridged stream crossings are common. For more complicated day trips and for overnights, it's a good idea to have a compass and be sure you understand and have planned for all the precautions mentioned in the "Backcountry information" handout (campfires permitted in metal rings only; take fire starter, high-energy food, first-aid; boil drinking water 5 minutes or filter or chemically treat it; learn to hang your food so bears can't get it).

Backcountry camping is permitted anywhere in the park provided it's not within 1/4 mile of a cabin or road. See under Porkies camping for details.

The **VISITOR CENTER** (906-885-5277) near the east entrance should be a visitor's first stop when it's open. That's from the May weekend before Memorial Day through October, normally from 10 a.m. to 6 p.m. It offers informative free handouts, detailed hiking and topo maps for sale, an **excellent bookstore**, and **interesting background exhibits**. The short **interpretive nature trail** here is a good introduction to area plants and animals. Helpful park rangers here can give information about trails, backpacking, canoeing, fishing (for steelhead, salmon, and trout), and more. A big, detailed relief map of the huge park helps orient visitors. An **excellent 15-minute multi-image slide show**, shown upon request, informs visitors about the area's history, wildlife and natural features, and recreational possibilities. Topical **evening programs** are held Monday through Thursday in July and August. (Usually they're at 7 p.m.; call for details.) Regular topics are black bears, wildflowers, peregrine falcons, owls, and bats. The daytime activity schedule includes interesting **hikes** with many themes. Hikes explore

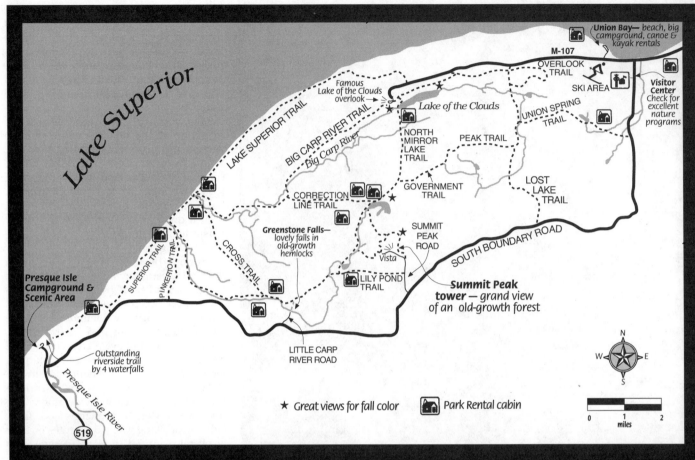

Union Bay— beach, big campground, canoe & kayak rentals

M-107

OVERLOOK TRAIL

SKI AREA

Visitor Center
Check for excellent nature programs

Lake Superior

Famous Lake of the Clouds overlook

Lake of the Clouds

UNION SPRING TRAIL

LAKE SUPERIOR TRAIL

BIG CARP RIVER TRAIL

Big Carp River

NORTH MIRROR LAKE TRAIL

PEAK TRAIL

GOVERNMENT TRAIL

LOST LAKE TRAIL

CORRECTION LINE TRAIL

SUMMIT PEAK ROAD

SOUTH BOUNDARY ROAD

Greenstone Falls— lovely falls in old-growth hemlocks

CROSS TRAIL

Vista

LILY POND TRAIL

Summit Peak tower — grand view of an old-growth forest

SUPERIOR TRAIL

PINKERTON TRAIL

Presque Isle Campground & Scenic Area

Outstanding riverside trail by 4 waterfalls

LITTLE CARP RIVER ROAD

Presque Isle River

519

★ Great views for fall color   🏠 Park Rental cabin

N
W E
S

0   1   2
miles

Porcupine Mountain Wilderness State Park
Amidst rugged hills, this vast expanse of virgin forest has lots of hiking trails, picturesque lakes, tempestuous rivers, and secluded cabins.

old mine sites and bear habitat and take visitors to **Michigan's record white pine**. **Stargazing** at Lake of the Clouds overlook is a real highlight for all ages. *Hikes and nature programs are held from mid June into early October, and then in winter, from late December into late March.*

SEEING THE OLD-GROWTH FOREST: A SHORT LIST FOR FIRST-TIME VISITORS

The essence of the Porcupine Mountains goes beyond seeing the celebrated scenic views. It means experiencing the heart of the **magnificent, old-growth forests** on foot. Here are a few recommended options for visitors with varying amounts of time and energy. Each trail includes a waterfall, river, or lake. For a wider range of hikes, consult the two guidebooks (above) or stop at the visitor center.

◆ **1-hour hike near a road. Beautiful OVERLOOKED FALLS** is in an area of old-growth hemlocks at the base of a gorge. The falls delicately drops into a

pool formed by mossy rocks. It's reached by a fairly level, 1/4 mile trail from the end of the dead-end Little Carp River Road off the west end of South Boundary Road. For a somewhat longer hike, **GREENSTONE FALLS** is a mile farther down the picturesque Little Carp River Trail. It's another graceful falls in a mossy glade within a dark, soft conifer forest. This is an interesting trail to hike because of its many small bridges and boardwalks, including a single 80' pine log across the Little Carp River.

◆ **3- to 4-hour hike**. From Government Peak Trailhead to **TRAP FALLS** and back, 2 1/2 miles each way. This hike goes through hemlocks, hardwoods, and a few big pine along the **BIG CARP RIVER VALLEY**, then proceeds uphill to the falls. It's a good, short hike despite some mud, hills, and obstacles.

◆ **All-day hike or easy overnight**. Parts of three trails combine to make a 10-mile triangle. Take Lily Pond Trail from

trailhead off the Summit Peak Road. Hike 3 miles to Little Carp River Trail junction. Hike 3 miles on Little Carp Trail to Mirror Lake. Take Mirror Lake Trail back to Summit Peak Road and down to the Lily Pond Trail trailhead. Trails are clearly marked, but hikers need to pay attention and use the trail map. You could camp off the trail. To do this 9 1/2-mile hike, your feet should be broken in and you should already be accustomed to a light pack if you're overnighting. A **nice, short detour**, especially for bird-watchers, is to take **Beaver Creek Trail**, a 1/8-mile dead-end boardwalk midway between Lily Pond and Mirror Lake.

◆ **Three- to four-day hike** (25 miles, 2 overnights at least). From near the end of M-107, take either the Lake Superior Trail (lake views) or Big Carp River Trail (cliff-top hiking) to the mouth of the Big Carp River. Follow the Lake Superior Trail one mile to the Little Carp River mouth, then take the Little Carp River

Canoeing & sea kayaking along Lake Superior

is increasing in popularity. **Rentals of canoes** and **open-cockpit kayaks** are available from the park concessionaire (906-885-5612) on M-107 just before the Union Bay campground.

The shore is an easy sandy beach all the way from east of Union Bay, the state park's lakeside campground on M-107, to Ontonogan. Most are lined with cottages. West of Union Bay, the shore becomes rocky, with steep bluffs and just a few places for small craft to pull over. Local enthusiasts like to find a quiet place to pull in and set up camp on park land or national forest land west of the park. They advise taking along a weather radio; conditions often change at Lone Rock, near the mouth of the Big Carp River. A good **day trip** is to start at Union Bay and paddle a few miles west to see the rocks. To do a long stretch of shoreline, it's best to go from west to east. The harbor at Black River Harbor is the easiest place to put in, but far away. The stairs down to the water at the Presque Isle river mouth are difficult portage but do-able.

Trail deep into the park, past lots of waterfalls. On your way to Lake of the Clouds (just off M-107 and close to both starting points) you'll pass Greenstone Falls, Lily Pond, and Mirror Lake.

◆ **North Country Trail** connections without interruption enable hikers to go west to the Black River waterfalls (not far from the Presque Isle River mouth) and east all the way to the Sturgeon River in Baraga County. Two **trailside shelters** have been built. More are being planned. The **high, remote section from around Norwich to Victoria is especially spectacular**; the entire route is quite varied. Excellent notes and photos are on the Western U.P. Peter Wolfe Chapter web site, www.north-countrytrail.org/ pwf/ (It notes that other routes through the state park are more scenic, but the North Country Trail is the most remote.)

OTHER FAVORITE DESTINATIONS

◆ Many people enjoy the **WATERFALLS along the PRESQUE ISLE RIVER**, on the park's far western edge, more than anything else they experience on an Upper Peninsula vacation. (Locals tend to say "Presk AISLE.") In their highly recommended *Guide to 199 Michigan Waterfalls*, the Penrose family, who seldom indulge in superlatives, say, "This is **one of the most beautiful stretches of river in the entire Upper Peninsula**. The pristine silence of the forest here is interrupted only by the water, a sound that is never far away." *These falls, close to CR 519, are some 30 minutes southwest of the Visitor Center off South Boundary Road. Park in the lot at the end of the road.*

The Presque Isle Campground is at the river's mouth. Within a mile's hike of the parking areas are **four waterfalls that stand out for their beauty and variety**. (It's just a short drive to the beautiful, easily accessible Greenstone Falls, see above.) A **boardwalk** along the river's west bank now makes the walk safer for anyone concerned about unsure, possibly slippery footing. Many people say the boardwalk is almost an attraction in its own right.

A **picnic area** is at the very end of County Road 519. Across a swinging bridge at the river mouth is Lake Superior. This is a busy place during spring steelhead and fall salmon runs. From the parking area, say the Penroses,

"a short walk leads to a network of stairs which drops to a trail. Just before the trail reaches the river, a boardwalk branches off to the right. [Return here later, but first] continue on the stairs to a suspension bridge. Just above it [is] a fascinating unnamed falls. . . . There the force of the powerful river. . . creates miniature whirlpools along the banks. The spinning action of the water has carved perfect half-circles into the stones which line the bank and polished them to a glossy black. . . . The best views of this effect come from the bridge."

Now go back and take the boardwalk upstream about 200 or 250 yards to the first overlook at **MANABEZHO FALLS**. To reach the second overlook at the brink of the falls, go upstream 150 yards more, up one stairway and down another. At the falls, the Penroses say, "a thick band of white, rushing water, which spans the 150-foot-wide river, drops about 20 feet over a rock shelf. The largest section is tinged with gold, and its heavy flow creates a blanket of foam which trails downstream." In another 100 yards, **MANIDO FALLS** is "a mass of white water" as it "descends over a network of gradually declining rock steps, then drops over a ledge of stone." Look up and down the river to see traces of the adjoining falls. The boardwalk ends at Manido Falls. Then the rugged

East/West River Trail goes another 1/4 mile to reach **NAWADAHA FALLS**, a 15-foot tumble across many rock steps that creates "a blanket of white foaming lace." To see the falls best, you need to take a side spur down to the river. Footing can be tricky here. The *Porcupine Mountains Companion* reports that the pool below Nawadaha Falls is "a good place to try for rainbow trout and brookies."

Here you are almost at South Boundary Road. If you want to hike a 2-mile loop and revisit all the falls from the more difficult trail on the river's east

Winter in the Porkies

There are lots of good reasons to plan a week of **downhill or cross-country skiing** here — just not between Christmas and New Year's, when it's really crowded and snow can be iffy due to the lake effect's moderating temperature. Later in winter the lake works in skiers' favor, creating lots of **white powder** that's **skiable into April**. Come in spring for the fewest weekend crowds at the popular downhill ski area.

The 641-foot drop is one of highest in Midwest. There are 14 trails and 11 miles of slopes at all levels, with the longest over a mile long. **Lift capacity** is 3,600 skiers an hour. 42 km of groomed **cross-country ski trails** *($6 & $8 adult trail fee, $3 and $5 ages 13-17, 12 and under free)* can be quickly accessed with a $3 one-ride tow ticket on the downhill lift. **Snowshoers** can use the one-way ticket to get up to use the hiking trails. **Lake Superior views** from both downhill and cross-country trail systems can be spectacular. Tow rates are low (currently $20 adults weekdays, $25 weekends, 12 and under free). The atmosphere is unglitzy and family-friendly. Where else, Jim Du Fresne points out, would the ski lodge let families have their personal crock pots cooking dinner while they're out skiing? (That may change in a few years, when the ski chalet concessionaire adds food service. Chalet expansion is first increasing space for the rental shop and skiers' lounge, however.) **Rentals of snowboards, downhill** and **cross-country skis,** and even **snowmobiles** are available, as are **lessons.** Call (906) 885-5612. For additional info on skiing the Porkies, call the park at (906) 885-5275. For area **snow reports,** call 1 (800) BSC-7000.

bank, cross on the bridge here. The trail, occasionally rough and hilly, passes some very large **old-growth pine, hemlock, and cedar**. It ends at the parking lots by the swinging bridge at the river mouth. &: none of these falls.

◆ Lake Superior's **UNION BAY.** Here is a **sand beach**, one of the few in the park and the only one accessible by car. Water temperatures vary in summer, depending on wind direction. It can be quite pleasant in late July, August, and September, disproving the myth that Lake Superior is too cold for swimming. *Along M-107 for 2 1/2 miles west from the main park entrance by Silver City to the Union Bay Campground and beach.*

◆ **LAKE of the CLOUDS OVERLOOK,** at the end of M-107, is **one of the state's most famous views** — and a **great place for fall color**. It looks down from a **dramatic rocky ridge** onto the **Big Carp River Valley**. From here the old-growth forests below seem like a distant green carpet. **Scenic overlooks** are near a parking lot, but not wheelchair-accessible. Expect a crowd of visitors in summer.

You can earn the drama of this overlook by approaching it on foot via the **scenic, popular ESCARPMENT TRAIL** along the high ridge. It reveals interesting rock formations along the dramatic escarpment. You can start at either the Government Peak trailhead four miles east of the Lake of the Clouds main overlook or at the Escarpment trailhead, two miles east on the south side of M-107. A shorter trail connecting a number of high scenic viewpoints is the Overlook Trail, a 3 1/2-mile loop. It also starts at the Government Peak trailhead off M-107 five miles west of the main park entrance.

If you're driving along M-107 to or from Lake of the Clouds, take time to stop at **MEAD MINE** along M-107. Here you can enter about **100 feet of an old copper mine shaft**. It's on the road's south side, just opposite the pleasant picnic area and historical marker on a hill overlooking Lake Superior. There's a **good sunset view of Lake Superior** from here.

◆ **SUMMIT PEAK OBSERVATION TOWER.** From the 40-foot tower at the **park's highest point** (1,958 feet above sea level), you're so high above the treetops of the forest, here in the park's interior, that you feel you're **floating above an undulating sea of green** — or of **fall color**, depending on the season. Come on a clear day (many are slightly hazy) and you can see all the way to the **Apostle Islands,** over 25 miles away. A panoramic sign points you to landmarks like the Copper Peak Ski Flying Hill and

Walks with park naturalist Bob Sprague are a highlight of a Porkies visit. Here among blueberry shrubs, prime bear habitat, he explains how bears eating their natural diet – berries, ants, larvae, acorns – must work hard to get enough calories. No wonder they quickly become addicted to garbage dumps and human handouts. Schedules of walks and other programs are at main campgrounds and the Visitor Center.

White Pine stacks. The **shady half-mile trail** up to the tower is pretty; the **view towards sunset is especially striking**. If you haven't exercised, you could huff and puff. The area just west of here suffered from the big windstorm of 1953, so the trees aren't nearly what you'd expect. Wayside **benches** invite you to sit and enjoy the forest. *It's a half mile from parking area to the 40-foot tower.*

For a little more of a hike, you can go out and back along the Beaver Creek Trail from the Summit Peak parking lot (about a mile each way). Or you could take the South Mirror Lake Trail from near the tower left to Mirror Lake (a mile each way) or back 1 1/2 miles to the Summit Peak Road (this is about 3/4 miles to the parking area). Midway on the South Boundary Road, 20 minutes from either end of the park, the asphalt Summit Peak Rd. penetrates two miles north to the parking area. &: no.

Porcupine Mountains State Park

logistics: The 20-mile-long park is in a little-developed area between Ontonagon and Ironwood. The park's visitor center and main facilities are off M-107, about three miles west of Silver City, where M-64 turns inland from Lake Superior to the mining town of White Pine. Silver City is more a collection of resorts than a town. Its general store can fill many visitor needs. Visitors to the park's western end and its waterfalls are closer to lodgings in Wakefield, Bessemer, and Ironwood. Park office phone: (906) 885-5275. TDD (906) 885-5278. Fax:(906) 885-5798. Visitor Center (906-885-5277) open from weekend before Mem. Day through Oct. Hours: 10 to 6 Eastern Time at least. State park sticker required: $4/$5 a day, $20/$25 a year. &: Visitor center, some campgrounds, some overlooks. Call.

PORCUPINES LODGINGS

See also Silver City. Expect higher rates Christmas week, New Year's, and Presidents' Day in February.

SILVER SANDS MOTOR LODGE
(906) 885-5748; www.exploringthenorth.com/silver/silver.html

The only private lodging facility within Porcupine Mountains State Park is this single-story motel. It's near the park entrance, across M-107 from Lake Superior and an **informal swimming beach**. 12 of the 23 rooms, all ample in size, have **lake views**; the others, popular in winter, face a **busy deer yard**. Air-conditioned; no phones. Queen beds. Color TV with 8 channels. Rates for ski season and summer (mid-June to color season): $58 (one bed) and $67 (two beds). Off-season: $54 and $58. Rates go by the room, not the number of people. Decor is simple. There's a **comfortable lobby with seating, a fireplace**, free morning coffee, a phone, and a **camp store**; a **lakeview picnic area with grills**; and a **basketball net**. *On M-107 just inside entrance to park. Closed April and much of May.*
H.A.: call. 👫👶: no extra charge.

PORCUPINE MOUNTAINS STATE PARK CAMPING

(906) 885-5275.
Reservations: (800) 44-PARKS; TDD (800) 605-8295; www.dnr.state.mi.us/

WILDERNESS CABINS/
(906) 885-5275

For many, the most desirable place to stay in the Porkies is in one of the **16 rustic cabins** deployed in **scenic spots** around the park. (For locations, see cabin icon on map.) Many are a mile or less from a road, requiring a modest hike with gear. Seven are on Lake Superior. The three on Mirror Lake come with rowboats. The **most remote** are the three on the Big Carp River, four miles in. Cabins are simply furnished, with bunks, table and chairs, and a wood stove. They have no electricity or indoor plumbing. Most sleep four and rent for $35/night. Four cabins sleep eight and one sleeps six; they rent for $45. Reservations (906-885-5275) are taken for the rest of the current year and all of the next year. Planning way ahead is necessary for best summer choices and for all winter weekend reservations of the three cabins that stay open in winter. &: one cabin. Call.

UNION BAY CAMPGROUND/
Porcupine Mountains State Park
(906) 885-5275; reserv.: (800) 44-PARKS.

95 modern sites are on a grassy area with few trees, overlooking Lake Superior, right next to the **park's best swimming beach** and **boat launch**. It's close to the rental concession and not far from the Visitor Center and other popular destinations. Not a choice for those who savor privacy. Reservations for coming year are taken starting Oct. Reserve for summer by Feb. & March. Usually open mid-May thru mid-Oct. *Just off M-107, 1 mile from park entrance.* &: showers, restrooms, 2 sites by showers.

PRESQUE ISLE RIVER CAMGROUND/
Porcupine Mountains State Park
(906) 885-5275.
Reservations: (800) 44-PARKS.

About 50 large, wooded rustic sites are on a 100' Lake Superior bluff, 1/4 mile from the mouth of the Presque Isle River. **Four dramatic nearby waterfalls** are on a 2-mile trail loop. It's at the end of the 16-mile Lakeshore Trail. The best sites overlook the lake, with **sunset views**. Perimeter sites back up onto woods for excellent privacy. Central sites are wooded with no privacy buffer. The need for infrastructure improvements put this popular campground on the DNR hit list for closure in 1998. Now it's here to stay, but as a much smaller rustic campground with hand pumps and vault toilets instead of flush toilets and showers. It has been downsized from 88 sites to around 50, so reservations for summer are strongly advised. *At the park's west end, 17 miles north of Wakefield at the end of CR 519 and South Boundary Rd. Go north from U.S. 2 at Wakefield's only light. $9/$12 a night.* &: no.

Inside one of the Mirror Lake cabins. The state park's 16 wilderness cabins are so popular that advance reservations for summer and winter are essential. Spring and late fall openings are more available, but be prepared for possible snow!

OUTPOST CAMPGROUNDS/
Porcupine Mountains State Park
(906) 885-5275

Fourteen drive-in campsites (no showers, flush toilets, or electricity) are in three rustic campgrounds off the South Boundary Road. Though the privacy is much better than at Union Bay, these wooded sites are not particularly choice. Sometimes they can be damp, and bugs are more of a problem than in breezier places on interior bluffs or the lakeshore. These campsites are not reservable. Prospective campers are advised to check them out or ask for tips at the Visitor Center. Register at park headquarters or Union Bay Campground. $6/$9 a night. &: no.

BACKCOUNTRY CAMPING/
Porcupine Mountains State Park
(906) 885-5275

Getting back into the **old-growth forest and back country**, away from vehicles and concentrations of people, is the best way to experience what makes the Porkies special. Backpacking may not be as difficult as you think. Park staff can advise you of walk-in campsites that don't involve too much of a hike (though of course they won't be as secluded). Do plan around the precautions in the "Backcountry information" handout, and

be prepared to deal with **bears** (see introduction.

These sites are not reservable, but registration for backcountry camping is required so that park personnel know who's out there in case of emergencies. Register at the Visitor Center (open 10-6 in season), or at the park headquarters (it's staffed mornings before 10; self-register after 6 p.m.), or self-register at the Presque Isle Campground or Summit Peak. The fee is currently $6/night/ group of 4. No advance reservations. Maximum group size is 12. Registering in person is especially advised for first-time back-country campers because it makes sure they get the best advice on trail conditions, etc. Fires are permitted only in permanent campsites with fire rings. Currently there are under **50 permanent campsites** on all sections of trail. They're readily apparent to hikers.

Silver City (pop. 75)

Today Silver City is mostly a collection of tourist-oriented resorts and other businesses along M-107 near the entrance to **Porcupine Mountains State Park**. But for three years in the 1870s it was a **silver mining boom town**. At the fur-trading post that was the first settlement here, stories circulated about silver found by Indians back in the woods away from Lake Superior. Homesteader Austin Corser actually found the silver on the Little Iron River in the 1850s. He kept quiet about it until he proved his claim. In the 1870s he revealed the silver, sold his land, and left. **Remains of his cabin**, and the **sweet williams** he planted, can still be seen by hiking up the Little Iron River from its mouth.

Soon some **30 mines** established claims, and three found enough silver to build a joint stamping mill to extract the precious metal. Daniel Beaser platted a town, naming its streets after Civil War heroes and the town after himself. No mines found enough silver to make any money, and eventually they closed. After Beaser died, the town's name was changed to Silver City. Today there's more to Silver City than meets the eye. Houses are on two back streets paralleling the lake but up the hill.

Peace Hill Concerts are **popular free outdoor summer performances** put on by a loose consortium of area musicians at the Great Lakes Trading Company (see below). Music covers a big range, from blues to Gershwin to folkish rock.

A **pleasant Lake Superior beach** in Silver City is at the mouth of the Iron River, just east of M-64 and the Holiday Inn. The cedars and stones between sandy beach and road make this a popular place to pull over, park the car along the road, and get out.

Silver Image Studio

In this **attractive studio/gallery** photographer Dan Urbanski sells posters, notecards, and photographs of his beautiful images of weather, waves, and other natural phenomena and wildlife in the Porcupines, the western U.P., and Isle Royale. Popular images and posters can also be seen and purchased through his website, www.quietlywild.com Click on the **wonderful "wilderness diary"** for words and photos of a series of outings in the vicinity.

Dan is a **good informal source of visitor information**, too, if he's not too busy. As a photographer he has explored the entire area, and he's a moving force behind the local chamber of commerce. He's also a self-effacing and straightforward observer, not cast in the competitive showman mode of many naturalists. A native Detroiter, he has loved the Porkies ever since he spent summers with his grandmother in nearby Wakefield. He turned his photography hobby into a career and moved up here

after his laboratory job moved south from Detroit.

Perched on the hillside in "downtown" Silver City. 885-5895. Open seven days a week from 10-5 in summer, evenings by chance, weekdays year-round. ♿

Great Lakes Trading Company

A **charming Arts & Crafts cottage** houses an eclectic collection of old and new: **pottery, antiques, and folk art featuring local artisans**. Here are welded sculptures, weavings, carvings, Tiffany-style lamps, and handmade jewelry. Look in at www.greatlakestrading .addr.com or call for this year's schedule of **delightful free concerts** held in the back on six Wednesdays in July and August.

On the east side of M-107 down toward the park. 885-5503. Open daily 11-7 from Mem. Day thru color season and by appointment. ♿: *no.*

Silver City General Store

The closest small **grocery** to the state park. Offers lunch meats, sausages, bread, and in summer deli items, plus **hardware, fishing and camping supplies**.

On M-107 in "downtown" Silver City. 885-5885. From mid-June thru color season: open 8 a.m.-9 p.m. daily. Otherwise open 8 a.m.-6 p.m. ♿

Bonanza or Greenwood Falls

In an area full of waterfalls, these are **unusual and compelling** enough to be worth a special visit, and they're not far from a main road. Thin layers of brown rock are tilted up at an angle to the wide riverbed, so water winds around the scalloped layers, but it's possible to walk across on the uplifted edges of rock. The **effect is dramatic**, whether or not there's much water flowing over the falls. About 600 feet downstream is a second, shorter falls.

Off M-64 about a mile east of M-107 on the way to White Pine. Turn west onto 2-track at stop sign. The road has been improved so it's possible to drive to a point near the falls.

SILVER CITY LODGINGS

BEST WESTERN PORCUPINE MOUNTAIN LODGE (906) 885-5311; fax (906) 885-5847; www.upbiz.com/mi/bestwestern.html e-mail: bwpml1@up.net

The **only full-service hotel in Ontonagon County** has a restaurant with Lake Superior view, a cozy separate

lounge, and a **sizable indoor pool** (44'; windows look out to the lake, but aren't placed so you can see the lake when swimming), with adjoining sauna, spa, and game room. The restaurant is open for three meals a day except in April and November, and always for dinner. On winter and spring weekends in ski season the bar has **occasional live music for dancing**. Back by the lake is a lawn with birch trees, a bonfire pit, and picnic tables. Benches and a gazebo are being added. **Bonfires on starry nights here are a real treat!**

Decor is pleasant but not luxurious. 71 rooms are on 3 floors with interior corridors. All have phones, cable TV with dozens of channels including ESPN and Disney, and 2 queens or 1 king. In-room coffee is coming. 2000 rates: $79 from mid-December through March and from mid-June through color season, $69 otherwise. Ask about rates for whirlpool rooms. Free continental breakfast in April and November. Though the hotel backs up on a rocky shore of Lake Superior, it's sited so no rooms are oriented to the lake. Some do have a view of the mouth of the Big Iron River across a parking lot. An **interesting park with woodsy shoreline** is a short walk away, on the river's opposite bank. Silver City's few shops are within walking distance along the road. *120 Lincoln/M-107 in Silver City.*

H.A.: entire facility is accessible; some rooms are ADA-approved ♿♟♙: 12 & under free; $5/extra person. 🐈: small pets but not cats; $10 extra

MOUNTAIN VIEW LODGES (906) 885-5256; www.mtnviewlodges.com

11 two-bedroom cottages, new in 1996, offer contemporary rustic style with just about every convenience except air-conditioning, which would very seldom be desired. Each has a **fireplace,** microwave, dishwasher, cable TV/VCR (video rentals are down the road), phone/fax, BBQ grill. Five cottages are **almost on the beach**, 6 are farther back but with **lake view**s. Rates for two: $109 in season; $89 between ski season and summer or between fall color and ski season. Cottages are sited to **favor privacy** and handy parking rather than common areas. Silver City's visitor-oriented businesses are an easy walk down the road (no sidewalks; can be busy). There are **fire rings by the beach**, and picnic tables are coming. Gary and Becky Andersen, resident owner-managers, took over the cottages in 1999. *237 Lincoln/M-107.*

A tucked-away gem on the north side of Ontonagon, Ontonagon Township Park has a mile of sand beach, a rustic campground beneath the pines, and a sunset walk to or to or from town on a paved walk.

H.A.: one cottage to ADA standards; good accessibility in all ♿👪: $10/extra person 🐕: dogs OK in 4 cottages; call.

LAKE SHORE CABINS
(906) 885-5318; www.yesmichigan.com

Shady, nicely landscaped grounds and a **sandy Lake Superior beach** distinguish this pleasant older resort. Of the six housekeeping cabins, five look out onto the lake. One new cabin ($108 in 2001) sleeps up to 8 in two bedrooms and a loft. It has a bath with shower, a cable TV, a **fireplace,** a microwave, and a **screened porch**. The other cabins are clean and cozy, rustic in style. Each sleeps 5 to 6 in two bedrooms. Each has a screened porch with swing, a gas heater, and half bath. (Showers are in the sauna building.) A charcoal grill and picnic table come with each cabin. No TV. Phone in office can be used in emergencies. Guests can make campfires on the beach, depending on conditions. Walk to restaurants, grocery. $69 year-round rate for two in 2001. 400 Lincoln/M-107 in Silver City, 2 blocks west of the Iron River mouth & Best Western. **H.A.:** call. Paved drive, sidewalks to cabins. ♿👪: $10/extra adult, $5/child. 🐕: call

White Pine (pop. 1,000)

This small company town, built in 1954, suffered an enormous blow when its reason for being, the **Copper Range mine and smelter**, closed in 1995. It was the last major copper mine in a region that was once the world's leading producer of copper. With huge quantities of South American copper closer to the surface and therefore less costly to extract, it's not clear that any of these U.P. mines will again open, even though enormous deposits remain **far underground.**

Nonetheless, an **exotic project** has resumed half mile down at White Pine. A company called SubTerra is using the deep mine's highly stable 48° F to grow a genetically-altered type of tobacco whose seeds may help treat cancer. Using 50 1,000-watt grow lights, they occupy 3,000 square feet for the plants. Ultimately, 25 acres of this highly controlled environment is available. Another advantage: it's quite secure from any potential eco-terrorists.

However, the fact remains that the three employees who run the underground tobacco-growing operation are a tiny fraction of the 3,000 miners working here when the Copper Range Company's operation was at its peak. By the time the mine closed in 1995, this number was down to about 900.

The **smelter**, used to heat and purify the copper ore, was installed in 1954 and had not been brought up to current pollution control standards. Its plume of smoke was a prominent local landmark, and it contained toxic mercury — a special concern being so close to Lake Superior. The Michigan United Conservation Clubs and other environmental groups had sued the Copper Range company to upgrade the smelter or shut it down.

With the price of copper so low, Copper Range's parent, the Inmet Mining Corporation of Canada, couldn't justify investing in the aging smelter. It closed both mine and smelter. (The mine's labor costs were high because the copper is so far underground. If open-pit mining had been possible here, the White Pine mine would be thriving.)

Some employment and future prospects are provided by the **Copper Range Company's refinery** that still operates here. It further processes smelted copper for customers who need a purer product. Currently it is now owned by White Pine Copper Refinery, which employs 67.

The Bad River Indians in nearby Wisconsin quashed hopes for a new, labor-saving method of using acid to extract copper from the mine's remaining rock pillars. It would have employed 400 for some years longer. But the Indians objected to rail shipments of acid over their land, partly for fear of derailments, partly out of environmental concern that the acid could affect Lake Superior.

By summer 1997 the generous government job re-training grants had run out, and the full impact of the closing on Ontonagon and Gogebic counties was finally being felt. Forty more jobs were lost by the 1997 closing of the Konteka Supper Club and motel, the town's social hub and one of the best restaurants in the western Upper Peninsula. Several small companies have re-occupied buildings once used by the mining company.

White Pine was planned and laid out in the 1950s as the **epitome of American suburbia in the middle of wilderness**, where bears are the reigning neighborhood nuisance instead of raccoons. Ranch houses line White Pine's curving streets. The town center is a sort of enclosed town square with supermarket (now closed), post office, barbershop, etc., surrounded by a parking lot. The noted Michigan architect **Alden Dow** designed the Konteka complex across the parking lot with a nod to his mentor Frank Lloyd Wright. Note: as we go to press, the motel and restaurant seem to be re-opening. Call (906) 885-5399 for current details.

Ontonagon (pop. 1,769)

Ontonagon is built on the site of an old Indian village where the **sizable, many-branched Ontonagon River** flows into Lake Superior. It has been an **important harbor** ever since the first European explorers came to the region in the 1600s. That's because it is the only safe Lake Superior port of any size between Eagle River 50 miles to the northeast and Chequamegon Bay far to the southwest in what is now Wisconsin. Such a refuge has been of no small importance, given the steep, high bluffs along most of the lakefront in this region of fierce Lake Superior storms.

Industry has shaped the town, especially the waterfront, where piles of coal have formed an unscenic backdrop to the **prim brick lighthouse**, built in 1866. (See below for lighthouse tours.)

Freighters still arrive at the harbor to deliver coal to fuel the huge **Smurfit-Stone Corporation paper mill**. In 1921 the original mill was built here on the lake just west of the Ontonagon River. The plant uses wood pulp from U.P. forests to make the crinkley inner layer of corrugated cardboard. The mill's 281 employees produce a staggering 801 tons a day and ship it out by rail and truck. Until 1996, freighters also brought coal here for the big White Pine copper mine, 15 miles to the southeast as the crow flies. The mine's closure put a well-paid workforce of 900 out of work. That has affected Ontonagon greatly, causing a decline in population and income for many local businesses.

Ontonagon's streetscape has a snaggle-tooth, workaday look that doesn't reflect the prosperity of the town's late 19th-century lumber boom years. That's because a **fire in 1896** destroyed the entire village and all its mills. The fire caused the permanent departure of the town's largest employer, the **Diamond Match Company**. Its two big mills had employed 500 and shipped 25 million board feet of lumber a year. After that disaster, the town's population of 1,500 declined, but rebuilt slowly to a peak of about 2,400 in the 1970s. Ontonagon is the county seat and home of the area hospital. Service jobs are a big part of the economy.

Ontonagon Lighthouse

In 1852, when the federal government responded to Ontonagon's **busy port** shipping copper and lumber, and built the first lighthouse on this site, it was only the fifth light on Lake Superior. The

The famous Ontonagon Boulder was from Victoria

From earliest times, white men traveling in this region heard rumors of the existence of a great mass of copper resting on the riverbanks nine miles upstream [from Ontonagon]. In 1667, Father Dablon, the French missionary-explorer, confirmed the authenticity of these rumors. The boulder, known as the Ontonagon Boulder, was inspected, hacked at, marveled over, and described by scientists, authors, and the merely curious until 1843, when, much the worse for wear, it was removed. It is believed that the Indians venerated the boulder. . . . Julius Eldred of Detroit paid the Indians $150 for absolute ownership of the boulder. The Federal Government granted Eldred permission to occupy the site for mining purposes but declared itself owner of the copper mass, which it sold to him for $1,365 in 1843. The story now becomes pure Gilbert and Sullivan. Eventually, the persevering Eldred and his boulder reached the river mouth, only to be met by War Department officials, who prepared to seize the prize and carry it off to Washington. They changed their minds long enough to allow Eldred to transport the boulder to Detroit, where, for a time, he charged a cash admission for the privilege of beholding it. But the Government again stepped in with orders that the boulder be shipped to Washington, where it now reposes in the Smithsonian Institution. In 1847, Congress allowed Julius Eldred the sum of $5,644.98 "for his time and expense in purchasing and removing the mass of native copper."

—From the 1941 W.P.A. guide to Michigan, *Michigan: A Guide to the Wolverine State*

present yellow brick lighthouse dates from 1866-7. Since then, south shore currents have piled up silt in front of it, so it sits a quarter of a mile inland. The **Ontonagon County Historical Society** has been involved in protecting and restoring the building since 1969 and has finally, through an act of Congress, wrested control of it from the Corps of Engineers. The society will eventually gain an easement so visitors can walk to the lighthouse, which is surrounded by the paper mill's gated private property. Eventually the coal piles that hide it from the road will be removed. The interior, though not restored, is in pretty good shape, and appropriately furnished with antiques from the society's collection. Its original fifth order Fresnel lens has been returned. The society's museum can show a videotaped **walking tour of the lighthouse**. **Lighthouse tours** by van are held daily from Memorial Day weekend through October 15. *Tours begin at the Ontonagon County Historical Museum downtown (see below) at 11 a.m. and 2 p.m. The tours are free (donations appreciated) but $2 is required for van transportation.* &: call ahead for van. Access with assistance to first floor, where a video of the second floor can be seen.

Ontonagon County Historical Society Museum

Like many local museums, this one had so much in its collections that the exhibit spaces were mostly a pathway between piles. Ruth Ristola, formerly in charge, saw that Ed Mustonen, now the manager, was gifted with a good eye for display. "Do whatever you have to to make it beautiful," he was told. "Arrange it as if it were your home." He has, and to good effect. True, the wallpaper behind some room settings may not be historically correct. But **it's fun to explore this place**. To learn the stories that go with the artifacts, ask for Bruce Johanson, museum leader and retired teacher, who instituted an ambitious local history program in the public schools. (He's now the local newspaper reporter and a **willing source of local facts and perspective**.) For info on people with roots in Ontonagon County, ask for Ruth Ristola, curator of genealogy and family history.

Here, in a large space that originally was a co-op grocery, are a great variety of interesting things along with room settings and period costumes that are the staples of local museums. Fans of **folk art** and crafts and Victoriana will especially enjoy what's here.

◆ a **harbor display** with **boat models** made in 1888, and memoirs to go with them

◆ **handmade instruments** including a Norwegian **langelaik** (akin to a dulcimer) and a Finnish **kantele** (a harp whose high place in Finnish culture was assured by its role as instrument of the gods in the national epic, the **Kalevala**)

◆ a large **panoramic artist's view of the Minesota Mine** operation in 1858

◆ a **watch collection**. One, an elaborately engraved silver watch, was presented to Captain Redmond Ryder in 1858 because the arrival of his ship kept the town from starving. His great-great-grandson showed up at the museum and asked whether they'd ever heard of Redmond Ryder. When the answer was yes, he donated the watch.

◆ a delightful miniature **peddler's wagon** with carved woodenware and horse. It looks like it came from the old country, but was done by Joseph Papineau for the museum in 1999.

◆ "**Risen from the Ashes**," a panoramic photographic portrait of Ontonagon in 1899.

The **gift shop** (no admission charged) is an attraction in its own right. Here are regional and ethnic cookbooks and foods, a Christmas shop, **Finnish imports** (linens, knives, Iittala crystal, sauna supplies); collector dolls; Dover Thrift Classics (great reading for $1 to $2): and the **best selection of children's and regional books around**. Ask for referrals to traditional rag rug weavers in the vicinity.

On River, Ontonagon's main street (also M-38 and U.S. 45) on the east end of downtown. Look for the lavender paint job. (906) 884-6165. Supporters get a quarterly newsletter. Open year-round, Mon-Fri 10-5, and on Saturdays 10-5 from Mem. Day thru Oct 15. Other times, including evenings, by appointment, often on short notice. $2 admission. &

Stubb's Bar & Museum

Taverns are a natural repository of memorabilia, but V. A. Nelson (called "Stubb" because he had one arm) conceived of his bar as a museum, starting with the usual mounted heads and a **mounted turtle with an unsettling stare**. Linda and Elmer Marks, who bought the place in 1973, continued the collection to the point that nearly every surface is covered and so much hangs from the ceiling (fish lures, guns, wagon wheels, lamps, and much more) that the ceiling itself is just about invisible. **Ancient snapshots** go back to logging days. Postcards from many times and places comprise the Wall of Fame. A chainsaw has created likenesses of Green Bay Packer heroes Brett Favre and Reggie White out of a single log. Recently commissioned scenes in clay show a hunter's cabin, Stubb's saloon, and Wild West and outhouse scenes. No food, just beer & booze.

500 River, downtown adjacent to the parking lot by the Ontonagon County Historical Museum. 884-9972. Open daily from 10 a.m. to closing, Sunday from noon. &

Ontonagon Township Park

Tucked away on the **beautiful Lake Superior shore** northeast of downtown, this simple park and campground enjoys a **beautiful setting** at the end of **Ontonagon's nicest old street**. The **public beach**, nearly a mile long, is sandy, with enough stones for interesting rock-picking. The park faces northwest, and a **wonderful sunset walk** can be had along the long sidewalk with benches by the street (&) or along the beach. There's a **picnic area with** tables and fire pits, and a **good view** southwest down to the **Porkies**. A **playground** and outhouses have been provided. The park is cleaner and more attractive than in recent years. Tip: for good driftwood, go to the beach's southwest end.

Take Houghton St. northeast from M-38 downtown. It turns into Lake Shore. Park is in 1/2 mile.

ONTONAGON RESTAURANTS

At the moment, far and away the **best food in town** is at Dennis and Audree Erickson's **CAPTAIN'S FAMILY REST-AURANT & LOUNGE**. It serves everything from early-morning breakfasts to Jilbert's ice cream cones to fresh fish and steaks that win praise from city people. The same kitchen and menu serves two separate but connected seating areas. To the left is the lunch counter and diner, to the right is the lounge with comfortable booths, now with an excellent ventilation system for smoke-aversive people who normally avoid bars. Broiled fresh fish dinners (mostly $8 to $10) include lake trout, whitefish, walleye, and sometimes salmon. Fish is one of many, many sandwiches, including burgers, hot dogs, and grilled cheese for kids. **Roast turkey is a real favorite** ($5 as a hot sandwich, $6.59 at dinner, or $7 for weekend dinners when there's a salad bar). Audree is known for her **great pie crusts**. Of the pies baked here ($1.69/slice), blueberry, raspberry, and apple are made with fresh fruit, not canned product. Tuesday is pasty day. No credit cards. Out-of-town checks OK. *227 River St. in downtown Ontonagon. 884-4475. Open daily. Kitchen open Mon-Sat 5 a.m. -10 p.m., Sun 7 a.m. to 10 p.m.* & 👫 Full bar

The prototypical small-town cafe and bakery, **SYL'S COUNTRY KITCHEN** (884-2522) offers a wide-ranging menu with something for everyone. Daily specials feature things like ham and scalloped potatoes, lasagna, cabbage rolls, or Swiss steak. The full-service bakery is known for **big, tasty cinnamon and pecan rolls**, **cinnamon toast** (bags of this crunchy dry toast are great for camping), and **nisu** (Finnish cardamom bread). Founder Syl Laitala (also a celebrated rug weaver) has finally retired and sold the place to her granddaughter Kathy Wardynski. No credit cards; checks OK. *713 River/M-38, downtown. Open 7 days 5:30 a.m.-10 p.m.*

ONTONAGON LODGINGS

Typical lodgings are small, owner-run motels and resorts on Lake Superior. Superior is quite shallow in this area, making for **warmer swimming** than in many places.

NORTHERN LIGHT INN B&B
(800) 238-0018; (906) 884-4290

This comfortable, updated turn-of-the-century house has 5 guest rooms with private baths (mostly $75 to $95). Three have **whirlpool tubs**. The private third-floor suite has a separate bedroom and 2-person whirlpool ($125). Ask about midweek off-season specials. An **adult, casual atmosphere** makes this a great place to unwind in a relaxingly private spot for stressed-out couples, or to socialize if they like. Common areas include a large living room with fireplace and games, and a big wrap-around porch. Innkeeper Dianne O'Shea fixes a **full breakfast** and is up on local happenings. There's an **electric sauna** and a big yard in a pleasant area of old homes. It's a block to a **driftwood beach**, a short drive to the beautiful sandy beach at ·the township park. Ask about two nearby fresh, fully equipped family vacation homes with cable TV and phone, 50 yards from the Lake Superior beach. *701 Houghton St. (runs north from M-38 downtown).* **H.A.**: no.

PETERSON'S CHALET COTTAGES
(906) 884-4230

Thirteen housekeeping cottages, mostly with Alpine trim, are in a **pretty, wooded, private setting**. It's a short walk through a woods to a **sandy Lake Superior beach**. Most sleep two to seven. 2000 rates for two, including taxes: $80-$120/night. $12/extra adult, $6/child. All have covered porches, grills, lawn chairs, 67-channel cable TV, and phones (each line is shared by two cottages). **Eight cottages have fireplaces, with wood provided**. Fully equipped kitchens, microwaves; linens.

There's a **canoe** and **paddleboat** to use, **snowshoes** to rent. The gift shop sells pop & pizza. Ask about vacation homes on other sites, that sleep 11 and 14. Reserve by May for summer choices. *287 Lakeshore, 1 1/2 miles west of Ontonagon, off M-64.* **H.A.**: call. 👫: $6/extra person

SCOTT'S SUPERIOR INN (906) 884-4866

This cozy, attractive, simple motel in 1960s Alpine style is in a **wooded setting** near a sandy Lake Superior beach. 12 rooms on one floor, air-conditioned, with phones, $49 and $61 (2 beds). Coffee, pastries. **Lobby with fireplace**. Refrigerator and freezer to use. Rec room with fireplace, **foosball, whirlpool,** and **sauna**. Five cabins (3 on beach, 2 new) are weekly in summer or $95-$150/night. Off-season discount. *277 Lakeshore Rd., 1 1/2 miles west of Ontonagon, off M-64.* 👫: one unit 👫: $10 for 5th person

SUPERIOR SHORES RESORT

(906) 884-2653; (800) 344-5355; e-mail: superior@up.net

This older 7-room motel and 3 attached "cottages" are situated on a small lot with **immediate beach access**. The two end motel units and all cottages have **lake views**. Fridges and tables are in motel rooms. Cottages have complete kitchens, sleep up to 8. All units have 67-channel cable TV, no phones, not air-conditioned. VCRs upon request. Phone and morning coffee in office. **Nightly campfires** in summer, conditions permitting. The picnic area has grills, tables, lawn chairs. Owners big on personal service. 2000 rates for two: $39 (motel room with one bed), $55 (two beds), $75 (cottage). Weekly rates year-round; midweek rates sometimes. *1823 M-64, 5 miles west of Ontonagon, 6 miles east of park.*

H.A.: call. 👫: 12 & under free. $7/ extra person (motel), $11 (cottage) 🐕: $7/night

ONTONAGON CAMPING

ONTONAGON TOWNSHIP PARK
(906) 884-2930, not reservable

This simple park and campground, tucked away northeast of downtown Ontonagon, enjoys a **long, sandy Lake Superior beach and beautiful views**. Campsites under big pines are big enough to accommodate 35' rigs, but don't provide privacy between sites. Electricity and water serves each site, but there are no showers or flush toilets.

There's a **playground** and a walkway to town. **Sunset views** from the walkway or beach are outstanding. This is a real find for **spur-of-the-moment vacationers** who haven't made reservations at the Porkies. Thus far, it only fills on holiday weekends. Not reservable. *Take Houghton St. northeast from M-38 downtown. It turns into Lake Shore. Park is in 1/2 mile. $8.50/night.* 👫: step into toilets.

RIVER PINES RV PARK CAMPGROUND
(906) 884-4600; (800) 424-1520; www.ontonagonmi.com/riverpines; e-mail: gladorp@up.net

Ontonagon's only modern campground has 32 modern sites ($17-$19/night for family of 4) on a tree-lined drive with full hook-ups; cable TV and phone hook-ups extra. **Shady tent sites** $12/night. The main house has one room to rent (sleeps 5); The rec room converts to a dorm room in winter. There's a rec hall, game room, playground, and small store and laundry room. The Ontonagon River is across the road with a dock for fishing and canoeing. Under 2 miles to town beach on Lake Superior. 600 River Road on west bank of Ontonagon River. *Take M-64 west out of town, but turn onto River Road just south of the marina. Open all year.* **H.A.** 👫 🐕

Rockland *(pop. 200)*

This **Victorian village** sits in the **beautiful valley** of the lower Ontonagon River, **surrounded by rocky hills**. Twelve miles east of Ontonagon on U.S. 45, it feels like **somewhere out of time**. Rockland was first settled in the 1840s when deposits of pure copper were discovered and substantial mines were dug here and at Victoria, three miles to the south. The Minesota Mine just southeast of town was one of the first U.P. copper mines to strike it rich. Following the traces of ancient Indian miners, the **Minesota Mining Company** found and removed a six-ton mass of copper in 1848 and soon followed a fissure vein of mass copper, extracting over four million pounds of copper a year. Irish and Cornish miners came. The Minesota Mine was played out by 1870. On U.S. 45 just east of Rockland, **interpretive markers** indicate the mine site. Inspired by the Minesota's immense profits, many companies continued to develop mines in Ontonagon County into the early 20th century. By the early 1890s Rockland had almost a thousand inhabitants. It was then the **epitome of frontier**

modernity and could even boast of having **Michigan's first telephone system**. (Ultimately Ontonagon County's fissure or mass deposits proved insignificant compared with copper in amygdaloid or conglomerate formations in the central Keweenaw.)

Rockland owes its 1890s Victorian architecture to a fire on July 4, 1892 that destroyed most of the town. A little girl whose parents told her not to use firecrackers managed to find one and lit it in her dining room. In a panic, she threw it out the window, igniting the lace curtains and, soon, quite a bit of Rockland as well. The fire spread unchecked because the townspeople were a mile and a half west of town dedicating the new cemetery. It took the girl a long time to get there and convince them to get back and help out. When Rockland rebuilt, it installed a state-of-the-art water system.

In the early 20th century, the mines closed down one by one. Finnish immigrants came here to farm. Rockland's population declined steadily —to 700 in the 1930s and under 200 today. Losing the elementary school really hurt. Today Rockland is a "**garden village**," as its civic leaders like to say. What with all the wildflowers and prominent flower and vegetable gardens, it's a **pretty place for a walk or bike ride**. Now all that's left in the way of commercial establishments are the **Rockland General Store** (which sells Jilbert's ice cream cones among many other things) and **Henry's Inn**, a popular bar and restaurant that draws visitors from far and wide.

Stop by Henry's on U.S. 45 in downtown Rockland. There Sally Gagnon — daytime bartender, co-owner with her husband Henry, cook, local historian and promoter extraordinaire — will fill you in on Rockland history. Ontonagon stole everything, she points out, including the famous boulder and the county seat. "But our history is still here, and the wonderful setting of our town," she proclaims. Property in Rockland today, however, "has no value," she says. That's how her daughter could buy up a vacant city block and turn it into a **beautiful big flower garden** right on U.S. 45. It's a striking sight from the highway because of the fanciful white archways and neo-rococo fencing, welded from steel reinforcing rods by Henry Gagnon in his free time.

Jessica Speer is among the artistic transplants to the area. She moved here from Wisconsin to learn from traditional Finnish weaver Syl Laitala of Syl's Restaurant in Ontonagon. Jessica's own

woven rugs, woven lace, **and throws** are contemporary. They are sold nationwide in galleries and shops. Call her to arrange a visit to her studio, **One of a Kind Weaving** (886-2672), or to find out about her occasional classes and workshops. The Rockland area has a lot to offer the visitor. Check out its new website, www.RocklandMI.org

Rockland Museum

The social history of everyday life in Rockland is effectively conveyed through roomscapes that are much more interesting than most local museums.

In the Rockland Activity Center and Library (formerly the school) on U.S. 45 at the south edge of town. 886-2821. Open afternoons during summer.

At Victoria Mine outside Rockland, company houses akin to this log home near Mass City have been restored for visitors. The Victoria Mine didn't allow additions like this one, which created more space for this family of 11.

ROCKLAND RESTAURANTS

The furnishings of **HENRY'S [Never] INN**, an old miners' bar, reflect many layers of Rockland history, and owner Sally Gagnon loves to talk about it. The original **Brunswick back bar** is from 1900. When Henry and Sally Gagnon first bought the place, he had to work at a job in L'Anse to make the payments — so Sally started calling it "Henry's Never Inn." Now Henry is the chief cook with a big reputation. The limited regular menu includes his **raved-about homemade soups**, and for very large sandwiches like the $4.75 stacked grilled ham and cheese or the Reuben. Wednesday is **build-your-own pizza night**. It wins high marks from a food-loving Chicago native who grew up on good pizza. Thursday is pasty night. On weekends **all-you-can-eat smorgasbords** ($9 to $10) of terrific homemade food draw crowds from as far as L'Anse, Houghton and even Rhinelander. Friday is the fish fry, of course, and Saturday Italian night with pizza and more. Expect some smoke. Cash preferred. *On the west side of U.S. 45 in Rockland. 886-9910.* &: several steps. Assistance cheerfully provided.

ROCKLAND LODGINGS

BUSSIERE'S BUNKHOUSE
(906) 886-2939 (evenings);
(906) 884-6053 (days)

Paul's Bar, once a happening place, has been totally renovated by former electrical contractor Howie Bussiere. Now it is a **spiffy lodging**, right in the center of Rockland, near Henry's Inn. The upstairs (3 bedrooms, sleeps up to 10, $125/day with a two-day minimum) has a full kitchen and dining area, two baths, a small sauna, large living room, and card room with a poker table. **Views of the countryside** are grand. Old dance photos evoke Rockland of the 1940s. The downstairs, a large motel-style room ($50/night), has two queen beds, coffee cart, and mini-fridge. Both units have phones and cable TV with 26 channels. Not air-conditioned. Groups often rent both units together. Hunting and snowmobile seasons book well ahead with repeats, but this place could be a fun summer hangout, too. *On U.S. 45.* **H.A.:** downstairs room. 👫👪: no extra charge

Victoria

If Rockland seems way outside the contemporary orbit, Victoria, three miles southwest, is even more so. To reach it from U.S. 45, you go over several **high ridges, heavily forested** in hardwoods. First you come to Old Victoria's **restored log miners' houses**. In another mile, a road to the right leads up a hill into the hamlet of Victoria, near another mine shaft. It's a collection of houses now used as vacation homes. Victoria Dam Road ends at the **impressive Victoria Dam and Reservoir**, built on the Ontonagon River's West Branch in 1931 to supply power to a copper mine. Today the dam and 405-acre impoundment are owned by the Upper Peninsula Power Company. The **boat launch** on the dam's north side gives anglers access to the almost **three-mile-long lake** with its good fishing for perch, northern pike, and walleye.

Old Victoria Restoration

Two miles south of Rockland is the Old Victoria Restoration, a **cluster of log houses built in 1899** around the shaft of the Victoria Mine. Restoring and furnishing the houses is yet another Rockland example of artfully improvised, bootstrap historic preservation, supported by visitor fees, a crafts fair the third Sunday in August, and **thimbleberry jam** made by caretaker/guide Chris Dolton. He gives **long, somewhat philosophical tours** about how hard life was here, especially for women. The restoration becomes more richly and accurately detailed each year, as information and donated artifacts from Old Victoria descendants are added.

Two houses are realistically furnished according to available historical information. The **Arvola House** is a rooming house, the upstairs crammed with beds as it might have looked in 1900. The single-family **Alexander House** reflects the life of a relatively well-off mining family in 1920. Mrs. Alexander (weaver Jessica Speer) may be at work at a large loom. The weaver's own rag rugs here are a higher caliber than the more utilitarian rugs she would have woven for others. One family researched and donated the entire kitchen contents that are authentic down to the rat trap.

The next house being put together is the **Erickson House**, a single-family house of an ordinary miner. Solid logs are being used from parts of ruined houses. Visitors interested in log construction may enjoy seeing the restoration and construction process in the works.

From Rockland, turn south just east of Henry's, go 2 miles south on the Victoria Dam Road. Open Mem. Day weekend thru color season, every day from 10 to 6. Also by appointment. (906) 886-2617. Currently $2/person suggested donation. More is always welcome. &: uneven ground outside, several steps into houses, narrow doors.

North Country Trail segment: Victoria to Norwich

The **12 miles of trail** here, part of a 130-mile continuous trail segment, go through **one of the most remote and rugged parts of the Upper Peninsula**, near several old mine sites. This stretch offers **numerous spectacular views** from bluffs and knobs, along with **beautiful stream valleys** and small waterfalls. The challenging terrain has lots of ups and downs. For many photos, detailed trail notes, and maps, look in on www.northcountrytrail.org/pwf/, the website of the Peter Wolfe Chapter, the local NCT chapter responsible for the trail between the Porcupine Mountains State Park and the Baraga Plains. (So far it goes east to the Sturgeon River.) And don't miss the interesting reminiscence about Peter Wolfe. (Note: the Adventure Trail he laid out to connect the North Country Trail to Mass City and Greenland is currently grown over.)

Doug Welker, webmaster and local contact person, suggests this strategy for a three-day backpacking round trip. Start at Victoria. Hike eight miles and find a **scenic campsite**; you'll use it for two nights. Then make a day trip to Norwich, leaving your camping gear set up to lighten the load. Hike back, spend the night, then go back to Victoria. The chapter has just built a **really comfy screened shelter with deck** a short distance from Old Victoria village, and so far it hasn't been much used. So you could start and end your trip right there. If it's in use, other campsites are nearby.

See the web site notes for the less spectacular but interesting trail sections east of Victoria, passing through the Forest Service's Bob Lake campground, traversing varied habitats. Work sessions are on the web site, and volunteers are always welcome. Caution: print out and read trail notes carefully, bring a compass, know how to use it just in case, and bring ample insect protection (a mesh veil over your hat can be a good idea), and be prepared for wet terrain or shallow fords at some times of year. In summer inland parts of the U.P. can be hot — or cold.

Greenland

Originally named "Grove City" when founded back in 1857, this **pleasant village** grew over the years to house the families of the 400 miners who trudged daily to work in the copper mine on nearby Adventure Mountain. Most of the original homes have disappeared, and those remaining remodeled to such an extent that their original austerity is no longer apparent. Today the major occupation is working in the surrounding forests, cutting and hauling softwood trees to the huge paper factory in Ontonagon.

There's a party store in Greenland, and a **colorful bar** where locals congregate. It's called "**Beer Belly Bob's**," and the proprietor does indeed have a considerable girth.The **cheeseburger** comes highly recommended.

Adventure Copper Mine

Now that the poetically named Adventure Mine has been reopened for tours, it makes an educational and **surprisingly scenic destination** that might come in especially handy on a hot or rainy day. (It's 47° in the mine; bring a jacket and closed shoes, not sandals, for stable footing.) Well-mannered, even-tempered dogs like golden retrievers or labs can enjoy this tour, too. The underground route is mostly level because the hill is so steep, giving easy access to the mine interior through a horizontal adit, instead of a vertical shaft. Visitors are taken up to the entrance in a vehicle. A bonus is the spectacular view to the east on exiting the mine, high above the treetops. Mine tours are given year-round and are **especially beautiful in winter**. The Adventure Mine is a popular snowmobile destination.

The guided tour comes in two parts, an underground tour of the mine itself, and an above-ground tour. Visitors see **pits made by ancient miners** from an unknown Indian culture and go past old adits and shafts, including the an "**ice cave**" created by cold air coming from an airshaft created to ventilate the mine. Each part lasts about 45 minutes, or an hour and 20 minutes for the combined tour. The **interesting gift shop**, in an A frame on the platform built for the hoist engine, could allow for another hour of browsing through its mineral samples, books on local history and minerals, and copper jewelry and other gifts. Kids with limited funds can have fun at this shop.

Developing the mine as a historical attraction was the dream of the parents of John Neph, who now runs things here with his wife, Winnie. He and his guides are able to provide a lot of perspective about this mine and mining in general, and they do it in a clear way that doesn't overwhelm. It's easy to imagine life in the mines, how hard the muckers and trammers worked loading rock into tramcars, ten hours a day, six days a week. Visitors get to see the mine stope (excavated mining area) by candlelight, and to imagine the sound of falling rock when the captain lit explosive fuses at the end of the shift. Formations of calcite, epidote (green), and feldspar (red) can be seen on mine walls.

John Neph's mother grew up in Greenland. When she took her husband back to visit in 1964, they fell in love with the property, which they were able to acquire. "The mine became my father's passion, replacing trout fishing," John says. Tours were conducted until 1986. John and Winnie Neph moved up from Gaylord in 1997 and reinstituted the tours.

The Adventure Mine, first explored in 1850, is typical of early Euro-American mining attempts that worked rich fissure veins charged with mass copper. They followed the traces of prehistoric miners who started mining surface outcrops of copper. The Adventure Mine tour shows where ancient miners built fires to heat surface rock, then threw hot water on it and beat it with hammers. Just who these miners were is a subject of debate. Could they have been Celts? **Prehistoric Celtic-type tools** have been found in the Porkies.

What the Yankee miners didn't realize was that fissure veins were unevenly distributed. Even the good ones could give out suddenly. The real profits in copper were made by companies big enough to afford the technology to extract copper from the less copper-rich but more widespread deposits around South Range, Hancock, and Calumet of amygdaloid formations (where the copper formed in bubbles of volcanic rock) and conglomerate formations (where copper minerals were formed from gasses that filled the small cracks and spaces in conglomerate rock). The first Adventure Mine investors, in 1850, were already among the lucky few who struck it rich in Lake Superior copper, at the Cliff Mine near Eagle River, another mass copper vein. Here at the Adventure

Mine, "they invested millions and never paid a dividend," says John Neph. "It always showed a lot of promise" — just enough to keep investors putting in a little bit more, in hopes of a payoff. Copper mined at this location was shipped by rail to the stamp mill at Edgemere north of Freda, then taken to the Quincy smelter.

Adventure Mine is on the east edge of Greenland, 13 miles east of Ontonagon, near M-26 at Mass City. 883-3371. Tours are regularly given from mid May through mid October and again from January through March from 9 a.m. to 6 p.m. Eastern Time. Just show up, you won't wait long. Otherwise tours by appointment when possible. 2001 rates: for underground (or above-ground) tour: $10/adult, $5 ages 12 and under. Combination tour: $15 and $8. &: only with great difficulty.

GREENLAND/MASS CITY AREA CAMPING

ADVENTURE MINE Campground
(906) 883-3371

So far, you can always find a spot at this **quiet campground** by the Adventure Mine. 25 **widely spaced sites** ($8 a night) have picnic tables and fire rings. No showers, no flush toilets. There's a central water source. The village of Greenland with a convenience store and bar with good food are a short ways away. *See above for directions. 883-3371.* &: call

COURTNEY LAKE
Campground/Ottawa National Forest
(906) 884-2411; TTY: (906) 884-6577

This 21-site rustic campground comes recommended as a **good family campground with excellent privacy** that's easier to get to than many national forest campgrounds in this area. The only time it might fill is on July 4. One area is for tent camping. Courtney Lake, about 30 acres, is managed as a trout lake. It's warm enough for good summer swimming and "still refreshing on the rare 90° day." It has a **white sand beach**, a **picnic area** and changing house, and a boat ramp.

8 miles east of Greenland, one mile south of M-38 on Courtney Lake Rd. $7. Open from late May thru mid Oct.

Mass City

This old copper mining village has a **splendid view of a big rock bluff** just north of town, the southern face of

Adventure Mountain. The **rock bluff**, viewed from town in the morning, seems to glow. It's especially handsome in the fall. Visitors can climb a path from the northern edge of Mass City up to the bluff, 600 feet above the city. The reward for this arduous climb is a **wonderful view of the region**.

Up through the 1940s, when there were still dairy farms in the region, there was a sizable maker of Italian cheeses, the Stella Cheese Factory, It is said to have been owned by a German count, whose workmen would throw the whey by-product down an abandoned mine shaft on Adventure Mountain. All that's left of the once-prominent cheese factory is its well, which you can still see down by the railroad tracks on the south side of town. Today the major employers for Mass City residents are independent logging companies.

Mineral collecting at the Caledonia Mine

Michigan's **only active underground mine** today is mined for the collector specimen market. Many of the minerals and copper slabs sold in gift shops come from here. Now Richard Whiteman, who owns the mineral rights to this and several other area mines, will take individuals or small groups on underground collecting trips by appointment. As at the nearby Adventure Mine, the hillside here is steep, so entrance is through a horizontal adit rather than a vertical shaft. Participants climb into stopes (enlarged mining areas, like rooms) where rock has already been broken. In places various minerals have formed in the interstices and bubble pockets of the amygdaloidal basalt here: **mass copper, datolite, quartz, epidote, calcite, feldspar,** and even **silver** can be found. Collecting trips are scheduled for a whole day, with a lunch break. A minimum of ten people (often from different parties) is required for a trip. Many participants are serious rockhounds, but novices could enjoy this, too. Richard supplies a hard hat and miner's lamp. He will advise about additional equipment — nothing too technical: a masonry hammer with chisel tip, a small 2-pound sledgehammer, a hand cultivator, folding shovel, safety glasses, and gloves. Wear boots and a jacket. The temperature is around 45°.

Richard had studied geology and mining engineering at Michigan Tech and worked for the White Pine Mine before developing this specialty niche in mineral specimens. Collecting trips to the Caledonia Mine have been a staple of the August **Red Metal Retreat** rockhound week, which Richard instituted. Now the Copper Country Rock and Mineral Club has taken on the responsibility of organizing the Red Metal Retreat, under the new name **Keweenaw Week**. (See www.geo.mtu.edu/museum)

The Caledonia Mine was first opened in 1863. Calumet & Hecla purchased it in the late 1930s, subsidized by war funding. From 1950 to 1958 a government-funded pilot project connected it with the Mass Mine and removed six million pounds of copper.

The mine is a **major hibernaculum for bats**. An estimated quarter million to half million of them come from up to 200 miles away to spend the winter here. The mine entrance has been redone to make it easy-in, easy-out for bats, and to reduce disturbance by humans and by hungry raccoons. The Caledonia Mine continues to cooperate with Bat Conservation International in preserving this important habitat.

Between Mass City and Rockland. By appointment only. (906) 296-9440. e-mail copper@red-metal.com $30/person. For ages 12 and above. Prefer to schedule trips on weekends. June thru October. &: no

ADVENTURE MOTEL (906) 883-3520

This **simple, clean spot** may fill the bill for rockhounds and travelers who appreciate its central crossroads location and proximity to the Caledonia mine and waterfalls. Owners Don and Nancy Withrow also run the pleasant adjoining cafe with pay phone, open 'til noon daily except Monday. Six small rooms are downstairs ($35); four larger rooms with newer furniture ($45) are upstairs, along with two housekeeping units. All have 19-channel cable TV. No phones. Fills during snowmobile and deer-hunting season. *1372 M-26 near the center of Mass City. Open year-round.* **H.A.:** call : $8 or $9/extra person

Bruce Crossing

A substantial village has developed at this major U.P crossroads, where M-28 heads east from Ironwood and U.S. 45 (the old military road) goes south from Ontonagon to Watersmeet and Eagle River, Wisconsin. Bruce Crossing has three restaurants, two motels, three bars, and a funeral home. There's now just a single grocery—actually more of a general store, **Settler's Co-op**, at the corner of U.S. 45 & M-28, It's got everything from propane and fish licenses to beer and farm feed. Residents of the area work in logging and at Smurfit-Stone Container in Ontonagon.

O-Kun-De-Kun Falls

This little-publicized waterfall is a **real treat for hikers**. It's reached by a 1.3 mile segment of the North Country Trail that goes through a tall pine forest, passing along the way **dramatic undercut rock ledges** and an unnamed waterfall that lets hikers go under the ledge and look out through the falling water. O-Kun-De-Kun Falls itself makes a long, straight drop over massive ledges. Just below the main falls, a **beautiful suspension footbridge** carries the trail across the Baltimore River and offers a fine view of the falls. Smaller falls upstream are also reached by the North Country Trail.

On U.S. 45 8 miles north of Bruce Crossing, sign and parking area are on east side. A Forest Service access road offers a more direct walk back. &: no

Agate Falls/ Bergland-to-Sidnaw Rail Trail

A steep, half-mile trail leads down from a **roadside park** and **picnic area** to this beautiful chain of cascades on the **Ontonagon River's Middle Branch**, as it emerges from a dense hardwood forest to tumble over chunks of dark, square rock. Hikers are rewarded with a pleas-

ant viewing area in a **cool, leafy glade** at the foot of the falls. Here they can look back up at the falls and the bubbling pool that spreads out at their base. The river below the falls has a **good spring steelhead run**, and some salmon in fall. Waterfall watchers in this area might want to visit Bond Falls, 15 miles southwest near Paulding. (See the Watersmeet chapter.)

The trail passes under the former railroad bridge that parallels M-28 and now forms the 43-mile, ballast-surfaced Bergland-to-Sidnaw Rail Trail for mountain bikes. Four bridges make this an interesting trail. Call the Copper Country State Forest, 906-353-6651, for details.

On M-28 (the road from Marquette to the Porcupine Mountains), stop 4 miles west of Trout Creek (or 7 miles east of Bruce Crossing) at the Joseph Oravec Roadside Park. It has picnic tables, drinking water, and vault toilets. Go north under the highway and railroad bridge to the falls. &: no

BRUCE CROSSING RESTAURANT

Good food and a **nice view** in back, looking out over a pond, has helped **GRAMMA GROOTER'S RESTAURANT & PUB** grow into a country-theme 120-seat restaurant featuring some 10 kinds of pie daily ($2.25/slice), giant sandwiches, daily lunch specials ($5.25), taco and fajita salads and such, and skillet breakfasts ($5.50) on hash browns, served any time. Dinners ($8 to $16) include fish, shrimp, steak, and marinated chicken, and come with starch and in winter soup or salad, in summer a salad bar. **Broasted chicken is a specialty**, as a dinner or in buckets to go ($10 for 8 pieces). *On M-28, 1/4 mile east of U.S. 45 in Bruce Crossing. 827-3413. Open daily 6 a.m.-10 p.m. year-round.* & Full bar

Keep in mind that all prices and hours of operation are subject to change. Lodging rates vary with supply and demand and are usually higher for spe-

Ironwood & the Gogebic Range

Its iron mines long closed, the far western U.P. now lives on tourism & timber, with dramatic waterfalls, scenic trails & four ski resorts.

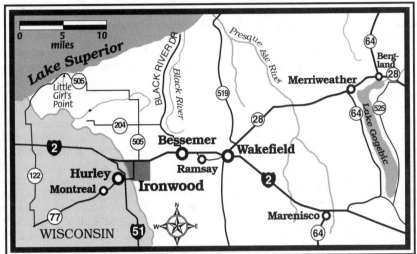

THE YEARS from 1910 to 1930 were boom times for the Gogebic Iron Range at Michigan's far western tip. Its best-known places are the twin county seats of Ironwood, Michigan, and its sister city across the Montreal River, the once-notorious Hurley, Wisconsin. The region's Ojibwa name, pronounced "go-GIBB-ick," means "where trout rising to the surface make rings on the water." The Gogebic Iron Range extends from Wakefield to Ironwood and into Wisconsin. The Oliver Mining Company, most recently owned by U.S. Steel, dominated the range. A defining event in local history was the last shipment of iron ore on August 15, 1967 to Granite City Steel in Illinois.

Today the mining scars are mostly covered over by vegetation. The **rugged landscape seems beguilingly scenic** in an unmannered, unpretentious way — when not interrupted by commercial sprawl. You see a **big sky** driving along U.S. 2 or the pristine **Old County Road** that connects Ironwood and Wakefield via Yale and Ramsay a few miles to the south. The sky is often remarkably beautiful, with wonderful effects of clouds and light, perhaps having something to do with Lake Superior-related weather patterns.

East of the mining range, most of Gogebic County's land is part of the **Ottawa National Forest**. This wild land was left to the government by logging companies that didn't want to pay taxes on it. National forest land includes **good fishing rivers and lakes**, miles and miles of hiking and snowmobile trails, and an exceptional network of **mountain bike trails** extending into Wisconsin on old logging roads. At the moment, the most visible active logging in the area was done by U.S. Steel prior to liquidating some 10,000 acres of its land. The canopy is gone from some previously forested and very visible areas, like the area along Black River Road by Copper Peak.

In the wake of widespread economic devastation as the iron mines began closing in the 1930s, area leaders worked to develop tourism. Tourist landmarks include **beautiful Gogebic County road signs** with Indian-chief silhouettes, erecting the **world's largest Indian** just outside Ironwood and building the world's highest manmade ski jump, **Copper Peak Ski-Flying Hill**.

The trappings of tourism, with their hype and pretense, are not found here, even though Michigan's Gogebic County and neighboring Iron County across

the state line in Wisconsin are heavily promoted during the ski season as **Big Snow Country**. Area lodgings have 10,000 rooms, largely because of the four ski resorts. Thousands of ski chalet units and condos cluster around the four big ski resorts: Indianhead (800-3-INDIAN), Blackjack (800-848-1125), and Big Powderhorn (800-666-9916) in Michigan and Whitecap (715-561-2227) in Wisconsin. The fifth Big Snow Country component is the beautiful natural ski hill by Lake Superior at the Porcupine Mountains State Park, less than an hour from Ironwood. See our **ski section** in front for details about these and other destination ski hills.

Waterfalls are the area's other major visitor draw. Gogebic County has 22 easily visitable falls, and 10 more are across the Montreal River in neighboring Iron County, Wisconsin. With so many waterfalls to choose from, visitors aren't as concentrated as in the Munising/Pictured Rocks area, also known for waterfalls. Fewer crowds make for a more enjoyable experience. Visit waterfalls before 11 or after 5 for best light effects and fewer other visitors. Here falls tumble quickly down from the highlands (the ancient, eroded Porcupine Mountains, actually) to Lake Superior. Water tends to be stained golden or brown by hemlock roots. The **best-known waterfalls** are on the **Presque Isle** and **Black rivers** within half a mile of Lake Superior. Far less celebrated, but even more spectacular when water hasn't been diverted, are **Saxon Falls** and **Superior Falls**, bordered by hundred-foot cliffs on the **Montreal River** forming the **Michigan-Wisconsin border**.

The Ironwood area is an interesting place to vacation because it's not just a tourist area. As in the western Upper Peninsula, the mix of people and cultures adds much to a visitor's experience. The population is composed largely of Finns and Italians who came to work in the iron mines, and Croats, Poles, and other Slavs from coal-mining regions of Eastern Europe. The latter had come earlier to mine what little coal was here.

People here are friendly. It's a pleasure to chat with the folks sitting next to you at cafés. And the food can be quite a surprise! Manny's in Ironwood still makes lasagna and ravioli by hand because their customers expect it. People can be stunningly generous if you're passably polite and forthcoming — like the family in a rattletrap

Central Time

All the Michigan counties along the Wisconsin border are on Central Time — that's the entire length of U.S. 2 in the western U.P. until it gets to Escanaba. Ironwood, Watersmeet, Iron River, Iron Mountain, and Menominee are all an hour earlier than Eastern time. If it's 5 p.m. in most of Michigan, it's 4 p.m. there. But Porcupine Mountains State Park, in Ontonogan County, is on Eastern Time.

pickup who offered to loan downstate visitors a flashlight and blankets so they could sit down on the beach by Superior Falls and watch the sunset. And the level of honesty and trust puts downstaters to shame. On Aurora Street in downtown Ironwood, still lined with remnants of taverns from the wild and wooly boom times, people who have bicycled downtown lean their bicycles, unlocked, by the entrances of stores, confident that the bikes will still be there when they come out. That's the kind of civilized lifestyle that still exists up here.

It's interesting how mining towns like Ironwood (and Iron River and Iron Mountain farther east) — unpromising places that began as bleak, artificial company towns where ethnic groups with no common culture were thrown together and fought — have become enduring communities that keep drawing their progeny back. Great natural beauty and cheap real estate help, no doubt.

Ray Crenna, a sixtyish opera singer and food lover who grew up in the area, comes back often from Chicago for sustenance. "You go away, and you come back, the hills are alive with music. It's cathedralish! It's a basilica of the four seasons! The trees have planted themselves. The gardens of wildflowers splash from heaven's paintbrush in swashes of color. It's like The Sound of Music. The music is in the landscape, like a woven tapestry, rough and smooth."

His Italian forbears came to Bessemer because some cousins came first and spread the word among their relations. "There was something very healthy about growing up here. You grew up with roots that you don't find very many places — roots that never leave you. This area just meshes, but you have to see it. People who have stayed here [without going away for awhile] are living in a jello mold and don't want to be shaken up."

In these gritty towns, wealth was extracted and quickly exported. Money didn't stay around and pay for too many fine offiice buildings and cultural institutions, the way it did in Houghton, Calumet, and Marquette. Here mining families experienced booms and busts, and saw legions of their children forced to move away. Many have managed to move back in retirement or after a first career. Many others have returned with their own children and grandchildren to spend summers here, spawning generations of Yoopers in diaspora. Much of the area's cultural energy comes from these returnees and transplants. To be in Wakefield or Bessemer at homecoming is to witness a sense of community that upscale suburbs could never match.

Note: points of interest have been arranged starting with Ironwood and going east along U. S. 2. Attractions on and near Lake Superior are placed according to where the motorist would turn north from the highway.

TO FIND OUT MORE: For tips and knowledge about the U.P. that's wide and deep, it would be hard to beat Pat Juntti and her helpful staff at the **MICHIGAN WELCOME CENTER** on U.S. 2 at Ironwood's west edge, just inside the Michigan line. They serve the entire state with vast amounts of printed information but make a point to be up on usual and unusual points of local interest. Ask about the new **Heritage Trail** program with things to see **off the beaten path in western U.P. counties.** Be sure to get the information-packed *Upper Peninsula Travel Planner*, a free glossy magazine. Open daily from 8 a.m. to 4 p.m. Central Time, to 6 in summer. (906) 932-3330. . . . Just across the state line where U.S. 2 meets U.S. 51 outside Hurley, the staff at **WISCONSIN'S HURLEY TRAVEL INFORMATION CENTER** is also exceptionally helpful and knowledgeable about attractions in the vicinity and the entire state. Wisconsin's state history agency sets up impressive mini-museums in state travel

centers. Here the subject is mining. Wisconsin leads the nation in bicycle tourism, with paved rails-to-trails bike paths (mostly in southern Wisconsin) that enable casual bicyclists to bike from town to town and stay in bed and breakfasts. Open year-round. From Mem. thru Labor Day open daily 8 a.m. to 6 p.m. Central Time. In May and Sept. open daily 8-4. Otherwise open Tuesday thru Sat 8-4. (715) 561-5310. . . . Online find lots of info on destinations and events in **HURLEY** and **Iron County** at www.ironcountywi.com, or call (715) 561-2922. . . . The **WESTERN U.P. CONVENTION & VISITORS' BUREAU** is a clearinghouse for travel info on all members, including every lodging over 10 rooms. It responds to phone inquiries and can steer prospective visitors to lodgings that meet their requirements. Call (800) 522-5657 or look in at www.westernup.com It posts snowmobile trail conditions and has a calendar of events that's extensive but not annotated. . . . . . . Small resorts line the shores of Lake Gogebic. For specific info on this area, call the **LAKE GOGEBIC CHAMBER of COMMERCE**, (906) 842-3611. . . . The **IRONWOOD AREA CHAMBER of COMMERCE** has its office in the Old Depot Park Museum downtown. (906) 932-1122 . . . Drop-in visitor info, handy for travelers coming from the east, is at the **WAKEFIELD CHAMBER of COMMERCE** at its chamber of commerce and a visitor center with local information and souvenirs on the south shore of Sunday Lake, where U.S. 2 and M-28 come together. (906) 224-2222.

LODGINGS TIPS: **Ski and snowmobile season** is the **busiest** time of year here. Christmas week and President's Day weekend, the busiest times of all, command premium rates. Six months' lead time isn't a bad idea if you want lodging with amenities like indoor pool, in-room whirlpool, trailside chalet, etc. . . **Summer brings bargains** at the ski resorts, especially for family accommodations with kitchens. Availability of highway motels is generally pretty good; it's another matter for cottages on and near water, which are mostly near the Porkies. Homecoming events on July 4 weekend fill area motels. So do the waterski championships held every other August on Sunday Lake in Wakefield. . . . **Reserve ahead for fall color season**, especially if you want more amenities.

PUBLIC LAND: The new supervisor's office of the **OTTAWA NATIONAL FOREST** on U. S. 2 is not only an information center, it's a nifty small **nature book store** with well chosen books for adults and children, plus detailed maps of the national forest for sale. Open Mon-Fri 8-4 Central Time. It's on the north side of U.S. 2 at the east edge of Ironwood, west of the figure of the giant skier and Big Powderhorn turnoff and just east of Grandview Hospital. 932-1330. The staff provides visitors with information and directions to less well-known Ottawa attractions that could make a delightful adventure out of the long trip across the U.P. on U.S. 2. &. . . There's much less state land in these parts than in some areas. The **MICHIGAN DEPARTMENT of NATURAL RESOURCES** field office in Wakefield is at 1405 East U.S. 2. (906) 224-2771. . . . Having so much public land in Gogebic County, Michigan, and Iron County, Wisconsin makes for outstanding **mountain biking**. Get the free bi-state trail map from either state's travel information center, from Trek & Trail on U.S. 2 in Ironwood, or by calling (715) 561-2922. 100 miles of easy trails connect the lakes around Marenisco south of U.S. 2. Challenging trails of the **Ehlco Mountain Bike Complex** are on national forest land just south of the Porkies near the Iron river. . . Most extensive is the system of trails in Iron County, mostly beginner to intermediate.

FISHING GUIDES: Two excellent outdoors stores are on U.S. 2 in Ironwood. For back-country fishing for many species, Bart Domin at **Black Bear Sports** (906-932-5253) guides and refers to other guides. He likes to teach and welcomes all levels of experience. . . . Dave Johnson at **Trek & Trail** (906-932-5858)is a flyfishing specialist.

EVENTS: Look in at www.westernup.com for an extensive but not complete calendar without annotations. The Ironwood Chamber of Commerce is in the process of preparing a website, too. . . . **Independence Day** means **homecomings** and parades in **Bessemer, Wakefield,** and **Marenisco**, with **fireworks** over Sunday Lake. . . . The free **Upper Great Lakes Renaissance Faire** brings fencing, games, music, parade in Renaissance garb, and lost arts to downtown Ironwood the second full weekend in July. The next weekend downtown Ironwood throws a four-day party for the **Ironwood Festival** with music and more. . . In and around **Hurley**, the **Iron County Heritage Festival** means three weekends of events from late July into mid August: homecoming, a memorable **living history tour** of **Hurley taverns**, dinners, dances, the county fair on the first weekend of August, and the **Paavo Nurmi Marathon** (a challenging course without many flat areas). See www.ironcountywi.com for details.

HARBOR with transient dockage: Outside Bessemer at **Black River Harbor** (906-667-0261; lat. 46° 40' 13" N, long. 90° 03' 00".W) with picnic tables, grills.

PICNIC PROVISIONS and PLACES:

See index for location and details on parks.

◆ There's no outstanding deli, making the top destination for picnic fixings the area's big supermarket, **Super One Foods** at 411 E. Cloverland in Ironwood. Or take out food from an area restaurant. In **Wakefield** (see Wakefield restaurants), **Randall's Bakery** has good pasties, and the **Korner Kitchen** has fried chicken and roast pork. In **Ironwood**, **Mike's** on U.S. 2 is the logical choice, with the **Royal Bakery** (good hard rolls) across the street.

◆ Handy to U.S. 2 in **WAKEFIELD** is pretty **Eddy Park** on the north side of Sunday Lake with a picnic area and warm swimming with a shallow area for little children.

◆ Off the beaten path in **RAMSAY** is the picnic area by the beautiful **Keystone Bridge**. Consider takeout pizza from the **Ore House Pub & Pizza** on the main street.

◆ **BESSEMER** has the absolutely idyllic **Bluff Valley Park**, where a creek winds by the playground and tennis courts. See distant hills as you hear the water. Turn south onto Moore Street at the main light, by the sign to Black River Harbor.

◆ The blufftop picnic area at **Little Girl's Point**, about 15 minutes northwest of **IRONWOOD**, looks out across Lake Superior. Just two miles south of town, Norrie Park on the Montreal River is a pretty picnic spot. Right in town, the flower-filled **Pocket Park** on Aurora at Suffolk has benches but no tables.

Ironwood (*pop.* 6,293)

Michigan's westernmost city is slightly farther west than St. Louis, Missouri, and about the same distance from Detroit as Detroit is from Albany, New York: 593 miles. Ironwood was the **pioneer city and business center of the Gogebic Range**. The Chicago & Northwestern Railroad platted Ironwood in 1885, the year the railroad completed its branch line through here to ship ore from the area's new iron mines. The name honors early mining captain and booster John Wood, nicknamed "Iron." By 1890 its population had grown to 7,745. Lumbering added to the boom town's fortunes once the railroad connection was in place to take forest products to market. But as a boom town Ironwood was relatively quiet because it had notorious Hurley, with its **many taverns and brothels**, just across the river in Wisconsin. Hurley drew off the wilder elements of the Gogebic Range. The powerful mining companies in Ironwood preferred its image as a wholesome, church-going community.

In 1930, when its mines were still going strong, Ironwood numbered 14,300, third in the Upper Peninsula after Marquette and Escanaba. By the 1940s, more accessible ore in Minnesota's Mesabi Range was being developed, and the Gogebic's star was beginning to fade. The vast amounts of money made from Gogebic iron didn't stay in the area. Today Ironwood is a plain, sprawling, somewhat faded place, though not without noteworthy preservation successes.

Central Ironwood

Hardly a shopper's paradise, Ironwood does have some **splendid vestiges of mining boom years**. Commerce has moved out to the highway to the point that downtown has far too many empty storefronts. Albert's, a wonderful old-time store known for its timeless outdoor

Mining towns grew up around mine locations. This 1890s photo looking south on Lowell Street towards downtown Ironwood shows in the distant shafthouses of the Norrie, **Ashland, Pabst, Aurora, and Newport mines. Between downtown and the distant mineshafts, undermining collapsed, causing a swath of town to be abandoned.**

At places like the Gogebic Range, mining and logging boom towns seemed to mushroom almost overnight, as seen in this 1886 photograph of Ironwood.

clothing, closed in 2001 after its owner died. Aurora and Suffolk streets, on Business Route 2, are the heart of the historic business district; Aurora continues west across the Montreal into Hurley (see below), where it becomes Silver Street and remains lined with bars to this day. Ironwood's residential "show street" extends east on Ayer, which is parallel to Aurora but one block north.

◆ **OLD DEPOT PARK MUSEUM.** The **handsome 1892 Romanesque Revival depot** houses the Ironwood area museum and research center. (The new genealogical society can be reached by calling 932-3934.) The first room deals with the area's railroad history, and can be opened upon request when the museum is closed by asking at the Chamber of Commerce, which now has space in the depot. More exhibits cover mining and life on the range. Good use has been made of **dramatic and poignant newspaper clippings**, for instance, about the 43 miners entombed by a 1926 cave-in at the Pabst Mine. A common kind of letter to the editor was from married women from the old country seeking husbands who had come to America seeking work and apparently started new families, abandoning their first wives. Much more material, including many photos and printed matter, is in files visitors can ask to see. Note: an informal archive of historic Ironwood area photos can be viewed — and prints purchased — from Gerald Kinnunen at Modern Portrait Studio, *222 E. Aurora, telephone 932-3800. Between Suffolk and Lowell, clearly visible to your right from Bus. Rte. 2/Suffolk just before you reach the center of town. 932-0287. Open daily from Mem. to Labor Day, noon-4. Otherwise by appt. (call 932-4142).*

Donations appreciated. &

◆ **FABRIC PATCH.** 3,500 bolts of fabric make this storefront a quilter's paradise, from beginners to experts. For inspiration there are **lots of examples of quilts, hangings, and garments**, plus books and patterns and helpful advice. Ask about one-day workshops. Rubber stamps are the store's other specialty. *121 N. Lowell, across from the depot museum. 932-5260. www.fabricpatch .com Mon-Thurs 9:30-5, Fri to 6, Sat to 4.* &: difficult. One step. Tight quarters.

◆ **IRONWOOD THEATRE.** Part Moorish, part Italian Renaissance, this theater was the **U.P.'s biggest picture palace** when finished in 1928. Recent restorations have gold-leafed the interior pilasters and proscenium and again revealed elaborate painted decorations, remembered by generations of local youth for their **alluring female nudes** and plump cherubs cavorting on clouds on the ceiling. (The decorations had been painted over in a misguided attempt to brighten up the place for the filming of Adventures of a Young Man, a 1962 movie about the young Ernest Hemingway/Nick Adams coming back from World War I. Critics called the film "overblown," "pretentious," and "embarrassing." The premiere in Ironwood, with stars Paul Newman and Jessica Tandy on hand, was a big, big local event.) Today the theater sponsors a successful arts series of chamber music, plays, and more, and hosts theater groups and traveling shows. *For events, call (906) 932-0618 or look in at* **www.ironwoodtheatre.org** *Friday afternoons in summer feature a variety of interesting free music. Sometimes the Barton theater organ is played. Stop by the office weekdays for impromptu tours. 107 E. Aurora, downtown.* &

◆ **DAN'S ANTIQUE MALL.** Three floors of old stuff that makes for **good browsing.** "Antiques" may overstate most of it, but you can find a lot from the 1940s and 1950s. *111 E. Aurora. 932-5002. Open 7 days a week, year-round, 9-5 Central Time.* &: main level.

◆ **ANNE MARIE'S ARTISTRY.** A small storefront in the Ironwood Theatre Building showcases Anne-Marie Batiste's smaller paintings and portraits, plus Nancy Ramsay's delightful pottery and some stained glass. Anne-Marie's work reflects her experience living in Africa as part of a mission. Freely painted, they're **alive with color and fearlessly personal.** Bigger murals fill the walls going down to the basement space where she conducts her art youth ministry. *Usually open Thursday through Saturday. No regular phone.*

◆ **POCKET PARK.** Fabulous flowers fill the gap left when a landmark sandstone bank building, badly deteriorated, was finally taken down. Photographer Gerald Kinnunen at the Modern Portrait Studio around the corner on Aurora led the landscaping effort. Benches let you sit down and enjoy the floral specatcle. The sandstone walls of the building, incidentally, have been reconstructed at Whitecap Resort outside Montreal, Wisconsin. *Downtown at Aurora and Suffolk.*

◆ **NORTHWIND NATURAL FOOD CO-OP.** This spacious co-op is good place to **find camping luxuries like good granola, trail mixes, juices, cheese, crackers, pancake mix** — and frozen organic dinners for motels with microwaves. It carries farm-fresh eggs and, in season, locally grown organic produce, including berries. Here are nutritional supplements and books, organic skin care products, and a fetch-

ing array of soaps, baskets, and pottery made by local people, plus some **Chinese teapots** imported by a local person from China. Nancy Ramsay's useful **pottery jars with druid-like faces** make unusual gifts at attractive prices. *210 Suffolk, just south of Aurora next to First of America bank. 932-3547. Mon-Sat 9-6.* ♿

◆ **IRONWOOD MUNICIPAL-MEMORIAL BUILDING.** Inside, this **lavish Beaux Arts pentagon** contains not only city offices but a swimming pool, gym, and auditorium. Local people raised $500,000 to commemorate their men who died in World War I; a wall of bronze tablets lists 1,580 names — a chilling number of deaths for a small area, illustrating how heavily the burden of wars weighs on working-class people. Scenic murals in the main entrance area depict dairying, lumberjacks, pioneers, Jesuits, and a wide landscape of hills punctuated from east to west by the headframes of the Norrie, Ashland, Pabst, Aurora, and Newport mines. Go up the grand staircase to see **stained-glass windows showing the Battle of the Argonne**, with airplanes flying above the town, shrapnel bursting in the streets, and heavy artillery firing from camouflaged positions. Flanking it, windows show the attack on Fort Sumter that launched the Civil War and the sinking of the Moro Castle in the Spanish-American War. Thanks to a recent restoration, the building's many decorative details can again be admired.

On Thursdays beginning at 5 or so, the auditorium is given over to **bingo** and refreshments, put on by Jaycees and Mary of Peace Catholic Church to benefit DOVE, a domestic violence program. *McLeod & Marquette, northwest corner. McLeod parallels Aurora a block to the south; Marquette is two blocks east of Suffolk/Business Route 2.* ♿: *call 932-5050.*

World's Tallest Indian

This fiberglass-covered Hiawatha was part of the area's energetic campaign to promote tourism as the iron mines were closing. The huge **eight-ton statue, 53 feet high**, takes the form of the stereotypical Indian chief. He stands in a hillside neighborhood in the Norrie location, site of one of the Gogebic Range's oldest and most productive mines, and surveys a long, undeveloped east-west valley that divides Ironwood. This is a **cave-in area**, cleared of buildings after some houses fell in when a mine shaft collapsed.

Rail connections enabled remote boom towns like Ironwood to leapfrog beyond existing settlements by providing markets for their minerals and timber. In 1892, just six years after Ironwood's founding, this handsome brick depot was built. Today it houses the historical society's museum and archive, and the chamber of commerce.

Hiawatha offers some good photo-ops for connoisseurs of roadside Americana. Pose the family in front of one of his giant moccasins. **Manny's,** a restaurant with **outstanding hand-made pasta**, is two blocks away.

From downtown Ironwood, go south on Suffolk/Bus. Route 2 up the hill about 1/4 mile. ♿

Norrie Park

Just two miles south of Ironwood, this wooded park down on the Montreal River is a **relaxing place to picnic** (there are picnic tables and grills) and to play tennis. The swimming used to be good, but lately bloodsuckers have been a problem, though some swimmers don't mind.

South of the Norrie location. Follow directions to world's largest Indian (above), but turn right onto Balsam before the statue. Park is 1 1/2 miles south on Balsam.

Mount Zion Scenic Overlook

High points from Ironwood to Wakefield offer some **grand views**, and this is one. Standing on the flat rock outcrop, you can see **unfolding ranges of hills**, forests, houses, farms, and cows. Use your imagination and you can see Lake Superior at the distant line where sky and land meet. This beauty spot is not much visited, and it's somewhat overgrown. Its south slope, back of Gogebic Community College, comes alive as a winter park, with a double chair lift, tubing, and night skiing.

From U.S. 2 at Greenbush (a block east of the light at Douglas Blvd.), turn north at Daisy's Motel, continue past Gogebic Community College, winding up the hill to the overlook.

Black Bear Sports

Fishing enthusiast Bart Doman sells fishing gear, fly-fishing materials, archery supplies, and guns and ammo.

He himself is a **guide with over 20 years of experience** and now has a referral service with other guides for fly-fishing, steelhead, smallmouth and largemouth bass, and lake trout and salmon. "Our service specializes in teaching as well as fishing, so all levels of experience are welcome," he says. "Our area has a lot of back-country fishing, which helps to get away from crowds. On many days we see no other fishermen."

100 W. Cloverland/U.S. 2, west of Bus. Rte. 2/Douglas, across from Mike's Restaurant. 932-5253. Mon-Fri 9-5, Sat 9-1 Central Time. Call for longer summer hours. ♿

Nature's Picks Rock Shop

Owner John Heikkinen, like many rock hounds, spent most of his life collecting. He started right here on the Gogebic Range. Now that he's retired, he opened a rock shop to share his enthusiasm for "rocks and minerals with true character." His unassuming store carries rocks and minerals from far and wide, including petrified wood, fossils, fluorescents, and Lake Superior agates and copper and iron specimens. Some jewelry is on hand, but this isn't a slick gift shop. The fun, unusual part is having lots of **affordable rocks**, minerals in interesting rock matrices, and slabs. Come here for tips on collecting locally. *600 W. Cloverland at Curry, across from Super One, west of the light at Douglas/Bus. U.S. 2. 932-7340. Open Mon-Sat 10-5 in summer at least. Call to confirm other hours.* ♿

Depot Antiques

Here in a frame freight warehouse on the Soo Line, Bonnie Gulan combines new and old, decorative and functional, with an **unusually good eye** that provides an appealing historic context to gifts and cards that would look less sincere in, say, a suburban mall setting. It makes for **great browsing** in a series of rooms. There are soaps, sweets, old magazines, new books and old, vintage costume jewelry, toys, puzzles, all sorts of gifts and antique furniture and collectibles, tending to the primitive/country casual. More browsing is across the street 318 North Lake St., *1 1/2 blocks south of U.S. on the east side of town. Turn south at the Holiday station. 232-0900. Open year-round. Mon-Sat 9-5. Call for Sunday hours in summer.* ♿ 2 steps up. Once inside, many but not all areas are accessible.

Pine Tree Gallery

This is a most **attractive gallery of original arts and crafts** of the Upper Great Lakes, a frame shop, and an impromptu visitor information center. Owner Phil Kucera is yet another Gogebic native who went south to find work (at O'Hare Airport, where he met his wife). But the lure of metropolitan life faded as Chicago sprawled and changed in the 1960s, just as Ironwood's mines shut down and tourism started developing. Eventually the Kuceras managed to move up here permanently, part of the back-to-the-land movement that brought a number of people here in the 1970s. Phil's longtime interest in woodworking led him to work with a Chicago restorer of antique frames, which introduced him to art sales.

His gallery and its changing exhibits regularly show antique maps and prints, pottery, paintings and original prints (but not limited-edition prints) of regional artists, including a number of Native Americans. Natural themes, including lots that involve fish, predominate. It's worth stopping by regularly whenever you're in the area. An added bonus: Phil is happy to sit down and **annotate the maps he gives out**, with directions and tips for backroads adventures here and in the Porcupine Mountains. Call about occasional talks.

824 E. Cloverland/U.S. 2, north side of road, a block east of the ligh at CR 505. 932-5120. Open year-round. From Mem. Day thru ski season: Mon-Sat 9-5, Sun 10-2. Closed Sun in spring. ♿

Trek & Trail

Dave Johnson, Ironwood native and silent sports enthusiast, offers equipment, accessories, and supporting maps and advice for cross-country and downhill skiing, mountain biking, snowshoeing, and fly-fishing. Now that the store

has moved out to a handsome log building on U.S. 2, there's room for kayaks and canoes as well.

Backpacks, outdoor gear, and functional casual clothing make up over half of Trek & Trail's business. The idea is to offer selection and quality better than that of big sporting goods chains, but not necessarily expensive. Brands include Sugoi cycling gear, Black Diamond backpacks, and Patagonia and Gramicci outdoor wear.

It's basically an active outdoor store, with a department for fly-fishing, Dave's passion. He himself leads guided fly-fishing trips on the Brule River in Wisconsin, a trout stream. Fly-fishing is a tricky business, what with 135 species of mayflies and with trout that have extremely selective conditioned responses to local insects. Local knowledge of insects and rivers is what small, personal shops like this have to offer, Johnson points out. (His local colleagues at Black Bear Sports down the road are also knowledgeable fly-fishing guides, he adds.) *1310 E. Cloverland/U.S. 2 next to Don & GG's restaurant, half a block west of the Kmart shopping center. 932-5858. www.trekandtrail.net Mon-Sat 9-6, plus Sun 10-4:30 in ski season and from July 4 thru Sept.* ♿

Ottawa National Forest Supervisor's Office and Book Shop

Here visitors can get knowledgeable individualized planning information and lots of handouts on recreational opportunities throughout the forest's million acres in the western U.P. **Detailed maps of the Ottawa** are for sale. There's also an **excellent nature book and gift store** run by the Ottawa Interpretive Association. Its profits pay for informational kiosks, visitor brochures, and such for the Ottawa National Forest. The children's books are quite appealing. This would be a good stop before a camping trip, to bone up on nature lore and campfire stories.

On the north side of U.S. 2 at the east edge of Ironwood. It's west of the giant skier and Big Powderhorn turnoff and just east of Grandview Hospital. 932-1330. Open Mon-Fri 8-4 Central Time. ♿

Little Girl's Point and vicinity

It feels like going off to the **edge of the world** — and **back in time**— to visit this simple, well-maintained Gogebic county park on a **high Lake Superior bluff** and

point. The trim stone bathhouse for the campground, the picnic pavilions, and caretaker's house are from another era. The bluff offers **long views off to the blue silhouettes of the Porcupines** on the northeast and to the Apostle Islands on the southwest. This is a **memorable place for a picnic**, with tables and grills. A pedestrians-only road and some stairs lead down the steep bank to a sandy beach with some stones, where kids have a grand time diving from a concrete structure brought to the site.

West along the shore, more **sandy beach** comes right up to the road, where you can park. The boat launch is at this part of the park. Continue west on CR 505 to get to Superior Falls (see below), a little publicized but don't-miss sight. *About 12 minutes northwest of Ironwood via Hemlock/Vanderhagen Rd, which becomes CR 505. From U.S. 2 on the west side of town, turn north onto Hemlock at the corner where Auto Body Glass is. 667-0411.* ♿ : call.

Little Girls' Point Honey

An interesting stop just east of Little Girl's Point is Amy and Claude Van Oyen's honey shop. The Van Oyens, who immigrated from The Netherlands in 1951, moved up from Grand Rapids after spending many vacations camping in the forest here. They lived simply but gardened big-time and got into honey to help send four children to college at once. They welcome visitors to walk the paths through the **colorful gardens** of their miniature estate. Children will enjoy its **picture-book look** and the **ducks and geese on the sunny pond**. Today their little home-based shop offers honey, maple syrup, beeswax candles (they burn longer), their daughter's **ceramic honey pots** and other pottery, and Amy's **four popular memoirs of their life in the U.P.** It also sells Claude's **garden tiles**, made with leaf prints and tracks. A few examples of Claude's wood carvings are around. He does them on commission. A glass-sided beehive on the deck by the house lets visitors see bees at work. You can still buy honey if no one's home. It's in the wishing well, sold on the honor system.

Amy would never have thought to write books, she says, if it weren't for the late Cully Gage, author of the beloved Northwoods Readers, drawn from stories he heard growing up in Champion. He found the story of the Van Oyens' lives so interestin he pushed and helped and criticized until Amy had produced several stories for Above the Bridge magazine. By

Ironwood area
Dramatic waterfalls, friendly people, and some very good, inexpensive food

Map labels:

Lake Superior

Little Girl's Point Park— swim, picnic, camp in a wonderful setting

elev. +1450 feet

Superior Falls— spectacular view of perhaps the most dramatic falls in the U.P.

505

505 Lake Superior Rd.

Lake Superior Rd.

Bald Mountain

Montreal River

MICHIGAN

Lake Superior Rd.

122

Saxon Falls— a majestic sight viewed from a bridge across the river

Airport Rd.

204

WISCONSIN

Peterson Falls

Michigan Welcome Center

2

Little Finland

Wisconsin Travel Info.

0   2.5   5
miles

Once infamous for its saloons, brothels, and rowdiness. Now known for restaurants.

Hurley

Iron-wood

77

2

Montreal— picturesque historic mning town

Montreal

51

---

then she was well on her way to finishing her first book, *Live It U.P.*, about how their large city family (four natural children and five Korean adoptees) adjusted to northwoods life.

If someone's home, knock on the door and come in for coffee. You're sure to learn lots. "I'm always giving lectures," laughs Amy, "planned and unplanned." *North off CR 505, 10 miles north of U.S. 2 and 5 1/2 miles east of Little Girl's Point. Look for the carved black bear by an old-fashioned beehive. Take driveway north about 1/2 mile. 932-4798. Stop by any time. Call ahead if you want to be sure the*

shop is open. &: a little assistance needed.

Superior Falls

This little-publicized waterfall is close to where the Montreal River empties into Lake Superior. The river forms the state line with Wisconsin. It's one of the **most dramatic waterfalls in Michigan** — more so, in some ways, than Tahquamenon Falls. Here the river is narrower, only 30 feet wide, wedged between steep rock walls of a deep gorge over a hundred feet down from the visitor's vantage point. The river turns into a thundering

column of foam, some 40 feet straight down, which soon settles into a quiet pool, turns, and flows between those towering and steep rock walls. The fracture lines go almost straight up and down, powerful testimony to the tremendous forces of uplift and tilting from the earth's early time. Wisconsin Electric Power owns this site and has built a viewing overlook and rail along the path from the parking area by a substation. The company uses nearby reservoirs, called flowages, to control the river's flow for producing electrical power. Occasionally there won't be much water going over the falls. If you want to be sure of seeing the full waterfall before setting out on this drive, call the Michigan Welcome Center (906-932-3330).

A very steep asphalt path descends from the parking area down to the river mouth and isolated, private beach. Local people like to come here and enjoy the sunset. It's a very steep walk back up!

About 22 miles northwest of Ironwood and 5 miles west of Little Girl's Point via CR 505. See directions to Little Girl's Point. Watch for sign and parking area near where 505 crosses the Montreal River and goes into Wisconsin. Or, for a more direct route through Wisconsin, take U.S. 2 for 11 miles west of Hurley, turn north onto W-122, go north about 4 miles, cross into Michigan, and go left to Wisconsin Electric Power station and parking area. &: no.

Saxon Falls

A couple of miles upstream from Superior Falls is another waterfall owned and controlled by Wisconsin Electric Power. When water levels are high, the effect of three sections of falls, juxtaposed with rocky pinnacles and pine trees in mist, is awesome. The falls are seen from a bridge across the river, reached by going down a long metal stairway from the electrical substation and parking area. Saxon Falls "was one of the most majestic and spectacular falls either of us had ever seen!," wrote Edna Elfont in *Roar of Thunder, Whisper of Wind*. For Wisconsin waterfall maps and more waterfalls in Iron County, Wisconsin, stop by the 24-hour Wisconsin Travel Information Center in Hurley where U.S. 2 joins U.S. 51.

From U.S. 2 in Hurley, Wisconsin, drive about 9 miles west to County Road B. Turn north (right) and go north on B. In 2.3 miles, B turns left, but you shouldn't. Keep north on Saxon Falls Rd. to its end. Opposite the road end is a substation. The falls is just upstream from it. &: no.

IRONWOOD RESTAURANTS

See also: Hurley, Bessemer and Wakefield restaurants

MULLIGAN & COMPANY in downtown Ironwood is part coffeehouse, part Irish pub (in a separate connecting space), and altogether a **pleasant place with a peaceful atmosphere**— a good place to talk. The limited menu features a breakfast wrap ($4.75 with coffee), a variety of wraps and sandwiches from healthy veggie or turkey to roast beef (about $5 with tortilla chips), and good soups. Cappucino and espresso drinks, smoothies with optional protein powder, malts, ice cream cones, fresh lemonade in season, and Harp's, Black and Tan, and Guinness on tap — this place really covers a lot of bases. Friday and Saturday nights it serves dinner, too, followed by varied live entertainment — sometimes Irish bands, sometimes alternative rock. Elegantly shuttered windows filter light; wicker seating is drawn up to the fireplace in the pub. *125 S. Suffolk/Bus. U.S. 2 at Aurora in the heart of downtown Ironwood. 932-4244. Open daily except Sunday. Coffeehouse open 7 a.m. to 5 p.m. Pub open 'til 2 a.m.* &

An updated diner, **MIKE'S** wins high

Little publicized but awesome, Superior Falls is where the Montreal River plunges into Lake Superior on the border between Michigan and Wisconsin. It makes a memorable outing, paired with a picnic at Little Girl's Point.

marks for just about everything: pizza, pasta, ravioli, chicken (fried or in casseroles) plus huge breakfasts and **homemade sausage. Portions are huge**, so senior portions are available. The popular **spicy Italian meatball sub** uses Italian hard rolls from the Royal Bakery across the street. A standout: **lasagna baked with meat sauce**, 5 cheeses. Sandwiches mostly $5, dinners $6-$12 including salad, bread basket, potato when appropriate. There's a big takeout business; the wait for pizza is no more than 20 minutes, and that's with everything on it. No plastic, no checks from over 200 miles away. *In Ironwood on U.S. 2, 4 blocks east of the Michigan Welcome Center. At Lowell St. next to Amoco station. 932-0555. Open daily, 7 days, at 7:30 a.m. to 8:30 in winter, 9 p.m. in summer. Closed 2 weeks around Thanksgiving, also 2 weeks around Easter.* &

Over the years since it began as a bar in 1938, **DON & GG's** has evolved into the **area's most ambitious restaurant**, though still a casual spot. It serves cappuccino and several vegetarian dishes, focuses on fresh ingredients, and offers little touches like homemade fries accompanying deli sandwiches ($3.79-$5.49). The all-day salad and sandwich menu includes homemade soups ($2.50/bowl), smoked trout or raspberry chicken salad on greens ($6), and Black Angus burgers. Dinners ($10-$14) include pastas, steaks (the grilled herbed ribeye topped with melted blue cheese is unusual), chicken, specials, and on Wednesday fresh Lake Superior trout with pasta ($11). There's outdoor seating with no particular view. *On East U.S. 2, half a block west of the Kmart shopping plaza. 932-2312 . Open Mon-Sat 10 a.m. to midnight, Sun noon-10 p.m..* & Full bar; many beers

The **handmade ravioli** ($10.45 at dinner) and lasagna at **MANNY'S** are **outstanding**, and the meat sauce, though nothing exotic, is pretty wonderful too. It's worth seeking out this comfortable, casual restaurant and lounge. It's way off the beaten path in the Norrie mining location. Dinners, including steaks, chicken, and stir-fries, are mostly $10 to $15, including soup and salad bar. Chicken pizza with white sauce ($10.25 for 12") is a hit. Vegetarian sauce is available on request. $6 Friday fish fries feature cod — beer-battered, steamed, or baked with parmesan. Burgers ($2.75-$6) and meatball subs are always available. Breakfasts have unusual touches, too, like pancakes with maple syrup ($3.75) and the $6.45 noodle omelet, a specialty. Lunch

The Tudor clubhouse of the Ironwood Country Club is open to the general public as the Elk & Hound restaurant.

specials ($5.50 including soup and salad bar) are a pizza buffet (Mon, Wed, Fri) and pasta (Tues & Thurs). Reservations or early arrival recommended for weekend evenings and Sunday after church. Smoke is permitted in the main dining room, and some smoke is evident in the non-smoking section. *316 E. Houk in the Norrie Location. See directions for World's Largest Indian, turn left at Indian. Manny's is just past ball field. 932-0999 . Mon-Sat 6 a.m.-9 p.m. Central Time, Sun to 2 p.m. Lounge open from 4 p.m. to midnight, later in summer..* &

Diners at **THE ELK & HOUND** can enjoy pretty good food in a country club setting at **reasonable prices**. The 1920s Tudor-style clubhouse sits on a hilltop. The big windows of the smoke-free main dining room have a **good view of the Gogebic Country Club golf course and hills beyond**. The atmosphere is come-as-you-are comfortable, but the **setting is rather romantic**. The sandwich and salad menu is available any time. Ten sandwiches are under $5 including fries (2000 prices); at $3.25 the 1/3 pounder competes with McDonald's yet in a much nicer setting. Lunch entrées and specials are $5-$6. The most popular dinner items are prime rib ($10-$16), surf & turf ($16), Friday fish fry ($7.25 or less) and ribs on Saturday. *On Country Club Road, which goes south from U.S. 2 on the east edge of Ironwood. Look for highway sign. Restaurant is a mile south of highway. 932-3742. Open year-round. Mon-Thurs 10-10, Fri & Sat 10-midnight, Sun 11-9.* & : yes, except no accessible restrooms in winter. Full bar

IRONWOOD LODGINGS

See also: Hurley, Bessemer, Ramsay, Wakefield

Two B&Bs are opening in the Ironwood area, one in a rural area north of town and one in-town, with a classical music theme. (The innkeeper is Austrian.) Ask about them at the Welcome Center or other visitor info places. Lodgings are arranged from west to east.

COMFORT INN   (906) 932-2224

This newer (1990) motel has a pleasant, medium-size indoor pool and whirlpool. A free deluxe continental breakfast (cereal, waffles, fruit, etc.) is put out in the lobby, along with coffee and tea any time. 63 rooms on 2 floors, with interior halls, include 12 one-room suites with whirlpool tub, microwave, refrigerator, and recliner. Rates vary widely ($50 to $125) with season, weekend, special events, etc. Near Pizza Hut, next to Country Kitchen. Bowling alley across street. Joggers and walkers will find quiet neighborhoods on both sides of the highway. *On U.S. 2 at Bus. U.S. 2/Douglas, 1 mile east of Wisconsin line.* **H.A.**   👫🚶: 18 & under free

SANDPIPER MOTEL   (906) 932-2000
www.westernup.com\sandpiper

The locational advantages of this **well-run family motel** with 25 units aren't immediately evident, but they are considerable. Right next door is Don & GG's, the area's most interesting and reliable restaurant. Two doors down is Trek & Trail outdoors store, with mountain bike, ski, and snowshoe rentals. A laundromat and the Breakwater Cafe are across the highway. Guests are welcome to use the microwave in the office, where coffee is available; a big continental breakfast is provided in ski season. Mini-fridges available upon request. The hot tub room is extremely pleasant; next to it is an **authentic Finnish sauna**, wood-fired, cedar-lined, with stones. Most rooms have two double beds. All have phones and cable TV. Rates are by the room in ski season (in 2000 they were $68 most weekends, $88 Christmas week). Spring through fall rates were $38 for two, $5/extra person. *1200 E. Cloverland/U.S. 2 east of Lake at the east entrance to Ironwood, but west of Kmart.* **H.A.**: call   👫🚶: $5/extra person in off-season   🐕: call

AmericINN MOTEL & SUITES
(906) 932-7200; reserv. (800) 634-3444; www.americinn.com

The AmericInn format (49 rooms at this location) comes off as comfort verging on luxury. Here there's a big lobby with cushy mauve sofas and chairs, the trademark fireplace, and breakfast area with any-time microwave and teas, where a generous continental breakfast is served. The pool room with vaulted ceiling, a whirlpool and adjacent sauna, looks onto grass, not asphalt. Don & GG's, the area's best restaurant, is

across the highway; a laundromat and family restaurant are next door. Snowmobile trail in rear. The rate structure changes with season, weekday/weekend, and occupancy. Sample ahead-of-time rates for a standard double (2 queens) for two, winter weekend, $105; for a July non-holiday weekend $91, weekday $75. Early reservations recommended for ski season weekends. *1117 E. Cloverland/U.S. 2 just east of Lake at the east entrance to Ironwood.* **H.A.**   👫🚶: 12 & under free

RIVER FALLS OUTDOORS
(906) 932-5638

Three guest houses are in a **charming, wooded setting** on the Montreal River at beautiful Peterson Falls. Owner Brian McGuire has the complex for sale. He's also a painter and paperhanger, and he's ready to slow down, but not super-anxious. So it may be run as it is for some time. This description was for 2000. You feel you're hovering over the falls out on the deck of the 4-room A frame that sleeps up to 10. (It rented for $150 a night in summer for 6, $250 in winter.) The bunkhouse and cottage were $75 in summer, $85 in winter. All guest houses have wood stoves, kitchens. Recreational extras include a 4' x 18' swimming pool, outdoor games and outdoor fire pit. Guests can use log cabin lounge and Finnish sauna, sleds for sledding hill, snowshoes. Stairs go down to the river. Intermediate x-c ski trails go 5 miles along river from here. *2 miles northwest of Ironwood. Call for directions. Reserve by May for best summer choices.* **H.A.**: call   👫🚶

IRONWOOD CAMPING

LITTLE GIRL'S POINT COUNTY PARK
(906) 667-0411 (not reservable except by the month or season)

One of the area's **truly tucked-away jewels** is this simple park: a long stretch of sandy beach on Lake Superior and a grassy bluff with a spectacular view above it. The campground, playground, and pavilion are on the bluff. It's a rustic campground (no showers, potable water available only at a central tank) that's just been upgraded with electricity. The 34 sites ($10/day for nonresidents) are used mostly by RVs, with some seasonal campers. They're in a grassy, partly shady area, with no screening between neighbors. Some directly overlook the lake. A caretaker stays on the site. So far the campground and overflow area only fill on the big July 4 weekend, but prospective campers can call ahead to see if it's close to full. The county parks

department is considering whether to add another 30 sites or so across the road. *About 12 minutes northwest of Ironwood via Hemlock/Vanderhagen Rd, which becomes CR 505. From U.S. 2 on the west side of town, turn north onto Hemlock at the corner where Auto Body Glass is. Open May through September.* **H.A.**: call   👫🚶   🐕

Hurley *(pop. 1,780)*

Today Hurley is a pretty placid place with a tourism-based economy and an **unusual number of bars** (including three with strippers, at the bottom of Silver Street). That's the only tip-off to its notorious past, unequaled in all the north woods. "Hurley, Hayward, and Hell," the saying went— though some people wonder if Cumberland shouldn't have been added to the list.

"Throughout the Middle West, wherever lumberjacks and miners congregated, Hurley was known as the hell-hole of the range," stated *Michigan: A Guide to the Wolverine State*, the 1941 W.P.A. guide. "Even Seney, at its worst and liveliest, could not compete with the **sin, suffering, and saloons** that gave Hurley a reputation unrivaled from Detroit to Duluth."

Hurley's rough, crude past was the subject of Edna Ferber's novel *Come and Get It* (1934). It's set during the Prohibition years when nearly 200 saloons, disguised as soda shoppes, lined downtown's streets, and when Chicago gangsters established resorts and gambling rackets in northern Wisconsin mining and lumber towns. Ferber described the fictionalized Hurley as "a sordid enough town. . . , with all the vices and crudeness of the mining camps of an earlier day, but with few of their romantic qualities. Lumber and iron were hard masters to serve. A cold, hard country of timber and ore. . . . A rich and wildly beautiful country, already seared and ravaged. . . . Encircling the town were the hills and ridges that had once been green velvety slopes, tree shaded. Now the rigs and shafts of the iron mines stalked upon them with never a tree or blade of grass to be seen."

A colorful true story from more recent times concerns a judge who ran a strip joint in which the stripper used a boa constrictor in her act. One fateful time she battered a heckling customer with it. Not long after that, the fire department got a call about a fire there, but arrived to find no smoke. Four or so hours later the place burned.

Hurley's colorful past comes to life on

a living history tour of Hurley taverns held during the Iron County Heritage Festival in late July and early August. For times, call (715) 561-5310 or visit www.ironcountywi.com

Iron County (Wisconsin) Historical Museum

Except for a big wine vat and a few other items, Hurley's rough, raw past seems remote and subdued here. Three floors of museum displays fill this splendid 1893 Romanesque Revival courthouse, a real landmark with a tall clock tower. The **courtroom** is a visitor highlight. With so much space, this has definitely become a community attic kind of museum well suited to explorer personalities. As we go to press, volunteers are working on organizing the collections. There's a logging room, a religious room, a mining room about the nearby Montreal Mine, a uniform room, an old back bar, a garment room, a barbershop — and that's just the top floor!

Volunteers disavow first-hand experience with Hurley when it was a wide-open town. "We're just transplants," said one. But it turned out she has been here since 1937 and had babysat for prostitutes' kids as a teen. (They were quite well behaved.) Her husband remembers "how [the prostitutes] used to roll lumberjacks and take all their money after they got them drunk."

The museum is largely supported by sales of rag rugs, a folk craft widespread among thrifty Finns. Iron County has lots of them! Visitors can see rag rugs woven here on four large, handcrafted looms. Rugs can be ordered, specifying color, end stripes, etc., or you can have your own old clothes woven into rugs, achieving a functional memento and exercising maximum artistic control. Pay by the inch: 50¢ for polyester, 55¢ for chenille, denim, and corduroy.

303 Iron at Third Ave. Iron intersects U.S. 2 two blocks south of W-77 on the south side of downtown. (715) 561-2244. Open year-round, from 10 a.m. to 2 p.m. Mon, Wed, Fri & Sat, except for holidays. Donations appreciated. &: call.

Wisconsin Travel Information Center

Wisconsin's state history agency sets up **impressive mini-museums** in state travel centers. In addition to loads of Wisconsin travel information, there's a lot here about mining and minerals, starting with the giant core samples out front and the drilling machine that extracted them. Mineral specimens relate to the area. Photographs illustrate the Cary mine, its drilling crew, tailing piles, the work life (including the respirator) of miner John Raffini, and more. Moreover, the staff here can field visitor questions about mining and minerals! *It's where U.S. 2 meets U.S. 51. (715) 561-5310. Open year-round. From Mem. thru Labor Day open daily 8 a.m. to 6 p.m. Central Time. In May and Sept. open daily 8-4. Otherwise open Tuesday thru Sat 8-4.* &

Iron County Farmers' Market

The **region's biggest farmers' market** — and one of Wisconsin's best — features produce, maple syrup, and crafts, all from the area.

Across from the Wisconsin Travel Information Center on U.S. 51, to your left as you enter Wisconsin on U.S. 2. (715) 561-3158. Depending on the growing season, it opens in mid-July and closes in late October. Market days: Wednesdays from 2 p.m., Saturdays from 10 a.m. &

Little Finland

A homey center of Finnish-American culture, Little Finland is one of those charming, completely unprofessional museums where the people — **exceptionally friendly people** — are the attraction more than any particular artifacts. The Harma House log farmhouse has been moved onto the site and furnished from the donor's memory. Here the tour guide may share the story of how her grandmother arrived at Ellis Island with a bunch of adventurous girlfriends who had all saved up to emigrate, and how she was recruited to be a maid in Wisconsin.

Numerous events are held throughout the year in Little Finland's large hall. Showcases hold photographs of Finnish immigrants and Old Country mementos they brought along. Delicious baked goods are for sale here with plenty of coffee — a continuing attraction for local people. In the basement there's a fine gift shop of Finnish imports: famous contemporary glassware, jewelry, folk-inspired table linens, candles, sauna items, Lapland dolls, striking Pokku hunting knives in many sizes, and woven hangings (often with animal or pine tree motifs) and rugs. There are also recordings of Finnish music, language tapes, and English-language books on Finnish-American subjects.

Special events include Laskaianen, a midwinter festival in February; the March 16 St. Urho's Day, invented in Minnesota to provide a Finnish-American counterpart to what St. Patrick's Day became among Irish-Americans; Mother's Day and Christmas choral concerts; music and a bonfire to celebrate Juhannus (a midsummer dance the Saturday closest to June 21); and an ethnic dinner during Hurley's August Heritage Days.

On U. S. 2, a little west of U.S. 51 just outside Hurley. Open Wednesdays and Saturdays 10 to 2 from April through December. (715) 561-4360. / Donation appreciated. &: main hall. Not gift shop. Log house with assistance.

Northern Great Lakes Visitor Center

If you're traveling in northern Wisconsin to or from the western U.P. on U.S. 2, a stop is in order just west of Ashland at this multifaceted information center. It focuses on the **human history** and the **natural world** of this part of **Lake Superior from Minnesota to Michigan**. The USDA Forest Service, National Park Service, University of Wisconsin extension, and State Historical Society of Wisconsin have teamed up here and use this dramatic building for group presentations, meetings, and school and other classes.

Get out and stretch on the 3/4 mile **interpretive walk** through a cedar and black ash **wetland**. (The staff hopes to have snowshoes to lend in winter.) There's a pet walking area and some picnic tables, too. For a **panoramic view** of Lake Superior, forest, and marsh, climb or take an elevator to the fifth-story indoor-outdoor observation deck (&). To zero in on birds, borrow binoculars at the front desk. **Hawk counts** are held here during spring and fall migration. **Nature programs** are scheduled; to time your visit, call ahead, or search for the upcoming website.

Inside, there's a **regional book and gift shop**, a historical research area for Wisconsin's nine northernmost counties, a touch-screen **interactive trip-planning** setup for the three-state Superior north country (no printouts, unfortunately), and many exhibits. A 10-minute audio-visual program with a **3-D effect** shows **how people have viewed the region over time**. A giant **interactive map** shows **glacial movements** and the **Ojibwa migration story and trade routes**. More interactive displays involve **iron-mine dynamiting**, Native American life in the area, logging, and fish and animal identification. Some live animals are on hand. *On County Hwy. G but visible from U.S. 2 just west of Ashland near where visitors turn north toward the Apostle Islands. (715) 685-9983. Fax 685-2680. Open year-round. Summer 9-7 Central Time. Otherwise 9-5.* ♿

HURLEY RESTAURANTS

THE BRANDING IRON STEAKHOUSE is most often recommended for steaks and BBQ ribs,. It's one of Hurley's **historic bars**, a place where margaritas come straight out of the tap. Customers or staff char-grill the steaks. 214 Silver St. (715) 561-4562. www.hurleywi.com/ *brandingiron. Open year-round except for vacation in April. Open 7 days, 5 p.m. to midnight Central Time.* ♿

Of all Hurley's historic saloons, the place that today draws visitors from far and wide is **FONTECCHIO'S BELL CHALET**, now expanded many, many times into a rambling and very popular Italian eating and drinking place. It scores for its **pizzas and homemade pasta**, its affordable prices, and its friendly, fun atmosphere. The copper-surfaced bar in front is what greets guests — that and garlicky scents of cooking — but this is definitely a place for families as much as for convivial groups of adults up for a ski weekend. The dining room is smoke-free. Lunch entrées are from $5 to $7, dinners are from $7.35 to $14.35 (for homemade linguini with seafood or shrimp). A large pizza with five toppings is $12. Pizzas get shipped all over. Reservations are often a good idea. *On Fifth at Division, a block north of Silver Street. (715) 561-3753. Mon-Thurs 11-2 and 5-midnight. Fri & Sat 5 p.m. to 12:30 a.m. Sun 5-11:30.* ♿

HURLEY-AREA LODGINGS

ANTON-WALSH HOUSE
(715) 561-2065; www.Anton-Walsh.com; fax (715) 561-9977; e-mail: info@Anton-Walsh.com

The exterior of this solid foursquare house from the early 20th century doesn't suggest how attractively it has been renovated and restored inside. The dining room, for instance, has **Craftsman-style wainscoting**, a coffered ceiling, and built-in cupboard. The comfortable parlor is a showcase of local history. Decorator themes have been attractively applied to the three upstairs guest rooms, all with private baths. (One has a screened deck, too.) 2000 rates for two: $89-$95 in ski season, $55-$69 otherwise. Innkeeper Gene Cisewski has returned to the area to pursue his own writing interests after years of working in

Washington, D.C. as a policy advisor on term limits and medical marijuana. His roots go way back and played a role in his winning an election to become the youngest Ironwood city commissioner by far in 1979. Now he's enjoying sharing the area with others. His breakfast specialties feature regional foods and dishes. The well-stocked upstairs guest library has cable TV, a phone, and fridge with soft drinks. There's a big front porch and a peaceful back garden with viney arbor trained on clothesline poles. Air-conditioning IS in the works. Shared phone and TV. *202 Copper St. (parallels Silver St. one block south) in downtown Hurley.* **H.A.**: no 👫👫:not suited to small children. Works out well with older kids and teens when a family takes the whole house.

WHITECAP MOUNTAIN RESORT
(800) 933-7669; (715) 561-2227; www.skiwhitecap.com

This full-service resort, family owned and managed by people who like good food, has done more to build year-round business than other resorts in the area. The summer section of its website isn't just an afterthought. The scenery is beautiful, there's a new 18-hole golf course, and there's an indoor pool — no restaurant in the summer, however. On spring-fed Weber Lake, a no-wake lake, there's swimming and fishing for trout, bass, and panfish. Rowboats, paddleboats, and a pontoon are for rent. Nearby Wisconsin waterfalls are another attraction. The stable offers **trail rides** (ages 8 and up) for $15/hour, basic instruction in western riding, "Horse Talk for Kids," and pony rides for younger children. Trail rides can be planned for all riding levels. Summer rates for condos start at $50/night for two. Lodging choices are varied. Some like the Davos Swiss in have a central gathering place with satellite TV for sports events. (This is too rural for cable TV.) *13 miles west of Ironwood, just north of Upson, Wisconsin.* ♿

Bessemer *(pop. 2,148)*

Bessemer, the Gogebic County seat, is at the midpoint of the Gogebic Iron Range. (Named for the Bessemer process of making steel of pig iron, it's locally pronounced "BEZ-muhr.") The town has some unusually attractive features. The well-built downtown, two blocks long, marches up the hill from the railroad tracks and U.S. 2 stoplight to a high point capped by the handsome, beauti-

A local woodcarving club makes the distinctive Indianhead signs to area attractions. Behind it is Bessemer's handsome high school building.

fully detailed Tudor-style Bessemer City Hall and Community Building. A WPA project from 1934, it includes a library and auditorium in addition to a firehouse and city offices. Display cases document its construction as a Depression-era make-work project and show off decades of trophies from local firefighters and athletic teams. The oriel window in the tower offers a grand view of main street (it's called Moore Street) and its many empty storefronts, with a backdrop of distant blue hills. Take Moore Street north across U.S. 2 at the light, and in two blocks you'll come to a most scenic recreation complex. A red rock cliff looms in the distance behind Massie Field (dubbed "Home of the Speedboys") on Moore Street, and Steiger Field, tucked in a natural bowl just west off Silver Street. Local signs proclaim it as "the **most scenic Little League baseball park in America**," and it just may be.

Residential streets around downtown Bessemer have some fine examples of classic bungalows and other early 20th-century Arts & Crafts architectural styles.

Today Bessemer's major employer is Bessemer Plywood, which uses the U.P.'s plentiful aspen and other trees to produce large quantities of plywood sheets. It's actually just north of the onetime mining village of Yale, on the beautiful Old County Road that connects Ironwood and Wakefield to the south. If you take that drive with children, they can play at the playground outside Bessemer Plywood's main office. (The mine owners must have had a connection with Yale the college, since the name of Yale's main street is Eli, as in Eli Yale the Connecticut merchant whose money gave Yale its start.) Another small firm, the Modern Case Company, makes cases for musical instruments.

Copper Peak Ski Flying Hill

The ski slide is the **highest man-made jump in the world**. It has a 580-foot vertical drop. The hilltop itself, reached by a chair lift, is over 350 feet above the land around it. The scaffolding of the ski slide rises another 280 feet in the air — visitors take an elevator 18 stories up. Brave souls can walk another 80 feet up to the upper platform. It's quite a view from the top: the Porcupines, the Apostle Islands, Minnesota, and maybe even Canada— a distant line below the clouds on the horizon. Needless to say, this excursion is not for those with fear of heights.

Some ski-flying slides are longer, but they are built along the mountainside with the jump at the end. This was built in 1970 for the first international ski-flying tournament in the western hemisphere. Ski-flying involves longer distances and uses different equipment from ski-jumping. The sport is much better known in Europe than in North America.

New concessionaires have added 12 miles of mountain bike trails on site, connecting with trails to Black River Harbor. There's a possibility that bikers will be able to hook their bikes to the chairlift, ride up in the chairlift and enjoy the view, then take any of several trails down on their bikes.

At the parking area, there's a gift shop, restrooms, bike rental facility, and a picnic area.

On CR 513 about 11 miles north of Bessemer. See directions to Black River waterfalls. 932-3500. Open from Mem. Day into early Oct., probably from 9 a.m. to 7 p.m. Not open in rainy weather. Rates for chairlift and elevator to top: around $8 (adults), around $6 (children).

Black River waterfalls & Black River Scenic Byway

Five beautiful and distinctive waterfalls are clustered within the two miles before the river's mouth, part of the **Ottawa National Forest**. They are among the most visited in the western Upper Peninsula. The Black River and

Lake Superior

Black River Recreational Area

Potawatami & Gorge Falls trails

Rainbow Falls
Sandstone Falls
Gorge Falls

(513)

Great Conglomerate Falls

Algonquin Falls

Copper Peak

Chippewa Falls

elev. +1550 feet

Black River

elev. +1380 feet

Black River Rd.

Big Powderhorn Mountain

(513)

Powderhorn Falls

Blackjack Mountain Ski Resort

(2)

Old County Road

Bessemer   Anvil

Yale   Ramsay

Scenic drive on a high ridge

Jessieville
Aurora

Black River

Black River

A scenic road to a Lake Superior beach & harbor passes Copper Peak lookout and 5 unusual waterfalls.

County Road 513 parallel each other for some 15 miles to Lake Superior from U.S. 2 in Bessemer. Passing Copper Peak Ski Flying Hill, CR. 513 winds through a high, rolling countryside of old farms and forests. The painfully bare slopes were lands recently logged by U.S. Steel before selling them. Some hills here are very high. In fact, these are worn-down

mountains, the westward extension of the Porcupine Mountains.

Mixed hardwoods and pines make the national forest land by the waterfalls **outstanding for fall color**. Most of the waterfalls require a substantial walk from a parking area off CR 513 to the waterfall and back again — a distance of 1/2 mile to 1 1/2 miles for each of the four falls. A good way for first-time visitors to experience these falls meaningfully is to plan two outings, separated perhaps by a picnic near the beach at Black River Harbor. It's not hard to overdose on waterfalls; see the introduction for advice on waterfall watching. Don't try to do them all, unless you choose to walk the five-mile trail that's mainly along the river.

Two falls that are both striking and easy to reach are accessed from the shared parking lot near Gorge and Potawatomi falls, about 13 miles from U.S. 2. The National Forest's wheelchair-accessible path leads to a picnic area, chemical toilet, and to the **unusually beautiful POTAWATOMI FALLS**. Seen in August, the falls' beauty relies on pattern and complexity rather than volume, drop, or force. According to Laurie Penrose's subtle description in *A Guide to 199 Michigan Waterfalls*, "The water passed over the rock in small tendrils of white angel hair, which separated and joined in complicated patterns before reaching the base of the gorge. The delicate picture of this falls — nestled in the gorge and surrounded by the deep greens of high summer — is extraordinary."

A quarter mile downstream, the quite dissimilar **GORGE FALLS** can be reached either by a **striking series of platforms and stairs** along the river (this is the more scenic path) or by going back to the parking area and taking the path and stairs to the falls. Neither way takes more than a few minutes. Here the water, constricted in a narrow gorge, has pounded on the stone to create a deep, smooth slide that ends in a mass of foam. The great, rounded stone, unsoftened by vegetation of any kind, is striking testimony to the power of water. This wall of red stone confronts you as you descend to the final platform.

GREAT CONGLOMERATE FALLS is some half a mile upstream from Potawatomi Falls. (It's the southernmost of this waterfall cluster near CR 513.) Here, over an extended stretch of river, water rushes around huge boulders and tears at trunks, felling several trees. It's a **wild, unsettling landscape**. The falls can be reached from a wide, smooth 3/4 mile trail from its own parking area. Or choose to take the west riverbank path from

At the unusual Gorge Falls, the Black River has pounded the conglomerate rock, creating smoothed, rounded surfaces. When visiting these waterfalls, avoid the crowds and dull light of midday. Walk along the river when possible. The North Country Trail follows the river's east bank.

Potawatomi Falls. This trail can be slippery, often steep with roots in the path, and sometimes not well marked. It is a 45-minute trek from Potawatomi Falls to the very beginning of Great Conglomerate Falls and back. First-time visitors might want to postpone this waterfall to a later trip, and save their time and energy to enjoy fewer falls in a more leisurely way.

Another quarter mile along the North Country Trail takes you to **SANDSTONE FALLS**, where the river makes leaps, first of five feet and then, passing between huge conglomerate rocks, dropping 20 feet.

Visiting **RAINBOW FALLS**, the northernmost of the five falls, seems more like a physical challenge than an invitation to pleasure if you look at the 200-step stairway that leads from the parking area just off CR 513. (That's a quarter of a mile down and then back up, all stairs, with no landings for a rest!) Fortunately the east bank offers a much more enjoyable way to reach this beautiful falls, named for the rainbows often seen in its mist. It allows you to conveniently see the nearby Sandstone Falls, too. Oddly, the elaborate national forest sign doesn't mention this route. Here it is: Park at the lot at the very end of CR 513 at Black River Harbor.

Take the swinging footbridge across the river mouth, look for the North Country Trail's triple blue diamonds in about 50 feet, and turn right. Follow the river upstream and up along the river wall on an earthen embankment made by the forest service. This trail reaches a plateau, then goes south past some massive old-growth hemlocks in the mixed old-growth stand on the way to the Rainbow Falls. Here, in early afternoon before the sun sinks too low, the **light effects can be memorable** as light on the mist rising above the pool creates a rainbow. Nearby the river has exposed layered sandstone, alternating gold and rose, for another colorful effect.

CR 513 turns north from U.S. 2 at the car dealership and school in Bessemer. The scenic byway part of CR 513 can also be reached from U.S. 2 by turning north onto Powderhorn Road at the giant skier sign west of Bessemer.

Black River Harbor

Today "the harbor" looks like many another resort of cottages. Early in the 20th century it was a fishing village based on abundant lake trout. Gogebic

County purchased some of the waterfront in 1924, and the village moved inland. Make-work Civilian Conservation Corps projects during the Depression developed the harbor park further. For decades after that, logging activity provided year-round customers for three taverns in the harbor. (One building survives as part of the Bear Track Cabin complex.) A bit of fishing history survives in **THE NET LOFT**, an **interesting antique shop** in the log and stone building on the road's east side, not far from the Bear Track Cabins. It's run by involuntarily retired commercial fisherman Doug Allen. He started trolling in 1938. The state put him out of business in 1968, with hardly any compensation, in its decision that it was in the state's best interest to encourage sport fishing over commercial fishing. "They said I wasn't in the business enough months a year. I practically gave my tug away." It's generally open from June through September from 10-5. 932-3663.

Black River Harbor/ Ottawa National Forest

This popular park and campground at the end of CR 513 (the Black River Scenic Byway) was developed on the site of a fishing village as a 1930s Civilian Conservation Corps project. In fact, the CCC improved the entire road from the vicinity of Copper Peak; it had been merely a wagon trail. By the parking area at the road's end is a marina and a **pleasant, shady picnic area** with a handsome stone and wood changing house and pavilion. A suspension footbridge (&) leads across the river mouth up to a **popular, sandy Lake Superior beach**. Kids love to jiggle and sway on the bridge. Crossing the bridge, turn left to reach the beach. Warmer river water mixes with lake water, so this is **one of the warmer places to swim in Superior**. The granite breakwall, used by walkers and fishermen, is another legacy from the CCC era, built to keep the harbor from silting up.

To get to Rainbow Falls (above), look for the North Country Trail's triple blue diamonds in about 50 feet and turn immediately right.

At the end of CR 513. For directions from U.S. 2, see Black River waterfalls, above. Free admission.

BESSEMER RESTAURANTS

Last-minute tip: **Kinda Kountry Kafé & Krafts** on U.S. 2 in town is recommended by a forester who works nearby and avoids fast food that comes out of the fry basket. Its **soups,** he says, are "really good — a meal in itself." 667-0725.

BESSEMER LODGINGS

Arranged from west to east. The lodgings along Black River Road, from Big Powderhorn to Black River Harbor, come first.

BIG POWDERHORN LODGING ASSN.
(800) 222-3131; www.bpla.com

Nearly 3,000 rooms in the lodge and various forms of condos and chalets (all with kitchens) are rented through the association. This far-flung development is done up in a generally Alpine style. There's a **big indoor pool** in the center. In summer expect a good deal; you should have a lot to choose from, too. The ski resort is about 13 miles to Black River Harbor and a Lake Superior beach with water that's not too cold. The five Black River waterfalls are a little closer. There's **outstanding mountain biking** in this area. *Two miles north of U.S. 2 between Bessemer and Ironwood. Turn by the figure of the giant skier.* : call

BLACK RIVER LODGE
(906) 932-3857; www: in the works

This informal, small lodge, aimed at families and groups, has a contemporary, rustic feel, and a friendly, casual atmosphere. It's in a **pretty, undeveloped rural setting**, just a few miles from the Black River waterfalls, Big Powderhorn ski area, and Copper Peak Ski-Flying Hill. Geared to skiing, in summer it's a **real bargain** and an **outstanding family vacation headquarters**. New owners Merwin and Jackye Hudson moved from the Twin Cities, but Jackye grew up in Ironwood.

There's a **big lobby with fireplace** and seating, morning coffee. Other common areas include a deck, an **indoor pool** (54' x 22') with a small sitting area, whirlpool, and **hot tub**; and a **70' lounge** with books and magazines, and tables for games. The **game room** has video games, pool, foosball, darts, and a juke box. The seasonal dining room offers **family dining** with a full menu, weekends in summer, more frequently in ski season. Outside are picnic tables, volleyball, a playground, occasional bonfires, plus trails for hiking, cross-country skiing, and mountain biking.

The 20 lodge units vary greatly in size. Off-season rates (from the end of ski season to Christmas) in 2000 were $35 (for a double) and $45 (for the two-room suite sleeping six). The same rooms in ski season were $87 and $98. No phones, anywhere, except for a pay phone in the lobby. A few units are air-conditioned. Seven units sleep 10, have kitchens, and rent for $190/night in ski season, $90/night otherwise. Of these, four are attached to the lodge; three are townhouses with fireplaces in a separate building. Substantially reduced rates for multiple nights. *On Black River Rd./CR 513, 8 miles from U.S. 2. Turn north at the sign of the big skier, by Powderhorn Rd. east of Bessemer.*

H.A.: two units. Reserve early. Rates are by the room. : call : no extra charge.

BEAR TRACK CABINS
(906) 932-2144

The original Bear Track Inn (now a year-round home) is a log cabin built as a tavern in the 1930s for loggers from lumber camps and mills still operating in the nearby woods. The setting, among pines and hemlocks, has a **real presence**. **Sandstone Falls** is across the road; Rainbow, Potawatomi, and Gorge falls are within half a mile. Over the years **three pleasant housekeeping cabins** (two sleep 4, one sleeps 6) have been built behind the old inn. Behind the cabins **trails** go back through the **dramatically dark hemlock forest** and connect with an extensive network of cross-country ski and mountain bike trails on old logging roads on national forest land. The cabins are furnished in casual, appropriately woodsy style, with lots of interesting touches, including handsome wood-burning stoves. Each has a grill and picnic table. A **Finnish wood sauna** is in a separate building. Innkeeper Norm Bishop **rents snowshoes** (and gets mountain bikes from Trek and Trail). He offers guide service for back-country skiing. Rates for two in 2000: $53 and $60 in summer, $65 in winter. The 7-person cabin rents for $130-$145/night. Call in August or earlier for good winter weekend availability. Summer use is more one-nighters, and better availability. *Near the end of CR 513, 1 mile from Lake Superior.* **H.A.**: call : $13/extra person over 3 years : call

EVERGREEN MOTEL (906) 663-4340

At this **delightfully homey** 1950s motel, faced with perfectly-arranged egg-shaped fieldstones, Art and Mary Ann Voss have individually decorated every room with interesting prints, vintage radios, rustic collectibles, and added thoughtful extras like refrigerators, coffeepots, well-chosen travel info, fans, cable TV with loads of satellite channels. Rooms can interconnect for families. $30 and $40 in ski season, $25 and $30 otherwise. (No air-conditioning here. Guests can use phone in office. *On U.S. 2, two miles east of Bessemer and 2 miles west of Wakefield.* **H.A.**: call.

TRAVELER'S MOTEL
(906) 667-0243

Among modest, older ma-and-pa motels this well-maintained 12-unit motel on the east edge of Bessemer stands out for lots of little reasons. Owners Donna and Mike Maslanka have steadily remodeled rooms with contemporary furniture and a bright, **cheerfully woodsy look**, often with knotty-pine walls. All rooms have mini-fridges, phones, and 67-channel cable TV. Bed configurations vary; ask about family rooms. 2000 rates for two were $32 in summer, $42 in winter, sometimes $55 on prime ski weekends. Picture windows look out to ranges of hills; the motel is set back from the highway, with picnic tables on the lawn. The side street connects with neighborhood streets, good for walking or jogging. Just east down U.S. 41 is a picturesque roadside park with wildflowers — a place where the hills really do seem to sing. It's called "Memory Lane," and there's a good view from the ridgetop (no real trails). **H.A.**: call : $5/extra person.

HEDGE ROW LODGING
(906) 663-6950; (800) 421-4995

This cluster of nine A frames combines the self-sufficiency of housekeeping cottages (rented by the night or week) with a central highway location on U.S. 2 between Bessemer and Wakefield. New owners have cleaned and repainted the chalets, but on my visit in summer 2000, little in the way of furniture or carpeting had been replaced. This is a meadow setting — no shade trees, and no outdoor furniture on my visit, either. But there's lots of **summer wildflowers**, big sky, and **beautiful vistas of ranges of hills**. The typical floor plan sleeps 6. It consists of a living/dining area with a kitchen on the back wall, then the bath, a back bedroom with a double bed, and a loft with a double and two single beds. Daily rates in 2000 (for two people): $45 in spring, summer, and fall. Winter rates (for four): $80 weekdays, $120 weekends. Ask about the 10-person chalet. Cable TV with 67 channels. Air-conditioned. No phones. No no-smoking chalets. Smoke, though detectable, wasn't a big problem on my visit. *On the north side of U.S. 2 between Bessemer and Wakefield.* **H.A.**: call. No hardened paths. : up to 2 children free;

$5/extra child

BESSEMER AREA CAMPING

BLACK RIVER HARBOR CAMP-GROUND/ Ottawa National Forest (906) 667-0261; reserv. 1-877-444-6777

At this exceptionally picturesque rustic campground on a bluff overlooking Lake Superior, 40 large sites have lots of privacy in a mixed hardwood-conifer forest. Summer campground host. On the North Country Trail, with network of side trails. Near boat ramp. A **sandy beach** is by the marina, across the swinging bridge to Rainbow Falls. Playground, concession. Flush toilets, but no showers or electricity. Make reservations for July & August to avoid disappointment. *At end of CR 513. $10/night for 2 adults, $5/extra adult. Open late May thru Oct 15, weather depending.* &

ALPINE TRAILER PARK CAMPGROUND
(906) 667-0737

This 48-site private campground on U.S. 2 has an **unusually scenic location**. Attentive hosts offer minigolf and fishing in a little pond. There's a playground. Hot showers. Cable TV hookups. Some sites are wooded. 16 tent sites ($14) are at the back overlooking the Black River. Most sites are about $18/night including hookups. *On the north side of U.S. 2, 2 miles west of Wakefield and 2 miles east of Bessemer. Open year-round. Water is turned off in winter, available at the service building.*

Ramsay

Originally a lumbering village, Ramsay was later redeveloped as a company town by the Eureka-Asteroid Mining Company. It built "white-painted, individualized houses" that were unique in the area. Today the town is predominantly a retirement community. One of the last remaining institutions, the Catholic church, closed in 1996. There remains a **tavern**, a post office, and the township hall. A **quaint old corner restaurant** on the main street has been reopened and spiffed up to good effect as **Ore House Pub & Pizza** (663-6331).

Keystone Bridge & Bessemer Township Memorial Park

There's a **pleasant little park with picnic area and beach** along the Black River as it runs through the village of Ramsay. It's a short walk just a hundred yards north to an unusual and picturesque keystone bridge, illuminated at night. The Chicago & Northwestern Railway built the bridge in 1891 for its branch line from the iron mines to the railroad's main line across the U.P. The bridge, built of carefully cut limestone, was constructed without mortar and locked in place by the keystone at the top of the arch. This is a very pretty place, but don't expect too much in the way of maintenance.

Ramsay can be reached from U.S. 2 by turning south east of Bessemer, at the intersection where the giant skier beckons north toward Big Powderhorn Resort. Or, for a scenic little backroads adventure, take Old U.S. 2 from Ayer Street in Ironwood. (See box this page.) *Park is on Old U.S. 2 on the river's west bank.*

The ANVIL HOUSE Bed & Breakfast
(906) 667-0788

The surroundings of this homestay B&B are beautiful and surprising, as seen from the road along on the high ridge through the Anvil Location on the old road between Ramsay and Yale. **Wildflowers and unfolding vistas** made for a Sound of Music experience. This **classic Craftsman bungalow** was built in 1918 for the superintendent of the Anvil-Keweenaw mine. It's not a fancy place; blocks of city neighborhoods were

For a scenic back road from Ironwood to Ramsay & Wakefield—

go east out Ayer, past the elaborate Spanish Baroque high school from 1925. Ayer turns into **Old U.S. 2**, once the main highway connecting the mining locations up the hill south of it. Now it's more like a country lane in a valley. Old U.S. 2 is beautiful in fall, with arching branches of color overhead, then opening onto a vista as it goes into Yale. For another beautiful view, turn south at the Jessieville location, two miles east of downtown Ironwood, and head up toward the water tower with the smiley face. This is near the **Newport Mine** (1874), first mine on the Gogebic Range, where Harvard geologist Raphael Pumpelly discovered iron. He named it after his Rhode Island home town in 1911, before Minnesota's Mesabi Range was fully developed, the Newport Mine was hailed as the world's deepest and most productive iron mine. To continue east, motorists will need to drive back to Old U.S. 2.

developed with houses like this. But it's pleasant, and in a quiet country setting. Candace Snyder has recently renovated the house with careful attention to historic details. Two first-floor guest rooms ($65 for two in 2000), furnished in **period antiques**, share a bath. Guests share use of the living room with fireplace; the dining room; the small, book-filled library where Candace has her upright piano; and the screened front porch with swing. Cable TV. A **hot tub** is part of the rear deck. The house sits on a large hilltop lot, so the yard is **quite private**, and **sunsets are spectacular**, especially in winter. "I am very proud of the area and have all kinds of useful information that will make your visit as enjoyable as possible," says Candace, who skis, snowshoes, and quilts. *15 minutes from three ski hills. N10330 Baraga Road, off Summit Drive just east of Anvil Road.* **H.A.**: call. 2 steps up to rear deck.

Wakefield (pop. 2,100)

Wakefield is the easternmost mining town of the Gogebic Range and the closest town to the west side of the Porcupine Mountains State Park. It spreads out south and east of Sunday Lake along M-28 and U.S. 2. Looking west across the lake from M-28 at sunset is a most **memorable sight**, especially when low clouds are backlit and the orange and purple sky is reflected in the lake, with the silhouettes of high hills unfolding in the distance. Indianhead ski resort takes advantage of these slopes.

Wakefield's population is declining, having been hit doubly hard recently with the closing of both the White Pine Mine as well as Connors, the biggest local private employer, which logged hard maples and ran a sawmill here. Smaller companies that log and haul timber are the largest remaining employers. Increasingly the base for the local economy is tourism, with many ski resorts and cottages in the vicinity.

The Eddy Park campground and beach on Sunday Lake's north shore offers modern camping in a shady spot, with swimming, and a playground. More swimming is at the park on the south shore, right where M-28 joins U.S. 2 by the state police post. Here too are a local information center and the huge head of an Indian brave, carved from a tree trunk by Peter Toth. His life work was to install one such figure in every state as a memorial to North America's first residents. The Gogebic Chiefs Ice Hockey Arena, a 1939 WPA project that used rough local stone in a 1930s moderne design, is also on the lakeshore on M-28.

WAKEFIELD RESTAURANTS

The **KORNER KITCHEN** is a homey spot with a cottagey-country atmosphere. It's famous for its **big hot beef sandwiches** ($6.20 with real mashed potatoes and salad or slaw). The full menu, which includes breakfast, ranges from spaghetti and burgers to roast beef, roast pork, and fried chicken, done from scratch right here. **Homemade cream pies** ($2) are a specialty. Consider takeout for a satisfying picnic. The Friday special is fried or baked haddock ($6.25) with potato and slaw. Limited no-smoking section; expect some smoke. *1207 East U.S. 2, about a mile east of downtown and the M-28/U.S. 2 intersection. 229-5311. Open 6 a.m.-6 p.m. daily, except closes at 2 p.m. Tues, stays open to 8 p.m. Fri & Sat. No credit cards; out-of-town checks OK.* &: requires assistance.

A storefront grocery in downtown Wakefield has been imaginatively transformed into the smoke-free **UPTOWN FOOD & DELI**. A few shelves have groceries for sale, artfully arranged with an eye for classic packaging. The six tables are quite a **popular gathering spot** for young and old: work crews, teens, women at lunch. The food is standard deli fare: subs served with complimentary chips and salsa, soups, taco salad ($4.25), chef salad ($3.50), hot dogs, and wraps. *Salads, meats, and some fruits are in the deli case. 501 Sunday Lake St. (south of the M-28/U.S. 2 intersection) in downtown Wakefield. 224-7421. Mon-Fri 9-4, Sat 9-2.* &: no. 3 steps.

WAKEFIELD LODGINGS

Expect higher rates for the weeks around Christmas, New Year's, and Presidents' Day.

REGAL COUNTRY INN & TREATS ICE CREAM PARLOR (906) 229-5122; www.westernup.com/regalinn

This unusual 18-room motel offers a bed-and-breakfast atmosphere **intended for adults**. There's a large central fireside room for evening relaxing, free continental breakfast with fresh cinnamon rolls, and a sauna. Ice cream parlor/sandwich shop is open year-round; hours vary with the season. Consult the extensive website for special packages, extra options like afternoon or evening tea, evening meals, **gourmet breakfast** served in historical theme rooms. **Enforced 10 p.m. quiet hours**. Rates quoted are cash or check; credit cards are $5 extra. All rooms have cable TV,

air-conditioning. No phones; guests can use front desk's. Basic motel rooms with a country look are $44 for two in summer, $60 in ski season. Victorian rooms with some antiques are $55-$59 in summer. $70-$75 in ski season. Historical theme rooms are $64-$69 in summer, $80-$85 in ski season. *602 East U.S. 2, a mile east of downtown and M-28 intersection.* **H.A.**: call.

INDIANHEAD MOUNTAIN SKI RESORT & CONFERENCE CENTER (906) 229-5181; www.indianheadmtn.com

An **unusually attractive setting** and facility makes this ski resort complex stand out. It's **built on top of a mountain**, so the massive ski lifts are less visible. See ski section for details on skiing. The 46-room main lodge, in an uncloying, vaguely Alpine style, is decorated in dark green and pine wood with Indian motifs. Some rooms have bunks; all have VCRs. The lodge is planned to separate noisy younger skiers from adults. In summer Indianhead offers lots of extras for family vacations at very attractive rates. Call for rates on lodge rooms and condos. In summer they start at $65 for lodge rooms, and $108 for a one-bedroom condo. The resort was closed for 18 months; new owners are tackling deferred maintenance.

The main lodge has an appealing bar/restaurant, an **extremely pleasant indoor pool**, **good game room**, exercise room sauna and whirlpool. In addition, there are **inviting outdoor terraces**, an outdoor pool, **nine holes of golf**, and **two tennis courts**. It's 17 miles to the waterfalls at the Presque Isle River mouth in the Porcupine Mountains State Park.

500 Indianhead Rd. north of U.S. 2 and west of Wakefield. **HA**: one room. Call on condos.

BINGO'S MOTEL (906) 229-5593

A real piece of **roadside Americana**, Bingo's is part of a complex that includes a wonderful vintage bar and a dance hall (now only used on special occasions) plus a gas station and garage. The garage and dance hall are now closed, but the 9 motel rooms ($30 for one bed, $40 for two in winter, 2001) and 10 one- and two-bedroom **kitchenette units** ($60) are a real find, nicely appointed and coordinated, with fresher decor and newer furniture than the vintage exterior suggests. Rooms have TVs, but cable doesn't come out here. Some units have air-conditioners. No phones — but calling cards can use the bar's phone. The bar is in a completely separate building, with a separate parking

lot, so noise won't be a problem. In summer Bingo's isn't as full as more expensive lodgings in Silver City. It's just about 13 miles, from the waterfalls at the beautiful "back door" of the Porcupine Mountains State Park along the Presque Isle River. Snowmobile season and hunting season are the busy times here. Owners Eugene "Bingo" Vittone and his wife, Charlotte, have the 97-acre property for sale. After 50 years, "It's time for a rest," Bingo says. But he won't break the property up, and he hasn't set a price. *On M-28, two miles east of Wakefield and about half a mile east of CR 519 that goes to the Presque Isle River waterfalls and Lake Superior.* **H.A.**: call 🚶🏃: $5/ child, $10/adult

WAKEFIELD CAMPING

EDDY PARK CAMPGROUND (906) 229-5131 for info & reserv.

The 94-site campground adjoining a Wakefield city park has some real plusses (hot showers, for one; a nearby boat launch, for another). It might serve as a good alternative to the rustic state park campground at the Presque Isle River mouth at Lake Superior, about 20 miles away via CR 519. The campground is next to a **pleasant, sandy swimming beach** on **Sunday Lake**, appreciated because it's reliably warm enough for swimming when Superior is too cold. A man from outside Houghton enjoys camping here because it's a quiet campground, "the kids are always going to catch something" and the water quality is good, "refreshing and not hot even on a warm day." Don't be put off by the harmless yellow color, caused by tannin from hemlock roots.

The campground caters to RVs. The main drive with 79 RV sites is on a peninsula, beneath shady maples. Sites have electricity and water. Many are taken by weekly ($60) and monthly ($200) campers, but space for overnight campers ($12/night) is usually available except on July 4 weekend and the biannual boat race. About 15 tent sites ($6) are in an open area along the entrance drive. *Off CR 519 on the north side of Sunday Lake. Open from Mem. Day thru bear season (early Oct.).* **H.A.**: showers, sites, paved walks through campground and park. 🚶🏃: no extra charge for extra people 🐕

Marenisco (pop. 300)

This village is on M-64 two miles south of U.S. 2 as it heading south toward Presque Isle and Manitowish, Wisconsin.

It's a small place, with a school, post office, grocery, and popular little restaurant. Most people drive west to the Ironwood area to work. Until early 1997 a substantial local employer, Norco Windows, was right in Marenisco, but new owners bought the company and consolidated its Marenisco operations with another plant.

On four of the many fishing lakes south of Marenisco are **four small (11-13 sites) rustic campgrounds** of the **Ottawa National Forest**: Bobcat Lake (with swimming), Henry Lake, Moosehead Lake, and Pomeroy Lake. For information about recreational opportunities in the national forest in this area, call (906) 667-0261.

Eight miles northeast of town is the south end of **Lake Gogebic**, the **Upper Peninsula's largest lake**, 12,800 acres and 12 miles long. A walleye planting in 1904 replaced one of the Midwest's finest bass fisheries with a walleye fishery that produces lots of small fish. Small resorts with lawns line most of the lake, which seldom has the wilderness feel that might be expected in this remote location.

Yondota Falls

This easily reached yet **secluded spot** on the Upper Presque Isle River is an unsung treasure for people who like their waterfall experiences unencumbered by signs, railings, and crowds. A local waterfall fan enjoys it more than the famous falls at the Porcupine Mountains' west end. About 15 miles east of Wakefield, it's not far from U.S. 2, so it makes a nice stop for Michigan vacationers starting the long drive back from the Porcupine Mountains.

A short, easy trail leads along the river through a deep woods to the top of the falls. It's about a five-minute walk. The river, already some 30 feet wide, constricts with a gush into a narrow gorge it has carved out of dark, pink-tinged rock. Then it spreads out to flow in three sections around boulders that are large, dry, and low enough that you can walk across them. For more of an outing, you can follow the trail along the river's east bank. It leads upstream some three miles to the

northern edge of Marenisco.
From U.S. 2/M-64 on the west bank of the Presque Isle River near Marenisco, take CR 523 north. In about 3 miles a bridge crosses the river. Drive over it and look to your left for a parking pullover where the trail leads downstream. ; : no.

MARENISCO RESTAURANT

FAIRFIELD'S FAMILY RESTAURANT serves up good food and ice cream and malts, too. It's the place for **big breakfasts** (homemade biscuits and gravy, smoked pork chops with potatoes and eggs) and $6 daily specials like home-**made gnocchi and meatballs**, or b**eef stew on biscuits**. Soups and chili are good, and so are the burgers. Chef, taco, and caesar salads are other options. The popular Friday night fish fry ($6-$7.25) offers a choice of pollack, walleye, perch, or butterfly shrimp with potato salad or potato pancakes. Windows look out on the wooded setting. The township park is across the street if you want to take out and enjoy the outdoors. *On M-64 in "downtown" Marenisco, a mile south of U.S. 2. 787-2220. Closed Mon. Open Tues-Fri 7 a.m. to 7 p.m., Sat & Sun 7 a.m. to 2 p.m.*

MARENISCO AREA CAMPING

LAKE GOGEBIC COUNTY PARK
(906) 667-0411

A 54-site campground, used mainly by RVs, is part of the 80-acre county park at the southern inlet to Lake Gogebic, on Ice House Bay. Most campsites ($10/day) are served by electricity and water, and visually open to neighbors. Many campers are monthly or seasonal, but so far it only fills on the July 4 weekend. There's a small tent area. No showers here, but campers are permitted to use showers at Lake Gogebic State Park, 6 miles away. *From the west, two miles east of the Marenisco turnoff, take M-64 northeast, watch for signs in 5 miles; turn onto East Shore Dr. From the east, about 19 miles west of Watersmeet, turn right (northwest) onto C.R. 525. Look for park signs as you near the lake.*

H.A.: *call*

LAKE GOGEBIC STATE PARK
(906) 842-3341; reserv.
Reservations: (800) 44-PARKS; (800) 605-8295 TDD; www.dnr.state.mi.us/

Walleye fishing is the big attraction for campers at this modern campground on Lake Gogebic, Michigan's **sixth-largest inland lake**. (Walleye eggs from here are used to stock other lakes. Walleye are small but plentiful; it's easy to catch the limit. Long ago Lake Gogebic was an outstanding yellow perch fishery before management programs meddled with nature and greatly reduced the number of perch.

Because the lake is fairly shallow, it **warms up early for swimming at the sandy beach area**. There's a large playground and picnic pavilion by the beach, with the boat launch south of that. M-64 runs close to Lake Gogebic's west shore, and the camping loops are wedged between the highway and lake shore. The park includes nearly a mile of shoreline; most of the lake is lined by cottages. Almost a fourth of the 127 campsites are right on the lake; none are very far from it. The campground is grassy, not wild, but generally shady. Current use patterns show the park filling on holiday weekends and occasionally during the first two weeks of August. A **three-mile trail** crosses the road to go back into the park's interior. It's a good place to see spring wildflowers and deer any time. *The park is on M-64, 8 miles south of M-28 at Merriweather or 10 miles north of U.S. 2 near Marenisco. State park sticker required: $4/$5 day, $20/$25 year. Camping $11/$14 night.* **H.A.**: showers, toilet, boat launch ADA accessible.

MERRIWEATHER AREA CAMPING

See **LAKE GOGEBIC STATE PARK** under Marenisco area camping.

Keep in mind that all prices and hours of operation are subject to change. Lodging rates vary with supply and demand and are usually higher for special events.

Watersmeet area

WATERSMEET LIES at the northern edge of the vast Wisconsin lake country. This area's economy has long been dominated by **fishing resorts** and **outdoor recreation**, as well as by forest products. The **Sylvania Tract**, 30 square miles of old-growth timber, was saved from logging in the 1890s and used as a fishing camp for iron magnates. Today all but its northern edge is managed by the Ottawa National Forest as the **Sylvania Wilderness Area**, a **motor - and machine-free wilderness area**. Most of the land in this area and much of Gogebic, Iron, and Ontonagon counties is part of the Ottawa National Forest. The area's **many national forest campgrounds** appeal to families, fishermen, and canoeists and kayakers of all levels. Adjacent to Sylvania, the **Cisco chain of 15 lakes**, largely under private ownership, is geared more to motorboats. Many small resorts and cottages are on its 270 miles of lakeshore.

The biggest news in recent years is the **Lac Vieux Desert Casino and Resort** north of Watersmeet, opened in 1996. The complex includes a 76-room AmericInn hotel and an 18-hole golf course, and it offers **headline entertainers**. The Lac Vieux Desert Band of Ojibwa takes its name from the productive lake on whose shore they have long lived and fished. (It's pronounced "LAHK view duh SURT.") After the treaty of 1854, some of the people from here pooled their winter hunting money, bought back some of their ceded lands here, and moved back from the reservation at L'Anse.

Thanks to the casino, Watersmeet now has amenity-loaded accommodations beyond small, personal mom-and-pop resorts that have been the area's mainstay. Still, the Watersmeet area seems **wonderfully undiscovered** compared with the go-kart tracks and tourist shops just 30 miles south at Eagle River, Wisconsin. Land O' Lakes, just across the border in Wisconsin, is much more developed and gentrified. Inside Michigan, there's a remoteness and wild beauty even along U.S. 2.

The name Watersmeet comes from the area's Ojibwa name. It refers to the fact, extremely important to Indians, that the waters of this rolling highlands drain in three directions: north into Lake Superior, south into Lake Michigan, and southwest into the Gulf of Mexico. The **Ontonagon River's Middle Branch** offers some beautiful **canoeing** (including some exciting whitewater) and two popular waterfalls as it flows north through undeveloped, often rugged forests to Victoria Dam, and then through farm country into Lake Superior. The mighty **Wisconsin River** begins in nearby Lac Vieux Desert and can be seen as a creek in a pretty little park just south of Land O'Lakes on U.S. 45. Downstream, the Wisconsin River shapes the Wisconsin Dells and provides electrical power for much of Wisconsin before joining the Mississippi at Prairie du Chien. The Brule River, born at Brule Lake 25 miles southeast of Watersmeet, forms part of the state line as it flows into the Menominee River and Lake Michigan.

TO FIND OUT MORE: The **WATERSMEET CHAMBER of**

Sylvania's old-growth forests and clear lakes, plus waterfalls and excellent canoeing and fishing

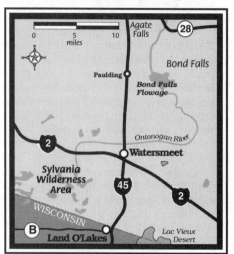

COMMERCE has a part-time secretary but no drop-in office. When you call (800) 522-5657, the Western U.P. Convention & Visitors Bureau sends visitor info for Watersmeet and contacts the Watersmeet Chamber so it can respond to inquiries. Visit the chamber website, **www.watersmeet.org** . . . The **Land O' Lakes Welcome Center** is in the conspicuous new log building on U. S. 45 at County Road B. It's run by the **LAND O' LAKES CHAMBER of COMMERCE** but also gives out information about the U.P. It's open year-round. From May thru Sept open Mon-Sat 9-4 Central Time, Sun 10-2. Otherwise open from 10-2 weekdays except Wednesday. Call (800) 236-3432 or (715) 547-3432. Fax (715) 547-8010. e-mail lolinfo@nnex.net **www.ci.land-o-lakes.wi.us**

PUBLIC LAND: Not just Sylvania but many other lakes in the area are included in this part of the **OTTAWA NATIONAL FOREST. www.fs.fed.us/ r9/ottawa/** (Currently a clearer map is on www.sylvaniaoutfitters.com). . . . Providing visitor information is the chief function of the national forest's **Ottawa Visitor Center** overlooking the southeast corner of U.S. 2 and U.S. 45 outside Watersmeet. Entrance roads are from both highways. It's open year-round, daily 9-5 Central Time from mid-May through mid-October. From Oct. 15 to May 15 open Wed-Sat from 9 to 5 Central Time. (906) 358-4724. . . . . On weekdays when the Visitor Center is closed, you can call or stop by the national forest **Watersmeet Ranger District office** on Old U.S. 2 East, just east of U.S. 45 in Watersmeet. Turn at the basketball court and gas station. This is the place for info on backcountry campsites outside the wilderness area. It's open from 8 to 4 Central Time. (906) 358-4551. TTY: (906) 358-4551. . . . The very eastern part of Vilas County, east of Land O' Lakes in Wisconsin, is part of the **CHEQUAMEGON-NICOLET NATIONAL FOREST.** Visit its informative website, **www.fs.fed.us/ r9/cnnf/** Phone (715) 479-1308. TTY (715) 479-2827.

GUIDED FISHING TRIPS and CANOE TRIPS: Compared with other parts of the U.P. Watersmeet has a host of guides for fishing and hunting. **Sylvania Outfitters** is a good referral source for all guides active in the area. **Fishing guides** include Tom Schwanke's **Wilderness Bay Guide Service** (906-358-9956; 906-358-4319; walleye a specialty), **Bruce Becker** (715-547-3100 or 906-358-9880), and **Al Knutson Guide Service** (906-544-2222). . . . Since 1983 **Rohr's Wilderness Tours** offers **guided canoe trips**, car spotting, outfitting, and cross-country ski and hiking events in the area, including the Ontonagon River and various headwaters of the Wisconsin River. They also offer **canoeing instruction** and certification at all levels. (715) 547-3639 or (815) 895-7635 (winter phone). www.RWTCanoe.com

EVENTS: Watersmeet and Land O' Lakes both have **fireworks** and **parades** over the **July 4** weekend. . . . . In Land O' Lakes, the fourth weekend in July brings the big Art Impressions **art and crafts show**; the fourth weekend in September celebrates fall with the **Top of Wisconsin Fest**; downtown merchants dress up for **A Dickens Christmas** and "A Christmas Carol" is performed; and on January's last weekend, local people build impressive **snow sculptures**. . . . Summer **evening programs** on natural history are held at the **Ottawa Visitor Center**.

PICNIC PROVISIONS and PLACES:

◆ In **WATERSMEET**, the **Clark Lake picnic area** (see text) at the edge of the Sylvania Wilderness Area provides drive-up access to a motor-free lake with swimming and hiking trails. Watersmeet's grocery, Nordine's, is more of a convenience and party store. Local people shop at Greg's in Land O'Lakes or in Eagle River (below) . . . Handy to U.S. 2 is the **Imp Lake picnic area** 6 miles southeast of Watersmeet with an interesting inter-

pretive trail.

◆ The **Bond Falls picnic area** is outside **PAULDING**.

◆ In **LAND O' LAKES**, the high-caliber community supermarket is **Greg's Foods** on the main street, County Road B. An interesting, readily accessible picnic spot is the **wayside park** by the **Wisconsin River's headwaters** on U.S. 45 just south of town.

◆ If you're coming from the east on U.S. 2, a stop at the fabulous **Angeli's Central Market** in **IRON RIVER** is in order. It's very large, contrary to what the old-timey name suggests. . . . Coming from the south, **EAGLE RIVER**, Wisconsin has two excellent big supermarkets, **Trig's** on Hwy. 70 East and **Bonson's Pick & Save** on U.S. 45

Bruce Crossing

See "The Porcupine Mountains & Ontonagon" chapter for **Agate Falls**, the Bergland-to-Sidnaw Trail, and **Gramma Grooter's Restaurant** in the Bruce Crossing area.

Paulding (pop. under 100)

This tiny place, surrounded by Ottawa National Forest land today, was once a **busy sawmill town** surrounded by logging activity. It still has a general store, a tavern, and a few other businesses and houses. Fishing and hunting are major pursuits today.

Bond Falls

The Penrose family's *A Guide to 199 Michigan Waterfalls* calls Bond Falls "breathtaking. . . . **one of the most spectacular [waterfalls] in the Upper Peninsula**." Seldom do the Penroses elevate one waterfall above others; they like them in different ways. Bond Falls is a rare exception.

Actually the much-visited waterfall on the Ontonagon River's Middle Branch is in two parts. The less spectacular first drop is over flat layers of dark rock, a little below the Upper Peninsula Power Company dam that creates the **Bond Falls Flowage**. Stepping stones lead across the river above the falls, and trails go down to the falls along both sides of the river, creating a **half-mile loop**. (Footing on the east bank trail can be difficult.)

The main trail leads down from the road along the river's west bank into woods of cedars and other conifers. The river then curves east and disappears, to be contained in a concrete channel that minimizes erosion and, some local peo-

ple point out, effectively spreads out the water for dramatic effect, making this an artifically enhanced waterfall. The concrete terminates in a viewing platform that permits a close-up view of the main falls. The river drops almost 50 feet in a wide series of stair-like boulders that make complicated, curvy spray patterns in many places. It creates a wide pool and then divides, forming an island. A bridge lets you cross onto the island, which provides a grand photo opportunity for capturing the falls' complex panorama against the sky, as if the photographer were standing in the river.

Another bridge leads to the steeper **east bank trail**. A **picnic area** and refreshment stand cater to Bond Falls' many summer and fall visitors.

In *50 Michigan Rivers*, fishing authority Tom Huggler says the five-mile stretch north from Bond Falls to Agate Falls is an excellent spot to fly-fish for **brook trout**. It's "shallow, fast water that stays cold, . . . with some deep pools and substrate of mostly cobble and

gravel." For **Agate Falls**, look under Bruce Crossing in "The Porcupine Mountains & Ontonagon Chapter."

From U.S. 45 in Paulding, go east on Bond Falls Road a little over 3 miles and park in the parking area. 1/4 mile walk north to falls.

"Paulding Mystery Light"

"While in Watersmeet, you should see 'The Mystery Light,'" advises a chamber of commerce brochure. "By tramping through dense woods to the summit of nearby hills, the mysterious light can be observed almost every night once darkness has descended on the northern wilderness. It appears to rise slowly out of the forest and then **hovers low in the sky** for varying intervals. . . . Some say it's the spirit of a long-dead mail carrier ambushed on the way to Green Bay over a century ago. . . . One woman thinks it's a mystical sign of religious significance." Another ghostly explanation is that an early railroad worker died on the tracks and returns to warn others with his lantern. Some fans of **paranormal experiences** make the trip up here to check it out, and it's definitely a **favorite teen party spot**.

One of the jokers who spread the buzz early in the 1970s has a simpler explanation. When US. 45 was rerouted, it meant that distant car headlights which used to be seen ahead on the road across the valley at Paulding are now viewed from this woods. The disorientation in getting off the road into this remote-seeming setting creates the stage for the mystery of an everyday phenomenon. But older people in the area say the phenomenon occurred before cars were so prevalent and lights so bright.

Still, Paulding's a place where telling tall tales is a favorite tavern pastime. Here are the directions, if you want to

45

Bond Falls—*dazzling 50-foot drops amid great scenery make this one of the UP's top waterfalls to visit.*

Ontonogan River

Paulding

BONDS FALLS ROAD

Watersmeet 7 mi.

Bond Falls Flowage

Engineering artifice enhanced Bond Falls and helped it become one of Michigan's most-photographed waterfalls. Decades ago a concrete channel upstream from the falls was constructed by engineers for the power company that owns the falls and impoundment behind it. The concrete channel reduced erosion — and also artfully directed the water so it spreads out across many boulders, making many leaping streams of spray.

investigate for yourself. Don't try to get there in the dark. Many logging roads make it easy to get lost.

From Watersmeet, go just over 4 miles on U.S. 45 and take the first left after the Eastern Time sign. That puts you on Old 45. Within half a mile, go left again onto Robbins Pond Road. In a few miles, up a hill, you'll see the well-worn spot. Look down the power line clearing on the path of the old railroad grade. Coming from the north on U.S. 45, about 5 miles south of Paulding look for the sharp turn to your right onto Old 45. Follow directions above. If you pass the Central Time sign, you've gone too far.

PAULDING LODGING

RUNNING BEAR RESORT
(906) 827-3208; e-mail rbearest@up.net

Families of hunters, anglers, and waterfall watchers will find lots to like about this unassuming place. Seven simple housekeeping cabins are arranged in a semi-circle, well back from the highway,

with a big back yard. The cabins aren't fancy — some have varnished chipboard ceilings — but they are clean and nicely coordinated. All have gas propane heaters. No phones. No TVs. Cabins sleep from two to eight. The photos on the bulletin board tell what this place is all about: proud kids with their catch, bear and duck hunters who "have been with me 30 years," according to owner Joseph Ursetti. "They drive a thousand miles from the Carolinas and say, 'You make it feel like home.'" The only common area is a pavilion with a giant smoker, scene of **September's bear party**, open to all. (The bear to smoke is contributed by whoever is lucky enough to shoot one.) The owner Joseph Ursetti was reluctant to nail down specific rates. *On the west side of U.S. 45, just south of the center of Paulding. Open from the last week of April thru November.*
H.A.: call   : call

ROBBINS POND Campground/ Ottawa National Forest

Three rustic sites are in this primitive campground on a small impoundment that's full of trout, in a shady area of mixed conifers, aspen, and birch. It's full of hunters in season, but otherwise not heavily used. Not a party spot. *About 5 miles north of Watersmeet or 5 miles south of Paulding, turn from U.S. 45 north onto Old 45. In less than half a mile, turn west onto Forest Hwy. 5230. Campground is in about 4 miles.* (906) 358-4551. *Currently no charge.* **H.A.**: no

Watersmeet *(pop. 600)*

This modest village of mostly ranch houses is north of the intersection of U.S. highways 2 and 45. Its "town center" is in the little strip along 45. Watersmeet has some 600 to 700 year-round residents, including many retirees. Unlike nearby Land O'Lakes, Watersmeet is **far from spiffy**, but

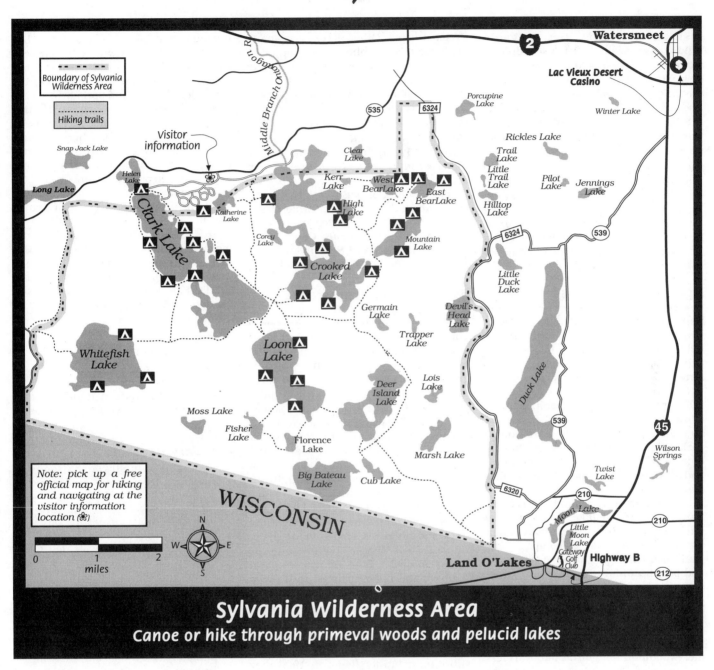

Boundary of Sylvania Wilderness Area

Hiking trails

Visitor information

Note: pick up a free official map for hiking and navigating at the visitor information location (✿)

0   1   2
miles

N
W · E
S

Sylvania Wilderness Area
Canoe or hike through primeval woods and pelucid lakes

things have been picking up since the 1970s. The new **casino** of the Lac Vieux Desert Band of Ojibwa, which opened in 1996, employs 350 from a radius of 30 miles and beyond. As one of the U.P.'s larger casinos (601 slots, a 500-seat bingo hall), it's the biggest thing to have happened here since a large sawmill was built in the 1970s and closed not long after. Everybody mentions the "$17.5 million casino complex" and its effect on the area. Still, what's the future in gambling, some people wonder. "I wouldn't want my kid dealing poker all his life," one man said.

Unlike many other U.P. townships,

the area around Watersmeet is growing in population, spurred not just by the nearby casino but the boom in lakefront property. Prices in the past five years have zoomed up, from well under $500 a

Topo maps

Get them for sure if you're going off-trail in Sylvania. They're also helpful in figuring out where you are on the unmarked trail system. For sale at the entrance A frame, at the Watersmeet Visitor Center, Sylvania Outfitters, and at the Ottawa National Forest office.

shoreline foot to an average of $1,000 a foot in 2001. Empty lots have become scarce. Now commonplace are tear-downs of older, modest cabins and resorts to build much bigger and fancier second homes and retirement homes.

Ottawa Visitor Center

A beautiful building houses the Ottawa National Forest information staff and contains an extensive **nature bookstore** geared to area plants and animals. The center provides an **excellent introduction** to the area. **Exhibits** illuminate the natural and human history of places within the national forest's Watersmeet District, including the **Sylvania Wilderness Area**. Call for schedule of **summer evening programs**, given weekly at least, typically on a Thursday. Don't overlook the 1/4 mile **nature trail** (&) that leads up from the parking lot. Its theme is the interconnectedness of the natural world: plants, water, deer, songbirds, watersheds, and human history.

Overlooks the southeast corner of U.S. 2 and U.S. 45 outside Watersmeet. Entrance roads from both highways. Open daily 9-5 Central Time from mid-May through mid-October. From Oct. 15 to May 15 open Wed-Sat from 9 to 5 Central Time. (906) 358-4724. www.fs.fed.us/r9 /ottawa/ &

Clark Lake, Sylvania

Adjacent to the Sylvania Wilderness Area where motors are prohibited, at the Sylvania Recreation Area at the north end of Clark Lake, the **Ottawa National Forest** provides convenient auto access to Sylvania's quiet and its natural beauty. There's a long, sandy **beach**, a **picnic area**, a refreshment concession, a changing house with **showers**, and a parking lot. Visitors in cars can enjoy a quiet, motor-free lake, old-growth forest and start to explore much of what makes Sylvania special.

An **8-mile trail** around Clark Lake, Sylvania's largest lake, gives an easy introduction to the area without camping or using a canoe or compass. The trail goes through groves of hemlocks and past beautiful wetlands. You'll probably see and hear the **haunting cry and yodel of a loon**. A pair nests on every Sylvania lake. You're likely to notice pileated **woodpeckers** at work on old trees looking for insects and hear summer woodland songbirds like warblers and red-eyed vireos. **Eagles** and **ospreys** perch over the lake, scanning for fish to swoop down on and catch.

Near the Clark Lake beach and picnic area is a gorgeous, 48-site **drive-in campground** with showers. Improved

Sylvania fishing regulations

Special fishing regulations for Sylvania are required because these mostly landlocked lakes have so few nutrients. (That's why they're so clear.) Rules change a little each year. Look for the Sylvania section on the official Michigan fishing regulations that comes with your license.

boat launch sites are on Clark and Crooked lakes. Other access parking is at Sylvania's periphery. (See map.) Of course, these more accessible areas are close to roads and not as quiet as the less accessible interior lakes and trails. But they're much, much quieter than comparable facilities elsewhere.

Day-use registration is required year-round. $5/day/vehicle use fee, or $20/season. A self-registration pipe is at every entrance. The main entrance off County Road 535, which intersects with U.S. 2 about 3 miles west of Watersmeet. The A-frame office is staffed from 8 a.m. to 5 p.m. to 6 p.m. Fridays, Central Time between May 15 and September 30. A-frame office: (906) 358-4404. &: *call.*

Sylvania Wilderness Area/ Ottawa National Forest

Thirty square miles of landlocked lakes among glacial hills, the Sylvania Tract is one of the very few expanses of **old-growth northwoods forest** to have escaped the logger's ax and the farmer's plow, as well as natural disturbances like forest fires and destructive windstorms. Sylvania won its reprieve by virtue of its great natural beauty and good fishing. In 1895 Albert Johnston, a Wisconsin timber cruiser, bought 80 acres here at the south end of Clark Lake, intending to cut its large, old pines. He decided instead to save the trees and build his home among them. He called his simple, picturesque log cabin Trossachs, from Tennyson's poem "Lady of the Lake." Three guests who worked for Ironwood's Oliver Mining Company (which soon became part of U.S. Steel) visited shortly after the house was finished. They liked the area so much that they asked him to buy the entire township for them. In 1900 they built the first lodge on the club property.

Over the years the lakes just beyond the Sylvania Tract became lined with resorts and cottages, dissipating their solitude and wilderness quality in the face of waterskiers and motorboats. But because Sylvania's generations of owners managed it as a fishing and hunting retreat with low levels of use and no logging, Sylvania retained the pristine beauty and wildness that Johnston loved. Today, as part of the National Wilderness Preservation System, most of the area is managed according to wilderness principles. On the north edge, near the main entrance A-frame, are a drive-in campground, beach, and two boat launches.

On these crystal-clear lakes it's not uncommon to hear not just loons but also the bald eagles who nest here, circling above, looking for fish. In the dense shade beneath massive hemlocks, the forest floor is open and springy with centuries' accumulation of needles. Nesting loons and eagles need to be left alone to reproduce. They flourish here because motorized boats are prohibited and because wilderness management techniques have kept water quality high.

Sylvania is also home to one of the shyest of all animals, the **wolf**. It's virtually never seen, but its howls can be heard. "The howl of a wolf is synonymous with wilderness and has a tremendous effect on anyone who hears it," writes naturalist Bonnie Peacock in her excellent short book, *Sylvania: Majestic Forests and Deep, Clear Waters* ($9.95 at the Visitor Center).

MAGNIFICENT TREES AND UNUSUAL PLANTS

The flora here in Sylvania are also interesting. The trees of this climax forest (yellow birch, eastern hemlock, and sugar maple) can live for hundreds of

Seasons at Sylvania

Spring is announced by loons returning from open water of the Atlantic or Gulf of Mexico. By May the woods are full of birdsong, establishing territory for nesting birds. Woodland wildflowers are at their peak in late spring, usually the end of May, before the leaf canopy shades the forest floor. Be prepared for the insects also out in force. (See introduction.) Later, into June, the woods bloom with fewer but showier flowers like the coralroot orchid and showy lady's slipper bloom.

Summer means the songbirds sing less, and all birds are busy gathering food for their growing young. This means eagles and other birds of prey are out over the water, looking for fish. Watch out for active **bear cubs** and the protective mama bears near them. A splendid time to visit is in early September and the last ten days of August, when weather is usually warm but family campers have headed home.

Fall is an intense time, neglected by campers. Everything is getting ready for winter. Leaves shut down chlorophyll production, change colors, and fall. Bears bulk up for the long winter. Squirrels store away vast food supplies. Loons head south usually at the end of September.

Banning motors from Sylvania's lakes makes them quiet, peaceful refuges for paddlers, swimmers, and nesting loons and eagles. Drive-up canoe launches give easy access to Crooked Lake (above) and to Clark Lake with its miles of sandy beach.

years in this environment, protected from high winds. No damaging fire or storm seems to have occurred here for many centuries. Undisturbed environments like these, with rotting logs and decaying leaf debris, suit mushrooms. The quantity of dead wood makes this ideal habitat for pileated woodpeckers, the largest of all woodpeckers.

Wildflowers, too, thrive at Sylvania, including lady's slippers that take years to reach blooming age. Many of the smaller of Sylvania's 36 lakes have bogs or encircling sphagnum mats with wildly varying plant associations, depending on the water's acidity level and the source of seeds that have become established there. These may include legally protected orchids and insect-eating pitcher plants as well as the leatherleaf common in acidic bogs. Some water bodies have become entirely covered over by sphagnum mats, turning into muskegs. These mats are best seen from the water. A footstep on these thin and fragile mats can destroy years of growth. People can fall through them, too.

FROM A RICH MEN'S RETREAT TO A PUBLIC TREASURE

The original three co-owners and four more U.S. Steel men formed the Sylvania Club for fishing and hunting. They owned and managed the land in common, built two lodges, guard cabins, and

caretakers' buildings. The club bought Albert Johnston's property from his widow after his Model T overturned and killed him in 1922. Some shares were sold to W. B. Thompson of Colorado, who had grown rich from copper investments.

Like many retreats in and near Wisconsin's north woods, during Prohibition Sylvania became less of a fishing camp and more of a place to drink, gamble, and party outside the law's reach. Thompson, an expansive host, was building a huge but quite plain lodge of hand-hewn western red cedar when he died in 1930. The lodge was completed by his daughter and her husband, Anthony Drexel Biddle, Jr., then an ambassador in the Hoover adminis-

Winter in Sylvania
offers ice fishing, winter wilderness camping, and cross-country skiing. Plowed parking is by the main entrance off CR 535. **Snowshoes**, for rent at Sylvania Outfitters, are an ideal way to explore Sylvania in winter. Deer, which can't move around in deep snow, make trails and yard up in the sheltering stands of hemlock in and around Sylvania. They feed on sugar maple saplings and cedar branches sticking up above the snow.

tration. But they spent little time there and eventually sold their shares to Detroit's Fisher brothers, who pioneered the enclosed auto body and made millions selling to General Motors.

Lawrence Fisher, the affable playboy who headed Cadillac Motors in the 1920s, owned three-fourths of Sylvania's shares through the 1940s and 1950s. A fishing enthusiast, he had caretakers create protected underwater habitats to produce trophy fish. Lake trout were introduced to Clark Lake. Smallmouth bass, native to these lakes, were (and are) the big attractions because they give such a good fight. The celebrities Fisher entertained are still the stuff of local lore: President Eisenhower fishing and golfing at the nearby Gateway Golf Course, Bing Crosby singing one Sunday at the Catholic church, Lawrence Welk regularly helping with dishes in the kitchen.

In the early 1960s, both Sylvania owners died. It was a rare opportunity for the government to buy a large tract of old growth timber and pristine lakes and let the public enjoy what had been an exclusive fishing club. In 1966 the U.S. Forest Service purchased it for $5,740,000 — the first major purchase of the federal Land and Water Conservation Fund Act. The money came from selling Golden Eagle entrance passes to national recreation areas. The lodges were dismantled and otherwise removed, so today the area feels more like it did in 1895 and not like a resort. Old roads are now hiking trails.

SYLVANIA'S WILDERNESS MANAGEMENT

Sylvania is a place for peaceful contemplation and fishing in the solitude of nature. It does not present the physical challenges that today's adventure-seekers have come to associate with the word "wilderness." Sylvania's hills at their steepest are like those in glacial lake belts near Ann Arbor and Kalamazoo. The lakes are placid except on windy days.

What makes Sylvania a wilderness area is the way it has been managed, preserving for the most part the undisturbed character of the land and water. Because the spring-fed lakes are landlocked, there's very little water exchange. (Crooked Lake, the headwater for the Ontonagon River's Middle Branch, is an exception.) "Anything put into these lakes will remain there a very long time," writes Bonnie Peacock. Rigorous management has kept water quality high. Motors of all kinds are prohibited, except on Crooked Lake. The lack of wakes and shoreline scouring is a great help for nesting birds, especially loons and eagles, which require quiet to nest.

(On Crooked Lake legal precedent permits electric motors. Two resort owners successfully sued the Forest Service, which had tried to ban all motors from Crooked Lake, too. If these resorts had promoted their unusual wilderness location, many local observers believe, they could have made lots more money than by fighting the Forest Service.)

The area is wonderfully quiet, except for the sounds of nature. Wilderness management is designed not only to protect natural resources, but to provide a wilderness experience for those people whose enjoyment of the natural world is ruined by the sounds of vehicles and by amenities common to most managed nature areas — things like railings, interpretive signs, and even simple directional markers.

Here at Sylvania visitors are allowed to make their own discoveries — and mistakes! *Choose Sylvania only if you are prepared to challenge yourself with primitive conditions and the elements you may encounter.* Group size is limited to 10 people while hiking or canoeing, and to five people per campsite to reduce the impact on other campers. (For more on camping at Sylvania, look under "Watersmeet Area Camping.") Non-motorized sailboats, bicycles, and portage wheels are all considered mechanical devices and prohibited as a result.

Canoes and kayaks are the ideal means for exploring these lakes, which are very different in character. Some of the lakes lie low, surrounded by marshes or bogs. Others are rimmed by steep hills. Clark and Loon lakes have lots of long sand beaches, making them great for peaceful swimming undisturbed by power boats. High Lake is 18 feet higher than neighboring Crooked Lake. Rentals are conveniently available from Sylvania Outfitters. (See below.)

Twenty-five miles of **hiking** and **portage trails** let hikers see 12 lakes, including all the larger ones. Portage trails give access to three more lakes. They range in length from about 200 feet to 3/4 of a mile. (Most Sylvania portages are 1,600 feet or under.) Twenty-one smaller lakes are reached by foot without trails.

FINDING YOUR WAY WITHOUT SIGNS OR MANMADE LANDMARKS

If you go off trail, be sure to have a compass, and consider getting a USGS map to steer you away from wetlands. Though the distances are short in these areas of glacial lakes, wetlands, and ridges, it's surprisingly easy to get turned around or to venture into an area

Nesting loons need solitude. Their nests, at water level, are damaged by boat wakes and by dams that change the water level. Loons thrive under Sylvania's wilderness management prohibiting motors.

where you're almost encircled by impassable wetlands. The challenge of canoeing in Sylvania is mostly in getting to your destination without helpful signs and markers showing you how to get to that portage across the lake. Once you're near a portage, the beaten-down path is easy to see. But most of these lakes have lots of inlets and peninsulas, and if you don't keep track of where you are on your small but accurate free Sylvania map, you could become easily confused and turned around. A compass is advised for canoeists and hikers alike. It's a good idea to leave word of your plans and whereabouts with someone.

*See map for **parking access points** to Sylvania. Day-use registration is required year-round. A self-registration pipe is at every entrance. New fees ($5/day/vehicle, or $20/year) are collected for use of improved parking areas by Crooked Lake and Clark Lake. Those parking areas are off County Road 535, which intersects with U.S. 2 about 3 miles west of Watersmeet.*

*For more info: The **A-frame office** by the main entrance is staffed from 8 a.m. to 5 p.m. daily (to 6 on Fri) Central Time between May 15 and September 30. (906) 358-4404. The **Ottawa National Forest Visitor Center** is open daily 9-5 Central Time from mid-May through mid-October; from Oct 15 to May 15 open Wed-Sat 8-5 Central Standard Time. (906) 358-4724. The **National Forest Watersmeet Ranger Station** on the north side of Old U.S. 2 just east of U.S. 45 in Watersmeet is open weekdays 7:30 to 4 p.m. year-round: (906) 358-4551. www.fs.fed.us/r9/ ottawa/*

Sylvania Outfitters

This year-round outfitters offers **canoe** and **kayak rentals** and **trips**. Rentals can be taken anywhere, but most are used on Sylvania's lakes and for the Ontonagon River's Middle Branch, a clear trout stream that's across U.S. 2 at a private canoe landing. River trips are

generally by reservation. The shop sells USGS and lake maps, tackle, bait, freeze-dried foods, and field-tested accessories like cooking kits, foam pads, paddles, clothing, etc. and makes referrals for area fishing guides.

Proprietor Bob Zelinski knows the area intimately. His father was a guide and caretaker at a fishing retreat just outside the Sylvania Tract. He himself has been an outfitter for thirty years. The website, www.sylvaniaoutfitters. com, gives a good map and overview of Sylvania that loads faster than the national forest website.

For Sylvania, lightweight Grumman canoes in four sizes, from 13 to 18 feet, rent for $20 a day, including vests, carrying yoke, and car-top carrier. Canoes can be both delivered and picked up for $10 (both ways). One-person kayaks rent for $20 a day. Two **Sylvania day trips** are offered: Clark and Loon Lake (no motors, isolated beaches, catch-and-release fishing) and Crooked and High Lake. Scenic, twisting Crooked Lake allows motors, normal fishing. Short, hilly portages connect with several other lakes, but so many twists and turns make good navigational skills a must.

River trips include the four-day trips described below, plus a two-day trip on the **Ontonagon's South Branch** between Ewen and Victoria Dam. (Bob Zelinski's four-wheeler gives access to an upper stretch for a three-day trip, too.) In *Canoeing Michigan Rivers,* Jerry Dennis and Craig Date write of this trip, "The South Branch may be the least-known and least-often-paddled of the major branches of the Ontonagon, yet we found it to be the most attractive and challenging." The last 1 1/2 miles of this trip involve Class II and Class III rapids that cannot be avoided. This trip is for experienced whitewater canoeists only!

Some canoeists rent car-top carriers or trailers to take Sylvania Outfitters' equipment to the Brule and Paint rivers near Iron River, which lacks an area

canoe livery. The Brule is well-suited for beginners and families.

Rentals for no-wax cross-country skis plus boots and poles are $5/hour, $15/first day, $10 each extra day. Reservations advised during busy times like Christmas week. Snowshoes & bindings are $10/day. The shop sells Iverson snowshoes, wax, and more.

On U.S. 2 and the Ontonagon River Middle Branch, 1 mile west of Watersmeet. (906) 358-4766. www.sylvaniaoutfitters.com ♿: call.

Watersmeet Ski Trails

During the ski season (typically from early December through most of March) Sylvania Outfitters (above) serves as the trailhead for the Watersmeet Ski Trails in the Ottawa National Forest. A 20-mile system of **groomed cross-country ski loops**, it's on Ottawa National Forest land leading up to the Sylvania Wilderness Area. Trails are groomed for traditional, diagonal-stride skiing. They go over varied terrain with lots of ups and downs, through Ottawa National Forest land. Though the flatter main trail is suitable for novices, the more interesting loops and the system in general are best suited to intermediate-level skiers. The trails go south to Jennings Lake, 160 feet above the starting point, so the return north has more downhills. The mixed forest includes many big hemlocks, pines, and maples. Beaver activity is evident, even in winter. The Raven Loop leads to the boundary of the **Sylvania Wilderness Area** and its ungroomed, unmarked trails. By Christmas other skiers will have established clear, packed trails in Sylvania. A map of Sylvania's trails, often over old logging roads, is available at the outfitters, the Visitor Center, or headquarters.

Hot drinks and snacks are served in a **warming room** with fireplace next to the Sylvania Outfitters ski shop.

Trails start at Sylvania Outfitters on U.S. 2, 1 1/4 miles west of Watersmeet. (906) 358-4766 for information. Donations pay for grooming. ♿: no.

Ontonagon River Middle Branch

Above the confluence with the East Branch, this pretty, relatively undeveloped stretch of river is **small and clear**, with **excellent fishing** for brook trout. Canoeing enthusiasts Jerry Dennis and Craig Date recommend it in their *Canoeing Michigan Rivers*. Refer to their book for detailed hints about how to run this and 17 other U. P. rivers. The stretch from Watersmeet to Bond Falls Flowage ("flowage" up here refers to a pond or impoundment) has water levels high enough for canoeing even throughout the summer. Above Mex-I-Min-E Falls and Burned Dam, the river has gentle rapids suitable for advanced beginners. The very popular stretch from the Forest Service campground at Burned Dam to the bridge at the abandoned townsite of Interior has a lot of whitewater in seven not-very-tricky rapids. It makes a **fine first whitewater trip** for intermediate canoeists. Wood turtles, painted turtles, and eagles are often seen.

Sylvania Outfitters on U.S. 2 1/4 miles west of Watersmeet, is well situated to begin these trips. Its **private canoe landing** on the Middle Branch is just across the road. Canoeists not using its services can put in at Watersmeet, on the river's north bank just east of U.S. 45. Sylvania Outfitters rents Old Town Royalex canoes, well suited for rapids, for $24 a day. Pickup charges cover from one to five canoes.

Sylvania Outfitters provides rentals and/or pickups for the following recommended trips on the Middle Branch:

◆ **Sylvania Outfitters or Watersmeet to Buck Lake Road** (second bridge). Two hours paddling with five small rapids. Moderate current. Some cabins. Limited parking at bridge. $6 pickup fee plus rental. Three-hour pickup time.

◆ **Buck Lake Road to Tamarack Creek.** A shortened version of the above trip, with no rapids. Moderate current. Very popular with customers. The pickup trip includes a brief visit to the falls at Burned Dam. $10 pickup fee.

◆ **To Burned Dam and campground.** The river slows through marshland after bridge, then narrows. The trip ends above Mex-I-Min-E Falls, called by Dennis and Date "a short, furious drop," or portage some 300 feet around them. The falls are a picturesque cascade, with a pool that's sometimes wadeable. Four hours minimum paddling time. $10 pickup fee. Limited parking at Burned Dam.

◆ **Burned Dam to Interior townsite.** Undeveloped stretch known for straightforward Class I-II white water (see above) not requiring tricky scouting or maneuvering. Two-hour paddling minimum. $16 fee for dropoff and pickup in 3 hours.

◆ **Burned Dam to Bond Falls Flowage.** (Incorporates previous trip.) After slower water and possible fallen trees, two difficult rapids before Little Falls require portaging for most canoeists. Pickup before impoundment. $16 spotting fee.

At scenic, popular Bond Falls, there's camping, a store, a park, phone, and plenty of parking.

Downstream from Bond Falls, canoe-

A lifetime of outdoor adventures in the Watersmeet area informs the tips given out by Bob Zelinski of Sylvania Outfitters. He knows things like which Sylvavnia lakes to paddle on a windy day, good spots to fish for trout or smallmouth bass, and interesting trails to hike.

ing the Middle Branch is really iffy. Upper Peninsula Power, which owns the dam and falls, diverts much of the stream's water in a flume that feeds through the Net River and South Branch into its huge dam at Victoria. Low water levels make the lower part of the Middle Branch rocky except sometimes in spring.

Mex-I-Min-E Falls and Campground

This is a scenic spot without crowds. A short, powerful cascade on the Ontonagon's **Middle Branch** is the focal point of a woodland spot that's so **picturesque** it's been painted and reproduced as a print sold at the nearby Ottawa Visitor Center, complete with mother bear and cubs. **Big conifers** surround the rocky little river, which makes downstream pools people like to wade in. There's a **canoe landing** and a ιwith vault toilet, picnic tables, and grills.

From U.S. 45 Just north of the U.S. 2/U.S. 45 intersection in Watersmeet, take CR 208/Old U.S. 2 east 7 1/2 miles. Campground is downstream from falls.

WATERSMEET RESTAURANT

The **PEPPERMILL CAFE & PUB** is what used to be Minnie's Restaurant. It too is all-around diner and separate lounge; it's the only real restaurant aside from the casino, and continues to be a gathering place for area people, truckers, and travelers. The signage is more tasteful than before, but the food's not as good, from reports in 2000. The **hot beef sandwich** (about $5.50) and **apple dumplings** are favorites. There's a Friday fish fry. Dinners ($7 to $15) are served family-style. One large dining area means it's hard to avoid smoke. *Northwest corner of U.S. 2 and U.S. 45, behind gas station. 358-4714. Open daily, 7 a.m. to 8 p.m. Central Time, to 9 weekends. 358-4714* Full bar

The restaurant at **Lac Vieux Desert Casino**, named **KITIKITEGONING** (the Ojibwa name for Lac Vieux Desert), is good enough to attract people from quite a distance who have no interest in gambling. There's a full menu, starting with breakfast, but most people order the daily all-you-can-eat theme buffet ($10 weekdays, $16 on Friday and Saturday when seafood and prime rib are featured). *On U.S. 45 about 2 miles north of U.S. 2 at the north edge of Watersmeet. Open daily from 6:30 a.m. to 9, to 10 weekends.* Full bar

WATERSMEET-AREA LODGING

See also Land O'Lakes, Paulding. Watersmeet lodgings are arranged from north to south.

AmericINN/Lac Vieux Desert Casino & Resort

(906) 358-4949; www.lacvieuxdesert.com
For vacationers and their children who require most every contemporary amenity, dining, and occasional big-name entertainment on site, too, this casino hotel, currently with 76 rooms, has more in one place than anyplace else in the western U.P. Furthermore, it's well done, with a friendly, together staff. The standard double rooms are a real bargain at $60, year-round. Whirlpool suites with pullout sofa, microwave, and fridge are $100, $109 weekends. Like other AmericInns, its lobby is a model of nouveau Northwoods elegance. It has a pleasant indoor swimming pool room with a medium-size oval **indoor pool**, whirlpool, and **sauna**. There's also a busy **video game room**, a gift shop, and, adjacent to the casino, in a restaurant with natural light, a **good restaurant buffet**. That's not to mention **9 holes of golf**, the casino's smoky bar, the **bingo hall/auditorium** where Johnny Paycheck, Janie Fricke, and George Jones have performed. The hotel has been so popular (snowmobilers book winter weekends a year ahead) that a 51-room expansion with child care area is due for completion in 2002. Nine more holes are being added to the golf course, too. *For summer at the moment, reserve a month ahead. On U.S. 45 about 2 miles north of U.S. 2 at the north edge of Watersmeet.* **H.A.** 18 & under free : call

WATERSMEET INN (906) 358-3058;
www.abrp.com/watersmeethtm Five **cushy suites** and a conference room have been created on the second floor of what was the Kelly Hotel in the 1890s. Decor is an elegant variant of Northwoods decor: lots of cranberry and dark green, fern and wildflower motifs, wreaths with twigs and grouse feathers. Developers Jack and Sandra Tadych own American Building Restorations in Franklin, Wisconsin, which makes stains and paints. They have a summer home in the area and thought snowmobiling plus cross-country skiing had created enough demand to warrant a project like this. The suites open onto a **lobby** with **fireplace** and Victorian reproduction furniture. Each suite has a **full kitchen**, cooking and eating facilities for four, a

sitting area and a queen bed, usually in a completely separate bedroom. All are air-conditioned, with cable TV with ESPN and Disney. Rates in 2000: $70 weekdays, $79 weekends for regular suites, $110 and $120 for the large, two-bedroom suite. There's a guest laundry. Ample parking for snowmobiles and trailers. On a trail. So far typical guests are mostly couples, but the arrangement works well for families and special events. In the works: landscaping. Smoking prohibited. *On U.S. 45 about a mile north of U.S. 2, across from a park. Open year-round.* **H.A.**: no : in larger room

SUNSET MOTEL   (906) 358-4450;
fax (906) 358-4258

The surroundings consist of a large parking lot abutting a gas station/convenience store, but the Sunset Motel offers attractive rooms, good service from locally knowledgeable owners, reasonable rates, and lots of amenities: cable TV, **refrigerators**, microwaves, phones, shower/tub combos, and a free **continental breakfast**. There's a freezer for fish catches, and fax and copy service. The Peppermill Restaurant (formerly Minnie's), a diner with a small bar, is the back-door neighbor. Rates, the same year-round, in 2000 were $41 for a double with sofa-sleeper, $50 for two doubles, and $70 for end-unit suites. *Northwest corner of U.S. 2 and U.S. 45.* **H.A.**: call : $5/extra person

VACATIONLAND RESORT   (906) 358-4380; www.westernup.com/vacationland; e-mail: wsmet@portup.com

Perhaps the area's most attractive resort is one mile from Sylvania in a wooded setting and a **long, sandy beach** on Thousand Island Lake. That's part of the **Cisco Chain of Lakes** so popular with boaters and fishermen, but quiet enough for **loons.** (Otters and eagles are often seen, too.) The 13 new or newish housekeeping cottages are on the lake. Most sleep 4 to 7 in two or three bedrooms. Typical rate in season (mid-June thru mid-August and Christmas week): $900-$1,050/week for 4 or 6 people. But most of it is booked from year to year. Waiting-list people can be helped if not tied to a particular week or cottage. Off-season rentals by the week or night; winter weekends and fall color season are busy. Examples in 2001: mostly $125-$140/night for 4 or 6 in Jan & Feb, late spring, fall color, and hunting season, mostly $85-$100 other times. See web

site for details. Pleasant interiors have knotty pine paneling, maple furniture, picture window, some fireplaces. Cottages come with **aluminum boat**, picnic table, grill, lawn chairs, microwave. No phones. TV with 5 channels (networks plus PBS).

The philosophy of owners Jan and Bill Smet is to encourage families to do things together, or just sit and watch the sky, so there aren't any organized activities except for a **weekly naturalist program**. There is a nice **playground**, a tennis court, **basketball** and volleyball courts, a **swimming raft**, **bonfire pit**, sauna, and fish-cleaning station, but no game room — though there are games and puzzles and good videos to borrow. An aluminum **fishing boat** comes with each cottage, and guests can borrow **kayaks** and **canoes** to explore the lake. Bill sails and enjoys teaching guests to **sail the Sunfish** ("You tip over a dozen times") so they can take it out. The pontoon boat, motors, and upgraded fishing boats can be rented. No jet skis. *Just off CR 535/Thousand Lake Rd. about 10 miles south of U.S. 2 Sylvania turnoff. Open year-round.* **H.A.**: one cottage. Call. ♀♂: Age 2 and under free. $10/night, $50/week/extra person. 🐾: in off season only. Call. $5/day.

WATERSMEET CAMPING

A primitive option on national forest land is the unusually scenic Burned Dam Campground with well-spaced, wooded sites near a prime canoeing stretch of the Ontonagon River a few miles northeast of Watersmeet.

CLARK LAKE Campground/ Sylvania Recreation Area

(906) 358-4724; not reservable; www.fs.fed.us/r9/ottawa/

The 48-unit drive-in campground between Clark Lake and Katherine Lake "abuts a wonderfully dark, springy forest of old hemlocks," we wrote in 1997. "What luxury, to look out into those majestic trees from your campground and still be able to enjoy a hot shower!" Today many of those trees are now stumps — a reaction to an incident in which a camper was killed by a falling tree at a nearby national forest campground. Was cutting the old trees a necessary safety measure — over 80% of the cut trees showed inner rot, a forester said — or butcher's work that went "goofy," in one local outdoorsman's opinion? Risk is part of life, he argues, and campers beneath mature trees incur less risk, say, than any highway motorist. At

any rate, the campground is visibly different—sunnier—and forestry personnel see some aesthetic merit to that. The campground is just beyond the boundary of the wilderness area, where no-motor restrictions apply; there threatening trees are being cut with cross-cut saws.

Showers (not ♿; one step, steep grade) are by the beach, about a mile by foot or car from the campground. With asphalt drives and grassy areas, the campground's roadside landscaping isn't the natural, wild look you might expect next to a wilderness area. And there are flush toilets to boot! Campsites are first-come, first serve, with a 14-day limit. They occasionally fill in July and the first three weeks of August. *On CR 535/Thousand Island Rd. about 7 miles south of U.S. 2. Clearly signed at intersection 4 miles west of Watersmeet. $8/night. Open from the last week of May through November.* **H.A.**: Restrooms on loops 2 and 3 are accessible except for grassy entrance.

SYLVANIA WILDERNESS AREA/ Ottawa National Forest

See below for phones; www.fs.fed.us/r9/ottawa/

The 29 wilderness campsites, nestled in the forest, are reached by water. (For canoe rentals, see Sylvania Outfitters.) Here too old-growth trees suspected of rot have been cut if near campsites, after the fatal incident at Imp Lake. (See Clark Lake campground.) Thirteen campsites are also reachable by land on defined hiking trails. An inconspicuous brown shoreline post marks each campsite.

Campsites are so artfully deployed that you can feel quite alone here, even when every campsite is full. Camp furnishings consist only of a big cast-iron fire ring and a wilderness latrine.

No-trace, low-impact camping is the rule here. Does camping mean listening to music around a campfire and socializing with other campers? Then the little disciplines of wilderness camping at Sylvania are not for you. The whole idea is to be quiet and inconspicuous, so campers in this restricted area can feel alone and listen to the night sounds of nature. Noise carries clearly across water. Quiet campers are far more likely to see and hear wildlife. Only five people per campsite are allowed. The maximum size for group travel (by water or by foot) is ten. Mechanical devices including bicycles, sailboats, and portage wheels are not permitted. Washing must be done at least 150 feet away from lakes and wetlands, using biodegradable soap

if soap is necessary. Baking powder makes a good biodegradable toothpaste. To reduce food debris that attracts bears to the campsite, strain dishwater and pack out all food scraps and garbage in your trash bag.

Wilderness camping means having the discipline and courtesy to be inconspicuous in this popular area. Wear earth tones when possible. Wearing soft-soled shoes like moccasins around the campsite is easier on the ground and more comfortable. Consider a fast, efficient lightweight stove instead of a campfire. Dead or downed wood, pine cones, and bark can be burned, but only within the fire ring. Collect firewood away from your campsite to reduce impact.

Water can contain harmful organisms, so it should be boiled, filtered in a .5 micron filter, chemically treated, or carried in. Water pumps are at the Crooked and Clark Lake launches and at the entrance station. Take precautions against bears. (See introduction.)

Reservations are taken for specific campsites between January 15 and May 15. After that, they're first-come, first-served.

Camping regulations: All overnight campers at Sylvania must camp at designated sites. Users must have with them at all times between May 15 and September 30 an overnight camping permit validated by Forest Service staff. From May 15 through September, get it in person at the A-frame entrance station off County Road 535. (See below.) From October through May 14, campers should self-register and pay at the A-frame or other trailheads. Camping fee per site per night: $10.

The A frame is on CR 535/Thousand Island Rd. about 7 miles south of U.S. 2. Clearly signed at intersection 4 miles west of Watersmeet. From May 15 through Sept 30, it's open daily from 8 to 5, to 6 Fridays, Central Time. (That's 9-6 Eastern Time.) A frame office: (906) 358-4404. Visitor Center info: (906) 358-4724. Off-season Ottawa National Forest office: (906) 358-4551. **H.A.**: call for tips. Requires assistance.

MARION LAKE Campground/ Ottawa National Forest

(906) 358-4551; not reservable. www.fs.fed.us/r9/ottawa/

This 39-site rustic campground (vault toilets, no electricity or showers) is nice because it's **quiet** but not far from Watersmeet or Sylvania, and about half the campsites are right on the 318-acre lake. One campsite loop is high, with lake views; two loops are on the lake; all are shaded by maples. In 2000 this campground didn't fill except possibly on holiday weekends. The lake has decent fishing for muskie, walleye, bass. The designated swimming beach has a log changing house built by the CCC in the 1930s. Group camping is in a separate area. *There's an open playfield for games. 5 miles east of Watersmeet on Marion Lake Rd., north off U.S. 2. Open mid-May thru Nov. $6/night.* **H.A.**: *everything but bathrooms. Vault toilets have a step.*

**IMP LAKE Campground/
Ottawa National Forest**
(906) 358-4551; not reservable.
www.fs.fed.us/r9/ottawa/

All the 22 private, shady sites here have lake views, and most are on 84-acre Imp Lake, where fishing for splake is good, trout fishing decent. There's an informal swimming area but not a designated beach with markers and signs. Vault toilets, no electricity or showers. The **pretty interpretive trail**, a 1 1/2 mile loop, starts at the picnic area, goes on a boardwalk past wetlands and a bog lake. Signs tell about hemlock, hardwood, and lowland conifers. It has been hardened, and the first part is accessible for wheelchairs and strollers. Steep grades make the last half difficult. *6 miles southeast of Watersmeet just south of U.S. 2. Open mid-May thru Nov. $5/night.* **H.A.**: *vault toilets have a step.*

Land O'Lakes (*pop. 500*)

This Wisconsin village of 500 lies about a mile west of U.S. 45 along Highway B. It's a picture of prosperity compared with Watersmeet, quite proud of its curb-and-guttered streets, redone downtown facades, and decorative lights and trees. The big Nagel lumber mill west of town is a mainstay of the local economy, as is tourism. In 2002 Conserve School, a private coeducational boarding school, opens on part of the 1,200-acre estate of the late industrialist James Lowenstine. His dream was to start a school that would emphasize environmental stewardship and ethical decision-making.

Until the early 1940s, Land O'Lakes was called State Line. The golf course and State Line restaurant actually straddle the line, as does Lac Vieux Desert, the big (4,300-acre) lake east of town. Known for its huge fish, it has yielded the world's record muskie and tiger muskie. Muskie fishing is catch-and-

release, but anglers can keep trophy fish over 45". For ice fishing there can be 400 vehicles on the lake at a time. Access to the trails and lakes of the **Sylvania Wilderness Area** can be gained on the northeast edge of town.

Gateway Lodge

This big log lodge was built as a vacationland showplace in 1938 by John King of King Broadcasting in Detroit. (Its home was in the impressive Maccabees Building on Woodward, now used by Detroit Public Schools.) The adjoining golf course and airport were part of the complex. A separate bar, now remodeled as the State Line Restaurant, was built to straddle the state line and circumvent local liquor laws.

The main lodge room with its huge stone fireplace, log rafters, and picture-book rustic ambiance is impressive, and the whole place is coming back after some hard times. Mementos look back on glory days and celebrity visits. The stylishly rustic dining room with fishing decor is well worth a look. It's now home of the King's Grille, a good restaurant with a varied menu including authentic Mexican dishes and some sophisticated touches. The surrounding terrain is flat and open, with few big trees. Adjoining the lodge are the Gateway Lodge Trap & Sporting Clay Ranges, the scene of many competitions. Call the lodge for details. *On Hwy. B at southwest corner of U.S. 45 intersection. (800) 848-8058.* &

Gateway Golf Club

Punctuated by **giant Norway pines** on fairly flat terrain, this 1940s-era 9-hole golf course starts with the first four holes in Wisconsin and finishes with five holes in Michigan. The slope rating is 123, and the hardest hole is the 559-yard number two (par 5). There's a small bar and restaurants.

From Michigan, take Highway 45 south. Just after you pass the Wisconsin line, turn right onto Highway B. The golf course is just before you reach Land O'Lakes. (715) 547-3929.

Glider and airplane rides

Just inside Wisconsin at the Land O'Lakes airport you can hire a pilot at Barry Aviation to take you up for an awesome view of the area's many forests and lakes. It's especially spectacular during the height of the fall color season. An experienced glider pilot will take you

up 2,000 feet for about a half hour ride. Soaring quietly on the air currents, you can see as far as Lake Superior and the summits of the Porcupine Mountains. Another notable landmark is the sizable Lac Vieux Desert, the lake from which the Wisconsin River originates.

You can also hire an airplane ride. Planes seat up to three passengers plus the pilot. The plane will take you literally anywhere you want in the U.P., from the Pictured Rocks to the Soo Locks. *Barry Aviation, Hangar One, Land O'Lakes Airport (just west of Highway 45), Land O'Lakes WI (715) 547-3759. Open summer and fall. Call ahead for an appointment.*

Wisconsin River Headwaters

It's thought-provoking to see such a **charming creek** at this pleasant roadside park and picnic area and consider how it gathers tributaries and becomes a big river flowing into the Mississippi and Gulf of Mexico. Author Holling Clancy Holling used a traveling turtle to trace the Wisconsin River's origins in *Minn of the Mississippi*, a companion to his classic *Paddle to the Sea* picture book. *On US 45's west side just south of Land O'Lakes.*

World's Largest Tiger Muskie

The area's claim to fame, now **stuffed and mounted**, is the star attraction at the **Minnow Bucket** bait shop east of town. *County Road E, about 2 1/2 miles east of U.S. 45. Open May-fall. (715) 547-3979.*

LAND O'LAKES RESTAURANTS

Arranged from state line south & west.

In 1996 Emilio Gervilla, who owned five tapas restaurants in Chicago and vacationed here, opened a sophisticated Chicago-style restaurant in the Gateway Lodge — too sophisticated to make it in the off season with local people. At **KING'S GRILLE** Alex and Susan Artega, who worked with Emilio, have a more widely appealing menu that includes basic burgers, personal pizzas, and gyros sandwiches but remains **far more gourmet** than anything in the western U.P. Here are salmon smoked on the premises in a salad or as an appetizer, char-grilled chicken, steaks, and tuna in a sandwich or as an entrée, and braised lamb shank over risotto (around $15). The soup and salad bar ($8 alone), with four soups each day, is very popular; so is rotisserie chicken with lemon pepper ($9 for 1/2 chicken), with roasted garlic potatoes. One Chicago transplant especially likes the authentic Mexican dishes. A perennial favorite is the house burrito grande (around $5.50) with grilled sirloin and green pepper, black beans, and cheese, with fresh salsa. Tortilla chips are housemade, too. Portions of Mexican are generous. Otherwise, she says, "portions may be too small for big appetites."

In the Gateway Lodge on Hwy. B just west of U.S. 45. (715) 547-3888. Open Thurs-Mon year-round, with likely breaks after Easter and Thanksgiving. Open for lunch (noon to 4 Central Time) and dinner (5-9:30). 🚻 👫👪 Full bar

The cute name notwithstanding, **T. J. GRIZZLY'S**, the popular local pizzeria, does have Italian roots, and it does a good job not just on its thin-crust pizza but on lasagna (around $5) and Italian subs and roast beef sandwiches ($5 and under). It's a tiny place with a few tables inside, picnic tables out front, and a big parking lot to accommodate all the take-out business. *On County Road B on the east edge of downtown Land O' Lakes, south side of street. (715) 747-3700. Closed Monday. Tues-Thurs 11 a.m. to 8 p.m. Central Time, Fri & Sat 11-9, Sun 4-9 in summer, 4-8 otherwise.* 🚻: no. Too crowded. 👫👪 Beer

LEIF'S CAFE in downtown Land O'Lakes is the **local hangout**, "where everybody goes." It has very good food, too. It's especially known for omelettes ($4-$6.25), chicken and dumplings ($6.35), and pies. Like the rest of town, it's all spiffed up, with exhibits from the Headwaters Art League. No credit cards. Out-of-town checks OK. *Downtown (County Road B), south side of street. (715) 547-3896. Open 7 days from 5:30 a.m. to 2 p.m. Central Time.* 🚻 👫👪

BENT'S CAMP (715-547-3487) is a century-old lakeside logging camp-turned-fishing resort with a lodge and popular pub. The vintage rustic decor (birch bark ceiling and walls) now has big windows overlooking Mamie Lake on the Cisco chain. Dock for boat-in customers. The bar may be smoky but the dining room isn't. Owner-cook Carol Peterson has introduced a nightly menu with **steaks** (a standout) plus specials. People stake out tables as early as 3:30 in summer for Friday family-style fish fry ($9, all you can eat) and **outstanding Saturday prime rib night**. Dinner entrées $9-$25. Any-time favorites: burgers, fried chicken platter, excellent deep-dish pizza ($12-$18 for 16"), Caesar salad with optional meat. *12 miles west of Land*

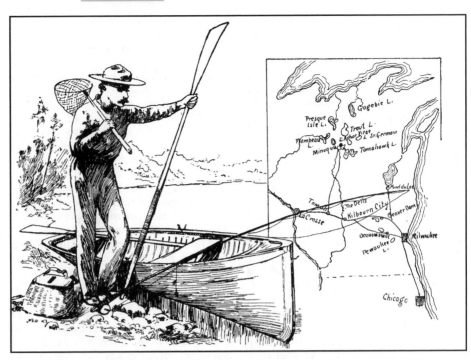

For over a century anglers have flocked to the lakes around Watersmeet and Land O'Lake, among the northermost of the many lakes forming the headwaters of the Wisconsin and Flambeau rivers. This illustration for a magazine article circa 1905 shows rail connections to Chicago.

O'Lakes on Helen Creek Road just off CR B. Open year-round except closed March and April. Open 11 a.m.-9 p.m., daily in summer, closed Tues. from Oct. thru Feb. **H.A.** restrooms not ADA accessible. 👫👪

LAND O'LAKES LODGINGS
Arranged from north to south.

PINEAIRE RESORT and MOTEL
(906) 544-2313; www.community.webtiv.net/innorth/PineaireNews

These seven cute, woodsy cottages (mostly $40/night in 2000) were erected by builders of the Gateway Lodge — for patrons' call girls, legend has it. Cabins are away from the road beneath fragrant big pines; the names, of Chicago suburbs, reflect owner Nick Kamieniecki's previous career as clerk of the Cook County Fourth District Court. Today they reek with **vintage charm** and homey touches— knotty pine, individual decor, mini-fridges, magazines in each room — but lack things like air-conditioning, phones, cable TV, a hot water system that immediately delivers hot water to each unit, and screen doors that don't slam. Regulars don't care. "Everybody likes it the way it was," says owner Nick Kamieniecki. "They're up here to hunt or fish; the only thing they need the TV for is the weather." Nick spent all his vacations in the area. The

Pineaire's old owners, friends of his father, called when they decided to sell. The 20-acre property has plenty of room for BBQ grills and screen houses with picnic tables— three of them — and a bonfire area. A path goes back among tall pines about a quarter mile to Moon Lake, a local family fishing lake where loons nest. Pineaire loans guests a canoe.

Regulars reserve many units from one year to the next, but some summer spots are open in January, and so far there's always space in May, late June, and October. Of course, cancellations always happen. But now that Nick and Jan have created an all-seasons website for area information, availability may change. Free continental breakfast is put out in the delightful morning gathering room when the motel is at least 40% occupied. Ask about suites, bed combinations. No non-smoking, but smoke was not noticeable a visit. Parking for boats, snowmobile rigs. *1/4 mile from major trail. On west side of U.S. 45 just inside Michigan line.* **H.A.:** call 👫👪: $5/extra person; teens enjoy camraderie; younger kids are bored. 🐕: pets welcome. "I'll take dogs over kids any day," says Nick.

The QUEST BED & BREAKFAST and Art Gallery (906) 544-2503
Retired Chicago-area art teacher Shirley Battin and her husband have made their

newish, air-conditioned log home a tranquil retreat. It's surrounded by pine woods and **gorgeous gardens**, and filled with quilts, other folk art, and lots of books on gardening and art. Shirley collects seeds from native wildflowers in the vicinity so she can propagate plants for her new meadow. Her serenity garden features little signs saying, "Listen" and, from John Muir, "In God's wilderness lies the hope of the world." The Quest is a low-key B&B, more like a personal English homestay.B&B rather than a heavily marketed inn. Shirley doesn't want it to interfere with her own art (her studio is in the barn), but she does encourage guests to gather in the family room, sit, and talk. Privacy for guests is not a problem, however. The upstairs is given over to two guest rooms. They share a pleasant hallway lounge and a bath; both are only rented to a group of family or friends; otherwise only one is rented. to avoid sharing a bath with strangers. The walk-out lower level suite sleeps up to five. It's a great place for families, with cable TV (ESPN and Disney), fridge, microwave, and wood stove. All rates ($65 for two, $15/extra person) include a full breakfast. Guests can use the Battins' phone. Easy biking distance to Land O' Lakes and to trails and fishing in Ottawa National Forest. Increasingly booked ahead in busy seasons. *On Crystal Lake Road, 1/4 mile east of U.S. 45 at the state line.* **H.A.:** call ♿👫: $15/extra

SUNRISE LODGE   (715) 547-3684; (800) 221-9689; www.sunriselodge.com' e-mail sunlodge@ newnorth.net

This well-known family resort, featured in many guides, offers lots of family summer activities and lodging in 22 cottages on 30 acres on Lac Vieux Desert, where there are **two docks with boats to rent** and a **shallow, sandy beach** area. There are nature hikes, canoe lessons, movie night, soccer, softball, volleyball and basketball games, tennis, an exercise trail and much more) Well-maintained grounds are more suburban than wild, though shaded by mature trees. Places like this are like summer camps for the whole family (no cooking required!), and often serve as family reunion headquarters. Kids' activities might let parents go off by themselves all day. Many regulars book a year ahead, so early reservations — six months or even a year ahead — are generally a must in summer and on winter weekends, though cancellations can happen. Fall and spring are busy, too, but not so full so soon. When full, Sunrise suggests

area alternatives. Two rec rooms in the air-conditioned lodge offer free games (ping-pong, pool), card tables, VCRs. All cottages have kitchens, color TV/VCRs; "executive units" have two bathrooms and various extras. Meals are served all year. Guests can choose from daily and weekly rates. In summer of 2001 the American plan (about $598/week for each of two adults, $36 or $59/week for each child) is by far the best deal; it includes all meals, which can be packed as box lunches for sightseeing expeditions. Spring and fall housekeeping rates for two with optional meals were $96/day. Call for winter rates, spring and fall packages focussing on fishing, fall color, holidays. Connects with main snowmobile trails. Consult the extensive website for details, lots of photos. The three-generation Mendham clan also runs the Stateline restaurant. *Open year-round. 5894 West Shore; turn east from U.S. 45 at the main intersection with Hwy. B.* **H.A.:** many cottages ♿👫: extra charge/child. 🐕: call

GATEWAY LODGE   (715) 547-3321; (800) 848-8058; www.gateway-lodge.com

Since 1993 owner/manager Bob Klager has been steadily working away at restoring its 1938 vintage charm to the common areas of this log-and-knotty pine northwoods showplace (see above), the victim of decades of ill-advised updates. Starting with the infrastructure of the naturally high-maintenance wood building, he's gotten to the point where that huge stone fireplace and big log rafters are more noticeable than the carpet, now a discrete 1940s pattern instead of the former smoke-saturated plaid. The wonderful beamed dining room, complete with knotty pine and original lighting, is now smoke-free, as are about half the 55 guest units in the rental pool, all with cooking facilities, cable TV, and phones. Ceiling fans; no air-conditioning. Room service from well-regarded restaurant under separate management. Guest units, under condo ownership, are individually decorated, so it's hard to generalize about them, but they tend to plywood paneling and laminated furniture. Studio units (a single room with small kitchen/sitting area) in 2000 were $50 weekdays, $70 weekends. Suites with separate bedroom were $60 and $80. The **indoor pool**, 30' by 70', and hot tub are in a rather plain room that also houses a sauna and exercise equipment. Guests and the general public can take shooting lessons and use the **shooting range**. Groups gathering at the Gateway on a given day may

include women without makeup in arty outfits, guys in gold neck chains, golfers, and over-50 motorcyclists in leather jackets. *On Hwy. B just west of U.S. 45, half a mile east of the center of Land O' Lakes.* **H.A.:** call. Some first-floor rooms are accessible. ♿👫: $8/extra person over 12

BENT'S CAMP RESORT (715-547-3487)

The **oldest area resort**, on one end of the Cisco Chain of Lakes, dates from 1896, when Charles Bent bought a logging camp and built a comfy, rustic log lodge. Today it houses a popular restaurant and bar that can draw crowds in summer. Grounds have big trees, lawns, grills, little privacy between cabins. Somewhat separated from the lodge are 11 housekeeping cabins of varying ages, all with front porches. Ten overlook Mamie Lake, southernmost of the Cisco Chain of Lakes. There's a swimming beach and raft, summer bonfires, and a playground. Fish cleaning station & freezer, tackle shop, boat launch; guide service available. Typical weekly rates: $450 to $700 (for 4 to 6). Daily rentals ($75-$100) except in summer. No phone (except in lodge), no TV, no towels. 14' aluminum boat comes with cabin. *12 miles west of Land O'Lakes on Helen Creek Road just off CR B. Cabins open May thru mid-October.* **H.A.:** call ♿👫: ages 10 & under free. $50/week/ extra person

LAND O' LAKES CAMPING

BORDERLINE RV PARK (715) 547-6169; e-mail border@newnorth.net

For RV campers and a few tent campers who want a convenient, shady campground with hot showers that often has a few last-minute sites, this small (around 20 sites) campground comes recommended by local resort owners. The owners carved out some space from a pine and popple woods that extends 400' back to the Wisconsin River, more of a **good-size creek** here. Paths connect the campground, which is close to the road but buffered by trees, to the river. Across the road is a Wisconsin state wayside with a boat landing and marker about the Wisconsin River headwaters. Modern sites with water, sewer, and electric are $19/night. A laundry connects with the bath house. *On Hwy. 45 1 1/2 miles south of Land O' Lakes. Open from May through October.* **H.A.:** wheelchair-accessible ♿👫: no extra charger 🐕

Keep in mind that all prices and hours of operation are subject to change. Lodging rates vary with supply and demand and are usually higher for special events.

Iron River, Iron Mountain & the Menominee Range

STRECHED OUT along U.S. 2 a few miles north of the Wisconsin border, the **lake-studded region** around Iron Mountain, Crystal Falls, and Iron River doesn't obviously showcase its charms to the hurried traveler. The old iron-mining towns are plain, except for Crystal Falls, and the well-known attractions are few. There's Michigan's **only underground iron mine tour** near Iron Mountain. And there are **two ski resorts**, Ski Brule (near Iron River) and Pine Mountain (near Iron Mountain). Less well known is the most **challenging whitewater** in the Middle West at Piers Gorge near Norway.

To serious outdoors-lovers the area is an alluring destination. **Real wilderness** is right outside towns that seem quite urban because of the compact streetscapes and ethnic mix of immigrant miners. Dickinson and Iron Counties, around Iron Mountain and Iron River, have **more wolves** than anywhere else in the Upper Peninsula, and **more good Italian restaurants**, too. The miles of unfolding forests of maple mixed with pine along U.S. 2 in Iron County are memorable. Beautiful vistas of nothing but trees accurately suggest that the highway and the mining towns it connects are but a thin strip of development in what remains largely a wilderness. The mines boomed in the late 19th and early 20th centuries and started closing in the 1930s. By the late 1960s active mining was largely over. Today this wilderness is managed for timber production.

Lots of brushy habitat make the area **famous for grouse**,

Wilderness reasserts itself in this old mining region, where wolves, eagles and homemade pasta aren't far apart.

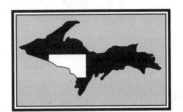

considered the king of game birds. When nationally prominent Michigan outdoor writer Tom Huggler and friends get together for their annual fall grouse-hunting trip, they go north of Crystal Falls, even though, Huggler says, he's written about the area so much that it attracts more hunters these days, even from the East Coast.

The great majority of this land is forested and remote, though interspersed with some hunting camps and logging operations. Vast wooded tracts are open to the public as part of the **Ottawa National Forest** and **Copper Country State Forest**, or as commercial forest reserve land, privately owned by Mead, Ford, Wisconsin Electric Power, and others. There are **few busy roads** to carve up this land into small areas. Big undeveloped tracts benefit large mammals at the top of the food chain. The **bear population** is the highest it's been in decades — a tribute to good habitat management.

Iron County alone, which includes the towns of Crystal Falls and Iron River, has over **2,000 lakes** and **900 miles of streams**. Just to the southeast, Dickinson County, though smaller, has a large, remote area of lakes and streams north of sprawling Iron Mountain. Fishing and canoeing are big draws. Of 15 U.P. rivers profiled in *Canoeing Michigan Rivers* (see bibliography), three are in Iron County: the Brule, Paint, and Michigamme. Most of these lakes and waterways are so **clean and quiet**, that canoeists and kayakers have very good chances of spotting bald eagles, loons, and other fish-eating

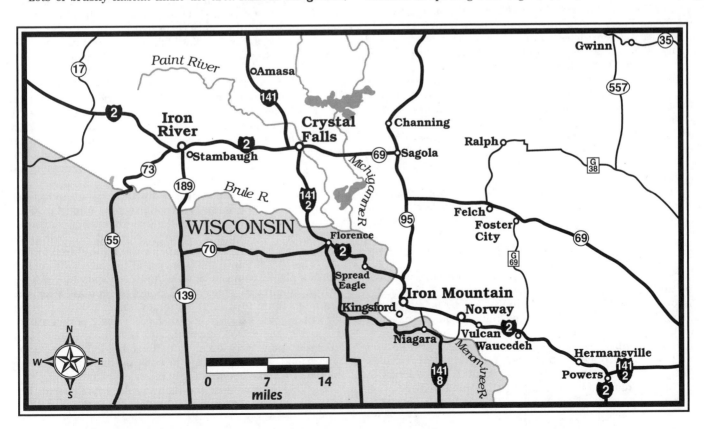

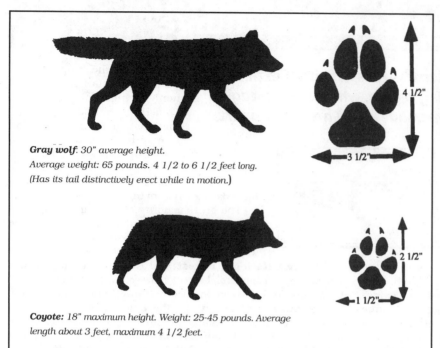

Gray wolf: 30" average height.
Average weight: 65 pounds. 4 1/2 to 6 1/2 feet long.
(Has its tail distinctively erect while in motion.)

4 1/2"

3 1/2"

Coyote: 18" maximum height. Weight: 25-45 pounds. Average
length about 3 feet, maximum 4 1/2 feet.

2 1/2"

1 1/2"

Wolves, often confused with the smaller coyotes, have fared well in northern Dickinson County (north of Iron Mountain) and much of Iron County (north of Crystal Falls) because deer are plentiful. Deer prefer inland areas with less snow than shoreline counties. Large areas of undeveloped land in northern Dickinson and Iron counties are good for wolves, who avoid human contact.

birds. With ideal habitat for fish-eating birds of prey, **Iron County has more nesting pairs of bald eagles** than any other county east of the Mississippi. Loons, especially sensitive to disturbances and chemical contamination, breed on many area lakes and visit others even in settled areas. To breed successfully, eagles and loons need clean water, a food supply of fish relatively free of pesticides, and few disturbances during the first twelve weeks of nesting.

Clear proof of the area's remote character is the success of the **wolf**. Wolves need to be left alone, and they need a good prey base. Wolves are known to exist in most of Iron County and the northern half of Dickinson County — a greater concentration than anywhere else except Isle Royale. "They're here in the U.P. all on their own, not introduced by wildlife specialists," points out wolf-lover Randy Gustafson, proprietor of Wilderness Adventures in Iron Mountain. "We must be doing something right." Wolves are here because they can avoid human contact and because of abundant deer. In these inland counties deer are more plentiful because there's less snow than in similarly wild counties near Lake Superior. Deer can't get around in deep snow because of their small hooves. Here they can browse more widely for food.

Seeing wildlife takes knowledge, time, and patience. Just finding evidence of the secretive wolf is a challenge. Discovering the charm of the north woods isn't an experience to be gobbled down quickly. Canoes, hiking, and snowshoeing are the ideal means to experience nature here up-close. Consider camping — back-country camping, even, so you won't be surrounded by busy campgrounds. **Northwoods Wildlife** by Janine Benyus is an outstanding introduction to watching wildlife by understanding their preferred habitats, seasons, and hours of activity. The Ottawa Visitor Center in

Watersmeet has an **excellent nature bookshop**. Wilderness Adventures in Iron Mountain has good outdoors books, too.

Waterfalls, unlike wildlife, afford a short, dramatic nature adventure that most able-bodied visitors can enjoy. This area has some **outstanding waterfalls**. Horserace Rapids is in a powerfully craggy setting near Crystal Falls. **Piers Gorge**, with its four Menominee River falls, is in an **awesome canyon surrounded by a beautiful pine forest** near Norway. Without intrusive development like railings, Piers Gorge is for **hiking and waterfall connoisseurs**, and it's not widely known.

The **Brule, Paint,** and **Michigamme rivers join** west of Iron Mountain to form the **Menominee River**. It was the major engine of early economic development in these parts during the 1860s and 1870s. Its watershed included prime forests, and it conveniently drained into Lake Michigan at Green Bay, not that far from Chicago some 300 miles to the south. Pine logs could simply be floated down the Menominee to the booming twin lumber towns of Menominee, Michigan, and Marinette, Wisconsin. Chicago's rail connections there made it easy to ship northwoods lumber to build the rapidly developing west. **Timber cruisers** were the first in many locations to discover the **iron deposits** that bestowed an intense burst of prosperity upon the Menominee Range from 1885 into the 1920s. Lumbermen active in the area were among the earlier investors in iron-mining operations. By 1900, Menominee Range iron mine ownership was consolidated under the Pickands-Mather and Mark Hanna conglomerates. Both were headquartered in Cleveland, Ohio, which was the chief beneficiary of the wealth the mines generated.

Juxtaposed to the area's wildlife and natural beauty is the idiosyncratic local culture of the western Upper Peninsula. First-time visitors are amazed at the **rich ethnic mix**. Finns, Italians, Cornish (builders of all those Methodist churches), Croats, and some Poles came to work in the mines. Here on the Menominee Range mining developed on an earlier base of logging and was done on a smaller scale, but over a longer period of time than on the Gogebic Range around Ironwood at the U.P.'s western tip. Germans, Swedes, and Norwegians first worked in lumber camps. The intermarried French and Indians go back to fur-trading days.

The Menominee Range has a different visual and ethnic character from the more-visited Keweenaw and Marquette ranges, where large, paternalistic Eastern mining companies and investors developed the communities and left their grand architectural stamp. In comparison, the typical architecture here is far less striking. The boom era in the early 20th century favored a plainer commercial style. And less money stayed here.

Iron Mountain enjoys a well-deserved reputation for **outstanding ethnic food**. Iron Mountain's intensely Italian north side offers some excellent Italian food: a spicy porketta roast and homemade ravioli, gnocchi, and lasagna swimming in a delicious spicy red sauce. Iron River has some estimable Italian food, too. A heritage of cooking for lumber camps accounts for some outstanding homestyle cooking.

The urban view from the highway does not charm. Iron Mountain snakes along nearly 10 miles of U.S. 2. Its vast new

Wolves vanished from the U.P. because they were aggressively hunted by farmers and bouny hunters like this man, photographed in Iron Mountain. Today public attitudes toward wolves in the Upper Peninsula have dramatically changed, partly because farming is diminished. Wolves now even grace the covers of local phone books.

eastside retail areas have created a headache of sprawl. But don't let these first impressions make you give up on these interesting places! They're full of surprises. Like the natural areas, the towns make visitors put a little effort into finding the nifty spots and reaching out to talk to local people. The reward is a travel mix that plays off natural and wilderness experiences with unusual, somewhat gritty real-life environments not covered up by the artificial veneer so common to tourist areas.

Today many jobs in these parts are related to timber in some way. **International Paper** (formerly Champion) is the region's biggest employer. It has a workforce of 583 in its Norway forest products division and its **state-of-the-art paper mill** in Quinnesec just east of Iron Mountain. There a 200-foot web produces 1 1/2 miles of paper every two minutes. It makes 314,000 tons of coated paper a year, used in magazines and catalogs.

Many more people work in small logging and pulp-cutting operations that supply big buyers of pulpwood and timber for furniture, building, and veneer. Trucks loaded with 100-inch-long logs are a common sight on area highways. Yards stacked with logs are along many highways and rail sidings.

Khoury Furniture, founded by members of Iron Mountain's good-sized Lebanese community, makes solid wood assemble-it-yourself furniture at its 250-employee Iron Mountain plant. The factory outlet on U.S. 2 on the north end of town has been closed, but occasionally you can find discounted seconds at the factory. Most sales are through retail locations throughout the country.

The area's central location in the Western U.P. creates more jobs, especially in Iron Mountain. It has a Veterans Administration Hospital, the U.P. mail processing center, and a growing retailing sector.

TO FIND OUT MORE:

For **Iron River, Crystal Falls, Amasa** and the rest of **Iron County**, contact the **IRON COUNTY CHAMBER of COMMERCE**. It's a clearinghouse for all kinds of information about the area, its recreation, lodgings, and culture, not just about member organizations. **www.iron.org** is an outstanding info source on events, culture, history, and much more. The super-helpful staff is happy to mail info. The physical chamber is just east of downtown Iron River, in the A-frame just south of U.S. 2 overlooking the river. *Open Mon-Fri 9-4 Central Time. (888) TRY IRON. (906) 265-3822.*

Visitor information for *all* lodgings and visitor attractions in **Iron Mountain, Norway**, and the rest of Dickinson County is handled through one combined super-source, the **DICKINSON CO. CHAMBER/ TOURISM ASSOCIATION** and economic development group, open weekdays 8-5 Central Time. (800) 236-2447; (906) 774-2002. The helpful staff fields questions and mails information. Its web site is **www.ironmountain.org** They share a building with the U.P. Tourism & Recreation Association, which publishes the information-packed *Upper Peninsula Travel Planner*, a free glossy magazine. The same office houses the **MICHIGAN WELCOME CENTER**, providers of heaps of printed info about tourism-related businesses throughout the state. *It's in downtown Iron Mountain on U.S. 2/Stephenson Ave. at A St. Open daily from 8 a.m. to 4 p.m. Central Time, to 5 in summer. (906) 774-4201.* &

PUBLIC LAND: Much of Iron and Dickinson counties is either federal or state land. The Michigan **DEPARTMENT OF NATURAL RESOURCES** administers the far-flung parts of the **Copper Country State Forest** through two offices, open weekdays from 7:30 to 4 Central Time. The DNR website is **www.dnr.state.mi.us/** The **Norway** office is on West U.S. 2. (906) 563-9247. The **Crystal Falls** office is on U.S. 2 just west of the intersection with U.S. 141. (906) 875-6622. . . . The **OTTAWA NATIONAL FOREST** has an office on Iron River's east edge, on Lalley Road just south off U.S. 2 by the state police post, near Angeli's Market. It's open from 8 to 4 Central

from 8 to 4 Central Time. (906) 265-5139. TTY: (906) 265-9259. **www.fs.fed.us/r9/ottawa/**

EVENTS: For **Iron River/Crystal Falls**, consult the calendar on **www.iron.org** or call (888-TRY-IRON). The biggest events are the U.P. **Championship Rodeo** in Iron River, the first full weekend in July, and the **Bass Festival** with a run, a parade, and fishing contests in early July. . . .In the Iron Mountain area, the **Pine Mountain Music Festival** in late June and July brings three weeks of high-caliber music, mostly classical music with some folk, jazz, and pop, to the U.P. The series always includes two operas and several workshops. Call (877)746-3999 or visit **www.pmmf.org**. . . . In February the **Continental Cup ski jump competition** comes to Pine Mountain.

PICNIC PROVISIONS and PLACES
Consult the index for details.

◆ **Angeli's Central Market** on U.S. 2 on the east side of **IRON RIVER** is the premiere gourmet stop for the entire western U.P.: outstanding wines, produce, baked goods, deli. Incredible!

◆ On a much smaller scale, **Sommers Sausage Shop** on the main street of **CRYSTAL FALLS** offers homemade sausages, sandwiches, soups, and a full line of groceries.

◆ Iron County picnic spots: outside **IRON RIVER**: **Lake Ottawa**, the **First Roadside Table** on U.S. 2. Near **CRYSTAL FALLS**: **Runkle Lake Park** east of town.

◆ **IRON MOUNTAIN** sets such a high standard for home cooking, the deli departments of the big supermarkets, **Super One** and **Econo Foods**, on U.S. 2 east of downtown are way better than average. But why not patronize the nifty little places like **The Gathering Place** downtown (sandwiches, deli items, breads, desserts), **Crispigna's Italian Pantry** on the North Side (see index; good meats, cheeses, and Italian wines) or **Monette's IGA** at 375 Woodward in Kingsford, with good hard rolls, meats, and bread.

◆ **Most distinctive picnic destinations**: Iron Mountain City Park in **IRON MOUNTAIN**, Fumee Falls roadside park in **QUINNESEC**, Strawberry Lake in **NORWAY**.

Iron River & vicinity

The big event in the Iron River area in recent years has been the consolidation of Iron River with adjoining Stambaugh and Mineral Hills. (Caspian citizens opted to remain an independent city.) The three-way consolidation, unprecedented in Michigan history, added about 1,500 citizens to Iron River. Stambaugh and Mineral Hills will disappear from future maps of Michigan. The consolidation was hotly debated, but ended up passing 2-1 in a July, 2000 election.

Historically, a string of five separate towns developed along the vein of high-phosphorous iron that was first mined here in 1879. Iron River, the oldest, is the commercial center of Iron County. A streetcar connected it with other towns clustered around mine shafts: Stambaugh (pronounced "STAM-bo"), up the hill where U.S. 2 bends by McDonald's, and Caspian and Gaastra to the south. Their downtowns thrived before cars were commonplace; now they're like ghost towns.

The area bears the architectural stamp of its boom times during the first two decades of the 20th century. Some neighborhoods have handsome, well-kept Arts & Crafts bungalows. The finest homes of mining company officials were on Iron River's south side, along Selden Avenue/M-189, a road now made ugly by random industrial and commercial development.

Mining communities spawned their own distinctive institutions. Two can be seen in Caspian. The Arts & Crafts-style **Caspian Community Center** at 404

Brady (the main north-south street, a continuation of Lincoln) was built in 1921 by the **Presbyterian Board of National Missions** as a library and center for social activities, art classes, and sports activities to foster assimilation of immigrants. The little **Italian Society Duke of Abruzzi Hall**, dating from 1914, has a dance hall, a wine-making and sausage-seasoning room, and a **bocce court**. To see it, get to Brady (a major north-south street) and take Morgan or Sawyer about three blocks east. The hall is on McGillis between them.

The high phosphorous content made iron from this ore more brittle and expensive to make, though it could be used in the hotter Bessemer process of steelmaking. Mines started closing in the 1930s. The last one closed in 1978. The hilly countryside is still beautiful and the northern half of Iron County is quite wild. Economic mainstays today are tourism and many second homes and retirement homes on lakes and near the Ski Brule ski resort.

Iron County Museum

Clustered around the Caspian Mine headframe is the Upper Peninsula's **largest outdoor "pioneer village" museum**. Some 20 buildings have been moved here. Eight barns, houses, and outbuildings are of **traditional log construction**. There's an early gas station; the **streetcar barn** and **streetcar** that once traveled from Gaastra through Caspian to Iron River; and the late Victorian house lived in by Carrie Jacobs Bond, then the mine doctor's wife. She became one of the first women to strike it

rich as a song lyricist. Her husband's bankruptcy from failed investments in the Panic of 1893, followed by his death, forced her to move to Chicago, where she tried writing music to support herself and her children. "I Love You Truly" was the most famous of her many hits. She looked back on her years in Iron River as the happiest in her life.

The most recent addition is the classical-inspired, **fresco-filled house** of the late Brandon Giovanelli. He was the shy, generous, and much-loved art teacher in local high schools and at Gogebic Community College. Greek mythology and Renaissance humanism prompted these sweeping paintings focusing on the human body, largely unclothed. Starting with two salvaged WPA construction warming shacks, he fashioned quite a classy home for his family: flat-roofed, with Greek entrance columns and a fabulous, statue-filled garden. But flat roofs are better suited to Mediterranean sunshine than to north country snowfalls. Here, after sustaining serious water damage, the house now has a pitched roof. There's a separate $2 admission to the Giovanelli house together with the **new art gallery** in the basement of the church next door.

Impetus for the museum came in 1963, when the Pickands-Mather Mining Company pulled out of the area and gave this property to the county for a museum. It had been the site of its offices (now demolished) and its most productive mine. Pickands-Mather's **recently restored Caspian Mine headframe** is next to the main buildings. Once such headframes dotted the landscape on Michigan's mining ranges and anchored

communities and memories. Now very few remain. To assemble this museum, then-high school teachers Harold and Marcia Bernhardt, who had already started a successful junior historians' club, launched dozens of successful fundraising projects. Evidence of their big hearts and attention to detail is everywhere.

Many of these buildings were threatened by demolition or neglect. In 1912 parishoners mortgaged their homes and took up shovels to build **St. Mary's Catholic Church**. Their descendants, dismayed when church authorities were about to demolish the surplus small church, were delighted to have it preserved here. Some buildings are furnished to approximate the everyday life of bygone eras. The **one-room school**, regularly used, is fully equipped, down to a full complement of slates. Other buildings contain exhibits ranging from humdrum to inspired. Many, many more exhibits are in a rambling complex of three new buildings.

It all makes for a most **impressive grassroots, nonprofessional museum**. It's an interesting place for exploring by unjaded kids who like poking around and by adults with some natural curiosity. Interpretation of local history to outsiders is low on the museum's priority list, however. There's an implicit assumption that most visitors are probably descended from local people and that they are already familiar with the basic outlines of local history, and ready to delve into details. Nevertheless, many summer visitors from afar enjoy this place and the people they meet here.

There's enough here to explore over several vacations — or a string of rainy days. Many large, flippable panels of local photos give a good look at the way each town looked in boom times. Detailed exhibits go into the **Menominee Range's geology**. Excellent crayon portraits bring local people to life. Pictures and memorabilia of area **brass bands**, accordions, and music teachers show the important function **music** played in adding gaiety and fun to a local life based on hard work. *Still more is back behind the big metal buildings:* mining equipment, a shop complex (print shop, fire hall, pop shop, barber shop), and the Carrie Jacobs Bond house.

Don't miss:

◆ A big, wonderfully carved folk-art model of a **logging camp**, known as the Monigal Miniatures.

◆ A **cubist mural of miners** drilling, painted by a Chicago Art Institute faculty

Iron River/Stambaugh/Caspian
These plain mining towns, decades after their booming heydays, contain surprising treats.

member for the old Iron Inn hotel's lobby.

◆ The late Joe Canale's realistic coin-operated **model iron mine** and **railroad**. An underground car picks up ore from the scraper drift, a skip lifts it to the surface, and a model train hauls the ore to Escanaba's smelters.

The museum has sponsored many noteworthy research projects, including one of Michigan's earliest and most comprehensive surveys of historic buildings. The **Mining Memorial** lists the names of 561 people killed in the Iron River area mines and has a **computer database**

Drilling in the Hiawatha Mine near Iron River. Mine shafts went so far underground they required huge pumps to keep them dry. Underground work was loud and dangerous. Note the ropes around these miners' waists, used to keep them from plunging to their deaths down a shaft. The Menominee Range alone produced almost 300 million tons of iron ore. The Iron County Museum has a computer database with information on every mine and miner. A video shows miners at work in the 1950s.

with information on every mine and miner in the area. A video monitor shows **"A Day in the Life" video of miners at work** in the 1950s. It uses not just the expected smooth promotional PR films but footage shot by an amateur photographer friend of many miners. It has the goofy, intimate feel of home movies.

Each year a wide array of **events** take place here: a summer **children's workshop** on nature; Italian and Scandinavian **ethnic festivals**; band **concerts**; various food and crafts **fairs**. The annual events schedule comes out in May and appears on the museum website. The people up here, unpretentious ind outgoing, are the area's untrumpeted travel secret, and these events afford visitors a good look at a

slice of community life.

The small **museum shop** sells publications about the area and gifts and collectibles that raise money for the museum. *In Caspian just northwest of downtown at Brady and Park. From M-189, south of Iron River, look for the sign at the Caspian Cutoff. Or (the more revealing route), from U.S. 2, turn south and go up the Stambaugh Hill on Washington, opposite McDonald's, between the church and the tavern. At First, turn left, go 3 blocks to Lincoln, then right. Follow signs. (906) 265-2617. Open June thru Sept, daily 9-5, Sun 1-5 Central Time. $5/adult, $2.50/child under 16. Family rates. $2 separate admission to the Giovanelli House and art gallery. ♿*

Lee LeBlanc Wildlife Art Gallery

Hollywood special effects artist and cartoon animator Lee LeBlanc (1913-1988) followed a career path typical of many of the U.P.'s bright, ambitious sons and daughters. He left Iron River to study art, worked and prospered in Hollywood for 25 years, then retired at 50 with his wife to move back home to fish and hunt. The wildlife art he created in his second career won honors, including the 1980 National Ducks Unlimited Artist of the Year. Sale of his prints raised millions of dollars for **Ducks Unlimited habitat conservation projects** in the Marquette area, Manitoba, Arkansas, and Mississippi. His **appealing paintings, mostly of ducks in marshes and lakes**, are suffused with a golden light and imbued with a lively peacefulness. It's also interesting to see products from LeBlanc's Hollywood career, from pinup girls to paintings used in the movies *Please, Don't Eat the Daisies* and *Ben Hur* as backgrounds.

Inside the Iron County Museum (see above). Admission included. ♿

Downtown Iron River

U.S. 2 bypasses by a block a surprisingly trim, comfy downtown. Until it lost its Penney's, it was a pleasant shopping contrast to the overwhelming, impersonal retail sprawl oozing east from Iron Mountain along U.S. 2. Small businesses and traditional downtowns are having a hard time holding on in the auto-oriented Upper Peninsula, where people are used to driving long distances. Downtown's future here may be in visitor-oriented businesses that build on downtown motels, restaurants, and the outstanding Central Arts and Gifts.

Along with several restaurants, two establishments deserve note:

◆ The **IRON COUNTY CHAMBER of COMMERCE** in the A frame overlooking the Iron River. A wide range of helpful area information is provided by a staff that enjoys answering questions about Iron County and the surrounding area. *50 E. Genesee St. in the heart of Iron River, just west of the river. (888) TRY IRON. (906) 265-3822. Open Mon-Fri 9-4 Central Time. ♿*

◆ **CENTRAL ARTS & GIFTS.** Andy and Lillian Busakowski's destination shop offers an **unusual mix of gifts**, collectibles, jewelry, and paints and hands-on art supplies. Andy does a lot of custom framing, and there's a gallery of lim-

ited edition prints and sculpture reproductions by artists from around the world. **Well chosen, colorful books** for children and adults reflect the area's nature, history, and ethnic threads. There's a **nice cookbook section,** too. **Collectibles** include **fabulous Russian porcelain** and Christopher Radko's **Polish glass ornaments**. A good place to head for on a rainy day. *216 W. Genesee downtown. (906) 265-2114. Mon-Fri 9-5 Central Time, to 4:30 Sat.*

Angeli's Foods/Plaza Cinema

Vacationing campers stopping by this large and super-spiffy supermarket at Iron River's east entrance will be astonished by what it offers: an **outstanding produce section** in which all greens are organic, ready to eat peaches and nectarines by mid May, giant cherries from a small grower in Washington, **an excellent wine selection**, certified Hereford

---

The Angeli ranch: an unusual immigrant success story

Alfredo Angeli, founder of the original Angeli's Foods, ran a grocery store as a sideline of his huge farm outside Iron River. Here's his twist on the typical immigrant success story. His father immigrated, worked in the coal fields of Pennsylvania, then stopped writing home and sending money. Alfredo, the oldest of ten children, came looking for his father and discovered him in the Upper Peninsula. Quite a sport, the father dressed well, played cards a lot, and had large debts. Alfredo paid off his father's debts, sent him back to Italy, and bought a farm — something almost impossible in the old country. Eventually it grew to 2,000 acres. He raised cattle, sheep, hogs, and chickens, had his own slaughterhouse, employed his adult children, some of whom who lived on the place, and hired a Chinese cook to handle cooking for family and staff. (Dinner for 30 was typical.) Good food was a big, big deal on the farm. Angeli set up all his own ten children in business and built supermarkets in Iron River, Marquette, and Menominee. But running a family business with ten equal owners proved unmanageable, and the chain split up. Grandson Fred Angeli, who grew up on the farm, operates **Angeli's Foods** in Iron River and Menominee.

---

beef, and organic baby food, for instance.

What's a place like this doing here in a county of only 15,000 year-round residents and an aging population loaded with thrifty Finns? Angeli's looks like a U.P. outpost of a sophisticated big-city chain. But it's actually a third-generation Iron River institution that grew out of one of the area's many neighborhood groceries. Owner-manager Fred Angeli is passionate about food. To spread his enthusiasm, he sends his department managers on trips to gastronomic hot spots like Zingerman's deli in Ann Arbor. His produce manager meets twice yearly with top produce people around the country. "If you don't get out and look around, how do you know what better is?" he says. "It's like raising the bar a little in high jumping." Some shoppers from Green Bay make special trips to the other Angeli's in Menominee.

Though the culinary exotica at Angeli's create a startling first impression, great attention has been paid to producing local home-cooking specialties. The store bakery's **crusty Italian bread** and **cornetti** (cross-shaped hard rolls designed to sop up sauces and juices) measure up to the most demanding local standards. Baking is basically from scratch, except for a very few things like croissant dough. Real butter is used whenever it makes a difference, as in the **bread sticks**. If you're heading home, you might put a frozen **porketta** in your ice chest so you can enjoy a home-cooked version of the area's outstanding spice-rubbed, garlicky slow-roasted pork.

Next door, Angeli's operates the **Plaza Cinema** (906-265-4070) because otherwise the county wouldn't have a movie theater at all. Riverside Plaza is a handy vacationers' stop because it also has a laundromat and pharmacy. *On U.S. 2 just east of Iron River in Riverside Plaza. (906) 265-5107. Open daily 7 a.m.-9 p.m. Central Time.*

Davis Music Center

The U.P. is full of surprises, and the unpromising town center of Stambaugh has two of them. At first glance, the whole downtown seems to have been closed and mothballed. Like downtown Caspian, it's too close to Iron River's bigger downtown to have survived into the two-car-family era of the 1960s. But a good bar like Kermit's, near the top of Stambaugh Hill, can develop into an area attraction, especially when it has good food, too. Across the street and

down a little, Keith Davis produces **hand-made violins**, **violas**, and **cellos** for members of the New Orleans Symphony, among other customers, and runs a **delightful general music shop** that appeals to country fiddlers, classical violinists, acoustic guitarists, and bagpipe players.

In the front room, there's likely to be a gorgeous old accordion from the iron range's heyday, along with assorted other stringed folk instruments. Musicians are welcome to drop in and "play the rack" (try out the instruments on hand). The coffee's always on — or, if it's gone, another pot can be brewed. There's music jewelry, select recorded music (mostly by ethnic performers), instructional videos, and, for the total novice, harmonicas, recorders, penny whistles, tiny fifes, and books on how to play them.

Keith Davis and his wife and partner, Diane, came up here from Indiana for his new engineering job in 1985. Three years later, when the job moved, his instrument-making business was worth turning into a full-time venture. In specialties like his, location doesn't mean much, he says, and fashion hardly matters. "UPS opens the world to us."

419 Washington, downtown Stambaugh. From U.S. 2 on Iron River's east side, turn south onto Lay opposite the McDonald's. (It becomes Washington.) (906) 265-2044. www.kdavisviolins.com Mon-Fri 10-4:30, Sat 10-2 Central Time. ⅃: one step.

Surprising downtown Stambaugh: violinmaker Keith Davis also has a wide-ranging music shop in a downtown that looks like a ghost town. The coffee's always on, and musicians are welcome to play used and new instruments for sale.

Lake Ottawa Park/ Ge Chi Ski Trail/ Ottawa National Forest

A **handsome lodge** built by the Civilian Conservation Corps is the focal point for this pretty, rather plush park on 551-acre Lake Ottawa. (See below for camping.)

The **extremely clear lake** is surrounded by mature maples and pines with no cottage development. A lawn leads down to the lake and an artificial **sand beach** and an accessible **fishing pier**. Walleye, bass, bike, and perch are caught here. This lake is oligotrophic (having few natural nutrients), so food fish have to be introduced, and fishing varies, depending on pressure and management success. Call for current fishing info.

Off a separate drive down to a **boat launch**, a **wigwam** covered in birchbark calls attention to the place's long history as a gathering place for native people. In 500 A.D. families spent summers fishing here. In the 1800s Ojibwa had sugar camps nearby.

The 10-mile **Ge-Che Trail**, a **hiking trail** that's also groomed for **cross-country skiing** by the nearby Covenant Point Bible Camp, begins at the boat launch parking lot. It goes through wooded and semi-open areas, connecting Lake Ottawa with **Hagerman Lake** across the road. It has several **loops** of various difficulty levels. Novices should take off their skis and walk at one point to get across to the other lake. Trail **maps** should be available at the trailhead by the boat launch, or stop at the National Forest office in Iron River.

About 6 miles west of Iron River. Take U.S. 2 west, in less than 2 miles turn at M-73. In about 1 mile, look for Forest Hwy. 101 and signs to park. (906) 265-5139. TTY: (906) 265-9259. ♿: fishing pier, day use building

Hiking path to "Treaty Tree" & Mile Post Zero/ Stateline Recreation Area

A 10- to 15-minute hike on this easy, secluded path leads to the spot at the head of the **Brule River**, where the **once-disputed Michigan-Wisconsin border** heads off in a straight line toward Lake Superior near Ironwood. This is a special spot for people who like history mixed with nature. The path starts at the Ottawa National Forest **picnic area** and **boat launch** on **Brule Lake**, headwater of the Brule River. The Brule and Menominee rivers form the state line east of here.

These woods and wetlands are quite placid, unlike the dramatic, rocky settings farther downstream. Hikers pass a log border marker in the young maple forest before reaching a more elaborate sign marking the site of the so-called **Treaty Tree**. Here in 1840, after Michigan had acquired the Upper Peninsula in the Toledo War, surveyor Captain Thomas Cram of the U.S. Corps of Topographical Engineers established **Mile Post Zero** of the straight, overland state boundary with Wisconsin. In 1847 the eventual boundary line was set by William Austin Burt, the U. P.'s famous surveyor who earlier had accidentally discovered the Marquette Range's iron riches near present-day Negaunee.

Though the U.S. had earlier acquired the Upper Peninsula and Wisconsin Territory by treaty with its Indian inhabitants, local Ojibwa still regarded their ancestral land as their own hunting land. Hence, Cram and Burt drew up more treaties, agreeing to give gifts in return for passage. For years Wisconsin contested the line Burt established. A joint boundary commission had it surveyed again in 1924, and Burt's survey proved accurate.

Follow directions to Lake Ottawa (above). Continue southwest on Forest Hwy. 101 about 4 miles to West Brule Lake Rd. Follow it 2 more miles to Stateline Recreation Area and parking. ♿

Ski Brule winter and summer

In the super-scenic hills southwest of Iron River, Ski Brule offers families the biggest variety of winter sports in addition to Alpine skiing: **23k cross-country skiing**, two snowboard parks, and ice skating. A distinguishing feature: it opens earlier in the season than other area ski hills, and stays open later. See ski section in front of book.

Summer activities feature mountain biking on-site with rentals ($5 trail fee); onsite **tubing, rafting,** and **canoeing** rentals on the Brule River; and one-hour guided **trail rides** on horses; and rentals onsite. The resort will arrange for **fishing guides** on nearby rivers and lakes, and for tee times at two **golf courses** 15 minutes away.

Lodgings are either condos or chalets. See Iron River lodgings section, or

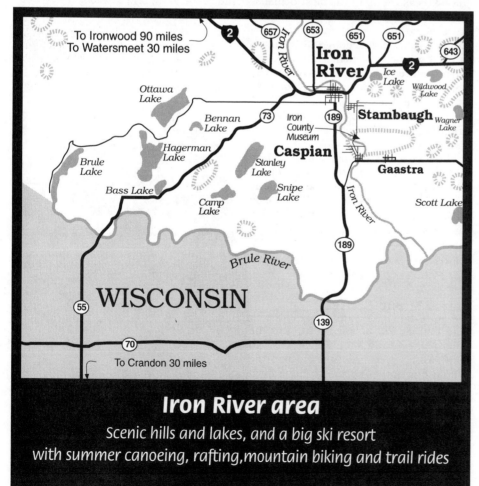

Iron River area

Scenic hills and lakes, and a big ski resort
with summer canoeing, rafting, mountain biking and trail rides

consult the website for winter rates.

7 miles southwest of Iron River. Take M-189 south, look for sign. (800) DO-BRULE. w w w . s k i b r u l e . c o m e-m a i l : skibrule@up.net

George Young Recreational Complex

This **plush golf course and indoor swimming pool**, opened in 1993, looks for all the world like a chic golf and ski resort in Colorado or on northwestern Michigan's gold coast. Yet it's quite affordable by the general public. This is yet another Iron County anomaly. The 3,300-acre complex, mostly undeveloped, borders three lakes. Golfers can see deer and eagles on the course. Foxes have been known to come up to golf carts.

Iron River native George Young struck it rich in Chicago as the owner of the Chicago Fire Brick company. (He married the boss's daughter). Young summered here and started this 18-hole **championship golf course** by adding a hole each year, modeled after his personal favorites from around the U.S. When he died, he left a large bequest to build the non-profit recreation center for members and day-use visitors. A board composed mostly of Chicago people directed the center's construction and oversees operations.

Inside, soaring log-beamed ceilings give a **luxurious sense of space**. Stylish 1990s takes on traditional lodge architecture are everywhere. There are trendily contemporary Native American motifs, Art Deco-inspired leather chairs, the requisite massive fieldstone fireplace, and elaborate antler chandeliers. The glass-walled lunchtime **restaurant** and **terrace** look out across the golf course into the woods. The **adjoining bar** is open 'til 9 p.m. Richly patterned tile walls enliven the downstairs **swimming pool** room. In winter, the center's expansive luxury seems the ultimate cure for cabin fever.

◆ **Golf** greens fees are currently $22 a day, and $20 extra for a golf cart (18 holes). The slope of the 7,049-yard Professional Course is 130, with a 74.3 rating. That of the 5,338-yard Standard Course is 118 with a 69.8 rating. In summer the course opens at 7:30 a.m., and on weekends at 6:30.

◆ For **mountain biking** there are **7 1/2 miles of trails** laid out over hilly terrain, with no trail fee.

◆ Hikers can use the beautiful 1 1 /2-mile **Wolf Track nature trail**.

◆ The swimming pool, sauna, and whirlpool are open from 10 to 9 daily

WISCONSIN

Crystal Falls/Chicaugon Lake area

Many streams and lakes, a luxurious public golf/ski/bike complex, and a handsome CCC-era state park.

(closed Mon & Tues in winter). Three wide lanes are about 49 feet long; a separate wading area slopes gently. Daily fee is $5, $3 for kids 12 and under.

◆ **Cross-country skiing** is on 10k of trails laid out for all abilities. Trails wind through woods and go to Wagner Lake. Grooming is for both diagonal stride and ski-skating. Trails are open from 10 to 4:30 Wednesday through Sunday. **Ski rentals** are $10 for adults, $5 for children. After skiing, the lounge stays open 'til 9 p.m. with beverage service.

Local people worried that this cushy behemoth would ruin small local golf clubs, but the membership fees here have discouraged many of this notoriously tight-fisted populace, and local golf clubs are regaining members. For vacationing visitors, the daily fees seem modest. Stay at the Chicaugon Inn a mile down the road, and you'll feel like you're at a fabulous resort in a wilderness area not overrun with rampant development.

On CR 424 at the southwest end of Chicaugon Lake between Iron River and Crystal Falls. 424 is reached by going east from M-189 at Caspian, by going

southwest from U.S. 2 via CR 639 just west of Bewabic State Park, or by going west from U.S. 2/U.S. 141 south of Crystal Falls. (906) 265-3401. ♿

Wolf Track Nature Trail

What makes this easy, **scenic 1 1/2-mile woodland nature trail loop** so unusual are the paintings and calligraphy by Marquette artist Carl Mayer and the simple, poetically written text by White Water Associates of Amasa. For example, the "Arctic Archive" display interprets a bog, where plants remaining from the area's post-glacial Arctic climate persist and slowly decay.

"Perpetual cheer in black and white" is the chickadee, called "a tiny dynamo with a racing metabolism. . . perpetually searching for its fuel of caterpillars, insect eggs, seeds, and berries." If you put seeds in your hand, a chickadee may feed from it!

Spring ponds, wolves, and the effects of glaciers on the U.P are among the other topics explored here.

The short drive to the trail is on the south side of CR 424 a little west of the entrance drive to the Young Complex (above). Visitors are asked to register at the complex clubhouse before using the trail. Free. &: probably, with a little help. One hill is near the loop's end.

Pentoga Park

Preserving an **Ojibwa burial ground** led to creating this pretty park at the southeast tip of Chicaugon Lake. Area Ojibwa had abandoned the cemetery when they moved west to Lac Vieux Desert to avoid the mining boom. Five thousand people turned out for the park's dedication in 1923. They witnessed Indian chanting and a procession in full regalia, the Caspian brass band, and a speech by a 90-year-old Ojibwa leader recounting his people's recent history. His band was delighted and grateful that the park had saved their old burial grounds from cottage development. The park manager continues, when time permits, to maintain and rebuild the cemetery's **spirit houses** (used instead of tombstones).

Today the park offers a **swimming beach**, **picnic area**, boat launch, an elaborate new **playground**, fish-cleaning house, and campground (see below). Supplies for **shuffleboard, horseshoes,** and **volleyball** are at the entrance booth. An old Indian trail leads to the Brule River three miles away. 1,100-acre Chicaugon Lake is **unusually deep** (115 feet) **and clear**. It's known for **walleye**, for **muskies** in June and September, and for **whitefish**, which spawn along the shore in November. If you're seeking peace and quiet, be advised that Chicaugon Lake is quite an active lake. It's quieter on the chain of lakes at Bewabic State Park, where local people don't like having to pay for the state park permit.

On CR 424 midway between Caspian and Alpha. From U.S. 2, take CR 639 south just west of Bewabic State Park. (906) 265-3979. Daily pass in summer $2, season pass $5. &

First Roadside Table

In a **stand of big trees**, this roadside picnic spot east of Iron River on U.S. 2 goes back to the very early days of auto touring in 1918. It was the first chapter in the Iron County Highway Department's very successful tourism and conservation campaign, launched by its history-minded young engineer, Herb Larson. In the 1920s, the rest stop idea quickly spread all over Michigan and beyond. Quite possibly this was the **first such rest stop anywhere**. Here's the story behind it.

Chief Edwards and his wife, Pentoga (left), and three others posed before a hogan at Chicaugon Lake. For some years after mining developed the area, they divided their time between Chicaugon Lake and Lac Vieux Desert to the west, near present-day Watersmeet. In 1891 Chief Edwards disposed of his people's lands in Iron County and permanently moved to Lac Vieux Desert. Today the Lac Vieux Desert Band owns the big casino-resort in Watersmeet.

Like many boys in the north woods, Herb Larson grew up listening to stories. Old-time settlers loved talking about the early days of iron mining and logging. He liked hearing Indians describe their old hunting grounds. He saw the barren wastes of pine plains where fire and erosion had followed the total logging-off of white pine. Because of all that, when he graduated from the University of Michigan School of Engineering, he had a fuller, more complex sense of environmental and social history than typical engineers of the era, with their can-do faith in progress.

Larson came back to Iron County to head its fledgling highway department just as lumber companies were busy harvesting the area's **magnificent hardwoods**. Hardwoods, too heavy to float down rivers like pine, had to be hauled to mills by rail. No tract of big pines remained in Iron County. But it seemed feasible to save what Larson envisioned as a **"living forest memorial of virgin hardwoods,"** he later wrote, "so that posterity could see and enjoy what nature had richly bestowed upon us."

Larson hoped to keep scenic wide strips of big trees along Iron County's principal roads. A man with a mission, he kept his ear to the ground about who was selling timber and land. When he learned that this prominently located parcel might be acquired, he went to the landowners, Cleveland Cliffs Iron, with

the support of the county board chairman, and bought it as a forest memorial public woods.

Larson's campaign to save old-growth timber along roadsides caught on with lumber firms owning local land. But it took a frustrating Sunday outing into the nearby Wisconsin lake country to inspire the **roadside table idea**. "In upper Michigan we could go where we chose," Larson wrote, "with no one to bother us." To a surprising degree this is still true today. But in northern Wisconsin in 1919, lake resorts were mushrooming. On that Sunday, everywhere Larson's party tried to have a cookout, they were asked to leave by a caretaker. The U. P. could soon suffer a similar loss of a much-loved activity, Larson feared. Why not provide picnic tables and grills at the forest memorial woods? This trend-setting roadside park soon attracted large gatherings — too large for the small picnic area. That success provided popular support for Larson's later projects: first, **Pentoga Park** and in the 1930s the beautiful Bewabic Park, now part of the state park system.

After eighty years, Herb Larson's legacy has generally endured. The U.S. Forest Service classifies roads as to their sensitivity, and visuals are considered in its timber sales.

On U.S. 2 four miles east of Iron River.

IRON RIVER RESTAURANTS

"Cucina de Mama" (mother's cooking) says the sign in front of **ALICE'S**. That's a picture of mama on the sign — owner Alice Tarsi's mother, Concetta. Her cooking was locally famous before Alice ever opened her restaurant. The mild red meat sauce is made the way Concetta did it — in the U.S., not in the Marches of central Italy, where she came from. All the **pasta is made fresh here each day**, and the **gnocchi (potato dumplings) hand-dimpled**. Favorites include spaghetti or gnocchi with a grilled pork chop ($10 or $11), meat or cheese ravioli dinner ($9.50), and a delectable cappelletti soup ($4/bowl). Dinners (up to $20 for steak tenderloin) come with salad or soup, starch, and a **basket of homemade bread**s. Half-portions are available. There's a separate **loung**e and a good selection of **Italian wines**. The interior is cardinal red, with a seasonally changing display of colored lights and artificial plants. Reservations taken, advised in summer and on weekends. No credit cards; out-of-town checks OK. *402 W. Adams/U.S. 2 on the west edge of downtown Iron River. 265-4764. Open Tues-Sun 4:30 p.m.-9 p.m. Central Time, to 10 p.m. from May thru Nov.* ♿ ⛄👫👫 Full bar

ZIPPEDY DUDA offers a varied menu, soup and sandwiches, homemade ravioli and gnocchi, steaks, shish keb ab, lobster, in a no-smoking, fine dining setting. There's a separate lounge. Dinner entrées, from $9 to $20, include a soup and salad bar. Early bird specials (from 4:30 to 6) are $7. Cream, fruit pies and cheesecake are homemade. The **Friday night buffet** ($9) has 7 kinds of seafood. *202 W. Genesee in downtown Iron River, one block south of U.S. 2. 265-6193. Closed Sun. Mon-Thurs 4:30-9, Fri & Sat 4:30-10.* ♿ 👫👫 Full bar

For breakfast, **HAPPY ITALIANS ROMA CAFE** on U.S. 2 just west of the river is a popular place — and just about the only breakfast places except for McDonald's. It also serves sandwiches, Italian food, and drinks in a family restaurant setting with big windows. *On U.S. 2 at West Adams in downtown Iron River. 265-9251. Open 7 days, 6 a.m. to 9 p.m.* ♿ 👫👫 Full bar

The **RIVERSIDE BAR & PIZZERIA** has enjoyed a **big local reputation for pizza** since 1946. Its crust is thin and cracker-like (a style encountered elsewhere in the U.P.'s iron ranges), its sauce spicy and made on the premises, and the sausage custom made. The limited number of classic toppings includes anchovies — "You

gotta have 'em." The only other foods in this **family-oriented sports bar** are the Friday fish fry ($6) and a foot-long hot dog ($3) that comes with homemade sauce and is available any time. No credit cards. Out-of-town checks OK. *On U.S. 2 in Iron River, a block west of McDonald's and just east of the river and downtown. 265-9944. Opens daily at 3 p.m., Sun at noon. Closes at midnight. Pizza served 4 p.m.-10 p.m.* ♿: one tiny step. 👫👫 Full bar

The menu at **KERMIT'S BAR, PIZZA PUB & GRILL** isn't ambitious, but what it does, it does well. This well-run bar is a regular lunch place for people who care about good food. Tasty char-grilled chicken breasts appear in a delicious chicken pita sandwich with cucumber dressing ($5), chicken Caesar salad ($6), and more. A spicy beef mix makes for good taco salad ($6), taco pizza with lots of toppings, and chili. There's a good steak sandwich ($7), breaded seafood dinners (mostly $6.25), nachos and bar food. A 1/3 pound burger is $3. That competes with McDonald's down the hill, and the atmosphere is lots nicer at this spiffy, unsmoky **sports bar** with **pool, darts**, and stacks of oak highchairs for little ones. *500 Washington at the south end of downtown Stambaugh. 265-2790. From U.S. 2 in Iron River, turn south onto Lay opposite McDonald's. Kitchen open Mon-Sat 11 a.m.-midnight Central Time unless it's so slow that Kermit's closes.* ♿ 👫👫 Full bar

Dancing, a favorite form of U.P. entertainment for a century, has largely disappeared on a regular basis. **THE LANDING,** a longtime restaurant on Chicaugon Lake, is one of the very few places where you can dine and dance — on a good hardwood dance floor. **Saturdays,** year-round beginning at 9, bring **classic rock and country**, with a band, deejay, or karaoke, for "the younger crowd" — baby boomers and younger. Friday dancing will be added in summer at least. **Sunday afternoons** year-round from 4:30 to 8:30 a band plays **polkas, waltzes**, and such for retirees and others who love the old dances.

The menu ranges from fine dining (steaks, chicken, pasta, fish) to sandwiches and burgers. The dining room has a good view of the lake. The new owner hopes to add a deck and gazebo. *Off CR 424 at the south end of Chicaugon Lake on the way to the George Young Recreation Center. 265-3343. Open year-round, at least Wed-Sun. Open 7 days starting late May into fall. Kitchen open 5-9, bar usually open to 2 a.m.* 👫👫 Full bar

IRON RIVER-AREA LODGINGS

Expect higher rates in deer-hunting season and ski season. An extra perk in the Iron River area is public access to the country-club-like George Young Recreation Complex (see above), with its beautiful golf course, cross-country and mountain bike trails, and big indoor pool.

Lodgings have been arranged starting with in-town, moving south and west.

AmericINN MOTEL (906) 265-9100; reservations (800) 634-3444

This **luxurious downtown motel**, finished in 1996, has been so successful that 24 more rooms are being added to its original 46 rooms. Regular rates for standard rooms in summer and ski season start at $94, higher on weekends and for special events. Whirlpool rooms and suites are more. Northwoods wildlife is the decorating theme. Masonry construction means quiet rooms. **Free breakfast buffet** includes hot cereal, fruit served in lobby with big **stone fireplace**, antler chandeliers, comfy sofas. Breakfast tables can become game tables. Hot drinks available any time. The **beautiful indoor pool** has big windows, a whirlpool, and a sauna. On snowmobile trail. *On U.S. 2 just east of downtown Iron River.*

H.A.: 2 rooms ADA accessible.
👫👫: 13 & under free

IRON INN MOTEL (906) 265-5111

The name of this basic two-story, 9-room motel recalls the landmark old hotel that once stood here. **Pleasant, good-size rooms** ($41 for two in 2000) are more attractively decorated than the exterior would suggest, and the owner-manager continues to make improvements (new carpeting most recently). All rooms have phones, air-conditioning, and cable TV with ESPN and Disney. A **good location** permits walks to downtown Iron River and its restaurants, and through an interesting turn-of-the-century neighborhood in the rear. On snowmobile trail. *On north side of U.S. 2 at west side of downtown.*
H.A.: 1 room ADA accessible 🐾: call
👫👫: 5 & under free, $5/extra person

LAKESHORE MOTEL
(906) 265-3611; www.iron.org/biz

A **lakefront setting**, **informed owner-managers**, and lots of extras make this motel special. All 20 rooms overlook **Ice Lake** just east of Iron River, half a block from Ice Lake Park. All rooms are air-conditioned, with cable TV and phones. Regular rooms are $33 (one bed) and

$45 (two beds), kitchenettes $45 to $70. Redecorating is in the works; the larger, upstairs rooms have been finished. Free coffee and **continental breakfast** are available in the office. Away from highway noise. Over 500 feet of shoreline has a **small sandy swimming beach**, a **boat launch** for guests, a dock and **picnic area.** Guests can **rent a rowboat or paddle boat.** Call at least 4 months ahead for best availability in July; advance reservations a good idea in August, too. *1257 Lalley Rd., 1 block south of U.S. 2 on the east edge of Iron River, 1 1/2 miles east of downtown.* **H.A.:** call. 👫🏻: rates by the room, not the person.

The CHICAUGON LAKE INN

(906) 265-9244; www.iron.org/biz

This very attractive newish 24-room motel on one floor is near the entrance to the spectacular George Young Recreation Complex (see above). Rooms have contemporary, Indian-inspired decor. All have phones and air-conditioning. No cable (it's not out here); TVs have 3 channels, but the big-screen TV in the comfortable lobby has 100 satellite channels for that important game. Standard rooms ($62 in 2000) have one king or two queens. Two whirlpool rooms ($79) have one king, a VCR, microwave, and mini-fridge. **Continental breakfast** is served in lobby. A **fish freezer** is available. Recent additions are a **volleyball court** and a **campfire area**, used on weekends. Next door is a **boat launch** on 1,100-acre **Chicaugon Lake** and The Landing restaurant with paddleboat rentals and weekend dancing. Close to Pentoga Park on the lake. About 10 miles from Ski Brule and Iron River. On main snowmobile trail. *1700 CR 424, about 5 1/2 miles east of Gaastra and 7 miles east of M-189.* **H.A.:** 1 room ADA accessible. Call on others. 👫🏻: 14 & under no extra charge. 🐕: 3 rooms. $10/night. Call ahead.

LAC O'SEASONS RESORT

(800) 797-5226; (906) 265-4881; www.webstruction.com/los/

Because it's somewhat larger than most lakeside cottage resorts, Lac O'Seasons offers many extras. There's a large **lodge** with **fireplace**, gathering area, **satellite TV,** and **kitchen** (a big plus for reunion groups that often rent cottages here). There's a big **indoor pool** with whirlpool, sauna, and a game room with video games, pinball, and pool. After dinner, many families come up to the lodge for **ice cream** (10 flavors) and socializing, while the kids swim in the lake or

pool. Stanley Lake is a **quiet lake**, known for walleye, with musky and large and smallmouth bass. The resort has over **600 feet of wooded shoreline** going down to the lake; sand has been moved in to create a **small beach**, protected by an L-shaped **swimming dock.** Two **swimming rafts** are farther out. **Kayaks, canoes,** and **fishing boats** are for rent, and a paddleboat free to guests.

Of the 15 housekeeping cottages, built over the past 25 years, 8 are on the lake. Typical rates for two bedrooms: $610/week or $90/day lakeside, $550/$80 otherwise. Some have fireplaces. All have TV/VCRs (just two channels on the TV), microwaves, decks. No air-conditioning. Rentals are by the week in summer, otherwise there's a two-night minimum. Summer availability is better than at smaller resorts. Call in January for best choices. *176 Stanley Lake Dr., 7 minutes southwest of Iron River, close to Ski Brule.* **H.A.** one unit.

SKI BRULE (800) DO-BRULE;

(906) 265-4957; www.skibrule.com; e-mail: skibrule@up.net

Of all the U.P. ski resorts, Ski Brule does the most to offer families a **variety of activities,** winter and **summer.** Lodgings are in the condos and chalets in this beautiful rural area near the Brule River Valley. There is no pool, indoors or out. Summer activities on the premises include **rafts, tubing,** and **canoeing, sporting clays** (shooting), guided one-hour **trail rides** on horseback, and **mountain biking. Fishing** is a huge area attraction. Outstanding golf and a beautiful indoor pool are 15 minutes away at the George Young Recreational Center outside Iron River. Summer rates start at $49 a night, $200 a week for two in condos, $59/$295 in chalets. Hot tub units start at $79/$395. Swimming at Lake Ottawa isn't far, either. Not air-conditioned. *7 miles southwest of Iron River. Take M-189 south, look for sign. Open year-round.* 🔥: call 👫🏻: no extra charge for 9 & under. $10/extra person over room rating. 🐕: call

IRON RIVER AREA CAMPING

GOLDEN LAKE Campground/ Ottawa National Forest

(906) 265-5139; not reservable
www.fs.us.fed.us/r9/ottawa

A mile north of U.S. 2 between Watersmeet and Iron River, this 22-site rustic campground offers convenient overnight camping on the developed site of **285-acre Golden Lake. One of the U.P.'s deepest lakes**, it's spring-fed and

cool even on hot days. Hemlock roots color the water golden. It's stocked with **trout.** Campsites are up above the lake, and many have a **view of the water.** Some are in a grassy, open area, others more shielded from neighbors and shaded by maple and hemlock. There's an adjacent **picnic area** and **boat launch** but no developed **beach,** though swimming is possible. Some summers a **campground host** is here. $6/night fee. *North off U.S. 2, 17 miles east of Watersmeet and 14 miles west of Iron River. Open May thru mid-Oct.* **H.A.:** paved sites. Toilets not accessible. 👫🏻 🐕

LAKE OTTAWA Campground/ Ottawa National Forest

(906) 265-5139; no reservations

This popular 32-site campground (with flush toilets but no showers) is on 551-acre Lake Ottawa, next to a pretty park and boat launch. (See above for park and fishing.) The **handsome log picnic shelter** with two large stone **fireplaces** was built by the Civilian Conservation Corps. So were the log restrooms with flush toilets. There's a **short trail** to the **sandy beach** at the day use area. Most sites have a **dense maple canopy** and **good privacy.** A **campground host** is usually here all summer. First-come, first-serve. Perhaps the Ottawa National Forest's most popular campground. Some years it's full most days in July, so call first and consider a backup. Or come early in the week. Paved spurs vary from 42' to 90'. *About 6 miles west of Iron River. Take U.S. 2 west, in less than 2 miles turn south at M-73. In about 1 mile, look for Forest Hwy. 101 and signs to park. Mostly $7 and $9 camping fee. Two larger sites are $12.* TTY: (906) 265-9259. *Open May 15-Sept 15.* **H.A.:** call. Accessible toilets by 2002. Accessible day use bldg. & fishing pier. 👫🏻 🐕: 6-foot leash

BLOCKHOUSE and PAINT RIVER FORKS Campgrounds/Ottawa National Forest (906) 265-5139; not reservable

These two tiny campgrounds (2 & 4 sites) are on the **Paint River**, a trout stream with **native brook trout**, canoeable early in the season. It's about 5 miles, maybe 2 to 3 leisurely hours. Blockhouse is **particularly pretty**, though maintenance isn't the best at these underused, remote spots. Therefore there's no fee charged. *Both are reached by taking C.R. 657 north from U.S. 2 (the junction is about 4 miles west of Iron Mountain) to Gibbs City (don't expect a city!) in about 10 miles.* **Paint River Forks** is less than 2 miles west of Gibbs City via 657, which turns west. *The road to Blockhouse is round-about: continue north from Gibbs City for almost 5 miles. Look for the sign and turn for another 5-mile drive via Forest Hwy. 2180. Open from May thru Nov.* **H.A.:** not really. Call 👫👨‍👧 🐕

PENTOGA PARK (906) 265-3979. Does not yet take reservations

In the 1920s this park on 1,100-acre Chicaugon Lake (see above) was created to preserve an Ojibwa burial ground. Park buildings of log and stone are handsomely woodsy. There's a **swimming beach**, picnic area, **new playground**, boat launch, fish-cleaning house, and 100 close-spaced modern campsites in a grove of **big oaks**. There's no privacy between sites. Sites are rented by the day ($12). Campsites fill for 6 or 7 summer weeks. Come Sunday thru Wednesday or Thursday and you'll probably get a spot. There's a **laundry** and pay phones. Supplies for **shuffleboard, horseshoes,** and **volleyball** are at the entrance booth. Group camping across the road. *On CR 424 midway between Caspian and Alpha. From U.S. 2, take CR 639 south just west of Bewabic State Park. Open May 15-Sept 30.* ♿: no

Crystal Falls (pop. 1,791)

Few Midwestern towns enjoy a more **spectacular site** and provide a clearer visual image than Crystal Falls. Where U.S. 2 turns from south to west, Iron County's memorable, tall-towered 1890 Romanesque courthouse sits at the crest of a steep hill and surveys the Paint River Valley. An undulating, uninterrupted vista of forest unfolds beyond. **"The Jewel of Iron County,"** as the courthouse has long been known, is at the very head of the main business street, Superior Avenue, which runs straight down to the river. In snowy weather, local motorists observe a practi-

cal parking tradition. Cars park on Superior's downhill (south) side to gain momentum, while vehicles with four-wheel-drive park facing uphill.

Crystal Falls actually stole the county seat — a fact widely remembered as an element of the east side vs. west side county rivalry that's still strong today. At Iron County's very inception, economic development on the county's east side, centered at Crystal Falls, was exactly mirrored by that on the west side, at Iron River. That coincidence set the stage for inevitable tension between booster groups for each area. 1875 brought the first iron ore prospectors and the first loggers to each area. By 1882 each town had a branch of the Chicago & Northwestern Railroad to serve its mines and lumber camps. At first Iron River received the temporary designation of county seat. In 1886 voters voted on the permanent location, but the ballots never got counted — why, no one knows. County ledgers were stolen at night and moved to Crystal Falls, and procedural strategies implemented to keep meetings and offices there. By the time a second vote on the county seat was conducted in 1888, Crystal Falls had legitimately won by nearly 100 votes. The striking vista afforded by the Crystal Falls courthouse site was used to help make its case for the county seat.

By 1890 Crystal Falls had grown to a population of 3,231. The booming town built a dam and electrical power plant on the Paint River. The **oldest U. P. dam**, it can be reached by taking Sixth Street north half a mile from the town center — a **scenic detour** that also passes the old log houses remaining from the **isolated Falls Location** mining settlement. (Some houses have been sided over.) Architectural legacies of Crystal Falls' boom times in the 1890s and the 1920s are the many handsome but not overwhelmingly impressive houses on Fifth, Marquette, and Crystal near downtown. A large population of Finnish immigrants still flavors the town today.

The city of Iron River and the county's west side would eventually overtake the east side, but only after 1900. It took that long for the Menominee Range to recover from the depression caused by the nationwide Panic of 1893.

Today Crystal Falls enjoys a reputation as a tight-knit town where natives and a considerable number of transplants and returning retirees work together on community activities from the arts and the environment to historic preservation. "You fall in love with the place," says Pat Sommers, a relatively

recent transplant who has a sausage shop here. "It's slow, it's easy-going. This is an interesting town, and you can be in the woods in three minutes. You can make a living here if you can live on $5 an hour."

In 1992 national media descended on this quiet place after a *Nature* journal research article proclaimed the existence of the **world's largest and possibly oldest known living organism**, an *armillaria bulbosa* or **honey mushroom** extending over 30 acres south of Horserace Rapids south of town. The "humungus fungus," as it was quickly dubbed, was discovered as part of a study of tree pathogens for the Navy by researchers at Michigan Tech and the University of Toronto. The study tested possible negative environmental effects of the Navy's ELF (extremely low frequency) underground antenna system to communicate with submarines. An ELF line is installed near Marquette to take advantage of its geology on the Canadian Shield which aids transmission. Their studies revealed that the underground filaments taken from a wide area were genetically identical, unlike previously known large fungal colonies, in which molds at intersecting edges were smeared together. This extremely large and successful individual organism, well adapted to its environment, was descended from a single spore probably over 1,500 years old, based on observed growth rates.

Crystal Falls' special status didn't last long. Other similar but larger fungi systems were discovered, including one in Washington state that's 40 times as large.

Economically, the town has stagnated for some years, its population in decline. But infrastructure has finally been installed in the city's 26-acre industrial park a half mile west of town at US 2 & 141. So far, there's been no luck in attracting businesses, however.

Iron County Courthouse

This splendidly sited Romanesque Revival courthouse from 1890 is perhaps **Michigan's most memorable courthouse**. Visitors can explore the interior of this well-preserved building and admire details like the oak wainscoting, carved oak balustrade, and decorative door hinges. The columns flanking the big entrance arch were quarried locally from outcrops along the Paint River. Look up before entering for a dramatic view of the towers and the galvanized metal **female figures of Law, Mercy, and Justice** over the entrance

A special point of pride is the **big,**

second-floor courtroom with its octagonal ceiling of decorative pressed metal and its **huge chandelier** with **muses** and **dragons** looking down from their perch of cast iron leaves. A window in the courthouse's second-floor stair tower frames the grand view down the main street and off into the forest in a striking manner.

Downstairs is a small **exhibit of county history** prepared by the Iron County Museum in Caspian, and a donated **geology collection** of regional rocks, some gorgeous minerals, and iron samples. The souvenir **courthouse mug** can be purchased at the County Clerk's office.

2 S. Sixth at the head of Superior, a block west of U.S. 2. (906) 875-3301. Open Mon-Fri 8-4 Central Time, closed 12-12:30. &: *rear entrance off parking lot.*

Downtown Crystal Falls

Just east of the courthouse lawn, at the head of Superior Avenue, are the Lutheran church and the **1935 post office**. In its **WPA mural** an idealized farmer and wife plow a field that certainly doesn't resemble the farms around here.

A good deal of Crystal Falls' commercial energy has migrated west of town around the intersection of U.S. 2 and U.S. 141. Superior Street has a number of noteworthy buildings and institutions. Lately some visitor-oriented businesses have opted for this charming setting. Highlights include (from hilltop to river):

◆ **The CRYSTAL FALLS CONTEMPORARY CENTER** holds **classes** for adults and children in yoga, dance, woodcarving, pottery. Of interest to summer visitors are **one-day drop-in sessions** like the $5 **open pottery studio** held some evenings and the summer **clay camp** and **art camp** for kids, two hours a day. *For a current schedule, visit www.crystalfalls.org and click on "culture."* 200 *Superior.* 875-4595. &

◆ **The CRYSTAL INN**, an **impressive three-story former hotel**, is now a senior citizens' home.

◆ The three-story brick building with a central tower at 401 Superior looks like an old brewery. It is actually the **CITY HALL**, built in 1914 as a community center with a fire house, an auditorium, and the **Crystal Falls District Community Library**, which is a good source of information on the area's mining history. *875-3344. It's open Mon-Thurs 9-7, Fri to 4, Sat 10-2.* &: *use side door.*

◆ **CRYSTAL THEATRE**. This small, 574-seat theater from 1927-28 has been restored through the Herculean efforts of

"The Jewel of Iron County": The 1890 Romanesque Revival courthouse is a spectacular building on a dramatic site. The front steps and a window in the stair tower offer a sweeping view down the main street of Crystal Falls out to miles of forest beyond. The lobby offers exhibits of local history and minerals. It took an act of theft for Crystal Falls to win the county seat from its arch-rival Iron River.

11 theater organ buffs. They repaired the abandoned movie/vaudeville theater, repainted its elaborate **multicolored geometric plaster work**, and installed a **21-rank Moeller theater organ**, much larger than a theater this size would originally have had. The summer pipe organ concerts draw from farthest away, but the June variety show sells out. Half the town's in it and the other half comes to see it. Traveling concerts, local theater groups, and a popular country and western show are booked. For **events info**, call (906) 875-3208 or (906) 875-6052 or visit **www.crystalfalls.org** and click on "culture." *304 Superior.*

◆ **Peninsula Title & Abstract** at Superior and Fourth has a leaded glass window bearing the name of the **CRYSTAL FALLS CO-OPERATIVE SOCIETY**. It was one of many co-ops common in mining districts, especially in Finnish settlements like Crystal Falls. Mines recruited heavily for workers in Finland. One local recruiting agent was so well known that letters addressed only to his name and USA would find their way to him in Crystal Falls.

◆ At **SOMMERS SAUSAGE SHOP & GROCERY**, Pat Sommers makes **outstanding snack sticks** and **fast-selling beef and chicken jerky**, both needing no refrigeration and thus a boon for campers. He prepares bacon, ham, smoked chicken, and more. Fresh sausages made here range from bratwurst, kielbasa, and their

new relation cheddarwurst, to Italian sausage, Cajun andouille, and chorizo. Sommers learned the trade from the founder of Lewandoski's Market on Grand Rapids' Polish west side.

Lunch specials, soups, **sandwiches**, and **deli items** are a welcome new addition. As yet there's no seating. *132 Superior. 875-6032. Mon-Fri 8-6:30, Sat 8-5.*

◆ **THE ART BARN.** A former feed barn houses the painting studio/gallery of Packy Eckola, an Iron Range native, Oakland County transplant, and local arts dynamo. She started the very popular and professional annual June variety show, now done by others. "You could go to any community and do something like this. Honey, there's talent everywhere," she says. Her new web site, packyeckolasartbarn@uplogon.com, conveys her publications and ideas about the importance of art as an alternative route to problem-solving, accessible to people of many intellectual abilities. *33 1/3 Fourth, behind Crystal Interiors. Open by appointment. 875-4179.*

◆ **BARGAIN BARN ANTIQUES**, after eight years on the highway, has taken over the old Nelson Hotel and installed its attractive (and attractively priced) mix of antiques and collectibles, large and small. With 22 upstairs rooms to fill, the proprietors are adding outside dealers. *60 Superior. 875-3381. Open Mon-Sat 9-5. In summer, could close on Wed and open Sun.*

Harbour House Museum

A really **unusual house** and a **hands-on policy** set this local house museum apart from others of its kind. Here visitors can play the piano, pick up the stereopticon, and leaf through old photo albums. It's a Queen Anne house with prominent gables and towers, but constructed of rough cement block, not wood. **Twin porches**, one upstairs and one down, wrap around the entire house, giving a **grand view** of the meadow and **Paint River Valley** to its immediate east. Builders of cement block houses before World War I were almost always progressive experimenters and innovators in many other respects. A local lawyer had the house built but never owned it, giving title to his secretary and her family in exchange for providing him with his meals. His law office and bedroom are furnished the way he had them. So are the downstairs rooms used by the secretary's family.

The upstairs rooms are given over to the Crystal Falls Museum Society's **exhibits on mining**, schools, military veterans, **children's toys** (including a miniature carousel), and clothing. The materials about area **Ojibwa culture** may be the best in the Upper Peninsula. Their curator is Earl Nyholm, a professor in Bemidji, Minnesota. His grandmother, **Pentoga**, was the Ojibwa chief's wife, after whom the village and park by Chicaugon Lake were named.

17 N. Fourth at Spring. Open Mem. to Labor Day, Tues-Sat 11-4 and by appointment. (906) 875-4341. Free. Donations appreciated.

Crystal View Golf Course

Golf's bygone simplicity still reigns at this **super-scenic and challenging nine-hole course** on the rather steep Paint River valley wall just east of town. The name was recently changed from Crystal Falls Municipal Golf Course, but the city still owns the course. Mature hardwoods along the valley floor frame a grand view of the little town from the fairway, culminating with the hillcrest courthouse and water tower. The trees and topography make for some blind spots that require golfers to ring bells to prevent accidental beanings on three holes. **Snacks** are available at the little white **clubhouse** from the 1920s. Men's course rating/slope is 35.1/124, women's is 37.2/125. 2000 fees: $13-$14 for 9 holes, $19 for 18 holes or all day, Mon-Fri. $100 for 10 plays any time.

Go east from town on Superior/M-69, turn left (north) onto Wagner right after crossing river. Watch for golf course entrance up the hill. 875-9919. Open from sometime in May into early Oct, weather permitting.

Runkle Lake Park

A **pretty, rustic-style park** from the 1920s affords swimming on Runkle Lake, barely a mile east of Crystal Falls. A **picturesque log shelter overlooks big red pines** and a lawn going down to the lake and **narrow sand beach**. There's a big dock, a wheelchair-accessible **fishing pier**, and a **boat launch**. Tennis courts, ball diamonds, and an enclosure with tame deer are nearby. See below for camping.

*From M-69 about 1/2 mile east of the Paint River, turn north at sign. Park is just ahead. (906) 875-3051. **H.A.**: good for wheelchairs but not paved*

Glidden Lake & Lake Mary Plains Pathway

A beach is near the 23-site rustic campground at Glidden Lake. A ten-mile **path** for **hiking** and **cross-country skiing** (groomed in winter) goes across flat to rolling terrain but doesn't actually reach Lake Mary. The first loop, 3.4 miles, includes a **boardwalk** across an interesting **bog**. Two other loops of 4.5 miles and 3.9 miles build on the first loop. The trail goes through pine plantations (some selective cutting does occur on this state forest land), pin oak uplands, and areas of aspen, blueberry, and birch. This area is part of the **Copper Country State Forest**.

Look for the sign to the campground a mile south of M-69, 5 miles east of Crystal Falls. (906) 353-6651. Free. ♿: no.

Horserace Rapids

The **rugged, romantic appeal** of this memorable place lies not so much in the rushing rapids down on the Paint River as in the **unfolding approach** to it. The path from the bluff top to the river 80 feet below is mostly paved for better footing. It leads down, gradually in many places, but with 86 steps in all. Soon you are twisting around massive boulders. First the rocks jut out among birches that catch the sunlight. Then the path descends into deep shade created both by towering dark pines and by the red-rocked bluffs on both sides of the river. The sound of the water grows louder as you go down. Ferns and mosses add to the feeling that this is a magical glen, a world of its own. Finally, walking

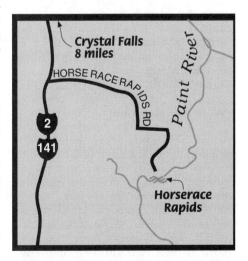

Horserace Rapids south of Crystal Falls is a magic, tucked-away place with an unfolding view of huge pines and roaring rapids as visitors descend from high bluffs into a shady canyon.

among the rocks, you reach the river's level and see how it rushes around more rocks as it flows west toward Paint Pond, the hydroelectric dam's impoundment of the Paint's last miles before it joins the Brule River near Florence, Wisconsin. In a few more miles the Brule and the Michigamme rivers join to form the Menominee.

On the east side of U.S. 2, about 6 miles south of Crystal Falls and 8 miles north of Florence, Wisconsin, look for the sign for the Iron County Airport and Horserace Rapids road. A good dirt road leads to the parking area in a little over 3 miles.

Bewabic State Park

An unusual mix of state park amenities at a convenient location is offered at this beautiful state park in a mature birch-maple forest. A handsome stone pavilion built by the **Civilian Conservation Corps** in the 1930s is the focal point of the **attractive, grassy picnic area** with a playground and **small, sandy swimming beach** on First Fortune Lake. A footbridge leads to a small island, also created by the CCC. Two **tennis courts** are the only ones in the state park system. A **boat launch** is nearby.

First Lake, the largest (192 acres) and deepest (72 feet), has **good fishing for bass and bluegill**. The entire four-lake Fortune chain of lakes can be canoed. Though the first and second lakes with their cottages and camps are seeing some noisy jet skis on weekends, First Lake is quiet enough for loons, which also nest on **Fourth Lake**, two miles from the boat launch. Eagles nest on Third Lake. Access to Mud Lake, just across U.S. 2 to the north, is limited to canoes by a low highway bridge. It has few cottages and good fishing for bluegill. **Canoes** can be rented at Fortune Lake Cabins (906-875-3736) at 116 Resort Drive, just east of the park. Michi-Aho Resort (906-875-3514) east of Crystal Falls on M-69 offers **canoe and boat rentals** and trailers.

The park owes its existence to Iron County highway engineer Herb Larson. In the early 1920s, buoyed by the success of his roadside park and picnic areas (above), he "tried to keep alert and ahead of the woodsman's axe," in his own words. On a train to Marquette he happened to meet the owner of this timbered land on Fortune Lake, who was about to sell to a lumber company. Larson talked him into selling it to Iron County for this park. Later Larson orchestrated WPA projects carried out by the CCC camp across the road.

Eventually Bewabic Park became too

much for the county to maintain. The state took it over in the 1960s. Many locals still resent having to pay to enter what they once enjoyed for free, so use is mainly by vacationers.

The park is on U.S. 2, 4 miles west of Crystal Falls and about 11 miles east of Iron River on the west side of First Fortune Lake. Open all year. Campground not plowed; plug-ins by the office are available. (906) 875-3324. State park sticker required: $4/$5 day, $20/$25 year. &: *buildings, being older, are not ADA accessible. People in wheelchairs will require assistance; others will probably do OK. Call.*

Chicaugon Falls

A mile hike leads to the top of this **striking, little-visited waterfall** that creates a dramatic deep glen among massive, dark boulders. The walk has some hills but isn't difficult. It's quite enjoyable, thanks to the dense forest along the way, and the huge and fragrant **cedars** along Chicaugon Creek. The trail crosses a tributary to a little **island** from which the water can be viewed as it drops a little, then turns and goes down a rock chute two stories high, before foaming over the boulders and falling again.

North off U.S. 2, .6 mile west of the entrance to Bewabic State Park. Take Long Lake Rd. north, winding east around the lake to its north side. In 3.3 miles look for a two-track on the right, by a yellow-painted stump. Drive in 1/4 mile. Park by gravel pit. More yellow paint marks 1-mile trail to falls. &: *no.*

CRYSTAL FALLS AREA RESTAURANTS

Formerly Club Felix, **SUE'S BORDER SUPPER CLUB** continues fine dining with an **exceptional soup and salad bar** included with all dinners. It's a favorite of guests at a Wisconsin B&B for the **"fabulous" Friday fish fry**, Saturday prime rib, and midweek specials. Tenderloin stuffed with mushrooms, garlic, and onions ($20) is a standout. Entrées range from $9 to $20. Pasta entrées for vegetarians. Diners can also order burgers and sandwiches à la carte. Currently smokers and non-smokers share a single space. That may change. *On U.S. 2 just inside the Michigan state line, 8 miles south of Crystal Falls and 4 miles north of Florence, Wisconsin. 875-3779. Mon-Thurs 4:30-9 p.m., Fri & Sat 4:30-10 p.m. Central Time.*
& &&&& Full bar

FOB'S FINE FOOD is the big, bustling **area gathering place**. Decor is comfy country. **Broasted chicken** (battered and fried under pressure) is a specialty. Breakfast is served all day. Prices stun city visitors: Fob's breakfast special (2 eggs, a piece of bacon or sausage, hash browns) for $1.39, daily specials like Swiss steak and rigatoni with salad or soup from $4 to $6 or so. Pies and soups are house made. *It's in the Williams Mini-Mall on U.S. 2 at 141, a simple strip mall with an enclosed sidewalk area. 875-4200. Open daily 5:30 a.m. to 9 p.m. Central Time.* & &&&&

CRYSTAL FALLS LODGING

See also Chicaugon Inn near Iron River.

EDGAR'S RIVERVIEW B&B
(906) 875-6213;
www.iron.org/biz/river/edriv.html

Richard Edgar's first wife finished decorating their dream house before her death. Afterwards, Richard decided to stay in the big house and become an innkeeper. The place enjoys a secluded setting in the woods on the Michigamme River within about 5 miles of two big impoundments. Feeders mean many birds and deer are constant visitors. All three guest rooms have river views, as does the deck. Edgar's is a blend of inn and homestay B&B. The three guest rooms ($85, $95, and for whirlpool room $105 in the year 2000) are in their own wing, with a separate entrance. Guests share most of the rest of the house with Richard and his new wife: the kitchen (they're welcome to use the fridge) and **fireside gathering room with big fireplace** and cathedral ceiling, decorated in successful mix of northwoods, country, and Native Americana. Full breakfast. Richard offers **canoe rentals** and **spotting**, and an informal **guide service** on his deck boat, for fishing and watching eagles. On snowmobile trail. *On south side of M-69 at Michigamme River, 6 miles east of Crystal Falls. Open year-round.* **H.A.:** call. Much is wheelchair-accessible. &&&: no extra charge

MICHI-AHO RESORT (906) 875-3514
This **fishing-oriented** roadside motel with cottages enjoys an unusual setting on the Michigamme River. A rear deck **overlooks a small pond** connecting to the river between two big impoundments. Rates go by the room. For one bed, $47 in winter (mid-Nov. thru March), $37 otherwise. Two beds: $57 and $47. Ask about rates for the three cottages. Reserve ahead for summer; not a bad idea for winter, either. It's been

open year-round since 2000-2001. The motel has **canoe** and **motorboat rentals** and spots canoeists on the nearby Michigamme, Paint, and Brule rivers. A tackle and **bait shop** are on the premises. *On north side of M-69 at Michigamme River, 6 miles east of Crystal Falls. Open year-round.* **H.A.:** call. : no extra charge

CRYSTAL FALLS AREA CAMPING

See also Pentoga Park near Iron River.

BEWABIC STATE PARK

(906) 875-3324.
Reserv.: (800) 44-PARKS; (800) 605-8295 TDD; www.dnr.state.mi.us/

This **beautiful state park** on a chain of four lakes offers swimming, tennis, and good canoeing and fishing. Most sites in the 144-site modern campground ($11/$14 a night) are in a heavily wooded area that enjoys **excellent privacy** plus electricity and showers. Foot trails and a drive connect the campground with the nearest lake, 1/4 to 1/2 mile away. The campground used to be near the lake, but the septic system failed. Use, though not heavy, is increasing; in 2000 Bewabic camping tended to fill on July and August weekends. The popular lakes may be busy on Saturday but are never crowded; Pentoga Lake is more heavily used. The two-mile **trail system** goes mostly through the mature hardwood forest of maples and birch. Canoeist-campers who'd like to avoid other campers altogether should ask at the office for the map to 40 acres of state land on Third Lake, on which they can camp informally. *On U.S. 2, four miles west of Crystal Falls and about 11 miles east of Iron River, on the west side of First Fortune Lake. Open all year. Campground not plowed; winter plug-ins are by the office.* State park sticker required: $4/$5 day, $20/$25 a year. **H.A.:** call. Buildings are not ADA accessible.

RUNKLE PARK and CAMPGROUND

(906) 875-3051

The 57 campsites at this **pretty lakeside park from the 1920s** have electricity, shade, and water hookups, but no privacy buffers. (See above for info on park.) Tennis courts and ball diamonds. Walking distance to Crystal Falls, golf. About $9/night without sewage hookup, $14/night with it. *Off M-69 about 1/2 mile east of the Paint River and Crystal Falls. Turn north at sign. Park is just ahead. Open from Mem. through Labor Day weekends.* **H.A.:** mostly pretty good, but not ADA accessible. Firm ground. Occasional tree roots.

PEAVY POND, BRULE RIVER and MICHIGAMME RESERVOIR/Wisconsin Electric Power primitive camping

The Wisconsin Electric Power company owns a great deal of land along the rivers and impoundments it uses to generate power. It has voluntarily developed small, primitive campgrounds on so-called "project lands" around dams that are licensed by the Federal Energy Regulatory Commission. These lands are required to be open to public access, with **boat launches** provided. Campgrounds have no electricity or plumbing. They are shady, with privacy buffers where terrain allows. Camping fee is $8/night. Most have four campsites or fewer. When larger, they provide wells and pumps. Campgrounds do offer road access, garbage collection, level sites for RVs.

Wisconsin Electric Power sites are mapped in its **"Wilderness Shores"** *pamphlet,* available at the Iron River chamber of commerce, Michigan and Wisconsin Welcome Centers (in Iron Mountain, Ironwood, Hurley, and Menominee). Or write Wisconsin Electric Power, 800 Industrial Park Dr., Iron Mountain, MI 49801. Attn: Hydroelectric Operations Division.

GLIDDEN LAKE Campground/ Copper Country State Forest

A **beach** and **boat launch** are near the 23-site rustic campground (no electricity or showers, vault toilets) at Glidden Lake. A 10-mile **hiking/ski path** starts here. Just a mile east of the Michigamme River, near Peavy Pond and its good walleye fishing. Look for the sign to the campground a mile south of M-69, 5 miles east of Crystal Falls. (906) 353-6651. $6/$9 night. **H.A.:** call.

Amasa (pop. 360)

The **wilderness village** of Amasa, once a mining and logging boom town of 3,000, remains a surprising place, even as its population has shrunk. Today it is sustained largely by employment in the forest products industry and by some second homes and retirement homes, on Fire Lake and elsewhere. (It's pronounced "AM-a-SUH" with the Finnish accent on the first syllable, though it's not a Finnish word at all, but the name of a relative of mining magnate Henry Pickands.) Amasa is not a place where you'd expect to find so many people on Friday night that you can't park on Main Street, or a well-known environmental consulting company, or a regionally celebrated musical group drawing on folk and classical music.

Three bars and a restaurant/grocery store/motel serve food that attracts people from all directions. The new **museum** of the **Amasa Historical Society** is in the old fire hall/city hall/jail. Downstairs display cases deal with local mining, logging, and more. The upstairs is divided to resemble part of a mine, a logging camp, a store, and such. It's open most days in summer, usually from 9 to 4, and by appointment. A list of volunteers is posted on the door; they can be called on short notice from the pay phone at the nearby Amasa Hotel, whose owner is a museum stalwart.

The town's energy is a tribute to the western Upper Peninsula's powerful magnetic pull, which reaches across generations to draw back progeny of miners, loggers, woodsmen, and frontier entrepreneurs. Dean and Bette Premo of the well-known music group White Water are a case in point. Their professors at Michigan State University, where they earned their Ph.D.s in environmental science in 1985, were incredulous to learn that their promising graduates were moving to Amasa to set up a consulting business rather than going into academia or joining an established firm. But Dean had spent many happy summers here at his grandfather Ralph Premo's house. He loved hunting and fishing with his granddad and his father. A folk singer himself, Dean fondly remembered his father's stories of the dances and fiddling at the farm social hall west of town on Town Line Road in a neighborhood of Finnish farms.

Dean's great-grandfather, George Premo, an Amasa pioneer in the 1890s, had been something of a northwoods legend as a teller of tales, a marksman, and the proprietor of the Hotel Premo, a famous boardinghouse and bar in the logging era. (For the Field Museum in Chicago, George Premo shot 160 whitetails to provide the 16 mounted specimens still on view in its "Deer in Four Seasons" exhibit.) George's father, Jean-Baptiste Primeau, had come as a fur trader to the Menominee River valley in the 1830s. Another Premo ancestor is Queen Marinette, the famous Ojibwa trader at the Menominee River mouth.

Dean and Bette knew that to earn a living in Amasa, they would have to follow the established pattern of living simply, diversifying, and relying on many skills and trades. In the old days, miners gardened and farmed. Loggers' wives cooked in camps. Mill hands' and miners' wives took in boarders. As tourism grew, many local people became guides and started small resorts. And everyone saved money for when the hard times came. Even today locals work on their own houses — only outsiders hire work out. In his lifetime Dean's grandfather Ralph Premo was a tailor, made radios, ran a barbershop, and was a postmaster when he retired.

"We realized we might have to do just about anything to live here," says Dean. In addition to building up their environmental consulting company, White Water Associates, Dean and Bette began taking their music more seriously. "We were willing to guide fishermen, or to make music for anyone who would hire us — festivals, fairs, schools."

Things have worked out remarkably well for the Premos. White Water Associates has grown to 20 employees. And Dean and Bette's eclectic folk music group has thrived. It's now a family affair with their children, Evan and Laurel, developing into accomplished musicians and performers in their own right. They've recorded five albums, and given many concerts in the Upper Midwest. (Their schedule and recordings are on part of their website, www.whitewater-associates.com) White Water Associates has grown by doing environmental impact statements, landfill and groundwater work, and educational programs for clients ranging from individual landowners to paper companies and foundries to Indian tribes, conservation groups, and local, state, and federal governmental units.

Dances are no longer held at the Amasa farm hall, but their spirit continues in the Second Sunday Folk Dance series held near Bewabic State Park. (See the music section for details on this popular, broad-based institution.)

North of Amasa, the impressive remains of the **Triangle Ranch** can be seen by taking the Triangle Ranch Road east from U.S. 141 a mile or so north of town. It is an unusually ambitious example of the many 1920s projects to develop cutover U.P. land. Judson Rosebush, an Appleton, Wisconsin paper manufacturer, bought nearly 9,500 acres and hired an experienced Colorado cattle ranch boss. His aim: "to test out exhaustively the practicability of large-scale, capitalistic manufacturing methods in agriculture," specifically, raising pedigreed Herefords. Five enormous barns were built, plus pens, corrals, and houses including a quite impressive manager's bungalow. But feeding the cattle over the area's six-month winters required more fodder than the ranch

could raise. Triangle tried other things. In 1927 it advertised itself as "the only dude ranch east of the Mississippi." It raised sheep and poultry. It attempted "fur farming" by fencing in wild muskrats and beaver. None of these worked. Eventually most of the land was sold to Kimberly-Clark and reforested for pulp production.

If you're driving north on U.S. 141 and are up for an adventure, you could take a side trip and have a pretty good chance of seeing moose. The **biggest regular concentration of moose** seems to be south of Covington and a little east of the highway along Tracy Creek, just inside the Baraga County line. Look under Covington in the Keweenaw chapter for details.

AMASA RESTAURANTS & LODGINGS

AMASA HOTEL (906) 822-7775
A plain clapboard place from 1891, the hotel hasn't changed too much since logging days — except for the growing collection of **Amasa memorabilia** on the walls. Half-pound hamburgers, a Friday-night **fish fry** ($6-$9), and occasional live music and dances are big draws to the downstairs restaurant. Homemade soups ($1.75/bowl) and chili go with the sandwich menu ($4-$5). Dinners ($7-$15) feature steak and chicken, include potato, salad, and sometimes dessert. Specials ($5-$7) are offered at lunch and dinner daily. Upstairs over the dining room, five cheerfully decorated **guest rooms** ($20/night) share a bath down the hall. No credit cards. Out-of-town checks OK. *On Amasa's main street, east of U.S. 141 12 miles north of Crystal Falls. Kitchen open from 11 a.m. to 8 or 9 p.m. Bar closes at 2 a.m. weekends.* **H.A.**: restaurant. Restroom too small. Upstairs inaccessible. 🚹🚻 Full bar

The **PINE CONE CAFE and TALL PINES MOTEL** is Amasa's other social center. The rambling A-frame complex incorporates the grocery store, a motel, and a café **known for good breakfasts and lunches**. Stars here are breakfast with omelets, fresh-ground coffee, and **homemade sausage and bread**, and lunch with specials (under $5) and soup. In summer it has been open for dinner, too. Each of the motel's eight rooms has two double beds and cable TV. All rooms permit smoking. Rates are $47 for two or more people. At the **Tree House bunkhouse** at the top of the A-frame, up to 8 people can save money by sharing a room. *On U.S. 141 at the north edge of town.* 822-7713. *Café open 7 days a week from 7 a.m. to 2 p.m. May serve*

dinner in summer. **H.A.**: 1 accessible room 🚹🚻: no extra charge 🐕: call

Iron Mountain (*pop. 8,154*)

The industrial powerhouses of the Western U.P. are the sprawling city of Iron Mountain, with its dispersed neighborhoods built around mineshafts, and its younger, trimmer sister city of **Kingsford** (population 5,549), built up around a Ford Motor Company complex in 1923. To the casual motorist on U.S. 2, the Iron Mountain area is unattractive, but it has its share of **tucked-away beauty spots** and some memorable people, restaurants, and small businesses.

Iron Mountain's earliest settlers arrived when iron was found here in 1879. By 1886 the population had skyrocketed to 8,000. Two years later Iron Mountain's mines, the Chapin, the Hamilton, and the Millie, employed 3,525 men, stated Mrs. Isaac Ungerer in a history given to the Iron Mountain Women's Club in 1914. She recalled the boom years from personal experience as the wife of a local retail businessman. "Times were good and the city prosperous and spreading out in all directions and the people spending money like water. Expense was no object and where a good was to be gained, the price was not considered."

Mrs. Ungerer recalled with pride various improvements befitting Iron Mountain's new prominence, tossing in an occasional comment on the **all-important social distinctions to be maintained** between miners and their betters. She reported that 1887 brought a pulp mill (to Quinnesec Falls, home of a giant paper plant today), the Bell Telephone system, a hospital "admitting such patients as were not acceptable at the Chapin Hospital," and the opening of a hotel celebrated by "a grand ball given for the aristocracy of Iron Mountain," followed by a party "for the less fortunate brothers."

By 1890 larger, better capitalized operators were buying up many mines throughout the iron ranges. Then the Panic of 1893 caused widespread layoffs and the threat of violence. Little note has been made of how ownership of Michigan iron mines, like many other spheres of American capitalism of the time, were controlled by the notorious monopolistic financial and transportation "octopuses" and trusts. These combined mining, shipping, rail, and financial interests provoked Frank Norris's muckraking novels and the trust-busting reforms of Theodore Roosevelt and the Progressive Era. The Chapin Mine and many other Menominee Range mines were bought at fire-sale prices after the Panic of 1893 by Mark Hanna, the Cleveland iron magnate and Republican Party boss so powerful that he engineered McKinley's presidential victory over the populist William Jennings Bryan in 1896 and became virtually the boss of the entire nation. In 1914 Mrs. Ungerer, the ladies' club historian, expressed gratitude about how "the Hon. Mark Al. Hanna came to our rescue, by taking over the Chapin Mine and putting 500 men to work."

While Iron Mountain mainly sprawls along its busy highways and around its old mine pits, **Kingsford** bears the stamp of **1920s subdivisions** familiar to anyone who grew up around Detroit. That's because the town developed around a complex of Ford plants from the early 1920s. **Henry Ford**, in his quest for industrial independence and self-sufficiency, wanted to **own the source of his raw materials**. The U.P. had both the iron used in steelmaking and the wood then used for auto bodies. Ford scouts, ever energetic, bought up vast amounts of timberland and created the first Ford sawmill, one of the world's most modern, on a farm Ford bought outside Iron Mountain. By 1923 the area was incorporated as the village of Kingsford, named after Edward Kingsford, the Iron Mountain Ford dealer who married Henry Ford's cousin.

Just as in Detroit, Kingsford's main street was **Woodward**, leading from Carpenter Ave./M-95 to the **Ford Airport** at Cowboy Lake. It's still one of the U. P.'s busiest and most attractive airports. Soon Ford's Kingsford complex included a body plant for Model T floorboards and frames; lumber kilns; a refinery; and a chemical plant that produced antifreeze, paint solvents, and **Kingsford charcoal briquettes**, **the world's first**. As in Dearborn, the residential areas planned for management and workers were clearly separated. Workers' housing was south of Breitung and the plants, while managers lived in **Kingsford Heights**, north of Woodward near the airport and golf course. Another older elite neighborhood is just to the east in the city of Iron Mountain, around Crystal Lake at the west end of H Street.

After Henry Ford died, his far-flung U.P. empire was scrutinized by Ford management for cost-effectiveness and gradually sold off. The briquette company eventually moved south but still bears the Kingsford name.

Iron Mountain and vicinity continues

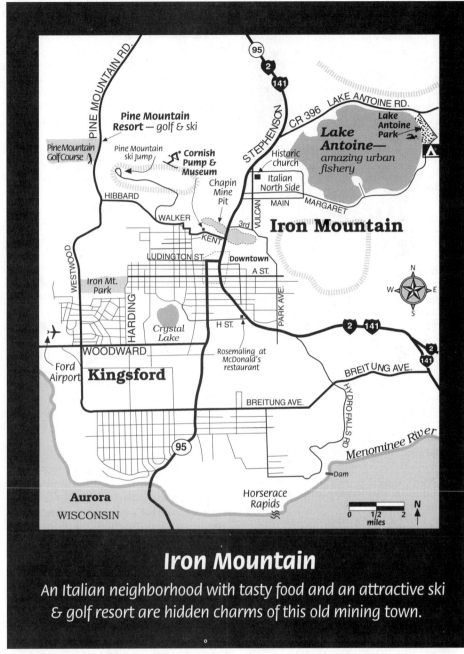

Iron Mountain

An Italian neighborhood with tasty food and an attractive ski & golf resort are hidden charms of this old mining town.

to have one of the strongest economic bases in the U.P. **Paper mills** are big employers: International Paper (formerly Champion) in Quinnesec (602 employees), StoraEnso (formerly the old Kimberly Clark Kleenex plant, more recently Consolidated Papers) in Niagara (450), and the Louisiana Pacific plant that makes 4x8-foot particle board in Sagola (178). Another large and fast-growing firm, Cable Constructors, has over 500 employees who install TV cable systems around the country. The large Wisconsin-based Grede foundry empire has a foundry in Kingsford with 485 employees. They make valves and other grey iron castings with complex internal shapes. Khoury's 150 employees make

do-it-yourself furniture kits. And there's even a company in Kingsford, Foley Martin, which makes fancy $750 stand-alone butcher block kitchen work tables sold all over the country.

The Italian North Side

It's not like it used to be in this tidy, tight-knit neighborhood that grew up just after the turn of the century north of the Chapin Mine and downtown. Today descendants of Italian miners have lost their language and intermarried. There are lots of non-Italian names among the parishioners of Immaculate Conception Church, built by Italian immigrant volunteers in 1902.

Bimbo and June Constantini contribute widely acclaimed porketta sandwiches and cappelletti soup to the fare at their popular North Side tavern next to their house. A former junior high teacher, Bimbo bought the tavern out of concern for his boyhood neighborhood.

But this trim working-class neighborhood has the feel of a **cherished way of life** where camaraderie and shared meals still mean a lot. New aluminum siding on these modest, well-kept homes is a point of neighborhood pride. A late summer bike tour reveals some **inspiringly serious home gardens**, with plum tomatoes staked and cut back for maximum growth in the precious summer warmth. Many small groceries remain, underscoring Iron Mountain's reputation for its ethnic food.

In March of 2000 the North Side of Iron Mountain basked in the national spotlight as its own Tom Izzo coached the Spartans of Michigan State to the national collegiate basketball championship. Izzo's Awnings and Izzo's Shoe Hospital, owned by relatives, appeared in Detroit papers. Newspaper stories professed amazement at how well the little guy from the U.P. and big black players from Flint meshed. The press, in its common way of not looking beyond the superficial stereotype, failed to see the similarities. Like Izzo, the "Flintstones" came from strong families with working-class backgrounds that emphasized team playing. True, the U.P. is entirely white except for Native Americans, but middle-aged people who grew up in the U.P. learned to deal with schoolmates from widely varying social backgrounds. Maybe that has something to do with the coincidence that another national coach, San Francisco 49ers' coach Steve Mariucci, was a grade school, high

school, and Northern Michigan University classmate of his friend Tom Izzo.

Vulcan, the north side's main street, parallels U.S. 2. Get there by turning east onto Third at Hardee's, or onto Margaret across from the A&W.

Highlights of the neighborhood include:

◆ **BIMBO'S WINE PRESS (L'Torchio di Vino)**, once a typical corner bar, has become a **center of local Italian-American culture and sports** with a limited menu of Italian specialties. See under Restaurants.

◆ **TOM BECCO'S MARKET** makes the **excellent Italian sausage** served at Bimbo's and prepares **porketta** to order, in addition to carrying **bulk olives** and a general line of meats. *100 West Main Street at U.S. 2. (Turn east by the Citgo station.) 774-2688. Mon-Fri 8-5, Sat 8-1 Central Time. &: no.*

◆ **CRISPIGNA'S ITALIAN MARKET** is a small grocery/liquor store that uses **old family recipes** to make its own ravioli (sold frozen), Italian sausage, and red sauce. It carries imported Italian food, candy, and wines. It's also a Western Union office and Greyhound depot. *On Margaret at U.S. 2, kitty-korner from the A&W. 774-0266. Open 10-5:30 Central Time. &: call.*

◆ **The IMMACULATE CONCEPTION CHURCH** is not to be missed on any north side tour. It's an **authentic bit of vernacular Italian architecture**, complete with big scrolled volutes on the front façade and an attached campanile (bell tower). This homemade elegance is the result of its unusual history. Father Giovanni Sinopoli, part of a Catholic order founded to minister to Italian immigrants, came to Iron Mountain from Italy in April, 1902. Immediately he set about organizing volunteers to construct a new church. Sandstone was quarried on nearby Millie Hill, just east of the Chapin Pit. A mere nine months later the church was dedicated. The stuccoed interior is peaceful and rather spare, not the heavily ornamented neo-Baroque style often seen in Catholic churches of that era. *500 Blaine at Vulcan. (906) 774-0511. Open 8 a.m.-8 p.m. or so, Central Time. Mass at 5:15 Tues, 12:10 Wed, 8 a.m. Thurs & Fri, 4 p.m. Sat, and 9 and 11 a.m. Sun. &*

Cornish Pump Engine & Mining Museum

Visitors with either an interest in mining or in the World II gliders made by Ford

in nearby Kingsford will find much of interest here. The **huge, steam-operated pump**, installed in 1893 to dewater the Chapin Mine, was then the world's largest mining pump. It's an awesome sight today with its **40-foot flywheel** moving **pistons over eight feet long**. It's called "Cornish" because the design was patterned after pumps from Cornwall, the mining region in the southwest of England. Cornwall exported master miners, engineers, and mining traditions directly to the U.P.

The Cornish Pump was built in Milwaukee by the E. P. Allis Company. Like many giants of the engineering world, it came on line at the end of an era. Electric pumps replaced it in 1913-14. This pump almost succumbed to a World War II scrap drive. But local sentiment saved it and eventually resulted in this museum, established by the Menominee Range Historical Foundation. The museum reopened in 2001 after being closed for a year and a half. An air shaft of the abandoned mine caved in right at the building's edge, requiring successive caps to stabilize and fill it. A **video** shows the damage and repairs.

Displays here focus more on mining techniques and geology than on the people and social history of the operators and miners. There's **mining equipment**, historical photos, and **geological specimens**. Displays of work clothes stained red with ore dust vividly evoke the everyday realities of iron mining.

There's also a lot here on Ford's **World War II gliders** and the fascinating role of gliders in **secretly deploying troops** behind enemy lines. That era comes to life with the help of an **8 1/2' glider replica**, videos of **gliders in motion**, and local photographs of the manufacturing operation.

Just south of the Chapin Pit and north of downtown Iron Mountain, turn west onto Kent St. and go a short way to the museum. 774-4276. Open daily from Mem. Day weekend thru Labor Day: Mon-Sat 9-5 Central Time, Sun noon-4. Call for spring & fall hours. Adults $4, ages 10-18 $2, under 10 free. Combined admission to both museums: $7 and $3. &

Pine Mountain Ski Slide

The ski slide, built in 1938, has seen **more competitive ski jumping than anywhere else in the U.S.** An international competition takes place each February. Skiers land mid-hill at 65 mph. Any time of the year, it's a **grand view from this hilltop**, looking out 30 miles and encompassing seven lakes.

From U.S. 2 in town, turn west onto Kent St. just south of the Chapin Pit, follow signs. In about 3/4 mile, look for Upper Pine Mountain Rd. which winds up to the hilltop. No charge.

Pine Mountain Resort

Frequent improvements and upgrades have turned this early (1938) ski resort into an attractive, full-service year-round resort with **beautiful landscaping** and a **gorgeous, light-filled indoor pool**. See Iron Mountain lodgings for the hotel and ski section in front of book for ski info. The 18-hole **championship golf course** designed by Jerry Mathews plays up the setting, with its boulders and mature pines.

About 2 miles northwest of downtown Iron Mountain off of Pine Mountain Road. From U.S. 2 in town, turn west onto Kent St. just south of the Chapin Pit, follow signs. From U.S. 2 north of town, turn south onto Pine Mountain Rd. just before the Menominee River and state line. (906) 774-9033; (800) 505-7463. &

Lake Antoine County Park

The park on spring-fed Lake Antoine (748 acres) is a **handy getaway spot**, thanks to its convenient location just east of Iron Mountain's north side and a **nice, long swimming beach** with a shallow dropoff. The views are of hills and suburban homes. "Although the lake is fully developed and fishing pressure is very high," writes Tom Huggler in *Fish Michigan: 100 Upper Peninsula Lakes*, "some consider it so be one of the best lakes in the western U.P. . . . .The west side is better for walleyes. . . . Overall the lake is a steady producer of largemouth bass." Bluegill, crappie, perch, northern — it's an amazing fishery in an urban area, partly because of DNR stocking, but quite possibly also because of all the minnows dropped by anglers. So speculates the county parks director. A seniors' park on the northwest shore offers shore fishing and a wheelchair-accessible **fishing pier**. There's a concession stand, camp store, volleyball, playground, and more. See Camping below.

On Lake Antoine Rd CR 396 east off U.S. 2 on the north end of Iron Mountain via Lake Antoine Rd. 774-8875. &

Iron Mountain Bat Mine

One of the **world's largest congregations of bats** — perhaps two million — winters in the abandoned Chapin Mine

You can walk right up the Pine Mountain Ski Jump any time of year. Wooden rungs make it possible. The view of surrounding lakes and forests is good at the base. Higher up, it's even better.

between downtown Iron Mountain and the north side. Usually in late September big brown bats and their small brown cousins gather here from a wide area. For a few days they hang on the awnings and overhangs of downtown buildings. When a cold spell kills off flying insects, the bats head for the mine.

The mine shaft drops 300 feet, creating a grand cavity for roosting. Most aren't seen until spring, when they emerge and fly off in short order. When the mine was closed, local officials had started to seal up the mine. An amateur spelunker alerted them to the presence of so many helpful bats. A grate was installed to keep people from falling in, yet let the bats fly in and out. Kids used to hurt and kill bats until successful **bat education projects** in elementary schools counteracted the practice. Today local people are quite well informed about the bats and their beneficial effects in eating mosquitoes.

To see the bat mine (but there's not much to see), take the East Side Cutoff from Third Street on the north end or from downtown take A Street up the hill and turn left onto Park Ave. Behind the Chapin Pit is a cement block building and a state police radio tower. Park there. The bat mine is behind the radio tower.

Menominee Range Historical Foundation Museum

The 1901 **Carnegie Library** building is home to the archives and collections of this historical society, focused mainly on Dickinson County. The lobby is a **well-stocked general store** from the turn of the century. Other displays move through the area's history, from indigenous peoples and fur-trading to **lumber camps** and **mines** that brought most of the populace to these parts. Many standbys of local historical museums are here, including gun collections; specimens of minerals, fossils, and mounted wildlife; and an unusual range of shops and professional offices: doctor, shoe repair, barber, pharmacist, etc., with an ice house, mine tunnel, barn, blacksmith shop, etc. in the basement. Appointments may be made to use the **archive**.

E. Ludington at Iron Mountain St. in downtown Iron Mountain. Open regularly from Mem. thru Labor Day, Mon-Sat 10-4 Central Time. Call for spring & fall hours. Adults $4, ages 10-18 $2, under 10 free. Combined admission to museum and Cornish Pump: $7 and $3.

Iron Mountain City Park

Having so much good takeout food in Iron Mountain suggests a picnic. A good spot would be the **picnic area** of this **hilly, picturesque city park** in the tall pines on a hillside west of downtown. There aren't many other places that have Italian **bocce courts** built of logs in the best northwoods rustic style. They're busy with league play in summer. Other attractions include **deer in pens**, **tennis** courts, **trails** for hiking, biking, and cross-country skiing, and a **sledding hill**. Short (around 1k each) hiking loops are groomed in winter for different levels of **cross-country skiing**.

From U.S. 2 downtown at the long yellow bank building, take A Street a little over a mile west to its end at the park. &*: restrooms.*

Rosemaling display at McDonald's

Customers have their Big Macs in a setting made cheery with rosemaling, that Swedish style of folk baroque decorative painting featuring colorful roses and leaves. In 1978, when this restaurant opened, McDonald's encouraged franchisees to have local themes. The owner at the time, part Swedish herself, hired Germaine Vincent, a noted Menominee rosemaling teacher, to decorate. (For more on her studio and classes, look in the Escanaba and Menominee chapter.) *On Stephenson/U.S. 2 at H St. just south of downtown Iron Mountain. 774-8430.* &

Northwoods Wilderness Outfitters & Adventure Store

An unusually wide variety of **area outings** is offered by Iron Mountain native Randy Gustafson and his wife, Molly. The Gustafsons are up on the very latest technological developments on outdoors equipment, and their **extremely well-stocked outdoors store** offers their favorites for sale and often to rent. For instance, there are Perception, Acadia, and Loon kayaks; We-No-Nah and Old Town canoes; both high-tech and traditional snowshoes; tents and equipment for camping and ice fishing; bait, tackle, and **extensive fly-fishing supplies**; and an excellent selection of **outdoors and nature books**, including many **geared to women**.

The Gustafsons are **dogsledding and skijouring enthusiasts**. Their store carries a wide range of dogsleds, skijouring sleds, and related equipment, probably the only U.P. retailer to do so at this time.

Check out **www.northwoodsoutfitters.com** for up-to-date **fishing reports** from guides, **river conditions**, and much more. **Fishing guides** are available for **bass, muskie**, and **walleye** on the Menominee River and its tributaries and flowages.

Outings include:

◆ **Kayak outings** on the complex backwaters of river floodings. The store uses stable, fun kayaks, easy to fish out of and ideal for beginners because no lessons are required. Lessons are needed before sea kayak touring, with its more complex watercraft.

◆ **Canoe trips** on the Pine and Brule rivers, ranging from 3 hours to 3 days. All have mild or mild to moderate current and no portages. Trips include drop-off, pickup, map, equipment, and notes on highlights. Trips are limited to six people to enhance quiet and opportunities for seeing and hearing wildlife.

◆ **Cross-country ski** and **snowshoe rentals** and advice on destinations.

Reservations advised. Weather may require canceling trips, with refunds. (The water and air temperature must add up to 100 for trips to be on.) A very pleasant, new log cabin near the store rents by the night.

Just north of Iron Mountain at the inter-

section of U.S. 2/141 and Pine Mountain Rd. Prominent sign. 774-9009. Open Mon-Sat 7:30 a.m.-6 p.m., Sun 8-4 Central Time. &

IRON MOUNTAIN AREA RESTAURANTS

Plain and old-fashioned, **JEAN KAY'S PASTIES** in Iron Mountain is where the highly regarded Marquette Jean Kay's began. Brian Harsch, the enterprising second-generation owner of Jean Kay in Marquette, built his business on the pasty recipe from his parents' original pasty shop here, named after his Cornish mother. The current owner uses Jean Kay Harsch's original recipe for its **classic pasty** ($3.25): cubed flank steak, *not* ground beef, plus optional rutabagas, and Crisco, not lard, in the crust. Brian believes that on the U.P.'s mining ranges, the deeper inland you go, the more people make pasties at home and the better they are. Jean Kay here also makes a vegetarian pasty ($4.25) involving cauliflower, carrots, broccoli, potatoes and more. *204 East B Street, half a block east of U.S. 2 downtown, a block north of the courthouse. 774-0430. Mon-Fri 9 a.m.-5:30 p.m., Sat 9-3 Central Time.* &

In the heart of gritty Iron Mountain it's a surprise to come upon **The GATHERING PLACE**, a **sourdough bakery** and sunny, **stylishly simple** no-smoking cafe. It's often packed; come before 11:45 for lunch. Founders Stretch and Carol Swigert, driving into town for the first time, saw this building as they stopped at a traffic light and felt divinely inspired to start a restaurant here, which they did two years later, in 1992. New owners continue their ambiance and successful menu, adding a porketta sandwich and burgers. Little touches

mean a lot. A bakery basket comes with breakfast specials like omelets, or country scrambled eggs with ham, cheese and vegetables ($3.75) or biscuits with Italian sausage gravy. Other possibilities: granola or oatmeal, pancakes and maple syrup, stuffed French toast, and express egg combos on biscuits or croissants. Lunches often come with choice of **tasty sides** like cornbread, fruit cup, bakery basket, muffins, cole slaw. Some examples: quiche ($4.25 with salad), deli sandwiches on sourdough bread ($4-$6, with fruit cup or potato salad or slaw), meal-size salads, half a sandwich and a cup of soup ($4). Lots of tasty sides can round out soup and make a meal. For dessert, there's homemade pie and carrot cake. Real cappuccino and coffee drinks. There's a big takeout business. For takeout, it's best to call ahead. *Downtown on East A Street, half a block east of U.S. 2. Turn at the long yellow office building. 774-875. Mon-Fri 7 a.m.-4 p.m. Sat 7-2.* &

BRUTOMESSO'S PIZZERIA, utterly plain and **locally beloved**, has for decades made a **celebrated pizza** with a **crispy, light cracker-like crust** and not much sau**c**e. The late Angelo Bruttomesso ruled the roost for years and kept kids in order. Now his widow Rose has retired, but the business has stayed in the family and remains the same. Prices start at $7.40 for a 10" cheese pizza to $12.85 for a large, with extra toppings from 60¢ to $1.60. Self-service. Ample seating. *305 N. Stephenson/ U.S. 2 at the north end of downtown Iron Mountain. 774-0801. Wed-Sun 5 p.m.-8 p.m. Central Time. From Mem. to Labor Day open Fri & Sat to 9.* &

BIMBO'S WINE PRESS/L'Torchio di Vino, once a typical corner bar, has blossomed into a **center of local Italian-American and sports culture**. A decorative wine press sits on the roof's corner. William "Bimbo" Constantini, who lives next door, bought the bar in 1978, when he was still teaching ninth grade. His reason: to protect the value of his property. He comes from a family of good cooks. He was already active in the Paesano Club, an Italian-American social group some 500 members strong. The parking lot has been fashioned into a semi-enclosed pavilion for Fourth of July Paesano picnics.

Bimbo's food offerings are the essence of simplicity. The menu was developed according to the baking schedule of the late, lamented Schinderle's Italian Maid bakery and its hard

roll. The **$2.75 porketta sandwich** is served all day Wednesdays through Saturdays. A thin-crust pizza is ready at 9 p.m. Wednesday through Saturday. June Constantini makes her famous hot beef sandwich for Friday and Saturday. What's left over from it is served Monday and Tuesday. Anytime items are cappelletti soup in chicken broth and homemade Italian sausage in a boat-shaped dish swimming in red gravy (the local term for tomato sauce) that's sopped up with chunks of Italian bread. *314 East Main at Vulcan. 774-8420. Friends stop by for morning coffee as early as 6:30 a.m. The bar closes at 11 or midnight weekdays, possibly longer. Vulcan, the main street of the Italian north side, parallels U.S. 2. Get there from the south by turning east onto Third near Hardee's. From the north turn onto Margaret across from the A&W.* ⚓ Full bar

A local Italian food-lover who grew up on good home cooking rates **EL KAPITAN** as his favorite area restaurant for its quality ingredients and careful preparation. The exterior of this third-generation family restaurant is unassuming; inside it's white tablecloths, burgundy, mauve, and lace. All the **pasta is hand-made** right here, as are the **gnocchi** (potato dumplings) and bread. The red sauce, made with meat drippings and not spicy like others in the area, simmers for hours for a smooth, untangy taste. There's also a white clam sauce, Alfredo sauce, and pesto. Beef is choice. Some dinner favorites: spaghetti ($9), ravioli (around $11 or $12), Italian Holiday sampler (around $12 or $13), shrimp in red sauce, 8 oz. beef tenderloin. Especially recommended: **tournedos alla Rossini** (tenderloin filet beneath Canadian bacon, sliced tomato, mozzarella, and mushrooms. Dinners come with good house salad, bread. *On U.S. 2 in Spread Eagle, Wisconsin, 6-7 miles north of Iron Mountain. 715-696-3493. Tues-Sat 5 p.m.-10 p.m., Sun to 9 p.m.* ⚓ 👫 Full bar

IRON MOUNTAIN AREA LODGINGS

Iron Mountain's newest motels are on the intensely developed commercial strip on U.S. 2/U.S. 41 east of town, near Wal-Mart and other new retailing but far from Pine Mountain ski slope and most other attractions. This stretch is so busy and so devoid of any local color or non-chain restaurants, we recommend other options. These are arranged from downtown north. Expect lodgings to be full for the Gus Macker Basketball Tournament (1st weekend of June), Summer Fest (last weekend of June), July 4 weekend.

THE TIMBERS MOTOR LODGE
(906) 774-7600; (800) 433-8533; www.thetimbers.com; fax (906) 774-6222.

The downtown location puts guests in easy biking and walking distance to interesting neighborhoods and restaurants, including the recommended Fontana Supper Club and Bruttomesso's Pizzeria across the street. 52 rooms on two floors have interior corridors. There's a medium-size **indoor pool** in a sunny, attractive space. Whirlpool, sauna, fitness center. Free continental breakfast with cereal and fruit. Friendly staff. Beneath the rustic, shingled ski look, designed by an architect owner, is an old railroad warehouse. Its beams can be seen today. Rooms have modem-compatible phones, cable TV with free HBO, Disney, and 90+ channels. Same rates year-round: for two, $44 (one bed), $50 (two beds). *200 S. Stephenson/U.S. 2 at Ludington.* **H.A.:** one room ADA accessible; call on others 👫👶: $5/extra person

COMFORT INN of Iron Mountain
(906) 774-5505; fax (906) 774-2631

A helpful staff, free deluxe continental breakfast, and big, new rooms (with teleports for business travelers) make this well-run 48-room motel stand out. Regular rooms for two are $56 ($7 less for one person). All rooms include a desk and either a recliner or sofa. Deluxe rooms (about $70 for two) have a sitting area, pullout sofa, microwave, and refrigerator. 100% satisfaction guaranteed. There's no swimming pool, and therefore no kids running around making noise, but there is an exercise room and hot tub. Business center has computer with printer, 2-sided copier/binder. Next door to Recreation Lanes bowling alley with pool tables. A block from Romagnoli's Italian restaurant and handy to Pine Mountain ski area. *On west side of U.S. 2 about 1 1/2 miles west of downtown Iron Mountain.* **H.A.:** 2 rooms ADA accessible. 👫👶: 17 and under no extra charge

PINE MOUNTAIN RESORT
(906) 774-9033; (800) 505-7463; www.pinemountainresort.com

This early ski resort, founded in 1938 by Milwaukee brewer Fred Pabst, has a convenient and **beautiful, wooded setting** in suburban Iron Mountain. The architecture and landscaping of the year-round resort are attractive. The lodge building has a handsome year-round restaurant and a **gorgeous, light-filled indoor pool** with adjacent sauna and whirlpool. The top-rated Timberstone Golf Course designed by Jerry Mathews is across the road. It plays up the setting, with its boulders and mature pines. The resort will arrange fishing guides for guests. See ski section for skiing details. Pine Mountain Resort reopened in November, 2000 under new ownership, including two on-site owner-managers with a community focus and local ties, after the previous owner's financial difficulties closed it for 17 months. The standard double lodge rooms, due to be refurbished, are currently quite a bargain at $44, winter and summer. Inquire about condos and other room configurations with sofa sleepers. *About 2 miles northwest of downtown Iron Mountain off of Pine Mountain Road. From U.S. 2 in town, turn west onto Kent St. just south of the Chapin Pit, follow signs. From U.S. 2 north of town, turn south onto Pine Mountain Rd. just before the Menominee River and state line. Open year-round.* ⚓

EDGEWATER RESORT & Country Cabins (906) 774-6244; (800) 236-6244; www.edgewaterresort.com

Nine appealing log cabins overlook the Menominee River in a beautiful, woodsy setting. Only road noise from U.S. 2 breaks the idyllic spell. The property is big enough to have **walking trails**. **Outdoor seating** overlooks the river in several places. A nifty **playground** and a **picnic area** also have good river views. There's a **basketball court**, a bonfire area with **bonfires** upon request (weather permitting), and a **weekly potluck** in summer. A **fishing boat** comes with every cabin, and there's a fish cleaning station and laundry, too. Most cabins have 2 or 3 bedrooms; all have kitchens, microwaves, cable TV (but no phones), and pleasant country decor. The cabins date from a 1930s WPA project in the city park and were moved here much later. The log exteriors have been preserved and refurbished. The interiors are quite modern. Rates for two-bedroom cabins with two beds are $370/week or $52-$90/day, depending on the season — a remarkable value for such attractive lodgings. The owners, transplanted Chicagoans, treasure the area's laid-back, undiscovered quality in comparison with places like Door County and Eagle River, Wisconsin. The smallest cabins, with one queen bed, are $315; the three-bedroom cabin is $480. Summer rentals by the week. Reserve a year ahead for peak summer season. *North U.S. 2 on east bank of Menominee River, 3 1/2 miles north of downtown Iron*

Mountain. Open April thru Nov. at least. Call for winter availability. ♿: 1 unit 👫👬 🐕 : call

LAKESIDE BED & BREAKFAST

(715) 528-3259; www.northern-destinations.com/lakeside; www.snowtracks.com/go/lakeside

Innkeepers Ronny McMullen, a former contractor, and his wife Rita designed and built this specifically to be a combination inn and home, so it was easy to design in extras like fireplaces and access to the shared **balcony** or **patio** from each room. By moving an existing house from the site, they were able to get a choice spot right at the east edge of Florence, Wisconsin (pop. 750), in the woods above **Fisher Lake**, 12 miles from Iron Mountain and 16 miles from Crystal Falls. Area people think highly of the Lakeside.

Ronny, an avid angler, will give guests **casting lessons** and tips on area fishing, which is varied and excellent. Several waterfalls are within 15 miles.

A **comfortable yet refined** country inn/northwoods lodge look is created by Amish quilts, antiques, wing chairs, a gun rack in the guest living room, and pine furniture. The two web sites clearly convey the interior. Big windows, decks, fireplaces, and a screened porch make for a place where some guests just hang around and read. The **full breakfast is an event**, with crystal and candles. The lower-level, walkout Florida room has a **hot tub** and **exercise equipment**. Down by the lake guests can use the hammocks, dock, swimming beach, raft, canoes, and paddleboats. A **footpath surrounds the lake**, where loons, eagles, and osprey can sometimes be seen. Six guest rooms are upstairs, one handicap-accessible room is on the first floor, and an extra-large room that sleeps up to four is in the walk-out lower level. Four rooms have lake views; the others face the road and parking area, which comes right up to the patio due to site constraints. Rooms are all $80/ night for two, as of spring, 2001; it's first-come, first-served for rooms with lake view, fireplaces, etc. Each guest room has cable TV. All are air-conditioned. The guest phone is in the hall. Reservations at least three weeks or a month ahead are recommended for summer, and longer ahead for fall weekends. Snowmobilers welcome; on a trail. *509 Furnace/U.S. 2 in Florence, Wisconsin.*

H.A.: one room is fully accessible 👫👬 : children can stay in large room

IRON MOUNTAIN AREA CAMPING

LAKE ANTOINE COUNTY PARK

(906) 774-8875; reservable

80 modern campsites ($15/night) at this convenient local park are closely spaced. See above for info on swimming and the outstanding **fishing**. A seniors' park on the northwest shore offers shore fishing and a **wheelchair-accessible fishing pier**. Reservations advised in July and August. *On Lake Antoine Rd./CR 396. Turn east off U.S. 2 on the north end of Iron Mountain near Romagnoli's restaurant. Campground is on lake in 1 1/2 miles. (906) 774-8875. Campground open Mem.-Labor Day.*

H.A. 👫👬 🐕

Norway *(pop. 2,959)*

Next to Crystal Falls, Norway is the **prettiest town on the Menominee Range**. It makes a good impression on visitors who pass through it on U. S. 2 on the way to Piers Gorge and the Iron Mountain Iron Mine. Norway has trim early 20th-century houses, tree-lined streets, and a tidy if not exactly affluent downtown just off U.S. 2. It's a welcome contrast to the massive commercial sprawl spreading east from Iron Mountain along U.S. 2.

Sizable models of a **Viking ship** greet motorists on both U.S. 2 entrances. Actually the area's logging camps and iron mines brought to Norway and its adjacent sister community of Vulcan not just Norwegians and Swedes but a lot of Germans, Irish, Cornish, English, Italians, and Poles as well. Still, Norwegian is the theme, and everyone promotes it. Next to each Viking ship is a sign announcing that Norway is **"The City of Trails."** It's an impressive accomplishment that a small group of energetic community leaders have raised tax dollars and grant money to build asphalt **bike and walking paths** connecting the town with outlying parks.

Norway's small-town charm also comes from the unnerving fact that the town has been moved — *twice*. Iron deposits were so extensive here that the town was undermined to the point that streets collapsed and houses sank. (You can see a **tilted but still occupied house** on Norway Street, parallel and just west of Main and north of U.S. 2.) Photographs from the 1890s show a much bigger and more impressive downtown where there's now a field, north of the present downtown. The first Norway was farther north on Main, up the hill, where a few streets of simple cottages remain between the two sunken pits.

Remnants of Norway's first phase survive in radically different forms. The **Aragon Mine** is now **Strawberry Lake and park**. (See below.) The farms and back roads here in the valley north of U.S. 2 are lovely. For a scenic shortcut to Iron Mountain's north side, turn north onto CR 396, which ends up at Lake Antoine.

By 1900, when the need for a third move had become obvious, Norway had matured beyond its rough and tumble boom years and was willing to plan for amenities of settled town life. Major buildings were built again over the next ten years. Two houses associated with Norway history are being preserved as part of the **Jake Menghini Memorial Museum** on U.S. 2 on the west side of town, near the viaduct and across from the new AmericInn. The two-room log house where Jake Menghini had his tidy private museum has been moved behind the unusual, European-looking house of Anton Odill, the Luxemburger who drilled the first tests for Norway's mines and stayed to build up the community. *The museum should be up and running in 2002. Call 563-7500 for hours.*

Today Norway's biggest employer is a label-printing factory, part of the Milwaukee-based North Star Print Group. The 95 who work here in Norway make millions of labels, many of them on metallicized paper, for beer bottles, household chemical products such as "Snuggle," and food cans.

Central Norway

Norway's Main Street runs perpendicular to U.S. 2, which is called Seventh Avenue in town. Go north on Main to reach Old Norway and Strawberry Lake. Here are some noteworthy specialty shops, arranged from west (where U.S. 2 joins U.S. 8) to east.

◆ **JERI'S QUILT PATCH & ANTIQUES.** This large Queen Anne house is full of interesting things: quilt fabrics and patterns, plus quilted items made by area quilters, rag rugs, glassware, stationery, other gifts, and antique furniture, linens, quilts, and more. Owner Jeri Giannunzio holds a **quilt show** with samples from pattern companies every year on the week ending on Labor Day. *Two blocks west of downtown at 703 Brown at U.S. 2 (northwest corner, behind Citgo station). Brown Street is U.S. 8 on the other side of U.S. 2. Park in alley off U.S. 2. 563-9620.*

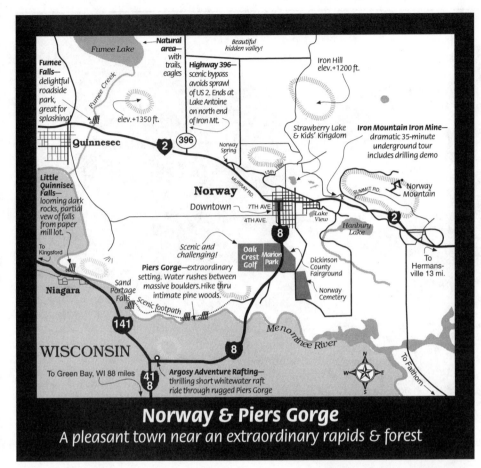

Norway & Piers Gorge
A pleasant town near an extraordinary rapids & forest

www.geocities.com/ gerisquiltpatch
Open Mon-Sat 10-5. &: ring bell at front.

◆ **NORTHERN EXPRESSIONS. Distinctive U.P. items** make this place stand out from other general gift shops that also carry lighthouses, Minnetonka moccasins, and popular lines of collectibles. Owner Judy Carlsen opened the shop in 1990 because she was annoyed that so little merchandise then in local shops reflected the natural beauty and historical richness of her native turf. Now regional gift shops are frequent, but Northern Expressions has had time to develop relationships with many U.P. craftspeople with limited outputs, like the Ojibwa women who make **porcupine quill boxes**. There's a careful selection of **regional books** and **recorded music**; ethnic heritage gifts including **rosemaling** by a talented local artist and intricate **Solje silver jewelry** from Norway; U.P. **pottery**, weaving, carving, **baskets**, and copper; driftwood ducks and fish; syrups and wild berry jams; wildlife art; and more. The **dreamcatchers** and **peace pipes** are made by Ojibwa from the eastern U.P. Don't miss the handpainted drums hanging from the ceiling! There's lots for collectors of loons and moose — and, suprisingly, for men: upper-end **knives**, hatchets, and com-

passes from **Marble Arms** in Gladstone. An added bonus: the staff is a wonderful source of **local information** on the Norway-Iron Mountain area. *640 Main just south of U.S. 2. 563-7172; 888-EH-MOOSE. www. northernexpressions. com Open Mon-Thurs 9-5:30, Fri to 6, Sat 10-4, Sun noon-4 Central Time.* &

◆ **NORWAY ANTIQUES MALL**. The friendly owners of this **pleasant, 34-dealer mall** in the old Ben Franklin are good at display and creative ideas for using old things. *729 Main, half a block south of Northern Expressions. 563-8246. Open daily Mon-Sat 10-5 Central Time. May thru Dec. also open Sundays noon-4.* &

◆ **SWEDISH PASSPORT.** Scandinavian imports — kitchen and dinnerware, glassware, and toys, not only from Sweden but from Norway, Denmark, and Finland — are featured, along with books on Scandinavian subjects. Embroidery is done right here. Sweatshirts with the Swedish horse (dala) are the most popular items. The shop occupies a house that served as the first hospital of the local mine. *626 Iron/U.S. 2, a couple blocks east of downtown and up the hill. 563-8200. Mon-Fri 9-5:30, Sat to 5, Sun noon-4 Central Time.* &: no.

◆ **CITY BAND SHELL.** A romantic painting of a Viking ship adorns the band shell, where **band concerts** take place at 7:30 p.m. on second and fourth Tuesdays from June through August. *On Main St. 2 blocks north of U.S. 2. Free.*

Strawberry Lake & Kids' Kingdom Playground

The caved-in Aragon Mine is now a **delightful pond** where loons stop and ducks congregate. The pond is stocked with trout; a wheelchair-accessible **fishing platform** by the parking area off 12th Avenue gives access. No fishing license is required for children and seniors. A small **picnic area** takes advantage of this pretty setting. A paved **trail loop** around the lake is well used by people from parents with strollers to kids on bikes and rollerblades to people in wheelchairs. A community-built **playground** offers swinging bridges, maze castles, slides, swings, and picnic tables.

Take Main north from U.S. 2 and downtown. Park entrances are on Central (playground area) and 2nd Ave. (fishing pier). &

Marion Park & Oak Crest Golf Course

A paved **bike trail** leads a mile south from Norway to this beautiful hillside park on the way to Piers Gorge. (The trail parallels Main two blocks to the west.) A canopy of majestic oaks makes this park special. A **picnic area**, playground, volleyball and horseshoe courts, and lighted **tennis courts** make this a good stop for visitors coming from Piers Gorge. The 18-hole **Oak Crest Golf Course** shares the park's hilly terrain and big trees. The clubhouse includes a restaurant.

Entrance to park and golf course is west off U.S. 8 a mile south of U.S. 2. In town, U.S. 8 is Brown St., 2 blocks west of Main. (906) 563-5891.

Piers Gorge

Along the Wisconsin border south of Norway, the big Menominee River has cut a **deep, dramatic gorge** where the river, normally 300 feet wide, is constricted to a narrow 80-foot channel, creating **powerful rapids of foaming water** as it rushes towards Green Bay. The Menominee River and its tributary, the Brule, form the **Michigan-Wisconsin border** from west of Iron River to its outlet on Lake Michigan at Menominee and Marinette, the lumber towns built by

Piers Gorge: a subtle, unfolding waterfall drama seen from a secluded path — a far cry from the crowds at Tahquamenon Falls during summer and fall color season.

logs the river carried. At Piers Gorge the river has created an **extraordinarily beautiful place** where steep-sided bedrock walls up to 70 feet high contain the rushing river for a mile and a half as it roars over a series of stone shelves in **four distinct waterfalls**.

Piers Gorge is a much subtler experience than the typical tourist waterfall. It's not at all a direct, well-trod path to a single overlook. The perspectives and views are constantly unfolding as you walk. Here you look down at steep rock walls, where rushing water undercuts islands below and tears at loose rock. Water tumbles over and smooths smaller chunks of rock lodged in the riverbed. The changing sounds of rushing water and smells of the forest envelop you. The power of water — and of natural forces — is everywhere evident. If a wild and lonely forest spectacle like Piers Gorge were in Germany, it would have been the subject of many Romantic-era poems of contemplation and spiritual yearning.

What with the drama of the water, rock, and forest, it's easy to overlook the area's big, fish-eating birds. Bald eagles roost and occasionally nest in tall trees along shore. **Eagles** and **osprey** can sometimes be seen scouting for fish in

the shallow water or soaring above. **Loons** frequent the quiet pools.

Despite the spectacular beauty, this isn't a big tourist spot, though local people love to **ski** these somewhat challenging trails. The road to the Piers Gorge parking lot is not plowed in the wintertime. Signs are few. The landowners, Champion International forest products and Wisconsin Electric Power, do provide some amenities like a parking area. And they cooperate with local groups which maintain the trail.

A relatively easy, relatively level **path** lets you look down at the river from the bluff's rim. It starts at the parking area, briefly passing through a **fragrant cedar swamp**. For part of the way wood chips are being added by a volunteer group to smooth over the small rock shelves and roots that can trip careless hikers. Farther on, *roots make footing occasionally uneven, not difficult for the reasonably healthy, but not for shufflers.* Short **side trails** branch off to the **gorge's rim**. The more adventurous can take trails that descend tortuously along the canyon walls to the river itself. In places it's possible to frolic in the gentler rapids – at your own risk, of course – or step across half of the wide river on the many

stones and boulders lying in the riverbed. The river banks are loaded with stones of all shapes and sizes, providing plenty of ammunition for stone-skippers.

A surprising crescent of **quiet beach** appears after the third pier. Shortly you emerge into a clearing by a power line. Follow the red ribbons to the fourth pier, avoiding the better-worn trail made by mountain bikes and ATVs. You might prefer to skip the fourth pier, more a rapids. Some years Argosy Adventures across the river offers guided **raft trips** at Piers Gorge. Call (715) 251-3886.

From U.S. 2 at Norway (that's 8 miles east of Iron Mountain) turn south onto U.S. 8 and drive 2 miles. Look for Piers Gorge Road on your right. Drive 1/2 mile to parking lot. If you cross the bridge and get to Wisconsin, you have gone too far. Go back 1/4 mile and look for Piers Gorge Road on your left. &: no.

Falls at the paper mill in Niagara, Wisconsin

The paper mill in Niagara, Wisconsin, offers another memorable but quite different look at the Menominee's spectacular bluffs in the general Piers Gorge area. Here a **massive wall of dark rock** forms the bank on the Michigan side. It looms over the little town and the mill. The rock creates a dramatic juxtaposition of humdrum everyday life with an impressive visual manifestation of powerful natural forces. Millennia of volcanic activity, compression, and uplift created these rocks, which water has shaped and chewed at for thousands of years. It's worth a side trip.

Part of the falls can be seen from the plant parking lot.

From Norway and U.S. 8, go south into Wisconsin. In about 3 miles, turn right onto U.S. 141 and go about 3 miles into Niagara. Take any side street to your right to reach the street that follows the river. Turn left and continue until you reach the paper mill. Park in the truck lot on the right just before the mill.

Iron Mountain Iron Mine

This **interesting and dramatic mine tour** of the former East Vulcan Mine goes through **2,600 feet of underground drifts** and tunnels to indicate what iron mining was really like. Visitors don raincoats and hard hats and ride the same **railway system** that took miners to their jobs until the mine closed down in 1945. They experience the **gloomy, drippy setting of a typical iron mine** and see some pretty things, like a fault of rose quartz, along the way. The 35-minute trip offers **spectacular views** of large manmade mine chambers called stopes. **Drilling demonstrations** show how loud, dirty, and dangerous the work was in earlier years. Miners typically started at the age of 11 and often died of black lung disease, caused by breathing rock dust, between 50 and 60.

The drama of going underground is what visitors remember about this competent tour. It's a nice break for families making the long trip from the Porkies to lower Michigan. The tight schedule doesn't really invite questions. The guide quickly discusses increasingly efficient drills and the tradeoffs they brought. Dangerous working conditions are detailed so frequently that visitors will walk away with a refreshed view of the importance of government occupational safety regulations. Also, it's a definite plus that most guides are local adults who grew up around miners. When listening to people from mining areas, it's always striking to realize the strong emotions bound up in this difficult, dangerous work: love and appreciation for parents' sacrifice, a good dose of realistic bitterness at the economic forces that determined the miners' lot, and an

immense amount of pride.

The interconnected mines here in Vulcan were among the earliest on the Menominee Range. When first ore was mined here in 1877, the incredibly rich ore was 85% iron. But it took three men 10 hours to dig just four feet by hand. The highest-paid miner was the blaster. Each of the Iron Range's many ethnic groups had its own job in the mines. The Cornish and Welsh, experienced in mining operations, were the bosses, bookkeepers, and engineers. Ethnic groups without mining expertise got the low-skilled jobs. Finns did the timbering – constructing the tamarack supports that held up the horizontal drifts. Italians were mostly drillers and blasters.

Deep shaft mines like this finally became obsolete when huge power shovels made open-pit mining much more economical.

Wear a sweater; far underground it stays a constant 43° F. year around. In addition to the **train ride**, the tour also involves some easy **optional walking** along pathways made smooth for visitors by concrete. Electric lights make the portion of the mine on tour far brighter than miners ever experienced. For a short while visitors are shown just how dark it was when the only illumination was with the candles or headlights on miners' lamps.

Kids and fans of roadside Americana will probably enjoy the tour's commercial trappings. The **gift shop** has lots of inexpensive **rock and mineral samples** in addition to souvenirs and regional books. There's a 40' wooden statue of Big John and a **freeform sculpture** made of pick axes and shovels assembled on a telephone pole. In the parking lot, Johnny Cash's ode to the heroic miner, "Big John," plays over and over. If you want a more leisurely overview of mining strategy and techniques, combined with an engineer's detailed perspective, tour the Quincy Hoist and copper mine in Hancock. If you enjoy mining lore, take both tours.

On U.S. 2 in Vulcan, 10 miles east of Iron Mountain and 2 miles east of Norway. (906) 563-8077. 35-40 minute tours late May to mid-Oct, daily 9-5 at least. Last tour at 4:20. Call for possible early morning summer tours. Adults $7, children 6-12 $6, under 6 free. &

NORWAY RESTAURANTS

Arranged from in-town to west of town.

A reader from Norway took us to task for overlooking **RIALTO LANES & RESTAURANT** — easy to do, since this fourth-

generation business hardly has a sign. It's a breakfast spot, a bar, a dinner restaurant, a **six-lane bowling alley that's straight out of the 1950s**, and a place for clubs to meet. "It is also a meeting place for all who have left our great little town and come back for a visit. The first stop morning or night is the Rialto." The menu includes hot dogs, burgers, Mexican, Italian, and steaks, plus homemade pies and, for vegetarians, gardenburgers and portobello mushroom sandwiches. Lunch entrées are around $6, dinners around $9. The **really good buffets** draw crowds: Friday fish ($11), Saturday evening ($9.50), and Wednesday at noon ($6). *In downtown Norway on Main St. just south of U.S. 2, next to Northern Expressions. 563-9919. Mon-Sat 8:30 a.m. to midnight.* & Full bar

THE CORNER HOUSE has long enjoyed a reputation for its **soups** (especially the egg dumpling soup) and its **pies** — fruit pies ($1.65/slice) and also cream pies and rich concoctions ($2/slice) like peanut butter luster (with a shell on top), walnut pie, and oatmeal pie. Hamburgers ($2.75 and up) and the sandwich menu are available any time, as is the soup and salad bar. $5.25 daily specials (served with soup or salad, starch, bread) may be chicken à la king, Swedish meatballs and noodles, gnocchi with red sauce, or lasagna. A regular dinner favorite is **roast pork and sauerkraut with homemade bread dumpling** ($8.25). There's a big breakfast and morning coffee business. Vegetarians order a la carte and have the gardenburger or the salad bar. *512 Seventh Ave./U.S. 2 a block east of downtown Norway. 563-5496. Open daily. Sun & Mon 7 a.m. to 8 p.m., Tues-Sat 7 a.m.-9 p.m.* & Full bar

THE THIRSTY WHALE BAR & GRILL, an old roadhouse on U.S. 2, has become a community hangout because of its personable hostesses, good sandwiches, and games — **volleyball** in summer, **trivia games** in winter. The menu is big on burgers (the legendary half-pounder is $3.75), club sandwiches, cudighi (that Italian sausage patty that originated outside Marquette), soups, and fish and chicken baskets ($4-$5), with a chef salad for greens. Of course, there's a Friday fish fry ($7.50). The nautical theme came inland from Escanaba. On a snowmobile trail. *On U.S. 2 just west of Norway, across from the AmericInn. Open Mon-Sat 11 a.m. to closing.* & Full bar

NORWAY LODGING

AmericINN (906) 568-7500

For visitors who want a **big, beautiful indoor pool**, hot tub, and sauna, and possibly whirlpool rooms, this new motel on the west edge of Norway, a short distance from that pretty town, is a pleasant alternative to the area's other motels with pools and whirlpools, caught up in the commercial sprawl east of Iron Mountain. The 45 rooms look out onto the town of Norway or, in back, onto woods. The **Thirsty Whale**, a roadhouse with good food, volleyball, and games in winter, is across U.S. 2. AmericInns are known for their soundproof construction and **big lobbies** with massive **fireplace**, comfortable seating, and tables used for the enhanced **continental breakfast** in the morning, and for cards and hot drinks in the evening. This one has some extra touches. Standard doubles in summer 2001 are from $67 to $91 (special events rate). *On U.S. 2 a mile west of downtown Norway.* **H.A.:** some rooms ADA accessible 🚺🚹: 12 & under free 🐾: call

VIKING MOTEL (906) 563-9245

This homey two-story motel is perpendicular to U.S. 2, adjoining a pleasant neighborhood near downtown. Its 20 rooms were $32 and $37/night for two in 2001. It's **tastefully appointed in a 1960s way**: plaster walls, Scandinavian modern/ northwoods decor, flower baskets. Phones in room. Air-conditioned with cable TV. Coffee in office. The owners' exotic accents aren't Norwegian; Frank and Gabriella Cescolini are Italian. 2-block walk to downtown restaurants. *On U.S. 2 at U.S. 8, 2 blocks west of downtown Norway.* **H.A.:** call 🚺🚹 : 10 & under free 🐾: call

Felch (pop. under 100)

A mining location at the edge of the Menominee Range, Felch developed in the early 20th century around a stop on the Chicago & Northwestern Railroad. Named after Alpheus Felch, an early Michigan governor much admired for his self-effacing honesty.

Bicycling along G-69 between U.S. 2 at Waucedah and M-69 at Foster City

This **excellent but lightly traveled road** through forests along the Sturgeon River Valley makes for great bicycling for medium-well-conditioned cyclists, says Dean Sandell, a state forest recreation planner.

Gene's Pond

Outstanding **bird-watching** and a remote quality make this impoundment of Dickinson County's Sturgeon River East Branch a favorite spot for serious outdoors-lovers. It's part of the **Copper Country State Forest.**

A **blue heron rookery** (nesting colony) is in the treetops near the state forest campground on the pond's north side. It's always a spectacle to see just one of those magnificent birds in flight over a river, its **six-foot wingspread** moving with stately deliberation. Imagine seeing several at once! The *Michigan Wildlife Viewing Guide* calls Gene's Pond "a jewel" for people who like to view large birds. **Loons** and **cormorants** can be seen on the surface, diving for fish, while trees by the shoreline provide vantage points for **bald eagles** and osprey on the lookout for their fishy prey. Boats are the best way to view wildlife here. Fishing isn't bad, either.

See below for camping. There's a **boat launch** (recently redone, with a new dock) but no beach; much of the shore is wetlands. A relatively easy **2.3-mile hiking trail** in two loops leads from the campgrounds to some **nifty overlooks** and around an old mine site. Good roads make it easy to get into the isolated, thinly populated area around the onetime mining communities of Felch and nearby Ralph in central Dickinson County, 25 miles and more north of U.S. 2.

From Felch go west 1/2 mile on M-69 to CR 581. In about 6 miles, turn west on Leeman Rd./CR 422, follow signs to Gene's Pond. (906) 875-6622. Free.

CAMPING NEAR FELCH

GENE'S POND Campground/ Copper Country State Forest 875-6622

See above for details about this isolated wetland area known for its water birds and fishing. The 14-space rustic campground vault toilets, no showers or electricity) has the sensitive design and big sites characteristic of most state forest campgrounds. There's a boat launch. A relatively easy 2.3-mile hiking trail leads from the campgrounds to overlooks and an old mine site. *From Felch (over 25 miles north of U.S. 2) go west 1/2 mile on M-69 to CR 581. In about 6 miles, turn west on Leeman Rd./CR 422, follow signs to Gene's Pond. $6/$9 night.* 🚹: no.

Foster City

Foster City, 20 miles northeast of Iron Mountain as the crow flies, is where G-69 (heading north from U.S. 2 at Waucedah) joins M-69. It's one of many, many U.P. lumber boom towns gone bust.

FOSTER CITY RESTAURANT & LODGING

MILL TOWN INN
(906) 246-3999; www.milltowninn.com

When Foster City's finest house, an ample place built in 1900 for the boss of the Morgan Lumber Company, was vacated by its longtime owners, they wanted Anita Mattson to have it. A substance abuse counselor, she was ready for a more upbeat occupation, and she loves to decorate. Furthermore, she felt the area needed a social center. The result is this cheerful, tastefully homey little café. Highlights with 2000 prices are Swedish pancakes ($3) for breakfast, home fries ($1.50) made from potatoes grown down the road, **excellent soups** ($2.25/bowl), and homemade cheesecake, muffins and pies ($1.75/slice). **Hearty breakfasts** include 3-egg omelets with home fries and toast ($3.50-$4.75). Lunch sandwiches ($3-$4.50) are served with choice of a side or soup. *Smokers in the small room make the environment not for the smoke-aversive.* This place is about inclusivity and a down-home atmosphere. "Loggers with dirty boots needn't apologize," says Anita. "We just sweep it out the door." There's an adjoining **ice cream parlor** in summer; in winter it becomes a **second-hand shop**. Recorded piano music makes for a relaxing mood. *Open 7 days, 6 a.m. to 4 p.m. Open later for summer ice cream. On M-69 in the heart of Foster City. From G-69 and the south, turn left.* 🚹 🚺🚹

MILL TOWN INN
(906) 246-3999; www.milltowninn.com

Upstairs over the cafe are two **surprisingly large, luxurious,** and smoke-free B&B guest rooms ($68/night including breakfast downstairs), charmingly decorated in outdoors themes. Each has an **in-room 2-person whirlpool, refrigerator,** and **sitting area** with sofa. **Gas fireplaces** are a new addition. The tiny swivel TV with poor reception is there more for the VCR and dozens of violence-free **romantic videos**. Anita and her husband, Al, discovered they had far more enjoyable vacations without watching TV news. Now some husbands who were initially upset that they couldn't watch the big game leave happy, saying they haven't talked so much with their wives in years. Guest rooms and the **front porch** offer good views. Though the inn is on a main snowmobile trail, most guests are quiet older people here to relax. There's nearby **fishing** on the beautiful Sturgeon River, bicycling along G-69, and **bird-watching** and hiking at Gene's Pond. **H.A.:** no 🚶🚶: no extra charge, rates are by the room. Rollaway and sofa-sleeper available.

Hermansville (pop. 500)

Picturesquely preserved like an insect in amber, this is the office for the company town that introduced hardwood flooring to the world in the 1880s. Until then, floors in homes had used softer pine. Hardwoods like maple and oak were too difficult to work and tended to warp. C. J. L. Meyer developed a kiln-drying process for taking the right amount of moisture out of hardwood and inventing machinery for making tongue-and-groove hardwood flooring strips. This process is still used today.

Hermansville is "one of the state's best examples of a wood products company town," writes Kathryn Eckert. She has canvassed the state in her work as state historic preservation officer and author of the monumental *Buildings of Michigan.*

The founder of the Wisconsin Land and Lumber Company established the town and mill here in 1878. Today, though Hermansville is rather lifeless, the town is pretty much intact. Laid out in a row on First Street, along the north side of the Chicago & Northwestern tracts, are the plain stores and public buildings from Hermansville's heyday, roughly between 1910 and 1930, when IXL hardwood flooring was in great demand. Between First Street and U.S. 2 are the company-built houses and school.

The large mill yard is still partially used by Lees Brown Furniture, makers of upholstered furniture. It's tucked away southwest of the IXL office and the railroad junction. Other Hermansville area industries are Brothers, welders of large storage tanks, and Wendricks Truss, manufacturers of roofing trusses. Rail lines through Hermansville are still in use. It's not hard to picture the town working full-tilt, especially if you can imagine the smell of sawdust and the high, piercing whine of circular saws and the screeches as they bite into wood.

Just five miles east of Hermansville is

Vintage industrial time capsule: the IXL Museum is a lumber mill office with original furnishings and records intact. The owners' elaborate upstairs apartment is a treasure trove of bourgeois German-American *kultur* of the 1890s.

a 6-acre **ginseng plantation**. The home of Gatien's Herbs is half a mile north of Powers, just off U.S. 2 on River Road next to the cemetery. Robert Gatien grinds the legendary tonic to put into capsules, which he sells for $15 a bottle (100 capsules, each with 535 mg. of ginseng). *N16323 J5 River Road. 497-5541.*

IXL Museum

For most of a century this **elaborate Queen Anne style office building** and apartment residence was the hub of the Wisconsin Land and Lumber operation and its **company town** of **Hermansville**. The office was completed in 1883; the company ceased operations in 1960.

Over the years little was changed here. A few things were added and very little removed, so it's **like visiting an office and apartment from the 1880s** with minor updates through the early 20th century. In the main office, old Burroughs adding machines and

inkwells sit on big oak desks, along with the mimeograph Edison invented. The original mechanical clock and crank telephones remain in place. Ledgers of pay records are here, too — a fabulous resource for labor historians. Businesses rarely leave such detailed records for public perusal.

Today it's not hard to imagine the company's 600 to 800 workers lining up at the paymaster's office to receive their weekly pay — in scrip to be spent at the company store. Wisconsin Land and Lumber built the entire town and owned the workers' houses until selling them off after World War II. Such corporate paternalism was common in Upper Peninsula mining and mill towns. Inexpensive housing was a great perk for workers, but being both landlord and employers also gave the companies extraordinary control over workers' lives. To give an idea of how workers lived in Hermansville, an **employee house** that remains unaltered when it was built (probably the late 19th century) has been moved next to the museum. Donors are being lined up to furnish it as it would have been in the early 20th century. It's hard to imagine a family of ten or twelve living in a three-room house like this, but they did, and without apparent hardship.

Some museum volunteers are older local people with roots in the town and its gossip. If one of them is your guide, your museum experience will be rich. Stay awhile and you may hear stories about how the owner advised the manager, when five men came into town asking for jobs, not to hire the German. Germans, he said, were trouble-makers. (IXL's founder himself was German!)

Details of architecture and decorating show that the owners indeed bought "the best of everything" for their headquarters, as the tour guides state. The brass doorknobs and the staircase's varied hardwoods are richly patterned. The owner's upstairs apartment for his sojourns here is quite grand. The parlor's **elaborate painted stenciling** has recently been restored. One bedroom is furnished to remember a beloved local schoolteacher who roomed here for decades. The memorable **attic** is laid out and organized as a storage area. One area is given over to massive gilt mirrors and huge framed engravings acquired on European trips. It's a treasury of bourgeois German-American *kultur*: scenes

from ancient history and images of then-current heroes, including Washington and Bismarck. Old trunks contain things that haven't yet been displayed.

C. J. L. Meyer established Hermansville to supply pine lumber for his big sash, door, and blind factory in Fond du Lac, Wisconsin, because Wisconsin pine was running out. He bought 50,000 acres of timberland around Hermansville, set up a sawmill here in 1878, laid out this company town, and built houses and rooming houses for its workers. At this stage of the lumber industry's development, it depended on unskilled immigrants for its work force. Hermansville's adult population was almost entirely foreign-born.

As the pine gave out here, too, Meyer turned his attention to the remaining hardwood. Here in the 1880s he first perfected machinery to produce hardwood flooring. Because of IXL, hardwood flooring became a prestigious home adornment. IXL ("I excel") was stamped in a circle on back of each strip produced.

Meyer was more an inventor and operations manager than a businessman. His son-in-law, Washington Earle, made IXL successful and bought the mill town at Blaney near Manistique to make more flooring. Credit for preserving the IXL Museum goes to his civic-minded descendants, including many U.P. residents.

Architectural historian Kathryn

Eckert writes that the office building is "one of the buildings that speaks most eloquently for the Upper Peninsula." It clearly shows so many themes that shaped the U.P.: the imported bourgeois culture of owners and managers; the polyglot immigrant workers; the lumber companies' meticulous organization and attention to detail in creating towns to support their enterprises; and the owners' characteristic sense of social responsibility and authoritative conviction that only they knew what was best.

Hermansville is on U.S. 2, 26 miles west of Escanaba and 15 miles east of Norway. Turn at the sign for the IXL Museum and go 4 blocks south. Museum is at southwest end of the main street. 498-2498 or 498-7724. Open daily Mem.-Labor Day 12:30-4 Central Time and by appointment. Annual admission (for as many visits as you like): $5/adult, $10/family. &: no. Six steps into the office; once in, the first floor is accessible.

Keep in mind that all prices and hours of operation are subject to change. Lodging rates vary with supply and demand and are usually higher for special events.

Escanaba, Menominee
& the shores of Green Bay

AROUND ESCANABA and Menominee is one of the Upper Peninsula's most **fertile and temperate areas**. It has been shaped by the lumber empires that harvested the timber riches along its rivers. **Escanaba**, **Menominee**, and its Wisconsin twin city of **Marinette** were **destined to grow rich** because of their locations at the mouths of the Escanaba and Menominee rivers, the longest good logging rivers that flow into Lake Michigan. The sawmills at their outlets were an easy sail away from **Chicago**, with its enormous appetite for lumber and its rail connections to growing towns and cities on the vast and largely treeless prairie. Logging along Lake Superior's more remote rivers occurred much later. The Escanaba area also benefitted from its rail connections to the Marquette Iron Range and, via the Soo Line, to Minneapolis and the Canadian Soo.

The **ethnic mix** here today largely reflects the immigrants in logging camps: Germans, French-Canadians, Norwegians, Swedes, and some Irish and Poles. There are fewer Finns, Italians, Croatians, and Slovenes than on the iron ranges.

Today, a hundred years after lumbering's heyday, its **grand architectural legacies** make Escanaba, Menominee, and Marinette interesting places to explore. The land has finally recovered from the devastation of clearcuts, forest fires, and the resulting erosion. Much of the land not suited to farming is part of the **Hiawatha National Forest** or the **Escanaba River State Forest**, managed both for recreation and harvesting timber. Many area rivers offer good trout fishing and scenic canoeing when water levels are high enough.

Of all the great logging rivers in Michigan and Wisconsin, only the Saginaw and Muskegon compared with the **Menominee River**. Wide and long, it forms much of the **Michigan-Wisconsin border** with its tributary, the Brule. Its watershed is the largest of any in the Upper Peninsula. The Brule's headwaters are west of Iron River over 120 miles from the Menominee's mouth. Much of the history and development is connected with the successful lumber barons who worked their way up the rivers to Iron Mountain, Iron River and beyond for new timber to cut. As the 20th century dawned, logging was waning. The last Menominee River logging drive was in 1917.

Good fishing and many bayfront parks in interesting old lumber ports, with unusual natural areas nearby.

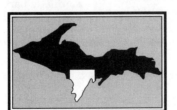

The area has been something of a backwater ever since the timber gave out. Escanaba and Delta County have grown a little in recent years, thanks to more industry and also to resorters and tourists. Menominee County has lost population for years, in part because it is in more direct competition with adjoining Wisconsin. Until Michigan's recent property tax reduction, Wisconsin enjoyed a competitive advantage in attracting new businesses.

Menominee County leads the U.P. in agriculture, because of its many **dairy farms.** Farming took hold early to supply lumber camps. Today Menominee County milk and cream is shipped north to Jilbert's Dairy in Marquette and south to Wisconsin cheesemakers. Local wags call this the **"banana belt"** for its temporate climate compared to places like Marquette. The mean annual temperature is 45° F., about the same as Big Rapids or Clare in the Lower Peninsula much farther south. The county also receives the U.P.'s least amount of precipitation, averaging under 30 inches a year.

Fishing is a major draw to this area. **Little Bay de Noc** was once rated by *USA Today* as one of the world's ten top fishing spots, especially for **walleye**. Professional walleye fishermen travel here on their tournament circuit. Deer hunters come here because the region, with its light snowfall, has the **U.P.'s greatest concentration of deer**.

TO FIND OUT MORE: For **Escanaba, Gladstone, Rapid River**, and **Nahma**, contact **BAYS de NOC VISITORS' BUREAU.** It serves area lodgings and promotes the area. It's also a source for information on **charter fishing.** Call (800) 437-7496, visit **www.deltafun. com,** or stop by weekdays between 8:30 and 5:30. The office is in Building 2 of the U.P. State Fairgrounds, directly west of the main gate on U.S. 2 at the west terminus of 12th Avenue. . . . Member businesses in the same area are served by the **DELTA COUNTY CHAMBER OF COMMERCE.** A membership organization, it's more about business than tourism, but the office at 230 Ludington across from the House of Ludington distributes visitor information, too. It's open weekdays from 9 to 5, to 5:30 in summer. (906) 786-1960. . . .The twin cities of **Menominee**, Michigan, and **Marinette**, Wisconsin, have loads of visitor information not just for their areas, but also for their entire states — and their broadly knowledgeable staffs will also *mail* information. . . . . The **MICHIGAN WELCOME CENTER** is on U.S. 41 at the foot of the Interstate Bridge, north bank of the Menominee River, across from downtown Marinette. (906) 863-6496. Open daily 8 a.m.-4 p.m. Central Time, year-round, possibly longer in summer. & If the small parking lot is full, continue on U.S. 41 to the adjacent M&M Plaza shopping center and take the stairs up to rear of Welcome Center. . . .Marinette County calls itself "the **waterfalls capital of Wisconsin.**" To find out more, stop at the **WISCONSIN TRAVEL INFORMATION CENTER**, turn right after crossing the Interstate Bridge on U.S. 41. It's in downtown Marinette next to the Stephenson Public Library. (715-732-4333). Open April through October, daily from 9 to 5, except in summer from 8 to 4. & . . . . For the local **chambers of commerce** call (906) 863-2679 for **Menominee** and (715) 735-6681 for **Marinette**, or visit **www.marinette county.com**

PUBLIC LANDS: There's a lot of public land in both Delta and Menominee counties. Extensive areas of land in the eastern part of Delta County, from the Rapid River area on east, are part of the **HIAWATHA NATIONAL FOREST**, which has a prominently located office and interpretive center, full of helpful handouts, maps, and a small nature bookstore, on the south side of U.S. 2 three miles east of Rapid River. It's open weekdays from 7:30 to 4. Call (906) 474-6442 or look in at **www.fs.fed.us/ r9 /hiawatha/** (Right now the forest service website isn't too well developed.) . . . . Considerable state land in Delta and Menominee counties, including lots of land on and near the shore of Green Bay is part of the **ESCANABA RIVER STATE FOREST**, with a management office in Gladstone at 6833 U.S. 2/U.S. 41/M-35 (906-786-2354).

EVENTS: For the ESCANABA area, consult the **calendar** on **www.deltafun.com** or call (800) 533-4386. The **Upper Peninsula State Fair** is the third full week in August. Exhibits are mainly farm-oriented, with the familiar rides and big-name country entertainers of typical state fairs. The **Great Lakes Championship Rodeo** is held each Father's Day weekend. There's a free **Civil War Encampment** in Ludington Park the last weekend of June. The first weekend of August brings the **Waterfront Art Festival** to Ludington Park. . . . For **MENOMINEE** there's the **Brown Trout Derby** at the end of July and the **Waterfront Festival** around the first weekend of August, with a big parade, fireworks, music, and more. . . .

MARINETTE County hosts the **Menominee River Century Ride** on the last Sunday in June (bike rides begin at 15k) . . . On a weekend in mid June country music fans in campers descend on a field in rural Porterfield, Wisconsin, 7 miles outside Marinette, for the **Porterfield Country Music Festival**, one of those events that just grew and grew. Around $75 buys a weekend of music by the likes of Suzy Boggs, Billy Ray Cyrus, and Willie Nelson, the 2001 headliners.

HARBORS with transient dockage: In **Gladstone** (906-428-2916; off-season 906-428-2311; lat. 45° 50' 15" N, long. 87° 01' 00" W) with showers. In **Escanaba** (906-786-9614; 906-786-4141; 800-700-9614; lat. 45° 44' 34"N, long. 87° 02' 05" W) with showers. In **Menominee** (906-863-8498; lat. 45° 06' 21" N, long. 87° 35' 58" W) with showers.

PICNIC PROVISIONS and PLACES:

◆ **Ludington Park** on the **waterfront** in ESCANABA is just about perfect. Most picnic areas are towards the park's south end. Pick up convenient, quality picnic fixings at **Gus Asp's**, 616 Ludington.

◆ The big supermarket in ESCANABA is **Super One Foods**. It's on the west side of North Lincoln/U.S. 41/U.S. 2, a couple blocks north of the M-35/U.S. 2 intersection as U.S. 2 heads north to Gladstone.

◆ **Picnic spots off U. S. 2** as it goes east between Rapid River and Manistique: Little **Bay de Noc Rec. Area** with giant hemlocks, remote **Peninsula Point** with its lighthouse tower, and the DNR boat launch at **Nahma**. Coming from the east? See Manistique chaper for its provisioning points.

◆ **MENOMINEE** is loaded with good takeout options. See our restaurant section for **Thai Cuisine** downtown and **Le Grapillon de Ore** French bakery/sandwich shop on the waterfront. Or stop at **Angeli's Central Market,** an amazing combination of supermarket and gourmet store. It's at the foot of the Interstate Bridge in the M&M Plaza on U.S. 41.

◆ In **MENOMINEE/MARINETTE**, three terrific parks on Green Bay are **Henes Park** off M-35 on Menominee's north side, the **harborfront park** on First Street in downtown Menominee, or **Red Arrow Park** in Marinette. **Stephenson Island**, the Marinette park off the Interstate Bridge, also has a picnic area.

◆ All the **parks along M-35** between Escanaba and Menominee have picnic areas and sandy swimming beaches.

Escanaba (pop. 13,140)

Sprawling Escanaba is one of the few U.P. cities to have a **well-balanced economy**. The metro area (over 20,000 including neighboring Gladstone and Rapid River) has retailing, manufacturing, tourism, some shipping, and, in the vicinity, fishing and farming. It also enjoys a **homegrown cultural life** centered on the Bonifas Arts Center, the 8th Street Coffee House, and local galleries. For the U.P., Escanaba is quite an urbane place, not the everybody-knows-your-name kind of small town depicted in movie star/Michigan playwright Jeff

Daniels' comic play and film, *Escanaba in da Moonlight*. Apparently Daniel couldn't resist the rhythmic possibilities of pairing Escanaba's name with the Finnish-ism of "da," though in truth Swedish, Norwegian, French, and German names are far more common in this area than Finnish ones.

A visitor's first impressions are of the unappealing commercial sprawl that extends along U.S. 2/U.S. 41 and the Little Bay de Noc between Escanaba and Rapid River for almost 10 miles, and of the flat, marshy areas south and west of town. But there is **surprisingly varied beauty** close at hand: in town along the lakeshore south of downtown and along

Little Bay de Noc; along the little developed stretch of M-35 south to Menominee, offering frequent glimpses of Green Bay; and along the area's many rivers and state and national forest land. For boaters, fishermen, canoeists, naturalists, hunters, and artists, the Escanaba area is an **attractive, low-cost place to live**. It shows up on national surveys of most affordable cities.

Escanaba's atypically mild U.P. climate and excellent shipping location combined to account for its relative prosperity. The city began as an **iron and lumber port** during the Civil War. Union armsmakers, railroads, and shipbuilders needed speedy delivery of U.P.

iron. In 1864 a railroad was built from Negaunee's iron mines to Escanaba, where the natural deep-water harbor made an excellent port. Most of the Little Bay de Noc is 50 to 70 feet deep. In the 1860s the Nelson Ludington Lumber Company of Marinette, Wisconsin, started to cut timber in the area. It platted the town, providing for its wide streets. In an act of unusual foresight, the company gave a mile of prime lakeshore for the new town's **beautiful Ludington Park.**

By the 1870s the park and the House of Ludington hotel (recently reopened) were destinations for tourists who arrived on steamships. In that decade the port got an extra boost when the Chicago & Northwestern Railroad connected Escanaba to the newly opened iron mines of the Menominee Range in Norway, Iron Mountain, and Iron River.

Being in the U.P.'s "banana belt" helped shipping and farming, too. Shielded from Lake Superior blizzards, the area gets an average annual snowfall of just 50 inches, a fourth of what's usual in many northern Lake Superior locales. In 1910, *Clover-Land* magazine's enthusiasm for promoting Upper Peninsula agricultural possibilities helped create the county fair that later became the **Upper Peninsula State Fair**. It attracts 130,000 visitors a year each August. (Michigan's disjointed geography means it's the only state to have two state fairs.)

Shipping iron ore isn't just a thing of the past. One of the most prominent present-day landmarks is the **mile-long, 300-foot high stockpile of iron taconite pellets** on the shoreline just south of the quarter-mile-long ore docks jutting out into the bay. These concentrated iron and clay pellets, created to transport iron ore more efficiently, are round and marble-sized. Not surprisingly, Escanaba's youth, having found them perfect ammunition for their slingshots, make regular trips to the mountainous heap to resupply their arsenals.

At one time most of the world's **bird's-eye maple**, harvested in forests up to 200 miles away, was shipped from the harbor docks, located just north of downtown. But today iron shipments dominate shipping activity here. Once Escanaba's port was second in importance to Marquette's, but their shipments are now at least equal, some 7 to 8 million tons a year. Iron ore from the Tilden and Empire mines near Ishpeming is moved by rail to Escanaba, bound for northern Indiana steel mills. Marquette docks load freighters going to Canadian steelmakers. Escanaba's big

ore-shipping facility is more modern than Marquette's. It uses huge 2,200-foot-long, high-speed conveyors to load taconite rather than dropping the pellets noisily into ships' holds from ore dock pockets, as it's done in Marquette.

The **huge Mead paper plant** just north of Escanaba, maker of coated paper for textbooks (some 60% of its business) and magazines, dwarfs all other companies in the region. Currently 30% of its wood comes from Mead-owned land, 15% to 20% from public land, and

the rest from privately owned land. Professional foresters work with landowners in developing a management plan, then contracting with independent loggers to supply trees and replant open areas. Mead employs 1,340 workers. That's in addition to the company's many independent logger-suppliers whose trucks are so common on U.P. highways.

The area's relatively low wages help several sizable machine shops who do contract work for national firms such as Caterpillar and Cummins. (89% of local

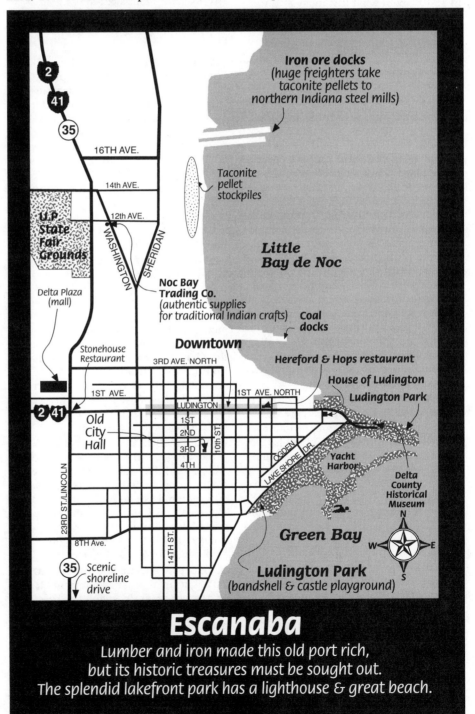

Escanaba

Lumber and iron made this old port rich,
but its historic treasures must be sought out.
The splendid lakefront park has a lighthouse & great beach.

machine operators earn under $10 an hour; 54% earn under $7 an hour.) The hottest company in town these days is **Engineered Machine Products**, west of town on 28th Street. In just a few years it has become the country's top manufacturer of **diesel engine cooling pumps**. Its 460 workers now generate $165 million in revenues.

Escanaba has managed to escape the boom-and-bust economy of most other U.P. towns of any size. The city's population grew from 9,500 in 1900 to 14,000 in 1940, about what it is today.

Downtown Escanaba along Ludington Street

What strikes a first-time visitor to Escanaba is just how long the downtown is for a city of 14,000 people. Ludington Avenue leads east to Lake Michigan from the highway junction of M-35 and U.S. 2 /U.S. 41. Its business district is all of 15 blocks long. A **sprinkling of vintage neon signs** across old storefronts and taverns makes Ludington Street especially impressive at night. The look is of the 1940s and 1950s, though some beautiful brownstone storefronts are much older. The architecture of **grand public buildings** and **churches** on **First Avenue South**, a block to the south, was often paid for by lumber fortunes. Ludington Avenue ends at a small point of land past the **lighthouse** that separates Green Bay (the body of water, not the city) to the south from the walleye fishing mecca of Little Bay de Noc.

These downtown highlights are arranged from west to east.

◆ **SAYKYLLY'S CANDIES & GIFTS. Celebrated hand-dipped chocolates**, made in Escanaba and shipped all over, are available at this gift shop. It also carries gifts like Waterford crystal, Hummel, and Dept. 56 collectibles, Swarvoski crystal, plush animals, and religious goods. It all started in 1906 when Lebanese immigrants Joseph and Mary Sayklly (pronounced "SAKE-ly') opened a grocery store. They had nine children; a son and his family started making candies, and two daughters ran the shop. Another daughter got into religious goods, which evolved into this gift shop. Sayklly's production facility at 910 Second Ave. North near the downtown waterfront now **ships 400,000 pounds of chocolate candy** a year.

Walk in and the candies are on your right — not only chocolates but Jelly Bellies, Juju coins, and such. Sayklly's most popular candy is called the "Snap-

Escanaba's name

"Escanaba" is a distortion of the Ojibwa term "land of the red buck." It refers to a once-famous hunting ground north of Escanaba that was crossed by a heavily-traveled deer trail. The region attracted Indians from hundreds of miles away because of its **abundance of deer**. Many paddled up the **Escanaba River** to reach it. The area remains a prime deer-hunting area of the U.P.

py," their version of the caramel- and chocolate-covered pecan "Turtle." Favorite souvenir gift: the **Yooper bar** ($1), a solid chocolate outline map of the U.P. Mail order is available. The new freestanding store with the bright red roof in front of Delta Plaza is open longer hours: 9:30 to 8 p.m. weekdays, 10-6 Saturdays, noon-5 Sundays. But this 75-foot downtown storefront is the visitor favorite. *1304 Ludington, north side of street. 786-6899 phone and fax; www.saykyllycandy.com; e-mail fudge@up.net. Mon-Fri 9:30-5, Sat to 4* ;

◆ **THE RECORD RACK.** This **highly diverse shop** carries used and new CDs, cassettes, and even vinyl, plus used VHS and DVD videos and video games. If there's any concentration, it's rock classics: the Beatles, Elvis, the Grateful Dead. Intermixed with merchandise are the **displays of a rock 'n' roll museum**, including a Buddy Holly high school yearbook, one of Ted Nugent's arrows, Beatle dolls, and a Robert Cray guitar. *1212 Ludington, north side of street. 474-6460. Open Mon-Sat 10-6.*

◆ **CANTERBURY BOOKSTORE** . This personal, general bookstore (new books only, for adults and children) has **especially good sections of Great Lakes and regional books and nature guides**. The small section of **Scandinavian imports** also stands out. *908 Ludington. 786-9751. Mon-Wed 9-5:30, Thurs to 7, Fri & Sat to 5.* : tight spaces.

◆ **THE 8th STREET COFFEE HOUSE** isn't just an ordinary storefront. It's an **extremely eclectic space** that occupies 10,000 square feet of the former Lauerman's Department Store, which makes for plenty of little nooks and crannies for meeting places and quiet study spaces. Groups that meet include writers, artists, Vietnam Vets, a camera club, and many more. There's a limited menu of the usual **coffee drinks**, **bagels**, and

muffins, plus **soups** and the $2.50 **cheddarwurst**, a sausage-cheese affair wrapped in bagel dough. The website details the rich and shifting schedule of performers who hold forth in the separate performing space. Every FRIDAY at 8 you'll always find free music scheduled by **The Delta Folks folk music association**, maybe hometown talent like bluesman Smiley Jim Lewis (his Shuffleaires are often heard at nightspots around town) or regional performers. SATURDAY at 8 there's **improvisational comedy** by the Eighth Street Irregulars. (The second Saturday is always open mike night.) Other nights have more impromptu performances that may not always take place: MONDAY (**bluegrass** with the Pickers & Grinners at 6, followed by the Bay Area Christian Ministry, with free pizza and movies or Monday-night football); TUESDAY (euchre); and WEDNESDAY (sort of **Dixieland-style brass**).

Proprietor Dave Van DeWyngearde drew on his coffeehouse memories from Ann Arbor to start the coffeehouse and seized the opportunity when this space became vacant. His model wasn't 1990s coffeehouse chic, but something much looser. Customers have followed suit and been inspired to donate furniture, pianos (three at the moment), art they have made, and even a 50" TV. *NOTE:* the entertainment's free, but if you come to the coffee house, *you are expected to BUY something.* It's not a cinch to pay the overhead on 10,000 square feet! *720 Ludington. 789-9174; www.geocities. com/eighthstreetcoffeehouse.com Open daily at least til 10 p.m. Mon-Fri from 7 a.m. Sat & Sun from 8 a.m.*

◆ **DELTA HOTEL** Breathing life into a large old hotel goes against the odds, but two local couples have done it. On weekends their Hereford and Hops brew pub/grill-your-own-steak restaurant often packs the front lounge and large rear dining rooms of this **1914 hotel**. The massive project also converted the upper floors to apartments. *624 Ludington at 7th St.*

◆ **JUST ASK GUS ASP BUTCHER SHOP.** The mysterious vintage neon sign alternates between the founding owner's name "Gus Asp" and "Just Ask." This **local landmark** is next to Hereford & Hops restaurant in the old Delta Hotel. Could "Just Ask" allude to the tobacco and newsstand's Prohibition-era reputation as a place to buy booze? Today, owned by the Moodys, half of the Hereford & Hops team, Gus Asp sells **fresh meat and cheese** in addition to the expected newspapers, candy, cigars, and party store items. *616 Ludington. 786-1881. Open daily 7 a.m.-11 p.m.* &

◆ **EAST LUDINGTON GALLERY.** Participating artists own and operate this **most attractive cooperative gallery**, where you can expect to find a wide variety of interesting gifts and art from $2 to $2,000. Current offerings include baskets, woven hangings, hand-blown glass, papier-maché, wreaths, jewelry, candles, scrimshaw, quilts, pottery, hand-forged iron accessories, stained glass, home accessories, greeting cards, and photographs, prints, and paintings. Some Christmas items are on hand all year round. Free gift wrap. The handsome red brick and sandstone building from the turn of the century was built to house the Masons' upper-story meeting rooms. *619 Ludington near 7th St., across from Hereford & Hops. 786-0300. www.delta mich.org/gallery Mon-Sat 11-5.* &.

◆ **DELTA COUNTY CHAMBER of COMMERCE.** Handy source of area info, next to Ludington Park. *230 Ludington Ave., across from House of Ludington. Mon-Fri 9-5:30, in summer also Sat 10-2. (800) 437-7496.*

◆ **HOUSE OF LUDINGTON.** First-time visitors to Escanaba often remember this **imposing old hotel** at the foot of Ludington Street. Ludington Park and the waterfront are so dominated by the House of Ludington that they seem to be its front yard. The hotel is a striking image, an authentic period piece, and a **characteristic example of the 19th-century Queen Anne resort hotels** that have mostly vanished. It goes back to the days when rather grand Great Lakes steamships disembarked here and Escanaba's waterfront park was a promenade and major visitor destination.

The hotel has been here since Escanaba's first years as a significant port. The current building dates from 1883, though it has been expanded and altered many times. Its days of greatest glory came after 1939, when the energetic and ebullient Pat Hayes, a Chicago Irishman, turned it into a legend with his good food and memorable personality. In the mid 1990s the hotel went bankrupt, and Escanaba ran the risk of losing its defining historic building. In 1999 Edward and Suzell Eichelberger from Mount Pleasant, scouting the U.P. for a somewhat smaller inn, came upon the abandoned landmark and decided to take on the job of bringing it back to life. They repainted the exterior in **lively Victorian colors**, redecorated, and reopened the grand old lady for dining and overnight lodging. Note: there's an **ice cream parlor** which serves cones, just the thing for a leisurely **evening walk by the bay**. For details, see below. *223 Ludington Ave.* &

Ludington Park

A **mile of lakefront parkland** begins at the foot of Escanaba's main business street, across from its landmark hotel. In a grand gesture of corporate paternalism, lumberman and Escanaba founding father Nelson Ludington had his chief engineer lay out this 120-acre park when he platted the town and its wide streets in 1863. It was an act of great foresight, here on the northwoods frontier, at a time when the urban parks movement was just being launched in the United States.

Today **five miles of paved pathways** within the park connect every attraction, making the park a preferred destination for people on wheels, from rollerblades and baby strollers to bikes and wheelchairs. One path begins in the park's north end, across from the House of Ludington, and extends along Lakeshore Drive to the park's south end. There, near the ends of Sixth and Fifth avenues, are a **band shell**, a large **fantasy-castle playground**, and lighted **tennis courts**. From mid-June through August **band concerts** are held here Wednesday evenings from 7:30 to about 9:30. Most **picnic areas** are in the park's south side, overlooking Green Bay and accessed by Lakeshore Drive.

Another paved **walkway** runs through the center of the park and over the bridge to Arnson Island. On the island are a **boat launch** and a **3,500' sandy swimming beach** that's hard to beat, with a bathhouse and **small playground**. There are good views across to the Stonington Peninsula and out into Green Bay. Beyond the swimming beach, the paved path extends to a protected **natural area** at the island's north tip. (The island creates a protected harbor for the **marina** on the opposite shore.) **Shore fishing** is allowed at all points in the park, including the municipal dock and in the natural area, and it is famous, especially for **walleye** but also for perch, trout, and salmon.

History-minded visitors who are extremely patient can read interesting, well-written **historical panels** deployed near the park's downtown end, in a garden across from the intersection of Lakeshore with Ludington. These panels go into considerable detail about key aspects of local history. Not far away are the Sand Point Lighthouse and the Delta County Historical Museum (see below).

The park extends south along the lake from the foot of Ludington Ave. downtown all the way to the foot of 7th Ave. (906) 786-4141. Free. &

Sand Point Lighthouse

This trim brick lighthouse, **dating from 1868**, has such a natural, settled look, it's hard to imagine that it's been drastically remodeled twice. In 1939 the Coast Guard discontinued the light, raised the roof, and made the building into a family residence for the Coast Guard chief. In the 1980s the Delta County Historical Society got a long-term lease on the disfigured local landmark. In "a marvel of renovation" (the words of the Penrose family in their *Traveler's Guide to 116 Michigan Lighthouses*), the society lowered the roof, reconstructed the tower's top, and conducted a successful search for a fourth-order **Fresnel lens** and an **authentic old lantern room** (found left on the ground at Poverty Island).

Inside, the **keeper's quarters** are furnished in a turn-of-the-century manner. Visitors can **climb the stairs** and look out from the **tower**.

In Ludington Park at the end of Ludington Avenue. Open from June thru Sept. Hours in June thru August: daily 9-5. In Sept: daily 1-4. (906) 786-3763. $1/adults, 50¢ under 13. &: no.

Delta County Historical Museum

The four-room museum of the Delta County covers local maritime history, the timber industry, railroads, and early life in Escanaba. There's a **model lumber camp**, too. Photographic and written archives are also here in what once was the Coast Guard's aids to navigation station.

About 100 feet southeast of the lighthouse (above) in Ludington Park, near the head of Ludington Avenue. Same hours as lighthouse. (906) 786-3763. Free. &

First Avenue South's historic architecture & shops

First Avenue South parallels Ludington Avenue a block south of it. Its striking turn-of-the-century churches, public buildings, and homes give a good idea of Escanaba's **glory days**. You'll see more, of course, if you walk or bicycle. Additional fine old houses are along Ogden Avenue, which joins First Avenue South at Second Street, behind the House of Ludington.

Here are First Avenue's highlights, arranged from the lake westward:

◆ **THE KITCHEN PLACE & VICTORIAN GIFT HOUSE.** The downstairs of this very large Queen Anne house is a **beautiful kitchen display showroom** where visitors can buy accessories, too — perhaps an afghan draped over a chair or a vase or framed picture. In good weather, there's something to drink while you sit on the **porch**. The house, full of nooks and crannies, has its **original woodwork, hardware, and lighting intact**. It seemed the perfect place for Dave and Judi Schwalbach to run their kitchen design business and live upstairs, too. Judi has always warmed up the kitchen cabinets with accessories and antiques, and customers always asked to buy them. So she decided to add a low-key gift shop. The store looks like a home — a home with a lot of kitchens. The large foyer with its elaborate woodwork really shines at Christmas, when five thousand lights decorate a 17-foot tree. *212 First Avenue South, behind the House of Ludington. 786-9595. www.victoriangift-house.com Mon-Fri 10-5, Sat 10-4. &: no.*

◆ **The former CARNEGIE LIBRARY, now a private home.** Historic public buildings are adapted to many new uses, but very seldom are they converted to single-family homes. That's just what contractor Paul Neumeier has done with Escanaba's grand, **neoclassical Carnegie Library from 1902**. He always liked the building, and the location is great, close to downtown and the park. The fiction stacks are his rec room, the reference room a living-dining area, the east wing a big eat-in kitchen. *Southeast corner, First Ave. South at 7th St., kitty-corner from the Bonifas Arts Center.*

◆ **BONIFAS FINE ARTS CENTER.** The U.P.'s largest towns have active arts groups. Escanaba's stands out for its beautiful and extensive facility here in what was built as the gym and auditorium of St. Joseph Catholic Church across the street at 709 First Avenue. A good deal of the lumber-based fortune of Luxemburger Bill Bonifas went to build a new church and this school gym and auditorium in 1937-8.

The Bonifas, as it's known, has galleries for **varied changing exhibits**, plus classroom and studio space and a theater. Local **theater** and **folk music** groups use it. Wide-ranging art exhibits run from regional shows of watercolors, baskets, and quilts to traveling Smithsonian exhibitions. Call or check the website to find out about **exhibits** and **events**.

The U.P. has a **surprisingly large number of working artists and craftspeople**. Probably, says one artist here, that comes from a strong strain of self-sufficiency, combined with the area's relative isolation away from the world of museums and other forms of imported culture and entertainment. *700 First Ave. South at 7th St. 786-3833. www.bonifasarts.org Tues-Fri 10-5:30, Sat to 5. &.*

◆ **ST. JOSEPH CATHOLIC CHURCH.** See the Bonifas Center for history. The church's towers and **unusual golden stone** make the exteriors striking. But the restrained neo-Romanesque style doesn't hint at the **sumptuous interior touches** like the church's **inlaid floors of four colorful marbles**, or its **mosaics** and **stained glass rose windows**. Mass is at 4 Saturday and 11:30 Sunday. Weekdays the church is generally open from 6:30 a.m. to 1:30 p.m., and visitors are welcome. *709 First Avenue South. 789-6244. &.*

◆ **BELLE PEARL/Old City Hall.** Escanaba's imposing Romanesque Revival city hall, built of red sandstone in 1902, has been renovated and restored by a construction company, one of several building tenants. Upstairs, partition walls have been removed from ornate council chambers to get back to the original woodwork and floor. Downstairs the attractive **Belle Pearl gift and antique shop** occupies one room. Antique furniture and small objects, new and old, including some locally made **handblown glass barrettes and necklaces**, are arranged with unusual design flair. *121 S. 11th St. at First Ave. South. Belle Pearl hours: Mon-Fri 9-3, Sat by chance (often 11-3 from spring thru Xmas) and by appt. (906) 789-0041. &: not yet.*

Noc Bay Trading Company

At powwows held throughout the Upper Great Lakes the splendid **Native American regalia** worn by participants is always a highlight. It's part of contemporary Indian culture for participants to make their own regalia as a way of reconnecting with traditions. Not every powwow participant has time to kill a deer and tan its hide, however, or to bring down a grouse to prepare a decorative ruff, or to make bone beads, so there's a real need for the quality traditional materials sold at this unusual shop.

Jewelry-making findings are also on hand. The focus is on Eastern Woodlands and Great Lakes Indian cultures; items about Plains or Southwestern In-

dian arts are quite peripheral. The small **showroom** is "a fascinating place," in the words of a local artist, with "a marvelous selection of beautiful things, well displayed." In addition to handcrafted traditional Indian objects, merchandise includes Pendleton Indian and muchacho blankets and jackets, and Leaning Tree and Finnish note cards. This is not the place to find rubber tomahawks. Some chemically dyed feathers are used in inexpensive kits for beginner projects, but most dyes are natural. **Glass beads** and other **trade goods** that became part of Indian traditions are sold here, too.

Loren Woerpel got into the business by accident some 20 years ago when local Boy Scouts took up the Indian crafts he taught with enthusiasm, thanks to a temporary hiatus in school athletics due to a school millage failure. He worked for the U. S. Forest Service then, so his wife, Donna, ran the Native American crafts supplies business along with her candle making. Now they have their own building, a 1904 storefront they have renovated. The Woerpels have no Indian ancestry, but some employees do. Most business here is through Noc Bay's **mail-order catalog**, and many if not most customers have Great Lakes Indian ancestry. Same-day or next-day shipping is a point of pride.

1133 Washington Ave., a block east of U.S. 2/U.S. 41 across from the U. P. State Fairgrounds. Turn east onto 12th Ave. at Bob's Buggy Wash & you'll see store at the next corner. (906) 789-0505. www.nocbay.com Open Mon-Fri 9-5, Sat 10-4. &.

ESCANABA RESTAURANTS

See also Gladstone. Restaurants here are arranged starting downtown and going west and north.

HEREFORD & HOPS has become a big hit and downtown anchor since two local couples founded it with a bang in 1994. They renovated the **1914 Delta Hotel**, putting 32 apartments on the 2nd through 5th floors and a **brew pub/grill-your-own-steak restaurant** on the first floor. Gus Asp, the liquor and cigar store next door, has become a **butcher shop**, too, selling the same beef served in the restaurant. The large restaurant is jammed weekends, so reservations are advised. A soup and sandwich menu (served all the time in the pub) and desserts invite anytime snacking. Not serving super-premium beef keeps prices in a range local people are happy to pay. Beers are brewed for broad appeal. Customers can choose to stand around a **big circular grill, fired by a ton of Tennessee hickory briquettes** a week, and grill their own steaks if desired with the help of a chef who directs the spectacle. A grill-your-own 18-20 oz. N.Y. strip steak sells for just $16, including baked potato, fresh bread sticks, and an **excellent salad bar** featuring tasty original variations on familiar themes. Alone it could keep vegetarians happy. There are also vegetarian pastas, pita, and large salads. Four homemade desserts a day. *Downtown at 624 Ludington at 8th Ave. 789-1945. www.herefordandhops.com Mon-Sat 11 a.m.-10 p.m., Sun 4 p.m.-9 p.m.* &: 8th Ave. door.

At the reopened **HOUSE OF LUDINGTON,** the more elegant of its two dining rooms overlooks the bay. The other is more casual. Both serve the same wideranging menu. At lunch, **strawberry-cashew salad** is a favorite, but you could get a hamburger, too, or one of many entrées. Dinners include pasta dishes, lamb, duck, wiener schnitzel, steaks, mostly from $13 to $20, with $14-$15 typical. In summer food and drinks are served outside on the patio facing the park. This is *the* place for a **pleasant after-dinner stroll**. *223 Ludington. 786-6300. Lunch Mon-Sat 11-2. Dinner Mon-Thurs 5-9, Fri & Sat 5-10. Closed Sun.* & Full bar

Many locals think **CRISPIGNA'S** has the **best pizza in town**. In addition to pasta with homemade sauces, it offers ample portions of homemade ravioli ($10 and $14), good steaks, and seafood. Dinners range from $7.45 to $18. It's a warm, personal place where owner Joe Crispigna visits with customers. Booths make it a good place to talk. Nice Chiantis, a good house dressing, and optional salad anchovies are welcome touches. **Reservations** accepted. *1213 Ludington. 786-8660. Open daily except holidays. Sun-Thurs 5-9, Fri & Sat to 10.* &: rear entrance Full bar

The **STONEHOUSE RESTAURANT and CARPORT LOUNGE** has long been a favorite for business lunches and nights out. It's one of the real culinary standouts in a town with surprisingly good food. **Broiled whitefish and perch** ($12-$15) are favorites, as is the baconwrapped shrimp appetizer ($7.50). Veal ($15) and prime rib are other specialties ($13 for a 10 oz. portion). Chef Rob Ekberg, who's been at the Stonehouse since 1985, has created **"Blackjack Ekberg"** ($19), a chargrilled New York steak flambéed with Jack Daniels and sautéed with green and black peppercorns in a demi-glaze. For vegetarians there are 2-3

entrées and a sandwich. Lunch entrées are from $6 to $10, with a $6.75 daily special and a $5.75 soup and sandwich or salad and fruit plate. *2223 Ludington at M-35. 786-5003. Mon-Fri 11 a.m.-2 p.m., Mon-Sat (and summer Sundays) 5 p.m.-9 p.m.* & Full bar

The **best chef in town**, by general agreement, is Robin Holmes at the **CARRIAGE INN** in the **BEST WESTERN PIONEER INN**, of all places. "I have been to some meals he has done that were just fantastic," comments a well-traveled executive. "The benefit dinners are events." As for every day, "ask what's good on the menu," he advises, and get the **spicy seafood dishes** when they're on special. He likes the rack of lamb, specialty steaks, salmon dishes, and jambalaya. The general public goes for his fish dishes ($12-$17), prepared various ways. The **huge Caesar and cobb salads** are lunchtime hits. Vegetarian and special diets by request — local doctors from India eat well here. In the evening the downstairs **pub** serves an **Italian menu** with pasts, pizza, and chicken pepperoni. Reservations suggested on weekends. *On Ludington/U.S. 2/U.S. 41 on the west side, one light beyond the intersection of M-35 and U.S. 2. 786-0602. Year-round hours: Mon-Fri for breakfast (7-11), lunch (11-2), and dinner (5-9), Sat dinner 5-9, Sun brunch (8-2). In summer also open for Sat breakfast (8-11) and Sun dinner (5-9).* & Full bar; extensive wine list

Broiled whitefish, super-fresh right out of the Bays de Noc, wins raves at **THE DELL'S SUPPER CLUB**. It's been in the same **vintage log building** since 1933, with an **88-foot U-shaped bar** and a **dance floor** that still gets used. (There's **dancing** to bands on most weekends, especially in summer, starting at 8:30.) A local fan supports the owner's claim to serve the **best salad bar in the U.P.** There are three salad bars, actually, all with homemade dishes. You can get a great meal by ordering the salad bar alone—a terrific bargain. Dell's also offers a full menu of steaks, prime rib, chicken, and seafood dishes. *Set back 300 feet off highway U.S. 2/U.S. 41, 5 miles west of town. 789-9250. Tues-Thurs 4:30-9, Fri & Sat to 10 p.m., Sun 4-9.* & Full bar

For great breakfasts at budget prices, try **DELONA'S** (786-6400), a family restaurant with bakery. It's in a house that grew into a restaurant, so the rooms are cozy. **Homemade pies** are a big thing here, along with daily specials (typically $4-5 at lunch, $5-8 at dinner) like fresh

smelt from late January through March. You can order off the soup and sandwich menu any time. *On the east side of U.S. 2/U.S. 41 between Escanaba and Gladstone. It's north of the Escanaba River between two motels. Open 6 a.m. to 8 p.m. daily, to 9 in summer.* &: no

ESCANABA LODGINGS

See also Gladstone. Many Escanaba motels, including the big **Days Inn** and **Super 8,** are in the heavily developed stretch of U.S. 2/41 just north of the M-35 intersection and Delta Plaza. Because this location offers no scenic or outdoor amenities and forces guests to depend on cars to get anywhere, we prefer the older motels that occupy prime locations near the bay. The **Best Western Pioneer Inn** on West Ludington/U.S. 2 (another piece of strip commercial development with no scenery) is a good choice for those who want to dine well, drink, and sleep in the same location because it's also home to the Carriage Inn, with the best chef and wine list in town. Check **www.deltafun.com** for information on other lodging options.

HOUSE OF LUDINGTON

(906) 786-6300; www.houseofludington.com; fax (906) 786-1985; e-mail: hol@bresnanlink.net

The 22 guest rooms at this refurbished landmark have been newly redecorated to feature themes (garden golf, country Victorian). All have private baths, cable TV, air-conditioning, and phones. Four room types: one double bed on the water ($75) or off the water ($65), two double beds ($85), two bedrooms and a connecting bath ($95). A **full breakfast** is part of the price. Two dining rooms, a pub, and an ice cream shop are on the premises. The location is ideal: **Ludington Park,** the bay, lighthouse, playground, and related attractions in one direction, and **downtown Escanaba shops** in the other. *223 Ludington.*
&: rates by the room

BROTHERTON'S MOTEL & COTTAGES
(906) 786-1271

A 4-unit motel and four cottages enjoy **lake views** and **considerable privacy** at this woodsy, well-maintained resort, started in 1936. **300 feet of sand beach** and **many tall pines** distinguish it from similar small resorts and attract a set of regulars and family reunions, so it's best to reserve early. But some vacancies develop even in July & August. Each unit has tongue & groove cedar walls, a picnic table, cable TV with ESPN and Disney. Phone in office. Motel for two people: $79 and $84/night, two-night summer minimum. 5-room cottages by the week in summer, $762-$966 in 2001. Ask for off-season rates. *5 miles south of Escanaba on M-35. Open from mid-May ice-out for fishermen thru hunting season.*

H.A.: call.   👫: no extra charge

ESCANABA CAMPING

PIONEER TRAIL PARK

(906) 786-1020; reservations accepced.

Used mainly by overnighters and anglers, this large modern campground is on the north side of the Escanaba River near its mouth. There's **shore fishing** and a **playground**. Its most striking feature, oddly enough, is the **nigthttime view of steam** emanating from the stacks of Mead Paper just up the river. Extras include **cable TV hookup** ($3/night). Camping fees are $15 for the 58 electric sites (36 of which have water), $10 for the 25 tent sites. *On U.S. 2/41 between Escanaba and Gladstone just north of the Escanaba River.*

H.A.: ADA accessible bathhouse

Gladstone (pop. 5,032)

This tidy, compact town near the head of Little Bay de Noc has attractive residential streets, Lake Shore Drive and Minneapolis Avenue, that look out to the bay across **beautiful Van Cleve Park** and its **swimming beach**.

Backers from Minneapolis of the Soo Line railroad founded the town as "Minnewasca Sioux" ("White Water") and established a flour mill here in 1887. But its main value was the **natural deep-water harbor**. Local leaders soon re-named it after British prime minister William Gladstone because British capital, raised through business interests in Canada to help develop their economy, helped finance the **Soo Line**. The railroad got its name because it connected Minneapolis-St. Paul with Sault Ste. Marie. Railroad engine repair shops and the harbor were built here, so the railroad could have a Lake Michigan port for shipping grain from Minneapolis.

Gladstone's economy has long combined tourism and industry. In the late 19th century **Cleveland Cliffs Iron**, which controlled iron mining around Marquette and Ishpeming, built a **blast furnace** and chemical plant along Lake Michigan on Gladstone's north end. Here kilns burned hardwood to produce charcoal for the smelting process, and extracted additional chemicals from the

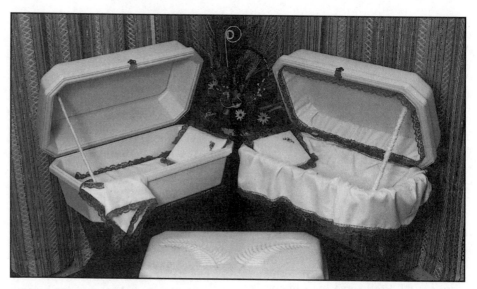

Perspective on the pet burial phenomenon is part of the tour at the world's largest maker of pet caskets, located in Gladstone.

wood, such as resins used in glue. By 1910 descriptions mentioned company houses extending "as far as the eye could see." Today three houses remain.

The place on the north end was named **Kipling** in honor of Rudyard Kipling, when he toured the North Country along the Soo Line — a trip arranged by its financial backers. The famous poet and novelist, author of *The Jungle Book* and *Kim*, asked what was the name of this industrial town. Actually it had no name — and, indeed, is no longer on the map. "Kipling" was the answer, just as "Rudyard" had been the response to a similar query in the eastern U.P. Later he wrote a poem entitled "My Two Sons in Michigan." The **Kipling House Bed and Breakfast** now occupies the last of Kipling's six big boarding houses.

Today Gladstone's harbor is used for recreational boats. Gladstone thrived with the railroad, then slowed down. But the population is now back up to its 1930s level of over 5,000.

Two unusual companies are in Gladstone. The decades-old **Marble Arms** makes rifle scopes for gun manufacturers like Remington, among other things. Its **hunting knives**, guns, and accessories from the past have become desirable collectors' items. Now a line of reproduction knives has been reintroduced. The Marble Arms **showroom** is open to the public weekdays from 8:30 to 4:30. It's in the big orange building just off the Kipling exit of U.S. 2/U.S. 41. Another uncommon firm, the thirty-year-old **Hoegh Pet Casket Company**, ships high-impact styrene plastic products all over the country. See below for tour and **pet cemetery** info.

Getting to the town of Gladstone from U.S. 2/41 is not as easy as you might assume because rail yards separate it from the highway. Look for the signs along the highway. The southernmost entrance is via Marble Avenue/ Lake Shore along the lake. The **main retail street**, Delta Avenue, intersects with U.S. 2 opposite the freight yard.

Hoegh Pet Casket Company

Here at the **world's largest pet casket factory**, Hoegh's (pronounced "hoig") actively promotes its products with **tours**. Groups and individuals are invited to "learn the **history of the pet burial phenomenon**. View casket manufacture and assembly. Stroll through the **model cemetery**, unique columbarium [like a mausoleum], the innovative memory wall and **colorful gardens**." The cemetery can be visited during daylight hours any time except winter. The caskets are also bought by amputees who wish to bury their severed limbs. Caskets aren't sold here at the plant, but they retail starting at around $15 at pet stores, pet cemeteries, and humane societies. A really plush crepe-lined coffin for a St. Bernard would cost over $350.

317 Delta Ave. just east of Fourth Ave, east of downtown Gladstone. Call (906) 428-2151 to arrange a tour, available year-round, weekdays 8 a.m.-4 p.m.

GLADSTONE RESTAURANTS

See also: Escanaba, Rapid River

The **LOG CABIN**, dating from 1933, is known for its **juicy pork chops**, ($12-$16), good whitefish, and its **wonderful**

hillside setting up above U.S. 2/41. Every table in the smoke-free dining room has a beautiful bay view. There's a full menu of beef, fish, and chicken dishes — not exciting, but consistent, with excellent service. Vegetarian by request. Lunches $4-$8, dinners $9-$23. The bar offers appetizers and a sandwich menu all the time. It has a deck by the pond in back where drinks and appetizers are served. Reservations recommended in summer. *On the bluff side of U.S. 2 & 41 & M 35 about 1 1/2 miles south of Gladstone, a little north of Terrace Bay. 786-5621, Open year-round for lunch (Mon-Fri 11-2) and dinner. May-Dec dinner Mon-Sat 5-10, Sun 4-9. Jan-April dinner Mon-Fri 5-9, Sat to 10, Sun 4-9.*

  Full bar

From the bread in sandwiches to the crust of fresh fruit pies, most things are **homemade** at **SOUTHWEST REFLECTIONS**. For years this smoke-free, renovated Queen Anne Victorian house has been an attractive, popular breakfast and lunch spot. Now, served from 4 to 8 p.m., owner Geri DeGraves has added dinner plates ($6.50 to $9) that reflect her own Mexican cooking heritage — mostly done just the way her grandmother in New Mexico taught her. Here are tamales, enchiladas, chimichangas, all with refried beans and rice. Lunch could be the **best-selling cashew-chicken-grape salad with a muffin** (about $6), wraps like spicy chicken with special BBQ sauce, fajita salad, or a cup of soup and half a sandwich or a daily special like Philly cheese steak or creamed chicken on a biscuit, or new things Geri likes to try out. Desserts ($1.85 to $2.50) include warm apple cake with lemon sauce, bread pudding and custard sauce, cheesecake, and ice cream with homemade sauce. *On the west edge of downtown Gladstone at 1016 Delta Ave. 428-1134. Mon-Sat 8 a.m. – 8 p.m.*

GLADSTONE LODGINGS

See also: Escanaba

TERRACE BAY RESORT BUDGET HOST

(906) 786-7554; (800) 283-4678; www.terracebay.com

The **best waterfront location between Escanaba and Gladstone** is used to excellent advantage here. Half the rooms have the **beautiful bay view** for just $5 extra in summer ($81 for bayside). Winter rates: $48. All the 71 large rooms have balconies and recliners. Also oriented to the bay: the big **dining room**, lounge, **terrace**, and a gorgeous **indoor**

swimming pool room with a small (30' or so) kidney-shaped **pool**. A spa, **sauna**, and **game room** are by the pool. (There's no swimming beach here on the west side of Little Bay de Noc, however.)

The original nucleus of the Terrace Inn was billed as "Escanaba's wonder ballroom" when it opened in 1933. The two-story motel wing on the north dates from the 1970s and has soundproof block construction. The older south wing is used when occupancy is high. Loads of good satellite cable channels are a bonus. A free **continental breakfast** is served in the comfortable large entrance area in the off season, from October through April. The motel is a block off the highway on a residential street that goes along the bay, so walks are possible. Less than a mile north, atop the bluff across the road, is the country club the resort has merged with. There Terrace Bay guests can enjoy **free tennis**, an outdoor **pool**, volleyball, a snack bar, and the area's 18-hole, top-rated **golf course** with driving range, putting green, instructors and free weekly golf clinics. Summer fees are $14 (9 holes) and $26 (18 holes). Free golf after Labor Day. *Sign is on U.S. 2 & 41 & M-35 about 2 miles south of Gladstone, motel sits back.*

H.A.: some ADA accessible rooms : under 16 free with adult; $5/extra person

SLEEPY HOLLOW MOTEL

(906)786-7092; (800) 473-3410; www.deltafun.com

Flower gardens and **spacious grounds** make this family-run motel stand out — that and the fact that 4 of the 18 rooms have **kitchenettes**. Another extra: it's one door down from the popular, affordable Delona's family restaurant. There's a **picnic area** with grills; **horseshoes**, shuffleboard, **croquet**, a swing set, **basketball**; and a **fish-cleaning station**. Rooms are nicely coordinated and decorated, with older furniture. Each has a phone, cable TV with ESPN and Disney, and in-room coffee. Rates are by the room, not the person: in 2000, tax included, $40 for one bed, $54 for two doubles, $59 for kitchenettes. *On U.S. 2/U.S. 41, a block in front of Terrace Bay (see above).*]

H.A.: some rooms ADA accessible : no extra charge : 1 pet room, $5 extra

BAY VIEW MOTEL (906) 786-2843;
www.baydenoc.com/bayview

A **woodsy location** back a ways from U.S. 2/U.S. 41 makes for a **pleasant picnic** and **BBQ area**. No bay view, con-

trary to the name. Delona's family restaurant (see above) is right next door. Most of the 22 handsomely furnished rooms are on ground level; some have refrigerators. All have phones, air-conditioning, and cable TV with ESPN and Disney. The newer rear building has less road noise. Summer rates for two: $49 (one bed), $60 (two). Winter $10 less. There's an attractive small **indoor pool** and **sauna**. *1 mile north of Escanaba River on U.S. 2/U.S. 41, next to DeLona family restaurant.*

H.A.: call : 12 and under free : call

KIPLING HOUSE (877) 905-ROOM;
(906) 428-1120; www.kiplinghouse.com

Kipling House is not just another romantic B&B, though it is that. Its guests can, if they choose, learn about everything from the **history of Kipling**, once the company town of a busy blast furnace and chemical plant, to details of dairying and timber operations in the U.P. to getting an overview of the U.P. economy. That's because Ann Miller, innkeeper with her husband, Ralph, is district legislative assistant for **State Representative Don Koivisto** — a position that developed naturally from her earlier life as wife of a dairy farmer near Bruce Crossing.

The Millers are intimately familiar with shrinking small communities, and they like people and entertaining. So it seemed quite logical to undertake the ambitious project of restoring this large house in a shrunken company town. They use it as their home, as a B&B, and as a place for receptions and putting up visiting dignitaries, from politicians to children's authors. They're all "folks" to Ann. Ralph, an army retiree from the area, loves to cook on a grand scale. He is also an upholsterer. The house, an impressive place with a **wide front porch**, was actually one of six boarding houses built by Cleveland Cliffs Iron. The Millers have collected historical material and photos about industrial Kipling, along with bits and pieces from other historic buildings in the area that have been demolished. Guests can borrow **bikes** to explore Kipling and Gladstone.

Kipling House is a homestay B&B, not heavily promoted, intended to be a comfortable place where guests can have as much or as little privacy as they like. Guests share the first-floor common areas with the Millers: **parlor with fireplace** and cable TV/VCR, dining room, morning room, front porch with six rockers and Chef Ralph's French Country kitchen. If the Millers are watching a video or game on TV, feel free to join in. An elegant **full breakfast** is served; so is a homemade **dessert**. On the second floor is one king room with private bath ($95) and two rooms that share a bath and sitting area with cable TV — an arrangement repeated in the two third-floor rooms. These rooms can be rented together (each room is then $75) or the larger room can be taken with sitting area and private bath (then it's $95). Some guest rooms are air-conditioned. Guests use the Millers' phone. Some guest rooms are a tailored version of flowers and lace, while others are more whimsical: sunflowers, lighthouses, and — the popular favorite — the tree house, with a tree painted on the ceiling. The two-person **rear cottage** ($150) has a downstairs sitting area with cable TV/VCR, and a cozy upstairs sleeping loft. Between house and cottage is a **gazebo** and **rock garden** with waterfalls.

Now that Michigan's bed-and-breakfast legislation allows B&Bs to serve other meals to overnight guests, Kipling House offers a **$150 getaway package** with a **five- or six-course dinner** that has proven very popular with area couples. The menu might include seafood bisque in puff pastry; French onion soup; a salad with pears, walnuts, and dried cherries, between-course sorbet; pork cutlet stuffed with ricotta and fresh spinach, dessert — maybe a cobbler or spongecake with fruit and crème brulée — all homemade, of course. *1716 N. Lakeshore Drive. From the north, turn at Rapid River sign. From the south, go through Gladstone.*

H.A.: no   👫👫: well suited to older children; 2 people/room

Rapid River *(pop. 325)*

Rapid River grew up around the dozen sawmills that sprang up here at the head of Little Bay de Noc, where the small Rapid River enters the bay. It's a mile or so west of the Whitefish River mouth. This village extends south off U.S. 2 near where U.S. 41 turns north to Trenary and Marquette. A popular gathering place is the **Swallow Inn** on Main Street.

Interpretive Center
Hiawatha National Forest

Excellent informational handouts and maps are available here, in person or mailed, about all national forest visitor attractions in the west unit, and some in the east unit by the Soo and St. Ignace. The west unit includes over half of the Hiawatha National Forest's **900,000 acres** in the Upper Peninsula: the wetlands and rivers of the Au Train basin north of Rapid River, a belt of lakes between Manistique and Munising with many campgrounds, stretches of Lake Superior shore, and much of the Stonington and Nahma peninsulas near here. In addition, there are **interpretive displays about area animals and archaeology**, and a **small nature store** with maps, posters, and books for adults and kids. Most popular item: Smokey the Bear doll. Source of greatest public confusion: conflict between Smokey's fire prevention message and the forest service's "let it burn" policy for fires caused by natural forces.

On the south side of U.S. 2, between the Whitefish River and the village of Rapid River. (906) 474-6442. Mon-Fri 7:30-4. ♿

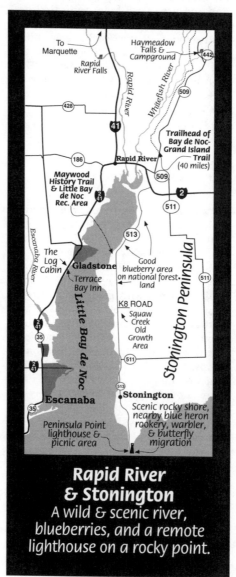

Rapid River & Stonington
A wild & scenic river, blueberries, and a remote lighthouse on a rocky point.

Rapid River
Cross-Country Ski Trail

Nineteen miles of loops through pine and maple forests offer something for everyone: easy loops of 1.2 and 2.7 miles (with a 20-foot variation from high to low), advanced loops of 6.4 and 10 miles that take good advantage of glacial hills, a 6.8 mile intermediate loop, and ski skating loops of 4.7 miles (intermediate) and 7.4 miles (advanced). The forested hills don't offer views, but the variety and challenge is enough to keep many area skiers coming back up to four times a week. The **Hiawatha National Forest** grooms this popular ski area.

From U.S. 2 in Rapid River, take U.S. 41 7 miles north. Look for signed parking area on left. Trail maps available at trailhead; maps on signboards are frequent. No fees as of press time. (906) 474-6442.

Rapid River Falls

This **four-tiered falls** and park along the Rapid River is a highlight of the trip along U.S. 41 from Escanaba through Trenary to Marquette. It's a short, easy walk to the falls on the smooth limestone alongside the river. The **beautiful riverside park**, with its **picnic tables**, grills, and **playground**, is an attraction in its own right.

From U.S. 2 at Rapid River, take U.S. 41 6 1/2 miles north to S-15, just before crossing the river. Turn left onto S-15 Road (the waterfalls are clearly marked). The park is in 1/3 mile. (906) 474-6442.

Bay de Noc-Grand Island Trail/
Hiawatha National Forest

Horses, hikers, and, in winter, dog sleds on part of the U.P. 200 race all use this pleasant and not overused trail, **40 miles long.** It parallels the **Whitefish River**, usually a half to two miles east of it. This corridor, the shortest distance from Lake Superior to Lake Michigan, was an **important canoe and portage route for Ojibwa traders**. The trail, however, stops short of reaching either lake.

Motorized vehicles are not allowed and have not been a problem. Hikers should plan on carrying water or be prepared to treat it for drinking. The only pump for potable water is at Haymeadow Creek Campground, 1 1/2 miles from the trail. Wells and vault toilets are at the assembly areas at the trailheads and mid way point. (See below.) **Primitive camping** is permitted anywhere on National Forest land; no permit needed.

A **map and trail description** with suggestions is available from Forest Service offices in Munising, Rapid River, or Manistique. Here's the Forest Service description of the trail: "Following the river bluff for a considerable distance, [the trail] offers the hiker many extended views to the west across the **Whitefish River valley**. The southern 1/4 of the trail winds through jack pine, red pine, and aspen timber, interspersed with grassy openings. The terrain is fairly level, broken only by an occasional stream crossing. As the trail stretches northward through the maple, paper birch, and beech forest, the hiker encounters the typical glacial terrain characterized by short rounded hills scattered in random fashion. These hilly stretches are occasionally separated by one- to five-mile stretches of flat land supporting pine and aspen."

The southern trailhead is on CR 509 1 1/2 miles north of U.S. 2 and 2 miles east of Rapid River. The northern trailhead is on M-94 10 miles southwest of Munising, on the north side of the road opposite Ackerman Lake. (906) 474-6442.

Haymeadow Falls

Haymeadow Falls and the nearby **Hiawatha National Forest** campground are for people looking for an **undemanding outdoor hiking and camping experience that's off the beaten path but not hard to get to**. About nine miles northeast of Rapid River, CR 509 crosses Haymeadow Creek, a tributary of Whitefish River. A half-mile trail leads from the road and parking area to the little falls, fifteen feet wide with a three-foot drop. At its base the water foams over a tumble of rocks. There a bridge crosses the little stream — a nice way to observe the falls.

The creek is a **high-quality trout stream** known for brook trout — an extra attraction for fishermen. The trail is "lovely," in the opinion of the Penroses, waterfall connoisseurs and authors. It goes "through a thick hardwood forest, over rolling hills and past tiny streams" to the creek. Ferns abound in places. Another **trail** continues a half mile to the campgrounds. Across CR 509 from the drive to the parking area, a half-mile connecting trail leads to the **Bay de Noc-Grand Island Trail**.

The two branches of the **Whitefish River** that converge not too far from Haymeadow Falls have been included as part of the federal **Wild & Scenic Rivers** program. This area is a **good place to**

In the 1890s this party had taken an excursion steamer across Little Bay de Noc to the Maywood picnic grounds. Today the Maywood History Trail at the Little Bay de Noc Recreation Area winds through a wonderful old-growth hemlock forest and interprets Maywood's history over centuries. Handsome illustrated signs provide fascinating bits of perspective, photos like this, and lively quotes from earlier eras.

see deer, waterfowl, and other birds, including bald eagles. The forest service gives out a **map** and description of 28 miles of canoeing on the east and west branches. In *Canoeing Michigan Rivers*, Jerry Dennis and Craig Date recommend and describe in detail a 13-mile stretch on the East Branch from Forest Road 2236, with an estimated four to six hours paddling. No canoe liveries serve this river because of insufficient water often in summer, resulting in too rough treatment of canoes.

From U.S. 2 about a mile east of the Whitefish River east of Rapid River, take CR 509 north 8 miles, taking care to follow the route at a left turn early on. After 8 miles, CR 509 takes the left (gravel) fork. Soon you'll pass the campground entrance to the right. The separate parking area and trail to the falls is in another 1/4 mile. (906) 474-6442. No fee. &: no.

RAPID RIVER RESTAURANTS

JACK'S RESTAURANT is the **consummate small-town diner** — and more. It offers very good food and good value, too, from the burgers and blueberry pancakes to the plate lunches (pot pie with

salad, and vegetable, for instance); $8 Sunday dinner of baked turkey or ham; and the Friday fish fry with vegetable, salad, potato, homemade rolls ($6 to $9 depending on whether it's beer-battered cod, fresh whitefish, or locally caught perch). Now in its 3rd generation, Jack's was founded in 1943 by Jack and Vivian Miller. (Her mother was a lumber camp cook.) The dinner menu changes daily. Many things are made on the premises: bread, desserts, wonderful soups. "Boiled dinner" soup (corned beef, cabbage, potato, carrot, onion) is terrific. Local people supply wild blueberries for pies. The counter dominates, but there's also a dining room. Bring cash if you're not from the U.P.! *Where U.S. 2/U.S. 41 meets Rapid River's Main St. look for the vintage neon sign. 474-9927. Open daily from 7 a.m. to 8 p.m. at least, longer on weekends and in summer. & except for bathrooms* ⚥ Beer & wine

Stonington Peninsula

The Stonington Peninsula extends out into Green Bay over 15 miles just east of Rapid River. It forms Little Bay de Noc to

its west and, to the east, Big Bay de Noc. Most of the peninsula is far enough from U.S. 2 to remain undeveloped. As farms are abandoned, **its interior is becoming wilder**.

In addition to campgrounds and beaches, Stonington offers visitors a scenic drive along County Road 513 to the point and lighthouse tower at its southern tip.

Maywood History Trail & Little Bay de Noc. Rec. Area

A **boat launch**; spacious, **private campsites**; and a **mile of sandy swimming beach** backed by grass and some shade trees are the most popular attractions at this **Hiawatha National Forest** recreation area close to Escanaba and Gladstone. A designated **swimming area** without a lifeguard is near the **picnic area** north of the rustic camping loops. (See below for camping.) **Sunsets** over the water, with city lights in the distance, are beautiful.

But what makes Little Bay stand out as a memorable place to visitors from afar is the **magical grove of giant, 200-year-old hemlocks**. The **Maywood History Trail** (&) winds through the grove. **Interesting interpretive signs** and illustrations take visitors on a time trip to see how this beautiful, sheltered spot has been enjoyed for centuries. They show how these trees escaped damage from the frequent forest fires that swept across the pine plains. The steep slope near the shore was created by the high lake level as the glaciers were melting 3,200 years ago. The name Maywood goes back to the 1880s, when the **"hemlock cathedral"** with its dense, high canopy made for a cool picnic and camping spot, soon joined by a small resort hotel with cabins. Steamers made moonlight excursions from Gladstone, and immigrant associations held dances at the picnic grounds. The history trail was constructed by high school volunteer members of the Student Conservation Association; the research and excellent writing are by Hiawatha National Forest archaeologist John Franzen.

The grove's sparse undergrowth and lack of leaf litter mean the small inhabitants of the forest stand out far more clearly than usual. **Little frogs** can be seen from a distance, and many kinds of **mushrooms** can be spotted on the tidy forest floor in August. The **cool shade** means **birds are active even at noon**. The rat-a-tat-tats of woodpeckers echo

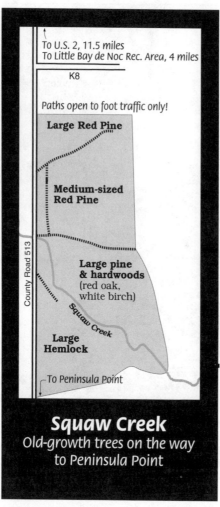

To U.S. 2, 11.5 miles
To Little Bay de Noc Rec. Area, 4 miles

K8

Paths open to foot traffic only!

Large Red Pine

Medium-sized Red Pine

Large pine & hardwoods (red oak, white birch)

County Road 513

Squaw Creek

Large Hemlock

To Peninsula Point

Squaw Creek
Old-growth trees on the way to Peninsula Point

as they search for insects. Other tiny sounds, scamperings and chirps, are wonderful — until the noxious whine of a jet ski breaks the spell.

Alas, Little Bay's convenience and proximity to urban areas can be a drawback. Jet skis are popular here, and parks close to cities can have weekend partying behavior not found at more secluded campgrounds.

Another trail, the attractive 1.2 mile **Bayshore Trail** (not wheelchair-accessible) goes along the shoreline from the southernmost camping loop to the **boat launch** at Hunter's Point on the developed recreation area's north end. (The water's so low in 2001 that the boat launch can be used only by small boats, if at all.) Looping off it, the 1.3 mile **White Pine Trail** goes through some big pines mixed with aspen and oak.

On County Road 513 6 miles south of U.S. 2. Turn south onto 513 at the Hiawatha National Forest Rapid River Ranger Office 3 miles east of Rapid River. (906) 474-6442. $3 day use fee. &*: all buildings & Maywood Trail.*

County Road 513 & Squaw Creek Old Growth Area

A 20-mile drive on CR 513 down the Stonington Peninsula and out to the Peninsula Point lighthouse is well worth while if you have the time. A good deal of the road is along the shore. Traffic is light, so it's a **good road for bicycling**. After the hamlet of Stonington, the pavement is occasionally gravel.

Ripe **blueberries** can be found and picked, typically from late July for three or four weeks, not far from the road up to Squaw Creek. (See introduction for more on U.P. blueberry picking.) During the 1920s and 1930s the area was a popular berrying destination for campers who would boat across from Escanaba, fish, and pick berries to can or sell to local merchants.

Having so many big old trees on this easily reached 64-acre stand is unusual. Few old-growth areas survived the logging era, and few of the surviving remnants are easily accessible from public roads. Here you'll find very large red and white pines, red oak, birch, and eastern hemlock, always especially impressive for their girth and dense canopy. This is not a virgin forest. But 19th-century logging spared a good number of sizable trees, now grown huge. In the 1930s local residents and Escanaba civic groups campaigned to include the area in the new **Hiawatha National Forest**.

Today the **Squaw Creek Old Growth Area** is not a marked and developed attraction, but it's worth seeking out. Existing two-tracks and logging roads are the only pathways. Take a **compass** if you want to explore off the paths. The **high, dense canopy** stunts understory growth and invites walking on the forest floor, springy with fallen needles. **Old Squaw Creek** angles across the area's southern half, and "adds its own special charm to the scenery," writes Tom Powers in his worthwhile *Natural Michigan* guide. "The fast-moving, red-tinged creek flows between high banks that twist and turn through the woods . . . . Huge trees grow along the banks and in many places tilt toward each other from opposite shores to form a green tent over the cool water."

3 miles past the Little Bay de Noc Recreation Area, look for Road K-8, the only significant road hereabouts. (There's no K-8 sign visible from CR 513.) Continue on CR 513. The old-growth area begins in 1/4 mile and continues for 1/2 mile along the road. Three old roads lead into the area. Park alongside CR 513. (906) 474-

6442. &: no. Some old-growth trees can be viewed from vehicles on CR 513.

Peninsula Point Lighthouse & Picnic Area

A 40-foot **light tower** is at the very tip of the Stonington Peninsula, 19 miles south of U. S. 2. It's part of the **Hiawatha National Forest**. The tower offers the leisurely explorer **splendid views** in many directions and a bird's eye perspective on the area's **rich bird life**. To the east, across the Big Bay de Noc, can be seen **Fairport**, the fishing village near the Garden Peninsula's tip. On a clear day, you can see the **offshore islands** extending southwest to the Door Peninsula. Look west across the Little Bay de Noc to see Escanaba. **Sunsets are spectacular**. Towards dusk, six miles offshore, can be seen the **Minneapolis Shoal Light**, which replaced the light here in 1936.

The lighthouse, whose restoration had been a prize-winning project of the local grange, was destroyed by fire in 1959. But the masonry tower was saved, and visitors can climb its **iron spiral stairway** to the top deck and lantern, big enough so a sizable group can enjoy the grand views. The grassy **picnic grounds** with rest rooms go back to a Civilian Conservation Corps project in 1937, just after the point became part of the Hiawatha National Forest. Those fallen cedars you may have noticed on the road to the lighthouse are evidence of the fierce windstorm that blew through in 1998.

This is a good place to view the **spring warbler migration**. There is a nearby rookery where **great blue herons** raise their young. It's an unusual number in one place of those dramatic birds. To feed their growing young, adults must keep active stalking fish in the shallow waters here.

The lighthouse here goes back to 1865, when Escanaba was starting out as a lake port and its busy shipping traffic demanded navigational aids to stay away from the shoaly point near the entrance to the Little Bay de Noc. **"The Devil's Ten Acres,"** sailors called it, "a trap with teeth of rocks set in a series of treacherous shoals."

A **one-mile trail** (not wheelchair-accessible) extends from the light tower along the shore and across a **cedar swamp via a boardwalk** to a parking area for RVs. RVs are too big for the picturesque narrow road that winds for a mile to the Peninsula Point through a grove of most interestingly twisted cedars. Though not a high-budget production, the trail is a pleasant attraction. **Interpretive signs** illuminate interesting aspects of the area, such as the

Monarch butterflies at Peninsula Point

Monarch butterflies from Upper Michigan and Canada stop at Peninsula Point in their spring and fall migrations to Mexico. The point reduces the distance they have to fly over water. Its dense **cedar trees protect resting butterflies** from the wind. And milkweed patches in clearings offer places for females to lay their eggs. After hatching, larvae feed on milkweed.

Since 1993 **butterfly research** has been conducted here as part of nationwide research projects to determine to what extent monarchs are endangered. Larvae on milkweed are counted, and adult monarchs are tagged. The Forest Service is always looking for **volunteers** to help out. Call (906) 474-6442 or 630-5188

and ask for volunteer extraordinaire C.J. Meitner. **The Great Monarch Chase** (a 10k run and 2.5 mile walk) raises money for butterfly research at Peninsula Point. It's held the first Sunday in October.

To observe migrating monarchs, conditions have to be right in August and September. They like to use northerly winds of **cold fronts** to speed their flight south. Bring your binoculars. When resting on trees, monarchs look like dead leaves. In August and September butterflies are also often seen in the parks along M-35 on Green Bay.

Look up the websites of **Midwest**

Participants in The Great Monarch Chase run gather at the Peninsula Point light tower. Visitors can climb the tower any time for a grand view.

Monarch Project (in Rochester, MN) and **Monarch Watch** (in Lawrence, KS) to find out more on the status of monarchs. Adult monarchs feed on wildflowers, and larvae feed on milkweed, so weed killers and loss of wild habitat poisons them and deprives them of food.

— adapted from pamphlet by Anne Okonek of the U.S. Forest Service Rapid River office

limestone bedrock at the water's edge, where fossils can be found from 400 to 500 million years ago. The shore here is too rocky and shallow for swimming, but it's a fine place for wading and beach-combing.

Take CR 513 to its end, 19 miles south of the junction with U.S. 2. (906) 474-6442. ♿: restrooms, picnic area.

STONINGTON CAMPING

LITTLE BAY de NOC Recreation Area/ Hiawatha National Forest

(906) 474-6442. Half the sites can be reserved at least 5 days in advance; call (877) 833-6777; TTY (877) 833-6777.

This **beautiful rustic campground** (no flush toilets, showers, or electricity) has 36 large single and double campsites on three loops, plus two group sites by reservation only. All sites have **lake views** and **trails** to the **sandy shore**. Those in wooded areas have **good privacy**, too. The **wooded Maywood Loop** is nearest the **boat launch** (with 2001's low lake levels suitable for small boats only). The Twin Springs Loop, open and grassy, is popular with jet skiers. The adjacent Oaks Loop is the quietest. It's set back farther from the **beach**. From mid-May through mid-September a **campground host** is here. For campers who don't insist on showers and similar amenities, the convenient location, beautiful setting, and outstanding trails (see above) make this a terrific camping spot, and except for some summer weekends, it usually has space. Be forewarned, however, that summer weekends can occasionally be noisy. *On County Road 513 6 miles south of U.S. 2. Turn south onto 513 at the National Forest Rapid River Ranger Office, which is 3 miles east of Rapid River. Fees $9 and $10/night, more for double sites. Open from May 15 thru Oct. 7.* ♿

VAGABOND CAMPGROUND & RESORT

(906) 474-6122; www.vagabondresort .com; reservations recommended, especially for holidays and cabins

With 60 sites, 28 acres of woods, and **sandy beach**, this friendly campground is a most attractive place, especially for anglers and for families with kids who want a lot of activities nearby. Sites come with water & electric ($16/night for 2), electric only ($15), or even with sewer ($21). $2/extra person. Rustic sites ($12) generally have more privacy. One building has restrooms, showers, and a laundry; another is a **rec hall** with video games, **ping pong**, foosball, and **pool**. Drives are gravel. Seven comfortable housekeeping cabins are rented by the week.

Owner Dan Figan, a longtime area resident, and his staff at the office offer coffee and sell sundries and bait. They're happy to give advice on what to do in the area. There are magazines, puzzles, badminton, inner tubes, and **games** to borrow (but kids must say "please"!). **Boat** and motors can be rented here. Pets on leashes are OK. Evening **bonfires** take place on the beach, where **sunsets** are outstanding. A mammoth, 400-foot **dock** serves for **fishing** (walleye are the big draw) and boating. A **natural area** and **trail** are on the premises; the trails of Little Bay de Noc Rec. Area are just 3 miles away. Jet skis, though permitted, are few, far outnumbered by fishermen. *2 miles south of U.S. 2 on CR 513. Open year-round. Electric sites are plowed. 3 Cabins are winterized.* **H. A.**: call.

Harris (pop. under 200)

This hamlet 13 miles west of Escanaba is best known as the home of the Chip-In Casino, or more recently the tropical-theme, Vegas-style **Chip-In's Island Resort Casino** . It now has a 113-room hotel, an indoor pool with **heated sand beach**, Harris itself doesn't even have a gas station. Three miles to the south of Harris, on Hannahville Road, is the **Hannahville Potawatami reservation**. Profits from the casino have allowed the tribe's members to increase their land holdings to some 5,000 acres and build a new school and clinic. 680 tribal members now live on the reservation. Kinship networks and community ties mean much more in Native American cultures than among the individualistic descendants of go-getting Yankee Protestants who are willing to move away from their families to follow their fortunes. Gambling has been a boon to Indians because it enables them to live together rather than going off to urban jobs. A small tribal-owned convenience store serves the local population.

The Potawatami, an agricultural people, are not native to the U.P. They gradually migrated westward from the Atlantic Coast over the centuries. **Michigan Potawatomi** lived mostly in the southwest corner of the state, where many live today. U.S. troops brutally forced most Potawatomi out of Michigan in the 19th century. But a Potawatomi band fled to a spot near the Cedar River. Eventually this small band came into conflict with white hunters and were rescued by a **Methodist missionary**, Peter Marksman, and his wife, Hannah (hence "Hannahville"), who allowed them to live

on their land until the land in Harris Township that became the present reservation was secured. They were later joined by other Potawatami who returned from reservations in Iowa and Kansas.

Now the Potawatami have taken advantage of their Indian status, once such a devastating problem, with Indian gambling. Their splashy **Chip-in's Island Resort & Casino** on U.S. 2/U.S. 41 opened in 1998. It is a major employer with 580 workers. 800-682-6040; www.chipincasino.com. The casino complex includes a conference center, a five-story 113-room hotel, two restaurants, three bars (one with live entertainment Thursday through Sunday), and big-name **headline entertainment twice a month**. There are over 840 slot machines, poker, roulette, Keno, bingo, and other games of chance.

The Green Bay shore

From Escanaba to Menominee M-35 parallels the lakeshore. It passes not only the usual cottages but also several parks, some with camping, and a number of small resorts. Behind the **sandy shoreline** in many places are natural areas full of plants like the tall, weedy *aurelia sarsaparilla*. These attract so many **butterflies**, they're often clearly visible

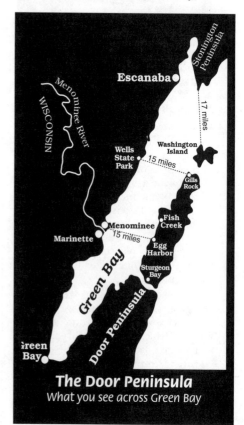

The Door Peninsula
What you see across Green Bay

from the highway in August. **Sawmill towns**, now dwindled to a few stores and buildings, grew up where **Ford River** and **Cedar River** empty into Green Bay.

For over 10 miles approaching Menominee, the bay is almost always in view. It's a **pleasant drive**, especially if you have time to **stop and picnic** or take a hike walk by the lake. **Wells State Park** has a **wonderful trail system**. Kleinke County Park now has a modern campground. Campers who don't need modern amenities and close quarters can try more primitive camping at Fox or Kleinke parks.

Portage Marsh Wildlife Area

Just south of Escanaba, a narrow spit about two miles long creates a protected small bay and wetland where migrating waterfowl like to stop, usually in April and October. Ducks, geese, herons, shore birds — they all come through. A simple **foot trail** goes out .6 mile toward Portage Point along the marsh-facing side. The **sand beach** on the spit's other side can be a good place to see shore birds, and to **swim**, too. This would be a peaceful, easy-to-reach place for **bird-watching**.

From M-35 four miles south of U.S. 2/U.S. 41, Portage Point Rd. leads to the trailhead, parking area, and boat launch (currently almost unusable because of low lake levels). &: path is too sandy, wasn't built for foot traffic. Parking area allows a marsh view.

Fuller Park

Here a **Lake Michigan swimming beach**, bathhouse, and **picnic area** are a short walk from the Bark River bank, a popular place for trout and bass **fishing**. A **boat launch** (for small boats only in 2001) allows handy lake access. A half-mile woodchip **path** crosses a **wetland**. This Delta County park has 82 mostly wooded acres. See next page for **camping**.

On M-35 at the Bark River mouth, about 18 miles south of the U.S. 2/M-35 intersection in Escanaba. (906) 786-1020. &

Fox Park

Over a mile of Lake Michigan shore with a **sandy swimming beach** and a **picnic area** is the main attraction of this simple, 60-acre Cedarville Township Park. There's a primitive **campground**, too (see next page).

On M-35 28 miles south of Escanaba, 7 miles north of Cedar River, and 25 miles north of Menominee. (906) 863-4721.

Cedar River

This old lumber village at the mouth of the Big Cedar River is now the center of an increasingly popular resort area. Only a couple dozen people live in the village itself. **Fishing** is big here, both in the river (stocked with trout) and in the bay, where walleye, smallmouth bass, salmon, and brown trout are plentiful. A **boat launch** on the north bank of the river's mouth provides river and lake access. The river can be boated in spring up to a rapids two miles from the mouth. A small **tackle shop** services sports fishermen.

Cedar River once bustled with a sawmill and pier where lumber was shipped to Chicago. Then the sawmill burned and most residents moved away. Two churches on the highway remain from the lumber village: the Catholic Church of the Sacred Heart (1887) and the Mission Chapel (1889).

Today Cedar River has two restaurants (Butch and Sue's is combined with a small motel) and a new convenience store. The largest local employer is **Ruleau Brothers fishery**, with about 50 employees. It's one of the few remaining commercial fishing operations of any size on the Great Lakes. Ruleau's uses several trawlers from the Cedar River docks to go after whitefish from late April to the end of September. Smelt is netted in the winter. The company's processing plant is in Stephenson, 12 miles due west of Cedar River. Although Ruleau's is a wholesaler, it will sell **fresh fish** to individuals from its Stephenson facility.

Wells State Park

This deceptively large park has much to interest naturalists, but you'd never know it from a quick look at the close-spaced modern campground or the popular developed **swimming beach**. **Impressive stands of old-growth hemlock** and **hardwoods** are part of the 350 acres donated for this early (1924) state park by the children of J. W. Wells. A onetime mayor of Menominee, he was one of the biggest lumber operators in the vast Menominee basin.

Today the park comprises 678 acres and stretches three miles north along Green Bay. State land that's not part of the park extends even farther north to include 1,400 feet along the south bank of the **Cedar River** at its mouth.

An outstanding, seven-mile system of **foot trails**, groomed for **cross-country skiing** in winter, makes the park's many

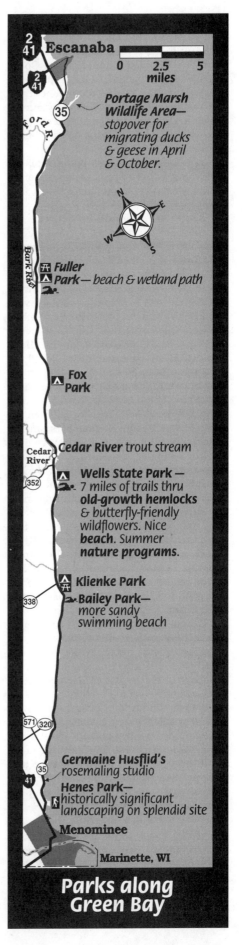

2 41 Escanaba

0 2.5 5 miles

Portage Marsh Wildlife Area—stopover for migrating ducks & geese in April & October.

35

Ford R.

Bark R.

⚑ **Fuller Park**— *beach & wetland path*

⚑ **Fox Park**

Cedar River

Cedar River *trout stream*

352

Wells State Park — *7 miles of trails thru* **old-growth hemlocks** *& butterfly-friendly wildflowers. Nice* **beach**. *Summer* **nature programs**.

⚑ **Klienke Park**

Bailey Park— *more sandy swimming beach*

338

571 320

Germaine Husflid's *rosemaling studio*

Henes Park— *historically significant landscaping on splendid site*

35
41

Menominee

Marinette, WI

Parks along Green Bay

interesting ecosystems easily accessible. The park is ornamented by handsome stone and log structures from Depression-era Civilian Conservation Corps make-work projects. CCC projects include a small rentable picnic shelter at the far end of the developed swimming beach and playground, trailside shelters, and **rustic rental cabins** by the beach in the less developed north part of the park. (These cabins are being replaced with a style that approximates the originals.) See next page for cabins and **camping**.

Shoreline wetlands lie between the low parallel sand ridges formed by old lakeshores. The many kinds of **summer wildflowers** in those wet meadows and dry ridges attract unusual numbers and varieties of **butterflies** and **songbirds**. The tall aurelia sarsaparilla is thick with monarchs from August into September. Behind this are thick stands of cedar and spruce. It all makes for **excellent bird-watching**, because of its grand variety of birds in a small area. Shorebirds and songbirds like the meadows. Birds that eat the insects found in the canopied needleleaf forest range from the big pileated woodpecker and its smaller blackbacked cousin to the tiny golden-crowned kinglet, constantly maneuvering among twigs looking for food. Birders come from afar hoping to see Blackburnian warblers in the old-growth ridge near the cabins.

A nice bonus for hikers is the fact that the northernmost trail, the **Cedar River Trail**, goes 1.7 miles from the campgrounds to the park's northern boundary at the hamlet of Cedar River, not far from the good food at the **Lighthouse Inn** or from **Butch & Sue's.**

Except for the developed swimming area, the **beach** is mixed with chunky limestone rocks, too sharp for swimming but fine for beachcombers looking for **fossils**. These fossils were formed 400 to 500 million years ago, when warm seas covered the center of North America. For a nearly solitary beach experience, just hike a quarter-mile south of the day-use area or north past the campground. From June through August **nature programs** (on constellations, building bat boxes, night walks, wetlands, etc.) are given. currently Tuesday through Saturday. Call to confirm schedule.

On M-35, 1 mile south of Cedar River, 30 miles south of Escanaba, and 23 miles north of Menominee. (906) 863-9747. Fax: (906) 863-6477. In Central Time Zone. State park sticker required: 2001 rates $20/year, $4/day. ♿: *day use facilities, 3 cabins.*

Cedar River Pathway/ Escanaba River State Forest

An eight-mile **trail system** of four stacked loops goes along the Cedar River, which is a **trout stream** for two pleasant miles near the trailhead, and through rolling, forested terrain. The trails are good for **cross-country skiing** (now groomed). **Mountain bikes** are allowed. This is a good place to see deer and occasional black bear.

Trailhead is at the campground northwest of Cedar River. From M-35, 1 1/2 miles north of the town of Cedar River, take CR 551/River Rd. 6 miles northwest. (906) 786-2351. ♿: *no.*

Kleinke Park

The sandy Lake Michigan swimming **beach** at this Menominee County park is at the **mouth of Fowler Creek**, which makes an especially good place for **wading** and **sand castle** projects. Most of the park's 24 acres are heavily wooded, with some grassy areas for play and picnicking. There's a **picnic pavilion** and **playground**, and a carry-down **boat ramp** and a 34-site **campground** (see next page).

On M-35 15 miles north of Menominee and about 8 miles south of Cedar River. (906) 753-4582. Free. ♿: *toilets.*

Bailey County Park

Almost **a mile of nearly pure sand beach**, on a point well away from the highway, makes this Menominee County park a popular place for local people to swim. **Low dunes** behind the beach give the area an extra natural dimension. There's a **picnic area** but no camping.

Just south of the park, work is progressing on the **West Shore Fishing Museum**, *due to open in 2007.* Visitors can use the **boardwalks** and watch work on the buildings every summer Sunday afternoon from 1 to 4 p.m. Exhibits and period rooms will illuminate fishing activities on this part of Green Bay, focusing on Native Americans before European settlement and also on commercial fishermen circa 1900. The Bailey family had a typical family fishing operation here from 1893 to the end of the 1930s. Having no heirs, they bequeathed their house and property to the county. Volunteer helpers are welcome; call (906) 863-3347 or e-mail bejj@cybrz.com

On M-35, 13 miles north of Menominee and about 10 miles south of Cedar River. (906) 753-4582. Free. ♿: *picnic area, toilets.*

Henes Park

A **gem of natural landscaping on a beautiful site** on Menominee's north side. See Menominee points of interest.

Restaurants along M-35

THE LIGHTHOUSE INN is known for **broasted chicken** ($7.25 for one-half chicken with potatoes and salad, $5.50 for a quarter chicken), Friday fish fry, and midweek seafood dished ($6.50 to $11). Burgers and lunch items are from $2.50 to $5.50. There's not much beyond salads for vegetarians. The setting, on the **Cedar River mouth** at **Green Bay**, is a big plus. **Otters** and many birds, including **eagles**, have been seen. Diners can eat outside in the **pavilion**, sometimes used for **fish boils**. *On M 35 in "downtown" Cedar River. 863-2922 Open year-round except Christmas week. Hours from May 15 through Nov: Tues-Thurs noon-8, Fri & Sat to 9, Sun noon, closed Mon. Winter hours: closes 1 hour earlier and on Sun.* ♿ 🚻👫 Full bar

Great homemade soup and **good breakfasts** — for instance, homemade biscuits and sausage gravy — make **BUTCH & SUE'S** the kind of local place people look forward to visiting again and again. Ask for the **homemade rye bread** at breakfast and on sandwiches. It's part of the the $3.75 patty melt. Daily lunch specials are $5.25. Half orders available. Broasted chicken is always on the menu; so is Hansen's Pizza from Green Bay, a standout among frozen pizzas. The Friday fish fry with Alaskan walleye is $9 with the salad bar. Sunday brings a breakfast buffet. For vegetarians, there's a garden burger plus the usual salads and sandwiches. *On M-35 in the heart of Cedar River, on the bay side. 863-9897. Open year-round. From April thru Nov open daily: Sun & Mon 8-2, Tues-Sat 8-8. In winter, open 8-2, closed Monday.* ♿

Camping along Green Bay

Arranged from north to south.

FULLER PARK
(906) 786-1020. Reservable.

This plush and very popular 25-site modern campground at this Delta County park enjoys a **quiet setting near the Lake Michigan beach** and boat launch (for small boats only in 2001). Bark River **fishing access** and a short **nature trail** across a wetland are other attractions. Fuller Park is extremely popular on summer weekends, but campsites have been available most weeks through Thursday. *On M-35 at the Bark River* *mouth, just inside Delta County. About 18 miles south of the U.S. 2/M-35 intersection in Escanaba and 16 miles north of Cedar River.* & *$15 or $17 (waterfront) a night.* **H.A.**: ADA accessible sites, restroom, showers, picnic site.

CEDAR RIVER Campground/ Escanaba River State Forest

15 well-spaced rustic campsites (no showers, vault toilets) are either on the Cedar River, a trout stream, or just across the drive from it. The natural areas and Lake Michigan beach at Wells State Park are only about 8 miles away. A good camping choice for people who like a quiet, rustic atmosphere. *8 miles northwest of Cedar River on CR 551/River Road, which joins M-35 just north of the village. (906) 753-6317. Self-registration, no reservations. $6/$10 night.* **H.A.**: with assistance for wheelchairs.

FOX PARK   (906) 863-4721

The 25-space campground, part of a Cedarville township park, is primitive (no showers or electricity, which means fewer users). The pines and oak make a **high canopy for shade**, but there's little vegetation buffer between the large sites. See above for info on park. *On M-35 28 miles south of Escanaba, 7 miles north of Cedar River, and 25 miles north of Menominee. (906) No reservations. Self-registration. $7/night.* &: no.

WELLS STATE PARK

(906) 863-9747. Fax: (906) 863-6477. In Central Time Zone. Reservations: (800) 44-PARKS; (800) 605-8295 TDD; www.dnr.state.mi.us/

150 close-spaced modern campsites on a single long loop are in a grassy, semi-open area right on Green Bay. (Some lakefront sites were removed so other sites could have better views and lake access.) The 22 most-requested sites back up directly on the bay. Some shrubby privacy landscaping is provided. Spur-of-the-minute campers can find places on summer weekdays. Advance reservations a couple of months ahead of time are enough to get a space most weekends. See above for details on attractions and events at this major state park. In a completely separate area, six **attractive rustic cabins** ($40 a night in 2001) have cooking hearth, pump, outhouse, double bunks, tables and chairs for 8 or 12. The **setting overlooking the shore is grand**, and **trails** are close at hand. *On U.S. 35, 2 miles south of Cedar River, 30 miles south of Escanaba, and 23 miles north of Menominee. State park*

sticker required. $20/$25 year, $4/$5 day. for stickers, $12/$15 night camping. **H.A.**: all modern toilet facilities are ADA accessible. Campsites are not yet.

KLEINKE COUNTY PARK

(906) 753-4582. $7. No reservations.

By summer of 2001 the campground of this Menominee County park will have flush toilets and showers. Of the 34 campsites, **half are on Green Ba**y, and half on the other side of the campground drive. 18 sites have electricity. All are shaded, with water views, but there's not much privacy between sites. Trees provide some screening from M-35, which isn't far away. Amenities include a sandy **beach**, carry-down **boat launch**, and **playground**. *On M-35 15 miles north of Menominee and about 8 miles south of Cedar River. $10/night with electricity, $8 without. Open year-round.* &: yes, but beach access is sand.

Menominee (pop. 9,131) Marinette (pop. 11.850)

Local people think of Menominee and its slightly bigger sister city, Marinette, Wisconsin, as the "twin cities." Fifteen institutions use "M&M" in their name, including the YMCA and a shopping mall. These **classic lumber towns** were shaped by their location at the mouth of the Menominee River, one of the largest watersheds in the north woods. First there were fur-trading posts here. French traders stopped as early as the mid-17th century to trade with the **large Menominee Indian fishing village** at the river's mouth. Marinette was named after Queen Marinette, the Ojibwa-Menominee woman married to two traders in succession. She lived here from the 1820s until her death in 1865, and managed her husbands' trading post and the real estate she acquired.

Beginning in the 1860s Menominee and Marinette boomed. Menominee was the biggest lumber port in the Upper Peninsula. Large-scale lumbering, financed by investors in Chicago, Milwaukee, and the East, meant that the port bustled with shipping activity until 1910, when the timber finally gave out. Since its turn-of-the-century high point, the cities have shrunk in size and importance. Menominee's population, 10% less than in 1980, continues to decline. Today it has about the same population it had in the 1890s.

The twin cities are unusual in having a **dredged ship channel** that permits

Lumber schooners brought lumber from Menominee and Marinette sawmills to markets in Chicago. The wind smelled of sawdust near these busy mill towns.

freighters to travel as far as one mile up the Menominee River. Marinette is home to **Marinette Marine**, located right on the river. One the few remaining major Great Lakes shipbuilders, it makes **tugs**, **minesweepers**, and **buoy tenders** for the Coast Guard and other customers. Big vessels also travel up the river to deliver scrap pig iron and pick up paper pulp from Menominee's new pulp factory, **Great Lakes Pulp & Fiber** at 701 Fourth Avenue. It supplies paper plants with recycled office paper, which it de-inks and bleaches, repulps and dries. It's shipped to Mead and other paper manufacturers in baled form.

You can get a view of the **colorful river traffic** from the **Hattie Street Bridge** two miles in from the lake. It's south off 10th Avenue in Menominee, or north off Riverside in Marinette.

The most interesting section of Menominee is **downtown** facing Lake Michigan — the Harborfront District along First Street. The historic downtown's striking buildings were erected from 1880 to 1910. They extend north and south of the **Great Lakes Memorial Marina Park**, site of the city's bandshell. The mills and docks that lined the shoreline have long gone, creating civic space for parks and lake views. The district declined as the lucrative lumber market dried up. Just a few years ago many of these storefronts were empty. In recent years the district has become over 80% filled with shops. (See below.) Summertime highlights are the **concerts** at the lakeside bandshell (see map) on Tuesday and Thursday evenings, where musicians play everything from big band to jazz to folk music.

Today most of Menominee's biggest employers are related to the paper in-

dustry, one of the major U.P. businesses due to the abundant supply of wood pulp. The 300 employees at **Menominee Paper** make waxed paper, sold under the name Wax-Tex. **Lloyd-Flanders Industries**, founded in 1906, made woven wicker furniture and won fame for its baby buggies. In the 1920s, when employees went on a lengthy strike, founder Marshall Lloyd circumvented the need for reed, and for weavers to hand-weave it, by inventing a loom which machine-wove a very durable wicker made of paper pulp rolled around wires. Today the factory, on U.S. 41/10th Street at 30th Avenue north of downtown, makes medium- to high-end wicker furniture. Its product line, which includes many outdoor pieces, is sold at some 2,000 stores across the country and abroad. You can call ahead for a **plant tour** at (906) 863-4491.

The city's largest employer is **Emerson Electric**, headquartered in St. Louis. The 500 employees at the Menominee plant make shop vacs and dehumidifiers sold at Sears across the U.S.

Henes Park

Nature and high culture come together in this **beautiful and unusual city park**. It's on a 50-acre point extending out into Green Bay on Menominee's north side. The entrance arch signals something special; the names of the wooded nature paths (Schiller, Goethe, Longfellow, Shakespeare, etc.) reinforce the point. German-American brewer John Henes (pronounced "HEN-iss") donated the park, built in 1907, a time when industrial uses dominated the waterfront. Residents of Menominee and Marinette welcomed having a destination for the **Sunday outings** that played an important role in **German-American culture**. A streetcar line soon extended out to the park. Germans typically loved trees, and Henes aimed to preserve in a natural way a choice part of the native landscape, in this case an **old-growth forest** of hardwoods, hemlock, and pine. Today new interpretive signs point out noteworthy trees along the woodchip paths.

The perfect proponent of the natural approach was the park's landscape architect **Ossian Cole Simonds**, an apostle of **"natural landscaping."** Simonds saw the landscape architect's role as selecting, framing, and highlighting choice parts of the natural environment — shores and old-growth forests, for instance — with viewpoints, paths, and buildings. He did not rearrange natural elements to enhance nature as a romantic composition. Simonds was well

Exploring lumber towns

One aspect of old lumber centers that makes them so much fun to explore is the continuing legacy of grand public gifts made by wealthy lumbermen competing for glory. A wealthy lumber town at a large river's mouth is likely to have at least some of these: beautiful turn-of-the-century **parks**; palatial **libraries**, and occasionally a fine theater or art gallery; fancy **churches**, sometimes with Tiffany windows; and, of course, a **residential show street** where the lumber barons erected their own elaborate homes. (Many of them now are used as gift shops, lawyers' offices, or bed and breakfast inns if they survived the destructive period when these grand homes were converted to uses like rooming houses and day care centers.)

Lumber towns needed foundries to supply saw blades and machine parts. So **heavy industry** arrived on the scene with lumber, and continued to develop, as civic leaders searched for an economic base to replace the vanished trees. Recruiting the low-skill workforce needed in the woods, sawmills, and later in the foundries and paper mills led to the other glory of lumber towns: the **ethnic mix** of immigrants whose descendants, now typically middle-class, treasure vestiges of their grandparents' customs and foodways. In the lumber towns around Lake Michigan, look for Polish and Swedish **bakeries**, occasional ethnic restaurants or dishes on the menu, Danish candymakers, wonderful big **Catholic churches** (if there was a large Polish population), and a clean, nature-based, folk-influenced Scandinavian design sense that's refreshing.

known for his designs for nature-based cemeteries, parks, and subdivisions. (The attractive Detroit subdivision of Palmer Woods, with its winding drives, huge oaks, and stately Tudor homes, was his work.) The original picturesque buildings he designed have been replaced by more utilitarian structures, but the effect of his plan remains.

Today the unusual park, a jewel of the twin cities, offers a **sandy swimming beach** with lifeguards, a new **playground**, **picnic spots**, and **fine views across the bay to Door County**. All radiate off the one-mile circle drive. Behind the second pavilion is a **picturesque**

pond with lily pads, fish, and frogs.

Entrance drive is on U.S. 35 just north of where it branches off U.S. 41 on Menominee's north side. (906) 863-2656. No fee. ♿: mostly.

Germaine's Husflid

This one-woman shop is filled with examples of **Norwegian rosemaling** (pronounced "rose-MAH-ling"), that colorful style of folk art painting based on rose-like flowers, scrolls, and leaves. Germaine Vincent says she loves wood, she loves painting, and she's been in love with rosemaling ever since 1963, when she first saw Violet Christophersen's work in nearby Marinette and at Vesterheim, the Norwegian folk museum in Decorah, Iowa. The three-dimensional shaded effect, she feels, makes rosemaling "the queen of folk arts." The traditional look consists of reds, blues, and greens that aren't too bright, plus black and off-white.

In addition to Germaine's own work (mostly on plates, bowls, and wood boxes called tinas), examples by other rosemaling painters are on display. Her 8" plates are about $25. She has studied several styles with dozens of teachers in the U.S. and Norway. Each region has its own style, and Swedish dalmaling is quite different from Norwegian rosemaling. *Husflid* (HOOS-flid) refers to Norwegian cottage industries. Germaine herself is not Norwegian but German and Dutch.

Also for sale: **supplies** and raw woodenware for others to paint. Vincent gives **lessons** two evenings, three mornings, and three afternoons a week. **Workshops** can be arranged for vacationers.

N-1194 North M-35, a mile north of Henes Park on Menominee's north side. Close to the road, in a white stucco building with a pine-stained upstairs. Coming from Escanaba, look for it after crossing Evergreen Rd. Open most afternoons or by appointment. (906) 863-3890. e-mail: husflid@mari.net. Fax: (906) 863-1218. ♿

Downtown Menominee on Green Bay

Centered on First Street between Tenth and Fourth avenues, **downtown's ornate storefronts** from the lumbering era line the Green Bay waterfront. Major government buildings and churches turn the corner onto Tenth Avenue and extend west to the impressive, **handsomely restored 1875 Italianate courthouse** between Eighth and Tenth streets. The 1905 **Spies Public Library**

(863-3911; &: use door on south side), at 940 First across from Tenth Avenue, is a **striking Beaux Arts concoction** with plenty of columns and arches, and a roof with balustraded parapet. Stop in to pick up a copy of a **walking tour** of the historic district.

The best view of downtown and old Menominee's skyline is actually from the lake, especially in the late afternoon, as the setting sun warms the brick buildings and picks out occasional towers and turrets.

Today First Street is undergoing a successful revival as a destination for **specialty shopping and strolling**. Downtown's browsing tone is set by the bookstore, arty accessory shops, antiques malls, a quilting shop, and some good cafés and The Landing restaurant, a highly regarded Marinette steakhouse which moved to a renovated historic building on the waterfront.

Fortunately Menominee's historic business blocks, mostly from the 1880s and 1890s, have survived virtually intact. Unravaged by parking lots or fires and little defaced by modernization, they have given restorers a lot to work with. Many of the brick buildings have handsomely ornamented Lake Superior sandstone trim for an earthily opulent effect. Block-long **Memorial Park** has been restored. The yacht club next door maintains the park and bandstand. The green open space acts as a window offering a view of the bay and the new **marina** below. Varied **summer concerts** are now Tuesday and Thursday evenings at 7 p.m., from mid June to late August. The marina attracts boaters from the summer-crowded Door Peninsula, just 19 miles across Green Bay from Sturgeon Bay.

Downtown's new energy comes after it long played second fiddle to Marinette's larger downtown. Then both downtowns were eclipsed by malls. Additional historic buildings are one street over, along Second Street. Interesting longer **walks** or **bike rides** go out to the lighthouse pier or over the Menominee River mouth to Menekaunee and Red Arrow Park. (See below.)

Downtown highlights, arranged from north to south, include:

◆ **ELEGANT EWE**. What started out as a yarns and stitchery shop has grown and evolved, now in a new storefront location. When the owner got involved in **ceramics**, that led to gifts, mostly ceramics, windsocks, and flags. There's a **huge inventory of yarns, kits, books**, and fabrics for **knitting, crochet, needlepoint, cross-stitch**, and more. Yarns

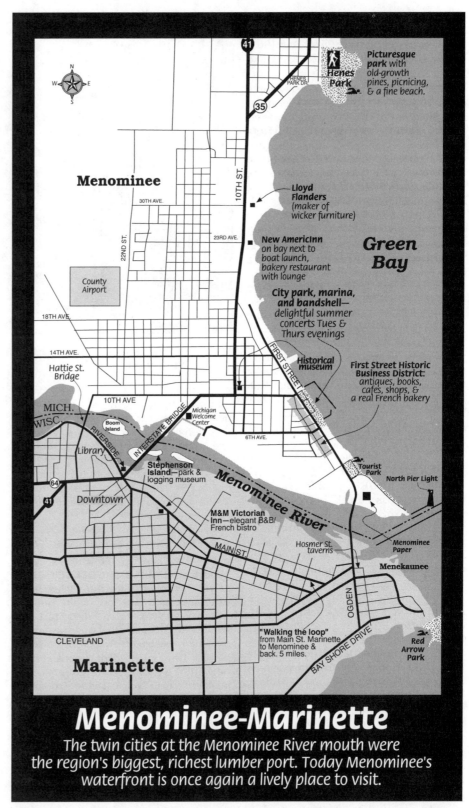

Lloyd Flanders (maker of wicker furniture)

New AmericInn on bay next to boat launch, bakery restaurant with lounge

City park, marina, and bandshell— delightful summer concerts Tues & Thurs evenings

Historical museum

First Street Historic Business District: antiques, books, cafés, shops, & a real French bakery

Michigan Welcome Center

Boom Island

Library

Stephenson Island—park & logging museum

M&M Victorian Inn—elegant B&B/ French bistro

Menominee River

Hosmer St. taverns

Menominee Paper

Menekaunee

Tourist Park

North Pier Light

"Walking the loop" from Main St. Marinette to Menominee & back. 5 miles.

Red Arrow Park

Picturesque park with old-growth pines, picnicking, & a fine beach.

Green Bay

Henes Park

Menominee

County Airport

Hattie St. Bridge

MICH. WISC.

RIVERSIDE

INTERSTATE BRIDGE

Downtown

MAIN ST.

CLEVELAND

OGDEN

BAY SHORE DRIVE

Marinette

Menominee-Marinette
The twin cities at the Menominee River mouth were the region's biggest, richest lumber port. Today Menominee's waterfront is once again a lively place to visit.

range from good-quality standard yarns to designer varieties with limited distribution. **Mail-order** is available. **Classes** are offered in knitting, stitching, and ceramics, along with ceramics painting and glazing. Examples abound. "I do it all," says owner Martha Tillson, a retired pathologist. "I paint in the daytime,

stitch at night, and knit when my eyes are tired." *501 First St. across from the library parking lot. 863-2296. Mon-Sat 9:30-5:30 Central Time. &: call.*

◆ **NORTHWOODS WILDLIFE GALLERY**. Limited-edition wildlife prints are set off to good effect by Marsha Bunting's **artful framing**. Her attractive shop also carries high-caliber reproduction decoys, animal brnozes, Santas, collector plates, and Hadley dinnerware. *515 First. 863-4000. Mon-Fri 10-5, Sat 10-4 Central Time.* &

◆ **ART RAGE.** Some two dozen artists contribute jewelry, glass, photography, and gift items to this **stunning contemporary gallery of original paintings and prints**. There's also ironwork, candles, ceramics, lamps, and other home accessories, in a price range that offers something for almost everyone. *601 First, across from the marina. 864-7243. Open Mon-Sat 9:30-5:30. Open some Sundays; call. Central Time.* &: call.

◆ **LE GRAPPILLON DE ORE BAKERY.** This **authentic French bakery**, a branch of La Grappe d'Or French bistro in Marinette, has been all the buzz since it opened in summer of 2000. Most business is takeout, perfect for eating in the nearby harborfront park. Its products are really wonderful, like nothing else in the region: baguettes, **real croissants** folded and refolded with no hollow spots, fancy pastries like cream puffs that look like swans and taste as good as they look, and an array of internationally inspired sandwiches ($4.50-$5.75). See restaurants for lunch details. *617 First St. 863-1032. Probably open year-round. Tues-Sat 8 a.m. to 2 p.m.* &: call.

◆ **AURORA BOOKS.** Booklovers Linda Murto and Ross Parcels have created a comfortable, personal general bookstore with **new, used**, and **rare books** for adults and children. It's strong on **poetry** and on the **Civil War**, with **large sections of regional and nautical books**. Used books range from popular recreational reading (the **mystery** section stands out) to serious nonfiction and **literary fiction**. The sitting area and ambiance measure up to the cozy ideal of an English bookseller. Interesting old things like elaborately framed portraits and a Civil War musket suit the historic building, which still has its tin ceiling. *625 First St. across from the marina. 863-5266. Open Mon-Fri 10-5:30, Sat 10-4 Central Time.*

◆ **QUILTER'S HAVEN.** Three quilting enthusiasts, frustrated at the lack of a convenient source for fabrics and supplies, joined together to start their own shop in summer, 1996. It's been a big success, and inventory has grown to 2,000 bolts, all 100% cotton. A quilter from Appleton comes here for the **good values on fabrics**. Examples abound, from large quilts to small projects like appliquéed sweatshirts and quilted totes. Some quilts are for sale, including Amish

In downtown Menominee by the harbor, interesting shops and cafés occupy renovated late 19th-century storefronts.

quilts. Bernina sewing machines are a new addition. The entire staff quilts, and they're happy to teach the basics to anyone. Their eclectic approach encompasses the gamut, from art hangings to traditional quilts to projects that recycle feed sacks. "We love fabric and try not to waste it," says Roxanne Baumgarten. Classes are offered. *707 First St. 864-3078. Open Mon-Fri 9:30-5:30, Thurs to 8, Sat 10-4, Sun 1-4 Central Time.* &

◆ **Lloyd's Theater/ TIMELESS TREASURES ANTIQUES & COLLECTIBLES.** In 1928 Marshall Lloyd of wicker furniture fame built this long white building with a vaguely Moorish facade to house his new department store and theater. Today, after most recently housing a Montgomery-Ward's, the department store is now the FNT Industries factory. That stands for **Fish Net & Twine**. One of the divisions here still makes **commercial fish netting**; the other makes **sports nets**.

The movie theater survived into the late 1990s. Today its 7,000 square feet of space, entered only from Second Street, is used by **Timeless Treasures**, a mall of 30 varied dealers, with furniture, collectibles (NASCAR items are one genre), paper antiques, and very few crafts. The new, leveled floor is removable wood, so the historic building could one day be converted back to theater use. Ask for directions to another antiques mall recently moved to Second Street. *Timeless Treasures is at 902 Second Street between Ninth and Tenth av-*

enues. 864-2412 . Open year-round. Summer hours (Mem.-Labor Day) Mon-Sat 10-7, Sun noon-6. Off-season hours: Mon-Sat 10-5, Thurs to 7, Sun noon-4. &: call. One step up. Mezzanine is inaccessible.

◆ **"English Cottage" GAS STATION.** Early gas stations were designed in architectural styles to blend with new neighborhoods of the era. Then in the 1930s a modernistic look took over, based on shiny contemporary surfaces. Today it's rare to find well-preserved examples of early, **quaint gas stations** like this one from the early 1920s. *823 First St.*

Menominee County Historical Museum

An **animated miniature circus**, complete with calliope music, is the star of this volunteer-run local museum. Push a button and the operating circus train moves around the periphery of the tents and staging areas. It's a close approximation of the Cole Brothers circus of 1929. Curator Bill King got the circus bug as a boy here in the 1930s from living near the train tracks where all the big circuses unloaded. At that time, a local man built models for a wealthy Indiana person who was assembling a grand and expensive model circus. Those attractive little circus wagons were occasionally displayed in local store windows before being sent off. King eventually took up the mission himself. He's one of perhaps 2,000 members of a nationwide circus modellers' association. Only about a hundred of their tiny circuses are on regular public view like this one.

A building as large as this museum has room for lots of interesting things. In a corner devoted to works by **local artists** are many carved wood animals, some winter scenes, portraits of interesting local characters, and a series depicting local buildings of significance. Two **very old dugout canoes** are in the large, recently refurbished **collection of Native American artifacts**. The next candidate for an upgrade is the fur-trading post. A new display uses artifacts, clothing, utensils, and photos to highlight the **Polish, Scandinavian, German,** and other non-Yankee families who came to the area. The large **logging collection** includes the usual tools, lots of photographs of camps and mills, and the business records of the **Menominee River Boom Company**, responsible for the initial development in much of Menominee, Iron, and Dickinson counties. Visitors enjoy the beautiful building itself, the former **St. John's Catholic Church**, built in 1921. On its balcony are displays of stores and offices: **shoe store**, doctor, printer, fashions with **bathing suits**, and more.

The adjoining building, open museum hours, houses the genealogical and other archives of the Michigan Anuta Research Center.

904 11th Ave., 1/2 block east of U.S. 41/10th St. Open Mem. Day thru last Sat in Sept: Mon-Sat 10-4, Sun 1-4 Central Time. Donation welcome. ᕳ: ground floor.

Michigan Welcome Center

This **charming log building** was first built in 1938 to give Wisconsin and Chicago vacationers a **memorable northwoods image of where Michigan begins**. It sets a high standard for log ar-

architecture that's small in scale but exceedingly picturesque. The 1982 rebuilding replaced deteriorated logs with ones equally huge and retained interior components like the original stone floor and wagon-wheel chandeliers. The details make the design work: logs extending out at the corners in the best Lincoln Log fashion, a wood-shingled roof, and two limestone fireplaces and chimneys. There's a small **picnic area** outside.

Welcome Center staffs are usually outstanding sources of information, both local and state-wide. Brochures are **mailed** upon request.

On U.S. 41 at the foot of the Interstate Bridge, north bank of the Menominee River across from downtown Marinette. Limited parking. If small lot is full, continue on U.S. 41 to the adjacent M&M Plaza shopping center and take stairs up to rear of Welcome Center. (906) 863-6496. Open daily 8 a.m.-4 p.m. Central Time, year-round, possibly longer in summer. ᕳ

A walk to the lighthouse pier

Walking or biking south along First Street from downtown presents options for two little adventures, first to a **pier** and then a**cross the Menominee River bridge** (see next entry). You can veer left and stay along the lake, passing some houses with nifty gardens before turning at **Tourist Park** (906-863-7652), opposite Third Avenue, and heading out Harbor Drive to the **North Pier Light**, about a mile away from downtown. Ferryboats of the Ann Arbor Railroad coming from Ludington once docked on land now used as parkland and a **public beach** without lifeguards. Here are **picnic tables and restrooms** (ᕳ).

A north **pier light** at the harbor entrance has guided boats to the Menominee River since 1877. This 25-foot light is a 1925 replacement for the original; the catwalk out to the light has been removed. Anglers frequent the pier, but there's no easy pedestrian access. It's necessary to step and pick your way across the rocky approach.

Menekaunee taverns and Red Arrow Park

If you continued south on First from downtown Menominee and passed the paper mill, you'd cross the Menominee River and an island in it. You'd then be in Wisconsin. On the south bank is the workers' neighborhood of Menekaunee (pronounced "MEN-uh-CAW-knee"), known for its **neighborhood taverns**.

Menekaunee, now part of Marinette, originated as a squatters' village. Millworkers, loggers, and fishermen built small houses on the shavings and sand that accumulated behind the breakwater built at the river's mouth by a lumber company. These squatters gained title to the land in a famous turn-of-the-century court case, in which the lumber company failed to reclaim its land.

Today a half dozen enclosed **fishing boats**, working remnants of Marinette's once-large fleet, tie up at a river slip near here. Menekaunee's **taverns**, all on Hosmer Street, remain a draw for people who want **authentic, unfussed-over local color**. College students home on vacation, for instance, join foundry workers, commercial fishermen, retirees, and occasional salesmen and merchant sailors who get together at **HELEN'S EDGEWATER INN** at 16 Hosmer, east of Ogden and within view of the water. *(715-735-9481)* Outsiders are welcome at this friendly bar, which serves only beverages, no food. It's the kind of place where customers give rides to Canadian sailors waiting while pig iron's being unloaded for the nearby Waupaca foundry so the sailors can get haircuts and buy sundries. Down the street at 32 Hosmer, **MIKE & JEAN'S** has a very popular Friday-night fish fry. Otherwise, from 11 a.m. to 9 p.m. daily except Sunday the food consists of burgers and, from the deep fryer, bar food and chicken breasts for sandwiches. *(715) 735-9804.* ᕳ

A **long sandbar** extends from Menekaunee for a mile out into the bay. At its base, **RED ARROW PARK** has taken outstanding advantage of this unusual location along both the river and lake. It's a **wonderful, hidden spot for walkers and joggers**. At the parking area a sidewalk with occasional benches extends north and west to the Ogden Street bridge across the river mouth. In the other direction, walk the mile out on Seagull Bar, a long sand bar in Green Bay, and you're almost surrounded by water. Before you get to the **sandy, unsupervised swimming beach**, there's a **picnic area** with grills and pavilion and a new **playground** (all ᕳ). A **boat launch** is on an inland bay of the park, where another **path**, not hard-surfaced, affords a view of the protected bay where herons and other waterfowl nest.

Historical note: the "Red Arrow" name goes back to the **32nd Red Arrow Division** formed of Michigan and Wisconsin soldiers in **World War I**. It earned its nickname for its swift attacks through German lines.

To reach Red Arrow Park from Menomi-

nee's First Street, go south over the bridge. First becomes Ogden. In 4 blocks turn east onto Leonard. Leonard becomes Bay View, which leads to the park. From U.S. 41 and the south, at the light past the mall, turn east (right) onto Cleveland. Stay on it (the name changes to Russell) all the way to Menekaunee. When it ends, go right on Red Arrow to the park.

A walking tour of downtown Marinette

The historic downtown retail district of this Wisconsin city is at the south end of the Interstate Bridge (U.S. 41) between Menominee and Marinette. The **impressive homes of lumber barons and merchants overlook the river** along Riverside (to the west) and Main Street (to the east). The mid-river park at Stephenson Island adds a natural dimension to downtown.

◆ **STEPHENSON ISLAND PARK and MARINETTE COUNTY LOGGING MUSEUM.** Until the last logging drive in 1917, Menominee River drives ended on this island. Here lumber companies sorted and sawed logs that had been floated from as far away as Michigamme and Iron River. Now the island is a park with a **picnic area**, boat launch, and **bandstand** where **free outdoor concerts** are held in summer from mid June through early August, on Tuesdays at 7 p.m.

The logging era is commemorated by the **museum** of the **Marinette County Historical Society** (715-732-0831), which can arrange for group tours out-of-season. Its centerpiece is a **miniature logging camp** meticulously constructed by Marinette woodsman and riverman John Mayer. There are other photos and artifacts about logging, like models of lumber schooners. Another display deals with Queen Marinette, the astute metis (French and Indian) trader whose influence was far-ranging from the 1830s to the 1850s. Outside the museum is a **skid of real logs**, drawn by **fiberglass horses**. Winter was when loggers moved logs from the woods to skidways and rivers on sleds like these, to be floated down the Menominee River to the booms right here. Employees of the boom company would identify each lumber company's logs from the logmarks on the ends, and maneuver them into each company's corral-like enclosure. Now that the water is so low, it's easy to see the rock cribs that anchored each floating enclosure. Marinette parks foreman Gary Kmiechk hopes that the park and historical society can set up the **1889 J. I. Case**

A team of fiberglass horses draws a skid of real logs outside the Marinette County Historical Museum on the island park in the Menominee River between Menominee and Marinette. In lumbering days, booms here held logs which were sorted to be sawn at each company's sawmill.

sawmill he found browsing the Harry's Engine website and give demonstrations. A beautiful thing with red daisies hand-painted on it, it had been used by a Wisconsin logging company not too far away. *Turn west off Interstate Bridge to get to the island by car. Or park at the Wisconsin Travel Information Center and take the new footbridge. Museum is open Mem. Day -Labor Day, Tues-Sunday 10-4:30 Central Time.* ♿

◆ **WISCONSIN TRAVEL INFORMATION CENTER.** For more info about Marinette County, stop in here. Marinette County, larger than Rhode Island, has many county parks developed around waterfalls. Often their shelters and bridges were built by the Civilian Conservation Corps in the 1930s to put young men to work and develop the area's tourism potential. Pick up a free **walking tour** of historic Marinette. *On Riverside next to the Stephenson Public Library. Turn right after you cross the Interstate Bridge; it's right there. 715-732-4333. Open April through October, daily from 9 to 5, except in summer from 8 to 4.* ♿

◆ **STEPHENSON PUBLIC LIBRARY.** Those who look inside this Neoclassical library, built in 1903 by donor Ike Stephenson, one of the powerful lumber clan, can see the rotunda's **stained-glass skylight** and other period touches. The nifty architectural details are hidden away in upstairs meeting rooms, reached through the upstairs stacks, now that the entrance is at ground level in the rear. The **history and genealogy room**, open library hours, can give interested users an idea of the city's early fur-trading history and lumber boom days; ask at the desk. *On Riverside at U.S. 41, to the right off the Interstate Bridge and across from the Best Western. Enter*

through newer wing in rear. *(715) 732-7570. Regular hours Mon-Fri 9:30 a.m.-9 p.m., Sat to 5. From Mem. to Labor Day, shorter hours: Mon-Fri 9-6, Thurs to 8, Sat 10-5.* ♿

◆ **RIVERSIDE AVENUE homes.** 1919 Riverside & 1931 Riverside were wedding gifts of super-rich lumber baron Isaac Stephenson to two daughters. More large homes are around the corner on State, a block west of Hattie. *Between Hall and Hattie, two blocks west of the bridge.*

◆ **The Lauerman Building/SIMPLY CHARMING.** The ground floor of the onetime Lauerman Department Store effectively displays antiques, often imported from Europe, and **fine furniture** in room settings for every room of the house, including kitchens. *(715) 732-9300.* Smaller antiques and jewelry are at a second store across the street, the **DUNLAP SQUARE GALLERY** (closes at 4 p.m., closed Tues & Wed). These two blocks of downtown are known as Dunlap Square. Today it's becoming even more of a visitor attraction, with **KATHY'S ON THE SQUARE bakery** and coffeehouse and a new educational toy store.

The block-long 1904 home to the old Lauerman Department Store has big upper-story windows — an innovation of the Chicago School of forward-looking architecture. Today a rehab project has successfully mixed retail with subsidized and market-rate apartments. *In downtown Marinette on the southeast corner of Main and U.S. 41 — the first intersection beyond the foot of the interstate bridge. Store hours Mon-Sat 10-5.* ♿

◆ **MAIN STREET HOUSES.** The **most elegantly restored** of the grand homes is the Queen Anne lumberman's house at 1393 Main, occupied by the **M&M**

Victorian Inn (715-732-9531) and **La Grappe d'Or French bistro** (see restaurants).

MENOMINEE/MARINETTE RESTAURANTS

After cooking at a number of Michigan and Wisconsin restaurants, Ron Berg ran the Flying Dutchman, Marinette's most respected steakhouse, with his father, Stan. In 1997 they launched **THE LANDING** overlooking downtown Menominee's harbor, where today Ron is the owner-chef. It's the **perfect combination of good food and a great setting**, with a **bayside patio** where cocktails are served. Sometimes there's **live piano music** on weekends. Specialties include a thick New York strip steak with garlic-bourbon sauce ($16) and broiled shrimp feast ($15). The menu features steak, chicken, veal, and seafood, often prepared the continental way, but a vegetarian could be quite happy here, too. Special touches include fresh bread sticks and a big, Olive Garden-style salad bowl. Lunches are around $7. **Reservations** recommended, especially in summer. *Downtown Menominee at 450 First St. (906) 863-8034 .Open for lunch Mon-Fri 11:30-2. For dinner Mon-Sat 5-9, to 10 Fri & Sat. From Mem.to Labor Day also open Sun 5-9.* &. ♦♦♦ Full bar

European bistros were the inspiration for the **very popular HARBOR HOUSE CAFE**. Its front porch and deck overlook the park and marina.The original owners have moved on, but their format of fresh, homemade soups, salads, sandwiches, and desserts in a smoke-free setting fits in with the food philosophy of new owner Tammy Nelson. Her fans at the University of Wisconsin-Marinette are sorry to see her go. Vegetarians can eat well here; so can hamburger eaters. No deep-fried fare. *1821 First St. in downtown Menominee. (906) 863-7770. In summer open daily from 7 a.m. to 9 p.m. Off-season hours: Mon-Sat 7-7.* &. ♦♦♦

Mostly this **real French bakery** is takeout, but a few tables inside and on the sidewalk make **LE GRAPPILLON DE ORE BAKERY** a very pleasant place to have breakfast, lunch, or just dessert with cappucino. "It's like a trip to Europe on the shores of Green Bay," raves one regular. (The name, which means " little golden grape," is pronounced "luh GRAPP-ee-yone duh ORE.") Delicious quiche or pizza is available by the slice (around $3). International-theme sandwiches ($4.50 to $5.75) on authentic croissants come with homemade chips (in a cute bag with bow) and slaw.

There's a French sandwich (smoked ham and brie), Mexican, Italian, etc. Eclairs, chocolate mousse tartes, giant strawberries dipped and swirled in white and dark chocolate — it's **like nothing else in the U.P.** or anywhere near it. Baking is done under the direction of two French chefs at La Grappe d'Or restaurant in a grand Victorian house in Marinette. *617 First St. in downtown Menominee. (906) 863-1032. Open, probably year-round, Tues-Sat from 8 a.m. to 2 p.m.* &.: call.

THAI CUISINE is an attractive little Thai-Chinese place with a **big takeout business**. It's a modest spot, but from-scratch cooking with fresh vegetables wins praise from some of the area's most discriminating cooks. Fans of Thai food should order it hot, otherwise it comes mild, geared to local tastes. Thai classics like lemongrass soup are available, but meat-and-potatoes types will probably be happy with dishes like garlic beef or shish-kebob. Pad Thai (rice noodes with sprouts and shrimp) is a favorite. There's lots for vegetarians. Typical price of a dish is $5-$6 at lunch and $7-$10 at dinner. *462 10th Ave. just west of downtown Menominee. (906) 863-6188 .Open Mon-Sat 11 a.m. to 2:30 p.m. and 4-9 p.m.* &.

SCHLOEGEL'S is a **local institution**, casual and family-oriented, where many service clubs meet. Generations of local people have gone to Schloegel's for dinner or after church. It's known for its good **New England clam chowder, Swedish pancakes, potato pancakes, and liver and onions**. The soup and sandwich menu is offered any time. Lunches $5-$7. Dinners $6-$10. The regular menu is online, and there are daily specials, too. Special diets accommodated. Pies, made with fresh fruit in season, and baked goods are also sold in the separate bakery and deli. *On the east side of 10th St./U.S. 41 on the north side of Menominee. (906) 863-7888. www .schloegelsrestaurant.com Open daily year-round. Mon-Sat 6 a.,m.-9 p.m., Sun & most holidays 7:30 a.m.-8 p.m.* &. ♦♦♦

At **LA GRAPPE D'OR BISTRO** (that's "golden grape" in English), a French chef from Bordeaux has trained a kitchen staff that turns out a changing menu of memorable French meals at a **price that will astonish** visitors from downstate Wisconsin and Chicago. The current $27 prix fixe includes seasonal offerings of an appetizer, entrée (it might be salmon, rack of lamb, rack of veal, Chilean sea bass), dessert, *and a* glass of wine. The appetizer might be authentic French

onion soup that starts with carefully caramelized onions, or Prince Edward Island mussels and cockles. (Cockles are scallops.) Or you can order a la carte and make a lighter meal of appetizers and dessert. The setting is an extra bonus: downstairs rooms and the enclosed porch in a **lumberman's Queen Anne mansion** with ornate woodwork and stained glass. Owner Jean Moore turned her childhood home into a bed and breakfast rather than have it sold. When she decided to do the 60-seat restaurant as well, she advertised in France because French-trained chefs never cut corners the way even the best American cooking schools train their graduates. "I feel totally transported!" raves a fan who's thrilled to be able to enjoy the products of a French patisserie and the U.P.'s natural beauty in the same urban area. In good weather there's **outdoor seating** in a French tent. **Reservations** recommended. No smoking. *1393 Main St. in Marinette. (See map.) (715) 732-9531. www.cybrzn.com/ victorian-inn/ Open year round except for late Jan & early Feb. Tues-Sat 5:30-10 Central Time.* &.: no except for tent in good weather ♦♦♦ Full bar

MENOMINEE/MARINETTE LODGINGS

Special events like the August Harborfront festival fill rooms a year in advance. There aren't all that many rooms in the twin cities, so sometimes events like a bowling tournament will fill up the town. Don't count on getting a room without reservations.

AmericINN MOTEL & SUITES
(906) 863-8699; (800) 634-3444

Rather than being isolated on a commercial strip, this luxurious 62-room motel, new in 1999, is within town *and* right on Green Bay. It has a real sense of place — and a boat launch, too. The **playground** and **picnic area** with grills have good bay views; so does an entire wing of guest rooms, including a dozen with **balconies** or **patios**. Rates start at $75 and vary with the season. The **indoor pool** is pleasant, with a cathedral ceiling and lots of natural light — an AmericInn trademark, along with the big, **comfortable lobby** with fireplace and generous "enhanced" **continental breakfast**, with sausage, even. Here it has a nautical theme. A **Perkins Restaurant & Bakery** with lounge is right next door. Ask about **one-room king whirlpool suites** and **fireplace suites**. You could walk to the waterfront, a little over a mile away, along First Street and only have two blocks along the busy road. Reserve ahead for weekends in season, starting in mid-May. *On U.S. 41/Tenth St. at 23rd Ave., a mile south of the Y junction of U.S. 41 and M-35, and just under a mile north of downtown, where U.S. 41 turns north.* **H.A.**: some rooms ADA accessible.

GEHRKE'S GASTHAUS   (906) 863-9005; e-mail: nagehrke@yahoo.com

This big, comfortable family home is **on the bay** three blocks south of the marina and downtown Menominee shops and restaurants. Guests have their own quarters. Three rooms in the main house ($68-$88) have private baths and use a large **living room** with **fireplace** and window with a **view of the bay**. Guests can play the **pump organ and baby grand piano**. Some decor reflects innkeeper Nancy Gehrke's involvement in theater. The attached but separate **"caretakers' quarters" suite** consist of two bedrooms, kitchen, and living room. The house is oriented to the street, but the big **back yard** has a **beautiful lake view and sandy beach. Big breakfasts**. No credit cards. *320 First St. Open May thru Oct., other dates by special arrangement.* **H.A.**: no   : call for extra person charge

BEST WESTERN RIVERFRONT INN
(715) 732-011

In downtown Marinette, this six-story, 120-room facility is the area's only full-service hotel with a restaurant and lounge. It's right downtown, across from the library, Stephenson Island, and the Interstate Bridge— a good location for walkers. Half the rooms have a nice river view. The **indoor pool** is about 36' long. Rates: $69-$85 depending on the view and season.1821 Riverside Ave., just to the west at the foot of the Interstate Bridge.

M&M VICTORIAN INN   (715) 732-9531; www.cybrzn.com/victorianinn

For **spare-no-expense elegance**, nothing around can match this bed and breakfast near downtown Marinette. It's in a large, beautifully restored Queen Anne lumberman's house — in fact, the very place where innkeeper Jean Moore grew up. The downstairs is given over to an **outstanding French restaurant** and bakery preparation area, except for one sitting room with fireplace for B&B guests. (Restaurant guests go through it to reach a restroom.) Five guest rooms, furnished with antiques, have private baths, phones, and cable TV. Check the website for photos. One guest room ($125, weekends $140) has a porch,

sleeper sofa for adults traveling together, fireplace, and two-person whirlpool. Another large room ($110/$125) also has a two-person whirlpool. The other three rooms are from $75 to $90, or $80 to $100 on weekends. Full breakfast. 1393 Main St. **H.A.**: no

MENOMINEE/MARINETTE CAMPING

See also: On the Shores of Green Bay; Peshtigo

RIVER PARK CAMPGROUND
(906) 863-5101; reservations advised

52 close-spaced modern campsites are down by the Menominee River right at the north end of the Interstate Bridge. Just up a stairway is M&M Plaza with the outstanding **Angeli's Central Market** and other services. There's **fishing** and a **playground.** This campground is so popular, many spaces are reserved a year ahead. Advance reservations a must in summer. $22/night, $132/week. *Open from mid May thru Sept.*

Peshtigo *(pop. 3,150)*

This rather plain Wisconsin lumber town and farm center developed near the mouth of the Peshtigo River seven miles south of Marinette. It's pronounced "PESH-tih-GO." It has continued to grow over the years, unlike many of its neighbors. The **Badger Paper Mills**, with some 200 employees, is its biggest employer. One of its papermaking machines produces coated papers that can be used for packaging for chewing gum and candy. Peshtigo manufacturers also produce document forms, store fixtures, and sausage casings. The lower reaches of the **Peshtigo River** are said to be well stocked yet lightly fished, resulting in excellent fishing for trout, walleye, smallmouth bass, and salmon. (Catch-and-release preferred.) Boat access is at the **Peshtigo Harbor Wildlife Area** at the river's mouth. Badger Park on the Peshtigo River has a 10,000-square-foot playground fort, plus camping for tents and campers. Contact the Peshtigo Chamber of Commerce, (715) 582-0327 or www.peshtigochamber.com

Peshtigo Fire Museum and Fire Cemetery

Seven miles from Marinette, a small local museum commemorates the greatest loss of life associated with the widespread forest fires that broke out in the north woods during the logging era. Log-

ging practices of the day left lots of combustible debris or "slash" in the woods. Tree tops, with their many branches and twigs, were left. When dried, this logging debris proved ideal for starting fires. Twigs and leaves provided tinder, with plenty of fuel for long-lasting combustion. When the weather was dry and the wind strong, fires could create devastation on a massive scale.

It had been a dry summer in 1871, and people near cutover land throughout the region worried about fire. Peshtigo was a busy sawmill town of 1,700 near the mouth of the Peshtigo River. Its woodenware factory was said to be the largest in the world. On October 8, the same day as the great Chicago fire, fires broke out in many other places. Much of Holland and Manistee, Michigan, were destroyed. Flames threatened Menominee and Marinette, but the wind changed before doing much damage to residential areas.

In Peshtigo, however, winds spread the fire so fast that many people weren't able to reach safe haven in the river. Some who did drowned. At least 800 people perished — more than in any other forest fire in U.S. history. Virtually the entire town was destroyed. The dead are buried in the **Peshtigo Fire Cemetery** next to the museum. Many are in a mass grave; the exact number of victims isn't known.

If you get out to look around, you won't soon forget this place. Here are the river where the people of Peshtigo sought safety, the cemetery where nearly half of them were buried, and the museum that commemorates the tragedy. There are large **murals depicting the fire**, some photographs of the devastation, and fire-damaged objects like melted coins. The museum also displays artifacts common in local museums such as tools and period clothing. Peshtigo was rebuilt promptly after the fire. The former Congregational Church that houses the museum dates from that rebuilding.

From U.S. 41 and Marinette, pass through downtown and turn right (north) onto Oconto before you reach the Dairy Queen. The church/museum is a block away at Oconto and Green. (715) 582-4492. *Open from Mem. Day weekend to weekend nearest to Oct. 8. During that time, open daily 9-4:30 Central Time. Free; donation appreciated.* : no. 10 steps.

Keep in mind that all prices and hours of operation are subject to change. Lodging rates vary with supply and demand and are usually higher for special events.

Manistique & the Garden Peninsula

Two interestingly isolated peninsulas, a ghost town, a dramatic spring, and a memorable lighthouse and park.

FOR NEARLY a century Manistique and surrounding areas on Lake Michigan's north shore have been among the Upper Peninsula's **most accessible vacation spots**, thanks to its location on the Soo Line between the Twin Cities and Sault Ste. Marie, Canada. Manistique is just 89 miles west of the Mackinac Bridge on U.S. 2, one of the two major east-west routes across the peninsula.

Both of the area's best-known visitor destinations have an **enjoyable low-key simplicity**. **Fayette,** on the Garden Peninsula just west of Manistique, is a picturesque and well-preserved ghost town. At **unforgettable Kitchiti-kipi (Big Spring)** a mighty underground spring gushes up into a deep clear pond, enchantingly green with moss. The motel row at **Manistique** enjoys a **Lake Michigan view** and access to a pleasant two-mile **lakefront pathway**. Indians camped all along this shoreline before the Europeans arrived because it was milder and calmer than the Lake Superior shore.

Scores of fishing lakes are northwest of Manistique. 8,659-acre **Indian Lake** was the early magnet for small resorts. Indian Lake, one of Michigan's largest inland lakes, is an extension of an e**normous surrounding stretch of marshlands**. Only five to ten feet deep in most places, it's home to lots of good-sized walleye, yellow perch, and smallmouth bass. Beyond Indian Lake a 25-mile stretch of **Hiawatha National Forest** extends nearly to Munising. **Fifty-two lakes** are in northwestern Schoolcraft County alone, and many more are in adjacent parts of Delta and Alger counties. See the Pictured Rocks chapter for information on this "Lake Country" area.

As in most of the Upper Peninsula, logging was a major part of the region's early development. Mills and ports were at Nahma, Thompson, and Manistique. An important legacy of the area's logging is the huge paper plant in Manistique. That city today offers more than meets the casual eye, thanks in large part to enterprising small businesspeople who have chosen to live and work in this relaxed little northwoods town. The new Traders' Point commercial and condo development takes good advantage of a fine harborfront site that used to be coal docks for the Ann Arbor carferry.

As the woods were logged off, the area reoriented itself to fishing-related tourism and to commercial fishing, too. Beginning in 1877 **Manistique's harbor** was used by steamships bringing vacationers to the area's hotels and cottages from Green Bay and, later, from Chicago and from lower Michigan via an Ann Arbor Railroad carferry from Frankfort. **Commercial fishing**, which has died out in most Great Lakes locations, still continues here at Garden and Fairport on the Garden Peninsula. At Fairport fishermen once caught and penned six-foot-long sturgeon, kept alive until sent to market in Chicago. "At times," reports the 1941 WPA (Work Projects Administration) guide to Michigan, "the sturgeon were frozen and piled on the shore like cordwood awaiting shipment."

Sand beaches, rocky limestone points and shoals alternate along the Lake Michigan shore here. The **Garden Peninsula**, a long limestone finger, extends 21 miles south into Lake Michigan, whose moderating waters give it a climate as mild as mid-Michigan. (Marijauna growers love its favorable climate and isolation.) Big deposits of **limestone** have played an important role in the local economy, beginning in the 1860s when it was used as a purifying flux in many small iron-making operations. Today the Port Inland quarry of Michigan Limestone Operations ships millions of tons of limestone from Seul Choix Point east of Manistique to steelmaking centers on the lower Great Lakes.

FOR MORE INFORMATION: Call for stop by the helpful **Schoolcraft County Chamber of Council** at 1000 W. Lakeshore/U.S. 2 just west of the harbor next to the new Big Boy. (906) 341-5010; **www.manistique.com** As a membership organization, it distributes info about its members and the area in general. Many businesses are linked with its website. Open year-round, Mon-Sat 9-5, and Sun 10-2 from June thru Sept. . . . . The **Manistique Area Tourist Council** serves the county's motels and resorts. It has no walk-in presence but mails visitor packets. (800) 342-4282; **www.onlynorth. com**. . . . The **Hiawatha National Forest** office at 449 East Lakeshore/U.S. 2 just east of downtown gives handouts and advise for camping, canoeing, and more on the area's extensive national forest land. It's open weekdays from 7:30 to 4 or so. (906) 341-5010. . . . For info on local bycycling or the beautiful **Pine Marten Run** (40 miles of mountain biking trails in the national forest), contact **The Bicycle Shop**, 315 Deer St./M-94, open weekdays and some Saturday mornings. (906) 341-5010

EVENTS: The second weekend in July **Folkfest** in downtown Manistique celebrates local ethnic heritage with live music and dancing, food booths, a 12k and 5k run, art show, and much more. Friday through Sunday. (906) 341-5010. . . At Fayette Historic State Park (906-644-2603) there's the **Blessing of the Fleet** on the third Sunday of July (the bishop of Marquette blesses fishing boats and pleasure boats, and on the first Sunday of August, costumed reenactments at **Heritage Days**.

HARBORS with transient dockage: In **Manistique** (341-6841; off-season 341-2290; lat. 45° 56' 41", long. 86° 14' 54") with showers. Limited dockage at **Fayette State Historic Park** (lat. 45° 43' 18", long. 86° 40' 15")

GUIDES: Great Northern Adventures has Garden Peninsula kayak tours. www.greatnorthernadventures.com (906) 225-8687.

PICNIC PROVISIONS & PLACES

◆ Off U.S. 2 on the harbor's west side, **Traders' Point** has a deli, Jilbert's ice cream, coffee house, and outdoor seating with **views** of Lake Michigan, the Manistique harbor, and the lighthouse (see restaurants).

◆ In a real hurry? **Get sandwiches** from **Hardee's** or **Subway**, both on U.S. 2 just east of the harbor, or **Burger King** just west of the harbor, and go to **Lakeshore Park** on U.S. 2 about half a mile east of the harbor.

◆ **Clyde's** (see restaurants) has fried baskets (perch, salmon,

chicken) and burgers. Take them to nearby **Roger's Beach** on Lake Michigan and U.S. 2 about 3 miles west of the harbor.

◆ **Grill your own.** Shop at a local supermarket. **Ken's Fairway Foods** is on M-94/Deer St. on the west side, **Jack's Super-Valu** is on Maple just east of Cedar, downtown's main street. Grills are at **Roger's Beach** and **Lakeshore Park** (see above).

◆ **Remote and beautiful:** the picnic area by the **Seul Choix Point lighthouse**, 8 miles south of U. S. 2 from Gulliver.

Nahma Peninsula

The Sturgeon River between Rapid River and Manistique (one of four Sturgeon Rivers in Michigan) has created the **short, marshy Nahma Peninsula — a delta**, really — where it empties into Lake Michigan between the longer Stonington and Garden peninsulas with their higher elevations. Nahma (pronounced "NAY-muh") means "sturgeon" in Ojibwa. At the river mouth the Bay de Noc Lumber Company created the company town of Nahma at the turn of the century. It had the trim, tidy look of a **well-planned company town**. Public buildings lined a rather **grand boulevard** with a median strip of lawn, leading to a cluster of mill buildings where the rail line neared Lake Michigan.

In 1951 an Indiana playground manufacturer bought most of the town, with big plans to turn it into a resort. **"Sold: One Town"** read the headline of a Life magazine article back then. However, the playground company didn't keep up with changes in play equipment, and it didn't have the money to develop the resort. Many of the buildings caved in, including the lumber sheds, the community building, and the school. Today people do live in Nahma — a mix of summer people and local people, some of whom seem to live on very low incomes. A residential development is slated to replace the school and the community building, which have been torn down.

In 1994 the three Groleau brothers, Warren, Pat, and Ron, who grew up in the tiny town, went in together, with their wives, and bought the hotel, the store, and half of the **attractive nine-hole lakeside golf course**. They refurbished the **Nahma Hotel** (see below) on the town's main boulevard and decorated it attractively. Having effectively revived their home town, they sold the hotel in 2000 to Carol Luft, a native of the Escanaba area. For 11 years she had managed the Thunder Bay Inn in Big

Bay — another remote place whose success has shown that out-of-the-way areas can thrive as low-key visitor destinations.

Millworkers were paid in scrip to buy at the company store. The Groleaus turned the **Nahma General Store** into a sort of **mini-museum, gift and antique shop with ice cream and groceries**, too. It continues to be open from Memorial Day to Labor Day. Call (906) 644-2648 for info on the **golf course**, still owned by Warren Groleau. It has small, 1930s-style greens and narrow fairways.

There's currently no public beach in Nahma, though there is a **small private beach** for hotel guests. The **DNR boat launch** gives access to **Big Bay de Noc**, with its **excellent fishing**. A real attraction, described in Tom Powers' *Natural Michigan*, is the wetland natural area along the **Sturgeon River**. He writes of "the **beautiful landscape — vast pine and hardwood forests, huge cedar swamps and black-spruce bogs**" and says, "If you catch even a glimpse of the swiftly flowing stream as it disappears around one of its ever-present bends, it will stay fixed in your mind." The river is easily accessible, because County Road 497 runs generally alongside it south from U.S. 2 at Nahma Junction. Most of the Sturgeon flows through Hiawatha National Forest lands. It is a beautiful, often productive, and **overlooked trout stream**. Fish habitat improvements will make fishing even better in the future. The Sturgeon has been designated a **Wild-Scenic River**. The tucked-away **Flowing Well picnic area** and **campground** north of U.S. 2 (see below) is a pretty place to enjoy the river.

Wildlife, not only waterfowl and fish but mammals, abounds in the area. A good way to see it is by **canoeing** down the river. **Canoes** can be rented at the NoNahMa Resort (906-644-2728) on the old mill site at the west end of the boulevard. They also **rent bicycles, jet skis,** and **paddleboats**.

Upstream on the Sturgeon River there's good fishing, says Tom Huggler in

his *Fish Michigan: 50 More Rivers*, in those places where there's good fish habitat without sterility-inducing sand.

GETTING TO NAHMA FROM U.S. 2: *The blacktop on scenic CR 497 is breaking up, so go slowly. Better roads are along the lakeshore: County Roads 495 (from Isabella) and 499 (from St. Jacques — the local pronunciation is Saint Jake's). They pass the cottages that line most of the Nahma Peninsula's shoreline. In places the lake is so shallow that land and water seem to merge in the shoreline grass. Bicycling groups have already discovered the low-traffic area and the pleasant accommodations at the Nahma Inn.*

Nahma Boat Launch

The DNR boat launch behind the Nahma Inn is virtually a park, with **fishing piers** and **picnic tables**. It gives access to Big Bay de Noc via one of the many artificial waterways dug by the lumber company.

Get to the town of Nahma via of CR 499, 495, or 497. At the Nahma Inn, on the south side of main street near the town's west end, look for boat launch sign. &

Nahma Marsh Trail

This easy trail through **prime wildlife habitat** in the **Hiawatha National Forest** consists of a **boardwalk** and hard surfaces from the parking area for about a third of a mile alongside the dammed marsh, ending at a double-decked **viewing platform**. Herons, muskrats, sandhill cranes, bittern, songbirds, and many waterfowl species are seen. The trail and platform are fully accessible for wheelchairs or strollers. Benches are frequent.

When the trail was constructed in 1993, "it weaved under a dense, dark cedar forest that concealed from hikers the wildlife of the marsh until they emerged onto the viewing platform," in the words of Forest Service supervisor Anne Okonek. In 1998 a windstorm with winds over 80 mph passed through the southern U.P. and flattened the cedars

lining the trail. Now that the Forest Service has reopened the trail, hikers have a much better view of the marsh! The area is slowly revegetating, as maples sprout up from stumps and balsam and spruce trees take root.

The trailhead is off CR 497 (the very bumpy road near the Sturgeon River) three miles south of U.S. 2 at Nahma Junction. (906) 474-6442. &

Flowing Well Picnic Area & Sturgeon River fishing

On the banks of the Sturgeon River, this small picnic area and campground, part of the Hiawatha National Forest, are a nice place for people who want to **avoid crowds** without getting too far from main roads. A **hundred gallons of water a minute** flow from an oil test well made in 1929. Today it provides drinking water, albeit hard and sulfurous. The mixed forest here is full of **wildflowers** in spring. "Many feel the **fishing** is terrific, but the brook trout, steelhead, and salmon here may be **wary and elusive**," warns the Forest Service handout. "The time of year may be critical for fishing success." For those with canoes, short (4 and 3 mile) **canoe trips** to and from Flowing Well can be taken by putting upstream at the 14 Mile Bridge of Forest Highway 13 or taking out downstream at CR 497 just south of U.S. 2. *From U.S. 2 at Nahma Junction, take Forest Hwy. 13 three miles north to the campground. (906) 474-6442. Free except for camping.* &: call.

NAHMA RESTAURANTS & LODGINGS

NAHMA INN

(906) 644-2486; www: nahmainn.com; e-mail thenahmainn @skyenet.net; fax (906) 644-2510

This architecturally plain hotel, built around 1910, is a most **comfortable place to hang out**, thanks to tip-top maintenance, big shade trees, a large **front porch**, and a cheerful **dining room** and **bar**. Of the 14 fresh and attractive guest rooms on 2 floors, 8 have private baths (2001 summer rates for two: $65 and, for a queen bed, $80), and 6 share two baths ($50 and $55). Rates include a free **continental breakfast**. No phone, and no TV. Guests can use the **private beach** within walking distance. Common areas include the **front porch** and a **sitting area** in the upstairs hall.

H.A.: one room wheelchair-accessible. Call on others. 👫: older children welcome; 2 people/room

As for the restaurant, new owner Carol Luft has expanded the menu offerings, and the full menu is available any time. There are more sandwiches (currently $4.50 to $6.50) and salads ($2 to $7.50). Dinners ($10 to $18) focus on pasta dishes and fresh whitefish and perch. Daily specials. Friday night brings all-you-can-eat fried whitefish. *May close in some of March and April. From May thru Oct, open daily noon to 10 p.m. Otherwise open daily, from 3 to 9 p.m. weekdays, noon to 10 p.m. Fri. thru Sun.*

H.A.: wheelchair-accessible
👫: children's menu   Full bar

NAHMA CAMPING

NO-NAH-MA RESORT

(906) 644-2728; fax (906) 644-2792; www.no-nah-ma.com; e-mail resort@nah-ma.com

This is the latest business to take over the old Nahma mill and its lagoon-like slips. It uses the former factory building to house the **rental bicycles,** sports equipment, and **boats**: canoes, paddleboats, fishing boats, and jet skis. Big Bay de Noc is a very short walk from everything here. The Nahma Inn with its good restaurant and lounge is just a block away. The noisy jet skis mostly are taken to inland lakes, so they aren't likely to be heard by campers, we're told. The six new **cabins** sleep up to six, with two bedrooms and a sofa-sleeper in the living-kitchen area, which has a gas fireplace. These rent for $575/week or $80/night. They face one of the slips; cedars block the view of Big Bay de Noc. All have limited cable TV with ESPN, and all permit smoking. Not air-conditioned. The phone in the office can be used when the office is open. Every cabin and campsite faces one of the slips, which connect to Lake Michigan via a channel by the silo-like tower where the mill burned wood waste. The slips do *not* connect to the Nahma River. The slips, full of lumber waste and some nails, can be quite shallow, and the lake can be choppy, so getting out on the water isn't a sure thing. The resort's **private beach** is around from the slips, by the Nahma River mouth.

The 50 **campsites** are in a loop along a finger that separates the other two slips. They aren't shady, though some cedars dot the area. All have the option of plugging into electricity and cable TV for $10/night. (They're $7 without electric.) Each has a fire ring and picnic table. At the moment two vault toilets — that's two holes, not two toilet *buildings* — serve the entire campground. Two

more may be added. Another hitch: there's no reliable shower. The showers in the rental building haven't been fixed as of spring, 2001. Campers can use a single shower in a cabin, provided the cabin isn't rented. Campers can pay to use private dump stations within a few miles.

About the rentals: only the jet skis come with their own trailer. Getting the canoe to the Nahma River, for instance, depends on whether you have a truck, or whether Mary is there, or the owner. (Mary, the all-around on-site presence, does have a truck with a trailer hitch.)

What does it all mean? This could be a great place to stay — depending on what all you want and need. If you're self-contained for camping, you'd have a lot of plusses here: camping right near Lake Michigan, with a good restaurant and bicycling nearby. The resort is where County Roads 495, 497, and 499 converge at the west end of Nahma. *Cabins are open year-round. Campground open from Mem. Day weekend through Sept.* **H.A.**: call   👫: no extra charge 🐕: call

FLOWING WELL CAMPGROUND/ Hiawatha National Forest

(906) 474-6442. Reservable.

Of 10 rustic campsites (no electricity, no showers), 7 are on the Sturgeon River. This small campground, used mostly by travelers on U.S. 2, isn't likely to be full, making for a more serene camping experience than at bigger, busier campgrounds. See info about the adjacent picnic area (above) for more about this place. *From U.S. 2 at Nahma Junction, take Forest Hwy. 13 three miles north to the campground. 2001 rates: $7/night. Open May 15-Dec. 1.* **H.A.**: call

Garden Peninsula

Fayette, the famous and picturesque iron smelting "ghost town," is toward the tip of the 21-mile-long Garden Peninsula, so called because the moderating waters of Lake Michigan all around it made it better suited for farming and orchards than most U.P. locales. The temperatures are more like that of mid-Michigan 200 miles to the south. Garden's best-known crop today is marijuana — an indication of how economically pressed and alienated some farm families have felt. Don't be surprised in early August if the normally quiet area swarms with state troopers and helicopters confiscating pot.

Lake Michigan is surprisingly seldom

seen from the Garden Peninsula's improved roads. But for people who really like to poke around, the peninsula is a **relaxing, congenial place** — the kind of place where you could be happy for days without going to a town big enough to have a supermarket. Here are some interesting spots, arranged from U.S. 2 at the north to the peninsula's tip.

◆ **GARDEN ORCHARDS.** Sweet and tart cherries and apricots are grown here, but the big crop is **apples, some 50 kinds**, often shipped in holiday gift boxes. The Honey Gold is the apple repeat customers line up for. It's a very tasty apple high in sugar, but with one major marketing limitation. Its skin is so sensitive that it easily shows pickers' fingerprints and bruises on the grading belt. Here gloved workers pick and handle the apples. The **market store** sells its apples, apricots in season, and samples of homemade preserves. **Cider** is pressed on the premises, and jam and honey are for sale. Orchards were common on Garden in the old days. But this large orchard dates to 1978-9, when 5,000 trees were planted here by the late Ed Mawby, a fruit farmer originally from Grand Rapids, and his son, Larry, now a well-known winemaker in Leelanau County. *In the 1950s former school on M-183 between U.S. 2 and Garden Village. (906) 644-2140. Open from cherry season (about July 10) to Christmas.*

◆ **GARDEN** is the peninsula's hub, on M-183 about 9 miles south of U.S. 2. It's a little **farming and fishing village** on the way to Fayette that has looked like a ghost town itself in recent years. As small farms and orchards decline, so has Garden's year-round population. The town's role as an important fishing center isn't immediately evident, since you have to drive down side roads to get to the water. Turn west off Van's Harbor Road just north of town and go down to the water to see the large facility of **Big Bay de Noc Fisheries** (644-2200). It's the only local fishery that sells retail, albeit in an informal way, without a real shop.

Many of Garden's quaint frame storefronts are empty. Cottagers and retirees bring some life to the place in summer. **Village Artisans and Garden Gallery,** an attractive little crafts gallery and consignment shop, sells works by over 50 area craftspeople. *It's open from Memorial Day through mid-October, daily from 10-5, Sun 12-5. 644-2025.* At the small, summer-only **Garden Peninsula Historical Museum,** genealogy, especially French-Canadian, is a specialty.

◆ Lake Superior State Forest's **PORT-**

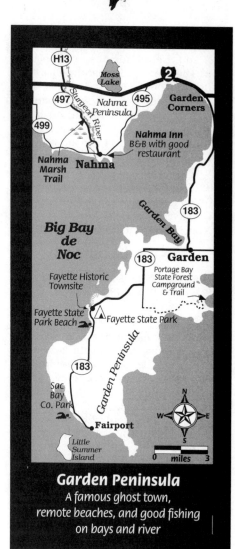

Garden Peninsula
A famous ghost town, remote beaches, and good fishing on bays and river

AGE BAY BEACH and campground (see below) can hardly be beat for their **low sand dunes, adjacent forests of mature pines, and peace and quiet**. The **nifty Ninga Aki Pathway** (that means "Mother Earth" in Ojibwa) begins at the far end of the campground loop. **Interpretive signs** show visitors 15 important plants used in traditional Ojibwa life. Loops are 3/4 mile and 1 1/2 miles. The **spring wildflowers** are so wonderful here in June that nature-lovers Lon and Lynn Emerick make an annual camping trip here a rite of spring. Lon describes it in *The Superior Peninsula,* his book of appreciative nature essays about the U.P. *From M-183 17 miles out the peninsula, past Garden, look for Portage Bay Rd., go 6 miles east on dirt roads to the beach. (That slow drive is what keeps the crowds away.) 452-6227.* &: *with assistance.*

◆ **FAYETTE HISTORIC TOWNSITE.** See below.

◆ **FAYETTE STATE PARK BEACH.** A **2,000-foot white sand beach** backed by low dunes is about a mile south of Fayette

Townsite, in a different part of Fayette State Park, reached by another road off M-183. There's a large **picnic area** and a changing house. *644-2603. State park sticker required; $4/$5 a day, $20/$25 a year.* &: *usable but not to code.*

◆ **SAC BAY COUNTY PARK.** This **beach** and **picnic area** is even **less crowded** than the state park's. They are off M-183 about five miles south of Fayette. The facilities are no match for those at the state park beach. But because it's a bit farther south, there's a more interesting **view**, off to the **islands** dotted between the Garden and Door peninsulas at the mouth of Green Bay. &: no.

◆ **FAIRPORT.** Almost at the very tip of the Garden Peninsula, Fairport is an active commercial fishing village, one of the few left in Michigan. Some old piers remain. Like most fishing villages, it has a plain, utilitarian air. The trailers probably belong to the summer people. Fishermen still in business today typically make good money, to the point that Fairport shows up as a higher-income blip when U.P. incomes are mapped. There's no store or restaurant here. If you look carefully on the drive out here, you can spot some houses and barns made of logs partly shingled over.

Fayette Historic Townsite/ Fayette State Park

This **picturesque industrial ghost town** curves around **pretty Snail Shell Harbor** on a bit of land jutting out into northern Lake Michigan. At its heart are the **great limestone stacks and beehive charcoal furnaces** of a charcoal pig-iron operation started in the 1860s. The silvery, weathered frame buildings and restored stone furnaces have been **preserved as ghosts**, not repainted and spiffed up as if they were new. From the main road and visitor center, visitors take an asphalt path down a **steep limestone bluff**. Here limestone was quarried for building and for flux to remove impurities in the iron smelting process.

Fayette is a peaceful place today, all green with leaves and grass. It's a far cry from its productive years in the 1870s and 1880s, when **soot and smoke, noise, mud, horrible smells,** and stockpiles of materials made one visitor compare Fayette unfavorably to Cleveland's worst slums. Imagine those quaint cabins surrounded by soot-covered children breathing air so dirty wives couldn't hang wash out to dry. (Managers' homes were thoughtfully located *away* from the soot and smoke.) The town boomed after

Fayette's smoky blast furnaces had been closed for a decade by about 1900, when this panoramic photo was taken. Not yet a ghost town, Fayette had already been transformed into a tourist destination from a crowded, dirty rural slum.

demand for high-quality iron escalated during the Civil War. It's named after its founder, Fayette Brown, general manager of the Jackson Iron Company, the pioneer of Upper Peninsula iron mining, based in Cleveland, Ohio. Brown studied how to reduce the tremendous cost of shipping bulk iron ore all the way to foundries on the lower lakes. He chose this place for a new blast furnace because the site had limestone to purify the molten iron and abundant hardwood forests to fuel the furnaces. Iron ore was shipped by rail from the Marquette Range to Escanaba. From there steamships took it 25 miles to Fayette's iron furnaces.

Fayette set production records during its heyday. But by the mid-1880s, nearby forests were depleted. Improved methods of making coke iron and steel were making charcoal iron too expensive to produce. The smelting operation here closed down in 1891. The **hotel** lived on as a **resort** for many decades. Fayette wasn't really a ghost town, strictly speaking, until it became part of the park. It survived for decades as a fishing village and summer place.

PLANNING TIPS. You have to plan a visit for Fayette to be a real highlight. The scenery won't automatically carry the day, though it is a beautiful view across the harbor to the exposed limestone bluffs, especially at **dusk**. *There can be lot of walking here, so plan what to see if your energy is limited.*

◆ *Come early or late in the day* when the slanted light is dramatic and there aren't many people. Sometimes a **morning mist** rising off the harbor gives a soft, romantic, ghostly look to the place. Evening **sunsets** are spectacular.

◆ *Stop at the visitor center.* Interesting, quick exhibits place the Fayette operation in the context of Michigan's iron industry. A big three-dimensional model orients you to the village down the hill. The 5-minute audio orientation is being upgraded.

◆ *Get a free townsite map* and consider buying the 48-page book *Fayette Historic Townsite* at the visitors' center

front desk. In its revised and improved version, it now unfortunately costs $10 instead of $3. The book is beautifully laid out, and contains an illustrated walking tour of the village, essays on ironmaking and archaeology at Fayette, plus one on children growing up at this remote company town, It's a good book if you like to sit, read, and decide what's worth your time before wandering around exploring and possibly getting tired.

◆ **Wander around** and **look inside the buildings**. Sophisticated, honest interpretive displays in the village are based on careful historical and archaeological research. The **hotel**, the **town hall** with its interesting **opera house** and **shops**, the superintendent's house, and one supervisor's home are furnished with satisfying period accuracy and detail, down to the suitcases of traveling salesmen. You really can have that window-in-time feeling if conditions are right and you have learned enough from the exhibits to flesh out your imagination. Some other buildings, like the **office**, are full of interesting and detailed exhibit panels. Read them, and you'll learn about subjects as diverse as the butcher business, medicine before the acceptance of antiseptics, ladies' entertainments, traveling shows, passenger steamers and excursion boats, and labor history. (When orders for iron were slow, workers didn't get paid — sometimes for weeks on end!) A display about **Fayette's children** and what they did is in a building across from the town hall.

◆ *After 11 a.m. the village will likely be filling up with tourists.* You can take a

A Door County bike trip from Fayette

Thursdays in summer a passenger ferry makes a day trip from Washington Island, at the tip of Wisconsin's Door Peninsula, to Fayette. That means bicyclists *could* take it from Fayette to Washington Island and spend a week bicycling in Door County without going around Chicago. Call (920) 854-2972.

worthwhile 25-minute **free guided tour** of Fayette's main street. The competent, college-age guides may well be descended from Fayette's laborers and commercial fishermen. That personal dimension makes history more vivid. These tours depend on park staffing and funding. They're offered in July and August, through Labor Day if possible. The **carriage tours**, contracted to a concessionaire, can be much less satisfying. The carriage top obstructs views, and the ride is horribly bumpy.

The interesting archaeological investigations of the area reveal much about workers' lives and daily activities that hasn't been recorded in surviving letters and diaries.

◆ *Scenic walks* are another attractive aspect of Fayette. The **cedar forest** by the superintendent's house feels like the forest primeval, a dark canopy offering occasional peeks at the lake. In fog the effect is eerie. Sounds of the unseen bell buoy are made louder by the fog. Big old **apple trees** behind some houses are bearing edible fruit by mid-August. You can walk inside the massive stone furnace walls by the harbor. Don't miss the **hiking trail** along the **limestone bluffs** east of the harbor. It's 1/4 mile each way. Four spots offer beautiful **views** of the village and look clear across Big Bay de Noc to the Stonington Peninsula to the west. The state park has seven miles of hiking trails in all.

◆ **Snail Shell Harbor** offers a transient marina (there's no pump-out station but it is a scenic setting for overnights), a boat ramp, and **fishing** for perch and smallmouth bass. It's a beautiful place at twilight.

◆ Two special **events** are held at Fayette. At the **Blessing of the Fleet**, on the third Sunday of July the Bishop of Marquette blesses fishing boats and pleasure boats. **Heritage Days** (the first Saturday in August) features costumed reenactments that might include 1880s baseball, bands, and a traveling medicine show.

Fayette Historic State Park is 16 miles south on M-183 from Garden Corners and

U.S. 2. (906) 644-2603. State park and grounds of townsite are open year-round; the cross-country ski trail goes through the townsite. Buildings & visitor center open 9 a.m.-5 p.m. from the 3rd weekend in May thru 2nd weekend in Oct. Fayette Townsite is open from 8 a.m. to 5 p.m., until 9 in July & August. State park sticker required: $4/$5day, $20/$25 year. &: only interpretive center. Planned for townsite: 2 accessible buildings, smoother paths. Call (906) 644-2603 for directions to drive down to townsite with handicap sticker.

Fayette State Historic Park

Fayette Townsite is only part of the 711-acre park. A **5-mile trail system** of several loops starts at the state park parking lot near the campground. It connects the beach, campground, and townsite, and winds through a **beech-maple hardwood forest**. Terrain is basically flat. Groomed for **cross-country skiing**, it's got to be one of the most interesting easy ski trails anywhere. The **beautiful sandy swimming beach**, 2,000 feet long, is backed by **low dunes**, with an adjacent **picnic area**. It is off a separate drive south of the main entrance but also off M-183. (See above for directions.)

Garden Restaurants

TYLENE'S RESTAURANT is a **classic roadside diner** on U.S. 2. It overlooks the head of Big Bay de Noc in Garden Corners. It's a **friendly place**, favored by a wide variety of locals from the Garden area. Overhearing their chit-chat is most interesting! Currently known for **big portions of home cooking and low prices**. Most breakfasts $4 and under. Lunches $4-5. Dinners $6.25-$11 include salad or, on weekends, salad bar. Sunday dinner specials are around $7.50. Pasties and fresh fish (caught by the commercial fishermen who eat here) are always on the menu. Vegetarian upon request. Desserts are homemade. Sunday dinners (around $7.50) The name comes from the original owners, Tyrone and Charlene. *1/4 mile west of where M-183 heads down the Garden Peninsula. 644-7115. Open daily from 7 a.m. to 8 p.m., weekends to 9; probably closed in winter unless owners find a buyer who wants to stay open longer.* & 👫👦

The food served at the **GARDEN HOUSE SALOON** in the village of Garden is limited to soups, sandwiches, and meat-based dinners with fries. The **prime rib** enjoys a big local reputation. Prime rib dinners (currently about $14) are Friday and Saturday nights, with leftovers appearing in sandwiches ($5.25 with fries). The atmosphere's distinctive, too. Diners are served in the barroom, dominated by a memorable back bar from the Dodge Main boom years of Poletown, near Hamtramck, "the capital of the world," in the words of "Polack Art" Paczkowski. *On M-183 in downtown Garden. 644-2844. The kitchen's open from 11:30 a.m. to 11 p.m., sometimes later.* &: rear entrance   Full bar

SHERRY'S PORT BAR & FAMILY RESTAURANT, strategically located opposite the entrance to Fayette State Park, is one of the many U.P. eateries that covers a lot of territory: ice cream shop, family restaurant, breakfast gathering place, bar. The garden room is non-smoking and away from the bar. Breakfasts are $4.25 to $5.25. Coffee free 'til noon. The whitefish basket with fries and slaw ($7) is the most expensive lunch item. Dinners (BBQ chicken, ribs, goulash) are mostly around $7. For vegetarians there are omelets, veggie pasties, typical meatless sandwiches. *On M-123 16 miles south of U.S. 2. 644-2545. Open year-round, daily 8 a.m. to 2 a.m.* & 👫👦   Full bar

Garden-Area Lodgings

TYLENE'S MOTEL
(906) 644-7163; www.manistique.com
This one-story, 12-unit motel from the 1950s faces U.S. 2. It has a **beach** at the head of Little Bay de Noc across the road. Simple, fresh rooms, pleasantly decorated, with newer furniture, are big enough for a table and two chairs. 2000 rates: $39 for two. Fans, not air-conditioning. Phone in office. New owners Brenda and William Searles moved up from Livonia to run the motel year-round. They bought it from Kay and Jerry Cousineau, who stayed here on their honeymoon and returned years later, after he was in construction in metro Detroit, to find it empty and going to ruin. He knew he could fix it up and urged her to give it a try at running it — which she did for nearly 15 years! They still run Tylene's Restaurant next door. On snowmobile trail. *On U.S. 2 in Garden Corners, about a mile west of M-183. Open year-round.* **H.A.** call. 👫👦: ages 8 & under free; $5/extra person. 🐾: call.

GARDEN BAY MOTEL   (906) 644-2258; e-mail: rimiller@upmail.com
At $44 ($265/week) for up to four people, these housekeeping units on Big Bay de Noc are a **tremendous bargain** for families, especially if they like to fish. Each has a common living/kitchen area and (usually) two small bedrooms. Each door is a different color (orange, yellow, green), accurately reflecting the original 50s ambiance. There's a **sandy beach**, fish cleaning house, **screen house**, and big lawn. Not many trees. There's a sturdy swing and slide set for kids. Some nights Don and Ruth Miller build a **bonfire** and join guests, who love the homey, low-key atmosphere. Being a mile south of the highway makes for a more laid-back clientele, including a steady number of foreign visitors who have this guidebook. Lots of returnees; summer availability is extremely limited, but cancellations do occur. Phone outside. No cable comes out here. TV has two channels, but "you're not supposed to come here to watch TV," says Ruth. *On M-183 a mile south of U.S. 2. Open year-round.* **H.A.:** call   👫👦 🐾: call. No large dogs that shed.

Garden Camping

PORTAGE BAY Campground/
Lake Superior State Forest

One of Michigan's **hidden treasures**. 23 large, rustic campsites in the pines are just behind low **dunes** from a **wonderfully natural, quiet sandy cove** on the east side of the Garden Peninsula — ample reward for giving up easy access and hot showers. This campground fills on summer holiday weekends, some other times in August. Two **hiking loops** are interpreted with info on plants used in traditional Ojibwa life.(See above.) *From M-183 17 miles out the peninsula, past Garden, look for Portage Bay Rd., go 6 miles east on dirt roads to the beach. (That slow drive is what keeps the crowds away.) (906) 452-6227. (906) 293-5131. Self-registration, no reservations.* **H.A.:** wheelchair accessible except beach area. *$6/$9 night.*

FAYETTE HISTORIC STATE PARK
(906) 644-2603. Reservations: (800) 44-PARKS; (800) 605-8295 TDD; www.dnr.state.mi.us/

61 semi-modern campsites (with electricity but not showers, flush toilets, dump station) are on three short loops, near Big Bay de Noc but not quite in view of it. If this were a modern campground with flush toilets and showers it would be full all summer long. Usage is increasing. In 2000, there were still a few spots even on non-holiday summer weekends. But you'd be smart to make reservations for late June through mid-August and avoid a chance of not finding a spot. The **boat launch** and beautiful

swimming **beach** are just about 1/4 mile away by foot trail but a long drive around to a different entrance. The park's 5-mile **trail system** of several loops connects the beach, campground, and townsite, and winds through a beech-maple hardwood forest. *Fayette State Park is 17 miles south on M-183 from Garden Corners and U.S. 2. State park sticker required; $4/$5 day, $20/$25 year. $9/$12 night camping fee. State park and grounds of townsite are open year-round.* **H.A.**: toilets. Call.

Thompson

Currently Thompson is little more than a crossroads at the intersection of U.S. 2 and M-149, the road to Indian Lake State Park and Kitch-iti-kipi. During the last decades of the 19th century, it was a busy fishing and sawmill village. Indian Lake's first resorts developed on the lake's southeast side, near Manistique. Today resorts and cottages virtually ring the lake, but the southeast shore enjoys the nicest setting, with the biggest pines.

Thompson State Hatchery

Here trout and salmon are "reared" — not just hatched, but fed and grown until they're big enough to be stocked in lakes and streams. That's 6 to 9 inches for trout and 3 1/2 to 4 inches for salmon. Visitors can see the indoor incubation room and tanks and the 12 outdoor raceways. Each holds about 85,000 trout or salmon. The necessary cold water comes from a 47° F spring and two 59° F deep wells. In spring and fall you might see fish being transferred to a truck (via a special fish pump; it reduces the stress of handling) that takes them to streams to be stocked. Each year this modern hatchery, built in 1977, produces about **800,000 yearling trout** (browns, steelhead, and rainbow), 600,000 **chinook salmon** for stocking, plus **10 to 15 million walleye fry** released in lakes or taken elsewhere to be raised in rearing ponds.

About 8 miles west of Manistique, just off U.S. 2 on M-149, just east of where U.S. 2 turns away from Lake Michigan. (906) 341-5587. Open daily 7:30-4, weekends and holidays 7:30-3:30. &

Kitch-iti-kipi (Big Spring)

Few natural sights in Michigan compare with the **beauty and mystique** of this enormous, bowl-like spring. Through a

Generations of tourists have enjoyed gazing down into the deep bubbing clear waters of Kitch-iti-kipi (Big Spring) from the rope-drawn observation raft.

storybook forest of cedars and pines, you come upon an amazing, emerald-green spring, oval and jewel-like, some 200 feet wide. Visitors pull a cable on a simple 18' x 20' **raft** to reach the middle, then gaze down through **45 feet of crystal-clear water**. Bubbling up from the bottom is a constant flow of about **10,000 gallons of water a minute** or more. **Huge brown trout** swim lazily around. Lime-encrusted logs, mossy and fallen to the sandy bottom, look like piles of sticks so close you could almost touch them.

The water here stays 45° F year-round, so the spring can be viewed in any season. If it's the off-season and the gate is closed, it's necessary to hike 300 yards to it. Summer is a good time to visit, though **fall color season** would also be nice. This **cool glade** is a delightful contrast on warm days. In the morning, mist hangs over the water and turns the surrounding woods into abstract, mysterious shapes.

Come either before mid-morning or near dusk to experience the serenity of the place. In mid-day it's a popular spot, much loved by children. The water is so green and clear, the fish so big — and a kid of six or seven can make the raft move! One enraptured toddler called out, "Hello, fish! Hello!. . . . I see a *humongous* fish! A see *five* of them!!" There's a pleasant **picnic** and **play-**

ground area and a well-run **concession stand** (open May 15 up into October) with snacks and gifts.

Kitch-iti-kipi (pronounced "KITCH-i-tee-KI-pee") is Michigan's biggest spring. Its name means "big cold water." It is not known where this enormous volume of water comes from. Hydraulic pressure forces the groundwater to the surface. The spring's bowl is similar to other sinkholes except it is connected with aquifers (underground streams). Sinkholes are created by underground water dissolving limestone bedrock to create caves. When the top layer of limestone finally dissolves, the cave collapses.

The state acquired this beautiful place in 1926, thanks to John Bellaire, owner of a Manistique dime store. He fell in love with the place, which loggers had used as a dump. Seeing its potential as a public beauty spot, he persuaded the Palms Book Land Company to sell the spring and 90 acres to the state for $10.

Palms Book State Park and Kitch-iti-kipi are northwest of Manistique. From U.S. 2, take M-149 8 miles north. (906) 341-2355. Open for day use only, 8 a.m.-10 p.m. State Park sticker required: $4/$5 a day, $20/$25 a year. &: only sidewalk to restrooms and raft. One high step onto raft. Accessible raft, improved walkway, and restrooms for 2002 or 2003, it's hoped.

Indian Lake Pathway

The **8 1/2 mile trail system**, part of the **Lake Superior State Forest**, is a series of three stacked loops, permitting short and long hikes. A **boardwalk** through a wetland to an **observation deck** is a highlight close to the trailhead. The terrain varies from gently rolling to hilly. Trail layout encourages **cross-country skiing**, and grooming is now provided. In the developed area around Indian Lake, the pathway offers a good opportunity for real exercise and **wildlife observation** away from people.

From U.S. 2 at Thompson, follow signs to Indian Lake State Park & Kitch-iti-kipi. Trailhead can be reached two ways. You can stay on M-149 for some 12 miles north of U.S. 2 and watch for signs before reaching Kitch-iti-kipi. Or you can take the CR 455 route that branches off M-149 closer to the shore of Indian Lake. Go past the state park. When CR 455 ends at the stop sign and the route to Kitch-iti-kipi goes right, you go left. Trailhead, clearly signed, is in about 1/2 mile. (906) 341-2355.

Indian Lake State Park

On Indian Lake, the Upper Peninsula's fourth-biggest lake (4 1/2 miles across), near Kitch-iti-kipi and Manistique. The south unit of Indian Lake State Park has **pier** and **boat launch** (both ⅄) and a developed **swimming beach**. There's **good fishing** for **walleye** and **perch**. The setting is more suburban, with lawns, rather than wild and natural. Indian Lake is quite shallow and therefore warms up sooner than most Upper Peninsula lakes. The new paved path and benches along the lakeshore are well used at sunset, and a big hit with people who can't negotiate bumpy terrain. Call for program times and topics of the popular **Adventure Ranger** program of hikes, games, etc., offered five days a week from June into mid-August. The quarter-mile **Chippewa Trail** next to the big South Shore Campground (see below) is due to get interpretive signs about wild foods used by the Ojibwa.

4 miles west of Manistique. From U.S. 2 at Thompson, turn north onto M-149; south unit is in 3 miles. Or from Manistique, take CR 442/Deer St. by continuing straight where M-94 turns north. (906) 341-2355. State Park sticker required: $4/$5 day, $20/$25 year.

Bishop Baraga Mission and Indian Cemetery

In 1832 a small log and bark mission was built here by the Jesuit Father Frederic Baraga, the legendary "Snowshoe Priest." He came to the Upper Peninsula, originally from Slovenia, to minister to Indians and founded many missions like this throughout northern Michigan before becoming the first bishop of Marquette. He came to Indian Lake with an Odawa man who had been an interpreter for the British in the War of 1812.

A group of history enthusiasts and the local Knights of Columbus organized to research the mission site by digging and finding sketches of the mission. They built the kind of **log structure** that would have been here. Other characteristic Odawa dwellings of bark have been constructed on the grassy area on Indian Lake. The **wood spirit houses** in the adjacent burial ground have been rebuilt with the help of descendants of those buried here who live in the area.

People are welcome to **picnic**, to walk in the woods, and **pick berries** and sweetgrass, that wonderfully aromatic grass Indians used in making baskets and in decorating bark objects. Signs interpret the site. The **chapel** is used for special occasions but is normally locked. Inside is a life-size wood carving of Father Baraga, done by a local man, and stations of the cross in tooled leather, a gift of local Indians.

The mission is on the east side of Indian Lake just north of the Indian River. From Manistique, take M-94 north through town, but turn west onto State Rd./CR 440 two blocks after M-94 turns north off Deer St. CR 440 ends at Indian Lake. Go right (north) over the Indian River, and in 100 feet turn left onto a dirt road. It dead-ends at the park. Call (906)341-2362 to arrange to see interior. Free. ⅄: no.

Rainey Wildlife Area

There's good **bird-watching** here from **boardwalks** and an **elevated platform** on the northeast side of Indian Lake. Especially during spring and fall warbler migration, **songbirds are plentiful** where Smith Creek creates a slough before entering the lake. The *Michigan Wildlife Viewing Guide* suggests calling warblers into view by standing still and softly going "pssh pssh pssh." There's a good chance of seeing bald eagles and ospreys from the observation platform spring through fall.

Take M-94 north from Manistique and

U.S. 2. In about 5 miles, turn left (west) onto Dawson Rd. In 11/2 miles you'll get the access road that goes north to the parking lot. (906) 452-6227.

THOMPSON LODGINGS

DRIFTWOOD SHORES RESORT & RV PARK   (906) 341-6266; (800) 788-3111; www.wmallory.com; fax (906) 341-8261; e-mail: wmallory@up.net

This **spiffy place** with **500 feet of Lake Michigan shoreline**, three blocks south of U.S. 2, is owned and managed by an avid birder, Diane Mallory, and her fly-fishing husband, Bill. He retired from designing technical training programs for Ford. Driftwood Shores caters to nature lovers who share their interests and love of peace and quiet. Their interesting **web site** details **fishing** opportunities and strategies, and lists **birds** sighted here, including many shore birds and some rarities in these parts like an occasional white pelican, wimbrel, and black-bellied plover. For two weeks toward the end of May, migrating warblers pass through and feed overnight in the brushy cover by the shoreline here. The resort name comes from **profuse quantities of driftwood** that wash up after storms. The sawmill that operated at the mouth of Thompson Creek built a tramway out into Lake Michigan so ships could load lumber without venturing into shallow waters near shore. For half a century slab wood and other mill waste was hauled out the tramway and dumped. Washed back as smooth driftwood, it's good for carving or painting. The resort is a mostly grassy, open area, without mature trees or shrubby buffers between campsites. All **campsites** ($16-$18/night for two; no tents) have electric and water, and lake views. A dump station, laundry, and shower building are on site. The **lodge** (actually a 5-unit **motel**) and two cabins also have sunrise water views, but RVs are between them and the lake. Everyone has access to the **sandy beach**, **benches** and **swings**, and the **picnic area** with fire pits and a big stone **fireplace**. All the five lodge rooms have log or pine walls, handsome snowshoe chairs, two queen beds, and private baths. 2001 rates for two are $52/night, $57 for the two kitchenettes. Rooms open onto a wide veranda with tables and chairs — a popular place to sit and chat. Smoking is allowed there. All lodge and cabin units have a TV/VCR, with free videos to borrow. TVs have only one channel. Cabins (rented for $62 for two, with a 5-day minimum) sleep 5 and 6. Smoking permitted in one cabin. No air-conditioning — it's not necessary.

All guests can use phone in office/ gift shop. Call in winter for good lodging availability; so far, a few campsites usually remain open on short notice (a day ahead, or that morning) even in summer. Driftwood Shores is a sociable place in a low-key way; October's "Survivors' Party," depicted on the web, draws regulars back.

On Little Harbor Rd., 3 blocks south of U.S. 2 at the center of Thompson. Open May thru Oct. **H.A.**: call 👫 : not really for kids. $5/extra person in lodgings, $1 for camping 🐕: call

AL-O-RAY MOTEL
(906) 341-2479

When Pete and Gert Hoholik owned this vintage 10-unit motel, it was a **classic piece of U.P. roadside folk art**: fabulous flowers flanking a memorable neon sign, driftwood for sale in front, a tiny café next door. Then Gert died and the motel stood empty until Gary and Dorothy Middlemiss bought it, and the flowers are back. I haven't revisited, but here's what I learned on the phone. The rooms, quite cozy and none too large, still have the knotty pine and the cozy, homey feel. Phone in office. Satellite TV with 100+ channels. A few picnic tables and a grill in a large yard. Winter is slow, and continued year-round operation is a question. Summer rates in 2000 were $40 (one bed) and $50 (2 beds). Probably no no-smoking rooms.Not air-conditioned. *On U.S. 2, about a mile west of Thompson and 6 miles west of Manistique.* **H.A.**: tight quarters 👫 🐕

THOMPSON/INDIAN LAKE CAMPING

INDIAN LAKE STATE PARK
(906) 341-2355;
Reserv.: (800) 44-PARKS; (800) 605-8295 TDD; www.dnr.state.mi.us/

Two very large modern campgrounds in grassy, rather suburban settings are near the Upper Peninsula's fourth-biggest lake. (See above for the day use area.) The modern **South Shore Campground** has 157 sites with little privacy. But it is right on the lake, adjoining the day use area, boat launch, and fishing pier. It fills on summer weekends and holidays, and sometimes during the week, too; to avoid disappointment in July and August, reserve in advance, a month or two ahead. It also has a big canvas **tipi** and two **mini-cabins** to rent. The semi-modern **West Shore Campground** has 144 secluded sites farther from the lake. It lacks

showers and flush toilets. but has electricity. It's rarely full, and available on a first-come, first-served, non-reservable basis. (For $2 per shower campers can shower at the South Shore Campground.) *A few miles west of Manistique. At Thompson, turn north off U. S. 2 onto M-149; park is in 3 miles. Follow signs to west unit. Or from Manistique, take CR 442/Deer St. by continuing straight where M-94 turns north.* (906) 341-2355. *Reservations:* (800)5432-YES. *State Park sticker required:* $4/$5 *day,* $20/$25 *year. Camping fees:* $15/$18 *in South Unit,* $9/$12 *in West Unit.* ♿: *South Unit & day-use area.* 👫 🐕

CAMP 7 LAKE Recreation Area/ Hiawatha National Forest
(906) 341-5666. 1/3 of sites reservable
www.fs.us.fed.us/r9/hiawatha

Equidistant to Indian Lake and the many resort lakes south of Munising off Forest Highway 13, this developed Forest Service campground has **41 wooded campsites** on 3 loops by a 60-acre lake with a **big, sandy swimming beach** and a fully accessible **fishing pier**, a popular place for kids. A **3-mile interpretive nature trail** begins near the **boat launch** by the picnic area and day-use beach. Fishing is mainly for **rainbow trout**. *Most easily reached by taking Forest Highway 13 north from Nahma, and turning east on hard-surfaced CR 442. From Indian Lake (about 12 miles), go west until you reach CR 437, then go north to CR 443 (gravel), then west 5 miles to Camp 7. Reservable. Camping fee:* $8-$12. **H.A..**: call.

Manistique (pop. 3,583)

This Lake Michigan port at the mouth of the Manistique River is architecturally an unprepossessing lumber and paper mill town. Because it was served by the U.P.'s major east-west railroad long before there were roads, Manistique also was center of a resort area of cottages and small resorts on nearby fishing lakes, especially Indian Lake. Recent improvements like the boardwalk along Lake Michigan and a new retail/ café-condo development at the river mouth have played up its scenic strong points.

Like many U.P. towns, Manistique has a smaller population than it had during its heyday. It boomed in the 1890s, thanks to its location on the Manistique River, its ice-free Lake Michigan harbor, and its station on the Soo Line railroad between Minneapolis and points east. Those factors led seven

brothers from Chicago to form the Chicago Lumber Company, build a great deal of company housing, and create subsidiary industries: a box factory, a broom factory, and a chemical plant. Manistique's most lucrative product, white pine, once poured out of local mills at the rate of 90 million board feet a year. Commercial fishing was another major industry.

After 1900, when the white pine gave out, the fishermen and resorters became a more important part of the local economy, and other industries moved in. Most important was the **giant paper mill**, Manistique Papers. It's been the biggest employer for many years, employing about 170 today. The publisher of the *Minneapolis Tribune* founded the plant as a controllable supply of newsprint. It's clearly visible from U.S. 2 if you look inland from the harbor. Papermaking requires immense amounts of water. The dam and flume the plant built in 1918-20 are what support Manistique's landmark **"siphon bridge"** (see below). Manistique Papers now uses recycled magazines to make newsprint and paper for business forms, magazine inserts, envelopes and such. Until recently the clay coating on magazine stock limited its potential for recycling, but now a process has been developed to remove the clay so the paper pulp can be reused. Call (906) 341-2175 for the date of the annual August **Manistique Papers open house**, when the public can see the paper-making process.

North Pier Light

This **splendid walkway** goes two miles east from the marina and lighthouse pier near downtown. It lets you walk from motels to town and back, enjoying the lovely beach and the view out across Lake Michigan all the way. The boardwalk is entirely wheelchair-accessible. The **beach** is varied — alternately rocky and sandy, in places backed by birches and cedars, in places next to wetlands where wild iris are profuse and ducks and redwing blackbirds nest. The nearby highway is usually not in sight, but always within earshot. **Lakeshore Park**, clearly visible across from the HoJo Inn, has a **picnic area** with grills.

The plain red **East Breakwater Light** is at the east entrance to the harbor and the Manistique River. The boardwalk goes right up to the breakwater's end. It's a simple, cheerful accent to the beach landscape, visible from afar. Walking out on the breakwater is done but not officially encouraged because when wind and waves are high, people could be easily swept off. You must climb over rocks to get out there.

Boardwalk parking at several places is designated by a special decorative sign. Some access points: by the marina; by the three-story apartments behind Hardee's; across from the Forest Service; across from the Colonial Motel; across from the HoJo Inn. No bikes. &

Traders' Point

This attractive complex includes a **café/bookstore**, **ice cream** and **fudge shop**, **antiques mall**, **auction house** with **interesting sales** about twice a month (644-4243), Warehouse Gym with **climbing wall** (341-4496), and residential condos. Traders' Point has an **outdoor eating area** that looks out onto Lake Michigan and across the Manistique River to the cheery red lighthouse. Developers Jim and Ginger Stark made excellent use of the site, once home to coal wharves and the Ann Arbor Railroad carferry that sailed across to Frankfort. All &. For current details on businesses and real estate in this unusual mixed-use development, check out the Traders' Point website, www.906thedoc.com/traders-web.html

Anchor businesses, owned by the Starks and their daughter and son-in-law, are:

◆ **UPPER CRUST CAFE and BOOK-STORE**. See "Restaurants." Also a bookstore. *Open year-round, at least Mon-Sat 9-5. Summer (Mem.-Labor Day) open daily 9-8. 341-2253* &

◆ **TRADERS' POINT ANTIQUE MALL** 15 dealers in antiques and collectibles include fishing lures and cottage furnishings. There are no country crafts. Developer/manager Jim Stark repairs and refinishes furniture on the premises. *341-7500. Open year-round. Mid May into Oct: daily 10-7. Winter hours: Tues-Sat 11-5.* &

***Traders' Point** is off U.S. 2 on the west side of the Manistique River mouth.*

Downtown Manistique

Manistique is too small to attract big chain stores, though fast food franchises like Big Boy and Subway are along U.S. 2. Awareness of tourism and its benefits has led to attractive improvements for a basically plain, simple downtown. Few grand legacies of the lumber era are here.

Cedar, downtown's main retail street, turns away from the lake at the flashing yellow light at Maple. Cedar parallels Maple one street to the west.

Manistique's beautiful two-mile boardwalk goes east from the lighthouse along the beach. In the background: the landmark water tower.

◆ **MUSTARD SEED**. A pleasant mix of books with coffees, chocolates, and local handcrafts. Now that it's moved into the onetime J. C. Penney store, there's lots more room for a mezzanine gallery of **local artists**. *237 S. Cedar/M-94. 341-5826. Mon-Fri 9-5, Fri to 6, Sat 10-5.* &

◆ **MERCADO IMPORTS**. This small, **colorful Latin American imports shop** in Manistique has a very wide selection of **sterling silver jewelry** from Mexico. Its offerings aren't what you'd expect to find in a paper mill town with just a modest amount of tourism. Here are leather handbags, hand-knit wool sweaters from Ecuador, rugs made by Zapotec Indians in pre-Columbian patterns, and colorfully painted **Oaxacan wood animals**. In 1986, on a family car trip to Guadalajara, Mexico, founder Dick Forstner was so taken with the folk art he'd found in towns along the way that he decided to chuck his work in construction in the Manistique area and go into importing. It wasn't easy at first, buying and making deals with his then-rudimentary Spanish. But he enjoyed traveling and kept at it, helped in the store by his wife, Trish, and daughters Ragen and Chloe. He gloried in his life, being able to live on Indian Lake, where he had spent happy summers as a child; working with his family; and getting to know local artisans from Peru and Bolivia to Mexico on his winter buying trips.

Now that Dick has died at a relatively young age, Trish runs the store with the help of a full-time manager, while she continues her career as a dedicated elementary school teacher and goes on buying trips, too. Working in the store is like staying in touch with Dick, she says, and even getting to know him better, by way of customers' fond reminiscences. "Dick loved people and traveling, and shared his pleasure. He's a person who believed in things and did them."

Far from being exploited, skilled artisans in traditional crafts in Mexico are able to make a good living within their indigenous rural economies. *217 S. Cedar, downtown. 341-6111. Mid-May to Christmas: open daily 10-5. In winter, open Fridays, Saturdays & by chance.* ⅄

◆ **FLORAL PHANTASMAGORIA. Antiques** and **works of area artists** are intermixed with **green plants**, **high-quality gardening tools**, outdoor containers for plants, and the flowers of a **full-service florist's** — all displayed with an artist's flair. The antiques and **rustic folk art**, some locally made like soapstone carvings, are things that would look good in cottages. The store moved to a larger, more visible spot on Cedar Street in 2001.

The shop is also the **studio** of co-owner Michele Earle-Bridges, who grew up in Newberry and went off to New York to get a BFA in illustration at the Parsons School of Design. After six years in New York, she and her husband Thomas, another U.P. native, decided to move back to the north country they love. When the local florist shop came up for sale, he decided to buy and run it, and combine it with her studio/shop. Friends from the East Coast ask Michele how can an artist work so far from any happening cultural scene, and she tells them, "I do here what I did in New York: get up and go to work in the morning." She's likely to be working on illustrations for an ongoing series of pet books for Barron's Educational Series. In what spare time she has, she does watercolor landscapes, largely scenes of forests and beaches in the vicinity. They are displayed here. *123 S. Cedar/M-94, across from the bank. 341-6262. Mon-Fri 10-6, Sat 10-3.* ⅄

◆ **CHRISTOPHER'S ANTIQUES.** A beautiful big storefront has room for a large and varied inventory to be artfully displayed. **Antique furniture** ranges from Victoriana to country and oak. Some really unusual larger pieces are typically on hand. There's also **vintage clothing**, linens, **jewelry**, fishing lures, **decoys**, and old **books**. The second floor is now also open, with antiques and **The Purple Lizard**, a one-room **gallery of local art,**. *211 Oak, around the corner from The Mustard Seed on Cedar. 341-2570. Open from April 1 thru Jan 31, Mon-Sat 9-5. From June thru Sept also open Sun 10-2.* ⅄*: ground floor.*

Siphon Bridge and Water Tower

Manistique's most prominent landmark is the 200-foot-high neoclassical brick **water tower** where M-94 crosses the Manistique River. It dates from 1921-22, when the municipal water system was installed. Apparently the presence of the new paper mill led the town to aspire to a kind of urban grandeur in the stylish design of this utilitarian structure.

The so-called **siphon bridge** here was once featured in Ripley's "Believe It or Not" newspaper series, as local publicists still love to mention. Here highway traffic is actually *below* the level of the water the bridge crosses, and the water supports the bridge. The 1941 Michigan WPA (Work Project Administration) guide gave an explanation of this unusual structure: "In 1916, when the Manistique Pulp and Paper Company was organized, engineers realized that a dam at the mouth of the river large enough to supply the needs of the mill would flood a large section of the city. If the shallow river banks were diked to hold the water, bridging the river would be expensive. The problem was solved by constructing a huge concrete tank lengthwise in the river bed; the sides of the tank provide artificial banks, higher than the natural ones. Concrete bulkheads, formed by the side spans of the bridge, allow the mill to maintain the water level several feet above the roadbed."

On M-94/River/Cedar at the north end of downtown.

Imogen Herbert Historical Museum

Writer Mary Blocksma loved the odd stuff she saw and the old-timer guide she met at this tiny house museum of the Schoolcraft County Historical Society. Among the museum's miscellaneous delights she described in *The Fourth Coast*, a description of her travels along the entire U.S. Great Lakes coastline: "a lampshade that closes like an umbrella, an 1883 quilt made completely of neckties, and a piano that got played so hard for so long that the ivories wore through to the wood. 'It's called the Gorsche Piano,' explains my kind docent, quoting, 'When the Gorsches thumped, Manistique did jump.'"

Many crisp, clear photographs show the Chicago Lumber Company and subsidiary businesses (a cannery, chemical plant, box factory, broom factory) that built up Manistique in the 1890s. Advertising memorabilia show, among other things, that Winkelman's, the Detroit women's wear store, got its start in Manistique.

The historical society hopes to get funds to repair the water tower and reopen it as exhibit space for the museum and for area artists. Meanwhile, Luella Olsen, in her 80s, born and raised in Manistique, is likely to be your guide. She's up on all manner of things, past and present. The **log house** in back was moved from the **Hiawatha Colony**, a communal agricultural colony founded in the 1890s by a socialist. The colony developed around a core of disgruntled Civil War veterans who had joined Coxey's Army and marched on Washington to claim benefits. The colonists were interrelated. Some 225 of them lived 13 miles north of town in Hiawatha Township until the experiment broke up in 1896. Most of the buildings were large, communal affairs. The cabin belonged to two brothers who refused to move into group quarters. Other colonists burned the first one, but they were ordered by the government to rebuild it.

M-94/River St., just west of the water tower and bridge. Open daily Mem.-Labor Day, from about 11 to 4. Call the Chamber of Commerce, 341-5010, for exact hours. Donations appreciated. ⅄*: cabin. House is too tiny.*

Roger's Beach

The area's best Lake Michigan swimming beach, unusual for having sand not limestone cobbles, is right on U.S. 2 between Manistique and Thompson. It also has a picnic area. *On U.S. 2 4 miles west of Manistique.*

Kewadin Casino, Manistique

This is another part of the sprawling casino empire run by the Sault Ste. Marie Tribe of Chippewa Indiana. It's got two blackjack tables, two Caribbean Stud tables, and 80 slots. There's a gift shop and combined deli and bar. Free drinks while gaming. Two miles east on U.S. 2 toward Manistique is the **Kewadin Inn**, with The Surf restaurant, where gamblers can stay for $40 a night.

Casino is 5 miles east of Manistique on U.S. 2. (906) 341-5510. Open 9 a.m. until 2 a.m., but table games are only played Sunday thru Thursday from 5 p.m. until 1 a.m. and on Friday and Saturday 10 a.m. until 2 a.m.

MANISTIQUE RESTAURANTS

TEDDY'S PUB & BISTRO has evolved over the years from a tavern known for pizza into a **fine dining restaurant** (the bistro) with adjoining **pub** that still serves **pizza any time**. Pan-fried walleye ($13) is the popular favorite among dinner entrées, followed by New York strip, BBQ ribs, and, on Saturday night and

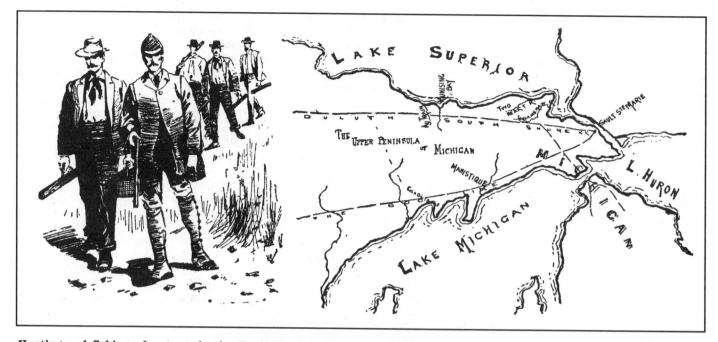

Hunting and fishing adventures in the North Woods were a magazine staple circa 1900. The article, "With Rod and Gun in Northwestern Woods and Waters" follows the exploits of Twin Cities gentlemen outdoorsmen of leisure who take the Soo Line from Minneapolis to Manistique for four weeks of camping, fishing, and deer hunting on Big Manistique Lake, then go to Trout Lake to take the Duluth, South Shore & Atlantic Railroad (top line) for more hunting and fishing on the Au Train River.

sometimes on Sunday, prime rib. All come with soup or salad and starch. For most vegetarians, there are pasta dishes, beginning at $6; strict vegans, call ahead. The four-page lunch menu includes burgers, hot dogs, salads, and specialty sandwiches like Chicken Italiano. Reservations recommended, especially in summer. *On the west side on M-94 at 100 S. Second, on the way to the state park and Munising. 341-8212; www.teddys.manistique.com Open daily year-round. Closed 'til 4 on Sun & Tues. Pub is open to midnight at least. Otherwise open for lunch from 11:30 to 2, for dinner from 5 to 9, to 10 in summer.* &: use bistro door. Rest rooms too small. Full bar. Good wine list.

UPPER CRUST CAFE and BOOK-STORE, a pleasant deli/bakery/café/bookstore, has lots of natural light and a **view of the lighthouse** across the harbor. The menu consists of soup, salad, over 30 sandwiches, and specialty desserts. **Outside tables** let you enjoy the exceptional setting on both the Manistique River and Lake Michigan. An **ice cream shop** is next door. *In the Traders' Point condo/retail complex off U.S. 2 on the west side of the Manistique River mouth. 341-2253. Open year-round, at least Mon-Sat 9-5. Summer (Mem.-Labor Day) open daily 9-8.* &.

Unreconstructed **1950s drive-ins** live on in the U. P. in the three Clyde's, founded

by Clyde Van Dusen in 1949 at the Soo. The Manistique **CLYDE'S DRIVE-IN**, on the west side of town, is open year-round. Each Clyde's still has **curb service** and a classic menu, including a light breakfast (this Clyde's is home to a regular kaffee klatsch), chili, lots of deep-fried baskets with fries and slaw (perch, for $6.75, salmon, and 4 pieces of chicken for $5.25 are very popular), a steak platter, a bison burger, and the famous C Burgers, in many sizes, made with fresh ground chuck as you like it. The quarter-pounder is $2.10. No credit cards. *From U.S. 2 and the west, take Chippewa/M-94 north before the harbor. From the east, take M-94/Cedar and turn left onto Chippewa about 3 blocks after passing the water tower. 341-6021. Open year-round. In winter (Dec-March) 9-7, in summer 9 a.m. to 10 p.m., otherwise 9-9.* &: no because of tight spaces. Curb service.

An area innkeeper regularly recommends **THREE MILE SUPPER CLUB** for its varied and **consistently tasty fare**: fresh fish, steaks, chicken, pasta, and shrimp and other seafood, prepared by the owner-chef. Cajun seasonings can spice things up. Most entrées are from $9 to $15, which includes soup and either a salad bar with homemade ingredients or the popular spinach salad with hot bacon dressing. The place has long catered to summer people and locals. Inside it has a vintage knotty pine interior, going back to when it was a dance destination. No reser-

vations. *On CR 442 three miles west of Manistique. From U.S. 2, follow M-94 through town (it is routed on Deer Street for some blocks) but stay straight and go west where M-94 turns north. 341-8048. Open year-round 4-9 weekdays, to 9:30 weekends. Currently closed Mondays.* &: 2 steps. Call. Full bar

SUNNY SHORES RESTAURANT (341-5582) overlooks Lake Michigan across the highway; very few other restaurants have a **Lake Michigan view**. It's big enough to handle tour busses but retains a personal atmosphere. This comfortable, unpretentious spot has personal touches like wood puzzle games on the tables. Expect competently prepared fare, from breakfast to whitefish dinners. *Closed from Dec. to April 15. On U.S. 2/East Lake Shore Drive on the motel strip east of town. (The Beachcomber is its nearest neighbor.) Open daily from about April 15 thru Nov. 6:30 a.m.-9 p.m.* &.

New owners at **FIRESIDE FAMILY DINING** are taking advantage of the **beautiful interior setting** (it has **three fireplaces**) to provide a varied menu in a fine dining atmosphere with a separate bar. Popular items on the dinner menu ($7.45 to $17, half portions available) include prime rib, whitefish, broasted chicken, and steaks, all with salad bar. Some dinner items are offered at lunch; specials are $5.25 to $6.25. Evening buffets on weekends ($11) may be expanded

in summer. There's also a $6.75 weekend breakfast buffet. Vegetarian by request. *341-6332.Open year-round, except possibly closed in March. Mon-Fri open from 11 to 10, possibly longer in summer. Sat & Sun open from 9:30 a.m. Closes at 10 Sat, at 9 Sun.* & 👫👫 Full bar

MANISTIQUE LODGINGS

See also: Garden Peninsula, Gulliver.

Many guests use Manistique as a base for day trips in the central U.P., from Tahquamenon Falls to Pictured Rocks.

Over a dozen motels are strung out east of town along U.S. 2 for some 4 miles. Almost all are across U.S. 2 from Lake Michigan but offer shore views. Some have beach and bonfire areas across the road. Many motels closer to town have access to the pleasant gravel **boardwalk** that leads east from the lighthouse area past birch woods and wetlands filled with dwarf iris and other wildflowers. Even on summer weekends, Manistique motels seldom fill entirely. You can't assume they're air-conditioned. *Note on locations:* motels are listed here from west (close to town) eastward along U.S. 2.

ELK STREET LODGE

(877) 341-1122; (906) 341-1122; www.manistique.com/ see B&B, Elk St.; fax (906) 341-8573; e-mail elkstlodge@bresnanlink.net

If you want a really casual, comfortable, and personal place with ample common space, you may want to consider this **offbeat and quite pleasant** lodging in what used to be the county poor farm. It does have shared baths, two for each room. It's in a quiet neighborhood a mile from Lake Michigan. "A comfort zone in sports lodging" is how it's styled. Each room has a gun rack for hunters, and there's a whole room for snowmobilers to store their helmets and dry their suits. The website gives a good idea of what it's like.

Years ago Barbara Lamb bought this handsome building and used it as an adult foster care home. Then she sold it on a land contract but got it back. The handsome building's best prospects seemed to be demolition by the nearby hospital. Barbara felt the building had value, and could envision running a B&B after she had burned out on adult foster care. She and her husband, Jack Nelson, remodeled and redecorated it in an attractive, lodge-like style, uncovering hardwood floors in the process. Real wood paneling and wallpaper make for a

warm look. One of the two large common rooms is the **breakfast** and **game room**, the only place smoking is allowed. The other is more of a living room with **cable TV** and **VCR**. The local art club uses the **gift shop** as a gallery. Of the eight guest rooms, four upstairs, not yet decorated, are currently $40 a night for two. Two downstairs rooms are $50. Two connecting rooms ($70) sleep four. No TVs except in common areas. Guest rooms have two double beds. Guests can take portable phones to rooms. Ceiling fans; air-conditioning seldom needed. So far summer has booked way ahead, by February, while fall and winter have been slow. On snowmobile trail. *906 W. Elk, west of the river and a block south of M-94 (Deer St.) as it winds west and north out of town.* **H.A.**: call 👫👫 🐈: well-behaved children & pets welcome

ROYAL ROSE B&B

(906) 341-4886 (also fax); www.manistique.com/

Even other area innkeepers enthusiastically recommend this **elegant B&B on an attractive residential street near downtown** Manistique and the harbor and boardwalk. Hosts Gil and Rosemary Sablack really do provide "the royal treatment." That, together with Rosemary's name, inspired the inn's name. A lawyer built the impressive frame house in 1904 and made it extra-generous so single schoolteachers could board there. The Sablacks grew up in Manistique and can field most any question about the area, historical or current. After retiring from careers in teaching and social work, they renovated the house and added bathrooms so each of the four pretty second-story rooms has a private bath. Not air-conditioned; fans and the location near lake make it seldom necessary. Guests can use phone in the office/gift shop. Direct TV (100+ channels) available upon request. One room ($95 for two) has a balcony. 2001 rates for the other rooms are $85 & $75.

Rosemary taught home ec and food service before she taught English and speech. "I love setting a nice table, with china and crystal," she says. The **full breakfast** is an event with candles and classical music. The inn is furnished with restrained elegance, combining new crystal chandeliers, romantic floral prints in guest rooms, and many antiques. Rosemary bakes cookies for guests and loves sharing cooking tips with guests and fellow innkeepers, including her former home EC student Carroll Harper at the Sandtown Farmhouse B&B near Engadine. She's

following up her cookbook for teens with a B&B cookbook. This is a homestead B&B, though one that affords a good deal of privacy. Guests share use of the **sitting room** with fireplace and Direct TV and a sun-filled **morning room** furnished in wicker, leading to a wraparound **rear deck**. *230 Arbutus (runs off U.S. 2 on both ends). Open May through Dec.* **H.A.**: no

COLONIAL MOTEL

(906) 341-6656

This motel has 22 drive-up units on one floor. Right across U.S. 2 is the east end of the beautiful one-mile boardwalk into town. Guests love the old-time northwoods ambiance: knotty pine, with some Rittenhouse log furniture. Rooms have phones, air-conditioning, and cable TV. Rates for two in summer are $52 (one bed) and $58 (two beds). Reserve ahead for July and most of August, when there's often a full house. In low season that's $38 and $44. At 7 a.m. guests can get a **thermos** of **coffee** from the office, and there are ceramic cups to drink it from. Owners Bob and Bonnie Vincent also own and operate the **Colonial Mattress Company showroom** next door, featuring "top of the line" Restonic mattresses made down the road in Escanaba. *On U.S. 2 at the east city limits. Open from March thru Nov.* **H.A.**: call. Log cottage with 3' door works well for wheelchairs. 👫👫: 12 & under no extra charge. $2/extra person 🐈: in designated pet rooms

BEACHCOMBER MOTEL

(906) 341-2567; www.manistique.com

This older motel's large, enclosed entry area is attractively set up as a **lounge** with magazines. New owners are furnishing it in wicker and serving a free continental breakfast. The 20 rooms, on ground level, are on the small side, with ceiling fans and a lake view. Rooms have two double beds, phones, and cable TV with ESPN and Disney. Rates for two in 2000: $36 for winter weekdays, $40 for weekends. In summer $56 and $60. Next door is the Sunny Shores restaurant. Across U.S. 2 is the **lake** and **boardwalk**, with a swimming beach within walking distance. *On U.S. 2/East Lake Shore Drive on the motel strip east of town.* **H.A.**: call 👫👫

STAR MOTEL (906) 341-5363

The only area motel with **direct Lake Michigan access**. Rooms have nice **views** from big rear windows. 1950s decor is memorably retro with modernistic furniture. Rooms are large and well-kept. Rates for two in summer 2000 were $52 (one bed) and $58 (two beds). Winter rates (on those winters when it's open) are $32 and $40. Rooms have phones and cable TV, fans instead of air-conditioning. There are only a few non-smoking rooms. Cement deer decorate the lawn. Plants flourish in the pleasant central **breakfast room**, where guests are served morning **coffee**. The longtime owner fusses over details. Most of the **beach** in back is rocky, driftwood-strewn, and rather wild, a fine place to walk. There's a small, sandy area suitable for **swimming**. The property goes back a ways and includes birches, cattails, and wildflowers. **Picnic tables**, a swing set, and a **bonfire area** by the beach encourage guests to get out, mingle, and enjoy the setting. The owner's son manages the Hiawatha Motel (906-341-2477) across the road. *1952 E. Lakeshore/U.S. 2. May close in winter.*

H.A.: call.　👪👦: no extra charge. $2/extra person.　🐕: call

BEST WESTERN BREAKERS MOTEL

(906) 341-2410; www.manistique.com

What makes this recently remodeled, 40-room facility stand out are a **indoor-outdoor pool** 60' long and a private **beach**, across U.S. 2 but set away from the highway, by an attractive natural area with big pines. Weather permitting, **nightly bonfires** are held there. Every room has a **lake view**, obstructed by parked cars on the ground floor. Second-floor rooms have a shared **balcony**. Decorating is recent. Extras include in-room coffee, desk, cable TV with free HBO, ESPN 1 and 2. VCRs, bikes, microwaves, fridges can be rented. Some rooms have **whirlpools**. Rates vary from around $69 to $119 in summer, $49 to $99 in winter. The Chinese restaurant next door serves American breakfast. *229 E. Lakeshore/U.S. 2 east of Manistique.*

H.A.: call　👪: 12 & under free with adult　🐕: call

MANISTIQUE CAMPING.

See also: Indian Lake.

Primitive dispersed campsites/ Hiawatha National Forest

Some of these undeveloped campsites on good fishing lakes have become so popular that reservation requests for most-demanded sites are honored in a lottery. Most requested of all is the 8-person cabin on Tom's Lake near Steuben. The wooded surroundings are remote and generally too small for large campers; some camping areas only have one campsite. Toilet facilities vary from

improved to primitive to none. A fat handout describes each area and camp-site, with its fishing, boating, and swimming possibilities. Get handouts from the **Manistique District Ranger Office**. 499 E. Lake Shore, Manistique 49854. (906-341-5666), and contact it in January to participate in the upcoming summer lottery. The Rapid River Ranger District office on U.S. 2 just east of Rapid River also has the handout.

Gulliver

Gulliver refers to both a township and a tiny collection of not-very-old buildings (two groceries, two gas stations, a bank, a lumber yard, a car repair shop, and some churches) near the blinker light on U.S. 2 where CR 432 turns south. CR 432 goes out to Seul Choix Point and Port Inland, passing between Gulliver Lake (almost 1,000 acres) and McDonald Lake (nearly 2,000 acres). Gulliver is a huge township, stretching north to Blaney and the Seney Wildlife Refuge. As a place name for a dispersed rural neighborhood, "Gulliver" encompasses the crossroads, the lakeside summer cottages, and the point where a fishing village once flourished.

The **Old Deerfield Resort** originally consisted of some 4,000 acres purchased from a logging company in the 1920s. The beautiful log restaurant on Gulliver Lake was finished as the Depression was taking hold, and the resort owners sold off parcels of their land, retaining the nucleus at the east end of Gulliver Lake.

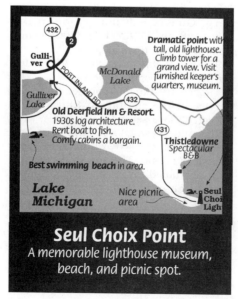

Seul Choix Point

A memorable lighthouse museum, beach, and picnic spot.

A trip to the Seul Choix lighthouse tower affords a memorable view of Lake Michigan's cedar-rimmed shore and Port Inland vessel traffic.

Seul Choix Point Lighthouse

This is an **unusually beautiful lighthouse museum** complex with a **tower** to climb. The Seul Choix Point Light is almost 20 miles east of Manistique. It's 8 miles off U.S. 2 on a dead-end road but well worth the trip. Seul Choix Point is near Lake Michigan's northernmost tip, surrounded by water. The name, pronounced "sis-SHWA," means "only choice" in French. Legend has it that voyageurs, caught in a storm, found safety in the bay behind the point that was their only choice. The light warns ships away from the limestone shoal that extends out from the point's south shore. The 78-foot **tower** (96 steps up!) offers visitors a **grand view,** all the way to **Beaver Island** on a clear day. It's also a good place to observe **freighters** being loaded at Port Inland, three miles across Seul Choix Bay. **Ships come in close to the light** as they head down for Gary. To find out when ships are scheduled to arrive, call (906) 283-3456 and choose the boat schedule option.

When the Coast Guard automated the lighthouse and then stopped staffing it in 1973, township residents worked to have the DNR purchase the surrounding 10 acres for a park. The park has **picnic tables**, restrooms (♿), a swimming **beach** and a **boat launch** on the sandy, protected Seul Choix Bay north of the light. **Trails** go through the rocky woods of fragrant cedars. At the same time the **Gulliver Historical Society** was formed with the idea of collecting local history and preserving the lighthouse complex as museum buildings. Its members have worked hard and successfully to garner

donations, income, and grants for restoration. Today the two-family, Romanesque-style **keeper's dwelling** by the tower has been restored. Most of it is furnished as it might have been when two families lived here in 1930. One bedroom, a small maritime museum, has a remarkable 1/10 scale **model** of the lighthouse, made with **30,000 tiny bricks** and a miniature Fresnel lens.

A second building, the third keeper's home, now contains the gift shop, library, and **video room** with continuous showings of two professionally produced, **award-winning videos**, both available for sale. One is on the history of Gulliver and its lighthouse. It includes film footage of the area when the first road was built. The other concerns spirits believed to be here and at three other Michigan lighthouses. (A former keeper died here; volunteers say he's been seen inside and out, that his image in a mirror has been captured on film, that whiffs of his cigars can be smelled, and that silver laid out on the table has changed position.) The **gift shop** is well stocked with clothing, books, and memorabilia of special interest to lighthouse lovers.

The **fog signal building** is a **museum** with **Coast Guard** and **local history** items, strong on logging and fishing. Here is an ancient dugout canoe photographed for *National Geographic*. The Gulliver Historical Society's next project is converting this building back to a boathouse, and displaying more boats here.

From U.S. 2 and CR 432 at the blinker in Gulliver, go south on CR 432 about 4 miles to CR 431 (gravel). Turn right (south) on CR-431 and go 4 miles to lighthouse. (906) 283-3169. Open daily from Mem. Day weekend (or a few days beforehand) through color season, 10 a.m. to 6 p.m. Donation appreciated. $2 charge for lighthouse tower climb covers insurance. &: fog signal building, gift shop, park restrooms, not keeper's house.

Port Inland/Michigan Limestone Operations

The limestone quarry and Lake Michigan port at Port Inland is at the end of County Road 431, three miles from the lighthouse. It was developed in 1930 by Inland Steel, one of the big steel makers near Gary, Indiana, to provide it with high-quality "quick lime" or calcium oxide used as a flux to remove impurities in steel-making. Now it's owned by Michigan Limestone Operations, headquartered in Rogers City near its giant quarry, a division of Oglebay Norton of

Cleveland, Ohio, a familiar Great Lakes fleet. The quarry's limestone products are now used as aggregates in concrete and asphalt, in steel-making, and as a filler in papermaking. Former uses were as quick lime used in water treatment and, when Pfizer owned it, as a component of talcum powder and pills. There's *no observation area on the property.* But shipping can be **observed from the swimming beach** and **lighthouse tower** at Seul Choix. To find out **when ships are scheduled to arrive**, call (906) 283-3456 and choose the boat schedule option.

GULLIVER RESTAURANTS

See also: Blaney Park

Fischer's OLD DEERFIELD INN serves up family-style dinners and sandwiches (burgers are $2.50, a hot beef sandwich $6) in a **picture-perfect setting: a vintage (1930) log inn** with big stone fireplaces, a long oak bar, and Rittenhouse rustic furniture. Glenn and Marilyn Fischer have the resort up for sale and have cut back the restaurant to dinner hours. Specials change, but you can count on **prime rib** ($15 for over a pound) on Saturday. *It's just off U.S. 2 on CR 432, overlooking Gulliver Lake. 283-3169. Open usually from mid-May into mid-October, 4 p.m. to 9 p.m. Closed Mondays* &: one step

GULLIVER LODGINGS

See also: Manistique, Blaney Park .

Fischer's OLD DEERFIELD RESORT (906) 283-3169.

110 acres. largely wooded, and 1700' of lakeshore and sand beach give guests at this 1930s summer resort plenty of room to spread out. Gulliver Lake is known for smallmouth bass and walleye. Each of the 20 cabins has a knotty pine interior, lakeshore location, and no phone or TV. Half, without kitchens, are rented like a motel by the day ($30-$40) or week. Half are housekeeping cottages, equipped with kitchens and supplied with boats. They're rented, by the week in summer, with a 2-day minimum in spring and fall, for $329/week (2-person efficiency), to $525 (3 bedroom, sleeps 10-12). Repeat guests reserve for summer vacation time up to 2 years ahead, but space is available in spring (the fishing is great in early June) and after August 20. The swimming beach has a gradual drop-off and 2 rafts. There's a playground, basketball, shuffleboard, horseshoes, and volleyball. The bait and tackle shop rents boats. Co-owner Marilyn Fischer is an authority about the area. She spear-

headed the Seul Choix Lighthouse restoration, and is the area's designated loon ranger. *It's just off U.S. 2 on CR 432, overlooking Gulliver Lake. Open May 15-October 15.* **H.A.**: call ⚇⚇ ⚇: no

THISTLEDOWNE at SEUL CHOIX
(800) 522-4649; (906) 283-3559;
fax (906) 283-3564;
www.bbonlline.com/mi/thistle/
e-mail: thistle@up.net

Far and away the U.P.'s most luxurious B&B— in an elegantly simple way — Thistledowne was designed as a contemporary inn to take advantage of its location on a sandy bay a few miles north of the lighthouse at Seul Choix Point. The architecture frames fine views and fills the house with natural light. The ground-floor guest rooms have gas fireplaces and private decks with access to Lake Michigan. The upper room has a good view of the bay and, in the distance, the lighthouse. All guest rooms ($195/night) have two-person whirlpool tubs, a TV/VCR (with 300 videos but just two channels), a sitting area, and queen beds. The spectacular tower room, used by all, has windows all around, with a wide bay view of Port Inland's freighters. The telescope lets you zero in on eagles or the distant Beaver archipelago. A sofa and desk make it a fine reading area. Downstairs, a full breakfast is served in the bayview breakfast room. The cozy Iroquois Room, where complimentary cocktails and hors d'oeuvres are served, opens onto a deck that leads to the shoreside gazebo.

After retiring from his job as residence hall director at the University of Michigan, innkeeper Bob Hughes decided to use his skills but on a somewhat smaller scale in designing the inn with his dream kitchen and separate quarters. He incorporated ideas gleaned from his years of travel with the U-M Men's Glee Club (he loves to cook, and likes to change table settings daily), and furnished the inn with books and art from his travels abroad. Reserve well ahead (from January to March) for specific dates — up to a year for color season. *6 miles southeast of Gulliver via CR 432 and Seul Choix Road. Open from May thru Oct.* **H.A.**: one guest room

---

Keep in mind that all prices and hours of operation are subject to change. Lodging rates vary with supply and demand and are usually higher for special events.

The Marquette Range

FOR WELL OVER a hundred years, **Marquette** has reigned as "Queen City of the North" – of Upper Michigan, at any rate. To a visitor it feels **more cosmopolitan** than anyplace else in the U.P., with far less local color and U.P. flavor than neighboring mining towns of **Ishpeming** (population 6,686) or **Negaunee** (4,576).

Iron made Marquette County the richest and most populous county in the Upper Peninsula. It was discovered by accident. After 1836, when the new state of Michigan acquired the western three-fourths of the Upper Peninsula as a consolation prize in the "Toledo War" border dispute with Ohio, it took years for surveyors to describe and map the vast northern realm above the Straits of Mackinac. In 1844 surveyor William Burt found nearly pure iron deposits at the surface at Teal Lake. That's the big lake seen just north of U.S. 41 in Negaunee, eight miles west of Marquette. Burt's magnetic compass fluctuated so suspiciously that he sent his men out to investigate. They returned with iron ore from rock outcrops. The next year native Ojibwa guided prospectors from Jackson, Michigan, to a place where iron ore was right at the surface, visible in the roots of a fallen tree. In 1847 that site became the Jackson Mine on the south side of Negaunee. It was the first mine of the Marquette Range, a band of iron deposits that prospectors eventually identified as extending some 45 miles from Gwinn, south of Marquette, through the mining centers of Ishpeming and Negaunee and west to Champion and Michigamme.

This beginning resulted in 40 mines in the Marquette Range by 1872. Miners extracted a million tons a year of the highest-quality iron ore available anywhere during the 19th century. The Marquette Range was home to the first of the enormously important Lake Superior mines that launched large manufacturing industries and helped create the wealth of Great Lakes cities from Milwaukee to Buffalo. Up to the mid 1870s the Marquette Range had the only important iron mines on Lake Superior. But by the end of the 1870s its rich surface deposits were becoming exhausted, and the Upper Peninsula's Menominee and Gogebic Ranges to the west were coming on strong with softer, somewhat less desirable ores.

The booming mines created **great wealth**. Though much wealth went east to investors in Cleveland, Worcester, Massachusetts, and elsewhere, a good deal of money stayed in the port city of Marquette and in Ishpeming, center of mining operations. The splendid late 19th-century sandstone architecture and the cultural institutions developed by the area's wealthy elite form the basis of the **beautiful, lively city** that

A rich old mining city and lively college town adjoins red rock lakeshore, rugged wilderness & choice trout waters.

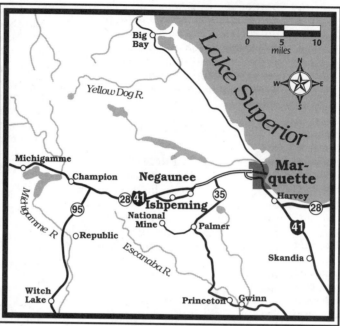

Marquette is today. Early on the area's energetic, politically savvy boosters gained Marquette two economic linchpins: the U.P.'s first state prison and its normal school for teacher training which became Northern Michigan University.

The mines recruited an immigrant workforce. In 1892 92% of all Marquette Range miners were foreign-born. The 1900 census showed Marquette County's foreign-born to come mainly from Great Britain (23%, represented by Cornish and some Irish), Finland (22%), Canada (20%), and Sweden (18% — Norwegians were included as part of Sweden at the time). Finnish immigration peaked in 1910, while Italian immigrants became a very large part of the ethnic mix between 1900 and 1920.

For the first and second immigrant generations, ethnic rivalry was typical, intensified by employment practices within the mines. Lumber camps were another important employment source, especially for French-Canadians. Indians intermarried with Marquette-area pioneers and later arrivals. One of Marquette's richest men, Louis Kaufman, was very proud of his Ojibwa ancestry. Today ethnic cultures, accents, homestyle cuisines, and genes have blended into a distinctive regional culture, and individual people with unusual backgrounds. A blond Finn and a dark Italian, for instance, may have dark-haired, pale-complected kids. The Cornish Methodists were at the top of the social ladder in mining towns (in Marquette the Episcopalians and Presbyterians were on top), while the Finns came in at the bottom and can be quite earthy. Those were the later Finnish immigrants, with more radical politics, the so-called "hall Finns," in contrast to the "church Finns," the equal of any Lake Wobegon Lutheran church woman in reticence and propriety. **Regional food specialties** aren't only pasties, a Cornish introduction. A Marquette-area food is cudighi (pronounced "COULD-ih-GI"), a spicy Italian pork sausage patty served on a bun with tomato sauce. Scandinavians developed winter sports and introduced Heikki Luunta (HEY-kee LOON-tuh), the Finnish snow god, now part of the local culture.

The Depression reduced mining employment. So did mechanization. After World War II, the underground mines started closing, replaced by huge open-pit mines using new techniques to extract small percentages of ore from vast masses of rock. Two of these newer open-pit mines, the Empire and Tilden mines near Palmer south of Negaunee, are still going — sort of. They employ a well-paid work force of 1,800 — an important component of the local economy. Mining operations were temporarily suspended in spring of 2001 because of the steel glut on the world market. The North American steel industry has been hurt badly by imports of semi-finished slab steel produced by countries from Asia to India and Brazil. (Automakers and other steel customers love the cheap steel, because they can manufacture their products for less.) On the very day suspension of operations at the Empire mine was announced, President Bush said he would seek restrictions on imports of cheap steel in the interests of national defense. So ore trains may again chug through Marquette to the ore dock near Presque Isle Park. It's an impressive spectacle, watching them back their cars out an ore dock extending 1,200 feet into Marquette Bay to deposit their heavy loads in waiting freighters.

Marquette County's population has been declining, from 74,101 in 1980 to 70,887 in 1990 and 64,634 in 2000. The 1995 closing of **K. I. Sawyer Air Force Base**, an B-52 base in Gwinn, 20 miles south of Marquette, has been a big blow to the area. With 6,000 people, it was the equivalent of Upper Michigan's fourth largest city. Sawyer meant more students at NMU, more skiers at Marquette Mountain, more kids in local schools. That shock ended any complacency on the part of local civic leaders. So far the county's K. I. Sawyer Development Department has found 63 businesses and agencies to occupy former Air Force space, with almost a thousand jobs. These include American Eagle's regional aircraft maintenance facility (247 full-time-equivalent jobs), a Louisiana Pacific sawmill (170 jobs) and CAN customer call center for a long-distance reseller (116 jobs). Sawyer International Airport uses some of the giant runways for Northwest/Mesaba and Midwest/Skyway feeder flights. Delphi Automotive Systems has a cold-weather test track. The Sault Tribe Property Management rents apartments in Air Force housing. Don Curto, owner of Marquette's New York Deli, started a conference center and restaurant in the former Bachelor Officers' Quarters. Aluminum extruders, potato processors, truckers, a day care center, veterinarians, psychologists — it's quite a varied array of tenants.

The chambers of commerce of Marquette and Ishpeming/Negaunee now work together as Lake Superior Community Partnership. Tourism, outdoor recreation, and visitor attractions are taken more seriously as an important part of marketing the area, not only to visitors but to businesses that might want to locate in the area.

The future of the iron mines, especially the Empire Mine, has become precarious as it becomes harder and harder to find handy space near the mines to put the immense overburden removed to get to the low-grade ore. Anyone driving east on U.S. 41 a few miles east of Champion can notice, on the distant horizon to the right (south), the stepped terraces of mine tailings. It's an impressive, totally unnatural sight akin to ancient earthworks; the *DeLorme Michigan Atlas* shows the extent of the mines and their tailings as big white blobs on a part of the map that's otherwise green. In Ishpeming, Suicide Hill, the venerable local ski and ski jump hill, is being relocated because CCI owns the land and needs it as a fill site.

The mines' continuing need for more and more land — a "desperate move by a dying industry," critics say — has become a hot political and legal issue. Mine employment has been a huge part of the area's psychic heritage, and the vast mining lands (and timber lands, too) are open to all for fishing and hunting under the Forest Reserve Act, in exchange for reduced taxation. Here and all over the western U.P., having so much seemingly public recreational land has, up to now, made people complacent about the reality that circumstances could change and the landowners could develop their land some other way. Now, with the loss of beloved spots like

Suicide Hill, and threats to Marquette's Presque Isle area in the not-too-distant past, it's easier for environmental groups to get some measure of public support. The **U.P. Environmental Coalition** has sued to prevent Cleveland-Cliffs Iron from filling in a lake. If it can't, CCI is threatening to close the Empire Mine. The head of the Coalition, NMU history professor Jon Saari, thinks that one factor in CCI's disposal strategy is to keep from piling up overburden in the same places, which could make Michigan's high point an artificial hill rather than Mount Arvon, none too high at 1,850 feet.

Despite the Marquette area's many touristic attractions, its economy has never been geared to tourism. Employment in the mines and in big bureaucracies, from the university and prison to government and the regional Marquette General Hospital, has been too good to encourage people to take up poorly paid, seasonal work in tourism. Local people generally tend to guard their favorite places from outsiders. (Perhaps this is an extension of passionate trout fishermen's secretiveness.) They underpublicize their publicly owned natural treasures — a striking contrast to the friendly sharing and local pride that's so striking in most of the western Upper Peninsula. That's beginning to change as local business leaders seek to diversify and build on their strengths, namely outdoor recreation close at hand. A nationally known planner led a symposium recently and offered some blue-sky possibilities that could make good sense, like Finnish telecommunications giants like Nokia setting up U.S. subsidiaries based in Marquette. After all, the city is already home to Carl Pellonpaa's "Finland Calling," **America's only Finnish-language TV show.**

A big part of the Marquette area's special charm is the way it intimately juxtaposes its twin sides of wilderness and relative sophistication. This old city, with its visual elegance, offers sophisticates more fine dining, entertainment, culture, and shopping than anywhere else in the Upper Peninsula. The steady flow of travelers across the U.P. along U.S. 41/M-28 provides customers not just for Marquette's revitalized downtown and its Third Street campus shopping area, but for a growing number of gift shops and galleries in Ishpeming, Negaunee, and the former mining village of Michigamme.

At the same time, great expanses of choice wild terrain begin right at the city's edge: to the north towards Big Bay, to the west (especially past Ishpeming), and to the south, where the upper reaches of the long Escanaba River challenge trout fishermen. Within minutes of town there are craggy granite outcrops of the Canadian Shield, celebrated trout streams, and rocky Lake Superior shoreline. "Come discover how civilized our wilderness can be" is the new motto of the combined area chamber of commerce and economic development organization, the Lake Superior Community Partnership.

Area visitor highlights include:

◆ Marquette's **museums, shops, restaurants, historic architecture**, and lakeshore **bike trail** and and parks.

◆ the rugged, rocky, and beautiful Lake Superior shoreline and inland streams and waterfalls between Marquette and Big Bay.

◆ mining-related sights including the awesome Tilden Mine tour, the outstanding Michigan Iron Industry Museum, the Presque Isle ore dock in operation, and the townscapes of Ishpeming and Negaunee.

◆ dogsledding opportunities and North America's leading mid-range dogsled race.

◆ wild, rugged country around Van Riper State Park, Craig Lake State Park, the McCormick Wilderness, and the Huron Mountains, where moose are thriving and might be glimpsed

TO FIND OUT MORE: For questions or to have local info mailed, including a helpful Marquette County Visitors' Guide with complete lodgings listings, attractions, events, and more, call **MARQUETTE COUNTRY CONVENTION & VISITORS' BUREAU**, (800) 544-4321 or visit www.marquettecountry.org. . . . The county-wide chamber of commerce/economic development group, **LAKE SUPERIOR COMMUNITY PARTNERSHIP** (888-578-6489) has a website, www.marquette.org A knowledgeable office staff may be able to field questions that tourism people can't. . . . The helpful new website of the **CITY of MARQUETTE**, including parks and camping info, is www.mqtcty.org.. . . The best place to pick up printed info about the area and the entire U.P. is the beautiful **MICHIGAN WELCOME CENTER** on U.S. 41/M-28 between Harvey and Marquette just east of town. It's open daily from 9 to 5, to 6 in summer. Call (906) 249-9066. . . . For local perspective, visit *Marquette Monthly* magazine's website, **www.mmnow.com** or look for a copy when you're in the area. . . .Some **BIG BAY** businesses are on the web at www.portup.com/bigbay/hmo/home.html

PUBLIC LAND: The **Escanaba River State Forest** is the managing agency for most of the public land in Marquette County, including the Little Presque Isle area, the Yellow Dog Plains,

The discovery of iron ore at Teal Lake in Negaunee in 1847 created the port of Marquette. This 1870 view shows ships being loaded at the ore dock in Marquette Harbor, with a memorial Civil War cannon at the left. Photographer B. F. Child documented the iron towns and wilderness; his photos live on in Superior View, photographer Jack Deo's archive/shop in downtown Marquette. Today iron mining faces an uncertain future — and Marquette County is responding pro-actively to the challenge.

some land east of Van Riper State Park, and the Escanaba River watershed around Gwinn. Some prime trout fishing waters are on this state land and in the Van Riper and Craig Lake state parks. The main **DNR** and **state forest office** is in Gwinn at 410 West M-35 (906-346-9201), with **field offices** in Ishpeming at 1985 U.S. 41 West just west of Westwood High (906-485-1031) and in Marquette (906-249-1497). Offices are open weekdays from 8 to 5. . . . The 17,000-acre **McCormick Wilderness** is part of the **Ottawa National Forest**, managed by its Kenton office (906-852-3500).

GUIDES, TOURS and RENTALS: Fishing in the Marquette area is famous. **CARPENTER'S SPORTING GOODS** in downtown Marquette (906-223-6330; www.carpentersoutdoor.com)

is a source of **fishing guides**. One guide is Brad Petzke (www.riversnorth.net). . . . Licensed charter boats can take anglers to **Stannard Rock**, famed for prodigious lake trout catches, and other places on Lake Superior. **KIMAR'S RESORT** (906-892-8277) in Shelter Bay has half- and full-day Lake Superior charters. **UNCLE DUCKY CHARTERS** in Marquette (906-228-5447; 906-228-307-; ww.uncleducky.com) offers deep-sea trolling, Stannard Rock trips, and inland fishing trips, plus lighthouse cruises to the distant Huron Islands. For a fuller current list of area **charters on rivers, inland lakes**, and Lake Superior, contact Marquette Country CVB (800-544-4321). . . . Bear hunting, deer hunting, upland game birds, trout fishing— you name it, if it's in the Big Bay/Yellow Dog watershed/McCormick Wilderness area, Big Bay native Jeff Ten Eyck and his **HURON BAY OUTFITTERS** (906-345-9265 or 345-9552) will take you there from May or June thru Novembe, satisfaction guaranteed. His half-day Big Bay-area waterfall tours ($35/person including lunch, appropriate poetry, and nature lore) are almost legendary. His company leads day trips and guided camping trips in the McCormick Wilderness and Huron Mountains area. An extra plus: handicap access is outstanding for many kinds of expeditions; one partner uses a wheelchair and goes just about everywhere. . . . Martha Bush and Ken Baker, proprietors of the Little Tree Cabins in Big Bay, and their children have a **FAMILY GUIDE SERVICE** (906-345-9535) to waterfalls and scenic spots in the Big Bay area. For a very modest fee they will consult at home over the kitchen table, mark up maps they give you, share tips, give directions, even take people out to area waterfalls, streams, and hiking and mountain biking trails — which are, alas, not easy to find on your own. On trips, Martha can tote a toddler in a backpack carrier. Skis or snowshoes can be rented for 2-3 day trips. . . . A staff of around ten experienced outdoorswomen and men leads tours in their specialties for **GREAT NORTHERN ADVENTURES** (906-225-TOUR; www.greatnorthernadventures.com) in the Marquette-Big Bay area and throughout the U.P. Adventures include dogsledding, kayaking, mountain biking, snowshoeing, and cross-country skiing. No experience required in most cases. These tours often combine physical exercise with rather luxurious meals and lodging. Custom tours and women's tours are available. . . . History buff Fred Huffman's **MARQUETTE COUNTRY TOURS** (906-226-6167) rents equipment and gives tours (on foot, by van or snowmobile, or on snowshoes or cross-country skis) of everything in the area, from mining and geology to Big Bay waterfalls and mountaintops. . . . Kayak specialist **NORTHERN WATERS** in Munising (906-387-2323; www.northernwaters .com) gives guided tours and instruction mainly in the Pictured Rocks area but also around Marquette. It rents kayaks to qualified people. . . . Cross-country skis and snowshoes can be rented from **WILDERNESS SPORTS** in downtown Ishpeming. It's also a good source of local fishing advice. . . . **COPE'S CANOE RENTAL** on U.S. 41 four miles west of Ishpeming, next to Lawry's Pasty, rents canoes for convenient use on area rivers and inland lakes. It's within 15 minutes of the Peshekee and Michigamme rivers and Lake Michigamme, Teal Lake, and Greenwood Reservoirs. Life vests and cartop carrier included with rental. Call (906) 485-4646 or visit www.upsell.com/ copes.htm . . . . Camping gear, canoes, kayaks, cross-country skis, and snowshoes can be rented from **NMU's Outdoor Recreation Center** from office 126A of PEIF (the Phys. Ed. Building next to the Superior Dome). Call (906) 227-2519. Limited hours. . . . **MAPLE LANE SPORTS** in Ishpeming's Country Village on U.S. 41 rents mountain bikes and snowmobiles. (906) 485-1636; www.exploringthenorth.

com. . . . Mountain bikes, canoes, pontoon boats, and fishing boats are rented at **MICHIGAMME SHORES Campground Resort** off U.S. 41. (906) 339-2116; www.michigamme-shores.com

HARBORS with transient dockage: In Big Bay (906-345-9353; lat. 46° 49' 45" N, long. 87° 43' 27" W, long. 87° 43' 27" W) with showers. In Marquette/Presque Isle (906 228-0464; winter 228-0460; lat. 46° 34' 20" N, long. 87° 22' 25" W) with showers. In Marquette/Lower Harbor (906-228-0469, winter 228-0460; lat. 46° 31' 56" N, long. 87° 22' 26" W) with showers.

EVENTS: Visit **www.marquettecountry.org** for details, dates, and a more complete events calendar. Theater, music, and other arts-related events, including popular **LAKE SUPERIOR THEATRE** summer productions based on regional history and music, are listed on the web at **www.marquettearts.org** Advance reservations are a must for the musicals, held in a converted boathouse. *Marquette Monthly* magazine has a good calendar, but you have to sift through the illness support groups and local clubs to find the interesting events. It's online at www.mmnow.com, or pick up a copy at the Michigan Welcome Center and area restaurants, bookstores, and museums. . . . JULY 4 is celebrated with fireworks at **Marquette's Lower Harbor** (which has an **International Food Fest** over the weekend), in **Ishpeming, Big Bay, Michigamme, Gwinn,** and **Republic**. . . . The third weekend in July brings the three-day **Hiawatha Music Festival** (see box). July's last weekend, **Art on the Rocks**, a two-day juried art show in Presque Isle Park, has some very high-caliber work from the area's professional art community. The site has to be one of the most spectacular art show settings anywhere. The unjuried **Outback Art Fair** is nearby at Picnic Rocks Park on Lakeshore Drive toward the lighthouse. . . . Marquette County hosts three nationally known winter events. The 53k **NOQUEMANON SKI MARATHON** starts in Ishpeming at 1,400 feet, goes up along ridges, then descends quickly to Lake Superior. The Superiorland Ski Club sponsors it; visit **www.noquemanon.com**. Non-marathon events include a snow-worthy outdoor art exhibit for the Glacier Glide on Saturday in Presque Isle Park. . . . Ski jumpers from around the world come to the **CONTINENTAL CUP SKI JUMPING TOURNAMENT** in Ishpeming, sponsored by the Ishpeming Ski Club. . . . The **U.P. 200 SLED DOG CHAMPIONSHIP** in mid February, the nation's leading mid-range sled dog race, is the centerpiece of a festive weekend. It's memorable to see and hear the dogs start off from downtown Marquette at midnight, go off to Chatham, and return to the Lower Harbor. Visit www.up200.org.

PICNIC PROVISIONS and PLACES: An excellent produce department and big deli section make for one-stop shopping **Super One Foods** on U.S. 41 just west of Westwood Mall (same side of road) heading out to Negaunee. Better bread, chewy and crusty, can be had at the **Huron Mountain Bread Company** (one bakery is on U.S. 41/South Front coming into Marquette; another is near the Ski Hall of Fame on U.S. 41 in Ishpeming). **Marquette Meats** (249-2333) has a big reputation for sausage, venison jerky, and meat. It's on M-28 in Chocolay Township, just east of where U.S. 41 and M-28 join. . . . In **MARQUETTE**, see Restaurant section for these picnic possibilities. **Babycakes Muffin Company** downtown and **Sweet Water Café** and the **Village Café** on Third Street bake desserts, muffins, and more. **Babycakes** also has salads, breads, filled croissants, and many picnic items. **Jean-Kay Pasties**, on the way to Presque Isle Park, bakes pasties all day long. Mexican takeout at **The Border Grille** is outstanding and vegetarian-friendly. The same owner's **Baja Bistro** in town offers rotisserie chicken and pork plus homestyle sides. . . . In **NEGAUNEE** fabulous pastries, brownies, cookies, and desserts are turned out at **Midtown Bake Shoppe**. See text. . . Good takeout subs and pizza can be had at **Paesano's Pizza** (after 4 p.m. only). It has a deck at the east end of Teal Lake. Paesano's has Italian dinners, too. . . In **ISHPEMING** on U.S. 41 **Ralph's Italian Deli** has takeout pizza, subs, and Italian wine from lunchtime on.

As for **PICNIC SPOTS**, a whole string of waterfront picnic areas are in **MARQUETTE**, beginning at the **Lower Harbor** and scattered along **Lakeshore Boulevard** all the way through **Presque Isle Park**. Another waterfront picnic spot is just behind the **Michigan Welcome Center** on U.S. 41 three miles south of town.. . . **BIG BAY** picnic areas are at **Perkins County Park** on Lake Independence and at the **marina**. Sack lunches at Sugarloaf, Squaw Beach, and Little Presque Isle are another possibility. At some point in the future, Gobbler's

Knob may become a picnic area. The **Corner Store**, across from the Lumberjack Tavern, makes good sandwiches in summer and has ice cream cones. Look for a bear on the porch and a moose on top. **Cram's General Store** has good BBQ chicken and better groceries than it used to. . . . In **NEGAUNEE** a new park on the north side of U.S. 41 has swimming in **Teal Lake**.

In **ISHPEMING** **Al Quaal Park** (see map) has a picnic area and swimming on Teal Lake. . . . East of **MICHIGAMME** the picnic area at **Van Riper State Park** is by the swimming beach. State park sticker ($5/day, $25/year) required. . . . An idyllic little Michigan Department of Transportation park and picnic area are along U.S. 41 along **Tioga Creek**, well west of Three Lakes — almost to the pointwhere M-28 splits off from U.S. 41. There's a pretty little **waterfall**. It's a wonderful place for a driving break before the last leg of a long trip to the Keweenaw or Porcupines.

Marquette (*pop.* 19,661)

This handsome city on Lake Superior stands out as the most affluent in the U.P. In part this is because of Northern Michigan University with 8,000 students and a staff of 1,000 as well as the U.P.'s largest hospital and only teaching hospital, Marquette General, with a staff of 2,500. Also, Marquette is the commercial center for the central U.P. and the Upper Peninsula administrative center for a host of state offices.

Marquette's historic **downtown**, on a steep hill just west of the **harbor is among Michigan's most memorable**. It is anchored by the **spectacular five-story Marquette County Savings Bank** at Front and Washington with its granite columns and clock tower. Locally quarried brownish-red sandstone (the brownstone of New York and Boston townhouses) gives Marquette buildings a look of stability and stature. Downtown Marquette is one of Upper Michigan's healthiest. **Interesting shops** are along the main street, Washington. More specialty shops are scattered along Third east of the NMU campus. Just northeast of downtown, **impressive historic homes** line East Ridge, East Arch, Michigan, and Ohio streets.

Many professional artists make their homes in Marquette, drawn by the natural beauty and the low cost of living. Their works are much in evidence in galleries, shops, and restaurants around town. The long winters and the self-sufficiency and geographical isolation foster their creativity, though they're no strangers to the art scenes in cities near and far. (Many U.P. residents are well traveled.)

The city is built in an area of rocky outcrops that at places create **dramatic** **100-foot-high formations and cliffs**. The city rises sharply from Lake Superior, affording **beautiful views of Presque Isle harbor and Marquette Bay**. Views are punctuated by dramatic landmarks: the **ore docks**, the old red **lighthouse,** and **Presque Isle Park**, a beautiful peninsula park whose craggy red rocks and tall pines jut out into Lake Superior.

The natural crescent-shaped harbor at downtown's eastern edge is the reason for the town's location. In 1857 the first of a succession of long docks were built to ferry iron ore out to ships waiting in Marquette Bay. This iron played a major part in industrializing America. Today iron is still being shipped from Marquette. It takes three or four trains, each with 120 cars, to fill a typical vessel with 20,000 to 30,000 tons of taconite pellets, a concentrated form of iron ore. These pellets go to make steel in Sault Ste. Marie, Ontario, Cleveland, or Dearborn. Today only the northern dock off Lakeshore Boulevard is used. The southern ore dock downtown hasn't been used for decades. These are giant structures rising up above any ship; the trains on top look small by comparison. In 2000 a waterfront development plan led to removing the railroad trestle that crossed over Front Street to the ore dock was taken down. Traditionalists were unhappy with the idea, but removing the trestle has opened up the shore south of the marina and made the ore dock loom larger above the water by taking away the horizontal line of the railroad bed.

Marquette is one of those frontier boom towns that developed because of the money and influence of Eastern investors. In 1849 — six years before the first Soo Locks opened — three men from Worcester, Massachusetts orga-

Seeing Marquette for the first time

All the commercial sprawl along U.S. 41/M-28 can induce a mind state of confused dullness and keep you from taking in Marquette's remarkable visual aspects. Here's how to avoid confusion as you come into town. Where U.S. 41/M-28 angles west and turns inland from Lake Superior, **take Front Street** north to downtown. Almost immediately to your right, you will see the small building of the Chamber of Commerce. Park here and walk north into the adjacent little **Marquette Park** where a bronze figure of Father Marquette is perched atop a red granite outcrop. This spot offers a fine view of downtown, the harbor, and the spires of churches on Ridge Street.

Walk north on **Front Street**. Many ornate downtown buildings have been restored a few blocks north, on Front at Spring. You might want to get an ice cream cone or cappuccino at Brew Bakers' coffeehouse, 320 South Front, or stop for refreshments at the 1893 **Vierling Saloon**, 119 Front at Main, whose rear window has a harbor view. Or go down to the harbor and out to **Presque Isle Park** by turning right at Washington, then head north along the lakeshore. (This route can also be biked via the scenic **Lakeshore Bike Path**.)

nized the second iron mining company in the Marquette Range and built a forge. Cleveland investors were behind three of the four large mining corporations that eventually bought out smaller operators and dominated the industry: Cleveland Cliffs, Pickands-Mather, and M.A. Hanna, the nationally influential Cleveland political boss.

Others made big money without having prior investment capital by being in at the beginning of the mining boom. Peter White, the grand old man of Marquette's first half century, came as a teenager to pioneer in one of the first mining expeditions. Then he parlayed 12 years of grassroots knowledge gained as Marquette's first postmaster into a fortune in timber and mining lands, and in banking. He remains honored today for his philanthropic and political support for Marquette institutions from hospitals and churches to Presque Isle Park and the public library.

Marquette's business powers chose many of the leading architects of Detroit, Chicago, Milwaukee, and Cleveland to erect their impressive edifices, according to Kathryn Eckert in *Buildings of Michigan*. Today Marquette attracts architecture buffs with its stock of elaborate 19th-century buildings. **Self-guided walking tours** are available at the Marquette County History Museum. Locals love to tell stories of the powerful people who shaped their city. It's hard to have a conversation about Marquette history without hearing about homegrown tycoons like Jewish merchant princes Louis Kaufman and Sam Cohodas, about the Huron Mountain Club (a summer retreat north of Big Bay so exclusive that Henry Ford couldn't get in for years), about the Cleveland-Cliffs mining and shipping empire, and about the Longyear mansion, the largest and grandest house in Michigan, dismantled, shipped to Brookline, Massachusetts, outside Boston on 190 railroad cars — the number of cars is always mentioned! — and rebuilt there for the Longyears' use.

Here are Marquette highlights, arranged starting downtown, circling back to the near south side, then moving north to Presque Isle Park.

Father Marquette Park/ Chamber of Commerce

Just south of downtown, a **quaint circular rock garden** surrounds a **dramatic red granite rock outcrop**, on top of which Father Marquette, the fearless Jesuit missionary, is depicted as he said

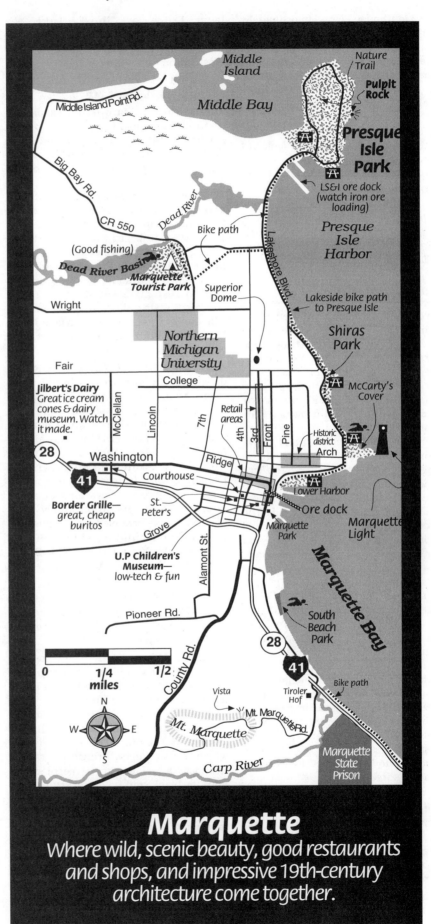

Marquette
Where wild, scenic beauty, good restaurants and shops, and impressive 19th-century architecture come together.

Mass at Lighthouse Point. Unfortunately, the footing here is a little tricky. But the little park and its benches offer a most **interesting up-close view of downtown Marquette** and the Soo Line **ore dock**. This is a fine spot to unwind from highway fatigue, pick up information and advice at the helpful chamber of commerce (now known as the Lake Superior Community Partnership), and look out at Marquette harbor, the ore dock, and **one of Michigan's most dramatic townscapes**.

501 S. Front/Bus. 41 at Rock. If parking lot is full, park across the street along Rock. (906) 226-6591. Chamber hours: Mon-Fri 9-5, and Sat 9-1 from mid-June into fall. &: park no, chamber yes.

Downtown Marquette

Centered on Washington between Front and Third, downtown Marquette is well worth exploring for its **interesting shops** and **striking architecture**. Washington Street has become much livelier in recent years, thanks to new specialty shops. It has a **critical mass for strolling, snacking, and browsing**. The densest center of shops is the 100 block of Washington between Front and Third. Restaurants and coffee bars are more on the edges, up or down Front Street. Two large new developments have brought to Front Street **real glamor**, an atmosphere generally in short supply in the U.P. The **Landmark Inn**, a vintage six-story hotel on Front Street that surveys town and harbor, has become a 61-room version of a bed and breakfast, with several restaurants, a piano lounge, and lots of personal service. Down the hill on Front, another developer has been pouring money into the **Rosewood**, a mixed-use complex of offices, specialty shops, and a nightclub/restaurant, **Upfront & Co.**

Most downtown retailing is on Washington. But the somewhat older buildings along Front Street, going up the steep hill paralleling the harbor, offer the most interesting streetscape. Non-monthly **PARKING** is in three places. In the first two, it's free for up to two hours. Saturdays, Sundays, and evenings parking is always free.

◆ **the lower level of the ramp between Washington and Bluff**. That's up from the main business block at Washington and Front. Drive into the ramp from Front or Third; a pedestrian walk in midblock leads from the ramp into Wattson & Wattson Jewelers on Washington Street.

◆ **the large surface lot behind the main block to the south**, on Main, entered from Front or Third. Take the elevator/stair tower to connect to Carpenter's Sporting Goods and other Washington Street shops.

◆ **the lot at Washington and Third, across from the post office**.

The Downtown Marquette Association administers Downtown Development Authority funds and organizes some downtown events. Call 228-6213 or consult its website, www.downtownmarquette.org

Downtown highlights have been arranged from south to north along Front Street on the assumption that you might want to begin with a Jilbert's ice cream cone from **Brewbaker's coffeehouse** at 320 South Front. It also serves sandwiches and soup; it's open from 8 a.m. to 10 p.m., seven days a week. If you begin your walk with ice cream, you will want to park on the surface lot on Main, just south of Washington, and walk south to Brewbaker's.

◆ **GETZ DEPARTMENT STORE**, a downtown **anchor**, carries brand name men's, women's and teens' clothing and shoes for many occasions, from work and outdoors (Carhartts and Columbia are in the basement) to casual and dress. **Teens love their second floor**, with denim, skate and surfwear, and fashion-forward footgear of the moment. A welcome extra: alterations done in-house. A third-generation family business, Getz has occupied this handsomely renovated building since 1900; it started in Michigamme in 1886. *218 S. Front. 226-3561. Open Mon-Thurs 9-6, Fri to 7, Sat 9-5:30, Sun noon-4. &*

◆ The **elaborate 1883 VIERLING SALOON** has a great view of the bay from its back windows. See Restaurants. *On Front at Main.*

◆ **WELLS FARGO BANK**. The Upper Peninsula's **most splendid temple of commerce**, this 1927 Beaux Arts building was designed to impress, starting with its massive columns and the 25' ceiling of the grand banking hall. The lavish and well-preserved interior is well worth a visit for its bronze doors and chandeliers (aglow from a recent cleaning), its black and gold travertine marble, and its **beautiful metal grilles**. There's also a **display of American money**: gold pieces, colonial currency, and more. Louis Kaufman and Sam Cohodas, illustrious Marquette banking magnates and builders of Granot Loma and the Michigamme Lake Lodge respectively, made this the flagship of their banking empire. *101 W. Washington at Front. 228-1203. Open Mon-Fri 9-5.*

◆ The **NEW YORK DELI and ITALIAN PLACE** is a favorite meeting and eating spot. It's in the historic Harlow Block, built in 1887 by Marquette founding father Amos Harlow of a type of variegated local brownstone "called 'raindrop' for its purplish brown iridescence," according to architectural historian Kathryn Eckert. See Marquette restaurants. *Northwest corner of Front at Washington. 226-3032. &*

◆ **PETER WHITE PUBLIC LIBRARY / MARQUETTE ARTS & CULTURE CENTER**. Renovating and expanding the 1904 library building was the focus of community brainstorming sessions that resulted in an unusual partnership. The public library's lower level is leased to other entities: a café and a city-supported arts organization with gift shop. The lower level is of greatest interest to the nonresident visitor. Here are the arts center's gallery with rotating monthly **exhibits** and classroom space. Call for occasional day-long workshops. The **shop** features art by local artists in many media (jewelry, copper, pottery, book art) plus children's books and some gifts from lines that sell nationally to art museum shops. *Exhibit galleries are open during library hours (see below). Shop hours are Mon-Thurs noon-9, Fri noon-8, Sat 10-5, Sun 1-5. &*

The lower level is also home to **BABYCAKES** at the Library, an abbreviated version of Babycakes, the popular downtown lunch and coffee spot. Here it serves scones, croissants, and muffins ($1.25); coffee, milk, juice, and more; a changing selection of soups, salads, and sandwiches (soup and half a sandwich is $3.25); and healthy after-school snacks like "ants on a log" (celery sticks with cream cheese and raisins) for 50¢. *226- 4326. Mon-Thurs 9-8, Fri 9-5, Sat 10-4. Closed Sun.* ⅄

Upstairs, in the library, visitors may enjoy seeing the **colorful children's room**, designed by children with a Lake Superior theme. Changing monthly exhibits are in the Huron Mountain Club Gallery. It was funded with a $50,000 gift from the extremely wealthy summer people at the exclusive and controversial enclave north of Big Bay, in an apparent move to win local support.

In 1904, benefactors of this grand library chose as a building material smooth white Indiana limestone, made fashionable during the Chicago world's fair of 1893. That architectural choice marked the demise of local red sandstone that now makes historic Marquette seem so handsome, earthy, and distinctive. The local newspaper noted in 1904 that the "beautiful whiteness. . . . has a distinctive air that would have been hopelessly lost had Lake Superior sandstone been used." *Front entrance is on Front just south of Ridge. Rear entrance is off Ridge. Library phone: 228-9510. Library hours: Mon-Thurs 9-9, Fri 9-6, Sat 10-5, Sun 1-5. Arts Center phone 228-0472.* ⅄: *rear entrance.*

◆ **RECYCLED ARTS** serves up an appealing, well organized mix of vintage clothing, antique furniture and "smalls", and crafts using recycled things. *110 W. Washington. 226-7775. www.recycledarts.comserves*

◆ **MICHIGAN FAIR** features an attractive selection of gifts of Michigan: shirts, candles, books, and pantry foods. Some examples: Norm Brumm's copper enamel, Michigan-theme tiles from Pewabic in Detroit, American Spoon jams and sauces, Mucky Duck mustard, Holland bowls, and shirt. *114 W. Washington. 226-3894. Open at least Mon-Fri 10-5:30, Sat to 5. In summer & Dec, also open Sun 12-4 and evenings.* ⅄

◆ **WATTSON & WATTSON JEWELERS** draws visitors with a **mine-like, walk-through exhibit** about the old Ropes Gold Mine in nearby Ishpeming. At this full-range jewelry store, a window looks

This splendid 1894 brick and stone building on Washington Street was long Marquette's city hall. It's one of many extraordinary downtown buildings here, a reflection of the great wealth created by iron mining. Local red sandstone (also called brownstone), favored by the nation's leading architects in the 1880s, gives them an earthy presence.

onto the back workshop where three jewelers work designing pieces, casting them using the lost wax process, setting stones, making repairs, and more. Another window looks onto the room where buffing and polishing takes place. The store's supply of Ropes gold is gone, but 14 karat gold is used in jewelry of regional interest: pins shaped like the U.P., tiny mosquitoes, and such. There's now a rock room like a museum store, with geodes, fossils, wind chimes made of agates, and other mineral items. Fossils led to a striking new curiosity, a **50,000-year-old fossilized skeleton of a Siberian cave bear**, over 6' high. *118 W. Washington. 228-5775. Open Mon-Thurs 10-6, Fri to 7, Sat to 5. From May thru Dec also open Sundays noon to 4.* ⅄

◆ **TOWN FOLK GALLERY** features accomplished **creations made out of vintage textiles** by owner Sandy Belt. Also for sale are the kind of vintage linens and furniture that inspire her, and contemporary "folk" art by other artists, including seven makers of Santas. Some of Sandy's patterns have been nationally publicized and distributed, beginning when she made dolls. (She no longer does.) Lately she's been using old buttons and bits of chenille bedspreads and other fabric as appliqué and accents, in one-of-a-kind pillowcases, jackets, and handbags embellished in a slightly funky style. She works on them while she minds the store. This is the third and last location for her gallery. If it doesn't work out, she'll still be producing — she has reps in upper-end handcraft retailing — so check out her website, **www.townfolkgallery.com** *121 W. Washington. 225-9010. Open Mon-Fri 10-5:30, Sat 10-5.* ⅄

◆ **BOOK WORLD**. This lively, well-stocked general book shop, part of a chain based in Appleton, Wisconsin, occupies what used to be the Nordic Theater. It has a good regional section, strong nature and children's books, and the best magazine selection in town. It also stocks premium cigars and imported cigarettes. *136 W. Washington. 228-9490. Open Mon-Fri 9-9 , Sat & Sun 9-5* ⅄

◆ **DONCKERS CANDY & GIFTS** goes back to 1896.The **vintage interior** is from around 1917. **Homemade fudge** is the big seller here, but a big variety of candy is sold by the pound, with a quar-

The Hiawatha Traditional Music Festival
Held at Tourist Park for 3 days the third weekend in July, this entertaining festival, run by the Hiawatha Music Co-op, has grown into a very popular, 3-stage event since starting in 1980. The eclectic music mix now includes blues and electric bands in addition to folk music. One tent has a **dance** floor. **Lectures and workshops** cover lots of ground: harmony singing, fiddle, mandolin, guitar, storytelling, crafts, songwriting, and more. "It's a wonderful environment where kids can wander around with their friends and learn new things," enthuses a mother. Each performing group does something for kids; the kids' tent has new activities every 2 hours. Weekend ticket prices in 2001: $30 advance, $40 gate, $2 for children 5-12.

Call (906) 226-8575 or visit www.portup.com /~hiawatha/festival.html

ter-pound minimum purchase: everyday bridge mix, sugar-free candy, upper-end chocolate truffles from Vermont, 18 barrels of hard wrapped candies, and realistic **"Lake Superior candy pebbles"** that enchant children. (They come from Colorado.) For nostalgic Detroiters, there's Sanders hot fudge. 625 square feet of gift basket items are in the back. *137 W. Washington. 226-6110. Mon-Fri 9:30-5:30, Sat 10-5.* ♿

◆ **SUPERIOR VIEW STUDIO.** Commercial photographer Jack Deo has a studio and gallery that sells his own landscapes and prints from his **vast archive of historic U.P. photos**. He started acquiring them in 1977 from old photo studios that had gone out of business. The historic photographs started increasing exponentially in 1997 when Jack opened his seasonal Mackinaw City branch, Views of the Past, in the Crossings, Bill Shepler's elaborate shopping and restaurant courtyard. That store exposed his business to thousands of people interested in donating, trading, or selling their own historic photographs from all over Michigan. Now Jack spends most of every winter cataloging the collection, presented in binders by category: maritime, hunting and fishing, trains, humorous, Michigan street scenes, gas stations, bicycles, and more. Sepia-toned photographic copies of historic photos are $12 (for 8" x 10"), $18 (for 11" x 14"), but they can be made in any size. It's easy to look up your home town. They're a good gift idea for the person who has everything. *137 1/2 W. Washington, over Donckers. 225-1952. Open Mon-Sat 10-5.* ♿: no.

◆ **CARPENTER'S OUTDOOR OUTFITTERS** is a welcome anomaly in modern America: a fishing and hunting store whose service and selection are specific to its own area. Furthermore, it is geared to a small city's wide range of customers and income levels. Owner Adam Carpenter came to Marquette as a NMU student because he loved the out-of-doors. He came back after an unhappy stint in a computer job outside Detroit when the owner of Lindquist's Outdoor Sport here, where he used to shop, decided to sell. Now he gets to advise other customers about his passions, from **fly-fishing** to **bird hunting**, deer hunting, and **canoeing**. Having a Gander Mountain in Marquette only makes it easier to focus on the local and/or the upper end. Here you can get flies and lures made by area people, Marble Arms knives from Gladstone, and Iverson traditional snowshoes from Shingleton, plus artisan-made gear like

Early frontier photographers: businessmen, artists & naturalists

Photographer Jack Deo sees himself as the grateful heir and keeper of a distinguished tradition of studio photographers who used great energy and artistry to chronicle the U.P.'s development and to preserve records of the natural world. Jack's archive of historic photos began in the late 1970s when, just out of NMU, he began collecting old cameras at auctions. He had a chance to buy up the extensive contents of the mothballed studio of the B. F. Childs Art Gallery, which had been in Ishpeming from the 1870s into the 1950s. There were wetplate stereo negatives from the trip Childs took around Lake Superior in the 1870s, using a Mackinaw boat with an Indian guide. His photos were very much like William Henry Jackson's

famous Yellowstone photographs: the same subjects (Indian life, natural landmarks, lake scenes), the same era, and the same attitude toward primeval nature.

"When I ran into the Childs collection, it was destiny," Jack believes. Everything came together for Jack: his interest in history, old photographic equipment, and printmaking; his central U.P. location in Marquette; and the synergies with his own growing photography studio. That find inspired him to buy the contents of many more studios. A year later, a fire destroyed the Childs studio building and its remaining contents.

"Those early photographers were all artists," says Jack. "They used light and shadow as part of their composition." In one of the most popular subjects, successful fishermen posing with their fish, Childs paid meticulous attention to the placement of subjects and their paraphernalia.

Today visitors to Jack Deo's **Superior View Studio** at 137 1/2 West. Washington in downtown Marquette or **Views of the Past** in the Courtyards at Mackinaw City can look through thousands of prints from Jack Deo's collections. They also include the negatives of pioneer wildlife photographer George Shiras III. Customers can have copies made of a vast variety of subjects and Michigan places. Some interesting old cameras are on display. If there's time, Jack relishes the chance to tell the stories of his photographer heroes.

Frank Signorino's handmade knives and Kim Troester's bamboo rods. The **archery** and **firearms** departments are more upper end (there are also used rifles), and the fly-fishing gear can get pretty sophisticated, with fly rods like St. Croix, G. Loomis, and Sage. But there's plenty of **inexpensive feathers and hooks** to get kids started tying flies, and sale bins for bargain-hunters. Ask about regular three-hour Wednesday-evening **fly-tieing classes**, limited to 10 participants. They are currently $10 for adults, $5 for students college age and younger — bargains compared with downstate classes.

Unlike anglers, retailers have an interest in helping newcomers find fish. Carpenter's offers free fishing advice, a guide service, and maps and compasses.

Adam says, "Fight the fish, not the crowds. That's our philosophy. There's so much untouched up here, if you're willing to do a little exploring, you can be rewarded." His staff is also savvy about Great Lakes fishing for lake trout and salmon. Watercraft here is geared to fishing. Adam points out that his store is also one of Michigan's biggest distributors of outdoors **socks**, including full lines of Wig Wam and Fox River. *131 W. Washington.www.carpentersoutdoor.com 228-6380. Open Mon-Thurs 9-6, Fri 9-8, Sat 9-5, Sun 10-4.* ♿

◆ **SNOWBOUND BOOKS**, around the corner and up the Third Street hill, is a large, well organized, and friendly general book shop (new, used, and out of print) with an **excellent regional and**

maritime section. Michigan and nature are especially well represented, and the U.P. section may well be the best anywhere, with antique U.P. maps in addition to books. This is the place to find first editons of Marquette's literary and fishing legend, John Voelker (a.k.a. Robert Traver, author of Anatomy of a Murder). Book lovers will enjoy the **eclectic, offbeat mix**. *118 N. Third. 228-4448; 800-247-8670. www.snowbound-books.com Open Mon-Sat at 9:30, to 6 p.m. most days except from Thurs to 7, Sat to 5.* ♿: no.

◆ The **DELFT THEATER**, the oldest of Marquette's three movie theaters, has a **nifty marquee** at 139 W. Washington. The entrance is actually in back by the parking lot in back. *Get there by turning south on Third from Washington, then turning east onto Main. 228-6463.*

◆ **ART U.P. STYLE GALLERY and GIFTS**. Paintings, pottery and sculpture by over a dozen area artists are featured at this attractive gallery/store that shares space with a frame shop and T shirt business. Many of the paintings, including proprietor Carol Papaleo's watercolors, are of landscapes and flowers pertaining to the U.P. Handmade gifts are from around the world. *149 W. Washington. 226-6154. Open year-round. From June thru Christmas open Mon-Fri 10-5:30, Sat 10-3. Closed Mon from Christmas thru May.* ♿

◆ **FEDERAL BUILDING/Marquette POST OFFICE**. This big impressive modernistic building from 1936 has some **nifty Deco touches** and a **WPA mural of Father Marquette exploring Lake Superior's shores**. *202 W. Washington at Fourth. 226-9963. Lobby open 24 hours.* ♿: *enter lower level from Washington, take elevator straight ahead.*

◆ Old **MARQUETTE CITY HALL**. Take a look at the elaborately ornamented **Romanesque entryway** and **scrolled iron grates** by the stairs. Nathan Kaufman was mayor in 1893, when the nationwide financial panic closed Michigan's iron mines. In *Historic Buildings of Michigan*, Kathryn Eckert tells how Kaufman, "known locally as a 'capitalist and progressive,' convinced the city council and citizens to issue bonds for $50,000 to build a city hall with local labor and local materials, thereby putting Marquette men back to work." Recently the city sold the building to a private developer who had the means to create an office center. *220 Washington.*

◆ **NEEDLEWORKS** is one of those won-

Why so many professional artists in Marquette?

Christine Saari, a major force behind the Oasis Gallery, explains. First, there's the **quality of life** of a small but rather cosmopolitan city close to **natural beauty**. Jobs aren't plentiful, but the **low cost of housing** makes it easier for artists to live off their art if they do national shows and have national gallery reps. Second, **Northern Michigan University's high-caliber art department** employs some artists and trains others. Third, Christine says, "The **isolation and climate** require people to draw from their **inner resources**. Creativity can flourish. Nature is all around you." Some artists (and writers) work better when spending their daily lives in isolated, sparsely populated geographical edge zones, without constant comparisons with the mainstream, intellectual, or academic art or literary worlds, their politics and connections. "Artists up here do travel and get their culture fix," says Nheena Weyer Ittner, founder of the Upper Peninsula Children's Museum. She herself was one such artist for awhile, selling her wearable art in many boutiques.

derful, helpful, **high-caliber fabric shops** that have become an endangered species in most of America, where women are too busy to sew. Alice Robinson and her daughter, Robin, love to sew and quilt and have time to help. In fact, you can use their cutting tables here to cut out and baste your project. Beginners, fear not! The Robinsons can help you find an appropriate project. The coffeepot is always on, and many customers stop by to get inspired and trade tips on a dull day. Here are **quality cottons** for quilting, and **good fabrics for outdoor wear**: Supplex, Polartec from Malden Mills, berber from Glenoit Mils, plus YKK zippers that hold up. Many samples of jackets, mittens, hats, lap robes, quilts, and wall hangings are on hand, with patterns and books to make them. Every third Thursday from 6 to 8, the drop-in **Thimbleberry Club** meets to get that popular quilt designer's new $1 pattern of the month. Supplies for **silk ribbon embroidery** are the store's other specialty. As for knitting, two stores are on farther down Washington Street. **Uncommon Threads** (225-1124) is two blocks down at 443 West Washington, and **Knit-N-Purl Yarn Shop** (225-0914)

is farther west at 1010 West Washington. *Needleworks is at 219 W. Washington across from the post office. 228-6051. Open seven days. Mon-Sat 10-5, Fri to 6, Sun noon to 4.* ♿

◆ **BABYCAKES,** a popular cappuccino bar and bakery, offers a rotating selection of 80 kinds of muffins and many delicious specialty breads, plus exotic bulk coffees and teas. See Restaurants. *223 W. Washington. Open Mon thru Fri 6 a.m.-6 p.m., Sat 7 a.m.-5 p.m. 226-7744.* ♿

◆ **OASIS GALLERY,** an exhibit gallery of contemporary art in many media, mounts stimulating, **wildly varied monthly exhibits** that may be thematic (the crow starred in one memorable exhibit), or a one-person show, or a group show like the annual high school show. Shows may highlight a technique. Oasis is a cooperative gallery, but not the typical kind intended mainly to showcase and sell members' art. Each Oasis member's main responsibility is to conceive of and curate one show a year, building on her or his own contacts to include works by artists from outside the area, sometimes from as far away as China. Organizer Christine Saari explains that the gallery can afford to show controversial and non-commercial art, like the show of belly casts of pregnant women, because its income comes from two successful annual fundraisers, the Holiday Sale and "Dinner by Artists," in which artists cook and perform for 150 people. The state of Michigan "Green Thumb" program pays a senior citizen to be a gallery-sitter. *227 W. Washington. 225-1377. Open Tues-Sat noon to 5.* ♿

◆ **MARQUETTE FOOD CO-OP**. Marquette's co-op hasn't evolved into the co-op as gourmet store, the way the Keweenaw co-op in Hancock has. Currently it carries no fancy cheeses, wines, or produce — but it's a good place to stock up on healthy snacks, granolas, trail mixes and nuts, juice, spritzers, soy milk, and such for camping, hikes, and travel. *325 W. Washington. 225-0671. Open Mon-Fri 10-7, Sat 10-5.* ♿

Marquette County History Museum

This **outstanding regional history museum** and research archive collects materials on the continuing history and cultural development of the central Upper Peninsula, and interprets them. Its subjects include the **social impact of fishing, shipping, logging, and mining**. Only a small fraction of its collections are on view. It's largely funded by the

Longyear Family Trust. John M. Longyear was an early landlooker from Lansing who found iron-rich land in Upper Michigan and later on Minnesota's Mesabi Range and leased them to mining companies. In this manner he became extremely wealthy.

This museum rates high in terms of **interesting old artifacts**. Don't miss the 1881 bird's-eye view of Marquette and its harbor. Several life-size exhibits focus on key aspects of area history. The audio-enhanced **Ojibwa family group**, designed with advice from area Ojibwa, shows a family, baby in cradleboard, with a cutaway wigwam and typical household objects. Trade goods, traps, and furs are in the fur trading post. You can meet the **Burt survey party**: a realistic representation of William Austin Burt, the heroically unassuming, unstoppable surveyor of much of the Upper Peninsula, with his compassman, using Burt's pride and joy, the solar compass he invented to set survey lines when iron deposits rendered conventional magnetic compasses useless. Burt's lines, run during extremely difficult conditions of bad weather, standing water, insects, etc., have proven accurate over the years. Here is the actual tamarack tree that marked Mile Post Zero, which established the straight, overland boundary with Wisconsin that runs from the headwaters of the Brule River to the mouth of the Montreal at Lake Superior, near Ironwood. Many museum visitors are school groups, especially since there are no weekend hours; the scaled-down street of shops organizes small objects for little people.

Two galleries are devoted to each year's changing exhibit. From April, 2001, through March, 2002, it is "The Lake Effect: Superior's Influence" from ecology to industry to art. An endowment from the John M. Longyear Family Trust means the museum can operate on a professional level with a staff of five, not having to depend on volunteers.

The **museum shop** has history-related gifts and good regional books, including its own re-publication of *Dandelion Cottage*, Carroll Watson Rankin's delightful popular girls' book from 1904, set nearby in a cottage on Ridge Street. (In it, plucky girls thwart a stuffy, negative minister and turn an abandoned house into their clubhouse.) Pick up easy-to-use **walking tour guides** of downtown and the Ridge-Arch Historic District, and an auto tour guide to outlying districts, for $1 each.

213 N. Front at Ridge, 2 blocks north of Washington. (906) 226-3571. www.mar-quettecohistory.org   Mon thru Fri 10-5, open 3rd Thurs to 9 p.m. Adults $3, ages 12-18 $1, under 12 free. &: call. Numerous interior stairways in this old building make access complicated.

Lower Harbor

This rich recreational area is just east of downtown at the feet of Washington and Main. Because downtown also links up with Marquette's near south side around the courthouse, Roman Catholic cathedral, and U.P. Children's Museum, it comes first in these next pages, followed by the Lower Harbor, Marquette Maritime Museum, Presque Isle Park.

Ridge & Arch Historic District and Third Street shopping

Descriptions of these come after the Lower Harbor, Maritime Museum, and Presque Isle Park.

Marquette's south side

The south side of town was home to early immigrants and Catholics and retains that makeup today. In this most class-conscious of U.P. cities, the south side still tends to be terra incognita to the academics, the gentry, and transplants. One of the city's treasured symbols, **Harlow's Wooden Man, a piece of antique yard art**, can be glimpsed in the back yard of 211 South Fourth. Southside highlights include:

◆ The **MARQUETTE COUNTY COURT-HOUSE** is a dignified 1902 Beaux Arts building whose stately dome surveys the town. It's a **don't-miss stop for fans of historic architecture** and for John Voelker aficionados. Most scenes from the 1959 classic *Anatomy of a Murder* based on his best-selling novel were filmed here in the elaborate second-floor courtroom where the real-life trial took place. The courthouse's grand entrance in front, off Third, has lots of steps and a **fine view of the city**, lake, and ore dock. The entry hall with its colorful tile floor has been restored with great respect. A display case is filled with memorabilia about courthouse history and Voelker's stories and novels inspired by local court cases. Peek inside the **elaborate second-floor courtroom**, trimmed with mahogany. Light filters in through stained glass windows at the base of its domed ceiling. *On Third at Baraga. Metered parking along Baraga. 225-8330. Open Mon-Fri 8-5.* &: use wheelchair-accessible entrance on

Baraga in new rear addition (it's signed).

◆ **ST. PETER'S CATHEDRAL**. In designing and later in remodeling this splendid edifice, the Catholic Church wanted to make a strong architectural statement to counterbalance the unusually large and elegant St. Paul's Episcopal Church on the northside hill at Ridge and Arch, near where wealthy Easterners lived. Building the twin-towered Romanesque cathedral took ten years before it was completed in 1890. Conspicuously sited on a hill surveying the town, it and the nearby courthouse dome form a **memorable southern skyline**. The church was rebuilt in part in 1935, after a fire. The **beautiful interior** may be visited weekdays. A simple wall treatment shows off the stained glass windows and woodwork. A side chapel is devoted to Perpetual Eucharistic Adoration, an old form of prayer promoted by Pope John Paul II as a powerful way of establishing peace on earth. An elaborate schedule of volunteers insures that the rosary is prayed around-the-clock in the presence of the consecrated host.

The Upper Peninsula's mid-19th-century bishop, Frederic Baraga, moved the diocesean headquarters from Sault Ste. Marie to Marquette in 1864. Today the **Bishop Baraga Association** is working to canonize the celebrated "snowshoe priest" who came from Slovenia (the northernmost of the former Yugoslav states) to minister to Indians on the northwoods frontier and started missions in the 1830s from near today's Harbor Springs to the Apostle Islands. He authored the first dictionary of the Ojibwa language, still in use, and worked to promote temperance — abstinence, in fact — among Indians. Attaining sainthood in today's Roman Catholic Church is no easy matter, however; it requires proof of two miracles, miracles that must be instantaneous, permanent, and without medical explanation. "In his time, people thought of Baraga as a saint," says Elizabeth Delene, the enthusiastic historian, archivist, and association director. Visitors can schedule a guided tour of the Baraga crypt (a simple marble room in the cathedral's lower level where many bishops are interred), the archive, and the house where he lived as bishop. Call (906) 227-9117. Many infirm people who have recently prayed to him to intercede for a miracle attribute their improvement to his help. Still, she says, "it's difficult to say that a chemical or drug didn't help."

Much later, hundreds of thousands of Slovenes immigrated to the Great Lakes area and worked in mines and factories. In 1930 Solvenian-American

Joseph Gregorich moved to Marquette from Oak Park, Illinois to advance Baraga's cause. His voluminous collections form the basis of the archive, open to any researcher, that also conveys a lot about U.P. life and connections with Catholic societies in Europe.

Today the Diocese of Marquette numbers some 100,000 of the total Upper Peninsula population of 300,000 — a sign of the size of the longtime French and Indian populations and the more recent, Catholic immigration — Italians and southeast Europeans who came to work in the mines, plus Irish (many Potato Famine refugees came to worked on the first Soo Locks). *311 W. Baraga at Fourth. Baraga intersects with Front/BR 41 just south of downtown. 226-6548. The church is open daily. Mass is at 8 a.m. and 5:15 p.m. weekdays, Sat 4 p.m., Sun 8 a.m., 10 a.m., 11:30 a.m.* &

◆ **D.J.'s BAKERY-DELI**, successor to Angeli's Bakery, still bakes **cross-shaped, crusty cornetti**, an Italian hard roll designed for dunking and sopping up pan juices. Their breakfast baked goods and pasties have a local following. Angeli's is a handy coffee and snack stop for anyone making a southside walking tour or visiting the U.P. Children's Museum next door. *At the bottom of the hill, at Baraga and First. 226-7335. Mon-Fri 6:30 a.m.-6 p.m., Sat 7:30 to 3.* &

◆ **BINGO at The Meeting Place/Women's Center** (225-1346) is a good place to witness and take part in this major U.P. leisure activity any night of the week. Games begin at 6:45 p.m. but players come much earlier. Each night benefits a different cause: Monday the Spouse Abuse Shelter, Tuesday a halfway house, Wednesday the IBEW Union charities, Thursday the local labor council political action and community service, Friday Women's Center Crisis Support, Saturday Marquette Co. Democratic Party, and Sunday Child & Family Services. For Sunday daytime games, come by noon. In the same building, the **WOMEN'S CENTER RESALE SHOP** (225-1103) is open weekdays 11 to 5, Thursdays to 6. *1310 S. Front, next to a gas station, about 4 blocks south of downtown.*

The Upper Peninsula Children's Museum

If slick, high-tech children's museums turn off the kids in your life — or you — and seem like too many buttons to push, you may well want to check out this **freewheeling, inventive place**. Rather than being educational in a dutiful way,

Improvising with donated materials helps account for the zany, creative atmosphere of the Upper Peninsula Children's Museum. Here floor man/educational director Jim Edwards poses with Rusty, the front-door Greet-o-Saurus. Inside at the Recyclo-Torium, kids make fun stuff from junk, building on a regional cultural habit of recycling that predates the ecology movement by generations.

this playful, handmade environment appeals to children's natural sense of **silly, icky, scary, creepy, and let's pretend**. The brochure reflects the tone: "Find Creature Kingdom — get in touch with some reptiles. 'Yikes!'" (This refers to a pond with turtles, and regular visits by a herpetologist and his very large snakes, which kids can touch.) "MicroSociety — it's a city, and it's just for kids. Stroll down the kid-sized street and shop at all the wacky businesses [including] the world-famous Fossil Rock Candy Café featuring such delicacies as Brontosaurus Burgers with Volcano Ketchup, Barney's favorite." Kids get a checkbook for the Reality Store, detail transactions, and consider financial and occupational goals and values. "Got trouble? Call SafetyVille Emergency 911 Dispatch!" Kids can jump into retired ambulance from Cedarville, ready to help. "Over the air. . . Be a pilot in a real plane" — the pretend control tower connects with the real fuselage cockpit.

The Go and Learn public restrooms (where boys get to **pee in a tree**) and "Where's your water" exhibit tackle the mystery of flushing the toilet. "Follow your tour guide and slide down the huge toilet, through the plumbing and into a septic tank. There separate septic components and learn about microbiology. Crawl through the drain field and into

an aquifer to explore life under a pond."

The museum's limited budget — limited by being in a county of 65,000, not half a million — and kid-based design process account for its **zany, cobbled-together creativity**, which happens to dovetail with the local culture of much of the U.P., where nothing is thrown away and home repairs are seldom hired out. The first seeds were planted in the early 1980s, after, when Nheena Weyer Ittner, who had grown up in the isolated and highly art-conscious city of Midland, moved to Marquette from Ann Arbor, where she had taught elementary school art. As the art teacher at Ishpeming High, she was excited about exposing her rural students to a wider world. Later, as a young mother, she became all too aware of how few places the area then had for parents to take their children. A trip to Shopko was tops for winter excitement. (Today, she hastens to add, it's altogether different.) With a grant from the Kellogg Youth Initiative Project, Nheena launched the Design-O-Saurus participatory design process in which kids contributed ideas around which the future museum built its "Investigation Station" areas. Meanwhile, in-kind contributions were sought locally, and a core staff emerged from volunteers. Seed funds came from outside the area; Marquette's business institutions were then much more likely to give labor and material stuff than money.

"It's a nice way to start a museum," she says, "looking within your community. We live in a daily sitcom. The people and the interesting dynamics — it's a hoot. You have to think creatively here." Grants for after-school programs and limited free passes help make the museum accessible to families without much money.

Call for regular happenings, such as one volunteer who comes in to pick up snakes and, changing gears, also talks about her mixed Indian heritage wearing her jingle dress of metal cones. (You need to have four dreams to make a jingle dress, which plays a role in healing rituals.) Groups visiting the U.P. might want to inquire about sleepovers at the museum. Parents and teachers, visit the website, **www.upcmkids.org**, for more ideas; some day Nheena hopes to have time to share her experiences on the web and in a book about the kid-focused museum design model.

123 West Baraga (the street the courthouse is on) just west of U.S. 41 on the south side of downtown Marquette. Park in the lot across the street. (906) 226-3911. Current hours: Mon-Sat 10-6, Fri to 8, Sun noon to 5. Admission $4.50/ adults, $3 ages 2 to 17. Ask about family memberships for parents and for grandparents. &

Lower Harbor

The Lower Harbor, Marquette's historic waterfront on Lakeshore Boulevard at the feet of Washington and Main streets, has become a **community focal point**. It has all the elements for an **after-dinner stroll** or a festive community event like the International Food Festival (July 4 weekend) and holiday fireworks, the Seafood Festival just before Labor Day, and the Labor Day Parade. The Lakeshore Bike Path goes all the way from here to Presque Isle Park. Much of this nearly five-mile distance is lined with parkland, and all is accessible from the bike path

Here are components of the Lower Harbor area, arranged from south to the Marquette Harbor Light at the north.

◆ **THILL'S FISH HOUSE** is the last commercial fishing operation of what was once a thriving Marquette-area fishery. Thill's two fishing boats dock here. Prices for fresh and smoked Lake Superior fish are lower than at supermarkets, and, of course, the **freshness can't be beat**. Thill's makes **smoked**

whitefish sausage, a smoked fish spread, and pickled trout, herring, and whitefish. It also sells a complete line of frozen seafood. *At the foot of Main, a block south of Washington, just north of the downtown ore dock. 226-9851. Open year-round, Mon-Fri 8-5:30, Sat to 3.* &

◆ **CINDER POND MARINA**, with 101 slips, serves seasonal and transient boaters and has a boat launch. Of relevance to rustic campers: it has **public showers**. It's the home of the well-regarded Uncle Ducky Charters and Cruises (228-5447). *Marina phone: 228-0469. Open May-Oct.* &

◆ **MATTSON LOWER HARBOR PARK** has a playground, picnic area, concession stand, restrooms, and fishing. Many events are held here, including sailboat regattas held each Wednesday evening and some weekends. Amateur sailors maneuver around the five-mile buoyed course. One Lower Harbor display that will long live on in local memory was the totem pole project by artist Mary Wright, the woman whose current career in masterminding community-made art projects was taken off. In her first project for celebrate Finnfest, the annual get-together of North American Finns held that year in Marquette, hundreds of old chairs painted in the Finnish national colors of sky blue and white lined the streets of downtown. Here at the Lower Harbor were over a hundred donated telephone poles transformed by families into family history totem poles, using paint, wood, metal, applied photographs and much more. One can be seen outside the Risaks' studio (below). *250*

Lakeshore. Open year-round. &

◆ **RISAK ART FORMS**. Ed and Julie Risak make **raku pottery** with a contemporary look but ancient origins in Japan. This is a working studio with a small display area. The raku process involves firing at high temperatures, which results in random patterns in the glaze that the artist can anticipate but not completely control. Ed has developed a clay body so that a thin-walled piece can withstand the thermal shock of taking pieces out of the very hot kiln and quickly cooling them, which creates the multicolored iridescence. Their rich copper glazes can include the full color spectrum, from greens and blues to orange, purple, and bright gold. Ed does mostly wheel-thrown pieces with hand-built embellishments. Julie does mostly hand-built slab pieces like the little moon boxes. Growing up outside Detroit, Ed was inspired by the famous iridescent copper glazes of Mary Chase Perry Stratton's Pewabic Studio in Detroit. Ed and Julie also use a traditional Japanese raku glaze, glossy which with random black crackles. The Risaks are among the best known of the many professional artists who make their homes in Marquette. *207 Lakeshore. 226-7720. Retail open year-round whenever the studio is open. Regularly open from May thru Oct and before Christmas. Typical hours Mon-Fri 10-5, Sat noon-5, Sun by chance. May be gone for shows.* &

◆ **MARQUETTE MARITIME MUSEUM**. See separate entry.

◆ **LAKE SUPERIOR THEATER**. A converted boathouse is home to original

Thill's, downtown at the Lower Harbor, is a great place to buy fresh just-off-the-boat whitefish and lake trout, or smoked fish. To the right is the old ore dock.

summer musical theater with regional themes based on U.P. history and music traditions. See www.marquettearts.org or call (906) 227-7625. Advance reservations advised for July and August.

◆ The **LOWER HARBOR BREAKWALL** is a very popular spot for fishing for coho, steelhead, lake trout, and whitefish. The breakwall is a **pleasant place for a stroll** on a nice summer evening. And it offers a **good view of the Marquette Lighthouse**, one of Michigan's most photographed lighthouses because of its handsome building and dramatic site atop sandstone bluffs.

◆ **MARQUETTE HARBOR LIGHT.** This picturesque lighthouses perches atop a rock bluff on Lighthouse Point. Guided tours of the lighthouse and grounds are offered by the Marquette Maritime Museum. See below.

Marquette Maritime Museum

The handsome old sandstone Water Works Building, not far from the lighthouse, is home to **one of the U.P.'s largest and most original maritime museums**. One highlight is the new McClintock *U.S.S. Darter-Dace* Memorial with memorabilia and a diorama of the WWII Battle for Leyte Gulf, one of history's largest naval battles, in which a Marquette submarine captain and many U.P. men served on the *Darter* and *Dace* submarines. Another highlight is the lens room with three **Fresnel lenses** and the rotating beacon from the Marquette Breakwater Light. It comprises the largest collection of lighthouse lenses on the Lakes. All are illuminated with beacons, creating a dazzling pattern of changing light and shadow. The lens from Stannard's Rock Lighthouse is a Second-Order Fresnel lens ten feet high that warned ships of Stannard's Reef. It is the farthest from shore of any Great Lakes lighthouse, 36 miles from the closet land at Keweenaw Point and 42 miles from Marquette. The Third Order lens from Big Bay (on loan from the lighthouse there) and the Fourth Order lens from Marquette Harbor, also here, seem small by comparison.

Large, colorful ship flags hang from the high ceilings. Children can pick up many things throughout the museum, including some ship models. They enjoy the **replica pilothouse of a 1900-era freighter** because they can turn the wheel, hit the bell, and blow the whistle and foghorn.

Only part of the collection is on display at any time. The very canoe used by

Swimming in and near Marquette
Lake Superior is at its warmest and gentlest, weather depending, at **South Beach Park** next to the Shiras Generating Plant south of downtown. It's a popular family beach because of the slope that's so gradual that a hundred feet out the water is knee deep. Get there from U.S. 41 by turning east onto Lake about a mile south of downtown. **McCarty's Cove** north of **Lighthouse Point** is the teens' and twenties' beach. The beach on the Dead River impoundment at **Tourist Park** is a protected, clean, and handy inland beach. For scenic beauty, it's hard to beat the beaches at **Little Presque Isle & Wetmore Landing**.

Charles Harvey for his personal transportation in supervising construction of the first Soo Lock can be seen. A typical Finnish fishing and hunting camp is up for another year. An exhibit shows how taconite pellets, a condensed form of iron ore, have made it more economical to ship iron. The well-stocked museum shop carries maps, photographs, T shirts, caps, all sorts of nautical and lighthouse gifts, and books, including half a dozen by Frederick Stonehouse, president of the museum's board of directors and a noted Great Lakes maritime author.

The museum is in the process of leasing the adjacent Mraquette Harbor Lighthouse from the Coast Guard. See below for guided tours.

300 Lakeshore Blvd. at the foot of Ridge, about 1/4 mile east of Mattson Park. Open daily from 10- to 5 from May 1 thru October. 226-2006. Current fee for the main museum: $3/adult, $1 kids 12 and under. Tour of lighthouse and grounds: $2. &

Marquette Harbor Light

The original light here, erected in 1853, was one of the first on Lake Superior because the Marquette Harbor became so busy with vessels shipping iron ore from the Marquette Range. This tower and keeper's house date from 1866; the house was enlarged with a second story in 1906.

As of sometime in 2001 the adjacent Marquette Maritime Museum is leasing the lighthouse as part of its museum. It gives a 25-minute guided tour of the lighthouse and grounds, including the

history of lightkeeping and Marquette Harbor. Visitors are escorted out on the six-foot-high catwalk extending a hundred yards out to the tip of Lighthouse Point. The **panoramic view of the city** and its environs is the best anywhere, all the way from Presque Isle and the Superior Dome to the prison, including the Lower Harbor, part of downtown, the courthouse, and St. Peter's Cathedral in between. (Because of the bluffs, visitors cannot walk the grounds unescorted.)

The Coast Guard station here is responsible for search and rescue from Big Bay Point to Pictured Rocks. Its other mission is law enforcement: checking vessels to make sure they comply with laws about life jackets, fire extinguishers, etc.

Off Lakeshore Blvd. about 3/4 mile northwest of downtown. Or take Ridge or Arch east to the lake. Museum phone: 226-2006. Lighthouse hours are same as the museum's, daily 10-5 from May 1 thru Oct. 31. $2 tour fee. Coast Guard phone: 226-3312. &: no.

Lakeside bike path from the Inner Harbor to Presque Isle

You can rent 5-speed bikes and take a pleasant bike ride along this **splendid shoreline bike path**. It extends 5 miles north from downtown to Presque Isle Park and then loops around the north and west perimeters of town via Hawley Street, an east-west street just north of the Superior Dome which leads to Tourist Park. Passing along Wright Street, the path turns south roughly along McClellan.

◆ **LAKESHORE BIKE.** This general bike shop on the bike path also rents bikes. *505 Lakeshore Boulevard just west of the lighthouse. 228-7547. Open Mon-Fri 10-6, Sat 10-4.*

◆ **McCARTY'S COVE** is the **favored swimming beach for young adults** just north of Lighthouse Point at the feet of Ohio and Hewitt streets. There's sand volleyball here, a picnic area with a lighthouse view, and a beach with a lifeguard in summer from noon to 8.

◆ **SHIRAS PARK.** Parkland continues a mile north of the lighthouse through Shiras Park. Here yet another picnic area is at the foot of Fair Street, looking out onto Picnic Rocks.

Lake Superior & Ishpeming RR Ore Dock

This steel-framed dock juts out almost a quarter of a mile into Lake Superior, 75

Awesome sight and sound: at Marquette's Presque Isle ore dock, railroad cars from the Tilden Mine empty iron-rich taconite pellets into the dock's 200 pockets. When a vessel pulls up to the dock, chutes are lowered from the dock into the boat's cargo hold. Loading is a noisy, interesting process to watch. Call (906) 226-6122 to find out when a freighter will be at the ore dock by Presque Isle Park — assuming that imports of heavily subsidized foreign steel are restricted and the mines reopen.

feet above the water. It's a **monumental sight** to see — and to hear, when loading is in process. The railroad approach is a mile-long earthen embankment. Railroad cars come from Cleveland-Cliffs Iron's taconite processing facility near their vast open-pit mines south of Negaunee, the Tilden and Empire mines. The rail cars continually move out along the top of the ore dock and empty taconite pellets down into the ore dock's 200 pockets. (Taconite is a concentrated form of iron-bearing rock, formed with clay into balls for compact, cost-effective shipment.)

Some 20 to 30 bulk ore carriers a month come to the dock to load. Chutes from each pocket are lowered into the vessel's cargo hold, and taconite thunders down into it. Then the ship shifts 20 or 30 feet (winches being tightened or loosened let it move), and new pockets empty into the hold. It's a noisy, impressive spectacle — a worthwhile opportuni-ty to view giant freighters in action. Vessels that carry taconite are usually older 600-footers. Thousand-footers usually come only to unload coal. This particular ore dock, built by a Cleveland-Cliffs subsidiary in 1912, revolutionized the shipping of iron ore. Its technology has been superseded by Escanaba's ore dock, which uses conveyors to load the ore.

The first vessel of spring is greeted with fanfare, a tradition that goes back to the early years when the citizens were isolated all winter and depended on ships to bring their food. To find out when an ore carrier will dock, call (906) 226-6122. Nearby is the giant, coal-fired generating station of Wisconsin Electric Power. It's the main electrical plant in the Upper Peninsula.

On Lakeshore Boulevard, shortly before the entrance to Presque Isle Park, about 4 miles northeast of downtown.

The Studio Gallery

The gallery and working studio of four artists, mostly with **national reputations**, is next to the entrance of Presque Isle Park. Kathleen Conover paints contemporary landscapes in watercolor, gouache, and acrylic. Maggie Linn's transparent watercolors are also landscapes, sometimes incorporating birds, flowers, and windows with reflections of other places, often her native Singapore. Vicki Allison Phillips mixes media in her jewelry. Much of it is fine jewelry in gold and silver incorporating glass, beads, and other materials. Typically jewelry is stored away when not being worn. Lately she's been making decorative tabletop sculptural assemblages in which component parts can be taken off and worn.

In 1994 Kathleen, Vicki, and Maggie started working together here. Recently Yvonne LeMire joined them. She welds scraps of laser-cut steel into large non-representational garden sculptures: gates, screens, wall hangings, and more.

Visitors enjoy being able to talk to the artists — two are always on hand — and the four women know each other's work well, so they can answer questions and talk about each other's work.

The Studio Gallery is part of a small complex that includes the old end-of-the-line **train depot** where townspeople from Marquette and Ishpeming got off for outings on Presque Isle. The depot now houses Presque Isle Station Gallery. The complex's owners intend to open a **chowder house** after they sell their house in Key West.

2950 Lake Shore Boulevard, just before Presque Isle Park. 228-2466. Open regularly from Memorial Day weekend to Christmas, but closed on holidays. Up to Labor Day open daily 11-5. After Labor Day open Fri-Mon 11-5. By appointment in winter. &

Moosewood Nature Center

Many presenters from varied backgrounds give **frequent programs for children on nature**, from geology to animal life. Programs are often fascinating and fun. The center had been based in a neighborhood school that closed. Now that the building has been sold, Moosewood has moved to Presque Isle Park — more visible for visitors, but too far from town to be convenient for locals. Call 228-6250 for programs, or — an easier option, scroll and scan the current month's calendar of *Marquette Monthly*, www.mmnow.com

In the Shiras Pool building in Presque Isle Park. (906) 228-6250.

Presque Isle Park

This rocky, wooded, and **extraordinarily picturesque peninsula** is a wonderful setting for an outing any time of year. When locals mention "the island," they're talking about Presque Isle (pronounced locally "presk AISLE"). A gazebo and picnic area on a promontory overlook near the entrance afford **excellent views out into the lake and back at the ore docks and harbor**. The green of pines contrasts with the red rock and great blue lake. Turnouts and footpaths lead off of the one-way, two-mile-long interior road at especially scenic points. Northwest of the peninsula are several craggy, dark islets and the Huron Mountains, blue in the distance. It's a **grand view, especially at sunset**. The high cliffs plunging into Lake Superior prove tempting — and **on occasion fatal** — for overadventurous rock climbers and divers.

Five miles of trails go up and down through woods of hardy conifers kept small by wind and rock. A resident deer herd includes some albino deer. Lacking protective coloration, albinos don't often survive in the wild, but in this protected place, they do. From December into March, four miles of groomed cross-country ski trails wind through the woods with occasional views past the ridges and peaks of lake ice to the still unfrozen lake. They are among the most beautiful places imaginable for skiing. The spring snowmelt comes earlier here than farther inland because of the lake's warming effect. The trailhead is at the entrance by the gazebo on the lake side.

The park's most developed part is on the neck near the entrance. A marina is on the south shore. On the north shore, shallow, protected Middle Bay makes the Lake Superior beach more tolerable for swimming. In this area too are tennis courts, shuffleboard, a playground, a concession stand, and a picnic area. Marquette's **huge Shiras Pool and a water slide**, open to the general public, are just inside the park entrance. A 1/4-mile paved Bog Walk Nature Trail is off the first parking lot past the entrance.

The Marquette City Band holds **summer band concerts** on Thursdays at 7 p.m. from mid June through the first Thursday in August in the bandshell right across from the picnic area and playground. Rain dates are Mondays.

Presque Isle Park is at the end of Lakeshore Drive, about three miles from downtown. (906) 228-0460. Open year-round. No fees except for pool admission and x-c ski trail fee. &

Ridge and Arch Historic District

Marquette's mining , shipping, and commercial magnates built their homes on a high bluff overlooking the harbor. The **dramatic site** and the **concentration of grand, well maintained historic homes** in an intact neighborhood make this a fine place for a leisurely walk. A $1 printed walking tour can be had at the Marquette County History Museum on Front Street, open weekdays.

Larger, older houses are on the long blocks of the east-west streets, starting with Ridge, and north of it, Arch, Michigan, and Ohio. Here are some architectural highlights, beginning at Ridge at High, with historical details from Kathryn Bishop Eckert in her *Buildings of Michigan* survey of historic architecture and her much more detailed *The Sandstone Architecture of the Lake Superior Region.*

◆ **ST. PAUL'S EPISCOPAL CHURCH.** Marquette's wealthiest congregation spared few expenses when they took St. Paul's Cathedral in Green Bay as the modeled for their **impressive Gothic Revival brownstone church**, finished in 1876. Kathryn Eckert wrote that its "high-style Gothic forms celebrate both the social and economic achievements of the parish and the city. . . . [It is] so elegant and splendid inside and out that some regarded it as out of character with this city in the wilderness." She called the architect, Gordon Lloyd, "one of the Midwest's most fashionable church architects." His work is familiar to most Michigan Episcopalians who worship in 19th-century churches.

Visitors are welcome to stop in at the church office on Ridge Street, pick up a tour pamphlet, and look inside. The brilliant stained glass windows, recently restored and releaded, are visitor favorites. Peter White donated the 1887 **Tiffany window** in the chapel, depicting the Resurrection. The "Christian Family" window (1922) shows Christ blessing the 11 children of Samuel and Juliet Graeveret Kaufman, one of whom built Granot Loma. *201 E. Ridge at High. 226-2912. The office is open at least from 9 a.m. to noon weekdays (closed Fridays in summer). Or you could come to 5:30 Wednesday evening prayer, or to Sunday services at 10:30 Sept-May, at 10 in summer.*

◆ The elaborate **1880 ITALIAN VILLA** at 410 E. Ridge. Its huge central tower makes it a sort of a **Charles Addams affair** in sandstone. It was built for Daniel Merritt, who made a lot of money first in a foundry and machine shop, then by investing in mining, banks, and land. He too was an Episcopalian. A master stonemason from Devonshire, England, designed the house and many of Marquette's leading buildings. Here he used variegated sandstone, reddish brown streaked with white, to good effect.

◆ The elaborate board-and-batten **GOTHIC REVIVAL HOUSE** at 450 E. Ridge built in 1867 in the picturesque style of Andrew Jackson Downing for Henry Mather. He came from Cleveland to buy iron-rich land and became the first president of the Cleveland Iron Mining Company, precursor of Cleveland-Cliffs.

◆ The 1875 brown sandstone **GOTHIC REVIVAL HOUSE** at 430 E. Arch, built for Andrew Ripka, from Philadelphia, who managed the railroad company dock.

◆ The newer homes east of Arch and Cedar, on the bluff overlooking Marquette Bay, mark the site of the James and Mary **LONGYEAR MANSION**, one of the largest and grandest houses in the Upper Midwest, which can now be seen in Brookline, Massachusetts, just outside Boston. It was a vast sandstone mansion in the round-arched, vigorous Romanesque Revival style, with landscaping designed after a site visit by no less than Frederick Law Olmstead, a father of the American parks movement. Longyear, from Lansing, parlayed the influence of his father, a Congressman and judge, into a fortune of millions, starting with surveying jobs. As a landlooker, he became familiar with U.P mineral lands, then made fortunes on the Gogebic and Mesabi iron ranges. "Longyear's shrewd ability to assess the region's mineral and timber resources and to deal with speculators, developers, and regulators aided his own transactions," wrote Eckert. The Longyears planned to donate bluffside property near here as a memorial park for their dead son. Other civic leaders rejected the plan and opted to build a railroad along the lakeshore. Rebuffed, the Longyears dismantled the house under the architect's direction — shipped it off on 190 railroad cars — this oft-told story is always embellished with "190 railroad cars" — and rebuilt it in Brookline, but continued to support local projects like the history museum. The rebuilt Longyear Mansion, after serving as a museum and archive for the Christian Science church headquarters, is now the clubhouse for an elite condominium project that adjoins it and respects its historic architecture.

◆ The **1887 SHINGLE STYLE HOUSE** at 425 Ohio, one of the few surviving houses designed by the important Chicago architect John Wellborn Root.

"The Village" shopping district on Third Street

A noteworthy retailing district that visitors might miss leads north up the hill from downtown toward the edge of Northern Michigan University. It's too spread-out to be ideally walkable. Here's where to find sport shops, campus hangouts, and popular restaurants like Sweet Water Café, Casa Calabria, and Vango's.

◆ **SWEET VIOLETS: A Feminist Bookstore**. Over the years the selection of books, gifts, and cards in Leigh Wall and Susan Graves' shop has evolved with customers' interests. The nonfiction section dominates, with a lot on women's health (physical and psychological) and philosophical and spiritual issues. Women's travel tales, books on journaling as self-discovery, and journals are

big sections. Especially germane to vacationing readers: *The Way of the Traveler: Making Every Trip a Journey of Self-Discovery* by Joseph Dispenz and *The Mindful Traveler: A Guide to Journaling and Transformative Travel* by Jim Currie. *413 N. Third. 228-3307. Mon-Fri 10-6, Sat to 5.* &

◆ **DOWN WIND SPORTS**. The staff is actively involved in all the sports the store deals with: climbing, kayaking and canoeing, mountain biking, downhill and **cross-country skiing** and snowboarding, **snowshoeing**, skijoring (a simplified form of dogsledding), and backpacking. They're happy to field questions from downstate paddlers, bikers, and hikers about good area destinations, whether or not a sale is involved. Each Tuesday evening in summer the store holds a **kayak demonstration** on a body of water that suits the weather; call for location. Similarly, every summer Thursday evening there's a **bike ride**, usually with a fast and slow group; call for location. **Annual events** include the Paddle Expo (1st weekend June) with clinics, speakers, etc.; and an **ice climbing festival** (1st weekend February). No guided trips. *514 N. Third between Michigan and Ohio. 226-7112. www.downwindsports.com. Mon-Thurs 9:30-6, Fri to 8, Sat to 5, Sun 12-4.* &

◆ **MAPS NORTH**. This unusual business combines a **wide-ranging map store** on the ground floor of an old house, and a **cartography lab** upstairs. Four partners (retired NMU geography professor Pat Farrell, his cartographer son Mike, NMU geologist Bob Regis, and NMU planner Jim Thams) felt the area could support a specialty map store, but they've been surprised at how well they've done. They carry every **USGS map of the U.P.**; maps, antique and modern, of the U.P. and Lake Superior; and regional guides of all kinds. The staff has a working knowledge of the area and of maps in general and the many digital maps and GPS (Global Positioning Systems) they demonstrate and sell. The back room has worldwide maps and guidebooks. Another room showcases wall maps and globes. *907 N. Third, three doors south of Vango's. Mon-Fri 10-5:30, Sat 10-1. Parking in the back. 226-6975. www.mapsnorth.com; e-mail benchmark@mapsnorth.com* &: in rear.

◆ **SCANDINAVIAN GIFTS**. All four Scandinavian countries are represented in Boli Soderberg's attractive shop. She herself comes from Finland's Swedish-speaking minority. Her new location has

classics of outstanding Scandinavian design: wool sweaters from Dale of Norway; crystal by Orrefors, Kosta-Boda, and iittala which again produces vases by the great architect Aalvar Aalto and practical glassware by his wife, Aino Aalto; and bronze and silver Kalevala Koru jewelry, both contemporary and traditional, based on medieval designs. Some silver jewelry incorporates spectrolite, a blue-green iridescent stone from Finland. The store's recorded **music** tends toward the folk tradition. Veikko Ahvenainen plays the accordion in contemporary, folk, and classical styles; he plays Bach so it sounds like an organ. Colorful Ekelund kitchen and **table linens** from Sweden have enthusiastic buyers who use the kitchen towels to make table runners, aprons, and curtains. The enlarged **food** section has jams, candies, coffees, cookies, and in the novelty department reindeer meatballs. The book selection is strong on cookbooks, coffee-table travel books, and translations of children's favorites like *Flicka, Dicka, and Ricka* and Astrid Lindgren's stories, from *Pippi Longstocking* to folk-flavored tales. Ask for the holiday mail-order catalog. *1025 N. Third. 225-1993. Open Mon-Fri 10-5:30, Sat to 5.* &

◆ **WINTERGREEN NATURAL FOODS**. This unusual natural food store emphasizes **products with traditional roots** rather than new age aspirations. For instance, there's Rumford Baking Powder with no aluminum; real cider vinegar made from apples, not grapes made to taste like apples; and witch-hazel soap. Only natural vitamins are stocked, and only products that have not involved animal testing. If your insect-repelling strategy is to try everything, as one experienced and highly allergic outdoorsman advises, this would be an ideal stop. A few **anti-bug tips**: the essential oils citronella and pennyroyal can be helpful. Pennyroyal is especially good with black flies. A dose of thiamine induces mosquitoes not to bite. (They still hover, however.)

Other specialties include medicinal and gourmet teas; wheat- and gluten-free products; dehydrated soups and meal-replacement bars of use to campers; non-dairy cheese; and soy dogs and burgers for the grill. *1015 N. Third in the Village Center strip mall. 225-1834. Mon-Fri 10-6, Sat 10-5.*

◆ **JACK'S IGA**. A handy grocery that caters to the college community. *1034 N. Third. 228-6487.*

Superior Dome/Upper Peninsula Heritage Center

Officials at Northern Michigan University had long campaigned to build an indoor football stadium to foster school spirit, improve attendance at games, and host other events. In 1991 this **five-acre facility**, 531 feet across, was completed to much ballyhoo as "the world's largest wooden dome," sometimes called the **Yooper Dome**. The bleachers seat 8,000. The artificial turf is said to be the largest piece of retractable turf in the world. From the inside you can see the wood framework of big Douglas fir beams, designed to be strong enough to withstand heavy winds and snow loads. State funds had been garnered by tying the dome to programs of an Olympic training center, which now has metamorphosed into the U.S. Olympic Education Center.

The dome has won a real place in the hearts and everyday lives of local people. Many trade shows and special events take place here. In a sports-crazy area, 20 high school games a season use the Dome. Games in the Superior Dome are a convenience when opposing teams are far apart — when Calumet plays St. Ignace, for instance. And crowds are bigger when weather is not a factor. In the land of ice and snow, the **walking and jogging track** has been a tremendous draw not just for athletes but for mothers and toddlers, seniors, and the general public — a step up from mall-walking, and a social center, too, with coffee and snacks available. In winter, 400 to 450 walkers show up weekday mornings when the track is open, at no charge, from 8 to 11:30 a.m. (There's a fee for evening hours.)

The joggers' outer concourse also houses the showcases of the ambitious **U. P. Heritage Center**, a project of history professor Russell Magnaghi and his U.P. history program. Each display window is over 30 feet long and 10 feet deep. "Legends of the Upper Peninsula" honors **John Voelker** (a.k.a. Robert Traver); the late State Senator **Dominic Jacobetti** of Negaunee, patron saint of the U.P. for all the regional projects he funded during his long career; Marquette **watercolorist Nita Engle**; and 1951 Nobel Prizewinning **nuclear chemist Glenn Seaborg**, who lived in Ishpeming until the age of 9, then moved to California. Son of a Swedish railroad mechanic, he co-discovered the transuranium elements numbered 94 to 102. Voelker's two sides are shown. Here is the desk where he wrote *Anatomy of a*

Olympic athletes in training

The U.S. Olympic Education Center at Northern Michigan University allows elite athletes in sports that don't have college teams to train while continuing their education at NMU or Marquette High School, instead of interrupting their education completely to prepare for the Olympics. The center has over 60 resident athletes in boxing, biathlon, Greco-Roman wrestling, short-track speedskating, and luge. A shining example is short track speedskater Cathy Turner who graduated with honors in computer systems and won gold and silver medals just two months later in 1992.

To find out about other NMU Olympians, visit www.nmu.edu/usoec

Murder and a model of his cherished fishing camp. Other cases feature "NMU Sports Championships," "The Natural World of the Upper Peninsula" (the mineral specimens are beautiful), and "Upper Peninsula **Ethnic Groups**," illustrated with riveting historic photographs.

History buffs may also want to ask to the Superior Dome student assistant to gain admission to the **Sam Cohodas Room** and learn about the life of that fabulously successful Jewish immigrant from Byelorussia who parlayed a pushcart into a regional produce wholesale business and ended up owning a bank. He expanded these businesses into a banking empire in the U.P. and Wisconsin, and orchards in several Midwestern and Far Western states. Cohodas was a major contributor to NMU. The room is a tribute to the Cohodas clan (Sam himself had no children), some of whom remain active in Marquette today. Artfully displayed items include apple juice cans, his K.I. Sawyer bomber jacket (he was a base supporter, not a pilot), birthday cards, poodle pictures, old Jewish coins and lamps, and early **Green Bay Packers memorabilia** (he was an original Packer Backer).

*Group tours are available upon request, or small groups can stop in and ask a student assistant for an impromptu tour. For a $5 **daily guest pass**, anyone can use the facilities here (for gold, tennis, exercise and weight training machines, and the track). The adjoining Physical Education Instructional Facility, also open to all for $5, has a swimming **pool** and other sports. Call for details.*

1401 Presque Isle north of Fair. (906) 227-2850. Open Mon-Thurs 8 a.m.-10 p.m., Fri to 5. Usually used weekends for special events. &

Mount Marquette Scenic Lookout

From the south side of town, see the city, bay, and lake from Mount Marquette. The road winds up the mountain from U.S. 41, leading to a parking area behind the rock outcrops at the summit. These offer a **spectacular view**. But picking your way up steep, irregular steps, over paths cut deep by too many mountain bikes, and over the rounded rocks is not for the infirm — or for anyone in high heels.

In winter, the road is closed to vehicles and open to snowshoers and cross-country skiers. One rugged man in his sixties comes here daily to run up and down on his special runners' snowshoes. **Directions:** Take Highway 41 South from town until you come to the Tiroler Hof hotel and make a right (that's west). The road will very quickly become a "Y." Veer to your left onto the dirt road (Carp River Drive) and follow the river for a half mile or so until you see a sign on your right that says "Mount Marquette." Turn and drive to the top where you will find space to park and paths to walk. Again in your vehicle, come down on the road on the other side of the mountain which will bring you to CR 553. On your left will be Marquette Mountain ski hill. Turn right to get back to Marquette.

Marquette Branch Prison & Hobbycraft Shop

This old prison, modeled after Michigan's Ionia House of Correction, looks something like a Victorian boarding school, what with the **picturesque towers** of its imposing central administration building and the beautiful flower gardens in front. In truth, part of the prison complex has always been a **maximum-security prison**, from the time it was finished in 1889. Marquette was a remote place where difficult prisoners were and are sent; it's one of the most secure prisons in the country, says a management staffer. Another portion of the prison has always been **minimum-security**; its inmates are the ones who maintain the grounds and have privileges to work with tools in the Hobbycraft Shop. Today the prison has some 800 inmates. Visitors are welcome to drive in, admire the flowers (grown in prison greenhouses) and the historic buildings, and then leave.

By the entrance, on U.S. 41, the **HOBBYCRAFT SHOP** sells crafts prisoners made. Mostly they are tooled leather goods — belts, key chains (some make mention of the prison itself), and wallets. The wallets wear like iron and don't cost too much. Typical motifs are eagles, western themes, and roses. Two current prisoners do cartoon characters. Jewelry boxes made of toothpicks and crosses and picture frames made of folded potato chip wrappers fall under the prison art subcategory of **"outsider art"** — a hot field in collecting. The quality of paintings and other stock varies with the prison population. Special orders are welcome; ask for extension 1243. Customers can have names, Masonic emblems, etc. put on anything in leather, from wallets and purses to gun holsters (!).

1960 U.S. 41 South, just south of the Carp River and Tiroler Hof motel at the south entrance to town. 226-6531. Hobbycraft Shop hours vary with warden and staffing. Currently they are Mon-Fri 9-4. Weekend summer hours a possibility. If key staff is sick, shop may be closed.

Michigan Welcome Center

Outdoor **picnic tables** look onto Marquette Bay behind this impressive log building. The Welcome Center houses a helpful staff and a vast array of travel pamphlets and state publications on attractions, lodgings, and subjects like golf, fishing, camping, snowmobiling, canoeing, antiquing, waterfalls, lighthouses, and more. Information can be mailed. Phone queries on many subjects are answered seven days a week. Works by area artists are on display.

On the east side of U.S. 41 as it enters Marquette. It's west of Harvey, and east of the 3 lakefront motels. (906) 249-9066. Open daily except winter holidays, 9-5. ♿

U.S. 41 road cut with ancient algal stromatolites

Conveniently located right across U.S. 41 from the Michigan Welcome Center is a section of rock exposed during highway construction that geology students come to study from afar. The geology department of Lawrence University in Appleton, Wisconsin, has prepared an interesting drawing and explanation that the Welcome Center hands out. In brief, it says that these rocks "are part of the eroded roots of a mountain system similar to alpine-type mountains" that may

have been **higher than the Himalayas** today. The rock was first deposited nearly two billion years ago, when "the earth's atmosphere was oxygen-poor and carbon dioxide-rich. One of earth's earliest forms of life, cyanobacteria, had the capability of consuming carbon dioxide and generating oxygen." The organisms, which still exist in oceans, formed sticky mats which trap sedimentary particles. In oceans today, they are eaten or obscured by invertebrate animals like corals. Here these structures, called stromatolites, are well preserved and easily visible.

As cyanobacteria proliferated, the earth's atmosphere became oxygen-rich — a devastatingly severe form of pollution for the primitive organisms. The cyanobacteria were oxidized and converted to **iron mineral**. That's the basis of the iron industry. The exposed stromatolites are on the right side of the road cut (assuming the viewer is looking at it from the Welcome Center), behind some trees just to the left of where the exposed rock comes close to the roadway.

This unusual surface appearance of stromatolites is at the easternmost part of the belt of iron deposits extending through Negaunee and Ishpeming to Iron Mountain, Crystal Falls, Ironwood, and Minnesota's Mesabi Range. *On U. S. 41 across from the Michigan Welcome Center on Marquette's south side.*

Marquette Mountain downhill ski area

See the ski section for details on this challenging ski hill where many competitions are held.

Blueberry Ridge Cross-Country Ski Trail/ Escanaba River State Forest

The Marquette area's popular, free cross-country ski area features 12k of regularly groomed trails in six loops of all difficulty levels. The three north loops have side-by-side diagonal-groomed tracks so people can ski next to each other. The 1.7 mile **lighted central loop** is groomed for both diagonal-stride and ski-skating, as are the south two loops. The Red Earth Loppet is held here in February.

Off CR 553 just south of CR 480, about 4 miles south of Marquette Mountain (see above for directions) and 7 miles south of downtown Marquette. (906) 485-1031. No fee; donation appreciated.

Jilbert's Dairy

Many dairy products distributed all over the U.P. come from Jilbert's Dairy, which prides itself on not buying milk from cows given hormones to increase milk production. Jilbert's plant, **ice cream parlor**, and store is also a very popular destination for visitors and locals alike. Increasingly, it's also becoming a kind of **dairy museum**. Glass windows let visitors see ice cream being made and milk being processed. The staff, including owner John Jilbert if he's around, is happy to answer questions. Walls by the office and window to the plant are covered with display cases of old milk bottles and vintage dairy advertising, from old U.P. dairies whenever possible. Recent renovations are extending the dairy museum out into the ice cream parlor, with space for select pieces of dairy equipment.

Ice cream connoisseurs marvel at the flavor of Jilbert's ice cream, which is not premium priced. John Jilbert attributes its "fresher, cleaner taste" to several factors, most importantly, that the cream is really fresh. As a small dairy (small by today's standards) Jilbert's processes milk in the same plant as it makes ice cream, and uses the very freshest of the cream it produces. Most ice cream is made in specialty plants that buy cream that's somewhat less fresh from dairies some distance away. Jilbert's Mackinac Island Fudge is a better vanilla, with a good, less sweet chocolate. **Yooper Mud Slide is a local favorite**: chocolate ice cream with fudge sauce and brownie pieces mixed in. Jilbert's is coming downstate to Frankenmuth via the new store of ice cream parlor at Mackinaw Crossing. Mackinaw City is Jilbert's only Lower Peninsula delivery stop.

Being a small dairy, and in an isolated area, also has helped Jilbert's in its decision to not use milk from cows given rBGH (bovine growth hormone). "It would be almost impossible for a huge dairy" to insist on hormone-free milk, John says. "We can pay a little more." To his knowledge, all Wisconsin dairies now take milk from herds given rBGH. The over 100 U.P. dairy farmers who sell milk to Jilbert's appreciate the money and the herd health benefits. Hormone-free cows live longer, on the average.

Why does Jilbert's ice cream parlor also have **U.P. specialty food products** and a Gordon Food Service outlet? Because Jilbert's sells to small groceries and convenience stores all over the U.P. Those customers can place small orders of Gordon groceries along with their weekly milk delivery. The U.P. specialty foods (Baroni's spaghetti sauce, many jams and jellies, maple syrup, etc.) showcase regional products and sell well to visitors. Sturdy round Wisconsin **cheese crates** with lids, used as sewing boxes, tables, and toy chests, can be covered with fabric. Helmi and Albert Hyrkas use unhomogenized milk from Jilbert's to make a sweetish, soft Finnish cheese, *juustuoa*, also known as **"squeaky cheese."** Juustuoa is good for breakfast with cinnamon toast and coffee. It is traditionally served to guests with pulla (sweet cardamom bread) and coffee. It also shows up at Finnish smorgasbords, where it's eaten with rye bread and salmon.

The Jilbert's Dairy building and grounds are attractions in their own right. **Jilly** the **giant Holstein cow**, adopted as Jilbert's mascot around 1990, has the brand resonance of a much longer history. One Jilly is perched on the silo. Another, on a trailer, goes on the road for parades and local events. The third and biggest Jilly is just waiting for a photo op of visitors seated on a milk pail by a **giant udder**. It's in a pretty little **garden** up the stairs opposite the ice cream parlor entrance.

Jilbert's impressive stone barn was built as the horse barn for the Upper Peninsula Brewing Company, as part of its elaborate, castle-like brewery complex. Most of the brewery was demolished for the D&N bank building. (The original brew master's office on Meeske, now surrounded by a fanciful garden, is the office of the local Big Boy franchisee.)

John Jilbert takes great pride in another historic preservation project in adaptive reuse: his own house, due to appear in *Architectural Digest*. He built it to incorporate the ruins of a picturesque stone and log pavilion built by the **Civilian Conservation Corps** in the 1930s for **Marquette State Park** west of town. The park was abandoned during World War II. After Jilbert's Dairy moved from Calumet to Marquette's more central location in 1984, John Jilbert bought the property, subdivided it, and kept three lots for himself. Visitors are welcome to drive by. Here's how to find it: from U.S. 41 just west of town, turn south onto CR 492 just east of Menard's. Drive south about a mile. Turn right onto Weiland Drive, drive around the circle to Bishop Woods Drive and look for the house.

Jilbert's Dairy is at the corner of W. Ridge & Meeske Ave. From downtown, take Washington out to Meeske (almost at U.S. 41, turn right). Or, take U.S. 41 to Business 41 (by the Holiday Inn); then take Business 41 north to Meeske. If coming from the west, it's easier to turn left just east of Shopko onto McClellan, go north and turn left again onto Washington. You can see the large fiberglass cow and red barn from U.S. 41. (906) 225-1363. Open daily including Sunday year-round. From mid April thru fall color season open 10 a.m. to 10 p.m. In winter open 10-6. ♿

Northwoods Supper Club gardens

Northwoods started out in the 1930s as a log cabin in the woods. Its owners were avid naturalists, as is the case with a good many Upper Michigan businesses. They developed **extensive terraced flower gardens** with many **wildflowers**, which can now be seen from the main dining room's large rear windows. Visitors are welcome to walk the trail through gardens and woodlands, past wetlands, a waterfall pool, and beyond to founder Fred Klumb's log cabin in the woods. From the parking lot you could walk around the front of the building to get to the garden, but it's easier just to go in and ask the staff to go out a back door.

3 1/2 miles west of Marquette, south off U.S. 41/M-28. Turn at large Northwoods sign. (906) 228-4343. ♿*: yes for restaurant; call for walk.*

MARQUETTE RESTAURANTS

Marquette offers more restaurant variety than anyplace else in the U.P. Fast-food restaurants and other chains are out on the highway. Except for the Border Grille and Northwoods Supper Club, all these recommended restaurants are either downtown or in "The Village," the campus-oriented area along Third Street and Presque Isle Boulevard.

Soups and salads at Babycakes Muffin Company downtown are exclusively **vegetarian**. Sweet Water Café on Third Street offers many **vegan** dishes for breakfast, lunch, and dinner. Both restaurants bake good bread, as does the Huron Mountain Bread Company at 1301 South Front/U.S. 41 on the south entrance to town.

After the Border Grille near U.S. 41 south of Shopko, restaurants are arranged starting with downtown, going north:

The **BORDER GRILLE** draws throngs with its fast, healthy, inexpensive neo-Mexican food, especially the **Border Burrito** (a 12" flour tortilla wrapped around sautéed vegetables with diced chicken or steak, melted cheese, sour cream— just $4.25 with Mexican rice, chips and tomato/onion/pepper salsa. A vegetarian forester recommends the veggie burritos that come with a salsa that looks like cheese sauce. Five different salsas are made right here. Good road food: the bite-size pieces of grilled quesadilla. At meal times, the Border Grille can get crowded, but it won't take over 15 minutes to get your food. *180 McClellan at Baraga, just south of U.S. 41 and Shopko. Sign is visible from U.S.41. 228-5228 . Open Mon-Sat 11 a.m.-10 p.m.* ♿ 👫👫

Traveling in England inspired Terry and Kristi Doyle to reinvent an **English pub** in Marquette. They began in 1985 by buying the 100-year-old **VIERLING RESTAURANT**, playing up its original back bar and evoking a clubby version of old world elegance. It became one of Marquette's most popular restaurants and meeting places. Ten years later they added the **Marquette Harbor Brewery**. Its full mash system turns out "proper" English-style beers, **heavy and malty porters, stouts, and brown ales** — no mild beers at all. Takeout customers can buy it in liter glass containers; it's served upstairs for $2 a glass, $4 for a 20 oz. English pint. The lower-level brewery can be seen in action through windows on Main Street.

On the main floor, stained glass separates the bar from the dining room, which offers a good view of the **harbor**. Lunch brings soups, meal-size salads ($5-$6.25), sandwiches and burgers. Soups, salad dressings, desserts are made on the premises. A specialty is **fresh whitefish** fixed six ways: with caper-tomato sauce, plain, Cajun, almondine, with tomato-lemon relish, and layered with seafood stuffing. "Never a bad meal," say regular customers, who rave about all-you-can-eat tempura-battered whitefish on Friday night. The dinner menu ($10-$15) includes rich dishes like shrimp in Bernaise sauce and light, HeartSmart entrées like chicken and vegetarian stir-fry. The wine list has about 80 selections. Reservations recommended on weekends. *119 S. Front at Main, 1 block south of Washington. 228-3533. Kitchen open Mon-Sat 11 a.m.-10 p.m.* ♿ 👫👫 Full bar

J.J.'s SHAMROCK IRISH PUB stands out for its **deck overlooking Marquette Harbor**. It advertises a fun and young atmosphere, the area's best bar food (including homemade onion rings and fries) and music to **dance** to. Expect some smoke. *113 S. Front downtown. 226-6734. Open Mon-Sat 11:30 a.m. to 2 a.m.* ♿ Full bar

UPFRONT & COMPANY, a **jazzy, arty restaurant and blues club**, is part of a block-long rehab/restoration project downtown that has spared no expense. (A NMU grad from not too many years ago, who owns a cable TV company in Indiana among other things, loves Marquette so much that he wanted to make it a livelier place for young adults.) The project includes handsome storefronts on Front just south of Main, offices, the lower-level restaurant, and a beautiful banquet hall overlooking the harbor. The restaurant interior itself is a work of art, a contemporary version of Art Deco with bright primary colors, glass block, some instrument motifs, dramatic spot lighting, with a mix of brick patterns and local stones. Menu offerings are a sophisticated take on proven favorites with a regional flair. 10" pizzas (mostly $11.50) and calzones ($8) are made from scratch and baked in a wood-fired oven. The house soup is **wild rice soup**, for instance, and the "Field and Stream" entrée featured pan-seared **steelhead** in a red pepper cream sauce and oven-roasted marinated quail ($20). Entrées also include oven-roasted chicken ($16), whitefish wrapped with leeks and a crab stuffing in filo pastry ($19), steaks, and vegetarian dishes. All come with bread from the Huron Mountain Bread company, soup or salad, and appropriate sides. Sandwiches, meal-size salads, and appetizers round out the menu.

Music starts around 10 — late for the area's many baby-boomer transplants who like blues and jazz — and there's a dance floor. Check out the website, www.upfrontandcompany.com, for the **music schedule**. *102 East Main, a block south of Washington, between Front Street and the harbor. 226-2824.* ♿

"Our customers have allowed us to seek out the finest," says Bob Green of **THE OFFICE SUPPER CLUB**. This **intimate, classic, white-tablecloth steakhouse and bar** is a special-occasion place, yet casual enough for boaters to feel comfortable walking up from the marina. A complete menu of meat and seafood dinners starts at $13 for chicken primavera and includes Black Angus filet mignon ($26 and $32), steaks, prime rib ($16), and Beef Wellington ($40 for two) and meats from far away, like New Zealand lamb rack, Atlantic salmon, and Australian rock lobster tails, all cryogenically frozen in 8 seconds so ice crys-

Mines in Marquette and the Western U. P. employed many ethnic groups which immigrated between 1900 to 1924, like these immigrants arriving at Ellis Island. As a result, the area has good Italian restaurants and food specialties typically found in big cities.

tals are too tiny to interfere with texture. Green became fascinated with top-quality meats when he took his Rib Chef controlled cooking system to restaurant trade shows across the U.S. Other uncommon meats are veal, ostrich fillets with portobello mushrooms and wine sauce ($23) and Cajun breaded alligator. Dinners come with a garden salad, followed by a sorbet, then the main course with starch and vegetable garnish. Smoke-free. Reservations advised on weekends. *154 W. Washington, downtown. 228-9335. www.kreative-koncepts.com Open daily 4 p.m.-10 p.m.* ♿: call. Full bar

KARMA CAFE is a downtown breakfast and lunch spot with a wonderfully **friendly** atmosphere. Prices for nutritious from-scratch homestyle cooking, both vegetarian and with meat, are **amazingly affordable**. The lunch special ($4.50) may be chicken lasagna, a veggie bake, or meat loaf with mashed potatoes and gravy. There are also rotating desserts, organic salads, a meat and a vegetarian soup, hamburgers and two veggie burgers, one with lentils, one with spinach and feta. Owner Denise Shebek named the café after her dog, and also because of her general philosophy that "what goes around, comes around. We treat everyone the same. That's what has made this place what it is." *130 W. Washington, beneath the Ben Franklin. 225-1823. Open Mon-Fri 9-5 and occasional Saturdays.* ♿: call ahead. Freight elevator. 🚻

The popular downtown cappuccino bar and bakery **BABYCAKES MUFFIN COMPANY** also offers salads and flavorful

soups ($2.89/bowl, also by the quart for $5.49). A big, tasty muffin is $1.25. Each day there's a rotating selection of 12 to 14 muffin varieties from the repertoire of 80, along with several **delicious specialty breads, scones, croissants, and dessert pastries**, from brownies and cookies, biscotti, and madeleines to tortes, cheesecakes, and tartes. Croutons toasted with olive oil, spices and butter are just $2.50 a pound. Homemade granola is a breakfast option. Everything's vegetarian. *223 W. Washington. 226-7744. Open Mon thru Fri 6 a.m.-6 p.m., Sat 7 a.m.-5 p.m.* ♿ 🚻

PORTSIDE INN combines a family-friendly atmosphere and menu with a full bar and a deck, one of the few places in town for **outdoor dining**. It even has a distant lake view. It's known for Mexican entrées (around $9), pizza, and seafood, from crab legs to pickerel. At lunch, sandwiches and salads are around $5. Root beer and floats are fun for children; so are bread sticks with pizza sauce. Thursdays at 8 in July and August there's **live music** on the deck, a vocalist with various styles of pop music. No cover. Reservations taken. *239 W. Washington downtown. 228-2041. Open Mon-Thurs 11 a.m. to midnight, Fri 11 a.m. to 1 a.m., Sat noon-1 a.m., Sun 2 p.m. to 10 p.m. Kitchen closes an hour before closing except for pizza.* ♿: side entrance on deck 🚻 Full bar

The **NEW YORK DELI and ITALIAN PLACE** is the very popular late-life project of Marquette native Don Curto, who came back to town after a newspaper career in New York and Washington. Inspired by his Italian background, his father's love of food and cooking, and his own wide-ranging travels, Curto has made it his mission to bring the necessities of the broader food world to Upper Michigan. He likes to say that his place is the **U.P.'s only Jewish deli**, with real nova lox, rye bread, pastrami and corned beef from suppliers to the best Jewish delis of Detroit; respectable bagels; and Dr. Brown's kosher soda. Chicken noodle soup ("attacks the mild illnesses") and matzo ball soup ("for the most serious seasonal germs") are always on hand, along with three selections from the repertoire of over 100 soups ($3/bowl with roll). Now that there's a liquor license, customers can have a beer with lunch or wine with pasta and other suppers (mostly $11 to $15, daily menu changes seasonally). Sandwiches are mostly around $5, or under $7 for the large version, both served with cole slaw and dill pickle spear. Meal-size salads ($4.50 to $7.25) are mostly Mediterranean-inspired. **Bread pudding**, brownies, and sour cream coffeecake are made here. Each month the *Marquette Monthly* features Don Curto's musings on food. *Front just north of Washington, west side of street. Alley access to parking ramp. 226-3032. Closed Sunday. Mon-Wed 11 a.m. to 8 p.m. Thurs-Sat 11-9.* ⅃: rear entrance 👫🕴 Full bar

The elegantly renovated **LANDMARK INN** downtown hotel has two dining rooms, quite traditional in an English *way, and a pub off the front lobby. It's at 230 N. Front at Ridge; phone 228-2580 or visit www.thelandmarkinn.com*

The Landmark's cozy, convivial **NORTH-LAND PUB** attracts regulars who work downtown. It serves a pub menu: personal pizzas, soups, burgers and other sandwiches, bar food from nachos to fried calamari, and a few main dishes like whitefish baked in a bag with brie.

The Landmark Inn's two fine dining restaurants started out "about 50 years ahead of the times up here," says a recently retired physician who's no stranger to fine dining in many places. As we go to press, they're searching for the right balance of food that's sophisticated without precluding a local market. Check the website for up-to-date menu info. Food reviews are mixed at this time.

The Landmark's main-level **HERITAGE ROOM** serves breakfast, lunch, and dinner and is known for seafood. Some popular dinner samplings: grilled yellowfin tuna with sautéed tomatoes and basil ($16), leek-wrapped salmon ($15). Reservations are suggested for the Friday seafood buffet ($22). Three vegetarian

entrées are offered daily. For dessert, the puff pastry swan stuffed with chocolate mousse, swimming in a raspberry coulis "pond" is a favorite. Lunch entrées are $6 to $8. Changing selection of 50 to 60 wines. *Open daily from 7 a.m. to 2 p.m. and from 5:30 to 10 p.m.* ⅃ 👫🕴 Full bar

The Landmark's reservations-only sixth-floor **SKY ROOM** is open for dinner on Friday and Saturday. The $35 prix fixe menu for the five-course meal changes each weekend. Lately lamb and veal have been featured along with a seafood and a beef entrée. The Sky Room looks south across the city and Marquette Bay to Marquette Mountain; the North Star Lounge looks north across the Ridge-Arch Historic District. The **views** are indeed fine; the trouble is, the 1928 window openings mean you have to be standing near them to see out and down to the city and lake. *Open Fri & Sat 5 p.m. to 10 p.m. by reservation.*

The sixth-floor **NORTH STAR LOUNGE**, a much quieter place than the Northland Pub, offers wines, beers, cocktails, and liqueurs and appetizers. Patrons can order food from the Heritage Room if they are prepared for an extra wait. (Its kitchen closes at 10.) *Open from Tuesday through Saturday, 5 p.m. to midnight.* ⅃ Full bar

BAJA BISTRO, from the same people who started the Border Grille, is more a meat-and-potatoes place geared to take-out, like the Boston Market chain but locally owned. Rotisserie chicken and pork are favorites, accompanied by garlic mashed potatoes, homestyle sides, and fresh salads. The **$5 combo with a quarter chicken** is better eating by far than a comparable meal at a burger joint. There's seating for 15 or 20. *547 W. Washington by 7th, across from Harlow Park. 228-0100 . Mon-Sat 11-8.* ⅃ 👫🕴

The **SWEET WATER CAFÉ** is a big, light, airy place, totally smoke-free, with a natural look and multicultural accents. It **smells great**, with espresso brewing, bread baking, exotic spices perfuming the air. Vegans can eat happily here, with several vegan entrées, sandwiches, and breakfasts. From-scratch baking and salad dressings are the rule. Four daily breads are satisfyingly chewy. **Breakfasts**, served to 3 p.m. weekends, include winter grain cereal ($4.80 a bowl) and the delicious $5.40 basic breakfast (2 eggs, several kinds of seasoned potatoes, toast, bacon). The **lunch** menu (currently $5.40 to $7.80, served all day) offers things like hummus and falafil on pita bread; a locally raised beef

or soy patty or chicken filet, served cajun, oriental, or "Midwestern plain"; and smoked chicken salad with grapes. Soup and sides are around $3 and under, available any time. **Dinners** (4-9 p.m.) include bread and soup or salad and rotating entrées like Indian dinners, chicken or vegetable lasagna, and fresh fish on Friday, baked, broiled, or pan-fried. Housemade cakes, cheesecakes, and cappuccino are for dessert. Beautiful china is a treat.

Owners Ursula Stock and Sean Murray met at Cornell's highly regarded hotel and restaurant school. Later they drove across the U.S. seeking the right place to start their ideal business. It had to have clean water, a college campus, and a population of under 300,000. They loved Marquette and Lake Superior. This onetime dance hall was bigger than they wanted, but they tackled it nonetheless. Reservations advised for groups over four. *517 N. Third between Ohio and Michigan. 226-7009. Mon & Tues 7 a.m.-3 p.m., Wed-Sun 7 a.m.-9 p.m. Reservations accepted. No smoking.* ⅃ 👫🕴 Full bar

A perennially **popular campus hangout**, **VANGO'S PIZZA & LOUNGE** has good, inexpensive food — a **great place to take kids**, despite the name. It's a plain place— the main decoration is a big-screen TV. Standouts include an **excellent Greek salad** and other Greek items; the 14" house pizza with lots of toppings; a healthy hero on pita bread with Swiss, sprouts; and cudighi (spicy pork sausage on French bread). Pizza dough is made from scratch. Typical lunch and dinner specials include chicken pilaf, sirloin tips, Friday fish fry. No video games. No credit cards. Out-of-town checks OK. Deliveries to motels. *927 N. Third at Park. 228-770s Mon-Wed 11 a.m.-midnight, Thurs-Sat 11 a.m.-2 a.m., Sun noon-midnight.* ⅃ 👫🕴 Full bar

The **VILLAGE CAFÉ** is one hard-working couple's favorite spot for lunch because of its **cozy, quiet atmosphere** and tasty, satisfying meals. Its **popular skillet breakfasts** ($6), omelets, and eggs benedict are served any time, as are quiches. Most come with a tropical fruit cup (guava, kiwi, papaya). **Chicken dumpling soup** is a signature item. There's always a vegetarian chili and eight meal-size salads made with lots of vegetables. The front case shows off the baked goods: several cheesecakes, muffins, and dessert bars, all made on the premises. *1015 N. Third. Open daily. Mon-Sat 7-3, Sun 8-3.* ⅃ 👫🕴

CASA CALABRIA is a casual, cozy, popular **Italian supper club** and pizza place with light, natural wood decor, a good wine list, and a separate **lounge**. All orders include homemade garlic bread. Standouts include **Calabrian chicken** (spicy Italian baked chicken, $8.50 with salad, around $11 with ravioli or gnocchi), cheesy lasagna, stuffed cheese shells with choice of 6 sauces, steak or pork tenderloin with a pasta side. All pastas come with choice of meat or vegetarian sauce. Dinners (mostly around $13) include minestrone or other soup, antipasto salad, ice cream. Pizzas are available in crispy thin crust, traditional, or deep dish. **Specialty pizzas** like Margherita (fresh tomato, oregano and basil) and Italian Chicken (Italian sweet-sour sauce, cheeses, and grilled chicken breast chunks) are standard priced — about $10 for large. *1106 N. Third between Magnetic & College, 2 blocks south of Superior Dome. 228-5012. Sun-Thurs 4:30-11 p.m., Fri & Sat to midnight.* &

In Marquette, the consensus is that the **best pasties** are from **JEAN-KAY'S PASTIES & SUBS**. It's strategically located near NMU, the Superior Dome, and Presque Isle Park. Jean Kay's traditional pasty uses cubed flank steak, not ground beef, plus optional rutabagas. Then there's the vegetarian option, using broccoli, cauliflower, celery, onions, carrots, potatoes, peppers, mushrooms, and low fat cream cheese and imitation shredded cheddar in a whole wheat crust. Each is $2.75. A fresh batch of pasties comes out every 45 minutes or so. For mail-order pasties year-round, call (800) 727-2922. Jean Kay's also offers pita sandwiches, wraps, and 13 different subs, from around $3 to $4.35). Bread bowl salads are around $4.35. Pasta salads are by the pound. *1639 Presque Isle at the Dome (Presque Isle is the northern extension of 4th St.).228-5310. Mon-Fri 10 a.m.-9 p.m., Sat & Sun 10-8.* &

Marquette's time-honored destination restaurant is the **NORTHWOODS SUPPER CLUB**. It's rustic, woodsy, traditional, and relatively inexpensive. The main dining room looks out onto a hillside **wildflower garden** laced with paths where the public is welcome to walk. The original building, a log version of Art Deco, dates to 1934-6. It now houses the lounge. Known for **steak, prime rib** (3 cuts are $16 to $24), fresh **whitefish** and **lake trout** (about $13). Meat is hand cut on the premises. Dinners include a soup and salad buffet, plus vegetable, potato, and roll. Tuesday-

night smorgasbord $11. Lunches (steak, whitefish, trout, or chicken entree plus potato and vegetable) are $8 and under. Salad bar & soup $4.10 at lunch, $8 at dinner. Thursday is pasty day, and we've heard they're very good. Homemade pies; call in advance for takeout. *On Northwoods Dr. 3 1/2 miles west of Marquette, south off U.S. 41/M-28. Turn at sign. 228-4343 Mon-Thurs 11-9, Fri & Sat 11-10. Current Sunday hours 10-2; may change.* & 🏃🏃 Full bar.

MARQUETTE LODGINGS

See also: Negaunee, Ishpeming, Big Bay

Most motels are on the busy, confusing commercial strip along U.S. 41/M-28 going west from town. A wide range of facilities are on the highway here, including most major chains and a number of good, inexpensive independent motels. However, this environment is entirely auto-dominated and without a view of Lake Superior. If you stay here, you'll need a car to go just about anywhere . That's a much less flexible situation if members of your traveling party have different habits and preferences. Our selections favor the few in-town locations and lodgings with a Lake Superior view.

The Marquette area has 1,200 rooms, which makes for good availability even in summer and on winter weekends, the premium seasons with higher rates. Advance reservations are advised in summer. Still, sometimes everything is full — say, for hockey tournaments at the Superior Dome — at times visitors wouldn't anticipate.

THE LANDMARK INN
(888) 7LANDMARK; (906) 228-2580; www.thelandmarkinn.com

Elegantly restored to much fanfare in 1997, the six-story, full-service downtown hotel, completed in 1928, has a wonderful downtown location on Front at Ridge. Rooms have been combined to create 62 larger rooms, each decorated individually with antiques. The **large and elegant** cherry and mahagony **lobby** with its **Italian marble floors** is a highlight.

23 rooms have gas or electric fireplaces, including each corner suite. Rooms on the south and east sides have a **harbor view**; the **town view** is also interesting. The original window opening means you have to be near the window to see the view. "Specialty rooms" have themes honoring local legends like Chief Kawbawgam or historian Fred Rydholm (this room has a lodge look) or famous

guests like Amelia Earhart. Check out the website for current rates and specials. As we go to press, they are $95-$104 (standard rooms), $105-$114 (specialty room with fireplace),$115-$124 (specialty lakeview), $125-$134 (specialty lakeview with fireplace), $169-$174 (Jacuzzi suite), $189-$194 (two room suite). A two-night B&B package including two breakfasts and a dinner is $223, or $261 in summer. There's no pool, but there's an exercise room, two 18-person whirlpools, and massage therapy on the premises. If the adjoining parking lot is full, valet parking is provided. The aim is to offer the personal style and service of a bed and breakfast. Food is served in the downstairs pub, in the Heritage Room (breakfast, lunch, and dinner), and the special-occasion Sky Room (weekend dinners only).

For four decades after its completion in 1928, the six-story Northland Hotel, perched near the top of the Ridge Street hill surveying Marquette Harbor, was the most elegant place in town. Renamed the Landmark, it continued operating until 1982, then stood empty while a succession of prospective developers checked it out. Bruce and Christine Pesola longed to resurrect the place but couldn't afford to do it. They went on to build and manage many rental units and commercial properties and to develop the successful Shiras Condominiums around the old quarry lake. In 1995 they bought the downtown landmark hotel and commenced to renovate it in style, drawing on Christine's cache of antique furniture and researching hotel history for the theme rooms. *Front near Ridge, two blocks north of Washington downtown.*

H.A.: some ADA accessible rooms
🏃🏃 : no extra charge; rates by the room

RAMADA INN   (906) 228-6000
This 113-room hotel on 7 floors is 2 blocks from downtown, 1 block from Harlow Park. Décor is contemporary. Some rooms have views of the city and lake; some look onto an atrium with a kidney-shaped indoor pool and whirlpool, with adjoining sauna, and game room. All rooms have La-Z-Boys. Two-person rates around $100. Some have refrigerators. VCRs and microwaves can be rented. Ask about in-room whirlpools, family suites. The lobby has coffee & a work center. The dining room serves breakfast, lunch, & dinner. Baja Bistro homestyle takeout is a block away. Rates: $67. *412 W. Washington, downtown.*

H.A.: accessible rooms   🏃🏃 🐕: call

VILLAGE INN

(906) 226-9400;
www.villageinnofmarquette.com

This convenient, pleasant 40-room, 3-story hotel is at the end of the Third St. shopping area, within three blocks of restaurants, NMU, the Superior Dome and its public recreation facilities, and the lakeshore bike path that goes to Presque Isle Park and downtown. It's a great location if you want to bike, exercise, and end the day with Italian food and wine at Casa Calabria down the street walk back to your lodging. Standard rooms for two are $57 in summer, kitchenettes are $65. Whirlpool rooms $110. Free morning coffee, donuts, and juice. *1301 N. Third, 13 blocks north of Washington.*

H.A.: some rooms ADA accessible 👫👣: 17 & under free ♿ $5/extra person

COMFORT SUITES   (906) 228-0028

An **extremely pleasant indoor pool**, a **big breakfast bar**, and large, new rooms that all have microwaves, minifridges, coffeemakers, irons, and hairdryers make this 60-unit hotel on the U.S. 41 strip a popular place with business travelers and families alike. The indoor pool and patio look out onto the woods behind the motel; there's a whirlpool, sauna, exercise room, and guest laundry. The lobby has a fireplace and seating area. Breakfast is served in the attractive **Shiras Club Lounge**, decorated with wildlife photographs taken in the area by George Shiras, "the father of wildlife photography." In the evening bar service is offered. Standard suites have a sitting area and partial room divider with two beds. Summer rates for two are $105. Ask about "king leisure suites" with two-person whirlpool. Hudson's Classic Grill Restaurant, a lively family restaurant/bar with a historic auto theme, is right next door. *On U.S. 41 on the west side of Marquette, just west of the Holiday Inn and half a mile east of Westwood Mall and Wal-Mart.*

H.A.: some rooms ADA accessible 👫👣: 18 & under free; $10/extra person

HOLIDAY INN   (906) 225-1351

The **largest indoor pool in the U.P.** attracts many families to this attractive 200-room hotel. Room refurbishing should be complete by summer of 2001. New rooms have three bed configurations: a king, king with sofa-bed, or two doubles. Summer rates: $82-$87 for up to 5 people, adults or children. Each room has a coffeemaker. The indoor pool room with whirlpool and adjoining sauna

looks out onto a wooded hillside with pond. Video games are in the same large area. There's a restaurant in the hotel and a Wendy's next door. *On U.S. 41 on the west side of Marquette, and half a mile east of Westwood Mall and Wal-Mart.*

H.A.: some rooms ADA accessible 👫👣: 12 & under eat free from kids' menu. 🐾: call

CEDAR MOTOR INN

(888) 551-7378; (906) 228-2280

Attractive rooms, nice landscaping, and a very clean, smallish indoor pool in a pleasant pool room make this independent motel stand out. A hot tub, sauna, and sun deck are in or off of the pool room. 44 units are in two buildings. Indoor corridors connect the rooms and buffer them from winter winds. All rooms have cable TV with free HBO, coffeemakers, and phones. Rooms in the pool building are larger and cost more. Sample room rates: $48 and $59 (one queen), $53 (one queen and La-Z-Boy), $55 (two doubles), $63 (two queens). Two efficiencies have fridges and microwaves. *2523 U.S. 41 West, fourth motel west of the Holiday Inn going up the hill.* **H.A.:** call 👫👣: 5 & under free; $3/extra person

Transplanted Austrians Sepp and Annemarie Hoedlmoser, now retired, built this onion-domed peace chapel in the woods behind their Tiroler Hof motel. The chapel can be visited; ask for the key at the motel.

TIROLER HOF MOTEL

(800) 892-9376; (906) 226-7516; e-mail tirol18.com (That's 18, the numeral)

This Austrian inn isn't the typical American fake Alpine look, but more like a newer hotel built in Europe. That's because it was designed and built by transplanted Austrians Sepp and Annemarie Hoedlmoser. (In 1997 they sold it to Goggi Schaub, a chef, and his wife, Bonnie. Now retired, the Hoedlmosers still live on the property.) A ski racer, Sepp came here to lay out Marquette Mountain's first ski trails in 1957-58. The inn became their summer income. It's built up on the hillside away from U.S. 41/M-28. Beautiful flowers and picnic tables encourage visitors to sit outside. The property abuts a **natural area** along Carp River valley, Marquette Mountain scenic lookout. **Wildflowers** and excellent morning and evening **bird-watching** are on **trails** through the Hoedlmosers' property in the woods, and by a **pond** in the valley, a favorite stopover for migrating birds. A charming walk winds up to and beyond the Hoedlmosers' delightful onion-domed woodland peace chapel that commemorates many world religions and recalls Sepp's home town of Strobel near Salzburg. Ask for the key at the office. Across the busy highway, a **bike trail** goes to Marquette in one direction and to Harvey in the other.

Room decor is simple and cozy. All are air-conditioned, with phones and cable TV with ESPN. $55/night year-round for two. First-floor rooms have patios, second-story rooms have balconies, all with distant Lake Superior views made possible by clearing some trees recently. A sauna and guest laundry are extra amenities. The restaurant with bar now serves three meals a day. *On U.S. 41 at the Carp River, 2 miles south of downtown.*

H.A.: call 👫👣: 12 & under free

BIRCHMONT MOTEL

(906) 228-7538; (877) 458-7805; www.birchmontmotel.com

Just about every room at this modernistic-style, 35-room two-story motel has a kitchenette and a balcony with a lake view. Rates: $38-$46 (one bed), $42-$52 (two beds). Four tiny rooms without kitchenettes are less. No air-conditioning. Full cable TV. The front lawn overlooking the lake is huge, with grills, picnic tables, and a small swimming pool. The bike path to town is across U.S. 41. Call ahead, especially for July weekends. *2090 U.S. 41 South, 3 miles south of downtown. Open May 1-Nov. 1.*

H.A.: call 👫👬: rates by room, not people 🐕: usually. Call.

SEACOAST at SAND RIVER
(877) 307-6710; (906) 343-6710; www.seacoastsandriver.com

On the other side of M-28 from where the short Sand River empties into **Lake Superior**, this nine-room motel extends back at right angles to the highway. The **beach** is **sandy**, and the location is midway between Marquette (16 miles to the west) and Au Train and Munising, 10 and 21 miles to the east. The remodeled, newly furnished rooms are very pleasant and thoughtfully appointed — "motel rooms with a cottage atmosphere," the managers like to say. Four are **kitchenettes** ($60 for two) with a queen bed and double futon. Most of the other five ($46 for two) have a queen and a double futon, plus a **mini-fridge**. Rates may be higher in winter to cover heat. Skiers like to stay here because they can cook for their special diets. All rooms have in-room coffee. Microwaves are available. There's a **picnic area** with gas grill. No air-conditioning; not needed. TV has three channels. Guests may use the office phone. By 2002 cottages are planned to be built in the back of the property, at which time one motel room may become a "hospitality room." Managers Chris and Cathy Staniek are **avid anglers** who make and sell fishing contour maps of inland U.P. lakes. Most rooms are non-smoking. *4012 M-28 East at Sand River, 16 miles east of Marquette. Open year-round.*

H.A.: call. Many wheelchair guests. 👫👬: 13 and under free 🐕: call.

MARQUETTE AREA CAMPING

See also: Champion, Big Bay.

MARQUETTE TOURIST PARK
(906) 228-in-season reserv. & info; (906) 228-0460 for off-season reserv. & info; www.mqtcty.org

This is pretty much the only campground convenient to both Marquette and the choice natural areas just north of it. The modern campground with showers, pay phones, paved roadways, etc. is hardly a wilderness experience, but it's quite pleasant. Shady sites aren't too close together. Tent campers have a separate, 38-site section and won't feel overwhelmed by the RVs, which have 62 sites. For convenience, the location can't be beat. It's right off CR 550 (the way to Sugar Loaf, Little Presque Isle, and Big

Bay), on a lake-size impoundment of the unfortunately named Dead River at the north edge of town. Actually the Dead River is good for **swimming** and for **fishing**. Pike is excellent, and trout and salmon can be caught downstream. Tourist Park also serves as an in-town municipal park. There's a good **swimming beach** with lifeguard and a playground and picnic area. **Bike paths** connect to Presque Isle Park and downtown. The NMU campus and Third St. shops and restaurants aren't far away. Tent sites are $9/day. Sites with electricity are $16; full hookup sites are $18. For one July weekend the Hiawatha Traditional Music Festival takes over. Drop-ins often available on non-holiday summer weekends. Reservations available; $4 fee. Call (906) 228-0465 in season. Off season, mail reservations to City of Marquette, Tourist Park Campground, *300 W. Baraga, Marquette 49855. Off Sugarloaf Ave. just south of the Dead River. From Washington St. downtown, take Fourth St. out to Wright, turn left, right onto Sugarloaf, follow signs. Open mid-May thru mid-Oct.*

H.A. 👫👬

HARLOW LAKE CABINS/Little Presque Isle State Forest Recreation Area
Info & reserv. (906) 485-1031

Six recent rental cabins are situated around 64-acre Harlow Lake, a **quiet lake** where only electric motors are permitted. The attractive rustic wood cabins are very simple, without indoor plumbing or electricity. Front **porches** overlook

Six state forest rustic cabins overlook Harlow Lake near Little Presque Isle. For just $35 a night, they lodge visitors near prime hiking, snowshoeing, and kayaking spots.

the lake. Firewood for the wood stoves is provided. Cabins sleep up to 6 on three bunk beds, rent for $35/night (2-night minimum), $225/week. Three cabins are on a peninsula in the lake, two are on a loop of the ski/hiking trail, and one is by itself on Harlow Creek. There's a wheelchair-accessible **fishing pier**. The lake tends to be weedy, but there are places off some rocks where people do swim. Prime hiking trails and an exceptionally beautiful Lake Superior beach are across CR 550 at Little Presque Isle. Reservations for the following year are taken starting in October. For example, bookings for 2003 are taken starting October, 2001. Winter is seeing lots of use, making year-ahead reservations essential. Summer isn't quite so booked. *Look for entrance road on inland side of CR 550, opposite drive to Little Presque Isle parking area, about 6 1/2 miles north of Wright St. (906) 485-1031.*

H.A.: 4 cabins, vault toilet, fishing pier are ADA accessible. 🐕

GITCHE GUMEE RV PARK & CAMPGROUND (906) 249-9102

"Ranger Jeff" Glass's little world, across M-28 from a beautiful **Lake Superior beach**, is more than an amenity-loaded 60-site RV park and tent campground — it's a **folk art environment** inspired by Hiawatha, Ojibwa lore, and a vision of the good life that includes both simple living and 68 channels of cable TV, brought to most campsites. In 1970 Jeff bought the original 52 acres (it's now 70) and began individually clearing camping spaces in the woods. Each year he has added little extras, so that today the entire campground is decorated with granite slabs and rocks, on which pictures and inscriptions have been carved. One example shows a log cabin and this poem:

"Throw all the waste into the fire.

Take home the cup and now aspire

To simpler life and greater giving.

You too will grow by simple living."

There's a handsome **log lodge** with handmade rustic furniture, where most of the time adults can get away from kids, linger over free coffee, watch a short movie on U.P. attractions, and borrow a book from the library. (Zane Gray and Cully Gage are favorites.) Around six p.m. the lodge is devoted to **Kids' Hour**, featuring free popcorn, a free bubblegum fudge cone, followed by a free movie. R-rated movies are shown later. Mrs. Fudge gives out free samples at the fort-like **fudge factory**, open evenings.

Bonfires on the beach are a simpler form of entertainment. There's a playground and a guest laundry.

"This campground, like camping in general, is made for people from all walks of life," says Ranger Jeff, who espouses a generous, non-judgmental populism. Vehicles range from the very simple to "million-dollar RVs like a 45' Spacecraft fifth wheel with four slides that's almost wider than my house."

Jeff believes in offering a lot for one price, rather than having lots of extra fees. All RV sites are **full hookup** with **cable TV**. Of course there's a shower building. Rates range from $18 (a basic site in an open area, say for gamblers who only want a place to sleep) to $28 for a very spacious site. The $28 family fee covers all immediate family members on a regular site. All sites are wooded except for the basic sites. Rustic sites are $22, with $2 extra for water and electric. One rustic cabin ($35-$45, no showers) has proven so popular that more are planned.

Reserve ahead for July. Cash only. Open year-round. On M-28 11 miles east of Marquette and 33 miles west of Munising. **H.A.**: showers, buildings, and many sites ADA accessible

On the way to Big Bay

The Marquette area's **best-loved natural places** — including Sugar Loaf mountain and the beaches near Little Presque Isle — are along County Road 550, which goes for some 27 miles from Northern Michigan University and Marquette Tourist Park to Big Bay, a Lake Superior sawmill town and getaway spot at the end of the road.

Though 550 is often close to Lake Superior, it's too far inland to offer lake views in this **heavily forested area**. In winter, the road is **famous for whiteouts** from snow blown in from the lake. Much of the land is open to the public because it's within the **Escanaba River State Forest** or owned by **Mead Paper**. The state has acquired 3,000 acres of prime shoreline land in a land swap with Cleveland-Cliffs Iron, which wanted 8,000 acres of state land, far less desirable for public recreation, for disposing of tailings from its Tilden Mine near Palmer.

Both Mead and the Michigan DNR have recently finished a number of projects around Little Presque Isle, Wetmore Pond, and Harlow Lake, building trails, creating **observation platforms**, and installing interpretive signs. An especially scenic section of the **North Country Trail** already connects these beautiful spots with Marquette (at Tourist Park). It looks as if some day a bikeway will join them with Big Bay.

Points of interest along CR 550 are arranged from Marquette and the south to Big Bay and the north.

How to get to CR 550 from downtown Marquette: go north on Front St. until it dead ends at Fair. Go left on Fair. In two blocks, turn right onto Presque Isle Ave. At the third blinking light turn left onto Wright St. Look for Sugar Loaf Ave./CR 550 on the right.

Phil's 550 Store

Get free maps of the Little Presque Isle area and trails plus the brochure and tape for the songbird trail ($20 deposit) at this **unusual convenience store**, fashioned along the lines of old-time country stores. Owner Phil Pearce, a Marquette native, always wanted to have this store, and now he does. He does welding and **blacksmith work** on and off the premises, sells locally made **crafts**, stocks an excellent selection of **wines** in his opinion, and carries **smoked fish** and worms. In summer he has sandwiches made up, and **Jilbert's terrific ice cream cones**.

On the east side of CR 550 before you get to Sugar Loaf, 2 miles north of Wright St. 226-9146. Mon-Fri 7 a.m.-10 p.m., Sat 8 a.m.-10 p.m., Sun 10 a.m.-7 p.m., to 8 in summer.

Sugarloaf Mountain

The summit of this **cherished local landmark** offers a **grand view** looking north and east to Lake Superior, and south to the city of Marquette with its steeples, and the green forests beyond. It's a 15- to 20-minute walk to the peak

A map for Little Presque Isle area hikes

19 miles of hiking and cross-country ski trails in many loops connect the area's natural features — not only the spectacular shoreline but Sugar Loaf and Hogback mountains, Wetmore Pond, Harlow Lake, and Potluck and Harlow creeks. The DNR trail map makes planning easy. Pick up a map at the 550 Store or the Michigan Welcome Center.

— a **view** best enjoyed when the **morning sky** is still dawn-rosy. The trail is well marked. *This half-mile climb is mostly stairway.* Rated "moderate" in difficulty, it is less strenuous than it might otherwise be, thanks to the steps built by the county, plus benches along the way and a **deck** at the **peak**. Today Sugarloaf is county property, but long before it was reached by a road, it was a favorite destination of Boy Scout hikes or paddles. The **stone obelisk** at the summit was erected by members of Boy Scout Troop 1 to commemorate their assistant scoutmaster, who died in World War I, with a monument his mother could see from her bedroom window on Arch Street. They carried stones up from the beach and caught rainwater with a tarp for the mortar. Troop 1 is among the claimants for first U.S. scout troop; when scouting was introduced from England, an already organized boys' club of the local Methodist church joined up immediately.

Sugarloaf was (and is) a special place to outdoors writer Jerry Dennis. He described it in his wonderfully evocative and well written collection of autobiographical sketches, *A Place on the Water: An Angler's Reflections on Home*: "Like many downstaters who attend Northern Michigan University, I was there for the country. . . . Even those places that were most popular gave access to a wildness that is rarely encountered in the Lower Peninsula. A few miles from campus, at the summit of a little mountain known as Sugar Loaf, you could stand on rock outcroppings and look north over the almost frightening vastness of Lake Superior, then turn south and see unbroken hills of forest tumbling inland toward the horizon like bunched rugs. It was country — and this is what I had come north to find — big enough to get lost in."

Sugarloaf Mountain is 6-7 miles north of downtown Marquette on CR 550. Get there by taking Front to Washington, turn west and go to Fourth Ave. Turn north onto Fourth, which becomes Presque Isle Ave. At Hawley turn west. It turns into CR 550. Look for sign by parking lot. Free. &: no.

Wetmore Pond/Mead Paper Co.

Short, unimproved paths lead from the parking area through **old growth forest** to a **spagnum bog** and observation **platform**. Or, if you choose, you can go to the left up into nearby red rocks. They offer a **grand view** of the entire scene: the bog below and Hogback Mountain in the near distance, across an abandoned rail bed now used as a non-motorized ski and bike trail. In spring and fall, migrating ducks and geese gather on the bog, making the rocks a grand vantage point for bird-watching.

Acidic bogs like this develop when wetlands receive little fresh water. Decaying plant materials make them acidic, so that they support only specially adapted acid-loving plants like sphagnum. Thick mats of floating sphagnum look solid but aren't. **Carnivorous pitcher plants** supplement the bog's low level of nutrients by attracting and digesting insects.

These rugged granite boulders and rock outcrops are southern manifestations of the Canadian Shield. These are popular places to picnic or even study. The rocks absorb heat and pleasantly radiate it in the cool spring air.

The trailhead by the parking area shows how to find the 1 1/2 mile trail west up Hogback Mountain, which offers yet another grand view of the lake and forest below. Mead Paper owns this land.

West off CR 550, about 5 miles north of Wright St. in Marquette. (906) 485-1031. ♿: no.

Little Presque Isle, Wetmore Landing & North Country Trail Segment

If this **gorgeous, rocky shore** and the adjacent **beaches** were a state park, they would be far better known and more visited. Local people treasure this area today. It is a good place for bird-watching during spring and fall migration.

Marquette-area hiking enthusiasts maintain that **one of the best trails anywhere** is the four-mile North Country Trail segment beginning at the parking area at Wetmore Landing. It continues south to Little Presque Isle and beyond, for another mile along Lake Superior before it turns inland and crosses CR 550 to end at Tourist Park on Marquette's north edge.

"With its blend of water, beach, rock outcroppings, and thick forest, the Little Presque Isle area is the quintessence of the lovely landscape of the Superior Peninsula," writes Lon Emerick in *The Superior Peninsula.* Much of the forest consists of old-growth hemlocks and red pine. Little Presque Isle and the sandy, popular swimming beach on the south side of [Presque Isle] Point are accessed by the Wetmore Landing parking area. South of them, Emerick writes, "a series of small coves and cliffs as high as 50 feet have formed, creating in miniature

George Shiras III and Wildlife photography's origins

As an 11-year-old from Pittsburgh George Shiras III started coming to Marquette to fish and hunt. He built on those experiences to become a pioneer of wildlife photography, prodigiously active from the 1890s into the 1940s. His grandfather first came to Marquette to fish in 1849, just as the city was getting started. George's father was a U.S. supreme court justice. George too became a lawyer. He made yearly pilgrimages to Marquette, drawn by its pristine waters and forests. Eventually he retired in Marquette.

After years of deer hunting with a gun, Shiras invented what's considered the first camera and flash designed for animal photography. With the encouragement of friend and fellow nature lover Teddy Roosevelt, he published *Hunting Wildlife with Camera and Flashlight.* He traveled the world photographing wildlife and even has a species of moose, which he discovered in Yellowstone Park, named for him. Shiras served as a congressman from Pennsylvania and helped enact many of the wildlife preservation acts we still live by today. The Shiras gun law prohibits carrying a gun out of season. He is buried in Marquette's Park Cemetery on North Seventh at Ridge, just a few steps away from another famous Marquette photographer, B.F. Childs. *—Jack Deo*

the layered and fluted formations found at Pictured Rocks National Lakeshore." Rims of ice around these little coves may last into May and June.

"North of the Point extends [another] sweep of sand beach punctuated only by Harlow Creek; each year the creek alters its winding course as it empties into Lake Superior," Emerick continues. "Back from the rock and sand beaches is a dense covering of tall red pines; shadbush and blueberry form the understory. The old beach lines can be seen as a series of low ridges further inland." The Little Presque Isle parking area affords access to this popular swimming beach. Kayakers can carry their craft a short ways to the beach to put in.

Little Presque Isle is a **striking focal point** for this shoreline hike. The island, about a hundred yards offshore, can be reached by kayaking or wading in hip-deep water — a **great place to enjoy solitude in a beautiful natural setting** where wind and waves have carved little coves in the rock,

The Wetmore Landing parking area is east off CR 550 about 5 1/2 miles north of Wright St. The Little Presque Isle parking area is a mile north. (906) 485-1031. No charge. ♿ no.

Songbird Trail

The 1.1 mile trail loop between Harlow Creek and Lake Superior, part of the Little Presque Isle State Forest Recreation Area, has ten stops with signs that interpret songbirds common in this area: sparrows, American redstarts, pileated and hairy woodpeckers, several kinds of warblers, merlins, thrushes, juncos, and gulls. A tape and tape player with headphones can be borrowed from Phil's 550 Store ($20 deposit), for visitors to acquaint themselves with the sounds made by these birds. May is the best time to see and hear lots of birds.

Park in the Little Presque Isle parking area (above) and cross the creek to get to the trail. (906) 485-1031. No charge. &: no.

Harlow Pathway/ Cross-Country Ski Trail

Two ungroomed loops totaling 5.6 miles offer easy to intermediate skiing here at the **Little Presque Isle State Forest Recreation Area.** For information on the six rustic state forest cabins on and near the lake, see under "Marquette-area Camping. "

Parking area for pathway trailhead is by a gravel pit west off CR 550, opposite the drive to Wetmore Landing and 5 miles north of Wright St. (906) 485-1031. No charge.

Granot Loma

The **rambling rustic private lodge** of banker Louis Kaufman rivals any Adirondack camp in its expense (an estimated $2 million spent over four years from 1919 to 1923), its size (the L-shaped main building is 215' by 300'), and its attention to detail. There are 60 fireplaces, one resembling a birchbark tipi. Though concrete and steel attach the house to a granite outcrop at Lake Superior's edge, the surface materials are primitive and hand finished: rubbed spruce logs, bark wall coverings of birch and cedar, and local slate (from the Arvon quarry in the Huron Mountains near L'Anse) and fieldstone. Indian motifs, Navajo rugs, and bright colors (oranges, greens, yellows, reds, and black and white) reflected Kaufman's pride in his Indian ancestry. His father, a Jewish immigrant who fared well in the clothing business in Marquette, married the daughter of a French trader and Ojibwa woman. Granot Loma is named for the first initials of Louis and Marie Kaufman's children: GRaveraet, ANna, OTto, LOuis, and MArie.

Granot Loma can be seen from the water, but *trespassing is strictly forbidden.* It can't be seen from a public road, but anyone can take Loma Farms Road past the barns, stable, creamery, pheasant house, manager's house, and office of Kaufman's showplace Loma Farms, originally devoted to raising prize cattle. Outsiders can go no farther than the

Henry Ford had the Thunder Bay Inn remodeled into a mill office with guest rooms in his typical Early American style. Its two big front porches look out onto Lake Independence and the sawmill Ford Motor once owned. The inn's restaurant is a popular destination for scenic drives.

fanciful, colorful postmodern/Native American security gate installed by the current owner, Chicago commodities broker Tom Baldwin — unless they want to plunk down a very **hefty fee** ($17,500 a day for ten or fewer people, $20,000 for 11 to 20 in spring, 2001). In that case, you can use the hiking trails, fishing stream, a fleet of ATVs, jet skis, mountain bikes, and more. Visit www.granot-loma.com Note: the original furnishings were mostly auctioned off years ago.

Loma Farms Road is off CR 550 about 7 miles past the parking area for Little Presque Isle.

Little Garlic Falls

A walk through **beautiful woods** and along a **wild, undeveloped river** are the highlights of this easy up-and-down trail of 2 1/2 miles to secluded Little Garlic Falls. The Little Garlic is a noted **trout stream**, home to brook trout all year. The spring and fall spawning runs of rainbow and brown trout from Lake Superior attract area anglers.

Parking area is off CR 550 on the road's inland side, just north of the Little Garlic River. About 12 miles beyond Wright St. on Marquette's north edge, or about 15

A spectacular fall color tour

from Marquette to Big Bay is a circle tour along county roads 550 (the main road past Sugar Load) and 510, the 35-mile, unpaved back way. Colors are usually at their peak from late September to mid-October.

miles south of Big Bay. Look for sign that says "Elliot Donnelly Tract" in honor of the donor of the falls property.

County Road 510 to Big Bay

CR 510 crosses the spring-fed Yellow Dog River and its tributaries, the Big Pup and Little Pup, all noted brook trout streams. They tumble down the cliffs and granite outcrops of this rugged part of the Canadian Shield, forming **several beautiful waterfalls** that can be found *by following directions carefully* on the waterfall and summer attractions **map** published by the Marquette Country Convention & Visitors' Bureau. CR 510 is easy enough to follow, though it winds so much that you're likely to be carsick unless you get out and walk to a waterfall or two. But road signs on the intersecting back-country roads are scarce. Consider contacting **guides** Fred Huffman (906-226-6167), Jeff Ten Eyck (a Big Bay resident who specializes in the area, 906-345-9265), or Martha Bush (another local person who enjoys sharing tips with families, 906-345-9535) for more remote areas.

To get onto CR 510 from U.S. 41/M-28, head west from Marquette. About 1 1/2 miles after the commercial strip stops, you'll pass under a railroad trestle. Look for the CR 510 turnoff on the road's north side just past the Northland Chapel Gardens.

Big Bay

For people who like to feel they're **away from it all**, this sawmill town at the end of the road is a favorite destination. The company-built lumber town on Lake Independence is tucked between the Huron Mountains and Lake Superior. Big Bay enjoys **ready access to the Yellow Dog River and other noted natural trout streams** that come tumbling out of the mountains and the high Yellow Dog Plains. Access from the west is cut off by the **Huron Mountain Club**, the summer retreat of extremely wealthy old-money families. The club raised local ire in 1995 by asking for a conservation tax break while still refusing public admittance to hunt or even hike on their extensive land holdings. In the U.P. the public has access rights not only to vast amounts of state and federal land but to mining and paper company lands as well. People here expect to have access to undeveloped land.

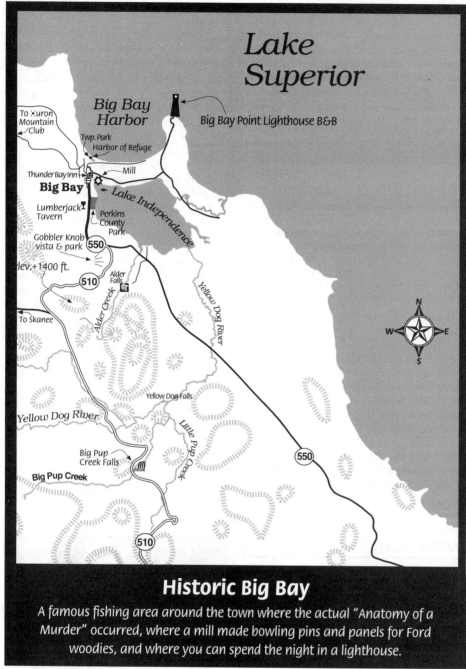

Lake Superior

Big Bay Harbor

To Huron Mountain Club

Twp. Park
Harbor of Refuge

Mill

Big Bay Point Lighthouse B&B

Thunder Bay Inn

Big Bay

Lumberjack Tavern

Lake Independence

Perkins County Park

Gobbler Knob vista & park

550

elev.+1400 ft.

510

Alder Falls

Alder Creek

To Skanee

Yellow Dog River

Yellow Dog River

Yellow Dog Falls

Little Pup Creek

Big Pup Creek Falls

Big Pup Creek

550

510

N
W E
S

Historic Big Bay

A famous fishing area around the town where the actual "Anatomy of a Murder" occurred, where a mill made bowling pins and panels for Ford woodies, and where you can spend the night in a lighthouse.

Founded in 1875 around a sawmill, Big Bay was connected to Marquette by a rail line. Logging camps supplied several sawmills, including a central mill complex so large it had four smokestacks. There **Brunswick** Lumber Company mill made **bowling pins** and hardwood flooring, among other things. In the 1930s, three large sawmills were built on the north edge of Marquette, a more cost-effective location. That spelled doom for Big Bay as a mill town. Brunswick closed its Big Bay operations in 1932; its company houses were sold for $35 each. The isolation of mill town life at the end of the lumber mill days around 1930 is portrayed in Mildred

Walker's fine first novel, *Fireweed*, written from first-hand observation as the company doctor's wife in Big Bay. Later Walker became a well-known regional writer in the west. The University of Nebraska Press has republished her well-received literary debut from 1934. It's a good read about the bright, energetic, Hollywood-infatuated daughter of a Swedish mill hand. Will she fulfill her dreams and enjoy the excitement of city life or get stuck in Big Bay after the lumber has run out?

Big Bay was close to a ghost town when **Henry Ford** bought the mill in 1942 and reopened it, shipping lumber to the Ford Rouge plant to make side

panels for his famous "woody" station wagons. Ford took a special interest in Big Bay and visited it frequently, since it was so close to his summer home at the Huron Mountain Club. He refurbished the old hotel in his best Early American style. Today it's known as the Thunder Bay Inn. The mill closed again in 1949, after Ford's death. To help make Ford Motor cost-effective, old Henry's grandson Henry Ford II eliminated most of his grandfather's cherished village industries, including this one.

In 1952 the owner of the popular Lumberjack Tavern in town was shot by an army lieutenant jealous over attention paid his wife. It is one of the country's most famous murders, immortalized by a local judge, John Voelker. Using the pen name of Robert Traver, he transformed the event in a best-selling novel and classic film, *Anatomy of a Murder*. Eight minutes of the movie were filmed in Big Bay, renamed "Thunder Bay."

Soon after World War II, Big Bay developed its current **split personality**. It has become a place for summer cottagers, largely from Marquette, and for retirees and visitors drawn by the wild trout streams, undeveloped waterfalls, natural beauty, and the mystique of the lighthouse B&B and the Thunder Bay Inn restaurant and inn. The late 1990s saw an influx of year-round residents, well-to-do commuters who built huge homes with big lawns going down to Lake Independence. Expect more pontoon boats, more cars on County Road 550, and better services. (The grocery now has an in-store bakery; the Thunder Bay Inn has more entrées on its regular menu.)

At the same time the village and the surrounding back country are home to people who have chosen to live very simply, on the fringes of society. In characteristic U.P. fashion, some locals stitch together a subsistence income from logging and seasonal jobs and live in old mill housing or in cabins in the woods outside town. The Lumberjack Tavern, still a **classic northwoods bar** with pool table and juke box, offers a window on this world.

Other proponents of simple living are transplants or offspring of Marquette professionals. They have created a community based on what could loosely be called New Age or ecology-based spirituality. Some home-school their children. They link up with organizations of kindred spirits in Marquette. Some have practiced simple living to a degree inconceivable to most Americans — like the family that lives two miles from their road and mailbox, without electricity or phone, and makes a living finding herbs and selling herbal remedies by mail.

Today Big Bay's only non-service businesses are three sawmills, two portable and one stationary. There's the famous old hotel and the infamous bar, **Cram's General Store** (formerly an IGA) with attached restaurant, the **Corner Store** (more of a convenience store with ice cream cones), a public school, some lodgings and gift shops, and, north of town, the Bay Cliff Health Camp for handicapped children. In winter Big Bay has snowmobilers, attracted by up to 25 feet of snow a year. Area businesses have banded together to groom snowmobile trails. Inquire at any lodging.

Juniper Shop/ Thunder Bay Inn

The Juniper Shop is an attractive small gift shop with good regional books and music, bird's eye maple handcrafts, and much more. Informal, self-guided tours are offered of the hotel/lumber company office complex renovated by Henry Ford and added onto for filming *Anatomy of a Murder*. It's fun to see publicity stills from the film with Jimmy Stewart, Lee Remick, Duke Ellington, and George C. Scott. Don't expect to see guest rooms after guests have checked in.

In the heart of Big Bay, where CR 550 turns west. (906) 345-9376. ♿: restaurant entrance on side has ramp.

North Shore Treasures

This rambling shop is charmingly furnished with **old country hutches** and other interesting pieces. The focus is the north country cottage look in pottery, metal accessories, throws, wool clothing, regional books, and jams, sauces, and other food gifts.

106 Bensinger/CR 550 by the south entrance to Big Bay. 345-9588. Open May-Oct daily 11-5. ♿

Big Bay Point lighthouse tour

Regular tours of this big brick lighthouse from 1896, now a bed and breakfast, give the general public a good look at the place, except for guest rooms after guests have checked in. The highlight is the **grand view from the parapet of the 65-foot tower**, 125 feet above Lake Superior. It shows off the site at the end of a peninsula jutting out into Lake Superior east of Big Bay. Just below you can see meadows, forests, Lake Superior's

rugged shore, and Lake Independence, with the Huron Mountains off in the distance to the west. During a big Lake Superior storm, it's an **unforgettable experience**. The fog signal house has an exhibit on the **lighthouse's history**. **Grounds** are **open to the public** from 10 a.m. to 4 p.m. daily at no charge.

Go through the town of Big Bay, take Dam Rd. to east around bay, take lighthouse road to point. 345-9957. **Tours** *given May through September, Tues, Thurs & Sun at 1, 1:30, and 2 p.m. $2.* ♿: no; difficult for crutches.

Lake Independence and Perkins County Park

Despite its popularity, this large (1,860-acre) lake offers **excellent year-round fishing** for most species of fish, according to Tom Huggler in *Fish Michigan: 100 Upper Peninsula Lakes*. The lake's weedy east end produces northern pike all year, there's a large walleye population, and perch fishing can be good in spring and fall at the mouth of the Yellow Dog River. Smallmouth bass is good, too. The **state record perch**, 3 lbs. 12 oz., was caught here in 1947. DNR netting has reduced suckers, so jumbo perch have come back. Independence Lake seems to be a naturally well-regulated fishery.

Furthermore, Lake Independence is **relatively warm for swimming**. The park has a **good beach** and **diving raft**, a barrier-free fishing pier, a fish-cleaning station, a playground, and volleyball area. (See below for camping.) .

On CR 550 at the south entrance to Big Bay. (906) 345-9353. ♿: yes, except beach.

BIG BAY RESTAURANTS

The **THUNDER BAY INN** serves as community gathering spot and popular destination restaurant, too. The large, pine-paneled pub was built onto the existing hotel for the main set of the bar in filming *Anatomy of a Murder*. The menu has expanded so that whitefish, steaks, walleye, and pork chops are always on the dinner menu ($8 to $15). Available any time: bar food, pizza, homemade soups and chili ($2.50-$3/bowl), meal-size salads (about $6), and good sandwiches and burgers. Several vegetarian sandwiches are always on the menu. *In the heart of Big Bay, where CR 550 turns west. 345-9376 . Open daily. Kitchen open Mon-Sat 11 a.m. - 10 p.m., Sun. noon -10. Closed for 3 weeks in April.* ♿: restaurant entrance on side 👪: kids' menu
Full bar

BIG BAY LODGINGS

BIG BAY POINT LIGHTHOUSE B&B
(906) 345-9957;
www.bigbaylighthouse.com

This seven-room B&B is one of two lighthouse inns in Michigan, and only around 20 in the U.S. Owner/innkeepers Jeff and Linda Gamble do all the little things to make this unusual lodging a destination where guests like to stay on the premises. The **cozy downstairs living room with fireplace** is well supplied with a beverage table, baked goods, and lots of games and books. The library VCR has good movies, including, of course, the locally filmed *Anatomy of a Murder*. The Gambles are ardent preservationists from Chicago. (Linda was the facility manager of the Frank Lloyd Wright home and studio in Oak Park.) They love to share lighthouse lore and stories. Linda bakes for the full breakfast. It's most fun to be here, they say, on those marvelous nights when the northern lights can be seen — November through March are the best bets — or when the sky is clear and the stars are out, or when the weather's really bad. Then you can sit in the **tower room** (a common area) and watch storms and lightning out in the lake. There's a **sauna** for guests, **trails** through the woods, and good early-morning opportunities to see birds and wildlife. Guests can borrow **snowshoes**. Three larger "keeper's rooms" with queen beds, fireplace, lake view are $183/night in season, May thru Oct., $160 otherwise. (Prices are from early 2001 and subject to change.) Two other rooms with queen beds, lake view are $143 or $125 off-season. Small rooms with a double bed and woods view are $123 and $99. For good summer availability, reserve 4-6 months in advance; for winter weekends, 4 weeks ahead. **Public tours** of common areas ($2) are given from 1 to 2:30 on Tues., Thurs. & Sun., May thru Sept. *Go through the town of Big Bay, take Dam Rd. to east around bay, take lighthouse road to point. Open year-round.*

H.A.: call on two first-floor rooms

THUNDER BAY INN (906) 345-9376;
www.thunderbayinn.com

The 1911 office/store/hotel/warehouse of the Brunswick Lumber Company surveys Lake Independence and the mill (now a residence) at the center of the sawmill village. When **Henry Ford** purchased the company to supply wood sides for Ford woody station wagons, he refurbished this building in his accustomed **Early American style** and turned the warehouse space into guest rooms.

Darryl and Eileen Small, owners since 1986, have made the place into a comfortable country inn and conference center furnished with antiques — a sociable base for exploring the back country. The two-story front porch is **great for relaxing**, as is the **big lobby with fireplace**. There's also a good **restaurant** with bar attached (see this page). Free continental plus breakfast. Of the 12 guest rooms, 7 have full baths, 5 have half baths with showers down the hall. All are on the second floor. No TV in rooms; no phones (phone is in lobby); no air-conditioning (fans instead). The satellite TV in the pub is often tuned into sports. A TV/VCR in the lobby lets guests see *Anatomy of a Murder* and more. Rates: May-Oct $65 for two (for rooms with half bath) and $85; Nov-March $30/person. Snowmobilers welcome; on trail. For good availability, book by May for summer, by August for fall color. *In the heart of Big Bay, where CR 550 turns west. Closes for three weeks in April.*

H.A.: no   👫♟: 12 & over

BIG BAY DEPOT MOTEL
(906) 345-9350; www.portup.com/~big bay/depot/

Five large, sunny, attractively decorated rooms ($55/night for two) include fully equipped kitchens. Free in-room coffee, teas, and such. No air-conditioning, and no phones; guests can call out on office phone, but only receive calls when owners are in. The grounds of this old freight depot aren't much for trees and landscaping, but the rooms and covered **gallery/porch** on the first and second floors offer a good **view** of Lake Independence and the old sawmill. Guests love to sit at the umbrella tables on the gallery and watch the sun rise. The picnic area and grills have a lake view, too. New in 2001: lake access via a stairway down the bluff to the beach. Color TV has 3 local channels. The tavern across the street has a satellite dish for big games. Walk to in-town businesses and Perkins County Park. Snowmobilers welcome; on trail. Phone in office that's always open. *CR 550 in Big Bay.*

H.A.: call. 2 rooms are downstairs 👫♟: no extra charge. $5/extra adult. 🐕

PICTURE BAY MOTEL (906) 345-9820
e-mail: turner@a1access.net (that's a, followed by numeral one)

This very clean, trim older motel has a **very pleasant seating area** in the back with a **view of Lake Independence**. Rooms have knotty pine paneling. Two

rooms have cooking facilities ($40 and $50/night). Two double beds are in each of the three sleeping rooms ($40). A phone is in the office. No air-conditioning; it's seldom necessary. Three TV has three channels. Snowmobilers welcome; on trail. *On CR 550 at the entrance to Big Bay, a mile from town. Walk to Perkins Co. Park and Lake Independence. Open year-round.*

H.A.: no   👫♟: no extra charge

LITTLE TREE CABINS
(906) 345-9535;
e-mail littletreecabins@portup.com

Four simple, tastefully furnished cabins are behind the **Independence Lake** home of Martha Bush, Ken Baker, and their children. They offer a worthwhile backcountry guide service for the families visiting the Big Bay area. There's a **200-foot stone and sand beach**, a community fire circle and picnic area, **nice hikes** up the **rocky, wooded hillsides** across the road, and **trout fishing** in the nearby Yellow Dog River. Independence Lake fishing is excellent (see above). Each cabin comes with a rowboat, picnic table, and fire ring. The cabins sleep 3 to 6; there's an extra charge for extra people, children and adult alike. Cabins have no water views. Two have screened porches. They rent by the week during summer ($325-$400), otherwise for $50-$75/day, with a 2-day winter minimum. This resort is geared to silent sports, rents a paddle boat, and has a bait shop. *On CR 550 about 3 miles southeast of Big Bay. Open year-round.* **H.A.:** call 👫♟

HIGH ROCK LODGE

(906) 345-9265 or (906) 345-9552
www.portup.com/~bigbay/hmo/home

Big Bay guide Jeff Ten Eyck and his partners Les Milligan and Jim Shattuck opened this mountaintop bed-and-breakfast in summer of 2001. It sits on a high point between the Yellow Dog River and Alder Creek a mile south of Big Bay as the crow flies. Guests park down below and are transported up to their lodgings; they can walk a mile down to have dinner in Big Bay, or an innkeeper will give them a ride, either way.

The partners constructed the log building in a more convenient spot, then hauled it up and built a deck around it, to take advantage of the **360° view** of Lake Superior and the Huron Mountains. Each guest room ($100 for two) has an excellent view. Two have private baths, and two share a bath. There's a living room with fireplace. A full breakfast is served. Jeff's **Huron**

Mountain Outfitters gives guided half-day **tours** (♿) of area woods and waterfalls.

H.A.: outstanding access. One partner, a builder and bulldozer operator, uses a wheelchair himself. 👫♟ 🐕

BIG BAY CAMPGROUNDS

PERKINS COUNTY PARK CAMPGROUND
(906) 345-9353; reservable

This modern campground on the west shore of Lake Independence is a nice place to camp, provided it's not the weekend for the annual softball tournament, or the second-Saturday-in-August pig roast at the Lumberjack Tavern. The grove of mature maples with some hemlock and pine makes for a **peaceful, shady, cool setting**. It's so shady, there's no understory for privacy buffers between sites. See above for fishing and swimming info. The campground is an easy walk into town. There are showers and flush toilets for all sites. Rates vary with services. 36 full-service sites (water, sewer, electricity) in 2001 were $15/night, $62 for 5 nights; 9 electric-only sites are $12/$50; 30 tent sites with no electricity $9/$38. The campground fills on weekends in July and the first part of August, so reserve ahead.

The campground area has had some famous residents over the years. The lieutenant who was the defendant in *Anatomy of a Murder* and his beautiful, bored young wife were among the dozens of army personnel who lived in trailers here in the 1950s while testing artillery anti-aircraft guns for the Army. (The lieutenant murdered the owner of the Lumberjack Tavern across the road.) The late Miss Perkins, the Queen of Big Bay, lived here in her youth, before she grew into a **600-pound hog** by consuming uneaten food from the local school lunch program and quaffing an occasional beer from the Lumberjack. Her owner, resident park manager Kim Bourgeois, then moved her to a spacious, wooded pen on adjacent private property. Miss Perkins died after an illness and was buried, not butchered. *On CR 550 at the south entrance to Big Bay. (906) 345-9353. Open May 15-Sept 15, and often into Oct.*

H.A.: some sites, all buildings, and a grass path to the water are wheelchair-accessible. 👫♟   🐕

Negaunee (*pop. 4,576*)

Negaunee's city seal prominently displays a tree stump. In a momentous discovery in 1844, Ojibwa guides led surveyors to a tree stump with bits of iron clinging to its roots. The spot became the **Jackson Mine** in 1847, the first of over 40 mines in the Marquette Range. Today it's marked by a **stone obelisk** at Miners' Park, on U.S. 41 at Mass Street at the east entrance to Negaunee.

The amount of iron in the Marquette Range turned out to be huge, enough to supply a significant part of the nation's burgeoning 19th-century iron foundries and steel industry. Today Negaunee continues to live off iron. More of its residents work at the nearby Empire and Tilden mines than anywhere else.

A blast furnace was built in Negaunee in 1858, the first of 25 in the U.P. But the lion's share of local ore was shipped to furnaces in the lower Great Lakes. This was no small feat. Completion of the locks at Sault Ste. Marie was essential, and they weren't finished until 1855. The path from Negaunee to Marquette's harbor 12 miles away was over high, densely forested hills, and it took six years to build a railway. Finally, the shallow Marquette harbor required a long dock, finished in 1859, to reach water deep enough for ships. By 1860 over 100,000 tons a year of iron ore were being shipped from the U.P.

But as the 20th century progressed, Marquette Range iron has become increasingly expensive to extract. All but two of the once numerous mines have

closed. These two big open-pit iron mines are near Palmer, about five miles south of Negaunee. At one time Negaunee had over half a dozen mines operating within its city limits alone. Whole neighborhoods were undermined. Areas in town have been cordoned off because of the danger of cave-ins from these underground shafts.

The **dramatic decline in iron mining over the decades** has had a visible effect on Negaunee. Its population, over 8,000 early in this century, is now under 5,000. As the mines closed one by one, little in the way of industry has replaced them. Most Negaunee workers commute to workplaces elsewhere, chiefly the county hospital, Northern Michigan University, and, of course, the two remaining out-of-town iron mines.

Exploring Negaunee and Ishpeming is fun for people who like distinctive places. These towns are at once plain and stately, the results of booms and busts endured through a large measure of simple living. The depressed downtowns have some **ornate buildings**. Many houses cluster around outlying mine locations, some in **amazingly picturesque spots**. Another visitor attraction is the swimming **beach** on **Teal Lake** just north of U.S. 41. Few public parks have such a spectacular backdrop.

U.S. 41/M-28 swings north of the

bluffs and rail lines defining the historic core neighborhoods of Negaunee and Ishpeming. The highway has drawn away most commercial vitality from the old downtown cores. Some enterprising history-lovers have established **antique shops** to take advantage of cheap space. In the Negaunee State Bank building (the bank went under in the 1930s) is Old Bank Antiques at 331 Iron Street. Down the street at 317 Iron is Midtown Bake Shoppe & Antiques which features made-from-scratch baked goods (carrot and cheese cakes are both popular) along side antiques, with a selection of lighting fixtures and garden fencing.

For a **scenic drive** through the old towns and environs, turn south from U.S. 41 onto **Business Route M-28**. It goes under the viaduct at the east end of Teal Lake. After passing through downtown Negaunee and going by its unusual 1914 city hall, BR 28 goes by Suicide Hill Road and enters southeast Ishpeming at Jasper Knob.

Michigan Iron Industry Museum

Overlooking a picturesque river valley near Negaunee, this fine little museum shows in **dramatic displays** how Upper Peninsula iron was central to America's industrialization.

The museum is in the **rugged, wooded hills** at the place on the Carp River where an **iron forge** was built in 1848, just four years after William Austin Burt discovered iron here. Red outcrops of conglomerate rock in this area are a stunning foil for the dark green of conifers. The forge converted ore directly into wrought iron used in things like nails, wire, and bolts. It took an acre of hardwoods to make five tons of iron. Little remains of the long-abandoned forge, but a **pleasant nature trail** leads from the museum past the 19th-century site. The delightful setting, fragrant with pine and meadow grasses in summer, makes this a nice place to linger and a handy rest and exercise stop for travelers heading across the Upper Peninsula.

An excellent, insightful tape-slide show, **"Life on Michigan's Iron Ranges,"** shows how hard the mostly immigrant work force labored — for 60-hour work weeks — and how much work the women did, gardening, cooking, taking in boarders and their wash. Upper Peninsula mining began before farmers and town developers had settled the area, so mining companies had to be community builders, too. It was in min-

Ishpeming & Negaunee

They pioneered the incredibly successful iron mining era that helped build the U.S. Now they have striking reminders of their historic past.

ing companies' interest that mining settlements quickly grow out of the raw boom town stage where saloons and brothels were the centers of social life. Companies successfully developed stability within their work force through low-cost housing rentals and various subsidies to churches and community centers. Corporate paternalism has been a big part of the history and townscapes of many communities on the iron ranges.

The museum does a good job of showing just how important the U.P.'s iron has been. **Almost half of the nation's iron from 1850 to 1900 was mined in this region.** In the 150 years since 1833, the California gold rush produced less than a billion dollars of minerals. Michigan lumber has produced almost $4.5 billion of wood alone. The Keweenaw copper ranges generated about twice that amount. But the riches from iron dwarf these, worth some $48 billion. Call for **special events** and **lectures** held at the museum.

From U.S. 41, 3 miles east of Negaunee and 5 or 6 miles west of the outskirts of Marquette, turn south onto M-35 for 1 mile, turn west onto CR 492 for 2 miles, then turn north onto Forge Road. Signs are clear. For information about special events at the museum, call (906) 475-7857. Open daily May thru October, 9:30-4:30. Free admission. &

Midtown Bake Shoppe and Antiques

Marybeth and Cory Rowe chucked the hectic life in Detroit's northern suburbs to pursue their personal passions. They have redeveloped a piece of downtown Negaunee in the process. Cory loves antiques. His shop has a general line; now that the bakery has expanded, he has moved his larger pieces into **Midtown Antiques 2**, across the street and down the block. Cory goes into **architectural antiques** in a bigger way than anyone else in the U.P. Here are fretwork, fencing, turned posts, hardware, stained glass, doors — the details and decorative touches that make such a difference in restoring historic buildings that have been remuddled.

Marybeth, a self-described chocoholic, worked for years as a pastry chef in **Chuck Muer** restaurants. She looked for space for an eat-in gourmet bakery in Marquette but found it too expensive. Then the Rowes hit on the idea of combining bakery, antique shop, and residence in this old frame building, covered

an vintage asphalt shingles. Cory has artfully covered the exterior walls with architectural items and plants. Marybeth and her staff bake **morning pastries**, cheesecakes, tortes, mousses, brownies, muffins, and **cookies** for individual customers, special events, and wholesale customers like the Landmark Inn. Wedding cakes are a big deal here. There are **tables** so customers can sit down and have a bite. No low-fat, low-taste substitutes here — she uses only butter and fresh whipping cream. The cheesecakes, **carrot cake**, and **hazelnut torte** are big sellers. Marybeth's personal favorite: banana cake covered with chocolate ganache (a heavy cream-chocolate mixture) poured over each piece of cake.

317 Iron St. in downtown Negaunee. From U.S. 41 outside Negaunee, turn south onto Teal Lake Rd. (under the viaduct), right onto Main, left onto Pioneer, and right onto Iron. Shop is in half a block. 475-0064. Open Mon-Fri 7-6, Sat 10-5, Sun noon to 4. &

Old Bank Building Antiques

Three stories of a general line of furniture and small items just down the street from Mid\town Antiques make Negaunee an antiquing destination.

331 Iron. 475-4777. Currently open year-round Mon-Sat 10-5, Sun noon-4.

The Depot Gallery/ Liberty Children's Art Project

Proprietor Marilyn Mutch has moved her gallery and studio from its namesake depot to Iron Street, Negaunee's historic downtown, which is becoming something of an **arts and antiques center**. Gallery artists number some of the Marquette area's most celebrated artists, including Maggie Linn, Paul Grant, and Nita Engle, landscape painter and the only Michigan woman to have received the American Watercolor Society's prestigious Artist of the Year award. (Call for info on occasional three-day **watercolor workshops** by **Nita Engle**.) Marilyn is often at work here, making her wheel-thrown functional pottery dinnerware and some freeform, fused glass jewelry .

Sharing the much larger space is the Liberty Children's Art Project, with inexpensive children's art classes for preschoolers to high schoolers, after school and, during vacations, one week long ($25 for five 1 1/2 hour classes).

442 Iron St., west of the Vista Theater. 475-4067. Open year-round, Mon-Sat 10-

5 or by appt. &: no.

NEGAUNEE RESTAURANTS

PAESANO'S PIZZA is mostly takeout with a few tables. It makes **good Italian pizza** and $5-and-under sandwiches: chicken, **cudighi** (Italian sausage patties), meatball, and steak. Pizzas average $12. Dinners (under $6) include spaghetti, ravioli, and meat and vegetarian lasagna. There's a deck with a **beautiful view of Teal Lake** and the hills beyond it. Smoke-free inside. *81 Croix on the east end of Teal Lake. Turn north at the stoplight (a Citgo and a Holiday gas station are on the corner) and go north a block. 475-6121. Open daily from 4 p.m. to 11 weekdays, til midnight Fri & Sat.* & 👪

SHIRLEAN'S, formerly Vango's II, now has a more American menu of breakfast, pizza, soups, hot sandwiches, burgers ($2.75), and Greek salad ($5) and other meal-size salads. It's about the only breakfast and lunch choice in downtown Negaunee. Friday fish fry is $7. No credit cards. *205 Iron in Negaunee Center downtown. 475-5045.Mon-Thurs 7 a.m. to 8 p.m., Fri & Sat to 10, Sun 7-3.* & 👪 Full bar

Part historic saloon, part sports bar, **TINO'S BAR & PIZZA** is one of those places where local cultures of different eras are layered. It's a local gathering place that attracts Marquette people, too. **Homemade cudighi** comes with onions, good sauce, and cheese ($4.25) or with green pepper and mushrooms too ($4.75). Large pizzas start at $8.75 plus toppings. *220 Iron in downtown Negaunee. 475-6832. Open daily. From Sun-Thurs 4 p.m. to midnight, Fri & Sat to 1 a.m.* &: one step 👪 Full bar

NEGAUNEE LODGINGS

QUARTZ MOUNTAIN INN
(906) 475-7165

This modest older motel is definitely one of Michigan's **most unusual**. Behind the building is a **prime rock-collecting area**. Rooms include phones and cable TV with HBO for $44 a night. The best part is the **terrific breakfast** served in the central common area by owners Jack and Nola McConaha, not just baked goods but fruit, sausage, scrambled eggs, and homemade oatmeal, along with Jack's perceptive, funny comments about life in the U.P. (As a Traverse City native, he's got an outsider-insider's view.) Though clean, comfortable, and predominantly no-smoking, the rooms are not fancy. Most of the 14 air-conditioned rooms are finished with plywood

paneling, and an enclosed hallway means they were dark when visited in fall, 2000. Ask about the six **apartment suites** with complete cooking facilities and beds for 4 to 5. Ask the owners about it. The current owners aren't rock collectors, but some samples and books from the previous owners are still around. Simple picnic facilities with a grill are on the grounds, but highway traffic is annoying. *On the south side of U.S. 41/M-28, 2 1/2 miles west of Marquette Co. Airport, 1 mile east of downtown Negaunee. Open year-round.*
H.A.: call 👥👥👥 🐕: call

Ishpeming (pop 6,686)

Ishpeming stands out from all other iron-mining towns because it developed as the U.P. operations headquarters for Cleveland-Cliffs Iron, one of Lake Superior's biggest iron-mining companies. The in-town skyline is punctuated by **three monumental CCI headframes** on Lake Shore Drive south of Lake Bancroft on the west side of town. These headframes housed the long hoist ropes wrapped around giant drums which carried miners and ore up from the mine shafts, some of them over a mile long. Two were built to resemble **huge Egyptian obelisks**, according to designs by the noted Prairie School architect George Maher. Those underground mines were closed when the Cliffs C Shaft, with the even taller, boxy headframe, was opened in 1955. It too is now closed. One of these striking structures is now illuminated at night as a reminder to motorists on U.S. 41 that there is a town — a quite interesting town — south of the highway.

Mining has been so big here that Ishpeming even had two blasting powder companies through the 1930s. Today mining remains the basis of Ishpeming's economy, what with CCI's U.P. headquarters and the 1,800 high-paying jobs at the nearby Tilden and Empire mines. As we go to press, the mines have closed because of the world glut of cheap semi-finished steel with which North American producers cannot compete. Things may change if President Bush gets restrictions on steel imports.

Few new industries have developed to replace lost mining employment. An exception is the booming Robbins Flooring Company on Greenwood Street just southwest of downtown. Using hard maple from U.P. and Canadian forests, it specializes in gym floors, **making the lion's share of basketball courts for**

The cultural icon of the U. P.

After *Anatomy of a Murder,* John Voelker's fictionalized account of a Marquette County murder trail, became a bestseller and hit Hollywood paydirt in 1959, he gave up his position on the Michigan Supreme Court to come home to Ishpeming and devote himself to flyfishing. Two utterly engaging books still in print, *Trout Madness* and *Trout Magic,* make even non-anglers want to take up flyfishing on area streams. The crusty, unpretentious author used the pen name Robert Traver. He lived in a big old house up the hill from Ishpeming's library and the Rainbow Bar and drank with the guys he'd grown up with.

The five-star movie *Anatomy of a Murder* comes across as remarkably fresh and contemporary today on account of its many outstanding performances from a star-studded cast, its crisp black-and-white cinematography, and its **Duke Ellington score**.

Director Otto Preminger heard about the book before it was published. After it spent 65 weeks on national best-seller lists, he acquired movie rights, came to visit Voelker, and decided to shoot some local scenes. He was so taken with the area and its people, he decided to shoot the whole movie in Marquette County — a big shot in the arm, monetarily and psychologically, for the economically depressed U. P. of the 50s. Preminger wanted to capture not only the look of

Judge/author/flyfisherman John Voelker (left, pronounced VOLK-er) and leading man Jimmy Stewart light up cigars during a break while *Anatomy of a Murder* was being filmed on location in Marquette County.

the place, he said. "I want the actors to feel it, to absorb a sense of what it's like to live here." The shoot was covered in national magazines. Locals loved it, starting when the cast arrived, mostly by train, at the snow-heaped Ishpeming depot: Jimmy Stewart as the defense attorney, Duke Ellington, co-star Lee Remick (Lana Turner had quit), Eve Arden (the people's favorite from her "Our Miss Brooks" TV show), Joseph Welch (the judge), George C. Scott, and Ben Gazzara. Paul Bonetti has put together the wonderful *Anatomy of a Murder Scrapbook,* full of meaty material on the filming and the author. It's $15 at local bookshops and at the Bonetti-owned **Congress Lounge & Pizza**, a mini-museum of Ishpeming history in downtown Ishpeming at 106 W. Main (opens at 4 p.m.). Other Voelker exhibits are in the front entry hall of the Marquette County Courthouse (page 194); and in the Superior Dome (page 201). Voelker's papers are in the NMU library. See the index for film sites.

Voelker's influence was widespread because he had so many friends. After he became famous, serious flyfishermen from around the world made the pilgrimage to Ishpeming, often invited to Voelker's secret fishing shack.

the **NBA and NCAA** as well as for Olympic competition. Robbins' 100 employees work overtime to keep up with demand, turning out four courts a day. Still, they have to compete for the prized higher-grade northern hard maple with six other flooring mills in a 250-mile radius, three in the U.P. and three in Wisconsin.

After remaining at a population of about 9,000 from 1890 into the 1950s, Ishpeming has steadily declined to its present size. Its once-vital downtown is now dwarfed by the commercial corridor along U.S. 41 to the north, along which 15,000 to 20,000 cars pass daily. "Country Village" is a strip mall several streets deep, in buildings so temporary and insubstantial in character that they look as if they could be hauled off at any moment to serve some more promising commercial opportunity.

Lately there's been more appreciation of Ishpeming's historic resources from many quarters. Rather than fading away, the memory of John Voelker (a.k.a. Robert Traver), trout fishing legend, author of *Anatomy of a Murder*, lifelong Ishpeming resident, and regular at the Rainbow Bar down the hill from his house, seems to be gaining steam. A **mini-museum honoring Voelker**, the movie, and all manner of local lore is downtown at **Congress Lounge & Pizza**. **Jerry Harju**, a retired engineering professor and comic storyteller in the vein of the great Cully Gage, has returned to the area to write six books and a regular Marquette newspaper column largely based on his adventures growing up in Ishpeming in the 1940s and 1950s. An Ishpeming Historical Society has been formed. The **ruggedly handsome stone 1891 City Hall** on East Division is being renovated. A summer **downtown walking tour** has been launched by a student in the popular, award-winning entrepreneurship class at Ishpeming High, the brainchild of business teacher Lisa Mongiat. (See below.) The class analyzes the community and its needs each year. It has prepared a feasibility study for the empty **Mather Inn**, the stately four-story downtown hotel, once a hub of activity at downtown's north end, on Canda at Main. Under its current owner, the hotel is in limbo, however.

Still in demand are the fine old homes up the hill behind the Mather Inn, built for mine managers near the turn of the last century. Some mine captains had tunnels connecting their homes with the mine shafts where they worked.

Ishpeming has long been associated with **skiing**. Downhill jumping contests,

begun by the local Norwegian residents, go back to the 1880s. The famous wooden **Suicide Hill ski jump**, 280 feet high and 860 feet long, was built in 1925 on Cleveland-Cliffs Iron land just east of town. It is still operated by the local ski club (486-4898), but it has been moved to Jasper Knob in town because the mining company wants to use the original site.

U.S. National Ski Hall of Fame & Museum

The local ski club started the hall of fame and museum years ago to draw attention to Ishpeming as the **birthplace of U.S. ski-jumping**. The roof, shaped like a ski jump, adds to the highway strip architecture outside town. Exhibits and a video emphasize **skiing history**, going back to prehistoric and medieval times. (Interested visitors can ask the friendly, helpful staff to see **other ski videos** from the listed collection of over 500 videos, including ski movies, Olympic competitions, and the 1989 **ski-flying competition** held in Ironwood — many people's only chance to get a look at that daring sport.) The museum's **ski research library** is one of the largest in the U.S. The annual Hall of Fame induction in late September is "a gala affair," we're told.

The museum tells the story of how downhill skiing developed from a minor sport brought to the U.S. by Scandinavians. In World War II the American ski assault team, which included many Upper Peninsula men, attracted national attention. Hollywood stars at the glamorous ski resort of Sun Valley, Idaho, popularized skiing in the 1940s and 1950s. Many returning soldier-skiers became resort managers when recreational skiing took off. A key to growth

was Michigander Everett Kirchner's artificial snowmaking machine, first used at his Boyne Mountain resort. Interesting biographies of Hall of Famers reflect the **far less commercial era** of skiing before the 1960s and 1970s. The display about disabled skiers is especially interesting. Visitors who are into contemporary ski racing won't find much of interest in the exhibit area.

On U.S. 41 between 2nd and 3rd about a mile west of Teal Lake. (906) 485-6323. www.skihall.com Open year-round, Mon-Sat 10-5. Closed major winter holidays. Adults $3, seniors 55 and older $2.50, students $1, children under 10 free. &

Artisans Gallery & Clay Studio

Owner Jean Waggoner makes her own ceramic ware in this working studio, and her small gallery shows original works in pottery, painting, weaving, wood, and glass by 15 to 20 craftspeople, all from the Upper Peninsula. A few, like raku potter Ed Risak, glassblower Rick Shapiro, and weaver and fiber artist Georgie Hurst, are well known to downstate buyers. Waggoner's own work has two looks: one-of-a-kind slab pieces in a contemporary style, and functional work well suited to camps and cottages.

On U.S. 41 a few doors east of Burger King and half a block east of the Ski Hall of Fame. Enter from side street. 485-1194. May-Dec: Mon-Fri 10:30-5, Sat 11-3 at least. Jan-April: gallery closed. &

Tilden Mine Tour

As we go to press, a summer shutdown of iron mining operations at the Tilden and Empire mines means no summer tours of the open-pit Tilden Mine in

For generations, ski jumping competitions have been held at Suicide Hill, on Cleveland-Cliffs Iron land outside Ishpeming. In Caroline Stone's girls' novel *Porcupine Mine* (1942), the plucky 13-year-old heroine wins a new pair of skis at Suicide Hill. Now the famous ski jump is being relocated because CCI needs the land to store the overburden removed in its massive open-pit mines.

2001. Call (906) 486-4841 for current info. We have revised but included our description of operations at the open-pit Tilden Mine because it gives a good idea of Lake Superior iron mining today. The reservations-only tour of the **vast open-pit mine** and **taconite-processing plant** has been quite popular. Many people find it one of the most memorable parts of their vacations. Not only does the tour provide an insightful look at a dramatic mining operation, it's also a memorable aesthetic experience, even if it wasn't intended to be one. Artists of industry like Diego Rivera and Charles Sheeler would have loved this place.

The U.P. iron industry today excavates iron ore in huge, 300-ton blasts. Now that the veins of richer ore have been mined out, Lake Superior iron mining remains competitive only because of a process that excavates greatly diluted ore and concentrates it into pellets of 64% iron with clay binding. These small round taconite pellets can then be shipped economically from the Michigan ports of Marquette and Escanaba to steelmakers around the Great Lakes. The Tilden mine began pellet production in 1973; it can produce 7.8 million tons a year.

If and when tours are being given, a bus takes tourgoers from Marquette and Ishpeming to the mine, where the tour lasts two hours. There's only one tour a day, so space is limited to the number the bus can hold.

Tour guides have been summer employees at Cleveland Cliffs Iron who have parents working at the firm. They have grown up around mining and are in all probability quite well informed and able to handle many questions. The tour, designed by CCI public relations person Dale Hemmila, gives outsiders a good overview of the precarious economics of U.S. iron mining today. Domestic iron mining and steelmaking have been hurt by dumping practiced by countries like Korea which have put a high priority on developing their own heavy industry. "Our biggest concern is the importing of unfairly traded semi-finished steel slabs," says Hemmila. "They use no domestic ore. We contend that much of [these imports] are being done so in violation of U.S. trade laws."

CCI has owned these iron ore reserves since 1865. Today CCI has partnered with two Canadian steel companies, Algoma and Stelco, who wish to control costs of their basic material. CCI manages the Tilden mine for the partnership.

Oddly, the huge open pit is less dra-

One of the most striking legacies of the iron mining era within the city of Ishpeming are the unusual concrete headframes (1919), inspired by Egyptian obelisks. A headframe housed the hoist that hauled mining cars in and out of underground mines. Here in the middle of its base of operations, Cleveland-Cliffs Iron departed from headframes' typical utilitarian design. This drawing was done by then-8th-grader Brad Cummins from an old photograph. It appeared in *Red Dust*, an annual oral history book published by junior high students in National Mine outside Ishpeming.

matic than the **plant interior**. The pit activity is far away. Blasts occur three times a week, in the morning, never at tour time. It's immediately apparent how enormously capital-intensive this operation is. Truck tires are 12 feet high, and they cost in the neighborhood of $20,000 each, tourgoers are told; a shovel would cost $9 million to replace. Mine operations never stop. The Tilden Mine employs around 815 skilled workers, from metallurgists, engineers, and computer operators to heavy equipment operators. Today the hematite pit is around 500 to 550 feet below the viewing area. There's enough ore to go down 800 feet more.

Inside the taconite processing plant, the noise from crushers and huge rotating mills makes it hard to hear. Signs explain steps in processing. A clearly written free souvenir booklet with color photos lets tourgoers review everything: business rationale, operations, environmental impact. The plant experience involves almost all your senses. It is quite warm — briefly — by the kilns. Occasionally the angled geometry of the chutes and towers strikingly frame outside views of the massive piles of rugged red waste rock and the precisely angled piles of pellets. Even in this monumentally unnatural environment, weeds and pine trees are taking hold, attesting to the power of living things.

The tour ends in the quiet control room, where experienced employees invite visitors' questions. Tourgoers leave with a free plastic goody bag including souvenir taconite pellets. It bears the

mining motto, "If it can't be grown, it has to be mined."

Incidentally, the Tilden Mine is named after **Samuel J. Tilden**, best known as the 1876 Democratic presidential candidate who gained national recognition as a reformer fighting New York's Tweed Ring but lost the election despite winning the popular vote. A New York corporation and railroad lawyer, Tilden (described as cold, secretive, and smart) grew rich from investments. He organized the Cliffs Iron Company in 1864. Much later he extended his Chicago and North Western Railroad from **Escanaba** to the Menominee Iron Range, increasing Escanaba's importance as a **"Iron Port of the World."**

Call to find out if tours are being given. Sign up in advance. Tours have nearly always been full. *In the past, there's been one tour per day mid-June thru late August, Tues-Sat, with busses leaving the Marquette Chamber of Commerce (906-226-6591) at noon, the Ishpeming Chamber of Commerce (906-486-4841) at 12:30. Bus seating is limited; call either Chamber of Commerce for reservations and for tips on appropriate dress (for example, no sandals allowed). Restricted to adults and children age 10 and up. Cost per person: $6. &: no.*

Da Yoopers Tourist Trap & Museum

Black flies, rusty cars, deer-hunting, saunas, bingo, beer, and other important aspects of U.P. life have been immortalized in the good-natured comedy sketches and satirical songs of Da Yoopers of Ishpeming. The group's "The Second Week of Deer Camp" and "Rusty Chevrolet" got nationwide air play in 1987. Simple pleasures are extolled in songs like "Fishin' wit' Fred": "It's a perfect day for fishin', drinking beer and telling lies. It's a little bit like Heaven when you're fishin' wit' da guys."

Da Yoopers have authentic North Country accents and a variety of musical styles to suit each topic, from Finnish accordion polkas to heavy metal. Da Yoopers can be earthy and crude, which some find hilarious. Others wince at their humor and complain that it stereotypes Yoopers as northwoods hillbillies. Judge for yourself! Their complex website, **www.dayoopers.com**, includes some tucked-away gems: a terrific section about rock and mineral collecting in the area and "Hoolie's Corner," **head Yooper Jim DeCaire's stories about growing up in Ishpeming** — more **comic realism** in the Cully Gage/Jerry Harju vein. Every neighborhood had its own personality, he explains, and in his neighborhood, everybody was a little bit crazy. Their unpredictability protected them from tougher kids.

A big Yooper theme is various embarrassments of the digestive tract. **Da Yoopers were in top form** on their 1987 **"Culture Shock"** album. "It's About Time" video ($10) features comic skits of "The Second Week of Deer Camp," "Camp Go-For-Beer," and "Why Do Girls Think I'm Scary?"

In 1990 two of the singing Yoopers, Jim DeCaire and Lynn Coffey, started the highway Tourist Trap as a free outdoor museum and gift shop, where people can get out, stretch, and take in a little local ambiance. Even if you have no interest in **gag gift items** and top-selling souvenirs like the tabletop two-holer outhouse, the museum and store is worth a stop. Da Yoopers' own $1 *Yooper Glossary: Understanding the Yoopanese Language*, read aloud, will enliven any car trip. The shop has some **terrific wood carvings**, an excellent section of books and tapes on Finnish-Americana, among other regional subjects. The new **ROCK KNOCKERS SHOP** for rockhounds has supplies (tumblers, hammers, polishers) in addition to samples, gifts, and displays of specular hematite, kona dolomite, and other collectible area minerals.

Outdoor museum highlights include a **life-size deer camp diorama**, a 60-foot model of an iron-mining drift, Ishpeming artist Kathy Waters' wonder-

Yucks galore are found at Da Yoopers Tourist Trap and free outdoor museum. In this scene, visitors witness a deer at his hunting camp playing cards, with a trophy human head proudly displayed on the wall.

fully detailed murals of scenes from local life, and metal-workers' art like a **10-foot mosquito.** There's a Model A Ford with a front-end bucket, made for snow removal long ago by a Mass City man, and the Guinness-record world's largest chainsaw, custom-made by a downstate craftsman.

Nationally known museum director Robert Archibald, an Ishpeming native himself, introduced his book *A Place to Remember: Using History to Build Community* by criticizing Da Yoopers' Tourist Trap as "an attempt to commodify and market a culture. I fear that it is an indicator of cultural debasement, a view of culture as exaggerated self-parody." Maybe Archibald has been away too long to recognize that Da Yoopers' humor is clearly part of a Finnish-American comic tradition, now spread into the whole region, that goes back at least a hundred years. Their self-parody has deep cultural roots.

On U.S. 41 just west of Ishpeming. Look for bill board. Mail-order available. (906) 485-5595. Open year-round. Summer

(Mem. to Labor Day): Mon-Fri 9-9, Sat 9-8. Sun 10-7. Thru Dec: open to 8 p.m. Jan-April: Mon-Fri 9-5, Sat 10-5, Sun noon-4. Call for May hours and to confirm winter hours. Free. &

Al Quaal Recreation Area

This **wild and natural 300-acre Ishpeming city park** on the north edge of town, overlooks Teal Lake. It hearkens back to the earlier, folksier, hardier style of winter sports brought by Scandinavians. Its **1,200-foot iced toboggan run** is great fun. Cost: $3 an hour including the park's rental toboggans; open Mon-Thurs 4-8, weekends 1-8. The adjacent downhill ski runs and a slalom run with rope tows are also lighted. Cost: $3. Open Wed & Thurs 6 p.m.-9 p.m., weekends 1-4. The **3k cross-country ski loop** (partly easy, partly intermediate) is wonderfully scenic. Part of it has been made into a snowshoe trail. The lighted outdoor ice rink is open Mon-Fri 4-8, weekends 1-8.

In summer, the park offers free swimming on Teal Lake, near a picnic area and lodge.

From U.S. 41, turn north onto Second opposite the Ski Hall of Fame, continue north 4-5 blocks. Take a right at the T. Park entrance is by a playground in 3 blocks. 486-6181.

Wilderness Sports

This widely known downtown outdoor store covers the gamut of local sports: hunting, fishing, archery, downhill and cross-country skiing, snowshoeing, and more. It's a **good source of local fishing and hunting information.** Fishing gear includes fly-fishing ties made by local anglers. Functional outdoor wear goes from traditional to fashion-forward. It offers cross-country ski and snowshoe rentals.

107 E. Division at Main, downtown Ishpeming. www.wilderness-sports.com Mon-Sat 8:30-8, Sun 9-5. 485-4565. & *one step.*

Ishpeming Walking Tours/Ishpeming High Small Business Center

Students in the second year of business teacher Lisa Mongiat's popular entrepreneurship class, having already analyzed the community and its needs and opportunities, have a chance to start their own businesses and use this downtown space and support facilities. High school senior Randy Smith, a charter member of the new Ishpeming Historical Society, launched a business conducting summer walking tours in summer, 2001. Call 485-6553 or 486-3962 to schedule a tour. Cost: $3/adult, $2.50 students. If the tours click, they'll probably continue. At the moment, other student businesses include two web page designers, a personal shopper, and a tennis camp. *203 S. Main. 485-6553.*

Lake Bancroft Park

On the west side of Ishpeming (see map), the park and picnic area has a good view of the mine shafts and town — a **dramatic landscape**. To see even more, climb up the hill behind it.
The park entrance is off Lakeshore Drive on the west side of Lake Bancroft.

Jasper Nob, Cliffs Cottage and vicinity

Jasper is a kind of dense, opaque quartz with crystals too small to be visible. Michigan jasper is a deep red. This **huge outcrop**, locally touted as **"the world's largest gemstone,"** forms a dramatic knob with a **good view on the southeast edge of Ishpeming**. The stately wall around it makes it look like a public park. Actually it's owned by Cleveland-Cliffs Iron, which does not encourage visitation because of liability. The public is allowed on the property, though footing is difficult here. *From downtown, take Division/BR 28 east to Jasper St., turn south. Nob is in one block.*

Back down a little on Jasper at Bluff, the entrance gate to the Swiss-inspired 1891 Cliffs Cottage can be seen. CCI president William G. Mather built it as his summer home. CCI uses it to entertain employees and guests. It's not visible from the street.

If you turn west onto Bluff, you can see one of Ishpeming's most interesting houses, a big, fanciful **Gothic Revival** affair at 112 Bluff. Inspired by Sunnyside, Washington Irving's Hudson River Valley residence, it took advantage of a grand view of town, now obstructed.

ISHPEMING RESTAURANTS

RALPH'S ITALIAN DELI, well stocked with Italian groceries, has a small eating area for quick meals. It's a convenient highway stop for pizza and for picnic and camping food. Crusty homemade rolls make for good subs (mostly $3.25 plus extras) in many varieties, including Italian spiced chicken breast, homemade

meatballs, and cudighi, the local Italian sausage patty, here in a turkey version as well as classic pork. Pizza is available from 11 a.m; a 14" cheese pizza is $8 plus $1-$2 for extra toppings. Large salads with antipasto toppings are from $4.75 to $6.75. There's good minestrone and spumoni ice cream. Many kinds of cold cuts, olives, prepared salads, and homemade frozen dinners are priced for local people, not gourmets. Packaged beer and wine builds traffic for this unusual specialty store. *On U.S. 41 outside Ishpeming across from the Ski Hall of Fame. 485-4557 From Mem. to Labor Day: Mon-Sat 8 a.m.-midnight, Sun 9 a.m.-midnight.*

A popular, pine-paneled downtown gathering place, **BUCK'S RESTAURANT** is known for its breakfasts, big portions, and daily specials, mostly $6 and under for lunch, $7 and under at dinner. Dinners include salad, potato, vegetable. Some examples: turkey, pork and beef that's always fresh-roasted, never pre-cut; on Friday beer-battered cod, fresh lake trout and whitefish, on Saturday steak and spaghetti. Mashed potatoes made from scratch. The extensive menu includes meal-size salads, 60 sandwiches from $2.25-$5. On display are many mounts of trophy deer and fish, plus local wildlife photos. *218 Main at Division/BR M-28, downtown Ishpeming. To get to downtown from U.S. 41/M-28, take 3rd (at Ski Hall of Fame) or Lakeshore south, jog and go south to Division, the main east-west road. 485-4534. Open daily 5 a.m.-9 p.m.: one step*

A local landmark, **CONGRESS LOUNGE & PIZZAS** is a family place and **popular gathering spot**. The bar has been here since an act of Congress repealed Prohibition — hence, the Congress name. Since 1957 it's been known for a **distinctive, thin cracker-crust pizza** with a tomatoey special sauce. A large pizza with the works is around $10. The only other food is cudighi (a spicy, wine-flavored Italian sausage patty) on a bun — $4 with tomato sauce, cheese, and mushrooms. Generations of local people have grown up on Congress pizza. If they've moved away, they stop in on vacations; it's packed here around the big July 4 homecoming. Now that Guido Bonetti has completely retired, his son Paul has assumed his role as informal local historian. If you show any interest in Ishpeming, he'll tell you a lot. The walls are decorated with a **museum's worth of local lore**, about John Voelker, hometown sports, mining, and more.

Paul created the interesting, revealing scrapbook on the making of Anatomy of a Murder (for sale for about $15). It reproduces his aunt's newspaper clippings from 1959, alongside interviews with John Voelker's widow shortly before her death. *106 N. Main a block north of Division/B.R. M-28 in downtown Ishpeming. Parking in rear off Bank. (906) 4896-4233. Open daily 4 p.m.-2 a.m.*: rear entrance. One step in front. Full bar

ISHPEMING LODGINGS

BEST WESTERN COUNTRY INN (906) 485-6345; reserv. (800) 528-1234; www.exploringthenorth.com/cvillage

An indoor pool, large rooms, and little extras make this 2-story facility, now grown to 60 rooms, an attractive place to stay. The lobby has a fireplace, free coffee, cookies, newspaper. The **indoor pool** is big enough for laps. There's a whirlpool, too. Very helpful, locally knowledgeable staff. Now that local retailing has pretty much moved out to the highway, into this "country village" surrounded by parking lots, there's a lot to do within walking distance: McDonald's, Country Kitchen restaurant, Jasper Ridge brewpub, a popular bowling alley, **movie theater**, and a strip mall with a **bookstore**. Just don't expect much in the way of authentic history; go downtown for that. Rates for summer thru fall: $78, with whirlpool rooms about $10 more. Plug-ins for snowmobiles; on snowmobile trail. The nearby **Best Western Jasper Ridge**, under the same management, offers family suites and business accommodations with office chairs and workstations but no indoor pool. *On U.S. 41 West a mile north of downtown Ishpeming.*

H.A.: some ADA accessible rooms; call for others : 17 & under free : in smoking rooms

Champion (pop. < 100)

This quiet village straddling U.S. 41 is a **pale shadow** of what it was from 1867 to 1912, when the famous Champion Mine was in operation here. Disguised as the isolated village of Tioga, Champion is known to thousands of enthusiastic readers of Cully Gage's Northwoods Readers, **humorous yet utterly realistic collections of character sketches and anecdotes**, based on life in Champion early in this century. The mines and logging had drawn together a

Dr. Van Riper, Cully Gage and *The Northwoods Readers*:

The old days remembered with humor and unflinching truth

As a kid from suburban Detroit, Ed Litwin loved coming up to the U.P. in summer. A big part of the experience was listening to the "old guys who hung out at the feed store, telling kids hair-raising tales of logging camp life and working in the mines." When Ed finally fulfilled his dream and moved to Marquette, sprawl had crept over the landscape, McDonald's and Domino's had arrived in the U.P., and the old guys were gone. Then he discovered the *Northwoods Readers*, based on the stories author Charles Van Riper ("Cully Gage") heard growing up in Champion before World War I. "Happily, I found that the old way of life was still around, if you took the time to look for it," Ed says. "Even better, I found a person who had lived in a small U.P. town, who had seen the boom and bust of the logging and mining days, and who wrote about it so clearly, and with so much feeling that you'd think you'd been there yourself."

Ed Litwin now gives occasional talks about Cully Gage and his father, "Dr. Van." "Dr. Paul Van Riper had come to Champion as a company physician for the Oliver Mining Company. He stayed after the mine closed, over his wife's objections, because he loved to hunt and fish." He also loved the variety and independence that came with being the only doctor in a vast area.

"He prepared pills in various colors to treat patients' self-diagnosed problems. (All were aspirin.) Dr. Van understood the value of that common drug and of the placebo effect. He came into contact with colorful home remedies. He made house calls by horse and buggy, when a trip to Michigamme, five miles away, could be an all-day ordeal. Veterinary medicine also went with his job, for to a logger his horse was his livelihood. Most families had a cow, chickens, and perhaps a pig. These, along with a potato patch and the abundant deer, fish, and partridge, were their means of survival. Dr. Van learned well the meaning of *sisu* [the esteemed Finnish value of endurance and guts]. He survived the flu epidemic of 1918, when his rounds lasted from before dawn to long past dark, and lived to be celebrated at the 1964 dedication of the state park that bears his name."

disparate group of people. Telling stories about each other was the chief form on entertainment. In real life **Cully Gage** was **Charles Van Riper**, son of Champion's longtime physician. "Dr. Van" had come here to work as the company doctor for the Oliver Mining Company, then stayed after the mine closed — because he loved to fish and hunt, and he liked the freedom, responsibility, and challenges of being the only physician in a remote area. Retired from a noted career as a speech pathologist, Charles Van Riper started writing for his grandchildren what became a long series of stories, using the Finnish nickname for Charles, Cully, and his mother's maiden name.

"Our little village," he wrote, "consisted of two little settlements, one inhabited mainly by French Canadians and Indians down in the valley, and the other atop a long, steep hill where the Finns and Swedes lived. A straggle of houses and log cabins containing other nationalities lined the hill road that joined them." When Champion Mine was booming, the villages of Champion and adjacent Beacon grew to a population of 2,500. Now the entire township has under 300, many of them of Finnish or French-Canadian ancestry.

Disaster in the form of a **cave-in** struck Champion in 1912, when "the ground shook, sidewalks cracked, and a dust cloud blocked the sun." A hole, a hundred feet deep and 300 feet wide, suddenly appeared and sucked in several homes. The Champion Mine collapsed and was shut down for good. By that time, mineshafts had penetrated over 2,000 feet into the ground, bringing up over 4 million tons of iron ore. The mine was southwest of town, just outside Beacon.

While some area workers commute to the Empire and Tilden mines to the east, a good many working residents are self-employed loggers. Four miles west of town Mead has a forestry office which manages 175,000 of the company's 675,000 acres of U.P. forest. This **Mead yard** is also a collection point for the most valuable hardwoods harvested by its contract loggers. These special logs, amounting to a million board feet a year, are resold to hardwood veneer plants. A mile away is an office of **Champion International**, the U.P.'s other papermaking giant. Its chief forester here manages 90,000 of Champion's 500,000 acres of U.P. hardwoods. Much of that wood goes to Champion's Quinnesec plant near Iron Mountain to make coated papers for the pages of *National*

Geographic, annual reports, and similar glossy publications.

Champion's chief claim to fame these days is as the "**Horse Pulling Capital of the U.P.**" The last weekend of each June a contest at the pulling ground north of the highway attracts thousands with workhorse competitions, mud drags, and other festive events.

Today you can almost count Champion's commercial businesses on one hand. They're all lined up on U.S. 41 to cater to passing motorists as much as to the local population. There's a sporting goods store, a small grocery store, Higley's Saloon, Bernie's Garage, and **Lou's Place**, a restaurant under new management where most everything is made from scratch, including the popular homemade wheat and white bread, homemade biscuits and gravy, soups, and pasties. The new owners have introduced Saturday evening porterhouse steaks and BBQ ribs.

Van Riper State Park

Many motorists pass this park's grassy beach and modern campground at the east end of Lake Michigamme. Perhaps they even know about the Moose Information Kiosk near the main

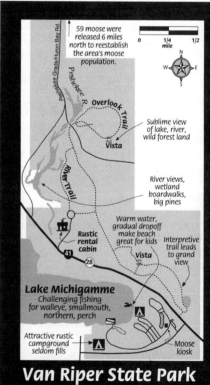

Van Riper State Park

A convenient park with scenic short trails, a moose kiosk, and good fishing & swimming.

Seeing a moose

The backcountry northwest of Marquette is **ideal moose habitat**, what with the tender shoots of regenerating forests, lots of lakes and beaver ponds full of aquatic plants for summer browsing, and older mixed woods with both tasty saplings and winter cover.

However, changes brought by the mining boom virtually eliminated the moose population in this century. Settlers overhunted moose. Eight times as big as a deer, a moose could feed a family for a long time in winter. Extensive logging encouraged whitetail deer, which carry a brainworm parasite usually fatal to moose.

By the 1980s, however, forest regrowth made conditions more favorable for moose, and wildlife biologists decided to reintroduce the area's biggest native creature. The 59 moose introduced from Canada in 1985 and 1987 had increased to over 300 by 1997. You might be able to catch a glimpse of these voracious half-ton vegetarians (they eat 50 to 60 pounds of browse daily) by taking the routes suggested in the moose section of the free Marquette Country's *Waterfalls and Lighthouses Guide* (call 800-544-4321 or stop by the Marquette Welcome Center) or by hiking in Craig Lake State Park. You're almost sure to see moose if you're willing to travel to a spot south of Covington (see Covington in the Keweenaw Chapter) at the right

time of day and hike in a ways.

In the outstanding *Northwoods Wildlife: A Watcher's Guide to Habitats*, Janine Benyus gives tips for spotting moose. Look for them "browsing the shrubs, especially at dawn and dusk, or wading in swampy wetlands to get sodium-rich aquatic plants. In a sea of vertical shrubs or trees, look for the horizontal line of deepest shadow, crowned with a rack of antlers. Males are usually alone and females are usually with a calf." Stay away from females, who are protective mothers. And keep clear of any moose during rutting season in October. Tracks are "large cloven prints, up to 6 1/2 inches long." Scat piles are like deer's, but much larger. The soft summer diet produces cow pies. Moose are not shy, incidentally.

---

entrance road. But they're probably completely unaware of the **extremely scenic, rugged, yet easily accessible natural areas** just north of the highway. To explore it, pick up a map at the contact station at the park's main entrance.

The most heavily used part of the park is around the main entrance and two campgrounds at the lake's east end. (See below for camping details.) The Van Riper after whom the park is named is Dr. Paul Van Riper, the village doctor in Champion and the father of Charles Van Riper (Cully Gage). The beach here was the **favorite swimming hole** for Champion residents. Dr. Van Riper, as a township commissioner, helped the town acquire the beach as a park. Local kids observed him in the act of changing into his swimsuit and memorialized the event by making up an unflattering chant about it. He then made sure that the new park got changing houses right away.

Here are park highlights:

◆ **Dramatic rock outcrops, hundred-year-old pines**, the Peshekee River, and Lake Michigamme can all be seen on a choice hour hike on the **OVERLOOK TRAIL**. It's reached by driving north almost a mile on Huron Bay Road, which joins U.S. 41/M-28 just west of the Peshekee River. Pay close attention, even looking back a little, to find Martin's Landing Road heading east across the river. As soon as you cross the river, park to your left and start the one-mile hiking loop up to the overlook. Stairs make the path easier, but you do need to watch your step over rocks; it's unfortunately not a hike for shufflers or the infirm. But it's a **sublime view**, so plan on lingering in this special place.

◆ On the opposite side of Martin's Landing Road, the **RIVER TRAIL** heads south along the Peshekee River valley. It begins on a boardwalk over wetlands,

then affords river glimpses before entering an area of big red and white pines.

◆ The **BEAVER POND TRAIL** north of U.S. 41/M-28 quite near the main entrance road has panels about plants and animals native to the area: grey wolf, eagle, bat, pileated woodpecker, pine marten, frog, salamander, sandhill crane. This loop of about two miles leads to another **scenic overlook** with another grand view; it hooks up with the more distant Overlook Trail. This too is a beautiful area, but highway noise detracts. For **cross-country skiing** and **snowshoeing** on a make-your-own-trail basis, park across U.S. 41 near the main entrance.

◆ The **MOOSE KIOSK** on the main entrance road south of U.S. 41/M-28 tunes visitors in to the **habits of moose**. It also tells the story of Operation Mooselift, the moose transplant operation that reintroduced the half-ton vege-

tarians to a release site six miles north of the park in 1985 and 1987. Since then the number of moose in the area has grown to over 300. One **video shows** moose in Canada's Algonquin National Park east of Georgian Bay being sedated, lifted by helicopter to a central area under the diligent supervision of wildlife biologists, put into crates, and trucked to a location near here, some eight miles north of U.S. 41 on Huron Bay Road. Another video shows "kiwi cowboys" from New Zealand, specialists in animal management, picking up moose here by helicopter to recollar them so their movements can be tracked. Smaller kiosks have displays about "Dr. Van," walleye, wolves, and the defunct Huron Bay Railroad built near here — a spectacular case of poor planning. Kiosks are in place from spring break-up through mid-October.

◆ **LAKE MICHIGAMME BEACH.** A favorite because of the **sandy beach has a very gentle dropoff and unusually warm water**.

◆ Fishing on **LAKE MICHIGAMME**. In *Fish Michigan: 100 Upper Peninsula Lakes*, noted angler Tom Huggler writes, "The lake has a long history of good fishing; however its great size [4,360 acres], abundance of structure, and dark color make it difficult to fish." He rates fishing opportunities for walleye, muskie, smallmouth bass, northern pike, yellow perch, and whitefish good or better. A boat launch is around on the south shore on the same drive as the rustic campground. **Boat rentals** are available from Michigamme Shores Campground (906-339-2116) or Cope's Canoe Livery (906-485-4646).

31 miles west of Marquette, 17 miles west of Ishpeming, and about 2 miles west of Champion on U.S. 41/M-28. (906) 339-4461. Winter weather providing, park stays open all year, with main road and some campsites plowed. State park sticker required: $4/$5 day, $20/$25 year. ♿: Kiosks now. Beach area sometime in 2002. See below for camping.

CHAMPION RESTAURANT

The popular **CROSS-CUT CAFE** at this highway restaurant/gas station/motel stop has a huge breakfast business based on **homemade cinnamon** and **caramel nut rolls**, muffins, and homemade American fries or hash browns. Good home cooking is the rule here. The $4 breakfast has eggs, potatoes, toast, 2 sausages. Homemade soups change daily. Homemade tapioca, rice pudding, and bread pudding are regular items.

Rotating specials are things like meat loaf, pasties (every Wed, $3.25 and $3.75 with slaw), **lake trout on Friday**. No credit cards; out-of-town checks OK. *On the north side of U.S. 41/M-28 at the intersection of M-95, 3 miles east of Champion. 339-2938. Open year-round daily from 7 a.m. to 7 p.m. ♿: call.*

CAMPING AROUND CHAMPION

VAN RIPER STATE PARK

(906) 339-4461; fax 339-4159
Reservations: (800) 44-PARKS; (800) 605-8295 TDD; www.dnr.state.mi.us/
Both the modern and rustic campgrounds are south of U.S. 41 close to **Lake Michigamme** with its warm swimming and good fishing. See above for descriptions of the park's excellent hikes and other recreational opportunities. Both campgrounds are in stands of tall pines, with mixed sunny and shady spots and little in the way of understory to provide privacy from neighbors. The 148-site **modern campground** ($12/$15 a night) also has two minicabins ($32/$35). In summer it's often full; reservations six months in advance are recommended. The nearby 40-site **rustic campground** ($6/$9 night) is more attractive in terms of natural beauty and privacy. Up to now it fills only on the July 4 weekend. Campers here can use the modern campground's showers by paying $10/night. A recently built **rental cabin** ($50/night; call 906-339-4461 to reserve) is by the Peshekee River off a drive leading north from U.S. 41 just east of the river. Furnished with table and chairs and a wood stove, it sleeps 10 on three bunks plus 4 cots. Book ahead for best selection of dates, especially in summer. *31 miles west of Marquette, 17 miles west of Ishpeming, and about 2 miles west of Champion on U.S. 41/M-28. (906) 339-4461. For reservations, call (800) 44-PARKS. Park open from May thru November, weather permitting. State park sticker required: $4/$5 day, $20/$25 year.*

H.A. (ADA accessible): rustic campground; beach sometime in 2001; modern campground sometime in 2002

Michigamme (pop. < 100)

Nestled on an inlet on the northwest shore of seven-mile-long Lake Michigamme, this old mining village, settled in 1872, had a population of 1,000 and two sizable hotels when several mines operated in the vicinity. (It's pronounced

"MICH-i-GAH-me.") The first and biggest, the Michigamme Mine, is just northeast of the village across Highway 41 on the western slope of Mt. Shasta behind the Mt. Shasta Lodge. The mine produced almost a million tons of iron ore until it shut down in 1900. Although the area around the mine is fenced off, rockhounds still like to sneak in and sift through the waste rock surrounding the mine shafts looking for once-plentiful "**black diamonds**," shiny garnets which are now hard to find.

At its peak Michigamee could boast of having in addition to its two hotels four general stores, eight saloons, two grocery stores, two "fancy" shops, two shoe stores, a big sawmill, and a broom factory.

The village avoided becoming a complete ghost town because of its location on the shore of 4,360-acre Lake Michigamme, known for fishing. Anglers occupied the homes the miners left, turning the village into a little fishing resort. Abe Cohodas of Marquette, who made a fortune in the produce business, built a big log lodge on the lake that was, until recently, operated as a bed and breakfast.

Henry Ford started another boom in the 1920s when he opened the Imperial Mine one mile to the west of Michigamme in a place still called Imperial Heights. It eventually closed in the 1930s.

Lake Michigamme, **one of Michigan's largest lakes**, reaches a depth of over **70 feet**. Its rocky 95-mile shoreline and underwater rocks make it good, if challenging, for fishing. It's especially well known for **big muskies**. A 40-pounder was caught in the 1970s. Smallmouth bass are also abundant here. Van Riper State Park, closer to Champion than Michigamme, provides access to the lake, its swimming beach, and convenient short trails in the rugged moose country just north of U.S. 41.

Michigamme shops & museum

The village's growing number of crafts, gift, and antique shops, often in charming historic buildings, cater to the resorters and travelers on U.S. 41/M-28. Most

---

Keep in mind that all prices and hours of operation are subject to change. Lodging rates vary with supply and demand and are usually higher for special events.

shops have common hours: *Open Thurs-Mon at least from May through November. Open daily June thru Sept. Hours: 10-5, sometimes longer, Sunday 12-5.*

Shops include**:**

◆ **A STONE'S THROW**. Bob Mercier, a Michigamme native who's spent his career teaching in Glen Ellyn, Illinois, started this, Michigamme's first shop, two decades ago with his wife, Mary. Hand-carved birds, pottery, rugs, baskets, watercolors, wood block prints, and more — largely with a natural theme. It's in a typical Scandinavian-style house. *On the east end of Main Street. 323-6356. Open July through September.* **H.A.**: several steps.

◆ **BEARY PATCH**. Bear enthusiast Jane Baxter has assembled an eclectic variety of antiques and handcrafted items on consignment (quilts, afghans, pillows, ceramics). Their common theme: unusual bears and moose made of fabric, plush, wood, and ceramics. *On Main at Brook in the heart of Michigamme. 323-6173.* &

◆ **MICHIGAMME HISTORICAL MUSE-UM**. This new museum conveys Michigamme's history with artifacts about logging and mining, fishing and hunting, and of course *Anatomy of a Murder*, a small part of which was filmed here. Life-size cutouts of Jimmy Stewart and Lee Remick make for a nifty photo-op. There are also reminders of the long time the area has been a vacation spot, with old outboard motors and vacation brochures to inspect. Soon a log house will be moved onto the site. Mines commonly built log houses for workers. *110 Main next to Beary Patch. 323-6608. Open Mem. to Labor Day, daily noon to 5. Free admission.* &

◆ **CHURCH IN THE WILDWOOD**. A handsome frame Swedish Lutheran church from 1877 now houses a gift shop that emphasizes hand-crafted U.P. things — pottery, twig and rustic furniture, birchbark baskets, and more. Few alterations have been made on the interior, which has stained-glass windows and walls covered in decorative pressed metal. *217 W. Main in the heart of Michigamme. 323-6144. Open May-Nov. In season: Mon-Thurs 10-5, Fri to 7:30, Sat & Sun 12-5. Call for off-season hours.* &: two short flights of steps.

Craig Lake State Park

Michigan's **wildest and least accessible state park** is a designated wilderness area with no interior roads and no motors permitted on lakes. It's "a fantastic place" for people who like really getting away. That's the enthusiastic opinion of Doug Barry, manager of Van Riper State Park. He's also responsible for Craig Lake. You're sure of **hearing loons**, he says, and possibly you can come upon a **moose feeding in shallow water**. Wolves have been seen here. Almost certainly you won't encounter another hiker all day. Doug has never seen more than seven cars in the parking lot at a time, and they have 7,000 acres to spread out in. The trail around Craig Lake is ideal for snowshoeing, but nothing is plowed, so it's necessary to park along U.S. 41 and snowshoe in. Also, state parks policy permits snowmobilers in this wilderness area, though snow depths mean they might easily get stuck. **Snow** is **so much deeper** and heavier than in nearby Van Riper State Park, that when it begins snowing people parked on interior roads are advised to get their vehicles out of the area to avoid being stuck there all winter!

Irregular lakes with **dramatic granite cliffs** make for interesting paddling — and very good fishing. The president of Miller Brewing used what's now the park as a specially managed fishing retreat and named the lakes after his children. The 7+ mile Craig Lake Trail means that if you stay near the lake, you can't get lost, even if you can't read a compass.

Be aware that Craig Lake State Park is unlike any other state park in its rugged access. The road to it — almost seven miles — is so rocky that it's *suited only to vehicles with high ground clearance. When loggers are active in the area south of the park* — and often they are — their roads are wider than the one-lane road to the park. Pay attention to informal signs painted on large rocks by the loggers to keep park visitors off of logging spurs. If you encounter a logging truck coming from the opposite direction, you are the one who has to back up until you can pull over. The logging truck is too big to pull over.

The park is worth putting up with the bad road. For canoeing, Craig Lake is **a lot like Boundary Waters** in northern Minnesota and Canada, but easier to get to, and with fewer people, according to park manager Doug Barry, who's familiar with both areas. Like Boundary Waters, Craig Lake has interconnected lakes, dramatic rock outcrops, and even a similar climate because this area, though much farther south than Boundary Waters, is so high and cold, with so much snowfall (over 300" in 2000-2001). **Get out in a canoe when the colors change and you'll not likely forget it.** Fall color peaks here in late September or early October.

Brewer Frederick Miller managed 307-acre Craig Lake to encourage muskie and northern pike. He instituted **special fishing regulations** still used today: catch-and-release muskie fishing and no live bait. It's an easy 1/5 mile portage from the parking area to Craig Lake. Getting to twisting Crooked Lake is a longer portage — about 3,000 feet — over a wide, fairly flat pathway without too many rocks. There you're really away

Craig Lake State Park's lakes are best enjoyed by canoe or kayak. In this remote area loons are heard and moose might be seen feeding in shallow waters like these.

from it all, Doug Barry says. Bass fishing there has been outstanding, well worth the extra effort. Most secluded of all, a favorite hangout of loons, is Clair Lake, with **good muskie fishing**. It's accessible by foot trail. The portage up a rocky, rugged trail is very difficult.

Miller built a simple lodge and a caretaker's house on the northwest shore of Craig Lake, a 1 1/2 mile hike from the parking area. Remodeled, today they are used as **rustic lodgings** rented to park visitors. The lodge ($50/night) sleeps 14 and has a big rec hall with a huge stone fireplace. The caretaker's cabin ($40/night) sleeps 6 in two bedrooms. There's wood heat and no electricity. Water is carried from a pump. These cabins, open from May 15 to October 15, are extremely popular. Sign up as early as possible in January of the year you want a reservation.

Clusters of tent pads are located on the sandy beach on Craig Lake's east shore, south of the portage trail, and just off the east end of the portage trail on Crooked Lake. *Camping is permitted, for backpackers only, everywhere in the park except around the two cabins.* It's $6/$9 a night, payable in the collection pipe by the parking area. The choicest spot — breezy, less buggy, and surrounded by water — is the little peninsula that sticks out into Crooked Lake not too far east of the portage trail.

The entrance road is about a mile west of U.S. 41/M-28 at the Michigamme Mobil station. **The park entrance is not marked;** *look for Keewayden Lake Road. Warning: rough, rocky roads are best suited for vehicles with high clearance. To get to the Craig Lake parking area, take the left fork of the Y in 2.7 miles. Parking is in another 3.9 miles. Drive carefully. Get maps, info at Van Riper State Park, about 7 miles east on U.S. 41. (906) 339-4461. Fax: (906) 339-4159. State park sticker required: $4/$5 day, $20/$25 year in 2001.* &: no.

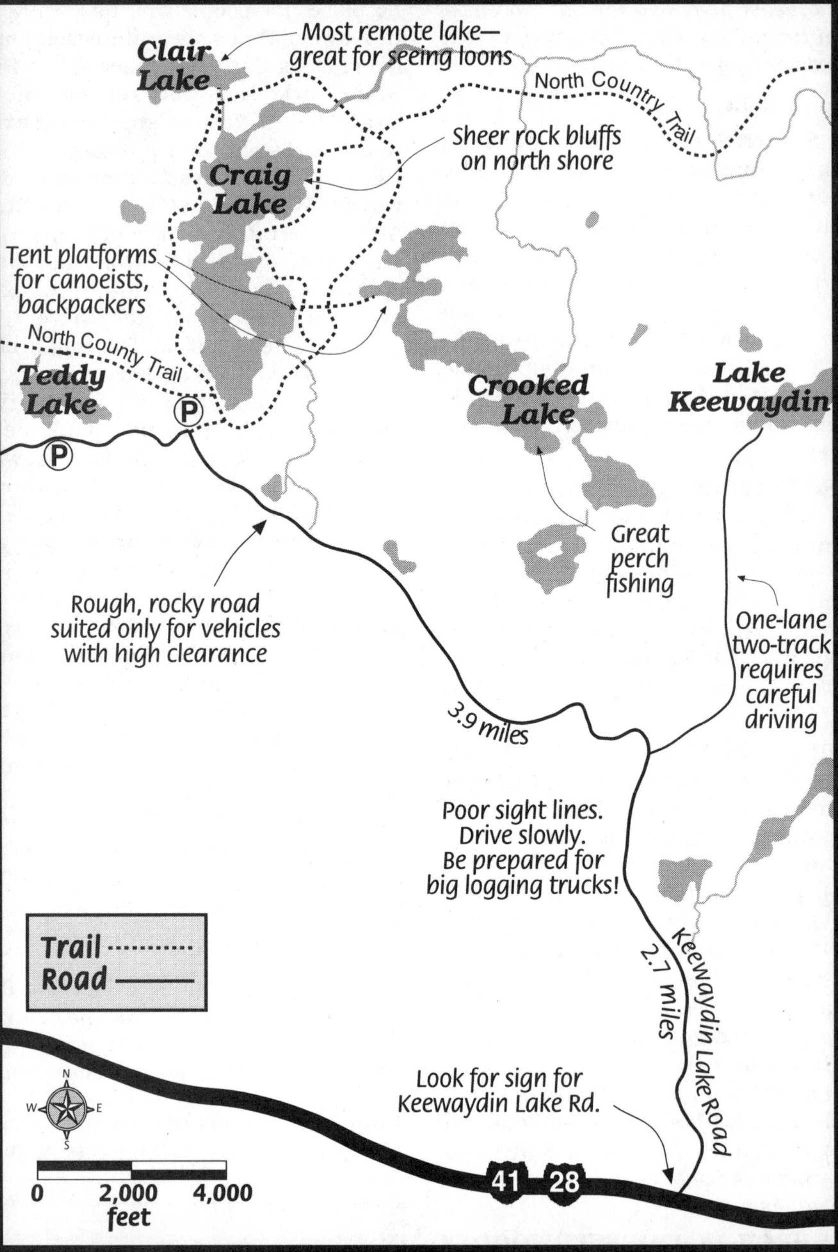

McCormick Wilderness

The 27 square miles of the McCormick Tract, about 10 miles north of Lake Michigamme and south of the Yellow Dog River, were assembled and developed as the wilderness hunting retreat of the Cyrus McCormick (who invented a successful reaper and developed his company into International Harvester) and his heirs. The high wetlands and lakes here are on the divide between the Lake Superior and Lake Michigan watersheds. In between some of the rugged rock outcrops are scattered **white pine perhaps**

Most remote lake—great for seeing loons

Clair Lake

North Country Trail

Sheer rock bluffs on north shore

Craig Lake

Tent platforms for canoeists, backpackers

North County Trail

Teddy Lake

Crooked Lake

Lake Keewaydin

Great perch fishing

Rough, rocky road suited only for vehicles with high clearance

One-lane two-track requires careful driving

3.9 miles

Poor sight lines. Drive slowly. Be prepared for big logging trucks!

Trail · · · · · ·
Road ———

Keewaydin Lake Road

2.7 miles

Look for sign for Keewaydin Lake Rd.

N W E S

0   2,000   4,000
feet

41 28

Craig Lake State Park

Wilderness managment means no motors on these delightfully secluded fishing lakes visited by loons, moose, and wolves.

300 years old. Mostly the area is maple with some oak and birch on the uplands, and spruce, balsam, and cedar in the wet areas. No trees have been cut for nearly a hundred years. McCormick was drawn to the area by its rugged and remote nature, by its remaining old-growth white pine, and by a positive evaluation from a Harvard botanist. His wasn't a fishing camp; there aren't many fish in these

nutrient-poor lakes and streams.

County Road 607 (the Peshekee Grade) cuts across the southwest corner, providing the only vehicle access to the McCormick Tract. Since 1987 it's been known as the McCormick Wilderness, part of the **Ottawa National Forest**. No trails effectively exist today except for one three-mile trail from the road to **White Deer Lake**, where the fantastic McCormick main lodge, one of several on the property, was built on an island. The paths that connected the McCormicks' wilderness retreat with the homes of their friends in the Huron Mountain Club by Big Bay are long grown over. Today this place is for **people who really want to get away from it all** — backpackers and snowshoers. (Winter is the best time to get around, because of course there are no bugs.) If you venture off the trail, bring a compass and USGS map and know how to use them, says forester Tom Strietzel. With swamps to go around, it's easy to get lost. *Leave-no-trace camping is permitted without a permit* unless there's a fire ban; campsites should be at least a hundred feet from a stream.

Ed Litwin of Marquette has a camp near here and read up on McCormick Tract history in preparing his talks about the Van Ripers. He writes, "In 1890, Cyrus McCormick, grandson of the inventor of the McCormick grain reaper and head of International Harvester, came to the area to camp and hike. Returning a few years later, he was shocked to find the virgin white pines cut off of the Baraga Plains. In an attempt to save the remainder, he purchased entire sections, forties, and even individual trees from the logging companies. Heir to a great fortune, he had several unusual log cabins built on an island on White Deer Lake off the Peshekee Grade. They were in the fashion of the great rustic resorts built in the Adirondacks by other wealthy families. Cabins, boathouses, dining hall, and lodging for help and guests were all handmade by the best log butchers, along with miles of hiking trails and footbridges.

"Dr. Paul Van Riper and his wife were frequent guests to his wilderness resort and enjoyed the reminders of a lifestyle far removed from Champion's. Dr. Van was frequently called to the McCormick estate to treat the elderly Cyrus McCormick and later his grandson, Gordon. Both Cyrus and Gordon (who had no heirs) were encouraged by Dr. Van to donate the estate to the state or federal government. This was eventually done. Although the forest service allowed the destruction of the magnificent log buildings, contrary to Gordon's request, the lakes and virgin timber stands are now open to the public as the McCormick Wilderness." Some of the disassembled log buildings do survive, but in a warehouse, we're told. *From U.S. 41 at the Peshekee River on the east end of Lake Michigamme, take CR 607 northwest about 12 miles to Baraga Creek and look for the trailhead. (906) 852-3501. TTY: (906) 852-3618. &: no*

Tioga River Roadside Park and waterfall

A lovely spot for a quick driving break, this park and **picnic area** is along the golden Tioga River. The river rushes around immense dark boulders and falls in short drops. A footbridge crosses the river just downstream so you can take in the beautiful scene.

On U.S. 41/M-28, ll miles west of Michigamme.

MICHIGAMME RESTAURANTS

MT. SHASTA RESTAURANT serves fresh lake trout and whitefish (around $11 at dinner or $8 for a smaller portion in a basket with fries), steaks (around $13 to $17), pork chops, liver and onions, and a limited Mexican menu in its vintage log lodge overlooking the highway and Lake Michigamme. Sandwiches and lunch entrées (about $5 to $8 with fries and salad) are available all day. Vegetarians can eat well here in summer. New owners do more fish, more specials, some holiday special events like a fish boil and pig roast. New for 2001: a deck. The log interior is decorated with oversize stills from *Anatomy of a Murder*, taken when a small but memorable part of the movie classic was filmed here. It's a thrill to imagine Duke Ellington at the keyboard of this very piano! Author John Voelker was a friend of the original owner. Ask to see scrapbook. The building was originally located north of Ishpeming. The logs were numbered, disassembled, and moved here, to the location of the Michigamme Mine. Mount Shasta is the name of the rock bluff behind the restaurant. *On U.S. 41 just outside town. 323-6312. Open daily, year-round, 11 a.m. to 10 p.m., bar open to 2 a.m. &: 2 steps   Full bar*

The **MOOSE CAFÉ of MICHIGAMME**, new in 2000, is a big, beautiful log building that's an impressive, even splashy addition to central Michigamme and a sign that there's enough of a market from second homeowners and shoppers to warrant this kind of investment. Reports say the food is good. Daniel Mattson, co-owner with his wife, Laura, grew up in Michigamme. The full menu includes many breakfast omelets (under $5), sandwiches, meal-size salads (around $5), and outstanding desserts from the Midtown Bakery in Negaunee. Though some foods are pre-prepared like eggrolls, corn dogs, and mozzarella sticks, much is homemade, including turkey, roast beef, breaded fish, and most pies. (Raspberry stands out.) The half-pound Mooseburgers (around $5.25)

are excellent, and the pizza is good, too. Dinners are mostly $6 to $8. No smoking! *105 Max at Main. From U.S. 41, take the Michigamme turnoff closest to Lake Michigamme. 323-1511. Open daily year-round, 7 a.m. to 9 p.m. &*

MICHIGAMME LODGINGS

See also: cabins at Craig Lake State Park and Van Riper State Park.

MOUNT SHASTA (906) 323-6312

Behind the vintage log restaurant, the much newer house of the former owners is now rented to visitors, either by the room or as an entire house. The four bedrooms share a separate living/dining/kitchen area with fireplace and cable TV with VCR. The recently remodeled house has no view. It's a comfortable set-up, appreciated by snowmobilers but open year. Serious rockhounds are probably aware that the hillside in back is a **prime collecting area for certain gemstones**. Rates for 2001: $40-$45/night per person, or $120-$140/night for the entire house. (Higher rate for weekends.) **H.A.:** call

PHILOMENA ON THE LAKE
(906) 323-6318;
www.travelup.com/philomena

Many improvements have been made by new owners Rob and Barbara Jamros to what had been a very simple resort in a wonderful location. A motel and four cottages overlook Lake Michigamme at the quiet south end of the village, away from the highway. There's not much in the way of trees, but lots of amenities: a sand beach and diving platform, boat dock and rentals (a pontoon boat, paddle boats, and a fishing boat), fish-cleaning station and freezer, outdoor grills and picnic tables, coffee on motel patio. All rooms have lake views. The motel now has two newly furnished two-room suites with two beds in the bedroom and a living/kitchen. Three motel rooms with older furniture are $49/night. No air-conditioning. Phone in office. All units have cable TV. No no-smoking rooms. Walk to tennis, shops. Summer books up way in advance, and rentals then are by the week: $450 for motel suites, $490 for cottages. In the off-season, suites rent for $75-$80/day, cottages $80-$85. The name comes from St. Philomena; a former owner prayed to her successfully for help in financing. *From U.S. 41 at Michigamme, follow signs. Open mid-May-mid-Oct.*

&: call.   : under 16 free   : $5/night

MAPLE RIDGE RESORT (906) 323-6334
www.mapleridgeresort.net

This attractive, newish resort on the north shore of **Lake Michigamme** consists of a long building built into a hillside, with 7 large, 1,000-square-foot apartments with knotty pine walls, each on one level. Park-like lawns with some birch trees lead gradually down to the lake, where a **harbor** has been created to protect docked boats from winds off the lake. 14' fishing boats and canoes may be rented. There's a **swimming beach**, a beachside deck with gas grill, a fish-cleaning house, playground, and horseshoes. The website gives a good idea of the surroundings and rental units. Most have two bedrooms and sleep a family of 5. Each has 30-channel cable TV; guests can use the office phone. Picture windows look out to the lake. The three upper units share a 90' balcony. Three-night minimum for the seven apartments; a smaller unit has overnight rates. Sample rates for two for three days from 2001: winter $250, summer $240. Ask about off-season rates. Near snowmobile trail. *Look for sign and turnoff about 2 1/2 miles east of Michigamme or 2 1/2 miles west of Van Riper State Park. .8 mile south of U.S. 41. Open year-round.*

H.A.: call. Not up to current code, but one guest in a wheelchair does well.

👫👤: under 4 free 🐕: dogs only. Extra fee

EDGEWATER MOTEL

(906) 323-6315; www.travelup.com

This simple, inexpensive waterfront motel isn't strictly in Michigamme but on U.S.41/M-28 in **Three Lakes**, 5 miles west. It faces the channel between Ruth Lake north of highway and George Lake to the south. Fish for bass, crappie, northern, walleye, perch. Many **picnic tables** and a playground take advantage of the pleasant setting. Four efficiencies in one-story wing are $40/night for two. Eight units in the two-story wing are $32 (two people, one bed) and $35 (two beds). The upstairs ones have a common balcony with view. All have **refrigerators**, new carpet, and a mix of old and new furniture. The color TVs get NBC and PBS. The interiors are nicer than the low rates and wide aluminum siding lead you to expect. No phones or air-conditioning. Free coffee, tea, and cocoa. Individually controlled central heat comes from an ingenious wood-fueled central furnace. **Rowboats** and **canoes** are free for guests. Near Craig Lake State Park, within 20 minutes of 32 waterfalls. Expect highway noise. *On U.S. 41 24 miles east of L'Anse. Open year-round.*

H.A.: call 👫👤: no extra charge 🐕

The strange story behind the Peshekee Grade wilderness road

If you're around Michigamme, you may hear reference to the Peshekee Grade, a rough road that follows the Peshekee River north from Lake Michigamme and penetrates some of Michigan's wildest, most rugged land as it heads to Lake Superior's Huron Bay near Skanee, south of the Slate River mouth. It's not a logical place to build a road requiring elaborate bridges and trestles — but there they are. Here's the story behind the Peshekee Grade, as related by Ed Litwin, who has a camp near it. He drew on research by the late Mac Frimodig. (You can drive along the Peshekee Grade in a four-wheel drive vehicle; how bad it is depends on recent weather.)

"Just west of Champion, the Peshekee River system empties into Lake Michigamme, which flows eventually to Lake Michigan. Its headwaters reach to the divide between the Lake Superior and Lake Michigan watersheds, which is the **highest land in Michigan**. The entire region was buried under a mile of ice ten thousand years ago, during the last glacial period. The massive runoff from the retreating glacier scoured out the Peshekee Valley, and it forms one of the only breaks through the east-west granite ridges found in that area. Long used for logging runs, the Peshekee River and valley were a natural northern route for the early loggers, trappers, and explorers.

"The Peshekee River valley was opened to road travel as the result of an expensive but poorly planned investment scheme. By the 1890s several iron mines were operating in the area of Champion, Michigamme, and Republic. Speculation was rife that gold, silver, lead, zinc, and copper would soon be found as well. Slate from the Arvon quarries, north of Michigamme, was considered to be some of the best in the nation. The natural harbor of Huron Bay [by Skanee] was only 25 miles north of Champion as the crow flies.

"Milo Davis, a downstate entrepreneur, proposed a railway linking Champion and Huron Bay to carry north the iron ore, timber, and slate being taken from the area. A group of investors formed, and the Iron Range & Huron Bay Railroad was founded. A thousand men were hired to build the grade, and the project was estimated to cost $15,000 per mile and take one year to complete.

"Work began in 1890 on the grade, and a huge ore dock, dwarfing Marquette's, was built in Huron Bay at a cost of over $250,000. It took 2 million board feet of lumber and 3,000 pilings driven into the lake bed to support it.

"Problems were immediately encountered on the grade. Bogs and swamps required long sections of trestles and built-up roadbeds. Many bridges were built crossing and recrossing the Peshekee. Several rock cuts, some as deep as 60 feet and 7 miles long, were laboriously hand-drilled and blasted from solid granite. Teams of oxen hauled off the rock. Typhoid fever hit the workers' camps, and the hospital in Champion over-flowed. Wagons hauled away the dead to communal graves each night. Cost estimates rose to $50,000, but more than $2,000,000 was spent to complete the project — a staggering sum in the 1890s.

Unknown to the builders, or ignored by them, was the fact that the grade crossed the highest land in Michigan [the path went between Mount Arvon and Mount Curwood], then dropped abruptly to the Lake Superior shore in Huron Bay. The estimated 25 miles were actually 42. But in 1895 the task was completed. Five thousand tons of rails were laid. Two locomotives, 20 flatcars, and other stock were purchased. With the project finally completed, a ceremony was held, and the first train left the Huron Bay ore dock bound for Champion. It was pulling several empty cars, due to the steep grade leaving the lake.

"It is now known that the grade was greater than 8%, too steep even for locomotives of today, loaded or not. Twenty miles up the line the roadbed gave way. 'The locomotive rolled on her side, and with that the great Iron Range & Huron Bay Railway ceased to exist.' So said Sam Beck, who was riding in the engine. He loved to talk about his '$2,000,000 ride.' Milo Davis and his brother escaped across the border with the few remaining funds. The ore dock was dismantled and the lumber shipped to Detroit. The locomotives, rolling stock, and rails were sold off. No ore ever made the trip."

Pictured Rocks/Munising/Au Train

THE TOURISM MAGNET of Pictured Rocks National Lakeshore is far from the only visitor attraction in the Munising/Au Train area. The Munising /Pictured Rocks area has **16 visitable waterfalls**. West of Munising, a beautiful shoreline stretch of M-28 through Au Train (pronounced "aw train") to Marquette passes right by sand beaches and big pines. **Several miles of beach** have been developed for public use as part of the **Hiawatha National Forest**. Much of Alger County is national forest land. In winter this same lakeshore stretch is notorious for sudden snow squalls and whiteouts. Many winter motorists favor the longer but less unpredictable inland route from Munising to Marquette via M-94 and U.S. 141, passing through Chatham and surrounding farm country.

In an area of memorable hikes, beaches, kayaking, waterfalls & shipwrecks, colorful cliffs meet clear, green Lake Superior.

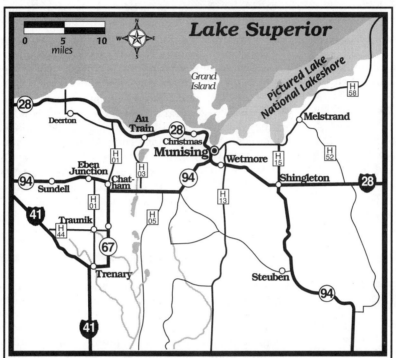

The Chatham/Trenary/ Skandia area, far from being in the middle of nowhere, as it might seem, is in fact in a handy commuter zone between Marquette and Escanaba, the U.P.'s two biggest employment centers. Several tiny agricultural communities have become known for unusual specialty businesses. Trenary has a **famous bakery** with a new restaurant. Chatham has a **good homestyle restaurant** and rooms in a **historic limestone hotel**. And the Slovenian four-corners of Traunik has a **delightful old-fashioned store**.

The **Au Train Basin** is part of the low-lying area of many lakes and streams extending south of Munising and Au Train to Rapid River and Manistique. In ancient times, going back to the Algonquian Noguet tribe, one of the most important trails in the Upper Peninsula followed the Au Train Basin near the Whitefish River. Today the Forest Service has reconstructed it as the **Grand Island-Bay de Noc Trail**. Today the area is studded with small resorts and national forest campgrounds and fishing lakes. At one time in the geological past the Lake Superior basin drained through this area into Lake Michigan and into the Mississippi River area at the present site of Chicago.

In winter Munising and the area south of it is alive with **snowmobilers**. It's on major east-west snowmobile trails across the peninsula. Today winter brings in more money to many motels and restaurants than the briefer summer season. Snowmobiling's huge economic impact in an area of small populations and incomes means that most restaurants of any size have tended to aim their business to the snowmobile market.

TO FIND OUT MORE: The **Alger County Chamber of Commerce** is now on M-28 next to Hardee's Restaurant at the east entrance to **Munising**. From May thru October it's open Monday thru Friday from 9 to 5. Possible Saturday hours. Reduced winter hours. (906) 387-2138. www .algercounty.com . . . . The **Pictured Rocks/ Hiawatha National Forest Visitor Center** answers questions and supplies printed information about the Pictured Rocks National Lakeshore, Grand Island, and the national forest land that makes up much of Alger County. The Visitor Center is also a **nature bookstore** with books about the area's natural and human history, and an extensive selection of nature guides and books for adults and children. It's in **Munising** on H-58 *just east of M-28, where the main highway turns to follow the lakeshore. Look for the brown signs.* (906) 387-3700. www.nps .gov/piro *Open year-round at least Mon-Fri 9-5. From mid June thru Labor Day open daily 8-6. From May thru Oct. open Mon-Sat 9-5.*

PUBLIC LAND: South of Munising and Au Train is mostly part of the **Hiawatha National Forest**. The visitor center (see above) supplies information, printed and oral, about the Pictured Rocks National Lakeshore and the entire Hiawatha National Forest, all the way east to Sault Ste. Marie and St. Ignace. . . . Overlooked amid the well-known federal recreation areas, **Lake Superior State Forest** has extensive land, pathways, and eight scenic rustic campgrounds on inland lakes and streams south of the Pictured Rocks National Lakeshore. They have excellent privacy and are less likely to be full. Get a map at the Pictured Rocks/National Forest Visitor Center, Michigan Welcome Centers, or call the DNR's Shingleton office on M-28, (906) 452-6227.

GUIDES: Guided **kayak outings** to **Pictured Rocks** and/or **Grand Island**, depending on weather, are offered by **Northern Waters** in Munising (886-GO-PADDLE; www.northern-waters.com) and **Great Northern Adventures** out of Marquette (909-225-TOUR; www.greatnorthernadventures .com). . . . Short guided hikes are part of the regular free programming at the **Pictured Rocks National Lakeshore**.

EVENTS: Munising celebrates **July 4** and homecoming in a big way, with fireworks at Bayshore Park, a parade, and more. Fireworks are on the Fourth, whenever it is. . . . The **National**

Park Service and **Hiawatha National Forest** hold **summer evening programs** at various locations, usually campgrounds. Get a schedule at the Visitor Center. . . . **Summer evening concerts** are Tuesdays at 7 from late June thru late August at Munising's downtown **Bayshore Park** at the foot of Elm, by the Pictured Rocks Boat Cruise dock.

HARBOR with transient dockage: In **downtown Munising** at Bay Shore Marina (906-387-2095 or 387-2275; 46° 24' 52" N, long. 86° 39' 06" W) with showers, picnic tables, launch ramp.

PICNIC PROVISIONS & PLACES: The place to pick up fruit, deli items, and groceries is **Glen's Market**, the huge 24-hour supermarket on M-28 at the east edge of **MUNISING** . . . . For more gourmet fare, consider calling ahead for takeout from the **Brownstone Inn** (892-8332) in **AU TRAIN**. . . . The **Trenary Home Bakery** in **TRENARY** bakes a full line of breads and rolls.

◆ **Sand Point picnic area** and **beach,** part of the National Lakeshore, is a wonderful destination, just five miles northeast of **MUNISING** on Sand Point Road, off H-58. It forms the entrance to Munising Bay and has an up-close view of Grand Island and its East Channel Lighthouse. The barrier-free **Sand Point Marsh Trail** crosses a wetland.

◆ Right in **MUNISING**, Bayshore Park at the foot of Elm

Street, across from the Boat Cruise dock, has picnic tables, grills, and a beautiful view.

◆ **Miners Castle**, 13 miles northeast of Munising, is the premiere **PICTURED ROCKS** sight. Picnic tables are scattered around the walk to the castle formation, but a staffer says the picnic area by the beach is even nicer.

◆ **Bay Furnace**, off M-28 just west of **CHRISTMAS,** has a picnic area by a sandy Lake Superior beach with a view of the charcoal iron smelter's ruins and Grand Island.

◆ At **AU TRAIN**, the Michigan Department of Transportation has a **roadside park** and picnic area by the low **Lake Superior sand dunes** off M-28, near where the warm, clear Au Train River empties into Au Train Bay.

◆ A picnic area and beach is on the southeastern shore of **Au Train Lake**, accessed off H-03/Forest Lake Road, the main road through **AU TRAIN** village. It's next to the Au Train Songbird Trail; see the main text for info on borrowing the tape recorder to hear birdsong in its environmental context.

◆ Another pretty **MDOT roadside park** off M-28 is at **DEER LAKE**, an inland lake with warmer swimming near Shelter Bay. It's about 8 miles west of Au Train and 20 miles west of Munising.

Munising (*pop. 2,539*)

Ringed by **dramatic high, forested hills**, Munising looks out across an attractive, often **sparkling-blue bay**. It has one of the most **beautiful settings** of any Michigan town, though many motorists might not notice it as they drive along the sprawling M-28 commercial strip. Motels and gas stations dominate the east entrance to town. Due north of town is huge, irregularly-shaped **Grand Island** with its **ancient lighthouse** and **steep bluffs**. Tucked just out of sight along the shoreline to the east is one of Michigan's most famous sights: the **Pictured Rocks**.

Going west from the sprawl, the highway passes the main downtown avenue, Elm Street, as it follows Lake Superior all the way to Marquette. Turn toward the water and you'll find the attractive new **marina** and **Bayshore Park** near the docks to the Pictured Rocks Boat Cruises. The park's picnic tables and benches are a good place to take a break and enjoy the often **sublime view** of the **harbor**, Grand Island, and the often misty interplay of light, clouds, and water.

Munising has been steadily losing population; it was over 3,000 in 1980, 2,783 in 1990, and 2,539 in 2000. It is finally making some strides in refocusing itself with Bayfront Park, a point of civic pride. Like Ontonagon, L'Anse, Che-

boygan, and Alpena, it has seen itself as an industrial town, with tourism an undependable extra. Historically towns like it have had a hard time making civic decisions based on scenery and appearances, and choice bayfront land has been taken up by uses that don't relate to the water or the view. The century-old buildings at M-28/Munising Avenue and Elm, a block up from the harbor drive, have been refurbished with a sense of history. Unfortunately two off the four are presently empty.

Munising's **superb harbor** is protected from Lake Superior's storms by 13,000-acre Grand Island. Long a pri-

"Our favorite season for exploring [Pictured Rocks'] many fascinating charms is spring, when wildflowers bloom in profusion along the shoreline footpath," writes U.P outdoorsman Len Emerick in *The Superior Peninsula.* Trillium grow in profusion here.

vate hunting retreat, Grand Island is now a national recreational area well suited to mountain biking and kayaking. The Grand Island ferry is off M-28 four miles northwest of town. For a great view of the island, harbor, and the city, there's a **Grand Island scenic lookout** on a mainland hilltop due south of the island west of Munising.

The **scenic sandstone cliffs** of Pictured Rocks and Grand Island contributed to the large number of **shipwrecks** here. Winds off the cliffs sometimes caused ships to sink or run aground, often as they sought refuge in Munising's safe harbor. The waters off Munising are now the **Alger Underwater Preserve**, with eight major wrecks within the 113 square miles. A worthwhile **shipwreck cruise** enables sightseers to visit three of them. Divers who enjoy exploring these wrecks take boats from Munising.

Groups of Ojibwa long made use of sheltered Munising Bay as a favorite summer camping grounds. The WPA guide to Michigan recounts, "The splendor of [the Pictured Rocks] cliffs and the thunder of the waves in the caverns filled the Indians with awe; the Chippewa, who controlled most of the Upper Peninsula and camped here each summer, believed that the gods of thunder and lightning lurked in the resounding caverns. They believed that Paupuk-keewis lived among the crags in the form of an eagle; and that many of the cliffs housed evil spirits that had to be propitiated at stated intervals. Hiawatha, their hero, hunted in these woods, stalked game along these cliffs, and waded past the palisades, indenting them frequently with his fist in its magic mitten."

The area's first important settlement was Grand Island, long used by Native Americans and later also as a fur-trading outpost, steamship fueling station, and destination for adventurous tourists. An iron blast furnace attracted permanent settlers to Munising in the 1870s. Sawmills, a tannery, and the Munising Woodenware Company, whose wide array of household products are represented in the local museum, furthered the town's growth. Today the Alger Maximum Security Prison, one of the U.P.'s many state prisons, is south of town. Built in 1990, it has a staff of 406 and can hold 532 prisoners. Sizable plants using U.P. timber are an even bigger part of the local economy. The **old paper mill**, started in 1903, dominates the shoreline just east of downtown. It's now owned by Kimberly Clark. With 460 workers, the plant uses U.P. hardwoods to make special papers such as the brown patch on the back of Levi's jeans, the little label on Chiquita bananas, and the labels on Elmer's glue bottles.

A **big sawmill** now owned by Oregon's Timber Products operates on M-28 six miles east of Munising. Fifty workers saw 70,000 board feet of maple a day. The best of the lumber is used by furniture- and cabinetmakers, while pallet makers buy the lower grades. Next to the sawmill Timber's planer mill has another 30 workers and a veneer mill has 140 workers who take top-grade maple, beech, and birch and peel off strips 1/36 of an inch at a time.

Hiawatha National Forest/ Pictured Rocks Visitor Center

The helpful staff here is happy to answer questions on the phone and fax or mail information sheets on activities and natural features upon request. They are equipped with a wide range of information not only on the national lakeshore but on the campgrounds, beaches, and fishing lakes of the less heavily used Munising District of the Hiawatha National Forest. Pick up a schedule of free nature walks and programs, held daily from late June through Labor Day.

*The Visitor Center has some displays of area recreational opportunities and an excellent small **bookstore** of relevant **nature** books and **area history**, plus*

The Pictured Rocks are 200' sandstone bluffs sculpted by wind and water and stained by mineral-rich seepage. They can only be seen from the water — usually from a tour boat, but also from kayaks *if* it's a calm day on Lake Superior.

USGS maps and trail maps for hiking and canoeing in the national forest and national lakeshore. The Visitor Center is at M-28 and H-58. Forest Service district office just east of downtown Munising. Look for brown signs. (906) 387-3700. Open year-round. Daily in peak season 8 a.m.-6 p.m.; otherwise Mon-Sat from 9-5 at least. Nov-April: closed Sun. ⟁

Alger County Heritage Center

For visitors to Munising Falls or Sand Point beach, it's easy to stop at this free

local history museum in a former school. Of greatest interest to outsiders are artifacts and materials about **Grand Island's Native American past**, curated by a descendant of the 19th-century Ojibwa band there; an **authentic fur trader's cabin**, moved from Grand Island to the museum grounds; and the **Munising Woodenware collection** from the factory that was a leading local employer in the 1920s. It made all sorts of things, from clothespins to tent pegs to pastry makers, rolling pins, meat tenderizers, and bowls, hand painted with flowers, ivy, and such. The fur trader's cabin, patterned after the carefully researched cabin at Michigan State University's museum, is furnished as it might have been in the 1830s, with trade goods (amulets, beads, food supplies, Hudson Bay blankets, calico fabric); pelts, snowshoes, and traps; and a birchbark canoe.

The Alger County Historical Society has taken the lead in the **East Channel Lighthouse Rescue Project** to restore Grand Island's picturesque frame lighthouse across Munising Bay three miles to the north. The museum archives (photos, records, clippings) are a useful genealogical resource.

On Washington St./Sand Point Rd. 1/2 mile north of H-58/Munising Ave. 387-4308. Open seasonally Mon-Fri 1-5. From June 1 to Labor Day usually open Mon-Sat 10-6, depending on volunteer staffing. Call for recorded hours. ⟁

Pictured Rocks National Lakeshore

These **famous sandstone bluffs** extend for some seven miles from Miners Castle to the Grand Portal. They have been sculpted by erosion and stained by seepage into **fanciful shapes and pictures**. The Pictured Rocks meet clear, green Lake Superior in a series of memorable views. **Ojibwa myths** attach great importance to these rocks and sea caves, which canoes had to traverse, up close and vulnerable to wind and storm. As early as the 1870s Pictured Rocks were a tourist destination of early Lake Superior steamship cruises into the wild north country. The Pictured Rocks form the core of the first National Lakeshore designated in the United States, in 1966.

Mostly the Pictured Rocks are only visible from the water, though the artful trails at Miners Castle give a good sense of the sandstone formations up close. The red and yellow sandstone bluffs, up to 200 feet high, have been shaped by wind, waves, and ice into **dramatic columns and watery caves**, then variously stained into colored "pictures" by mineral-rich water seeping between sandstone layers. The colors of the sandstone cliffs are subtle. Blues and greens are created by copper, the reddish hues by iron. In midday on a glary day they can look washed out. **Five waterfalls** are formed when short streams (characteristic of the Upper Peninsula) tumble down the escarpment near the lakeshore.

Typically visitors see the rocks on the Pictured Rocks Boat Cruise. Northern

Programs on nature and history at the National Lakeshore and nearby National Forest

Check at the visitor centers on either end of the National Lakeshore for the Park Service's schedule of frequent free talks, tours, and other interpretive programs given by staff and volunteers. Popular programs include predators and bears, Lake Superior, and shipwrecks. One program explores streams to find caddis flies, mayflies, and other food for fishes. Another explains the results of research on streams and lakes that monitor water quality with baseline date on temperature, acidity, and insect populations.

Waters Adventures' kayak instructional excursions, requiring no previous experience, provide a quieter, more intimate view of the awesome bluffs. Great care is advised to any people without experience on Lake Superior who are considering an excursion in their own boat. Lake conditions are famous for changing quickly.

The entire National Lakeshore

extends 43 miles east from Munising Falls just outside Munising to Grand Marais. Its 70,000 acres encompass two sizable lakes, waterfalls, several stream mouths, Twelvemile Beach, and the spectacular Grand Sable Dunes. The North Country Trail (formerly Lakeshore Trail, goes the National Lakeshore's entire length. A shuttle bus from Munising gives hikers a ride back or allows them to hike parts of the trail without making a round trip.

The National Lakeshore is a **four-season destination**. Its highlights attract considerable crowds in summer and fall color season, while its diverse charms are subtle enough to bring back nature-lovers, waterfall enthusiasts, and backpackers again and again all around the year. Lon Emerick gives Pictured Rocks an entire chapter of *The Superior Land*, his book of appreciative nature essays. He hikes the North Country Trail here (Lakeshore Trail) each spring for its wildflowers.

The 43-mile stretch of National Lakeshore, acquired parcel by parcel, seldom extends inland over five miles. Often it's quite narrow. No road directly connects destinations within the

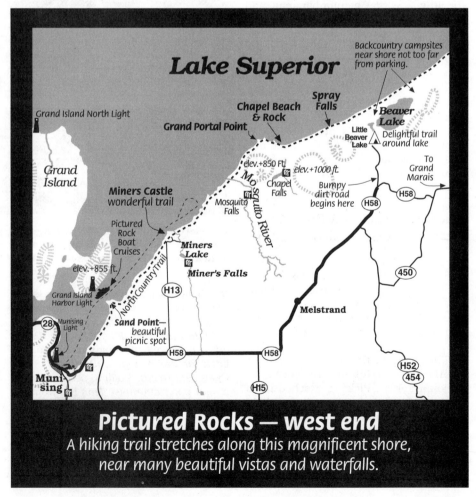

Pictured Rocks — west end
A hiking trail stretches along this magnificent shore, near many beautiful vistas and waterfalls.

National Lakeshore. That creates difficult logistics. Access to popular destinations like Miners Castle and Chapel Falls is via entrance drives extending north off County Road H-58. H-58 twists and turns for about 50 miles from Munising to Grand Marais through backcountry, often well south of the lakeshore. It's now paved for over 23 miles, with five miles recently paved east of Melstrand, up to Little Beaver Lake Road. Beyond that it turns to gravel that can be very rough and washboarded. H-58's rough sections keep extremely long RVs from using the national forest's campgrounds.

PLANNING A VISIT TO PICTURED ROCKS NATIONAL LAKESHORE

Lack of a good road divides the lakeshore into two sections for all practical purposes. One section is best accessed from Grand Marais, the other from Munising. It looks as if H-58 might some day be completely paved (who knows when?) as a compromise solution to a bitter controversy over building a shoreline road through the National Lakeshore. For the time being, you need to carefully plan visits to the national lakeshore to minimize driving.

Scope out what interests you and plan to stay or camp at the end that suits you best. The isolated Grand Marais area is detailed in the "Tahquamenon & Seney, Grand Marais & Whitefish Point" chapter. A good many naturalist-writer-artist-academic types prefer Grand Marais' less developed, less conventionally touristy personality. Munising, however, offers easy access to the pretty Au Train area with its accessible Lake Superior beaches, the Big Island Lake Wilderness Area, and Marquette, just an hour west on scenic M-28. It has one outstanding restaurant in the Brownstone Inn near Au Train.

Plan your visit with the knowledgeable free help of the **Hiawatha National Forest/ Pictured Rocks National Lakeshore Visitor Information Center** in Munising (906-387-3700). Check there for the schedule of free interpretive programs held from late June through Labor Day.

Here's a summary of sights of greatest interest along the shore, arranged from Munising to Grand Marais. In summer these points of interest may also be the busiest, so you may want to include other spots accessible only by foot.

◆ **MUNISING FALLS**. This slender, exceptionally attractive waterfall has a **dramatic 50-foot drop** into a small, rocky canyon. In winter the sight is equally spectacular when the column of

Up close and quiet — experiencing the Pictured Rocks the way Ojibwa canoeists did. Even kayak novices can take Northern Waters or Great Northern Adventures trips to the Pictured Rocks or Grand Island and their sea caves.

water is frozen. A pleasant, 800-foot path (&) leads to the falls. The **excellent interpretive center** at the parking lot gives historical perspective on the region's geology and logging history. It's next to the site of an 1868 blast furnace

Pictured Rocks' and Grand Island's cliffs and sea caves via kayak

Kayakers say the experience of entering sea caves like these is deeply affecting in a multidimensional way, as the waves echo and resonate over your head and you enter a watery, dark environment like a dimly remembered womb. The sounds vary from cave to cave, and depend on the amount of waves on the lake surface. The wet rocks have an elemental smell. No wonder Ojibwa creation tales are set right here at Pictured Rocks! **Northern Waters** offers **guided kayak excursions for beginners**. Kayaking along Pictured Rocks is only for experienced paddlers or guided groups because the rocks are so exposed to Lake Superior's fickle weather. Grand Island's bluffs and caves by Trout Bay are sheltered from typical winds and more accessible from a nearby beach. They are wonderful places to kayak, simpler and safer.

which made 16 tons of pig iron a day. *On H-58 about 2 miles east of downtown Munising and the intersection of M-28 and H-58. The unstaffed center is open May 1 through Oct. 31, daily 8:30-4:30.* &

◆ **SAND POINT** and **BEACH**. This point of land jutting out toward Grand Island offers a good view of the island and the city of Munising. In the evening there is a distant view of the Pictured Rocks. (They're shaded in the morning.) The beach just south of the point is one of the warmer swimming spots in Lake Superior. This is a grand place for a picnic, an easy drive from town. Local swimmers point out that once you get acclimated to the chilly water, you don't feel the cold. The half-mile **SAND POINT MARSH TRAIL** (&) crosses a scenic wetland that's alive with waterfowl, herons, and water-loving songbirds. Signs explain what you're looking at. Beaver lodges can be seen. Come near dawn or dusk to glimpse the nocturnal creatures themselves.

Plan enough time for a stop at the interesting **Alger County Heritage Center** on Washington on the way to Sand Point. The authentic fur trader's cabin from Grand Island, furnished as it would have been in the 1840s, is alone worth a detour. *East of Munising a little over a mile on H-58, then left on Washington St. 1/2 mile to Sand Point Rd. North 2 miles.* &: entire trail.

◆ **MINERS CASTLE** and **FALLS**. A **spectacular view** looks down at an emerald-green Lake Superior cove from high upon a **majestic, castle-like cliff**, a single great stone some nine stories tall. The water's clarity lets you see the rocky bottom even at considerable depths. The Pictured Rocks cliffs can be seen from land here, but the orientation means the light is never right for a good view. Still, if you only have time for one Pictured Rocks excursion, this should be it — the setting is so beautiful and the short trail so artful in the way it reveals the striking landscape. Another trail well worth taking leads to a **gorgeous long beach** and **picnic area** just northeast of Miners Castle. (It's also possible to drive down to Miners Beach.) Farther inland is **Miners Falls**. It's off Miners Castle Road and accessible from the road and parking area via a steep half-mile trail and stairway (64 steps). There is no trail along the Miners River. At the falls, water drops some 40 feet, with spray bouncing off the rock shelf, and forms interesting shapes in the stone at its base. Towards the end of the trail to it is a **panoramic view of Lake Superior** in the distance.

A recent addition is the new **Miners Castle Visitor Center** by the parking area. The staff can provide information about the National Lakeshore and Hiawatha National Forest, but it doesn't give permits. It's open in summer, from Memorial Day to Labor Day, from 9:30 to 5:30. &

Take H-58 east from Munising. In about 7 miles, turn north on Miners Castle Rd. for 6 miles to Miners Castle. &: overlook platform and trail to Miners Castle.

◆ The 43-mile **NORTH COUNTRY TRAIL** within the National Lakeshore (previously known as the **LAKESHORE TRAIL**) is the only route that follows the shoreline. It connects major sights with spurs to campgrounds. Several designated backcountry campsites are along the way. Permits, available by reservation by phone and from either visitor center, are necessary for this. Reservations are taken starting January 15. They must be made by two weeks before the trip. Group campsites are busiest. Individual sites fill up on summer holidays. Reserve at least a couple of months ahead.

Trailheads are at Sand Point or Munising Falls at the Munising end, and at the Grand Marais Visitor Center. Typical hiking time: three nights and four days. Anyone planning on hiking this train should get Olive Anderson's

---

Hiking tips for Pictured Rocks
The National Parks Service passes these along.
◆ Always wear sturdy **footgear**.
◆ If you plan to be out an extended time, carry a **snack** and a canteen of **water.** Save more than half your energy for the return walk.
◆ Because local weather is modified by Lake Superior, dress for **cool conditions** and carry **rain gear.**
◆ If you are hiking in unfamiliar terrain, carry a **map** and **compass** and know how to use them.
◆ **Stay away from cliff edges.** Rock within the Lakeshore is soft, crumbly sandstone and often covered with gravel.
◆ Tell someone where you're going.
◆ **Pets** are allowed only on specific trails. Check a bulletin board or ask a ranger.
◆ Bikes are not allowed on hiking trails.

Pictured Rocks National Lakeshore: A Guide available at the Visitor Center.

Alger County's **Altran shuttle** runs Monday, Thursday, and Saturday with a 10 a.m. pickup at Munising Falls and 11:30 a.m. pickup at Grand Marais. It's $10 a person. Call in advance if you're planning to use it. *The shuttle will drop off hikers at any point along H-58.* No bicycles are allowed on trails. Hikers might well consider hiking part of the trail — say, from the Munising trailhead to Sand Point and Miners Castle (about 6 miles) and an additional mile through the woods to Miners Falls, for a 12-to-14 mile round trip. Or time your hike so the Altran bus can take you back. (Call 906-387-4845.) You might even ask if the shuttle could drop you off somewhere else. Shuttle service from Munising to Little Beaver requires a 24-hour notice.

◆ **CHAPEL FALLS and MOSQUITO FALLS.** These two waterfalls are on either side of the Grand Portal that's a highlight of the Pictured Rocks. They are

---

Scuba diving in the Alger Underwater Preserve
Unusually clear waters and eroded underwater "caves" are other area attractions in addition to shipwrecks. Call the Alger Chamber of Commerce, (906) 387-2138, for a **dive brochure**. Dives are easily arranged through Capt. Pete Lindquist's **Grand Island Charters** (906-387-4477).

---

reached from the same parking area. **Mosquito Falls** is the less visited and probably the **more charming**. "The Mosquito River here slides, then cascades over layers and shelves of black rock, leaving small pools in its wake," write the Penroses in their extremely helpful *Guide to 199 Michigan Waterfalls*. "You can wade in the water, and the ledges are a perfect place to sit and soak under the spray." The new, volunteer-built Mosquito Falls Trail makes a 4-mile loop to the three sections of falls, a Lake Superior beach, and back, with several vistas on the way. Follow the general National Lakeshore trail map to see how it all goes together.

The 1 1/3 mile trail to Chapel Falls is so wide, it's almost like a road. The falls is seen from a bluff with a **panoramic view** down on the falls and forested river canyon. The same trail passes through a good blueberry area and in another 1.8 miles leads to Chapel Rock and a **beautiful crescent beach** on Lake Superior. It's another mile and a half via the North Country Trail (Lakeshore Trail) to delightful, isolated **Spray Falls**, which makes a **dramatic 70-foot drop** from the forest directly into Lake Superior.

◆ Some local hiking aficionados mention the **WHITE PINE TRAIL area** around Beaver Lake as their favorite regular hiking destination. **Loons** and **eagles** are sometimes seen along the self-guided nature trail. The 8-unit rustic Little Beaver Campground enables hikers to make this a base camp for hikes in two directions. Inquire at the Visitor Center for details.

◆ **AU SABLE POINT LIGHTHOUSE**, Hurricane River Campground, Log Slide, **GRAND SABLE DUNES**, Sable Falls, and the Grand Marais Maritime Museum are all most easily accessible from Grand Marais. Descriptions are in the "Tahquamenon and Seney, Grand Marais and Whitefish Point" chapter after Grand Marais.

Pictured Rocks National Lakeshore's helpful main visitor center is at the junction of M-28 and H-58 in Munising. See above for hours. Open year-round. Call (906) 387-3700 to get a general or backpackers' visitor packet. The Grand Marais visitor center is on H-58 about 5 miles west of Grand Marais. open from late May thru mid September. Currently there are no fees for the National Lakeshore except for developed campgrounds and backpackers' permits.

Pictured Rocks Boat Cruises

Most people see the Pictured Rocks by taking a three-hour boat cruise from Munising. Late-afternoon light is best for seeing the colors. The 5 p.m. cruise in July and August is recommended. Arrive early to get a seat on the top deck, the best place to view the scenery. If you do, take a windbreaker. The cruise begins by passing 14,600-acre **Grand Island**, once the private retreat of Cleveland-Cliffs Iron Company, now part of the Hiawatha National Forest. (See below.)

The tour competently illuminates key facts and shows passengers the Pictured Rocks' scenic highlights, from Miners Castle to Pulpit Rock, the Grand Portal, and the dramatic Chapel Falls. However, the engine's background noise can be annoying. Narrations vary from one captain to another. Some are pretty hokey. You may find it annoying to be asked by the narrator, "Isn't it beautiful?" and having interesting formations labeled with such names as "the battleship" and "the flowerpot."

An attractive alternative to the tourist boat is to take a **beginner's kayak tour** of these famous rocks. In a kayak, more stable than a canoe, you're low on the water and can quietly get right up to the massive cliffs and look up at rock sculpted and stained by centuries of wind and waves. Even on a calm day, a kayak allows one to **feel exposed to the power** of this greatest of all lakes. (See below for kayaks tours.)

Pictured Rock Boat Cruises leave from downtown Munising from Friday before Memorial Day thru October 10, weather permitting. From Mem. Day weekend thru June: leaves at 10 a.m. and 2 p.m. From July 1-August 19 there are seven trips a day, at 9, 11, noon, 1, 2, 3, and 5. In late August there are five trips a day, at 9, 11, 1, 3, and 5. From Sept. 1 thru Oct. 10 leaves at 10 a.m. and 2 p.m. (906) 387-2379. Adults $24, children 6-12 $9, 5 and under free. The 37-mile trip takes 2 hours and 40 minutes. &

Northern Waters Sea Kayaking

Proprietor Carl Hansen has led guided sea kayak trips on Lake Superior since 1987. He and his staff of experienced paddlers offer **guided half-day and day trips** and longer excursions to the Pictured Rocks, the sandstone cliffs, sea caves, and shipwrecks of Grand Island, or Isle Royale. Grand Island's cliffs and caves are like Pictured Rocks, but on a smaller scale. The island has become a **premiere kayaking destination**. All guided trips include instruction for people with no previous kayaking experience. A mix of solo and tandem kayaks is used.

The **one-day guided trip** ($79/adult, $65/youth) goes either to Pictured Rocks or Grand Island, depending on lake condition and the group's abilities and requests. There are discounts for groups of seven or more. Reservations are required. It may be possible to make day-trip reservations the night before. For longer trips it's best to reserve two weeks in advance, especially in August and for holidays. The three-day Pictured Rocks or Grand Island camping trip ($319/$255 complete, including tents, gear, and food) involves more training, possible hiking, and a more leisurely exploration of Lake Superior's scenery. Overnights allow for seeing sunsets on the water, possible moonlight paddles, stargazing, and, if you're lucky and up late enough, seeing the Northern Lights.

Sea kayaks can be rented for unguided Lake Superior trips after a four-hour safety course. Instruction includes learning paddle strokes, braces, and rescues (you will get wet!), followed by dry-land instruction on how to enjoy kayak camping. Other kayaks can be rented for use on inland lakes and slow streams after just 15 minutes' instruction. These are stable enough for families, fishing, and dogs. Visitors are welcome to stop by and see a free video on sea kayaking. Northern Waters sells a wide variety of kayaks and accessories for fishing, hunting, whitewater rivers, small lakes, and circumnavigating the Great Lakes.

Contact information: (906) 387-2323; (866)GO PADDLE. www. northernwaters.com e-mail: paddling@northernwaters.com

712 W. Munising/M-28 in the quonset hut between the high school and the American Legion, west of downtown. (906) 387-2323. Open from May through September. Daily 10-5 at least. &: *call.*

Glass Bottom Boat Shipwreck Tour

This intelligent, well-thought-out tour does everything a good tour should do. In two hours it shows you things it would be difficult to see on your own. It provides perspective on what you see. And it gives a clear introduction to shipwrecks without being tediously detailed. You leave having seen things in a new way — no trivial accomplishment in our jaded times. Check out the interesting website, www.shipwrecktours.com

Captain Pete Lindquist, a Munising native and a onetime Air Force diver in Okinawa, has been in the dive business since 1981. His son, Joe, and daughter, Kate, are part of his enthusiastic staff, now grown to 11. The shipwreck tour has become so popular that it now uses a much bigger, 101-passenger boat, 60' long, formerly used for the Pictured Rocks cruises. It's been customized with two large 4'x10' viewing wells. A second boat, specially designed for shipwreck viewing and for divers, is being added.

On the way to the shipwrecks the boat passes close to the weathered East Channel Light and sand cliffs on Grand Island, and it offers a distant view of the west side of the Pictured Rocks.

Although Munising Bay is well protected from Superior's storms, **32 shipwrecks** occurred in the area as ships sought its refuge but failed to make it. Most wrecks occurred in November, mainly between 1860 and 1929.

The shipwreck tour takes you to three shipwrecks and passes over each one three or four times. To help you understand what you're looking at, the experienced narrator passes out diagrams of how the wreck lies in the water and photos of the vessel's original appearance. Information is delivered naturally and intelligently; this is not a wind-up, rote tour. Narrators are good at encouraging and answering questions. The iron ore carrier *Burmuda* [sic], an **intact wreck from 1860**, is seen from on top. The **wooden steamer *Herman Hettler*** went off course in a 1926 storm and struck a reef off Grand Island's Trout Point. It is on its side. The third wreck, actually discovered by a tour customer, is an **anonymous scow schooner** whose sinking went unrecorded. Scow schooners, in a pre-Civil War design unique to the Great Lakes, had rounded, barge-like prows instead of pointed hulls.

Kids love this tour. They get excited about finding little things like pop cans and other recent trash on the lake bottom, and they really enjoy speculating about wrecks. A high point is when everyone under three feet is invited to the pilot house and allowed to wheel the ship.

From Mem. Day weekend into mid October, weather permitting, shipwreck cruises leave from the tour dock by the public boat launch at 10 a.m., 1 p.m., and 3 p.m. This dock is off M-28 at Division St., about a mile west of downtown and

just west of a park. It is not the same dock as the Pictured Rocks cruise dock downtown, or the Grand Island ferry dock. Reservation info: visitors are encouraged to reserve places on the 2-hour cruise the day before. Call (906) 387-4477. $22 for adults, $9 for ages 5-12, free for ages 5 and under. Lindquist also takes divers out to wrecks (there are nine). Group tours upon request. ♿

Grand Island Scenic Overlook

It's well worth stopping at this Michigan Department of Transportation rest area and park, perched high above M-28 west of Munising. The overlook platform offers an **excellent view of the shoreline and Grand Island**, along with a relief map and interpretive display about the island, so you can understand what you're looking at. Get there by the short path through the beech woods. Back by the parking lot are picnic tables and grills and a rest room.

Look for sign, access road up a steep hill off M-28 just opposite Tourist Park, 2 1/2 miles west of Munising. Look for the blue and yellow "Scenic turnout MDOT" sign. Closed in winter. ♿

Grand Island National Recreation Area

Protecting the entrance to beautiful Munising Bay is **unspoiled Grand Island** with its remarkable scenery: a **spectacular shoreline with colorful 200-foot sandstone cliffs, two light-houses, and sea caves**. It is not a wilderness area, but it is managed with very limited development as part of the **Hiawatha National Forest**.

In season (from Memorial Day week-end into early October) Grand Island is reached by a three-minute ferry ride from the dock on M-28 three miles west of Munising, almost in Christmas.

Both the Pictured Rocks Cruise and the Glass-Bottom Boat Shipwreck Tour offer good views of Grand Island's **color-ful sandstone cliffs** on the south shore. Passengers can see the picturesque, pri-vately owned East Channel Lighthouse, its wood weathered to a dark gray. The Alger County Historical Society is spear-heading efforts to preserve the light-house.

Otherwise, kayakers, hikers, and mountain bikers are in the best posi-tions to appreciate the island's dramatic scenery, which is mostly along the shores. (See map on next page.) Protected Munising Bay, with its many

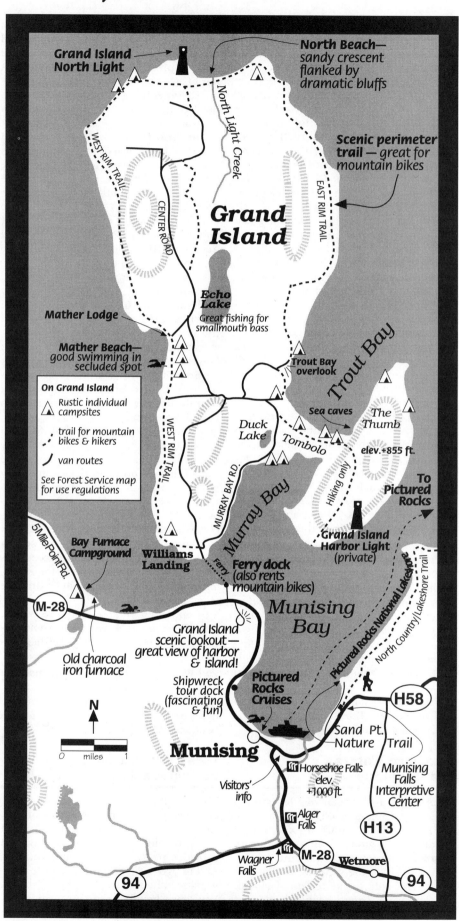

This 1867 engraving from *Harper's Magazine* **shows Williams Landing on Grand Island at that time. Abraham and Anna Williams and their big family arrived in 1840 and built log buildings next to the birchbark lodges of the island's Ojibwa band. According to oral tradition, the Indians had invited him to settle so they could make use of his services as a trader and blacksmith. Here, as at Beaver Island in Lake Michigan, the area's oldest settlements were island-based, eclipsed only when railroads developed the mainland.**

Anna Powell, the Williams' daughter, interviewed in 1906, recalled, "I'll never forget how the island looked the first time I saw it. I was 12. It was raspberry season. The bushes were loaded down with them. Mother put up lots of them. [The Indians] did everything they could think of to show how friendly they were. They were always giving us children little mococks [birchbark containers] of maple sugar."

interesting shipwrecks close to the surface, is ideal for sea kayaking. Many campsites have been developed with sea kayakers in mind. **Mountain bikes** may be **rented** ($12 a day) from the Grand Island Ferry; see below. Cars, trucks, and ATVs are banned from the island from mid June through early October. Ten permits a day for vehicles are issued at some other times. Roads and trails are now clearly signed, with "You are here" maps of the island.

To make the island more accessible to the general public, there is a 2 1/2 hour **Grand Island van tour** (&), which has some real drawbacks. It focuses on the island's natural and human history. Stops include the beach and overlooks at Trout Bay, Echo Lake, and Mather Beach. However, most of the time is spent driving on bumpy roads through young maple forests in cutover land. It's

easy to get carsick, and you hardly see the sandstone cliffs. Vehicles are far from the ideal way to see the island, The tour is offered daily, currently from early July into September. The $20 cost includes the ferry ride. Kids 12 and under are $11. Call (906) 387-4845 weekdays for reservations; otherwise call (906) 387-3503.

For up-to-date info sheets (rules for camping and mountain biking are subject to change) and a helpful personal orientation annotated on a map, stop by the Pictured Rocks/ National Forest Visitor Center. One essential piece of advice provided to bikers and hikers: "Know your pace and keep track of the time" so you can meet the ferry on time. The north-facing shores are for experienced kayakers only; weather can develop in a hurry in the Munising area.

Winter brings some cross-country

skiers out to the island, crossing on the ice bridge from the ferry landing. Far more plentiful are snowmobilers. The ice bridge is usually safe from mid January through February, but circumstances can change. Seek local information. The National Park Service/Forest Service will not give advice about crossing the ice. Ice formations hanging from the sandstone cliffs at Trout Bay, contrasted with the blue of open water, are beautiful. Trout Bay is also a popular place for ice fishing.

These areas in particular stand out as destinations for day trips and camping.

◆ **WILLIAMS LANDING** is where the ferry docks today. **Excellent panels** at the small visitor center here give a good overview of the island's thousands of years of use. There's a **picnic area** by the dock. This was the hub of island activity when Abraham Williams, fur trader and tourist guide, had his trading post, farm, overnight lodging, and fueling station here.

◆ North of Williams Landing, the **Murray Bay Road** goes past the site of the Grand Island Resort. The big hotel is gone, but the tennis courts and white hotel annex, now privately owned, can be seen from the road. About a mile and a half north of the ferry, well beyond the private cottages, the road passes the **STONE QUARRY COTTAGE**, one of the island's oldest buildings, circa 1847. The Forest Service has rehabbed it as a future interpretive site. North of it is the Williams-Powell family's cemetery. It's near the **MURRAY BAY BEACH**, where there are campsites and a picnic area which has one of the island's few indoor toilets. (None have running water.)

◆ **TROUT BAY** is where a tombolo or **sandbar** connects the main part of Grand Island to what was another, smaller island on the southeast, now called the **"Thumb."** Here are a beach and, on the Thumb, colored sandstone bluffs and sea caves, like Pictured Rocks only not as high. Currently six primitive campsites are here. Trout Bay is an ideal place for kayaking, and a wonderfully evocative one, says Dean Sandell of the DNR Forestry Division. "In the sea caves the water comes in in swells, making wonderful sounds — higher pitched than other sea caves. It's quite a treat. The wet rock smell is very organic. There are tiny beaches of pearl-like round stones . The water over those stones, perking down through them, makes subtle sounds. It's a place that slows you down to absorb those great experiences. I could spend a lot of time on Trout Bay."

◆ **MATHER BEACH** is at the outlet of Echo Lake Creek on the island's west shore. Rock shelves dominate the scenic lakeshore here. The beach is reached by a stairway; it's a **wonderful place to swim**. Mather Lodge can be seen across the creek. It was the personal hunting retreat of William Gwinn Mather, the chief operating officer of Cleveland-Cliffs Iron in Marquette. CCI owned the island from 1901 until his death in 1951. Nearby **228-acre Echo Lake**, shallow and alkaline, less than a mile away down a dirt road, offers the **best fishing for smallmouth bass** of anywhere in the Hiawatha National Forest.

◆ **NORTH BEACH** is a crescent beach at the outlet of North Light Creek, nestled between two high points with 200-foot sandstone cliffs. The **dramatic lighthouse**, still in use, is one of the Great Lakes' highest. It's on the northwestern

point, clearly visible from the water but hard to see from the beach below.

Though there are some very old and large hemlocks in the island's northern part, people mistakenly expecting a wilderness will be disappointed. For most of the first half of this century Grand Island was owned by Cleveland Cliffs Iron and managed according to the conservation-minded wishes of its president, William Gwinn Mather. He used the island as a hunting retreat, game ranch, and resort. Large-scale logging of the interior occurred from the 1952, shortly after his death, to the late 1980s. Powerful windstorms have taken down more big trees.

Grand Island has a **nearly 5,000-year history as a Native American fishing and hunting ground**. Indians also came to the island to get **quartzite**, a hard, shiny rock that can be chipped to make cutting and scraping tools. Oral tradition depicts the island as Kitchi Minissing, "Grand Island," a special place in their legends and memories. In

Cleveland-Cliffs Iron, based in Ishpeming and Cleveland, owned nearly all of Grand Island from 1901 to 1988. CCI operated a resort complex north of Williams Landing from 1904 to 1959. The resort and Grand Island Forest and Game Preserve were promoted as low-key getaways with hunting, fishing, boating, tennis, and hiking. The hotel shown in this ad is gone, but the annex (rear) and some cottages remain.

VACATION AT
GRAND
ISLAND
MUNISING, MICHIGAN

HOTEL
WILLIAMS

the 1790s British fur trader John Johnston from Sault Ste. Marie noted that "Grand Island is the summer residence of a small band of Indians who cultivate maize, pumpkins, and potatoes. . . . Grand Island Bay forms the largest and safest harbour upon the lake. . . . The south end of the island is low and sandy but covered with herbage; on it, and on the adjoining hill, the Indians have their huts. The bay is directly opposite where they go spearing every calm night with flambeaux."

Illustrated plaques about the island's history, part of the visitor center at the ferry landing, were written by National Forest Service archaeologist John Franzen. One notes, "Location was everything in the fur trade. In the early 1800s, American Fur Company traders and their competitors built small log cabins in or close to Indian settlements on Grand Island and the mainland. Government survey parties and missionaries also visited frequently during this period. European and Native American cultures often mixed during the fur Trade era." One of the 1840s traders' cabins has been moved to the grounds of the Alger County Heritage Center and authentically furnished. It's east of Munising near Munising Falls.

"In 1984 Grand Island was put on the real estate market," explains another plaque. "With the support of many other organizations, the Trust for Public Land, a private non-profit group, bought the Island in 1989 for $3.5 million. Congress authorized federal purchase and Grand Island became part of the Hiawatha National Forest in 1990." Owners of cottages retain their rights to continue to use their property. After much debate on a development plan for Grand Island, the National Forest Service has opted for very limited development focused mainly on the shoreline. (Grand Island's 27-mile shore is bigger than Mackinac Island's.)

CAMPING on Grand Island: There are currently 16 designated campsites for four to six campers each, two on Murray Bay and four on Trout Bay. At this time they are first-come, first-serve, with no fees or permits necessary. They have metal fire rings and nearby vault toilets. Two group campsites for from seven to 25 are reservable. **Random camping is allowed** according to these guidelines: no fires, not on tombolo, use Leave No Trace techniques, and stay over 100 feet from private property, trails, inland lakes and creeks, the research area at the island's north end, and from Lake Superior or cliff edges.

NOTES: Mosquitoes and **black flies** can be very bad, typically from mid May thru early or mid July. Visitors are advised to bring insect repellent and a head net (always a handy item).

Concerning **archaeological artifacts**: unauthorized digging or collecting artifacts on federal land is illegal. (It's actually illegal to take away anything, including rocks and wildflowers.) If you find artifacts or observe illegal digging, contact the U.S. Forest Service in Munising.

Grand Island Ferry operates from Memorial Day weekend into early October. The ferry leaves from Grand Island Landing one mile west of Munising on M-28. It's a three-minute trip, with almost immediate return trip from Williams Landing. Departure times are at least 9 a.m., noon, and 3:30. Thru June there's a 6:30 departure. From July thru Labor Day there are also round-trips at 10, 11, 2:30 and 5:30. (906) 387-3503. Reservations advised. $10 round-trip for adults, $5 ages 6-12, $3 bike. Entry fee to the island: $2/person. Request a current map and info sheet from Pictured Rocks/National Forest visitor center, (906) 387-3700. &: *ferry, restrooms on island.*

Central Munising

Munising has a real downtown, though you may not notice it driving through town on M-28/Munising Avenue. Look for the four-corners at Munising and Elm, where there are **four historic two-story buildings**. The handsome stone bank was originally a bank. The stylishly restored frame storefront is where the Charing Cross bookshop used to be. (The owners did so well selling their used and rare books online that they moved back to their hometown of Cleveland, Ohio, closer to sources of supply. It's another loss of a face-to-face retail business to the Internet.) The block of Elm Street just south of M-28 is the traditional downtown's chief business block. Stores and service businesses extend around the corners onto Superior, especially down East Superior towards The Dogpatch Restaurant on the corner of M-28.

Munising Bay is one of Michigan's most **beautiful landscapes**, and the renovated **Bayshore Park** is a fine place from which to view it. There's a gazebo, picnic area with grills, and a memorial to Vietnam veterans. It's at the foot of Elm Street, across from the docks of the Pictured Rocks Boat Cruises.

Other noteworthy spots for visitors, arranged from east (M-28) to west, include:

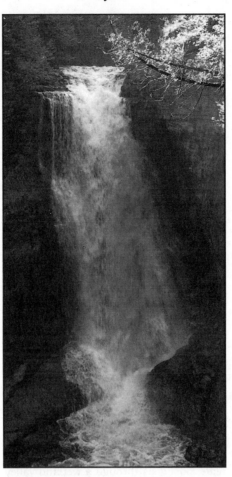

Munising Falls, just two miles east of downtown Munising, combines a pleasant trail (very busy in the daytime in summer) with an interpretive center about the area's geology (responsible for the many waterfalls) and history.

◆ **THE GIFT STATION** occupies a **picturesque brick building**, a former Mobil service station from the 1930s, now painted dark green. It's a multifaceted general gift store with an extensive stock of collectible lines, crystal, and theme gifts: fishing and hunting, north woods, lighthouse decor and books, nautical, and unusual Magic Motion clocks that play many kinds of melodies on the hour. The T-shirts and sweatshirts are unusually attractive. *101 Cedar at M-28, east of downtown. 387-3013. Open 7 days, year-round, 9 a.m.-6 p.m. at least. In summer open to 9 or later.* &

◆ **THE BAY HOUSE**. In the time-honored U.P. tradition of making a living by doing a lot of different things, the Bay House has evolved into a **locally popular café** with a salad/soup/sandwich menu, ice cream, coffee specialty drinks, jewelry, and — in the rambling rear rooms — garden accessories, **rocks and minerals**, and local paintings, pottery, and more. Sit down at a table on the

are one of the area's big attractions. Several are almost in town. Look at the Munising side of the Chamber of Commerce map for popular Munising Falls (water drops down the same multicolored sandstone formation as Pictured Rock at **Horseshoe Falls** (the centerpiece of a private attraction with a pleasant streamside garden and nature trail), **Alger Falls** (right on M-28 east of town), and **Wagner Falls**, more secluded and more powerful, a short walk from M-94. Eight waterfalls (the best-known being **Miners Falls** and **Chapel Falls**) are within the Pictured Rocks National Lakeshore. Contact the Visitor Center for a map. Two of the most charming are on the east edge of town, part of the Michigan Nature Association's **Twin Waterfall Plant Preserve**. To see them, take East Munising Ave./H-58 1 1/2 miles east from the M-28 turn and strip. About 400 feet past a Y, look for a staircase and parking area. Climb the stairs, go through a muddy area, and follow the canyon trail to **Olson** or **Tannery Falls**, cross the bridge in front of the falls, and return on the canyon's other side. **Memorial Falls** are reached more easily. From H-58 perhaps 1/4 mile east of the stairway, turn east on Nestor St. In a block, find signs. Follow the trail through a woods to the top of the falls. A side trail follows the canyon fall down to the falls; it continues to **Olson Falls**.

front porch of this onetime hotel for a **leisurely view of small-town Munising**. *111 Elm. 387-4253. Open 6 days a week, year-round. From Mem. Day thru fall colors, 8 a.m. to 9 p.m., In the off-seasons, 8 a.m. to 5 p.m.* :& *not really. About 5 steps up.*

◆ **PUTVIN HEALTH MART** This large, exceptionally helpful downtown drug store also offers gifts, summer fun accessories, Radio Shack, and many special services, including 24-hour emergency prescription service. *119 Elm at Superior. 387-2248. Mon-Sat 9 -6.* &

◆ **MAMA BEAR'S DEN** carries supplies, yarns, and fabrics for knitting, crocheting, tatting, quilting, and porcelain dolls, with examples of these to inspire and instruct. One specialty: **"Bear Wool" yarn from sheep in the nearby Eben area**. Now owner Glynne Ellen offers week-long classes for summer vacationers. The store also offers custom printing of photos and art, scanned while you wait, printed onto T shirts, mugs, etc. *206 E. Superior, 2 blocks west of The Dogpatch. 387-1570. Open year-round, Mon-Sat 10-6.* &

◆ **THE HEN HOUSE** gift and home accessories shop has moved into one of Munising's **nicest homes**, a turn-of-the-century frame house with leaded glass windows. Owner Debra Crommel has arranged lamps, pictures, rugs, etc. into vignettes — country, Victorian, woodsy, etc. There's a year-round Christmas room and **fudge**, made fresh right here — a new addition to Munising. Debra, a new fudge franchisee, says this is the best fudge she's ever eaten, and it comes in 100 flavors. Her favorites: pumpkin and a fudge version of the Almond Joy idea. *231 W. Munising/M-28, next to the Dairy Queen on downtown's west edge. Enter in rear. 387-4866. Open year round. Daily in summer 10-9. In the off-season open Mon-Sat 10-5.* :& too many steps.

◆ **KIDS' CONNECTION PLAYGROUND.** Volunteers built this impressive **castle-like linkage of play equipment**. *Varnum at Court, one block west of Elm. Open daily 8 a.m.-10 p.m.*

◆ **MUNISING RANGE LIGHTS.** One form of navigational aid for vessels coming into a harbor was having two lights. Lining them up kept the vessel on course. Here the front range light is a white conical tower set back a little on M-28/Munising Avenue at the foot of Hemlock Street, five blocks west of Elm. Looking up Hemlock, you can see the rear range light perched on a hill with a woods behind it. Because it's up, it's much smaller, and looks like a backyard ornament of some sort.

Valley Spur
Cross-Country Ski Trails

Because Valley Spur is **artfully laid out**, meticulously groomed most days of the week, and less well known — therefore less crowded — than Pictured Rocks trails, the 38-mile trail system in the Hiawatha National Forest three miles south of Munising is a **favorite destination** of many dedicated cross-country skiers from above and below the bridge and from Wisconsin, too. Heavy snows make for a **deep base** and for skiing from December into April in most years. Dick Fultz of the Cross-Country Ski Shop in Grayling inspired a Traverse Magazine article that's posted on the web (www.traversemagazine.com/WDIV — that's for "winter diversions").

A **wonderful variety of scenery**, including hardwood forests, hemlock groves, small lakes, make all Valley Spur's 11 loops interesting. The B beginner's and warm-up loop, 2.8 miles starting at the parking lot, is perhaps the most scenic of all. The first stretch follows an old logging railroad grade, the namesake "Valley Spur," crossing a creek (here a narrower snowshoe trail is between the ski trail and creek) and following the upland edge of a swamp. *Traverse Magazine* writer Jeff Smith waxed rhapsodic. "Criss-cross a sleepy black-bottom creek. Catch the glint of sun off the rivulets. Trace your eye along the pillows of snow that edge the stream as it widens and necks down — a dark serpent weaving through the hemlock and snowy marsh."

Forest Service planner Dave Worel laid out the trails starting in 1978 to take advantage of the gentle slopes and varied topography of this glacial landscape, on an end moraine and its small hills. "The difficulty on the expert trails comes not from speed but turns," he says. "The winding valleys mean you have to step around corners at some speed. Skiing is supposed to be fun. It's no longer fun if you're frightened at the top of a hill. My intermediate trails tend to be fairly easy; nobody wants to be a beginner. The H loop [a 4.4 mile intermediate loop] goes through a wetland valley

Outstanding cross-country skiing and good mountain biking near Munising

The area benefits from having the National Lakeshore and National Forest with so much public land in a central location. Get information from the Pictured Rocks/Hiawatha National Forest Visitor Center at (906) 387-3700 or the chamber of commerce (906) 387-2138. Groomed areas are the 10.7 k **Munising Cross Country Ski Trail** between Munising Falls and Sand Point ("Should not be missed," says hiking guide author Dennis Hansen), the 38k Valley Spur system just south of town with rentals and a warming cabin. Ungroomed trail networks are on **Grand Island** and, in the Hiawatha National Forest south of Munising, the 11.7 k **Bruno's Run** and the 12k **McKeever Hills Ski Trails** south of Pete's Lake. The **McKeever Cabin** can be rented for about $35/night; call (906) 387-3700.. One concern: winter storms come up with unusual suddenness here. Skiers should always be informed about weather fronts.

and an **old-growth eastern hemlock stand** that's probably 300 years old."

For Dave, Valley Spur has been as much a labor of love as part of his Forest Service job. He's often one of the the volunteer out at the cozy log warming cabin on weekends. The Clinton administration's quiet cutbacks and downsizing of the federal government have meant the Hiawatha National Forest has fewer staff (130, contrasted to 169 in the early 1990s) doing the same amount of work. Valley Spur's operating budget is less than a third of what it was during the first Bush Administration. Skiers are now asked to pay, and Friends of Valley Spur has been organized to maintain the trail system. Another problem is its Munising location when the area's population center, Marquette, has other cross-country trails closer to town. The annual catered **Taste and Glide** ($15 including trail fees) on the first Saturday in March promotes Valley Spur.

For skiers who want well planned ski trails that are an alternative to highly groomed trails, there's **McKeever Hills Ski Trail** that winds among the lakes on Hiawatha National Forest land south of Munising. Its 6 1/2 miles of loops are mostly intermediate, with one challenging loop around Wedge Lake. It's on H-13 13 miles south of Munising. Parking is south of the turnoff to Pete's Lake Campground.

Note: on winter weekends, Munising lodgings can fill up fast with snowmobilers. Book ahead, try to take off during the week, or get a room in Marquette or Escanaba, where lodgings are plentiful. (If you do stay in Marquette, use M-94 and not M-28 to avoid sudden snowsqualls off the lake.)

On M-94 3 miles south of Munising. Typically open from sometime in December into April. (906) 387-2512. TDD: (906) 387-3371. $5 donation requested.

MUNISING RESTAURANTS

Few Munising restaurants serve reliably good, fresh meals, which may seem surprising, considering the volume of visitors in summer and snowmobile season. The trouble is, there are too many people wanting food at certain limited times, making for slow service. But there's no population base to sustain a year-round business and keep a good cook. The result: restaurants that depend on Gordon Food Service (and that's not necessarily bad food at all), the grill, and the deep fryer. The Navigator, a seasonal restaurant in a beautiful downtown loca-

tion with a water view, couldn't make it. The area's best food comes from places where an owner who cooks does most of the cooking.

In a nutshell, for really good food, go to **The Brownstone Inn** in Au Train. For unpretentious home cooking, go to **Country Connection** or **The Golden Heart** (Chinese-Thai). For speedy service in a beautiful setting, go to **Glen's Market** and then have a picnic, supplemented perhaps by your favorite breads and cheeses from home.

People who ordinarily wouldn't set foot in an old-time bar like the **COUNTRY CONNECTION** rave about the **pasties** ($4.50 with slaw or gravy) and 1/3 pound burgers ($2.75). The home-cooked food here is eclipsing the alcohol, anyway. "We're progressing it into a restaurant," says Phyllis Brock. She owns the downtown spot, originally a roller rink, with her husband, Chum. Breakfast is served any time if it's not too busy. Lunch brings soup, specials ($5 to $6), fried chicken baskets ($6 for 3 pieces). For dinner there's whitefish, fried or broiled ($9) and T bone or ribeye steaks ($10.50). Dinners come with soup, salad, and potato. Friday fish fry ($8-$9.75) brings out the salad bar, too. There's an outdoor patio. *208 N. Superior between Maple and Birch, 2 blocks west of the strip. 387-4839 . Kitchen open Mon-Sat 9 a.m.-closing, Sun noon-closing.* Full bar

GOLDEN HEART RESTAURANT, mostly Chinese with around eight Thai dishes, is a good choice for travelers who want fresh green vegetables and non-fried food. True, the locally popular dishes here like sesame chicken are often breaded and deep-fried, then served in sweet and sour sauce. But healthier options abound, like cashew dishes with snow peas or Chinese vegetable dishes. For kids who are picky eaters, there are egg rolls and chicken rice soup. Lunch dishes are under $6, dinner dishes from $6.50 to $11. *Downtown at 202 Superior at Maple, across from Main Street Pizza and a block south of Subway. 387-5445. Open daily year-round. Mon-Sat 11-9. From spring thru fall, open Sundays from noon to 8. In winter, open Sun 4-8.* **H.A.:** call. Tight quarters.

DOGPATCH has been the year-round visitor favorite for decades. According to local reports, the food is usually consistent, but it's possible to have a very disappointing meal. Still, it's a place with a full menu and a pleasant atmosphere (the Dogpatch/L'il Abner theme goes back to Al Capp's comic strip) where you

can get a drink with your meal. The 26-item soup and salad bar is another plus. There's fresh fish (around $13 as dinner entrées) and homemade fruit cobblers. Not much for vegetarians except the salad bar. *On Superior at M-28 in downtown Munising. 387-9948. Open year-round from 7 a.m. to 10 p.m.* Full bar

CHERRYWOOD LODGE at the Best Western motel east of Munising offers three meals a day in a **pleasant, history-minded atmosphere** that combines a bar, fireplace, ample natural light, a varied menu. Same food, prices, owner as Dogpatch. *On M-28 three miles east of town. 387-5400. Open from Dec. thru March and June thru Oct. Open daily 7 a.m.-9 p.m. at least, later on weekends* Full bar

MUNISING LODGINGS

See also: Au Train, Lakes Region, Marquette.

The sprawling commercial strip of busy M-28 is at the east edge of the compact little town of Munising. They are within easy walking distance of the waterfront park and downtown, but in an environment dominated by vehicles and truck noise. Most of our choices are elsewhere. In-season rates typically apply in Munising from July through fall color season (usually early October) and in snowmobile season (mid-December through February and into March).

Motels are arranged from north (in-town and closer to Lake Superior) to south.

DAYS INN   (906) 387-2493

This large (66-room, 2-story) motel, on the town side of busy M-28, has a **kidney-shaped indoor pool** of 30 feet or so plus **whirlpool** and **sauna** in a pleasant, sunny pool room. **Large rooms** with contemporary decor have many bed combinations. Rates for two people in a standard room in high season (summer and snowmobile season) $66 (one bed) and $98 (two beds). *Next to Sydney's restaurant. Across from Glen's supermarket. M-28 on the strip, 4 blocks southeast of downtown. Rear faces Cedar St.*
H.A.: many rooms fully accessible
18 & under free : call; small pets

TERRACE MOTEL   (906) 387-2735; www.exploringthenorth.com

This older motel is in a **quiet residential neighborhood** two blocks away from the highway and a 9-block walk from downtown. Some of its 18 rooms open onto

each other for family use. The **game room** has a **kitchen,** pool table, air hockey, and darts, all free. There's also a sauna. Snowmobilers can use a heated garage for repairs; the trail starts here at the parking lot. Current winter & summer room rates: $48 and $52. Off-season: $36 and $40. *520 Prospect. From M-28, turn south (up hill) onto Brook at the Citgo station, then right on Prospect.*
H.A.: call : rates by the room
: medium-size pets in smoking rooms

SUNSET MOTEL   (906) 387-4574; www.exploringthenorth.com/munising; e-mail: sunset@chartermi.net

This two-story motel enjoys a **beautiful setting on Munising Bay**. Of its16 rooms, six have kitchens ($8 extra). Current rates from mid-June to Labor Day for two people in a room with one queen: $51, with two queens $55. Otherwise $38 and $42. Rooms have extended cable TV. Over half are knotty pine. There's no air-conditioning — right on the water, it's very seldom needed. A pay phone is outside. There's a gorgeous view across the bay, with nice light effects at dusk. The motel has a **dock, seawall, and beach**. There's room for shuffleboard and a playground. Book at least a month ahead for good summer availability. *1315 E. Bay just north off East Munising Ave. about 1 1/2 miles east of town. Open May thru Oct.*
H.A.: call : under 5 free. $4/extra person : one dog per room, $5 extra

BEST WESTERN MUNISING
(906) 387-4864; www.bestwestern.com

The area's **only full-service motel**, 80 units, sits back from M-28 three miles out of town. The large lawn has a playground, outdoor pool, and picnic area with BBQ. In rear is a **large, very pleasant indoor pool** with big windows, now connected with each lodging building. The **attractive Cherrywood Lodge restaurant and lounge**, run by the same people who own The Dogpatch, are open in snowmobile season and from June through October. Rates for a standard double: $69 to $89 in summer, $99 and up in snowmobile season. Deluxe room with microwave, refrigerator, freezer, lounger: $69- $99 in summer. *Three miles east of town on M-28.* 3 units : rates by the room

MUNISING AREA CAMPING

See also: Au Train, Christmas, Inland Lake Country in this chapter. For campgrounds in and near the east end of Pictured Rocks, look under Grand Marais

Bay Furnace, a peaceful, almost church-like stone tower with arched openings, is by a picnic area, campground, and beach near Christmas. It alone remains from a noisy, smoky 1870s iron-making complex. Here iron ore from the Marquette Range was fed into the roraring charcoal-fueled blast furnace, producing streams of molten iron that flowed into sand molds.

in the "Tahquamenon & Seney, Grand Marais & Whitefish Point" chapter.

Most camping in the Pictured Rocks National Lakeshore is closer to the Grand Marais end and therefore found under Grand Marais in the "Tahquamenon & Seney, Grand Marais & Whitefish Point" chapter. Handouts on those rustic campgrounds can be had at the Visitor Center. Not far to the south of the National Lakeshore are several attractive rustic campgrounds of the **Lake Superior State Forest**, usually with excellent privacy between sites. For them also see Grand Marais camping. Good bets for finding a campsite when other campgrounds are full: Island Lake and Widewaters, two inland campgrounds south of Munising in the **Hiawatha National Forest**.

LITTLE BEAVER LAKE CAMPGROUND/
Pictured Rocks National Lakeshore
(906) 387-3700; not reservable

8 rustic campsites on the shore of Little Beaver Lake are closer together than the other two National Lakeshore campgrounds. Because this campground is so small and so well located, it is the most likely to be full. Have some backup campgrounds in mind. On the beautiful White Pine Trail, with interpretive signs, around the lake. **Good location for day hikes**. The road down to the campground is so steep, big RVs can't make it back up. $10. *About 20 miles east of Munising on H-58, then 3 miles north on Little Beaver Lake Rd. Open from May 10 thru Oct. 31.* &: 1 site.

WANDERING WHEELS CAMPGROUND
(906) 387-3315

This 89-site private campground scores high for a **wooded setting and pleasant atmosphere**. It has many kinds of sites, from various hookup combinations to

none at all and sites for tents. Hot showers. Laundry. Grocery store. Group sites for tents. Lots of extras include heated pool, rec hall, basketball, volleyball, horseshoes, badminton, and (for a fee) minigolf. Reservations recommended. *On M-28, 3 1/2 miles east of Munising. Open May thru mid-Oct.* &: call.

BACKCOUNTRY CAMPING
along Pictured Rocks'
North Country/Lakeshore Trail
Permits required from the Visitor Center; (906) 387-3700

13 dispersed primitive campsites, to be used by hikers and kayakers, are along this popular trail. Most are at stream mouths or near lakes. Mosquito River, Chapel Beach, and Beaver Creek campsites are below the bluff, near beaches. Call (906) 387-3700 to request a reservation form and map with locations and mileage between sites. The required permits are in such demand that you should sign up as soon as possible after January 15 if you're considering July and August, or if you'd like group reservations at other times. If you reserve by mail or fax, do so at least two weeks ahead of your visit. Cost: $15/permit (up to 14 nights) for groups up to 6; $30 for groups from 7 to 20. All that's provided is a fire ring and bear poles from which food must be hung. **Leave-no-trace** camping practices should be observed, and backpacking stoves instead of fires are encouraged.

Primitive camping at DISPERSED
CAMPSITES/Hiawatha National Forest
Some of these undeveloped campsites on good fishing lakes have become so popular that reservation requests for most-demanded sites are honored in a lottery. The **wooded surroundings are remote**,

and generally too small for large campers; some camping areas only have one campsite. Toilet facilities vary from improved to primitive to none. A good number of these are in the Steuben area, in Schoolcraft County but closer to Munising than Manistique. Most requested of all is the **8-person cabin on Tom's Lake** near Steuben. A fat handout describes each area and campsite, with its fishing, boating, and swimming possibilities. Get handouts in person or by phone from the Manistique District Ranger Office. *499 E. Lake Shore, Manistique 49854. (906-341-5666). Contact it in January to participate in the upcoming summer lottery.*

Christmas (pop. 400)

Christmas, an unincorporated area with a few motels and resorts, was given its name by the Munising man who, in 1938, started a roadside factory to make holiday gift items. The factory soon burned, but the name survives. So do the roadside Santas it inspired. A **big Kewadin Casino** (387-5475) is along M-28 here, open from noon to midnight. It's a branch of the five-casino empire of the Sault Ste. Marie Tribe of Chippewa Indians. The Christmas casino is right on the highway, so it's handy for a pit stop to use the restrooms and get a free soft drink or coffee. Now a 40-room **Paradise Inn motel** is being built next to the casino.

Bay Furnace Picnic Area

Here are a **picnic area** and **small beach** across from Grand Island. Down the drive is the 50-site **Bay Furnace Campground**. The area is part of the Hiawatha National Forest. Next to it the sandstone ruins of a charcoal-fueled blast furnace are interpreted for visitors. Between 1869 and 1877, iron ore from the Marquette Iron Range was converted to pig iron and shipped from a dock that once was here. The village of Onota, with about 500 people, occupied the site until fire destroyed it in 1877. Small northern furnaces like these were superseded by big steel-making centers around Chicago and Pittsburgh.

From M-28 at Christmas, look for sign to Bay Furnace campground. It's not far north of the highway. (906) 387-2512. &

CHRISTMAS RESTAURANT
FOGGY'S STEAKHOUSE & LOUNGE features the popular **grill-your-own-steak format** while offering a full menu,

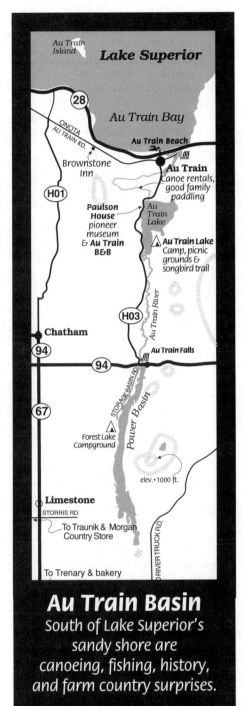

Au Train Basin
South of Lake Superior's sandy shore are canoeing, fishing, history, and farm country surprises.

including sandwiches ($4.25 to $5.75) any time. Nestled along creek, it has expanded into huge place with a log cabin façade — a **hot spot for snowmobilers**. Fun atmosphere, good food, says a woman who works at a local gift shop. This being Christmas, there's a fair amount of year-round Christmas decor. All steaks are $16, from an 8 oz. filet to a 22 oz. top sirloin. Dinner entrées ($8 to $17) usually come with soup and salad bar and soft-serve ice cream. Lunch items include subs, Mexican, Rueben, fish, pizza. *On M-28 in Christmas, kitty-*

corner from the Kewadin Casino, on lake side of the highway. 387-3357. Open daily year-round, from 11 a.m. (noon on Sunday) to 10. May open for breakfast in summer and snowmobile season. **H.A.** 👫🚶 Full bar

CHRISTMAS CAMPING

BAY FURNACE Campground/ Hiawatha National Forest
(906) 387-2512; not reservable

50 rustic campsites (no showers or electricity) are on two asphalt loops close to Lake Superior. Some sites are **wooded,** others open. Surprisingly, some sites are usually available in summer. Come early in the week in late July-early August to be sure. There's a **small beach** and **beautiful views across to Grand Island.** This campground is a favorite of divers exploring nearby shipwrecks. *From M-28 at Christmas, look for sign to Bay Furnace campground. It's not far north of the highway. $8/night. Open May 15-Sept. 30.* ♿ : 2 sites.

Au Train (*pop. 300*)

Located just south of where the Au Train River finally makes its **sandy, serpentine union with Lake Superior**, Au Train has long been a summer resort. The hamlet is centered on the Au Train-Forest Lake Road that runs south from M-28 at Au Train Bay. The population swells by 50% in summertime. Au Train has also become a popular retirement community.

The **sand beach** here along Lake Superior extends for miles and offers beautiful views across the bay. **Scenic highway turnouts** make it easy to get out **and walk the beach. Charming Scott Falls** is right on the south side of M-28 two miles east of Au Train. Park at the roadside park on the opposite side of the road to get out and explore it.

Au Train's preferred swimming spot is in the **warmer Au Train River** by the highway bridge, just before it enters the lake. The sand piled up here led to the name Au Train, according to Walter Romig in *Michigan Place Names:* "The river carried so much sand into the lake here as to form a shoal over which the voyageurs would drag (trainerant, in French) their canoes to make a short cut." This site was also popular with Ojibwa, who camped here while they hunted and fished nearby. Later Au Train became a dog-team stop on the northern U.P. mail route.

Canoe rentals in Au Train
are for use on the peaceful Au Train River, Au Train Lake, and the long basin south of it. Two liveries are just south of the little town on Forest Lake Road: **Northwoods Resort** (906-892-8114) and **Riverside Resort** (906-892-8350). The placid Au Train River twists and turns a lot on its way to Lake Superior. One popular trip takes three hours to go 7 miles through national forest land. Another takes an hour or two longer to get through the wide water just downstream from the popular riverside swimming beach.

Paulson House Museum

For many years this 1884 log house, an unusual example of **Swedish log construction** in Michigan, was the centerpiece of the Avery family's outdoor museum of pioneer crafts. Then the museum complex was sold off. Susan Larsen, born in this very house and now a cartographer for half the year in California, has carried on and enhanced the place's tradition as a **pioneer museum**. The downstairs serves as a **gallery space** for a changing display of **quilts** from the past century. There's no more shop area, but a few favorite items will be offered online at www.autrainlake.com, including some U.P. cookbooks, wood carvings, and quilts.

Upstairs, room settings of antiques recreate pioneer-era living spaces, including the schoolroom that actually was in this house. **Historical gardens** reflect what the house might have been like in 1900, with a **big late-May daffodil display** followed by lilacs, lilies, and many perennials. There's also wildflower test garden done with the Forest Service's help to see how plantings of native wildflowers fare.

On Forest Lake Rd. south of Au Train, 2 1/2 miles south of the M-28 blinker light. or 6 miles north of M-94. 892-8892. Open July & August, noon-6 p.m. Earlier and later visitors might be shown around. Call for spring and fall hours. ♿: ground floor of house.

Au Train Songbird Trail/ Hiawatha National Forest

By borrowing a tape player, audio interpretive guide, field guide, and binoculars, beginners can sample an unusually helpful **introduction to bird-watching** on an easy two-mile hiking trail. The

tape features 20 species in their likely habitats: woods, bog, field, and the lakeshore, where ducks, shorebirds, and maybe an eagle or osprey may be seen from an observation tower. Sometimes the birds may sing back to your tape! Morning is the best time for birdsong, followed by dusk. Rent the audio kits for a $10 deposit ($8 will be returned) from either grocery on Au Train Forest Lake Road in the center of Au Train, or from the Paulson House Museum.

Songbird Trail is by Au Train Lake Campground east off H-03/Forest Lake Rd. 4.5 miles south of M-28. (Look for national forest signs). Trail starts by campsite #11. (906) 387-3700 . &: call.

Bay de Noc-Grand Island Riding & Hiking Trail

Used largely by horses and riders, this **40-mile trail**, part of the Hiawatha National Forest, roughly follows an **ancient Ojibwa canoe and portage route** used as a direct inland route from Lake Michigan to Lake Superior. The Whitefish River almost connects Au Train Lake with the head of Little Bay de Noc at Rapid River. The trail begins at M-94 south of Au Train and follows the Whitefish River valley along the river bluff, with some good views. It passes Haymeadow Falls and campground north of Rapid River. (See Escanaba chapter.) The northern part has some hills, separated by level stretches.

Conflicts between horsemen and hikers, which can be difficult in heavily-used public land near large metropolitan areas, apparently aren't much of a problem here.

The northern trailhead is on M-94 south of Au Train. Park north of M-94 by Ackerman Lake. (906) 387-2512. A brochure is available from all Hiawatha National Forest offices. &: call

AU TRAIN RESTAURANTS

Excellent and interesting food, prepared from scratch, served in a **charming setting** — that's what brings local people and visitors back to **THE BROWNSTONE INN** again and again. This distinctive fieldstone building seems like a northwoods version of a comfortable European inn, mellowed by age and use. Homey lace curtains and a Victorian crazy quilt are played off against the stone fireplace and original Rittenhouse rustic furniture. A former Detroit cop built the place in 1946, using local rock and a good deal of salvage like factory windows from a

Munising plant. The mahogany wainscoting may come from the Ford glider plant at Kingsford.

The chance to buy the distinctive building was what drew the owners east from California. Jeffrey Van Bremen, burned out from too much intense, Silicon Valley-style problem-solving on the job, had been taking restaurant cooking classes. He runs the kitchen. He's an anti-snob, says his wife. The menu and specials combine the expected (whitefish, steak, prime rib, bar food like wing dings and poppers, Friday fresh fish) with the inventive and the gourmet. Currently Jeff enjoys making interesting salsas to go with fish and pork, sometimes blackened, and inventing different lasagnas. (Shiitake, oyster, and crimini mushrooms make a great lasagna with white sauce and zucchini.) Sometimes wild salmon caught in British Columbia show up on the menu. The fresh local whitefish ($12 at dinner) is prepared many ways, including Jamaican and (for $1 extra) Rocky Mountain-style (with bell peppers, poppyseed). Customers call and ask, "What's Jeff doing interesting tonight?" Portions are generous. Dinners include salad, potato, vegetable, potato rolls. An excellent selection of wines and beers is available to go.

On the lunch menu, served any time, are charbroiled hamburgers conventional and exotic ($4.50 to $5), fresh whitefish sandwiches, home-cut fries, and meal-size salads. The smoky burger comes with smoked Gouda cheese. The Laughing Whitefish salad ($9) , served hot with jerk seasonings, stands out among salads, available with nine homemade dressing. Homemade desserts, cappuccino and coffee drinks served any time.

Dinner reservations recommended, especially weekends. Call-ahead takeout orders are encouraged. Come early for yellow lake perch (Friday). Sunday barbecue often sells out by 2. In this small, 60-seat place, there's often a wait between 6 and 8 p.m. Jeff's wife, Deb Molitor, runs the bar and budget; her past years as a special ed teacher "translate really well to bartending," she says. "It's all about individual needs." *On M-28 two miles west of Au Train blinker. 892-8332. July-Labor Day: Mon-Sat 11 a.m.-10 p.m., Sun noon to 9 p.m. In June may close earlier if it's slow. Otherwise Tues-Thurs 11-9, Fri & Sat to 10, Sun noon-9.*

&: yes but not restrooms &&& Full bar

AU TRAIN LODGINGS

NORTHWOODS RESORT (906) 892-8114; www.exploringthenorth.com/northwoods/resort.html

13 well-kept housekeeping cottages are either near a **sandy beach** on Au Train Lake or in a **heavily wooded area** across the road. The grounds slope gently to the lake, which has a swimming dock here. **Nightly bonfires** are held on the beach, weather permitting. Tuesday potluck in July & August. The resort **rents boats, motors, canoes, and ride-on-top kayaks**. The **sauna** is fired up nightly — a hit with kids. A small game room is off the sauna. Old logging roads from back go into national forest land — an hour's hike along the winding Au Train River. Near 10-mile mountain bike loop. Duck blinds available. Near a main snowmobile trail.

All cottages have picnic areas with grills. Many have decks. Bedrooms vary from 1 to 5. Cable TV upon request. Courtesy phone in laundry. Typical weekly rates in season $375-$800. Nightly rates in off-season typically $55-$150. *From M-28, go two miles south on Forest Lake Rd./Co. Hwy. 03. Open year-round. &: call.*

AU TRAIN LAKE BED & BREAKFAST (906) 892-8892; www.autrainlake.com

Behind the Paulson House Museum (see above), proprietor Susan Larsen has a pleasant little B&B in the adjacent A-frame on **Paulson Lake**. It's a short walk across the road to Au Train Lake. The 3 guest rooms ($75 and $85) are not large but comfortable, furnished with antiques in a fresh, eclectic style. There's a sitting area and large deck. No TV; radio/CD players in guest rooms. Bring phone card to use phone. The **full buffet breakfast** often has a regional flavor. The downstairs guest room has private bath; upper rooms share a bath. The front room has **gorgeous lake view**. See directions for Paulson House. Ask about separate, antique-furnished housekeeping cottage (open floor plan) that sleeps up to 4, with cable TV, $600/week. *Open late May through Sept.*

H.A.: call &&&

ROCK RIVER BEACH RESORT (906) 892-8112

Right where the Rock River tumbles into Lake Superior, a **charming waterwheel** catches the eye of most every motorists on the way to Marquette. It's part of this trim little resort. Its eight cottages, the little dam, and the first waterwheel date from the 1920s. But the resort's origins go back decades before that. The grandfather of the present owners, as a young man, rowed down from Marquette to work for his uncle, a lumberman who was cutting the area's white pine. Young C.C. clerked in his uncle's store in the village of Rock River and decided that some day, when he had a chance, he would live at the Rock River mouth. He fulfilled his dream when he built these rental summer cottages for certain residents of Munising and Marquette. The dam generated power for its electric lights. His son-in-law Byron Braamse continued the **picturesque landscaping** tradition with stonework. Byron's son Peter and grandson Jack carried on the look with their own embellishments.

Today the two-bedroom housekeeping cottages, finished in **knotty pine**, are mostly booked in summer by repeat weekly guests, but availability is good from April through early June and again from September into November. They sleep from two to eight and currently rent for $265 a week plus gas, or $65 a night with a two-night minimum. These are simple getaways, tastefully furnished but without TV or planned diversions. Four have **stone fireplaces**. Expect to hear road noise. "The patio," built on the foundation of a house that burned, is a gathering place with rustic chairs where guests watch the sun set. One side of the **beach** is sandy with a few pebbles, the other stony. In good weather it's possible to canoe out to Au Train Island, 3/4 mile from the nearby point, and see the interesting striped formation of Jacobsville sandstone. *On M-28 at the Rock River mouth, about 6 miles west of Au Train. Open from April thru Nov.*
H.A.: call 👫👶: no extra charge 🐕: well mannered pets & attentive owners welcome

AU TRAIN CAMPING

See also Christmas. The Pictured Rocks/National Forest Visitor Center can advise campers of the availability of many area campsites and their suitability to individual preferences. Stop in for handouts and the latest availability information.

AU TRAIN LAKE Campground/ Hiawatha National Forest

(906) 387-3700; not reservable

830-acre Au Train Lake, largest in the area, is popular not only for fishing (for northern, walleye, and perch) but for **water-skiing**. Of the 37 shady rustic sites (no showers, vault toilets, first-come, first-serve) on two asphalt loops, 11 are right on Buck Bay, on the lake's

east side. A boat launch and picnic area with swimming beach are adjacent. The **2-mile songbird trail** (see above) starts here. Canoes and boats can be rented locally. *Just east off H-03/Au Train-Forest Lake Rd., 4 miles south of M-28 at Au Train and 3 miles north of M-94. Look for National Forest sign at Forest Rd. 227. Open from May 15 to Sept. 30.* &: not currently.

Chatham (pop. 231)

Chatham, named after the Ontario city, is on the east edge of a **sizeable farming area** that extends to Skandia, Traunik, and Trenary. Chatham was first developed in 1896 as a lumber camp. The lumber camp was gone by 1899, when the railroad came and the State Agricultural Experiment Station (now part of Michigan State University) was established in 1899. The **striking, three-story limestone hotel**, now home of the Village Traveler restaurant, was built as the Pacific Hotel in 1904. It was one of the few buildings to survive a fire in 1925.

Today Chatham is most widely known for its role on the route of the U.P. 200, one of the nation's most important **dogsled races**. A fair number of the area's old 80-acre Finnish farms are now devoted to dogsledding.

Rock River Falls & Rock River Canyon Wilderness Area

People who love waterfalls for their otherworldly magic and not their been-there, done-that touristic appeal may want to seek out Rock River Falls. This recently designated wilderness area is along the canyon of the Rock River, some **150 feet deep**. The path down to the falls from the nearest road is well used, about 3/4 of a mile long. It is not marked, but not hard to follow either. It goes through a deep woods before reaching the river above the falls. In *A Guide to 199 Michigan Waterfalls*, the Penroses, who have just about seen them all, say it's one of Alger County's **most beautiful falls**, and certainly one of the most **remote**. After dropping about 20 feet over a limestone ledge, "the water catches on the steps of the ledge, creating progressively smaller streams, which form feathery trails from top to bottom." Wear waterproof footgear or expect to have wet feet.

See the Penroses' book for directions and details for another beautiful, out-of-the-way waterfall in the same wilderness

area, Silver Bell Falls. Silver Creek also forms a 150-foot canyon, but the waterfall is quite different.

As a wilderness area, Rock River Canyon Wilderness has no signs, no waste containers, no planned improvements. You won't get lost if you follow the trail to the falls. If you want to explore further without following the river, you'd do well to get a **USGS map** of the area from the **Pictured Rocks/ Hiawatha National Forest Visitor Center** and know how to read it and use your compass or GPS device. Take out your trash. Bury human waste in a 6" deep hole. Note: the **"ice caves"** near Eben, a favorite but now forbidden snowmobile destination, are within the wilderness area, but most people would have to trespass on private land to get there. *From M-94 Chatham, go north on Rock River Rd. where M-94 makes its right-angle turn. Go 3.6 miles, crossing the Rock River, to take USFS Road 2276. Turn west (left) and go about 4.3 miles. Look for a pullover on the left and the path to the falls.* &: no.

CHATHAM RESTAURANT

The **VILLAGE TRAVELER** is a cheerful, completely unpretentious restaurant that's a center of local life, open for breakfast, lunch, and dinner. Lunch specials ($around $4) may be soup and a sandwich or a plate. The full dinner menu is mostly $5 to $6, served all day. Vegetarian by request. *Open daily year-round. Sun & Mon 7 a.m. to 5 p.m., Tues-Sat 7 a.m. to 8 p.m. 439-5509. N5298 Rock River St./M-94 in downtown Chatham.* **H.A.:** 3 steps. 👫👶

Sundell

Sundell, eight miles west of Chatham on M-94, was once a rural railroad stop with its own post office. Its first postmistress, Selma Harsila, got to name it and used her maiden name, the Swedish Sundell.

Laughing Whitefish Falls Scenic Site

This is one of those memorable waterfalls which **materializes suddenly**, without an audible announcement, from an insignificant-looking creek. You walk gradually downhill, first through an old field studded with wildflowers, then into the second-growth **hardwood forest**. When you reach a stairway, you're looking at a **dramatic hundred-foot wall of**

water cascading over vertical limestone shelf. The stairway descends alongside the limestone canyon wall, where water has sculpted little hollows. It's a 20-minute walk each way. Unlike most waterfalls, this one is best visited at mid-day. The ravine is so steep, it's too dark at other times.

The falls, though out of the way, is well signed. From M-94 in Sundell, go north on Dorsey Rd. In about 2 miles, turn right to the access road. The parking lot is in half a mile. &: no.

Limestone

This little place on M-67 between Chatham and Trenary was founded in 1889. and named after the limestone bed of Johnson Creek about three miles north of town. Everything in town pretty much lines up along M-67 — the convenience store in the Limestone Mini-Mall, the Limestone Baptist Church, Old Joe's Bar, a few houses, and the herb farm.

Limestone Herb Company

Owners Tim McAvinchey and Danita Rask have decided to take a year off in 2001. Call 439-5448 about 2002. It's quite possible that they'll be back to business, with their pretty shop full of dried flowers, herb books, essential oils, and such, and the **beguiling mix of plants** they grow from seed or cuttings: wildflowers, everlastings, perennials, and herbs — all hardy for Zone 4, which includes most of the U.P.

Meanwhile, the beautiful, big cottage display garden in front of their house is there, and visitors are welcome to stop and see it.

N2690 M-67 one mile south of the Limestone Mini-Mall.

Traunik

In the decades around 1900 many Slovenian peasants came from their homeland around Ljubljana, bordering Italy, Austria, and Hungary to work in Upper Peninsula mines and lumber camps. Michigan was **well known in Slovenia** because of the energetic activities of many Slovenian missionaries, beginning with Father Frederick Baraga, the **legendary snowshoe priest**. Slovenes who had worked in lumber camps settled in this neighborhood. Their Slovenian hall, cemetery, general store, and tidy two-room school remain today, neatly arranged around the inter-

Traunik time trip: the main elements of a Slovenian rural community (school, social hall, cemetery, store) are perfectly preserved. Old-time classic merchandise is for sale at Morgan's General Store. The upstairs apartment, where the household goods of original storekeeper Louis Mikulich were left, is a museum commemorating the early 20th-century general store.

section of Limestone-Traunik Road (H-44) and Eben Depot Road (H-01). Coming upon Traunik you can feel you've fallen into a time warp. Storekeeper and postmaster Louis Mikulech commemorated his native village in changing the settlement's name to Traunik (pronounced "TRAW-nik") from Buckeye Landing, named after the Buckeye Land & Lumber Company, active in the area.

Morgan's Country Store & Museum

Louis Mikulich's general store and upstairs apartment live on in Dee Morgan's tribute to the **old-fashioned general store**. She used to visit a store like this with her grandpa when she was growing up in the Keweenaw mining town of Mohawk. Physically the building is little altered from when Mikulich built in 1922. So many furnishings were left in the upstairs living quarters that Morgan has added to them and turned them into a **museum of life in the early 1900s**. On the tour ($2 for adults, $1 for kids 12 and under), a costumed guide shows visitors around the place and tells the story of the country store in America.

"We like the simple life," writes storekeeper Dee Morgan. "We believe that our customers do, too. Days past had a quiet charm and warm trusting simplicity that today's world has largely lost." Downstairs there's a real store with

antique reproductions and all sorts of **old-fashioned, practical things** for sale from agateware pottery bowls to donut cutters, penny candy, towels and table-cloths, leather goods, and old favorites like Grandpa's Pine Tar Soap.

At the main four-corners where H-01 meets H-44 in Traunik, 4 1/2 miles north of Trenary and U.S. 41. Open May-Dec, Mon-Fri 9 a.m.-5 p.m., Sat 10 a.m.-5 p.m. 446-3737. &: store only, not upstairs museum.

Trenary

Originally a **sawmill town**, Trenary grew into a large enough farming community to have two groceries, three bars, and a movie theater. Now many of those are gone, but the Trenary Home Bakery has put Trenary on the map for Yoopers across the U.S. The **Trenary Outhouse Classic**, held the last weekend in February, has gained Trenary more national publicity because it's one of those colorful, easy newswire stories that harried editors find hard to resist. Centerpiece of the weekend is an out-house race. Requirements: build an out-house of wood or cardboard, install a toilet seat and TP roll, mount it on skis, and push it 500 feet to win. Subcategories include "People's Choice," "Most Original," and "Most Miles Traveled."

Trenary Home Bakery Plus

The old Finnish bakery favorite of **cinnamon toast** (korpu) has been so successfully marketed and distributed by this small-town bakery that, far and wide, it's simply known as "Trenary toast." Slightly sweeter than ordinary bread, it's coated with a cinnamon-sugar-spice mix and baked again, slowly. The resulting toast is great for dunking in coffee. With a shelf life of five months, it's ideal for hunting and camping.

In the 1950s Hans and Esther Hallinen started delivering brown paper bags of toast to stores in Escanaba, Marquette, and Munising. Success led them to upgrade the bag, but customers insisted on going back to basic brown paper. Today Trenary toast has become a quintessential U.P. regional food item and a sentimental favorite among those who have moved away. A 10-ounce bag (10 to 12 pieces) currently sells for $2.65. **Mail-order sales** through an 800 number (800-862-7801) are UPS'd to every state. Now it's on the web as well. The Trenary Home Bakery also bakes a

full line of breads: Italian loaves, long and round; buns and sub rolls; a traditional Finnish rye called limpu (it's $2.75 for a 1 1/2-pound loaf); and popular new white and rye breads shaped like the pans they're baked in.

Building on the bakery's success, Bruce and Maureen Hallinen have combined bakery retail sales with a little restaurant in a separate building, the former Red Owl grocery. Maureen, also a Trenary native, lived quite awhile in Racine, Wisconsin, which styles itself "the most Danish city in America." Racine's famous regional food item is the kringle, a wide disk of a coffeecake made of layered pastry and fruit filling, akin to a Danish but thinner. Now Maureen has introduced the U.P. to **kringles, sold by the slice or whole**, thanks to a nearby baker who trained under Racine kringle makers. The bakery restaurant has a 1950s look with red and black checkerboard floor and local history on the walls: old metal signs, the Trenary train station sign, license plates, and more.

On M-67, three buildings east of Trenary's main four-corners. From U.S. 41 19 miles north of Rapid River and 35 miles southeast of Marquette, go east 1/2 mile to Trenary. 446-3000. Same hours as restaurant: winter Mon-Fri 7 a.m. to 6 p.m., Sat 9-3, closed Sun. Starting in May, open Sunday, 9-3 at first. Starting in May, open 7-7. Summer hours: 7 a.m. to 8 p.m., Sat & Sun 9-6. &

TRENARY RESTAURANTS

TRENARY HOME BAKERY PLUS uses the famous bakery's fresh breads (see above) in its sandwiches, bread bowls filled with soup of the day, and many kinds of subs like the popular turkey sub. The evolving format offers breakfast items like bacon and egg or ham croissants and fresh donuts. It also serves Jilbert's ice cream. No credit cards; out-of-town checks OK. *Same hours, location, and setting as retail bakery (above) 446-3000. Winter Mon-Fri 7 a.m. to 6 p.m., Sat 9-3, closed Sun. Starting in May, open Sunday, 9-3 at first. Starting in May, open 7-7. Summer hours: 7 a.m. to 8 p.m., Sat & Sun 9-6.* &

In the cutover old fields and pastures around Trenary, Traunik, and Sundell, scenes like this once were common. They, like many communities in the central Upper Peninsula, began as logging villages. Cutover land was sold to immigrants eager to have farms of their own.

Shingleton (*pop. 250*)

This little village is where M-94 intersects with M-28 at the west end of the Seney Stretch. That arrow-straight 30 miles through flat swampland may be Michigan's **most boring highway**. Shingleton was named for a old shingle mill from the 1880s. Today a **sawmill** operates just outside of town. Its 12 employees make maple boards for furniture-makers and eight-foot railroad ties of beech and maple, wholesaled to railroads for $10 apiece. This mill, like others in the U.P., is finding it harder and harder to get good quality maple logs from mature trees over 60 years old. Another local forest products company, Bell Timber just south of downtown, logs red pine from nearby forests and makes them into telephone poles some 50 feet long. Other local residents work at Camp Cusino, a mile west of town on M-28 at Percy Road. Unlike many U.P. prisons which house some of the state's most dangerous criminals, Cusino is a minimum-security state prison with no armed guards and largely prisoners with non-violent offenses such as writing bad checks. Nonetheless, concertina wire was added to its fences after an escapee killed someone several years ago.

Iverson Snowshoes

Iverson's is **one of only two wood-frame snowshoe factories remaining in the U.S.** In this age of high-tech, lightweight metal snowshoes, traditional wood snowshoes, derived from Native American designs, are out of fashion except for décor.

However, Iverson's snowshoes are the most practical. So says a U.P. man who spends much of his time in winter working outdoors in the snow. "It's not a matter of snowshoe weight," he says. "You have to add the snow that gets lifted on the tops of new-style snowshoes. Traditional snowshoes with tails were designed for long distances. The weight

of the snowshoe slides off the tail. Iverson's bearpaw, with the rounded back, is a wonderful stable platform to work off of. The high-tech snowshoes just punch holes in the snow."

At Iverson's workers take long strips of white ash, steam them to increase their flexibility, bend them around a form, and dry them in a kiln overnight. The labor-intensive job includes hand-lacing with traditional rawhide or more durable neoprene. Visitors can drop in and watch, if it's not too busy or if cutting isn't going on.

Snowshoes are easy to use and practical. Iverson's makes nine models for different purposes. Rustic, **snowshoe-style furniture** and fishnets are also made on site and displayed in the retail shop. The $300 rocker is functional and attractive. Check out the online catalogue at www.iversonshowshoe.com

From M-28 in Shingleton, turn north on Maple St., two blocks west of Shingleton's only blinker. (906) 452-6370. E-mail snowshoe@jamadots.com. Open Mon-Fri 8-3:30. Large groups should call first. &*: call first, narrow passages.*

Inland Lakes of the Hiawatha Nat'l Forest

Between Munising, Manistique, and Rapid River is a low-lying area of over a hundred lakes and **numerous streams**. Most of it is part of the Hiawatha National Forest, but there are many private cottages and fishing resorts around the lakes. The **40-mile Bay de Noc-Grand Island Trail National Recreation Trail**, following the Whitefish River, is used mainly by horseback riders. (It's described at somewhat greater length in the Au Train section.) The trail follows a canoe route that was one of the Upper Peninsula's most significant.

Hunting, fishing, boating, snowmobiling, four-wheelers on some places in summer — the area appeals to all sorts of active recreation. It's a real **U.P. hub for snowmobiles**. "You can ride forever," one resort owner pointed out. **Valley Spur's outstanding cross-country ski trails** south of Munising aren't far away, either. The ungroomed **McKeever Hills Ski Trails** are in this area.

Many National Forest campgrounds and developed beaches, boat launches, and picnic areas are here beyond the ones described in this book. The Pictured Rocks/National Forest Visitor Center (906-387-3700) has maps and handouts for those facilities and for many hiking and cross-country ski trail systems. So do other Hiawatha National Forest offices, including the ones in nearby Rapid River and Munising.

Another attraction National Forest offices can provide details about is the **Big Island Lake Wilderness Canoeing Area.** There's no road access to these **23 small lakes**, from 5 to 149 acres, which are linked by waterways or by marked portage trails. Motors are banned, though motor noise from nearby lakes in this developed cottage area can sometimes be heard. At Big Island canoeists can camp in designated spaces or choose their own sites. Abundant wildlife includes eagles and many loons. **Canoe livery service** is provided by Hiawatha Resort on Forest Highway 13, phone (906) 573-2933. Canoe and kayak rentals and multi-day trips can be arranged through Northland Outfitters in Germfask. Call (906) 586-6684. Complete outfitting (tent, gear, etc.) is available.

Big Island is east of Forest Highway 13 and northwest of Steuben.

Indian River Canoe Trail

The Indian River, a designated **wild** [i.e., undammed] and **scenic river**, flows from Fish Lake, 15 miles south of Munising near the bigger, better known Pete's Lake, to Indian Lake near Manistique. These 36 miles have been marked as a canoe trail. The Indian River is the most-used recreational river in the entire Hiawatha National Forest. It's a gently flowing river, usually some 30 to 50 feet wide and one to three feet deep. The trip goes through hardwood forests, mixed conifers in the low areas, and marshlands good for seeing wildlife. Brown trout top the list of fish species. "Keep in mind that there are many windfalls," advises the Forest Service brochure, "and that the river is not cleared from bank to bank. Look for the canoe slots well in advance of reaching downed trees, and be prepared to get your feet wet."

The Forest Service has been busy reconstructing canoe access sites and rehabbing areas damaged from over-use, according to recreation planner Anne Okonek. Improvements have been made at Widewaters and Indian River campgrounds, the two streamside campgrounds. Widewaters Campground 13 miles south of Munising on Forest Highway 13 would be a good place to start a short trip. **Canoe livery service** is provided by Hiawatha Resort (906-573-2933) on Forest Highway 13.

The northern trailhead is at Fish Lake. From Forest Highway 13 look for the drive to Widewaters Campground but go a little farther. The trail ends at Palms-Book State Park, near Kitch-iti-kipi (Big Spring). Forest Service offices and info centers in Rapid River, Manistique, and Munising can provide the helpful brochure. Or call (906) 341-5666 (TDD 341-3514) or (906) 387-3700 and it can be faxed or mailed. No fee. &: call.

Pine Marten Run Hiking and Horseback Riding Trail

Five loop trails with interconnecting spurs go around 11 small lakes and alongside the Indian River for a short way. The entire trail system, part of the **Hiawatha National Forest**, is **26 miles**. Loops vary from 3.8 miles to 7.2 miles, which makes for many possibilities for short or long excursions. Trailheads are along three different roads, so hikers and riders can easily return to their vehicles. **Glacial lakes** like this are fun to explore because they vary so much in terms of their topography and plant communities.

Three **Adirondack shelters** (available on a first-come, first-served basis) allow for easy overnights. Reservable **dispersed campsites** are on several of the lakes; some are highly sought-after, and advance reservations are a must in summer. Call (906) 341-5666 for a map-brochure and reservations.

The area is southwest of Steuben, in the west corner of Schoolcraft County, between the two major north-south roads that go into this lake-studded area of the Hiawatha National Forest. Riders are said to be pretty good about cleaning up after their horses.

The trails are just northwest of the intersection of CR 437 and 440, with a trailhead on each road. Another trailhead is off Forest Road 2258. (906) 341-5666; TDD (906) 341-3514. & : call.

LAKE COUNTRY RESTAURANTS

New owners at **The CAMEL RIDER'S RESTAURANT** are building on a long reputation for good food, in a gorgeous setting overlooking a Deep Lake, part of an all-sports chain of lakes in the Hiawatha National Forest. Open for dinner only, they offer lots of fish (whitefish, lake trout, perch, and walleye) and even some vegetarian stir-fries and kebobs in addition to specialties like one-pound pork chops, marinated and stuffed, and steak for two. Entrées mostly from $11 to $15. Dinners include soup, salad, potato, and garlic bread or a bread loaf.

On CR 440 about 3-4 miles east of Forest Hwy. 13. About 22 miles south of Munising and 24 miles north of Nahma Junction on U.S. 2. Well signed. 573-2319 From Mem. Day into fall open Tues-Thurs 5 p.m.-9 p.m., Fri-Sun 2 p.m.-9 p.m. Otherwise probably open noon-9 p.m., closed Mon. Call to confirm hours. Closed from April to Mem. Day. &

LAKE COUNTRY LODGINGS

See also Munising, Au Train.

TIMBER RIDGE LODGE
(906) 387-3790;
www.timberridgemotel.homepage.com

Snowmobilers have discovered this **wonderful, wooded getaway** 10 minutes from Munising. A motel/lodge has nine recently built two-room housekeeping suites (starting at $44/night in the off-season). Each suite has **ample individual decks** that seem to hang in the treetops looking down at **Hovey Lake**. How is such a deal possible? Mike Nolan and Terry Nolan, co-owners with their wives, are builders. Their wives, Jan and Mary Sue, are well informed about area recreational opportunities, including bird-watching. Kitchens include microwaves and coffeemakers. Each unit has a TV (2 channels), queen bed, and queen sofa sleeper in the living room. Suites sleep 4 and there are extra cots for more kids. Phone in office. No air-conditioning. Stairs — 56 of them — go down to the lake and **dock.** Guests have free use of rowboat, paddle boat. There's a sauna, **rec room** with pool table, and heated garage for snowmobile repairs. A four-bedroom **rental lodge** is on the lake. Call well ahead for winter weekends (some guests reserve a year ahead) and summer. The lodge would be beautiful in fall color season. *On Buckhorn Red. 1/4 mile north of Buckhorn Restaurant, between M-94 and FH 13. Open year-round.*
H.A.: call

CAMEL RIDER'S RESORT
(906) 573-23, look under resorts

Four **widely spaced hillside cottages** in the trees overlook Deep Lake, an all-sports lake that's part of a chain of lakes. All have TV (two channels), microwaves, fire pits. Each cottage comes with a boat. They sleep from four to eight and rent by the week in summer, by the weekend otherwise. The beach, playground, outdoor sitting area, and dock are reached by stairs. There's a fish-cleaning station. Rentals range from $400/week or $80 a day in summer to $570/week. $50 more in winter to cover heat. *On CR 440 about 3-4 miles east of Forest Hwy. 13. About 22 miles south of Munising and 24 miles north of Nahma Junction on U.S. 2. Open year-round except for April.*

H.A.: call. Beach access is nearly impossible.

HIAWATHA RESORT
and CAMPGROUND
(906) 573-2933; www.algercounty.org/chamber/lodging/

Six housekeeping cottages are on an unusual, 30-acre piece of property that scores high in outdoor amenities like **big trees**, a **quiet lake** (Blue Lake), and **paths through woods**. Two gazebos have been built on the lake to enjoy the sunsets. The nearby Indian River offers **good canoeing**. The resort offers boat and canoe rentals, a fish-cleaning station, horseshoe pits, and a heated workspace for snowmobile repairs. Nature-loving owners Sherry and Bill Hagerty are good sources of advice on the area's recreational possibilities. Cottages sleep from four to eight. They now have new carpets, beds, bedspreads, and drapes. Rates go by the person. For two people they would be $300 to $360/week and $50-$60/night, with a two-night minimum. The 14-site **roadside campground** has little privacy between sites, but it does have a shower/laundry building and complete hookups ($14/night). $12 for tent campers. *On Forest Hwy. 13, halfway (about 16 miles each way) between U.S. 2 at Nahma Junction and M-28 at Wetmore/Munising.* **H.A.**: call : first 2 under 5 are free; $6/extra person

LAKE COUNTRY CAMPING

See also Rapid River, Munising, Manistique, Thompson. The Pictured Rocks/National Forest Visitor Center (906-387-3700) has maps and handouts on the six lakeside campgrounds in this area. The two main roads to penetrate this area are the north-south roads, Forest Highway 13 from Wetmore outside Munising to U.S. 2 at Nahma Junction, and M-94 from Shingleton to Manistique. East-west roads through twist and turn around so many lakes that a detailed local map would be helpful. Campgrounds are arranged according to easy access from major north-south roads. *Hiawatha National Forest Manistique office 906) 341-5666*

COLWELL LAKE Campground
(906) 341-5666; (reserv.: 877-444-6777)

This very popular 35-site rustic campground has been reconstructed to be

Tom's Lake Rustic Cabin is a very popular rental cabin ($35/night) on a small lake in the Hiawatha National Forest between Manistique and Munising. The Manistique office (906-341-5666) handles reservations and the waiting list for it and for scattered primitive campsites on small lakes in the same area.
To make up for cutbacks and year-to-year uncertainties in federal and state recreational funding, U.S. Forest Servic and Michigan DNR recreation planners are reaching out to form partnerships with communiity groups, youth groups, and businesses. Rapid River Rustic Homes donated the cabin package for Tom's Lake Rustic Cabin.

fully accessible to wheelchairs and strollers. Some sites have electricity. A scenic 1.6 mile **hiking trail** with benches goes around 145-acre Colwell Lake. There's a swimming beach, boat ramp, and fishing for northern pike, largemouth bass, perch, and panfish. Group sites available. A **fishing pier** (&) is planned for 2001 or 2002. *About 9 miles south of Shingleton and M-28 via M-94. $6 and $9/night. Open from May 15 thru Oct. 7.* **H.A.:** fully ADA accessible.

INDIAN RIVER Campground
(906) 341-5666; not reservable

Proximity to M-94 makes for some road noise at this 5-site rustic campground, but the **fishing is good**, and so is canoe access to the Wild and Scenic Indian River and canoe trail. There's also a picnic area here. (See above.) *About 13 miles south of Shingleton on M-94. $7/night. Open from May 15 thru Oct. 7.* **H.A.**: call.

LITTLE BASS LAKE Campground
(906) 341-5666; not reservable

On 84-acre Little Bass Lake, this 12-site rustic campground has no swimming area, and as a result, few children and less noise. Lightly used, the campground is enjoyed by people who want to be **away from noise**, boating activity, and development. There's carry-in boat access only. Fishing is for largemouth bass, pike, perch, crappie, and bluegill. *Take M-94 11 miles south of Shingleton. Turn west on CR 437, then south about 2 1/2 miles on Bass Lake Road to campground. $7/night. Open from May 15 thru*

Oct. 7. **H.A.**: call

DISPERSED CAMPSITES
Permits required. Call the Manistique office for maps, info, and reservations: (906) 341-5666. Lottery is in February; sites are reservable after that.

For people who'd like to feel they're pretty much all alone on a **peaceful northwoods lake**, with no amenities (that means no toilets or drinking water), the primitive, dispersed campsites on 17 small lakes in the vicinity of Steuben, between Munising and Manistique, are considered choice. Six lakes have only one campsite on them; five have two campsites. Large campers are not suitable because of narrow entrance roads. The Forest Service's info sheet indicates which campgrounds have back-in boat access and which are only carry-in. Though certain lakes get reserved early, there are quite a few sites left by early June, and some will be available on short notice. **H.A.**: call.

CAMP 7 LAKE Campground

See "Thompson/Indian Lake Camping" in Manistique chapter.

Accessed from Forest Highway 13 between M-28 at Munising/Wetmore and U.S. 2 at Nahma Junction

Keep in mind that all prices and hours of operation are subject to change. Lodging rates vary with supply and demand and are usually higher for special events.

Tahquamenon & Seney, Grand Marais & Whitefish Point

FOUR MAGNETS of Upper Peninsula tourism are located in this area: the spectacular **Tahquamenon Falls**, the dramatic **Great Lakes Shipwreck Museum**, the eastern part of the **Pictured Rocks National Lakeshore** west of Grand Marais, and the **Seney National Wildlife Refuge**. Legendary trout and canoeing streams rise from the spring-fed wetlands around Seney, most notably the **Two Hearted** and the **Fox**. And there are the three **Manistique lakes**, including the 10,000-acre Big Manistique Lake. These lakes, although largely developed with cottages, are excellent fishing spots. In the middle of it all is **Newberry,** a sleepy old lumber town.

The northern part of the Eastern U.P. between Grand Marais and Paradise contains some of the most **remote and inaccessible land** to be found in the eastern United States. In this age of exotic ecotourism, its relative proximity to downstate population centers and its flat to rolling character detract from its wilderness allure. But there it is — a place to be alone, and a challenge to hikers who can't count on coming to a highway or bridge to find their way if lost. The skeleton of a hunter wasn't found until two *years* after he was reported missing. A DNR field forester recalls the time it took his crew *two hours* to drive seven miles *on a road* to fight a forest fire along the Two Hearted River south of Pretty Lake.

The wilderness portion of the Eastern U. P. doesn't have mountains, but it does have Lake Superior. Its most remote areas are good places for people who really want to get away from civilization — within two hours of the Mackinac Bridge. Better-known visitor destinations have seen tremendous real estate activity, however. In places the road from Paradise to Whitefish Point seems to bristle with "for sale" signs and even a few showy gated entrances, the greatest affront to indigenous U.P. culture among people who grew up freely roaming the woods and streams from their back doors. The breathless ads of North Coast Realty (http://north-coast-realty.com/) allude to "prestigious Whitefish Bay" and "exclusive living on the Lake Superior shoreline, . . . high in desirability as well as providing remoteness and sophistication." The latter refers to a widely despised subdivision of trophy homes east of Grand Marais. For 80 hard-to-reach acres 15 miles from Paradise as the crow flies, $75,000 was the asking price in fall, 2000: "plenty of high ground, yet patches of standing water swamp adds to the charm. Old trails access the property."

This wild, lonely area is home to a famous waterfall, legendary fishing rivers, agate beaches, superb birding, and many shipwrecks.

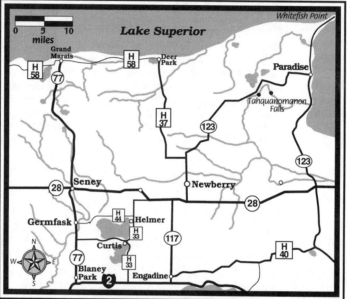

The entire Lake Superior shore from the Au Sable Point lighthouse to Whitefish Point is good territory for **agates**, though some places are better than others and the shore is constantly changing. There are probably fewer agates to be found than decades ago, when fewer rockhounds were combing the beaches. New agates are continually being moved onto shore from the lake bottom. (Scuba divers able to comb the bottom enjoy better pickings!)

Most of the interior terrain in these parts is low-lying and marshy. An exception is some clusters of glacial hills south of Grand Marais at the headwaters of the Sucker and Two Hearted rivers. There a hilltop reaches almost 600 feet above Lake Superior.

This is one of the least productive agricultural areas in the U.P. Much of the area was pine forests before the lumbering era, and much of the soil is sandy or wet. Aside from logging and the new prison in Newberry, tourism is the major economic activity these days, from fishing and sightseeing in summer to snowmobiling in winter.

TO FIND OUT MORE: For **SENEY, BLANEY PARK**, and **GERMFASK**, contact the helpful **Schoolcraft County Chamber of Commerce** in **Manistique** at 1000 W. Lakeshore/U.S. 2 just west of the harbor next to the Big Boy. (906) 341-5010; **www.manistique.com**. Open year-round, Mon-Sat 9-5 and also on Sunday 10-2 from June thru Sept. The **Manistique Area Tourist Council** mails visitor packets. (800) 342-4282; **www.onlynorth.com**. . . . For **CURTIS** and the **MANISTIQUE LAKES**, contact the Curtis Area Chamber of Commerce, (800) 652-8784 or (906) 586-3700; www.exploringthenorth.com/-curtis/home.html. The handy, free 88-page area directory, *Lakes of the Northwoods*, is a most useful info source. . . . **GRAND MARAIS** has two local websites, www.grandmarais-michigan.com and www.natureinabundance.com, established by artists and small businesses. Call (906) 494-2447. . . .For **NEWBERRY** and **Luce County** the **Newberry Area Chamber & Tourism Association** has an office in a little log house on M-28 at M-123 south of town. It's open weekdays. Call (906) 387-2138 or visit www.exploringthenorth.com/newberry. . . . For **PARADISE** call (906) 492-3219 or (906) 492-3927.

PUBLIC LAND: Much of the area between Lake Superior and the Tahquamenon River is part of **Lake Superior State Forest** or **Tahquamenon Falls State Park** (see point of interest). The State Forest area office in Newberry has lots of visitor informa-

tion — also about the extensive state forest land between Pictured Rocks National Lakeshore and Seney. The Newberry office is on the east side of M-123 north of M-28 before you enter town. Open weekdays 8 a.m. to 5 p.m. (906) 293-3293. www.dnr.state.mi.us/. . . . There's also a good deal of land from Seney to Blaney Park that's part of the **Hiawatha National Forest**. Call or stop by the **Manistique office** at 449 East Lakeshore/U.S. 2 just east of downtown. Open weekdays from 7:30 a.m. to 4. (906) 341-5010; www.fs.us.fed.us/r9/hiawatha. . . More **Hiawatha National Forest** land is around Hulbert, administered by the **Sault Ste. Marie office** on I-75 Business Spur, not far from the I-75 exit. (906) 635-5398. Each office and the **Michigan Welcome Centers** at St. Ignace and Sault Ste. Marie carry the **complete range of Hiawatha handouts** and advice on camping, canoeing, hiking, and other recreational opportunities.

GUIDES: Mark's Rod & Reel on M-123 north of Newberry is the best source of info on new **fishing guides** in the Tahquamenon area. (906) 293-5608. . . . For fishing the Seney area you might try **Big Cedar Campground and Canoe Livery** on the Manistique River. (906) 586-6684. . . The **Fish and Hunt Shop** (906-586-9531) in Curtis is another good info source. . . . The **Whitefish Point Bird Observatory** offers guided **birding tours** from mid-April through June (see www.wpbo.org or call 906-492-3596) and **winter owl tours** in the Eastern U.P., booked through the Sault chamber, (800) 647-2858.

EVENTS: The village of **CURTIS** goes all out for **Independence Day** on Sunday of the weekend. **Arts on the Lake** is on Labor Day weekend. **Winter Carnival** is sometime in February. . . . In **GRAND MARAIS** Independence Day is celebrated with a parade, games, fireworks, and a street dance on July 4. The eclectic **Grand Marais Music & Arts Festival** (blues, rock, bluegrass and more) is at Woodland Park is the second full weekend of August. . . . **PARADISE** has its Blueberry Festival in early August. . . . **NEWBERRY** holds lively **old-time festivals** at the Logging Museum on the fourth weekends of June (**Polka Festival**), July (**Old Time Music Jamboree**) and August (**Lumberjack Days**). **Dog sled races** are in February, and the **Tahquamenon Nordic Invitational** is in March.

HARBORS with transient dockage: South of **Paradise** at the Tahquamenon River mouth and the Tahquamenon Falls State Park (906-492-3415; lat. 46° 45' 31" N, long. 84° 57' 52" W.

Near **Whitefish Point** and Little Lake (906-658-3372; off-season 492-3415; lat. 46° 43' 06" N, long. 85° 21' 48" W). In Grand Marais at the Burt Twp. Marina (906-494-2381; lat. 46° 41' 05" N, long. 85° 58' 15" W) with launch ramp.

PICNIC PROVISIONS AND PLACES

◆ Supermarkets are few and far between in this sparsely populated area. The **Curtis IGA** on Main Street in **CURTIS** caters to a more affluent clientele. In **NEWBERRY Mac's Big Owl Market** is in the shopping plaza M-123/Newberry Ave.

◆ Just south of **Germfask** on M-77 is an MDOT highway **picnic area** on the Manistique River.

◆ West of **Seney** on **M-28** is a big new **highway rest area** and log-cabin style restrooms. It's not super-scenic but it's in just the right place for a break before driving the boring Seney Stretch.

◆ **Grand Marais'** most scenic in-town picnic area is next to the bungalow museum on the bay side of **Coast Guard Point.** Go through downtown, then curve east along the shore of West Bay. There's also a picnic area by the **Pictured Rocks Visitor Center** on H-58 a few miles west of town. There's a **downtown grocery** store. The **West Bay diner** has outstanding breads and deli salads, meats, and cheeses, but it's often crowded. Mid-afternoon it's less busy.

◆ At **Deer Park** on H-58 east of Grand Marais there's a picnic area by the beach at **Muskallonge Lake State Park**.

◆ Just north of **Newberry**, the **Tahquamenon River Logging Museum** has a picnic area near M-123. The interpretive path back to the river is beautiful.

◆ At **Tahquamenon Falls State Park** the picnic area is by the main parking lot at the Upper Falls. You are welcome to bring a bag lunch to the beautiful **outdoor deck** by the **Camp 33** restaurant and takeout snack bar with good burgers. Travelers are advised to stock up on terrific sourdough bread at **North Star Bakery**, on M-123 nine miles west of the Upper Falls.

◆ **Sawmill Park** in Paradise is just north of the blinker light on Whitefish Point Road. More spectacular is the picnic area overlooking Lake Superior at the **Tahquamenon River mouth**, part of the state park. There's a small grocery in town and Brown's Fish House, whose smoked fish and fish dip are excellent.

◆ **Whitefish Point** has no designated picnic area, but a brown bag lunch on the benches at **Hawk Hill overlook** would be memorable. Or bring a blanket and take a foot trail from behind the **Whitefish Point Bird Observatory** to the beach.

Blaney Park

This is the town that was sold all at once. Twelve miles south of the Seney National Wildlife Refuge on M-77, the town of Blaney Park began as the company town of the Wisconsin Land and Lumber Company. In 1909 the townsite and some 33,000 acres were acquired by the Washington Earle family, descended from the designer of the machinery that first produced tongue and groove flooring. It was sold under the IXL trademark — "I excel." (The IXL company headquarters/museum at Hermansville, west of Escanaba, is a fascinating and rather opulent Victorian time capsule. Look under Hermansville in the Menominee Range chapter.)

The Earles stopped logging in 1926 and considered other possibilities for Blaney, including cattle ranching, forestry, and agriculture. The best possibility seemed to be recreation based on hunting and fishing. The Earles remodeled existing buildings and in 1927 opened the **Blaney Park Resort** — 33,000 acres of cutover land with many small lakes and streams. Old logging roads became hiking and riding trails. Eventually Blaney Park's appeal was broadened with a restaurant, tennis, golf, and riding. Various motels and cottages were built. The mill-town-become-resort never had the lush landscaping associated with resorts today. Hunting and fishing in the back country was always its big attraction. A private air field enabled guests to fly in.

The resort thrived into the 1950s but then declined. The Earles auctioned off the land in 1984 and town buildings in 1985. Many family members remain in the area. They are regarded highly, and affectionately, by local people and by the subsequent owners of Blaney Park, a diverse crew, mostly urban refugees, who breathed new life into the town.

BLANEY PARK/U.S. 2
RESTAURANTS

The **BLANEY INN**, built in 1935 in an informal colonial style, was once the clubhouse and main dining room for the extensive Blaney Resort. Today it's a delightful restaurant and a surprising, **memorable dining experience**, with cocktails, good food (the varying soups and bread basket are outstanding), and period touches (knotty pine, original lighting, XL hardwood flooring, and vintage maple furniture). It's a peaceful place catering to a sedate older clientele. There's a beautiful **view** onto bird feeders and the lawn that once was the golf course. **Old postcards** in the entrance area show the Blaney Resort in its prime. The **vintage 1930s barroom** is a cocktail lounge northwoods-style. Backlit color photographs are of the Blaney area. There's a full menu (steaks, fish, pork chops, pasta dishes). Seafood fettucine and fettucine Alfredo are favorites. Dinner entrées ($10-$17) include soup, salad, starch, and bread basket. Sometimes private parties book the entire facility, so **call in advance on Friday and Saturday** to make sure the dining room is open to the general public. *On M-77 at the south end of Blaney, east side of road. 283-3417. Open for dinner from Father's Day through Labor Day at least, Thursday thru Sunday, and sometimes into fall. Hours: 5 p.m. to closing.*
  Full bar

A simple diner and bakery connected to a motel, **DREAMLAND** is known for **big portions of home cooking**. Ray and Bern Troxler make their own pork sausage, bread, and jam, so the $5 sausage, egg, potato, and toast breakfast isn't just average fare. The combined lunch and dinner menu features daily specials and favorites like pasty and slaw ($4.25), whitefish dinner, ham steak ($8), liver and onions ($7), and T bone steak ($12-$13), and homemade pie ($1.75), with fresh fruit in season. The soup and salad bar of homemade items comes with steaks, for $1 to $2 extra with other entrées, or for $5 separately. Friday and Saturday evenings bring buffets. *On U.S. 2 two miles west of M-77 (near Blaney) and 7 miles east of Gulliver. 283-3122. Open from May thru Nov. daily from 7 a.m. to 8 p.m. In summer open to 9 p.m.*
  Full bar

A dramatic log building makes **The POOR BOY Restaurant** a familiar landmark for U.S. 2 motorists between Gould City and Blaney Park. Hands-on owner-cooks Al Morrison and Bob Brotherton

Where to Fish
In and Around
Blaney Park

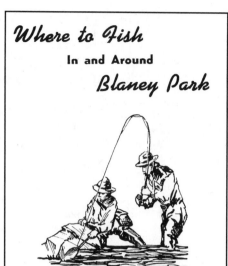

Fishing was the chief attraction of the Blaney Park Resort, established on cut-over land in 1927. This pamphlet, by guide, photographer, and philosopher Harrison Beach, demystifies trout fishing on the Fox at Seney, where the young Ernest Hemingway fished. No need for fancy flies, Beach advised. "Truthfully, 98% of the trout caught here are taken with worms and a spinner."

make the food equal to the setting. There's **no smoking** anywhere — unusual for a large place in this area. The Poor Boy is known for **omelettes and big breakfasts** (served any time except for pancakes and French toast), good soups, pasties, walleye and perch, and the big, fresh, homemade soup, **salad and dessert bar** ($7 alone), put out Thursday through Saturday from 4 p.m. to closing. (Seafood salad and desserts like chocolate mousse and cake stand out.) Dinner entrées are from $9 to $15. Sandwiches and meal-size salads are served any time. The $6 daily lunch special may be soup and a sandwich or a plated special. *On U.S. 2 outside Gould City. Open year-round except from after snowmobile season into April. In summer open Sun-Wed from 7 a.m. to 3 p.m., Thurs-Sat 7 a.m. to 8 p.m. In fall and spring closed Tues & Wed. After hunting season closes at 3 Thurs, so winter hours are Sun, Mon & Thurs 7-3, Fri & Sat 7 to 8.*

BLANEY PARK AREA LODGINGS

Arranged from south (U.S. 2) to north.

BEAVER BAY RESORT
(906) 477-6793; www.exploringthenorth. com/beaverbay/resort.html

This small resorts stands out because of

its **quiet, wooded lakeside setting** and its five charming, beautifully maintained **vintage cabins**, all with knotty pine interiors, locally made rustic furniture, and screened porches. 1,956-acre **Milakokia Lake** is known for bass, walleye, perch, and northern pike. **Trails** go through the 58-acre property. In summer the five older two-bedroom cottages rent for $300 a week for 4 people. In off seasons they're $75 a day with a two- or three-day minimum. The duplex and three-bedroom cottage are winterized, more modern, and rent for more. All cottages are on the lake. Each comes with a 14' aluminum boat, gas grill, and fire pit. Bring linens. No air-conditioning. There are **swings, volleyball, badminton,** and **horseshoes**. Most summer spots fill up with repeat guests; call by March for openings. The off season is less busy, and September is a glorious month here. *Just south of U.S. 2 near Blaney Park, 25 miles east of Manistique and 60 miles west of the bridge. Between M-77 (to Blaney Park) on the west and H33 (to Curtis). Now open year-round.*

H.A.: 4 steps to each cabin   : call

BLANEY PARK MOTEL (906) 283-3205

This clean, simple six-unit motel dates from an earlier era of the Blaney Resort. It provides good, inexpensive accommodations for a night or two with picnic tables outside but not much in the way of landscaping. TV gets 1 to 3 channels. Phone in office. *East side of M-77 at U.S. 2 . Open from sometime in May thru October*

H.A.: one step, small bathrooms.
  : $5/extra person

BLANEY LODGE (906) 283-3883
www.blaneylodge.com

Recent freshening has made the lodge, built as a hotel and boarding house for Wisconsin Land and Lumber in 1895, an attractive choice for travelers on a budget or with an interest in offbeat places. Rooms are **remarkably inexpensive**: $29 for a room with one double bed and private bath, $39 for two connecting doubles with one bath. The price includes a **continental plus breakfast** with homemade muffins, cereal, and fruit and, in the evening, **pie**. There's a front sun porch where breakfast is served, and a comfortable lobby with fireplace, once the front desk for the entire Blaney Resort. An **air strip** with paved runway is right out back. One group of pilots comes back to Blaney Lodge regularly. You can fish off the bridge at the bottom of the hill. Now for the caveats: when the lodge is close to

The Blaney Park Resort built these charming Cape Cod cottages in 1938. As today's Blaney Cottages, they're rented by the night.

full, water use can outstrip the current well's pumping capacity. And if it's hot and the room air-conditioners on the south-facing rooms are all on, the electricity may short. This can happen with large groups. Normal occupancy isn't high enough to create these problems, which will eventually be solved. Rental cabins are in back. *On the west side of M-77 in Blaney Park.*

H.A.: not lodge. Ask about cottages
👫 🐕 : in back cottages

CELIBETH HOUSE Bed & Breakfast

(906) 283-3409; www.celibethhouse.com

Built in 1895 as a residence, Celibeth (pronounced "SEAL-uh-beth') was used by Wisconsin Land and Lumber as its Blaney headquarters, then turned into a tavern and inn for the Blaney Park Resort. It's a **gracious, comfortable place**, with an living room with fireplace, library, and eight guest rooms (mostly $85), five downstairs and three up. Each is furnished with antique and vintage furniture, with a private bath. One large room ($100) accommodates four adults. There's no TV anywhere. Guests can use the business phone. Elsa Strom, who started the bed and breakfast, sold it in 2000. One of the new owners has done even more with flower gardens, hummingbirds, benches, and statuary. It now offers what's billed as a full gourmet breakfast. The **afternoon tea**, open to the public and guests by reservation for $12 a person, consists of sandwiches, berries in clotted cream, and dessert, A wonderful bonus: **trails** through the 85-acre property with its meadows, beaver ponds, plentiful wildlife, and **fishing** in Lake Anne Louise, formed by a logging dam. *On M-77 at the north end of Blaney Park. Open May thru Oct.* **H.A.**: call

BLANEY COTTAGES (906) 283-3163

Thirteen **charming cottages with fireplaces**, built in 1938, are rented by the night. They make for about the coziest motel experience possible. They've been revamped with La-Z-Boys, sofas, and oak and brass accessories. They don't have kitchens. VCR and videos. TV gets 1-3 channels, weather depending. Guests use phone in office; room phones may be installed. Breakfast (coffee, juice, muffins) may be brought to rooms when it's slow, or put out in a common area. The Blaney Park Resort, centered a mile north on M-77, built the complex to have a presence on busy U.S. 2.

Not only is the lawn and interior drive nicely landscaped with flowers, but there are 40 acres in the back where a **walking path** leads a quarter-mile to a creek and pond with beaver dam. **Bonfires** are held many evenings. There's a small **playground, volleyball, horseshoes,** and a p**icnic area** with gas grills and tables. Sample rates: $40 to $45 for a one-room cottage, $65 for a queen bedroom and living room with queen sleeper sofa. Ask about off-season discounts. *On U.S. 2 just west of M-77. Open year-round.*

H.A.: call 👫 : 12 & under free 🐕 : call

Germfask *(pop. under 100)*

This small two-street town on M-77 just east of the Seney Wildlife Refuge used to be called "The Dump" because lumbermen once dumped logs into the Manistique River here to float them down to mills in Manistique on Lake Michigan. The name has a Scandinavian ring. Actually it is made of the initials of the last names of the eight men who settled the township in 1881.

Seney National Wildlife Refuge

For people with an interest in wildlife, the enormous 95,212-acre Refuge southwest of Seney is a **magical place** where it's easy to get an intimate look at **many different northwoods wildlife habitats**. Motorists driving along a special road built on dikes may see bald eagles, trumpeter swans, and loons in their natural habitats. Bicyclists use the nearly sixty miles of mostly flat backcountry roads. Signs of elusive wolves and moose who use the Refuge may be seen in the back country. Birders intent on expanding their lists of rare or uncommon birds sometimes drive thousands of miles to spot the yellow rail or black-backed woodpecker found here. Seney may be the very best place to see woodcock in the entire United States.

Hints for finding wildlife to watch are conveyed through excellent **interpretive displays** in the Visitor Center and through signs along the trails and wildlife drive. Knowledgeable staff and volunteers can direct visitors to unusual habitats such as bogs and recently burned areas. Common birds include mergansers, ring-necked ducks, trumpeter swans, goldfinches, and pine warblers, which can often be heard along the tour route.

THE REFUGE STORY

The story of the Seney National Wildlife Refuge is told in a well-written display at the Refuge's Visitor Center. The Refuge is a vast (150 square miles) and peaceful wetland between Munising and Seney that drains into the Manistique River. From 1881 to 1900 the area was logged off. Fires swept many cutover lands, including the Great Manistique Swamp, part of which is in the Refuge. A decade later, land speculators started to drain the land to develop it for farming. They failed and left. Most of the land reverted to the government for nonpayment of taxes during the Depression.

In 1935, an intricate system of **dikes** and **spillways** created thousands of acres of **open pools** for waterfowl at the Refuge. The project was accomplished with funds from duck stamp purchases and labor from the Civilian Conservation Corps (CCC) and Works Projects Administration (WPA), two make-work projects of Franklin Roosevelt's administration. CCC crews planted aquatic plants favored by ducks and geese: pondweed, bulrushes, duck weed, wild rice, wild celery, and more.

Today the Refuge is managed by the U.S. Fish and Wildlife Service to encourage waterfowl production. Controlling water levels creates wet and dry cycles that mimic nature. (Because the pools are manmade, wet-dry cycles can't occur naturally.) Controlled fires imitate the beneficial effects of lightning-caused fires. For instance, fire is used to prune back and maintain sedge meadow habitat for the secretive yellow rail. The heat of fires causes jack pine cones to open and release seeds, thereby allowing new growth.

Though wildlife management is the Refuge's main purpose, much has been done for visitors. The **Visitor Center** and seven-mile **Marshland Wildlife Drive** have become popular Upper Peninsula attractions. The Refuge's back roads and dikes have been opened to hikers and bicyclists. Fat-tire bikes work best. Nearly 60 miles of biking and hiking trails are ideally suited for viewing wildlife. Canoeing is encouraged along the Manistique River.

PLANNING YOUR VISIT

Plan your visit to the Refuge so you'll be able to view wildlife in the *early morning or evening*, when birds and mammals are most active. The wildlife drive and trails are open from sunup to sundown. Over 200 species of birds and 50 species of mammals, including the eastern timber wolf, have been recorded here. The outstanding Visitor Center is open from 9 a.m. to 5 p.m. seven days a week from May 15 to October 15. A **bird list** is available at the Visitor Center, along with a **map** and **guide** to the Refuge. **Brochures** are available after hours at the display in the Visitor Center parking lot. *In the off-season,* information is available at the main office next door.

MAIN VISITOR ATTRACTIONS

◆ **VISITOR CENTER.** Excellent displays, a knowledgeable staff, and the Seney Natural History Association's small **bookstore** make this a good first stop for orientation. New **exhibits** include an interactive mural where viewers look for hidden wildlife (kids love this challenge), a display on refuge management techniques, tips for wildlife observation, and **"The Sounds of Seney"** with 32 wildlife sounds. A multi-projector **slide/tape introduction** to the Refuge, 14 minutes long, tells visitors what they can expect to do and see at Seney. The **loon exhibit** invites visitors to hear the loon's four main calls while seeing a beautiful diora-

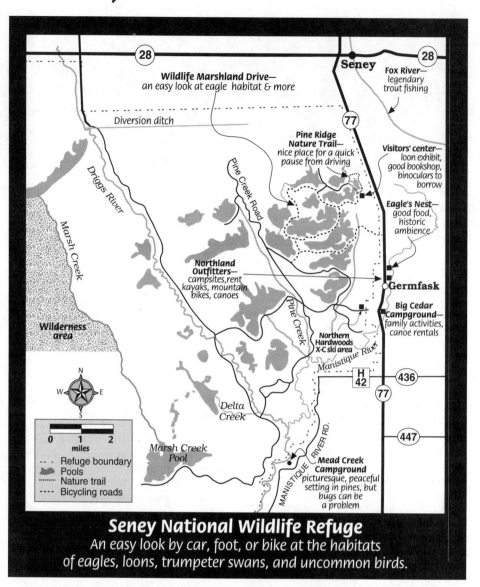

Seney National Wildlife Refuge
An easy look by car, foot, or bike at the habitats of eagles, loons, trumpeter swans, and uncommon birds.

ma of a loon with a chick on its back. A short **video** shows loons in action. Loons are plentiful in the Refuge because it meets their three main requirements: 1) clean water; 2) quiet, undisturbed nesting islands; and 3) a good supply of fish to eat.

Free **brochures** describe the Refuge's policy and **opportunities for hunting and fishing**. Northern pike, bullheads, and perch offer anglers a challenge. Get information on the nature trail, wildlife drive, and back roads (closed to vehicles). Visitors can **borrow binoculars,** a **bird guide**, and a **flower guide at** no cost. *Open May 15-October 15, 9 a.m. to 5 p.m. (906) 586-9851. Free admission.* &: marginally.

◆ **PINE RIDGE NATURE TRAIL.** A 1.4 mile loop with interpretive signs takes visitors along high, dry pine ridges that weave through the pool system. It's an easy walk, but there are some low hills and uneven ground. A **boardwalk** tra-

verses a marshy area that's excellent for viewing songbirds. Spring and summer **wildflowers** are abundant. It's a peaceful experience except for nearby road noise. New panels show how wildlife uses plants along the trail. *Begins at Visitor Center. Parking at the Visitor Center and nature trail is plowed through late March.* &: no

◆ **MARSHLAND WILDLIFE DRIVE.** This seven-mile **self-guided auto tour** on a one-way gravel road connects three **observation decks** in favorite habitats where trumpeter swans, loons, osprey, and bald eagles can sometimes be seen. Deer, beaver, turtles, waterfowl, and wading birds are also plentiful. **Spotting scopes** are provided at each observation deck free of charge. **Binoculars** can be borrowed at the visitor center. Interpretive signs are quite informative. The **fishing loop** adds 1 1/2 more miles and one **fishing platform** to the drive. The speed limit is 15 mph. Narrow clearances and car traffic on the drive make it more enjoyable for **bicyclists** to use back roads instead. They'll see more wildlife on back roads, too. *The Wildlife Drive starts near the visitor center and ends on M-77, just south of the main Refuge entrance. It's open from May 15 through October 15, daylight hours only.) During nesting season the drive is closed to motorized vehicles to leave birds undisturbed, but not to walkers or bicyclists. During peak migration season some areas may be closed to all visitors. Check for info at the Refuge office.* &: decks and scopes are barrier-free.

◆ **BACKCOUNTRY PATHS** along dikes and service roads offer hikers and bicyclists nearly 60 miles of prime wildlife viewing. Intersections are clearly marked so users can easily plot their routes and see where they are on the Refuge map. Surfaces are varied. Hard-packed gravel and sand work fine for bikes with narrow tires in most conditions, but mountain bikes would be better, especially after rain.

◆ **NORTHERN HARDWOODS CROSS-COUNTRY SKI AREA.** Ten miles of **groomed trails** are usually skiable from mid or late December through March. Trails are normally groomed just before and after the weekend. *Trails start at the parking lot 1/2 mile west of M-77, 1/3 mile south of the blinking light in Germfask. For snow conditions, call (906) 586-9851.*

◆ **SNOWSHOEING** is permitted anywhere except on the ski trails. It's not a good idea to snowshoe across pools.

◆ **CANOEING** can be done on the Refuge's rivers. The Manistique River is the only conveniently reachable stream section that can be canoed during the allotted daylight hours. Canoeing is not allowed on the Refuge pools or marshes.

Canoe rentals are available at Big Cedar Campground (586-6689) on M-77 just south of Germfask, and at Northland Outfitters (586-9801) on the north edge of Germfask off M-77. (It also rents kayaks and **mountain bikes**.)

There are three popular **places to put in**: Northland Outfitters (see above; it also rents canoes and kayaks); Big Cedar Campground (see above), and the pretty **picnic area** on M-77 about a mile south of Germfask. (The latter site is very steep.) People with their own canoes are welcome to put in at the canoe liveries, for a $5 fee if they leave their cars there.

Canoeists end up at the 10-campsite **Mead Creek Campground** of Lake Superior State Forest on County Road 436 south of the Wildlife Refuge (see

The Seney National Wildlife Refuge's wetlands are managed to provide plenty of fish for bald eagles and other fish-eating birds and mammals. Visitors have a very good chance of seeing bald eagles.

below). NOTE: in summer, the numbers of canoeists keep wildlife away, notes one frequent user. *For best wildlife viewing in summer, get out early in the morning.*

Although there are no picnic tables, grills, or trash cans on the Refuge, **picnicking** is allowed. Bring a blanket, take your trash home with you, and don't light any kind of fire.

The main entrance to the Refuge is on M-77, 2 miles north of Germfask and 5 miles south of Seney. (906) 586-9851. The website is part of the U.S. Fish and Wildlife Service website: www.midwest .fws.gov/seney/index.html Between May 15 and October 15: Marshland Wildlife Drive open between sunrise and sunset. Visitor Center open 9- 5. <u>*Visitor use of the Refuge is limited to daylight hours.*</u> *In* **winter,** *the visitor center parking lot is plowed through late March. The entrance to ski trails is off the parking lot west of M-77, half a mile south of Germfask. Free admission.* &: *visitor center, viewing platforms along wildlife drive, indoor & outdoor toilets.*

Canoeing the Manistique River

The Manistique River near Germfask is well serviced by canoe liveries — perhaps too well serviced if seeing wildlife is your objective and you're out at a popular, busy time in summer. Get on the river early in summer to improve your chances of seeing wildlife in the popular stretch through the Seney National Wildlife Refuge. In *Canoeing Michigan Rivers*, Jerry Dennis notes that downstream from the confluence with the Fox,

just east of Germfask, the Manistique is "wide, with slow current and sand bottom, and is well-suited to combined camping and fishing trips by paddlers of all abilities. . . . Fishing is primarily for pike, bass, and walleye, with some trout in the upper reaches."

Canoeing Michigan Rivers maps the Manistique and 44 other rivers, 17 in the U.P., with extensive notes and tips. It divides the 67-mile river into 3 segments. Putting in at Seney and paddling to Germfask is a two-day trip covering a prime fishing part of the legendary Fox and the Manistique. (Both area canoe liveries offer this trip.)

The most extensive outfitters in the central U.P., **NORTHLAND OUTFITTERS** rents perhaps 50 canoes, plus kayaks and mountain bikes. New owners Tom and Sally Kenney offer short two- and four-hour trips on the Manistique River ($27 and $35). They can arrange and outfit canoeists for long, multi-day canoe trips on the **Manistique and Fox rivers** and at the **Big Island Lake Wilderness Complex** south of Munising. New in 2001: sales of Old Town canoes and kayaks. *On the north edge of Germfask just east off M-77, 1 1/2 miles south of the Refuge entrance. 586-9801.* &: *call*

BIG CEDAR CAMPGROUND on the Manistique River offers various trips. It rents 12 canoes and 8 kayaks. The owner fishes frequently. The popular four-hour trip through the Seney Wildlife Refuge is $20. A shorter trip is also available. *On M-77 just south of Germfask, opposite entrance to Northern Hardwoods Ski Area. 586-6684. Open May through November.*

GERMFASK RESTAURANTS

A vintage colonial-style building, once the headquarters building of the wildlife refuge, houses the **EAGLE'S NEST**. This family-oriented restaurant, popular with locals and tourists alike, overlooks a pond. The menu, a shortened version of that at the owners' Zellar's Village Inn in Newberry, tends to hearty homestyle cooking, but is varied enough to offer veggie burgers and stir-fries for vegetarians and fare for other special diets. Favorite meals include cinnamon rolls at breakfast; whitefish, broiled or deep fried (about $10 with potato, soup, salad bar), and the Zellarburger at lunch, half a pound of beef with bacon and cheese. There's fresh fish when available. Soup and salad bar only: about $5. Check out the Fireside Room for interesting **historic photos** of the wildlife refuge under construction. *It's on M-77 at the north*

end of town. 586-6444. Open daily, May through November, 8 a.m. -9 p.m.
& ♿♟♟

The **JOLLY INN** is a **lively bar** going back to 1937. The look is rustic, with a pine-sawn interior. The back room, converted into a dining room, has become a **popular gathering place for locals and resorters**. It's known for its good and substantial food and low prices. A smoke-eater is a recent and welcome addition; so is breakfast, starting at 8. Specialties include a half-pound burger ($3.50), pasties ($4.75), and dinner specials like the $8 all-you-can-eat Friday fish fry and Saturday's prime rib ($9.50 and $14.50) and BBQ pork ribs ($9 and $14). Dinners come with salad bar and potatoes; the soup and salad bar alone is $4. The sandwich menu is served any time. Despite all the meat, vegetarians won't starve; there's always a meatless soup, veggie sandwiches to order, and the salad bar. The first Saturday of every month there's a live country band and plenty of room for dancing. *On M-77 in the heart of Germfask. 586-3334. The kitchen's open 365 days a year from 8 a.m. to midnight, on Sunday from noon.*
&: new this year ♟♟   Full bar

GERMFASK LODGINGS

JOLLY MOTEL   (906) 586-6385

This newish 10-room motel, next door to the Jolly Inn, is geared to snowmobilers in winter. Rooms, all on one floor, have knotty pine or log interiors, cable TV, and 2 double beds made of logs. Rates are by the person: in 2001, $27 for one, $48 for two, $5/extra person. Reservations are recommended a month ahead in winter, more in hunting season, 1-2 weeks ahead in summer. Pay phones are outside and in the Jolly Inn. *On M-77 in "downtown" Germfask.*
& ♟♟:10 & under free =: $5/night

GERMFASK CAMPING

NORTHLAND OUTFITTERS 586-9801
www.northlandoutfitters.com

Fifteen large, shady modern campsites (showers, flush toilets) for RVs and tents are near or on the **Manistique River** in a **pretty, grassy spot**. Rates: $16 (rustic with showers), $18 (riverfront rustic), $20 (electricity, water, and cable). Even more popular are four rustic **overnight cabins** (no plumbing or indoor cooking, but bedding, electricity, heat, and in three cable TV). They rent for $45 to $60/night and sleep four. Reserve these well in advance. New owners Tom and Sally Kenney **rent canoes, kayaks,** and

mountain bikes and have an extensive **camp store** and **gift shop**. Next door to the Eagle's Nest restaurant. *On the north edge of Germfask just east off M-77, 1 1/2 miles south of the Refuge entrance. Open May thru Oct.* **H.A.**: bathhouse is accessible. Sites are grassy but not hardened.

BIG CEDAR CAMPGROUND
(906) 586-6684

On the site of CCC Camp 3626, this 20-acre private campground on the Manistique River has 53 mostly wooded sites with water, electricity, and a modern bathhouse. Each campsite's neighbors are clearly visible. **Canoes** and **kayaks** can be rented here. Laundry, small store on premises. There are horseshoes, a **playground**, volleyball, **badminton**, and short **trails** along the river. The owners are fishing enthusiasts. *On M-77 just south of Germfask, opposite entrance to Northern Hardwoods Ski Area. Open from May 1 thru March 1. $16/night, $13 for tents. $2/extra person.* **H.A.**: call.

MEAD CREEK Campground/ Lake Superior State Forest
(906) 452-6227; www.dnr.state.mi.us/

10 rustic campsites (no showers or flush toilets, water pump) are on a creek next to a fork of the Manistique River at the south end of the Seney National Wildlife Refuge. Expect large, shady sites with good privacy from neighbors. Not heavily used. *From M-77 2 miles south of Germfask and 7 miles north of Blaney Park, turn west onto H42/CR 436/ Manistique River Rd. Campground is in 5 miles. $6/$10 night.* **H.A.**: call.

Seney (pop. 275)

Once the Upper Peninsula's **most raucous lumber town**, Seney today is the quiet crossroads of M-28 and M-77 next to the Fox River. Now it's best known to most vacationers as the starting point of the **Seney Stretch**, that mind-numbingly monotonous 30 miles of M-28 between Seney and Shingleton that's the most direct route from the Mackinac Bridge to Pictured Rocks and Marquette. Here the highway is straight as an arrow and flat as a pancake because it's crossing a swamp. The **scraggly, flat, boring landscape** can get burned into a motorist's brain and mistakenly become representative of the entire U.P. interior.

Unprepossessing today, Seney is **legendary for its fishing** and for its repu-

tation as one of the roughest lumbertowns in the north woods. The "**Big Two Hearted River**" in Hemingway's famous story was actually the Fox, not the Two Hearted, and he fished it near Seney. The Fox's fishing fame was revisited in an August, 1997 *National Geographic* article.

Forest fires destroyed Seney. Today's little array of gas stations, restaurants, and motels spread out along M-28 doesn't reflect its previous configuration. **Andy's Seney Bar** is the town's remaining tavern. But once Seney was a teeming collection of drinking, gambling, and whoring establishments. (A downstater who loves visiting U.P. bars calls Andy's one of the best.) Andy himself came up in 1978 from Traverse City to buy the old bar. The combined IGA grocery market and Golden Grill restaurant is now the town's biggest employer. Its owners and some employees are members of the Seney Mennonite Church. A company that makes wood trusses for homes is the last remaining major lumber-related company.

Seney's colorful past, and the exaggerations which embellished it, were recounted in the 1940 W.P.A. guide to Michigan: "Tales of license and corruption brought to Seney an investigating committee of newspaper reporters, among them one of the few women reporters of the day. Unimpressed by the gambling, fighting, drinking, and prostitution, she began her reports with a story of the 'Ram's Pasture.' Yes, she wrote, the rumors from wild Seney were true—and more, the place was a hell camp of slavery! Strangers were being 'shanghaied' on the frontier, shunted into camp, held in chained peonage, and tracked by fierce dogs when they attempted escape. Forced to work in the forest by day, they were marched into camp at nightfall and held in the 'Ram's Pasture,' a stockade unfit even for dumb animals. The place was so overcrowded that the chained men were forced to sleep in shifts.

"This story made headlines in metropolitan dailies throughout the country. A congressional committee was kept out of the district only through efforts of Wall Street lumbermen and Michigan politicians, who denied the story indignantly, stating that a hoax had been played upon the newspaperwoman by obliging practical jokers who wanted her to find what she was looking for. They declared that the 'fierce dogs' were mastiffs raised by a local saloonkeeper for the general market; that the 'Ram's Pasture' was the main floor of a crowded hotel, where the manager permitted men to sleep in 8-

hour shifts on payment of regular rates in advance, and that the 'armed guards' merely insured the prompt removal of sleeping men. There was no slavery, no shanghaiing, no stockade.

" . . . [But] the lawless reputation of Seney was not unearned. Few places of its size ever had quite so many picturesque characters as this mad community. The most notorious figure of the group was the section-hand Leon Czolgosz, who later assassinated President William McKinley. Another was P. J. Small, better known as 'Snap Jaw,' who regularly earned drinks and food by biting off the heads of live snakes and frogs. Extending his talents one day, he snapped off the head of a lumberjack's pet owl, and the woodsman laid him low with a peavey handle. 'Stuttering' Jim Gallagher left his mark—mostly with rough hobnail shoes—on the faces of those who found his speech amusing. 'Protestant Bob' McGuire was a peaceful man with thumbnails like miniature bowie knives; he seldom fought, but, when he did, his opponent was left from the combat with gaping wounds across his face.

"'Stub Foot' O'Donnell and 'Pump Handle Joe' met incoming trains, stood strangers on their heads and shook out their loose change. 'Old Light Heart,' who liked raw liver and slept in two sugar barrels turned end to end, eventually lost his toes by frostbite."

Trout fishing on the Fox River

Both the East Branch of the Fox River above M-28 and the entire Main Stream pass through undeveloped state land and offer good fishing, says Tom Huggler. He maps and describes the Fox from a fisherman's perspective in *Fish Michigan: 50 More Rivers*. Fishing is better in some years than others. What makes Fox fishing so good? There are no steelhead and chinook salmon to compete with trout, he says. "The system is constantly charged with an ample supply of groundwater, which provides for stable, year-round flows that rarely warm above 68°. The overall difficulty of access helps curb fishing pressure. The DNR releases yearling brook trout to the Main Stream to augment native reproduction." State forest campgrounds on the East Branch and Main Stream provide good river access.

Huggler writes that the East Branch "has larger and bigger trout than the Main Stream" — largely because more of it is unreachable. Watch for probable DNR regulations to keep fishing quality up.

After describing the river's various sections and passing along numerous tips, Huggler summarizes, "The Fox River is a beautiful, pristine trout stream largely unchanged from the days of Hemingway's visit. But it is not an easy stream to either fly fish or canoe. Those with some skills at both pursuits, however, will be amply rewarded."

Fox River Pathway

A 27-mile trail along a famous trout river through a remote area not two hours from the Mackinac Bridge — the Fox River Pathway (part of the **Lake Superior State Forest**) sounds more exciting than it is. After awhile the open country is boring to hike through. There's no potable water except at the campgrounds on either end. Even the weird and poetic **stump fields** — acres of big charred stumps remaining from long-ago forest fires — aren't fascinating after an hour or so of hiking through them. For the story behind stump fields, look for the Kingston Plains Burns in the Grand Marais section of this book. They extend northeast from the junction of Kingston Lake Road and the Adams Truck Trail.

Still, this is a place to get away from civilization, and the DNR was able to brush and remark the trail in 2000. There's good **fishing**, and **blueberry crops** can be heavy, depending on the year. Hiking is rated moderate to difficult because of the up-and-down terrain. The **Fox River Campground** is five miles northwest of Seney off County Road 450. Here six rustic sites are along the river and accessible by canoe. Two miles northwest of the campground the eerie **stump fields** begin. At Stanley Lake there's a striking **overlook** but no longer a campground. Regular confidence markers let hikers know they're on the trail. Farther on, stump fields are also found on the **Kingston Plains**,

The trail starts at the Seney Township Campground and follows the Fox River to the Kingston Lake state forest campground off H58 on the southern edge of Pictured Rocks National Lakeshore, about 4 miles south of Twelvemile Beach. (906) 239-5131. &: no.

SENEY RESTAURANTS

The **GOLDEN GRILL** is a big, bustling, unpretentious place, long known for ample portions of home cooking at breakfast, lunch, and dinner and a big salad and dessert bar. It's a place where tourists and locals come together. The lunch special (about $5.75 including

soup) always has one meat (maybe a chicken dish, roast beef, or meat loaf) with the extensive salad and dessert bar. There's a big smorgasbord put out every day at 4 p.m., always with fried chicken, on Friday with fish and shrimp also, and Saturday chicken, BBQ ribs, and swiss steak. In summer, hunting season, and snowmobile weekends there's a big breakfast bar ($5 with meats, pancakes, and much more) from 6:30 to 10 a.m. *In Seney, south side of M-28 adjoining the IGA. 499-3323 Open Mon-Sat 6 a.m.-8 p.m., to 8:30 in summer.* &

SENEY CAMPGROUNDS

EAST BRANCH OF FOX RIVER CAMPGROUND/Lake Superior State Forest
See Grand Marais section on camping

Curtis/Helmer/McMillan

Two of the largest U.P. lakes are **Big Manistique Lake** and **South Manistique Lake,** separated by a narrow isthmus where the village of Curtis is located. **Big Manistique Lake**, over 10,000 acres in size, is the shallower of the two, in many places just five or ten feet deep. It's known for **yellow perch fishing**. During the 1920s and 1930s, tons of fish caught here were iced and shipped south to Chicago. **South Manistique Lake**, 4,000 acres, never gets deeper than 30 feet. It

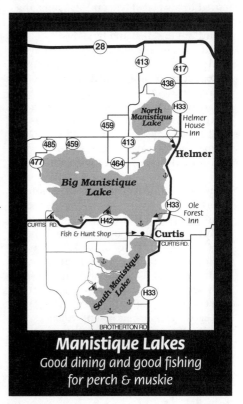

Manistique Lakes
Good dining and good fishing for perch & muskie

Fishing a legend in Hemingway country

Trout fishermen who have read Hemingway often feel drawn to follow in the footsteps of Nick Adams in "Big Two-Hearted River," best known of all Hemingway's Nick Adams stories. Here's lifelong trout fisherman Jerry Dennis describing his own pilgrimage to the river Hemingway made famous writing from his book of delightful fishing essays, *A Place on the Water: An Angler's Reflections on Home*. The river is actually the Fox; the name of the nearby Two-Heart was appropriated for its sublime name.

"'**Big Two-Hearted River**' brought to life a cherished fantasy of discovering lovely rivers filled with large, surface-feeding trout. . . . The Fox even today has a reputation for brook trout of a size rarely encountered elsewhere in the United States. Fish fifteen to twenty inches long are taken with fair regularity, primarily by locals with a knack for drifting night-crawlers through the deep pools downstream from Highway M-28. Some of those blunt-bodied trout, their spots highlighted with hobby paint, have been mounted and hung on the walls of area service stations and tackle shops. . . . Such trout can still be found in the Fox, though not in the numbers of even a few years ago. The predations of those local trophy hunters have had an impact."

"I had expected the river [the Fox at the M-28 bridge a quarter mile west of town] to be clear and lively, bubbling over bright cobblestone. Upstream would be a stretch of meadow water where large trout rose to grasshoppers and, beyond it, the river, would disappear into a dark swamp that promised even larger trout."

Instead the Fox was small, choked with fallen trees, and flowed sluggishly through dense growths of tag alders. The water was discolored, a blend of silt and swamp drainings, and passed with little vitality over a bottom of soft sand.

The Fox's dark color comes from tannic acid from the roots of trees in the waters it drains. The dark water is clear, not muddy, and clean. There's a clear line where brown water joins blue at the Fox's confluence with the Manistique just west of the north end of Big Manistique Lake. Not only Hemingway but Henry Ford fished this spot, where anglers can catch the cold-water trout and warm-water fish from Big Manistique Lake.

On Dennis's pilgrimage to the Fox, on a humid June day, he was routed by insects — and ended up camping on Lake Superior, where the wind usually blows away the bugs. It was a good thing he brought Hemingway's *In Our Time* along.

---

is has a large, underfished population of large **muskie**, some of them 40 to 45 pounds. South Manistique also has a lot of smallmouth bass. Walleye have traditionally been plentiful, but heavy fishing has depleted their numbers. In 1997 walleye numbers have begun to increase again.

Resorts and lodges took hold here in the 1880s as the loggers moved on and the railroad sold lots to replace the lost lumber business with vacationers. Curtis's railroad hotel lives on after being moved to a wooded site on Big Manistique Lake. It's now the popular **Ole Forest Inn** restaurant and bed and breakfast.

Helmer is a wayside hamlet on H-33 at the northeast bay of Big Manistique Lake, six miles from McMillan and M-28. There the **Helmer House Inn** (see below) hearkens back to Helmer's earliest days around 1880. A Presbyterian minister built it as a mission, then sold it to Gale Helmer, who turned it into a resort hotel and added a post office/general store, now a gift shop. Today both lakes are lined with many cottages and small resorts. There's enough marshy shoreline to provide good cover and food for fish. Ice cream shops, gift shops, and bait shops are Curtis's strong suits. A good place for advice, bait, tackle, **boat rentals**, and fishing-related T-shirts and such is the **Fish and Hunt Shop** on Main Street in Curtis (906-586-9531). Owner Dan Duberville is a former fishing guide.

RESTAURANTS

Arranged from south (Curtis) to north.

Fresh, made on the premises sauce and dough account for the excellent reputa-

tion of **PIZZA STOP**. Subs and hoagies, served warm, are also very popular. Owners Cecilia and Richard Rapin do all the cooking themselves, so it's consistent. There are seats for 21, and a window for soft-serve ice cream in summer. *On Main Street near H-33 in Curtis. 586-6622. Open year-round daily except Tuesday from 4 p.m. to 10 p.m. In summer open to 11 p.m. Fri & Sat.* ♿ 🚻

CHAMBERLIN'S OLE FOREST INN is known for ample portions of food that's often very good, served in a **gorgeous setting**. The big, comfortable old hotel was moved from its original site by Curtis's train station to a wooded bluff overlooking Big Manistique Lake. **Sunsets** over the lake, framed by large trees, are enjoyed from the dining room and wrap-around porch, where cocktails, appetizers, and desserts are served. (There's no problem with having dessert without dinner.) There's also a lounge with cable TV and a lobby with a big stone fireplace. Dinner favorites are planked whitefish ($16), oven-roasted prime rib, and lake perch when available. Dinners include a fresh-baked bread basket, potato, and soup or salad. Many weekends there's easy-listening entertainment. Breakfast specialties include omelets (mostly around $7), homemade biscuit with sausage gravy, and French toast ($3) at breakfast. Sandwiches, meal-size salads, and homemade soups are served at lunch and in the off-season in the evening, too.

Bud Chamberlin, co-host with Mary Gordon, came upon the abandoned resort while out snowmobiling and

decided to restore it. Snowmobilers are the primary winter clientele. **Reservations** requested; in summer, there's excess demand. *On the south shore of Big Manistique Lake, on H-33 mile north of Curtis. H-33 connects U.S. 2 (8 miles south of the inn) with M-28, about 9 miles north. (800) 292-0440; (906) 586-6000. www.chamberlinsinn.com Open from 8 a.m. to 9:30 p.m. all year, except for April.* ♿ 🚻 Full bar

HELMER HOUSE, another good restaurant in a historic building, has a warm country look. The enclosed front porch of the 1880 house overlooks **Big Manistique Lake**. The grandson of the second postmaster-innkeeper revived the place, turning the abandoned house into a restaurant and **bed and breakfast**. Local whitefish, bluegill, perch, and shrimp head the restaurant's wide-ranging menu ($7 to $15) that includes pasta, chicken, and steak. There's always an oven special for $7. The attached general store gives a good idea of what constituted a village center in the years when simple fishing resorts first developed in this area. *On H-33 in Helmer, 6 miles south of M-28 at McMillan and 6 miles north of Curtis. 586-3204. Open from around Mem. Day weekend thru mid Oct, Mon-Sat 4-9. Closed Sunday.* ♿: call 🚻

Good service and good food recommend the **TRIANGLE RESTAURANT** on M-28 east of McMillan. The big windows look out not only onto the highway but to the woods and wetlands by East Lake. The full menu appeals to travelers and locals

alike, with baskets and sandwiches served any time. Daily lunch plates (mostly $6 and less, served for supper, too) may be beef stew, spaghetti, or whitefish. Whitefish dinners (around $10) are served any time. Fridays bring the all-you-can-eat fish special. *On M-28 where it curves and intersects with Manistique Lake Road east of McMillan. 293-8469. Open daily 7 a.m. to 9 p.m., in summer 8-8.*

CURTIS/HELMER-AREA LODGINGS
Arranged from south to north.

J. T. GORDON'S at Portage Creek
(906) 586-6033

The four rooms in this long shingled cottage enjoy an **idyllic setting** facing shady Portage Creek between the two Manistique lakes, in the middle of Curtis but back from the road. Each room opens onto the long porch facing the water. They're delightfully furnished, more like a tailored bed-and-breakfast than a motel or cabin. Rooms can interconnect. Two are efficiencies with two double beds (currently $65/night) and a sitting area, and two have one double bed ($35/night). Don't be misled by the low rates; these are very pleasant — and they don't have to be rented by the week in summer. All have cable TV; no phones or air-conditioning. (Seldom needed.) Owner Tom Gordon, retired from teaching in Saudi Arabia, has an antique shop farther back on the property, part of his family's resort. This year (2001) his niece has opened a coffee shop in the front office. *On Main Street on the channel in Curtis. Probably open year-round.*

H.A.: one room accessible call

GORDON'S RESORT (906) 586-9761;
www.in the works

Sally Gordon Gibbons has two new log-sided cottages on Portage Creek, across from her brother's resort, and a remodeled cottage across the road on South Manistique Lake. It's a fine setting, on the water yet in town, which kids love. The two-bedroom cottage on the creek sleeps up to six; it's $250 for three nights or $500 a week. The four-bedroom lakeside cottage with a bunk room and whirlpool is $450 for three days or $950/week. By the week in summer. Ask about off-season rates. *On Main Street on the channel in Curtis. Open year-round.*
H.A.: call.

NORTH SHORE COTTAGES
(906) 586-9833; (800) 589-9833

Right in the center of Curtis, a bustling place in summer, four clean, two-bedroom housekeeping cottages face Big Manistique Lake. Each has a cable TV, a sofa sleeper, a grill, and a 14' fishing boat. They sleep 4 to 5. Most are from the 1940s, with knotty pine paneling and a lakeside screened porch (glassed-in in winter). There's space for a nice yard, trees, a fish-cleaning station, and a bonfire spot. The resort is on the **riverside boardwalk**. Rented by the week in summer, otherwise with a two-day minimum. Currently $450/week, $65 a day, except in snowmobile season with four adults $75-$85 a day. *On Main Street near H-33, behind co-owner Lori Rushford's North Shore Beauty Salon and Gift Shop. Open year-round.*
H.A.: no

CHAMBERLIN'S OLE FOREST INN
(800) 292-0440, (906) 586-6000;
www.chamberlinsinn.com; e-mail: chamberlin@portup.com

The hotel's guest rooms over the restaurant are bigger than those at many old hotels. They're largely furnished with turn-of-the-century antiques and reproductions. Some rooms (mostly $100) have private baths, and some ($80) share baths. Some have cable TV. One has a jacuzzi. None have phones, but there's a pay phone in the upstairs hall. The third floor has been remodeled into a suite ($125). A hearty breakfast is included. Since the guest rooms are over a bar and restaurant at the top of an open stairway, evening noise is to be expected. Common areas include the big lobby with fireplace and a great front porch. In fall color season the wooded setting overlooking **Big Manistique Lake** is particularly beautiful. There's good **fishing** for walleye, pike, bass, and perch, a dock for small boats, and a swimming beach. A **deck** and **stairway** down to the lake has several landings with benches for sitting and watching the sun set. *See restaurant for location.*
no : welcome. $10/extra person

INTERLAKEN RESORT
& BURNT ISLAND (906) 586-3545;
www.interlakenresort.org

Multitudes of recreational amenities are provided at this year-round family resort. It's on a wooded hillside going down to the north shore of **Big Manistique Lake**, a very large lake with no crowding of boats. Eight modern two-bedroom and three-bedroom housekeeping cabins come with microwaves and TV/VCRs with a large library of videos to borrow. (If you have Direct Satellite

System TV, bring your own box and hook in.) Each cabin has a picnic table, grill, outdoor furniture, and covered porch with a water view. Nine-person **hot tubs** are in two enclosed gazebos, one for children, one for adults. There's a guest laundry. Guests have complimentary use of canoes, paddle boats, **pontoon boats**, a tanning booth, and a fishing boat with motor. The grounds have plenty of room for an elaborate playground, a lakeside pavilion and **picnic area**, volleyball, and horseshoes. There's a **game room** with many free games. Cottages are rented by the week from mid June to Labor Day, otherwise daily or weekly. Call for rates.

The resort owns all of **Burnt Island** and two rustic cabins on it, which guests can use without additional charge. A weekly summer highlight is a complimentary steak or lobster dinner, occasionally with live entertainment. On a snowmobile trail. 8 miles from mountain-biking or cross-country skiing at Seney National Wildlife Refuge. *On H-44 a little west of Helmer. Open year-round.*
H.A.: 2 cabins ADA accessible
: call

SANDTOWN FARMHOUSE
Bed & Breakfast
(906) 477-6163; www.sandtownfarmhouse.com; e-mail: charper@portup.com

This comfortable, unpretentious 1920 farmhouse, 12 miles east of Curtis and 5 miles north of Engadine, is much more like a trip to grandma's than it is a visit to the fantasy elegance associated with B&Bs. All four guest rooms do have private bathrooms and individual heat control, but Caroll Harper usually bakes and cooks the full breakfast on a cast-iron range, tends a big garden, and makes rag rugs on her grandmother's loom. She grew up in Engadine, and she and her husband, Tom, were thrilled to move back after retiring early from their jobs as food service director and junior high math teacher in fast-growing Howell outside Detroit.

Their 80-acre farm is in the middle of what had been potato and dairying country, with sweeping vistas of an austere landscape punctuated by occasional small barns and Lutheran churches. The big sky makes sunsets and storms most dramatic. The property goes back to a woods, where Tom keeps some three miles of trails mown for walking, cross-country skiing, and snowshoeing. Hunting is allowed, and snowmobile access is good. The large front porch wraps around to a deck with hot tub in

back — a great place to unwind on a starry night. Antique-furnished guest rooms range from $45 (under the eaves, bath across hall) to $60 (ground floor) to $80 (double tub, panoramic view, king bed). Not air-conditioned. Satellite TVs are in the parlor and kitchen. Sandtown Road zigs and zags through woods, wetlands, and fields, past the Sandtown Cemetery and Mennonite church, to Curtis and the Manistique Lakes. *On Sandtown Rd. just east of M-117, 8 miles north of U.S. 2 at Engadine.*
H.A.: call

CAMPING

SOUTH MANISTIQUE LAKE
Campground/
Lake Superior State Forest
(906) 477-6048.Not reservable.

This popular 4,000-acre lake is known for walleye, yellow perch, pike, and bass fishing with some bluegill. This campground is a convenient location for visiting Seney Wildlife Refuge, the Straits and Mackinac Island, Lake Michigan beaches on U.S. 2, and the Soo. Of 36 rustic campsites (no running water or electricity), at least a third are on the water, and they are more open. Others are shady, with good privacy. This popular campground fills with the bass opening in May and at other times, too, but many campers just stay for a day, so openings do occur. 6 miles southwest of Curtis via S. Curtis Rd. and Long Point Rd. From the east, go through Curtis, take the turn to the south, circle back south around lake. *From the west, take M-77 to CR 447 between Blaney Park and Germfask, east on 447, then north (left) and east (right) onto S. Curtis Rd. $6/$9 night. No reservations.* **H.A.**: call.

Grand Marais (pop. 400)

The remote, simple little village of Grand Marais enjoys one of the U.P.'s finest sites. It's located on the only natural harbor of refuge along the 90 miles of beautiful but treacherous Lake Superior shoreline between Munising and Whitefish Point. Grand Marais is the gateway to the **eastern end** of the **Pictured Rocks National Lakeshore**, with the eerie, impressive Grand Sable Dunes, charming Sable Falls, and the Au Sable Point Lighthouse, where remains of several shipwrecks are visible on the nearby shore.

Today Grand Marais makes for an intimate, out-of-the way base from which to explore the unspoiled forests,

dunes, Lake Superior shoreline, lakes, and streams around it. It's at the end of a single blacktop road, M-77 from Seney 25 miles to the south.

This village is really at the end of the line. Roads do go east and west, roughly along the lakeshore for a ways, but they are unpaved and often very bumpy. The worst is H-58 going west to Munising, skirting the south boundary of Pictured Rocks National Lakeshore. Driving the whole distance without stopping can make you carsick. Don't plan to use one end of the Pictured Rocks area as a base and make frequent forays to the other end, or you'll spend two unpleasant hours each day in the car. That's why we have divided the Lakeshore between the Munising and Grand Marais chapters. Camping in the National Lakeshore's central area, at Hurricane River or Twelvemile Beach, works somewhat better as a single base for day trips.

The harbor offered such good protection to 17th-century French explorers that they gave it the name "marais," pronounced "muh-RAY." Its literal translation is "marsh," but the voyageurs used it to mean a sheltered inlet or harbor of refuge, whether marshy or not. The village went through successive booms: first as a port for the lucrative early 19th-century beaver pelt trade; then lumber, which was depleted by 1910; and then commercial fishing, which had a more gradual death. When the timber that supported most of Grand Marais ran out, the railroad tracks that were the only overland connection to the rest of the world were pulled up. The population dropped from around 4,000 to under 300 in a few months. Families who stayed here eked out a subsistence living into the modern era.

Grand Marais became a federal har-

bor of refuge in 1896 when the government built two long, parallel jetties out into the lake to serve as an entryway to West Bay. Attached to the base of the eastern jetty was a huge timber breakwater that extended 5,770 feet to the east. The Army Corps of Engineers maintained the breakwater until World War II, but then neglected it, leading to its eventual destruction. As a result, the shoreline is eroding and the harbor, once 50 feet deep, is only half that depth today and filling in rapidly. Residents and summer people have attempted t to get the U.S. Congress to appropriate funds to remedy the situation.

The older houses in Grand Marais date from its boom years between 1860 and 1910, when it was an active fishing and lumber port full of saloons and sawmills. Since then, tourism, hunting, fishing, retirees, and recently snowmobiling have joined together to sustain the local economy. The village really fills up in summer and in fall color season, and again on winter weekends. In town, aluminum-sided ranch homes now seem to outnumber the simple older homes. It's possible to think you've seen the entire town and be unaware of the pier, the beach, and the former Coast Guard station at the interestingly windswept point at the end of the peninsula that forms West Bay and the harbor.

The idea of developing a paved scenic road along the National Lakeshore has aroused great controversy. Many area businesses favored it, but people who appreciate the natural quality of the undeveloped shoreline fought it. A compromise has been worked out to pave H-58, which generally is well away from the shore. So far it's paved from Munising as far as the turnoff to Little Beaver Lake.

Grand Marais has an idiosyncratic local culture because of the coming-together in such a small, out-of-the-way place of such a variety of people: indigenous Yoopers, largely descended from turn-of-the-century loggers and fishermen; serious trout fishermen drawn by the area's many trout streams and their own secret little spots on public land; hunters; retirees, including military personnel; and many nature-loving artists, writers, corporate refugees, and affluent people from the northern Lower Peninsula who are well aware of the area's special quality. (These categories often overlap.) Often they vacationed here as kids, sometimes visiting grandparents, and are drawn back in later life. A number of artists and writers live here, seasonally or year-round. Novelist and poet Jim Harrison escapes to his cabin near here when his home turf around Lake Leelanau gets too busy with summer visitors. The lakeshore near here has its share of trophy homes, which doesn't sit well with the simple living people.

Grand Marais used to be its most tranquil in winter, but now snowmobiles make it a jarring time to visit. The noisy machines converge here on weekends, and lodgings and restaurants do as much business as during the height of summer. Winter weekdays are a good deal quieter.

Note: points of interest have been arranged from south to north in town, and then out from town west along Lake Superior in the Pictured Rocks National Lakeshore.

The Teenie Weenie Pickle Barrel Cottage

This former summer cottage, a local landmark, is made of giant pickle barrels. William and Mary Donahey, creators of the band of elfin characters who starred in the 1920s Teenie Weenie comic strip, summered on Grand Sable Lake. The Monarch Pickle Company, which used Teenie Weenies in its advertising, surprised the Donaheys with a gift of life-size versions of the pickle barrels inhabited by the advertising characters. One big barrel is the foyer and a two-story one forms the house. For laminated **Teenie Weenie cartoon placemats**, stop in across the street at the Superior Hotel.

Alas, the Pickle Barrel Cottage is in jeopardy as we go to press. It has sat unused and unmaintained for years after serving as a shop and tourist information center. Local people are seeking expert help in wood preservation.

In town on Lake/M-77 at Randolph, next to the Sportsman's Restaurant.

Superior Hotel

This is a trip back in time — back maybe to the 1940s, when this simple hotel was already over 50 years old. The soda fountain is no more, but townspeople come to pick up their newspapers and have a cup of coffee, starting at 7 a.m. If you sit around, you'll overhear a lot about town life. Proprietress Isabelle "Bess" Capogrossa has an unusually detailed take on the local scene — and a long perspective. She herself first came to Grand Marais as a toddler in 1924. Her parents bought the hotel around 1938. She was born in Canada and has

lived as an adult in other places, but her view of Grand Marais is unparalleled. She can tell you — if you want to ask — about what kids did here for fun when the north woods were really remote, about earlier eras of tourism, about when the telephone came to town and who had what ring, and about how the lumberjacks, grown old, still came in from the woods and squandered six months' pay in the bars. It's hard to believe — but true — that her son Rick is responsible for the breathless real estate copy of North Coast Realty, alluding to "prestigious Whitefish Bay." He also spins out the rambling tales in the widely distributed, free *Grand Marais Pilot.*

The nine hotel rooms upstairs (see under lodgings) are plain, comfortable, and clean, and the mattresses are terrific. *125 Lake at Randolph. 494-2539. Opens around 7 a.m. for coffee.* &: no.

The Marketplace

This cooperative shop and activity center is the showroom for some two dozen members of **Grand Marais Cottage Industries.** There's a lot here — photographs, handknits, lamps, novelties, art glass, carvings, and more, all juried and all made in Grand Marais.

This grassroots economic development organization has cultivated a lot of surprising talent and spun off several independent stores and studios. Its website, **www.natureinabundance.com**, gives an excellent view of the area and events, in addition to showcasing cooperative members and programs.

Funshop is a series of **art** and **nature programs** for visitors and local people, young and old, on topics like water color painting, stained glass, dune walks, and other events like the **dulcimer workshop**, held the third weekend in August. Funshop activities are concentrated in summer but given year-round.

On the east side of Lake Street as you come into town, next to the white Methodist Church. 494-2438. Open from the end of May thru December. Up to October open daily 10-5, to 6 in July and most of August. From Oct. thru Dec. open Sat & Sun 10-5 or by appointment. &

Gitche Gumee Agate & History Museum

Skills and wisdom handed down from one generation to another— that's the hidden story behind many of the best U.P. places that visitors can see today. For all the summers Karen Bryzs spent

in Grand Marais, visiting her grandparents, she loved visiting Alex Niemi and his Gitchee Gumee Agate Museum the most. Agates and learning to recognize them were only part of the attraction. There were the stories — about how, in 1910, when the Alger & Smith Company finished logging, the last thing they tool with them was the railroad to the outside; how the stranded employees who decided to stay (largely Finlanders) used their ingenuity, thrift, and a good measure of *sisu* (that Finnish quality of toughness and endurance) to build self-sufficient lives here. (The lumber company gave them some land.) The Niemis built three fish tugs to make a living off the lake, while raising most of their own food to feed their family of six children.

Alex Niemi sold his fish tug in 1953 and started the Agate Museum the next year, as a sideline to his job managing the Woodland Park campground. Karen was among the kids who was fascinated with his stories, his music, his puppet Nutty Buddy, and his knowledge about rocks and minerals. In 1994 she and her husband moved to Grand Marais, bought the Dunes Saloon and turned it into a restaurant, brewpub, and rockhound visitor center. Her dream was to pay tribute to Alex Niemi by reopening the museum — which she did in 1999. When she bought his former house, she discovered boxes or Grand Marais artifacts and enough original furniture to turn the back part of the museum into a house museum of everyday life. She tracked down the *Shark*, the Niemis' last tug, deteriorating in a field near South Haven, and was given the tug. The cost of transporting it to Grand Marais was considerable. The *Shark* is now outside the museum, still awaiting restoration.

The museum is about Lake Superior minerals (fluorescents, copper, and more) and agates. Karen says it has the largest collection of Lake Superior agates ever displayed. It's also about history and how people made a **self-sufficient life** in Grand Marais with **very little cash**, growing and processing food, making clothes on a knitting machine, using a pig boiler to steam-bend wood for the *Shark*. "If kids learn something about history," Karen says, "they get a rock." Karen is interested in giving workshops "about our geologic and historic past." People are invited to help the museum by volunteering their time (one day a week would be great!) or skills and by donating cash. *E21739 Braziel St., around the corner from the Lake Superior Brewing Co. and opposite the entrance to Woodland Park. 494-2590. www.gitche-*

gumee.com *In July & August open daily from 4 to 9 p.m. Open some weekends in spring and fall. $1 admission; donations appreciated.* ♿ call

Harbor entrance, range lights, pier & beach

Drive out the short peninsula that forms West Bay and you'll come to a parking area by low **dunes**. The windswept **beach** at Coast Guard Point is on the other side. A long stone **pier** juts out into Lake Superior, intended to protect the harbor entrance. **Coho, steelhead,** and **whitefish** can be caught off this pier. Sometimes in spring and fall, when the wind happens to come from the north-northwest, there are so many whitefish that the pier is crowded with fishermen day and night.

On the pier is the **front range light,** consisting of a room perched on a steel skeleton. The **rear range light** on shore behind it is similar but with an octagonal lantern. By lining up the lights, vessels are guided into the harbor. Range lights aren't warning lights, they're welcoming lights, says lighthouse fan Pat Munger, an active member of the local historical society. Its museum is in the light keeper's house across the road. Next to it, a **picnic grove** is behind the monument to fishermen drowned in Lake Superior.

A hundred-year-old breakwall on the other side of the harbor entrance, unre-

You can glimpse aspects of the life of a working-class U.P. family circa 1900 at the Grand Marais historical society's museum. It's in the former lighthouse keeper's house by the beach and pier.

paired for years, has succumbed to storms. Without it, the harbor is silting in.

Light Keeper's House Museum

Near the range lights, built by the Coast Guard in 1899, this bungalow houses a folksy local museum. The **Grand Marais Historical Society** has furnished it as a working-class home using artifacts from the area. Members have recorded a lot of oral histories from old-timers, resulting in tours that include some good stories that go with things in the museum — like one of the bicycles, driven by gears, not a chain. It was used by a local couple who, around 1900, bicycled on

Indian trails and country roads from South Dakota to Grand Marais, long before highways. As a **hands-on museum**, nothing is behind cases. Kids can play the piano (it's out of tune because the museum isn't heated), use an old hand coffeegrinder to grind a few beans, crank the phone, and ring the "blueberry bell." Picking blueberries was an important source of income. Families would camp in the cutover areas where blueberries flourish. Children had to stay within hearing distance of the blueberry bell.

Take Lake Ave./M-77 through town. Just before it ends at the beach, turn right onto Canal/CR 702 and go east past Welker's Restaurant. Open daily 1-4 from July 4 thru August and in Sept. on Sat & Sun, 1-4. **Other times by appointment,** *which can be spur of the moment. 494-2404. Free. Donations welcomed.* ♿: *except second floor.*

Grand Marais Maritime Museum

This small museum, part of the Pictured Rocks National Lakeshore, is in the former Grand Marais **Coast Guard station**, an impressive two-and-a-half-story affair topped by a tower room (not open to the public). Displays are done in the minimalist style typical of the National Parks Service, which spotlights a few objects such as a breeches buoy used by lifesavers. There are some photos of local fishermen and the lifesaving station here. The toilet in the ladies' room is in almost the very place where the Coast Guard radioman last made contact with the *Edmund Fitzgerald.*

Take Lake Ave./M-77 through town. Just before it ends at the beach, turn right onto Canal/CR 702 and go east past Welker's Restaurant. Museum is on left. **Museum hours vary** *from year to year, depending of National Parks Service staffing and volunteers. Call 494-2660 or 387-3700 for current hours. Free.* ♿

Agate Beach

Go west along the shore from the harbor breakwater pier, or go down the bluff at **Woodland Park**, to come to another beach extending miles to the west. At this well-known agate beach, even novices might find the variegated, translucent stones of quartz while strolling along the shoreline looking through the clear water, especially in spring or after a storm.

Karen Brzys (center) and the Gitche Gumee Kids, her steadfast helpers, at the agate Gitche Gumee Agate Museum founded by her mentor, Axel Niemi. Resurrecting the museum has fulfilled her longtime dream. To the right is the *Shark*, the Niemi family's handmade fishing tug.

Banded agates are formed by liquid quartz in cavities of preexisting rock. Their exterior may have a pitted, potato-skin texture. Most common are shattered pieces with distinctive agate banding. (The colors are formed by different impurities.) Other interesting stones like jasper, puddingstone, and banded chert can also be found here.

A one-mile walk down the beach and you'll be at the mouth of **Sable Creek**. A short path along the creek leads up to the delightful **Sable Falls**. (Camping hint: stay at Grand Marais' modern Woodland Park Campground for ready access down to the agate beach.)

Goewey's Garage

Fish carvings by Lee and Betty Goewey (he does trout, she does panfish) are in such demand in this hot collectible field that there aren't too many on hand for visitors to see. The Goeweys also make art glass windows, mostly with natural or maritime subjects. Demand is such that not too many of them are likely to be around, either. All the Goeweys' work now is commission work, but they enjoy having an **open studio** and meeting visitors and prospective customers. Art glass is opaque and variably colored. Often the glass itself suggests a landscape or scene, like the Grand Portal, the northern lights, or a crossfox (mixed red and gray) that comes into their yard.

From M-77, turn east at the Pickle Barrel Cottage onto H-58/Randolph St., north (lake) side of road. Look for sign. From Mem. Day thru Sept usually open Fri & Sat 10-4. sometimes Wed. Otherwise open by chance or by appointment. Call first. 494-2312. (888) 629-7099. www. natureinabundance.com/gifts/goewey's garage &

Crystal Pine Cone

Dorothy Woropay loves to paint scenes — beaches, autumn trees, waterfalls, lighthouses, freighters — on beach stones and saw blades. Her daughter Peggy turns rocks into animals and people. Their **studio/gallery** is in a cabin among the pines. Their work comes highly recommended by other area artists.

Off M-77 just south of town. At the hill crest, turn west onto Westridge. Road. Crystal Pine Cone is at the end of the road at the top of the hill. 494-2610. Open May thru Thanksgiving, typically 11-6 in summer, may close earlier at other times. &: no.

Creative Enterprises

Set in the woods near the artists' home, this **interesting studio/shop** features a very wide variety of mostly nature-inspired crafts from Upper Peninsula craftspeople: pottery, jewelry, hand-blown glass, baskets, T shirts and sweatshirts with floral and lighthouse designs, notecards, and their own photographs and paintings. Bob and Nancy Weston, who took early retirement from jobs as a metallurgist and a teacher, responded to the challenge of local naysayers who said it would be well nigh impossible to launch a successful crafts business on a self-sustaining scale. They decided to not to skimp but to "do it right" in building their studio home. Bob is a scenic photographer. Nancy paints and draws — on paper, stones, gourds, fabric, printing plates. The store mats and frames the varied watercolors, drawings, and prints offered here. Often the Westons can be seen working on projects during store hours. Call about **occasional workshops** offered here.

On M-77 about 3 miles south of Grand Marais. 494-2744. Open May thru October daily 11-6, otherwise by chance or appointment. &

Sable Falls

A delightful half-mile walk and stairway take you through a forest to the falls, part of **Pictured Rocks National Lakeshore**. The falls and Lake Superior are revealed in tantalizing glimpses before finally you look down on the entire cascade from the rocky shelf at its precipice. Stairs with occasional benches continue down and along Sable Creek to a **rocky beach**.

To extend this adventure, walk right (east) along the shore. This is known as a good stretch for **agates**, though its accessibility makes for slimmer pickings than at more remote areas. In a mile you'll be at Woodland Park, in another mile at the Grand Marais harbor entrance.

The parking lot for the trails to Sable Falls and Grand Sable Dunes is off H-58 about a mile west of Grand Marais Free. &: no.

Grand Sable Bank & Dunes

These vast banks and dunes along Lake Superior are a highlight of **Pictured Rocks National Lakeshore**. Seen from the trail's vantage point midway up their height, the dunes look dramatic and overwhelming. They are entirely bare and blindingly blank on a sunny day, slanting into Lake Superior at the steep, 35 ° angle of repose common to all piles of dry sand. When the **sun is low**, the effect is more **beautiful and mysterious**, as the dunes shade into purples and pinks. The banks stretch west for five miles, down to the Log Slide. Don't be tempted to walk down to the lake here unless you're up to a difficult half-hour spent walking back up the sand, slipping and sliding with every step.

"Grand Sable" (pronounced "SAAH-bl") means "big sand." These banks are a huge formation, up to 275 feet high, created during the last ice age when sand and gravel filled in a deep rift in the glacier. Atop the gravelly banks, sand dunes rise another 80 feet. These are **"perched dunes"** because they are perched on top of another landform. They were probably formed when wind and waves piled up sand at the edge of Lake Nipissing, forerunner of Superior.

The half-mile **trail** passes through an old orchard, over a creek, and through a jack pine forest, then enters a bleak dunescape where only a few hardy plant pioneers like marram grass can take hold. Excellent **interpretive displays** explain the principles of plant succession in the beach's harsh, dry, nutrient-deficient environment, which alternates suddenly from hot to cold after sunset. You can also see a small **ghost forest** of trees overwhelmed by sand.

The parking lot for the trails to Sable Falls and Grand Sable Dunes is off H-58 about a mile west of Grand Marais. Free. &: no.

Grand Sable Visitor Center

Free information on the **Pictured Rocks National Lakeshore**, including campgrounds, day hikes, and historical destinations, is provided at the official visitor center at this remodeled farmhouse. **Displays** are about recreational opportunities. A small **bookstore** focuses on the area's natural and human history. A two-mile **trail** through a deeply shady beech-maple forest begins at the parking lot here and leads to old farm fields and what's left of a logging camp.

On H-58 about 5 miles west of Grand Marais. (906) 494-2660. Open from mid-May thru September at least. Hours depend on staffing. They are usually 10-6 daily. Extended hours during summer season. Call to confirm hours. Free. &

Log Slide Overlook

This high point of the ridge along Lake Superior, part of the **Pictured Rocks National Lakeshore**, is almost 300 feet above the water. The overlook platform offers wonderful **views** — especially around sunrise and sunset — looking toward the **Au Sable Lighthouse** to the west and, to the east, looking down the length of the **Grand Sable Dunes**. In the late 19th century loggers rolled and slid logs down this sharp incline on a wooden slide, to be loaded on lumber schooners. **Outdoor exhibits** convey

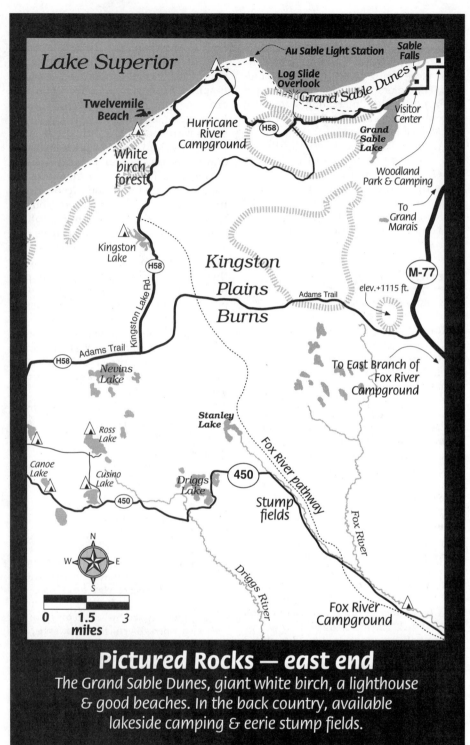

Pictured Rocks — east end
The Grand Sable Dunes, giant white birch, a lighthouse & good beaches. In the back country, available lakeside camping & eerie stump fields.

that historical scene. Bring your binoculars to pick out details!

Off H-58 about 8 miles west of Grand Marais and 24 miles east of Munising. &

North Country Trail/ Lakeshore Trail

Hike a section of this famous trail connecting the most prominent sights within the **Pictured Rocks National Lakeshore**, and you'll really experience them rather than just taking in a quick view. You could start farther east, at Woodland Park in Grand Marais and hike along the beach to Sable Falls, then hike up alongside Sable Creek to the Visitor Center. See the Munising/ Pictured Rocks chapter for the box on hiking pointers and for points of interest at the trail's Munising end. The Lakeshore Trail is part of the North Country Trail.

The North Country Trail

Hike **from Marquette to St. Ignace** over 200 miles along the completed sections of the North Country Trail. It goes from Marquette through the Pictured Rocks and Muskallonge State Park on Lake Superior and then through the Hiawatha National Forest, passing by the Upper and Lower Tahquamenon Falls.

Visit its extensive website, **www.northcountrytrail.org** for trail notes, a general map of the entire trail, info on ordering trail guides, interesting stories of trail adventures, and more. Eventually the trail will extend from the Appalachian Trail in New York State to North Dakota.

The trailhead for what was formerly known as the Lakeshore Trail is at the **Grand Sable Visitor Center** *on H-58 about 5 miles west of Grand Marais.*

Au Sable Point Lighthouse

Part of the **Pictured Rocks National Lakeshore**, the dramatic red brick lightkeeper's house and attached white cylinder of a tower sit atop picture-perfect red sandstone rocks. The lighthouse, finished in 1874 and enlarged in 1909, has been restored to its 1910 condition. Its lantern again houses the Third Order Fresnel lens, six feet tall. The functioning automated light is on a separate tower outside the lighthouse. To avoid auto congestion, **access is only by foot** via an easy 1 1/2 mile road (3 miles round trip).

From July 1 through Labor Day free **tours** are held every hour, Thursday through Sunday, if staffing is available. The tour guides, volunteer and professional, are well informed about lighthouse life and lore. For an **amazing view** of the **Grand Sable Dunes**, visitors can climb the 87-foot **tower**, ten at a time. The dunes are most striking when the sun is low. *Call (906) 494-2660 to check tour times, which are subject to change.* Climb down the rocks from the lighthouse (be prepared to scramble), go west a ways along the beach, and you'll come upon two **shipwreck skeletons** sticking out of the sand. The sand moves constantly, so in some years more of the wrecks is visible than in others. A third shipwreck is close to the Hurricane River Campground. Many ships were wrecked on the busy stretch of coast between Munising and Grand Marais. The light

warned them to stay away from the shallow sandstone shelf.

Interpretive signs on the lighthouse grounds and along the access road inform visitors about the functions of various buildings in the lighthouse complex and what the National Park Service is doing to restore it. Visit the Grand Marais Maritime Museum in town to learn more about area shipwrecks and lifesaving installations.

Take H-58 to the Hurricane River Campground. (That's 13 miles from Grand Marais or 39 miles from Munising.) It's a pretty 1 1/2-mile walk to the lighthouse from the lower campground over a flat, easy access road through a forest. Alternate route if you're agile: walk along the beach (follow the sign to the shipwrecks), enjoy the scenery and greater solitude, and climb up the bank to the lighthouse. Free. &: no. Too sandy.

Twelvemile Beach & White Birch Trail

This long sand and pebble beach, part of the **Pictured Rocks National Lakeshore**, is approached from H-58 through a beautiful white birch forest. Swimming here can be awfully cold, but the **beach** is fine for picnics. The two-mile interpretive **nature trail** takes you from the east end of the Twelvemile Beach Campground through the beautiful and unusual **White Birch Forest** of large birches. White birches are normally sun-loving pioneers after forest fires and cutting. They're soon shaded by more adaptable maples. Here they have thrived longer, thanks to moist soils and plenty of sunlight. (The birches can also be seen from H-58.)

Take H-58 (unpaved) about 15 miles west of Grand Marais or about 37 miles east of Munising and turn into the drive to the Twelvemile Beach campground. Park by picnic area or along the access road. &: no.

Kingston Plains Burns

This area, part of the **Lake Superior State Forest**, is the best-known of the **eerie, striking stump fields**. They were created when forest fires burned off so much of the soil's humus that the forest couldn't regenerate as it usually would. Some stumps here had been cut and burned later. In other cases, fire killed the trees, whose trunks broke off irregularly at different levels. Most but not all fires were associated with the wasteful practices of the logging era, when slash (treetops, cut limbs, etc.) was left in the

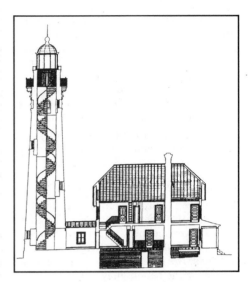

The 87-foot tower of the AuSable Point Lighthouse affords a grand view of the nearby dunes.

devastated woods. When dried, it was easily ignited by sparks or lightning.

Some stump fields were caused by forest fires before loggers came. Lightning could strike a very tall tree and kill it, or a windstorm could topple many trees. When dried, these dead, resinous pines would easily ignite.

Pine resins within stumps have preserved pine stump fields, which provide an unusual **visual record** of the density and size of the **presettlement old growth forests** here. It's not uncommon to see big stumps, two feet in diameter, every ten feet. The north part of the **Fox River Pathway** (see Seney section) passes through these stump fields.

In the Kingston Plains today, **lichens** are the principal living plant. Reindeer lichen "can form large mats carpeting the ground," wrote Richard Holzman in *Scenic Highlights at the Pictured Rocks National Lakeshore*. "Walking on the lichens is like walking on sponges in wet weather or potato chips on a dry summer day. **Spring** is the most colorful season here, when everything is green with fresh growth touched by spring flowers. By **summer** the porous soil is dry, and browning vegetation most evident. Grasshoppers can be especially abundant, hundreds fleeing with each step."

A reliable, detailed trail guide to the National Lakeshore

is Olive Anderson's *Pictured Rocks National Lakeshore: A Guide*, available at the National Lakeshore visitor centers.

Slowly the land will recover, and future attempts to replant these areas will meet with more success than similar projects in the past. Some state foresters are working to preserve stretches of stump fields as visual records of the pineries that provided so much of the basis for Michigan's later industrial wealth.

Where H-58 turns west, south of Kingston Lake and the campground there, take the Adams Truck Trail east two miles.

GRAND MARAIS RESTAURANTS

There aren't many restaurants in this very small place, and in summer they can be overwhelmed. As we go to press, things are looking up. It appears that Welker's, the good-size motel and restaurant near the beach, may have new owners and an infusion of new energy. The Sportsman, a classic northwoods bar-restaurant in the heart of town, is for sale. Year-round offerings in Grand Marais depend somewhat on who feels like cooking.

What used to be the Earl of Sandwich has grown into the 52-seat **WEST BAY DINER**, a diner, deli, and bakery. People rave about Rick Guth's big club sandwiches ($5 to $8) on Ellen Airgood's fresh bread, and the whitefish sandwiches and fresh fish ($8-$10). Ellen bakes very good muffins, cinnamon rolls, and monster cookies loaded with raisins, nuts, chocolate chunks, and more. The big breakfasts, including the efficient $7 buffet in summer, have a huge following. There are cappuccino and espresso drinks and ice cream, too. The burgers ($3 to $6) come in three sizes and three meats: beef, buffalo, and ostrich. Part of the restaurant is an original **1948 Paramount diner**, one of the New Jersey manufacturer's smallest models, with a view of the bay. It all adds up to a very busy place. **Deli customers** who want the good bread, meats, and cheeses and the salads (tuna, potato, pasta, slaw, etc.) have been trained to **call ahead for afternoon pickup**. No smoking. *Past the post office on the corner of Veterans and Woodruff on the bay. 494-2607. Open some winters. Always open daily from mid or late May thru color season. Opens at 7:30, breakfast served starting at 8. In summer generally open 'til 8 or 9. After color season, closes in the afternoon.*

&: ramp by rear parking

LICKETY SPLIT is a little fast-food place that serves sandwiches, subs, burgers, and, from Memorial Day through color season, **Jilbert's ice cream**. Mary and Ray Gage have been open for breakfast and lunch all year in years when with no other restaurants having breakfast hours. The **picnic tables** outside have a nice view of the bay. *Downtown on the west side of Lake Ave. next to the grocery, across from the bank. 494-2266*

LAKE SUPERIOR BREWING COMPANY, formerly the Dunes Saloon, is a restaurant and a brewpub. The tavern part and its bar go back to the logging boom circa 1900; the **family dining room** is in back. What the restaurant offers depends partly on the season. In summer, fresh whitefish, locally caught, is the big seller, as a very large sandwich with fries ($6 or $7), or as a dinner ($13 or so) with potato or wild rice and the salad bar. Sandwiches, meal-size salads ($6-$7), and homemade **pasties** and **pizza** are available year-round. Winter means no fish but steaks, ribs, and homemade soups. **Scotch egg** is a tasty appetizer that goes well with stout: a hardboiled egg in wrapped in sausage, then dipped in egg, rolled in bread crumbs, and baked.

Alcoholic beverages are not the only focus here. Excellent **cream soda**, orange soda, and **root beer** are **made on the premises.** As for the **brewpub**, brewer/owner Chris Sarver got into home brewing before the current craft beer boom. In the early 1990s he rebelled at having to pay $16 for a six-pack of his favorite English beer if he could get it, and decided to duplicate it himself. When the Dunes Saloon was up for sale, he and his rockhound wife, Karen Brzys, bought it. He didn't have to buy a new brewing system. It wasn't hard for him and his father to make one from scratch, adapting used equipment. After all, they were already pros designing automation systems for automotive assembly lines. The brewery's stainless-steel tanks are on view to diners. Beers appeal to a wide variety of tastes, from people who love Bud Light to aficionados who value distinctive flavors. A few staples are augmented by a changing variety of other brews. Two favorites: Agate Amber (medium-bodied, "combining malty richness with the perfect amount of hoppiness") and Cattail Ale, a light golden ale with medium hops flavor and citrusy finish. **Tours** available upon request.

Downtown on the west side of Lake Ave./M-77. 494-2337. Open year-round, daily from noon. Kitchen closes at 10 except for pizza. Tavern closes at 2 a.m. or whenever. May close for maintenance in April or November.

&: entrance from south parking lot.
Full bar

GRAND MARAIS LODGINGS

At peak times in winter and summer there's way more demand for rooms than supply in this little town. New owners at Welker's, the large motel on Coast Guard Point, could improve the lodgings picture. **Note**: a small **beach** on West Bay behind downtown means that visitors staying at the Dunes Motel, Alverson's, and the Superior Hotel have a very short walk to a relatively warm swimming beach.

ALVERSON'S MOTEL (906) 494-2681; www.natureinabundance.com

Every one of the 14 large rooms in this two-story motel has a view of Grand Marais Harbor. Owners Richard and Colleen Grove have redecorated the rooms with creative touches like hand stenciling to match the bedspreads. All have cable TV, phones, and either one queen and a sofa bed or two double beds. Rooms in summer and fall are under $55, $5 extra person. Snowmobile season $5 more, $6/extra person. Call for off-season rates. A **picnic table** and grill are in the back. Downtown restaurants and shops are a block away. *On Randolph a block east of Lake/H-77. Turn at the Pickle Barrel Cottage. Open year-round.*

H.A.: call : under 2 free

SUPERIOR HOTEL (906) 494-2539

A wonderful anachronism, this plain, century-old hotel has nine clean, comfortable rooms with bedside lamps, easy

---

*Where to stay
for a Pictured Rocks vacation*

If you want to stay in a town but be close to nature for a leisurely Pictured Rocks vacation, **Grand Marais** has it all over Munising, which is affected by a busy highway and commercial development. Grand Marais' location is isolated. It's a good spot for people who want to really get away. The Fox River and fishing lakes of northern Alger and Schoolcraft counties are close at hand, and the Seney Wildlife Refuge is an easy day trip. On the other hand, **Munising** is centrally located for energetic sightseers. It not only is close to the big attractions of Pictured Rocks, but it's near Grand Island, Au Train's beaches, and a good restaurant, The Brownstone, and just a 45-minute drive to Marquette.

chairs, and excellent mattresses. Decor is a utilitarian version of the 1950s. At the end of the hall are two bathrooms and one shower. There's no TV except in the lobby, and no phones — but guests can use the owner's phone. The rates can't be beat — $25 for two if they stay a night, $20 if they stay multiple nights, and $5 less for a single person. Some guides and websites have keyed into the atmosphere without checking the facts. Prospective guests call expecting an antique-filled country inn or B&B. "Sometimes I can stop them fast. I explain that I only have two bathrooms and they're at the end of the hall," says owner Bess Capogrossa. "I'll hear them take a breath and a little gasp."

Don't think the hotel is closed if there are no lighted hotel signs at night — that saves electricity. It's all part of the owner's clearly articulated business philosophy that anyone deserves a vacation. *125 Lake downtown.* &: no.

DUNES MOTEL   (906) 494-2324; e-mail: jhubbard@jamadots.com

This small, well-run motel perches on the hill at the south entrance to town, but should be able to go on a vacation and have a break. She makes enough for a comfortable living, she says — so why should she raise her rates? *125 Lake at Randolph, a short walk to restaurants* trees now block a lake view. The large rooms have big picture windows and1960s contemporary decor with leatherette headboards. All have refrigerators, in-room coffee, and cable TV. Guests may use the office phone. "Reasonable rates," says the owner. Two two-bedroom kitchen units. *On M-77 on the south edge of Grand Marais. Open year-round.*

H.A.: call ♿👪🐕

VOYAGEURS MOTEL (906) 494-2389; www.grandmaraismichigan.com

This newish two-story, ten-room motel sits up on the bluff overlooking West Bay, near the school and about a two-block walk to town. Each room has a large rear window with a water view. Rooms have cable TV, minifridges, and coffeemakers. Peak season rates for two: $70. $66 in the off-season. Ask about three-bedroom rental house. The community room with hot tub and sauna has a microwave for guests' use. There's a BBQ area with a good view. *On Wilson St. east off M-77 at the south edge of town. Open year-round.*

H.A.: some ADA accessible rooms
♿👪: 12 & over $8 extra
🐕: short-haired only

Strollers enjoy Sable Beach at the foot of the Grand Sable Dunes. Dogs are allowed on trails and in campgrounds of all Michigan's national and state parks except for Isle Royale, but they are required to be on a six-foot leash.

WOODS' COTTAGES (906) 494-2366

A find from an earlier era. Four vintage housekeeping cabins (mostly two-bedroom) with pine paneling and nifty **rustic furniture** are nestled down in a cedar grove with nice views of low **back dunes**. A **walkway** crosses what remains of the Sucker River to reach the Lake Superior **beach**. Guests can make beach fires, weather permitting. Cabins have cable TV. Towels and linens are furnished. The down-to-earth, unpretentious owner appreciates the serenity of this special spot. Smoking OK. Only 1 picnic table. Rented by the week in summer. $50/night or $336/week. Limit: five people per cabin, including children. Make reservations by spring at the latest. *On north side of H-58 about 1 1/2 miles east of town. Open from May thru mid October.*

H.A.: call ♿👪: $3 for fifth person

SUNSET CABINS   (906) 494-2693

Four beautiful housekeeping cabins with views of Lake Superior have been gutted, winterized, and finished in a woodsy style, with tongue-and-groove paneling and **rustic furniture**, vintage and new. From H-58 the access drive goes 400' through the woods. To reach the Lake Superior beach, it's necessary to row across a pond or walk around it. Formerly the Sucker River flowed through this low area. All cabins have cable TV, full kitchens, and grills. The two one-bedroom cabins sleep up to 4 on a king bed and queen sofa-sleeper. They currently rent for $450/week or $75/day, year-round. Weekly rentals in summer, otherwise three-day minimum.

Other cabins have two and three bedrooms. Guests can use office phone. By 2002 all will have decks. *On H-58 about 1 1/2 miles east of town, past Woods' Cottages. Open year-round.*

H.A.: call 🐕
♿👪: flat rate/cabin except in winter

CAMPING AROUND GRAND MARAIS

WOODLAND PARK

(906) 494-2381 for info, reservations; www.natureinabundance.com

On a grassy, wooded bluff between a Lake Superior agate beach and a Grand Marais neighborhood, this municipal park offers **beach access**, a playground, and a modern campground with a new shower building. 125 campsites have electricity, cable TV for an extra fee, and not much privacy. Rates are $16 for lakefront electric, $15 oterhwise. Non-electric sites ($11) include 20 drive-up tent sites and, on the beach. It's an easy walk to restaurants, shops, and Coast Guard Point. Space is usually available, except for July 4, the last week in July (kayak week), and the second full weekend in August (music festival). The Gitchee Gumee Agate Museum, designed for kids, is just across the street. *Take Lake St./M-77 through town, turn left on Braziel, right into park. (906) 494-2381. Open May 15-Oct. 15.* &

HURRICANE RIVER CAMPGROUND/
Pictured Rocks National Lakeshore
(906) 387-3700. No reservations.

22 shady rustic campsites in a mixed forest are divided between a high bluff above Lake Superior and a lower level, a

short walk to the **beach**. A **campground host** is here in summer. Privacy between sites is good. This campground is closer to a town (12 miles to Grand Marais) than other National Lakeshore campgrounds. Shipwreck skeletons in the sand and the 1 1/2 mile trail to the **lighthouse** are special attractions, especially for kids. Coho fishermen camp here in spring to fish in the river.

Availability tips: All the National Lakeshore campgrounds here fill up on holiday weekends and between mid-July and late August. There are no reservations. Prospective campers are advised to arrive late in the morning or early afternoon, and to have alternate camping plans, including state forest campgrounds not in the visitor center information base. *On H-58 12 miles west of Grand Marais. $10/night. Open May 10-Oct. 31.*

H.A.: one site ADA accessible

TWELVEMILE BEACH CAMPGROUND/ Pictured Rocks National Lakeshore
(906) 387-3700. No reservations.

38 shady, private rustic campsites sit in a beautiful birch woods on a bluff overlooking the Lake Superior. The setting is more picturesque than Hurricane River, and the lake seems closer. Privacy between sites is good. A **campground host** is here in summer. The two-mile **White Birch Trail** loop goes up from the campground into a rare stand of very old and large white birches. Availability tips: see Hurricane River Campground.

On H-58 about 15 miles west of Grand Marais. (906) 387-3700. Open May 10-Oct 31. $10/night

H.A.: two sites ADA accessible.

BACKCOUNTRY CAMPSITES on North Country Trail/Lakeshore Trail/ Pictured Rocks National Lakeshore

Of the 13 very popular primitive camp-

> ### Camping on Lake Superior? Prepare for cold!
>
> No matter if it's July and air-conditioning weather a few miles inland, when the north wind blows off the lake, it can get cold. Campers are well advised to bring a sleeping bag, cool-weather jacket, and layerable sweaters and such — no matter what the month. A U.P. state forester recalls the naive surprise of visiting managers from Lansing who came totally unprepared for bone-chilling cold on a June camping trip by the big lake.

> ### Bug strategy: be flexible, try everything
>
> Generally lakeshores are breezy and bug-free by midsummer, but if it's been humid and the wind is out of the south, stable flies that normally remain inland can be blown onto the beach. In that case, it may be a good day to stay in town.

sites, 4 are on the lakeshore's Grand Marais end: at Sevenmile Creek, near Twelvemile Beach Campground, between the lighthouse and the Log Slide, and at the west end of the Grand Sable Dunes. For reservation info, see "Backcountry camping" after Munising in the Pictured Rocks/ Munising/Au Train chapter.

KINGSTON LAKE Campground/ Lake Superior State Forest
(906) 293-5131. Not reservable.

This is one of the choice state forest campgrounds in the central Upper Peninsula because of its location in mature hardwoods on an inland lake with swimming and fishing — just five miles from Pictured Rocks' Twelvemile Beach. "It's a great lake to kayak or canoe," says a woman who puts this campground on her short list of favorite spots. This campground is the northern terminus of the **Fox River Pathway** (see after Seney), which goes through the eerie stump fields of the Kingston Plains. Michigan's **state forest campgrounds**, always rustic, are an unheralded treasure because of their typically scenic locations and private campsites. Kingston Lake has 16 sites, some on the lake. This campground occasionally fills in summer, especially in July. *On H-58, about 20 miles west of Grand Marais. $6/$10 night.*

H.A.: fire rings and gravel to harden surfaces are yet to come.

EAST BRANCH of FOX RIVER Campground/ Lake Superior State Forest (906) 293-5131. Not reservable.

Because it's on a prime trout stream, this 19-site rustic campground (vault toilets, no showers, no electricity) fills in June and on holidays, and sometimes other times in summer. Come between Tuesday and Thursday and you'll probably get a site. Two levels of campsites are both on the river; 4 other sites have river views. A campground host is sometimes here in summer. The pine canopy provides shade and scenery but little privacy between sites. Expect some bugs

because of the river setting. A quarter-mile path leads to a fishing platform (&) overlooking the old ponds of a former fish hatchery. *Just west off M-77, 8 miles north of Seney. $6/$10 night.*

H.A.: now ADA accessible

For state forest campgrounds along the **Blind Sucker River and Lake Superior** 14 miles east of Grand Marais via a gravel road, see after Deer Park.

Deer Park

No trace except a huge pile of sawdust remains of the small sawmill town of Deer Park, on the site of the current-day state park. **Muskallonge Lake** was the holding pond for logs brought from the nearby area by narrow-gauge railroad. Finished lumber was shipped from the Lake Superior dock.

Here the Lake Superior shore is unaffected by nearby roads, yet easily accessible to hikers along the **North Country Trail.** The long hiking trail goes along and near the lakeshore for some 30 miles east of Grand Marais, past Muskallonge Lake and the mouth of the Two Hearted River. Unusually **varied rocks**, including agates, attract rockhounds. The woods are a diverse mix of species, with good **fall color** added by oak and maple. **Wild blueberries** flourish on the sand ridges.

This area is an **overlooked jewel** for many local people and outdoors-lovers who feel pressed-in by the summer crowds of visitors attracted to the more spectacular and famous beauty spots at nearby Pictured Rocks and Tahquamenon Falls. No wonder people were incensed when Massachusetts developer Ben Benson (now Shelter Bay Forests) erected his trademark white fencing along his New England-style lakeshore development in Luce County along H-58 east of Grand Marais. That fence hit all the hot buttons of any self-respecting Yooper. It flaunted private ownership of land that everyone regards as the public domain, open to all, and it paraded upscale Eastern ways in a region that's assertively low-key and unassuming.

North Country Trail: Grand Marais to Mouth of the Two Hearted River

Far less used than the North Country Trail section through Pictured Rocks, this section, part of the **Lake Superior**

State Forest, goes near the Lake Superior shore in an area known for **agates** and an unusually rich mix of rocks in general. Though the trail is just a mile or so from the gravel road H-58, it has a real wilderness feeling and a lot of interest and variety. It goes up and down steep, forested sand ridges of 50 or 100 feet, so it's rated moderate to difficult. **Views** of the lake and shore alternate with areas through the ridges' pine and oak.

The 3-mile **Blind Sucker Pathway** lets hikers make a **7.6 mile loop.** The path uses an old railroad grade, not especially scenic, that parallels the Blind Sucker Flooding and connects Blind Sucker Camp grounds #1 and #2 with the Lake Superior Campground and **beach.**

Trailheads are east of Grand Marais along H-58, in the Lake Superior State Forest Campground, Muskallonge Lake State Park, and Two Hearted River Mouth State Forest Campground. Look for the blue and gold compass shield. (906) 293-5131. Free. &: no.

Lake Superior Campground beach

Here, part of the **Lake Superior State Forest**, is convenient access to a beautiful **agate beach**, not overused, that's not just rocks but sand, too. On the North Country Trail segment that makes a 7.6-mile loop with the Blind Sucker Pathway (see above).
Just off H-58 12 miles east of Grand Marais or 7 miles west of Deer Park. (906) 293-5131. &: vault toilets, tables & fire rings. No fee for day use.

Blind Sucker Flooding canoeing & fishing

A small **boat launch** by the Blind Sucker #2 campground (part of the **Lake Superior State Forest**, like all this area) lets canoeists put in. They can explore the river flooding, pass **bass fishing** stumps, and get out on its south side to **pick blueberries** on exposed sand ridges. There are six miles of good, easy **canoeing** from the short river's mouth to its source in a marsh to the west. The flooding was created years ago as habitat for Canada geese. When they're migrating in May and September, the area is alive with activity. **Fall color** is good, too. **Swimming** in the river is possible here, though there's no real beach area. **Fishing** for pike and yellow perch is excellent. Bluegill and rock bass are also in these waters. Nearby Blind Sucker Campground #1, by the dam, has more sun and a bigger swimming area.

Just south of H-58, 13 miles west of Grand Marais and 7 miles east of Deer Park. (906) 293-5131. Free. &.

Muskallonge Lake State Park

Here a developed **swimming beach** on a **warmer-water inland lake** is just a quarter mile from a **beautiful Lake Superior beach** where some pebbles may be agates. But the 191-site modern campground and large areas of lawn lend an oddly suburban look to this remote area. Turn into the campground drive to reach the Muskallonge Lake beach. Lake Superior can be reached from a stairway that leads down from H-58 to the beach. Resorts outside the park rent boats and motors. The best **fishing** is for pike and walleye, with perch providing a good fishery for kids. There's more to this park than meets the eye. Pick up a map and ask about Cranberry Lake, **Trout Creek**, and other parks of the park.
18 miles east of Grand Marais on H-58 (gravel), or 23 miles north of Newberry via M-123 and H-37. (906) 658-3338. State park sticker required: $4/$5 a day or $20/$25 a year. &: in process. Call.

Pretty Lakes Quiet Area path and canoeing

This area, part of the **Lake Superior State Forest**, rates very, very high as an ideal camping and day-use activity loca-

Earl lumbermen expected Michigan's vast white pine forests to last 500 years. Instead, they were gone in half a century because of three technological innovations: the big wheel, an improved saw, and flexible narrow-gauge railroads, which permitted year-round logging. (Before that, winter snows enabled sleds to move logs out of the woods to rivers for spring river drives.) This photo, circa 1900, shows Newberry lumberman D. N. McLeod's Blind Sucker RR east of Grand Marais. Pine logs were hewn and squared off in the woods. "Waney pine" logs were hewn leaving rounded corners, allowing for more saleable timber from each tree.

tion, in the opinion of one experienced outdoorsman with high aesthetic standards. Five small lakes are linked by **canoe portages** which stand out clearly as pathway openings. A short (about 2/3 mile) hiking path connects three of the lakes. **Canoe campsites** are at every portage and one other location, and an 18-unit rustic campground is at Pretty Lake.

From H37/CR 407 about 5 miles south of Deer Park or 23 miles northwest of Newberry, take CR 416 about 3 miles west to campground road. (906) 293-5131. No fee for day use. &: main campground.

Deer Park Camping

LAKE SUPERIOR Campground/ Lake Superior State Forest

(906) 293-5131. No reservations.

This attractive rustic campground (no showers or electricity) offers convenient access to a beautiful **agate beach**, not overused, made of rocks and sand. The campground is some 300 feet from the beach, separated by low **dunes** forested with oak and pine. They help shield the campsites from a wind off the lake that can be very, very cold indeed. It's a direct walk from most of the 18 shady campsites to the beach. Some sites are perched up on the hillside. It can be cold here on a day where motorists a few miles inland turn on the air-conditioner. *On the North Country Trail segment that makes a 7.6-mile loop with the Blind Sucker Pathway. Road noise can be heard from nearby H-58. Just off H-58 12 miles east of Grand Marais or 7 miles west of Deer Park. Serviced May thru Nov. $6/$10 night.*

H.A.: tables, fire rings, vault toilets.

BLIND SUCKER #2 Campground / Lake Superior State Forest

(906) 293-5131. Not reservable.

This 32-site rustic campground is desirable because of its shady, scenic setting along the flooding of the Blind Sucker River, close to Lake Superior but away from its often cold winds. A small **boat launch** lets canoeists put in to explore the river flooding, pass bass fishing stumps, and get out on the river's south side to pick **blueberries** on exposed sand ridges. **Swimming** in the river is possible, though there's no real beach area. About 20 sites are on the river. **Fishing** is for pike, bass, and perch. Nearby Blind Sucker Campground #1, by the dam, is more open and less scenic. *Just south of H-58, 13 miles west of Grand*

Pretty Lakes Quiet Area
A delightful place to camp, canoe, fish & hike — just 10 miles from Lake Superior.

Marais and 7 miles east of Deer Park. Serviced May thru Nov. $6/$9 night.

H.A.: ADA accessible.

MUSKALLONGE LAKE State Park

(906) 658-3338. Reserv.: (800) 44-PARKS; (800) 605-8295 TDD; www.dnr.state.mi.us/

171 modern campsites (with all the amenities: hot showers, electricity, playground, etc.) are in a surprisingly suburban setting, with lawns and planted trees. A few sites look out into 217-acre **Muskallonge Lake**, while others are near the cove with the **swimming beach**. A 1.5-mile **trail loop** goes from the campground along Lake Superior and back, connecting with a beautiful stretch of the **North Country Trail**. Reserve by mid-May for a good selection of summer dates. *18 miles east of Grand Marais on H-58 (gravel), or 23 miles north of Newberry via M-123 and H-37. State park sticker required: $4/$5 day or $20/$25 year. Open from mid-April to first snow, usually mid-Nov. Before May 15 and after Oct. 15 it is semi-modern (bathhouse is closed).* **H.A.:** call. ADA accessible new building to be completed by summer 2002, it is hoped.

PRETTY LAKE Campground/ Lake Superior State Forest

(906) 293-5131. Not reservable.

Of all the fine rustic state forest campgrounds on inland lakes in northern Luce County, Pretty Lake stands out. It

enjoys an especially beautiful, serene setting in a mature pine and hardwood forest on Pretty Lake, with its sandy **beach**. It's especially beautiful in **fall color** season. The 18 rustic campsites (no running water or electricity) are very secluded, and over half are on the lakeshore. There's usually a **campground host** in summer. A large, open area is for group campfires. Pretty Lake is a **quiet area** — canoes only, no motors. It's planted with brown trout. **Five small lakes** are linked by short canoe portages. Clusters of three canoe campsites are at every portage and one other location on Beaver House Lake. **Lake Superior** at Deer Park is under 10 miles away, with pristine, secluded public lakeshore close at hand. No wonder the campground often fills up in summer. More spots open up Tuesday through Thursday. Availability is good in September, and fall fishing and duck hunting is excellent. *From H-37/CR 407 about 5 miles south of Deer Park or 23 miles northwest of Newberry, take CR 416 about 3 miles west to campground road. Serviced May thru Nov. $6/$10 night.* **H.A.:** ADA accessible.

Between the Tahquamenon and Two Heart River mouth

The interior north of Newberry and the much-visited Tahquamenon Falls is

some of the Upper Peninsula's most remote land. Mixed forests of maple, birch, and conifers, and many wetlands make for outstanding **fall color**. Most land is part of the **Lake Superior State Forest**, and loggers are active in some areas. Of the scattered sawmill villages established during the bygone lumber era, none has developed into a permanent community.

The western part of this area is drained by the four branches of the **Two Hearted River**, made famous by Ernest Hemingway, who appropriated its poetic name for his short story about fishing on the Fox. Totaling over a hundred miles, the **Two Hearted** is a designated **wilderness river** under the state's Natural Rivers Program, which defines a wilderness river as "a free-flowing river, with essentially primitive, undeveloped adjacent lands." Reliable water levels and **fishing** for steelhead and trout make it popular enough as a **canoeing stream** to warrant a canoe livery/campground/motel at its mouth.

The area east of the Two Hearted is largely drained by the **Shelldrake River**, which empties into Whitefish Bay north of Paradise. This land includes the extensive, wild portion of **Tahquamenon Falls State Park**. For poetic descriptions of the remote Lake Superior shoreline and vicinity, read the Penroses' *Guide to Michigan Lighthouses* on the Crisp Point Lighthouse and naturalist Jim Rooks on the Michigan Nature Association's Lake Superior Sanctuary. This part of the shore is prime **agate-hunting** territory, too. See the Grand Marais section for pointers on finding them.

The land here is low. Small **sand dunes** are along the Lake Superior shoreline and forests, marshes, bogs, and swamps in the interior. Much of the land is open to the public for hunting, fishing, and recreational use, as state land that's part of the state park or the **Lake Superior State Forest**. The State Forest has three campgrounds along the Two Hearted, and three on nearby lakes. Some remote and rather rough sections of the **North Country Trail** pass through here. The trail is less difficult near the lakeshore from Grand Marais and Deer Park to just east of the Two Hearted's mouth. Then it turns south and heads for Tahquamenon Falls, going through some challenging areas. Visit **www.northcountrytrail.org** for tips and some recent details. There's an amusing account by two determined women who, when the trail was less clearly marked than now, hiked for many miles before finding themselves on the private side of a gate.

The Two Hearted River's poetic name

derives not from a personality of changing moods but from the more mundane circumstance of the river's configuration. For four miles or so its North Branch and West Branch run parallel, a short distance from each other. An 1884 gazetteer called it "the Double Hearted (or Twin) River," but the Two Hearted name soon came into general use.

Mouth of the Two Hearted River

Fishermen flock here and fill the campground, part of the **Lake Superior State Forest**, from April through fall, with a lull in July. Opening week of the trout season in April is crazy, no matter how much snow remains. **Fishing** in the lake is for steelhead, salmon, and menominee. The entry road leads to a parking lot by the simple dirt **boat launch**. West of the lot is a campground and a footpath to a nifty **swinging suspension bridge** across the river mouth leading out to a scenic little point in Lake Superior. There's **canoeing** on the river and hunting not only for agates but for flat, dark stones prized for water gardens.

From Newberry, take M-123 19 miles northeast to CR 500. In about 7 miles, turn left onto CR 414. Follow signs to the nearby Rainbow Lodge and the campground, over various turning gravel roads for 12 or so miles. (906) 293-3293. &: campground facilities.

Canoeing and fishing the Two Hearted River

The entire Two Hearted River is a trout stream. Most of it can be fly fished. Fishing pressure, generally low to moderate, is highest at the Reed & Green Bridge and at the river mouth in spring and fall. Tom Huggler's large-format *Fish 50 Michigan Rivers* details fishing opportunities on all the Two Hearted's branches. As of spring 2001 there's no guide service to the river. **TWO HEARTED CANOE TRIPS** at **Rainbow Lodge** (658-3357) offers up-to-date fishing tips and complete **spotting service** on all river branches from its Rainbow Lodge. It has several **canoe trips**. A very popular and easy **half-day trip** from the Reed & Green Bridge State Forest Campground to the river mouth is around $32, and a longer **two- or three-day trip** from High

Bridge Campground is around $62 to $95. On the longer trip, fallen trees present problems for less experienced paddlers. For families with small children, there's a **1 1/2 hour** trip to the river mouth ($27). The half-day trip combines the virtues of family canoeing in an area that's largely wilderness, except for a few cabins.

"The river is 35-45 feet wide, and depth is two to four feet over a bottom of gravel and scattered large rocks or sand," writes Jerry Dennis in *Canoeing Michigan Rivers*. "Low hills of oaks, birch, pines, and spruce rise away from the river's occasionally short, steep banks. . . . Toward the end of this section, dunes appear. The Lake Superior surf can be heard long before the end of the river. . . . Numerous **sandbars** make convenient resting and picnic stops."

"Basic paddling skills are sufficient to handle any of the Two Hearted's light riffles, except in early spring when extremely high water creates hazards," Dennis says. "Early and midsummer plagues of black flies are legendary and should be prepared for."

Directions to Two Hearted Canoe Trips (**www.exploringthenorth.com/newberry/rainbowlodge**): *From Newberry, take M-123 19 miles northeast to CR 500. In about 7 miles, turn left onto CR 414. Follow signs to Rainbow Lodge.*

Crisp Point Lighthouse

This handsome, tall (58'), rounded brick tower was built in 1902 because, says lighthouse historian Charles Hyde, "many vessels heading for Whitefish Point had deviated slightly from their course and were wrecked at Crisp Point." Crisp Point, really just a slight bulge on a map, is **on a remote stretch** of **Lake Superior**, between the virtual ghost towns of Vermilion and Two Heart, and about eight miles from each. Today an automated light makes use of the tower. The tower is all that remains of the light station complex.

"Because of its isolation and difficult access," wrote the Penroses in *A Traveler's Guide to 116 Michigan Lighthouses*, "this lighthouse is rarely visited, and you will probably have the beautiful area entirely to yourself. . . . The sandy shoreline is unbroken — no houses, harbors or docks — in both directions as far as they eye can see. A dark line of forest follows the strip of sand; beach grasses and low bushes provide other greenery; and the beach is littered with gnarled **driftwood**."

Today it has become easier to visit

the lighthouse, thanks to Luce County's improvements to the seasonal road. The Crisp Point Light Historical Society, led by Nellie Ross of Paradise, has tackled the preservation problem on every level, starting with sandbags to stabilize the shoreline at this exposed point. The society received the *Lake Superior Magazine*'s 2000 Achievement Award. "Using a potent mixture of elbow grease, determination, and partnerships, society members have created a model for how to save the aging towers that once guided our inland seafarers," said the magazine's editor, Paul Hayden.

The society's efforts are detailed on www.crisppointlight.org, its extensive website. Click on "history" for many interesting historical photos documenting the light tower and its battle with the elements.

About 8 miles east of Culhane Lake Campground and thus some 37 miles northeast of Newberry. Access roads are seasonal and open only from approximately mid May to mid October. Do not attempt to go here other times. You may get stuck and need a wrecker to get out! If in doubt about road conditions, call Rainbow Lodge, (906) 658-3357. Directions: from M-123, take County Road 500 all the way to Little Lake Harbor. Take CR 412 right (east) and pay close attention to CR 412 signs to stay on the right road. In 4 1/2 miles, CR 412 turns north. After that, the last 2 1/2 miles have been widened and improved with gravel.

Two Hearted Lodgings & Camping

Tip: Showers ($2) at Rainbow Lodge are available to all.

RAINBOW LODGE (658-3357; www. exploringthenorth.com/newberry/rainbowlodge

In this remote area Richard and Kathy Robinson's place has grown from a spring and fall fishing retreat into a big, year-round place catering to campers, snowmobilers, hunters, anglers, and rockhounds. *Only in snowmobile season* the Two Hearted Café offers breakfast and lunch (chili, burgers, pies, soups — all homemade) daily. The **grocery store** supplies campers with groceries, alcoholic beverages to take out, camping supplies, tackle and bait. There are two motel rooms and four housekeeping cabins ($42-$95, depending on size). The 45-site **primitive campground** next to a grass airstrip costs the same as the state forest campgrounds. **Showers** ($2) are available to campers and non-campers

alike. This is not an old, picturesque lodge nestled in a mature forest. Built in 1967, it's in a jack pine forest. *From Newberry, take M-123 19 miles northeast to CR 500. In about 7 miles, turn left onto CR 414. Follow signs to Rainbow Lodge.* **H.A.**: 1 cabin accessible. Call on others.

RAINBOW LODGE (906) 58-3357; www.exploringthenorth.com/newberry/ rainbowlodge

45-site primitive campground. *See above.*

MOUTH OF THE TWO HEARTED RIVER/Lake Superior State Forest
(906) 293-5131. Not reservable.

Fishermen fill this remote campground from April through fall, with a lull in July. Snow is bulldozed off the campground for the crazy, intense opening week of the trout season. The entry road leads to a parking lot by the simple dirt boat launch. The 39 rustic sites (no running water or electricity) are in two loops. The smaller loop, west of the lot, is more open. Here the attraction is a swinging suspension bridge across the river mouth leading out to a scenic little point in Lake Superior. Over half the sites are east of the lot, in a grove of red pine separated from the lake by a wall of cedars and pines, which protect it from winds. There's canoeing on the river, and rock-hunting. *From Newberry, take M-123 19 miles northeast to CR 500. In about 7 miles, turn left onto CR 414. Follow signs to the nearby Rainbow Lodge and the campground, over various turning gravel roads for 12 or so miles. Serviced May thru Nov. $6/$10 night.* **H.A.**: ADA accessible.

CULHANE LAKE Campground/ BODI LAKE Campground Lake Superior State Forest
(906) 293-5131. No reservations.

These are for people who like to be away from it all in a wild, unspoiled natural area within two miles of a beautiful, remote, and little-known stretch of Lake Superior. The 22-site campground on 60-acre **Culhane Lake** is in a stand of very large pines. The nearby **Bodi Lake Campground** has 20 sites in a stand of mature pines and oaks. Fishing in both lakes is for panfish. A 1.25 mile **hiking trail** loops by Bodi Lake and over a bog. The Crisp Point Light is within 10 miles, and it's a 17-mile day trip to Tahquamenon Falls. Other area attractions: shipwrecks, agate-hunting, blueberry-picking. Both campgrounds are well shaded in red pine and maple. Sites

enjoy good privacy from neighbors, and still aren't too heavily used because of their remoteness. Half are on the water. *Culhane Lake is about 3 miles east of the mouth of the Two-Heart (via unimproved roads) and 30 miles northeast of Newberry. From Newberry, take M-123 19 miles northeast to CR 500, which twists and turns over 11 miles to Culhane Lake. Bodi Lake is about 2 miles farther, on CR 437. Serviced May thru Nov. $6/$9 night.* **H.A.**: call.

McMillan

At the south edge of the timber-rich swampy headwaters of the Tahquamenon River, McMillan sprang up as the Duluth, South Shore, & Atlantic Railroad was beingconstructed here in 1881.

McMillan Restaurant
See Curtis/Helmer for a description of the **Triangle Restaurant.**

Newberry (pop. 2,686)

This old lumber town, the only town of any size in Luce County, was processing lumber from surrounding camps as early as the Civil War. Unlike lumber boom towns like Flint, Saginaw, Muskegon, or Menominee/Marinette, Newberry did not have the resources to to develop into a manufacturing center, though a state mental hospital, aggressively sought by local civic leaders, created steady employment through much of the 20th century. The variety of tree species in the Tahquamenon basin did enable the local forest products industry to survive into the present day.

Newberry village was founded by some of the men who had built a railroad in the 1870s from St. Ignace to the Marquette Iron Range. It connected with the Lower Peninsula railroad being built north up to the Straits of Mackinac. These investors, from Detroit and the East, established the Vulcan Furnace Company, akin to the operation at the much-visited Fayette State Historic Park, to make charcoal iron. Vice-president John S. Newberry named the main streets after family members (Newberry, Truman, Helen, Parmalee, John, etc.) none of whom ever lived here. Rising Republican politicians Truman Newberry and James McMillan, soon to become U.S. Senators, were honored with especially prominent streets. The charcoal iron plant lasted until 1945.

Newberry's low point occurred in 1990 when the sprawling **state mental hospital** south of downtown, which at its peak housed some 1,800 patients, was shut down. The stately, impressive Georgian-style campus of cottages and a receiving hospital covered 900 park-like acres on M-123 on the south side of town. At that time, "you could stand on our main street, throw a rock, and not have a chance of hitting a soul," says one longtime resident.

The economic blow after the psychiatric hospital closed was greatly softened when in 1995 the west part of the hospital site was used to build the **Newberry Correctional Facility,** a medium-security state prison. The facility houses 930 prisoners and has a staff of over 300, adding $28 million a year to the local economy. Rolls of glinting silver razor wire top the prison's 16-foot perimeter fences, creating a less than heartwarming visual entrance into town. Opened in 1996, the prison has been one of Newberry's few economic boosts in recent decades. Another is the impressive **Louisiana Pacific** plant just southeast of town. Using state-of-the-art pollution controls, the plant's 125 employees make 100 million board feet a day of exterior siding out of Canadian aspen. Finally, the surge in snowmobiling has turned the winter doldrums here into a beehive of activity, with many motels filled to capacity on weekends.

In a county without a stoplight (Luce County has only 7.7 people per square mile; only Keweenaw has less), Newberry is the only place you'll find a Pizza Hut or fast-food restaurant between Sault Ste. Marie on the east and Manistique or Munising on the west. It has become the principal lodging center serving Tahquamenon Falls, which draws up to 750,000 visitors a year. Downtown Newberry also has a few interesting **antique shops** and a **Country Gallery**, a big multifaceted gift shop. **Doc's Place**, a coffeehouse with desserts and antiques, was started by the dentist next door.

Luce County Historical Museum

The 1894 **sheriff's house and jail** that houses the museum looks like a lumber baron's mansion. Its many stone arches, its turrets, its **stained glass windows**, and the rich textures of pressed brick, red sandstone, and shingles make for a lively composition in the Queen Anne style. The building is worth a visit in its own right. Despite some later wallpaper, it's pretty much intact, with its original parlors, kitchen, dining room, and bedrooms — and original jail cells, too.

In the 1970s, when modernizers sought to replace the entire courthouse complex, the newly formed historical society managed to save the grand sheriff's residence but not the courthouse, which also resembled an overgrown Queen Anne mansion. The iron fountain with a crane was part of the courthouse's park-like grounds.

For kids, the museum highlight is the sparsely furnished jail cell, a grim place clad in iron — the perfect place to take a photo of dad. Other highlights of this unpretentious museum of the Luce County Historical Society depend on the visitors' interests. There's a lot here, usually without much in the way of captions or interpretation, but if you ask, you'll get the story behind the objects — or the town. Some people like the details of home life: how the cream separator and the butter churn worked, how irons were heated, how the ice box was drained, items in the country store, toys kids played with, quilts made from recycled fabric, the collars and buckles women used to make old dresses look new. Collections are here and there: bottles, fans, a striking **hat collection**, African artifacts, and Swedish and Indian baskets.

Some rooms have approximate period furnishings. Others are more archival storage areas with photographs, maps, books, scrapbooks, yearbooks, and the archives of the late Charles Sprague Taylor, who loved the area's woods and rivers and history. Here are transcripts of his many interviews.

Maps locate the important **archaeological sites** located by Taylor with University of Michigan archaeologists in the 1960s near **Naomikong Point**, based on pottery fragments and points washed up in Whitefish Bay and found by Taylor and his son. The site proved to be one of the most significant of the **Middle Woodland Period** of Upper Great Lakes Culture between 200 B.C. and 800 A.D. If your guide is his widow, Carol Taylor, you can hear this exciting story first-hand and gain a knowledgeable perspective on the lumber era, too.

411 W. Harrie St. at Court, 4 blocks west of M-123/Newberry Ave. and a block north of McMillan. 293-5946. Open from July 4 weekend thru Labor Day, Tues, Wed & Thurs 2-4 or by appointment. Free admission; donations appreciated. &

Canoeing the Tahquamenon

The only canoe livery on the Tahquamenon, **Mark's Rod & Reel Repair** and **Canoe Livery,** offers very beautiful **two-hour paddles** from the Dollarville Dam (west of town) east to the Tahquamenon River Logging Museum in Newberry. **Longer trips** go farther down the river into the gorgeous, wild country below the dam. It's a four-day or so trip to the falls, with camping anywhere you can find a clear spot. This is **easy, flat water, with no portaging**, well suited to beginners with good camping skills. Cost: $25 (slightly higher for distant points) for spotting (that is, taking you and your canoe to the put-in point) plus $20/day canoe rental fee. Mark Yeadon doesn't rent canoes when the water's so high that the river channel can't be seen. There's **good fishing** for pike, muskie, walleye, and panfish. At the livery, **bows** and **bow repair** are also available. **Bicycle repair** is a new addition. Mark is happy to direct cyclists to lightly traveled roads.

The generally placid Tahquamenon doesn't make for exciting canoeing. But it does inspire rhapsodies among people who grew up fishing and hunting along it. In *Tahquamenon Country: A Look at Its Past*, for instance, Sprague Taylor wrote about its wilderness character and its contrasts. "For a hundred miles. . . , it flows through plains and heavy timber, marshy flats and thickets. It is a river given to the woods, yet where the plow has made brief contact near its banks, the scene is almost pastoral."

Mark's Canoe Livery is just north of Newberry, at M-123 and CR 462. (906) 293-5608. www.exploringthenorth.com/ Open year-round. Opens daily at 8 a.m. in summer. Stays open to 5 at least.

Tahquamenon Logging Museum and Nature Study Area

Unassumingly housed in an old farmstead, this grassroots local museum is a real treasure. The **local history displays** in the onetime farmhouse are excellent. An interesting **interpretive nature trail** leads back through a woods and swamp to a scenic **Tahquamenon River overlook**. It gives a remarkably clear explanation of northwoods tree species. If you can see the top-notch **logging video** done by Wendell Hoover, Hartwick Pines' former logging historian, you'll gain a new appreciation of the social history of logging and the lives of shanty boys.

In Newberry's Tahquamenon Logging Museum, lumber camp life is illuminated. This photo shows some of the crew at Robert Nelson's camp near Whitefish Bay around 1905. Many Michiganders can trace their ancestors or their fortunes to northwoods timber. A century ago the investment capital for Detroit's fledgling auto companies largely came from lumber.

Some things here aren't so interesting. The displays of tools and equipment can be tiresome without vitalizing ideas or stories. Fortunately, however, this museum is one where the volunteers — mostly retirees from some aspect of the logging business —have been part of the story. "They're up on everything," says museum member Gus Walker.

New areas are being added all the time: a restored log house, circa 1880-1900; a building with artifacts from CCC days (the **Civilian Conservation Corps**, a Depression make-work project); and a stationery sawmill that should be operating by midsummer, 2001.

Lively **old-time festivals** are held on the fourth weekends of June (**Polka Festival**), July (**Old Time Music Jamboree**) and August (Lumberjack Days). All feature logging contests and Saturday breakfasts at the cook shack. At all events, the music starts about noon and lasts until everyone gets tired.

On M-123 at Tahquamenon River, 1 1/2 miles north of Newberry. (906) 293-3700. Open 9-5 daily from Memorial thru Labor Day. $3/adults, $1.50/kids 6-12, 5 and under free. &: museum buildings and the trail up to the river.

NEWBERRY RESTAURANTS

TIMBER CHARLIE'S FOOD 'n' SPIRITS a quite popular spot, consistently recommended. It has evolved from a bar and grill into a full-service restaurant with a big menu ranging from steaks and lobster to Italian, Mexican, pasties, whitefish battered or broiled, and meal-size salads. Knotty pine walls, a terrazzo floor, ruffled curtains, and mounted animal heads give the place its old-timey character, carried over by a menu with a lumberjack's glossary of food terms (Irish apples are potatoes, biscuit shooter for waitress). Now there's a Timber Charlie's gift shop, too. The restaurant is known for BBQ baby-back ribs ($11 and $14 at dinner in 2000). Dinners ($8 to $18) include potato, and salad. Soups are a specialty: four a day, always including French onion and a tasty, meaty vegetable beef soup. $2.65 buys a crock of soup, along with a roll, crackers, and a pickle — enough for a meal. The $5 grilled chicken salad is also good. *110 Newberry Ave./M-123 at the north end of downtown, by the tracks. 293-3363. Open Mon-Sat 10:30 to 9 at least, to 10 or 11 weekends. Sun opens at noon.* &.

ZELLAR'S VILLAGE INN is Newberry's other popular restaurant, a place that does everything from hearty breakfasts to Mexican, hot dogs to prime rib, homemade pies and pizza, buffets, and dancing with DJs and occasional live music in its lounge. Daily lunch specials are $5. Daily dinner specials are currently pork chops (Mon.), spaghetti (Wed.), liver and onions (Thurs.), fresh fish (Fri.) and prime rib (Sat.). Breakfast buffet on weekends. Dinner entrées are $7 to $16, with Friday fish fry ($10) with fresh fish when available and Saturday prime rib ($11). There's a veggie burger and omelets for vegetarians. *Connected with the Best Western on the east side of South M-123 at the bottom of the hill from M-28. 293-5114. Open daily 6 a.m. to 10 p.m.* & 👫👫 Full bar

In addition to very good pizza, **PIZZA PLACE** has a spiffy eat-in dining area and **patio** that take advantage of the good hillcrest view. Among the specialty pizzas, the chicken fajita with roasted peppers, onions, bacon, and olives is a standout. Non-pizza menu items include chicken strips and subs. Delivery available. *On the west side of M-123/S. Newberry Ave. as it enters town from the south. It sits back from the road up on a hill. Look for the penguin on the sign. 293-5551. Open daily, year-round, 11 a.m. to 11 p.m.* & 👫👫

A popular local institution is the **Friday night all-you-can-eat fish fry** at the **ELKS' CLUB**, with whitefish and menominee dinners. *It's downtown at 109 Newberry Ave./M-123, across the street from Timber Charlie's. 293-8321. The fish fry starts at 4:30 and lasts until 8 or so.*

NEWBERRY LODGINGS

Newberry is 25 miles from Tahquamenon Falls. It makes a convenient hub for day trips through the wilderness on the Toonerville Trolley, to Seney National Wildlife Refuge, the Two Hearted River Mouth, and the Grand Marais end of Pictured Rocks. As the area's only town, it offers way more services (groceries, late dinners, laundry) than other area lodging choices. For other lodging options, see Paradise, Hulbert, Trout Lake, and Brimley.

Motels are arranged from in-town to beyond.

ZELLAR'S VILLAGE INN
(906) 293-5114

For people who want everything under one roof — a competent restaurant, **Z's Lounge** with **dancing** on weekends, darts, and pool, and a motel — this popular local gathering place is the right choice. There's no indoor pool, but guests can use the **indoor pool** at the adjacent Super 8 when it is finished in late 2001. The motel has 20 units plus two duplexes on one floor. Rooms are pleasant and up to date, with cable TV, phones. If quiet means a lot, ask for rooms away from Z's Lounge, especially on Wednesday (karaoke night) and weekends. There's room in back to walk dogs. Not far from the in-town street system, a plus for walkers and joggers. *On M-123 at the south edge of town.*

H.A.: some ADA accessible rooms 🧍🧍: under 16 free 🐕: $10

SUPER 8 of NEWBERRY Opening winter 2001-2; call Zellar's (906) 293-5114

The Zellars, who own Zellar's Village Inn, are building a 40-room Super 8 with indoor pool next to their existing motel, restaurant, and lounge with entertainment. It will have four Jacuzzi units. Rates and such have not been determined as we go to press.

GATEWAY MOTEL (906) 293-5651; exploringthenorth.com/gateway/motel/html

Each of the 11 pleasant rooms in this single-story motel is individually furnished with books to read, a rocking chair, and prints and paintings of natural subjects. The exterior is adorned with wood carvings: largemouth bass, eagle with fish, snowmobiler, hummingbird, logging truck, and more. Rooms have cable TV and either one queen ($52 for two in season) or two queens ($62). Ask about low off-season rates. *On west side of M-123, 1/4 mile south of Newberry.*

H.A.: call 🧍🧍: under 12 free; $4/extra person 🐕: call

BEST WESTERN NEWBERRY
(formerly Days Inn)   (906) 293-4000

Newberry's biggest (66 rooms on 2 stories) hotel is, as we go to press, the only one with an **indoor pool**, plus sauna and whirlpool. (The new Super 8 will also have an indoor pool.) Rooms have either queen or king beds, cable TV, phones. Summer rates: $88 standard, $146 for a one-bedroom room suite with microwave, refrigerator, cooktop (sleeps 4), $161 for a two-bedroom suite that sleeps 6. Off-season rates are substantially less. Small free continental breakfast. *South of Newberry on M-28 a mile east of M-123.*

H.A.: some rooms ADA accessible 🧍🧍: 12 & under free

The MacLEOD HOUSE
Bed & Breakfast   (906) 293-3841; www.macleodhouse.com; e-mail: fcicala@up.net

When a bank expansion threatened to destroy one of Newberry's real lumber baron mansions, Cheryl and Frank Cicala moved it out to a pretty rural location not far from town, restored it, and fashioned a third-floor apartment for themselves.

The 1895 house has the big front porch that's a hallmark of the Queen Anne style. Interior period details are in excellent condition: parquet floors in four woods, paneling in the parlor and stair hall, fireplace and mantel. Appropriately **Victorian furniture**, lighting, china, and window treatments — and a parlor organ, that workhorse of bourgeois culture in isolated areas — create a **convincing turn-back-the-clock effect.** Three attractive guest rooms, shown on the website, are all on the second floor. 2001 rates: $69 to $95, depending on the room. Two side porches and a deck are outdoor sitting areas with pleasant rural views. A full breakfast is served. *On CR 441 southwest of Newberry but north of M-28.*

H.A.: no   🧍🧍

HALFWAY LAKE RESORT
(906) 658-3579; www.explor ingthenorth/halfwayresort

Eight new housekeeping cabins and a private, 64-acre spring-fed lake make this 400-acre resort quite unusual. No gasoline motors or outside boats are allowed on **pristine Halfway Lak**e, surrounded by hardwoods, to avoid introducing weeds, exotic species, and pollution. Quiet reigns; loons nest on the lake. A fishing boat comes with each cabin, and electric motors can be rented

to use on the lake. Pike and perch reproduce naturally; walleye and trout are stocked. Guests are welcome to catch dinner, but otherwise it's catch-and-release except for trophy fish. No fishing license is necessary. Lake Superior at Deer Park is 12 miles away.

All cabins have two bedrooms; seven have lake views from their picture windows. Each has a TV with 2-3 channels in summer, 5 in winter. The covered porches are too small for more than one chair. Cabins sleep up to 8. Rates start at $100/day in season, $75 otherwise, or $650/week for parents and their children under 16.

Reservations in prime time are for minimums of Saturday thru Monday or Wednesday thru Friday. Ask about **delux cabins** with gas fireplaces. There's a small **sand beach** for swimming. By the road away from the cabins are a **game room** with **sauna** and **hot tub**, volleyball, basketball, and horseshoe pits. It's an easy mile to a snowmobile trail. *12 miles north of Newberry on CR 407. Turn west at Four Mile Corner.*

H.A.: call   🧍🧍: 16 & under free with parents   🐕: call

Soo Junction

This tiny hamlet in a low, wet cutover setting was once important as the junction of a logging railroad with the old Duluth, South Shore and Atlantic Railroad, known as the Soo Line. The Toonerville Trolley is run by a descendant of the original lumberman who started the rail line. It takes the same route through the forest (now regrown) to the river.

Toonerville Trolley and Riverboat Trip

Taking a trip through a real **wilderness** by train, and perhaps also by boat, is as much the point of this longtime excursion as getting to the **Upper Falls of the Tahquamenon**, the destination of the all-day train-riverboat trip. Passengers often see wildlife — not just deer but sometimes **bears** in their natural habitat, and eagles and sandhill cranes. Serious **bird-watching** is possible on the river cruise. For **rail fans**, the 24" **narrow-gauge track**, one of the longest stretches in the U.S., is an attraction in itself. It's now possible to do just the train trip, in 1 3/4 hours, though we'd recommend the relaxing all-day trip if you have the time. It's a good choice if you're stuck in the area on **rainy day**, though days when the sunshine sparkles on the water would be nicest of all, especially in **fall color** season.

Lumberman Robert Hunter (great-grandfather of Kris Stewart, who today owns and runs Toonerville Trolley with his wife, Dixie) put in the rail line, originally standard gauge, from his river sawmill, by today's boat dock, to the Soo main line at Soo Junction, where the train trip begins. By 1927 the trees were logged over but no road had been built to the falls. A retired conservation officer in the area teamed up with Hunter to offer this very sightseeing trip after receiving frequent calls from downstate dignitaries wanting to view the falls. At first Hunter rigged up a model T Ford as a makeshift rail runner. The Toonerville Trolley proved such a success that in 1933 Hunter needed a longer train. He purchased equipment from the narrow-gauge mining and logging rail lines then going out of business and switched to narrow-gauge track. Recently the Stewarts bought the boat and the business of the other Tahquamenon boat cruise company.

A five-ton diesel engine, originally used in mines, pulls the train through an interesting mix of northwoods habitats: spruce (both scrubby and majestic), tamarack, and birch and young maples. It's a bumpy, noisy ride (just like an old-time railroad), 35 minutes each way. Passengers are handed a tree guide with numbers corresponding to numbers marked on trees they pass. The river part of the trip (4 hours altogether) passes mature second-growth forests and a few cottages; the wide river is the main attraction. The 250-passenger, double-deck riverboat is quiet, without disturbing vibrations. It's easy to hear the knowledgeable narrator/pilot, a longtime local resident who's good at wildlife identification. He highlights local **Ojibwa lore**, the history of **Tahquamenon logging**, and, above all, nature and wildlife. There's food and bar service; the grilled hamburgers are excellent. The atmosphere on this leisurely cruise is congenial. You may learn a lot of Michigan history from the mostly older crowd.

The boat docks quite a ways upstream from the falls. A 5/8-mile **nature path** goes through a beautiful old conifer forest and looks down on the river. This walk goes up and down through the forest before visitors descend down stairways along a dramatic sheer cliff to the falls overlook platform. Roots and other irregularities have been smoothed over on three-fourths of the pathway.

However, tour-goers with problems in walking, breathing and heart functions are advised to stay behind in the boat. This view, from the south side of the Upper Falls, is less complete or dramatic than that from the state park on the river's north side. That's a minus. A plus is approaching the falls by foot, having experienced the river in its placid state.

Here's the schedule for the **all -day train/boat trip** in 2001. *June 15-30:* Monday-Thursday only. *July 1-August 24:* daily except Sunday. *August 25-October 6:* Friday-Sunday. Cost: $25/adult, $12 ages 6 to 15; under 6 free. Train leaves at 10:30 a.m. Come by 10 or so to be sure of a seat. 2001 schedule for the **train ride only**: June 15-30: Friday-Sunday. July 1-August 24: Tuesday thru Sunday. August 25-October 6: Mon-Thurs. There's a short stopover at the landing, with the second boat available for restrooms and food service. Train-only tours depart at noon. Come earlier to be sure of a seat.

Train leaves Soo Junction (about 2 miles north of M-28 and 12 miles east of Newberry). Big signs on M-28 mark the turnoff. Operates daily, approximately June 15-October 6. (888) 7-TRAIN (year-round); (906) 876-2311; (906) 293-3806 (winter). Reservations recommended for holiday weekends. $18/adult, $9 children 6-15. Under 6 free. &: no, but help is available to climb in and out of train cars and boat, which can't accommodate wheelchairs. Boat trip need not involve steps. Walk to falls is not accessible.

Hulbert

Being near an established area of vacation homes and some small resorts has helped make Hulbert more attractive than many similar old logging villages. Worth a look is the **Hulbert Methodist Chapel**, an ingenious combination community hall and chapel. It's at the corner of Maple and Third in the village. It's a charming rustic affair of cedar logs and beach stones built in 1935 with money from the Depression-generated Federal Emergency Administration of Public Works. A Methodist minister from Newberry who served a dozen far-flung northwoods churches orchestrated the project for the "Little Church in the Big U.P." It's full of decorative touches inside and out: a pulpit made of a log, a fireplace by the stage, a combination chimney/bellcote of carefully ordered stones, stained glass memorial windows. Reversible seats let the audience face

either the pulpit on one end or, in its community hall guise, the fireplace and stage at the other.

A rugged ridge runs south and east from this village, located just south of the East Branch of the Tahquamenon River. Vast expanses of swampland surround the town. Especially from May through June, the black flies and other insects make venturing out into the hinterland an uncommonly painful experience. One fly-fisherman came back saying he looked like he had been the victim of multiple ice pick stabs. Nonetheless, downstaters have bid up prices for available land to where it would be hard to find anything for less than $1,000 an acre.

HULBERT RESTAURANTS

The **TAHQUAMENON HOTEL** is a community institution in Hulbert. A relic of logging days, it began life as the boarding house and office of the wooden bowl factory, then became a post office, ice cream parlor, and dance hall. Today it's a favorite gathering place for breakfast (8 a.m.-11 a.m.), cocktails, and dinner (5-8 p.m. except 8 a.m. to 2 p.m. Sundays). The menu ranges from hamburgers (around $3 for a quarter-pounder) and homemade soups (around $2.25/bowl) to fresh whitefish dinners ($12 when available). The food's better under the current owners than it had been. *From M-28 at Hulbert Corners, take the main street through Hulbert; tracks and hotel are around two turns on the west edge of town. 876-2388. Closed April & May.* &: yes, but restrooms are upstairs.

The rustic dining room at the **HULBERT LAKE LODGE** is now open to non-guests for breakfast and dinner without reservations almost all year long. The vintage lodge is in an attractive setting on a quiet lake, with a **walking path** throught the woods. Home cooking is varied but always good. Breakfasts are around $6-$7. Very popular: fresh whitefish or perch. Dinner entrées ($12-$14) include salad, potato, and homemade bread. Sandwiches (around $6) are also available. *South off M-28 about a mile east of Hulbert Corners, and 6 miles west of M-123. 876-2324. Currently closed only in mid March (whenever snowmobile season is over) and April. Open Wed-Sun from 8 a.m. to 11 a.m. and from four to 8 p.m.* &: no

HULBERT LODGINGS

SNO-SHU INN (906) 876-2324; www.snoshuinn.com

Five cabins with wood stoves, an apartment, and an "inn" unit with three bedrooms and two baths are on wooded, grassy grounds at one of the major intersections in Hulbert. All have TVs, but only with three local channels. Some have cooking facilities. The resort is very well maintained. There's a phone in the office and a **picnic area** with grills. **Hiking** and snowmobile trails on National Forest land are across the road. Guests can have **access to Hulbert Lake**, rent fishing boats, and use the hiking path and beach at the owners' Hulbert Lake Lodge two miles away (see below). One-room cabins with two double beds rent for $65-$70/night; the inn that sleeps 14 to 20 is $330-$350/night. *Hulbert Rd. at Maple St., 1 mile north of M-28 and Hulbert Corners.*

H.A.: call

HANDSHAKE MOTEL & RV PARK
(906) 876-2378

Reminiscent of the time when city people took farm vacations to relax, this quaint four-unit motel forms the front farmyard. With some kitchen units and a central location for touring, this could make a good base for a vacationing family. The owners live in the picturesque farmhouse. Tom Weaver is a local constable. Roni Israel-Weaver does custom quilting, mostly on quilts others have pieced, in a sunny room next to the farm

garage. Big old maple and apple trees and **adjacent natural areas** make for a beautiful setting. Paths and a snowmobile trail on the other side of the road go into the woods for miles. (Much of this land is part of the **Hiawatha National Forest**.) The four pleasantly decorated motel units have knotty pine walls, a mix of older furniture, and TVs with 5 or 6 channels. Guests can use office phone. Summer rates: $45 for one double bed, $50 for two rooms with a connecting bath (sleeps four), $80 and $90 for two-bedroom units with living room-kitchen that sleep up to 6 and 8. The RV park in back, hardly visible from the motel in front, is $15/night for full hookups, without showers or restrooms. *On M-28 near Hulbert. Open year-round.*

H.A.: call. Tight bathrooms.

HULBERT LAKE LODGE
(906) 876-2324;
www.hulbertlakelodge.com

Good food in the lodge dining room and a quiet location on private, 3-mile-long Hulbert Lake make this well-kept, vintage resort the favorite summer getaway for a nature-loving artist. "**Fishing** [for lake trout, pike, smallmouth bass, and panfish] can be fantastic," he says. "Birding is fabulous, with eagles, osprey,

and loons. And the hosts are wonderful folks." The Hulbert Lake Club owns a thousand acres around the lake; hunting is excellent. **Motors are restricted** to 10 h.p. **Swimming** and **sailboats** are encouraged. **Boat rental:** $25-$45/day. **Hiking trails** are in the nearby woods. A sociable atmosphere reigns in the dining room. Five cabins without kitchens are in a woodsy setting on the lake. No TVs — the lodge is nature-oriented! However, the planned rec room for kids by the lake will have a TV and games. A phone, fireplace, and coffee are in the lodge. There's a picnic area with grills. Cabins sleep 2 to 7. Reserve early for summer! Sample daily rates: one-room cabin: $60/$75, two bedroomf for four $85/night. Ask about larger units with multiple baths. *South off M-28 about a mile east of Hulbert Corners, and 6 miles west of M-123.* **H.A.:** call.

Tahquamenon Falls

Tahquamenon Falls State Park

Most Michigan waterfalls are attractive but puny affairs when compared with the mighty waterfalls of the world. Michigan's one really substantial waterfall is the Upper Falls of the Tahquamenon River. The falls are nearly 200 feet across. As much as 50,000 gallons of water a second plunge 48 feet into a canyon below. The sandstone shelf of the falls is compressed beach sand from when this was a seashore in late Cambrian times, 500 million years ago. The sand was the eroded particles of ancient mountains deposited by streams and sifted by wave action.

Tahquamenon Falls has been an important landmark and attraction at least since before the time of the Ojibwa. In Longfellow's poem based on Ojibwa legends, Hiawatha builds his canoe "by the rushing Tahquamenew."

Park visitors are concentrated so intensely at the Upper Falls and the Lower Falls four miles downstream that it's easy to forget that this 40,000-acre park is Michigan's second-biggest state park, laced with 17 miles of **hiking trails.** The park stretches 13 miles west from Whitefish Bay at the Tahquamenon River's mouth. Most of it is a designated wilderness area where you won't see a power line or hear a car. **Maps** —and **consultation**—are available at the fee stations at the Upper and Lower Falls or at park headquarters on M-123 between them.

The most memorable vantage point

If anything, the view of the Upper Tahquamenon Falls is even more spectacular in winter, when mist from the plunging water forms huge icicles on the nearby cliffs. The long walk to the falls from the parking lot shields visitors from the sounds of the many snowmobiles that flock here on winter weekends.

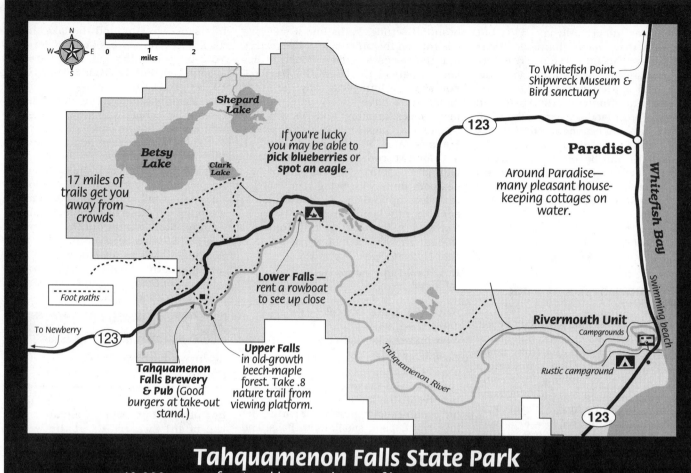

N
W E
S

0   1   2
miles

Shepard Lake

Betsy Lake

Clark Lake

17 miles of trails get you away from crowds

If you're lucky you may be able to **pick blueberries** or **spot an eagle**.

Foot paths

To Newberry

123

Tahquamenon Falls Brewery & Pub (Good burgers at take-out stand.)

Upper Falls in old-growth beech-maple forest. Take .8 nature trail from viewing platform.

Lower Falls — rent a rowboat to see up close

Tahquamenon River

123

To Whitefish Point, Shipwreck Museum & Bird sanctuary

123

Paradise

Around Paradise— many pleasant house-keeping cottages on water.

Whitefish Bay

Swimming beach

Rivermouth Unit
Campgrounds

Rustic campground

Tahquamenon Falls State Park

40,000 acres of natural beauty, home of bears, coyotes, otter, deer, fox, porcupine, beaver, and mink. 17 miles of hiking trails connect the two magnificent waterfalls with old-growth forest and wild back country.

at the **UPPER FALLS** is reached by a stairway. Find it by turning right as you go from the parking lot to the falls. The state park has constructed an exciting **platform** that allows you to stand right at the brink of the falls, so you can take in the dramatic contrast between the serene meanderings of the upper Tahquamenon River and the roaring foam below the falls. A wheelchair-accessible viewing opportunity, not so dramatic, is a longer, .4 route down the same path. The river is darkened by tannic acid from the many hemlocks, cedars, and spruces along its banks, which gives the initial spill of water an interesting brownish hue. From this same viewing platform you see, far downstream, the once-again peaceful river as it flows between reddish bluffs another 20 miles towards Lake Superior's Whitefish Bay south of Paradise. The **left trail** from the parking area leads to a less spectacular view of the falls from the lower river.

A .8 mile interpretive **nature trail** leads from the platform at the Upper Falls. The entire area around the falls is a **beech-maple climax forest** that has been developing since the retreat of the last glacier. Some of its trees are about 300 years old, but visitors focused on the falls miss out on this unless they

When to visit the falls—

In midday in July and August, the crowds and cars by the Upper Falls can be overwhelming. In color season it's also a well-trod tourist path.

If you don't like being part of a herd, consider coming in the off-seasons. Early May, with its active birds and wildlife, is nice. (Black flies can be a problem from late-May through the third week in June; mosquitoes can always be bad if it's been damp.) Another nice, quiet time is the end of October, when some leaves are

think to look up.

At the Upper Falls parking area, visitors are greeted by an unusually striking log building that offers a good selection of souvenirs and regional and nature books. Its name, **Camp 33**, recalls the large area logging company whose owner bought 200 acres near the falls and sold that land to the state as part of the park. (He kept a two-acre inholding.) The concessionaires who erected Camp 33 and run the store are his descendants. The high-ceilinged, post-and-beam timber-frame structure was built with oak posts and beams (no nails), which are exposed on the interior. The buildings and seating of the **picnic area** and **takeout restaurant** look out into the surrounding forest of big trees, well separated from the massive parking area. It's a beautiful place to sit and eat, when it's not too crowded. The takeout restaurant serves pasties, cooked-to-order hamburgers, and similar fare.

Energetic and fit hikers might well

The Lower Tahquamenon Falls are less dramatic than the Upper Falls, but more complex and just as beautiful. You can rent a rowboat and explore the falls close up.

prefer avoiding the busy parking lot and approaching the Upper Falls by foot from downstream, for maximum dramatic impact. An up-and-down **riverside trail**, recently improved, follows the Tahquamenon River for four miles upstream from the trailhead at the Lower Falls to the Upper Falls, crossing smaller streams on boardwalks along the way. Once at the Upper Falls, of course, you would need to walk four miles back.

The **LOWER FALLS,** four miles downstream, is smaller but, in its own serene way, equally impressive. Here the Tahquamenon River drops 22 feet in a series of cascades that surround a sizable island and a series of boulders. You can view the series of falls from a high bluff, but for around $2 a person you can **rent a rowboat** from the concession. That takes you much closer. A footpath goes right up to the falls. There's a **picnic area** along the river, a restaurant by the parking lot, and two **modern campgrounds** (see below). Below the Lower Falls, the Tahquamenon River offers the park's best fishing: perch, northern pike, muskies, and walleye. Fishing pressure is considerable, however.

Spectacular **fall color** peaks here well into October, later than in much of the U.P. A mix of maple, birch, and conifer makes for rich yellows and reds contrasted with dark green. An easy, flat trail into the forest is the four-mile **Giant Pine Loop** that begins at the brink of the Upper Falls and passes by some very old white pines. This trail cuts through the **fourth-largest old-growth forest** in Michigan, a never-harvested

Tahquamenon Falls State Park in winter

The Giant Pine Loop is groomed for **cross-country skiing** in winter. Skiers are welcome to make their own trails elsewhere. **Snowshoers** often take the trail between the falls, and use the Clark Lake Loop into the back country. **Ice fishing** is another attraction. In his book of meditative U.P. nature explorations, *A Superior Peninsula*, Lon Emerick highly recommends an all-day visit to the waterfalls in midwinter, when most of the falls have frozen into huge daggers and the colors at close range are breathtaking. **Winter camping** and visits are becoming increasingly popular. Be aware, though, that **snowmobiles** now noisily descend on the new brew pub/restaurant, echoing through

community of American beech, sugar maple, yellow birch, and Eastern hemlock, interspersed with some white pine.

North of M-123, trails up to 13 miles long enable hikers to get away from the crowds in the **BACK COUNTRY.** Trails pass through many habitats, including conifer forests, sandy ridges, and boggy lakes typical of the eastern Upper Peninsula. A series of three **wilderness lakes** with northern pike and perch can be reached by an access road to Clark Lake and a half-mile portage to Betsy Lake.

Staffing limitations mean the trails north of M-123 haven't been marked in years, though use has made them clear enough to follow. Expect to have to climb over windfalls in places. Except for the Giant Pine Loop, these trails are moderate to difficult. *Park staff is happy to recommend hikes to suit your interests.* The **North Country Trail** passes through the park, going east to the Rivermouth Campground and picnic area. North beyond the park, the North Country Trail has many wet areas as it goes up to Lake Superior near the mouth of the Two Hearted River. Waterproof footgear is recommended.

The four-mile **trail connecting the Upper and Lower Falls** (a section of the

North Country Trail) now has boardwalks, bridges, and steps on slippery hills.

A third developed area of this vast park is the **RIVERMOUTH UNIT** south of Paradise, where the Tahquamenon empties into Whitefish Bay. It has rustic and modern campgrounds, and a beach and picnic area on Whitefish Bay just off M-123. The shallow bay can warm up nicely when the weather is warm and sunny.

Interpretive programs on topics like logging history, Native American history, black bears, and old-growth forests are given at the park from mid-May through September. From July 4 through Labor Day weekends there are two programs a day, including Junior Ranger programs for kids.

The park hub (2 falls, 2 campgrounds, Headquarters) are in the same general area on M-123 12 miles west of Paradise (Lower Falls) and 21 miles east of Newberry (Upper Falls). The Rivermouth Unit is on M-123 4 miles south of Paradise. (906) 492-3415. Open year-round. State park sticker required; $4/$5 day, or $20/$25 year. &: concession buildings, toilets at Upper Falls, path from parking to Upper Falls, boardwalk at Lower Falls.

North Star Bakery

Nine miles west of Tahquamenon Falls on M-123, it's a tremendous surprise to come upon this bakery in the middle of the woods, turning out **crusty loaves of European sourdough bread** in two wood-fired brick ovens, often without the aid of any electricity at all. (This property, built as a motel, and most of the surrounding area is off the grid. The only electricity comes from a gasoline generator.) Paul and JoAnne Behm had long been interested in European bread. When they met a 70-year-old man from Fairview, Michigan, who helped them plan and build the oven, the pieces fell together and they opened the bakery in spring, 2000. The bread's crisp crust, chewy texture, and flavor measure up to the best downstate breads in every way but price. (To build a local year-round business here, prices can't be too high.) Among the breads baked here, depending on the weekly schedule, are Italian, French, raisin-walnut or date-walnut whole wheat, a very popular multigrain, caesar bread (with anchovies!), and several cheese breads — Asiago-jalapeño, sharp cheddar, blue cheese. It's worth planning several picnics based on this good bread. Stop at Brown's Fisheries

coming into Paradise for smoked fish or spread.

On M-123 9 miles west of the Upper Falls or 13 miles northeast of Newberry. 658-3537. E-mail: northstarbakery@mail.com Probable summer hours 9 a.m. to 8 p.m. daily except possibly Sunday. Call to confirm morning hours. &: call

TAHQUAMENON RESTAURANTS

TAHQUAMENON FALLS BREWERY & PUB enjoys the deserved reputation of serving the **area's best food**. The brewpub and full-service restaurant, owned and operated by Lark Ludlow and her brother Barrett Ludlow, is in the prime location at the parking area to the Upper Falls. Their grandfather had a restaurant here before selling much of his land to the state, retaining these two acres. The DNR didn't want alcohol served at the park, but the Ludlows were legally entitled to do so. Their restaurant continues the quality and style of their Camp 33 store and snack bar. The $3.25-a-glass price for handcrafted beer doesn't exactly encourage drinkers to load up. Sandwich and dinner menus are offered all day. Whitefish (about $13 in 2000), almost always fresh, heads a dinner menu that also includes steaks, shrimp scampi in garlic butter sauce, and pastas (several vegetarian). Entrées ($13-$17 in 2000) come with soup or salad, fresh bread, and potato or rice pilaf. The beer-battered fries are excellent. For lighter appetites, there's a whitefish sandwich (about $6) or charbroiled yellowfin tuna sandwich ($6.50), several burgers, meal-size salads with charbroiled chicken or smoked fish, and pasties ($7.25). Wild rice soup and brew pub cheese soup made with aged cheddar and smoked ham (both $2.75 in 2000) are hearty and distinctive. Windows look out onto a forest. In winter there's a fire in the big **stone fireplace**; food is served on a **deck** in summer. *At the Upper Falls parking lot. 492-3341. Open daily year-round (except for April and November), 11 to 8:30, to 9 on Saturday.* & 🚻 Full bar

TAHQUAMENON LODGINGS

See **Paradise**, 12 miles east of the Lower Falls and **Newberry**, 21 miles west of the Upper Falls.

TAHQUAMENON FALLS CAMPING

See also **Paradise**, Newberry, Strongs, and Bay Mills. People who prefer more space between campsites should consider the state park's rustic campground at the river mouth and the state forest

campgrounds north of Paradise.

RIVERBEND CAMPGROUND/
Tahquamenon Falls State Park
(906) 492-3415. Fax: (906) 492-3590. Reserv: (800) 44-PARKS. (800) 605-8295 TDD; www.dnr.state.mi.us/

This shady, close-spaced, very popular 87-site modern campground ($14/$17 night) is closest to the Lower Falls, just before the day-use parking lot. Stairs permit river access. There's easy access to the hiking **trail** between the falls. Campsites are gradually being consolidated to eliminate too-small sites. Reservations taken six months ahead; early reservations advised for peak summer times. **H.A.:** now completely ADA accessible.

OVERLOOK CAMPGROUND/
Tahquamenon Falls State Park
(906) 492-3415. Fax: (906) 492-3590. Reserv: (800) 44-PARKS. (800) 605-8295 TDD; www.dnr.state.mi.us/

This modern campground ($14/$17 a night) is also shady and closed-spaced, with about 90 sites is a quarter-mile walk from the Lower Falls and as a result less likely to fill than Riverbend. A few sites are plowed for **winter camping**. See above for advance reservation info.

Both campgrounds are at the Lower Falls, off M-123, 12 miles west of Paradise. State park sticker required: $4/$5 day, $20/$25 a year.

H.A.: call. In progress. Not technically in compliance with current ADA standards.

Paradise (pop. 510)

This remote village on Lake Superior's Whitefish Bay has become such a popular tourist spot in recent years that in peak seasons restaurants and lodgings are hard-pressed to keep up with demand. Getting a meal in Paradise can be a challenge in busy times, and in the off-season your only choice after 8 p.m. may be a burger and fries at the Yukon Bar. Visitors are advised to stock up on groceries and pick up some outstanding bread at the North Star Bakery west of the Upper Tahquamenon Falls.

Paradise was founded in 1925 specifically as a resort community and named by an apparently zealous promoter to attract visitors. The population swells in summer when resorters return to their cottages. You can **fish** for walleye from the end of June to mid-July off the local boat launch dock or at the mouth of the Tahquamenon River south of town. Muskies are prevalent here in the spring. Because of the increasing popularity of snowmobiling and cross-country skiing, Paradise is as busy these days in winter as in summer. Round-the-clock **snowmobile grooming** has made Paradise an especially popular place for that noisy recreation. At any one time in the winter you may find as many as 500 snowmobiles parked in town. In summer, many divers stay in Paradise who explore the underwater shipwreck preserve to the north.

Paradise has several motels, resorts, and restaurants strung along M-123 where it parallels Whitefish Bay, before it veers west to Tahquamenon Falls. Many resorts overlook Whitefish Bay. Due north is the Great Lakes Shipwreck Museum at Whitefish Point. Its billboards, aided by the lighthouse craze, create a steady stream of traffic headed for Whitefish Point in peak summer months.

All this activity has created a boom of sorts for Paradise. There's a new credit union, a new Best Western on the lake, and an impressive new community library, along with a True Value hardware store and IGA grocery store. Retirees comprise the biggest category of new residents, but some have moved to the area as part of **Companions of Christ the Lamb**, a Catholic "private association of the faithful" who run a **wilderness retreat center** outside Paradise. It was started by Father Jack Fabian of Newport, Michigan, between Detroit and Monroe. Open to people of any spiritual persuasion, the retreat center draws on the long Christian tradition of withdrawing to the desert for contemplation (real deserts in the case of Jesus, John the Baptist, and St. Anthony and the Desert Fathers, metaphorical deserts for St. Francis of Assisi). Individual retreatants camp by themselves or stay in

cabins and family housing, built by Companions community members. Retreats can also be arranged for groups, and there is a beautiful chapel whose glass wall brings the outdoors in. But simplicity and **solo wilderness** retreats, usually along the Betsy/ Shelldrake River, are what it's all about. Under those conditions retreatants have to trust more. There's no electricity, just a generator used for construction projects. Retreats are not to be confused with nature identification, birding, or fishing, either. The informational brochure advises retreatants to leave their binoculars and nature guides at home. Suitable books are few: a journal, a Bible, a book of common prayer. Retreats occur year-round but are mainly from May through October. Companions of Christ the Lamb never seek publicity but respond to requests for information. Contact Chuck or Kathy Rollent at (906) 492-3815. The retreat center is reached by going on M-123 four miles west of the blinker light, then taking Farm Truck Road north and following the signs.

Steve Harmon of Birchwood Lodge (see below) sees the area from an outdoorsman's perspective. Here's his interesting take on Paradise — and fishing — in fall. "After Labor Day the pace in Paradise lessens somewhat. The nights become cooler and the fishing picks up. While those with the bigger boats fish the Bay for whitefish and lake trout, the Tahquamenon River . . . provides the most varied fishing for the average fisherman. The river supports walleye, pike, tiger muskie, perch, and bass. . . . Brook trout streams are available for those who like the bush and hate crowds. Nice rainbow and brown trout are caught at the Upper and Lower Tahquamenon Falls."

Color season is, of course, very beautiful and very busy. **"Mid-November** can be a **very stormy time**, and it's now that the Bay gets really **interesting**," Harmon writes. "It's not an uncommon sight to see ocean-going freighters anchored temporarily a half mile off shore from our resort. The winds blow and the trees bend to the snapping point. You can hear the steady roar of the lake as you walk through town. The skies turn steel gray and the town waits. It's this month that has sent more ships to the bottom of the bay than at any other time."

Sawmill Park

This pleasant park is along a stream right in Paradise. There are **picnic**

tables, grills, vault toilets, and a **nature walk** along the creek.

On the west side of Whitefish Point Rd. (away from the lake) on the north edge of town, across the road from Birchwood Lodge. ♿

Rivermouth Picnic Area and Beach/ Tahquamenon Falls State Park

The sandy beach just south of Paradise slopes gently into the bay. Here (and in few other spots north of here) the bay is accessible to the general public. It's hard to imagine that this area was once occupied by the busy lumber port and sawmills of the **ghost town of Emerson**, and later by commercial fishermen whose nets and tugs added a picturesque note to the bay. In the 1930s a local landowner gave the state over 2,000 acres at the Tahquamenon mouth as part of the state park.

Off M-123 just north of where the Tahquamenon River empties into Whitefish Bay. State park sticker required: $4/$5 aday, $20/$25 a year. ♿: no.

PARADISE RESTAURANTS

In season Paradise restaurants are often too crowded. Out of season, even in fall when visitors are still out in force, it may be hard to get a meal on some days of the week after 8 p.m. except at the Yukon Inn. In the real off seasons, The **Penguin** restaurant (492-3390) south of town on M-123 is most likely to be open, especially for breakfast and lunch. It's a good idea to come to Paradise prepared: bring a well-packed cooler, supplemented with smoked fish from Brown's and the excellent bread from North Star Bakery west of Tahquamenon Falls. Tahquamenon Falls Brewery & Pub, at the Upper Falls, has very good food and stays open most of the year. At busy times it too is likely busy.

You might think you'd seen Paradise and miss **BROWN FISHERIES Restaurant & Market** because it's on the west edge of town. It's a pleasant place inside, with nifty paintings of local fishing boats. The only trouble is, if one customer is smoking, it gets smoky. Whitefish comes fried (3 pieces for about $8) or broiled ($10), with fries or baked potato. The tomato-based whitefish soup (about $3.50 a bowl) is delicious. A whitefish sandwich with fries and slaw is $5. Fish is maple smoked in back, and smoked fish is used for a dip that would make fine picnic fare. Commercial fisherman Buddy Brown is a part owner of the Howard

Johnson Inn and loves to golf, incidentally. No credit cards. Checks OK. *On M-123 1/4 mile west of the light. 492-3901. Open from some time in May thru October. Fri & Sat only 'til June 15. Then open Mon-Sat, noon to 8.*

A good all-around bet in Paradise is the **PARADISE RESTAURANT**. At Norma DeLong's family-run restaurant, four generations help out, and grandkids are waiting tables. It's known for whitefish dinners, Swiss steak, and cinnamon rolls. Also popular is the deep-fried chicken. Dinners come with salad bar and potato. Don't be put off by the "insured by Smith & Wesson" sign at the door; the staff and service is friendly. No credit cards; checks OK. *On the lake side of M-123. Closed from mid-Oct. to mid-Dec, mid-March to mid-May. Open daily except Thursdays from 7:30 a.m. to 8 p.m., to 9 in summer. 492-3424.* &: call

Some folks who clearly aren't counting their cholesterol make a B-line for the Yukon Burger, an amalgam of ground beef, ham, bacon, and cheese, at the fabulously rustic **YUKON INN**. This is the quintessential log tavern, built in the 1930s. Log buildings like this are susceptible to all sorts of exterior maintenance problems, but don't be put off by the deteriorating logs outside. Inside, the logs and rafters and rustic furnishings just glow. This popular Paradise bar is self-described as "the friendliest bar in the north," and the moniker does seem well deserved. Alas, as for vegetable nutrition, the onion rings and ketchup are just about it. *Right in town on M-123. 492-3264. Open year-round, daily at noon. Kitchen open 'til 10.*

&: call   Full bar

The only restaurant with a full bar, where you can get a whitefish dinner with beer or wine in a smoke-free dining area, is the cheerful **LITTLE FALLS INN** adjoining the **Red Flannel Saloon**. The rustic log building was a ballroom in the 1930s, part of the Cedar Lodge complex. It offers a full menu at breakfast, lunch, and dinner. *On M-123 in the center of Paradise. 492-3529. It's generally open from 8 a.m. to 9 p.m., closed Wednesday in summer, Monday and Tuesday in winter, and closed altogether at weather-dependent slow times in spring and fall.*

& &: Full bar

Paradise Lodgings

Paradise offers the closest accommodations to Tahquamenon Falls, 15 miles to the west, and to Whitefish Point, 12 miles north. The point is home of the Whitefish Point Bird Observatory and is increasingly busy with visitors to the Great Lakes Shipwreck Museum. Paradise had long been a charmingly pokey place where many little resorts back up to Whitefish Bay. The gently sloping, sandy beach here has water that's not too terribly cold for Lake Superior. In the distance you can see the hills of Canada. Paradise, 60 miles from both Sault Ste. Marie and St. Ignace/Mackinac Island, is well located for a pleasant week's vacation with day trips to major eastern U.P. sights. Noisy snowmobiles dominate the winter here; advance winter weekend reservations are advised. High season rates typically apply from mid-June through Labor Day, sometimes through color season, and from mid-December through mid-March. Reserve in advance for good summer and fall weekend availability. Many motels offer Audubon Society Members discounts.

CLOUD NINE COTTAGES
(906) 492-3434

This small resort has a pleasantly woodsy feel, a quiet family atmosphere, and almost 300' of **sand beach**. Three of the four attractive, pine-paneled housekeeping cottages have water views. Each has two bedrooms, a microwave, and a TV/VCRs. $65-$90/night for two people in prime season; 25% off at other times. There's no cable in Paradise; TVs get about 5 channels. A collection of family videos is at the office, along with a phone guests can use. Furnishings are 1970s rustic. Cottages come with picnic tables, grills, and lawn furniture. Guests have free use of a **pedal boat**. Reserve early; lots of repeat customers. *Half a mile south of downtown Paradise on M-123.* **H.A.:** call : $5/extra person

CEDAR LODGE   (906) 492-3310

An unusual 1950s design combines the common gathering areas of old-fashioned lodges with six motel units overlooking Whitefish Bay and six cabins without water views. The lobby has a big stone fireplace, books and games to borrow, and a view of the bay. It's all very old-timey — all except for the plush, stuccoed three-story Best Western Lakefront Inn that longtime Cedar Lodge owners Jim and Shirley Stabile have erected next door. Guests of the six-room motel now share use of the 430' of beautiful **sandy beach** below the 20' bluff, the beachside deck, the outdoor fireplace and portable grills. The convenient location is right in town behind the owners' Little Falls Restaurant, but well back off the road on the lake. The two-bedroom knotty-pine cabins have full kitchens and two queen beds. They sleep two adults. Some have fireplaces. 2001 rates: $95/night in spring and fall with a two-night minimum, $100/night in summer (one-week minimum) and snowmobile season. The roomy, soundproof motel units have coffeemakers. They are sided in cedar, with open rafters. They rent for $95/night in summer, $85 in spring and fall. All rooms & cabins have been completely renovated and refurnished within the past 10 years. All rooms have satellite TV with 9 stations. Phones are in office. *On M-123 slightly south of the main intersection in Paradise. Lodge closes after hunting season. Cabins usually stay open in winter.*

H.A.: call

BEST WESTERN LAKEFRONT INN & SUITES (877) 538-2313; (906) 492-3770; www.bestwestern.com/paradise

It's more Mackinaw City than what Paradise has known up to now: a cushy hotel with an impressive lobby, breakfast area with a lake view, indoor pool, and luxurious rooms, richly decorated in burgundies and deep blues, with balconies overlooking Whitefish Bay. It doesn't just have phones but dataports and satellite TV (9 stations; that's a lot for Paradise). At 41 rooms, the hotel, owned by the longtime owners of Cedar Lodge and Little Falls Restaurant, isn't as big as it seems, and the indoor pool isn't all that large or lavish. Currently there's a limited continental breakfast. The rooms are wonderful, and so is the location: 430' of beautiful sandy beach below the 20' bluff, a beachside deck, an outdoor fireplace, and small picnic area. All lakefront rooms have a **balcony** or **patio**. Rates in summer, 2001 were $155 for lakefront rooms (two queens) with a water view, currently $138 for the same room without the view, and $165 for **lakefront suites**. These one-room suites have a living area with upholstered chairs and pullout sofa, and a king bed. There are no whirlpool rooms. Shoulder season rates in 2000 were $109 (no view), $129, and for suites $139. Consult the Best Western website for possible off-season specials. *On M-123 slightly south of the main intersection in Paradise. Open year-round.*

H.A.: some rooms ADA accessible : rates go by room, not occupancy

CURLEY'S PARADISE MOTEL
(906) 492-3445; www.paradise.com

You wouldn't guess it from the road, but

this one-story motel has 26 quite modern rooms and many resort amenities: a lakeside **picnic area** with grills and fire pits, 500 feet of **sand beach**, a tennis court, a pinball and video game room, a heated garage for snowmobile repairs, and a small exercise room with weight machines, rowing, and ski machines. Ten motel rooms have picture windows with a lake view, though parked cars may be in the way. Five comfortable, attractive cottages and a good-size house are almost on the beach; some have decks. All rooms have phones, TV (6 channels), and in-room tea and coffee. Typical rates for most seasons: $70 for one queen, $90-$95 for two. Some rooms have kings. Guests can use the microwave and refrigerator in the office. Décor and furniture is a standard, updated motel look. Proprietors Bill and Lynda Ferguson stayed here on their honeymoon in 1962. For divers, who usually charter boats from Capt. Pete Lindquist in Munising, an air station is on the premises and a dive shop next door. *In "downtown" Paradise, opposite where M-123 turns west. Open year-round.*

H.A.: some rooms ADA accessible 👫: under 16 free 🐕: call

HARMON'S BIRCHWOOD LODGES
(906) 492-3320; www.harmonsbirchwoodresort.com

The ambiance is woodsy and unfussy at this vintage family resort on Whitefish Bay with eight housekeeping cabins. Host Steve Harmon, a 20-year resident, knows a lot about the area's recreational possibilities: bird-watching, fishing, shipping, and more. His collection of rental videos (each cabin has a **VCR** along with 9-channel **satellite TV**) is most interesting. Guests are provided with lots of extras: **inner tubes**, adults' and kids' **bikes** to loan, **badminton, volleyball, horseshoes, shuffleboard**, tetherball and a rope swing. There's a stone fireplace, a screened **beach house** with a grand view, and stairs going down to the sandy beach. It's an easy walk to the center of Paradise. The cabins are gas-heated and well insulated, with knotty pine interiors, 1970s-style rustic furniture, and microwaves. Guests can use office phone. One cabin has a lake view. Cabins sleep from 2 to 6 and are generally rented by the week in summer. Typical summer rates for 4 people in 2000: $480-$625/week, $80-$95/day. Winter rates slightly less. Ask about spring and fall discounts. *Down a drive off Whitefish Point Rd. on the north edge*

of town. Open year-round.

H.A.: call. Sandy ground, 👫: $10/extra person 🐕: no

FREIGHTERS VIEW RESORT
(800) 236-3277; (906) 492-3266; www. In the works

The six fresh, tastefully furnished units here should appeal to people who like things new. Five units overlook Whitefish Bay; the sixth, a cabin is in the woods with a partial water view. Two buildings are duplexes with one kitchenette unit ($65-$70/night) and one motel room without cooking facilities ($55 to $60/night). 25% off-season discount. *There's a four-person maximum occupancy, including children.* Each unit has a TV/VCR with about 5 channels and videos to borrow. Guests can use phone in office. There's a **shared deck** by the lake, a dock, two kayaks to borrow, horseshoes, volleyball, and a fire pit. Sand has been added to build up the **beach** below a sea wall; it's good for wading way on out. The resort is quite close to Whitefish Point Road, which is busy and audible from 9 a.m. or so 'til 7 p.m. in summer. *Two miles north of Paradise on Whitefish Point Rd.*

H.A.: call 👫:

PARADISE AREA CAMPING

RIVERMOUTH UNIT/
Tahquamenon Falls State Park
(906) 492-3415. Reservations:
(800) 44-PARKS; (800) 605-8295 TDD; www.dnr.state.mi.us/

A 76-space **modern campground** ($14/night) and a 55-site **rustic campground** ($6/night) nestled into the wooded lowlands on a bend of the Tahquamenon River just before it empties into Whitefish Bay. Reservations are advised for July and August, a week ahead, and more than that for holidays. There's a river launch site for canoes and boats; ask about fishing. A bayfront **picnic area** and **sand beach** are across M-123 just north of the river's mouth. Some **interpretive programs** and junior ranger programs are held here. This is a popular, heavily fished area for pike and muskies in early spring, and for walleye and smallmouths to July, says Tom Huggler in *Fish Michigan: 50 Rivers. 4 1/2 miles south of Paradise just west off M-123. State park sticker required: $4/$5 a day, $20/$25 a year.* ♿: In progress. Doesn't comply with current ADA standards, but facilities are used by people in wheelchairs.

ANDRUS LAKE Campground/
Lake Superior State Forest
(906) 293-5131. Not reservable.

Close to Whitefish Point, 25 rustic campsites are spread out around a lake with a beautiful, **sandy beach**. This campground is a popular alternative to the close-spaced, modern campgrounds of nearby Tahquamenon Falls State Park. Availability is best in spring, or after school starts. A back-up choice is nearby **Shelldrake Dam Campground**, two miles farther west on Vermilion Rd. Shelldrake isn't not on a lake any more, but it has its low-key charms, set on a ridge forested by jack pine and red pine. The water was drawn down because the dam needs to be repaired. The project is caught in a dispute between two branches of the DNR. Fisheries doesn't want the dam at all; it prefers to see more rivers go back to their natural flow. The Wildlife Division doesn't have funds to repair the dam. Public sentiment favors repairing the dam. *6 miles north of Paradise, turn west onto Vermilion Rd. Campground is in 1 mile. Serviced May thru Nov. $6/$10 night.* **H.A.:** call.

Whitefish Point

Whitefish Point forms the entrance to Lake Superior's Whitefish Bay. The bay's geography concentrates both ships and migrating birds at Whitefish Point. Here where the straits are narrow, birds flying along Lake Superior's shoreline often cross north into Canada, which makes Whitefish Point a major destination for serious birdwatchers.

Marked to ships by the light at Whitefish Point, Whitefish Bay is the funnel for ships entering and leaving Lake Superior via the St. Mary's River at Sault Ste. Marie. That busy river leads to Lake Huron and the lower lakes. Whitefish Bay is protected, but the open expanse of water to the north is called "the graveyard of the Great Lakes." It bears the full force of winds from the north and west. Many vessels have sunk there, making the area a magnet for divers. The most recent and dramatic wreck was the *Edmund Fitzgerald* in 1975, but many more wrecks occurred in the late 19th century, when vessels on the lakes were smaller and far more numerous and navigational aids were more primitive.

Shelldrake once stood at the mouth of the Shelldrake River three miles north of Paradise. As a sawmill town it had unusual amenities. It had a hospital and homes for 1,000 with plaster walls and bathrooms with hot water heated by the sawmill burner. Today no trace of Shelldrake remains easily visible.

Centennial Cranberry Farm

In the 1890s cranberries were one of Whitefish Point's exports, and several farmers were in the area. This farm was the first, where an enterprising fisherman, noticing that Native Americans sold wild cranberries and blueberries to Lake Superior schooners, successfully tried farming them in the marshes here. Wisconsin is where most Midwestern cranberries are raised today, and it's where farmers Loren and Sharon House and his daughter, Susan Sikora, take their wholesale crop to market. With all the visitors passing by their side road on the way to Whitefish Point, it made sense to open the farm to visitors. The **self-guided tour** consists of a video about cranberries, their culture and harvest. It's a wet process that uses unusual machinery. (Indians harvested cranberries from their canoes.) The tour gets visitors off the beaten path on rural roads they'd never visit otherwise. A gift shop is a new addition in 2001. **Harvest** begins sometime in mid October and lasts for a week. Cranberries are sold here by the pound through the end of the month. Phone or e-mail in early October for more exact harvest date.

10 miles north of Paradise on Whitefish Point Road to Wildcat Road. At sign, go 2 miles west. 492-3314. E-mail: shouse@ jamadots.com Open from around Mem. Day thru October, daily noon to 6. $5/car. ♿

Great Lakes Shipwreck Museum & Whitefish Point Light Station

The former Coast Guard complex at Whitefish Point forms the core of this dramatic and extremely popular museum. As the lighthouse craze gets bigger and bigger and the museum markets itself more aggressively, the large parking lot can by full by 11 a.m. with cars of visitors from many states — a surprise if you expect end-of-the-road isolation. Come at 10 to avoid crowds. Touring the museum, seeing the presentation in the theater, visiting the lighthouse, and walking around the site can easily take at least two hours. The **paths to the lakeshore** by the bird observatory are not to be missed!

To gain a good sense of this significant place, you might want to see the

Shipwreck Museum founder and creative force Tom Farnquist (right) and board member Jene Quinn posed before their 2 1/2-hour dive to recover the *Edmund Fitzgerald*'s bell. Their Great Lakes Shipwreck Historical Society sponsored and carried out the 1994 expedition.

museum first, then purchase the excellent photo guide, *Whitefish Point Light Station 1849* (currently just $5), and go up to a bench on the **Hawk Hill overlook** behind the museum to read it and take in the point, the light tower, and its natural surroundings. Follow the boardwalk back between museum buildings. The **Hawk Hill overlook**, up 28 steps, is used for bird counts during migrations. Looking out onto the light station and Whitefish Bay, it's easy to see how the shore between Whitefish Point and Munising, unprotected from weather systems, had become known as the **"Shipwreck Coast"** as early as 1846. The influential New York newspaperman Horace Greeley visited Lake Superior and mounted a campaign to protect ships with navigational aids. A lighthouse here, Lake Superior's first, was built in 1849. The first stone light tower was already suffering from erosion as the Civil War loomed on the nation's horizon. President Lincoln authorized the current "iron pile" skeletal tower, which has held up ever since 1861.

The light station and Coast Guard complex, now owned by the well-heeled Shipwreck Museum, is in a tip-top state of preservation. It's not easy to distinguish historical buildings from completely modern buildings that look historic, like the large and attractive **museum**

store (888-397-3747; www.Shipwreck Museum.com). **New wings** to the original museum are in the works, one for exhibits and the *Edmund Fitzgerald* Memorial, one for a new theater. More restrooms will be added.

The interior of the main museum building uses eerie, somber music and dramatic lighting in an otherwise dim room to convey the **haunting world of underwater shipwrecks**. Models of boats which have sunk in Superior are juxtaposed with items brought up from the depths, such as a ship's bell from the schooner *Niagara*, sunk in 1887, or a carved eagle from the steamer *Vienna*, sunk in 1892. Narrative text describes causes of shipwrecks (excessive speed, anchoring inadvertently in a shipping lane, violent storms) to add to the drama. The centerpiece is a giant second-order **Fresnel lighthouse lens** 12' high, dwarfing ones typically seen. Its light casts irregular patterns on the dim floor and ceiling.

The *Edmund Fitzgerald* exhibit caps the museum. The museum spearheaded the bell recovery project. A ship's bell symbolizes the connection of crew and ship. Some relatives of the dead sailors felt that raising the ship's bell would draw attention to their pleas to divers to leave in peace the wreck and its bodies, preserved by Superior's cold water. The Fitzgerald's bell is now on display here. Now there's concern on some relatives' part that too much publicity for Fitzgerald dives by the museum and others only turns the shipwreck and gravesite into another potential tourist attraction. Then there's the issue of commercial exploitation of tragedy through Fitzgerald souvenirs — sold here and just about everywhere in the region.

The theater now occupies what was the Coast Guard chief's quarters. It currently shows an excellent film about the *Edmund Fitzgerald* 1995 bell recovery, including the ceremonies and the families' emotional responses to the recovery.

In the lighthouse, the duplex lightkeeper quarters have been carefully restored to mint, like-new condition. The quarters of Keeper Robert Carlson, who served from 1903 to 1931, have been restored to the time period of 1920 with remarkable accuracy, thanks to the detailed memories of his granddaughter, Bertha Endress Rollo, who grew up there. Lighthouse life is vividly conveyed not only by the visual details but in the text of displays in the other side of the duplex. Life was meticulous in routine and upkeep. Families were necessarily close-knit. Reading and nature study

were natural activities. "It is a lonely life, but also in a way, a noble life," wrote Keeper Carlson.

A sizable Coast Guard Station developed around the lighthouse here. In 1985 much of the Coast Guard station became the home of the Great Lakes Shipwreck Historical Society, founded by diver Farnquist, then a Sault Ste. Marie junior high biology teacher. He and other Great Lakes divers, concerned about the loss of shipwreck artifacts, wanted to share the excitement and history of shipwrecks with a wider public. In the museum's early years he adroitly marshaled volunteers and grants to develop the museum and the related Great Lakes Shipwreck Historical Society into nationally prominent organizations. The society continues to look for new shipwreck sites and to organize diving projects. That's in addition to the museum's role as an outstanding visitor attraction.

Farnquist had also become expert at underwater photography. Mysterious, evocative photographs of dives have been enlarged as backgrounds for exhibits. They make this museum unusually compelling. An exhibit designer for the prestigious Milwaukee Public Museum was so taken by the shipwreck museum that he worked regularly with the society.

Take M-123 north to the end of Whitefish Rd., 11 miles beyond Paradise. (906) 635-1742. Open from May 15 thru Oct. 15, daily 10-6. Adults $7.50, children $4.50, families (2 parents and children) $21.50. &: museum but not theater or lighthouse.

Whitefish Point Bird Observatory

"Whitefish Point is a phenomenal concentration spot for migrating birds," explains the introductory pamphlet of the nonprofit, year-round WPBO research facility here. Birds fly along the shore and use the point extending out into Lake Superior to minimize flying over open water. The bird observatory was established in cooperation with the Michigan Audubon Society in 1979 "to document and study migratory bird populations and their habitats in the Great Lakes region." **Bird banding** is its **most powerful tool**. Banding "determines both the composition and pathways of migrating raptors [hawks, owls, and other birds of prey]. Birds are caught using fine-mesh nets locating in the woods at the Point, or at a blind using lures." Information is gathered about age, sex, weight, pesticides in the bird's

Migration: what to expect when

By the Whitefish Point Bird Observatory

SPRING: Spring migration through Whitefish Point begins in mid-march and peaks in mid-May. Early spring highlights include Bald Eagles and Northern goshawks, followed by 15,000-25,000 other **raptors**, with Sharp-shinned Hawks and Broad-winged Hawks being most common. Other raptors include Golden Eagle, Osprey, Rough-legged Hawk, Peregrine Falcon, Merlin, Turkey Vulture, Northern Saw-whet Owl and occasionally Great Gray Owl. By diligently searching through the thick jack pines in late April, fortunate individuals may find a Boreal Owl.

The impressive **spring waterbird migration** (20,000 to 45,000 birds) begins in mid-April. It features a large variety of loons, grebes, ducks, shorebirds, gulls, and terns, with many rarities found each season. Common and Red-throated Loons and Red-necked Grebes are frequently seen, as well as scoters and an occasional jaeger.

More excitement is provided by an excellent **songbird migration** that begins in April with finches, and peaks in May when warblers arrive in great numbers. Spring is a good time for beginning birders because many migrants are singing and displaying their breeding plumage.

FALL: Mid-August through October is a wonderful time for birding at Whitefish Point. Fall highlights include a **spectacular migration of 50,000-100,000 waterbird**s, with occasional single-day counts of several thousand loons, grebes, geese, and ducks, occasionally punctuated by a jaeger or unusual gull.

August and September are excellent months to test your birding skills by viewing large numbers of "fall-plumaged" songbirds. Many species stop to forage before journeying southward.

blood, and more. To estimate the fat beneath each bird's skin, banders blow the feathers on the bird's belly. All this information is entered into a nationwide computer database. If the bird is caught and rebanded or recovered by a citizen, the bird's migration can be mapped. Banding data can assess the health of various species' populations. For up-close profiles of Upper Peninsula bird researchers in action, read Sheryl De Vore's interesting book, *Northern Flights:*

Tracking the Birds and Birders of Michigan's Upper Peninsula, a $12 paperback.

Whitefish Point has become a visitor destination during spring and fall migrations. The **extensive WPBO website**, www.wpbo .org, has visitor information, current conditions and migrations, news about Michigan Nature Association land acquisitions in the area, and interesting, lengthy profiles of featured birds, their natural history and their distribution and status, world-wide and at Whitefish Point. New members of Whitefish Point Bird Observatory are always welcome.

Low, windswept dunes, **miles of undeveloped beach**, and the fun of watching ships make Whitefish Point a fine place to spend the day whether or not many birds are around. There are usually some shorebirds in summer.

For an excellent **map of the point's trails**, and for helpful tips for bird-watching at the point, stop at the observatory's **gift shop**, a treasure trove for bird lovers. and buy the observatory's checklist. (The map is in back.) In the same building, a small **indoor nature center** interprets the area. Just south of the building feeders and shrubs attract birds, and a bench lets birders sit and observe.

Don't miss the trail to the **hawk dun**e and overlook (behind the Shipwreck Museum) and the trail to the point (north of the observatory center). Here the dry forest of jack pine and lichens meets the wind-shaped dunes and beach. It's a glorious place to linger and spend the day watching birds and looking at Lake Superior's colorful beach stones. Birders are advised to bring warm clothing year-round for this windy, cool environment.

Free w**eekend programs** are offered on most weekends **from mid-April thru May**: guided **birding tours**, a guided **owl walk** at dusk, and, when possible, **"Raptors Up Close,"** with owls from the previous night's banding. Call to confirm.

*The WPBO gift shop and nature center are in a small building on the east side of the parking lot at the Point, also used by the Shipwreck Museum. (906) 492-3596. Open daily from mid-April thru mid-October. Minimal hours: 10-4. From mid-June thru Labor Day open 10-6 daily. **Mail-order** available in season. &*

Lake Superior Nature Sanctuary/ Michigan Nature Association

This remote and beautiful stretch of shoreline, backed by bogs, forests, and

Whitefish Point's natural setting is a highlight overlooked by many visitors to the well-known Great Lakes Shipwreck Museum. The Hawk Hill Overlook, pictured above, looks out over the area's characteristic jackpine forest to the 1861 Whitefish Point light tower and Lake Superior. Other trails lead from the Whitefish Point Bird Observatory to the beach along Whitefish Bay.

meadows, should first be visited with a MNA volunteer guide. It's an all-day trip because it takes a long time to drive there (over rough roads leading from Whitefish Point Road) and then hike in.

Jim Rooks, well known to many U.P. vacationers as the proprietor/guide of Bear Track Tours in Copper Harbor, regards this 369-acre sanctuary as "the **perfect wild corridor**. . . . Its native residents include deer, bear, and coyotes. Wolves and moose have roamed its trails. Here is wilderness by any test!

"Not a single person lives year-round in the township, and only a few people in neighboring townships," Rooks continued. "A few poor roads point toward the area from south, east, and west, but none quite reach it. A half mile of impenetrable bogs separate the **beach** from a high, wooded **ridge** that offers beautiful **views** of Lake Superior.

There's just one way through the spruce bogs to the beach — hence the need for a guide. Rooks waxes eloquent about the opportunities to get to know

this pristine area. "Faint trails descend . . . over broad plains of departed seas and lead to beach and dunes along Superior's shore. There are magnificent trees to be examined and wildflowers; cool hollows of land and sunbaked blueberry plains. The smell of the north woods is all around.

"I have heard thrush, vireo, parula, blackburnian, and black-throated green warblers; seen twinflower, twayblade, arbutus, and anemone, yew and striped maple; ruffled grouse, barred owl, hooded merganser, sandhill crane. . . . I have seen a bobcat and followed bobcat tracks on the beach. With all these still living in this wilderness, the wilderness traveler can ask for little more."

The **Michigan Nature Association** is a charitable trust that has purchased over 8,000 acres of natural land as permanent nature sanctuaries in 51 Michigan counties from southern and southeast Michigan to the Peninsula. It continues to add nature sanctuaries in the Whitefish Point area. Call the Michigan Nature Association at (810) 324-2345 to contact the local person to guide you to the sanctuary, or to ask about buying its big $29 *Nature Sanctuary Guidebook*, packed with maps, descriptions, photos, and interesting information tidbits about its sanctuaries — over 30 in the Upper Peninsula and 49 below the bridge.

Keep in mind that all prices and hours of operation are subject to change. Lodging rates vary with supply and demand and are usually higher for special events.

Sault Ste. Marie

The Soo Locks, top boat-watching & fishing, gambling on a grand scale, and some memorable scenery & architecture in two countries.

SAULT Ste. Marie is the U.P.'s second largest city, with a population of some 15,000. It's the business and government administrative center of the eastern Upper Peninsula. The Sault has **long been a tourist attraction** because of the Soo Locks at Lake Superior's outlet. It is a **mecca for serious boat-watchers**. But the huge, glitzy Las Vegas-style Kewadin casino and its entertainment is now a much bigger visitor draw than the locks.

The city is also a visitor hub for a **beautiful natural area** that extends west along the forested shores of Whitefish Bay and north into Canada. Connected by the International Bridge, the much larger **Sault Ste. Marie, Ontario** (population 79,000), is the point of departure for the Algoma Central Railroad's **popular Agawa Canyon excursion train** (in winter it's known as the **Snow Train**); for the drive along the **spectacular red Lake Superior bluffs** to Wawa; and for **Searchmont,** a ski resort with the second-biggest vertical drop in the Midwest after Mount Bohemia in the Keweenaw Peninsula.

Sault Ste. Marie, Michigan, is the **oldest continuously settled place in the Middle West**, going back to a trading post in the 1650s and mission a decade later. The southern (now American) riverbank was higher and more habitable. Long before that, Ojibwa (also called Chippewa) Indians lived on Sugar Island and fished in the whitewater rapids of the St. Mary's River, teeming with whitefish. They called the place "the rapids" — "Sault" in French, "Bawating" in Ojibwa (pronounced "BOW-ding," rhymes with "cow").

The **rapids,** rich in many species of fish, have always been the basis of the local economy. During the fur trade, from the 1600s into the 1800s, portaging around the rapids was necessary. (Today's Portage Avenue by the locks is along that old portage route.) The pressing need to ship valuable cargoes, first of copper, then iron, and later grain, to the Lower Lakes motivated the construction of a succession of **locks** which would eventually permit even huge 1,000-foot freighters to pass from one lake to the other.

There's little in the way of manufacturing and no mining in this part of Michigan. Across the river in Sault Ste. Marie, Canada, the imaginative American industrialist Francis Hector Clergue put together cheap power (generated by the fall at the St. Mary's River) with the iron and timber in the Canadian hinterland to create an industrial powerhouse that today dwarfs the older American Sault in population. Much of the land in Michigan interior here is marshy, though some of the

best Upper Peninsula farmland is around Pickford and Rudyard, 20 miles to the south. Two **automotive test tracks**, Continental Teves near Brimley and Smithers near Raco, take advantage of the area's cold, snowy weather and relative accessibility to Detroit via I-75. The big prison complex at Kincheloe and the casino are the biggest employers in a region that used to have one of the state's highest poverty rates before the Sault Ste. Marie Tribe of Chippewa Indians led the way to community economic development on an impressive scale through gambling.

Between Sault Ste. Marie and Whitefish Point, **Lake Shore Drive along Whitefish Bay is beautiful and most interesting**. At Brimley, it offers **terrific Lake Superior views** looking out onto shipping lanes. Going west along Lakeshore Road through Bay Mills, motorists pass the Bay Mills Casino and Resort (the first casino to take advantage of a prime scenic location and market itself as a destination resort with golf) plus a lighthouse museum with a **stunning view from its tower**, a **remarkable scenic overlook**, a **fish hatchery**, and a **beautiful short section** of the **North Country Trail** with a swinging bridge. The **Hiawatha National Forest**, which includes much of this land, has several picnic areas, campgrounds, and **beaches in prime settings**, often with very large trees spared during the logging era.

It all makes for a lovely day's drive, **especially magnificent in fall color season**, when maples, birches, and dark green conifers make rich color contrasts. If you're going between Tahquamenon Falls and Sault Ste. Marie, it's well worth the extra time to take Lake Shore west from Brimley as an east-west scenic route, instead of the direct but dull M-28.

TO FIND OUT MORE: For lodgings info and a travel guide to the entire area, including Brimley, with helpful itineraries, call **SAULT CONVENTION & VISITOR BUREAU**: (800) MI-SAULT, (906) 632-3301; www.saultstemarie.com. Its office is at 2581 I-75 Business Spur, in the circular building where the road turns north into town. Open weekdays 8:30-5:30. . . . . The **MICHIGAN WELCOME CENTER** is by the last I-75 exit in the U.S., at 943 Portage Ave. West. (Take Portage west of I-75.) It's full of printed information about the entire state, but especially strong on area and U.P. attractions. Open daily 9 a.m. to 5 p.m. (906) 632-8242. &. . . . At the Canadian end of the International Bridge, the **ONTARIO TRAVEL INFORMATION CENTER** is an extremely helpful source of all kinds of travel information, from customs and rebates and local info to provincial and national parks. Info can be mailed. The *Algoma Country Travel Guide* pulls a lot into one publication about the area. For an excellent guide to Sault Ontario events, get *Welcome! Sault Ste. Marie The International City*, a newsprint magazine published by *This Week* community weekly. Look for the Ontario Travel Info sign to your right coming off the bridge. (705) 945-6941; call collect to avoid international long distance. Open daily year-round, at least from 8:30 to 5. From mid June thru Labor Day open 8-8. In spring and fall open 8-6. . . . . For **free trip-planning info on CANADA'S NATIONAL PARKS and HISTORIC SITES**, call (888) 773-8888. . . . Traveling with **pets**? To enter Canada, their proof of vaccination is required.

PUBLIC LANDS: Most public land near the Michigan Sault is part of the **HIAWATHA NATIONAL FOREST**. Its office is at 4000 Bus. Spur I-75, out between the State Police Post and Cascade Crossing Mall. Open weekdays 8-4:30. The 24-hour lobby also has a complete range of handouts for the entire Hiawatha National Forest. (906) 635-05311. . . . The **MICHIGAN DEPARTMENT of NATURAL RESOURCES** Sault office is at 2001 Ashmun. (906) 635-5281. . . . . In Canada, two provincial parks are near Sault Ontario: **PANCAKE BAY PROVINCIAL PARK** and the very large **LAKE SUPERIOR PROVINCIAL PARK** on the way to Wawa. Get information about them by calling or stopping at the **Ontario Travel Information Center by the International Bridge**. (705) 945-6941. They accept collect calls.

GUIDES and GROUP OUTINGS: (This is a partial list.) Guided day trips and custom vacations kayaking, canoeing, or riding are offered by **Algoma Adventures**. Call (705) 945-5032 or visit www.algomaadventures.com. . . . **Experience North Adventures outdoor store** offers wilderness trips and natural history tours guided by **naturalists** via sea kayak, canoe, and foot to many natural areas. (705) 254-3899.. . . . The **Sault Naturalists of Ontario and Michigan** meet regularly and take monthly field trips. For upcoming outings and recent sightings, call the **Border Birder Hotline** at (705) 256-2790. . . . **The Saulteaux Club** of the Voyageur Trail Association schedules over 30 hikes, and bushwhack ski and snowshoe outings a year along its trails. For upcoming outings, call (705) 253-5353 and choose message 9999. Or visit www3.sympatico.ca/voyageur.trail

EVENTS: In **SAULT MICHIGAN** The **International I-500 Snowmobile Race** in early February. . . . **Engineer's Day** and **Soo Locks Festival** in late June and early July with music, games, and a chance to walk across the locks. . .The **Sault Tribe's Traditional Powwow** over July 4 weekend, with grand entries, open drum, and lessons. . . . The **International Bridge Walk** on the Saturday between Canada Day and July 4. It starts from Lake Superior State University at 9 a.m. July 4 brings a parade and fireworks. . . .The **Sugar Island Old Time Music Festival** in early August, with rustic camping. Call

(906) 632-8750. . . .For more details consult www.saultstemarie.com or call (800) MI-SAULT. . . . **SAULT ONTARIO** puts on one of **Ontario's largest winter carnivals, Bon Soo**, with fireworks, a professional snow sculptures, contests and dances at the Roberta Bondar Pavilion, traditional winter sports, snow volleyball, snowpitch, and a **Polar Bear Swim**. . . . **Canada Day**, July 1, is celebrated with music, children's activities, and fireworks along the river boardwalk. . . In early September native people from across America travel to the **Batchewana First Nation Annual Pow Wow** on the Rankin Reserve. . . . .One of the world's richest pro curling events, the **Regal Capital Curling Classic**, comes to Sault Canada usually in early November. . . . For details, contact **ONTARIO TRAVEL INFORMATION CENTER** . Call collect (705) 945-6941

HARBORS with transient dockage: In **Sault Ste. Marie** the **Charles Harvey Marina** south of Mission Point and the Sugar Island Ferry, east of town (906-632-6741; lat. 46° 28' 15" N, long. 84° 18' 00" W) with showers, launch ramp. Also, the **George Kemp Marina** in town on Portage Ave. by the S.S. *Valley Camp* (906-635-7670; lat. 46° 29' 57" N, long. 84° 20' 21" W) with shower, launch ramp, grills, laundry, long-term parking.

PICNIC PROVISIONS and PLACES

◆ In **SAULT MICHIGAN** the giant **24-hour Glen's Market** is the convenient all-around provisioning stop with a big deli section. It's on I-75 Business Spur at the newish Cascade Crossing center with Wal-Mart. . . . More sophisticated deli fare can be had in town at **Penny's Kitchen** and **Cup of the Day**. See **Restaurants**.

◆ Along Lake Superior's **Whitefish Bay** near Bay Mills and Brimley, choice picnic spots are the **Big Pine Picnic area**, Monocle Lake, and Brimley State Park. The **Wilcox Fish House** west of Bay Mills sells fresh fish and a whitefish dip. Find them through the index.

◆ In **Sault Michigan**, picnic tables at **Locks Park** and **Mission Point** are pretty whether or not there are ships to watch. Mission Point has grills, too.

◆ In **SAULT ONTARIO** the easy visitor choices for picnic fare are in the **big Station Mall** on Bay Street near the river. There's a produce market and good takeout fare at **Tim Horton's** (famous for soups and good sandwiches) and **Gourmet Stop**. Tim Horton's has other locations around town.

◆ The picnic tables at the **Sault St. Marie Canal National Historic Site** are a wonderful place to linger. The perimeter walk around St. Mary's Island affords the **best view of St. Mary's Rapids**.

◆ Benches & picnic tables are **all along the St. Mary's River Boardwalk** from the locks to the Bondar Pavilion and beyond.

◆ For ideas about more distant picnic destinations **on the Lake Superior drive** north from Sault, Ontario, ask at the Ontario Travel Information Center.

Sault Ste. Marie, MI
(*pop. 16,542*)

Located on the south shore of the St. Mary's River, across from its much larger Canadian sister-city of the same name, the Sault overlooks one of the most **strategic links** in Great Lakes shipping, the Soo Locks that make it possible for **giant freighters** to pass between Lake Huron and Lake Superior despite the rapids and 21-foot change in elevation here. ("Sault" means falls in French.) The **attractive park** and viewing stand at the locks is a magnet for boat-watchers and tourists of all stripes. Sault Ste. Marie is Michigan's oldest continually occupied settlement and one of the oldest in the U.S., thanks to the ancient portage around the falls of the St. Mary's River.

For centuries the rapids were an important Indian fishing spot in the region. The was first visited by a

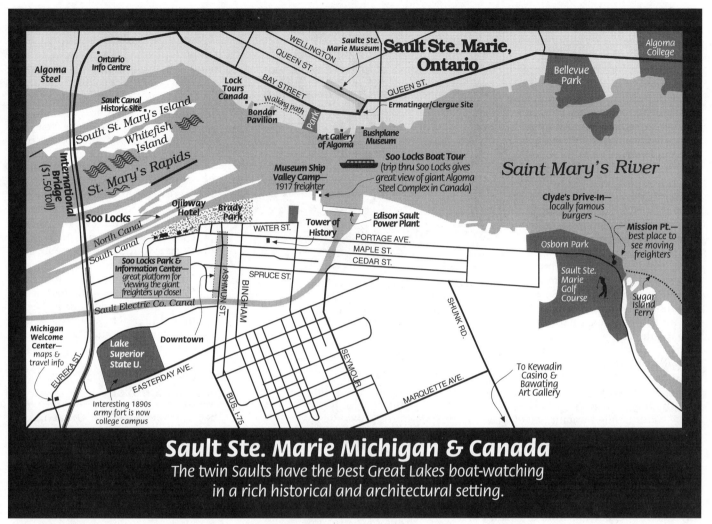

Sault Ste. Marie Michigan & Canada

The twin Saults have the best Great Lakes boat-watching
in a rich historical and architectural setting.

European in 1618, when Etienne Brulé, Champlain's scout, was on his search for the fabled Northwest Passage to the Orient. A **French trading post** developed here in the 1650s. Father Jacques Marquette established one of his Jesuit missions here in 1668. By the 1730s Sault Ste. Marie's importance in the fur trade had been eclipsed by Fort Michilimackinac at the northern tip of the Lower Peninsula.

Even though the city is located at such a strategic spot and over 100 million tons of cargo passes right by its downtown every year, Sault Ste. Marie has remained commercially rather static over the decades. It reached a low point in the late 1970s and early 1980s, when the state's economy was floundering and **the Air Force closed its Kincheloe air base** south of town. (Built to defend the strategic locks, it's pronounced "KIN-shul-OH.") A radar base closed as well. But the economy has picked up since the late 1980s, due to the **giant Kewadin casino** outside Sault Ste. Marie, two smaller casinos in nearby Bay Mills, and the **big new Kinross and**

Chippewa prisons at Kincheloe.

Gambling is the linchpin for the **Sault Ste. Marie Tribe of Chippewa Indians'** multifaceted, long-range **plan** under longtime tribal chairman Bernard Bouschor to build a self-sufficient employment base, educational and social services, and health insurance for all tribal members. Before gambling, many houses on the reservation had no indoor plumbing. Now the tribe has become a benefactor for the whole area. The tribe has developed its flagship Kewadin Casino in Sault Ste. Marie into a **spectacular entertainment/lodging/ cultural complex**, complete with a gallery of native Woodland art.. It sets a high standard for

To be sure to see
a ship in the locks—

find out what boats are expected when by calling the information desk at the Soo Locks Visitor Center: (906) 932-1472. The center is open from 8 a.m. to 10 p.m., and in summer from 7 a.m. to 11 p.m.

Midwestern casinos. Years ago the tribe, ever aware that the gaming industry is fast-changing and increasingly competitive, started to diversify with its gambling earnings. It now owns two construction companies, a charter air service, a manufacturer of driveshafts for the automotive aftermarket, several motels in and beyond Sault Ste. Marie, and a cleaning company.

The **Kewadin Casino** finished building the biggest convention center in the Upper Peninsula in 1997 with an eye to making the city a broad-based destination. It added a 16,000-square-foot bingo hall, three restaurants, a nightclub, a convention room seating 530, the 1,300-seat Dreammaker Theater, and an extra four stories on its Clarion Hotel, enlarging it to 300 rooms. The **Bawating Gallery** displays a large collection of contemporary **Woodland native art**, some of it for sale. **Demonstrations** of beadwork, basketmaking, and painting are usually on Saturdays. The casino is southeast of town on Shunk Road north of Three Mile Road. (see map). For information, call (800) KEWADIN, (906) 635-4917, look in at www.kewadin.com, or contact Tickets Plus (800-585-3737) for headline entertainment that has recently included Kenny Rogers, Culture Club, Gordon Lightfoot, and Loretta Lynn.

Gambling earnings have provided the wherewithal to develop educational and social service programs that emphasize traditional Ojibwa spirituality, traditional culture, and youth sports as effective tools in fighting substance abuse. The tribe's **well-written and substantive newspaper**, *The Sault Tribe News*, is worth seeking out. It gives revealing glimpses of community life, including activities at the charter elementary school and the Big Bear Arena, which brought ice hockey facilities in the American up to Canadian standards, with year-round ice and more.

Prisons, viewed in toto, are perhaps the largest industry of all in this region. The **Kinross** and **Chippewa correctional facilities** which house some 3,000 prisoners and pump $80 million a year into the local economy. The huge Kincheloe prison complex to the south handles another 4,000 prisoners and employs over 1,000.

Until the steady decline of the Canadian dollar (in 2001 worth only 64¢), another boost to the local economy had been the sizable number of Canadians crossing over the International Bridge to buy much cheaper gasoline and dairy products on the Michigan side. The bridge, over two miles long, once averaged 10,000 vehicle crossings a day because it is the only U.S.-Canadian bridge between Port Huron, 345 miles to the south, and the Ontario-Minnesota border, almost 600 miles to the northwest. But the daily vehicle count now numbers less than 9,000, and Americans going north to bargain-hunt in Loony-land now outnumber Canadians going south.

A conspicuous sight crossing the border into the U.S. are **big logging trucks** bringing cheaper timber from Canadian forests, where environmental restrictions are less stringent than in the U.S. Another common sight are trucks with big loads of steel from the giant Algoma plant, a looming sight across the river.

In the late 19th century, there were plans for Michigan's Sault Ste. Marie to become a major northern metropolis by using the St. Mary's River as a power source. **Francis Clergue** from Maine pursued this dream but went bankrupt in developing the impressive **sandstone hydroelectric power plant**, a quarter mile long, where the waterpower canal meets

Completion of the Sault Locks in the 1850s was a momentous event for the Upper Great Lakes. No longer did boats have to portage through the town.

A Chippewa fishing village and a portage town

For two hundred years [from 1668 to 1855] Sault Ste. Marie was a one-street town, straggling along the portage trail beside the mile-long rapids in the St. Mary's River. . . . The sound of the rapids was a constant voice. For miles the shore was dotted with the camps of the Indians. Their fires gleamed at the water's edge, and constant as the rapids came the drone of Indian drums.

There was a permanent village of Chippewas who lived by fishing and making sugar on the maple islands. In the spring thousands of other Indians gathered there to trade their furs at the big warehouses beside the portage trail and to gorge on whitefish from the river. Two men in a canoe could obtain five thousand pounds of fish in half a day. They dipped them out of the rapids—big, rich whitefish, weighing six to 15 pounds—with a scoop net on a pole. They feasted around their campfires, and for miles the wind carried the savory odor of roasting whitefish.

— From *The Long Ships Passing: The Story of the Great Lakes* by Walter Havighurst, (1942)

the river, on East Portage two-thirds of a mile east of Ashmun. The three-mile long power canal effectively created an island of downtown Sault Ste. Marie, which is connected to the rest of the city by five bridges. It's all too easy for visitors to miss seeing the **grand churches** and **public**

buildings from this exuberant turn-of-the-century era. They are along Bingham Avenue, which parallels Ashmun two blocks to the east.

The new industries so eagerly anticipated by Clergue never came to the Michigan. Clergue went bust, and Sault Ste. Marie, Michigan, is today not another Minneapolis but a town of less than 20,000 residents. Despite Clergue's ultimate financial failure, deals and alliances he had made earlier with Canadian investors did transform Sault Ste. Marie, Canada into the major **industrial center** it is today. Clergue helped create the **Algoma Central Railroad** (the famous Snow Train), St. Mary's Paper, Algoma Steel, and Algoma Central Marine. His story is poignantly told at the Tower of History on Portage Avenue in Sault, Michigan, and at the Ermatinger/Clergue Historic Site in the Canadian Sault.

Soo Locks Park & Visitor Center

A key link between the Great Lakes, the Soo Locks give a **close-up view of giant freighters**. They are on the American side of the river. (There's also an interesting visitor center at the smaller and older **Canadian lock**, now used for pleasure boats, on an island near the foot of the International Bridge.) The St. Mary's River connects Lake Superior to Lake Huron, then to the lower Great Lakes, and ultimately to the Atlantic. The locks, four in all, enable vessels to bypass the St. Mary's Rapids, a gradually descending drop of 21 feet. (So much water has been diverted by the locks and power canal that the rapids are far less impressive than they once were.)

For watching big boats up close, there's hardly a more dramatic place anywhere than the **elevated viewing stands**. They are in front of the visitor center operated by the **U.S. Army Corps of Engineers**, which constructed and maintains the locks and operates them toll-free. You can **look down onto the main deck of each massive vessel**, barely six yards away, as they move into the MacArthur Lock, the closest to shore. You see the crews of the locks and the ship moving about as the valves in the lock's floor open to let in or release water and the ship floats slowly up 21 feet to the Superior level or down to the Huron level. (It's all done by gravity; no pumping is required.)

At 800 feet long, the MacArthur Lock

The *Roger Blough*, 858' long and 105' wide, squeezes into the Poe Lock with inches to spare. A laker and a saltwater vessel are in the upper approaches to the MacArthur Lock at left.

The International Bridge and the Wisconsin Central railroad bridge are in the background. Photo & caption from *The Soo Locks Visitors Guide* by Roger LeLievre.

(built in 1943 and named after the controversial general Douglas MacArthur because of his Corps of Engineers connections) can't handle the current generation of thousand-foot vessels. They lock through the Poe locks farther north. "Discussion continues about building a **new, even larger U.S. lock** in the space now occupied by the Davis and Sabin locks," writes Roger LeLievre in *The Soo Locks Visitor's Guide* (24 pp., about $7), the clearest and most authoritative guide to the locks, past and present. A new lock "would relieve the pressure on the Poe, the only lock able to handle vessels more than 730 feet long and 76 feet wide. Cost of such a lock was estimated at $225 million in 1999, and would be paid for by the Federal government and the states surrounding the Great Lakes."

Alongside the locks, the **Soo Locks Park** is a **beautiful, peaceful place** to linger when it's not too crowded. It has the **air of a European park**, with its benches and neatly planted rows of same-size trees. The park is **especially pleasant in the evening**, when lights reflect on the water and illuminate the trees. Recorded music plays, and **colored lights illuminate the fountain**.

Often the Sault is foggy in spring and fall, giving it a haunting atmosphere. In an age known for its speed and instant connections, Locks Park is an entry point to the **slow-moving world of shipping**, and it has a real allure for visitors. Some people find it so relaxing that they hang around for days.

Each Wednesday evening from late June through August the **Superior Concert Series** brings to Locks Park **acoustic music**, often pertaining to the area's maritime and ethnic heritage: **voyageur** ballads, folk, Celtic, **sea shanties, plus bluegrass, barbershop,** and **country swing**. Bring lawn chairs or blankets.

Nowadays you should expect to wait a while to see a big boat pass through the locks, or plan your visit for the

Cold spot
Sault Ste. Marie is chilly even by U.P. standards. The winds sweeping off Lake Superior create average winter lows of just 5° F and average summer lows of 52° F.

arrival of a ship. Call (906) 932-1472 for a **recorded message of ship arrivals**. One big cargo ship comes through the locks every hour and a half on the average, though ships sometimes bunch due to bad weather and waits to go through the Poe Lock can be lengthy. Only 180 U.S. and Canadian cargo vessels are registered on the Lakes — down from 300 in 1886. That's largely because efficient, high-volume thousand-foot bulk carriers are gradually replacing 600-footers with the same number of crew but less than half the capacity. Also, the collapse of the Soviet Union means much less Great Plains wheat is being shipped overseas.

The Corps of Engineers' **elaborate and interesting Soo Locks Visitor Center** is open long hours from mid-May through mid-November. (See below.) In 1995 it doubled in size and added new displays. The locks' story is told with brochures and diagrams (quite helpful to boat-watchers) and with interesting photographs going back to construction of the first American lock in 1853-5. (A very small lock had been built on the Canadian side in 1797.) By 1853 the Upper Peninsula boom in copper and iron mining had created a pressing need for efficient shipping. The area's remote frontier location made it hard to get a federal land grant to be able to fund lock construction. Senator Henry Clay scoffed that a canal here would be "a work quite beyond the remotest settlement of the United States if not in the moon."

Visitors can see a **short video on the locks' history** and operations. As ship traffic and vessel size have increased, new locks have been built over the decades. Also on view is a **large working model of the locks** and a display about the environment of Lake Superior. An **arrival schedule** on the wall tells which freighters are due the next two to three hours.

Nine thousand vessels pass through these locks each year. About one half are huge cargo vessels, some carrying as much as 70,000 tons. In summer an average of over thirty freighters a day go through. Of the **85 million tons of cargo that passes through the locks each year**, over half is **iron ore** from the U.P. and Minnesota. **Coal** sent up from the lower lakes makes up another 15 million tons. **Minnesota wheat** accounts for 9 million. Other downbound vessels take iron taconite pellets from the iron ranges to steel plants on the lower Lakes, while upbound Great Lakes freighters are most likely to be carrying coal, stone, steel, cement, fuel oil, and road salt.

Most of the boats you see going through the locks are strictly Great Lakes vessels. But there are also ships that come from all around the world. These **oceangoing vessels** are easily recognized for their salt stains and three angled masts. The principal cargo of these "salties" coming from Lake Superior is grain grown in the North American heartland that feeds people around the world. To **identify the owners of every ship** on the lakes, consult *Know Your Ships* ($14.95), the boatwatcher's bible.

Locks Park extends east to the ends of the Poe and MacArthur locks, permitting a **dramatic view of the massive gates opening and closing** around the vessel locking through. The 1896 stone Administration Building with its observation tower gives a stately presence to the scene. A **wonderful aerial view** of the falls and locks is afforded by going over the impressive International Bridge to Sault Ste. Marie, Canada.

See **Ontario attractions** for background about the Canadian locks, once busier than the American locks. For speedy access to the interesting websites about the Canadian and American locks, go to www.locktours.com and click on "Canadian locks" (very interesting, done by Parks Canada) and "American Locks" (done by the Corps of Engineers).

To reach the locks, *take either I-75 Business Loop exit and get on Ashmun St., which is downtown. At the T intersection, turn left (west) onto Portage. Locks are in one block.* ***Dates of opening*** *and closing the locks vary. Currently the shipping season has been from mid or late March through mid-January. Park along Portage or adjacent streets. If space is tight, look west on Portage.* ***Corps of Engineers information center*** *is open mid-May through mid-November, 8 a.m. to 10 p.m. Extended hours, 7 a.m.-11p.m. from mid-June through Labor Day. (906) 632-3311.* ♿.

Portage Avenue shops

The relaxed scene at Locks Park contrasts to the clutter of tourist shops on the other side of Portage Avenue. (Portage Avenue is so named because it was the route over which ship cargoes were portaged or carried from Lake Superior to Lake Huron before the locks were built.) Some of the shops across from the locks continue to be among Michigan's most uninspired tourist traps, while others are competent, fun souvenir shops aimed at the mass market. Note: The Twin Soo Tour Train, a recommended visitor attraction, has been discontinued.

More **upscale year-round shops** are in the 200 block of Portage, across from the entrance to the Ojibway Hotel. A number of bars with occasional **bands and dancing** are in this block, too. The locally owned **MOLE HOLE** (632-3540) is at the corner of Portage and Osborn. At the **SHIPWRECK COAST MUSEUM STORE** at 223 W. Portage, (888) 800-7270, sales benefit the Great Lakes Shipwreck Museum at Whitefish Point. Here nautical models, gifts, and clothing plus Iverson snowshoe furniture are displayed with the same drama seen in the Great Lakes Shipwreck Museum. Visit it online at www.lssu.edu/shipwreck/ The **GREAT LAKES ART GALLERY** at 215 W. Portage, phone 632-9814, shares space with the **Portage Avenue Ice Cream Parlor** and its soda fountain. The gallery and frame shop has an extensive display of limited-edition prints of vessels and lighthouses include local and regional maritime scenes by Pat Norton in a distinctively misty, moody watercolor style. A few books and videos are sold here too, and some videos can be previewed here on a monitor. Far and away the area's **best selection of maritime books, maps, and gifts,** however, is at The Ship's Store a mile east off Portage next to the museum ship *Valley Camp*.

Past the west end of Locks Park and a short way down Ferris, Alberta House (635-1312) is the home of the **Sault Area Arts Council**, which mounts monthly exhibits. Its juried **gallery shop showcases pottery, watercolors, and prints** by some of the area's many active artists. It's open Tuesday through Friday, noon to 5, and Saturday 12-4 in summer.

A riverfront walk along Water Street and Brady Park

It's easy to visit the locks and remain unaware that there's a most attractive walk along Water Street. It's behind the six-story Ojibway Hotel that marks the apparent end of Soo Locks Park. Water Street leads to another **beautiful park** that offers a **close-up view of any upbound vessels** waiting to enter the locks.

Brady Park is on part of the site of the first Fort Brady, built in 1823. Interestingly, though the British had been defeated in the War of 1812, they did not quit this area until forced to by Michigan's territorial governor, Lewis Cass, in 1820. Cass claimed the Sault for the United States "with reckless courage that almost precipitated a massacre by pro-British Indians," according to historian Willis Dunbar.

Between the street and the river is a **history walkway** of flower gardens and interesting markers, new and old, that illuminate further aspects of the Soo's rich history. A **bust and bas-reliefs of scenes from Sault history** commemorates the outdoors-loving Chase Osborn, onetime publisher of the Sault Evening News. He was one of Michigan's more interesting governors and the only one from the U.P. A progressive Republican, he believed in using government to benefit society and its less fortunate members. He was Michigan's chief game & fish warden. From 1899 to 1903, Michigan commissioner of railroads. As governor from 1911 to 1912 he worked to enact Michigan's first workmen's compensation and successfully lobbied nationally for the free trade in the Reciprocity Agreement of 1911 with Canada, over the opposition of U.P. lumber, pulp, and farm lobbies. (He never won later bids for governor and U.S. senator.) Later he became a militant prohibitionist.

The core of Brady Park is on a **knoll capped by a red granite obelisk monument**. In 1905 it commemorated the 50th anniversary of opening the locks. The designer was no less than Charles McKim of **McKim, Mead and White**, the New York architecture firm that was the most prestigious of the time. It's an impressive Beaux Art touch from the turn-of-the-century era, when the citizens of the Soo aspired to greatness. Between the obelisk and the river is a **palisade of wood stakes** constructed on a small part of the original line of Fort Brady when it was here.

Overlooking the park are **several impressive homes**. One is the Water Street Inn bed and breakfast. The **site of Father Marquette's mission** is commemorated by a marker across Water Street from the park at the corner of Bingham.

River of History Museum

The ambitious River of History Museum in the **old Beaux Arts post office building** is an interesting change of pace from typical local history museums. Spoken stories at a few compelling **life-size dioramas focus** on key periods of area history and prehistory, beginning with a recreated scene of ancient people who speared whitefish by the rapids. The idea is to build on the stories handed down by native peoples, so visitors hear things like Bawating (the St. Mary's River rapids) saying, "I am old but ever young. Used but ever abundant, filled with life and alive with energy."

Gradually, as funding permits, the current director is adding to permanent and changing exhibits to make this less of a cruise-through museum aimed at school groups and children with short attention spans. Here kids can step into a **French fur trader's cabin** and try on clothes and other hands-on items. A room in British trader John Johnston's house has been recreated. Some exhibits change from year to year. Going through all eight of the museum's galleries takes about 30 to 45 minutes. It's a **good rainy-day destination**, with a **fine museum shop** of educational materials and local crafts.

209 E. Portage, a block east (right) from Ashmun/Bus. I-75 downtown. Park in rear. (906) 632-1999. Open mid-May thru mid October. By appt. in winter. Basic hours: Mon-Sat 10-5, Sun 12-5. $5/adult, $3.50 seniors, $2.50 ages 8-16. 7 and under free. $15/ family. &: use rear entrance by parking.

Bingham Avenue historic buildings

It's easy to see all the major visitor destinations in town and yet, if your head's not turned toward the monumental courthouse, you can miss this **avenue of**

The Chippewa County Courthouse anchors Bingham Avenue with its grand late 19th-century buildings. In front is "The Crane of the Sault" by Ralph Wolfe and William Morrison. The crane is the paramount totem or clan emblem of Sault-area Ojibwa.

impressive buildings. It vividly conveys the confidence in the area's destined greatness felt by local leaders in the late 19th century. Facing Bingham at the corner of East Portage is the **grand CHIPPEWA COUNTY COURTHOUSE of 1874**. It's made from limestone quarried on Drummond Island, trimmed with Marquette brownstone and capped with a large mansard-roofed clock tower.

History fans might want to end their walk with a visit to the **BAYLISS PUBLIC LIBRARY** (632-9331) at the end of Court Street, by the Power Canal. It's not an old building, but visitors may be interested in the space for rotating exhibits and in the Judge Steere History Room, which has materials from the Chippewa County Historical Society. *Open Tues-Sat from 9-5:30 except Tues & Th to 9, Sat to 1 or 3. &*

Of the avenue's **fine churches**, one of the most interesting is **SAINT JAMES EPISCOPAL CHURCH** (632-2451; &), at 533 Bingham at Carrie. Finished in 1903, it's on the **prestigious National Register of Historic Places**. In *Buildings of Michigan*, architectural historian Kathryn Eckert writes that the Late Gothic Revival church "resembles the small parish churches found on the Eastern Seaboard that were influenced by the English Ecclesiological movement." Local stone enhances "the look and flavor of the English parish church," she says. Chase Osborn, the newspaper editor who later became Michigan's only

governor from the U.P., gave the **11-bell carillon**, because the church was the only place in town large enough to hold the bells. They are heard each Sunday morning around 9:30. Visitors are welcome to see the interior. The evangelists, Matthew, Mark, Luke and John, are represented in **four carved figures** and again in the **beautiful front Tiffany stained-glass window**, said to be the third largest stained-glass window in Michigan. *Sunday services are at 8 a.m. and 10 a.m. Or, any weekday morning between 9 a.m. and noon, just ring the doorbell at the side entrance off the parking lot.* Today it's a challenge for a small parish to maintain this beautiful building, so donations would be appreciated.

In July and August St. James and four other churches cooperate in presenting a daily series of interesting free programs about each church's music, history, or art at 2 p.m. St. James is Tuesday, **St. George Greek Orthodox Church** at 511 Court is Wednesday, **Central Methodist** at 111 E. Spruce is Thursday, and **St. Mary's Catholic Churc**h is Friday. First Presbyterian at 309 Lyon had been Monday, but a fire in May, 2000, virtually destroyed it and it hasn't yet been rebuilt. Pick up a schedule here or at the chamber or visitors' bureau.

Bingham parallels Ashmun one block to the east. See map.

Tower of History

For an **outstanding overview of the area geographically and industrially**, visit the **weird but worthwhile** Tower of History. This **21-story concrete tower**, in an architectural style of the 1960s known as Brutalism, was built as the bell tower for the monumental, never-built church planned by the parish priest to replace the existing church next door. The project was intended to commemorate the role of missionaries in settling the Upper Peninsula. In 1967, after the $660,000 tower was finished, the governing Catholic bishop said enough already to the grandiose parish project. So the 1880s church remains next door at 320 East Portage. (See below.)

Le Sault de Sainte Marie Historical Sites turned the ill-fated tower into a museum. The best part is the **amazing 360° view from the tower's open-air deck** down onto the locks, the town below, the St. Mary's River, the Canadian Sault riverfront, Lake Superior, and the Laurentian Highlands beyond. It's one of those views where the real world looks like an aerial photo. Bring binoculars — and a windbreaker if it's at all cold or windy.

Also memorable is the **video** shown in the museum theater about the fruits and failures born of the **vision of Francis Clergue**, the man from Maine who put together the deals that created not only the monumental Edison Sault Power Plant just east of here but also the economic foundations of the Canadian: the vast Algoma Steel plant and St. Mary's Paper across the river. Other exhibits, limited by the tower's small base, deal with logging, Sault-area Indians, and Bishop Baraga.

326 E. Portage, 3 blocks east (right) from Ashmun/Bus. I-75. (906) 632-3658. Open mid-May thru mid-Oct, 10-6 daily. $3.25 adults; $1.75 ages 6-16. ♿: 3 or 4 steps lead into the museum. Once inside, wheelchairs can go on an elevator to the tower deck. Tight spaces make the rest of the museum inaccessible.

St. Mary's Pro-cathedral

The honorific name of "pro-cathedral" refers to the Roman Catholic parish's early role as the home of **Upper Peninsula's first cathedral**, founded by Bishop Frederick Baraga. He later moved the cathedral to Marquette. The 1880s church survived the attempts of a priest in the 1960s to replace it with a monumental concrete church in a style akin to the 21-story bell tower (now the Tower of History) next door.

The **stunning interior** got a high-caliber restoration in the 1990s. The rich blues, reds, and greens of the stained glass are echoed in the columns, carpet, and most memorably in dark blue walls with a delicate gold accent pattern. Local people are awed at the transformation. **Weekend masses** are Saturday at 5:15 and Sunday at 9:30 and 11:30 (11 in summer). Visitors are welcome to come in weekdays. Use the side door; look for a pamphlet about the church. Come between 10 and 4 to be sure of not interrupting Mass.

In the **Mary Room**, a separate space entered from the same entry hall, can be seen an acquisition from Bishop Baraga's tenure here: a **stained glass window of the 19th-century Belgian Blessed Virgin Mary**.

St. Mary's cooperates with four other churches in presenting free 2 p.m. **summer weekday programs of church music, art, and history** in July and August. Its day is Friday. See St. James Episcopal on Bingham (above) for details. *320 E. Portage. 632-3381.* ♿

Schoolcraft, Johnston and Baraga houses

Three of the earliest and most significant houses in the Upper Peninsula's history have been moved to Water Street to avoid demolition on their original sites. They are just west of the Valley Camp and new marina. The nonprofit Le Sault de Ste. Marie Historic Sites owns them and is looking for grants to complete their restoration. Eventually the organization would like to have them open as a sort of living history, akin to the Ermatinger-Clergue site on the Canadian side. During the Engler administration, state funds for historic preservation projects have withered, however.

Plaques identify the surviving portion of the simple dormered cottage of John Johnston and the small, **two-story house built by Bishop Baraga** when the Upper Peninsula's Roman Catholic diocese was in Sault Ste. Marie. He moved it to Marquette in 1864.

Elmwood, the Federal-style headquarters of U.S. Indian Agent Henry Rowe Schoolcraft, is where he collected materials for his books of **Ojibwa legends that Longfellow drew upon** for his wildly popular narrative poem *Hiawatha*. Elmwood's main house and connecting wings formed the center of Indian affairs for the upper Great Lakes from 1827, when it was finished, until 1833, when

---

John Johnston:
British loyalist and Michigander

"A native of Ireland and a Protestant, John Johnston (1762-1828) arrived on the Lake Superior frontier in the early 1790s. He married the daughter of a powerful Chippewa chief and settled here in 1793. Johnston's knowledge of the Chippewa and the Great Lakes region made him a central figure in the development of this frontier. His original house was a hospitable meeting place for explorers, trappers, traders, and Indians. Loyal to the British, Johnston aided them in taking the American fort on Mackinac Island in 1812. In retaliation, American troops burned Johnston's house in 1815. He soon rebuilt it. This surviving portion, erected about 1822, in part to house his daughter Jane and her husband, Henry Rowe Schoolcraft, is a reminder of Johnston's pivotal role in the area's transition from British to American control."

*— State Historical Marker
in front of the Johnston House*

---

the Indian Agency was moved to Mackinac Island.

The **energetic, opinionated Schoolcraft**, an explorer, scholar, administrator, and **self-promoter**, was a key figure in Michigan's territorial era. He explored the northland as far as the headwaters of the Mississippi to help assess the area's possibilities and advise on negotiating treaties with Indians.

Here in Sault Ste. Marie Schoolcraft met and married Jane Johnston, the bright, pretty daughter of the area's most important fur trader and his Ojibwa wife. Jane passed along the legends and stories that became the basis of *Hiawatha*. Despite Schoolcraft's status in literature and Michigan history, he's no local favorite. "He lied like a trooper," says Yvonne Hogue-Peer, Native American genealogist, granddaughter of chiefs (she's also descended from 17th-century Scottish immigrants), and past vice-president of the Chippewa County Historical Society. "He was self-taught, he had an inferiority complex, and he was out to impress. He made up a lot. Neither white nor Indian historians here like him because they don't know what to believe. He could have been an outstanding ethnologist because he had so much material to work with."

Schoolcraft's credibility was affected, it's widely agreed, by his **dislike of Indians** and his **desire to moralize** about their lack of ambition. Indians weren't allowed inside his mansion. When his wife's relations had to spend the night, according to oral tradition corroborated by physical evidence, they stayed in a pit dug under the house. Jane's considerable abilities as a storyteller and cultural interpreter went unacknowledged. (Schoolcraft himself did no field work.) He was no kinder to others. Eager to hog the limelight, he misled the young botanist who went along on his expedition and wanted to write a joint account of the trip. He belittled the early painter of Native American cultures George Catlin. And he publicly humiliated Bishop Baraga.

Schoolcraft designed Elmwood as a **grand mansion** for his residence and office. On its original site in a grove of spruces it faced the river, and its elegant elliptical windows and fanlights can be seen if you walk around to the back. **"Nothing matched it in the whole territory of Michigan,"** says Lake Superior State University history professor Bob Money, who worked for decades to research, save, and move the house. "Schoolcraft always had his eye on greatness. He had to have a house larger than his father-in-law's." The veranda was a hundred feet long, and the house and its furnishings elegant beyond anything else on the Upper Great Lakes.

Elmwood was the center of social life when winter cut off the village and Fort Brady from the rest of the world. The long winters help account for Schoolcraft's prodigious literary output here. Later Charles Harvey stayed at Elmwood when he was superintending the first lock's construction. A lumber baron bought Elmwood from the federal government and remodeled it beyond recognition into a Queen Anne mansion, full of picturesque gables and chimneys. Bob Money followed his hunch that the Victorian showplace concealed Schoolcraft's late Federal-style house. When expansion by the Edison Sault power plant threatened to demolish it, a generous and careful builder helped the grassroots preservation group move it. The electric company wouldn't drop its lines, so the house was floated in two pieces on a barge to its present location.

At some point in the next couple of years, at least some of these historic houses will be open to the public. Call the *Valley Camp*, (906) 632-3658, for current info.

Water Street is parallel to Portage, a block to the north. From Portage, take Bingham or Johnston to Water.

George Kemp Marina

There's a **nice picnic area** with grills at this beautiful new marina on the site of the onetime Kemp Coal docks, right next to Elmwood and the other historic houses. It's convenient for visitors coming to or from the *Valley Camp* or Soo Locks Boat Tours.

On Water Street at the foot of Johnston, next to the Valley Camp. ☐

Museum Ship *Valley Camp*

The Museum Ship *Valley Camp* is an unusual **blend of museum ship and Great Lakes maritime museum**. It's a 1917 steam-powered Great Lakes freighter, 550 feet long. Its large cargo holds have been converted into a museum with historical exhibits, two video theaters, aquariums of fish from the St. Mary's River, ship models, and more.

In one cavernous space the **Edmund Fitzgerald display** and the video "The Mystery of the *Edmund Fitzgerald*" effectively capture the eeriness with which that huge freighter disappeared suddenly from the view of a trailing freighter in that

The *Edmund Fitzgerald* display, video, and two wrecked lifeboats are highlights of the *Valley Camp* museum ship in Soo Michigan; more is at the Shipwreck Museum at Whitefish Point. The mysterious 1975 sinking occured just 16 miles from the protection of Whitefish Bay. The 729-foot *Fitzgerald*, launched to much fanfare in River Rouge, Michigan in 1958, was the first "maximum Seaway-size freighter" built for the new St. Lawrence Seaway to the Atlantic. Though soon surpassed by fifteen 730-foot vessels, the *Fitzgerald* remained a boat-watchers' favorite.

famous November storm in 1975. Captain Jimmie H. Hobaugh, USCG retired and now the museum's director, says that despite 25 years of investigation and many dives, "We're no closer to knowing what caused her to sink than we were when I conducted the Coast Guard search for the *Fitzgerald* in 1975." Many visitors come just to see the **Fitzgerald's two torn lifeboats**, among the very few remnants of the wreck to surface.

Another video theater gives a general history of the Great Lakes. These and other videos are for sale in the excellent **SHIP'S STORE** next door, managed by Le Sault de Sainte Marie Historical Sites, of which the Valley Camp is a part.

The superstructure lets visitors see **how the crew lived** on a bulk cargo carrier typical of those on the lakes between 1917 and the 1970s. The *Valley Camp*, under the ownership of Republic Steel, carried her last cargo, from Minnesota's Mesabi Range to the lower lakes, in 1966 before becoming a museum. **Especially interesting is its pilothouse**, which contains one of the lakes' first radar systems. Visitors can look in at the captain's quarters, the quarters of the other officers and crew, and the mess hall and galley. Until you **walk the deck**, it's hard to understand just how long 550 feet is. Even harder to take in is the increased carrying capacity of the thousand-footers that now set the standard for Great Lakes vessels,

with four times as much cargo space as the *Valley Camp.*

Interns in maritime history have reworked the faded lettering and out-of-date exhibit text that hurt the museum's credibility in the past. A new exhibit relates to the career of the late "Skipper" Manzutti, an independent ship builder, owner, captain, and maritime surveyor who was well known and well loved in the port of Sault Ste. Marie.

Tip: this place is so big, it's important to look at the **overview diagram** of the museum handed out to each visitor, in order to pick out what's likely to interest you most. Don't underestimate the **enthusiastic young female guides**, who have been rigorously trained by Capt. Hobaugh himself. They can answer questions authoritatively. This is a great place to visit on a rainy day.

Park by the dock off East Portage, 1/2 mile east of Ashmun and just west of the Soo Locks Boat Tours and the Edison Sault Power Plant. Open mid-May thru mid-Oct., daily 10-5. In July & August open 9-9. (906) 632-3658. Adults $7.25, kids 6 thru 16 $3.75, 5 and under free. ☐: partly. Museum and balcony in hold is accessible. So is main deck (via a ramp) but not bridge or crew quarters.

Ship's Store

The **excellent shop** of the Museum Ship **Valley Camp** is in a separate building by the parking lot with a **fine view of the river**. Its collection of books and videos on Great Lakes maritime subjects is outstanding. Here too are books on more general subjects like navigation and knot-tying, boat-related children's books and cookbooks, nautical brass, plus T shirts, sweatshirts, and maritime gift items. Visitors can **preview specific videos** on its in-store monitor.

Same parking area and hours as Valley Camp. 632-3658. Open mid-May thru mid-Oct., daily 10-5. In July & August open 9-9. &

Soo Locks Boat Tour

The Soo Locks Boat Tour offers a **dramatic ship's perspective of the locks**. Come early to get seats at the front of the boat if possible. The two-hour excursion takes you through the locks up to the level of Lake Superior, passing under the 2.8-mile-long International Bridge to Canada. The tour boat goes through both the Canadian and American locks. You are treated to a rather **surrealistic view of Canada's huge riverfront Algoma Steel**, with thousands of employees and five blast furnaces. On its wharf are enormous piles of purplish taconite pellets from Lake Superior's iron-mining regions. Across the river, you see downtown Sault Ste. Marie, Canada, and its waterfront. The narra-

tive, like that in many tours, involves too many statistics and too few ideas to make the statistics meaningful. But most visitors love the tour. *Note: The locks tour from the Canadian side has a fresh narration, rewritten at the behest of local historical groups. It might be worth a try.*

The slightly longer **sunset dinner cruise** ($38.50 for adults, $29.50 for children) gets you out on the water at a beautiful time, what with the light effects and the reflected blaze of the Algoma Steel furnaces on the water. The **dinner buffet**, with whitefish or roast beef entrée, is **quite good**.

Boat tour docks are along East Portage east of Ashmun/Bus. I-75 and the locks. One dock is next to the Museum Ship Valley Camp on Portage, half a mile east of Ashmun; another is 1.7 miles east of Ashmun, beyond the Edison Sault powerhouse. Regular season is from mid May into mid October. At the least, tours are at 11:30 a.m. and 2 and 4 p.m. In July and August boats leave hourly or more often between 9 a.m. and 5:40 or 6:40 p.m. For the complex, changing schedule, call (800) 432-6301 or pick up a brochure — they're everywhere. Buy tickets ahead of time. Adults $17, ages 13-18 $14.50, ages 4-12 $7.50, age 3 and under free. &

St. Mary's River Lighthouse Cruise

This new four-hour cruise, offered occasionally, takes visitors up through the locks to offer a sailor's view of the much-

visited Point Iroquois Lighthouse on Whitefish Bay that marks the entrance to the St. Mary's River, passing some **interesting and little-known navigational aids** along the way. The route is weather dependent, but the 8:30 a.m. departure time is more likely than afternoon to have favorable conditions.

The cruise passes an **impressive keeper's residence** at Birch Point near Brimley, now in private hands, and the remains of an abandoned lighthouse on Round Island. The cruise boat crosses to the Canadian side, passing the Gros Cap Reefs Light, going by the Point aux Pins beaches, and passing various navigational aids. Extra bonuses: you may get to see a lot of freighters coming in and out of the St. Mary's River, and you necessarily go through locks. The tour boat usually uses one lock on the American side and the Canadian lock.

Call (800) 432-6301 for dates. Reservations a must. Cost: $36. Leaves from Dock # 2 at 515 East Portage.

Edison Sault Power Plant & Alford Park

The distinctive Edison Sault Power Plant, a **major visual landmark** of the city, extends a quarter-mile along the St. Mary's River east of downtown. The project, completed in 1902, was pulled together by the visionary entrepreneur Francis Clergue. He hoped to use the power generated by the 21-foot drop between Lake Superior and the lower river to spawn new industries and transform Sault Ste. Marie, Michigan, into an industrial powerhouse. The hydroelectric plant attracted just one industry. But today it **generates 26,000 kilowatts of power**, helping to serve the electric needs of residents here as well as users as far away as Mackinac Island. The plant was constructed of the red-brown sandstone excavated when the power canal was dug. The looping cross-city canal supplies the water to turn the

The Soo is a good place for birding and fishing. Rarely seen this far south, Arctic-bred gyrfalcons (above) hang out by the Edison Sault plant in winter, feeding on unlucky ducks. The Whitefish Point Bird Observatory and gift shop, a popular day trip from the Soo, sells an inexpensive area bird guide and many birding books. This print by Gary Wright is among its decorative items. For Sault-area outings and sightings, call the Border Birder Hotline, (705) 256-2790.

plant's 69 turbines. "This wonderful building is the very essence of man and nature at work in northern Michigan," wrote architectural historian Kathryn Eckert in *Buildings of Michigan*.

Adjacent to the plant on its eastern end is Alford Park, an extraordinary location from which fishermen catch giant salmon each fall.

Mission Point, Aune Osborn Park & Sugar Island Ferry

The riverside park at the east end of Portage Avenue is **"the #1 place anywhere in the Great Lakes for boatwatchers to see boats in motion,"** says Roger LeLievre, editor-publisher of *Know Your Ships*, the annual boat-watcher's bible — and he's been just about everywhere on the lakes. "Vessels come closer there than pretty much anywhere else." Generations of local boat-watchers have enjoyed spur-of-the-moment outings driving down to the park to see what's coming at this point where the St. Mary's River bends south on its way to Lake Huron. One hitch: sometimes there are so many boatwatchers (they come here from all over the Great Lakes) lining the riverbanks and taking pictures that they obstruct the view.

A nice bonus: Clyde's Drive-In, right by the park, a Soo institution since 1949, known for its fresh grilled C burgers, trimmed as you like. A burger from Clyde's is "a must thing" for Roger on every visit to his home town.

The **Sugar Island Ferry** (635-5421; $4.50/car round trip) runs year-round and makes two round-trips an hour. The new *Sugar Islander II* leaves the mainland on the quarter hour and leaves the island on the hour and half-hour. It's larger than the old ferry, and better suited to withstand icy conditions.

Sugar Island

Sugar maples dominate the forest of this 15-mile-long island in the St. Mary's River. They made it a favorite Indian sugaring spot for many hundreds of years. Many Ojibwa lived here in recent times. The **Sault Ste. Marie Tribe of Chippewa Indians** bases its **tribal membership** on being able to trace ancestry to those **Sugar Island bands**. Cottages and small fishing resorts dominate the island today.

When the sugar maples turn red and yellow in fall color season, a drive around the island is a **spectacular experience**. There's a **café** and **ice cream shop** at

Mission Point at Osborn Park is "the best place on the lakes to see boats in motion," according to Great Lakes shipping authority Roger LeLievre. An added plus of the location: grilled-to-order hamburgers from Clyde's.

the ferry and a **bar with food** two miles up the hill on 1 1/2 Mile Rd. A **small township park** is on the North Shore Road. Get a map at the Sault Chamber of Commerce on Bus. I-75 (800-MI-SAULT). There's no perimeter road except along the north shore and part of the west shore. The downbound shipping lane is along the west shore, by the Michigan mainland. The upbound lane is on the Canadian side and not as close to shore.

For a vacation experience by the woods and water that's close to town, consider investigating Sugar Island resorts, especially if you like to fish or boat. They're open from sometime in May through sometime in October. Resorts are on the east shore, on Lake George, some 6 to 10 miles across. Boats are often included with accommodations. We have arranged the resorts from north to south: **Hay Point Hideaway** (906-632-6928), **Mountain View Resort** (906-635-0573), **Bennet's Landing** (906-632-2987; also boat rentals, tackle shop), and at the island's southeast tip with a good view of upbound shipping, **Island View Resort** (906-632-7976), and **Rainbow's End Resort** (906-632-6082).

New Fort Brady/ Lake Superior State University

With some **3,300 students**, almost all of them undergraduates, Lake Superior State University — or Lake State, as it's known locally — is **Michigan's smallest public university**. Personal attention is

one of its well-deserved selling points. Best-selling author of ancient prehistoric fiction Sue Harrison (*Mother Earth, Father Sky*) attributes her success to professors here who encouraged her through years of rejections from publishers. Wildlife management, business management, and criminal justice are some of Lake State's biggest programs. A fair percentage of its students commute from Canada. LSSU began after World War II when Michigan Tech in Houghton was flooded with returning G.I.s going to school on the **G.I. bill.**

Programs were set up here on the campus of **Fort Brady**. The fort dates from 1892-3. It was relocated to this high point to better guard the Soo Locks and its strategic iron shipments, essential for military production in wartime. Today the **possibility of attack** seems far-fetched, but it wasn't. Over 20,000 troops were stationed here at one time. Fort Brady was most active during World War I and just before American involvement in World War II. During that war the fort bristled with antiaircraft gun emplacements protecting the locks. Some of the late-Victorian fort's buildings were built as multi-gabled barracks, others were officers' quarters and offices that resemble Queen Anne houses with porches, overgrown and simplified. They're arranged around a **parade ground** akin to a collegiate quadrangle. Pick up an **interesting annotated map** and **self-guided walking tour** at the admissions office in Hillside House. (See entrance sign for directions or stop at security office for a map.) The university added new buildings starting in the 1960s. The Chippewa County Historical Society and LSSU are developing a small Fort Brady museum in the former stockade. Call LSSU (below) for details. **Custom campus tours** are by arrangement; call 635-6696 or (888) 800-LSSU and ask for admissions.

Students and faculty participate in a **first day of spring** celebration that's probably unique. To lift spirits when weeks of snow cover remain, they **burn a papier-mâché snowman** while passing out flowers and reading poems about spring.

Internationally, LSSU is best known for its **Word Banishment List**, released by newspapers on January 1. Most-nominated picks for 2000: chad, speaks to, celebrate, fuzzy math, the redundancies "manual recount by hand" and "final destination," factoid, diva, dude, and "have a good one." **To nominate words** or see the whole list, visit www.lssu.edu (it's also a treasure trove of historical info) and scroll down to Word Banishment List. The list is compiled not by the English department but by the public relations office from thousands of nominations, mostly from the U.S. and Canada. Inspired by the Queen's Honor List of new knights, the Word Banishment List was the brainchild of the late Bill Rabe, a metro Detroit PR man who spent the last two decades of his career at LSSU. He devised it to give his school some media visibility and released it on January 1, a slow news day. "It's so popular, the press calls us if they don't get their copy by mid-December," says current PR staffer Tom Pink. He and his coworker compile the list in between their other, more central duties by getting help from faculty and students in weeding through the nominations.

LSSU is north off Easterday, a major east-west artery that is the last exit off I-75 before the International Bridge. Go east from I-75 or west from Ashmun to reach it. The main entrance is Meridian. www.lssu.edu (888) 800-LSSU or 632-6841.

International Bridge

Before this long, imposing bridge was completed in 1962, it took a ferry to cross the St. Mary's River, which meant that residents of the Twin Saults on either side of the border got to know one another much better. The International Bridge, planned and financed by the governments of Michigan and Ontario, connects two of the most important highways on the North American continent:

the **5,000-mile Trans-Canada Highway** and **2,000-mile I-75**, which goes all the way to southern Florida. Next to the International Bridge is an **unusual jackknife railroad bridge built in 1919** and still in use. It folds up on both sides to allow freighter traffic through. Rail cars most frequently are loaded with logs bound for paper mills.

The International Bridge is nearly three miles long including approaches. It's a worthwhile sight in its own right. It offers passengers in motor vehicles **splendid views west to Lake Superior**, down onto the sprawling Algoma Steel plant and fly fishermen on Whitefish Island, and east to the Soo Locks.

Once a year, on the Saturday before July 4, pedestrians can walk across the bridge as part of the **International Bridge Walk** celebrating Canadian and American independence (June 29 and July 4). It starts at Lake Superior State University, north off Easterday on the hill overlooking the bridge, at 10 a.m. *Terminus of I-75. $1.50/auto, 75¢/bike. Bicycles can cross any time, in a regular traffic lane.*

SOO MICHIGAN RESTAURANTS

Arranged from the locks outward.

Across from the locks park at 329 W. Portage, The **LOCK VIEW Restaurant** isn't just for tourists. Local people regard its **whitefish** as the best, and the soups are good, too. Whitefish ($11 at dinner, including Friday's all-you-can-eat fish fry after 4 p.m.) is prepared five ways: pan-fried, broiled, deep-fried, cajun, and lemon pepper. Other attractions are the $3.45 breakfast special with eggs, meat and hotcakes; Heart Smart items at every meal; $6 basket specials at lunch, burgers, and fried clams. The owner spends winters making various kinds of locks-related nautical decor for tables, walls, etc. When it's busy, the second floor is open (in summer this is often Thursday through Saturday), which gives a view of the locks through trees. *329 W. Portage. 632-2772. Opens sometime in late April or early May, weather depending. Closes mid Oct. Open daily 7 a.m-8 p.m. at least, weekends to 9, in season to 10 p.m.* 🚫 🚶🚶 Full bar

FREIGHTERS, the restaurant at the **Ojibway Hotel**, next to Locks Park, is in transition — to what it's not clear — as new owners seem to be trying to figure out how to seek the right balance. Freighters had offered Soo Michigan's most sophisticated and expensive fare, but lost business to Soo Ontario's top restaurants due to inconsistency in the

kitchen under previous owners. The new owners haven't stinted on investing in the property. In the winter they cut back on restaurant hours and service. What will the summer bring? If it's anything like last year's menu and quality, expect very good dinner entrées in the $16 to $23 range, with dishes like rack of lamb and veal marsala in addition to the usual whitefish. Seafood was a specialty. Vegetarian by request. In any case, the dining room here is a very pleasant space. The glass-lined back wall **overlooks the locks**. Last year the hotel's cozy **CAPTAIN'S PUB & GRILL** featured not only a full bar but ice cream, cappuccino, and a light sandwich menu. In summer it opens at noon, otherwise at 5. The pub has a gas fireplace and looks out onto Locks Park. Ask about **possible entertainment** on weekends. *240 W. Portage. 632-4100. Daily 6 a.m.-9 p.m. From June through mid Oct to 10 p.m.* 🚫 🚶🚶 Full bar

Tucked away on a downtown side street, **PENNY'S KITCHEN** has grown from a caterer into a bustling, very successful smoke-free coffeehouse, deli, **bakery**, gourmet, and **kitchen specialty shop**. A bright, casual atmosphere reigns in the café (with table service), which opens early for fresh bagels, muffins, and scones (75¢ to $1.50) and entrées like blueberry pancakes ($2 and $3.45), omelets ($5 and up), filled croissants, and $4.75 egg/cheese scrambles served in bread bowls. For lunch there are many deli sandwiches (mostly $5 to $6), **wonderful soups**, and prepared salads. This is the place for **special picnic takeouts**. *On Spruce, 3 blocks south of Portage and half a block west of Ashmun. 632-1232. Mon-Fri 7 a.m.-6 p.m., Sat 8-5, Sun 8-3.* 🚫

CUP of the DAY Coffeehouse & Deli in the heart of downtown offers public **Internet access** and a wide range of coffees, cheesecakes, fountain sodas, smoothies, raw juices; entrée salads ($5-$6); over 30 specialty wraps, panini, and sandwiches (mostly around $5); and soups. There's lots for vegetarians. House specialties are **chicken gumbo soup** and **grilled California panini with turkey, avocado, and cheddar**. The owner/chef, who heads the downtown business group, promotes lunch meetings, so this is an especially good place to observe local cultures in process. *406 Ashmun. 635-7272. www.cupoftheday .com. Summer hours: Mon-Fri 7 a.m. to 8 p.m., Sat 8-6, Sun 9-3. Regular hours: Mon-Fri 7:15-6, Sat 8:15-3.* 🚫 🚶🚶

Perhaps the best-known restaurant in the Michigan Soo is **THE ANTLERS**, a family restaurant (15 years ago it would have been called a bar) in an old building made of sandstone rubble. The draw is the decor: **dozens of deer antlers cover the walls and beams**, intermixed with **stuffed beasts**, from a big polar bear to deer and beaver. Sometimes these mounts form the centerpieces of **wildlife scenes**. The Antlers has gradually evolved after an Irishman from Detroit's east side bought it in 1948 and went for the hunting motif. It's still in the family, and the mounted animals number over 300. **Bells** and **whistles** fill the air every hour or more, when there's a touchdown or a customer with a birthday — or just upon request. The wisecracking 8-page menu ($4 to $25) features burgers, Mexican dishes, steaks, chicken, and seafood, along with homemade soups. *804 East Portage across from the Edison Sault power plant. 632-3571. Opens daily at 11 a.m., except noon Sun. Kitchen open to whenever.* & ♯♠♠ Full Bar

Generations have grown up on various sizes of the C Burgers, from baby to the 3/4 pound Big C, made fresh on the grill and served as you like at **CLYDE'S DRIVE-IN**. Hearkening back to an earlier era of burger joints (1949), Clyde's offers eat-in and **curb service** and remains very much a diner serving breakfasts, chili, soups, and baskets of fried chicken, shrimp, and perch. An extra plus for boatwatchers: it's at Mission Point, the **best place on the Great Lakes to watch freighters in motion**. No credit cards. *At the Sugar Island Ferry dock on Riverside Drive. That's the extension of East Portage, about 2 miles east of Ashmun. 632-2581. Open from May into mid-October. Open 7 days, 9 a.m.-10 p.m., Fri & Sat to 11 p.m., later in summer. Curb service from 11 a.m.* & : curb service only ♯♠♠

STUDEBAKER'S RESTAURANT and LOUNGE is a local favorite, especially for breakfast. It's a competent all-around restaurant with a wide-ranging sandwich, salad bar, and dinner menu (Mexican, pasta, steak, seafood, chicken). Most dinner entrées are from $7 to $10. The sandwich menu is served any time. The big breakfast menu features good 3-egg omelets ($5 and under) and a **weekend breakfast buffet**. It's fun to see an owner's collection of **Studebaker memorabilia**, highly evocative for people who grew up in South Bend. *3583 I-75 Business Spur next to Days Inn out by Kmart. 632-4262 Open daily 7 a.m.-9 p.m., to 10 in summer and on Fri & Sat..* & ♯♠♠ Full bar

For **pizza** and a full menu, **ANG-GIO'S RESTAURANT** stands out. It's a weekly destination for the families of many working mothers. The sandwich menu is served any time. Weekdays bring the lunchtime pizza buffet from 11:30 to 2. Dinner entrées are from $9 to $11. *By the Ramada Inn on the west side of Bus. Spur I-75. 635-3046. Open daily from 11 a.m. to 10 p.m.* & ♯♠♠ Full bar

SOO MICHIGAN LODGINGS

See also: Soo Ontario

NOTE: Motel row is mixed in with shopping plazas and fast-food on Business Route I-75. It includes older, independent motels in town but up the bluff and too far to walk to the locks. Large facilities, closer to the I-75 exit, are from 60 to 100 rooms and most likely to have indoor pools: the Days Inn, Best Western Colonial, Hampton Inn and Holiday Inn Express. The Comfort Inn is adjacent to Cascade Crossing, anchored by Wal-Mart, that has the movie multiplex.

Casino business helps fill rooms everywhere in the Soo, of course. Many motels offer **free casino shuttles** and special casino packages. Some offer **Agawa Canyon train packages.**

Kewadin Casino's growth fueled a long lodgings boom here, but more new facilities were being built just as competition increased from other casinos in Mount Pleasant and Detroit. As a result, there may be 300 rooms too many — good for visitors, bad for the local lodgings industry.

From the perspective of environments that have a sense of place, the **most interesting locations** by far, are those **by the waterfront** — either near the locks or within walking distance to the waterfront parks. Ships move through the locks and down the river at all times of day and night. It's fun to take an evening stroll and watch a giant vessel passing by, with its superstructure lit up like a party boat.

Area motels can fill up from gamblers and special events, but with so many rooms, turnover is high and summer availability is better on short notice than in smaller vacation areas. Book early (April or May) for special events.

Consult the convention and visitors' bureau or AAA for a wider range of lodging possibilities. Motel selections here are arranged from the locks and river out Bus. Spur I-75. See also: **Soo Canada.**

ASKWITH LOCKVIEW MOTEL
(906) 632-2491; (800) 854-07455; www.lockview.com

The well-run motel is across from the locks' visitor center. A few of its 47 mostly drive-up rooms have limited views of the locks; most don't. But this is an **ideal location for boatwatchers** who want to be where the action is at a moment's notice. The motel is really a collection of attractively remodeled tourist cabins and motel buildings. The lot has room enough for cars and some small lawn areas. A **little terrace with tables** is in front. Hanging flower baskets and good maintenance make up for the cramped site. The ample rooms are rather elegantly furnished. All have cable TV, air-conditioning, and phones. Many bed configurations. Complimentary coffee and **continental breakfast** is served in the office. The Lockview Restaurant is next door. Free shuttle to casino. Sample rates for two from 2000: $58-$64. Less before mid June. *27 W. Portage right across from the Soo Locks Information Center. Open from last weekend of April to October 15.*
H.A.: some ADA accessible rooms ♯♠♠: $3/extra person

LONG SHIPS MOTEL   (906) 632-2422

This pleasant family-run place across from the locks has 23 attractive drive-up rooms on one floor. All rooms have cable TV and air-conditioning. Some have phones. Morning coffee is available in the office. Various bed configurations: one queen, one double, two doubles. *427 W. Portage, opposite the west gate of the Sault Locks Park. Open from May thru mid October.*
H.A.: call ♯♠♠: under 10 free; $5/extra person

RAMADA PLAZA HOTEL OJIBWAY
(800) 654-2929; (906) 632-4100; www.ojibwayhotel.com

This **elegantly renovated six-story hotel**, built in 1928, enjoys an excellent location next to Locks Park. Of the 71 rooms, those on and above the fourth floor on the north side, above the nearby trees, have **good views of ships**, though the vintage windows are smallish. There's a comfortable lobby, **cozy bar**, **small indoor pool** with sauna, spa, and fitness room. Freighters restaurant and Captain's Pub are in the hotel. New owners are doing even more, with new wallpaper and new carpet for starters. All rooms have dataports and voice mail plus standard features like cable TV. Rooms vary from small but luxuriously decorated to large, elaborately furnished two-room suites with spas, king beds, and wet bars. Standard summer rates: $139, or $225 for suites. Ask about possible packages and AAA, AARP discounts. The hotel is frequently full on winter weekdays because of G.M. technicians who come up to test vehicles under arctic conditions. *240 W. Portage just east of Locks Park.* &

WATER STREET INN B&B
(906) 632-1900; (800) 236-1904

The **setting is terrific**: a **circa 1900 Queen Anne mansion**, built by a lumber dealer who included all the trimmings: stained glass windows in the grand stair hall; marble fireplaces; and original woodwork. It's perched up so the wrap-around front porch and the gazebo offer a **good view across attractive Brady Park to the river and passing ships**. It's easy walking to the locks, historic downtown areas. Innkeepers Anna and Duane Henion are here in part because of his job with the International Bridge. They keep up with destinations and restaurants on both sides of the border. 4 rooms ($75-$105) have private baths. *140 Water, across from Brady Park.*

H.A.: no

DORAL MOTEL   (906) 632-6621

A **pleasant outdoor pool area**, picnic tables, and a **good view of passing ships** from the second floor are special attractions at this two-story, 20-room motel circa 1970. The building of the Soo Locks Cruises somewhat obstructs the ground-level view. Rooms have phones, cable TV, and air-conditioning. In-season rates in 2000 were $66 (2 doubles or one queen), or $72 for the larger family room. Morning coffee in lobby. The Antlers restaurant and *Valley Camp* are within two blocks. Reserve at least a week ahead for summer weekends. *518 East Portage across from the Soo Locks Cruises parking lot. Open from late April thru October.*

H.A.: call 👪: free with parents; $5/extra person

RIVER-AIRE MOTEL (906) 632-8342
off-season (616) 946-2921;
e-mail riverair@torchlake.com

Totally off the beaten path, this **charming four-room motel** is south of Mission Point and a 10-minute drive to the locks. The property extends **back to the St. Mary's River**, where a **picnic area** and benches offer a serene place to watch boats and have **evening bonfires**, weather permitting. Each room, paneled

in knotty pine, has a king bed, a **minifridge** and microwave, and a sofa bed. Rooms have cable TV and air-conditioning. Guests can use the office phone. Rates are currently around $50 — an incredible value, made possible because a facility like this is too small to advertise. Owners Joanne and Reg Fischer put out sweet rolls and coffee in the office each morning. Reserve early (by April at least) for summer. It's 1 1/2 miles to Clyde's, which serves breakfast and famous burgers. All no-smoking. By reservation only. *On Riverside Drive just south of Three Mile Road, 1 1/2 miles south of Mission Point. Generally open from Mem. Day thru mid Oct.*

H.A.: call   🐕: call

HAMPTON INN
(906) 635-3000; (800) 426-7866

Based on scouting around in fall of 2000, the Hampton Inn has the **most attractive indoor pool and lobby area** in Soo, Michigan. For some families, that's quite important. Next to Abner's restaurant, not far from Ang-Gio's and Studebaker's. **3295 I-75 Business Spur. H.A.**: some ADA accessible rooms.

KING'S INN MOTEL
(906) 635-5061; (800) 424-4875

This friendly, owner-operated 16-room motel has a lot to offer travelers with pets, who won't find accommodations in big, new facilities. The five-acre property has **space to walk dogs** in back and some picnic tables. Rooms are individually decorated and pleasantly homey. All have direct-dial phones, cable TV, air-conditioning, and in-room coffee. Rates for two in season: $48-$52. Many bed combinations. Smoking rooms have microwaves and minifridges. There are some no-smoking rooms where pets are permitted, and some allergen-free rooms with no smoking and no pets. Note: smoking rooms had noticeable smoke on a visit in fall, 2000. *On snowmobile trail. Near Studebaker's restaurant. 3755 I-75 Bus. Spur a little north of Three Mile Rd. Open year-round.*

H.A., call   👪: free with parents
🐕: with permission

PLAZA MOTOR MOTEL
(906) 635-1881;
www.plazamotormotel.com

Fabulous English-style gardens and **beautiful rooms** the equal of any bed and breakfast make this 21-room motel almost unique. A relaxing atmosphere in this adult getaway is paramount, and rooms are designed for **cocooning**, with **minifridge, microwave**, and coffeemak-

er with Godiva coffee. All have phones and cable TV. Even the smaller rooms seem luxurious, thanks to Waverly fabrics and furnishings that underscore the English country look. Each room is different; the king rooms have four-poster beds with canopies. Because the market here is so competitive, rates are amazingly low — currently $49 to $61. Owner-managers Jim and Lori Anderson have had the motel since the late 1980s, and every year they add to the garden, a mix of perennials and annuals. **Benches** and a **gazebo**, furnished in wicker, encourage guests to enjoy the gardens. The **fountain** helps mask road noise. It's hard to believe that Wal-Mart and the cineplex are just around the corner. *3901 I-75 Bus. Spur, exit 392, just north of Three Mile Rd. Open year-round.*

H.A.: call

HOLIDAY INN EXPRESS
(906) 632-3999; (800) 632-7879

This five-story, 97-room facility has an unusual location away from the other chains, right near Lake Superior State University and the last Michigan exit of I-75. It has an **indoor pool, exercise room**, and some rooms on upper floors have a **view** of the **St. Mary's River** and **International Bridge**. It would be the best year-round choice for people who like to walk or jog near their lodging. Listed rates for standard rooms for 2001: $69-$99. There's a free continental breakfast and an attractive lobby.

Just south of Easterday at I-75 exit 394

H.A.: some ADA accessible rooms. 👪

KEWADIN Hotel & Convention Center
(800) 539-2346; (906) 635-1400;
www.kewadin.com

This vast 24-hour Las Vegas-style complex, the flagship of the Sault Ste. Marie Tribe of Chippewa's casino empire, not only has the casino and bingo hall but an **indoor pool, gallery of Native American art**, weight room, and **live entertainment**, including frequent headline performers. Many tribal facilities including the Big Bear Arena are nearby. Consult the website or call for current packages and room rates at the 320-room hotel. *2186 Shunk Rd. east of town. See map.* & 👪

SOO MICHIGAN CAMPING

AUNE-OSBORN CAMPGROUND
(906) 632-3268; not reservable

Right **on the St. Mary's River** just east of the Edison Sault Power Plant, this modern city-owned campground has 100 close-spaced sites, 57 with electric and water. It's mostly used by RVs, but tent campers are welcome. Rates are $18/night, or $20 for a few sites on the water. Don't expect much in the way of shade. There's a **playground**, dump station, and boat launch. The campground's leasee-manager, Chuck Stevenson, is a retired lockmaster, and he's a great resource on shipping and Soo History. He worked for Cliff Aune (pronounced ON-ee), the area engineer for the Corps of Engineers, and remembers when Stella Osborn, the adopted daughter and widow of ex-Governor Chase Osborn, lobbied to have her husband's name included in a public facility. Sites open up daily. Checkout time is noon. Come then and you'll most likely get a site. *1225 Riverside Dr. (Portage). Open from May 15, probably earlier, to Oct. 15.*

H.A.: shower buildings ADA accessible

SHERMAN PARK CAMPGROUND
(906) 635-5075 (office), (906) 635-5341 (city parks & rec). No reservations.

This 25-site rustic campground is on the Upper St. Mary's River west of town and I-75. The campground is next to a park with a **nice sandy swimming beach** that stays shallow way out, a **boat launch**, horseshoe pits, and playground. The campsites themselves are shady, without water views or shrubby buffers between sites. The campground normally doesn't *fill. $12/night. West of I-75. Take Easterday west to Fourth Ave., turn north to campground. Open from May 15 to Oct. 15.*

H.A.: not really

Sault Ste. Marie, Ont.
(pop. 79,000)

This Canadian steel-making city dwarfs its older American counterpart across the St. Mary's River. The Ontario city of Salute Ste. Marie is home to giant Algoma Steel, a complex that dominates the view up the St. Mary's River from the Michigan side. The steel mill was created shortly after 1900 as part of American entrepreneur Francis Clergue's idea to use power generated by the Falls of the St. Mary's to turn the twin Saults into major industrial centers. He got more investors on the Canadian side than the American. The same Canadian investors built the Algoma Central Railway north into the wilderness to ship iron ore for the new steel plant and to develop the forest resources of the hinterland. The

The Sault Ste. Marie National Historic Site in Canada features the reconstructed 1895 lock, now used by pleasure boats. Once it was deeper and more important than the American lock. A trail goes alongside the St. Mary's Rapids. Lock Tours Canada offers tours through the Canadian and American locks.

Algoma Central still hauls freight and timber but is more famous as the Agawa Canyon Tour Train (the Snow train) taking visitors to look at the wilderness in fall and winter.

Algoma Steel is **Canada's third largest steelmaker**, with 4,000 employees. Rolled steel for making auto bodies is a major product, as is structural steel plate for construction. Although much bigger than any plant in the U.P., Algoma once was much larger. It had 12,000 employees in the 1970s before being downsized because of the same pressures from Japanese steelmakers that decimated Pittsburgh's steel giants.

Now Canada's largest employee-owned company, Algoma is repositioning itself. It is abandoning the production of what the industry calls "shaped products" like steel rails and tubes to concentrate on making rolled steel, a mainstay of the auto industry. But the com-

pany is still struggling, bitterly complaining of the steel dumping practices of countries from Brazil to China to Bulgaria.

The American and Canadian boat tours through the Soo Locks provide visitors with an almost **surreal, up-close view** of those portions of the **sprawling Algoma complex** that are on the riverfront.

The steel plant attracted many Italian immigrant workers early in the century. Today **Italians make up over one third of the city's population**. Their most visible presence is the **many Italian restaurants**, some of them quite good (see below).

The Canadian Sault's other big company is 400-employee St. Mary's Paper, just east of the International Bridge along the river. Clergue founded it as a pulp mill in 1896. Into the plant by train come tons of logs daily, and out come approximately 660 tons of the shiny paper used in advertising supplements for customers like Kmart and Target.

Kids today can still get excited about visiting Canada — a foreign country — and noticing foreign coins, kilometers instead of miles, different spellings and words on signs, and different cereal, candy, and crackers in the supermarket. Canadians still celebrate **Queen Victoria's birthday** (May 24) on the nearest day that makes a three-day weekend. A number of restaurants offer **afternoon tea**. And from October to mid-April they play **curling**, a very slow

Changing money

To get the best rate of exchange, the Sault Ste. Marie Canada visitor office recommends **exchanging currency before shopping**. U.S. money can be changed at any bank, at the Ontario Visitor Centre on Queen Street as you get off the bridge, and the NorCam Currency Exchange, 303 Cathcart. $1 U.S. = about $1.30 Canadian. All major U.S. credit cards are accepted in Canada.

game involving sliding a stone on ice. Call the Soo Curlers Association (705-945-6174) for details. Add a souvenir with a Canadian maple leaf for a lasting memory! It can be interesting for adults, too, to see the differences between the two North American countries, from styles of residential construction to bookstores and radio stations where the government's insistence on Canadian cultural content can be seen and heard.

Now there are **great bargains** for shoppers whose American dollar buys over $1.40 in Canadian merchandise. Station Mall downtown has over 125 stores. One-of-a-kind shops and restaurants are on Queen Street between between East and Gore. See below. **Charity gambling** was introduced in 1999 to give gamblers at Kewadin Casino a reason to cross the river and gamble in Canada. The casino, first of its kind in Ontario, is strategically located next to the Ontario Travel Information Center (705-945-6941) at the International Bridge exit.

The Canadian Sault is also the point of departure for **canoe, kayak, and fishing** trips to **Lake Superior's scenic north shore** and the **Algoma Highlands**. **Spectacular red cliffs** join Lake Superior at the edge of the rugged Canadian Shield, North America's oldest rock. Rocks and lake make a trip along the shore road to **Wawa**, 120 miles northwest of Sault, Ontario, a memorable experience for the most seasoned traveler — especially during fall color season. Wawa is an iron-mining and resort town of 5,000. Agawa Bayou and Lake Superior Provincial Park are popular places to stop along the way; fishing, kayaking, and beaches are big draws. **Ancient petroglyphs** add a cultural dimension. The Sault Michigan CVB's free travel guide has a good itinerary for a one-day drive along Superior's Canadian shore. For guided trips and group outings, see "To Find Out More" in the chapter introduction.

Here are many of the attractions of most interest to American visitors, starting with info about the Agawa Canyon Tour Train and then along the riverfront, starting with the Canadian locks moving east to the landmark Roberta Bondar Pavilion (the tent-shaped gathering space) and downtown Queen Street.

The Agawa Canyon Tour Train and Snow Train

The tour train of the hard-working Algoma Central Railroad heads north into the **mostly roadless wilderness** toward **Hearst**, a mostly French-speaking lumber town dubbed "the **moose capital of**

Peak fishing seasons in the Sault area

Walleye—May 15 -June 15, Aug 15-Oct 15, Dec 15-Jan 15.
Yellow Perch—March 1-May 15, Sept 1-Oct 15
Northern Pike—May 15-June 30, Sept 15-Oct 30
Muskie—May 15-Aug 15, Sept 15-Oct 30
Whitefish—May 15-July 30
Smallmouth Bass—June, Sept-Oct
Brook Trout—May 1-June 15, Sept
Brown Trout—July, Sept 15-30
Steelhead—May
Pink Salmon—Aug 15-Sept 30
Chinook Salmon—Aug 15-Sept 30
Atlantic Salmon—June 15-Aug 15.

—*courtesy Sault Convention & Visitors Bureau*

Ontario." The very popular one-day excursion goes 114 miles, about a third of the way to Hearst, allowing passengers to view the wilderness from the comfort of a passenger train. It takes you "over towering trestles, alongside pristine northern lakes and rivers, and through **awesome granite rock formations and mixed forests of the Canadian Shield**," according to the brochure. "The same vistas and panoramas . . . inspired the Group of Seven to create some of Canada's most notable landscape art." The train descends to the Agawa Canyon floor, where passengers can get out. It has a park with gravel walkways, four waterfalls, and a lookout platform, a 300-stair climb. Box lunches can be eaten here, or breakfast and lunch, beer and wine are served in the dining car. **Fall color is especially beautiful.**

Recently **premium dome car service** has been introduced, for a premium price almost twice the usual fare. It does include a continental breakfast, light lunch, and steward. Dome passengers spend half the trip in the upper dome and half in the lower lounge. Reserve early for these limited seats.

The **Snow Train** takes the same trip in winter, "as snow laden trees give way to panoramic views, **snow-choked rock cuts** and **waterfalls transformed into fantastic ice sculptures** by the cold breath of winter." The snow precludes the two-hour layover and walk in the park. Some passengers say staying all day on the train without exercise gets a bit much, no matter how dramatic the view.

The Algoma Central's **information-packed website** presents the **railroad's history** and other **passenger options** in interesting detail, including "Lodges along the Line" and "Tour of the Line" for

rail fans with an overnight in Hearst. Hearst is a starting point for canoe and fishing trips and a snowmobile hub. It offers visitors a mill tour, an art gallery, hobby farm with moose, eco-museum, and more.

Reservations advised. Many area lodgings offer tour train packages. (800) 242-9287. The train station is at the west end of Station Mall on Bay St., clearly signed from the International Bridge. The tour train runs from late May through mid October. It leaves at 8 a.m. and returns at 5 p.m. Current rates in Canadian/approximate American dollars: in summer, adults $56/$40, over 60 $48/$34, students 5-18 $18/$13, under 5 $13/$9, babies free. **Dome cars** *(all ages) $115/$82. Fall fares: adults $75/$54, students $45/$32, children $20/$14. Snow train fares: same as summer.*

Sault Ste. Marie Canal National Historic Site

The canal here, opened in 1895, was the last link in an all-Canadian water route from Lake Superior (source of Canadian iron and steel) to the Atlantic. Prime Minister Sir John MacDonald "believed that **Canadians must not rely on U.S. transportation systems**," according to *The Border at Sault Ste. Marie*, an interesting little book by Canadian history professors Graeme S. Mount and John Abbott, available at The Ship's Store by the *Valley Camp* and at bookstores on the Canadian side. (The Canadian Pacific Railroad, memorialized in Gordon Lightfoot's "Canadian Railroad Trilogy," was part of the same dream.)

The canal and island it's on are interesting to visit today for many reasons. The **interpretive Attikamek Trail** ("attikamek" means "whitefish") goes around the perimeter of the island for 1.37 miles, affording an **outstanding up-close view of the St. Mary's Rapids**. The rapids attract many anglers today. For information on **fishing and guide services** on the Canadian side, contact Sport Fishing Development, (800) 361-1522.

The canal's technology, advanced for its day, remains unchanged, so it's like a **museum of bygone technologies**, which guides explain. The locks are used by pleasure boats and operate frequently. The handsome sandstone administration building, power house, and stores building have a quaint look today. The Friends of the Sault Ste. Marie Canal sell gifts and snacks here.

When built, the locks were deeper

than the American locks. In 1910 they were busier, in terms of tonnage shipped, because large carriers of iron and coal locked through here. But they were never expanded. Later, Great Lakes passenger ships preferred the less busy Canadian locks. Eventually the locks languished. Damaged by an accident, they were reconstructed within the original locks and reopened in 1997.

Why did Canada build this canal when the American locks were already there? As a colony and later a dominion allied with British interests, **Canada felt vulnerable to attack**, from potentially discontented elements within Canada (the French and Métis minorities and others) and from without. In the Fenian movement in the 1850s, Irish-American famine refugees in the U.S. "regarded British North American border communities as legitimate targets," according to Mount and Abbott. A quick read-through Canadian history uncovers a lot of relevant events most Americans are completely unaware of, beginning with the **Mackenzie and Papineau rebellions** of 1837, loosely comparable to a delayed version of the American War of Independence. The rebellions failed, but many of their supporters fled to the U.S. (A fair number settled in Michigan's Thumb, where Canadian-style Gothic Revival farmhouses dot the countryside today.) During the 1870 Louis Priel rebellion in Manitoba, the U.S. threatened not to let the Canadian militia pass through the Soo Locks, but relented after Canada countered with talk of denying access to the Welland Ship Canal around Niagara Falls.

For speedy access to the websites about the Canadian and American locks, go to **www.locktours.com** and click on "Canadian locks" (very interesting, done by Parks Canada) and "American Locks" (done by the Corps of Engineers).

From the International Bridge, take a right onto Huron (toward the river), go straight, cross tracks, turn left onto Canal Drive. (705) 941-6262. TTY: (705) 941-6205. The outdoor site and island is always open. The visitor center is open year-round. The canal operates from May 15 to Oct. 15 from 10 a.m. to 8 p.m. at least, from 9-9 in summer. Visitor center summer hours from early June thru Labor Day: 10-8 daily. Other times open Mon-Fri 8:30 to 4:30 p.m. ♿: visitor center, perimeter trail, picnic area. Not historic buildings.

Lock Tours Canada

The Canadian lock tour operates on a smaller scale than the American tour, with one boat, and a shorter season. Both tours take the same route on their two-hour trips, going through locks on both the American and Canadian sides, going under the International Bridge, and passing Algoma Steel. Local historical groups have worked with Lock Tours Canada to improve the narration, which most likely gives it an edge over the American tour as it was in 2000. Because the tour starts on the Sault Ontario waterfront, you see more of it up close. There's also a **dinner cruise** ($46 Canadian, $32.35 U.S.) that gets you out on the water at a beautiful time, but distracts from the view. Bring a jacket if you want to enjoy the view from the open-air upper deck.

Call (877) 226-3665 for schedule and reservations. www.locktours.com The dock is downtown by the Bondar Pavilion. Operates from June into mid October. 2001 rates (with approximate U.S. dollar equivalent): adults $20/$14.30, ages 13-18 $15/$10.70, child $10/$7.15. ♿

St. Mary's River Boardwalk

A **beautiful downtown boardwalk**, dotted with **fishing platforms** and interpretive markers about key events in area history, extends along the riverfront for a mile. The entire route is suitable for wheelchairs, rollerblades, strollers, etc. The boardwalk goes east past the striking Ojibwa-inspired tent roofs of the **Roberta Bondar Pavilion**, named for Canada's first woman astronaut, a Sault native. One claim to fame is the **world's largest back-lit mural**, in which 10 area artists have depicted local landscapes and cultures with key events in area history and pre-history. The Pavilion is the scene of **summer concerts** on Tuesday and Thursday evenings and of **farmers' markets** Wednesdays and Saturdays. *It starts near the ship canal and locks on St. Mary's Island beneath the International Bridge and continues a mile to Brock St., almost to Pim. ♿*

Downtown shopping

With over 125 businesses, a food court, a produce store, and three sit-down restaurants, **Station Mall** between St. Mary's River Drive and Bay Street represents mostly a cross-section of Canadian chain stores. **Tim Horton's sandwich shop** in the food court is said to have

excellent **soups and sandwiche**s. The Gourmet Stop is also recommended. Station Mall also has the **12-screen Galaxy Multi-Plex**, a giant 2,400-seat **cinema** and **game center** with an interactive TV that lets moviegoers review movies. The mall website, www.thestationmall.com, has info about each store. Regular mall hours are somewhat shorter than in the U.S.: weekdays 9:30 to 9, Sat to 5:30, Sun 1-5.

The **traditional downtown** along Queen Street East from Pim to Gore is sometimes called Queenstown. Queen Street runs one way from east to west; coming off the bridge, head for Bay Street nearer the water. It goes east. There's two-hour free parking at six city lots. Storefronts date from 1910 or so into the 1920s, so Queen Street is **trim and tidy, not Victorian quaint**. Here you'll find upper-end women's apparel shops such as First Impressions, Hill Tribe Designs, and Fashion Shop. For men there's Art Gabriel's and Bishop's. In the old Cornwall Building is a shop featuring fine handmade items from pottery to clothing to giftware. **Experience North Adventures** (705-254-389) at 488 Queen St. East stocks skis, snowshoes, **sea kayaks**, canoes, and hiking and **camping gear** and offers **rentals**, instruction, and **guided trips**. .www.exnorth.com Antiques, local crafts, and antique reproductions are at the **Clock Tower Gift Shop** of the Sault Ste. Marie Museum at 690 Queen Street East. More contemporary art-related gifts and original art is at the shop of the Art Gallery of Algoma, at the foot of East Street on the river.

Fireball Coffee 'n Arts House at 746 Queen St. East is **part coffeehouse**, part artists' co-op and exhibit space, **part arts center** and **music store**. It even has its own label, Fireball Records, to promote local talent. People are welcome to bring their lunch. Call or check the website for upcoming programs of live muisc (alternative, folk, jazz, and blues — often original), and spoken word nights. (705) 949-8756.

Four museums are within a one-block radius of Queen and East: the outstanding Canadian Bushplane Heritage Center, the unusual Ermatinger-Clergue Historic Site, the Sault Ste. Marie Museum in the striking historic post office, and the Art Center of Algoma. They offer a **"4 Culture" passport** for $10 a person, a savings of $2.50. (Admissions needn't be on the same day.)

Bushplanes are interwoven with the history of Canada's northern wilderness. They are showcased at the Canadian Bushplane Heritage Centre.

Canadian Bushplane Heritage Centre

Seaplanes enjoy an **illustrious Canadian heritage** of adventure and **heroic fire-fighting** service, flying to wilderness lakes. It all started right here on the Sault waterfront. The Ontario Provincial Air Service began here in 1924 to send out planes to fight fires. It devised the water-bombing technique. Later seaplanes were used to get to lumber, mining, and hunting camps.

When the planes became amphibious and land-based, float plane veterans took over this impressive 1940s waterfront hangar as their museum. Here they work restoring planes and organizing bushplane history materials and historical displays. They're the guides, too, and able to speak from experience.

The museum is "really well done," says an American visitor. It appeals to "most anyone with any interest in history," not just to airplane fans. The **introductory slide show is excellent**. Exhibits include a life-size scene from a firefighters' bush camp, a hands-on engine test cell, a radio lab, a fire station, and vintage survival gear. There's a **big aviation gift shop**, too. The extensive website, www.bushplane .com, is replete with many historic photos and text, **floatplane events**, and links with related sites.

On Pim St. at the water, reached via Bay St. about half a mile east of Station Mall downtown. (705) 945-6242. Open daily year-round. From June thru Sept. open 9-9. Otherwise open 10-4. $7.50/adult, $3.75/students, $1.50/ child. &

Ermatinger/Clergue Heritage Site

Now part of downtown, next to a Chinese restaurant and real estate office, is the **oldest stone house west of Toronto**. It was built in 1814 as the home and trading post of Charles Ermatinger, an important independent fur trader, and his wife, Mananowe, daughter of an Ojibwa chief. They lived here until 1828, when they both moved to Montreal to conduct his merchant business. Ermatinger defied custom among traders, which called for turning his native wife over to the incoming trader upon departure.

Visitors are treated as if they have entered the **home of a wealthy gentleman** and his native wife. There's often food being prepared and something in the oven, and visitors can help stir — or open the book lying on a table. Costumed interpreters may be working in the garden — the yard and orchard go back to the river — and visitors are welcome to join in and weed or turn the trenched compost pile. The herbs and **survival plants** — tough flint corn, root crops, medicinal herbs, dye plants— grow in a **"tangle garden,"** almost as if they were in the wild, says site director Daphne Poirier. People who are fascinated with Colonial Michilimackinac will likely enjoy this, related to Mackinac but from a slightly later era than the mainland fort. The **gift shop** carries hand crafts, books, cookbooks, and souvenirs relating to the site.

The **Clergue blockhouse** layers the Canadian Sault's industrial era on this early site. The visionary American industrialist Francis Hector Clergue, a native of Maine, moved across the river upon building the giant hydropower plant in the American Sault. On the site of the St. Mary's paper mill he found the stone ruins of an early 19th-century powder magazine of the North West Company. He romanticized the fur trading era and decided to rebuild the blockhouse and live there at the paper mill, surrounded by his industrial empire. The blockhouse was moved to the Ermatinger site in 1996. In early 2001 Clergue's papers were discovered in an old warehouse. The ledgers, other business records, and photographs will reveal more about the business and social life of this eccentric visionary.

831 Queen St. East. (705) 759-5443. Open from mid April until mid Nov. and by appointment for groups as small as 10.

Current hours: from mid April thru May Mon-Fri 10-5, from June thru Sept daily 10-5, from Oct thru mid Nov Mon-Fri 1-5. Admission $2/adult, $1.50 for children under 12, $5/family. &: ground floor & summer kitchen, grounds.

Sault Ste. Marie Museum

"Ontario eclectic" is the architectural label for this former post office with its bulbous corner clock tower. It was built between 1906 and 1912 of sandstone excavated when the Canadian locks were dug. No building like this will likely be found in the United States. **Interior details** like the staircase and the three-story skylight are interesting in their own right. At the museum are a First Nations **birchbark dwelling** (the Canadian term for Native Americans), maritime and other history exhibits about the Algoma District, a hands-on children's Discovery Gallery with a vintage dress-up corner, and galleries for art shows and changing exhibits. The **Clock Tower Gift Shop** with antiques, reproductions, and handcrafts is here.

690 Queen St. East at Pim. (705) 759-7278. Open year-round. From late May thru Sept open Mon-Sat 9:30-5, Sun 12:30-4:30. Off-season hours Tues-Sat 10-5. $3/adult, $2/children, $8/family (Canadian dollar). &: rear entrance. Ring bell.

Art Gallery of Algoma

There's a growing permanent collection and some 24 exhibits a year at this art education center, where workshops, classes, and other programs are held. The shop has art-related gifts, and the **sales gallery** features **original art**, mostly by local artists. At the foot of East St. at Bay, on the river next to the public library. *From the bridge, take Bay St. east. (705) 949-*

9067. Open daily. Mon-Sat 9:30-5, Sun 1-5. Free admission. &: mostly

SAULT ONTARIO RESTAURANTS

It's not surprising that much larger Sault Ste. Marie, Ontario has a better array of restaurants than its Michigan sister.

One of Canada's best restaurants, some say, is **A THYMELY MANNER** in an **elegant 1920s house** downtown. Since 1972 Rosetta Sicoli and her mum, Maria, have been cooking and serving continental cuisine and homemade breads and desserts in a comfy, cozy, somewhat Victorian setting. Favorite dinners include fresh Lake Superior trout broiled in wine, herbs, and garlic ($16 Canadian), Thymely Veal (sautéed veal cutlets with portobello mushrooms and peppercorn sauce, $20 Canadian), and rack of lamb with fresh herbs ($27). Entrées include pasta. Vegetarian and special diets by request. Many appetizers, pastas, and sides are meatless. Patrons are also welcome to stop in for dessert (mostly $5). Reservations recommended, especially on weekends. *Downtown at 531 Albert St. East. (Go left off the bridge; Albert is the first right. Continue on thru 6 or 7 lights.) 705-759-3262. Open for dinner Tuesday-Saturday from 5:30 to around 10.* &: no ♿♟♟ Full bar; good wine list

"Wonderful," says a well-traveled retired international Ford executive about **ADOLFO'S SEAFOOD & STEAK HOUSE**. A husband-wife team from Italy are the owner-chefs of this small restaurant, which has a Victorian atmosphere. The continental dinner menu emphasizes seafood and steaks. Dinner entrées start at $11 Canadian for the daily pasta special and go up to $33 for surf & turf with lobster tail and crab. Most dinners are in the $17-$20 range; all include salad, soup, beverage plus starch and fresh vegetable. Lunches are $7 to $9 Canadian. Soup and sandwich menu available any time. Four vegetarian entrées are made daily; everything's prepared fresh, so it's easy to deal with special diets. Reservations recommended. **Afternoon tea** ($5-$9) is from 2:30 to 4. *920 Great Northern, the extension of Pim downtown. (It's on the east side of the road, just beyond the G.M. dealer and the first drive past the light.) 705-254-4578; www.adolfos.net Open daily except Sunday, 11:30 a.m. to 10:30 p.m., to midnight Fri & Sat.* &: ♿♟♟ Full bar

As for Italian restaurants, a favorite is the **NEW MARCONI Restaurant**. One **popular tradition** in Sault Canada is

ordering dishes **family-style**. At the New Marconi, the "family style" dinner ($18 Canadian) consists of a soup, a pasta, meatballs, barbecue ribs (a house specialty) and chicken, and salad. Other specialties are osso bucco (braised veal shank, $19), homemade pasta and gnocchi (mostly $12 Canadian), lots of shellfish and fish, and the only Black Angus in the Canadian Sault. Some vegetarian dishes. Lunches from $7 to $16. The homemade spumoni is said to be "exquisite." Reservations recommended, especially on weekends. *At 480 Albert West, in the west end, two blocks west of Huron (the first street off the bridge) near Algoma Steel. 705-759-8250; 888-498-4299. Open Mon-Sat from 11:30 a.m. to 10 at least, to 11 Sat. Closed Sun.* &: very low curb ♿♟♟ Full bar

GIOVANNI'S is another good Italian reestaurant, with homestyle pastas, family-style dinners, steaks, fresh fish ($12-$14 Canadian), and pizzas, too. Lunch specials $5-$9. Dinner entrées come with unlimited garden salad. *516 Great Northern Rd./Hwy. 17 a little north of Second Line East, well north of downtown. Open daily from 11:30 a.m. to midnight. (705) 942-3050.* &: ♿♟♟ Full bar; better than average wine list

SAULT ONTARIO LODGINGS

Especially for kids who haven't become blasé, visiting a foreign country — any foreign country, even Canada — and picking out all the little differences can be fun. We recommend staying near the waterfront, or in a homestay B&B, or at a family-oriented Ramada Inn with a 5-story indoor waterslide. The exchange discount has varied in recent years between 27% and 30%, so deduct 30% to get American rates.

HOLIDAY INN
(705) 949-0611; (800) HOLIDAY)

Every room here has a **striking view of the waterfront** looking out over Michigan — either up (toward the locks) or downstream. The 8-story, 195-room hotel is downtown right **on the river** and the Boardwalk, next to the Roberta Bondar Park (scene of concerts, farm markets, and more). A large mall is across the street. There are river views from the **indoor swimming pool** and whirlpool, the **outdoor patio**, and the **restaurant and lounge**. Rates: $139-$150 Canadian (summer), $154-$170 (fall), $120 (Nov & Dec), $129 (winter & spring). Newly redecorated rooms have dataports, coffeemakers, cable TV, pay-per-view movies. *Downtown at 208 St.*

Mary's River Dr.
&. ♿♟♟: under 18 free, under 12 eat free from kids' menu ⚞

RAMADA INN FUN CENTRE
(705) 942-2500; U.S. (800) 228-2828)

For families this place is a great bet, especially in winter. It combines a 211-room hotel in a 7-story tower with what amounts to a vast indoor resort. There's a **5-story waterslide** (free for guests), a 9-hole "wilderness" miniature golf course, **pools indoors and out**, a fitness center with sauna and whirlpool, a **game room, restaurant, lounges**, and a tunnel to a **24-lane computerized bowling alley**. Rates are $104-$124 Canadian, with a free game of bowling and minigolf. Ask for packages. 3 whirlpool rooms. Reserve at least a month ahead for fall; otherwise a week ahead is usually OK. *5 minutes north of downtown at 229 Great Northern Road (the northern extension of Pim downtown).*

&. ♿♟♟: under 18 free with parents 🐕

TOP O' THE HILL B&B
(705) 253-9041; (800) 847-1681; fax (705) 946-5571; www.sympatico.com/brauerb/index.html

Gardeners are especially apt to enjoy this rambling, antique-filled house. After they built it (by themselves!) on a bare hillside around 1960, owners Bernt and Margaret Brauer created all kinds of interesting nooks: **patios**, an **orchard**, a **lily garden**, **fountains** and **goldfish ponds** outdoors and in, **bird-feeding areas**, a **tree house** and **mountain hut** for kids to play in.

The house sits up and away from a busy road, and offers **good views of distant hills**. Two guest rooms ($65 Canadian) share a bath. (One has twin beds.) An air-conditioned king room ($95) has its own bath. *On Second Line Rd. some 3 miles northwest of downtown. Open May into early October.*
H.A.: no ♿♟♟: ages 5-15 $15 extra

Brimley (pop. 900)

Brimley is today divided into two parts: a **resort hamlet** where the Waishkey River empties into Lake Superior, and the **village** a mile south on M-221, which joins Lake Shore just west of the river. (The name Waishkey was recently changed from Waisko, which was apparently a corrupted transliteration of the name of an Ojibwa chief. The correct local pronunciation is "waa-ISH-kuh.")

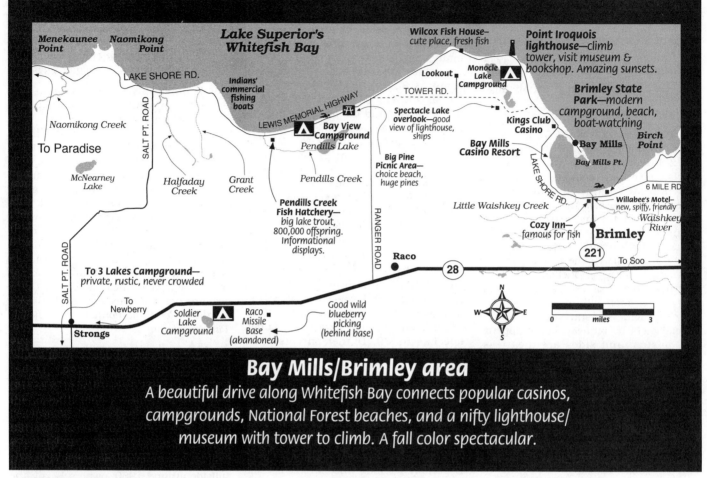

Menekaunee Point   Naomikong Point

Lake Superior's Whitefish Bay

Wilcox Fish House— cute place, fresh fish

Point Iroquois lighthouse—climb tower, visit museum & bookshop. Amazing sunsets.

LAKE SHORE RD.

Lookout

Monocle Lake Campground

TOWER RD.

Indians' commercial fishing boats

LEWIS MEMORIAL HIGHWAY

Spectacle Lake overlook—good view of lighthouse, ships

Kings Club Casino

Brimley State Park—modern campground, beach, boat-watching

Naomikong Creek

SALT PT. ROAD

Bay View Campground

Pendills Lake

To Paradise

McNearney Lake

Halfaday Creek

Grant Creek

Pendills Creek

Big Pine Picnic Area— choice beach, huge pines

Bay Mills Casino Resort

Bay Mills

Birch Point

Bay Mills Pt.

LAKE SHORE RD.

6 MILE RD.

Pendills Creek Fish Hatchery— big lake trout, 800,000 offspring. Informational displays.

RANGER ROAD

Little Waishkey Creek

Willabee's Motel— new, spiffy, friendly

Waishkey River

SALT PT. ROAD

Raco

Cozy Inn— famous for fish

Brimley

221

To Soo

To 3 Lakes Campground— private, rustic, never crowded

28

To Newberry

Soldier Lake Campground

Raco Missile Base (abandoned)

Good wild blueberry picking (behind base)

N W E S

miles
0   3

Strongs

Bay Mills/Brimley area

A beautiful drive along Whitefish Bay connects popular casinos, campgrounds, National Forest beaches, and a nifty lighthouse/ museum with tower to climb. A fall color spectacular.

Brimley is the beginning point for a **beautiful drive along the south shore of Whitefish Bay** for at least 20 miles, or all the way to Paradise and Whitefish Point if you want to go that far. The east part of this area, right by Brimley, is affected by the twin influences of cottage/small resort development and by the Bay Mills Indian Community, a long-time area fishing community which pioneered Indian gambling in the region.

Once a **bustling lumber and commercial fishing town**, today Brimley is more of a bedroom community, home to a good number of the personnel who work at the big state prison 20 miles south in Kinross. Downtown Brimley has a combination hardware/convenience store, a bank, and not a whole lot more.

The region around Brimley is rich in **tasty wild blueberries**. Picking is permitted anywhere on National Forest land. See the introduction for hints, and ask local Forest Service personnel for suggestions. Sadie Tinsley picks 500 quarts a year. You can buy them from her home on M-28 at Tilson Road, a mile west of the turnoff to Brimley via M-221. But if you want to pick them yourself, a **locally famous spot** is the area behind

the old missile base near Raco, about ten miles west of Brimley on M-28. In a typical season, the blueberries ripen the fourth week of July and last for about a month.

Backroads route from Sault Ste. Marie to Brimley

This way gives a better, more interesting sense of the area than the busier route along M-28. And it's shorter, too.

Take Bus. I-75/Ashmun/Mackinaw Trail out of Sault Ste. Marie. You might want to stop to pick up brochures and information sheets at the **helpful Hiawatha National Forest office** on Bus. I-75 (906-635-5311). Do not turn onto I-75. Instead, continue south on Mackinaw Trail and turn right (west) onto Six Mile Rd. at the blinker and cemetery. In seven miles you might enjoy stopping at well-known Great Lakes marine artist **Mary Demroske's Mushroom Cap Studio and Gallery** (906-248-6632; by chance or by appointment. Baskets, pottery, and her own prints and cards of freighters and lighthouses are for sale. Look for the gray garage on the north side of the road.

After eight miles on Six Mile Road you will reach Lake Shore Road and Brimley.

Brimley State Park

Boat-watchers love this tidy, 151-acre park with a mile of Lake Superior shoreline. The picnic area has an **outstanding view of freighters** heading to and from the Soo Locks. The **beach** here is one of the **warmest places to swim in Lake Superior**. The park and modern campground feels suburban, not at all wild.

Entrance off Six Mile Rd. just east of Brimley. (906) 248-3422. State Park sticker required. $4/$5 a day, $20/$25 a year. ♿: toilet/shower building at the camp ground.

Wheels of History Museum

Trains of the Duluth, South Shore & Atlantic RR once brought logs to the mill town of Bay Mills and took finished lumber to distant markets. The Bay Mills-Brimley Historical Research Society, instrumental in restoring the Point Iroquois lighthouse, has now turned its attention to the local history of **railroad-**

ing, **fishing, logging, milling,** and early telephones, all richly represented in this tiny museum. It occupies a turn-of-the-century wooden coach from the Algoma Central Railroad. The photos of the sprawling, smoke-belching Bay Mills townsite, now almost completely vanished, gives rise to contemplation of the transience of man's endeavors. The **gift shop and info center** is in a **caboose**.

3221 at Depot St. From Lake Shore, turn south onto M-221 just west of the river mouth. (906) 248-3665. Open mid-May thru mid-Oct, Sat & Sun 10-4 at least. From mid-June thru Labor Day open Wed-Sun 10-4. Donations appreciated. &.

BRIMLEY & BAY MILLS RESTAURANTS

Arranged from Brimley west to Bay Mills and beyond.

Locals and people from as far as Newberry stop at the **COZY INN** for its **whitefish dinners**—2 pieces of fried fish, cole slaw, and potato for $6.50. Often it's fresh whitefish caught by local commercial fishermen, when available. A soup and sandwich menu is also served all day. This is a bar and a family restaurant. *On Lake Shore Drive, just down the hill from the heart of Brimley on the left corner. 248-5131. Open year-round, 7 days. Kitchen open noon to 8 p.m. Bar open 'til 2 a.m.* & 🕴🕴 Full bar

The Bay Mills Casino restaurant, known as **SACY'S**, overlooks Whitefish Bay. It's super-spiffy in a very decorator way, and the food's good enough to attract local resorters, not just gamblers. This **luxurious environment** connects up with tribal roots via **large**, beautifully framed **photos** of **tribal old-timers** at work as **commercial fishermen**. (They catch the whitefish served here on weekends.) The full-service restaurant is open 24 hours a day, with buffets at breakfast ($6), lunch (around $7) and dinner ($9 or on weekends $11). A few tables are outside on the **deck** with a view of Waishkey Bay, and diners can take their meals outside. *It's on Lake Shore Dr. about 2 1/2 miles west of M-221 coming from Brimley. 248-3617.* & 🕴🕴 Full bar

Four generations of Wilcoxes have fished in this area. Ralph and Shirley Wilcox sell the fish they catch — fresh, smoked, and cooked at their bright, cheerful **WILCOX'S FISH HOUSE & RESTAURANT**. The menu is simple: whitefish, lake trout, or herring, lightly floured and fried, served with french fries, slaw and rolls. A one-piece dinner is about $6, all you can eat is $9. Their **smoked fish spread** comes in half-pound tubs. *On*

---

3 ways to get helpful handouts on Hiawatha National Forest outdoor recreation

◆ Call (906) 635-5311 Mon-Fri 7:30-4:30 and ask to have handouts mailed.

◆ Stop by any **Ranger Office.** The lobby of the Soo office (p. 288) is open 24 hours. The St. Ignace office 3 miles west of the bridge is open weekdays from 8 to 4.

◆ Stop in the **Michigan Welcome Center** as you get off the Mackinac Bridge at St. Ignace and look for the Hiawatha National Forest center and staff person.

Lakeshore Drive at the Dollar Settlement, two miles east of the Bay View Campground, about 10 miles west of Bay Mills. From M-28 just west of Raco, take Ranger Rd. north. 437-5407. Open daily from May thru Oct, 11 a.m. to 8 p.m. Closed Nov & Dec. After Jan. 1, open Fri-Sun until May. & 🕴🕴

BRIMLEY LODGINGS

WILLABEE'S MOTEL
(906) 248-3090; fax (248-3169

New in 1998, this 36-unit motel on two stories is on the bank of the Waisheky River near its mouth. Next door is a restaurant with lounge; between the buildings, stairs go down to a **boat dock** on the river and fish. Coffee and hot drinks are available in a comfortable, **homey lobby decorated in antiques**. Rooms are large, with queen or kind beds and sometimes a pullout sofa. There's cable TV and phones with data ports. Sample rates for summer 2001: $64 tax included on weekdays, $70 on weekends. Brimley State Park is two miles to the east, Bay Mills Resort and Casino two miles west, and the Cozy Inn is just across the road, by the gas station/convenience store. On snowmobile trail. *6615 Six Mile Rd. where it joins M-221 in Brimley.*

H.A.: some rooms ADA accessible 🕴🕴: 18 & under no extra charge 🐾: call

BAY MILLS RESORT & CASINOS
(888) 422-9645; www.4baymills.com

The brochure styles the resort as a "unique gaming getaway" for people who may enjoy "hearing the clanging of a paying slot machine" or the "quiet lapping of waves." There aren't many lodgings in this beautiful area. This is large (144 rooms), attractive, and just about

---

the only place on the lake east of Paradise as we go to press in 2001. Every room has at least an **angled lake view**. Rates in summer, 2000 were $69-$79 tax included for a standard double, $99 to $109 for jacuzzi suites. Off-season rates were as low as $32-$38. The decor is terrific and the service is friendly in a down-to-earth way. Cushy leather sofas flank a big stone fireplace in the lobby, where it's often so quiet, you'd never dream the noise and cigarette smoke of a casino were a short walk away. (Friendliness is something gamblers really care about, Bay Mills's marketing surveys indicate.) There's a **pub** with pizza, a **restaurant** with an all-you-can-eat café, and a **quiet lounge**. No-smoking rooms are available. Ask about per-person golf and gaming packages. There's a driving range and golf pro at the 18-hole **Wild Bluff golf course**. *On Lake Shore Dr. about 2 1/2 miles west of M-221 at Brimley.*

H.A. Some ADA accessible rooms. 🕴🕴: 18 & under free

BRIMLEY AREA CAMPING

BRIMLEY STATE PARK
(906) 248-3422. Reserv.: (800) 44-PARKS (800) 605-8295 TDD; www.dnr.state.mi.us/

See above for park amenities. Good for boat-watching. Spaces in this big, modern campground are **unusually large**, but without shrubs or trees between sites for privacy. Half are sunny, half shady. A few sites are close to the lakeshore. A round of expected improvements in 2001 or 2002 will upgrade electric and add pull-thrus, reducing the number of sites from 270 to around 235 in the process. This is the only modern campground (with showers, electricity, etc.) on the lake, close to many beautiful spots in the Hiawatha National Forest and well located for day trips to the Sault, Straits area, and Tahquamenon and Whitefish Point. With the expected site reduction, it's expected to fill every prime summer month. So reservations are definitely advised! Most campers here are Canadian, and economic changes mean they've been vacationing less on the American side. As a backup in the same area, you might check out **Minnow Lake Campground** (906-632-6980) three miles east at 6101 W. Six Mile Rd. *The entrance to Brimley State Park is off Six Mile Rd. just east of Brimley. State Park sticker required. 2001 fees: sticker $4/$5 day, $20/$25 year; camping $12/$15 night.*

H.A.: toilets, 1 shower bldg. (continued) minicabin are ADA accessible. Picnic tables, fire rings are not. Flat sites. Seems to work OK for wheelchair campers.

MONOCLE LAKE CAMPGROUND/
Hiawatha National Forest

(906) 635-5311; not reservable
www.fs.us.fed.us/r9/hiawatha

The campground offers 39 rustic sites (picnic tables, fire ring, pit toilets, hand pump).A cold-water shower is at the day-use area. The campground fills only on summer weekends. No sites are actually on the water, but some overlook it. Lake Superior and the Point Iroquois lighthouse are just a mile away. See the description of Monocle Lake under Bay Mills for more on the 2-mile trail, boardwalk, picnic area. *From M-28, take M-221 to Brimley, go west on Lake Shore 7 miles. 1 mile east of Point Iroquois. $10/night. Open May 12-Oct 16.* **H.A.:** as far as possible in a rustic campground. Tables, fire rings, lantern posts, toilets, and first part of trail are ADA accessible. Electricity to recharge wheelchair battery is at the pump house.

BAY VIEW CAMPGROUNDS/
Hiawatha National Forest

(906) 635-5311; not reservable

Here 14 of the 24 rustic, private campsites (picnic tables, fire ring, vault toilets, hand pump) are steps away from the **sandy Lake Superior beach** in an area of mixed pines and hardwoods. Watch ships. Look for **agates.** There's nearby fishing at creek mouths. It's a mile from popular Big Pine Picnic Area. This campground fills on some summer weekends and sometimes during the week in hot weather. *About 16 miles west of Brimley on Lake Shore Dr. From M-28 at Raco, take Forest Road 3154 to Dollar Settlement, turn west (left) 2 miles. $10/night. Open May 12 to Oct. 16.* **H.A.:** call

Bay Mills

Once Bay Mills was a bustling, smoky factory village of 1,200 at the tip of the long point extending out into Waishkey Bay. Around the turn of the century it handled huge amounts of timber, turning logs into boards, doors, and boxes. By the 1920s the timber was exhausted and the town had pretty much shut down. (The Dollarville place name down the road was for a lumberman named Dollar who was active in the area, and not named for American currency, incidentally.) Today the town of Bay Mills no longer exists, though the much older **historic center of the Bay Mills Ojibwa community** can still be seen. It's at the Mission Church and Bay Mills Indian Cemetery on Lake Shore Drive, right at the base of Bay Mills Point and not far from the small King's Club Casino, now a kind of branch casino. Indiana University Press has just published Charles Cleland's illustrated narrative history of the tribe, *Place of the Pike* ($18.95.)

The township of Bay Mills, home of the **reservation of the Bay Mills Indian Community of Chippewas**, is thriving. Its 2000 population almost doubled over the past decade to over 1,200. The tribe has grown to over 400 as its lucrative casino has provided employment for younger tribal members who had moved away to find jobs. **The Bay Mills Casino and Resort** (888-422-9645; www.4 baymills.com) on the shore of Waishkey Bay has given a new, forward-looking twist to the typical casino-hotel complex. It claims to be "America's first tribally run casino." The resort has been planned as a destination for non-gamblers, too, with an 18-hole **championship golf course** on the bluff (the views are outstanding) and a restaurant and deck with a bay view. The hotel, now expanded to 144 guest rooms, is the only lodging between the Sault and Paradise to enjoy a lakefront location and a full-service restaurant. As in Sault Ste. Marie, gambling revenues have fueled a new self-sufficiency, with social services and education that are tribally funded and controlled, rather than depending on the complexities of federal funding and distant politics. **"Gambling today is our whitefish,"** says one tribal member, putting the phenomenon in the context of the traditional communal livelihood.

The tribe's **Bay Mills Community College** (248-3354) serves tribal members and others. It has an opens admissions policy and about 300 students, typically over 70% tribal members. The two-year college offers courses in applied fields like accounting, computer graphics, medical billing, and native studies like Ojibwa language, tribal government and economic issues, and Native American art. In 2001, a multi-million-dollar skilled trades building is being built to provide more courses in skilled trades such as construction and auto maintenance. For many students the two years spent here provide a helpful transition to four-year colleges. Those who complete two years at tribal colleges such as Bay Mills have a 90% comple-

tion rate at four-year colleges, compared to 10% who don't receive this initial preparation. The college library houses donor James O'Keene's **outstanding collection** of vintage beadwork, buckskin clothing, headdresses, and other **traditional art from many Indian cultures** from the Pacific Northwest and Great Plains to the Eastern Woodlands.

The **Bay Mills Indian Community's Honoring Our Veterans Powwow** (906-248-3241) is a two-day affair held each year on the first full weekend of June. Dancing and drumming are in the afternoons with a grand entry in the evening. There's a supper feast on Saturday, plus breakfasts each day. There are activities for children and crafts vendors. Powwows have always been joint celebrations with other communities, to which outsiders are welcome.

Mission Hill/
Spectacle Lake Overlook

This **delightful spot**, part of the Hiawatha National Forest, offers one of the **most memorable scenic panoramas of the entire Upper Peninsula**, unfortunately marred by a limited amount of vandalism at the site. Here a steep sand dune dramatically towers over the Lake Superior shore. To the left, the white tower of the Iroquois Point lighthouse stands out among the dark pines and hardwoods. If you're lucky, you can see some freighters heading in and out of the Soo Locks, visible to the far right. Behind the locks are the Algoma Steel stacks and, blue in the distance, the rugged Laurentian hills of the Algoma Region of Ontario. Just below is Spectacle Lake. A plaque remembers Herman and Frances Cameron, an inspiring, community-minded Ojibwa couple from Bay Mills who liked to come here "for contemplation and renewal." Follow their example. Don't hurry from this serene spot. The **homemade funerary art in the cemetery** back from the overlook is poignant.

If you continue due west along the bluff, you will arrive at the Dollar Settlement on Whitefish Bay in five scenic but bumpy miles through the woods.

The inconspicuous turnoff from Lake Shore Drive to Mission Hill is a little west of the Bay Mills Indian Cemetery.

Monocle Lake

The centerpiece of this **attractive natural area** in the Hiawatha National Forest is **172-acre** Monocle Lake, stocked for

A magnificent view of Whitefish Bay can be had from the Point Iroquois light tower, some 25 miles by car southeast of Whitefish Point on the scenic shore road to Sault Ste. Marie. The nearby Spectacle Lake Overlook offers a similar view, with a foliage foreground that's beautiful in autumn.

fishing with walleye, bass, pike, and perch. There's a **beach, boat launch**, and **picnic area** with charcoal grills. Lots of improvements, including a **floating fishing dock** and hard gravel paths, make the area about as wheelchair-accessible as a rustic camping area can be.

A **two-mile hiking trail** loop starts at the picnic area and goes through natural hardwoods that are intermixed with some very old white pines and hemlocks. The trail's first 1,100 feet are fully acces-

sible, including the boardwalk that carries the trail across a wetland and **beaver dam**. The industrious beavers, which grow to 40 to 60 pounds, make use of the boardwalk, too. The interesting, fun-to-read *Northwoods Wildlife: A Watcher's Guide to Habitats* says that beavers "are quite punctual, leaving the lodge every day at dusk to feed. Most of their work is done at night, except in the fall, when they may be seen during the day catching their winter source of tree

limbs by the lodge." Beaver lodge entrances are underwater to avoid predators. Ospreys (also called fish hawks) have a nest in the area, so it's not unusual to see them catching fish in the wetland shallows.

When the trail comes to a bench in a quarter mile, a spur leads left up the **bluff overlook for a grand view of the shipping channel**. See under Brimley-area camping for campground description

From M-28, take M-221 to Brimley, go west on Lake Shore 7 miles. 1 mile east of Point Iroquois. (906) 635-5311. Free day use. &

The Point Iroquois Light Station & Museum

This complex, part of the Hiawatha National Forest, brings together all the elements that create the **lighthouse mystique** for so many people. The site is memorable. It's in a woods just back from a **beautiful beach** with ample deposits of **driftwood** and **colored rocks**. A new boardwalk now makes the beach accessible to wheelchairs and strollers. At the lighthouse, weather permitting, visitors can climb the spiral iron stairway in the **65-foot tower** (that's 72 steps) and get a **fine view of the busy shipping lanes** at the St. Mary's River entrance. Often several freighters can be seen at once. The view is especially memorable in fall color season and at sunset when a number of vessels are on the sparkling water, silhouetted against the colored sky.

As for the museum, one apartment of the 1870 lighthouse has been furnished to give an idea of the lightkeepers' everyday lives. Other museum rooms show lighthouse technology, the **history of navigational aids**, and photos from the lighthouse from the 1890s until its closing in 1962. This important light station housed three families. At one time, a small school was held here, too. Betty Byrnes Bacon, who grew up here, recalled her life at this self-sufficient homestead in the 1920s in a delightful book, *Lighthouse Memories*. It's available at the **attractive small museum shop** run by the Forest Service. The shop is well supplied with not only with books on lighthouses and Great Lakes maritime matters but with bird guides and other nature books, plus Smokey the Bear in various forms. The Bay Mills-Brimley Historical Research Society worked with the Forest Service to renovate the lighthouse and develop this museum.

On Lake Shore Dr. 5 miles west of Brimley and east of Paradise. 437-5272. Open from May 15 thru October 15 daily

from 9 a.m. to 5 p.m. Often the tower but not the museum is open until 7 or 8 p.m. Free admission. Donations appreciated. ċ. no. 3 steps into lighthouse, tight spaces. Boardwalk loop through woods to beach is accessible.

Big Pine Picnic Area

Sault residents often cite this picnic area, part of the Hiawatha National Forest, as their favorite place in the entire area. Loggers left some **good-size pines** here. Now, a hundred years later, they have grown are very large indeed. There's a popular Lake Superior beach, sandy enough for lounging but with interesting colored stones (including some agates) for **good rock-picking**. Bring binoculars for a better view of **ships entering the St. Mary's River**. Picnic tables, grills, and benches make this a fine place to linger and watch sunsets in an especially scenic spot.

On Lake Shore/Curley Lewis Hwy. just west of Dollar Settlement and Ranger Rd. (which joins M-28 near Raco, 6 miles south). About a mile east of Bay View, 9 miles northwest of Raco. Free. ċ.

Bay View Beach

Except for campers, the sandy Lake Superior beach is virtually empty, and the forest behind it has some really big red pines. It's part of the **Hiawatha National Forest**.

From M-28 at Raco, take Forest Road 3154 to Dollar Settlement, turn west (left) 2 miles. (906) 635-5311. Free day use. ċ: no.

Pendills Creek National Fish Hatchery

Lake trout stocked in the Great Lakes each year come from this hatchery and its subsidiary National Forest hatchery at nearby Raco. Long tanks called raceways are covered with galvanized steel roofs. Eggs go into egg-seeding programs in lakes Michigan and Huron. In Lake Superior native lake trout have been reproducing naturally well enough that stocking is no longer necessary. Here fry are reared for a year, until they are five to eight inches long. Then they are released. Visitors can enter the tank buildings and look down at the **masses of little fish**. The big, dark brood fish that used to be here have been moved to the Raco hatchery.

Displays and pamphlets show eggs developing into fish. They tell the story of

how **parasitic sea lamprey** from Lake Ontario nearly destroyed the Upper Great Lakes fishery in the 1930s before being partially controlled by lampricide chemicals and natural predators like the coho salmon.

On Lake Shore Rd. 4 miles west of Dollar Settlement and Forest Rd. #3154. (906) 437-5231. Open Mon-Fri 8 a.m.-4 p.m. Weekend outdoor visitation allowed, but visitor center is closed. Free. ċ.

Indian Fishing Historical Marker & roadside park

This spot offers a **sweeping view**, a **sandy beach**, and the interesting story of a 1981 Supreme Court case brought by Big Abe LeBlanc of Bay Mills. The nation's highest court confirmed his contention that in an 1836 treaty Michigan Indians gave up their land but not their rights to fish and gather. As a result, Indian commercial fishermen can continue to fish while state policy otherwise severely limits commercial fishing in favor of sport fishing. There's **good fishing for lake trout and salmon** at the mouth of the many rivers and creeks in this area that are bridged by Lake Shore Drive.

On Lake Shore at "the narrows," where the road almost touches the lake, a little west of the Pendills Creek Hatchery.

North Country Trail Segment

Casual hikers enjoy making a 1 1/2-mile round trip on this short and **especially scenic** part of the long, multi-state hiking trail. From the parking area it's a quarter-mile hike to the **swinging bridge**, and another half mile to Tahquamenon Bay.

Look for the unmarked parking lot on Lake Shore Drive just west of Naomikong Creek (signed), a little over three miles west of Salt Point Rd.

BAY MILLS RESTAURANTS, LODGING & CAMPING

See under Brimley, above.

Raco

During the Depression, Civilian Conservation Corps camps near Raco and Strongs gave employment to young men from Hamtramck and Detroit working on projects like pine plantations, tourist campgrounds, fire towers, road-building, stream projects, fish planting, and fire suppression. A handout map-

ping and describing a self-guided **CCC tour** of places near M-28 between Strongs and Raco can be obtained from the Hiawatha National Forest headquarters in Sault Ste. Marie or at the St. Ignace Welcome Center.

Two **National Forest campgrounds** (see just below) that almost never fill are handy to M-28 and enjoy a good central location for touring to the Straits and Mackinac Island, the Lake Michigan beaches along U.S. 2, the Soo Locks, Tahquamenon Falls, Whitefish Point, and the Seney National Wildlife Refuge.

RACO AREA CAMPING

SOLDIER LAKE CAMPGROUND/ Hiawatha National Forest (906) 635-5311. Not reservable.

Right off M-28 but away from highway noise, this campground is used mostly by overnighters. It hardly ever fills up, even on holiday weekends. 44 non-reservable, rustic sites (no showers, electricity, or flush toilets) almost surround a small 15-acre lake, on which motors are prohibited. This is a place where campers who want seclusion can hardly see their neighbors. 24 sites are virtually on the water, not separated by a road, and all are close to it. **Sandy beach**; picnic area. The large, partially enclosed **log shelter** from the CCC era has a fireplace for cold weather. A trail winds around the lake. A quarter-mile connector between sites 38 and 39 leads to the **North Country Trail**. *South off M-28 via an entrance drive 5 miles east of Strongs or 7 miles west of Raco. $9. Open May 15-Oct. 16.* **H.A.**: call

THREE LAKES CAMPGROUND/ Hiawatha National Forest (906) 635-5311. Not reservable.

A central but peaceful location on **19-acre Walker Lake** is the chief asset of this 28-site campground. Its liability: more bugs than usual early in the season. From July through September it's better. 21 sites have immediate lake access. Anglers are the chief users. **Perch** are caught in Walker Lake. No motors are allowed. A picnic area is across the lake from the campgrounds. West across Forest Rd. 3142 is **Whitemarsh Lake**, with perch, pike, bass, and bullheads. *On Forest Road 3142, 2 miles south of M-28 at Strongs. $9. Open May 15-Oct. 16.* **H.A.**: call

Keep in mind that all prices and hours of operation are subject to change. Lodging rates vary with supply and demand and are usually higher for special events.

Les Cheneaux, Drummond Island & the St. Mary's River

Amid rocky isles & points, marshes and northwoods forests, an unhurried paradise for fishermen, sailors, nature-lovers & boatwatchers.

ROAD VIEWS don't showcase most of the many low-key delights of the quiet corner of the Upper Peninsula east of the Mackinac Bridge. The land is flat to rolling — no mountains, no waterfalls. Striking views occur where close-to-the-surface limestone bedrock meets the waters of northern Lake Huron in a vast variety of forms: islands, rocky points, offshore rocks, bluffs, deep fjord-like inlets, and rocky coves rimmed with an occasional sand beach. **The area's beauty is on the water**, not just the Lake Huron shore but along the St. Mary's River and on inland lakes and marshes. In the old resort areas of Les Cheneaux (pronounced "LAY-shen-OH"), DeTour, and Drummond Island, visitors must seek out the scenic spots pretty much on their own. An exception is highway **M-134 between Cedarville and DeTour**. Here the road affords views of a series of rocky points and little bays, some with sandy beaches and low dunes, others with marshes full of wildlife. So much state land abuts M-134 (it's part of the Lake Superior State Forest) that the highway seems part of a beautiful, magically under-used park. **Frequent pulloffs** make it easy to stop and **watch birds**, or to **swim**, or to beachcomb for the area's plentiful limestone **fossils**, or to walk into the low natural areas of birch, cedar, and hemlock.

Although there's no separate bicycle path, M-134 has extra-wide, two-foot paved shoulders that make for good **bicycling**. There's not very much traffic here, and summer resi-

dents are often seen walking along the shoulders enjoying the pristine scenery. Another plus for out-of-shape cyclists: it's quite flat. **Mountain bikes** would allow additional adventures, taking the often rough, unimproved roads south off M-134 out to the points, or on Drummond Island. For a delightful, lazy day, wear your swimsuit or shorts and good wading shoes, and bring binoculars for watching birds and boats.

The local culture in this area is a down-to-earth, pleasantly conservative blend of long-time summer people and local people, who are largely descended from the area's farmers, sailors, quarrymen, and fishermen. Many have some French-Canadian and/or Indian heritage. Both groups share a love of fishing and the outdoors.

An unusual variety of habitats and native flora and fauna characterizes the Les Cheneaux-Drummond area. Botanist Ellen Weatherbee finds the islands of northern Lake Huron and the St. Mary's River endlessly fascinating. The **spring warbler migration** as seen on Drummond Island's south shore is an undiscovered attraction for birders. And the **fish**! As noted outdoorsman Tom Huggler explains in 50 *More Michigan Rivers* (see the bibliography in the introduction), the **St. Mary's River**, which forms the border between the eastern U. P. and Canada, is "**one of the most diverse fisheries in North America** . . . . home to more than 80 species of fish, at least 44 of which spawn in the system's four distinct fish

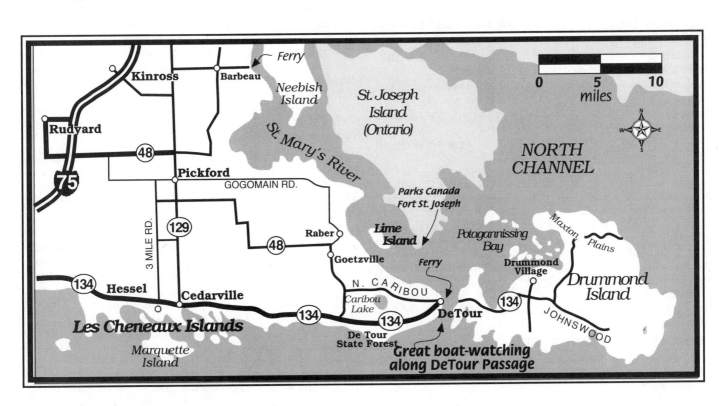

Great boat-watching along DeTour Passage

habitat types: emergent wetlands, sand-gravel beaches, open waters and bays, and the St. Mary's Rapids. Besides fish native to the system, the river hosts migrants — everything from smelt to sturgeon — from lakes Superior and Huron. This incredible body of water is home to **world-class Atlantic salmon fishin**g in the rapids, outstanding herring and whitefish angling, and many other gamefish species, including some in the trophy class."

The river is "the drain plug for Lake Superior," Huggler explains. It "carries a tremendous volume of water south for 68 miles to northern Lake Huron. . . . It ranks **No. 8 among American rivers for rate of flow**." Fishing isn't quite what it once was, Huggler adds, due to the impact of freighter traffic, Indian gill-net fishing, and cormorants eating too many perch.

The St. Mary's River and the North Channel into Georgian Bay were key parts of the ancient Great Lakes highway from the Atlantic into the heart of the north woods. That **canoe route** was used by **native peoples** and by the **voyageurs** who brought the forest animals' furs to Quebec and then to European markets. Today the river, artfully depicted in the 1930s children's classic *Paddle-to-the-Sea*, has become one of the **world's great shipping highways**. (During Prohibition it was known as "Whiskey River," though there were far fewer rumrunners here than in the other Whiskey River —the Detroit River). **DeTour, Raber,** and **Barbeau** offer boat-watchers **views of huge lakers** carrying up to 60,000 tons of Lake Superior iron ore or almost two million bushels of wheat a year loaded in Duluth or Thunder Bay. It's fun to bone up on Great Lakes shipping and then bring your binoculars to take in the details of the slow-moving giants. (*Steamboats and Sailors of the Great Lakes* and *Know Your Ships* are highly recommended primers for boat-watchers. See the bibliography in the introduction.)

The **North Channel** is a premiere destination for North American **sailors** and **boaters**. They love its **protected waters**, and the **ever-changing vistas between the islands**. It extends for 120 miles between St. Joseph's Island at the lower end of the St. Mary's River and Georgian Bay. The channel, mostly in Canada, is formed on the south by Drummond Island in Michigan and, in Ontario, by Cockburn Island and long, irregular Manitoulin Island.

TO FIND OUT MORE: For **Les Cheneaux**, call the **LES CHENEAUX CHAMBER of COMMERCE**, (906) 484-3935, stop by the **Les Cheneaux Welcome Center** on M-134 between Hessel and Cedarville (north side of road, a mile west of the blinker light). Look in on the area's outstanding website, **www.lescheneaux.org** for a wide variety of information on businessess, cultural institutions, nature, and more . . . For **DeTour** call **DeTOUR CHAMBER of COMMERCE** (906) 297-5987 and leave a message, or visit www.detourvillage.com. . . . For **Drummond Island**, call the **DRUMMOND ISLAND CHAMBER of COMMERCE**, (800) 737-8666 or visit **www.drummondisland.com** North Haven Rentals & Gifts, on M-134 not far from the ferry, functions as an informal information center. (906) 493-5567. Open daily in season. . . Mike Lilliquist and his crew at the **MICHIGAN WELCOME CENTER** in **St. Ignace** by the Mackinac Bridge exit are a font of helpful information and background, with hundreds of free pamphlets and often free phone books of U.P. areas. (906) 643-6979. Open daily, year-round, 9-5, in summer from 8 to 6. The center *can* be reached from the U.P. side of the bridge.

PUBLIC LAND: The **LAKE SUPERIOR STATE FOREST** administers a great deal of state land along Great Lakes waterways near DeTour, on Drummond Island, and along the St. Mary's River. Contact the DNR's Sault Ste. Marie office, open week-days from 8 to 5 at 2001 Ashmun. (906) 635-5398. . . . A few areas in Les Cheneaux are part of the **HIAWATHA NATIONAL FOREST**, (906) 643-7900. Its complete range of handouts is stocked at the Michigan Welcome Center by the Mackinac Bridge exit in St. Ignace. The National Forest's St. Ignace adminsitrative office, an attraction in its own right, is on the north side of U.S. 2 six miles west of the bridge. It's open weekdays 8-4:30. . . . **THE NATURE CONSERVANCY** is actively supported by private funding in the Les Cheneaux area and has an office in Cedarville in a Victorian house on Meridian Road across the street from the museum. 484-9970. Generally open weekdays 9-5. As private landowners donate land to the Conservancy, more land in the area becomes available for public use, on a leave-no-trace basis. **Nature preserves** open to the public are described in some detail on **www.lescheneaux .org/nature.html**

GUIDES AND CHARTERS: In **Les Cheneaux,** Jim Shutt's Dreamseeker Charter & Tours and Norman Perkins Les Cheneaux Island tours are Great Lakes fishing charters and scenic cruises. Jim Patrick gives guided kayak tours as North Huron Kayak Company (484-3466). The Great Outdoors on M-134 (434-2011) is a local hunting and fishing store. . . . The local outdoors store in **DeTour** is North Country Sports (906-297-5165) downtown. . . . **Great Northern Adventures** offers Les Cheneaux kayak tours. (906) 225-8687. www.greatnorthern adventures.com . . . .**Drummond Island** Yacht Haven (906-493-5232) is a good source of fishing guide referrals. Botanist Ellen Weatherbee (734-878-9178; e-mail eew@umich.edu) does half-day trips through The Nature Conservancy and holds a Drummond spring weekend. (Expect intense botanical identification, not loosely appreciative nature observations.). . . Capt. Jack Behrens of DeTour does fishing charters and custom cruises for up to six on **Drummond's north shore** and along the **St. Mary's River** (including Lime Island). Call (800) 206-8079 or visit www.michcharterboats.com/island queen

EVENTS: Consult **www.lescheneaux.org** for details. The area's big event is the **Wooden Boat Show** on the second Saturday of August in Hessel. Les Cheneaux school children provided the impetus for the mid May **Frog Festival**. North of Cedarville, **Creekside Herbs** (www.TheEnchantedForest.com/ CreeksideHerbs/) offers a full schedule of interesting **workshops** and some day-long free special events featuring children and artists. **Les Cheneaux Historical Museum** holds occasional evening programs. Two **summer theater** productions of the Les Cheneaux Education Foundation pack in crowds at the high school in Cedarville.

HARBORS with transient dockage: In **Hessel** the Clark Twp. Marina (906-484-3917; off-season 484-2672; lat. 46° 00' 05" N, long. 84° 25' 30" W) with showers, launch ramp, laundry. In **DeTour** (906-297-5947; off-season 906-643-8620) with showers.

PICNIC PROVISIONS and PLACES
◆ **Cedarville** has the area's only big supermarket, **Cedarville Foods**, on M-134 at M-129. Its deli section is better than it used to be. Pammi's Restaurant and Cheryl's Place (see restaurants) do a big take-out business; so does Ang-Gio's for pizza. The prime picnic spots are the picnic tables at the **marinas** in downtown **CEDARVILLE** and **HESSEL**.
◆ Serene picnic areas with beach, woods, and dunes close at hand are along **M-134** between Cedarville and DeTour. 18 miles **east of Cedarville** there's a beautiful Michigan Department of Transportation **roadside park**. Four miles beyond that is the **DeTour Picnic Area** on state land.

◆ In **DeTOUR** itself there are benches and a gazebo in the **Dr. Shula Giddens Memorial Garden**, overlooking the DeTour passage and its occasional freighter traffic. DeTour's grocery, **Sune's**, is on Ontario Street, the main drag that parallels the waterfront.

◆ **DRUMMOND ISLAND** lends itself to outings on or near the water with a good sack lunch. A formal picnic area in the heart of Drummond Village (north on Bailey Road) is the **Betsy Seaman Park**, right on the water with a playground. The island has a grocery, Sune's, right on the four corners. A short ways beyond it on Johnswood, in part of a house, is a very good all-around gourmet deli and wine shop, **Gourmet Gallery** (493-5507).

Les Cheneaux Islands

An untrumpeted treasure of the eastern Upper Peninsula is the Les Cheneaux Islands area, with its **rocky islands and peninsulas**, its **wildflower meadows**, and its cedar shores and wetlands. Within just 45 minutes of the Mackinac Bridge and Sault Ste. Marie, this **old resort area** makes a fine base for a week of relaxation that could be augmented with some sightseeing as far away as Tahquamenon Falls and Whitefish Point. This region along the northern shore of Lake Huron has tended to attract some of the U.P.'s more affluent nature lovers, so it's no accident that seven nature preserves have been donated and/or purchased through The Nature Conservancy, which now has its Northern Lake Huron Program office here. Birdwatching, wildflower walks, sailing and most of all fishing are favorite activities.

The second Saturday of August the **Antique Wooden Boat Show** at Hessel puts the area in the spotlight. Otherwise, Les Cheneaux is off the beaten tourist track. There's not a big golf resort or shopping district to be found — and that's the way local residents and the people who have summered here for decades want things to stay. About the only obvious signs of recent development are the big Cedarville Foods supermarket, a two-story Comfort Inn in Cedarville, and a small strip of shops on Island View and M-134 in Hessel. Increasing numbers of retirees and urban refugees are making their permanent homes here.

Les Cheneaux means "the channels" in French. Glaciers formed the rocky fingers of limestone, sand, and gravel that stretch out southeast into Lake Huron's most northwestern waters. These long fingers break up into a series of 36 islands along 12 miles of shore. At the heads of two island-filled bays are the onetime fishing villages of **Hessel** and **Cedarville**.

Some islands are quite large. Others

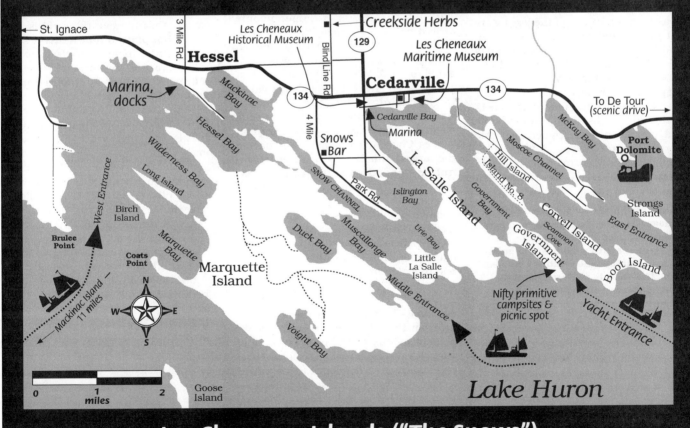

Les Cheneaux Islands ("The Snows")
A simple, civilized world of rocky islands and protected bays.
Famous for its wooden boats.

are big enough for just a few cottages. Tiny **Dollar Island** in the Snows Channel is a perch for a single fantastic house that extends its verandas and docks out into the water and seems to float without terrestrial support.

The **sheltered bays** and **channels** make for ideal **sailing** and **boating** since small craft are protected from the Great Lakes' winds and much bigger waves. **Constantly changing vistas** created by the complex shorelines of many islands and inlets make for interesting boating even at very slow speeds — in a rented fishing boat with an outboard motor, or in a **canoe** or **kayak**. (A paddler in good shape can canoe from Hessel to Cedarville in two hours.) The area's idiosyncratic shoreline architecture adds interest to paddling and cruising. Wonderful old **boathouses**, elaborately rustic like the big summer houses they are connected with, line long-established areas such as the east shore of Marquette Island and the mainland peninsula facing it.

The Snows have been a favorite summer retreat since the late 19th century. It was then, at the end of the logging era, that older Middle Western cities were establishing themselves as industrial and commercial powerhouses and centers of great wealth. Hay fever relief and escape from city heat led many wealthy people from Chicago, St. Louis, Pittsburgh, and especially Ohio to build rambling summer houses here, modestly referred to as "cottages." Favorite locations were the largest islands: **Marquette Island**, offshore from the vil-

Famous for wooden boats: the Les Cheneaux Islands Antique Wooden Boat Show (advertised in this poster) celebrates the area's tradition of building, maintaining, and restoring wooden boats. The show is at Hessel on the second Saturday of August.

Antique Wooden Boat Show & Art Festival Hessel, Aug. 10, 1996

Interesting plants bloom on Lake Huron's limestone shores

Bunchberry and bearberry carpet wide areas. Twin flowers, trillium, ground hemlock, and pyrola adorn the deep woods. Orchids, the joy of every flower lover, are found wild and undisturbed. Present everywhere is a variety of trees, shrubs, ferns, lichens, moss, and fungi.

— *Hiawatha National Forest*

---

lage of Hessel, 6 1/2 miles long and 3 1/2 miles wide, and 4-mile **La Salle Island** off Cedarville. Tucked away on these wooded islands, the summer homes aren't as ostentatious as their counterparts on Mackinac Island or Harbor Springs. Les Cheneaux has always enjoyed a very low-key charm. The area's good fishing, natural beauty, and tranquillity also attracted artists, academics with free summers, and fishermen from many walks of life.

Boats have always been, of necessity, the primary form of transportation here. Through the 1930s, summer people arrived by D&C steamer from Detroit or Cleveland. (Into the early 1960s the old route of M-134 from St. Ignace was just a gravel road.) Today, there are no cars, just golf carts, on any of the islands not linked to the mainland by roads. Summer islanders use motor boats to get to the mainland, where marinas park their cars.

Les Cheneaux is famous for having the **largest number of restored wood-hulled boats in the United States**. Being in storage nine or ten months a year spares a lot of wear and tear on summer people's boats. Thanks to family tradition, nostalgia, and natural thrift, it's *de rigueur* in these parts to keep that old mahogany Chris-Craft for 40 years and to maintain it in excellent condition. **Mertaugh's Boat Works**, on the waterfront in the center of Hessel, is the **oldest Chris-Craft dealer in the U.S.**, dating from 1925. New owners have given it a contemporary look. Another source of vintage wood boats was the local boat-building trade. It developed to serve fishermen and was kept alive by purchases from summer visitors.

All this makes for a pleasant little paradise for environmentally-conscious sailors and fishermen who hate the noise and posturing of powerboats and the macho boaters who go with them. At the **municipal marinas** at Cedarville and Hessel during July and August, wooden boats can be seen in all directions, with more and more sailboats all

the time. The attractively designed marinas have **gazebos** and plenty of benches that make them nice places to linger.

Les Cheneaux doesn't have the tourist traffic that typically goes with Indian gambling. There's long been an Ojibwa community around Hessel. Today the Sault Ste. Marie Tribe of Chippewa has built its smallest **Kewadin Casino** (484-2903) on Three Mile Road north of town, not far from the tribe's development of ranch homes.

Viewed from water or land, the shoreline of Les Cheneaux makes for a tranquil landscape. White boulders and mostly gravelly beaches are played off against a blue summer sky, the bright greens of poplars and birches, and the contrasting dark cedars and spruces. In late summer, splashes of goldenrod and purple asters create a simple beauty that's an ideal antidote to overstimulated lives. **Fall colors**, more yellow than red, stand out against the evergreen and water. If you can't use a boat to explore the area, take beautiful M-134 east to DeTour, stopping frequently along the way.

This sense of sweet simplicity and harmony with the natural world is captured in ***Hollyhocks and Radishes***, the delightful and hugely successful cookbook inspired by author Bonnie Mickelson's many summers in the Snows and by the generous, life-loving spirit of the late Julia Chard. For years Mrs. Chard dispensed fresh vegetables, coffee, cooking tips, and country wisdom from her front-yard produce stand near Hessel. Her observations on life and the world around her give the book a wonderful depth. Stop by the Hessel office of Pickle Point Publishing (it's in the Weekly Wave building on Pickford Avenue between a bar and the Hessel Bay Inn). There you can get *Hollyhocks and Radishes*, autographed by the author if she's around, which she often is between May and September.

Hessel

This small village is at the head of the bay by the west entrance to Les Cheneaux. Like its larger neighbor Cedarville, in the 1880s Hessel grew from a loose settlement of Indian fishermen in the area into a lumber port with a post office. Logs were brought here to be loaded onto lumber schooners in spring. Today the busiest places in town are the marina and docks where residents of Marquette Island and the smaller islands come and go to their summer homes.

Seeing beautiful old boathouses like this, photographed by Andrew Tanner in 1906, adds to the fun of boating in Les Cheneaux.

The 1930s WPA guide describes Hessel as having a "simple, unstudied charm." The guidebook points out, "In earlier days, Hessel found winter the busiest season, when the air was vibrant with the noises of lumbering activity; now it is summer that brings excitement to the village, and the turning of the leaves signals the closing of at least half of its houses. On several points of land nearby, marking the sites of Indian villages, is the Indian grass, long and tough-fibered, that was worked with split ash in basket weaving, giving a peculiarly sweet, characteristic odor to the baskets. . . . Hessel was considerably embarrassed, years ago, when sheriff's officers fell asleep while guarding a group of suspected kidnappers, who could see no reason, under the circumstances, for remaining. Because of the escape, a jail was erected in 1906, a tight little building, secure against future prison breaks. Ironically, the building has never been called upon to fulfill its purpose, but serves as a polling place, its single cell now a woodbox."

Note: points of interest have been arranged from west (coming from St. Ignace) to Hessel at the east.

Search Bay Beach & St. Martin Hiking and Ski Trail

At the end of FR 3436, about 1 1/2 miles south of M-134, is a mostly sand **beach** on Lake Huron's Search Bay, part of the **Hiawatha National Forest**. It's popular with local people. Not many others know about it. A few **picnic tables** are at this beautiful, out-of-the-way place. Small boats can be launched at the **boat launch** here if water levels are high enough. Two non-reservable **dispersed campsites** encourage primitive camping (no toilets, no water) here. Campers are asked to follow the principles of no-trace camping and leave the area as clean as it was when they arrived, or even cleaner.

Two easy, groomed **cross-country ski loops** in a figure-eight pattern, 1 1/2 miles each, go through the woods and wetlands at the base of the little peninsula going out to St. Martin's Point. From the trailhead a little south of M-134, the first loop starts in frozen cedar swamps, then comes up to a

July-blooming dwarf lake iris grow only in wetlands by the shores of the northern Great Lakes. Artist Oliver Birge's wood engravings of it and other wildflowers are sold at the Les Cheneaux Historical Museum.

spruce and balsam woods broken with occasional wildlife openings of aspen — the same habitat of the second loop, which is basically dry in summer. The second loop also makes a **pleasant hiking trail** that offers a good chance of seeing deer, grouse, bald eagles, hawks, and perhaps even a porcupine or bear. Get there by going down Forest Road 3436. Hikers should take the trail where the second loop crosses the road twice.

On M-134 6 miles west of Hessel and about 10 miles east of I-75. Look for "Ski Trail" sign. (906) 643-7900. Free.

Birge Nature Preserve

The Nature Conservancy has received many gifts of land in Les Cheneaux area. This 168-acre preserve of cedar wetlands, hardwoods, and Lake Huron shoreline gives the public easy access via a quarter-mile path and **boardwalk** to **Loon Lake**, where eagles, beavers, osprey, and other wildlife can be seen. Oliver Birge, donor with his wife Edna, is well known in the area through his art. He has made woodcuts of many of the wildflowers that grow here, including orchids, ladyslippers, gentian, iris, Indian paintbrush. For directions and details on the growing number of nature preserves in Les Cheneaux, see **www .lescheneaux.org/nature.html**

From M-134 about two miles west of Hessel, take Point Brulée Road about 1/4 mile south. Look for sign. The preserve is on both sides of the road.

Hessel Home Bakery

Under previous owners Bill and Marge Ackerman, this full-line bakery developed an **excellent local reputation for scratch baking and good pasties**. There are cinnamon rolls and sticky buns, potato rolls, onion buns, hard rolls, lots of pies, cookies, a French pastry, and a variety of breads. (The supermarket now sells good bread, too.) Tangy salt-rising bread is baked on Friday.

On M-134 a short way east of the blinker light outside Hessel. Open from mid-March thru Thanksgiving. From Mem. to Labor Day open Mon-Sat 6:30 a.m. to 3 p.m. Otherwise open Tues-Sat 6:30-3. (906) 484-3412. &: one step.

HESSEL RESTAURANTS

The **HESSEL BAY INN** has served as the **local gathering spot** for years, with fresh fish in sandwiches and dinners and a full menu (everything from scrambled eggs at breakfast to prime rib and lobster for dinner). It's up a ways from the harbor, but with a **water view** from inside or the **front deck**. *From M-134 at Hessel, turn south at the blinker light and proceed to the center of Hessel. 484-2460. Closed Nov & Dec, plus March 15 or so to April 15. Otherwise open daily, 8 a.m. to 9 p.m., to 10 Fri & Sat* . & ⅋₸⅋ Full bar

HESSEL LODGINGS

SUNSET RESORT

(906) 484-3913; www.lescheneaux.org

Six winterized cottages are on extensive, grassy grounds at the west end of the Hessel waterfront. There's a **nice view of the islands** across Hessel Bay. The location is quiet but convenient. All cottages have two bedrooms, small porches, and plain exteriors. Microwaves and cable TV/VCRs have been added. The knotty-pine interiors are fresh, clean and homey, with new carpeting and a mix of updated and older furniture. All cottages

---

---

have **water views**, picnic tables, and charcoal grills. The dock, a **small sandy beach**, and a bonfire ring are across the drive. There's a volleyball net, playground, lots of space for games, and for anglers a fish-cleaning house and freezer and a deer pole. *Summer rates: $595/week. $75-$85/day off-season rates. West end of Lake St. in Hessel. Open year-round.*

&: 1 step, older bathrooms 🐾: $10/day
⅋₸⅋: 4 people/cabin. $10/extra person

HESSEL CAMPING

National Forests allow free-of-charge **dispersed camping** almost anywhere you want within its boundaries. In the Hessel area there are two cleared areas near the Search Bay beach; most of the St. Martin's Point area is within the **Hiawatha National Forest boundary**. See camping section in introduction. (906) 643-7900.

Cedarville

Like Hessel, Cedarville began in the 1880s as a lumber and fishing port and soon became the provisioning point for summer islanders at the head of the Middle Entrance to Les Cheneaux. Since the 1950s, when Cedarville got a branch bank and hardware store, it has become the area's shopping center, with a large supermarket.

Traditionally **Pickford** had been the area's business center. That inland farming community still has an interesting old store, **Pickford Dry Goods**, with classic outdoor clothing and shoes. **Mackinac Island's many horses** spend their winters around Pickford, incidentally.

Les Cheneaux Historical Museum

The general museum of the Les Cheneaux Historical Association deals with the area's social and natural history. (See below for the society's maritime museum.) Summer people and year-round residents have created a **remarkable range and quality of videos**. Visitors can ask to see several different videos about Les Cheneaux's birds, geology, plants, and history. (They're also for sale for $28.) **"From Ice to Islands"** is a natural history that explains the unusual glacial action that resulted in the islands' northwest-southeast axis. **"Les Cheneaux en Bateaux"** deals with the islands' social history, with a special

---

emphasis on locally built wooden boats for fishing and resort transportation. Gorgeous close-up photographs of local flora and fauna may well succeed in inspiring visitors to slow down and observe the beautiful natural world around them here.

Displays are organized to show the development of Cedarville and Hessel since their settlement in 1884. There are **local limestone fossils** of unusual interest, **Indian crafts and dugout and bark canoes**). Photographs and artifacts depict lumber camp life, the hotel and tourist era, and the area's famous wooden boats — from fishing boats to mahogany Chris-Craft runabouts that summer people still use to reach their island homes. The boat models are beautiful.

The museum's glory is its **collection of photographs,** contemporary and historic. A very precise and industrious amateur photographer, Andrew Tanner, recorded the simple joys of resort life from 1885 to 1920: fishing and boating, picnics, and fish fries. Hundreds of his large, detailed glass-plate negatives resurfaced in recent years and are used in museum videos and displays.

Real students of natural and human history could happily spend a rainy day here without the least regret. Impatient kids are likely to last about 10 minutes, however. The **museum shop** is strong on books and note cards of local interest. Inquire or look at the website for occasional **Monday-evening programs**. Summer Wednesdays bring **featured artists** from the area, one from 10 a.m. to 1 p.m. and one from 1 to 4 p.m.

On Meridian Rd. in Cedarville, one block south of light and supermarket at M-134 and M-129. 484-2821. www. lescheneaux.org (see culture). Open from Memorial Day weekend thru the first week after Labor Day. Open daily 10-5, except Sun 1-5 and closed Sun & Mon in

June. $2/adult, $5/family. ♿

The Nature Conservancy Northern Lake Huron Program office

Thanks to private and non-profit local funding, The Nature Conservancy of Michigan has an office in Cedarville that undertakes the environmental education, land trust, ecological research, and sustainable economic development functions that are the hallmarks of the Conservancy's integrated approach to environmental stewardship. Some day its activities will include involvement in ecotourism, which so far is growing on its own here in any case. By avoiding partisan politics and taking positions on political issues, the Conservancy is able to work in the wide area of environmental concern shared by people from many political points of view. The number of **local nature preserves** donated by private landowners is increasing. For details on visiting them, look in on **www.lescheneaux.org/nature.html** Stop by to pick up an interesting brochure about the area's distinctive shoreline ecosystem.

On Meridian Road across the street from the museum, in a Victorian house shared by The Pine Cone shop. 484-9970. Generally open weekdays 9-5. Sometimes closed in summer when staff is in the field.

The Great Outdoors

Brian Harrison's outdoor shop deals with **hunting, fishing**, and **kayaking**. Here are **kayaks for rent**, and sea touring kayaks and general recreational kayaks for sale. **Knives** are another specialty. Brian himself makes and refurbishes knives on the premises, and serious knife collectors often stop by. In another part of the store Brian's wife Anna makes baskets and gives **basket-making lessons** in many styles. This area has become quite a social gathering place. Anna's Native American ancestry (from both the Upper Great Lakes and the Sonoran desert) led to her interest in traditional crafts. She also does beadwork and quillwork.

On M-134 just east of the blinker light, across from Cedarville Foods. 484-2011. Open year-round, Mon-Sat 9-6. ♿

Safe Harbor Books

This small, pleasant full-service bookstore is on a side street, tucked behind the Great Outdoors on M-134. In addi-

Island cottagers depended on boats for transportation and fishing. That kept local boat shops busy long after commercial fishing declined. This 1906 photograph shows photographer Andrew Tanner, his wife, and son in their Mackinaw boat. Interesting videos of Les Cheneaux resort life, drawing on Tanner's photographs, can be seen at Les Cheneaux Historical Museum.

tion to general reading for children and adults it has good **regional, Great Lakes maritime**, and **nature** sections — and local information as well. **Journals** and **rubber stamping supplies** make for good vacation pastimes. There are always signed copies of best-selling historical fiction by nationally known author **Sue Harrison**, who lives just up the road in Pickford. Her curiosity about the origins of her Native American neighbors led her to research and imagine their ancestors' lives in the Aleutian Islands nearly 10,000 years ago. *Mother Earth, Father Sky* kicked off the Ivory Carver trilogy; now she's finishing up the second trilogy, *The Storyteller.*

On King St., one street east of the blinker at M-134 and M-129. Look for the big highway sign and the blue awning. Go south on King, turn in drive immediately behind shopping strip. (906) 484-3081. Open year-round. From Mem. Day thru Xmas: Mon-Sat 10-6. Winter: Mon-Fri 10-5:30, Sat to 4. ♿

Les Cheneaux Maritime Museum

A relocated 1920s boathouse contains many boats and boat-related items. The new addition dwarfs the original building and permits more boats to be displayed. There are sailboats, rowboats, Old Town canoes, and many historic photos of the area boating scene. Viewing windows let visitors see restoration and **boat-building activities** in the boat-building shop. Volunteers have built a **replica of a Mackinaw boat**, the standard means of transportation before roads were improved. Its double-ended design allowed boats to be easily beached in storms.

In Cedarville, on M-134 two blocks east of the light and just east of the high school. (906) 484-3354. Open from Memorial Day weekend thru the first week after Labor Day. Open daily 10-5, except Sun 1-5 and *closed Sun & Mon in June. $2/adult, $5/family.* &

Government Island

Picnicking and camping are available on this **beautiful, uninhabited island**, just off La Salle Island and an easy 4 1/2 miles straight out of Cedarville. Of all the 26 Les Cheneaux Islands, it's the only public land because a Coast Guard Station was here from 1874 to 1939. Today it's part of the **Hiawatha National Forest**. The pilings from its dock are on the cleared site at the island's northwest end. Today, says the U.S. Forest Service, "the island is being managed to preserve the natural wilderness condition favorable to plant and animal life." Birch and conifers dominate the two-mile-long island. It's been a **popular day-trip destination** for the area's many boaters.

The shore in general is surprisingly rocky and steep, though small boats can be beached at two places. The first landing seen from a boat coming from Cedarville is readily apparent on the island's east shore. After beaching the boat, walk up the hill into a meadow where you'll see two small outhouses. The cleared **campsite**s and some **picnic tables** are nearby. Each campsite has a picnic table and fire ring. A second landing at the island's south side is also readily apparent. It too is near a **picnic area**. The **view** here looks out into the expanse of Lake Huron. Camping is permitted only on designated campsites. None are reservable. Campers are asked to follow the principles of leave-no-trace camping and leave the area as clean as it was when they arrived, or even cleaner.

A **sandy beach** stretches along the west shore for a third of a mile. Local Girl Scout troops help maintain the island. *(906) 643-7900. No charge or registration for camping.*

Creekside Herbs

Wendy Wagoner, helped by her sister, Tammy Patrick, has created a **beautiful, multifaceted place** that's part **herb farm** with **display garden**, **culinary and medicinal herbs,** and essential oils for aromatherapy; part teaching space; part gallery of handmade things from regional artists; and part "green" home and garden shop (with casual clothes of organic cotton and hemp, for instance). It's all based on contemporary spiritual thinking from many sources, largely from Wendy and Tammy's Native American heritage. "Our goal is to promote a sense of connection and integration through our

community, to live and do business in a way that demonstrates our priorities."

Display gardens include a sculpture garden, traditional herb garden, medicine wheel garden, and children's area. Behind them is a **spiritual trail** through the woods, with eight stations, starting with "Healing ourselves and the planet," "Visioning," "Meditation," "Being fully present," "Giving thanks," and "walking our talk through demonstration." "Sitting on the porch overlooking a winding stream, you will enjoy a northwoods afternoon. Read a book, have lunch, or just meditate," invites the brochure. "Perhaps you'll catch sight of a blue heron or beaver. Silently join nature's celebration of life."

Potted herbs, perennials, everlastings and scented geraniums are outside on the big deck, under the shop's eaves, along with garden supplies and containers. Creekside sells over 200 **herbs and perennials suited to the U.P.**, including many **native plants**. Sweetgrass, that evocative accent to Indian crafts, can be purchased here. It's somewhat invasive, so a little, planted in a separate area, can go a long way.

The newly formed **Northern Wild Plant & Seed Cooperative** gives sclasses and provides seeds and cuttings of native plants.

Other **classes** include **yoga, massage, Reiki** (a laying on of hands healing technique), and one-day herb and garden workshops. Call or visit the website for these classes and special days: Artists' Festival, annual **Kids' Festival** (theme for 2001 Ojibway storytelling and dance), and native plant and garden tours.

Local and regional artwork makes for a **gallery/shop** that's far more personal

and sincere than gift shops which purchase standard lines. Here are hand-blown glass, baskets, fiber, jewelry, and Native American art and pottery, plus skin care products, specialty foods, and books on Creekside's subject areas.

1 mile north of Cedarville and M-134 on Blind Line Rd. Turn north at the car wash, west of the blinker light. (906) 484-2415. www. TheEnchantedForest.com/ CreeksideHerbs/ Closed Jan-March. From May thru Sept open Wed-Sun10-5. Sept thru Dec Fri & Sat 10-5. &

North Huron Kayak Company

Jim Patrick, who also gives guided kayak tours, displays the kayaks and canoes he sells at Creekside Herbs.

See Creekside Herbs, above. 484-3466.

Michigan Limestone Operations Cedarville Plant

Freighters take on loads of limestone at **Port Dolomite** in McKay Bay, on the eastern edge of Les Cheneaux. Outsiders can't come in the compound, but it's easy to pull off M-134 and watch. Call the main office in Rogers City to track vessel movements: (517) 734-2117.

On M-134, 4 miles east of Cedarville.

Prentiss Bay marsh

Here Prentiss Creek forms a **wide marsh**. The scores of nesting boxes are for **tree swallows**. Some 300 such boxes have been deployed in the area. Longtime resident Harry Harris, a former gunsmith, a birder, and a dedicated ecologist, made them from scrap. Each

Harry Harris, one of many nature-lovers in the Snows area, has made over 300 nesting boxes for tree swallows. Each spring he sets them out in the Prentiss Bay Marsh. This drawing shows one of many local scenes from Bonnie Stewart Mickelson's wonderful *Hollyhocks and Radishes* **cookbook, a homey paean to gardening, seasonal food, and**

spring he sets up the boxes from his boat; each fall he takes them in. Many of his **exceptional photographs of birds** are on display at the Les Cheneaux Historical Museum.

On M-134, 7 miles east of Cedarville, just inside Chippewa County.

Bailey Park

See DeTour for details on this beautiful Michigan Department of Transportation picnic area and beach.

DeTour Picnic Area and Beach

See DeTour for this hidden treasure.

CEDARVILLE RESTAURANTS

Arranged from west to east. As we go to press, the bank that holds its mortgage is about to take bids on The Landing, the prominent waterfront restaurant with good view and a deck.

Vintage rusticity and a congenial neighborhood atmosphere reign at the **SNOWS BAR**. With knotty pine paneling, original Rittenhouse furniture, and a painted mural of the islands, it's a real **period piece**, dating from the repeal of Prohibition. Regulars still talk about Margaret Crawfuss. The **$6 Snowsburger**, a huge affair that comes with fries and homemade cole slaw, is seasoned and garnished with an olive just the way she did it. Originally the place was down by the water, but during a period of high lake levels, it was moved up the hill across the road. Boaters can dock at Les Cheneaux Landing across the street. Dinner favorites include **fresh walleye** (currently $12) and **broasted chicken** ($10). Both are among the attractions of the all-you-can-eat buffet ($14) on summer weekends. New this summer: a vegetarian platter. *On Four Mile Block Rd. between Cedarville and Hessel. Look for large directory sign, turn south, go 1 mile. 484-3370. Open daily, year-round, from 11 a.m. (noon on Sunday) to close, midnight at least.* &: thru kitchen or via side ramp. Full bar

Pizza, pasta, and ample, good breakfasts like the Italian special (eggs, Italian sausage patty, American fries, around $5) are the big attractions at **ANG-GIO's** (484-3301). This versatile place offers an any-time steak and eggs or sandwich menu. A salad bar comes with dinner entrées. Every night there's a different special (around $9). The **pizza buffet** is Tuesday, Thursday, and Saturday nights. *On M-134, 1/4 mile west of the*

For current events in Les Cheneaux
Pick up a copy of the *Weekly Wave* edition of the *St. Ignace News* for informative, personal local journalism of a high caliber rarely encountered today. Boating in Les Cheneaux and Drummond's Potagannissing Bay can be fun, but tricky navigating. Is that an island ahead, or a point? A channel or a bay? You have to keep track of where you are! Every motel and resort has a map.

blinker light in Cedarville. Open daily year-round from 7 a.m. to 9 p.m., to 10 in summer. & Full bar

PAMMI'S RESTAURANT started as a coffeehouse and sandwich spot. Now Pammi Harrison is adding dinner entrées, including a very popular all-you-can-eat Friday fish fry combo ($11): locally caught walleye, whitefish, and lake trout, lightly breaded. Her light, cheerful place won a following with espresso and cappuccino drinks, desserts like homemade Brownie Obsession, and a fresh menu for this conservative area, featuring wraps ($5-$6) like **portobello chicken** (with fresh spinach, provolone, and tomato). She makes her own sauces, so the olive burger ($4.59 with chips) stands out. All sandwiches come with a **deviled egg** — her mother's idea, and customers love it. *On the northwest corner of M-129 and M-134. 484-7844. Open year-round. In summer 10-10 daily. Otherwise open 11-7 at least, to 8 in spring and fall.* &

CHERYL'S PLACE offers pizza made on the premises, Jilbert's ice cream cones (40 flavors in summer), homemade soups, burgers, and subs, and some salads in a tiny downtown spot. It's across the street from Cedarville's **marina park**, where **picnic tables** let people enjoy a beautiful setting with their meal. **Mushroom soup** has lots of fans. *Across from The Landing restaurant. Used to be Pop's Deli. Summer hours: Mon-Sat 11 a.m. to 2:30 a.m., Sun 11-11. Otherwise Mon-Sat 11-8:30 or so, Sun noon-6.* & : no

CEDARVILLE LODGINGS

Arranged starting with in-town locations.

CEDARVILLE COMFORT INN

(906) 484-2266; (800) 222-2949; www.home.northernway.net/~comfortinn

This tastefully decorated, 49-room motel is the only mainstream chain lodging in the far eastern U.P. outside St. Ignace and Sault Ste. Marie. It offers large rooms with phones and many extras: a **40' indoor pool** with **hot tub** in a light, airy space; an exercise room; video games; VCR rentals; and a **guest laundromat**. A free **deluxe continental breakfast** is served in the attractively furnished lobby with fireplace, TV, card tables, coffee, and a microwave. 1 block to Ang-Gio's restaurant, 100 feet to Pammi's Restaurant. Summer rates for a standard double are typically $99, more for special events; fall and spring rates $79. Ask about winter rates. On 100-mile snowmobile trail. *On M-134 about 1/4 mile west of the blinker outside Cedarville.* **H.A.**: some rooms ADA accessible : 18 & under free :$10

WATERLAWN COTTAGES

(906) 484-2456

Six totally remodeled cottages, very spiffy in an updated rustic way, have new appliances, cable TV/VCRs, picnic tables, quilts, and decorative stained-glass touches. They're on a narrow 1,200-foot peninsula **in Cedarville Bay** at the east edge of town — surrounded by water, with **good views of islands from the covered porches**. Each cottage has two bedrooms and sleeps six easily with a pullout sofa. There's a flotation docking system and fish-cleaning station. Fishing boats are available. There's a **tiny sand beach** and no room for trees, but there's a gazebo and cheerful flowers in window boxes. Waterlawn is near the high school athletic field with jogging, basketball, tennis, and a playground. Seldom available in July, August. Phone in office. About $660/week. *On Grove St. 1/4 mi. east of post office. Look for sign made like the back of a boat.*

H.A.: a few steps into each cottage. Call. : included

SPRING LODGE COTTAGES

(906) 484-2282; (800) 480-2282.

This vintage resort, beautifully maintained, enjoys a **shady, quiet waterfront location** on the Snows Channel, 1/4 mile from the Les Cheneaux golf course and across the road from the popular Snows Bar restaurant. The extensive grounds with wonderful trees go down to water. The common room in the quaint lodge is open to guests. There's a **sandy swimming beach** and **beach bonfires**, weather permitting. Many kinds of boats are for rent. There's a freezer for anglers, and fish cleaning tables. Most of the 20 cottages overlook the water. They typically rent for $650 to $800/week for 4 people. Six older cottages without views are around $400 for 4. Small log cabins for two are less. Cottages, built over many years, are continually updated. All come with microwaves, coffeemakers, cable TV, and lawn furniture. Call early for best summer availability. Walk-ins and daily rates possible in spring and fall. *On 4 Mile Block Rd./Park Rd. between Hessel and Cedarville. Look for big group sign on M-134. Open May 1-Nov. 1.* **H.A.**: call 🚶👫🐕

LES CHENEAUX LANDING

(906) 484-2558; (800) 466-5061

11 architecturally attractive older cottages with knotty pine or log interiors are on or near the Snows Channel, close to the Snows Bar restaurant and Les Cheneaux golf course. The **setting is pleasant**: woods by the road, lawn by the water. Year-round owners Mark and Esther Engle have a **nifty little bait shop** and store behind their house, where guests can borrow games, puzzles, and books. There's a horseshoe pit, swing set, basketball and volleyball courts, picnic tables & BBQ grills. A bonfire area is on the small beach. **Boat rentals** $17-$44/day. 2000 rates: two-bedroom cottages that sleep four begin at $400, four bedrooms (sleeps 10) $775. For daily rate in off-season, divide by 5. *Just down from Spring Lodge at 1158 S. Park Rd./4 Mile Block Rd. between Hessel and Cedarville. Look for big group sign on M-134. Open mid-April to mid-November.* **H.A.**: call 🚶👫: $5/extra person 🐕

LES CHENEAUX INN B&B

(906) 484-2007; www.laketolake.com

This totally remodeled older house is on a corner lot in the center of Cedarville. The downstairs public dining room serves a **gourmet breakfast in summer**, open to the general public and B&B guests. **Dinners** are **by reservation only** for groups of 10 or more. Two upstairs guest rooms ($70 and $80) share a bath and sitting room. The front one has a water view. The carriage house ($90) has 2 double-bed rooms, a sitting room and bath. Decor is updated traditional decor. There's a **pleasant small side terrace**. One block to marina, restaurant. *Hodeck St. across from Krupa's Cottages. Open May thru mid-Oct.* **H.A.**: no

DeTour (pop. 400)

The simple village of DeTour overlooks the DeTour Passage. Here the St. Mary's

River that leads from Lake Superior and Sault Ste. Marie empties into Lake Huron. As a fishing community DeTour goes back to French-Canadian times. It became an important firewood fueling station with the opening of the Soo Locks in 1855. "DeTour" means the turning place. Here voyageurs' canoes and, later, ships turned sharply from the river to head for Mackinac and the Straits. The word, if pronounced correctly in the French way, would have the accent on the second syllable — "de-TOUR." But everybody says "DEE-tour."

Two parks along the DeTour Passage are **ideal for watching up-close the big freighters** that come by every hour or so. Fogcutter Bar & Grille by the Drummond Island ferry has an even better view of all boat traffic.

An idyllic 24-mile stretch of M-134 between DeTour and Cedarville passes a series of **bays and rocky points** to the south, and state forest land to the north. It's a **beautiful drive or bike ride**, perfect for frequent stops to **swim**, **walk**, and **enjoy the views** and explore the interesting habitats, from dunes and woods to wetlands.

Today tourism and retirees sustain the pleasant, unassuming place. Two shops worth seeking out are **RIVER THREADS** (T shirts, sweatshirts, etc.) and **THE HEN HOUSE** (quilts, wood bowls, and other folkish accessories).

DeTour's chamber of commerce recommends **goose- and duck-hunting** and touts DeTour as the "best-kept secret of the eastern U.P." and "gateway to the North Channel," that long, protected body of water ending at Georgian Bay

that's so popular with boaters.

Note: points of interest have been arranged from DeTour Village west along M-134.

DeTour Passage Historical Museum

Opposite the ferry dock, this small museum has a little bit of everything about DeTour: pioneer farming, Indian history, early local institutions, and, of course, the ferry and other local marine operations. Its pride: the **big Third Order Fresnel lens** from the DeTour Reef lighthouse.

104 Elizabeth St. From M-134 as it comes into town, look for the sign down to the ferry. (906) 297-3404. *Open Mem. to Labor Day 1-5, except Sat 10-5.*

DeTour Point Lighthouse Preservation Society

In 1998 this energetic non-profit group formed and took possession of the lighthouse that marks the DeTour Passage at the southern end of the St. Mary's River. The DeTour Light had been built in 1931 at the end of the DeTour Reef, a mile from shore at its nearest point. The society has been selling sweatshirts and lighthouse memorabilia to raise matching money for grants. It's been helped by having a captive audience of people waiting for the ferry. By 2001 it had garnered almost all the $1 million required to restore the concrete lighthouse and turn it into a museum. A donated tugboat will take passengers out to the light when the project is complete. *On Elizabeth St./M-134 next to Fogcutter Bar & Grille.* 297-8888. *From Mem. to Labor Day open daily from noon to 7 or so.*

Dr. Shula F. Giddens Memorial Gardens

A **sunny park and gazebo overlook** the De Tour Passage and resemble an ambitiously landscaped front yard that's colorful with flowers. Benches let you sit and enjoy the view, which occasionally includes freighters. *South side of M-134 on west edge of De Tour village.*

Caribou Lake beach

The shores of Lake Huron are mostly rocky through this area. They don't encourage much swimming and splashing. The informal public beach at Caribou Lake four miles west of DeTour offers **warmer swimming** and a **gradual**

sandy beach. Never crowded.

On S. Caribou Rd. Either take southernmost DeTour east-west street west or, east of Cedarville, turn north from M-134 onto M-48, then east onto S. Caribou in about 2 miles.

DeTour beach, picnic and cross-country ski area

The former De Tour State Park, now part of **Lake Superior State Forest**, is a real find for picnickers, swimmers, and campers who don't require a lot of conveniences. Out of sight of the highway, towards St. Vital Point, are a **nice, sandy beach** backed by a **mature coniferous forest**. There are a few picnic tables, a **hand pump**, vault toilets, and 21 large, private campsites. An ungroomed cross-country **ski loop**, 3.3 miles, goes through the mature pines.

On M-134, 6 miles west of DeTour and 3 1/2 miles east of M-48. (906) 293-5131. Self-registration. &: no.

Bailey Roadside Park

This is much more than the Michigan Department of Transportation's typical roadside park. There's a **beautiful, sandy beach**; a **shady, grassy picnic area** with lots of picnic tables and grills; plus vault toilets and a water pump. The beach is beyond some birches and cedars and over some low dunes. The view is accented by occasional offshore rocks and, blinking in the distance when it's dark, the square **Martin Reef Light** seven miles to the southwest. It warns boaters away from shallow water.

18 miles east of Cedarville and 10 miles west of DeTour. 1 mile east of M-148. &

DeTour Restaurants

Right by the Drummond Island ferry, **FOGCUTTER BAR & GRILLE** offers **excellent whitefish** (fresh daily, prepared several ways) and **waterfront dining** that's up close to the shipping channel. A **deck** brings boatwatchers even closer to giant freighters gliding by. There's a full menu at lunch ($6-$9) and dinner ($12-$18), with steaks, ribs, and more, but the fish and the outstanding salad bar are what draw diners from Cedarville and beyond. Friday is all-you-can-eat whitefish ($14), Saturday is walleye (also $14). Tom, Barbara, and Tyler Snider gutted the place when they bought it in 1997. Reservations recommended in summer and on weekends. *On Elizabeth St./M-134 at the ferry. 297-5999. Open year-round except closes for*

roughly a month in mid-March if the snow is gone. From Mem. to Labor Day open daily 11 a.m. to 10 p.m., otherwise open daily noon to 9 p.m. & ♯♦♦ Full bar

The **DOCKSIDE CAFÉ** is at the center of DeTour life in every way. Located at the village's main intersection, it's the **year-round gathering spot for morning coffee-drinkers**. Specials are an attraction, at lunch and, in summer, at dinner ($9-$11). Things like roast ham with potato salad and homemade baked beans, are a big draw, along with homemade pies and soups all year long. So are **hearty breakfast dishes** ($5-$7) like the sausage omelet with homemade sausage gravy, or stuffed hash browns with eggs, onions, and cheese. Turkey for the hot turkey sandwich is roasted fresh here, and fish is from the Barbeau Fisheries down the way. No alcohol. Vegetarian dishes upon request. *At the blinker on Ontario (DeTour's main street) and Elizabeth. 297-5165. Open year-round daily from 7 to 3. From Mem. to Labor Day open to 8, except closes at 3 Sunday and Monday.*

&: yes, but not restroom ♯♦♦

Boaters in DeTour favor the **MAINSAIL** because it's an easy walk from the public docks and it has a lounge and full bar in addition to an extensive menu and consistent food. *On Ontario 2 blocks north of the main four-corners. 297-2141.*

& ♯♦♦ Full bar

Dick Hanson, videomaker turned Great Lakes maritime gift store chain owner, has taken over the popular spot at the north end of DeTour Village by the marina that had been known as **FORTINO'S PIZZERIA and THE COW BARN** ice cream shop. He hadn't come up with a new name by spring of 2001 but expects to run it as it has been, at first, anyway. A sit-down restaurant, it's been known for **good grinders**, burgers, a soup and salad bar, and lake perch dinners. It offers a **good view of waterfront activi-**

ties, including docks where **river pilots** get on and off of ocean-going vessels that require pilots to navigate the St. Mary's River. *297-2132 .Open daily in summer noon to 10. Otherwise open Wed-Sat 3 p.m. to 9 p.m.* & ♯♦♦

The **ALBANY SUPPER CLUB** is a **vintage period place**, hardly changed since the 1950s. Once dancing was part of its attraction; now it's the **fresh fish dinners** ($9 with potato, soup, juice, and salad). It's a place, the owner says, "where you know everybody who walks in the door." More than a few summer people fantasize about buying it and bringing back dancing. *On M-134 just west of DeTour, north side of road. 297-8321. Open daily 5-9:30, perhaps later.*

&: call ♯♦♦ Full bar

DeTour Lodgings

DeTour VILLAGE MOTEL
(906) 297-5165

This 8-room older in-town motel wraps around the Dockside Cafe (see above) and its parking area. It's not fancy but clean, convenient, and open year-round. Rooms have cable TV. $49 for two in fall, 2000. It's best to call a month ahead in summer. No air-conditioning or phones. *On Ontario at Elizabeth in the center of DeTour.* **H.A.:** not bathrooms. ♯♦♦
🐾: $5 extra

ODY'S CARIBOU LAKE COTTAGES
(906) 297-6397

Four cottages and one three-bedroom trailer on quiet Caribou Lake come with kitchens, microwaves, picnic tables, charcoal grills, and boats. Guests can **swim off the dock** or go to the sandy, uncrowded public beach 1/4 mile down the road. Caribou Lake, known for walleye, bass, panfish, and pike fishing, is visited by loons nesting on a nearby marshy lake. Deb and Ody Odykirk are most hospitable hosts. They have opened a small convenience store next door. Cottages have TV but cable doesn't come out here. Phone in office. Reserve by Feb. or earlier for prime summer rentals. Cottages are around $250 to $275 a week, $50 or so a night in the off-season. *On S. Caribou Rd. Either take southernmost DeTour east-west street west or, east of Cedarville, turn north from M-134 onto M-48, then east onto S. Caribou in about 2 miles* **H.A.:** call ♯♦♦ 🐾: call

DeTour Camping

DE TOUR Campground/
Lake Superior State Forest
(906) 293-5131

This **beautiful, 21-site rustic campground** has a lot to offer for people who can forgo hot showers, flush toilets, etc. Set in a mature pine forest, close to a sandy Lake Huron beach. The area is of unusual natural interest, and just 45 miles east of the Mackinac Bridge. Come early in the week in summer for the best sites. This campground fills on holiday weekends. *On M-134, 6 miles west of DeTour and 3 1/2 miles east of M-48Serviced May thru Nov. $6 /$10 camping fee. Self-registration.* **H.A.**: *call.*

Drummond Island

"There's so much to do on Drummond Island, but you have to know where to go," say one veteran visitor. From the road, the island can seem like merely a lot of trees because few roads offer views of its interesting shoreline. Full of coves and bays and little limestone islands, the shore, when open and sunny, is studded with wildflowers all summer long. The many **inland lakes** aren't readily visible. And there's not a lot of planned entertainment here. **Fishing** has long been the mainstay of the resort economy, and before that of resident Ojibwa. Once subsistence farms, often Finnish, dotted the island. Today the limestone quarry on Humms Road south of the ferry provides some good-paying jobs. The island's year-round population is growing steadily, from 746 in 1980 to 835 in 1990 and 992 in 2000, due largely to retirees.

Drummond Island is the **largest U.S. island in the Great Lakes**. The **British** built a **fort here** in 1815, having lost their Mackinac fort and fur-trading center to the Americans at the end of the War of 1812. (A reconstructed chimney and other artifacts from the fort can be seen at the island museum.) The Treaty of Ghent that ended the war agreed to appoint a joint commission to survey the boundary between the U.S. and Canada, using the **main shipping channel** as the **international border** in the case of islands in the Detroit and St. Mary's rivers. Thus Drummond became American, and the British abandoned their fort in 1828.

The island's commercial hub extends along Townline Road from the M-134 four-corners north to **Drummond village** on the north shore and island-studded Potagannissing Bay, with its waterfront park and playground and historical museum. (This long word is pronounced "POT-uh-GAN-iss-ing.") **A nine-hole public golf course** and two **tennis courts** are

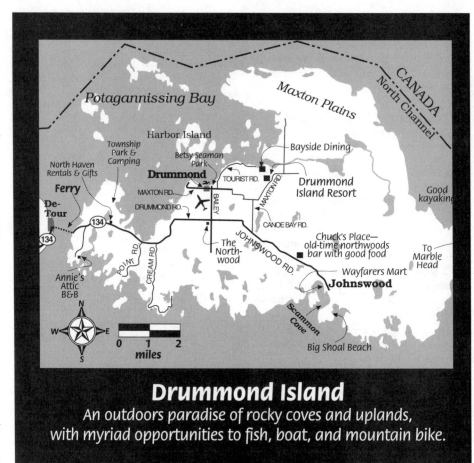

Drummond Island
An outdoors paradise of rocky coves and uplands, with myriad opportunities to fish, boat, and mountain bike.

west off Townline Road by the airport.

In winter there's a **skating rink** by the town hall. **Ice bridges to Canada** from Potagannissing Bay are marked by Christmas trees. They link Drummond with St. Joseph Island and Thessalon, Ontario, the only two places where U.S. snowmobilers can legally cross into Canada.

The Drummond Island ferry operates year-round. Between April and December it runs regularly around the clock, leaving DeTour at 20 minutes before the hour and Drummond at ten minutes after the hour. When demand is high, the ferry runs more often than that. From January through March it runs from 6:10 a.m. to 11:10 p.m., and at 1:10 and 1:40 upon request. The ferry can run at other times for an extra $25 plus fares. The trip itself is 10 minutes. The regular **fare** is $10 round trip for a vehicle and driver, plus $2 for additional passengers. Six-month **ticket books** are $24 for 10 vehicle round trips, and $7 for 10 passenger round trips.

Some **70% of the island is state land**, much of which is quite wild and not easily accessible. Some 5,000 people are on the island in summer, but they're so dispersed, it doesn't feel crowded. Though fishing, boating, and hunting form the basis of the resort economy, Drummond Island's attractions aren't limited to those pursuits. The protected coves and interesting, ragged rocky shoreline make for really **interesting kayaking** and **canoeing**.

Here the same limestone escarpment that forms the Garden and Door peninsulas is at the surface, not overlain by much glacial till. The thin alkaline soils make for unusual soil conditions that encourage specialized plants. With so many habitats — marshlands, cedar swamps, ridges of mature maples and pines, popple, plains and meadows, inland lakes and a marshy river — the island is a **dream to botanists and naturalists**. There are **ferns** and an **unusual variety of orchids**. Loons and an occasional bobcat and moose can be seen. Wolves are in residence on the island. (Drummond has no skunks, possums, or porcupines, however.) Far from cities, the **night sky** is very dark. **Maple syrup-making** continues to be a big

thing on the island. So is **morel month** in May. As in so much of the Upper Peninsula, **berry-picking** is a special pleasure. Wild strawberries and raspberries typically ripen in mid-June and mid-July respectively. The **May warbler migration** is spectacular. The entire south shore is full of warblers that have flown across Lake Huron and stopped to rest and eat blue flies.

Drummond Island is ideal for people who like to explore interesting habitats by **kayak, canoe, mountain bike**, or **hiking.** But the island isn't all neatly signed and interpreted. To get out and explore the wild areas, you can take interior roads that turn into two tracks, then get out and walk. **North Haven Rentals & Gifts** on M-134 and Fairbank Point Road, 2.7 miles east of the ferry (see below), is a handy place to stop for local information. It rents canoes and kayaks. (Drummond Island Outfitters went out of business because of health problems.)

It's a misconception that the island was wrecked by pizza magnate Tom Monaghan and his 3,000-acre golf resort, the subject of much negative publicity in the late 1980s. Monaghan's enthusiasm and grandiose projects inspired much controversy. Monaghan sold the resort to Clif Haley, retired CEO of Budget Rent-a-Car, and the Bailey family, longtime Drummond residents and the owners of Yacht Haven. Renamed **Woodmoor** and, more recently, **Drummond Island Resort and Conference Center,** it has a famous golf course and sponsors a variety of interesting activities.

North Haven Rentals & Gifts

In two years Jim and Sue Kelley have grown their multifaceted Drummond businesses into an **impressive 1,700-square-foot log lodge** that's an **upscale northwoods gift shop** (but not so upscale that kids can't afford some things). It also rents **canoes**, **kayaks**, and **pontoon boats**, with mountain bikes probably coming soon. It also sells maps and serves as a good first stop for Drummond visitors in need of orientation and advice on possibilities for excursions. The store is also the main office of their property management company and **vacation home rental** business. (See lodgings.) Coming soon: a laundry and other businesses across the road.

On M-134 at Fairbank Point Road, 2.7 miles east of the ferry. (906) 493-5567; www.drummondrentals.com. Gift shop & rentals open from April into early January. From May into early Sept open 9-6 daily. Other times closed Sun & Mon. ♿

Drummond Island Historical Museum

This local museum emphasizes artifacts of **Indians**, **Finnish farmers**, and **Yankee settlers** from the island's early historical period. Other displays cover the British Fort Drummond, the lumber era, sporting camps, ferry boats, and the island's rich fishing and boating history. A new building made of hand-hewn logs replaces the museum building that burned. The fireplace is from the stones of a chimney at Fort Drummond.

In Drummond Village, 10 miles from the ferry. Take M-134 east about 8 miles, turn north (left) at the island's main four-corners, proceed to village, then take shore road left about 1 block to museum. (906) 493-5746. Open daily 1-5 from Mem. Day into mid October. 1-5. Donations appreciated. ♿

Drummond Island Yacht Haven

This **big marina** offers fishing tackles, scuba refills, **hot showers** for campers, a **laundromat**, and the usual charts and marina supplies, **guide referrals**, plus a very wide range of **boating rentals**. Sample daily rates: fishing boat with motor $75 a day/$375 a week; 24' pontoon boat $150/$750; runabouts $75-$185; 17' Boston Whaler for water-skiing $190/$950, skis $20/day.

On the west edge of Drummed village. (906) 493-5232. Open April 15-Nov. 15, 8 a.m.-6 p.m., often 'til 8 p.m. ♿

Drummond Island Resort & Conference Center

The resort and corporate retreat built by the various inspirations of pizza magnate Tom Monaghan are interesting even to people who don't stay there. In 1991 a group of mainly local people bought the whole place, 2,000 acres, for pennies on the dollar of what it cost to develop. **The Rock, designed by Harry Bowers, is one of Michigan's most beautiful and unusual golf courses**, carved out of the wilderness and studded with rock outcrops. Golfers can see deer, eagles, and an occasional bear. A driving range and the Halfway Shack are on Maxton Rd. almost a mile west of the lodge. Rates for 18 holes including carts range from $39 in spring and fall to $69 in summer. Call (906) 493-1006 for tee times.

Monaghan's longtime fascination with Frank Lloyd Wright shows itself off in the resort's most beautiful area on Potagannissing Bay. The expansive Monagahan originally envisioned Domino's Lodge as a retreat for his corporate families, where they could bond, relax, and at the same time think about pizza and Tiger baseball. Successfully imitating Wright's mature style, Monaghan designed (often on napkins) three of the cottages built here. One was for himself and his chief executives, one for former U-M football coach Bo Schembechler, then the Tigers' general manager, and one for Sparky Anderson,

then the Tigers' manager. Many of these **wonderful vacation homes can be rented** (for not outrageous sums) by anyone who needs to accommodate groups from four or eight to 18. See "Drummond Island lodgings." Monaghan learned Wright's knack for creating alternately cozy and expansive spaces and integrating outdoors and indoors in a special way. It can be experienced in the **beautiful Bayside restaurant,** in the heart of the onetime Domino family compound. The restaurant is open to the public from June through September and weekends in winter. See "Drummond Island Restaurants." The main dining room's walls were built twice, after Monaghan changed his mind — something for which he was famous in these years (the 1980s). Many islanders reaped the rewards of a trip to the dump, scavenging high-quality plywood and other building materials ripped out from projects Monaghan deemed unsatisfactory. Across the road down to the water is an **outdoor chapel** designed by well-known architect Gunnar Birkerts, which can be booked for weddings.

Monaghan's intense focus on the details of fast, hot pizza delivery had made him very rich and given him the time and money to indulge his passions, principally for architecture, and to treat his friends and business associates lavishly. But things quickly got out of control at Domino's Lodge. Some of his corporate family members wanted more to do than just fish and boat, which led to the golf course, which was way over budget, which lead to the idea to invite the public to golf there — while at the same time keeping outsiders well separated from the Dominoids. (Today Monaghan devotes his time, energy, and money to conservative Catholic projects in Nicaragua and in Ann Arbor, including the new Ave Maria Law School. He has radically simplified his life — his style always vacillated between poles of luxury and austerity — and is determined to die a poor man.)

On Drummond Island, Monaghan invited the late Charles Moore, once the prominent head of Yale's architecture school, to design a resort hotel up near the golf course. It was completed in 1990. Moore, known for his high-spirited and playful contextual approach to design, took his design cues from the northwoods sawmill that had been on the site. **Woodmoor Lodge** used massive logs accented with splashes of bright color and lots of metal details like rafter brackets and corrugated siding. It has a much more industrial look than the archetypical northwoods log lodge. Today the bright colors have been replaced with additional logs. The hotel building materials (logs, native sandstone, and corrugated metal) related to local building traditions. The **lodge interior is an attractive, striking place**, in a dramatic, decorator sort of way, with Navajo-style rugs, cowhide rugs, and other stylish rusticana of the day. Anyone expecting the characteristic Wrightian integration of outdoors and indoors will be disappointed. The asphalt parking comes almost right up to the hotel. Alluding to simple northern Michigan sawmill towns, the related areas (pool, bowling alley, tennis courts, gym, etc.) form a main street and town square linked by walkways.

Getting around Drummond by land and water

The automobile is the worst way to see anything interesting on Drummond Island. The island is an outstanding place to hike, mountain bike, canoe, kayak, or boat, however. Two good sources for maps, charts, and equipment rentals, and for information about guide services are **Drummond Island Yacht Haven** and **North Haven Rentals & Gifts.**

People interested in focusing on the island's unusual natural areas are well advised to go on the annual **botanical habitat trip** led by Ann Arbor botanist **Ellen Weatherbee**, who owns property on the island and spends lots of time here. The convivial 4-day trip takes people to way out-of-the-way places, shows what to look for and how to get around with plat maps. Call (734) 878-9178 for info, or e-mail her at eew@umich.edu She also gives half-day trips for The Nature Conservancy. She says you can learn a lot by driving around the island with a good map that shows state land. When you find it, park, take your compass, and get out and explore.

The **public PINS BOWLING CENTER**, next to the lodge, was also designed by Moore. Its exposed rafters and posts are painted bright colors, intensifying the playful mood established by corrugated metal towers with wood decorations. (These were inspired by Russian churches.) Pins' eight lanes are open from 11 a.m. to 11 p.m. in season. Call extension 1004 for lane times. **Pins Bar and Grill** (see Restaurants) is one of the island's recommended eateries.

THE CEDARS SPORTING CLAYS course is also open to the public in season from 10 a.m. to 6 p.m. by advance reservation. It's about 3/4 mile from the lodge, by the golf course driving range on Maxton Rd. Call (906) 493-1006. The course "was built to simulate the countless types and angles of shots an avid upland bird hunter or waterfowler may encounter. . . 12 different stations [are situated along] a winding path . . . among Drummond Island's beautiful cedar and birch-maple woodlands." Rates are $20 per person per round of 50 targets, shells not included. Shotguns can be rented for $20 extra. Instruction available; groups welcome.

Most parts of ***Drummond Island Resort*** *(lodge, golf pro shop, bowling alley, Pins restaurant) are on Maxton Rd. about two miles east of Drummond village. It's clearly signed from Johnswood Rd. and from Drummond Rd.* ***Bayside Fine Dining*** *is on Tourist Rd. on the water. (800) 999-6343. (906) 493-1000 Fax: (906) 493-5576.* ♿: most of the resort, including the lodge.

Big Shoal Township Beach

A tucked-away **sand beach and small park** enjoy an **otherworldly setting** on Big Shoal Cove on Drummond's peaceful south shore.

At the end of Big Shoal Rd. From the 4 corners and M-134, take Johnswood Rd. straight and right, through Johnswood. Look for sign. No charge.

Back country adventures

For **maps**, stop at **North Haven Rentals & Gifts**. A map showing state land will keep you from inadvertently trespassing. Take along a compass and drinking water, too. For further local information, ask the staff of wherever you're staying. Many local people are quite knowledgeable.

Here are some popular backcountry destinations, arranged from southeast to north.

◆ **GLEN COVE**. This is a **good camping destination for kayakers** because the primitive road gets you right up to the water. At Johnswood, some 15 miles from the ferry on the main interior road, turn northeast and get onto Kreetan Road and then Sheep Ranch Road. (Some maps call these "Glen Cove Road.") Take them some seven miles toward the water (it will become quite rough). At the intersection known as

Corned Beef Junction, turn left and you'll soon be at the cove.

◆ **MARBLE HEAD. Dolomite cliffs a couple hundred feet high** descend to the North Channel in steps. View Cockburn Island across a narrow passage. See Glen Cove, but turn right toward Glen Point at Corned Beef Junction. When you can't go any farther, get out and walk along the shore east perhaps three miles around Marble Head.

◆ **POTAGANNISSING RIVER.** A kayak or canoe trip can take you into some **remote areas** where **loons** nest and **wild rice** grows. The river connects four lakes. Water levels, controlled by a dam, can be too low to be navigable. On a map, the chain of lakes looks easy to navigate through, but in fact it's **full of false channels**, complicated by heavy growth of summer vegetation. So it's a good idea to hire a **guide** to go back here, unless it's duck-hunting season. Heavy use makes channels obvious then.

◆ **MAXTON PLAINS.** Here the limestone bedrock is right at the surface, almost like pavement in its flat expanse. Plants grow in the cracks, creating four to eight inches of **spongy soil** on top that supports the **rare alvar grasslands and alpine plants.** To survive here, these plants must be alkaline and able to withstand sudden alternations from dry to soaking conditions. These boring-looking grasses can burst into bloom within a day, turning into a sight of great if subtle beauty. **Alvar grasslands** exist in only a few places in the world including nearby Manitoulin Island, Pelee Island, and Latvia. Much of the plains is Nature Conservancy property. Mountain bikers are prohibited from biking on the fragile, thin soils. *From Drummond village, take Maxton Rd. east and then north into plains.*

◆ **FOSSIL FORMATIONS.** Fossils, commonly found in the exposed limestone of the eastern U.P. and Straits area, are especially abundant on the beach about a mile east of Poe Point on Drummond's north shore. See a good map.

◆ **POTAGANISSING BAY and HARBOR ISLAND.** There are over 30 islands in this protected bay. The uninhabited ones without cottages are fun for kayakers and boaters to explore. Large Harbor Island with its **big interior cove** is public land where boaters like to swim, fish, pick berries, and see beaver lodges along the shore. No campfires or camping are allowed here. The cove, seven feet deep, is a popular place for boaters to drop anchor and spend the night.

In an old warehouse, the Wayfarers' Mart offers lodgings and much-praised dinners by reservation. It overlooks Scammon's Cove on Drummond Island's remote south shore. The island's fascinating shoreline makes for ideal kayaking.

DRUMMOND ISLAND RESTAURANTS

CHUCK'S PLACE, the **quintessential old-time northwoods bar** with mounted hunting trophies and **pool table**, also serves **really good food**. It's a favorite local hangout year-round. Daily specials include generous tacos ($3.75 for two) on Monday night, unlimited Friday fish fry ($7), and Saturday seafood specials ($10-$16). The regular menu ranges from burgers, bisonburgers, and a very popular **cheesesteak hoagie** ($3 to $4.50) to pizza, a 16 oz,. porterhouse ($14), and ribs. One large room may be hard for the smoke-sensitive. *On Johnswood Road 6 miles east of the four corners, opposite the country store. 493-5480. Open year-round except Christmas Day. Kitchen open from noon to 10 p.m., later in summer. Bar open at least 'til midnight.* &: side door, slight hump Full bar

The local year-round breakfast gathering spot is the **BEAR TRACK INN**. It also serves lunch and has a motel next door. *It's on Town Line Rd. between the four corners and the village, across from the school. 493-5090. Open daily year-round. Mon-Sat 7 a.m. to 2 p.m. Sun 7-noon, breakfast only.* &

PINS GRILL at the Drummond Island Resort's bowling center is the resort's breakfast spot and a popular eatery. **Pizza** is a big draw; 16" classic, Mexican, chicken fajita, and veggie pizzas run around $15. Dinner entrées like chicken breasts, whitefish, or sirloin steak run from around $11 to $16, including soup or salad and starch; Southwestern entrées are $7 to $9. Then there's a big sandwich menu ($5 to $7,

served with fries), homemade soups, salads, and nightly specials. Expect a wait. *On Maxton Rd. about 2 miles east of Drummond Village. Follow signs from Johnswood Rd. or Drummond Rd. 493-1003. Open daily from Mem. Day through September. In May and October open weekends for breakfast and lunch, nightly for dinner.* & Full bar

BAYSIDE DINING at Drummond Island Resort offers fine dining in a **lovely setting overlooking Potagannissing Bay**. Tom Monaghan designed the space in the mature style of his idol, Frank Lloyd Wright. It served as the dining area for his corporate retreat. Entrée samplings: whitefish Niçoise with risotto primavera ($24), sautéed pork loin medallions stuffed with Brie over apple and verde vegetable julienne with chive mashed potatoes ($24). All come with soup or salad. Ask about special wine dinners. Reservations advised, especially in summer: (906) 493-1014. *At the junction of Maxton Rd. and Tourist Rd. Open daily 6-10 p.m. from Mem. Day weekend through September, weekends in Oct, Jan, Feb and March.* &

By the time you get to **WAYFARERS MART** at Scammon Cove and Johnswood, 16 miles from the ferry, it's easy to feel you're entering another sphere, well beyond Michigan — maybe somewhere like Nova Scotia, and maybe several decades into the past, too. The Wayfarers Mart is a charming, idiosyncratic place — a two-room bed and breakfast that's also a **destination restaurant by reservation only**.

It's in a plain but charming wide red frame building perched near the water.

The building originally served as the company store for the sawmill town that once was here. The Wayfarers Mart name dates from a sporting goods store here in the 1940s. Carol Martin came upon the empty building for sale in 1991, on her first trip to Drummond Island from metro Detroit. "Normally I'm not an impulsive person," she recalls, "but I was just smitten." She quit her job of 18 years and has been here ever since. Recently she took over from fellow innkeeper Anne Stadler as editor of the interesting monthly *Drummond Island Digest*.

Carol cooks **highly praised dinners** year-round with 24-hour reservation. They're served in a former tearoom with a stone fireplace and windows looking out onto the cove. In warm weather drinks and dinner can be enjoyed on the **deck**. The first caller chooses two entrées from several possibilities ranging from $19 to $26 (a price that includes soup, salad, dessert, and beverage). Baby-back ribs in a mustard glaze ($24) and rack of lamb ($25) have been popular. Vegetarian (usually a morel fettucine) by request. Bring your own wine or liquor; Carol provides setups and can tell you where to buy wine on the island. Dinners are not appropriate for children. *36000 Johnswood Rd., 3 miles east of the Country Store, about 15 miles from ferry. (906) 493-5935* &

DRUMMOND ISLAND LODGINGS

YACHT HAVEN
(906) 493-5232; fax (906) 493-5229; www.diyachthaven.com; e-mail: yachthaven@northernway.net

20 attractive cottages with picture windows and decks are sited to take advantage of **excellent views of Potagannissing Bay** and its many islands. Some cottages are on the water. Others are perched on the wooded hillside behind it. The 3-bedroom cottages with big stone fireplaces are especially nice. Two **small, sandy beaches** are next to the cottages. Extras include outdoor grills and picnic tables, horseshoes, croquet, basketball, volleyball, and hiking trails nearby. The cottages are set apart from the owners' busy Yacht Haven marina, where fishing boats and motors, pontoon boats, runabouts, and water-ski boats can be rented. Weekly/daily rates: 2 bedrooms $500/$100; on the water $620/$124. Three bedrooms (some on the water) $905/ $181. Reservations accepted a year in advance; it's best to make them by year's end at least. The Baileys are descended from old island families and have seen and

done a lot on the island themselves. Today they are also co-owners of the Drummond Island Resort. They're good to talk to when things aren't too busy. *At the west edge of Drummond village. Open year-round.* &

DRUMMOND ISLAND RESORT
& Conference Center (800) 999-6343; www.drummondisland.com

Lots of little extras make this an attractive destination for people who like the outdoors. Guests have free use of mountain bikes, cross-country skis, snowshoes, canoes, kayaks, and sailboats. 12 miles of **hiking** and **groomed cross-country ski trails** in nearby woods include a 3/4 mile interpretive **nature trail**. There's an **outdoor pool**, **hot tub**, **tennis**, a **gym**, and **sauna** on the premises. **Fishing** in the **trout pond** is free to guests. Owners and managers hope to build on nature-related activities. Guests can borrow binoculars and guides from the bird-watching library. **Bowling** is available for a fee. So is the **sporting clays course** ($20/round). **Boat rentals** and **fishing charters** can be arranged. **The Rock golf course** is 1.2 miles from the lodge via a paved cart path. Ask about golf packages, couples' retreats, lodging & Bayside dining packages.

At **WOODMOOR LODGE** 40 log lodge rooms with rustic decor come with refrigerators, satellite TV/VCRs, phones with voice mail. Half are loft rooms with cathedral ceilings and an upstairs loft with queen bed. Rates are $150 in summer, $114 on off-season weekdays, $85/$95 in winter. A casual restaurant is next door at Pins bowling alley.

The resort evolved from the corporate retreat of Domino's Pizza founder Tom Monaghan. The **COTTAGES in the FRANK LLOYD WRIGHT style,** designed by Monaghan, are nestled in the woods near the water, either on **Potagannissing Bay** or overlooking a pond. For anyone who likes the Wright approach and his artful way of manipulating spaces and integrating nature and indoors, these are **very special places**, though not without their eccentricities. Many cottages have double bunk beds, for instance. Though the cottages are often privately owned, guests can rent some time slots for many in the rental pool. Call for times and rates. The rental pool includes Monaghan's own house (five bedrooms, five baths a big room for entertaining) sleeps 18. The Boathouse (big room out on the water, sleeps four), and three- and four-bedroom houses on the pond. *Winter special: stay two nights,*

get the third night free. Guests here can use all resort facilities by the lodge. **H.A.:** lodge is accessibe. Call for cottages ⚥: 12 & under sleep and eat free. 🐕:call. $50/stay

ANNIE'S ATTIC (906) 493-5378
Close to the ferry and on the island's south side, away from other resorts, Anne Stadler, portrait photographer and former editor of the island's monthly newspaper, has **three antique-filled guest rooms** in her family's 1911 cabin and in the attractively remodeled carriage house behind it. There's a stone fireplace and lawn with a **grand view of Whitney Bay**, its islands, and **freighters** beyond it. Birds, butterflies, and wildflowers abound here as on much of the island. There's a canoe for guests to use. In the main house, two guest rooms ($55/night) share one bath. The carriage house is $65/night. All guests are served a full breakfast. *On Humm Rd. (the first right east of the ferry off M-134), over the hill from the quarry.* **H.A.:** no ⚥: in carriage house

WAYFARERS MART B&B (906) 493-5935
Two **casually charming bedrooms** ($55 and $65), furnished with antiques, overlook Scammon Cove in this delightful homestay B&B. Big breakfast. They share a bath. Each has a TV, but there's no cable or satellite, so stations are few. There's a **cozy living room. Wonderful dinners** are available upon request — see restaurants. The dining area is quite separate from the lodgings. A **deck,** lawn chairs, and a picnic table let guests enjoy the **otherworldly view**. Guests can use the refrigerator, and they can **fish from a pier** on the property. The peaceful setting encourages guests to do nothing. 1 1/2 miles to swimming **beach**. *Directions: see restaurants. Open year-round.* **H.A.:** call ⚥ 🐕

NORTH HAVEN RENTALS
(906) 493-5567; www.drummondrentals.com

This rapidly expanding property management firm rents furnished vacation homes that each has a **water view** and access, a waterside deck, TV/VCR with 75 videos, fire pit, gas grill, and other extras. One-week minimum in summer, otherwise 3-day minimum. Just specify what you want: sunset view, fishing, freighter view — and the Kelleys will match you up with a property. *On M-134 2.7 miles east of the ferry. Open year-round.* **H.A.:** call for individual homes. 🐕: call

DRUMMOND ISLAND CAMPING

DRUMMOND TOWNSHIP PARK
(906) 493-5321

About 40 rustic sites (vault toilets, no showers) enjoy a private, pretty wooded setting near the water, with one of the island's **few sand beaches for swimming**. Some sites have electricity. The convenient location is not far from the village, ferry, or commercial four-corners. There's a boat ramp. This is a good place for kayakers and canoeists to put in. This first-come, first-serve campground is a very popular place in summer. Spots are more likely to open up during the week. Failing that, campers can almost always find spots at several **resort campgrounds**: Four Seasons on Tourist Rd. (493-5291), H&H in the village (493-5288), and Johnson's Resort on Scott Bay (493-5550). *Just north off M-134, 7 miles east of the ferry. Currently $8/night, $9.25 with electricity.*

Raber & Lime Island

Raber is a tiny place, just a public dock, some houses, a summer-only motel, some resorts, and a small store-gas station-laundromat. The village is known for the Raber Bay Bar & Grill, a **very popular waterfront bar and restaurant** and for fishing in Raber Bay, especially for herring beginning around July 4, for smelt whenever they happen to run in summer, and for walleye in winter and at ice-out.

Hiking and boat-watching on Lime Island

Three and a half miles offshore from the Raber dock, closer to St. Joseph Island in Canada, is Lime Island, long a fueling station for ships. The island's onetime company town sits in a clearing in what's a **rather wild island**, much less disturbed by man than nearby Neebish Island. It is state forest land today.

Here the state DNR has designed a **getaway experience without cars, shops, phones, and constant electricity**. You have to have a boat to get here or be able to afford two charter trips. Capt. Jack Behrens out of DeTour conducts **custom cruises** for up to six people along the St. Mary's River, including Lime Island. Call (800) 206-8079 or visit www.michcharterboats.com/island queen For other charter possibilities, you could also call the chambers of commerce at DeTour and Drummond Island.

Visitors can camp or stay in newly refurbished workers' cottages, hike its trails, boat-watch, and fish. "If you need to escape the predictable schedule of everyday life and experience the calming effects of Michigan's northern woods and waters, we have the place for you," states the brochure. "Rustic cabins and cottages in remote, calm, and beautiful surroundings can be yours in Michigan's state forests." See below for details about camping and cottages.

Lime Island was most recently owned by Consolidated Coal, which supplied fuel to coal-burning steamers and, later, to diesels. The island village, which once had its own school, had become a deteriorating ghost town by 1982, when Consolidated Coal offered to donate the island to the state.

In an age of tight budgets and decreased funds for camping and visitor facilities, state DNR officials thought long and hard before even accepting the gift. Then they devised an extremely successful plan to transform the deteriorated village into a nifty yet simple and easy to maintain getaway.

"What happened on Lime . . . should become a classic example of a government agency doing just about everything right. Lime is a great example of accomplishing more with less," wrote Jack Edwards in an article in *Great Lakes Cruiser* entitled "Lime Island: Miracle in the Lower St. Mary's." The underfunded Forest Management Division of the DNR took on the project and formed a citizen advisory board, then worked to minimize costs by using helpers who worked for free. Some were at-risk youth referred by

the courts; National Guard men and women on annual training maneuvers; and local volunteers, including summer people and DNR employees from DeTour and Sault Ste. Marie, who worked for free many Saturdays to get the job done.

Visitors can explore many interesting relics of island history, starting with the **huge, 900-foot coal dock** at the island's northwest side. It forms the breakwall for the **boaters' harbor.** No amenities are here, but there's no docking fee, either. *Boaters are advised to be careful entering and leaving the harbor.* A shipping channel is just 200 feet to the west, and freighters' bow waves can powerfully affect the course of small craft. The dock area has become a **picnic area.** Near the dock is a **large Victorian house** once used by superintendents of the coal refueling facility. Visitors can look in the restored **one-room schoolhouse,** then see the **ruins of lime kilns**, most of which operated here between the 1880s and the early 1900s. Earlier lime kilns here had provided mortar used in building the Soo Locks, and lime for nearby Fort St. Joseph, too. A few **interpretive signs** tell about the island's lime history. The kilns are 1/4 mile north of the docks.

A walkway lets viewers look into the **archaeological site** excavating historic and prehistoric activities here. In the early 1700s the island was home to French involved in the fur trade. **Four-thousand-year-old copper points** have been discovered on the island.

Several miles of hiking trails are on Lime Island. One starts behind the schoolhouse and leads to the flat sand

As part of the state forest's Lime Island visitor project, abandoned Consolidated Coal workers' housing has been turned into cozy, rustic overnight cottages for rent. The island, accessible only by private boat or charter, is an ideal place for people who really want to get away from it all, watch birds fish, and explore its trails and archaeological sites.

bars on Lime's south and east sides, where Indians rendezvoused and played lacrosse. The trails show visitors wildflowers, wetlands, wild berries, and birds. Blue herons nest on Lime's northeast tip, and eagles and osprey are seen — also bears. Volunteer **campground hosts** live on the island from spring through fall. They're happy to advise and help visitors. *For questions, call (906) 635-5281.* **H.A.:** There's a steep bluff from the boat slips up to the cabins and trails. Most of the island is flat. If campground hosts are near the slips, they can provide transportation in their van.

RABER & LIME ISLAND RESTAURANTS

The **RABER BAY BAR & GRILL** packs in hungry diners from all around to a rather remote spot on the St. Mary's River overlooking Lime Island. Delicious all-you-can-eat fresh fish dinners (around $11 and up) with a good soup/salad/dessert bar are the big attraction. There's also a full menu from burgers to steaks, with fresh fish in baskets or as sandwiches. The vintage bar dates from Prohibition's repeal in 1933. Now it's greatly expanded, with good views of passing vessels. *In Raber. Raber is about 2 1/2 miles north of Goetzville; where M-48 turns west, continue north on Gogomain Rd., the area's main street. Or take Gogomain east from Pickford, where it is the east road at the main four-corners. 297-5701. Open year-round. May to December, open daily 11-11, Sun noon to 9. Open Thurs-Sun in the off season.* Full bar

RABER & LIME ISLAND LODGINGS

LIME ISLAND COTTAGES/ Lake Superior State Forest

Two- and three-bedroom coal workers' cottages accommodate up to 8. They sit on a bluff overlooking the St. Mary's River, 1/4 mile up from the dock. Each renovated cottage has a knotty pine interior, a custom-made rustic pine table, chairs, and bed platforms, and a wood stove. A solar collector supplies electricity during the day. Vault toilets; water pump. No showers except for solar showers with a privacy screen. Guests should bring a light for evening, cook stove and equipment, bedding, and sleeping bags. Available spring through fall. $45/day, $250/week (Friday-Friday). No pets. **Reservations required;** call (906) 635-5281. **H.A.:** cottages are ADA accessible, and the island is flat, except for the bluff leading up from the boat slips. Campground hosts will drive disabled

visitors up, but they aren't always around. Call.

SEVERAL SMALL RESORTS have frontage on Raber Bay and nearby Munuscong Bay, a similar fishery. They are: **Fisherman's Point** (906-297-6671), **Jack's Landing & Karen's Rustic Cabins** (906-297-6355), **Water's Edge Resort** (906-297-2191), and **Glen's Cove** (906-297-5042). **Raber Bay Landing** (906-297-5812) offers year-round cottages, camping, boats, and dockage.

RABER & LIME ISLAND CAMPING

LIME ISLAND Camping/ Lake Superior State Forest
(906) 635-5281; no reservations

Tent platforms are about 400 feet from the harbor dock. Tent tie-downs are built into the decks. Bring a stove or portable grill. Vault toilets. Water pump. Solar shower. Take precautions about bears; see introduction. Additional tent platforms are on the island's southeast side, accessible by water or by a 2.2 mile trail from the harbor. *Open spring thru fall. Call (906) 635-5281 to check availability or to make reservations for group camping. $6/$9 night.* **H.A.:** call : no

Barbeau

A hamlet of resorts, a convenience store, and a restaurant is on the St. Mary's River near the Neebish Island ferry. The inland dot for Barbeau on the state highway map marks the location of the post office at an isolated rural intersection.

Freighter Alley

Here at the Neebish Island ferry in Barbeau, where watercolorist and maritime artist Pat Norton had her riverfront studio, Dick Hanson has set up the laid-back shop and headquarters for his small northern Michigan retailing empire. He's starting with gift shops here, at DeTour, in Northport, and in Traverse City. It seems like it would be a stretch — or a shock — to move from Traverse City (where he still owns Island View Vineyards) to Barbeau. But here he is. Whitney, his King Charles spaniel, has become well known to ferry passengers. Dick is a photographer and writer for travel videos and magazines. His career really took off when he did some videos for Bo Schembechler, former University of Michigan football coach and Detroit Tiger general manager.

At the Neebish Island ferry landing on 15

Mile Road. (906) 647-2033. Seasonal. **H.A.:** two steps

BARBEAU RESTAURANT

Tiny Barbeau is fortunate to have **SHIRLEY'S COZY CORNER**, a spacious, friendly place. Shirley's homemade soups and lunch specials ($3.50-$5) are tasty. Fish, chicken, and steak dinners currently range from around $8 to $11. The place looks out onto the downbound shipping land. There are pool tables, and a big wood stove for winter. *3 miles east of Barbeau's post office, at the end of 15 Mile Rd. a mile north of the Neebish Island Ferry. 647-8014. Open year-round. Current hours: May-Nov: 11 a.m.-11 p.m., Dec-April 11 a.m.-10 p.m.*

Neebish Island (pop. 77)

Neebish Island remains wonderfully undeveloped. Even though only four of its 21 square miles are state owned, people have not built many cottages here, as they have on Sugar Island to the north.

The island has been settled since the 1880s. Its name is an Indian word for "where the water boils," referring to the once-furious rapids along its western side. Today those rapids are greatly diminished, due to a deep channel dug in 1908 to permit freighter traffic. During World War II, the Coast Guard had a camp here, and before that there was a busy sawmill at Johnson Point. A couple who live on the island operate the ferry. It takes cars and people from Barbeau ($8 round-trip for car and driver, $2 for passengers over 12 years old) until the ice bridge forms just upstream after the Soo Locks shut for the season January 15. Ever since the little convenience store burned down, there is no place to buy food on the island. That can be a problem when the Coast Guard

> ### The British fur-trading fort on the St. Mary's River
>
> At the south tip of St. Joseph Island, the big Canadian island on the St. Mary's River, **Fort St. Joseph National Historic Site** has an excellent outdoor museum on the fur trade and British-Canadian history. Call (705) 949-1231 for season and hours. The rest of the island is a major Canadian visitor destinatiion, with shops, resorts, and inns. Call Ontario Travel Information (705-945-6941) for a map-guide.

comes through in late March with an ice breaker that demolishes the half-mile-long **ice bridge** to the mainland. Often this is done so early that ice quickly again forms, too thin to walk on but thick enough to prevent the ferry from operating, thus stranding the islanders, sometimes for two weeks until a permanent water channel is reestablished.

The Coast Guard's eagerness to open the water channel is because the giant freighters must carefully maneuver around Neebish Island in order to move through St. Mary's River to the Soo Locks and into Lake Superior. Boaters and ferry passengers can see the sheer limestone rock of "The Cut" if they look south from the ferry dock. The Corps of Engineers first created The Cut around 1900 to open up a second shipping channel, and has widened it to accommodate longer and longer freighters. The original channel was on Neebish Island's east side. Today it handles the upbound traffic and its western side the downbound traffic. Neebish is also known for **unusual birds**. A family of great grey owls, much bigger than most owls, lives here. There are also snowy owls, northern hawk owls, red- and white-winged crossbills, northern shrike, and rough-legged hawks.

NEEBISH ISLAND LODGING

GAINES RESORT (906) 632-3956

Tucked in the southeast corner of the island is an old resort with remarkably inexpensive cabins. The Gaineses live in a

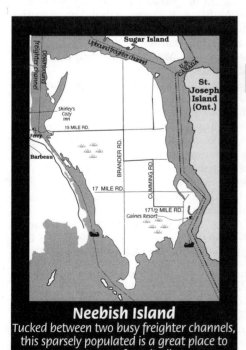

Neebish Island
Tucked between two busy freighter channels, this sparsely populated is a great place to get away from it all.

converted 1890 barn. This place and all its cabins have views of the east (upbound) shipping channel. Deer hunters, duck hunters, and fishermen are guests in spring and fall, but many summer guests are families with children. Each cabin has a heater, refrigerator, stove, hot and cold running water, and comes with a 14-foot aluminum boat with oars. Two little one-bedroom cabins overlook the water, with a view of Rock Island, a slender island made by the Corps of Engineers from waste rock created when the St. Mary's River shipping channel was widened. The cabins rent for $175 a week. Each has its own bathroom in a separate building in a little adjacent bathhouse. Another one-bedroom cottage with inside bathroom is $190/week. A three-bedroom sits by itself a little up the hill. It's $300 a week or $60 a night. *Write: HC 51, Box 382. Barbeau, Michigan 49710. Open from May 15 thru deer season.* **H.A.**: no 👫👫 🐕: no

---

Kinross

This small town has an airport just to its south with a runway over 2.5 miles long. It and the runway at the former K. I. Sawyer Air Force Base south of Marquette are the longest runways in Michigan. A legacy of the cold war, they were built to accommodate B-52s and giant re-fueling tankers. The Kincheloe field here has been renamed the Chippewa County International Airport. Its enormous size is weirdly out of proportion to the air traffic it now generates.

Just east of this cavernous, underused airport is another massive site: Michigan's biggest prison, Kinross, whose 113 acres hold over 1,200 prisoners. (Jackson Prison, long the world's largest walled prison, has been subdivided into smaller, more manageable

units.) Another prison in the vicinity, Hiawatha, on Marshall Road, incarcerates another 930 prisoners.

The town was founded as a station on the Minneapolis, St. Paul & Sault Ste. Marie Railroad (the Soo Line) in 1891. It was named after a town in Scotland by the Scottish settlers who had moved south from Canada. By the 1930s Kinross straddled the old highway (superseded by I-75 a couple miles east). Nearby farms grew hay, grain, and vegetables to market in Sault Ste. Marie.

Kinross Heritage Park

Here near one of the Upper Peninsula's main farming areas, the volunteer museum of the Kinross Heritage Society commemorates **pioneer farming** and the logging that preceded it. Displays include a blacksmith shop, shoe repair shop, and barber shop. An 1882 **log cabin** and a 1902 one-room schoolhouse are outside. There's a half-mile **nature trail** through 20 acres of mature pines, maples, and oaks. Much of the fun of visiting the U.P. is meeting old-timers at museums like this. Here people can tell you about the impact of the now-closed Kincheloe Air Force Base across the way, and the prison that followed it.

On Tone Rd. about a mile east of I-75, across from the Chippewa County Fairground. (906) 495-7110. Open Mem. to Labor Day, Thurs-Sun 1-5 and by appointment. Donations welcome. ♿

Navigating the St. Mary's River with its twists and turns is a challenge for increasingly large freighters. Special river pilots come aboard from DeTour to the Soo. Just south of Neebish Island is "The Cut," where the Corps of Engineers created a second shipping lane by excavating bedrock. This vintage postcard shows The Cut and the lookout station, superseded by radar. Abandoned, the lookout can still be seen just south of the Neebish Island ferry.

Keep in mind that all prices and hours of operation are subject to change. Lodging rates vary with supply and demand and are usually higher for special events.

U.S. 2 from St. Ignace to Naubinway

THE EASTERN GATEWAY to the Upper Peninsula is St. Ignace and the Straits of Mackinac between lakes Michigan and Huron. It's unusual in America because its recorded history goes back for centuries, yet it has not been overlaid with a thick layer of development. Here it is possible to experience the **natural landscape of several centuries ago**. This part of Michigan is **virtually without industry** except for tourism and some limestone quarrying. The year-round population is sparse. Much of the land is part of the **Hiawatha National Forest** and **Lake Superior State Forest** which reverted to government when logging companies, having harvested the timber, didn't pay property taxes. Tourism is such a big part of the economy here that unemployment soars from under 5% in summer to over 20% in the winter off season.

When the first French explorers came here, Ojibwa, Huron and Odawa peoples had long fished in the Straits area's productive waters and met to trade on Mackinac Island. Named for its prominent turtle shape, the island holds a prominent place in the Ojibwa people's creation myth.

Recorded history of the Straits area goes back to 1634, when Jean Nicolet passed through the Straits trying to find a route to the Orient. Soon French fur traders and their voyageur agents had superimposed a far-flung fur-trading system on the preexisting Indian trade networks. The fur trade's center was first at Michilimackinac (now Mackinaw City) and later on Mackinac Island. Jesuit priests were troubled about the harm done to native peoples by the fur trade and by trade goods, especially alcohol, for which Indians had not developed a genetic tolerance. Jesuits were legendary in their determination to spread their faith. Father Jacques Marquette established a Jesuit mission at St. Ignace in 1671 and named it after their order's founder, St. Ignatius Loyola.

The area's economic bases during the17th and 18th centuries—hunting and fishing—are still important today. History, natural beauty, hunting, and fishing drive the tourism economy that sustains the area. **Mackinac Island**, a carless survival of Victorian tourism that is being transformed into a kind of nouveau Victorian stage set, is Michigan's top destination for overnight travel. **St. Ignace** today is **shaped by Mackinac Island ferries** and the many motels serving tourists to the island. The ferry trip is shorter, the lodgings less expensive, and the pace slower than at Mackinaw City.

Tourism in the St. Ignace area got a huge boost in 1957 when the Mackinac Bridge was completed between the two peninsulas. It replaced a cumbersome carferry which resulted in summer waits of one to two hours and backups of up to five hours in hunting season.

A visit to St. Ignace can illuminate the area's **350-year**

Just north of the bridge, long sand beaches, good camping, easily accessible natural areas, and 300 years of Ojibwa, French, and American history at the Straits.

recorded history. Here a substantial portion of the native-born locals are descended from a mix of Native Americans, French trappers and voyageurs, and fishermen and loggers from various backgrounds, most visibly the Irish. About 85% of the school population has some Indian heritage.

U.S. 2 parallels Lake Michigan for most of the 42 miles between the Mackinac Bridge and Naubinway. Naubinway is the little fishing village at Lake Michigan's northernmost tip. The highway passes alongside long, **sandy beaches** and **low dunes** alternating with forests and marshes and stony points. It's punctuated with **overlooks** and dramatic vistas. Much of this area, including inland fishing lakes, wetlands, and much of Lake Michigan's northernmost shoreline, is public land, part of the Hiawatha National Forest or Lake Superior State Forest. Rustic campgrounds invite visitors make this centrally located area a base camp. The **North Country Trail** heads north toward Tahquamenon Falls from St. Ignace. Hikers could arrive by bus and hike off conveniently into the back country, though the trail sees few such "through hikers."

VISITOR INFORMATION: Call, stop by, or visit the website of the helpful **ST. IGNACE CHAMBER of COMMERCE** (800) 338-6660; (906) 643-8717; www.stignace.com The office is in town next to the Museum of Ojibwa Culture and Marquette Mission Park at 560 N. State. It shares a building with the museum's outstanding shop of books and Eastern Woodland Indian art. Hours are weekdays from 8 to 4. Summer hours are weekdays 8-6, Sat 9-5. . . . . Mike Lilliquist and his crew at the **MICHIGAN WELCOME CENTER** in St. Ignace by the Mackinac Bridge exit are amazingly knowledgeable about the area and the Upper Peninsula. The Welcome Center gives away many hundreds of free pamphlets and magazines (ask for the wide-ranging *Upper Peninsula Travel Planner*). It often has stacks of free phone books to U.P. communities. The 24-hour lobby has restrooms and a weather station — two video monitors, one with national weather, one repeating local, U.P. and state conditions, road reports, and forecasts. Displays include a big model of the Mackinac Bridge, a majestic black timber wolf and a bearskin. The center is just north of the Mackinac Bridge toll booths. Open daily, year-round, 9-5, in summer from 8 to 6. (906) 643-6979. It *can* be reached from the U.P. side of the bridge. Turn left before the change booths.

PUBLIC LAND: The Michigan Welcome Center at the St. Ignace side of the Mackinac Bridge stocks a complete array of handouts about recreational opportunities in the **HIAWATHA NATIONAL FOREST**. The Forest Service also has serves visitors through its beautiful new office on the north side of U.S. 2, six miles west of the bridge. Its demonstration garden of **native plants** is worth a look any time, and it has a few picnic

tables, too. It's open weekdays from 8 to 4:30 year-round. (906) 643-7900. . . . A few choice areas are part of the **LAKE SUPE-RIOR STATE FOREST**. The nearest DNR office is on U.S. 2 East in Naubinway. (906) 477-6262. Open weekdays, 7:30 to 4.

EVENTS: Consult www.stignace.com or call (800) 338-6660 for details. Three big auto events are the biggest deals in **ST. IGNACE**. The car show and Bridge Walk fill all rooms and requiring advance planning or day trips from elsewhere. The last weekend in June, the **St. Ignace Car Show** fills the area in one of the nation's largest all-make, all-model shows. . . . The previous weekend, **Antiques on the Bay** features original and restored classic and antique autos. . . . The third weekend in September semis with custom art, light displays and more come for the **Richard Crane Memorial Truck Show**. . . . The **Labor Day Bridge Walk** is a Michigan tradition. Thousands of walkers join the governor and other politicians walking the five miles from St. Ignace to Mackinaw City, the only day pedestrians are allowed on the bridge. The two days before Labor Day are of special interest for the **Native American Art Show & Sale** and **Michinemackinong Powwow** with crafts, storytellers, and music. . . .St. Ignace's rich mixed cultural heritage is celebrated with storytelling, boats, music, crafts, and children's activities at **Culturama**.

HARBORS with transient dockage: In **St. Ignace** (906-643-8131; off-season 643-6876; lat. 45° 51' 58"N, long. 84° 43' 06" W) with showers. In **Naubinway** the Garfield Twp. Marina (lat. 46° 05' 12" N, long. 85° 26' 25" W) with showers, launch ramp.

PICNIC PROVISIONS and PLACES

◆ The big 24-hour **Glen's supermarket** on U.S. 2 as you come into **ST. IGNACE** is the easiest and best bet for deli foods plus meats. 643-9636. It's right near the excellent **Mackinac Fish Market**, where fresh and smoked fish and beef jerky are packed for travel at no extra cost. Smoked whitefish pâté makes the simplest picnic elegant. 109 Elliot next to Family Dollar. 643-7535.

◆ Picnic spots abound in town. In **St. Ignace** along the boardwalk are the **marina** and **Kiwanis Beach**. (See map.) **Dock #3** is a public park south of downtown by the old ferry docks.

◆ Right outside town off of U.S. 2 by the Mackinac Bridge exit, the **Father Marquette Memorial picnic area** offers a grand view of bridge and straits, plus an interpretive trail.

◆ The **Hiawatha National Forest** office on U.S. 2 six miles west of the Mackinac Bridge has a couple of picnic tables by its pretty garden of native plants.

◆ All along **U.S. 2** to Naubinway, 42 miles from the bridge, are many picnic areas built by the **Michigan Department of Transportation**, the U.S. Forest Service, or the state forests that either overlook Lake Michigan or give access to good swimming beaches. Consult the text for picnic areas at **Gros Cap**, the **Lake Michigan Campground**, M-DOT parks at **Brevort, Cut River,** and **Epoufette,** and **Hog Island** (less impacted by traffic). . . . .The **Hiawatha National Forest** picnic area on Brevoort Lake offers warmer swimming and canoe and kayak rentals. . . . The **Mystery Spot** has a pretty wooded picnic area.

St. Ignace (pop. 2,568)

St. Ignace overlooks crescent-shaped Moran Bay, an **ideal harbor**. It's directly northwest of Mackinac Island, which is five miles out in the Straits. St. Ignace is the closest mainland town to the popular resort island. In summer **passenger ferries** almost constantly shuttle passengers from St. Ignace docks to Mackinac. State Street, the town's main thoroughfare, has become **four miles of motels** and other tourist-oriented establishments. Today its role as a point of embarkation for Mackinac Island is St. Ignace's major livelihood, though it is also Mackinac County seat and the eastern U.P.'s second-largest community after Sault Ste. Marie. Its intelligently edited local newspaper, the *St. Ignace News,* is the envy of many a larger place.

For Mackinac-bound visitors, St. Ignace has some real advantages over **Mackinaw City**, depending on one's preferences. In recent years Mackinaw has been slicked up and refashioned according to the **Disney and Branson brand of tourism**. It has a court of restaurants and shops, a multiplex theater, a long row of amenity-loaded motels, and the crowds and prices that

go with all that. St. Ignace still has quite a bit of old-time tourist kitsch, but it is a year-round town with a pleasant harborfront boardwalk, a big Glen's supermarket, and other useful services. **Sand beaches, dunes,** and other natural areas are close at hand. It's hard to find a native of Mackinaw City, while St. Ignace has a **tremendous sense of rootedness**.

Downtown gets lost in a jumble along State Street, but St. Ignace churches, schools, and the courthouse are in the trim and tidy neighborhood up on the bluff. Go up along Portage, or along Goudreau just north of the Municipal Building, and you'll find the **hidden town**. The 1920s brick Tudor house on Portage, the **biggest house in town**, was built by Prentiss Brown, owner of the Arnold Ferry Line and a U.S. Senator.

"Mackinac" and "Mackinaw" are **pronounced the same way**. The letter "c" is silent, so the last syllable is **"naw."** "Mackinac" how the French spelled the Indian word, "Mackinaw" is the English way. It's never right to say "MACK-i-NACK," whether you're referring to Mackinaw City, Mackinac Island, or the Straits of Mackinac.

On the south end of downtown, Spring Street climbs the hill past the library to the big red brick **St. Ignatius Loyola Catholic Church** at Spring and Church. The **Catholic cemetery** is an interesting place for its numerous old Irish monuments, its French, Irish, and Ojibwa names, and its many angels, Blessed Virgin Marys, and little American flags. To find it, turn south from Spring onto Chambers at the athletic field, "Home of the Saints" and go south a few blocks.

Once St. Ignace played a more important role in American history. After Father Marquette built a mission here in 1671, the French built a fort to defend it. It remained active until 1701, when it was deliberately burned to the ground. In that year Cadillac, commander at Michilimackinac, left to build a fort far to the south that would control the entrance to the upper Great Lakes. That fort was Detroit.

After 1701, the forts at Michilimackinac and later Mackinac Island protected the French and then the British fur trade at the Straits and provided a source of law and order in this remote part of the world. Commercial fishing got its start in the 1800s with French Canadians who moved here from Canada. Lumber also built up the local

Before the Mackinac Bridge was built, it took a carferry like the *Vacationland* (above) to get a vehicle from the Lower to the Upper Peninsula. During the hunting season, lines of waiting cars approched five miles long.

economy at St. Ignace. Though the settlement was not at the mouth of any significant logging river, it was near the mouth of the Carp. Fishing remained important into the 1930s, when two million pounds a year of whitefish and trout were still being shipped. In 1881 the rail line arrived that connected St. Ignace with Wisconsin to the west and with the Lower Peninsula (linked by rail car ferry) to the south. A year later St. Ignace became the seat of Mackinac County. But until the Mackinac Bridge was completed in 1957, St. Ignace remained quite isolated. It was the last place in Michigan to have three-digit phone numbers. Well into the 1950s it received only a few hours of television each night. A Coast Guard retiree who liked St. Ignace so well he stayed comments, "If Alaska is 30 years behind the times, as my wife says, St. Ignace is 50 years behind." He says the names you read in histories from the 1800s are same names as the people on city council today.

A transplant who married a local man says, "Kids from the area like the anonymity of college but [usually] come back after getting their degrees. Some don't have a desire to go elsewhere and are happy to clerk at a motel. It can be nice to have everybody know your name. I joke with my husband that it's a good thing he married me. They needed a little fresh blood in their blood line."

A motel on north of town has been transformed into the **Kewadin Shores Casino**, owned by the Sault Ste. Marie Tribe of Chippewas, the Upper Peninsula's masters of economic development through gambling. It's nowhere as big or fancy as the Soo casino and

convention center with its headline entertainment, but it does help fill motel rooms on the north side of town. It's at 3039 Mackinac Trail, just east of I-75 exit 352. (906) 643-7071. Following the huge success of the tribe's Little Bear Ice Arena in Sault Ste. Marie as a center for area hockey teams, the tribe funded **"Little Bear East" Ice Arena** &

Visiting Mackinac Island

It's been a key place for centuries: the trading center for Great Lakes Indians and later for the 18th and early 19th-century fur trade; then a Victorian resort with grand cottages; now not only a popular getaway but the scene of important state political meetings at the Grand Hotel. (Horses and carriages are picturesque draws today. But practical reasons led to cars being banned in the 1920s. The automobile's destructive potential for affecting the island was clear by then. How could a small island handle too many cars?)

Don't get completely caught up in the tourist shuffle. A little reading up can help you plan a better-balanced trip that combines walks along the quaint back streets; bicycling around the island and to the interior's dramatic rock formations; visits to historic sites; and dining and snacking in glorious settings. Free tourist info from the Welcome Center or island chamber can get you started. Our website, www.huntsguides.com, will include a carefully considered 13-page overview of the island and 10 more pages on attractions along and near the south side of the Straits of Mackinac.

Conference Center in downtown St. Ignace next to Marquette Mission Park. It changes into a conference center when it's not skating season. Call the St. Ignace Rec Department (643-8676) for public skate times.

Points of interest have been arranged from the Mackinac Bridge into town and then north of town. After that comes the section along U.S. 2 starting just west of the bridge.

Mackinac Bridge

Michigan's two peninsulas are separated by four miles of water at the Straits of Mackinac between Mackinaw City and the limestone bluffs south of St. Ignace. Before November, 1957, getting to the U. P. from down below took a 45-minute carferry ride plus extra time for waiting and loading that ranged from an hour to waits of three and four hours in busy summer times and five hours and five-mile backups in hunting season. The Mackinac Bridge turned the trip into a ten-minute drive — and bestowed upon travelers a memorable landmark and experience. It also kicked off a new era of Upper Peninsula tourism and spawned a host of motels along U.S. 2 west of the bridge.

Choicest camping and outdoor recreation spot south of the bridge: **Wilderness State Park** (231-436-5381. **Legs Inn** (231-526-2281) is a masterpiece of northwoods rustic folk architecture — with beautiful gardens, a fine lake view, and good Polish food. It's 20 miles southwest at Cross Village, not far from the south side of scenic Wilderness State Park. Open from late May thru mid-October.

An excellent guide to Mackinac Island is longtime summer resident Amy McVeigh's **Mackinac Connection.** It covers everything from the horses to history to what it's like to live on the island to lodgings and restaurants.

For visitor info on the three interesting historic sites of the **Mackinac State Historic Parks,** call (616) 436-5563. There's the late 18th-century fort on the island, a less dramatic but in many ways more interesting recreation of the earlier **Michillimackinac** fort and trading center at Mackinac City, and a sawmill and appealing natural area at Mill Creek, a few miles south. Together they bring to life the fur trade and its mix of cultures (Indian, French, British, and American).

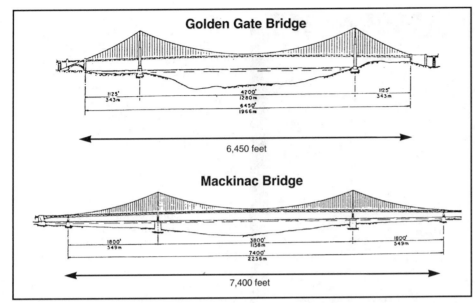

Golden Gate Bridge

1125'
343m

4200'
1280m

6450'
1966m

1125'
343m

6,450 feet

Mackinac Bridge

1800'
549m

3800'
1158m

7400'
2256m

1800'
549m

7,400 feet

Completion of the Mackinac Bridge in 1957 had an enormous impact on tourism in the eastern U.P. The bridge spans almost 1 1/2 miles. Its roadway deck, 155 feet above the water, offers a grand Straits view.

The view from the bridge is remarkable, especially coming from the north. You see Lake Michigan to the west and Lake Huron to the east. The vast expanse of water, peninsulas, and islands is even more riveting when there's a huge freighter passing under the bridge, 155 feet below the roadway deck. Best of all is **ice-out in late March**, when the broken ice forms fascinating chunky swirls as it moves. It's a special treat to look down and see the Coast Guard icebreaker *Biscayne Bay* from St. Ignace.

Don't worry about safety. If you stay within the speed limit (normally 45 mph) and obey special weather-related instructions on the lighted display board, you'll be fine. In cases of cars going over the guard rail and plunging to the lake, drivers were speeding. One was ruled a suicide; the other involved a tiny Yugo automobile in very bad weather.

As a dramatic landmark, the bridge helps sell motel rooms with bridge views. At night, thousands of lights outline the graceful parabolic cables suspended from the **552-foot towers**. It's a grand sight — the **elegant simplicity** of the towers and cables, played off against the random patterns of distant car lights on the roadway.

The **best places to view the bridge from the U.P. side** are the parking area at the foot of Boulevard Drive, the picnic area at Father Marquette National Memorial just west of the bridge, and Curio Fair, a vintage roadside attraction with a tower on West U.S. 2. **Mackinaw City** has several pleasant parks with

bridge views. One extends east of Colonial Michilimackinac (the reconstructed 18th-century fort just west of the bridge's southern base) to the Old Mackinac Point lighthouse. Four miniparks on Lake Huron are at the east ends of every street north of Central.

Talk about a Straits bridge first came up in the 1880s, at the time when three railroads joined to operate the first railroad car ferry across the Straits (1881). Completion of the Brooklyn Bridge in 1883 fueled the idea of a Straits bridge. In 1921 the bridge engineer who promoted the Detroit-Windsor bridge proposed an **island-hopping bridge route**, 24 miles long, with a series of relatively short bridges connecting Cheboygan to St. Ignace via Bois Blanc, Round, and

---

Diving in the Straits area

Some 14 wrecks are buoyed for divers, and another 11 can be found with sonar. Still more are described in Chuck and Jeri Feltner's authoritative, interesting *Shipwrecks of the Straits of Mackinac* . . . . . For a dive brochure, call (906) 643-8717. For more info and for reservations on the 42-foot dive boat ($75/day to visit 2 wrecks), call Straits Scuba Center. In season it's open at the Star Line main dock, 587 N. State, when the staff isn't on a dive; phone (906) 643-7009. Get info any time from its parent shop, Macomb Scuba Center in Warren, (810) 558-9922. Ask about off-shore dive sites.

Mackinac islands. In 1934 the first bridge authority asked for federal Public Works funds for that project, but it was rejected.

A 1940 proposal for a suspension bridge with a 4,600-foot span was abandoned after the ill-starred Tacoma Narrows Bridge, a similar bridge by the same designer, was destroyed by high winds that same year. Momentum for a bridge lost steam because of World War II and objections from the state's auto ferry service between Mackinaw City and St. Ignace. In place since 1921, it had developed its own political constituency.

Credit for reviving the bridge idea, according to industrial historian Charles Hyde in *Historic Bridges of Michigan*, goes to William Stewart Woodfill, the energetic, political, promotion-minded president of Mackinac Island's Grand Hotel. Woodfill's group effectively lobbied for a new bridge authority. Its feasibility study led the state legislature to authorize bonds for the project and start construction.

Building the bridge was a monumental story. It begins with the piers, constructed by sinking huge steel caissons into the mud, driving them into bedrock, and removing the mud to pour in reinforced-concrete piers. The story is best told at the free **MACKINAC BRIDGE MUSEUM** (231-436-5534) on the main business street **in Mackinaw City**. An ironworker who helped build the bridge started the museum over his **Mama Mia Pizzeria**, at 231 E. Central at Henry, where it remains today. The displays aren't professional or slick, but the project has both intelligence and the heart of grassroots history. There are hundreds of workers' personalized hardhats, before-the-bridge photos of huge lines of cars waiting for the ferries during hunting season, and an excellent half-hour **film** about designing and building the bridge.

Fare for the I-75 Mackinac Bridge is $1.50/car (driver and passengers), $1/motorcycle, $2.50 or $3.50 for cars with trailers or small motor homes. **Bicyclists** *and* **pedestrians** *must request to be transported (for $2 a person) by calling the Mackinac Bridge Authority at (906) 643-7600, or stopping at the office by the St. Ignace approach to the bridge. $30 commuter books for 24 trips save a little time and 25¢/trip.*

U.S. Coast Guard Cutter *Biscayne Bay*

Visitors are welcome to tour this busy vessel when it's docked here at its home port. (Summer is the best time to find it in). This relatively new class of icebreak-

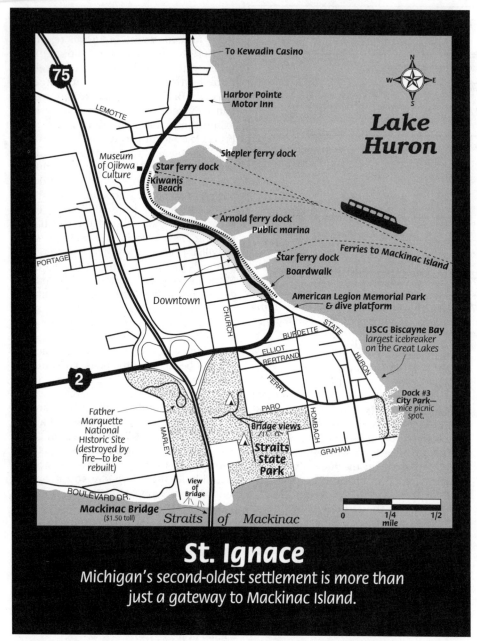

To Kewadin Casino

Harbor Pointe
Motor Inn

Lake
Huron

Shepler ferry dock

Museum
of Ojibwa
Culture

Star ferry dock

Kiwanis
Beach

Arnold ferry dock
Public marina

Star ferry dock

Ferries to Mackinac Island

Boardwalk

Downtown

American Legion Memorial Park
& dive platform

USCG Biscayne Bay
largest icebreaker
on the Great Lakes

Dock #3
City Park—
nice picnic
spot.

Father
Marquette
National
Historic Site
(destroyed by
fire—to be
rebuilt)

Bridge views

Straits
State
Park

View
of
Bridge

BOULEVARD DR.

Mackinac Bridge
($1.50 toll)

Straits of Mackinac

0   1/4   1/2
mile

St. Ignace

Michigan's second-oldest settlement is more than just a gateway to Mackinac Island.

ing tug uses a wider beam and greater horsepower to break more ice, and a "bubbler" lubrication system to do it more efficiently. The ship's round-hulled bow slides up on the ice and then crushes down through it. (In case it gets stuck, ballast tanks enable it to shift and break the ice.) The bubbler system forces air out into the water through ports in the hull, thus keeping broken ice away from the ship and avoiding friction.

At the Coast Guard Station is at 1075 S. Huron south of downtown. From downtown, follow State St. southeast along the shore at American Legion Park, where Bus. I-75 branches west and goes up the hill. Turn east onto Bertrand or Paro to reach Huron. Call (906) 643-6435 to arrange a tour. ⅊: call.

St. Ignace Boardwalk

Improvements like gazebos, picnic tables, and benches are continually being made to this **mile-long path** along the harbor. It has become a good place to get in touch with Moran Bay and St. Ignace history, as conveyed in **10 or so interpretive signs** on subjects from shipwrecks to commercial fishing to the meeting of French and Native American cultures. Look for the *Edith Jane*, a **Mackinaw boat from 1899**. The double-ended design, adapted from Indian vessels, proved the ideal work boat in shallow waters because it could easily be pulled up onto the beach.

The continuous walkway begins at the **MARINA** just north of the Mackinac Grille. Here are a **gazebo** and **picnic**

tables.

On Friday evenings from late June into late August, free **BAYSIDE LIVE concerts** take place here, featuring many kinds of music. Check with the chamber or its website for performers: (800) 338-6660, (906) 643-8717, or www.stignace.com. Soon the marina will be adding 130 slips. After that project, the boardwalk will be connected to the south to American Legion Memorial Park, another waterfront park.

The boardwalk ends at **KIWANIS BEACH.** Here are **picnic tables**, a gazebo, and a **sandy beach** — a fine place to swim, though not as busy as it once was. This was the "Old Mill Slip" by a lumber kiln. Logs were corralled by chain booms so that wave action could peel the bark. Some bark remains on the bay bottom in this vicinity. The city of St. Ignace adds sand here each year. *Continuous walk extends from the marina to Kiwanis Beach across from Marquette Mission Park and the Museum of Ojibwa Culture.* ⅊

Downtown St. Ignace

Downtown is one of those places that looks confusing to passing motorists but can be quite a pleasant place once you get out and walk, especially if it's not high season when State Street traffic is at its worst. Downtown has gained greatly from continuing improvements made to the harborfront parks and boardwalk. Tourist shops are like Mackinac Island's ten years ago — not anything very distinctive. Many carry popular collectible lines. If upscale shopping in a beautiful setting is what you want, go to Petoskey or Harbor Springs, within an hour's drive.

Noteworthy points of interest have been arranged from south to north, first on the built-up side of the street, then along the harbor.

◆ **BOOK WORLD.** This well-stocked general book shop, part of a chain based in Appleton, Wisconsin, has a **good regional section**, **strong nature and children's books**, and the **best magazine selection in town**. For those hooked on *The New York Times*, it's "a godsend," says one summer resident. It also stocks **premium cigars** and imported cigarettes. *52 North State. 643-7569. Open year-round. Summer hours Mon-Sat 9-9, Sun 9-5. Otherwise Mon-Sat 9-8, Sun noon to 5.* ⅊

◆ **COFFEE SOCIETY at the Colonial House Inn.** The inn, a **classic revival** affair with a two-story portico and

In a former Catholic church in St. Ignace, the Museum of Ojibwa Culture shows how indigenous people survived the harsh winters on the Straits. It's on the site of Father Marquette's Jesuit mission founded in 1671.

columns, sits up and back a little from State Street, which makes its porch a nice place to sit, relax, and look out at the harbor. The coffeehouse, in a side wing, has a **big horse chestnut tree and beautiful shade garden** in front of its deck. It serves teas, coffee and espresso drinks, smoothies, French sodas, and desserts. *99 N. State. 643-6900. Typically open daily from mid May through color season. Summer hours 8 a.m. to 10 p.m. to Labor Day at least. Otherwise open daily from 10 to 5.* &: through back door.

◆ **THE EMPORIUM. Antique lighting** is a specialty at this large, general line antique shop with lots of furniture. The owners do upholstering, too, and sell at retail **upholstery fabrics**. *110 N. State. 643-6565. Open year-round, Mon-Sat 9-5, Sun by appointment.* &: one step.

◆ **JUSTRITE BAKERY. Cinnamon rolls** from this old-time bakery are a St. Ignace tradition. *312 N. State. 643-8144.*

Museum of Ojibwa Culture/ Marquette Mission Park

This intelligently done small museum, owned by the city of St. Ignace, is in a former Catholic church. The front gallery focuses on the **subsistence culture of the Ojibwa people,** early inhabitants of the upper Great Lakes. Exhibits depict their ingenuity in surviving in a cold, harsh climate and getting the necessities of life from the water and land around them. In the rear gallery, the exhibit **"Currents of Change in the Straits"** deals with the arrival of the Hurons, the Odawa (Ottawa), and in the 1760s and

1770s the French, who sought beaver fur for fashionable hats. The museum takes the viewpoint of native people and shows how they allied with the French against their common British enemy.

The museum and church occupy the very **site of Marquette's Jesuit mission** (1671-1701). Here, too, in this vicinity were villages of Huron and Odawa people, driven from their homes in southern Ontario in the 1640s by the hostile, expansionistic Iroquois.

A **memorial to Father Marquette** occupies the park by the museum. Significant archaeological digs have occurred here. A Huron **longhouse** and other **outdoor exhibits** describe how Huron and Odawa refugees adapted their cultures to this new land. At that same time French traders and voyageurs were introducing changes that would forever destroy native peoples' way of life, which was difficult but ecologically balanced.

Crafts demonstrations and workshops are held frequently; call for upcoming events. The museum's **NATIVE AMERICAN ART SHOW & SALE** is held on Labor Day weekend, Saturday and Sunday from 10 to 8. In addition to demonstrations and booths featuring many artists represented in the museum store, there are foods and music.

500 North State/Bus I-75 at the north end of downtown St. Ignace. (906) 643-9161. Open from Memorial Day thru mid October. Hours up to late June: Mon-Sat 11-5, Sun 10:30 to 5. Summer season: daily 10 to 8. From Labor Day to closing same hours as June. $2 adults & teens, $1 elementary, $5/family. &

Behind the courage of Father Marquette and the Jesuits

"It is difficult for us to comprehend the . . . flaming zeal of the French missionaries to save the souls of the 'savages,'" commented the late historian Willis Dunbar in his *Michigan: A History of the Wolverine State* (1965). "They regarded life as a torture, and death as a great release. They not only endured hardship, they courted it. . . . It did not matter to the Jesuit how hopeless it might seem to convert the Indians to Christianity. . . . His job was to carry out the will of God, to forgo all bodily pleasures, and to labor unceasingly to convert the Indians . . . .. When a man has not the slightest desire to live any longer than God ordains, he is not only unafraid to brave danger but he welcomes it."

The traditional powwow held each Labor Day weekend at the same time as the Ñative American Art Show and Sale is like a family reunion. Purists hunt the animals whose feathers and hide is used in regalia.

Ojibwa Museum Gift Shop & Artisans' Guild

Museum director Molly Paquin and Ron Paquin, whose skills in traditional Native American crafts range from birchbark canoes and baskets to antler carvings and knives, have developed the museum shop into a real destination. It clearly has the Upper Peninsula's **largest section** of **books and music** about **Eastern Woodland Indians** and the **best selection** of **locally made**, certified **Native American art and craft**, both traditional and contemporary. It's a peaceful place that shows the results of knowledgeable selection and a good eye for display. The **French history of the Straits** is another theme of the shop. The notebook on artists tells about the artists and their involvement with their work. Here are black ash baskets, porcupine quill work, antler and bone carving, birch bark containers and cutouts, dreamcatchers, paintings, and books by local authors, including *Not First in Nobody's Heart*, Ron's memoir of his boyhood and his dreadful yet all-too-common experience in Indian boarding schools, in his case the one in Harbor Springs.

Many workshops taught by the shop's contributors are part of the **Anisnawbe Practical Crafts and Living Skills series** from June into October. Many but not all participants come from native backgrounds and seek to acquaint themselves with their culture, which had been effectively suppressed for generations in most families. Ask for a flyer, and register early. Topics include appliqué techniques, beadworking, ground-fired clay pottery, an Ojibwe language introduction, and birch bark containers. *566 North State, at the north end of downtown, across from the Star ferry dock and Kiwanis Beach. (906) 643-9161. Open from Memorial Day thru mid October. Hours up to late June: Mon-Sat 11-5, Sun 10:30 to 5. Summer season: daily 10 to 8. From Labor Day to closing same hours as June. Free admission.* &

Indian Village

A classic of picturesque tourism. "Neon and wooden teepees attract motoring tourists to this colossal souvenir warehouse," writes Kathryn Eckert in *Buildings of Michigan*, the monumental survey of historic buildings. "The long metal building is faced with cedar bark, [and inside] wallpapered with birch bark decorated with pictographs of arrows, animals, canoes, and headdresses." The 1977 building resembles the landmark building from 1927, which it replaced. Inside are rubber tomahawks and other longtime staples of the tourist trade.

499 N. State, across from the Ojibwa Museum. 643-8980. &

Horseshoe Bay Wilderness Trail/Foley Creek Campground

The best, least crowded beaches are the ones you have to hike to get to. A good hike gets you away from annoying boom boxes, jet skis, etc. This **one-mile hiking trail**, easy for a wilderness area, leads to a **sandy, secluded Lake Huron beach**, backed by coastal wetlands where **many shore birds, ducks, and great blue heron can be seen**. Bald eagles sometimes perch in the tall pines nearest the shore, scanning for prey. Most of the Horseshoe Bay area is part of the **Hiawatha National Forest**. The trail goes through the 3,800-acre Horseshoe Bay Wilderness. The first section is a **boardwalk** that passes over a fragrant **white cedar swamp** where pitcher plants and morels have been found. Bring insect repellent for this moist area. Hunting is permitted in much of the area; call for details (to participate or avoid). See below for camping info; the campground is accessible by car.

Trailhead is at the north end of the Foley Creek Campground, on H673/Mackinac

Trail, 2 miles north of I-75 exit 348. Or, from the north and the I-75/M-123 exit and road to Cedarville, turn south onto Mackinac Trail and go about 1 1/2 miles to campground entrance (on left). (906) 643-7900. No fee. **H.A.:** a person on crutches could deal with the first part.

Carp River Canoe Trail

Within 15 miles of St. Ignace, this easy and **beautiful stretch of the Carp River** winds past logging rollways and forests of pine, maple, and birch that are a proposed wilderness area. It also goes under I-75. The river is rated for beginners; the entire stretch shown on the map is a two-day trip, and canoeists are allowed to camp at undesignated spots along the river. The Carp River is also a second-quality trout stream where brook, rainbow, and brown trout are in river pools and steelhead and salmon are near the river mouth. The Carp River ends at the rustic Carp River Campground and Lake Huron's St. Martin Bay.

One forest service recreation specialist says that canoeing and camping here is one of her very favorite activities in the entire area. Pick up a Forest Service map of the canoe trail, put-in points, and the few rapids. There's no canoe livery in this vicinity. For parties with two cars, it

would be easy to leave one car at the campground and canoe to it.

Get the Canoe Trail map and brochure from the Forest Service display at the St. Ignace Welcome Center or at the Hiawatha National Forest office on U.S. 2 west of St. Ignace. Or call (906) 643-7900 to have one mailed or faxed.

Castle Rock

The nucleus of this vintage roadside attraction is a **dramatic limestone stack**, eroded by water and wind to form a "castle." Mackinac Island's nearby stacks and arches have attracted tourists for over a century. Here, for 50¢, visitors can climb to the observation platform at the top of the rock and take in an **interesting view to the east and southeast**. They'll see (from left to right), St. Martin Island and, on the horizon on a clear day, Marquette Island in Les Cheneaux, St. Ignace, ferries coming to and from Mackinac Island, and, finally, the towers of the Mackinac Bridge peeking up above the bluffs. It's a **stunning view at sunset** and in **fall color season**. A **big, old-fashioned souvenir shop** is at the base of Castle Rock. Note: watch out for luxuriant poison ivy that may occasionally extend past the chain link fence into the edge of the walkway.

North of St. Ignace on the extension of Bus. Loop I-75. Or from I-75, take Business Loop 348, follow signs. (906) 643-8268. Open from May thru color season from 9 to 6 at least in spring and fall, from 8:30 to 9:30 from late June thru Labor Day. & : no.

ST. IGNACE RESTAURANTS

See separate section for restaurants west of Mackinac Bridge. Arranged from south to north.

The **MACKINAC GRILLE** manages to combine a **sophisticated menu** for this area and an interior that's attractive and historic in a decorator kind of way, and still keep the small-town atmosphere so it has a year-round local kaffee klatsch and Sunday after-church breakfast buffet. The Sposito brothers, who own and run the Driftwood and two Mackinac Island restaurants, teamed up with the Star Ferry owners on this appealing project. The main dining area is the depot from the old **merchandise dock** where freight from the Soo Line was loaded onto rail car ferries that crossed the Straits to connect with the New York Central and Pennsylvania railroads. Seating in a **railroad car** is near the entrance. And the bar offers a **beautiful view of Moran Bay**. Soups are exceptionally good and hearty. **Whitefish** is prepared in unusual ways, like the baked whitefish dip appetizer with garlic bread sticks (around $7), good with soup for a light dinner. Of the dinner entrées (mostly $11-$15, including soup or salad, fresh bread, and potato), specialties are whitefish Rockefeller (baked, then served under creamed spinach) and "poor man's whitefish," steamed in foil with potatoes, broccoli, mushrooms, tomatoes, and onions. **Personal pizzas** and pastas make for an adaptable menu for many diets. **Reservations** recommended in summer. *251 S. State next to the marina. 643-7482. Open daily year-round. In season hours: 8 a.m. to 10 p.m., to midnight Fri & Sat. In the off-season closes at 9 weekdays, 10 weekends.* ♿ ⛹ Full bar

The **VILLAGE INN,** one of Mackinac Island's most reliable and affordable restaurants, now has a year-round St. Ignace spinoff on the south end of downtown. Here too it's known for **pizza and whitefish**, though it has a full menu. Planked whitefish (about $13) comes prettily surrounded by dutchess potatoes and a side salad. During the week the **$6 all-you-can-eat burger bar** from 11 to 3 is an incredibly good deal for big appetites: burgers, chicken breasts, hot dogs, and some kind of pasta salad or such. Seafood chowder is a weekend favorite. Video games keep kids entertained. *250 S. State. 643-9511. Open 7 days a week year-round, 10 a.m. to 2 a.m.* ♿ ⛹ Full bar

In town next to the Arnold Docks, **THE GALLEY** covers all the bases between May and mid-October. It has a **good harbor view**, lounge, reliably good food, and a wide-ranging menu for breakfast, dinner, and sandwiches and meal-size salads (served all day). The **breakfast special** (under $3) is an especially good deal. Specialties are **broiled whitefish**

and lake trout ($12 as a dinner, $6 as a sandwich with fries and slaw) and fried perch. So is prime rib. Dinners come with soup and salad, potato, and rolls. The soups are very good. There's not much for strict vegetarians. *241 N. State. 643-7960. Open from May thru color season. 7 a.m.-10 p.m. daily. (May close at 9:30 early and late in the season.)* ♿ ⛹ Full bar

A fourth-generation downtown diner, **BENTLEY'S CAFE & DAIRY BAR** has been refurbished to play up its **classic soda fountain** and vintage look. Now there's a juke box, checkered tiles, and loads of Coca Cola memorabilia plus interesting old stuff from the attic of this 19th-century building. What's always been the same are the ten o'clock coffee crowd of local businesspeople; **big, made-from-scratch shakes and malts** (now $3); homemade soups; and $5 lunch specials (soup and sandwich, served until 5). Fried whitefish dinners are around $8 including potato and soup or slaw. The takeout window in front offers 24 flavors of ice cream cones with a special kids' price (89¢ for 12 and under) to make taking the family out for ice cream more affordable. *62 N. State, across from the Arnold Dock. 643-9031. Open year-round. From Mem. Day thru Nov., open daily including Sunday 6 a.m.-10 p.m. Closed Dec & Jan. From Feb up to Mem. Day open daily 6 a.m. to 2:30 p.m.* ♿ ⛹

HURON LANDING is worth a try because of its good view of Lake Huron, its year-round hours, its lounge, and its wide-ranging breakfast, lunch, and dinner menus. *441 N. State, downtown between the Arnold Dock and Marquette Mission Park. 643-9613.*

St. Ignace Lodgings

See separate section for lodgings west of Mackinac Bridge. Here lodgings are arranged from the bridge into town and then north.

St. Ignace proper has some 40 motels, nearly all deployed on the 4 miles of Bus. Loop I-75/State St. that curves along the Lake Huron shore between exit 344B and exit 348. That number doesn't include the many extremely inexpensive small motels west of the Mackinac Bridge along West U.S. 2, largely dating from the years just after the bridge was finished in 1957. The area has 2,000 rooms. It can completely fill in July and August and car show weekend. But there's a lot of turnover from short stays. If you don't want to commit to a long stay in a place you

haven't seen, you might call to get a reservation for the first night, then look around.

To the casual motorist, these motels can all blur together, but there are real differences. Some are on the water. Often the older, plainer places have the best sites. In general, the chains charge the most and have the newest facilities. Larger, newer motels with water views are north of downtown and up the hill. Room rates fluctuate with occupancy and go way up for holiday weekends and the big Antique Auto Show the last weekend of June. Motels with State St. addresses of 740 N. State and below are in town, close to its homey amenities and possibilities for walks. Lodgings with addresses of 899 N. State and above are isolated on the highway, where walking would be unpleasant.

Busiest times, when advance reservations are imperative, are the car show weekend (last week in June), July 4, and Labor Day. Most lodgings have casino packages. Ask for details.

MORAN BAY MOTEL   (906) 643-9790

Perched on the hillside on the way into town, this well maintained single-story motel stands out for its big front deck and picture windows with a **grand view of the St. Ignace harbor**. Most of the nine pleasantly decorated rooms are air-conditioned, and all have cable TV. No phones in room. Normal weekend rates for two in summer are from $50 to $65. In spring, rates start at $32 for two. The cross street allows for nice walks up into neighborhoods up on the bluff. *500 West U.S. 2 at Keightly. Open from May thru color season.* **H.A.:** call ⛹ : 10 & under free; $4/extra person 🐕 : call

COLONIAL HOUSE INN Bed & Breakfast (906) 643-6900;
www.colonial-house-inn.com

This Classic Revival house in downtown St. Ignace is a familiar presence to generations of summer visitors. In recent years owner Elizabeth Brown and her attentive staff have made steady small improvements so that the inn now sits among **gorgeous gardens**. Now that she has retired as a professor of music education at Central Michigan University, she is planning to revamp the adjacent **11-room motel** as an adult bed and breakfast getaway with romantically decorated rooms furnished in antiques. Air-conditioning is coming. The motel is set back behind a **garden**, and its second floor has a balcony entry area. All rooms have cable TV. Current in-season rates are $49-$59 for rooms with one queen bed, $59-$69 for two beds.

The inn, with six guest rooms, is intended as a romantic getaway for couples. Most rooms in season are $79 to $99 weekdays, $99 to $119 weekends. Ask about two-room suites for two, and ask about off-season rates. All rooms have cable TV and private baths. Some are air-conditioned. A **coffeehouse** in a side wing enables more people to enjoy this attractive place without affecting the common areas of the inn, a parlor and breakfast room. Upstairs all guests have use of the **balcony overlooking the water**. The house and its wrap-around veranda sit up from the street and afford a **nice view of the harbor**. The antique-filled inn is a satisfyingly quaint place. A full sit-down **breakfast** is served on flowered china. Some old wallpaper and clawfoot tubs give the inn atmosphere; if you want a quick morning shower, make sure you get an appropriate room. Also, some beds may be too short for tall people. Front rooms have a grand view but some road noise. *90 North State. Now open year-round.* **H.A.:** no for inn; call for motel

The BOARDWALK INN

(906) 643-7500; www.boardwalkinn.com

A smoke-free 12-room **bed and breakfast** occupies a hotel **built in 1928**, right downtown and across from the boardwalk, as the name implies. It's a personal place, managed by owners Steve and Lanie Sauter, and it has **large common areas**: the ground-floor lobby and on the second floor a sitting room and fireside breakfast area where a **continental plus breakfast** is served. Most guest rooms have been enlarged. Some are two-room suites. All are air-conditioned with cable TV. All are freshly decorated with white or light walls, wallpaper borders, generally romantic motifs, and antique furniture from late Victorian to French Provincial. A photo of each room is on the website with each season's rates for each room. Summer rates for most rooms are $54 to $74 weekdays, $74-$94 weekends. Winter rates are mostly $54 and $64. *316 N. State.* **H.A.:** no : $5/extra child, $10/extra adult

The DRIFTWOOD MOTEL

(906) 643-7744; (906) 643-7299

The location isn't picturesque, but this 20-room, single-story motel is **convenient,** directly across from the Shepler and Star Line dock and a half a block to the museum, picnic area, and boardwalk. Furthermore, a competent full-service restaurant and sports bar is part of the motel complex. (The same family runs the Mackinac Grille.) The Driftwood could prove ideal if you're looking for a good rate for a room with significant extras: phone, fridges, coffee, and air-conditioning. Two people, one queen: in season $46, otherwise $30. Two people, two beds: $54 and $36. There are some no-smoking rooms. On snowmobile trail. *590 N. State. Open year-round.*

H.A.: call : under 5 free, $4/extra person

HARBOUR POINTE

(906) 643-9882; (800) 642-3318; www.harbourpointe.com

This big four-building complex (150 rooms in all) enjoys St. Ignace's best combination of amenities: decor, along the waterfront, Mackinac Island view, and attractively landscaped grounds. It really is, as promoted, a "resort atmosphere." It's on an **unusually large 11-acre site** at the north edge of town. In its front office building by State Street there's a large, **sunny indoor pool** and hot tub. A free **continental-plus breakfast** is served in a large breakfast area with vending machines and hot drinks available any time. It has a water view, as does the **sun deck** by the heated **outdoor pool** with whirlpool and wading pool. A **video game room** is in a separate building with the **guest laundry.** A **playground** and horseshoes are near here. The back three buildings form a grassy court with some trees, **volleyball**, badminton, and a BBQ and **bonfire area**. The **800' beach**, like most in the area, is gravelly. It's possible to walk to restaurants, but not generally convenient. The terminus of the boardwalk is a 10-minute walk away. Rooms face away from road noise. All have refrigerators. Most rooms in the Huron Building and virtually all in the posh new Ontario Building have **excellent water views and balconies**. Rates vary with the size and location of rooms. Sample summer rates for rooms with two double beds: $98-$110. For two queens: $125-$169. Off-season rates start at $55. Ask about spa rooms. VCRs can be rented. *797 N. State. Closed Nov. into mid April.* **H.A.:** some rooms ADA accessible : kids free with parents

K ROYALE MOTOR INN

(906) 643-7737; (800) 882-7122

This three-story 1960s-era motel has **600' of beach**. (Beaches here have gravel; don't expect great sand.) Each of its 95 rooms has a **lake view** — and each unit has a refrigerator, phones, and cable TV. The lower level looks out on the parking lot, but the top two floors have balconies. The best summer rates for non-special weekends are obtained by making reservations before June 20. In 2000 these ranged up to $98, depending on floor. Back from the beach is a lawn with some play equipment, benches, BBQ grills, and picnic tables. There's a 40' heated **indoor pool**, whirlpool, **game room** with video games, and a **guest laundry**. **Free continental breakfast** (juice, rolls, donuts). Some two-bedroom units sleep 7. *1037 N. State, a mile north of downtown. Open mid-April thru most of Oct .*

MELODY MOTEL   (906) 643-9272

This very clean 21-room courtyard motel **on Lake Huron** is a delightful spot for people who like the **50s look**, replete with picture windows, decorative concrete block touches, and plastic flamingos in the beautiful flower beds. It has a **nice 300' beach** and **playground,** but alas, today's children expect more in the way of electronic amusements. Coffee in rooms. No air-conditioning. Phone in office. Summer rates around $40 — what a deal! *1421 Bus. I-75 at Evergreen Shores, about 1 mile south of Exit 348 and Kewadin Casino. Open May thru mid Oct.* **H.A.:** call : small pets. Call.

ST. IGNACE AREA CAMPING

See also: U.S. 2 West, Brevort, Epoufette, Naubinway

STRAITS STATE PARK

(906) 643-8620. Reserv.: (800) 44-PARKS; (800) 605-8295 TDD; www.dnr.state.mi.us/

If you want a modern campground with showers, electricity, etc. that's convenient to Mackinac attractions, this is your place, closer to Colonial Michilimackinac and the Mackinac Island ferries than any other modern campground. It would be a 1 1/2 mile walk north through residential streets to the town center of St. Ignace. The 52-acre park is just east of the north approach to the Mackinac Bridge — making its **overlook** near the **picnic area** a good place for a view of the bridge and Straits. The overlook is off a separate drive from either camping area. Traffic noise from the bridge is the down side of this location.

The park has two big campgrounds, used mainly for short stays by people visiting Mackinac Island. The **upper campground**, better for campers with big rigs, has about 150 large, open, grassy sites. The lower campground, with about 125 sites, is in a more natural area of cedar and birch, dense enough to provide privacy but also to obstruct the Straits view. Its loops are close to the beach, where campers like to come at dusk to watch boat traffic through the Straits and see the changing evening sky and the colored lights that outline the great bridge. The park fills every night in July and most of August, but it turns over frequently, too. In the past, if campers arrived early in the day, they'd find a spot. In 2001 the reservation system lets campers reserve until noon the day of arrival; it may change availability. *From I-75 and U.S. 2, just north of the bridge, go east on U.S. 2 less than half a mile to Church St. Turn south onto Church go three blocks to park. Open year-round; plowed for winter camping. State park sticker required: $4/$5 a day, $20/$25 a year. Camping fee $14/$19 a night.*

H.A.: shower/toilets and some ADA accessible sites in east loop of lower campground, Buildings 1 & 2 in upper campground.

FOLEY CREEK CAMPGROUND/ Hiawatha National Forest
(906) 643-7900;
www.fs.us.fed.us/r9/hiawatha

The Lake Huron **beach** here is **sandy and secluded**, a mile from the campground (via the **Horseshoe Bay Trail**, which goes through a small but **fascinating wilderness area**). That distance has kept the 54-site rustic campground (vault toilets, no showers) from being full, except on the July 4 and possibly car show weekends — even though the campground, nestled among large white pines, is shady, quite private, and convenient to St. Ignace and area attractions. **Campsites are on a bluff**; **Foley Creek** runs along the south end. A **campground host** is usually here in summer. *On H673/Mackinac Trail, 2 miles north of I-75 exit 348. $10/night. Open from early May thru Sept.* **H.A.**: 3 sites ADA accessible

CARP RIVER CAMPGROUND/ Hiawatha National Forest 643-7900
This campground, in a **scenic spot** convenient to St. Ignace, fills only on the car show weekend and some holiday weekends, so it's a boon for last-minute campers. For people who like a **peaceful place**, this is a favorite area camping spot. Here 44 campsites are laid out under big trees in two loops on the bluff above the Carp River, classified as a wild and scenic stream. See the Forest Service handout, available at the St.

Ignace Welcome Center, about Carp River canoeing. Stairs go down to the river where rainbow and brown trout can be caught. The forest service handout has more **fishing** tips.There's a **campground host** most summers. *On Mackinac Trail/H63, about 3 miles southwest of exit 359 at M-134, and 13 miles north of St. Ignace. $10/night. Open from mid-April thru Nov.*

H.A.: 2 sites.

U.S. 2 from the Bridge to Pointe aux Chenes

Father Marquette Memorial and Museum

In March 2000 a fire caused by lightning completely destroyed the Father Marquette Museum, focused on the achievements and spiritual motivation of Jacques Marquette (1637-1675), who founded Sault Ste. Marie and discovered and mapped the Mississippi River in his nine short years in North America. Preliminary planning to rebuild the museum is underway.

Most objects that had been on exhibit were museum reproductions. Archaeologists located several archaeological artifacts that had been displayed. Most, damaged or transformed by the intense heat, will be preserved.

Meanwhile, the **picnic area** with a **panoramic view** of **Mackinac Bridge** and the public restrooms remain open. The interesting, 15-station **interpretive trail** focuses on the 17th and 18th century environment of the Straits area and how that environment was used by native peoples and by the newly arrived Europeans. At the **bridge overlook**, panels bring to mind the 1673 canoe exploration of Father Marquette and fur trader Louis Jolliet, a skilled navigator and map maker, as they passed below en route to the Mississippi. In the 17th century the Straits were vitally important to international politics and economics.

The popular free **evening interpretive programs** will continue to be held here outdoors at 7:30 Mondays and Wednesdays for seven weeks from after July 4 weekend into late August. **French Heritage Days** are presented here in summer. Call Straits State Park, (906) 643-8620, for events schedule.

The memorial/museum is south off U.S. 2 just west of I-75 and St. Ignace. State park sticker required: $4/$5 a day, $20/$25 a year. &: pathway, picnic area. Restroom probably too narrow.

Boulevard Drive/ Point Labarbe Road

Here the shore road out of town **avoids the commercial distractions of U.S. 2** just west of St. Ignace. You'll see **sweeping views of Lake Michigan** with an occasional freighter. The most dramatic views of the Mackinac Bridge are from the parking area at the foot of Boulevard Drive. In a few miles the shore road joins U.S. 2. About a mile west of where Point Labarbe Road joins U.S. 2, you can turn south onto Gros Cap Road and follow the shore for another four miles or so.

To reach the shore road from U.S. 2 just west of I-75, turn south onto Boulevard Drive at the Howard Johnson's/ Marquette Memorial Drive. Boulevard Drive is gravel for a mile or so. To continue onto Point Labarbe Road, turn right before you get to the parking lot and stay along the shore.

Curio Fair

Another **old-timey tourist trap**, this fantasy **encrusted with seashells** and rocks was built just after the Mackinac Bridge opened in 1957. The style hearkens back to a much earlier era. Here too, as in St. Ignace's Indian Village, birch bark and twig Indian pictograms wallpaper the inside. The **tower** (8 stories up) has a **grand view of the bridge** and Straits to the south and woods to the north — **especially beautiful in fall color season.** It's 50¢ to climb the tower and worth a stop any time.

About 1 1/2 miles west of the bridge/I-75. 643-8626. Open mid May thru mid Oct. Hours: at least 9-5; 9-9 in season. &: curio shop but not tower.

Totem Village

To passing motorists, Totem Village — part museum, part gift shop, part zoo — may not seem any different from Curio Fair or Indian Village, themed tourism done by amateurs with a primarily commercial intent. If you come inside and explore, however, it's clear that it's informed by a **sincere spirit** that **respected Ojibwa life** as he came to understand it, at a time when very little had been written about it. The late Ralph McCarry's roadside attraction, started in the 1950s, falls in the category of **folk art** or **outsider art environment** by a **visionary artist** who uses images and words to preach his (or very seldom her) message. A heart attack meant that McCarry, in his late 40s, couldn't hold down a job. He became fascinated with

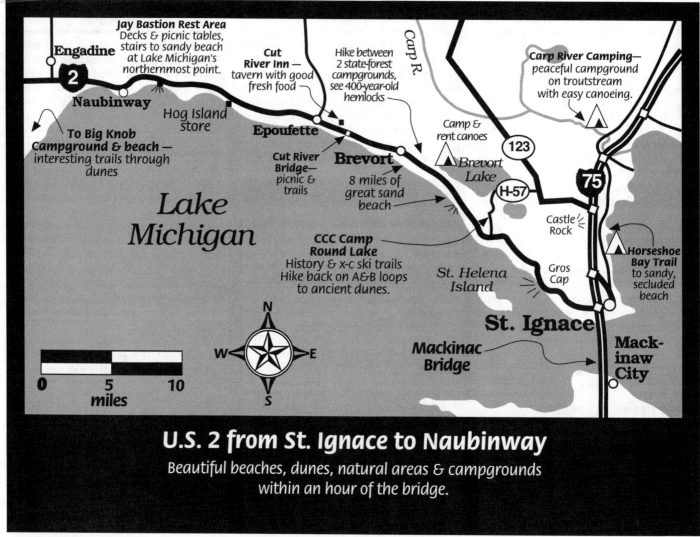

U.S. 2 from St. Ignace to Naubinway
Beautiful beaches, dunes, natural areas & campgrounds within an hour of the bridge.

wood carving and started to research and study subjects from lumber camps (he had worked on Tahquamenon logging crews) to early forts to Indian life. His efforts and collections grew in scope and scale and did provide a living for him and his family. Contemporary sophisticates can fault him for blending Ojibwa philosophy with totem poles from the Pacific Northwest. McCarry's approach predated by decades any hint of political correctness. "He was part Indian himself and saw Totem Village as an educational tool to restore pride in the heritage," says proprietor Nancy Dandona, who readily points out that totems were not indigenous to the area. Local Native Americans, pleased to be subjects of *any* favorable publicity at the time, honored McCarry with the name "White Wolf of the Chippewas" and held spring and fall feasts at Totem Village.

Kids, who don't expect museum-caliber labels of provenance, are open to experiencing this rambling place. And kids like it that a few dollars can go far in the **gift shop**, too. It also has a good selection of books and music mostly about Eastern Woodland Indians, and crafts like quill boxes. Peaceful pipe music accompanies the museum experience. It starts with **beautiful beadwork, pipes, arrowheads,** and other artifacts from many native cultures, displayed in a dark, confined log corridor. Then the museum opens up to areas of **life-size dioramas** and, finally, the big, 40' by 60' totem pole building, over 20' high, with a replica of an **Ojibwa medicine lodge**, strewn with juniper boughs. Here are meticulous scale models of a lumber camp, Fort Fond du Lac, and the first Soo lock, McCarry's primitive paintings, and **hand-lettered philosophy** such as "Be not puffed up but kneel and pray with your brother" and his Chief's Prayer: "Before I condemn a brother, let me walk in his moccasins for 3 months." Beyond the lodge paths lead outside, where bobcats, sprightly **sika deer**, peacocks, and **thunder foxes** are in large enclosures beneath cedars.

Nancy and Fred Dandona bought Totem Village in 1969. "I feel we're its caretakers," says Nancy. "People expect my museum to be like a state museum. That hasn't been my intention." The Dandonas have gone to great lengths to preserve the vulnerable totems, which suffered in an outdoor environment. For years they thought they'd have to move the whole place for a highway reconstruction project, that was eventually cancelled.

Two miles west of the Mackinac Bridge on U.S. 2. 643-8888. Open from May thru Oct. In season open 9 a.m. to 10 p.m. Otherwise open 10 a.m. to 6 p.m. Admission to museum: $2/adult, $1/child, $5/family. &: Museum is fine. Assistance needed outside on one hill.

Gros Cap Cemetery

Cemeteries always provide a window on a community's past. This one (it's pronounced "grow cap") is unusually interesting and old for the area. After shifting sands began to cover old burial places in

Moran Township, this cemetery was established in 1889, and some older burials and monuments were moved here.

About 3 miles west of the bridge/I-75.

Hiawatha National Forest/ St. Ignace Info Center and administrative unit

Stop in at this beautiful new building or call for lots of free handouts and helpful advice, not just on campgrounds, fishing, and hunting but on good berry-picking spots, wilderness areas, and many outdoor recreation opportunities. Handouts cover the entire national forest, not just this area. **Picnic tables** are by the beautiful entrance **garden** of **native plants** with interesting interpretive signs. The plaza's concrete pavement has animal footprints in it — a fun introduction to tracking skills. Now that the units of 13-state Forest Service Region 9 have funding for outdoor recreation planners or interpreters, **off-site educational programs** can be scheduled from this office.

1798 West U.S. 2, north side, 6 miles west of the bridge. (906) 643-7900. Open year-round, Mon-Fri 8-4:30. ♿

Deer Ranch

Behind the extensive moccasin and leather goods store, three large pens have been fenced off for placid-looking, relaxed deer. They have enough space to feel comfortable. The pens are in a cedar grove. This is a good way to see deer up close — Michigan whitetail, and also some white whitetail from Pennsylvania. (They aren't really albinos because they have brown eyes.) Visitors are warned that "Fawnee bites" — because Fawnee has been bottle-raised and reflexively chomps down on anything put into her mouth. "Put your fingers in any deer's mouth at your own risk."

North side of U.S. 2 West, 4 miles west of the bridge. 643-7760. Usually open from 2nd week of May (snowmelt permitting) through October. Open daily at 10 to 4 in spring, to 5 in June, 6, in July and August 9-9. $3/person, under 4 free. ♿

The Mystery Spot

"Can you solve the mysteries just waiting for you? You will experience optical contractions and physical sensations here that are hard to believe." The Mystery Spot's enticing I-75 billboards have been tempting kids and irritating parents since 1955. Today Dan McCarthy, one of the kids whose dad never would stop here, now owns the place. It's a part-time seasonal job that enables him to ski several months a year in Colorado. He has built up the once-rundown business and added miniature golf, a game arcade, and a stockade fence maze. **Picnic tables** take advantage of the pretty, wooded setting.

Still, the Mystery Spot's heart remains the radically slanted wood building. It's toured in 20 minutes. Elizabeth Edwards of *Traverse* magazine toured it in 1995 with her 7- and 10-year-olds and their friends. "Before we could ask too many questions," she wrote, "[our guide] hustled us inside where he rolled a ball uphill — without pushing it. We all got a chance to try it. Next, we stood on a level platform and found our bodies cantilevered out into midair. We walked up a wall and tilted precariously into the air but didn't fall. We sat in a chair with its back legs balanced on a beam, front legs suspended in the air. When I asked the inevitable 'why?' . . . the queasy feeling we all left with was more believable than his explanation. It was the kind of sick you get from reading in the back seat of a car."

Here are the rates. **Just the Mystery Spot**: $4.50 for kids 5 to 11, $6 for adults. Kids 4 and under free. Combo ticket for **maze, minigolf, Mystery Spot:** $6 and $8. (Can be divided over two different days.) **Maze alone** (takes about 10 minutes) $1.50 kids and adults. **Minigolf**: $3.

On U.S. 2, about 4 miles west of the bridge, just west of the Deer Ranch. (906) 643-8322. Open from early or mid May thru 3rd weekend of Oct. Open 9-7 in the off-season, 8 a.m. to 9 p.m. in season. ♿: can see first and last portions of Mystery Spot. No charge.

Gros Cap roadside park and Helena Island overlook

This **blufftop park and picnic spot** take in a fine view of **St. Helena Island** two miles offshore. (Note: the local pronunciation is "St. Helene.") French fishermen from Gros Cap (the shoreline village that once stood below the bluff here) established a prosperous village on St. Helena in the 19th century. It grew to around 225 people. The **natural harbor** on the beautiful island's north shore made it an ideal fueling stop for wood-fired steamships. Later it became a pleasant destination for outings by boat or sleigh. In bad weather it remains a harbor of refuge — and weather can get so bad, so suddenly, that a number of St. Ignace people today have memories of pleasure trips to the island where their stay was extended involuntarily.

On the southeast shore is a **classic, tapered lighthouse** with a brick keeper's dwelling, built in 1873 and abandoned by the Coast Guard in 1923. Ongoing restoration and site improvements since 1986 by scouts and other volunteers have been directed by the well-connected GLLKA, **Great Lakes Lighthouse Keepers Association**, based in Mackinaw City. Look in on its website, currently at www.gllkakeepers.virtualave.net for information about its events, including occasional three-day work sessions on St. Helena, for which participants pay $190. Shepler's Mackinac Island Ferry conducts a number of very popular scheduled **Straits-area lighthouse cruises** each summer for $45.50 per person, children under 5 free. Call (800) 828-6157 for details. Or look in on www.sheplers.www.com Reserve well in advance. The westbound cruise goes by St. Helena and several reef lighthouses out in Lake Michigan. On the 5-hour **St. Helena Walkabout** ($145/person, limit of 20), participants are dinghied to the island village. Shepler's also offers custom cruises to suit various groups' interests.

St. Helena Island makes a **fine destination for small boats**, provided the water is calm. With rocky limestone shorelines, forests and wetlands, meadows and sandbars, the 266-acre island offers much variety in a small (1 mile by 1/2 mile) space. It is privately owned and currently for sale. Drawbacks for adventurers: snakes and poison ivy.

6.3 miles west of the Mackinac Bridge, 1/2 mile east of Cheeseman Rd.

Pointe aux Chenes River Marsh

Just east of Pointe aux Chenes, this river's many twists between Round Lake and Lake Michigan form an **unusually large and undisturbed marsh**. It's inaccessible, except by canoe during high water. Loons, osprey, eagles, and terns live there. An osprey nest is visible from the road near the river bridge. A wide shoulder lets motorists pull over and observe. *On U.S., 2 about 7 miles west of St. Ignace.* ♿: visible from car

CCC Camp Round Lake Interpretive Site /Sand Dunes Cross-Country Ski Trail

This trail-laced area, part of the Hiawatha National Forest, offers **15 miles** of **trails** and an **excellent outdoor exhibit** (taken in during the winter)

about the **Civilian Conservation Corps** and the camp that was here in the 1930s. Here was one of 2,650 camps across the U.S. set up to put unemployed young men to work during the Depression. The CCC employed 600,000 men in 1935. Flat gravel walks connect large, engraved metal signboards marking the sites of various camp buildings. **Well-written interpretive signs** by Hiawatha National Forest archaeologist John Franzen convey what camp life was like for jobless young men here. They worked on CCC reforestation projects, made trails, and built many of the Michigan State Parks' most beautiful rustic buildings — all for $30/month plus food and clothing.

"City boys surrounded by trees," says one sign. It describes typical CCC crews as "boys that didn't know an ax from a baseball bat." At Round Lake some 200 young men built roads, planted trees, made the dam and campgrounds at Brevort Lake, and cleared logging debris to prevent fires. The site is now a meadow, filled with wildflowers in late summer. The **philosophy** and **politics** behind the CCC are clearly conveyed through excellent writing and graphics. This is an inspiring place, in a quiet way.

Six **trail loops** (each a couple of miles) go through open areas and wooded old oak forests on the backs of dunes. *Mountain bikes are not allowed. Stay on the trail in this fragile dune environment.* In summer, loops A, B, and C offer more stable footing; D, E, and F go through more bare sand. Though the trailhead is in an open field, they lead to some beautiful natural areas, according to outdoor recreation planner Lori Crystal: ancient sand dunes that offer beautiful views of mature hardwood forests — beech, birch, and red maple, beautiful fall color. "The further back you go, the more secluded it feels. After a mile, you don't hear the highway noises." Loop A, the easiest, takes you through gorgeous waist-high ferns; continue into Loop B a ways for a nice hike that's not too long — a good break from highway driving.

The **cross-country ski** season here usually lasts from early December through March. Trails are groomed on Mondays and Fridays, and there's firewood for building a fire at the **warming cabin** by the entrance. *Half a mile north of U.S. 2 on H-57/ Brevort Lake Road. Call (906) 643-7900 for trail conditions.* &: interpretive site fully accessible. Toilets no. Trails no.

U.S. 2 RESTAURANTS

Hearkening back to an earlier era of burger joints, **CLYDE'S DRIVE-IN No. 3** offers eat-in and **curb service** and remains very much a diner. It serves light breakfasts and chili, soups, and baskets of fried chicken, perch, and shrimp. Its **regionally famous C Burger**, made fresh on the grill, is served as you like. Malts and shakes are made the old-fashioned way, too. The Clyde's concept premiered in Sault St. Marie in 1949; Clyde's #2 is in Manistique. *On the north side of U.S. 2, just west of the Bridge. 643-8303 . It's open from April into November, weather permitting, 9 a.m. to 10 p.m.* &: interior is too small; curb service is fine 🚹🚺🧒

SUZY'S PASTIES is a spiffy, trim spot that's well positioned for takeouts for picnic stops along U.S. 2. Or you can eat in. Here are all the U.P. tourist classics: pasties (around $4) in beef, turkey, and vegetable variations, smoked fish, slaw to go with it, and fudge for dessert. A man from Iron Mountain, a town known for its pasties, rates these high, though they're made with ground meat. (Purists insist on cubed flank steak.) *On the north side of U.S. 2 one mile west of bridge, just west of Burger King. 643-7007 Open from sometime in May-mid-Oct 10-7, possibly longer in July & August.* &.

LEHTO'S PASTIES, which innovated the pasty as road food in the late 1940s, serves only its original-recipe classic (ground sirloin with rutabaga in addition to the usual potatoes and onions), and only to go. The price in 2000: $4.25. The recipe is for sale for $5. Pasties are baked throughout the day. John and Katherine Lehto came to St. Ignace from L'Anse because he got a job working on the ferries. On the weekends he built a little roadside shop from cedar logs out of a swamp. A cement truck broke down outside, and that supplied the foundation. One July 4, explains his granddaughter Katherine, "he made beaucoup bucks, and the rest is history." Lehto's fame prompted a swing into the North Country from food writers Jane and Michael Stern. *On U.S. 2 about 4 miles west of the Mackinac Bridge. 643-8624. Open from around Easter thru Dec. 1. Hours from 9 a.m. to 6 p.m. or until pasties are gone, sometimes as early as 2.*

U.S. 2 LODGINGS

See also: St. Ignace, Brevort, Epoufette, Naubinway

SUPER 8 of ST. IGNACE
(906) 643-7616

This 56-room motel was finished in 1997, taking advantage of the property where the Million-Dollar View Motel used to be. The lot extends way back from the highway on the bluff; behind it, a golf course slopes down. Half the rooms have balconies and an **excellent view of the Mackinac Bridge**, which is especially picturesque at night, when lights outline the suspension cables. There's an 18' x **30' indoor pool**, a lobby with a **free continental breakfast**, and a **guest laundry**. AAA listed rates for non-special events summer season: $89-$109. *1/4 mile west of bridge on U.S. 2.* **H.A.**: some rooms ADA accessible 🚹🚺🧒

STRAITS VIEW MOTEL
(906) 643-9355; (800) 401-1813

The hidden surprise of this 16-room, single-story motel is the beautiful, **park-like area** in back with a great **view of the Mackinac Bridge**, the **Straits** from Waugoshance to St. Helena, and **sunsets** and passing ships. Four rustic swings, four picnic tables, and a bonfire pit

Four generations of Lehto Pasties on U.S. 2. From left to right: co-founder Katherine Lehto, her grandson Dan Smith, daughter Katherine Babock (who has made pasties here for the past 30 years), and granddaughter Cassandra Darnell.

encourage guests to linger and take it all in. The motel consists of two buildings parallel to the highway so rooms have neither the bridge view nor direct highway noise. New owners Mary and Ivan Wolfe have put new furniture, new carpet, and new bedspreads and curtains in each attractive room. Rooms are air-conditioned with cable TV and phones. At $70 for summer weekends, $65 weekdays for two queens, $67 and $61 for one queen, they are a very good value for anyone looking for a pleasant room and convenient but striking setting. Ask about spring and fall rates. Coffee and donuts in office. *1177 West U.S. 2 about 2 miles west of the bridge and just west of Curio Fair. Open from May probably thru Nov.* **H.A.:** call : rates by room, not person

POINT LaBARBE INN & CABINS
(906) 643-8566

A piece of vintage roadside Americana, this motel and cabins (formerly the Wagon Wheel Motel) are styled to resemble a fort with blockhouses. The interiors, recently redecorated by a new owner, are a surprisingly attractive blend of old and new. The nine cabins are **especially charming** with their **knotty pine** walls, checked curtains, and original rustic furniture. Car access is from the rear, on the grass, so the front yard, which sits up above the highway, has a **nice view of Lake Michigan** and St. Helena Island in the distance. A few picnic tables take advantage of the view. The cabins, not air-conditioned, have fans. The 10 air-conditioned motel units are also nicely decorated, taking their cues from the dark green and burgundy in the wallpaper borders with pheasant and duck motifs. Sample rates for two people, one bed in summer: $38 weekday, $48-$55 weekends. A phone and free coffee are in the office. Some **kitchenettes** and refrigerators are available. *On the north side of U.S. 2 three miles west of St. Ignace. Open from May thru Oct.* **H.A.:** call

SILVER SANDS RESORT
(906) 643-8635; (888) 706-0092

This well-run old-fashioned family resort has **750' of Lake Michigan beach**, gravelly but with sand hauled in for a children's play area. Fourteen well-spaced rustic housekeeping cabins, dating from the **1920s**, have been freshened and maintained. One row faces the water; another row is behind them. All are far away enough from the highway that the sound of waves would likely be louder than highway noise. All cabins have

small covered porches. Some have screened sleeping porches, and two have **charming stone fireplaces**. Each house has a picnic table, charcoal grill, and bonfire ring, but no TV. The exception is the single much newer cabin ($805/week) with a jacuzzi, washer, dryer, TV/VCR, and microwave. The front cabins are rented by the week in season, mostly for from $560 to $665, which sleep five to seven. The back row of cabins sleep four and rent by the night ($60) or week. Bring linens and towels. *On the lake side of U.S. 2 four miles west of the bridge, across from Deer Ranch. Open April thru October.* **H.A.:** call

The BALSAMS RESORT
(906) 643-9121; (313) 791-8026 (Labor Day to early June);
www.balsamsresort.com

Behind the simple six-unit motel facing U.S. 2 are 9 little **log cabins** designed in the best picturesque vernacular of the 1920s, the heyday of rock gardens and wishing wells. They are in a **cedar forest**, perched **along the Moran River** (actually more of a creek bridged by footbridges). Artists Orr and Eva Greenless designed and built the cabins over two decades starting in 1927. The housekeeping cabins have loads of little nooks, outside and in — tiny terraces, bay windows, alcove beds — and sometimes a stone fireplace. Four have handmade tables with designs under glass made of birch bark, peacock feathers, and dried plants. Interior walls are log or knotty pine. The cost of keeping everything in a charming time warp for decades has been the deterioration of basic infrastructure. New owners, a group of four metro Detroit families with young children, fell under The Balsams' spell and are determined to restore the place, but with new electrical, plumbing, and water and up-to-date bathrooms. One, a mother of five, has designed a nifty new playground. Five cabins grouped together are ideal for family reunions. The website has planning suggestions for a week in the area, with tips on mountain biking in the adjoining **Hiawatha National Forest**, wildflowers, and much more. Cabins sleep from 2 to 6 and rent for $600 a week or $100 a night in season. Each has a picnic table and grill. Everything but towels is provided. Ask about spring and fall specials.

The **stream** and **trails** meander through the wooded, 40-acre property, where the Greenlesses constructed little rapids and waterfalls. Wildlife abounds in this natural setting — ducks, mink,

deer, fish, great blue heron, and more. Eagles and pileated woodpeckers have been seen here. Some guests stay for days just taking it in. Across U.S. 2 is a sandy, private **Lake Michigan beach.** There's a **bonfire area** on the beach and one behind the motel.

All **motel rooms** are on the large side, with picture windows looking out onto Lake Michigan across the highway. Motel rooms come with a minifridge and microwave. Motel guests have access to the grounds and have a picnic area, too. Current rates: $65/night in summer, $40-$54 in the off season. Phone in office. No air-conditioning —not necessary. Reserve early for best summer availability. *On West U.S. 2, 5 miles west of the bridge. Open May thru mid-October.* &: call. **H.A.:** call. Plans are for fully accessible cabins. : call

U.S. 2 CAMPING
See also: St. Ignace, Brevort, Epoufette, Naubinway

KOA KAMPGROUND
(906) 643-9303

The 145 modern campsites along these gravel drives are more widely spaced than at many private campgrounds, so the campground doesn't seem as large as it is. Campsites are among cedars yet mostly open and sunny. Some have water and electric ($26 for two), some also have sewer ($29 for two). Tent sites in a separate area are $20/night for two. Maintaining a functioning water system in this area is a challenge, necessitating extra-person charges for children. There are showers and a playground. The same owners operate the delightful **Totem Village** next door. *On U.S. 2 two miles west of the Mackinac Bridge. Open May thru Oct.* **H.A.:** showers, restrooms, some sites ADA accesssible : $2 for kids over 5; $3/extra person

Brevort area

Today's Brevort, an unincorporated area, has become for most U.P. visitors a short patch through which they must slightly slow down as they barrel down U.S. 2 to points west. (The pronunciation is "BREE-vort.") The settlement dates to 1875, when the Mackinac Lumber Company built a warehouse for logging supplies. Swedes came to work in the lumber camps and stayed. Some took up fishing. **Trinity Lutheran Church**, up on a hill off the highway, raises a **midsummer pole** in the Swedish tradition on the third Sunday in

June at 9 a.m. Visitors are welcome to come as they are. As we go to press, many of Brevort's better-known businesses are closed and/or for sale.

Lake Michigan beach from Pointe aux Chenes to Brevort/

U.S. 2 passes right along eight miles of **beautiful, sandy, wide beach** just east of Brevort. This public land is part of the **Hiawatha National Forest**. Wide shoulders make it easy to pull over and stop anywhere. There are no picnic or restroom facilities here, but in warm weather hundreds of people stop and swim here. Low dunes lead back from the north side of the highway and invite exploration by nature-lovers. The low, wet spots in the dunes between here and Brevoort Lake are a **good place to find blueberries,** typically in late July through mid-August.

Dunes like these are stabilized by a succession of plants that follow the principal pioneer, American beach grass. Its long, deep roots grow down to find moisture in the sand, and the grass blades can withstand being buried by sand. Once the dunes are stabilized, juniper, oak, and pine will follow. Eventually enough soil will be formed to support a forest like that on the old dunes on the south shore of nearby Brevoort Lake.

Between H-57/Brevort Lake Road and Ozark Road in Brevort.

Lake Michigan beach & picnic area

Low dunes separate the sandy **beach** from a shady, mature forest on the stabilized dunes, all part of the **Hiawatha National Forest**. The **picnic area** and restrooms are on the drive to the popular rustic campground. *On U.S. 2 about 6 miles west of Brevoort Lake Road and about 3 miles east of Ozark Road. (906) 643-7900. No fee.*

Brevoort Lake

The **4,233-acre** lake, part of the Hiawatha National Forest, has a manmade spawning reef that has helped create a **good walleye fishery**. Fish Michigan: 100 Upper Peninsula Lakes details and maps fishing opportunities in this heavily managed and stocked lake, which also has pike, muskies, panfish, bluegills, and crappie.

Spencer's Landing an **extraordinarily helpful camp store** on the entrance drive before the main campground, rents

canoes and fishing boats (bring your own motor) and **kayaks**. Tackle, bait, groceries, and snacks are for sale. Nearby is a **sand beach on Brevoort Lake** and a **lakeside picnic area** with tables and grills.

20 miles northwest of St. Ignace off U.S. 2. Turn north onto Brevoort Camp Road for 1 mile to park. 292-5471. Store is usually open from mid May through last week of September. Hours: 8 a.m.-9 p.m.

First Edition Books

Mary Carney runs an i**nteresting used and antiquarian bookstore** and the Black Letter Press from her country home north of Brevort. First Edition's main specialty is **Michigan and Great Lakes history**, but there's lots of good general reading on hand, plus assorted printed ephemera, maps, and some unusual T-shirts and sweatshirts. Black Letter Press reprints **out-of-print books on Upper Peninsula history**, and some Michigan railroad material, too.

461 Worth Road. From U.S. 2 in Brevort, turn north onto Ozark Road. Go half a mile until you reach Worth Road; shop is at the corner. (906) 292-5513. Open from April thru September. Open daily 10-6, evenings by appointment. ᕦ: no.

BREVORT CAMPING

See also: St. Ignace, U.S. 2 west of bridge, Epoufette, Naubinway

LAKE MICHIGAN CAMPGROUND/ Hiawatha National Forest

(906) 643-7900. Not reservable.
www.fs.us.fed.us/r9/hiawatha

Of 35 rustic campsites (no showers, vault toilets), 16 have direct access to **Lake Michigan**, and most have **lake views**, too. There's a nice, sandy **beach** below the dunes, with **sunset views**. Good privacy between sites; some tent sites are between small dunes. Very popular because it's so close to the beach. Road noise can be heard. In summer, come in midweek for best chance of a site. Consider Foley Creek or Carp River, under "St. Ignace Area Camping," as backup alternatives. 2 miles from **Brevort Lake**, with warmer swimming and good fishing. A **campground host** is usually here in summer. *Just off U.S. 2, 5 miles east of Brevort and about 18 miles west of the Bridge. $12/night. Open mid-May through early Oct.* **H.A.:** toilets, 2 campsites ADA accessible

BREVOORT LAKE CAMPGROUND/ Hiawatha National Forest

(906) 643-7900; not reservable

This extremely popular rustic camp-

ground (no electricity, no showers) enjoys **two scenic, wooded locations near a prime fishing bay**, on a lake managed for good fishing. (See above.) **Boat rentals**, groceries, and advice is available from Spencer's Landing store outside the campground entrance. A small peninsula has a good swimming **beach** and one loop of 48 campsites, 35 with direct water access. A 22-site loop is nearby, near the boat launch. **Good privacy between large sites**. Campground host. Some flush toilets. The 20-minute **Ridge Trail** interpretive walk begins just outside the campground and goes up a sand dune with a Lake Michigan view. The **North Country Trail** passes near the campground; a trail marker is by the campground entrance. Close to **Lake Michigan** Campground swimming beach. Generations of campers have come here and developed a real sense of camaraderie, sort of like a summer resort. This campground routinely fills in summer. To get a spot in summer, check with the **campground host** for tips on who's leaving when. May and September after Labor Day aren't too busy.

Off U.S. 2, 20 miles west of St. Ignace and about 4 miles east of Brevort, north off Brevoort Camp Rd. Not reservable. $12/$14/night. Open mid-May thru early Oct. **H.A.:** restrooms, showers and some sites ADA accesssible ♿ 🚻 🚹 🐕

LITTLE BREVOORT LAKE Campgrounds/ Lake Superior State Forest

(906) 643-7900. Not reservable

Of these two popular rustic campgrounds, the 20-site north unit fills first. The 12-site south unit, set in **rolling hills among hardwoods** and some big hemlock, is in some ways nicer. Get in by 6 p.m. Friday, and you'll probably find a spot! Both units have **swimming, boating,** and **fishing** (though this small lake is vulnerable to heavy pressure; catch-and-release is advised). Because this is a designated natural area, *boat motors are restricted.* The lake is an embayment formed during a higher stage of Lake Michigan. **Hemlocks some 400 years old** grow in the moist back dunes of the old, forested dunes. The diverse terrain means every kind of north country tree grows within this limited area. A **one-mile hiking path** connects the two campgrounds and takes visitors through this interesting natural area. An ORV trail is nearby. *Watch for signs on U.S. 2, 1 1/2 miles southeast of Brevort. Campgrounds are north of U.S. 2. Serviced May thru Nov. $6/$9.* **H.A.:** vault toilets not up to ADA code. Level sites.

DISPERSED CAMPING/
Hiawatha National Forest

Of the eight attractive, isolated, quiet individual campsites in the Brevoort Lake area, something is just about always available. Three wooded sites are on the south shore of Brevoort Lake. Five sites, open with **river views,** are on and near the **Carp River.** It's a trout stream, off Forest Road 3332, which goes north and south between the two Brevoort lakes. Some campsites are near the Carp's Rock Rapids. Two sites are near **Round Lake,** where the CCC camp trail is. All these sites are primitive. They have no picnic tables, water, or outhouses, and there's no fee to camp here — no reservation system, either. Pick up a **map** at the Forest Service on U.S. 2 west of St. Ignace, or call (906) 643-7900. **H.A.**: no.

Epoufette

French fishermen established the unincorporated village here (pronounced "EE-poo-FETT") in 1859. The lumber era held sway in the 1880s. Today there are a few houses by Epoufette Bay west of U.S. 2. Commercial activity is on the highway.

Cut River Bridge & picnic area

Motorists on U.S. 2 notice the striking, deep **limestone gorge** formed by the Cut River as it empties into Lake Michigan. But the **attractive, shady picnic area** at the bridge's east end isn't quite so obvious, nor is the paved **path** and **stairway** that descend 147 feet to the river. A striking stretch of asphalt path (&) goes under the dramatic stone bridge supports to the splendid stairway. The stairs are in flights, with large landings and overlooks to make the trip back up less arduous and more interesting. As you descend, the sound of waves replaces highway noise. It's beautiful to look down through the treetops and glimpse the beach and water below. This would be especially dramatic in **fall color** season. From the bottom, it's an easy walk along the river to the **sandy beach.** Kids enjoy diverting water to make their own channels and lagoons.

Spectacular as the walkway is, the DNR Wildlife Division's *Michigan Wildlife Viewing Guide* (Michigan State University Press, $9.95) says that "the real beauty of this site lies hidden among the rolling, forested **dunes** of the Lake Superior State Forest. Hike these trails in May to view **spring wildflowers** such as trout lily, trilliums, and Dutchman's breeches. Spring is also a good time to view migrating warblers and other songbirds." Look up to see **interpretive markers** identifying plants.

It's not altogether obvious how to find these **attractive trails,** each about 1/4 mile. On the east side of the bridge, walk along above the river back from the parking area to find a wide dirt trail with wood chips. It leads down the valley wall to the river mouth by the beach — a 10- to 15-minute walk out to the lake. A footbridge down by the lake, some 50 to 100 yards in from the shore, lets you cross the river and take the other **trail up the west side** of the river valley. That trail down to the lake begins at the north end of the parking area by the west side of the bridge.

You can make a loop by going down on one side of the bridge, up the other, and then walk across the high **U.S. 2 bridge** on a pedestrian walkway. **The view down is terrific.** Be advised that the sway and vibration from big trucks may be thrilling — or alarming.

On U.S. 2 about 4 miles west of Brevoort. Vault toilets are by picnic area. &: *first part of walk to stairway from east picnic area.*

Hog Island Country Store

Co-owner Gino Farone loved his childhood Upper Peninsula vacations so much, he was determined to preserve the funky, idiosyncratic local color of this small clapboard store and trim white cottages. (See below for lodgings here.) Inside there's much more than liquor: a surprising line of groceries, bait, gifts, **smoked fish** and other **regional products** (maple syrup, wild rice, beef jerky, etc.), displayed with nostalgic retro panache. Pick up an occasional **newsletter** about the area and local happenings, or check out the website.

On U.S. 2 at Hog Island, 8 miles east of Naubinway and 7 miles west of Epoufette. 477-9995. www.portup.com/ ~farone/index.htm Open April thru Dec. 1. &: *a few steps.*

Hog Island Point

A **sandy Lake Michigan beach** has picnic tables, vault toilets, and a shady, spacious rustic campground, all part of **Lake Superior State Forest.** Highway noise is audible. *Half-way between Epoufette and Naubinway south off U.S. 2. (906) 293-5131.*

EPOUFETTE RESTAURANTS

The **CUT RIVER INN** has evolved from a roadside tavern into a family restaurant. Sandwiches, served any time, include fried whitefish and perch ($7.25), chicken salad on foccaccia, and burgers ($5.75). The owner's husband is a commercial fisherman in Naubinway, and the inn is **known for fish,** though steak and ribs are on the menu as well. Dinner entrées (around $12) come with salad bar. Specials are Friday night fish fry ($11), Saturday BBQ ribs, Sunday baked chicken. *1 mile west of Cut River Bridge in Epoufette. 292-5400. Open year-round except closed for first 3 weeks of December. Mon-Sat 11 a.m.-9:30 p.m., Sun noon-9:30.* & ♯♀♂ Full bar

At the **SKYLINE RESTAURANT** travelers can stop for breakfast or dinner and admire the effects of the changing light on Lake Michigan, seen from this blufftop vantage point. It's a **simple diner with a grand view.** For dinner there's whitefish, deep fried ($9) or broiled ($10). There are lunch specials (about $6), a breakfast buffet on weekends ($7 for adults, $4 for kids), and soup and sandwiches any time, plus pies and sometimes cakes made on the premises. *On U.S. 2 a mile west of the Cut River bridge. 295-5556. Open daily year-round. From Mem. Day weekend thru Nov. open 7 a.m. to 8 p.m. daily. Otherwise open Mon-Thurs 8 a.m. to 2 p.m., Fri-Sun 8-8.* & ♯♀♂

EPOUFETTE LODGINGS

See also: St. Ignace, U.S. 2 west of Mackinac Bridge, Brevort

WONDERLAND MOTEL
(906) 292-5574

This one-story, 10-room motel is on a hill across from Lake Michigan, so the **views from the picture windows or the benches outside are wonderful indeed.** A scenic pullout and picnic area are right across the highway. The motel was closed for the season, so these notes are based on looking in the windows. Maple furniture and ruffled spreads are from an earlier era. The carpet is new. Rooms have phones and TVs, but not air-conditioning. (Probably it's seldom needed.) Rates for 2000 for two people in one bed were $38. *On U.S. 2 east of Epoufette. Open from sometime in May through color season.* **H.A.**: call ♯♀♂

SKYLINE MOTEL
(906) 292-5556

Simple, fresh, clean rooms have picture windows in back looking out onto **Lake Michigan** from the high bluff along the highway here. Rooms rent for $40/one bed, $45/two beds. The owner operates

Commercial fishing tugs waiting for the spring thaw in Naubinway. Whitefish is by far the biggest catch of Great Lakes comercial fishermaen and the most popular dinner in U.P. restaurants.

the Skyline Restaurant next door. Neighbors are the Cut River Store and Deli, and, across the road, the Cut River Inn. *1 mile west of the Cut River Bridge, between Epoufette (3 miles) and Brevort (5 miles). 25 miles west of Mackinac Bridge. (906) 292-5556. Generally open year-round.* **H.A.:** call 👫🧍: no extra charge; $4/extra person 🐕: $4 extra

HOG ISLAND COUNTRY STORE & COTTAGES (906) 477-9995

Don't be alarmed by the big roadside signage on this tidy, old-fashioned store and tourist cabin complex. It's part of Gino Farone's vision of historic preservation — keeping things in the same vein as in those wonderful childhood U.P. summers he spent here in the 1950s. The housekeeping cabins ($40/single, $48 double) are clean and cozy. The 7 cottages sit well away from the road, separated by a **big lawn with old fashioned wood swings and chairs**. Each cabin has a **picnic table** and **grill**. A private **Lake Michigan beach** is a short walk away. Ask about the nearby rental house ($600/week, or $125/night) with more amenities. The store sells smoked fish, milk, groceries — most of what you'd need for a short stay. Ask for the newsletter on area activities. *On U.S. 2 at Hog Island, 8 miles east of Naubinway and about 7 miles west of Epoufette. 35 miles west of Bridge. Open April thru hunting season.* **H.A.:** one step, tight quarters. 👫🧍: no extra charge

EPOUFETTE CAMPING

See also: Brevort, Naubinway, U.S. 2 west of Mackinac Bridge, St. Ignace

HOG ISLAND POINT Campground/ Lake Superior State Forest

A **sandy Lake Michigan beach** is served by vault toilets, picnic tables, and a shady, spacious rustic campground. Of 58 sites, many are on the water. Used mostly for overnights, not extended stays. A **campground host** is usually here. Highway noise audible. *Half-way between Epoufette and Naubinway south off U.S. 2. (906) 477-6048. Serviced May thru Nov. $6/$10. No reservations.* **H.A.:** *some gravel sites.*

Naubinway

Another blur for many motorists hurdling along U.S. 2, Naubinway was once a busy lumbering and fishing village. There's more to the actual village, south of the highway near the Lake. In the harbor on the eastern end of town fishing tugs can be seen (some are still active) with their distinctive boxed-in silhouette.

Settled by French-Canadian fishermen in 1880, Naubinway boomed in that decade. Lumbering and fishing grew together and 1,500 people lived here. Six hundred men worked at a sawmill; 34 fishing tugs employed many others. By 1898, two years after the mills closed, only six families remained. Naubinway stayed focused on fishing, however, through the devastating 1940s lamprey invasion that decimated the fish population, and into the 1960s, when the state DNR's decision to favor sport fishing in most Great Lakes waters put many smaller commercial fishermen out of business. Court decisions in the 1980s have enabled Indians to continue fishing, since they never gave up their rights to hunt and gather when they sold their land.

GarLynFarm Zoological Park

Visiting this small zoo was a **surprisingly pleasant experience**. It could make a good travel break for families making a long drive across U.S. 2. The animal enclosures are in a mostly shady pine forest back on a drive from the highway. To the casual observer, the animals seemed relaxed yet alert; only the wolf was pacing. Without exploring extensively the complicated ethics and situations of domesticating wild animals, zoos in general, and these animals in particular — which ones have been injured in some way and unable to survive in the wild, it seems fair to say that it's better to feed animals in a zoo setting like this than to make deer in the wild dependent on human food sources that might be withdrawn. If people are set on observing a black bear on their trip to the U.P., it's far better to feed an apple to the bear here than to help create wide-ranging nuisance bears by feeding bears around campgrounds or patronizing restaurants that leave garbage out for bears.

Children are likely to enjoy the intimacy of this small woodland zoo, where animals are never far away and peacocks and other ornamental fowl wander about. Many adults will enjoy it, too. They can feed sika deer, llama, goats, ducks, and chickens. A fox, wolf, and bear native to the area are here. So is a reindeer and a wallaby from Australia. New animals are added every year. For books and gifts about animals and nature, the gift shop is the equal of many a city zoo shop. Owners Gary and Lynn Moore are good at fielding questions about the animals.

On U.S. 2 just east of Naubinway, 38 miles west of the Mackinac Bridge. Open from April up to Christmas. 477-1085. From May thru Oct, open daily 11 a.m. to 7 p.m. In April open Fri-Sun 11-7. In Nov & Dec open Sat & Sun 11-5. $4.75/adult, $3.75 kids 4-16, 3& under free. $17/family maximum ♿: *assistance required on some slopes*

Jay Bastion Rest Area

Here at the northernmost point of Lake Michigan the state Department of Transportation has constructed a really impressive new rest stop: a log cabin-style building with restrooms, and two decks by the parking area with steps leading to the **beach**, where some people like to swim. **Picnic tables** are on the deck and by the parking area. If you go down by the beach, you can avoid the sound of truck engines idling. Plants near the beach include some protected species unique to the Straits area, such as dwarf iris, Pitcher's Thistle, Lake Huron tansy.

On U.S. 2 about two miles east of Naubinway. ♿: *everything but stairs*

Peninsula Shores Gallery

Framed photos of Upper Peninsula wildlife (bear, loons, bobcats, owls, and more, all photographed in the wild) and scenery are displayed in Jim O'Neil's **handsome gallery**. Jim says he's winding down from keeping regular hours and doing more on the Internet. The image that keeps gaining steam is his photograph of an electrical storm over Lake Michigan, in which a great bird has been "designed and sculpted by lightening," as he says. This connects with the role of the thunderbird in Indian stories; it's led Jim to explore his own Native American ancestry.

On the south side of U.S. 2 at the west end of Naubinway. (906) 477-9877; (906) 477-6303. Open by chance, 25-30 hours a week in season. &

Big Knob Pathway & Crow Lake Pathway

These interesting short pathways, part of **Lake Superior State Forest**, make for nice little adventures for campers at the beautiful Big Knob Campground and for motorists driving across the U.P. on U.S. 2. The highway is just 3 1/2 miles north of both trailheads. The **Crow Lake Pathway**, a 2 1/2 mile loop, climbs along a **dune ridge** with a **view of Crow Lake** in 3/4 mile. Then it descends into a flatland of ferns, with **lots of blueberries** in August.

Interpretive displays tell about the marsh hikers pass before climbing low dunes and reaching a stand of old-growth white pine. Kids will enjoy the dramatically shorn trees damaged by lightening. To complete the loop, the path goes along Big Knob Road for about half a mile. The **trailhead** is at the south end of the flooding; the sign faces north. Parking area is on right (west) side of road.

The 1/4 mile **Big Knob Pathway** leads up the side of a wooded sand **dune**, unusually high for this area, to an **overlook** which looks out onto Knob Lake and the surrounding marshland (but not to Lake Michigan). Canada geese flock here in spring and early fall, making for a lively, noisy scene. The trailhead is across the road from Crow Lake trailhead and parking area.

From U.S. 2 about 4 miles east of Gould City or 1 1/2 miles west of Engadine, look for the sign to the state forest campground and Big Knob Rd., a dirt road that twists. Take it 3 1/2 miles south. Park by the Crow Lake trailhead on the west side of Big Knob Road. (906) 293-5131. & *no.*

Marsh Lake Pathway & Big Knob beach

A **1 1/2-mile path** leads west into **lakeside sand dunes** from the parking area by the Big Knob campground and **beach**. Then it crosses **interdunal ponds** on a small bridge and winds back through marshes before connecting up with Big Knob Road for about 1/6 mile roadside walk back to the parking area. This is part of the **Lake Superior State Forest.**

Now that the state has purchased 11,000 acres south of Gould City going all the way to Scott Point (see below), Big Knob connects up with a stretch of **sand beach** that goes west for miles and miles. Low **dunes** behind it make it like the beach along U.S. 2 by Brevort, but without the cars. "What a beautiful beach!" exclaims a longtime forester who's just about seen everything in the eastern U.P. The Nature Conservancy bought this land first, until the state found funds to acquire it.

See directions for Big Knob Pathway but continue south 6 miles from U.S. 2 to the parking area. (906) 293-5131. &: no.

Scott Point

Scott Point is the closest mainland point on either peninsula to the **Beaver Archipelago**, which is clearly visible on the horizon. **Squaw Island** and its **lighthouse** are barely 10 miles offshore, and Beaver Island is another six. This area is part of the **Lake Superior State Forest.** The wide, sandy **beach** descends so gradually into the water that adults can wade out for a hundred feet without getting their knees wet. **Shore birds are abundant** in this idyllic and remote place. Wetlands behind the beach dunes provide more good habitat for birds. A state forest **picnic area** with grills is in a cedar grove at the road's end.

The DNR has acquired the shore and land going east of Scott Point to the Lake Superior State Forest Big Knob Campground (see below). That means virtually all of the Lake Michigan shore from Port Inland to Big Knob is public land. It's a **beautiful beach**, tucked away, not affected by auto traffic, and it seems to go on and on forever. Walk it for miles, and you'll feel you're in another world.

From U.S. 2 at Gould City, go south about 10 miles on Gould City Rd. Park is at road's end. (906) 293-5131. Free. &: vault toilet.

NAUBINWAY RESTAURANTS

SHIRLEY'S COVE BAR, the only bar in town, has been purchased by Gino and Ellen Farone, who had previously owned the Hog Island Country Store and run it with good-hearted retro panache. The bar has been here "forever," Ellen says, and Shirley was nice enough to let the Farones use her name. They are doing more with homemade soups and daily lunch specials, as opposed to fry-basket cooking, and say they serve the best burger in the area (around $5 with fries). The Cove Bar looks out to the water, with a **partial view of the cove** and marina. There's a grassy area with horseshoe pits out back. There's also a small dance floor, and more **live music** is in the works — country, cajun, rock, a real mix. Last winter Jim Rorie, the Farones' friend from Memphis, stayed all winter and played his country-blues music each weekend. He wrote some songs about the U.P., too — they may appear soon on a tape. *Turn south at the blinker light in Naubinway. Bar is on the water. 477-6061. Open daily, 11 a.m. to 2 a.m., Sun from noon.* &: call.

NAUBINWAY CAMPING

BIG KNOB Campground/
Lake Superior State Forest
(906) 477-6048. Not reservable.

A destination beach and campground that's *really* off the beaten path, but not inconvenient. The 23-site rustic campground is at the end of a road that winds at least six miles through forest and wetlands. Campsites in the **low, forested dunes** behind the beach and marshes are **pleasantly separated** if not quite invisible to neighbors. See above for info on the **beach** and three **hiking trails** in this interesting natural area.

See directions for Big Knob Pathway but continue south 6 miles from U.S. 2 to campground. Serviced May thru Nov. Camping $6/$10 night. **H.A.:** *call. Beach access may be difficult.*

> ***Keep in mind*** that all prices and hours of operation are subject to change. Lodging rates vary with supply and demand and are usually higher for special events.

INDEX

To provide many access points to a long book and a varied place, we have come up with many subject headings. The index is not comprehensive, and some inconsistencies and omissions have occurred. We hope this index helps readers use our book and plan trips.

All **cities**, **towns**, **villages**, and **islands** are **boldfaced**.

CATEGORIES (canoe rentals, bookshops, copper mining, etc.) have been capitalized.

Most shops except for museum shops have been subsumed under towns. Look up those towns, or start with **SHOPPING**.

Each county's source of tourism info has been referenced by county name. The U.P.'s six **Michigan Welcome Centers** are referenced under that name.

Restaurants, **lodgings** and **campgrounds** have been indexed by regions corresponding to chapters in this book. See page **355**.